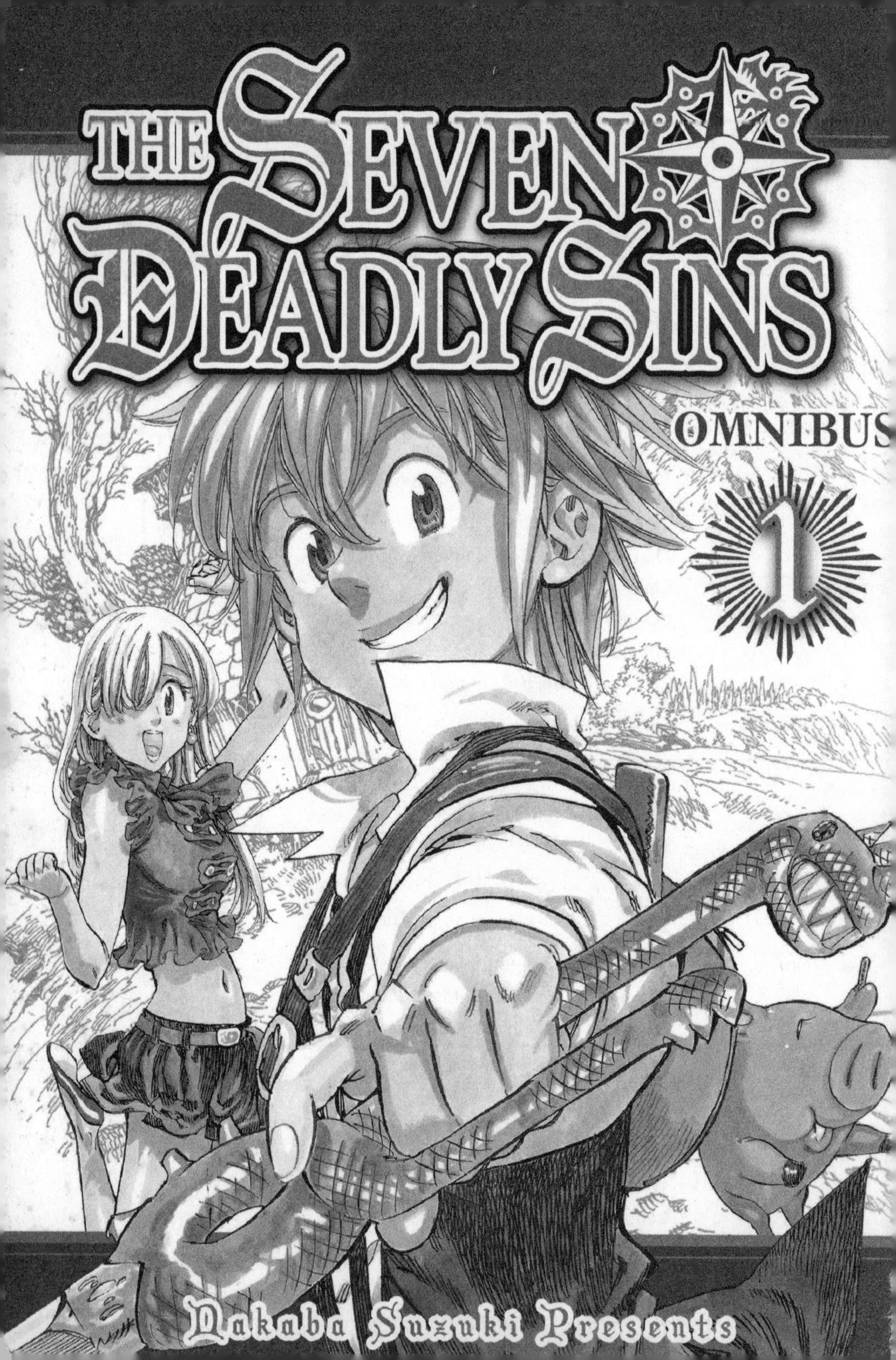
THE SEVEN DEADLY SINS
OMNIBUS
1
Nakaba Suzuki Presents

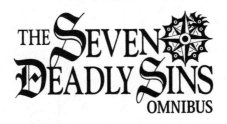

OMNIBUS

NAKABA SUZUKI

Table of Contents

Chapter 1 – The Seven Deadly Sins ··· 3

Chapter 2 – The Holy Knight's Sword ··· 69

Chapter 3 – What One Must Do ··· 109

Chapter 4 – The Sin in the Sleeping Forest ··· 139

Chapter 5 – Dark Memories ··· 160

Chapter 6 – The Holy Knight Gilthunder ··· 195

Chapter 7 – Dark Prisoner ··· 215

Chapter 8 – A Girl's Dream ··· 235

Chapter 9 – No Touching ··· 260

Chapter 10 – An Unseen Malice ··· 281

Chapter 11 – Even If You Died ··· 301

Chapter 12 – A Chaotic Party ··· 321

Chapter 13 – Ready to Sacrifice ··· 341

Chapter 14 – Explosion ··· 361

Chapter 15 – Caught in the Reunion ··· 385

Chapter 16 – The Poem of Beginnings ··· 406

Chapter 17 – Storm's Brewing ··· 428

Chapter 18 – A Touching Reunion ··· 449

Chapter 19 – The Sin of Greed ··· 473

Chapter 20 – Two Paths ··· 493

Chapter 21 – Revenge Knight ··· 513

Chapter 22 – A Pursuer to Fear ··· 533

Bonus Chapter – Nothing Wasted ··· 559

nakaba suzuki presents

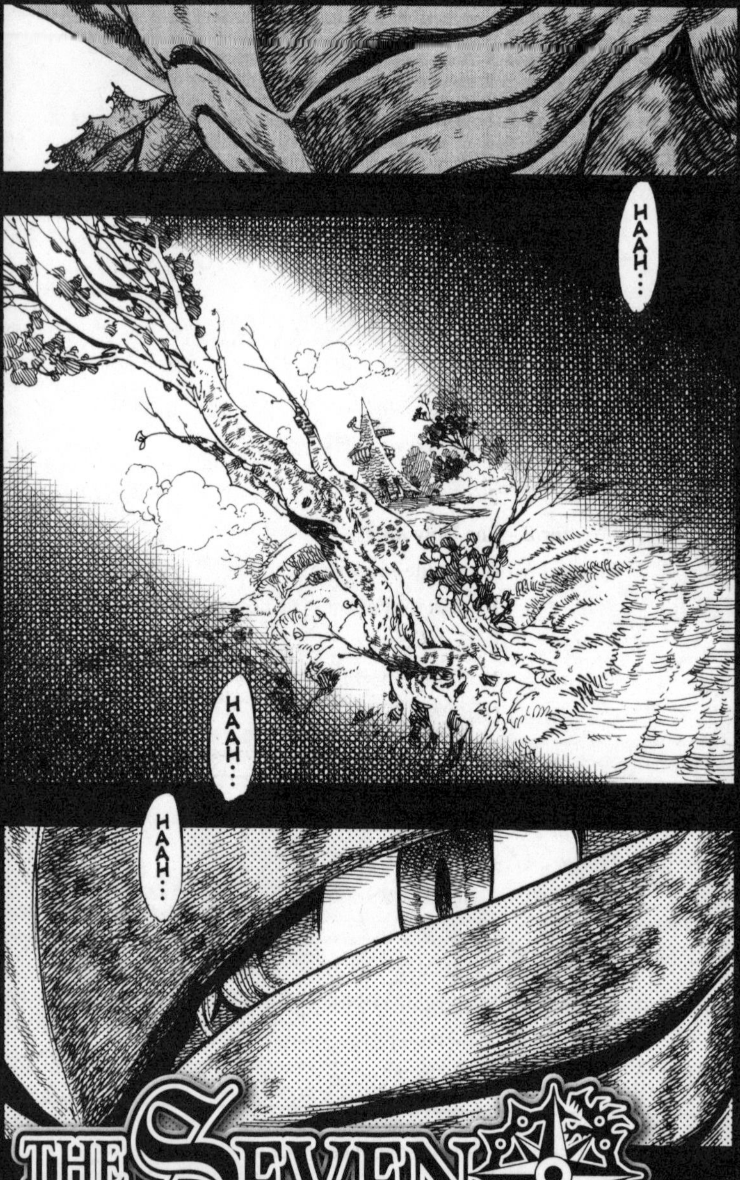
HAAH...
HAAH...
HAAH...

THE SEVEN DEADLY SINS 1

Nakaba Suzuki

THE SEVEN DEADLY SINS

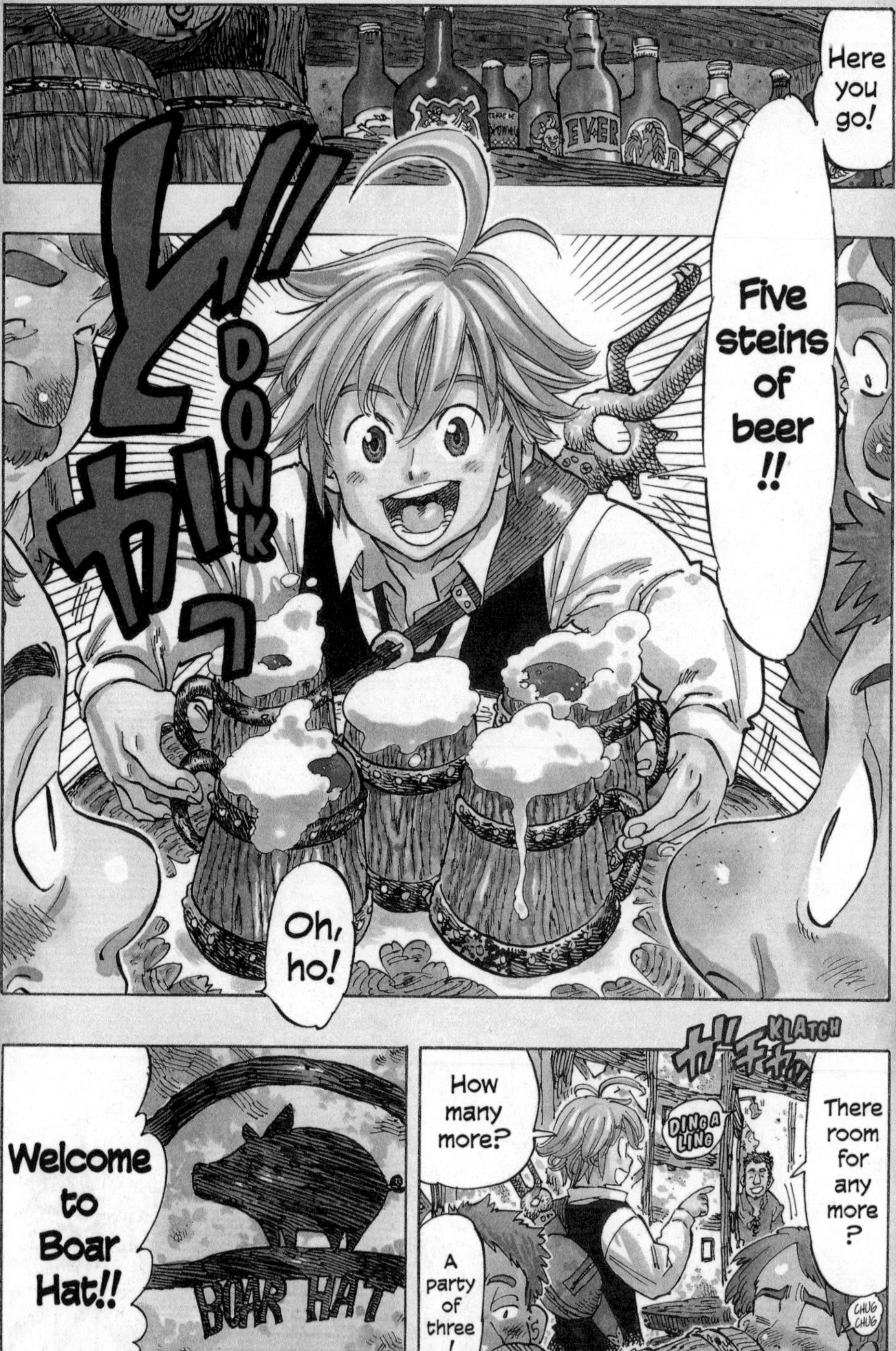

Here you go!
Five steins of beer!!
DONK
Oh, ho!
KLATCH
DING A LING
There room for any more?
How many more?
A party of three!
CHUG CHUG
Welcome to Boar Hat!!
BOAR HAT

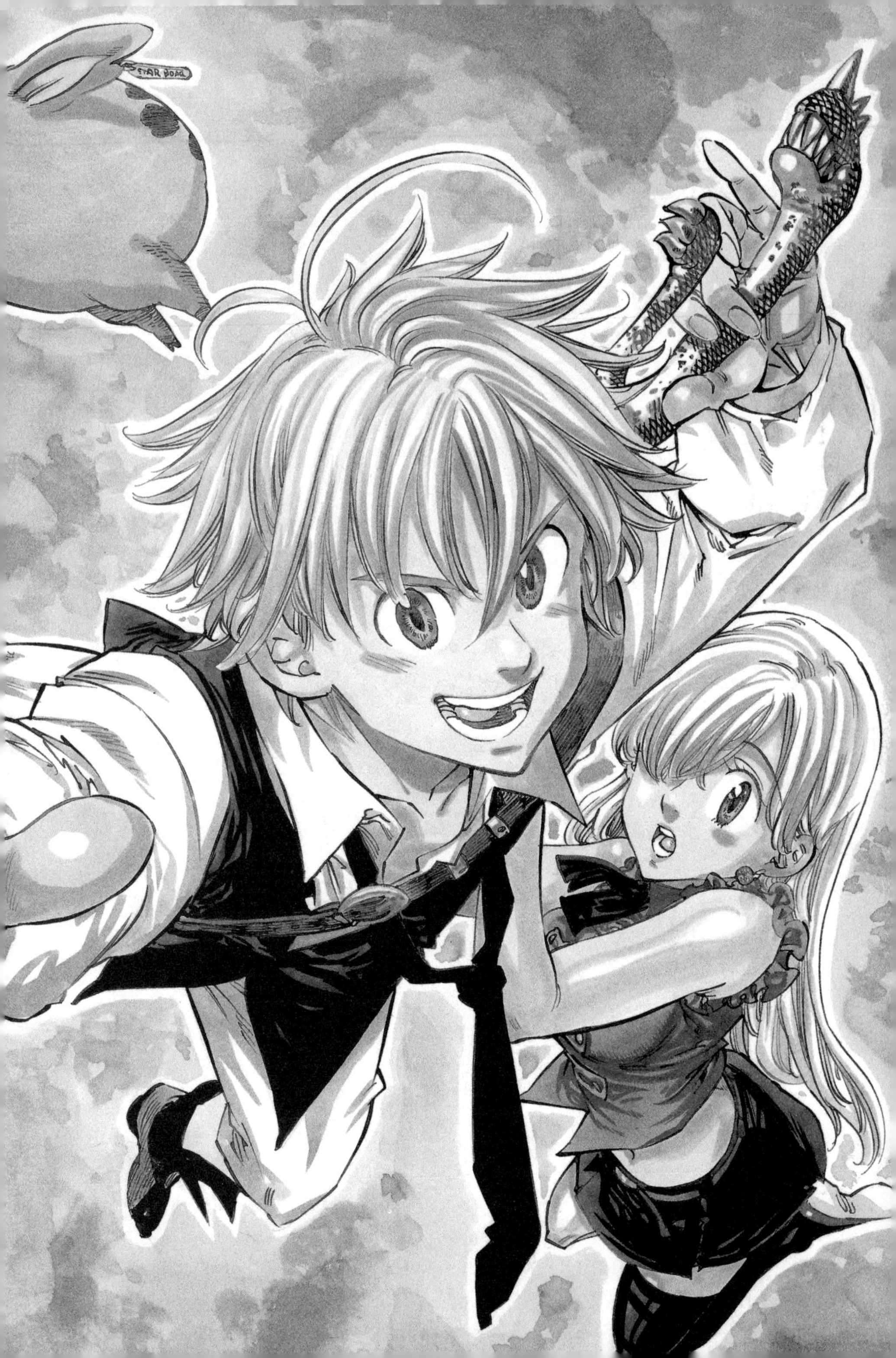

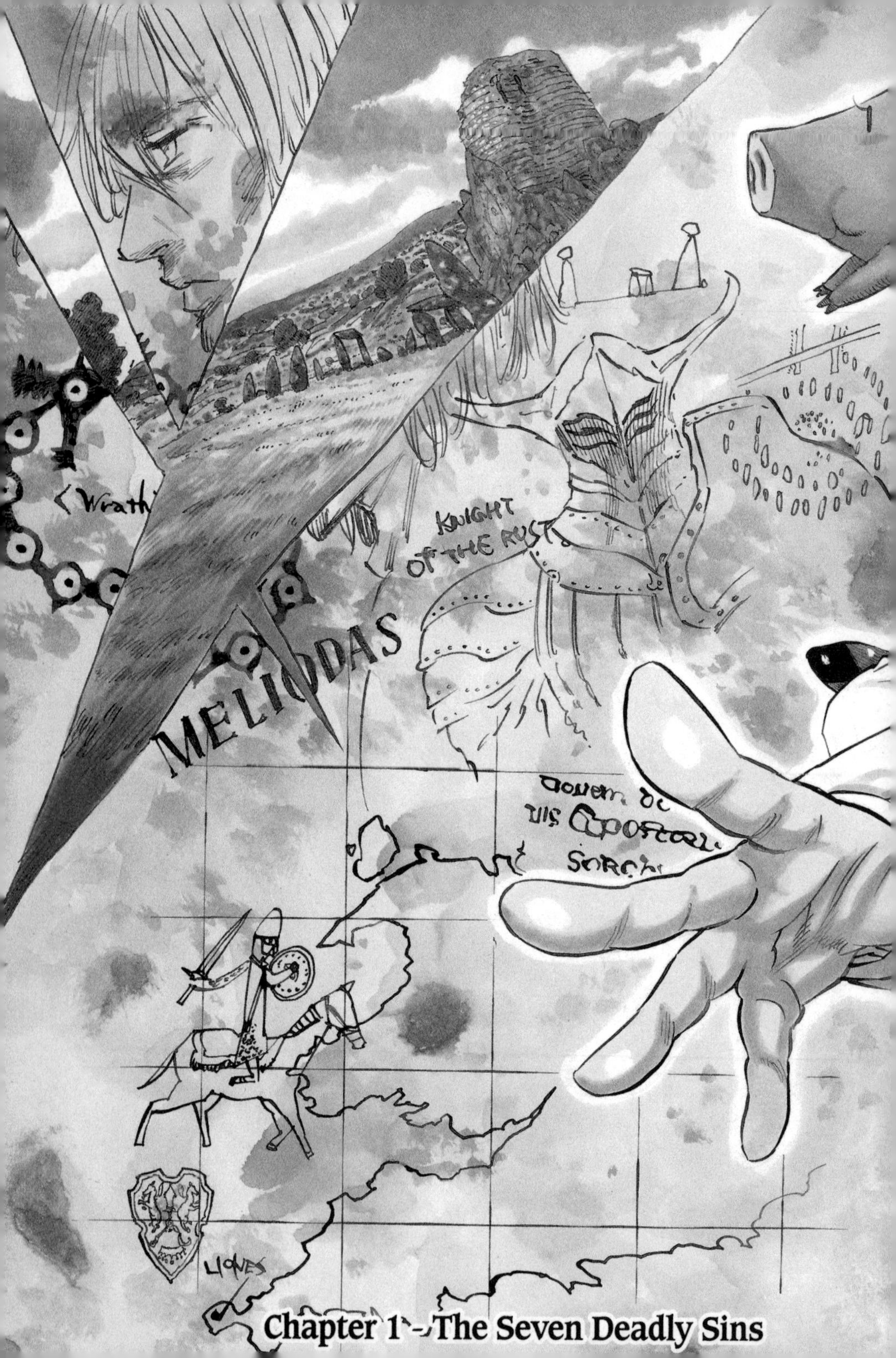
Wrath
KNIGHT OF THE RUST
MELIODAS
LIONES

Chapter 1 - The Seven Deadly Sins

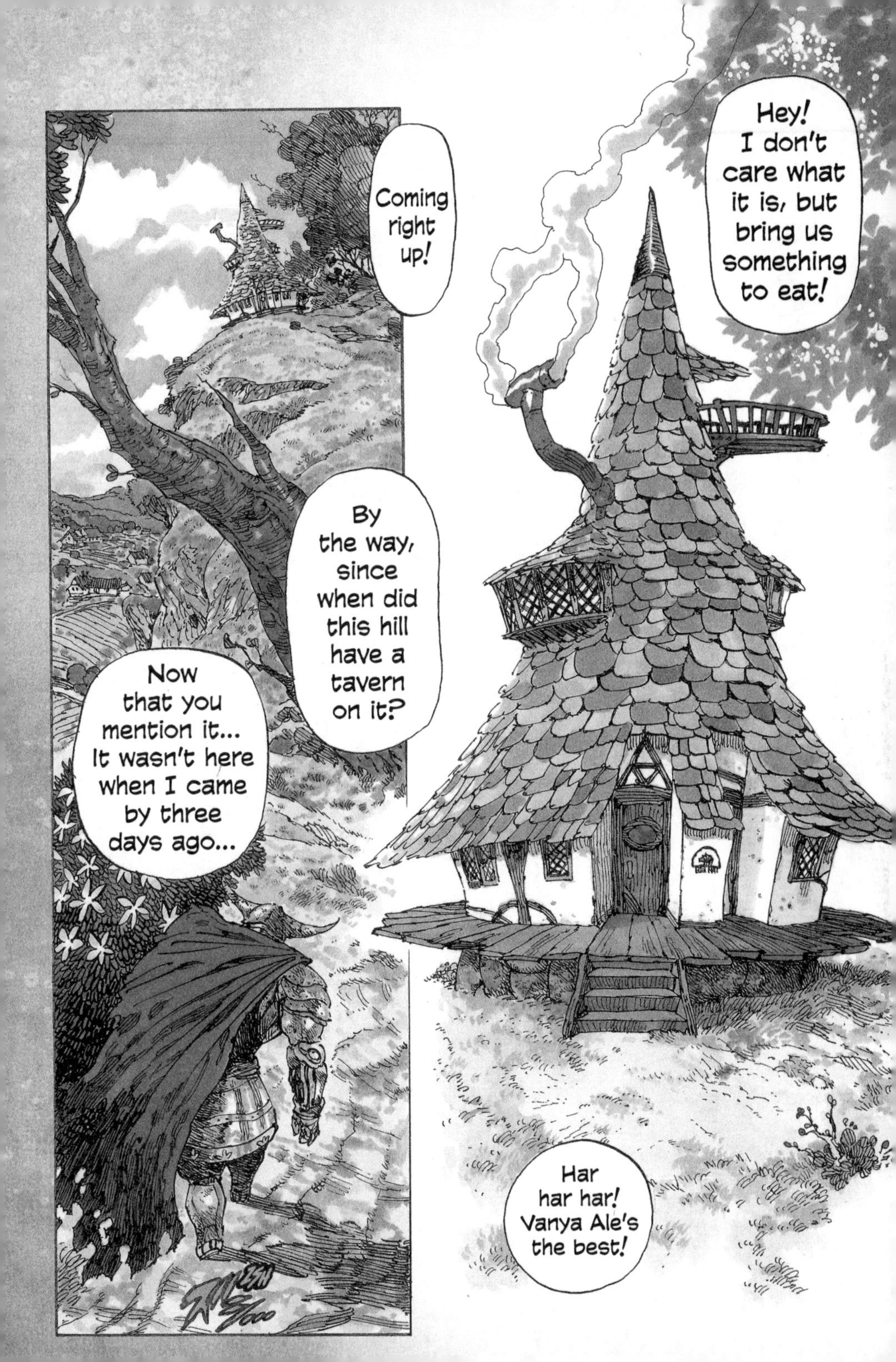
Hey! I don't care what it is, but bring us something to eat!
Har har har! Vanya Ale's the best!
Coming right up!
By the way, since when did this hill have a tavern on it?
Now that you mention it... It wasn't here when I came by three days ago...

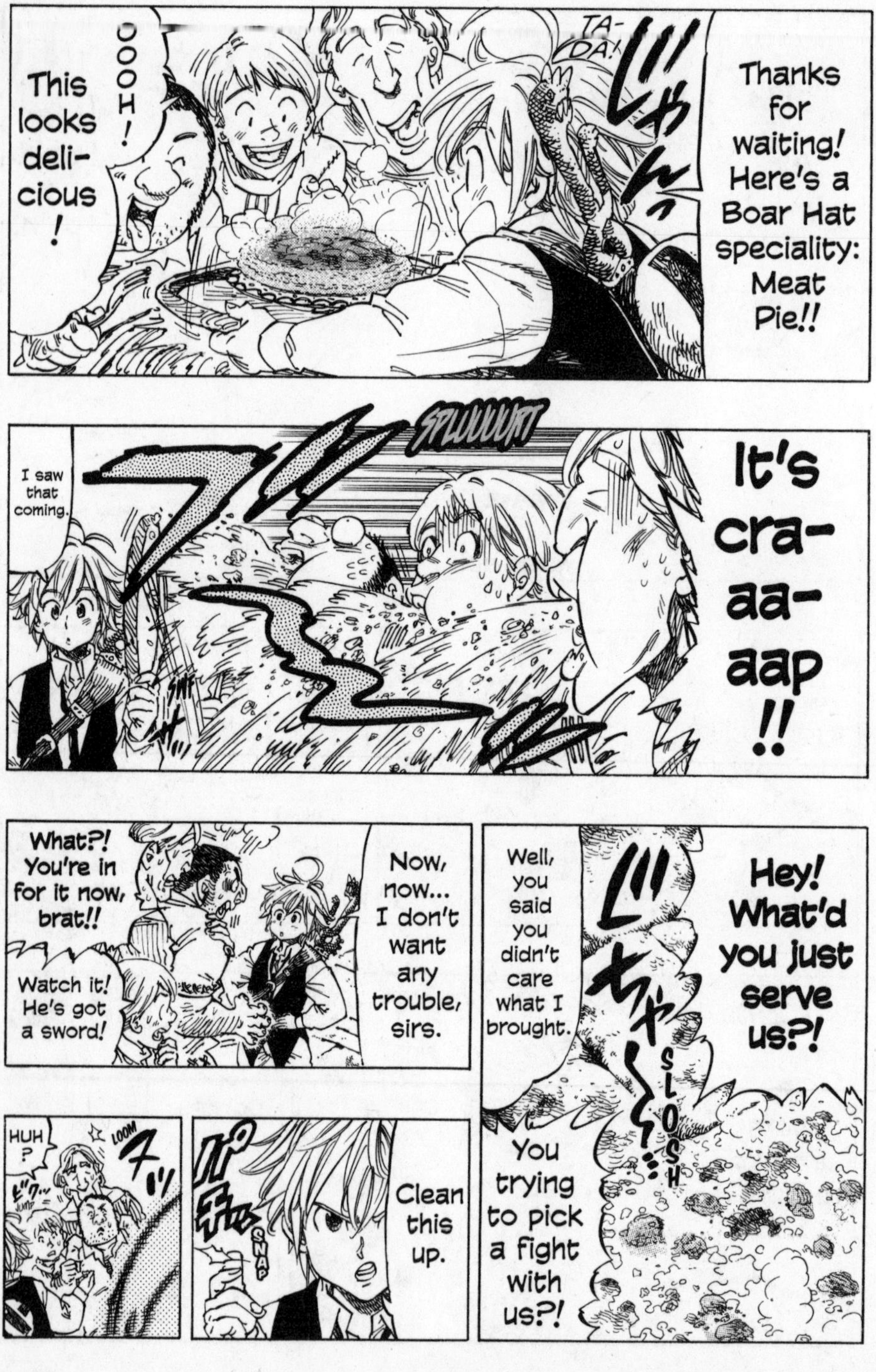

Thanks for waiting! Here's a Boar Hat speciality: Meat Pie!!
TA-DA!
OOOH!
This looks deli-cious!
It's cra-aa-aap!!
SPLUUUURT
I saw that coming.
Hey! What'd you just serve us?!
Well, you said you didn't care what I brought.
SLOSH
You trying to pick a fight with us?!
Now, now... I don't want any trouble, sirs.
What?! You're in for it now, brat!!
Watch it! He's got a sword!
Clean this up.
SNAP
LOOM
HUH?
JUMP

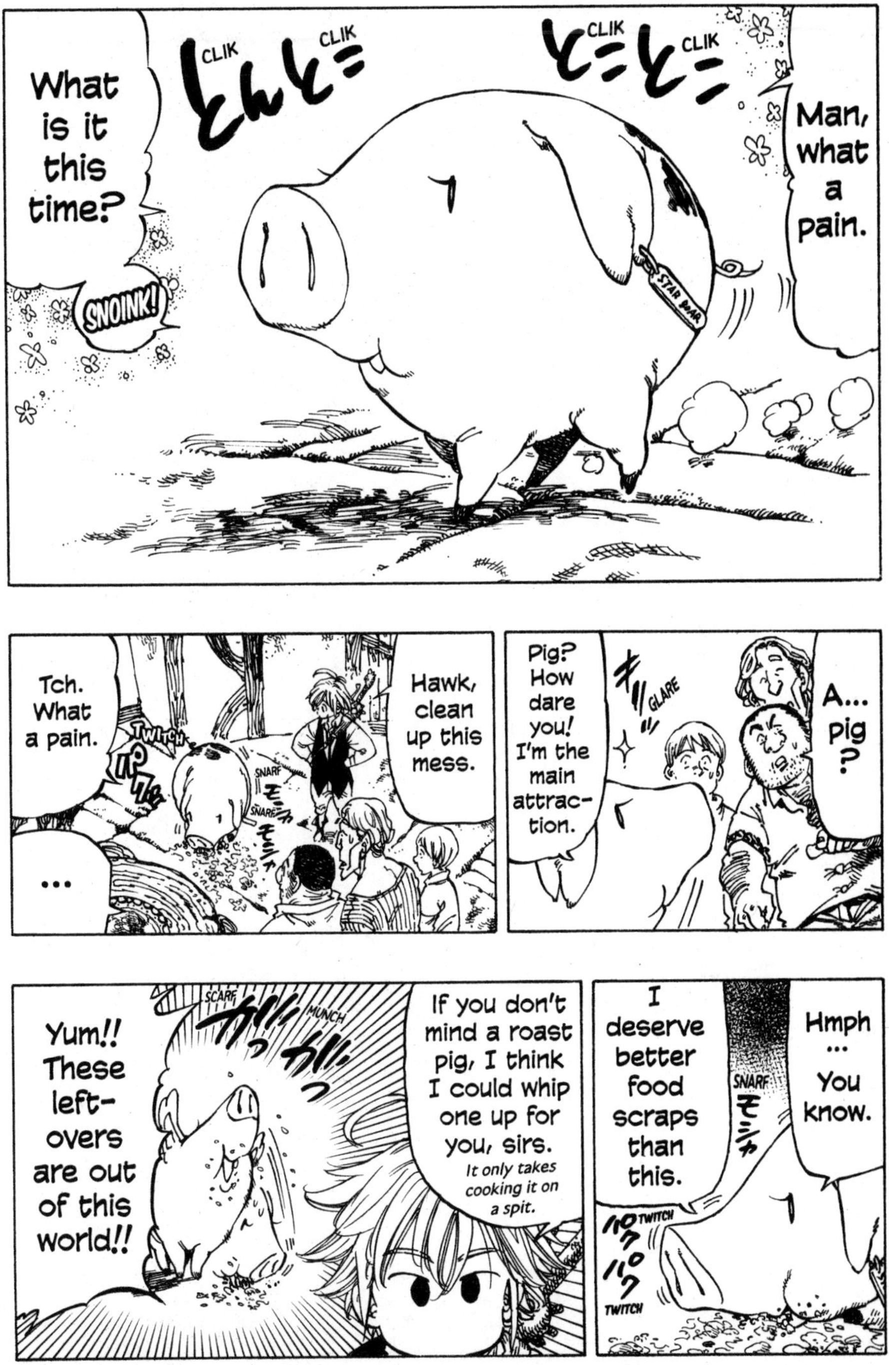
Man, what a pain.
CLIK CLIK
CLIK CLIK
What is it this time?
SNOINK!
A... Pig?
GLARE
Pig? How dare you! I'm the main attraction.
Hawk, clean up this mess.
SNARF
SNARF
TWITCH
Tch. What a pain.
...
Hmph... You know.
SNARF
I deserve better food scraps than this.
TWITCH
TWITCH
If you don't mind a roast pig, I think I could whip one up for you, sirs.
It only takes cooking it on a spit.
MUNCH
SCARF
Yum!! These left-overs are out of this world!!

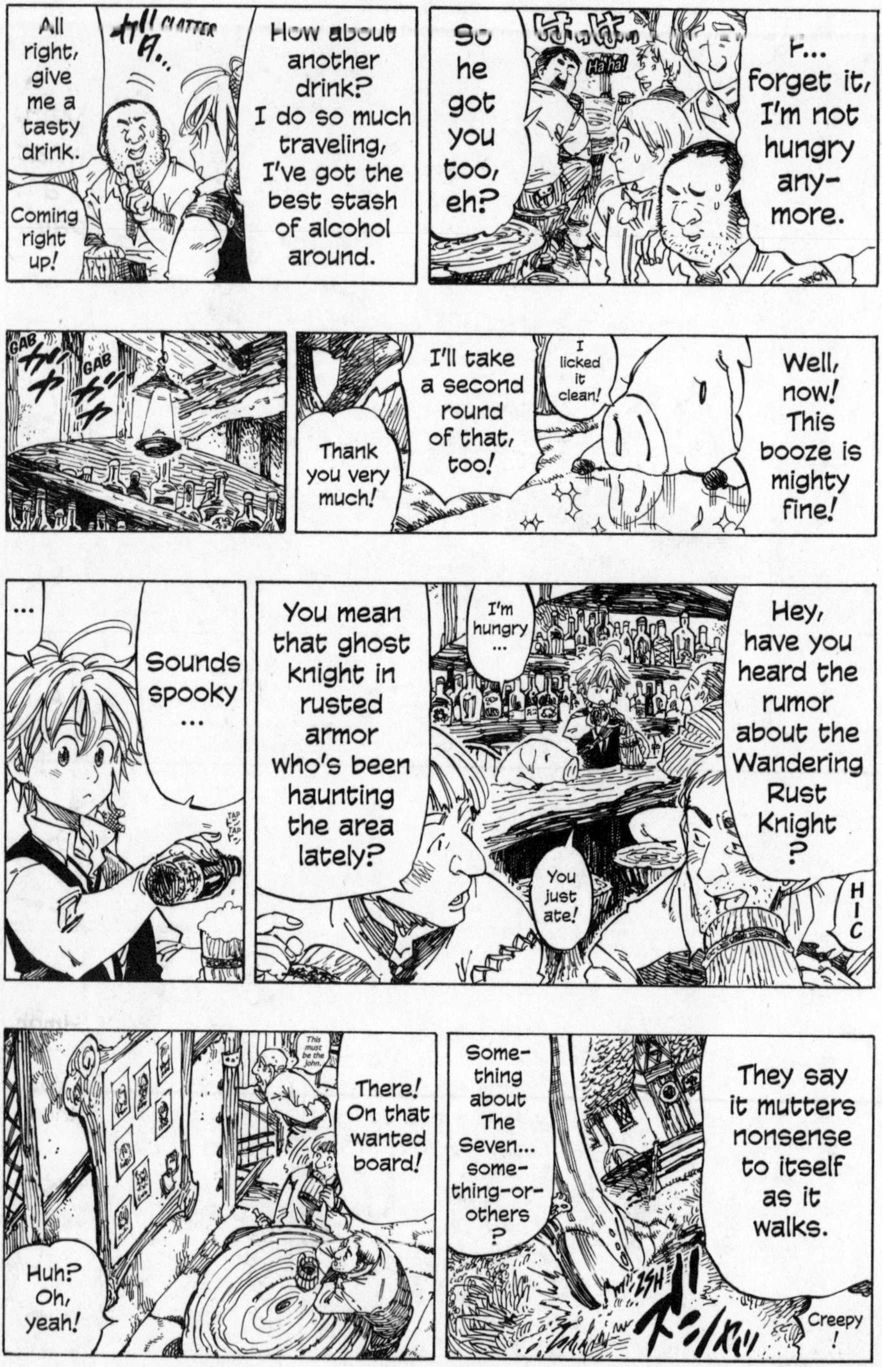
F... forget it, I'm not hungry any-more.
Ha ha!
So he got you too, eh?
How about another drink? I do so much traveling, I've got the best stash of alcohol around.
CLATTER
All right, give me a tasty drink.
Coming right up!
Well, now! This booze is mighty fine!
I licked it clean!
I'll take a second round of that, too!
Thank you very much!
GAB
GAB
Hey, have you heard the rumor about the Wandering Rust Knight?
HIC
I'm hungry...
You just ate!
You mean that ghost knight in rusted armor who's been haunting the area lately?
...
Sounds spooky...
TAP TAP
They say it mutters nonsense to itself as it walks.
Something about The Seven... some-thing-or-others?
Creepy!
This must be the john.
There! On that wanted board!
Huh? Oh, yeah!

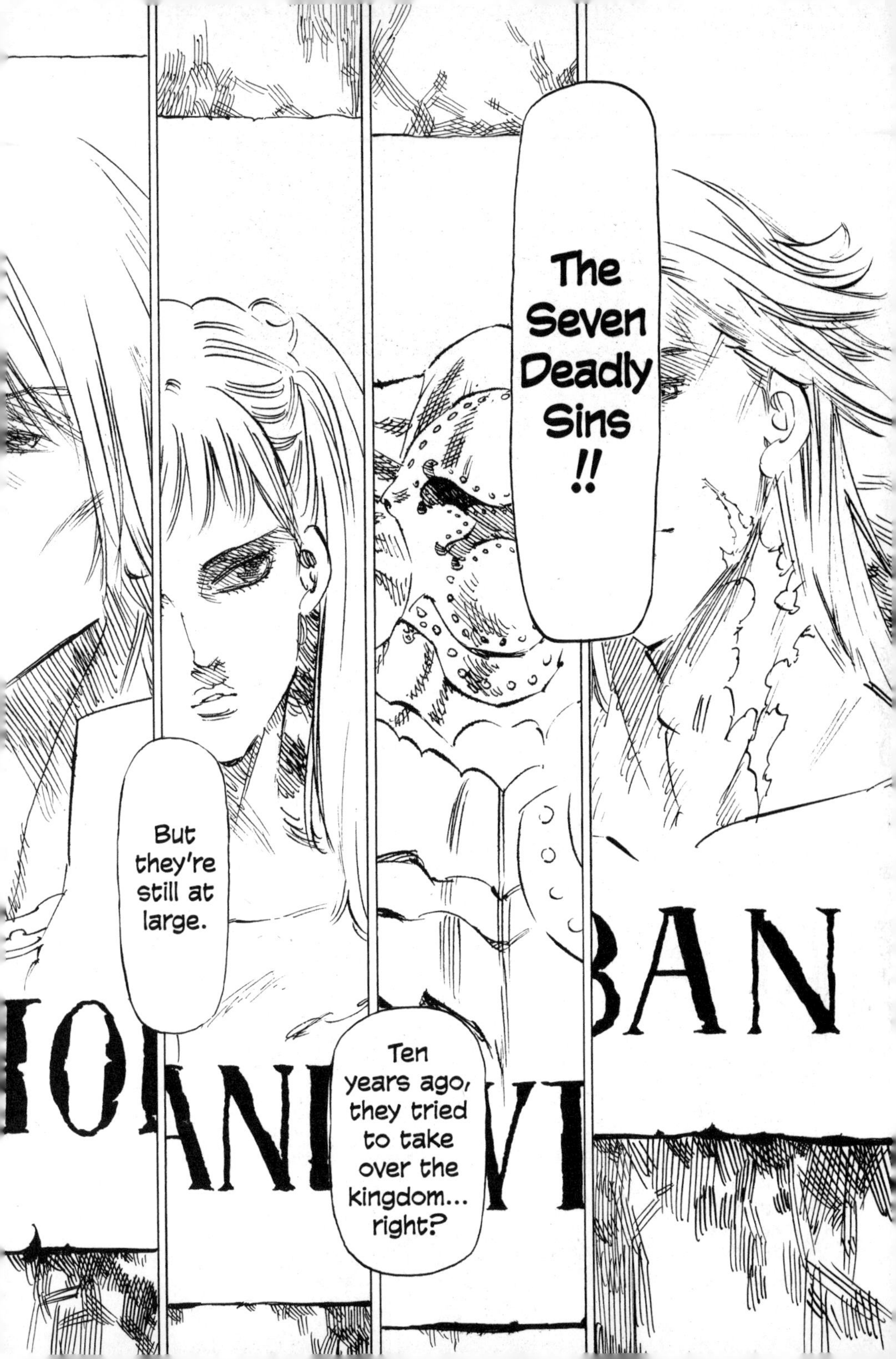

The Seven Deadly Sins!!
BAN
Ten years ago, they tried to take over the kingdom... right?
But they're still at large.

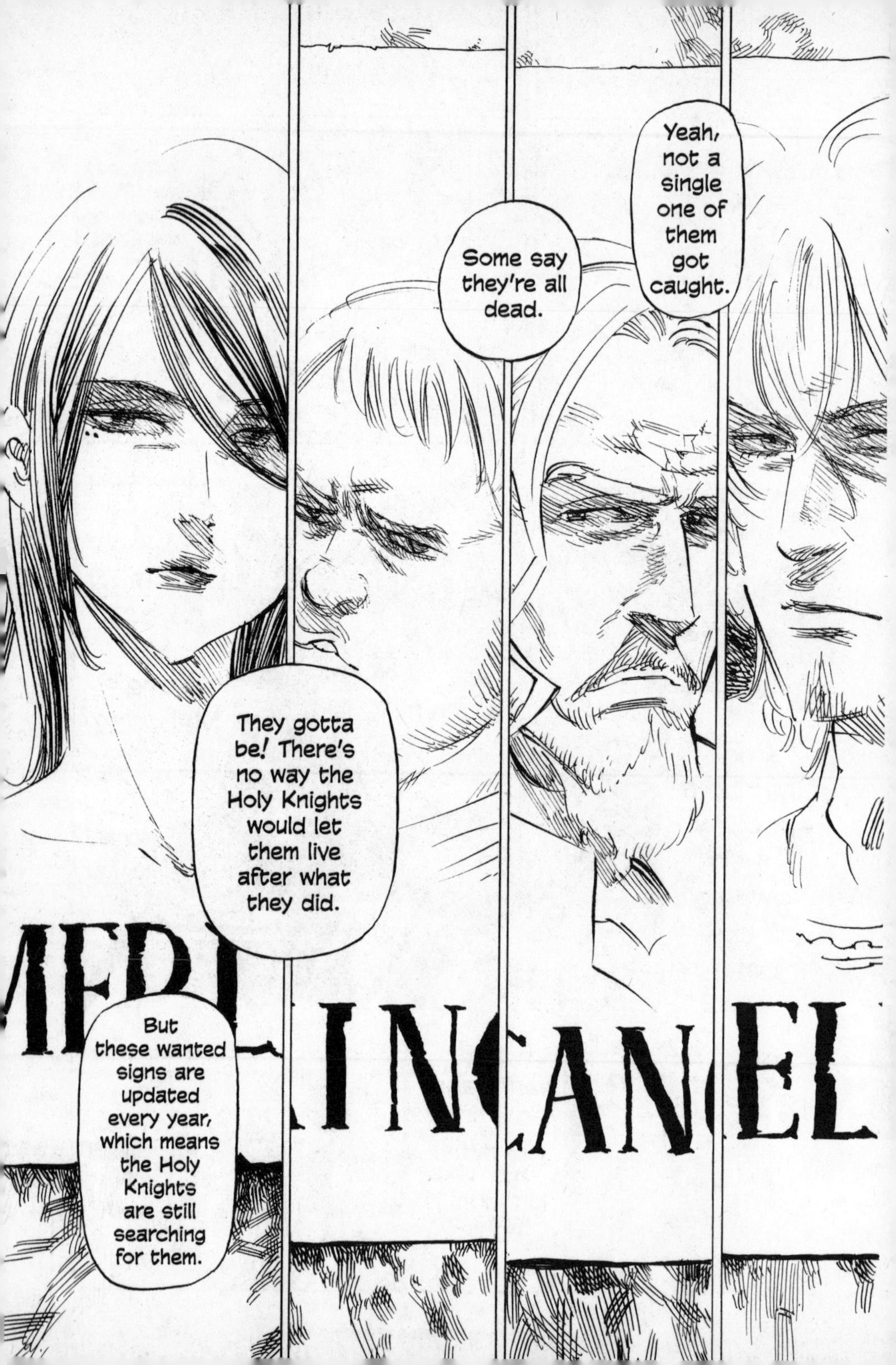
Yeah, not a single one of them got caught.
Some say they're all dead.
They gotta be! There's no way the Holy Knights would let them live after what they did.
But these wanted signs are updated every year, which means the Holy Knights are still searching for them.

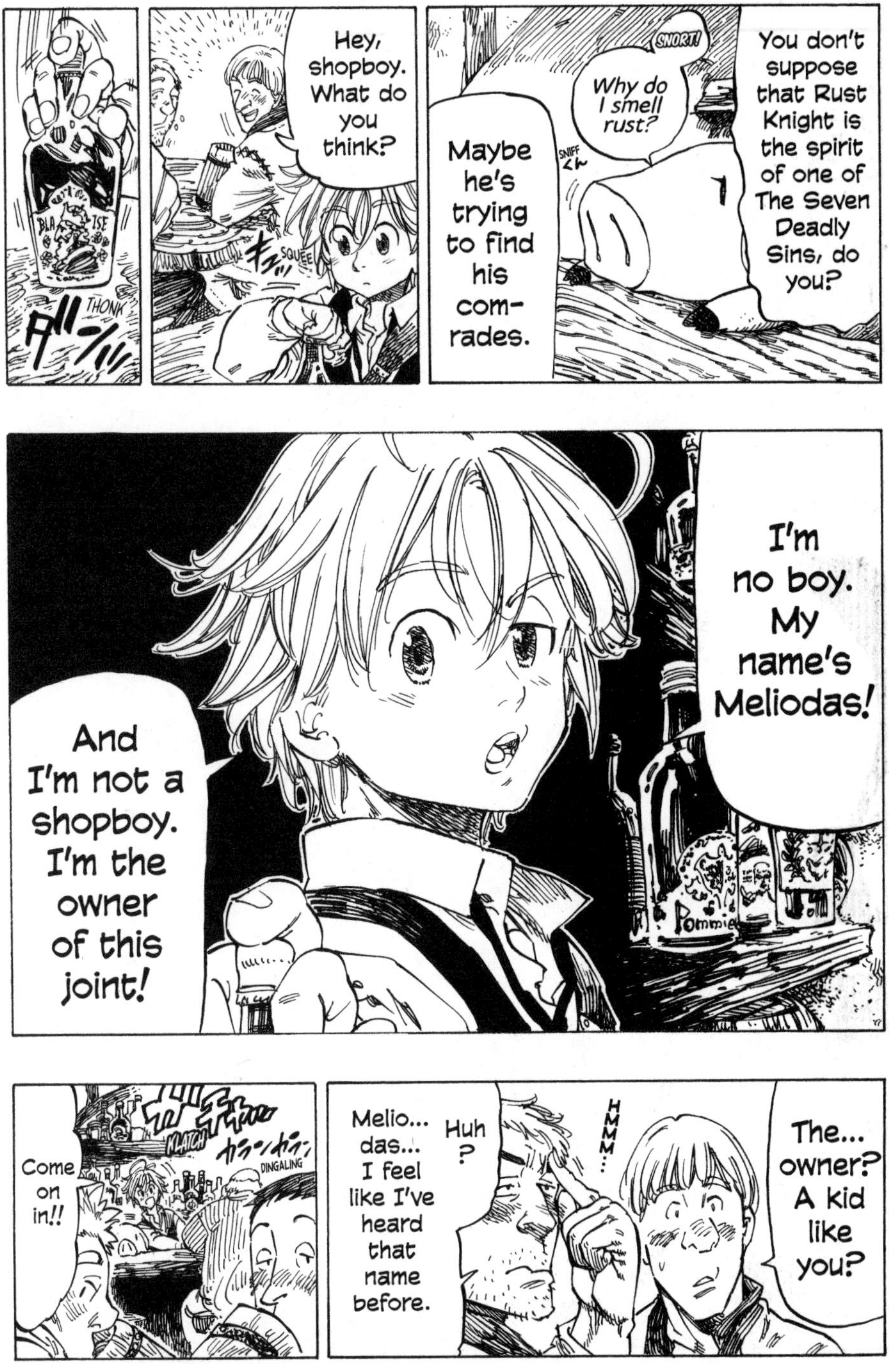
You don't suppose that Rust Knight is the spirit of one of The Seven Deadly Sins, do you?
SNORT!
Why do I smell rust?
SNIFF
Maybe he's trying to find his comrades.
Hey, shopboy. What do you think?
SQUEE
THONK
I'm no boy. My name's Meliodas!
And I'm not a shopboy. I'm the owner of this joint!
The... owner? A kid like you?
HMMM...
Huh?
Melio... das... I feel like I've heard that name before.
KLATCH
DINGALING
Come on in!!

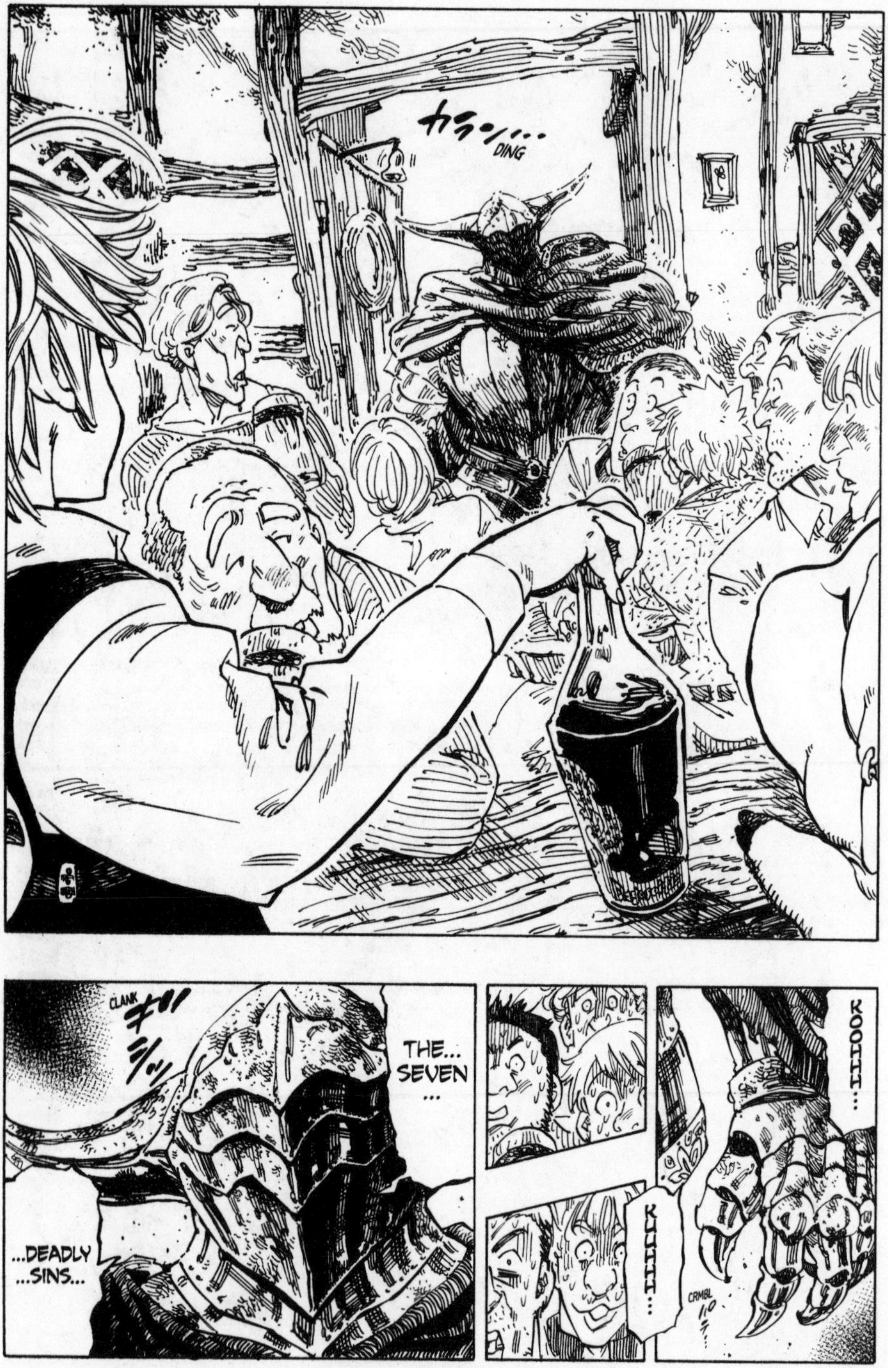

カラン…
DING
KOOHHH...
CRMBL
KUHHH...
CLANK
THE... SEVEN ...
...DEADLY ...SINS...

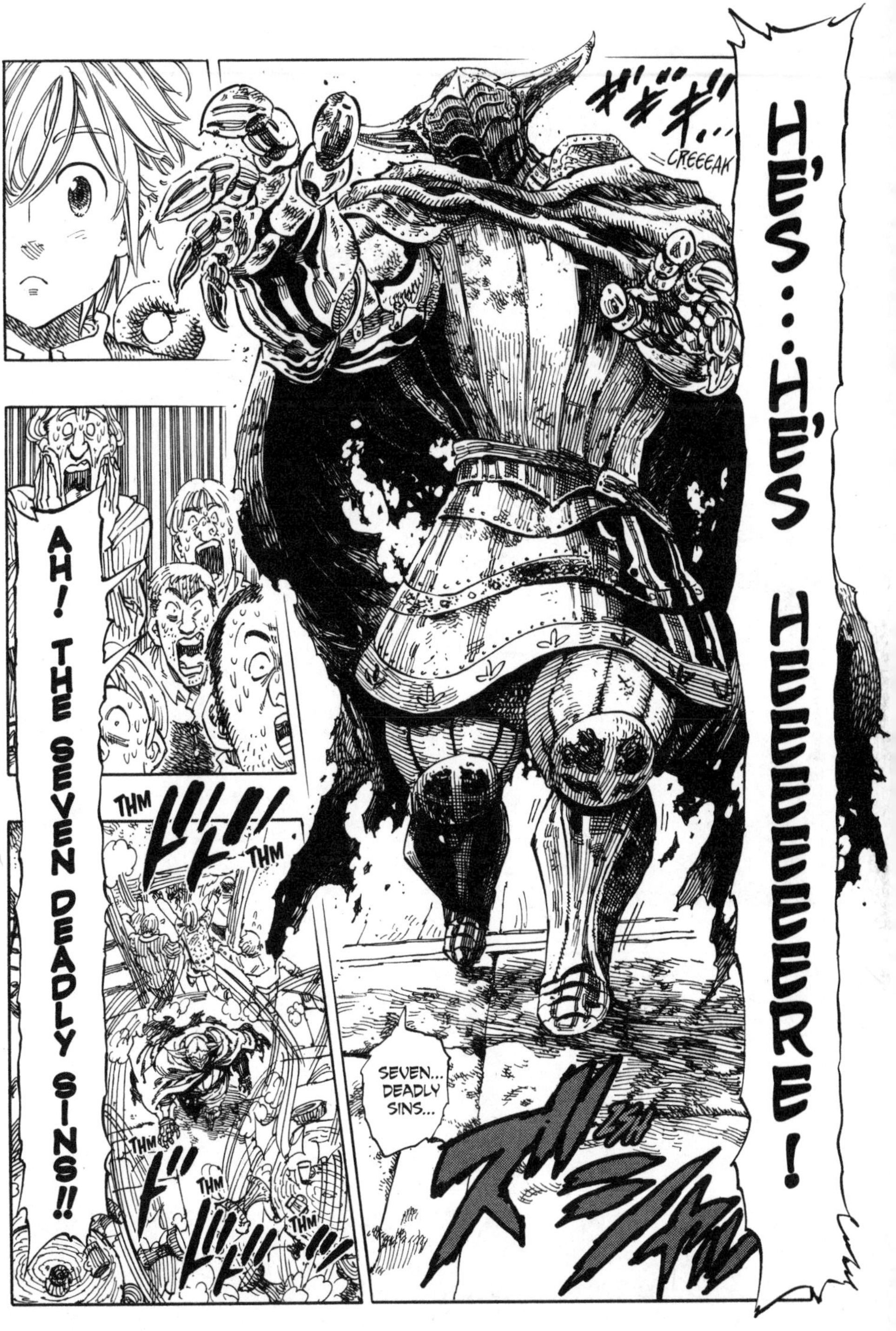
HE'S... HE'S HEEEEERE!
CREEEAK
AH! THE SEVEN DEADLY SINS!!
THM
THM
THM
THM
THM
SEVEN... DEADLY SINS...

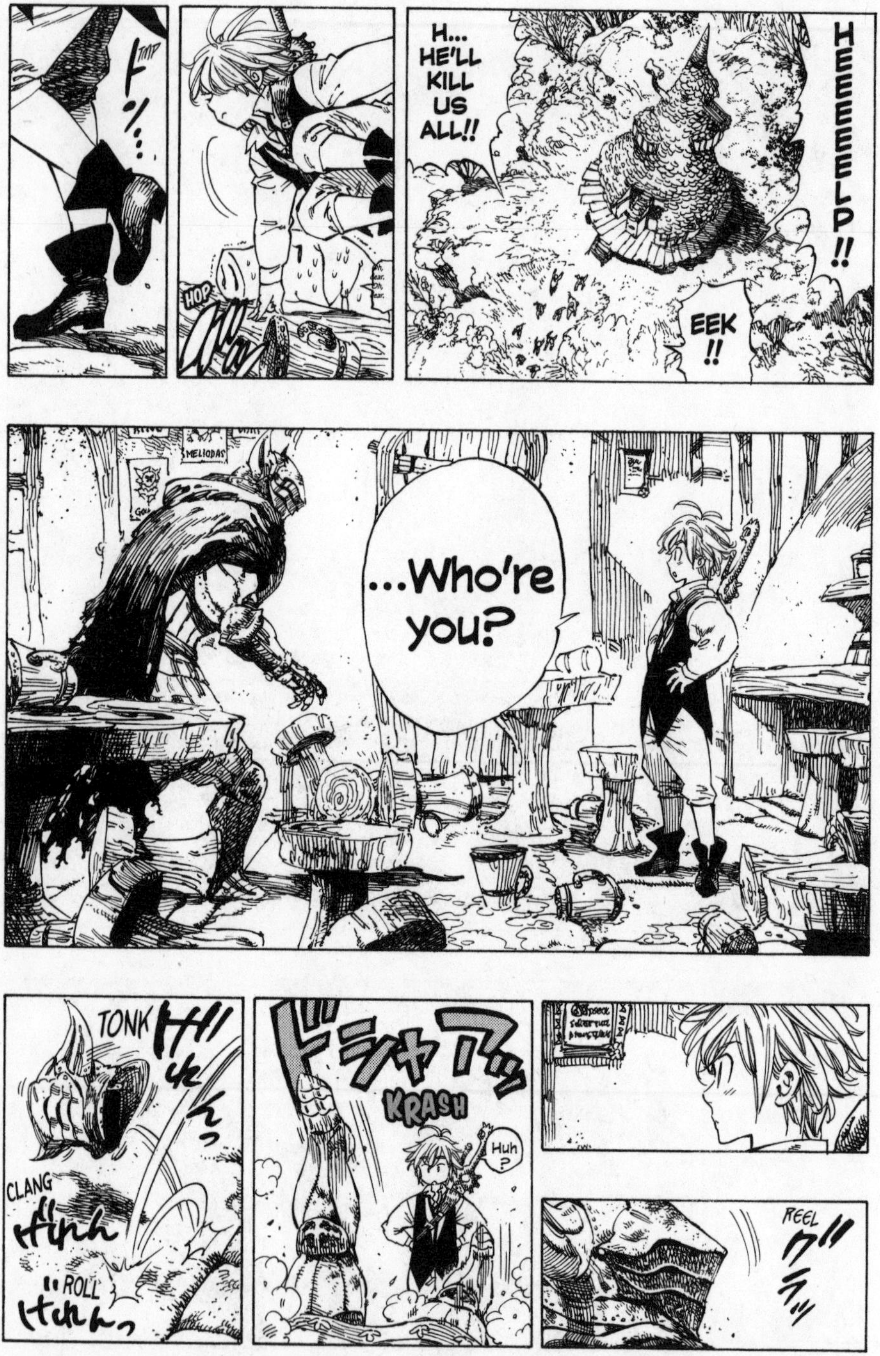
HEEEEELP!!
H... HE'LL KILL US ALL!!
EEK!!
HOP
TMP
...Who're you?
REEL
ドシャアッ
KRASH
Huh?
TONK
CLANG
ROLL

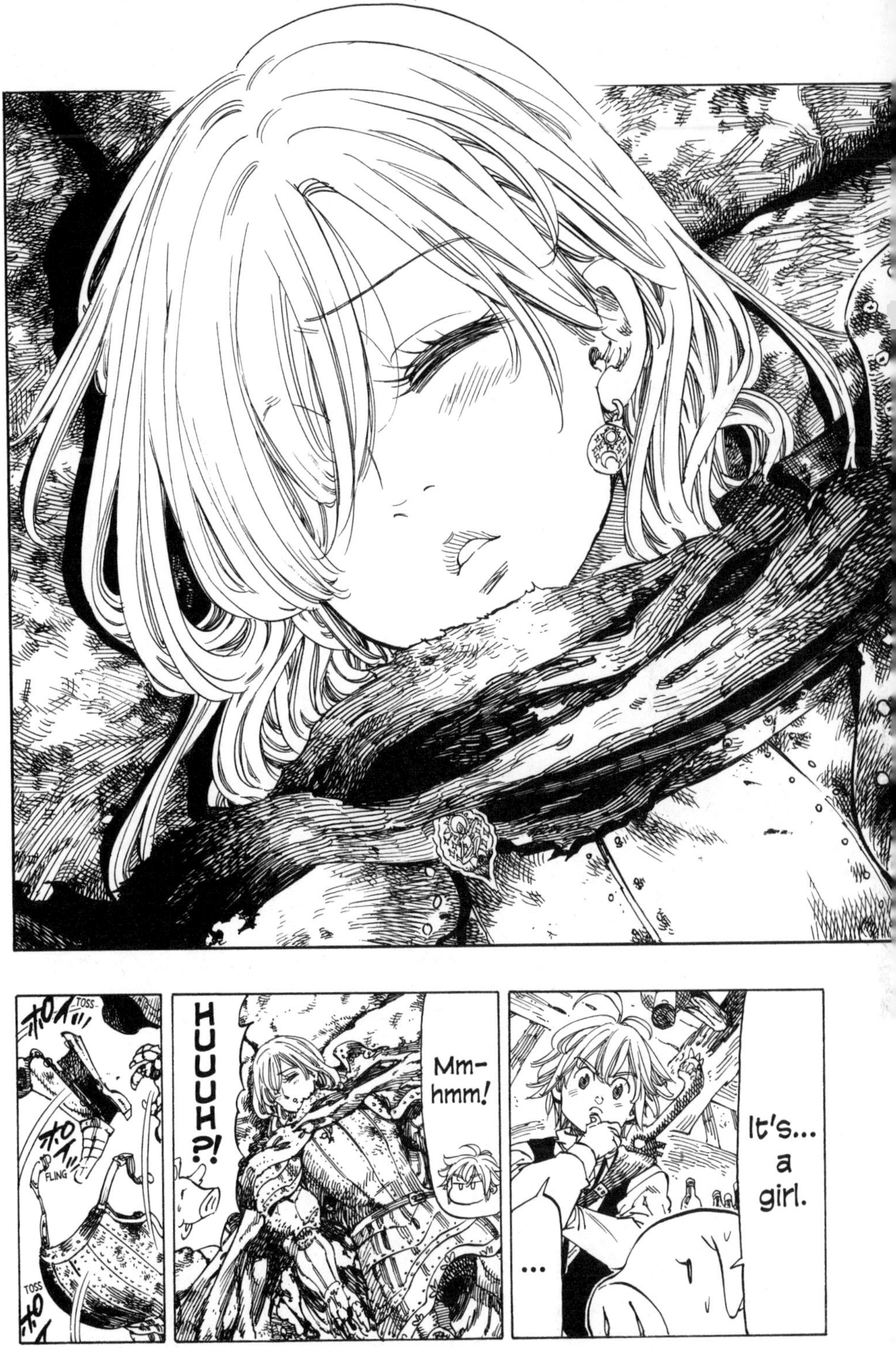
It's... a girl.
...
Mm-hmm!
HUUUH?!
TOSS
FLING
TOSS

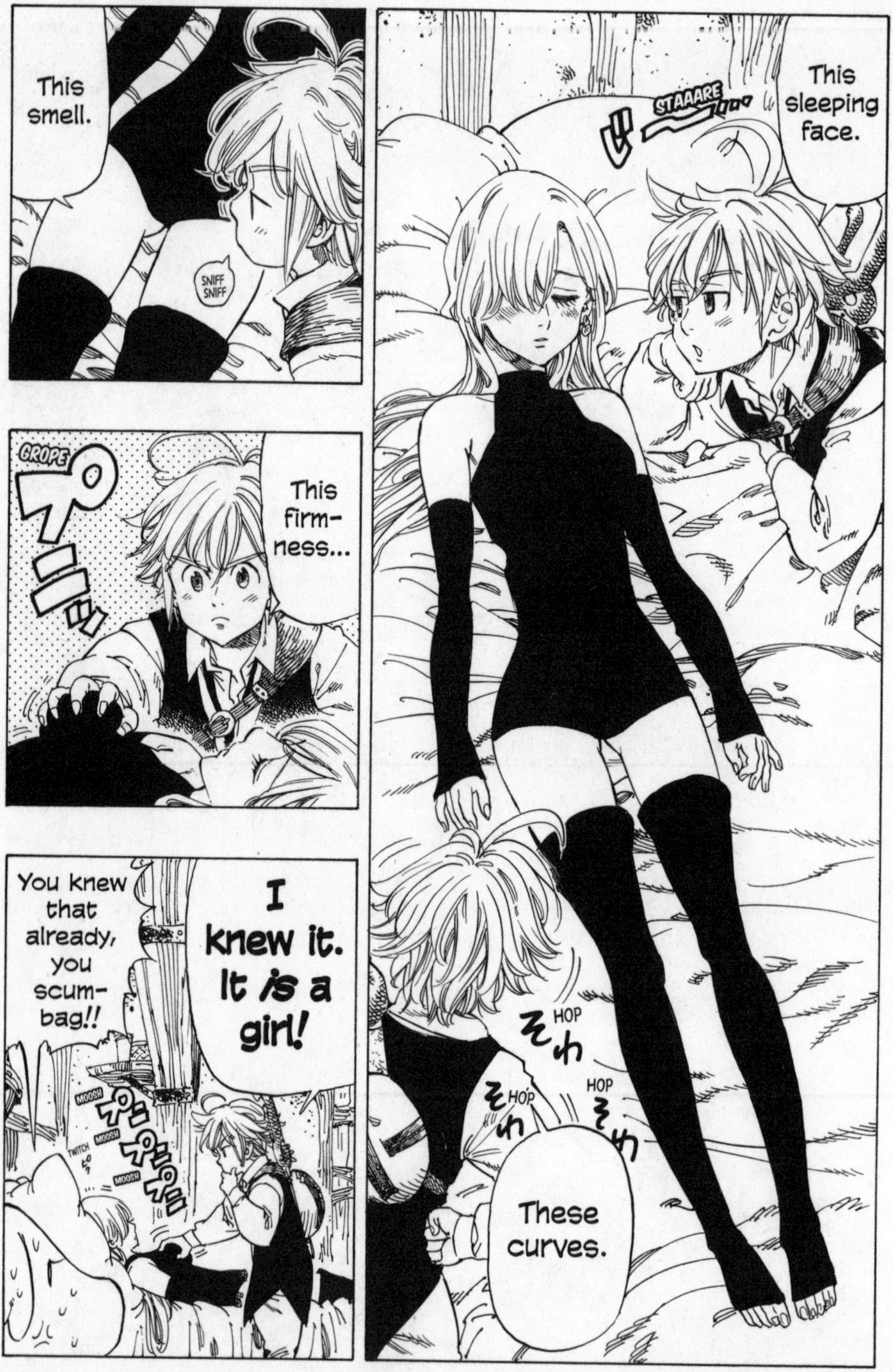
STAAARE
This sleeping face.
HOP
HOP
HOP
These curves.
This smell.
SNIFF SNIFF
GROPE
This firmness...
I knew it. It *is* a girl!
You knew that already, you scumbag!!
MOOSH
MOOSH
MOOSH
TWITCH

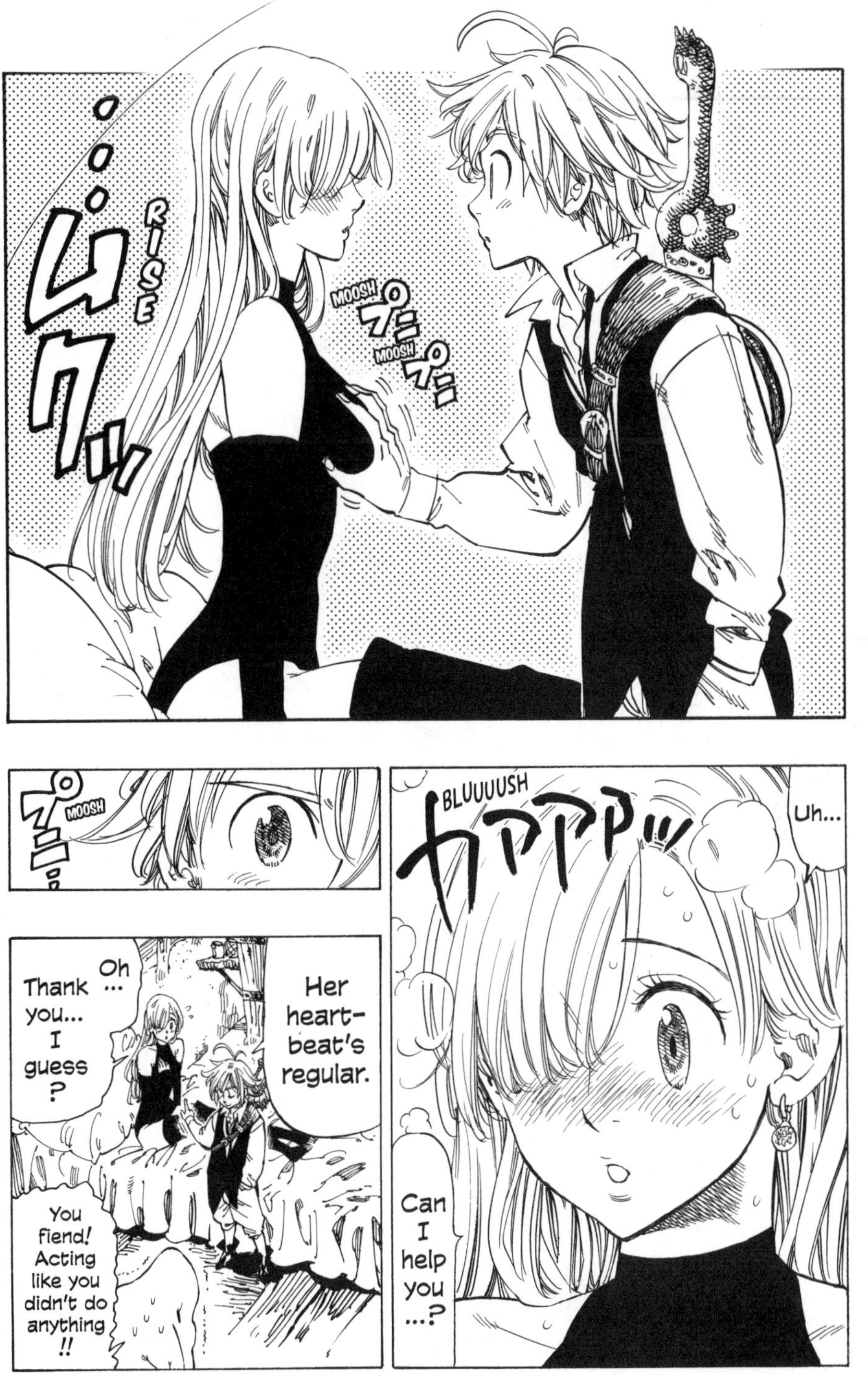
MOOSH
MOOSH
RISE
Uh...
BLUUUUSH
Can I help you...?
MOOSH
Her heart-beat's regular.
Oh...
Thank you... I guess?
You fiend! Acting like you didn't do anything!!

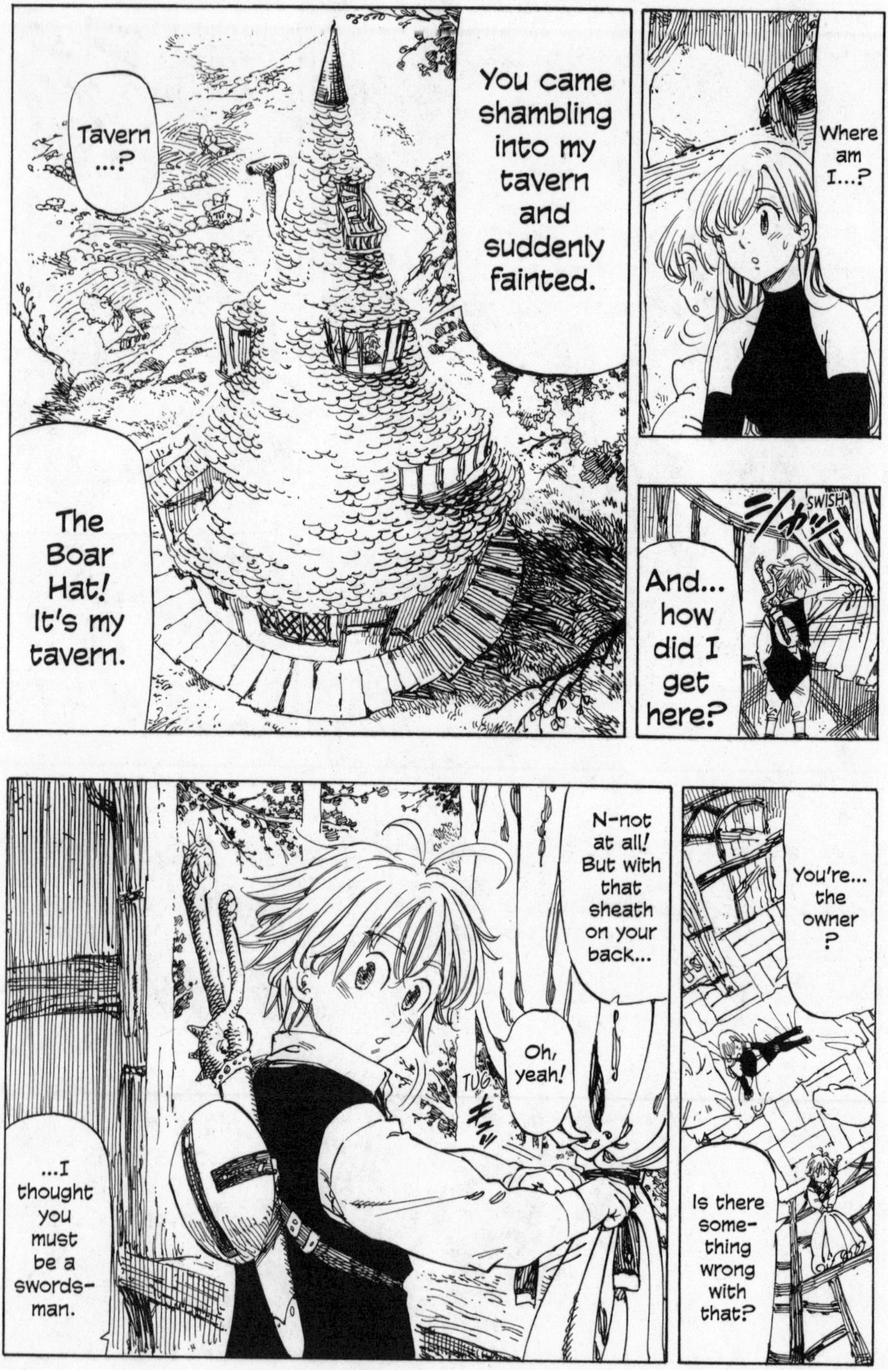

Where am I...?
SWISH
And... how did I get here?
You came shambling into my tavern and suddenly fainted.
Tavern ...?
The Boar Hat! It's my tavern.
You're... the owner?
Is there some-thing wrong with that?
N-not at all! But with that sheath on your back...
Oh, yeah!
TUG
...I thought you must be a swords-man.

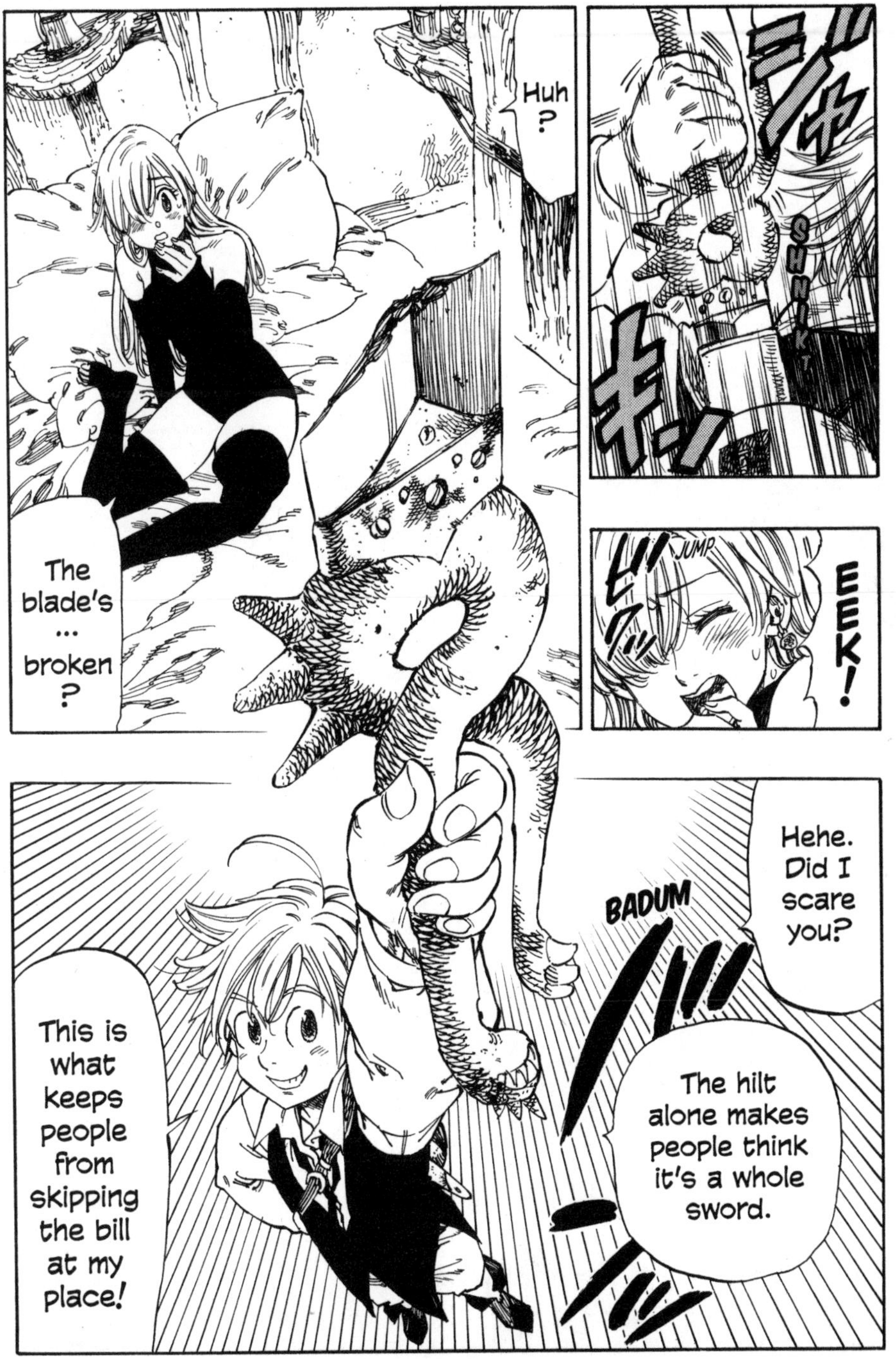
SHNIKT
JUMP
EEK!
Huh?
The blade's ... broken?
Hehe. Did I scare you?
BADUM
The hilt alone makes people think it's a whole sword.
This is what keeps people from skipping the bill at my place!

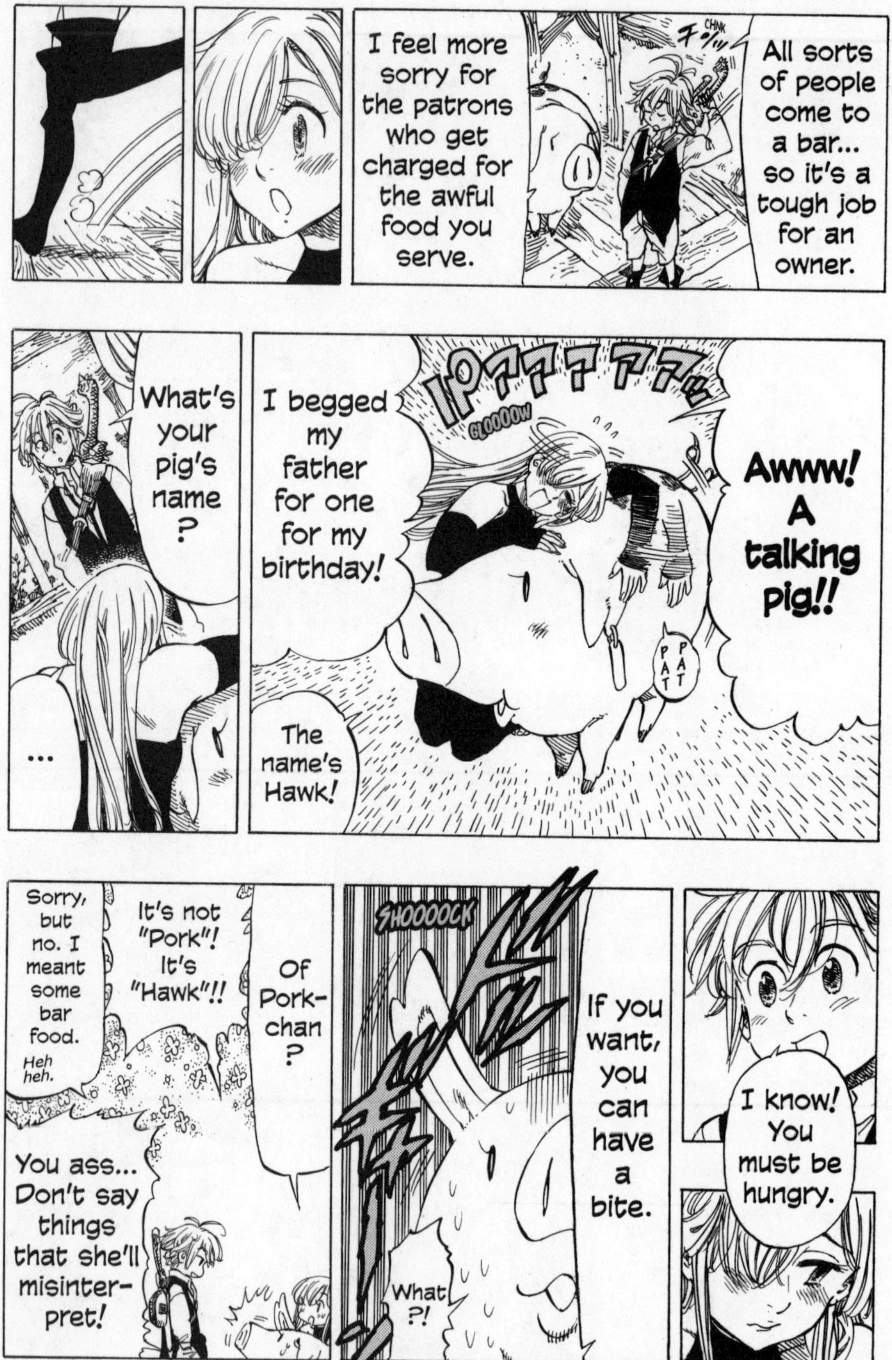

All sorts of people come to a bar... so it's a tough job for an owner.
CHINK
I feel more sorry for the patrons who get charged for the awful food you serve.
Awww! A talking pig!!
GLOOOOW
I begged my father for one for my birthday!
PAT PAT
The name's Hawk!
What's your pig's name?
...
I know! You must be hungry.
If you want, you can have a bite.
SHOOOOCK
What?!
Of Pork-chan?
It's not "Pork"! It's "Hawk"!!
Sorry, but no. I meant some bar food.
Heh heh.
You ass... Don't say things that she'll misinterpret!

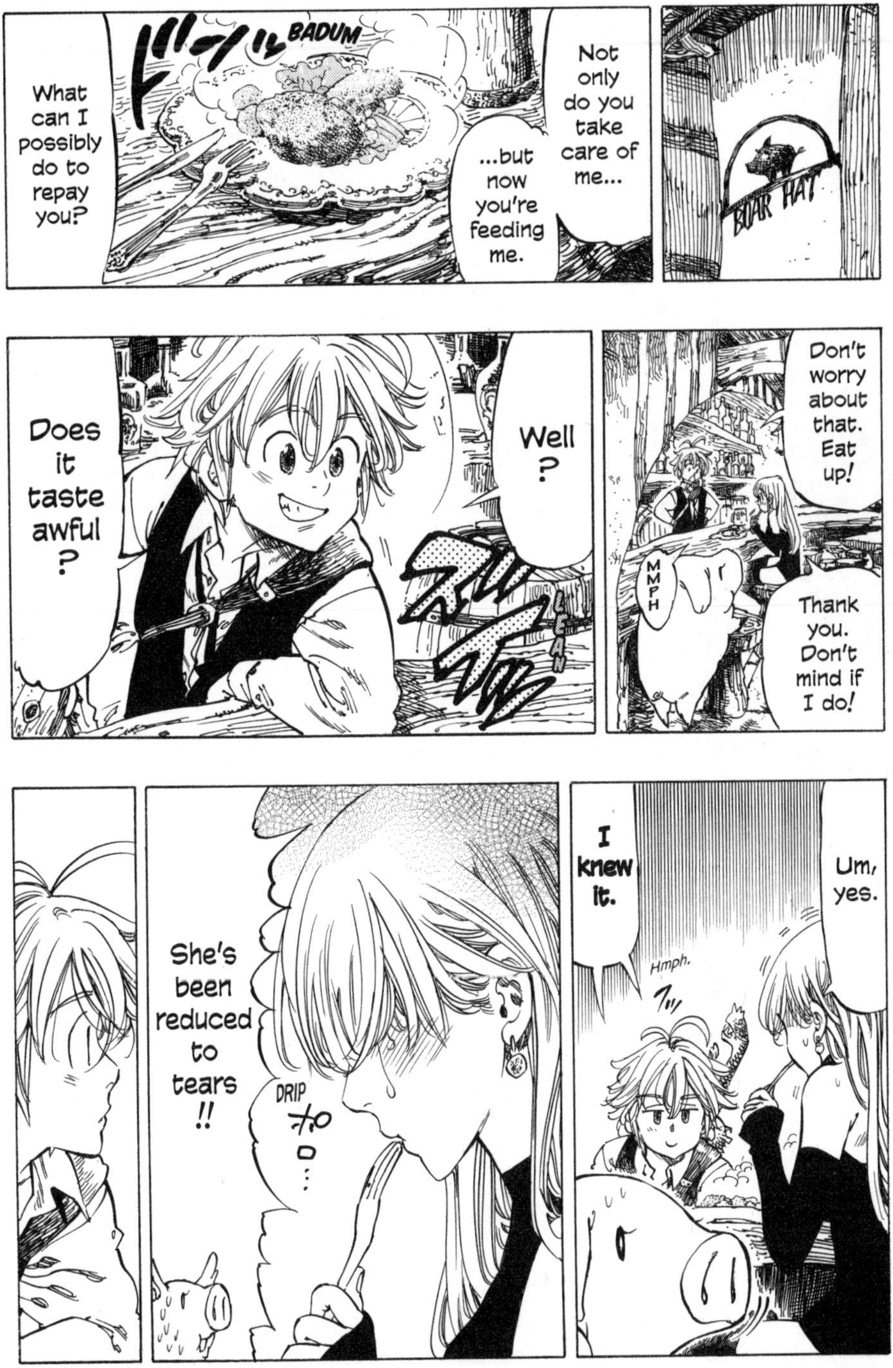
BOAR HAT
Not only do you take care of me...
...but now you're feeding me.
BADUM
What can I possibly do to repay you?
Don't worry about that. Eat up!
MMPH
Thank you. Don't mind if I do!
Well?
LEAN
Does it taste awful?
Um, yes.
I knew it.
Hmph.
DRIP
She's been reduced to tears!!

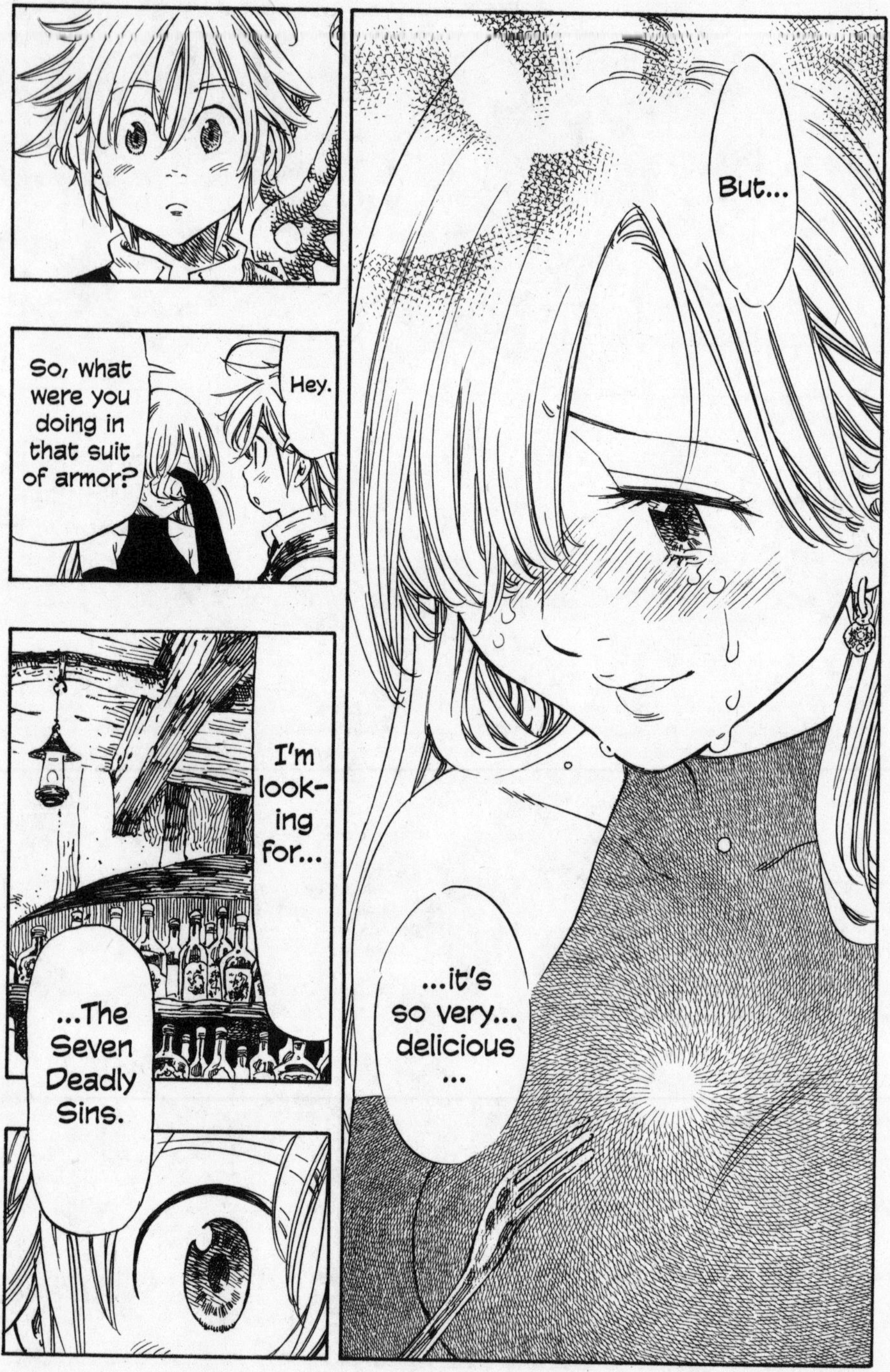
But...
...it's so very... delicious ...
Hey.
So, what were you doing in that suit of armor?
I'm looking-ing for...
...The Seven Deadly Sins.

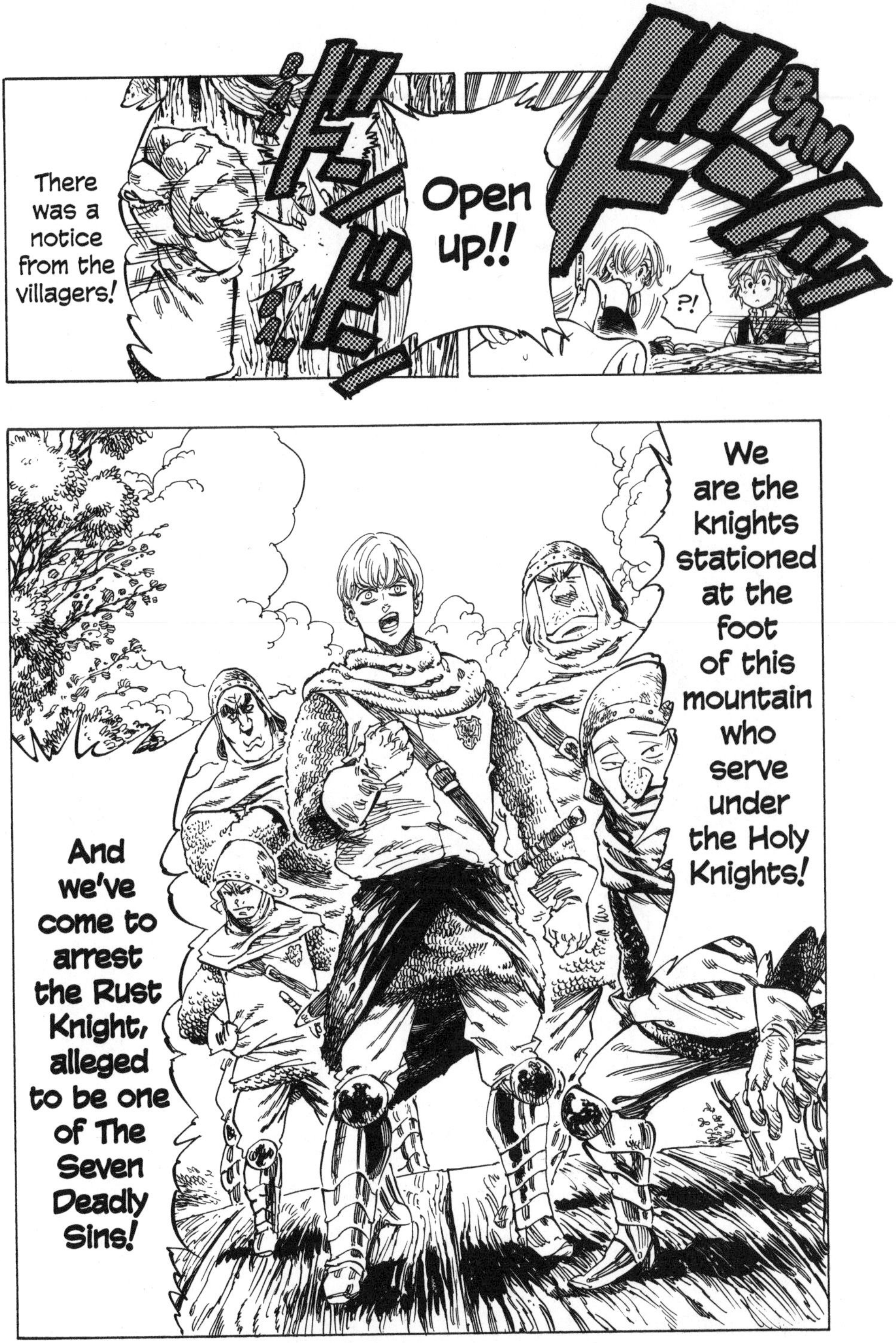
BAM!
?!
Open up!!
There was a notice from the villagers!
We are the knights stationed at the foot of this mountain who serve under the Holy Knights!
And we've come to arrest the Rust Knight, alleged to be one of The Seven Deadly Sins!

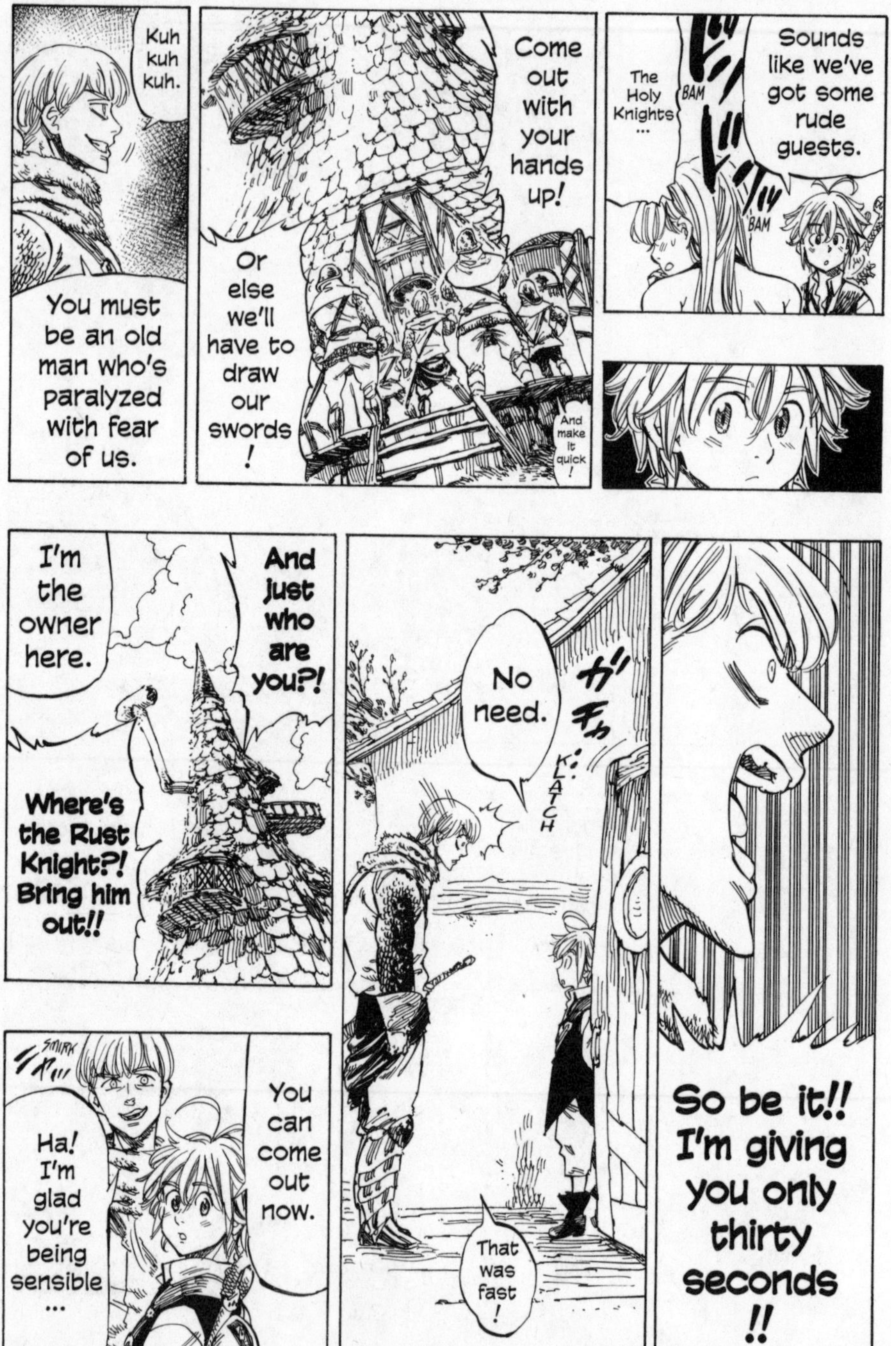
Sounds like we've got some rude guests.
The Holy Knights...
BAM
BAM
Come out with your hands up!
Or else we'll have to draw our swords!
And make it quick!
Kuh kuh kuh.
You must be an old man who's paralyzed with fear of us.
So be it!! I'm giving you only thirty seconds!!
No need.
KLATCH
That was fast!
And just who are you?!
I'm the owner here.
Where's the Rust Knight?! Bring him out!!
You can come out now.
SMIRK
Ha! I'm glad you're being sensible...

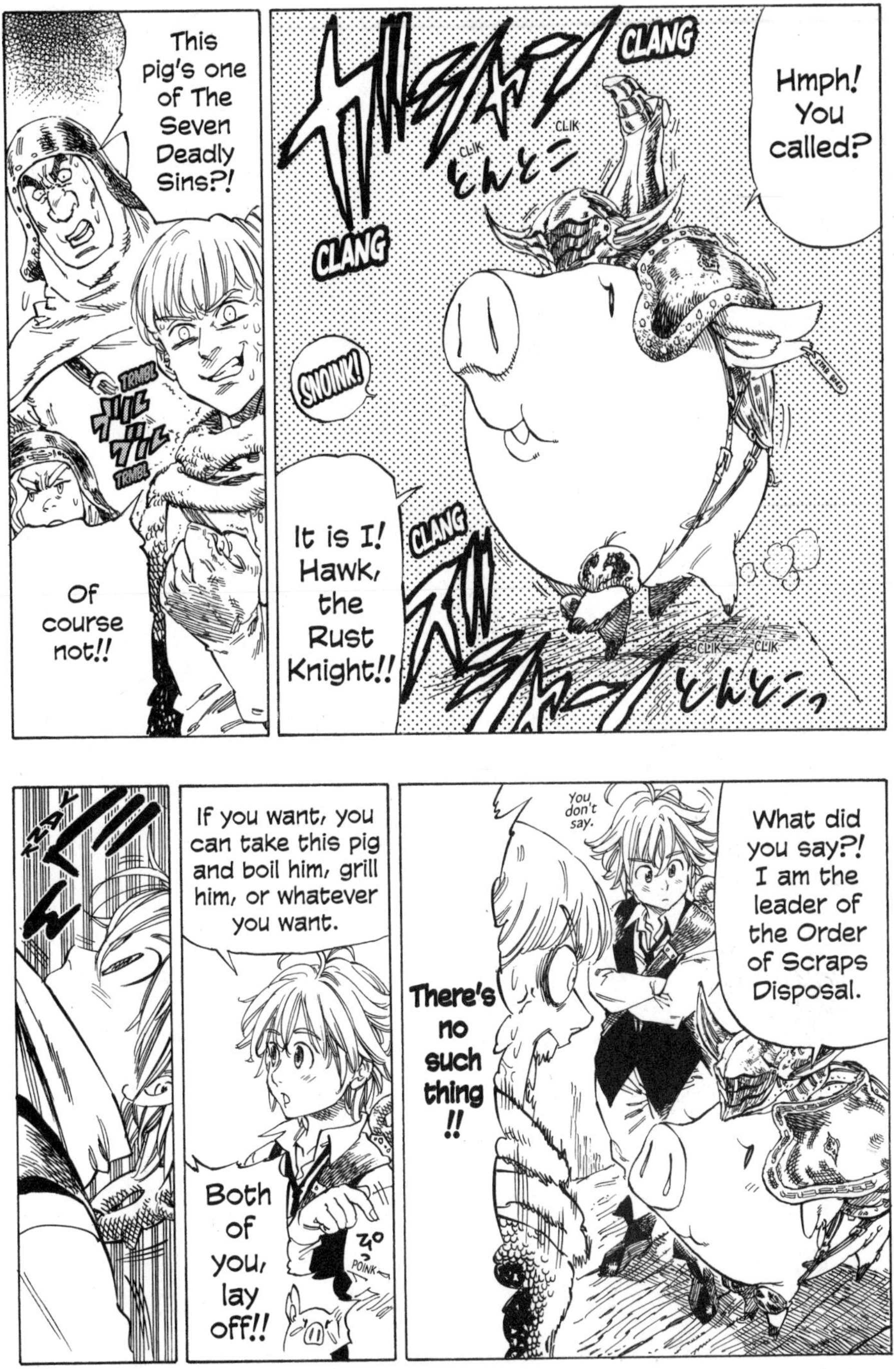
CLANG
Hmph! You called?
CLIK
CLIK
CLANG
SNOINK!
It is I! Hawk, the Rust Knight!!
CLANG
CLIK
CLIK
This pig's one of The Seven Deadly Sins?!
TRMBL
TRMBL
Of course not!!
What did you say?! I am the leader of the Order of Scraps Disposal.
You don't say.
There's no such thing!!
If you want, you can take this pig and boil him, grill him, or whatever you want.
Both of you, lay off!!
POINK

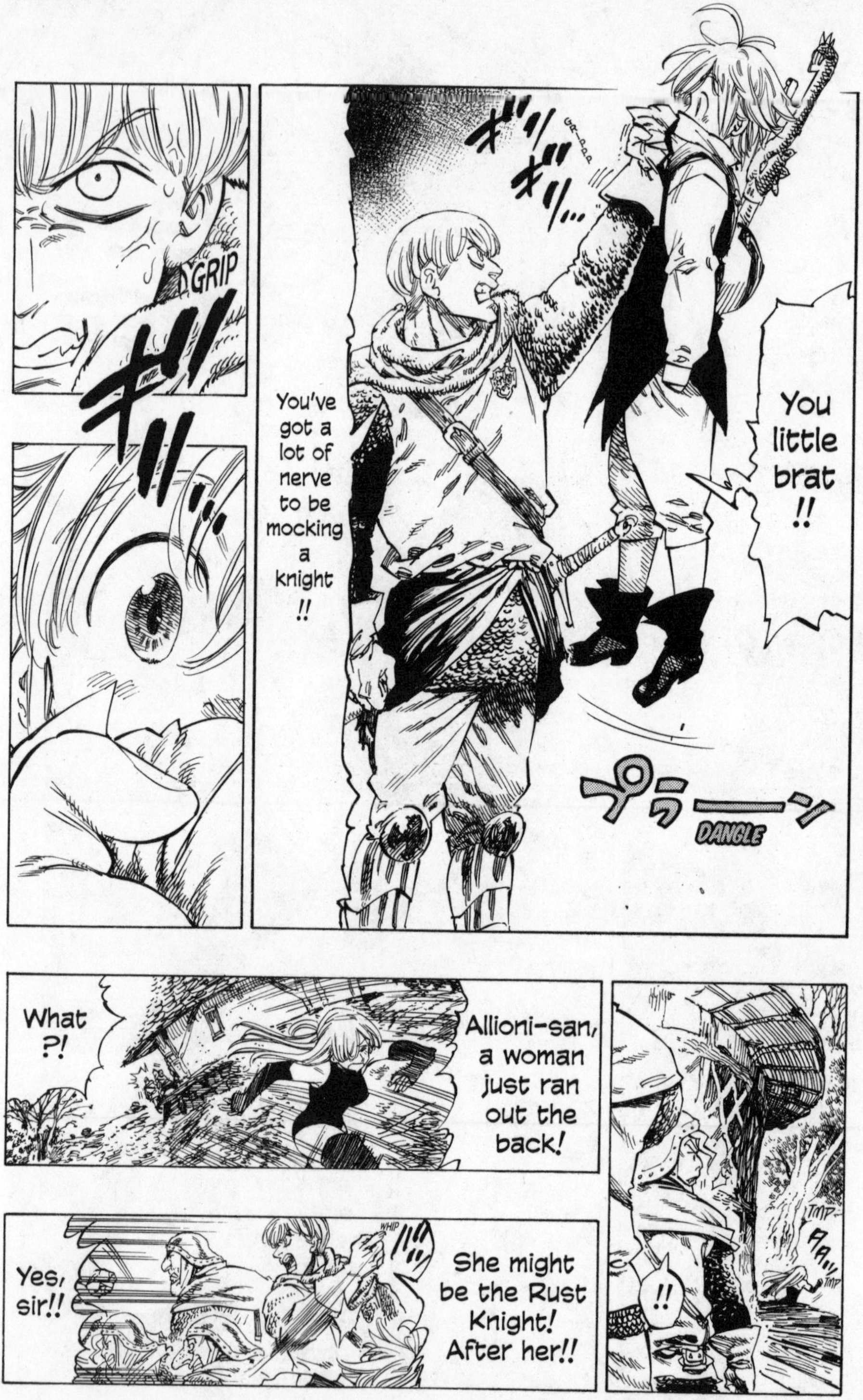

You little brat!!
You've got a lot of nerve to be mocking a knight!!
DANGLE
GRIP
!!
TMP
TMP
Allioni-san, a woman just ran out the back!
What?!
She might be the Rust Knight! After her!!
WHIP
Yes, sir!!

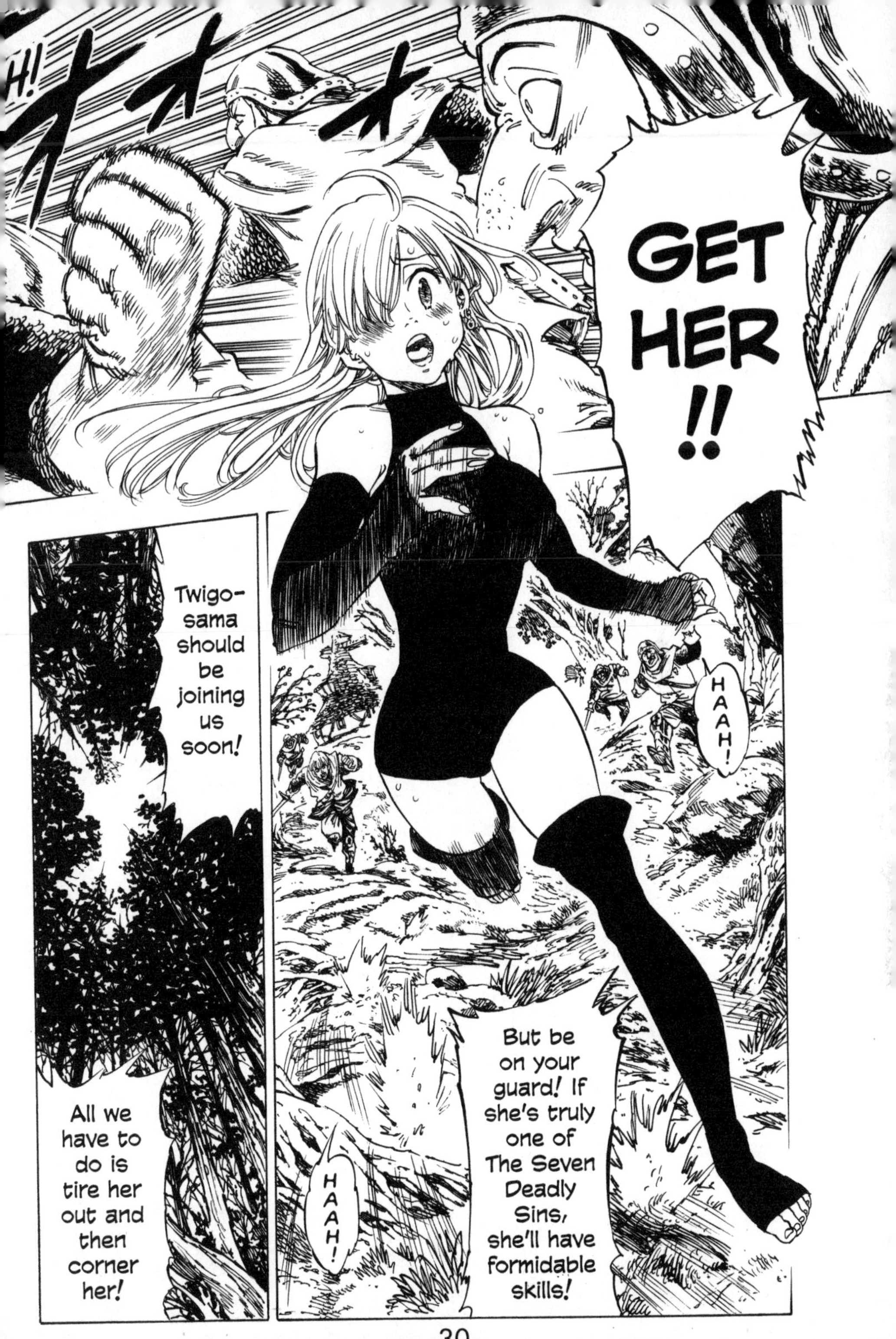

GET HER!!
H!
HAAAH!
But be on your guard! If she's truly one of The Seven Deadly Sins, she'll have formidable skills!
HAAAH!
Twigo-sama should be joining us soon!
All we have to do is tire her out and then corner her!

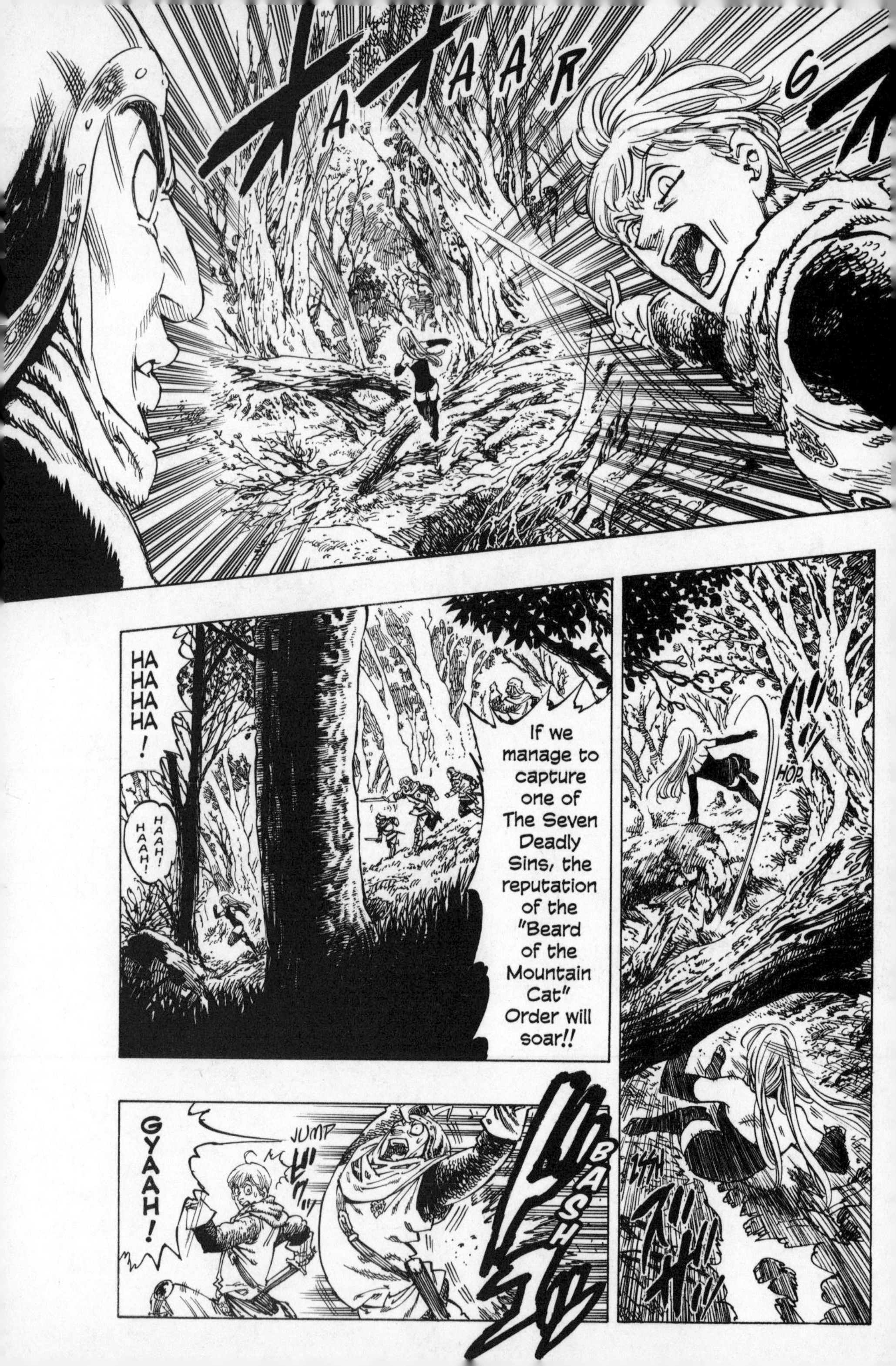
AAARG
HOP
If we manage to capture one of The Seven Deadly Sins, the reputation of the "Beard of the Mountain Cat" Order will soar!!
HA HA HA HA!
HAAAH! HAAAH!
BASH
JUMP
GYAAH!

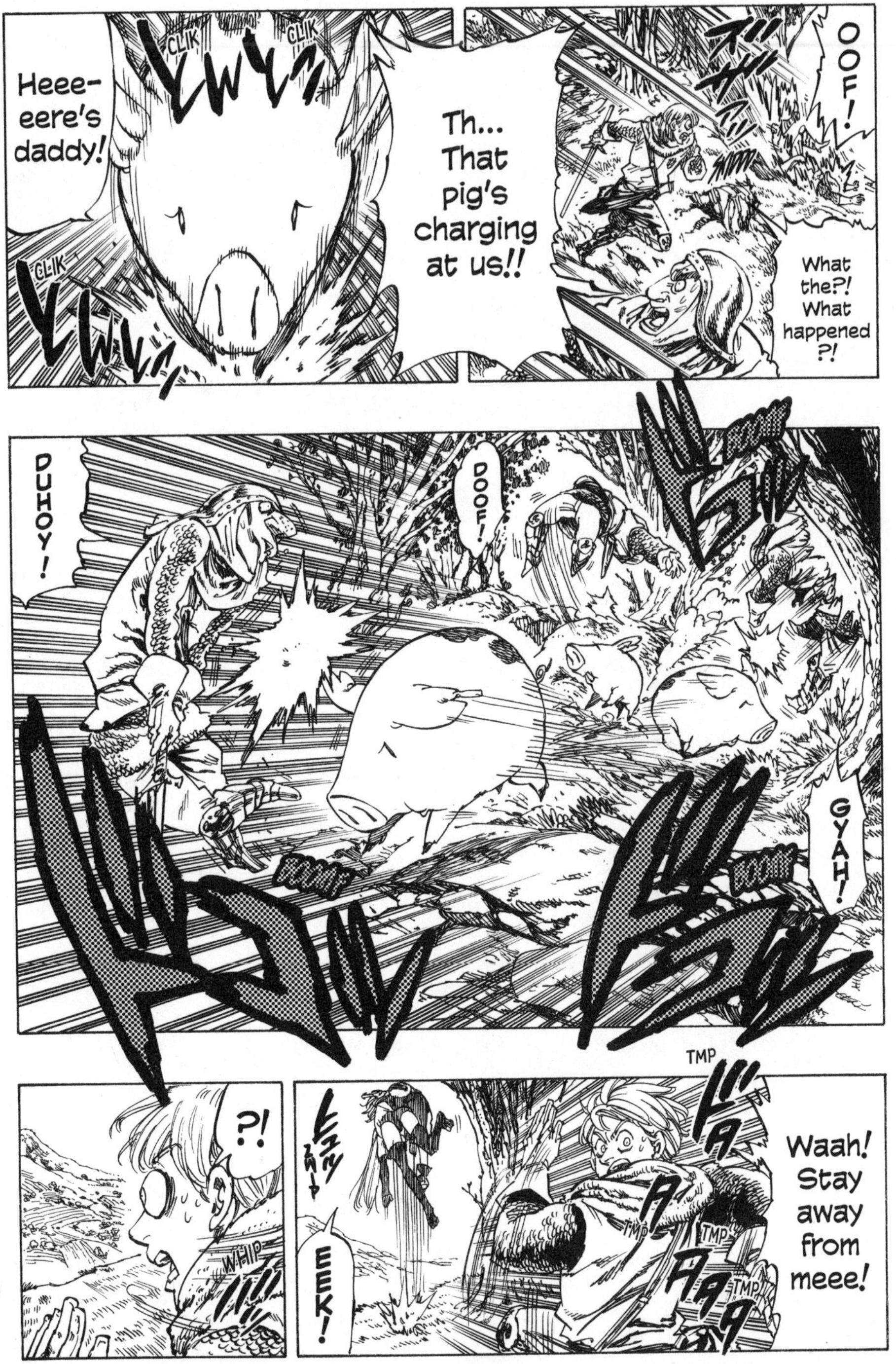
OOF!
What the?! What happened?!
Th... That pig's charging at us!!
CLIK
CLIK
Heeee-eere's daddy!
CLIK
GYAH!
DOOF!
DUHOY!
TMP
Waah! Stay away from meee!
TMP
TMP
TMP
ZWIP
EEK!
?!
WHIP

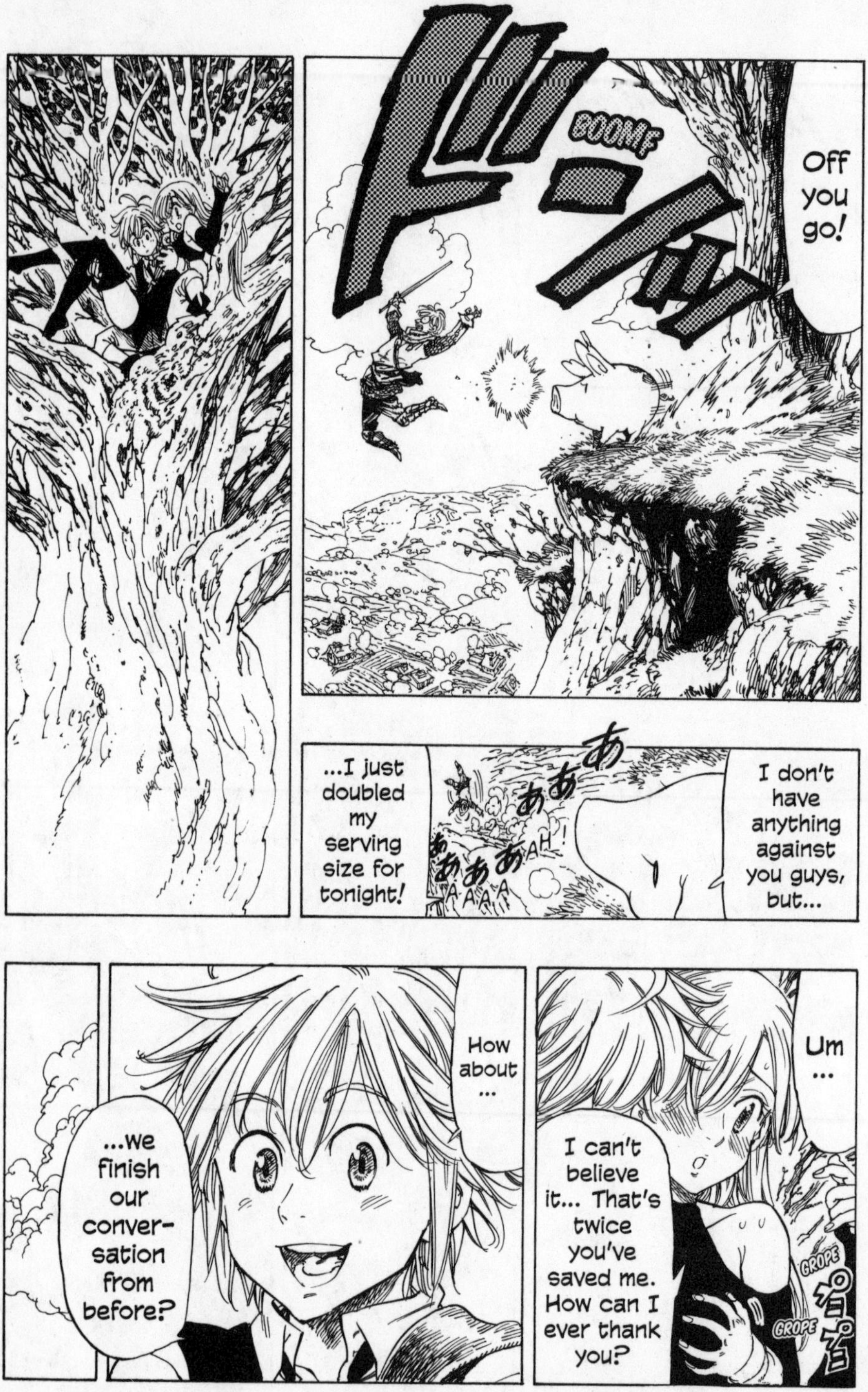

ドーン
BOOM!
Off you go!
I don't have anything against you guys, but...
AAAAH!
...I just doubled my serving size for tonight!
Um ...
I can't believe it... That's twice you've saved me. How can I ever thank you?
GROPE
GROPE
How about ...
...we finish our conversation from before?

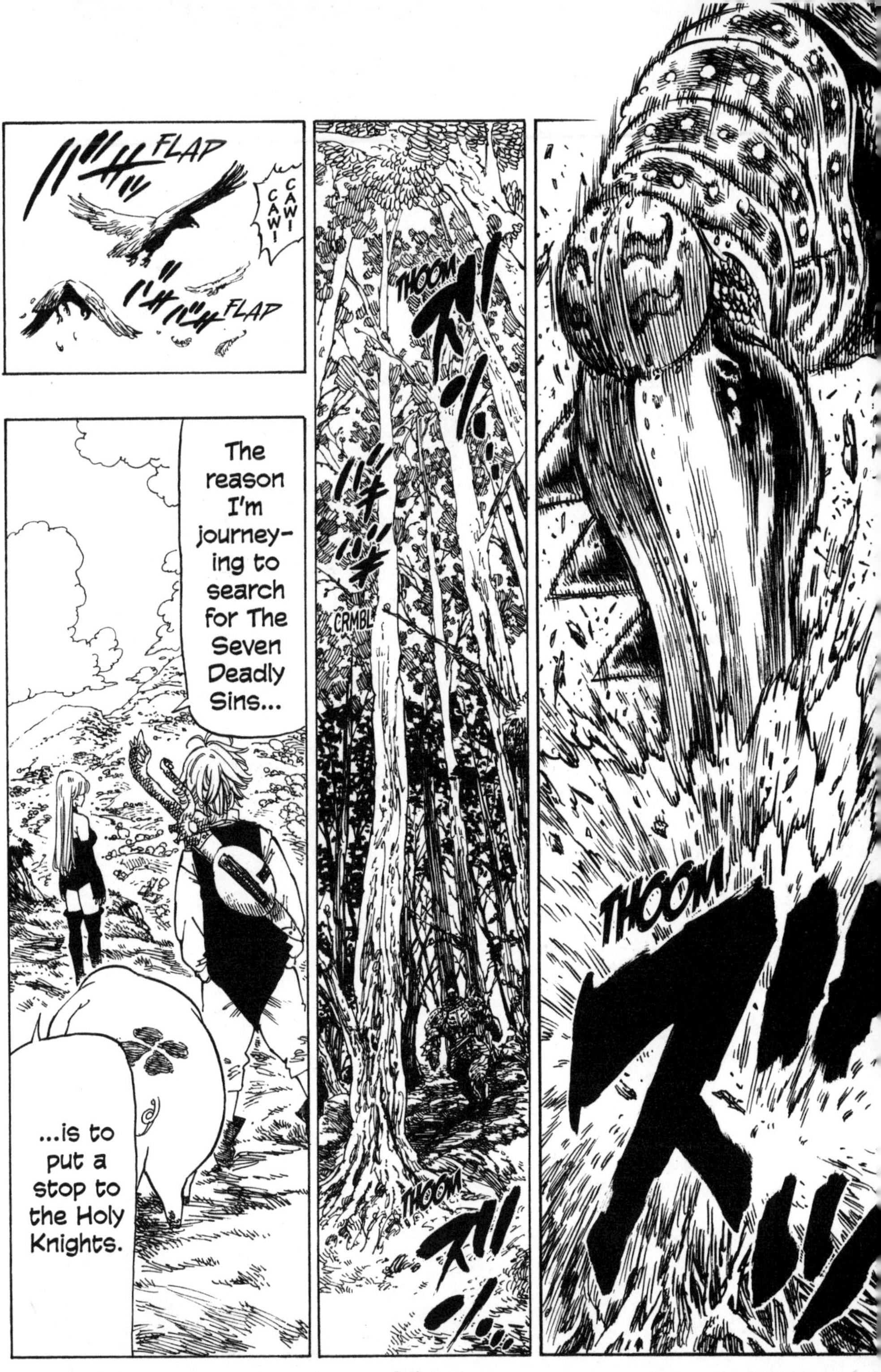
THOOM
THOOM
THOOM
CRMBL
THOOM
FLAP
CAW! CAW!
FLAP
The reason I'm journey-ing to search for The Seven Deadly Sins...
...is to put a stop to the Holy Knights.

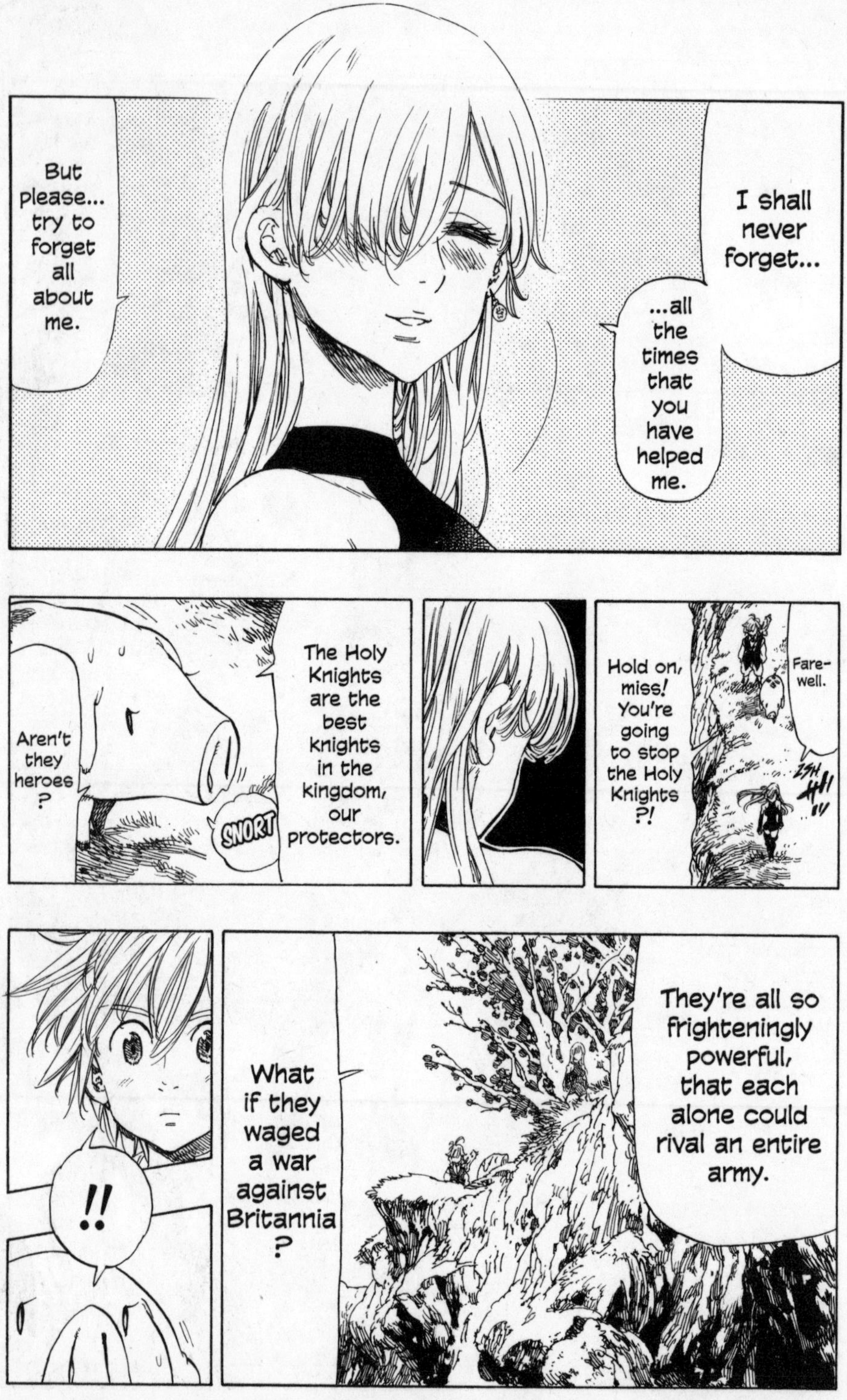

I shall never forget...
...all the times that you have helped me.
But please... try to forget all about me.
Fare-well.
Hold on, miss! You're going to stop the Holy Knights?!
The Holy Knights are the best knights in the kingdom, our protectors.
SNORT
Aren't they heroes?
They're all so frighteningly powerful, that each alone could rival an entire army.
What if they waged a war against Britannia?
!!

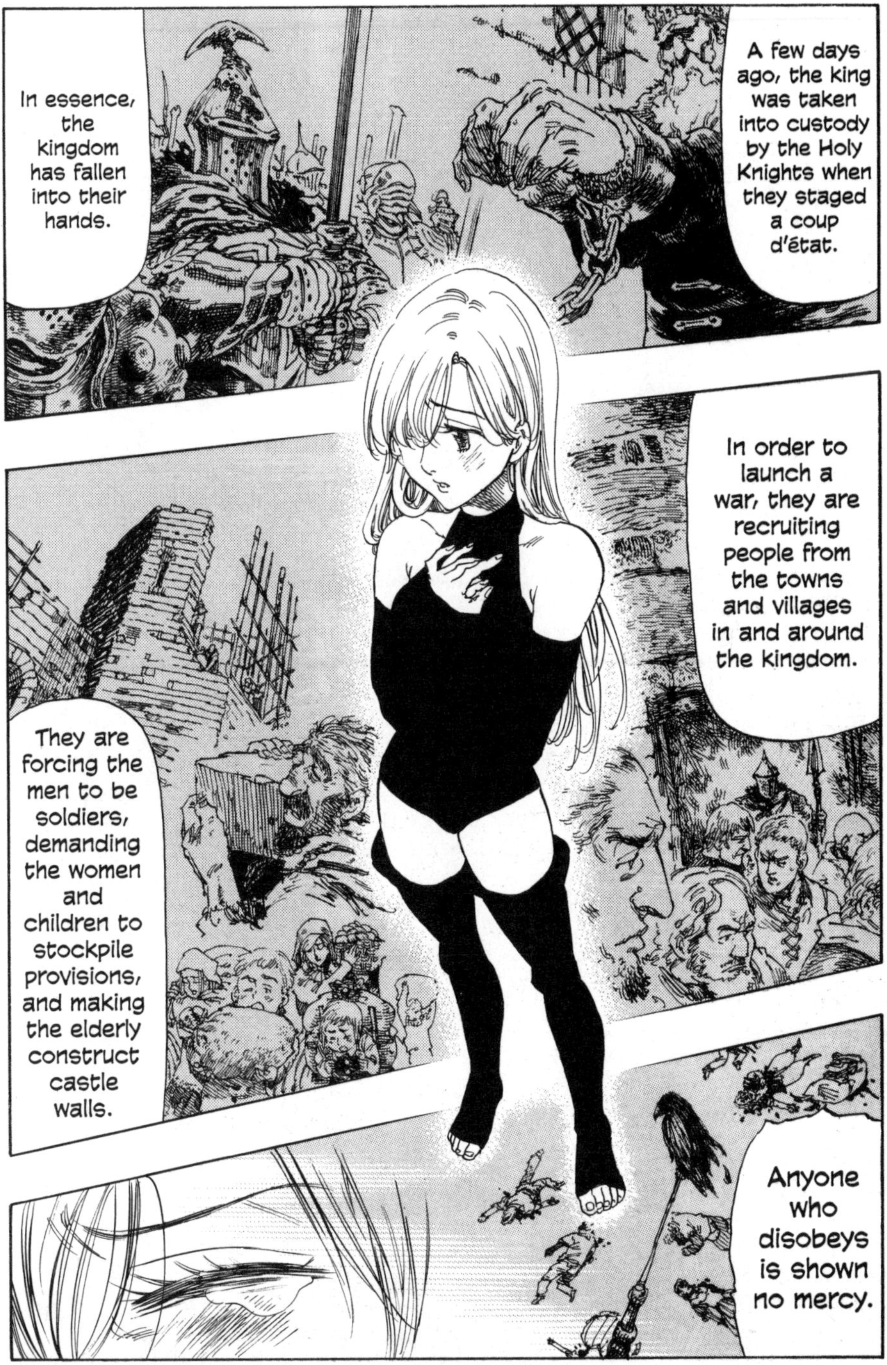
A few days ago, the king was taken into custody by the Holy Knights when they staged a coup d'état.
In essence, the kingdom has fallen into their hands.
In order to launch a war, they are recruiting people from the towns and villages in and around the kingdom.
They are forcing the men to be soldiers, demanding the women and children to stockpile provisions, and making the elderly construct castle walls.
Anyone who disobeys is shown no mercy.

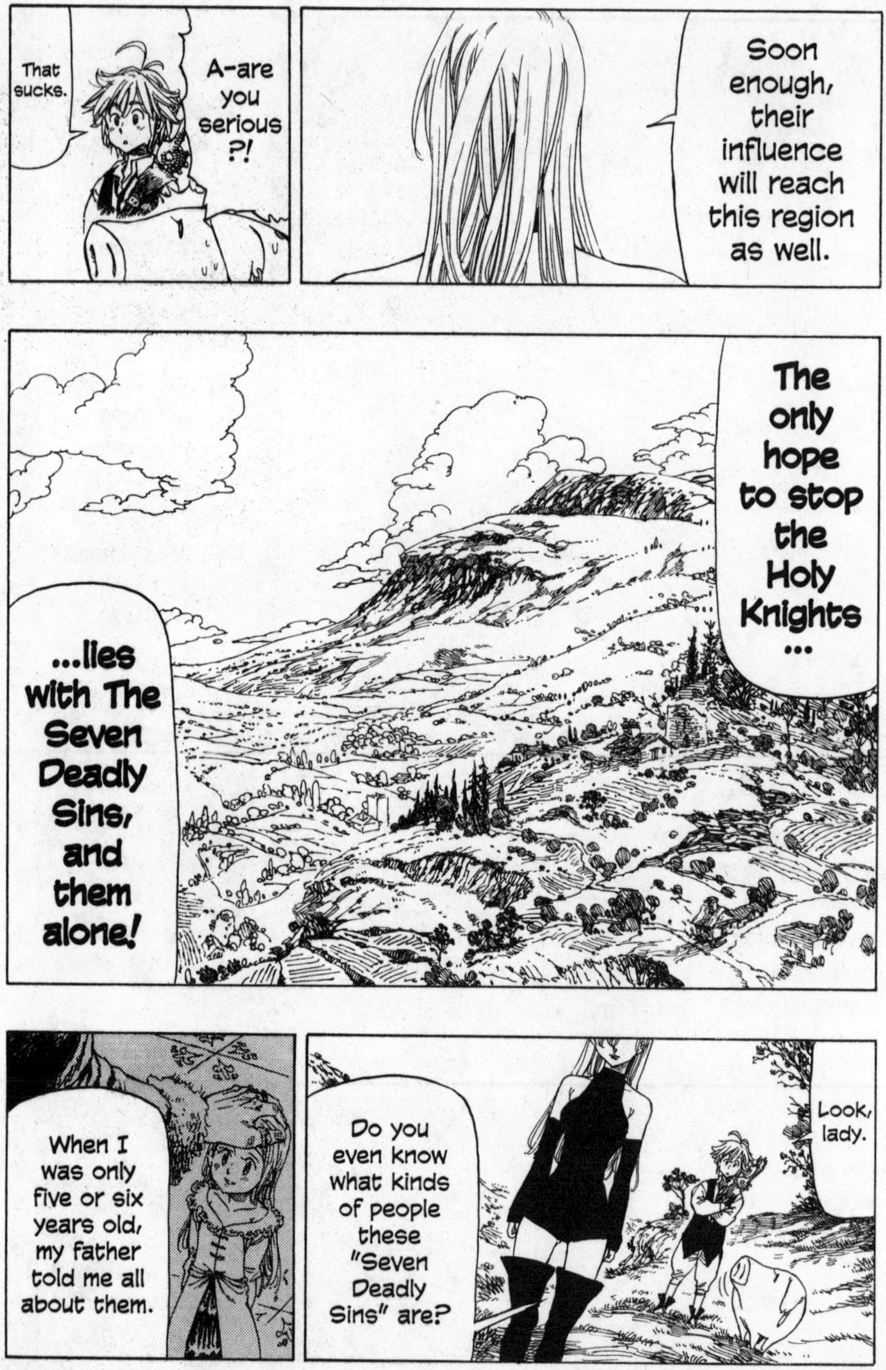
Soon enough, their influence will reach this region as well.
A-are you serious?!
That sucks.
The only hope to stop the Holy Knights...
...lies with The Seven Deadly Sins, and them alone!
Look, lady.
Do you even know what kinds of people these "Seven Deadly Sins" are?
When I was only five or six years old, my father told me all about them.

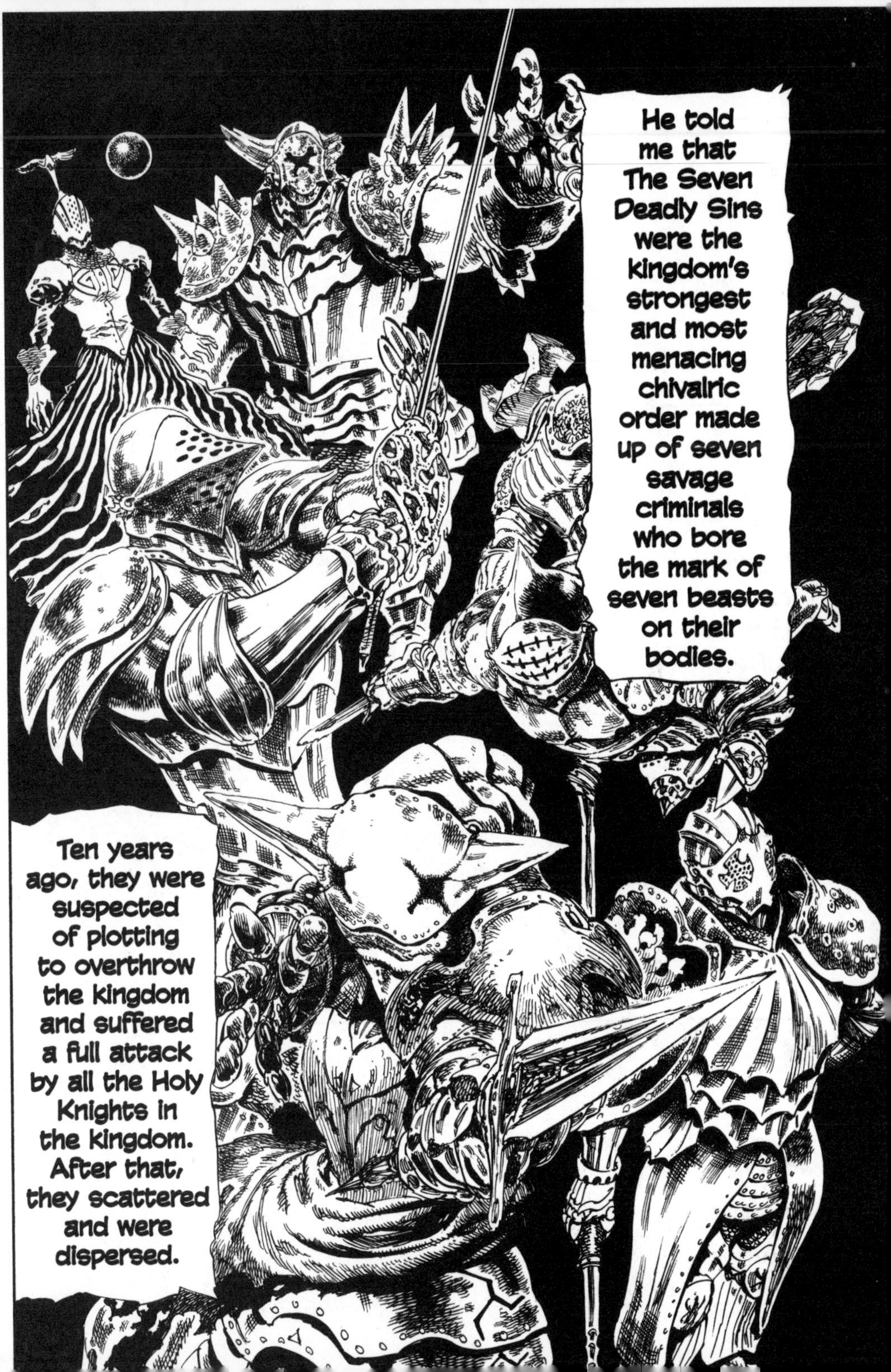
He told me that The Seven Deadly Sins were the kingdom's strongest and most menacing chivalric order made up of seven savage criminals who bore the mark of seven beasts on their bodies.
Ten years ago, they were suspected of plotting to overthrow the kingdom and suffered a full attack by all the Holy Knights in the kingdom. After that, they scattered and were dispersed.

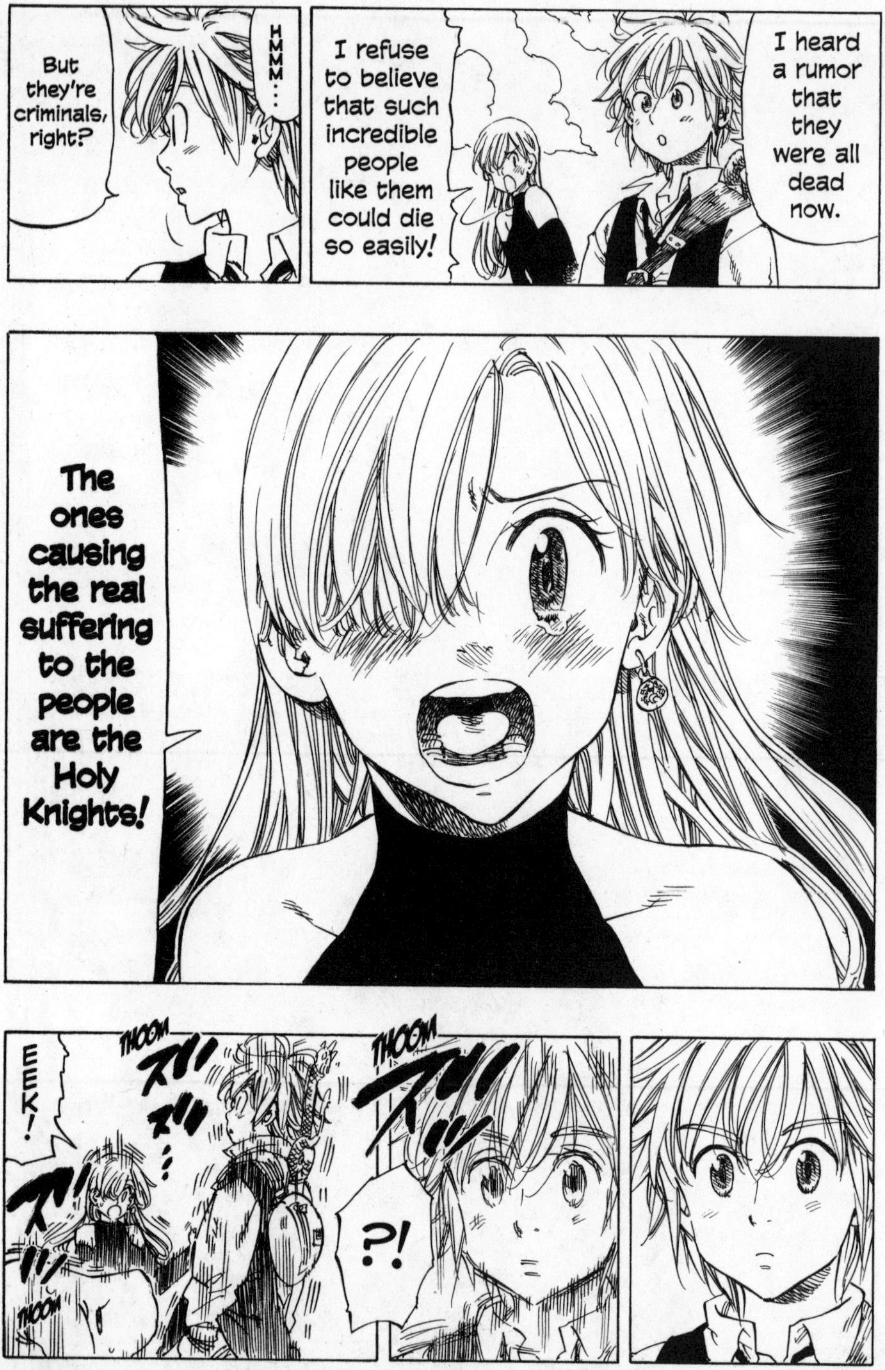
I heard a rumor that they were all dead now.
I refuse to believe that such incredible people like them could die so easily!
HMMM...
But they're criminals, right?
The ones causing the real suffering to the people are the Holy Knights!
THOOM
?!
THOOM
EEK!
THOOM

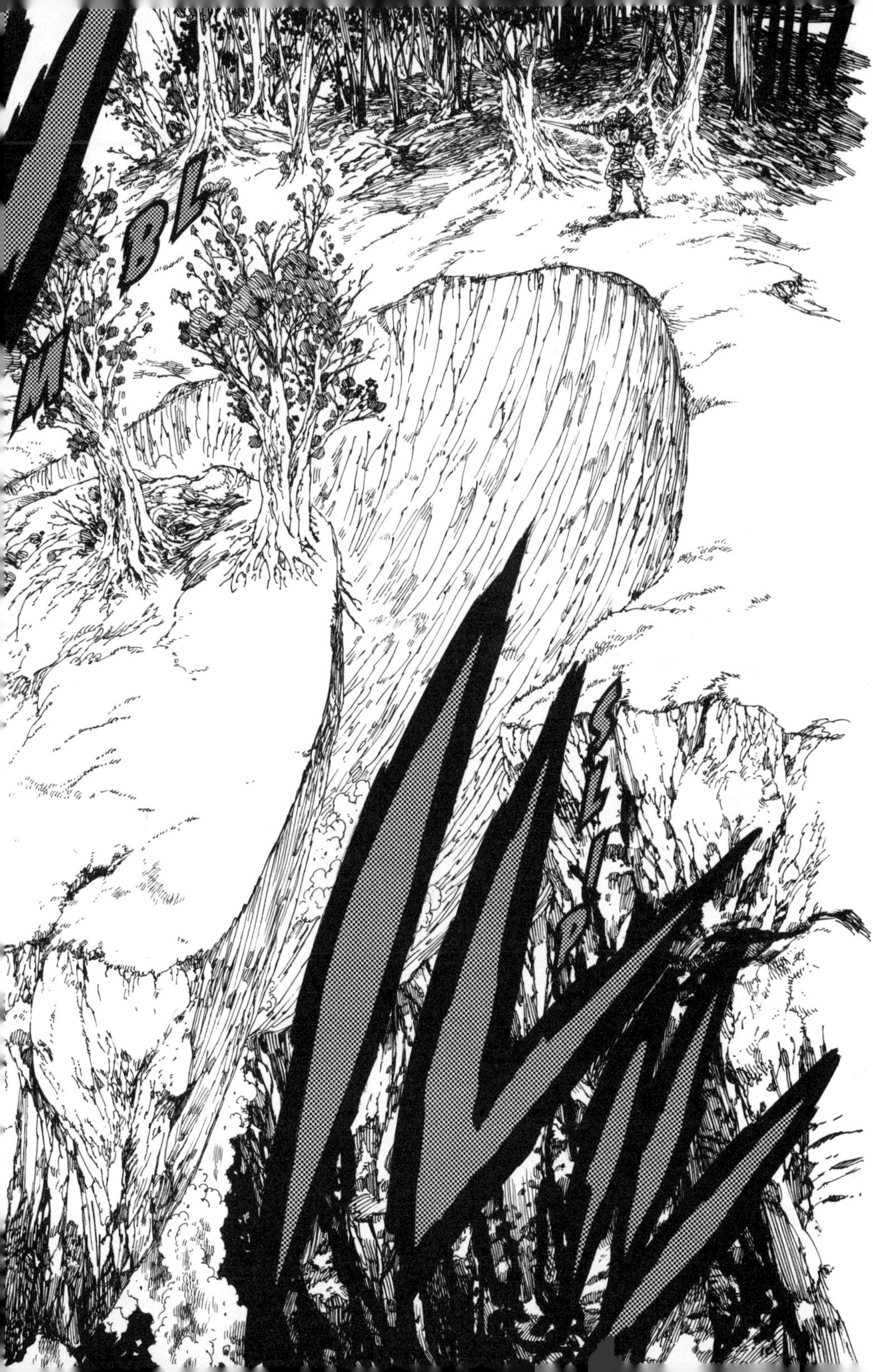

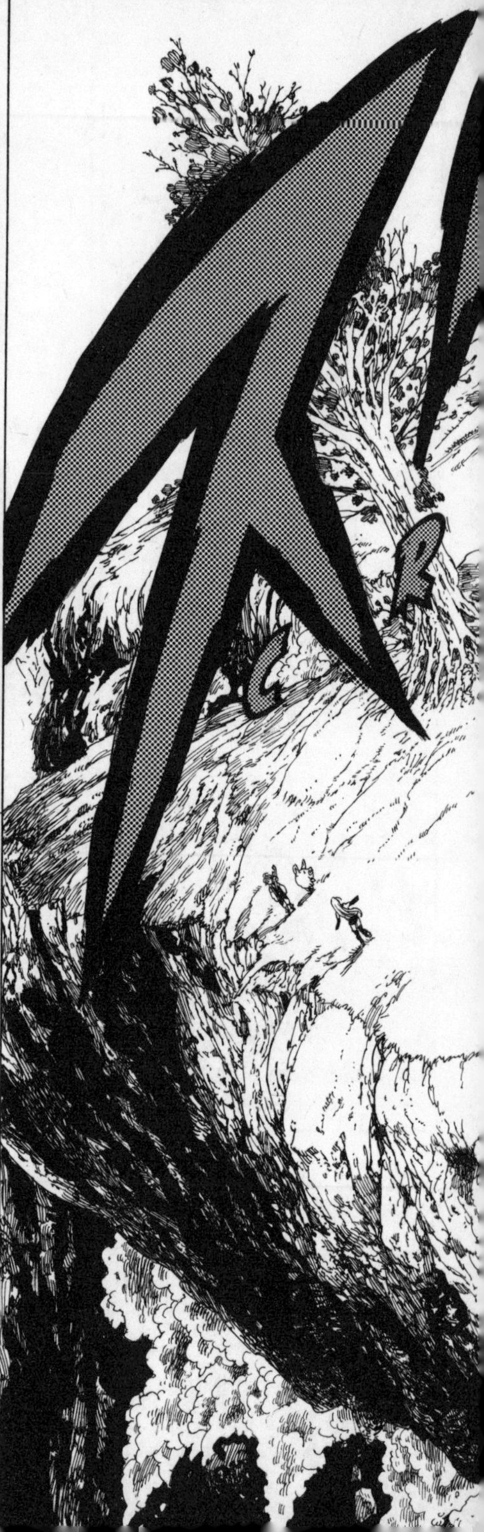

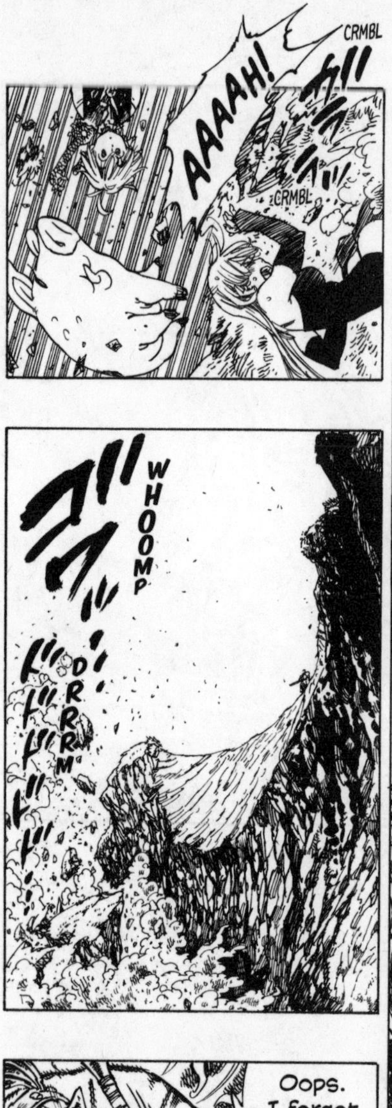
CRMBL
AAAAH!
CRMBL
WHOOOMP
DRRRRM
Oops. I forgot to check if they were the people from the report or not.
CHINKT

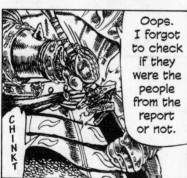

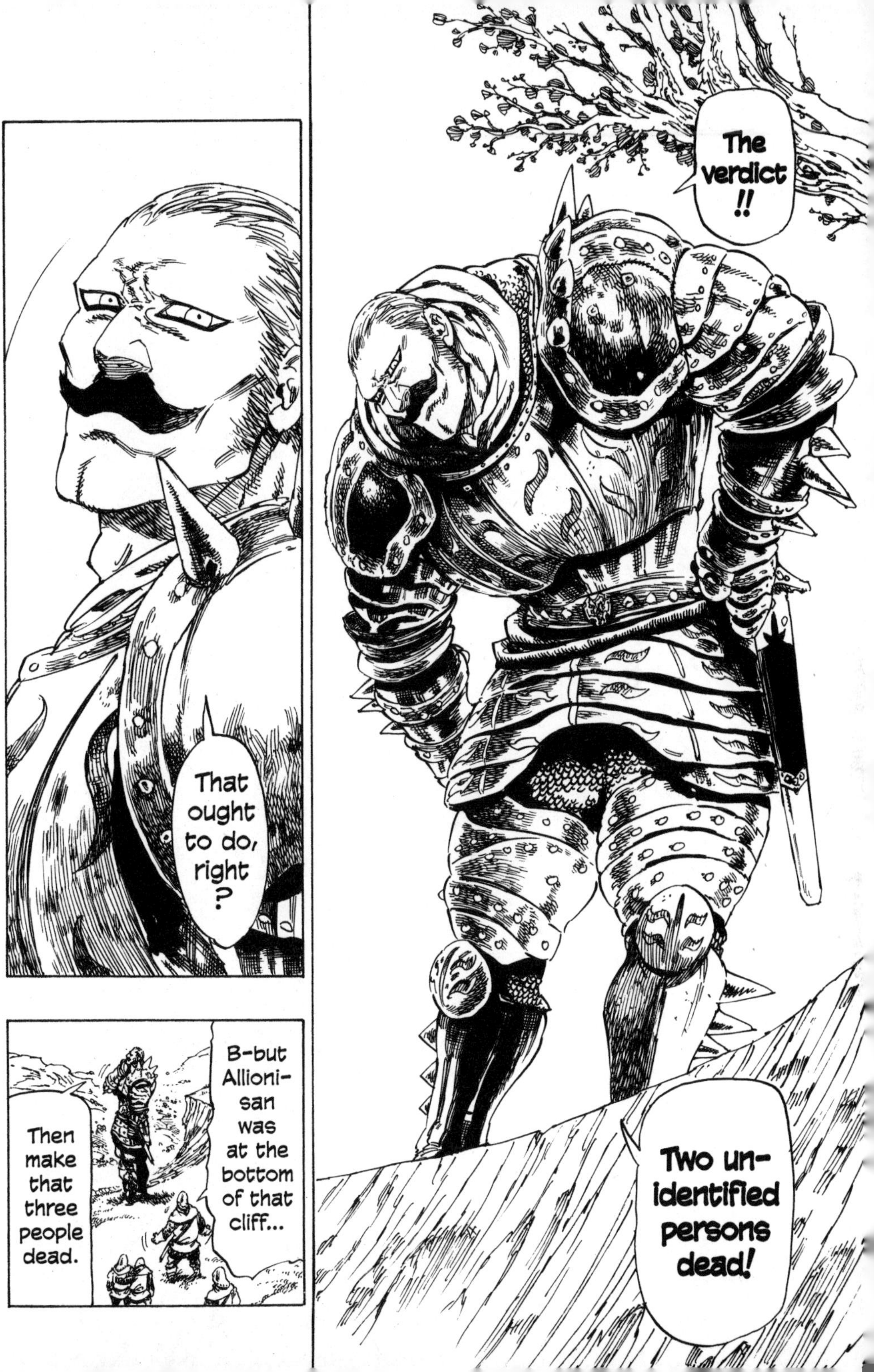
The verdict !!
Two un-identified persons dead!
That ought to do, right?
B-but Allioni-san was at the bottom of that cliff...
Then make that three people dead.

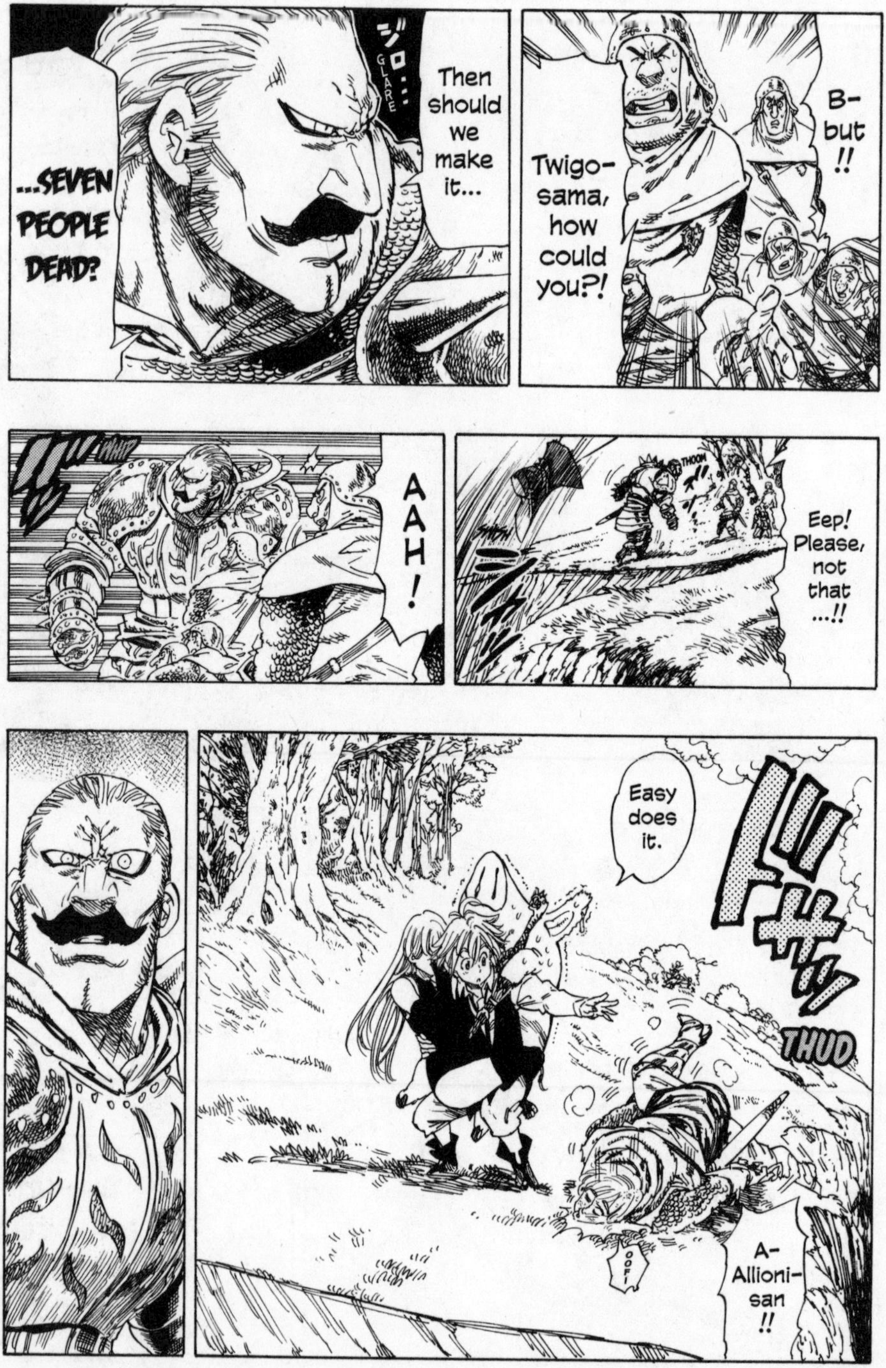
B-but!!
Twigo-sama, how could you?!
ジロ…
GLARE
Then should we make it...
...SEVEN PEOPLE DEAD?
THOOM
Eep! Please, not that ...!!
WHIP
AAH!
THUD
Easy does it.
OOF!
A-Allioni-san!!

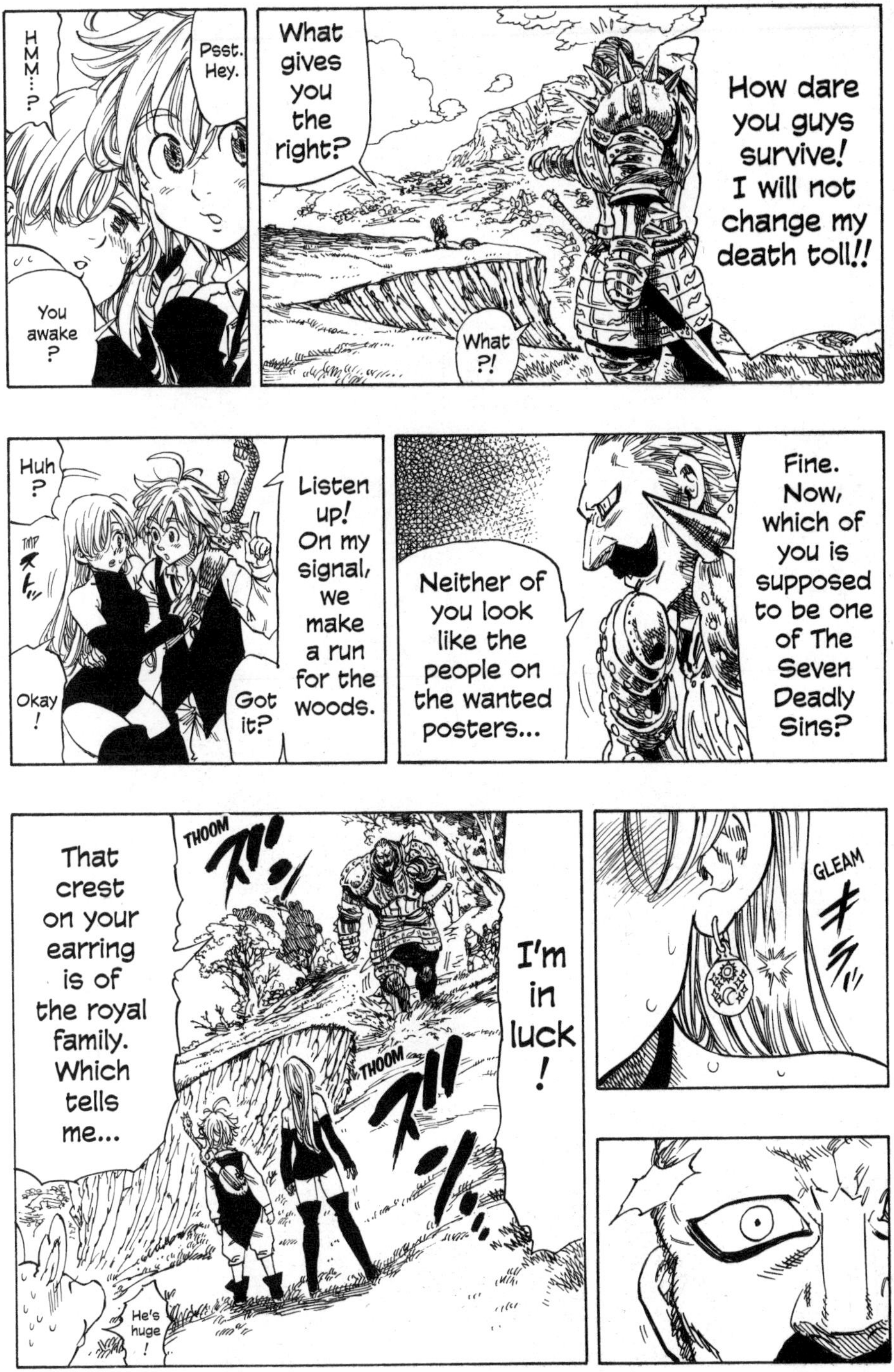
How dare you guys survive! I will not change my death toll!!
What gives you the right?
What?!
Psst. Hey.
HMM...?
You awake?
Fine. Now, which of you is supposed to be one of The Seven Deadly Sins?
Neither of you look like the people on the wanted posters...
Listen up! On my signal, we make a run for the woods.
Got it?
Huh?
TMP
Okay!
GLEAM
I'm in luck!
THOOM
That crest on your earring is of the royal family. Which tells me...
THOOM
He's huge!

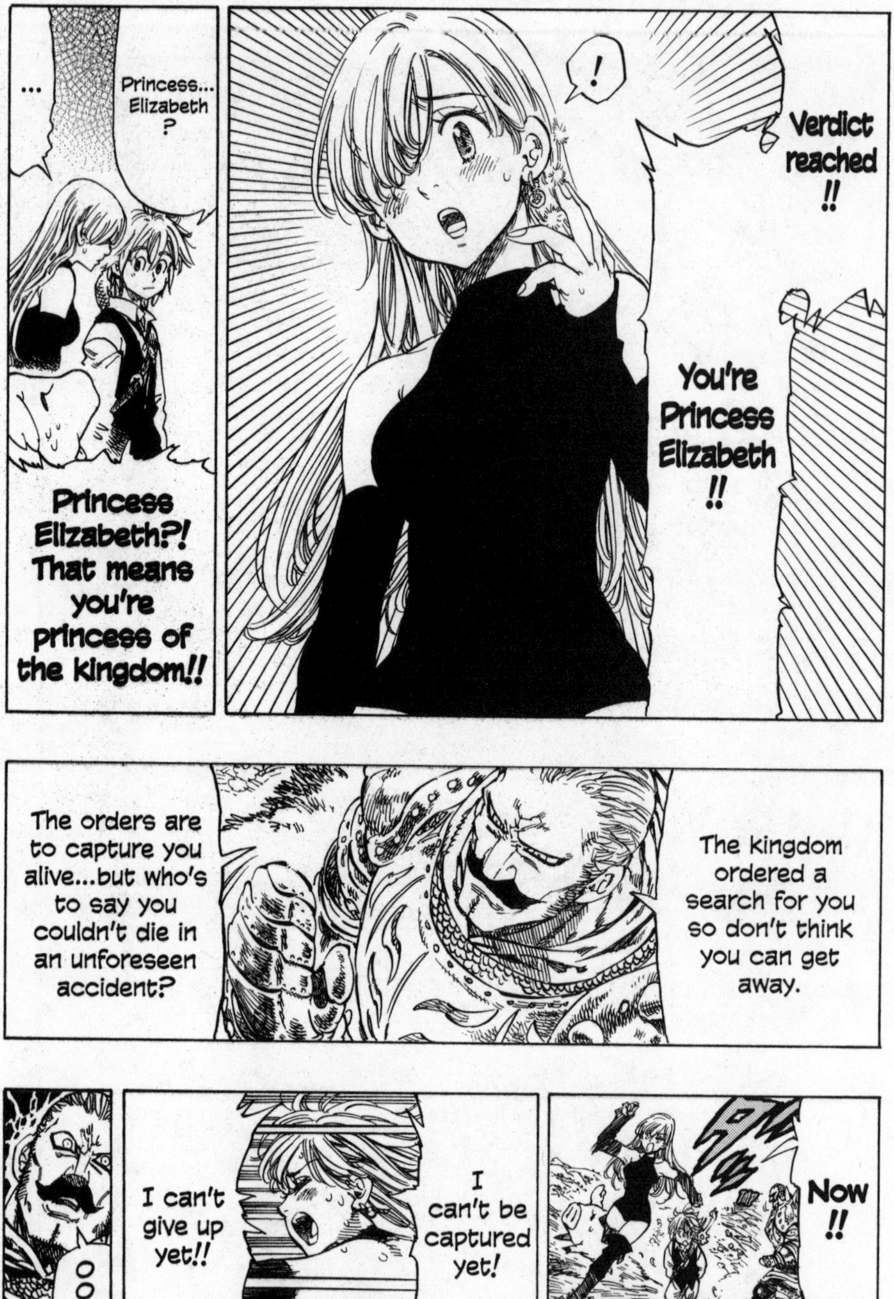
!
Verdict reached!!
You're Princess Elizabeth!!
Princess... Elizabeth?
...
Princess Elizabeth?! That means you're princess of the kingdom!!
The kingdom ordered a search for you so don't think you can get away.
The orders are to capture you alive...but who's to say you couldn't die in an unforeseen accident?
Now!!
I can't be captured yet!
I can't give up yet!!
OOH...

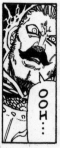

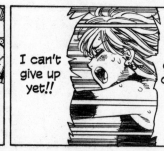

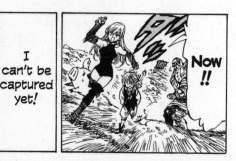

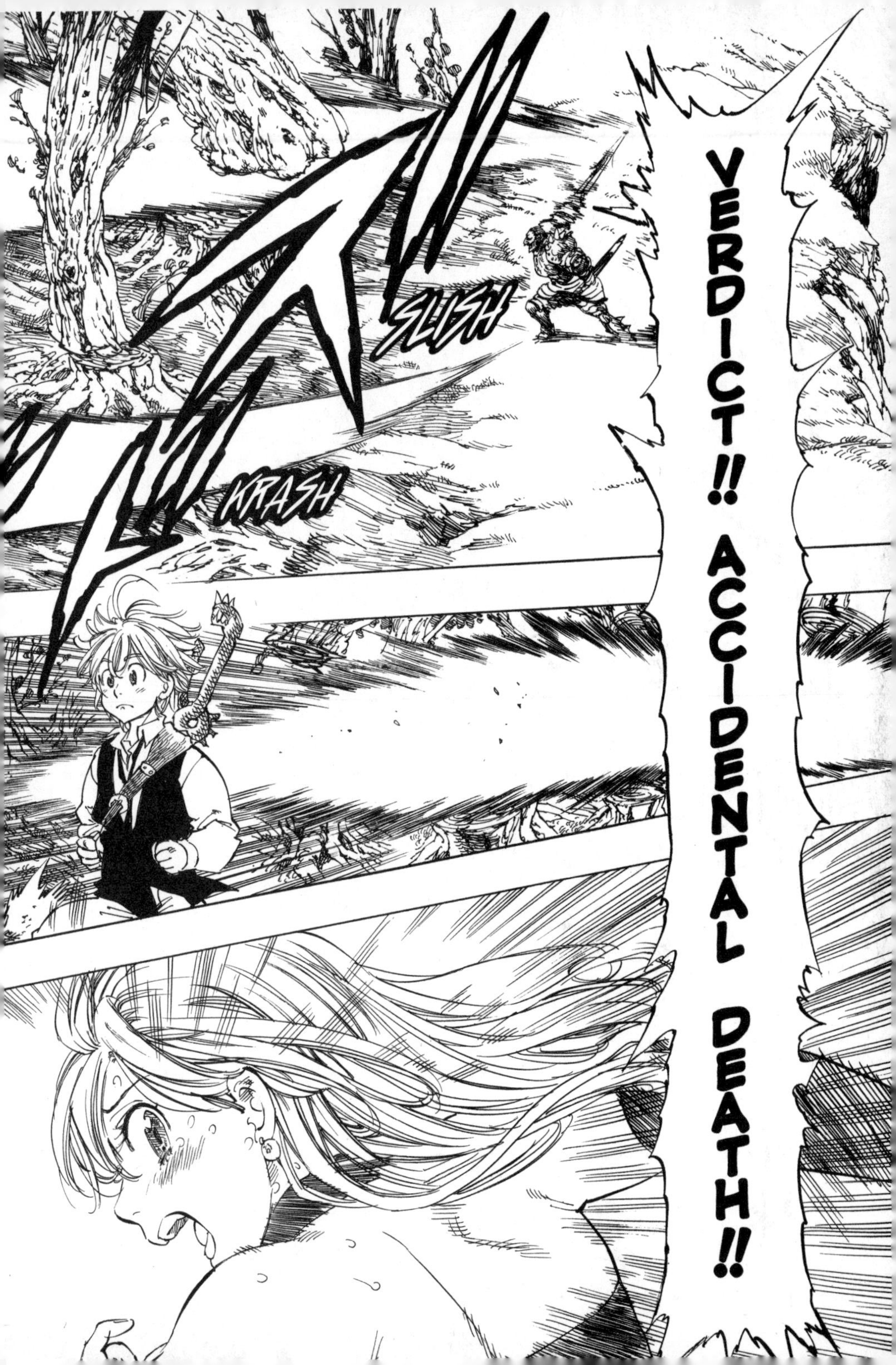
VERDICT!! ACCIDENTAL DEATH!!
SLISH
KRASH

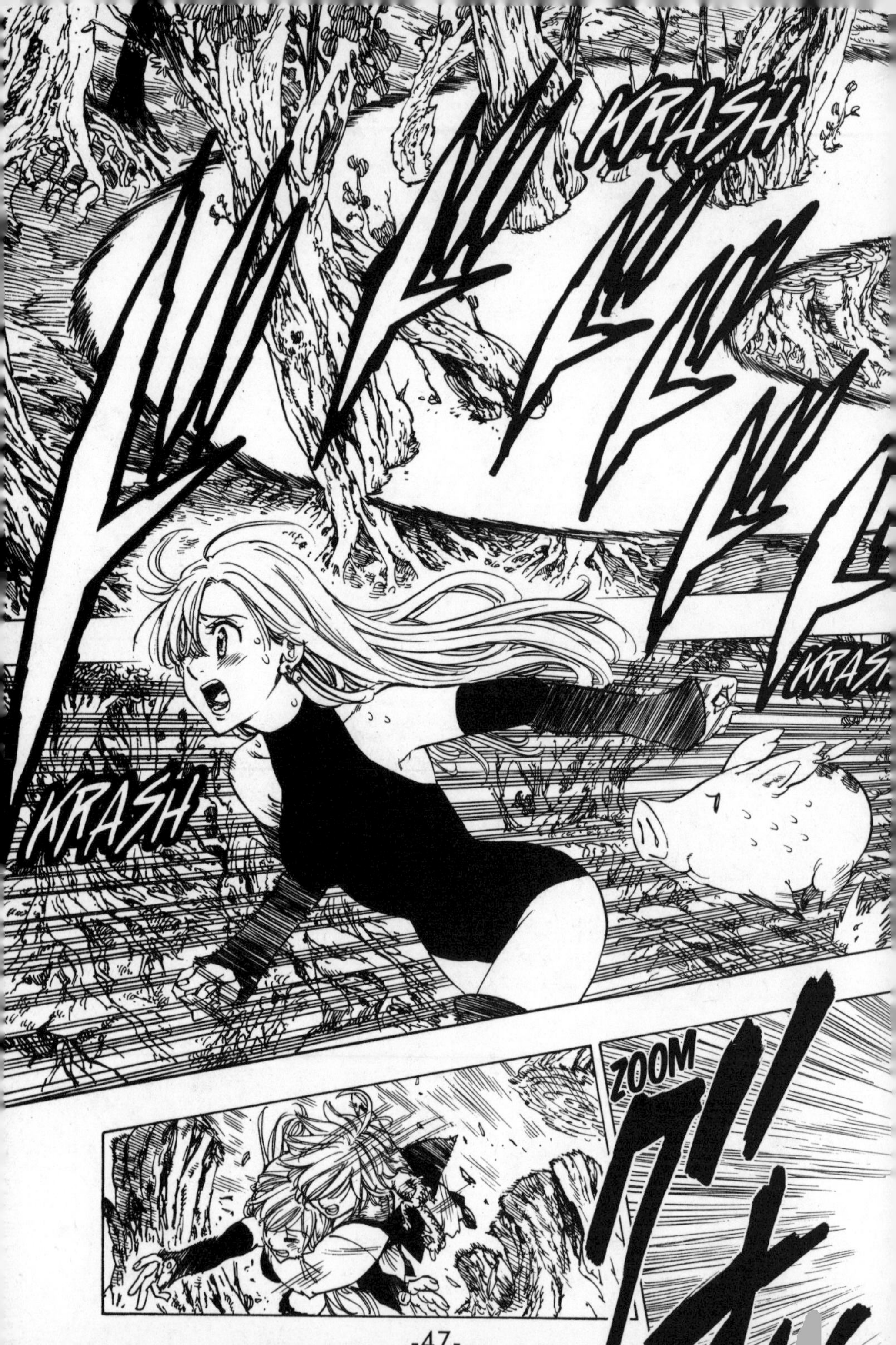
KRASH
KRAS
KRASH
ZOOM

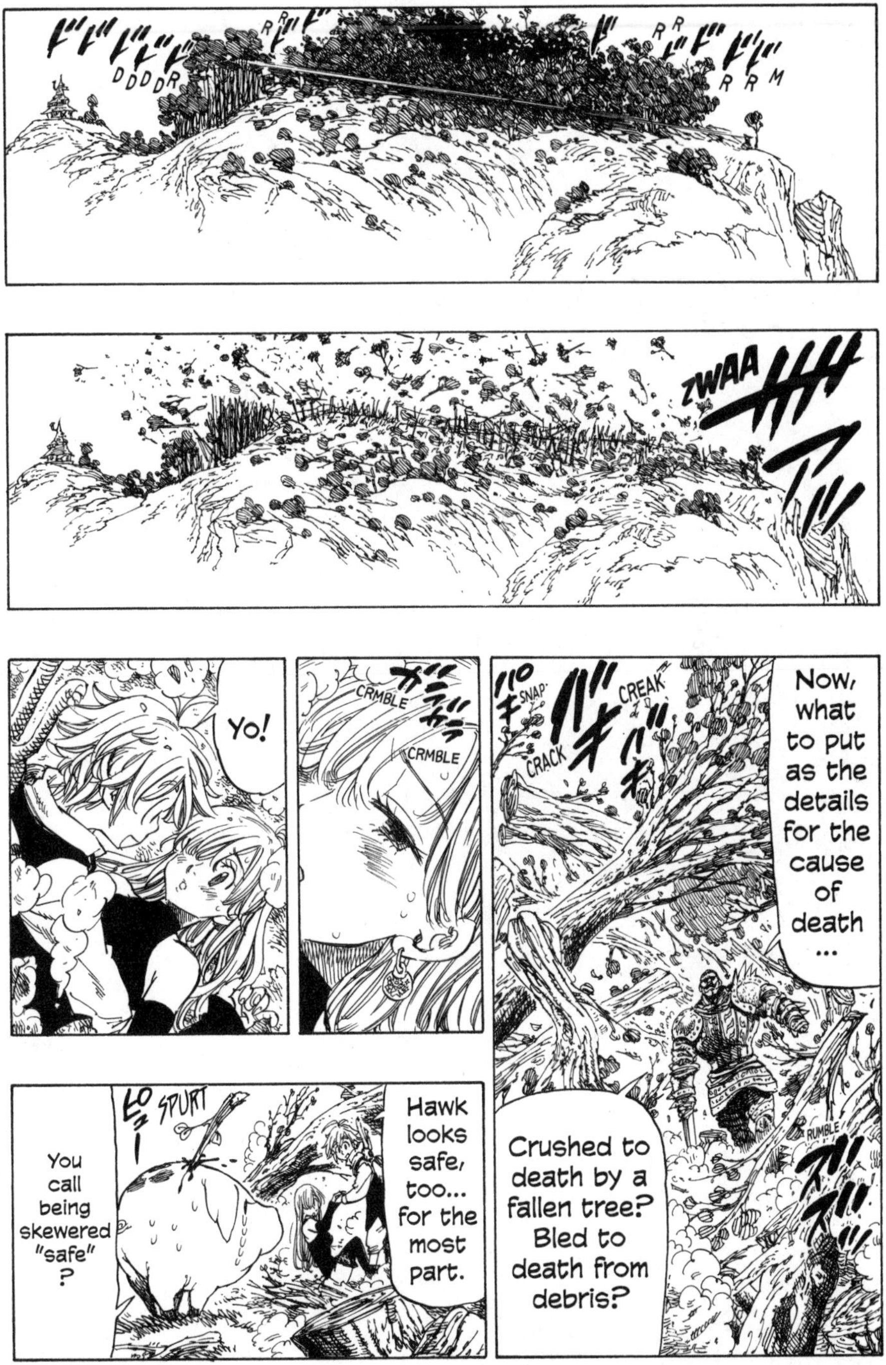
DDDDR
RR
RRM
ZWAA
SNAP
CRACK
CREAK
Now, what to put as the details for the cause of death ...
RUMBLE
Crushed to death by a fallen tree? Bled to death from debris?
CRMBLE
CRMBLE
Yo!
Hawk looks safe, too... for the most part.
SPURT
You call being skewered "safe"?

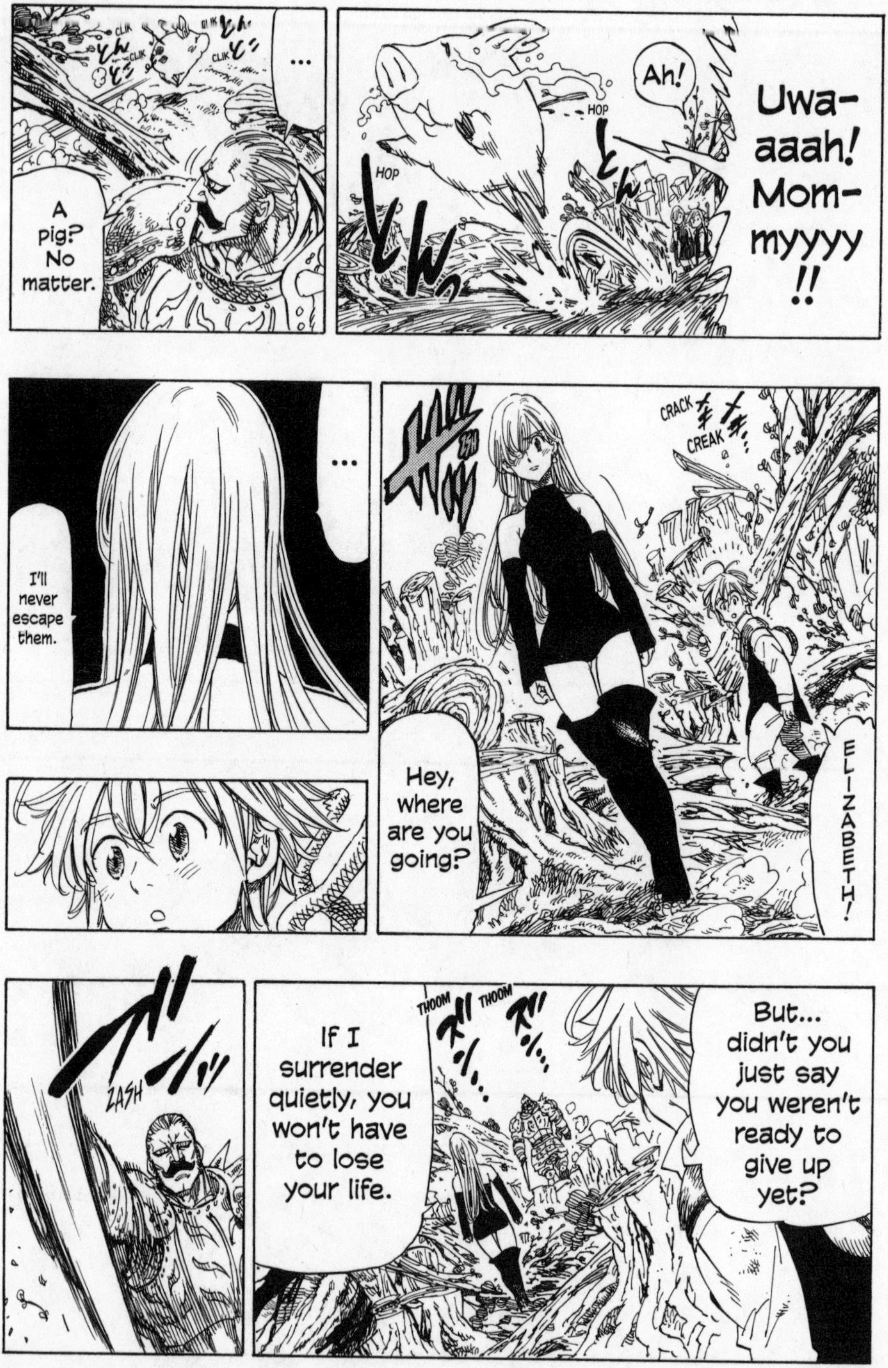

Uwa-aaah! Mom-myyyy!!
Ah!
HOP
HOP
...
CLIK
CLIK
A pig? No matter.
CRACK
CREAK
ELIZABETH!
Hey, where are you going?
...
I'll never escape them.
But... didn't you just say you weren't ready to give up yet?
THOOM
THOOM
If I surrender quietly, you won't have to lose your life.
ZASH

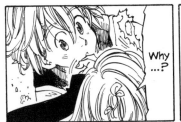

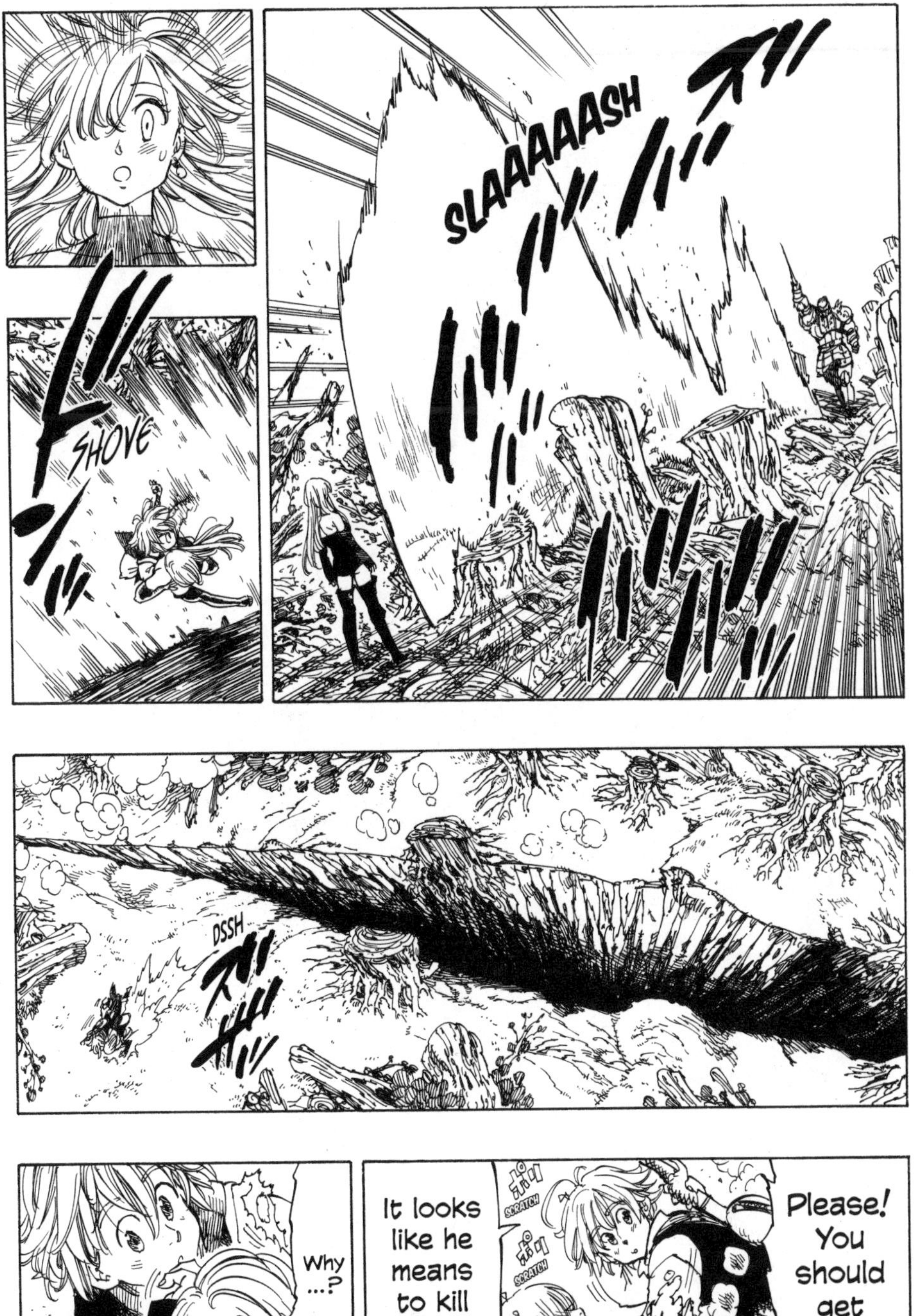
SLAAAAASH
SHOVE
DSSH
Please! You should get away!!
SCRATCH
SCRATCH
It looks like he means to kill us both.
Why ...?

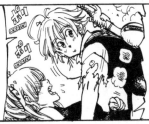

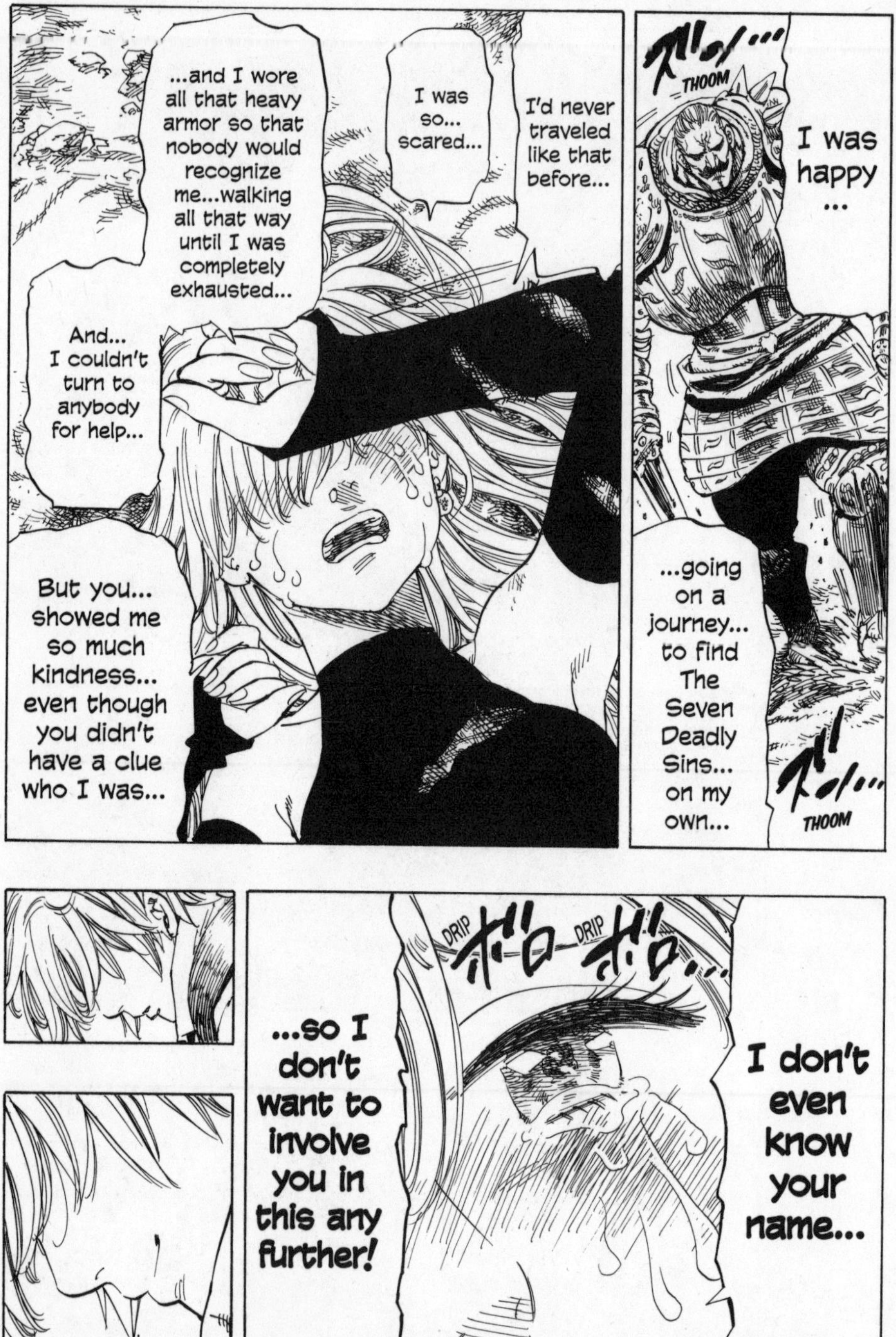
THOOM
I was happy...
...going on a journey... to find The Seven Deadly Sins... on my own...
THOOM
I'd never traveled like that before...
I was so... scared...
...and I wore all that heavy armor so that nobody would recognize me...walking all that way until I was completely exhausted...
And... I couldn't turn to anybody for help...
But you... showed me so much kindness... even though you didn't have a clue who I was...
DRIP DRIP
I don't even know your name...
...so I don't want to involve you in this any further!

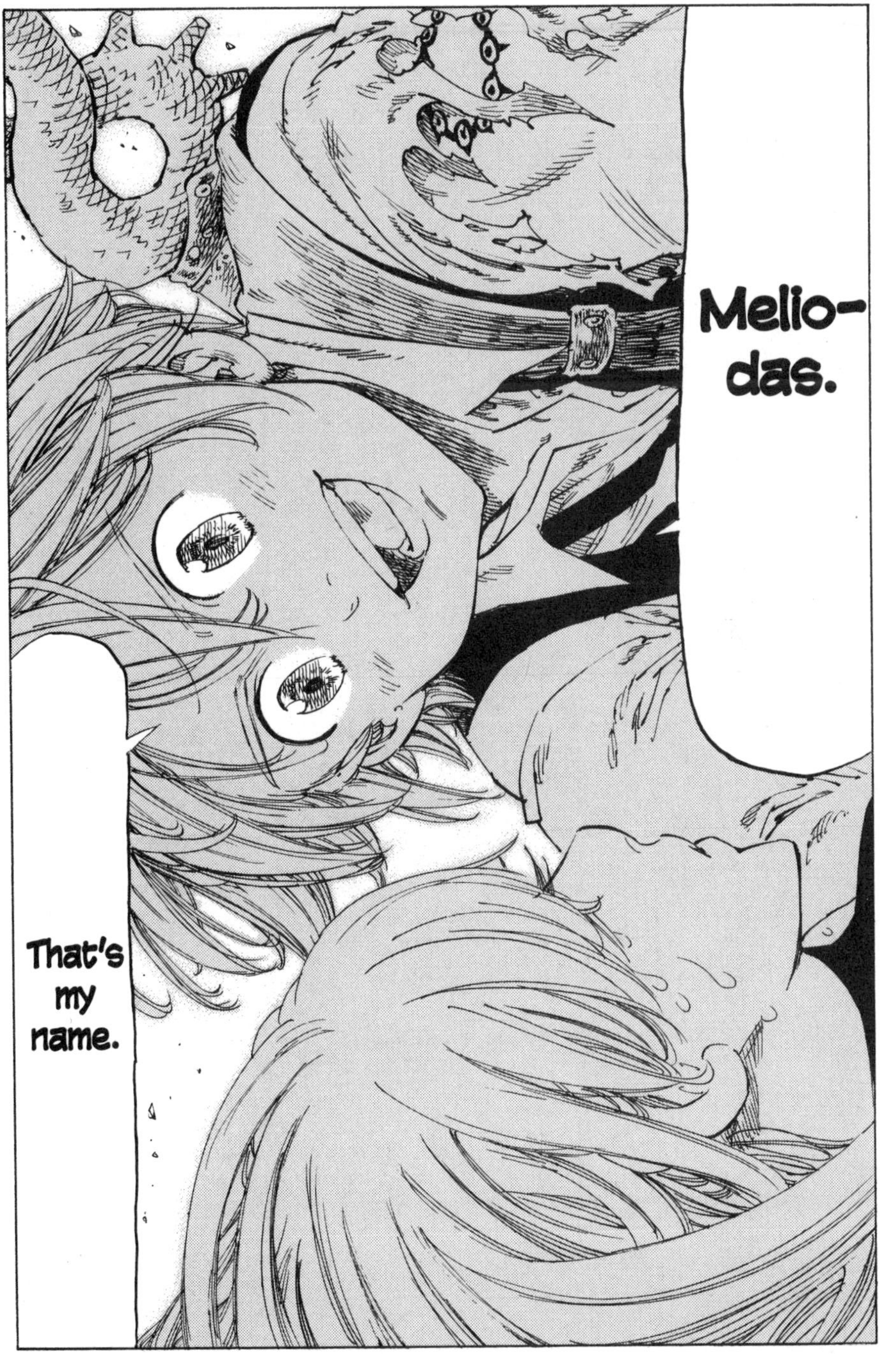
Melio-
das.
That's my name.

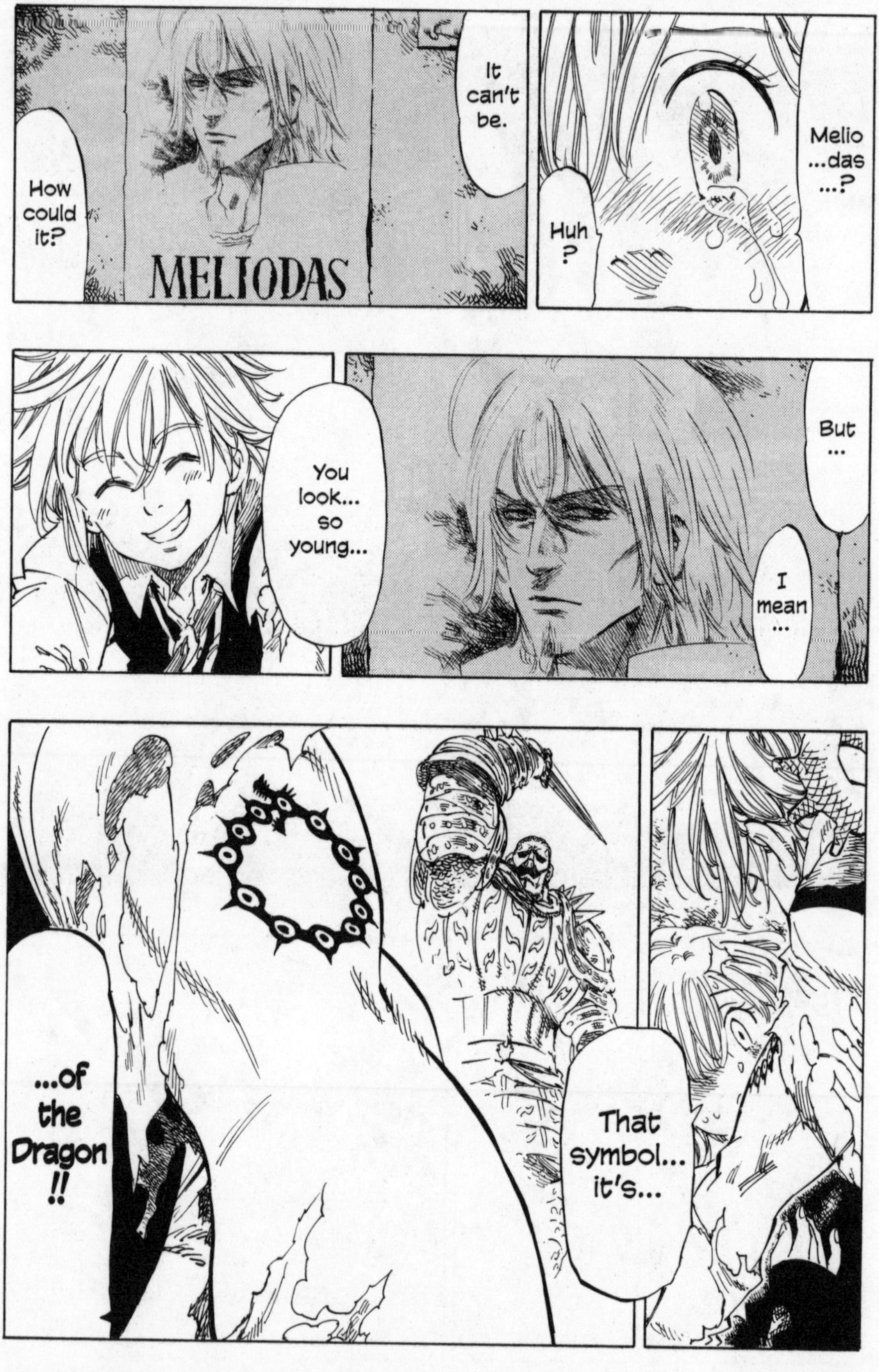

Melio ...das ...?
Huh ?
It can't be.
MELIODAS
How could it?
But ...
I mean ...
You look... so young...
That symbol... it's...
...of the Dragon !!

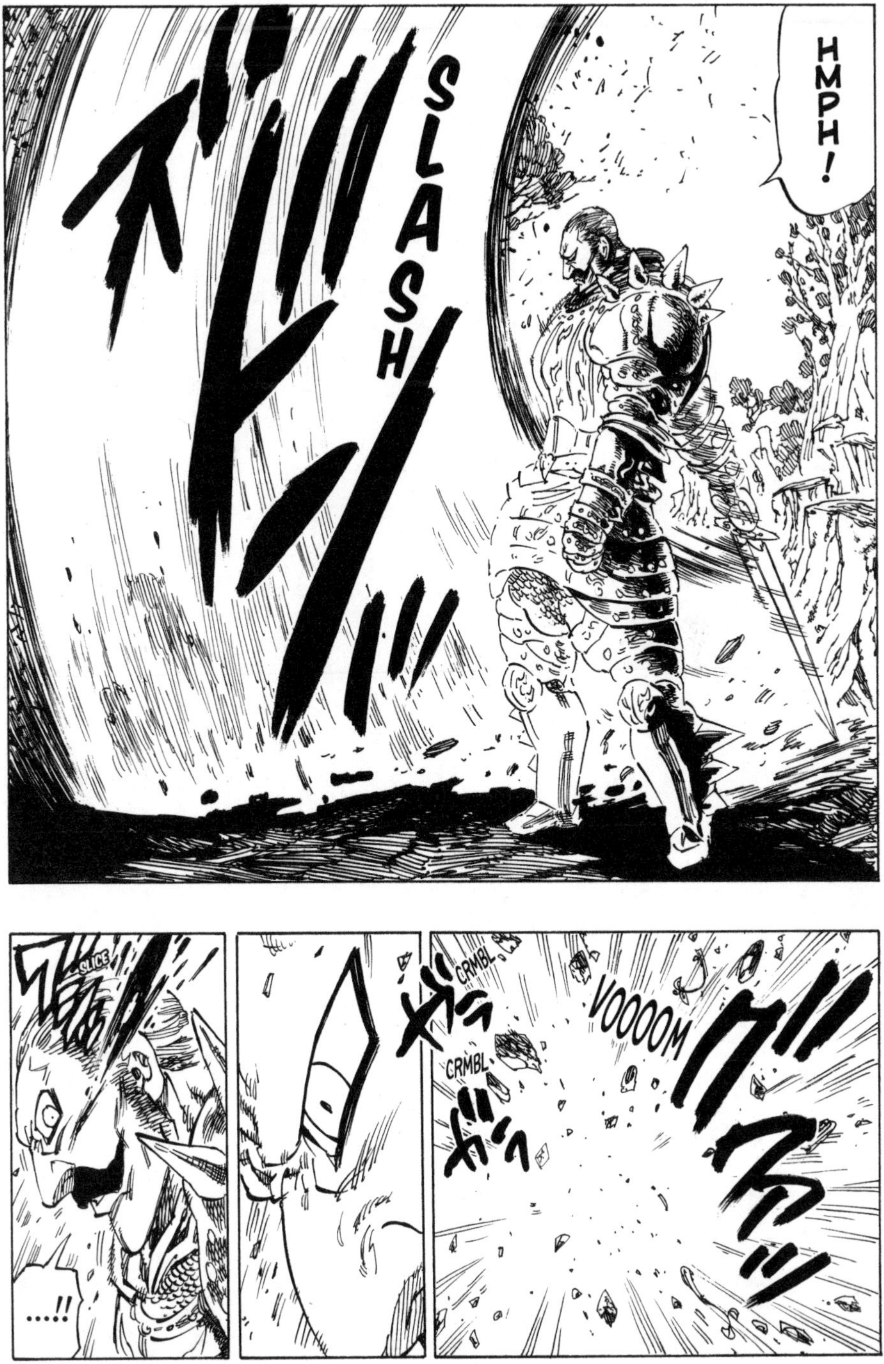
HMPH!
SLASH
VOOOM
CRMBL
CRMBL
SLICE
....!!

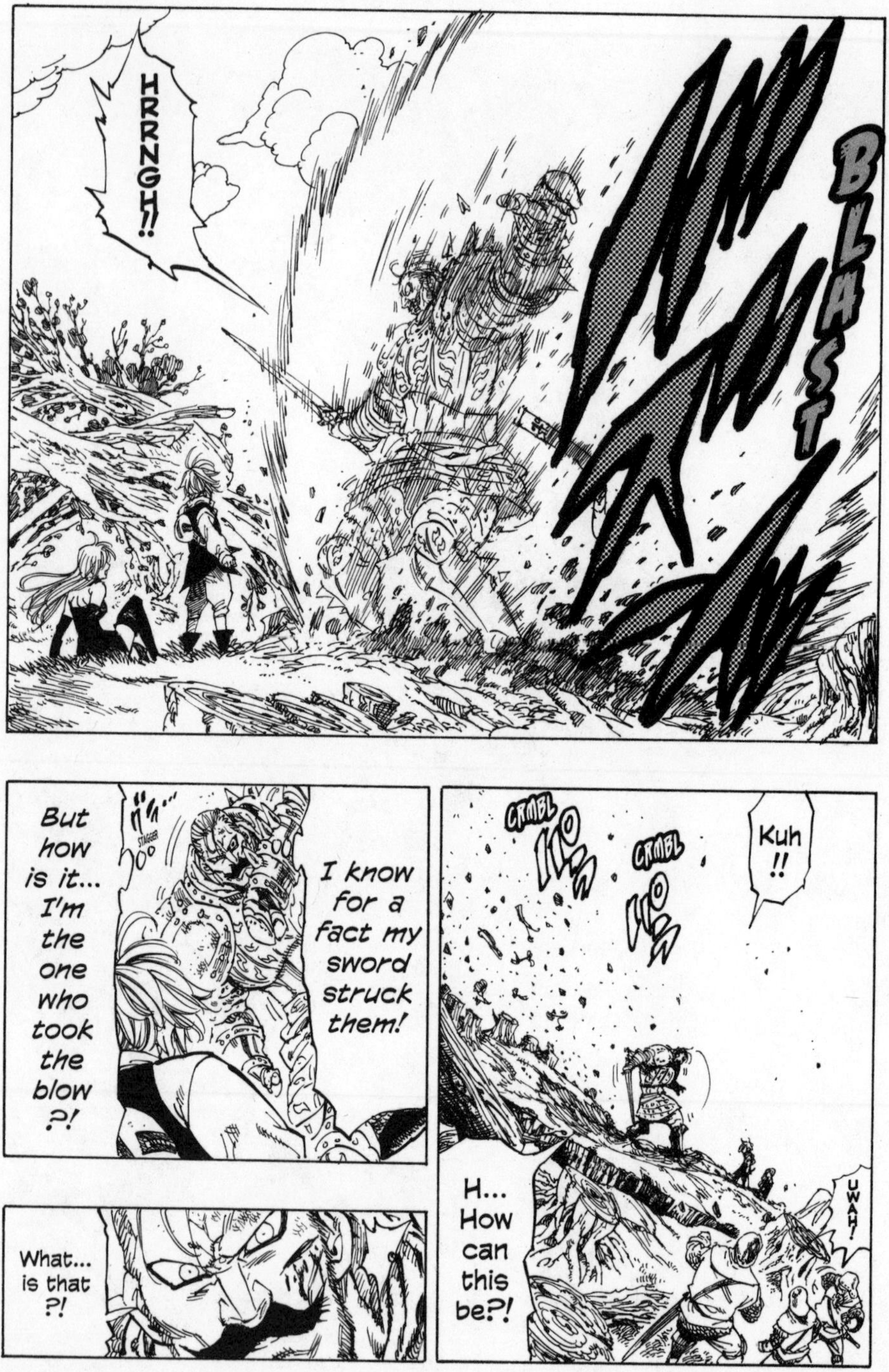
BLAST
HRRNGH?!!
Kuh!!
CRMBL
CRMBL
UWAH!
H... How can this be?!
I know for a fact my sword struck them!
STAGGER
But how is it... I'm the one who took the blow?!
What... is that?!

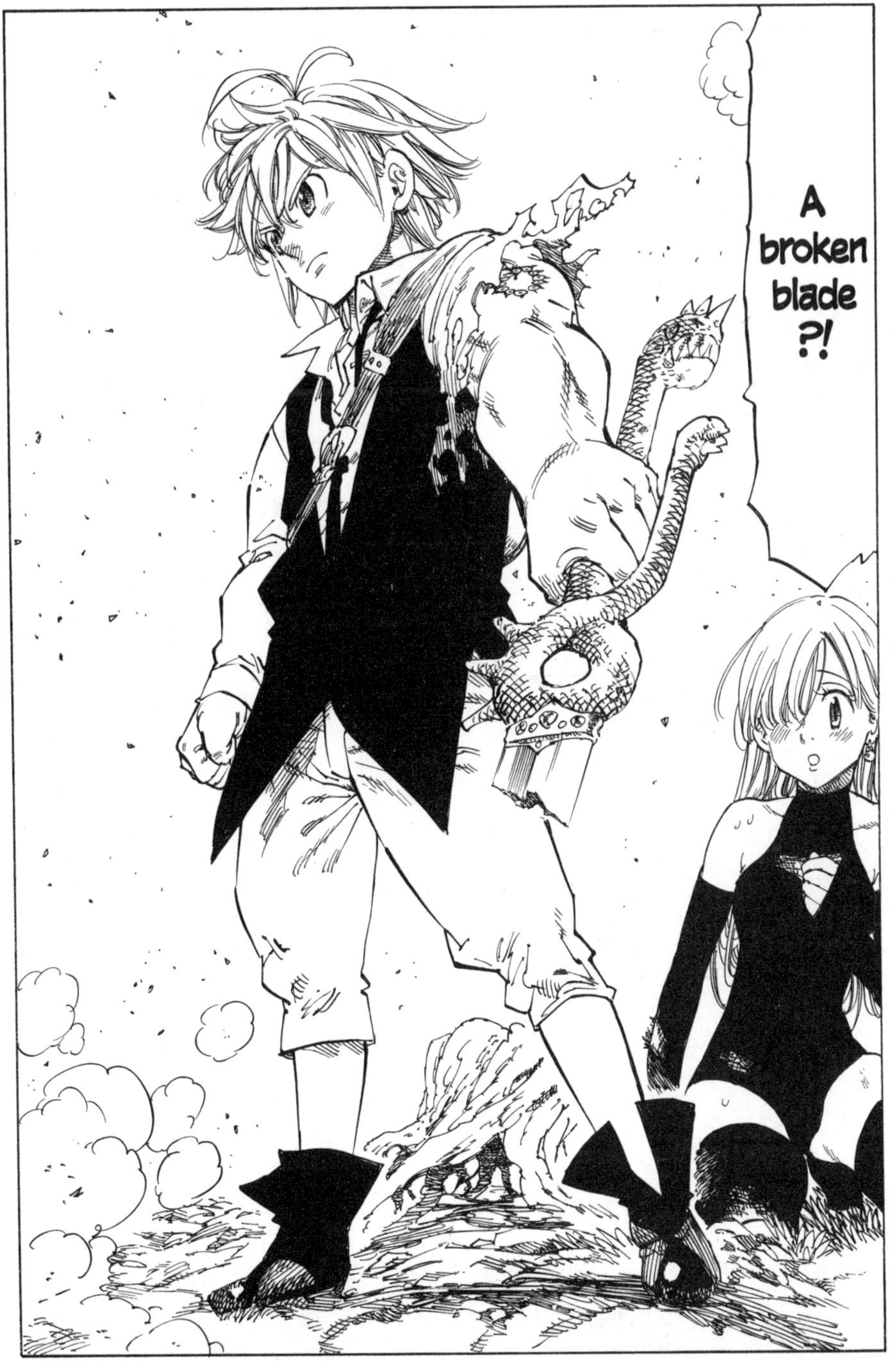
A broken blade ?!

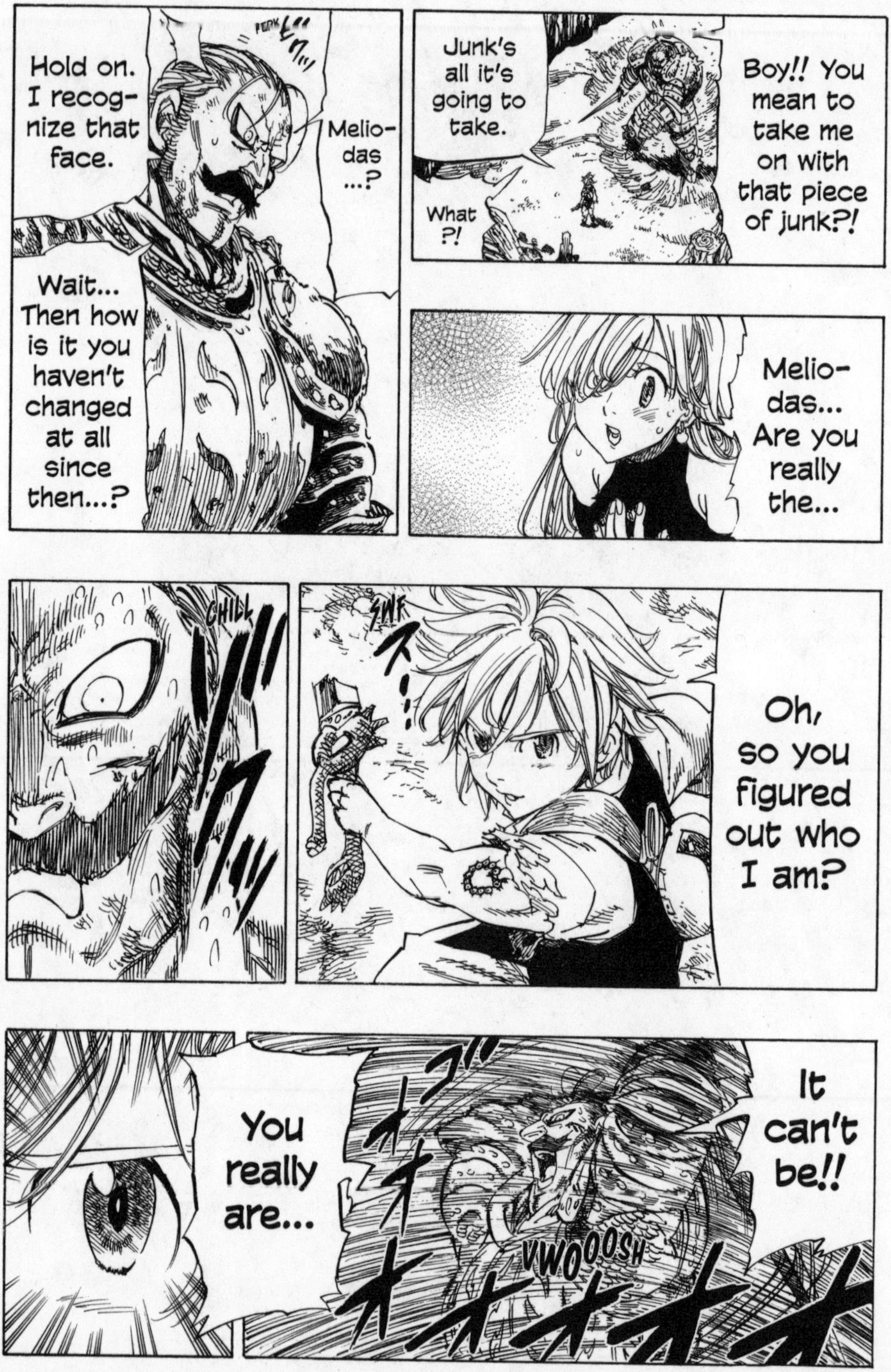
Boy!! You mean to take me on with that piece of junk?!
Junk's all it's going to take.
What ?!
Melio-das... Are you really the...
PERK
Melio-das ...?
Hold on. I recognize that face.
Wait... Then how is it you haven't changed at all since then...?
SWF
Oh, so you figured out who I am?
CHILL
It can't be!!
VWOOOSH
You really are...

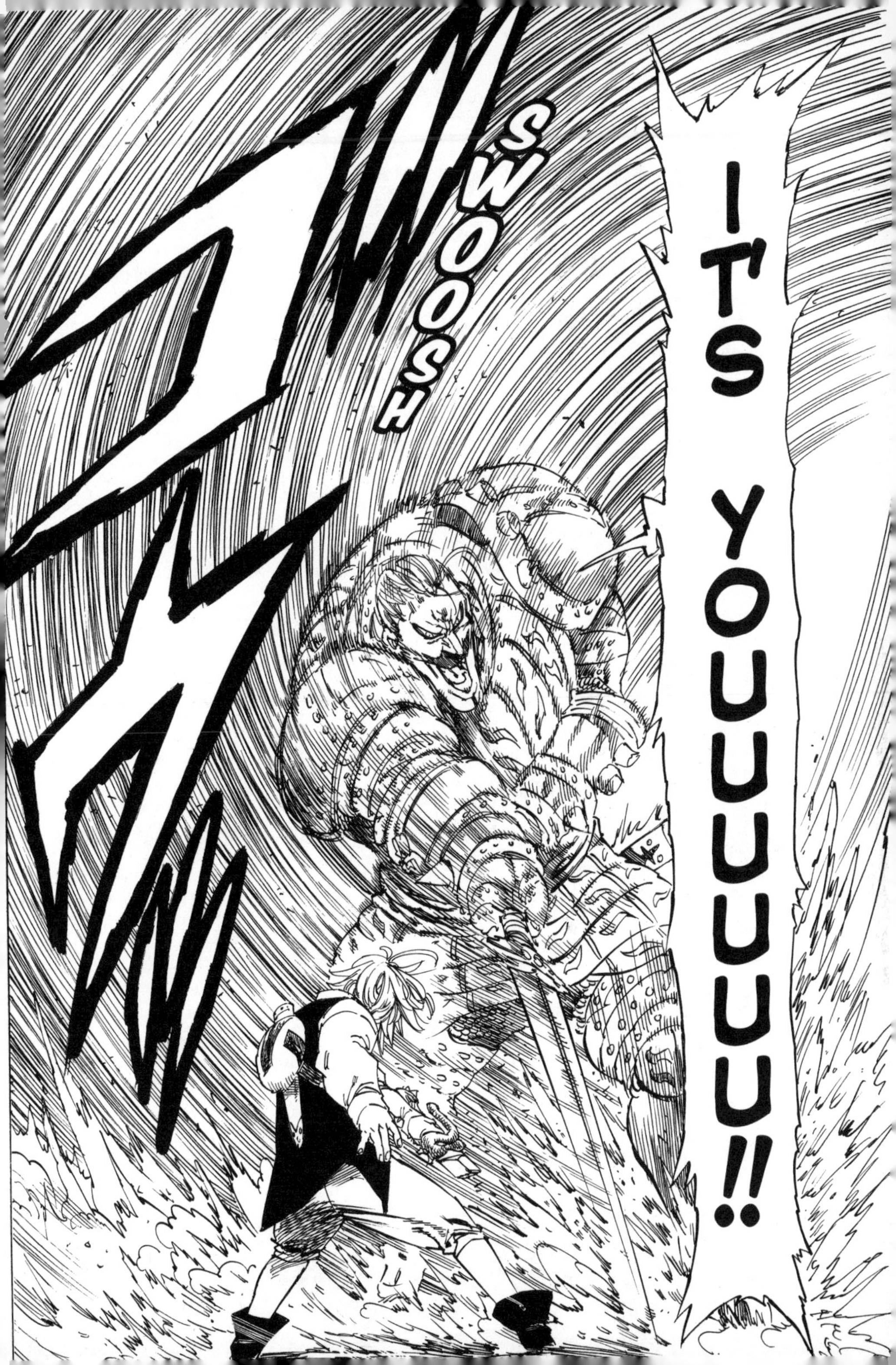
IT'S YOUUUUUU!!
SWOOSH

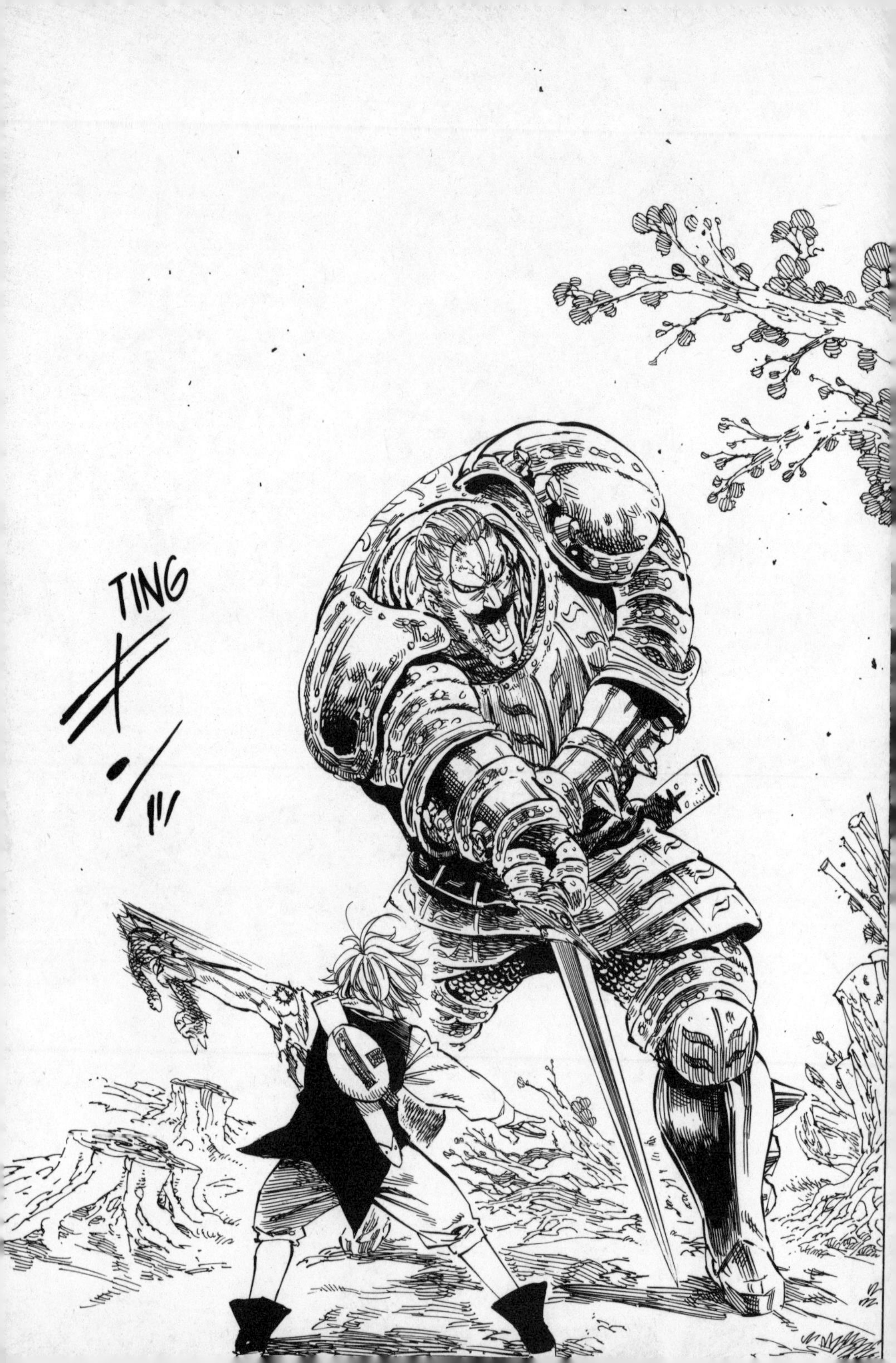
TING

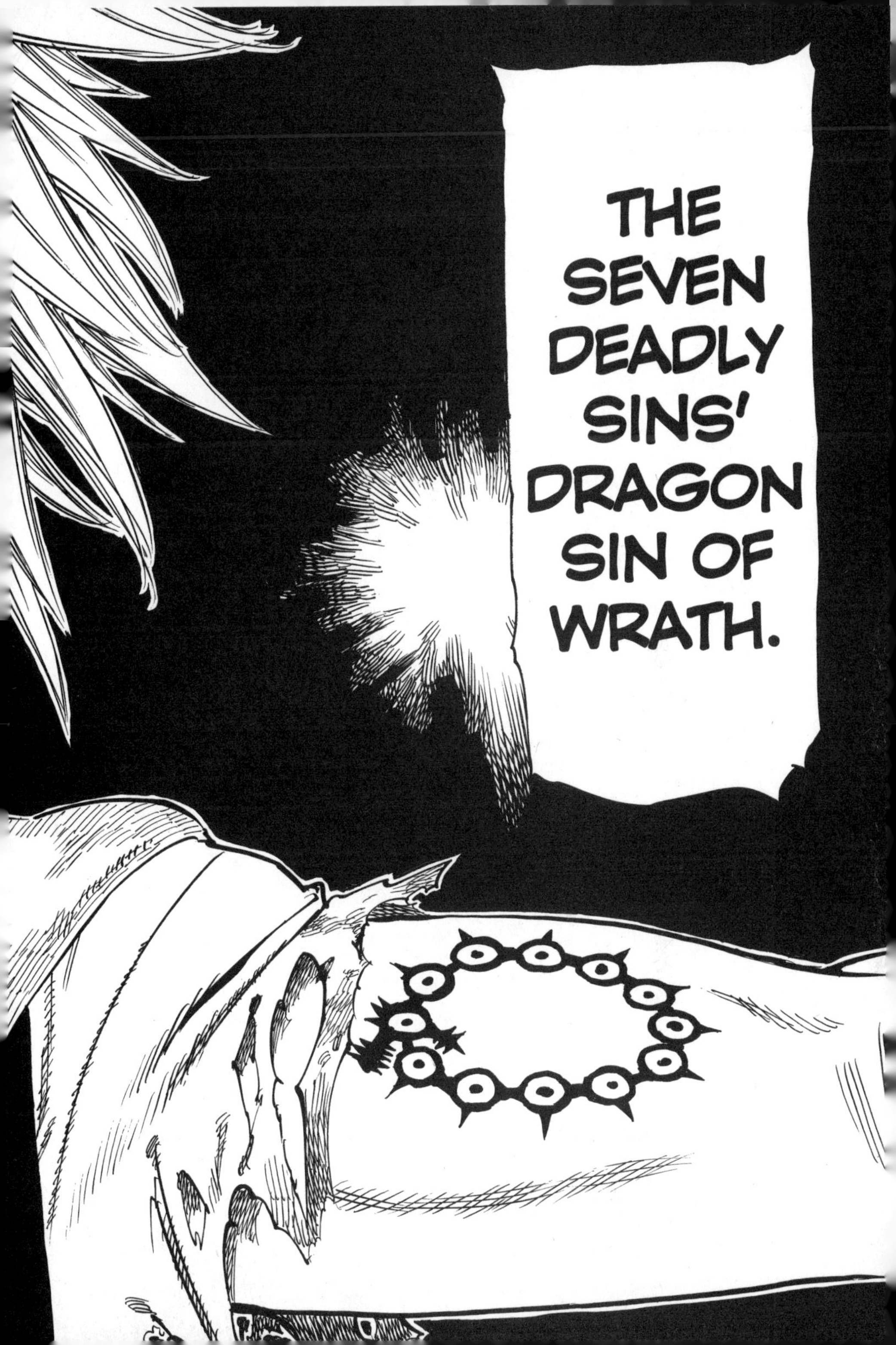
THE SEVEN DEADLY SINS' DRAGON SIN OF WRATH.

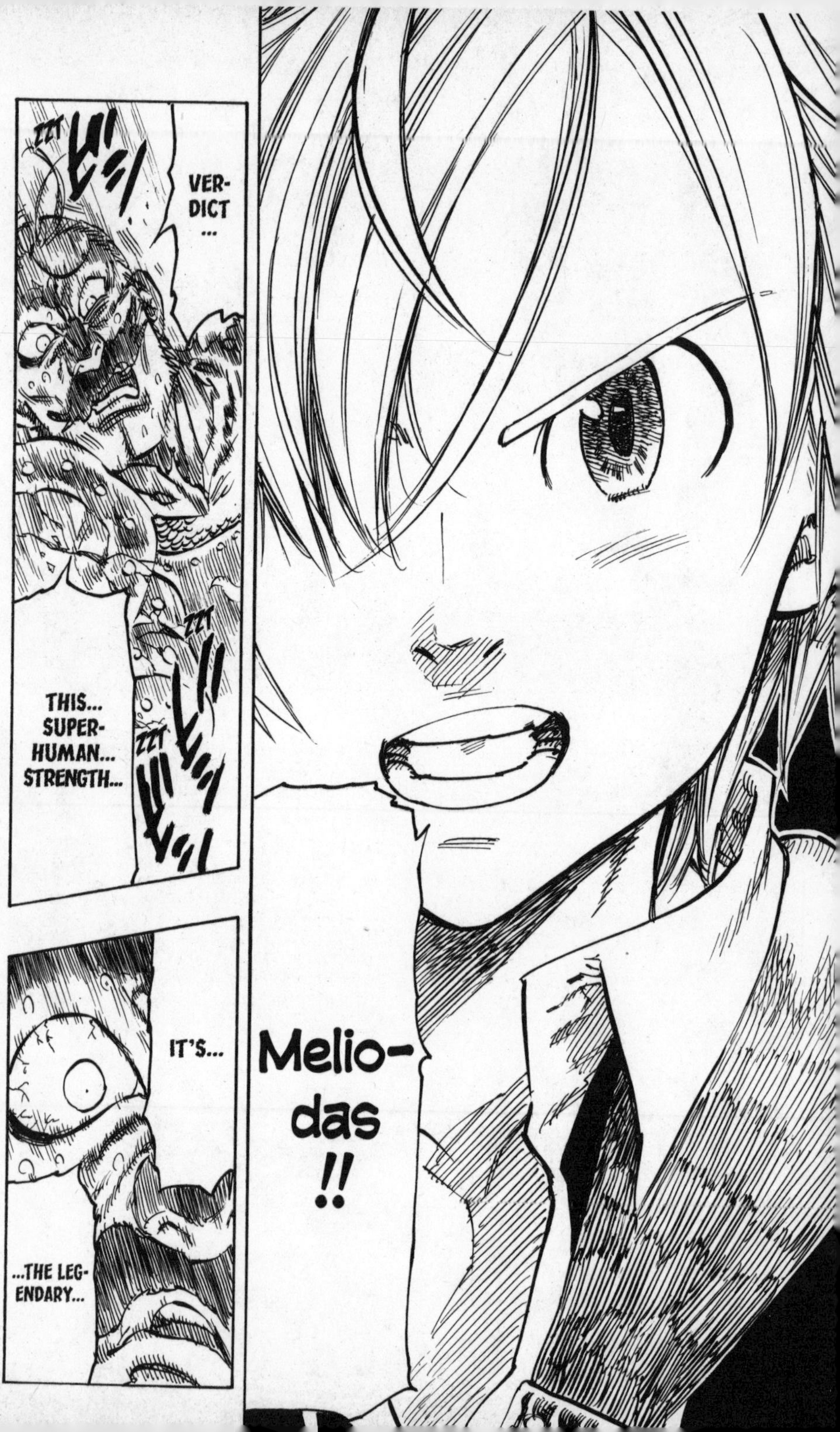
ZZT
VERDICT...
THIS... SUPERHUMAN... STRENGTH...
ZZT
ZZT
IT'S...
...THE LEGENDARY...
Meliodas!!

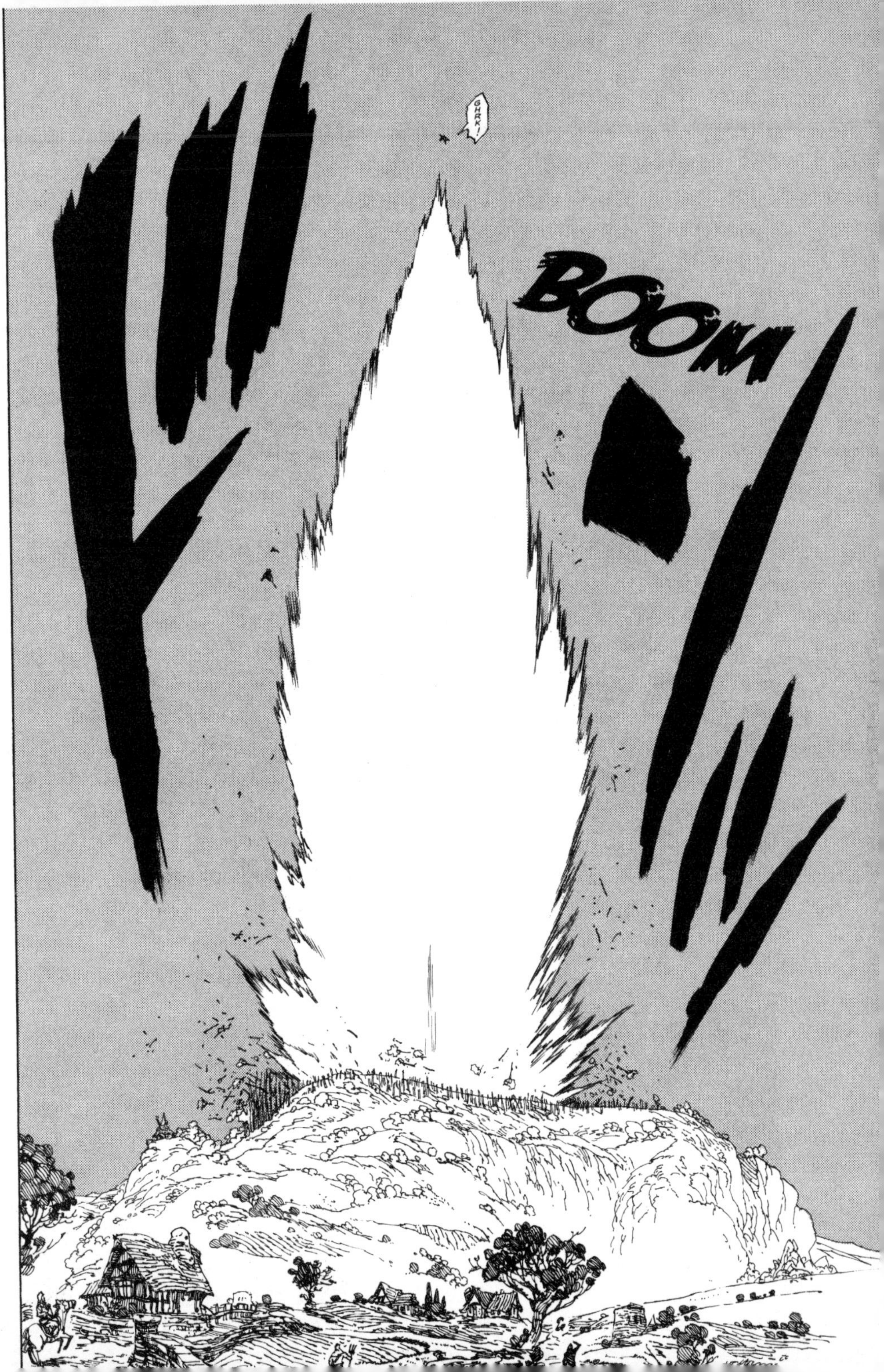
GHRK!
BOOM

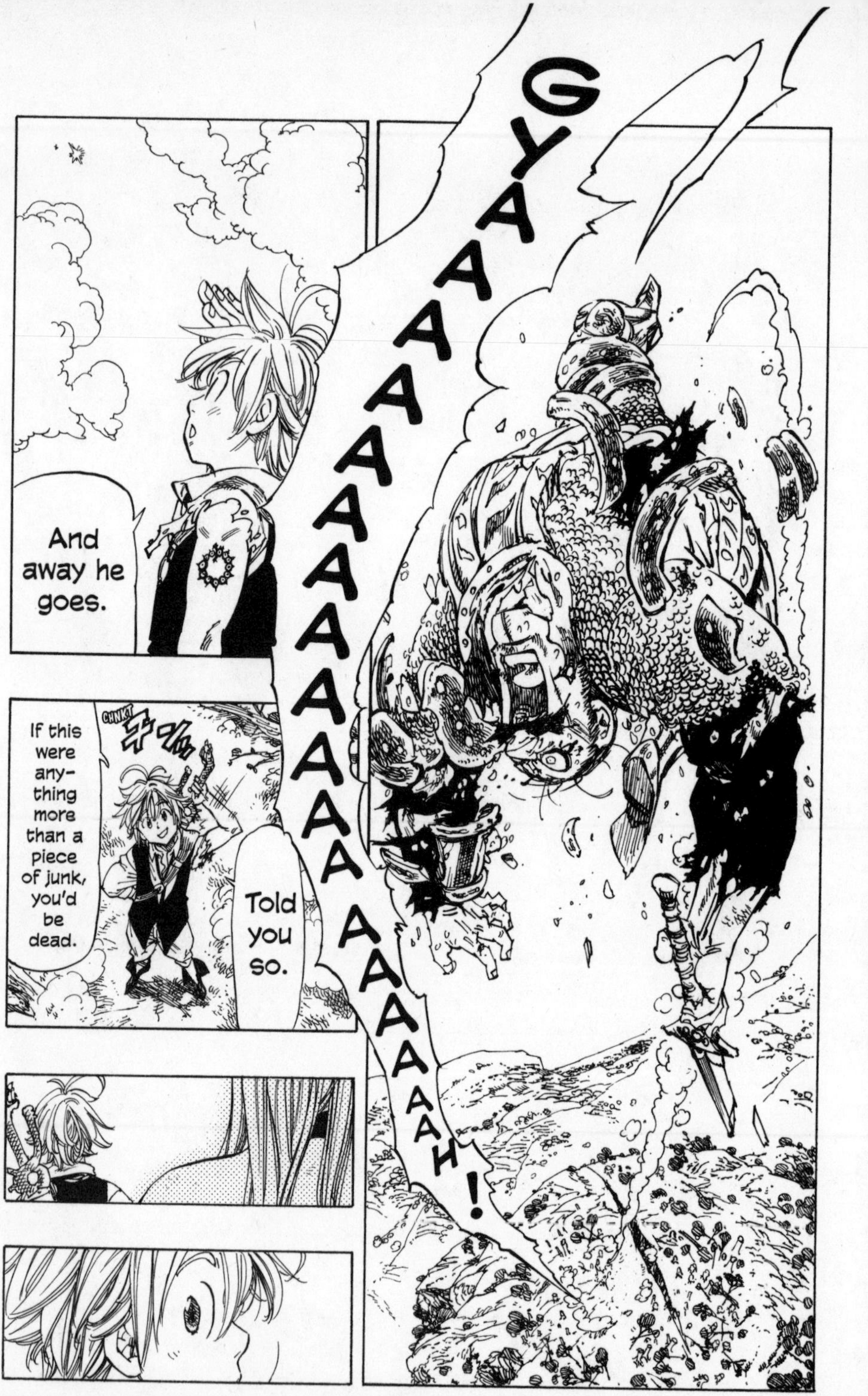
GYAAAAAAAAAAAAAAAAAAH!
And away he goes.
Told you so.
CHNKT
If this were anything more than a piece of junk, you'd be dead.

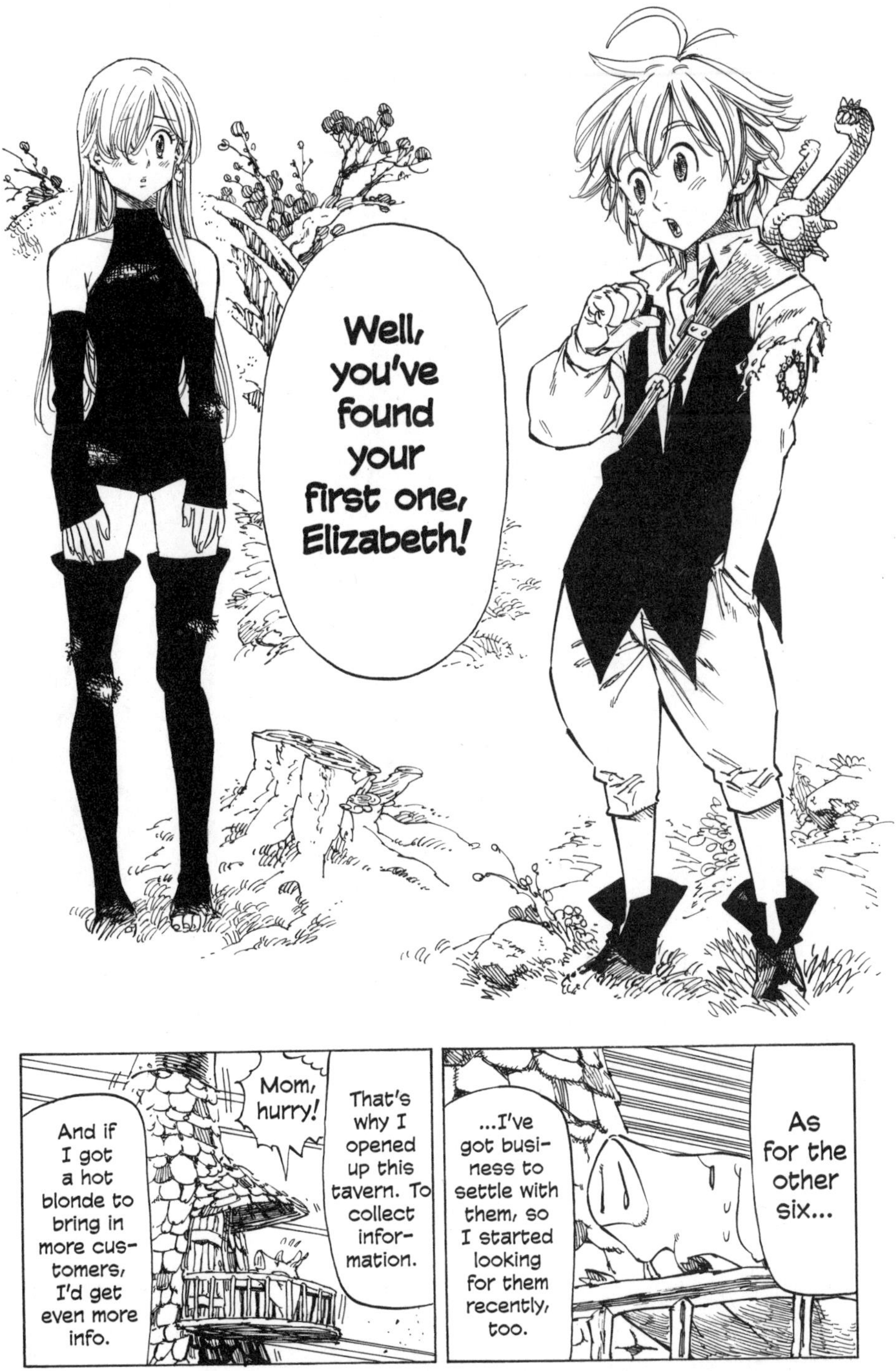

Well, you've found your first one, Elizabeth!
As for the other six...
...I've got busi-ness to settle with them, so I started looking for them recently, too.
That's why I opened up this tavern. To collect infor-mation.
Mom, hurry!
And if I got a hot blonde to bring in more cus-tomers, I'd get even more info.

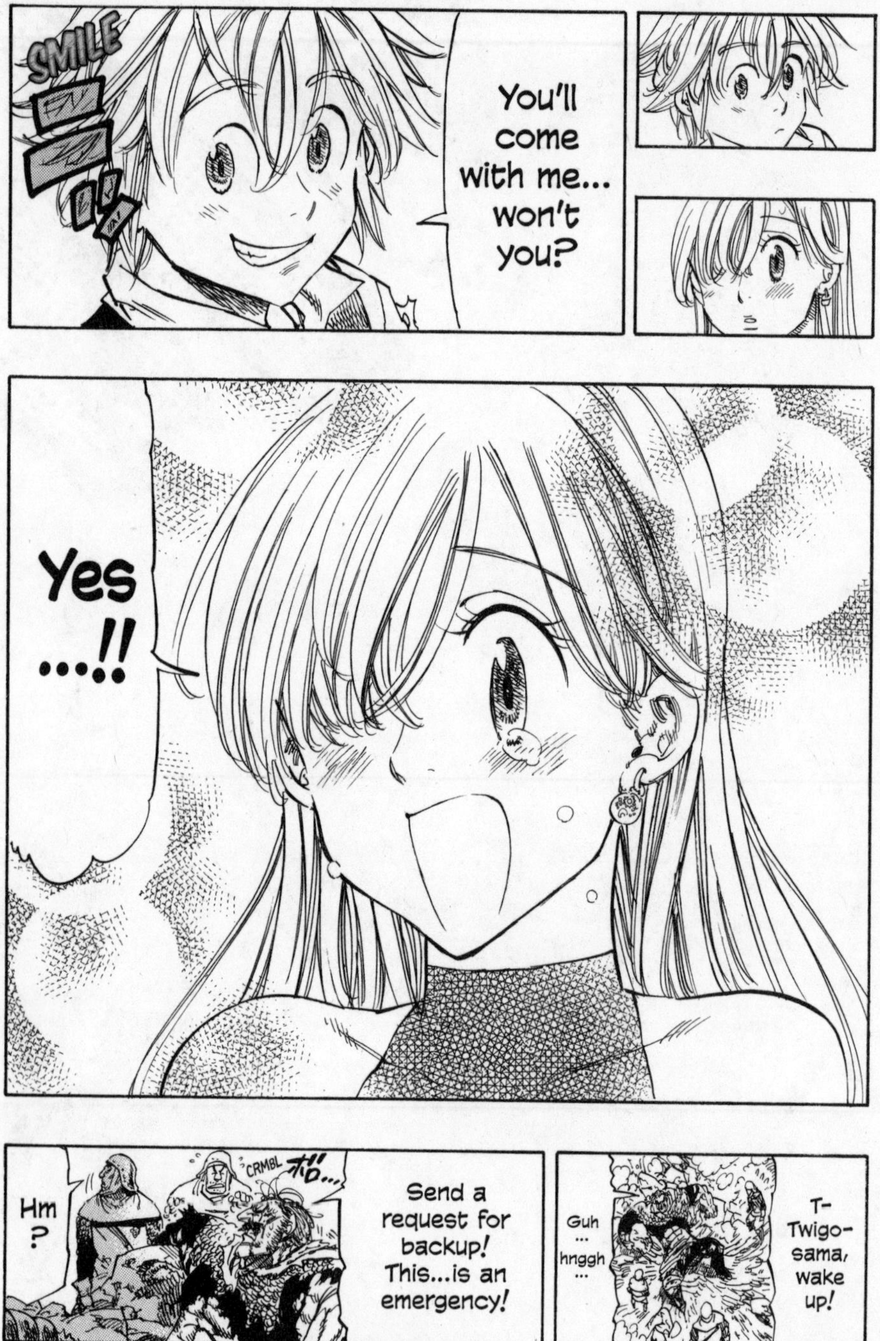
SMILE
You'll come with me... won't you?
Yes ...!!
T-Twigo-sama, wake up!
Guh ... hnggh ...
Send a request for backup! This...is an emergency!
CRMBL
Hm ?

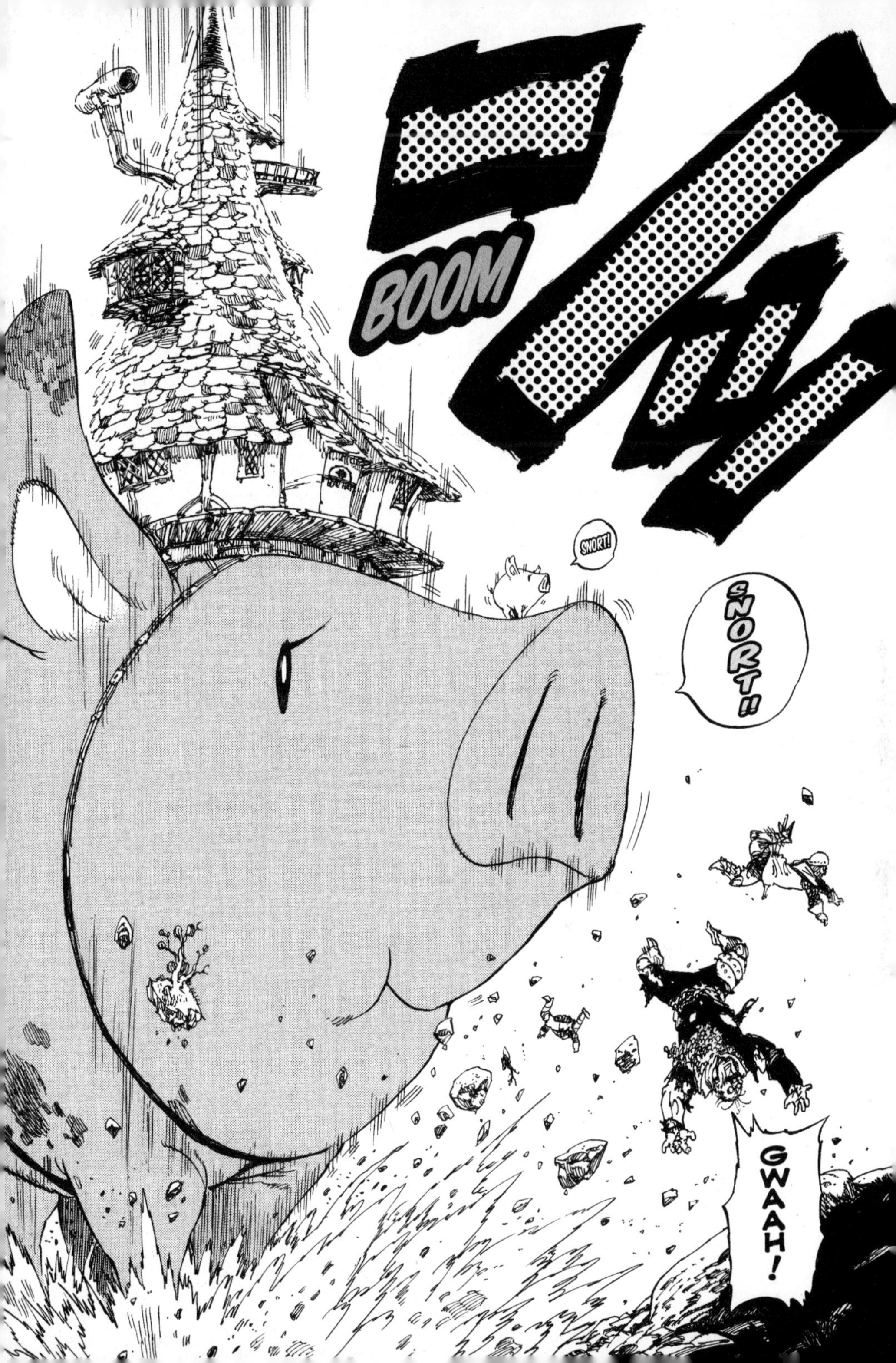
BOOM
SNORT!
SNORT!!
GWAAH!

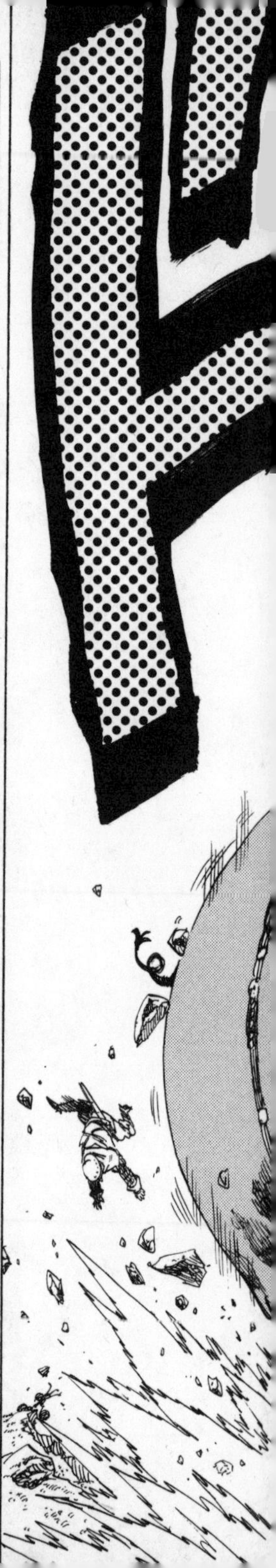

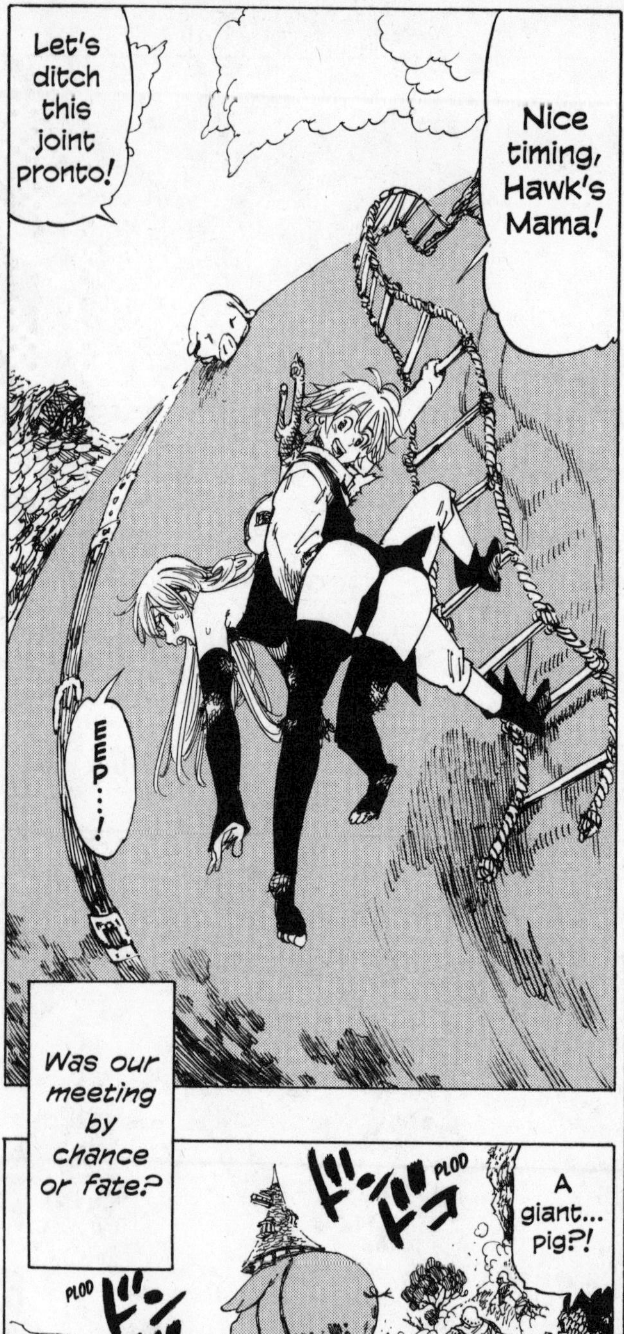
Nice timing, Hawk's Mama!
Let's ditch this joint pronto!
EEP...!
Was our meeting by chance or fate?
PLOD
A giant... pig?!
PLOD
PLOD

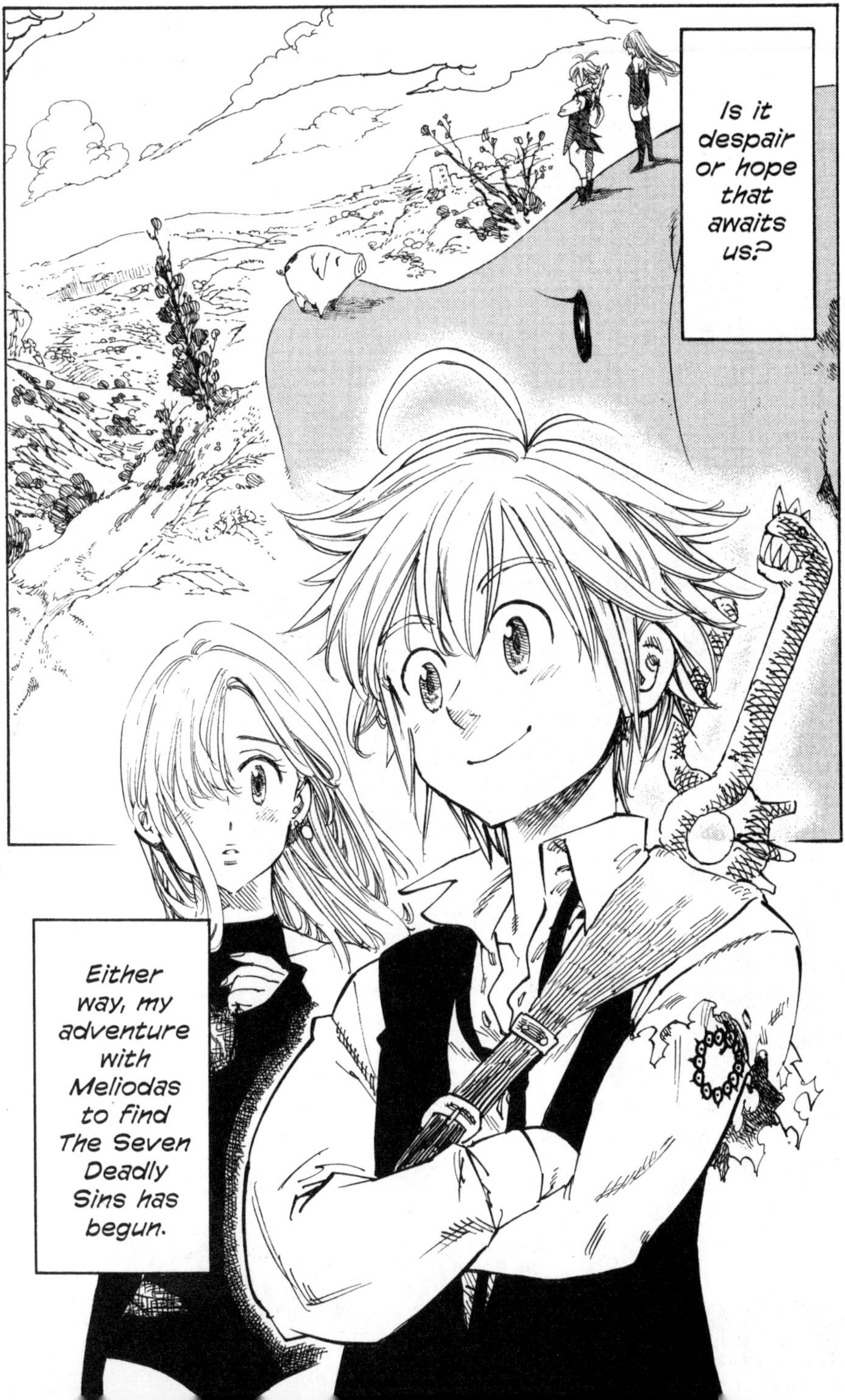
Is it despair or hope that awaits us?
Either way, my adventure with Meliodas to find The Seven Deadly Sins has begun.

Chapter 2 - The Holy Knight's Sword

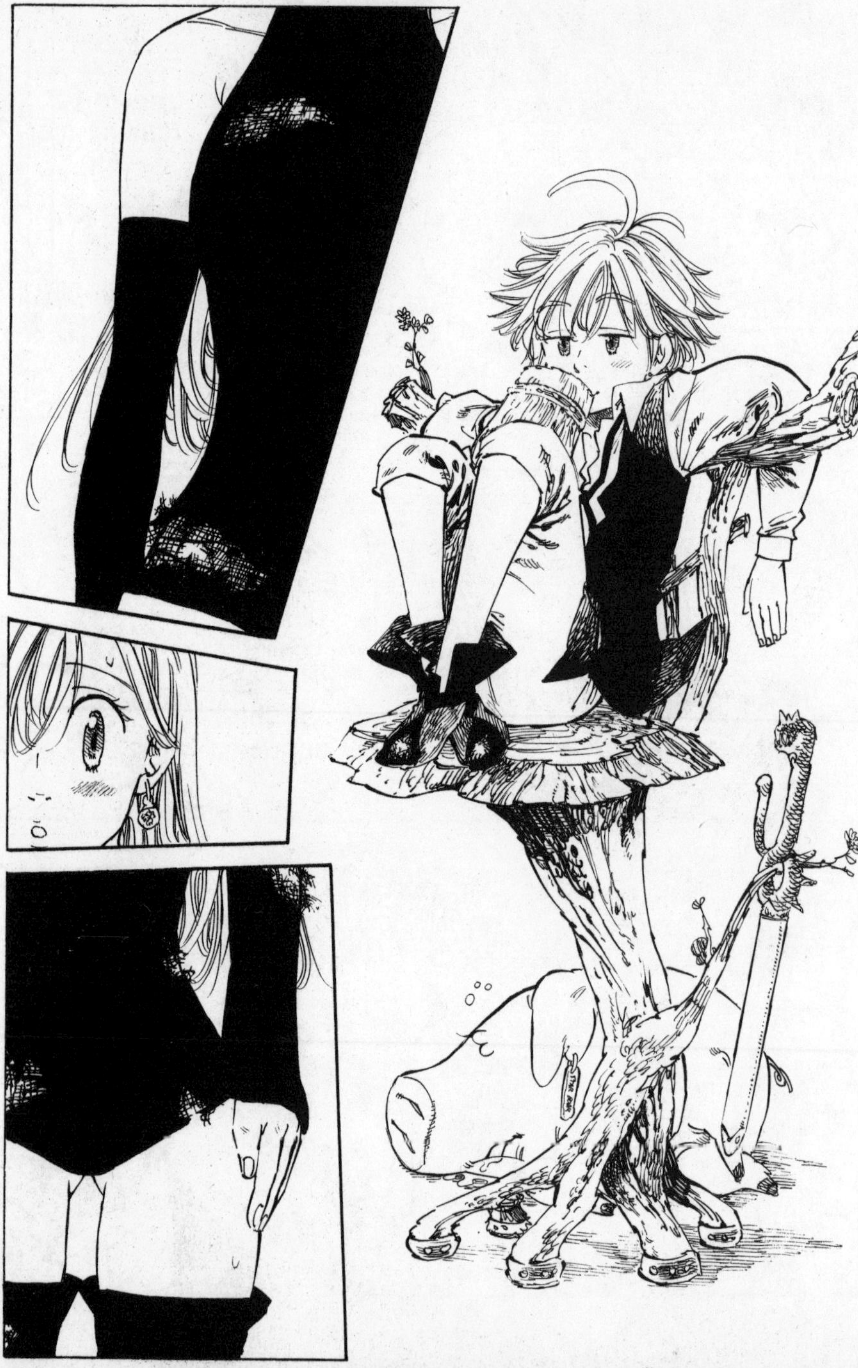

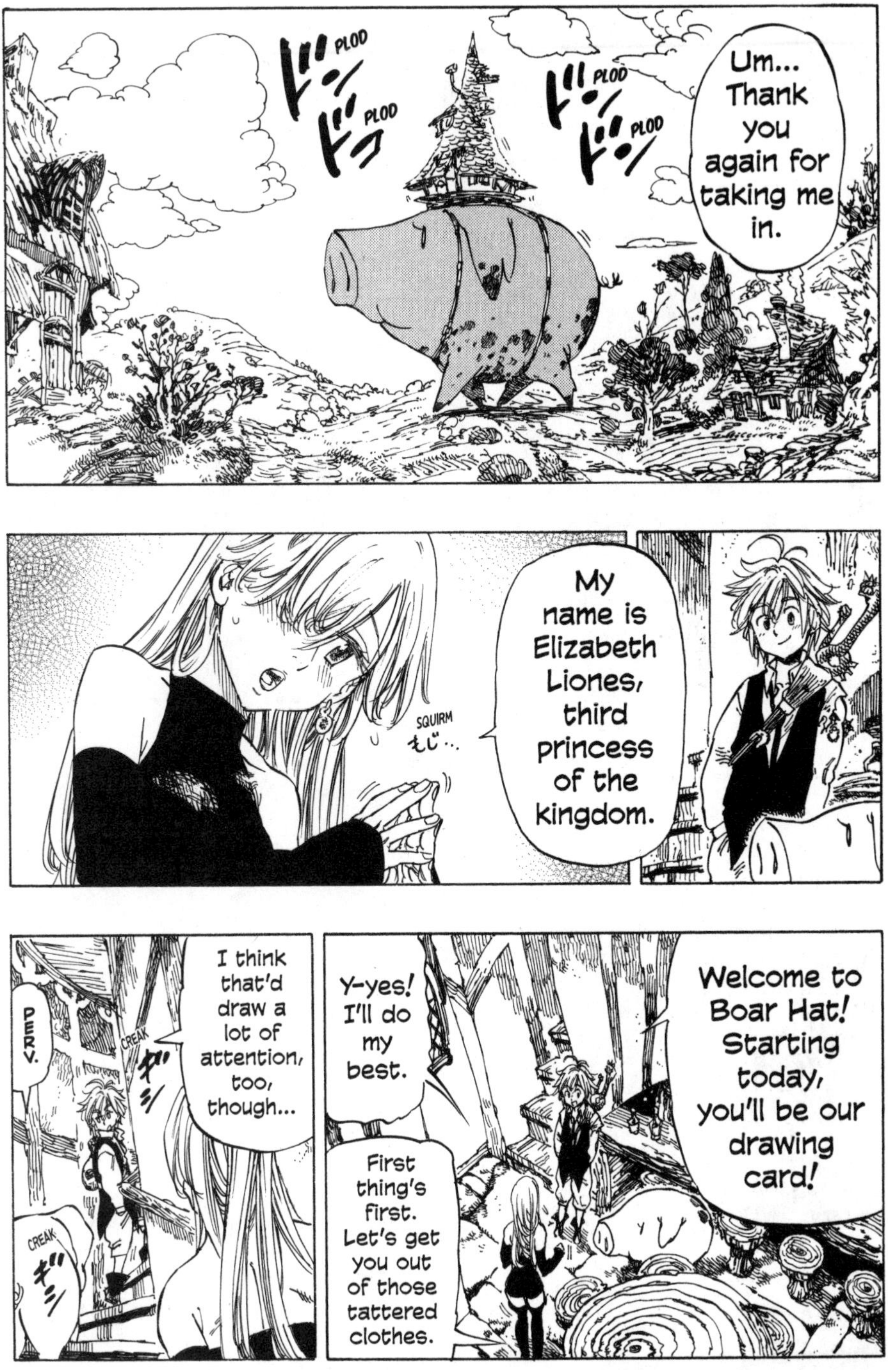
Um... Thank you again for taking me in.
PLOOD
PLOOD
PLOOD
PLOOD
My name is Elizabeth Liones, third princess of the kingdom.
SQUIRM
Welcome to Boar Hat! Starting today, you'll be our drawing card!
Y-yes! I'll do my best.
First thing's first. Let's get you out of those tattered clothes.
I think that'd draw a lot of attention, too, though...
CREAK
PERV.
CREAK

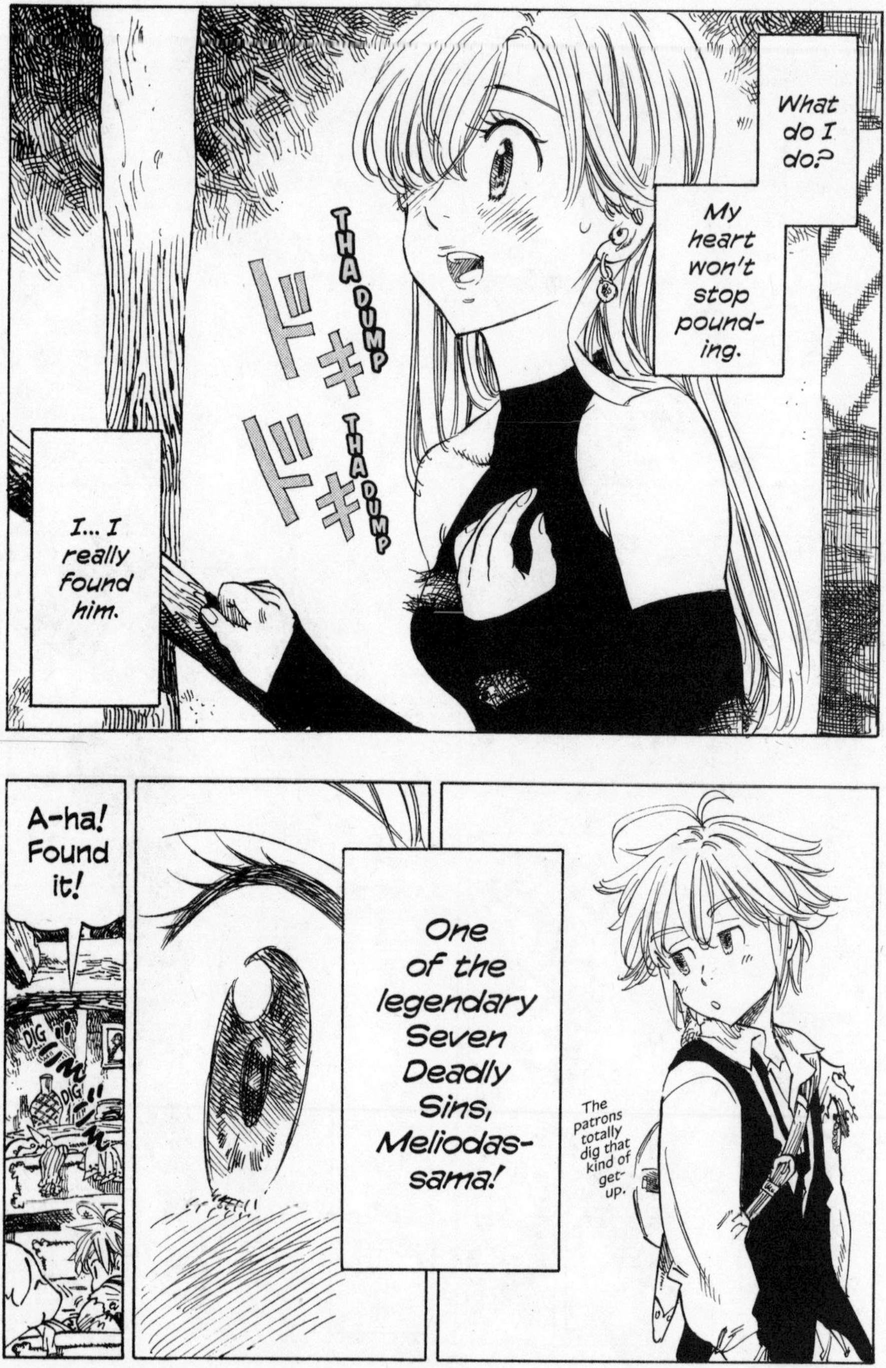
What do I do?
My heart won't stop pounding.
THA DUMP
ドキ
THA DUMP
ドキ
I... I really found him.
The patrons totally dig that kind of get-up.
One of the legendary Seven Deadly Sins, Meliodas-sama!
A-ha! Found it!
DIG
DIG

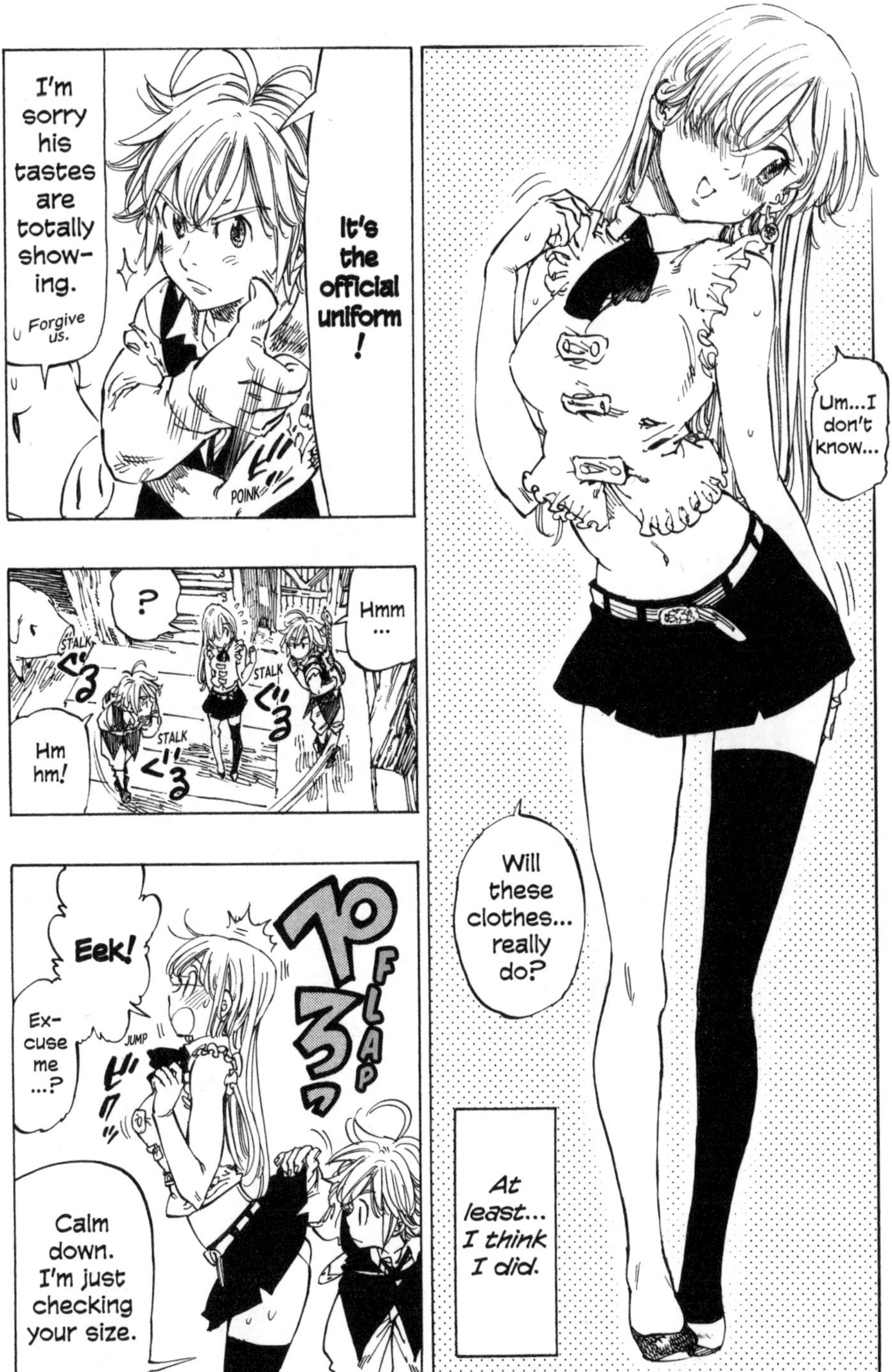
Um...I don't know...
Will these clothes... really do?
At least... I think I did.
It's the official uniform!
I'm sorry his tastes are totally showing.
Forgive us.
POINK
Hmm ...
STALK
?
STALK
STALK
Hm hm!
FLAP
Eek!
JUMP
Excuse me ...?
Calm down. I'm just checking your size.

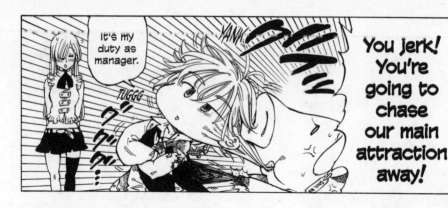

You jerk! You're going to chase our main attraction away!
TUGGG
It's my duty as manager.
Um... Melio-das-sama?
Uh... I have some-thing I want to ask you.
Hrm.
Sure. Ask away!
Don't act like a big-shot!
Are the Seven Deadly Sins...and you included, really the terrible criminals that society says you are?
KING
BAN
And if you are... then what crime are you guilty of?
I believe that society has you all wrong! I mean, you rescued me even before you knew who I was!
What crime... you ask?

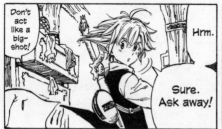

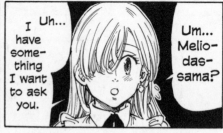

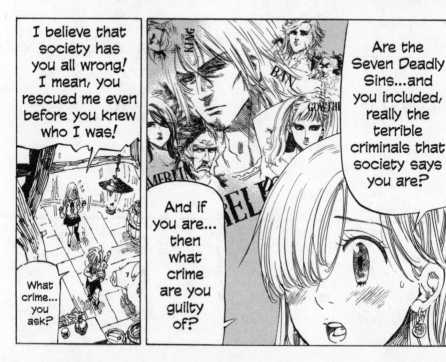

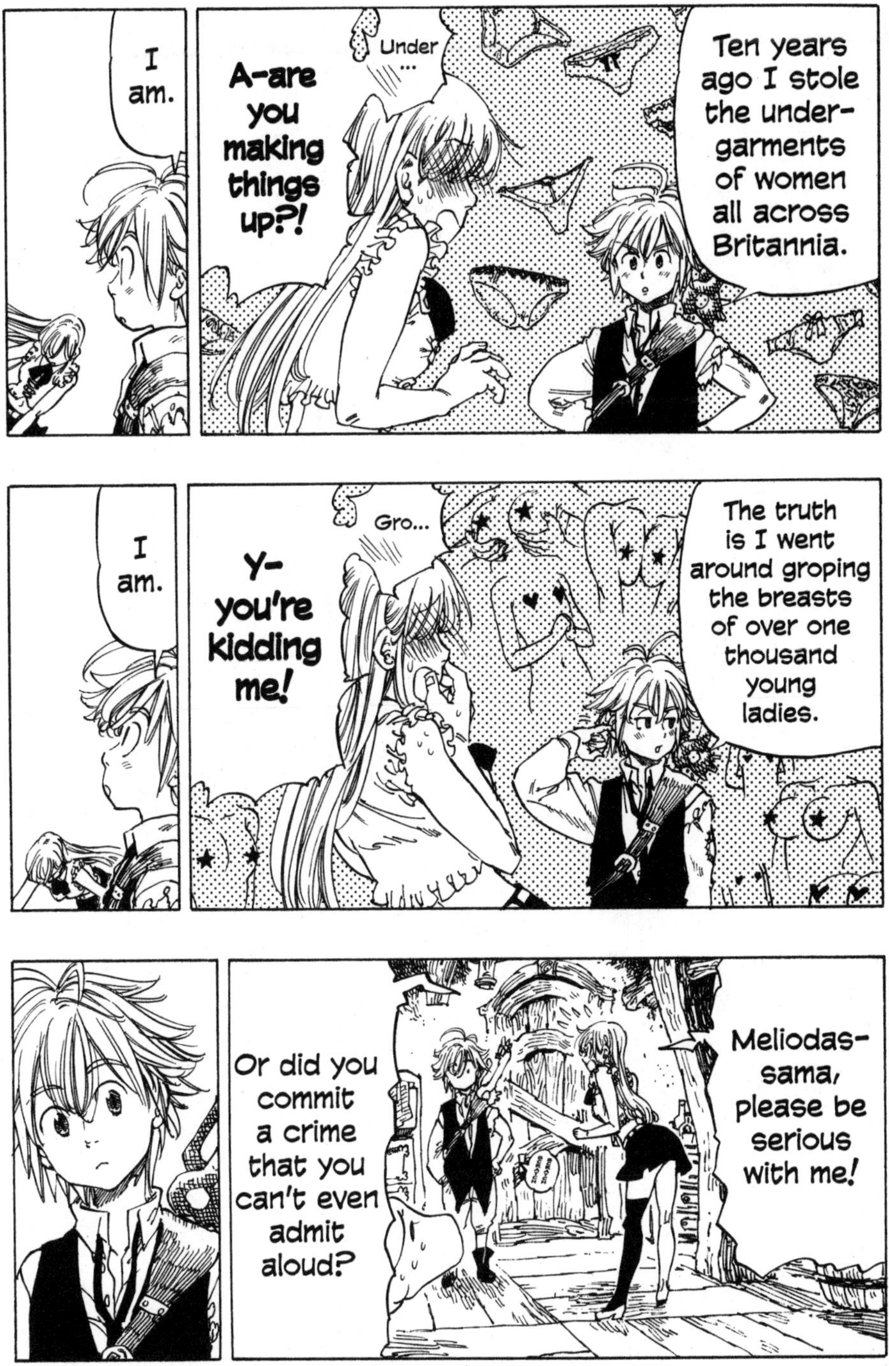
Ten years ago I stole the under-garments of women all across Britannia.
Under ...
A-are you making things up?!
I am.
The truth is I went around groping the breasts of over one thousand young ladies.
Gro...
Y-you're kidding me!
I am.
Meliodas-sama, please be serious with me!
Or did you commit a crime that you can't even admit aloud?

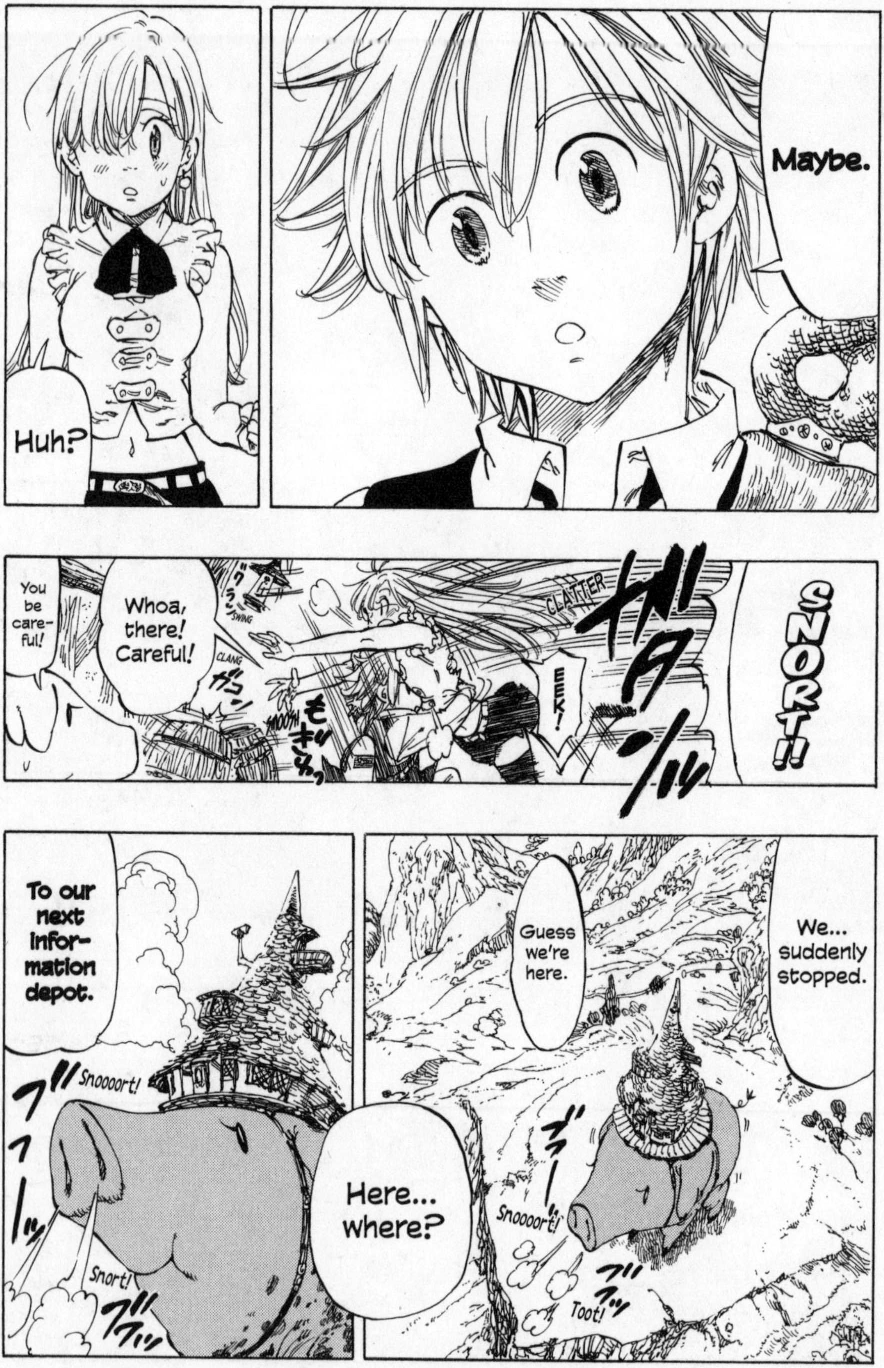
Maybe.
Huh?
SNORT!!
CLATTER
EEK!
SWING
Whoa, there! Careful!
CLANG
You be care-ful!
We... suddenly stopped.
Guess we're here.
Snoooort!
Toot!
To our next information depot.
Snoooort!
Here... where?
Snort!

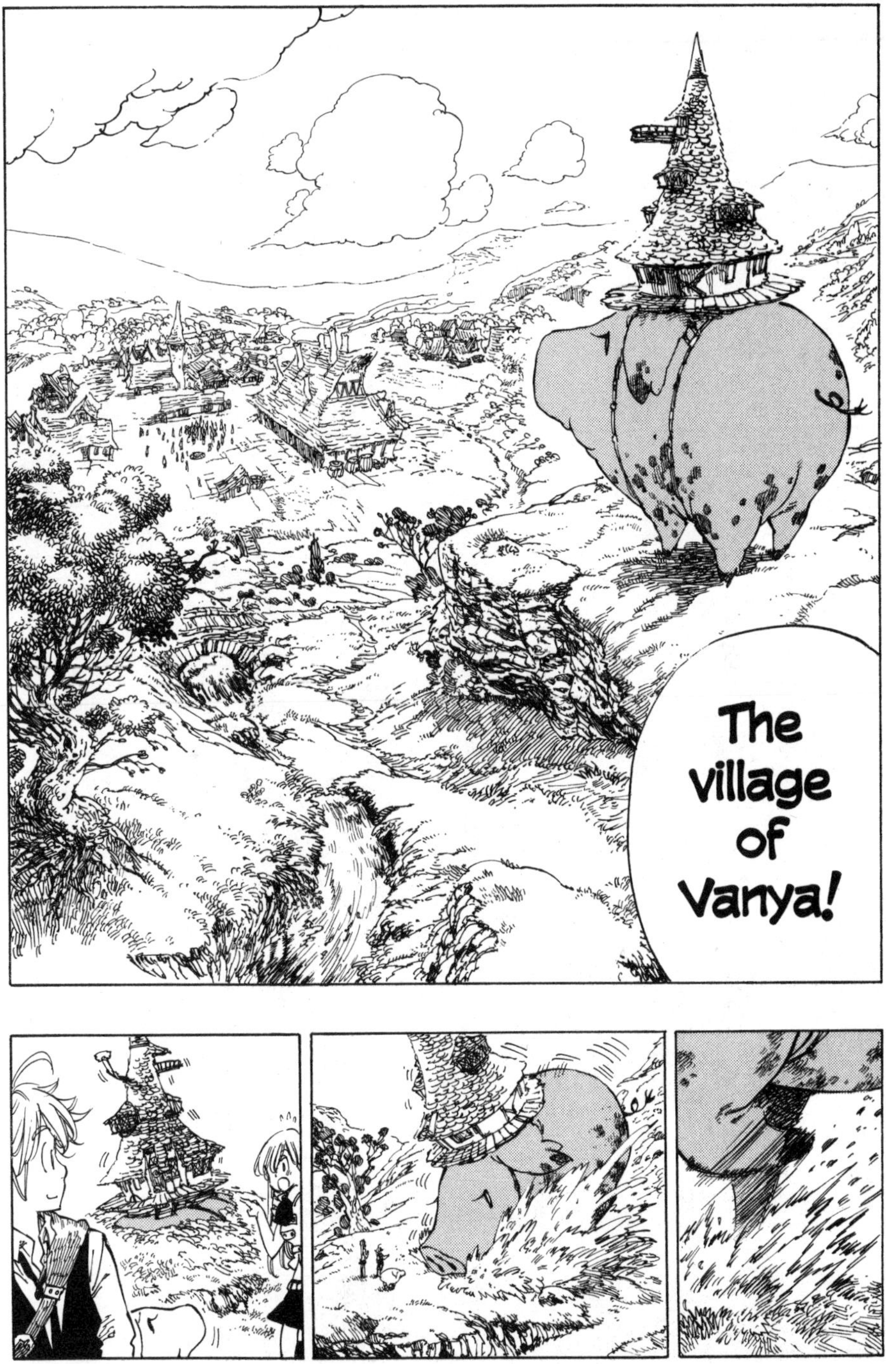
The village of Vanya!

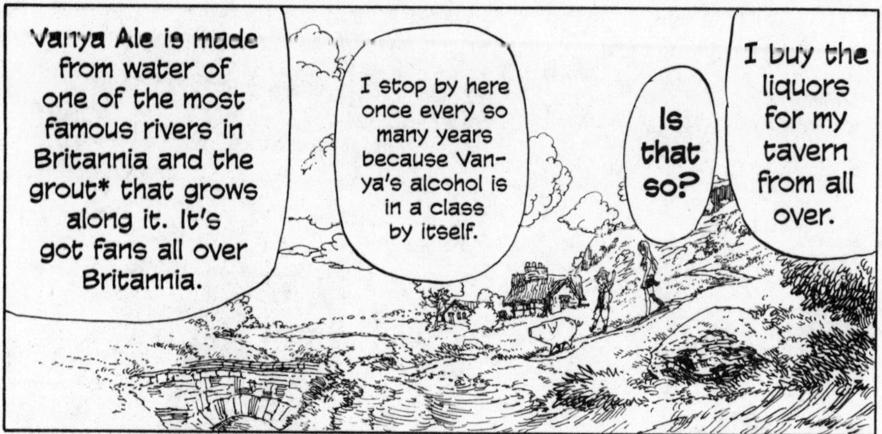
I buy the liquors for my tavern from all over.
Is that so?
I stop by here once every so many years because Vanya's alcohol is in a class by itself.
Vanya Ale is made from water of one of the most famous rivers in Britannia and the grout* that grows along it. It's got fans all over Britannia.

* Grout - a kind of herb used in ales (beer) in the old times

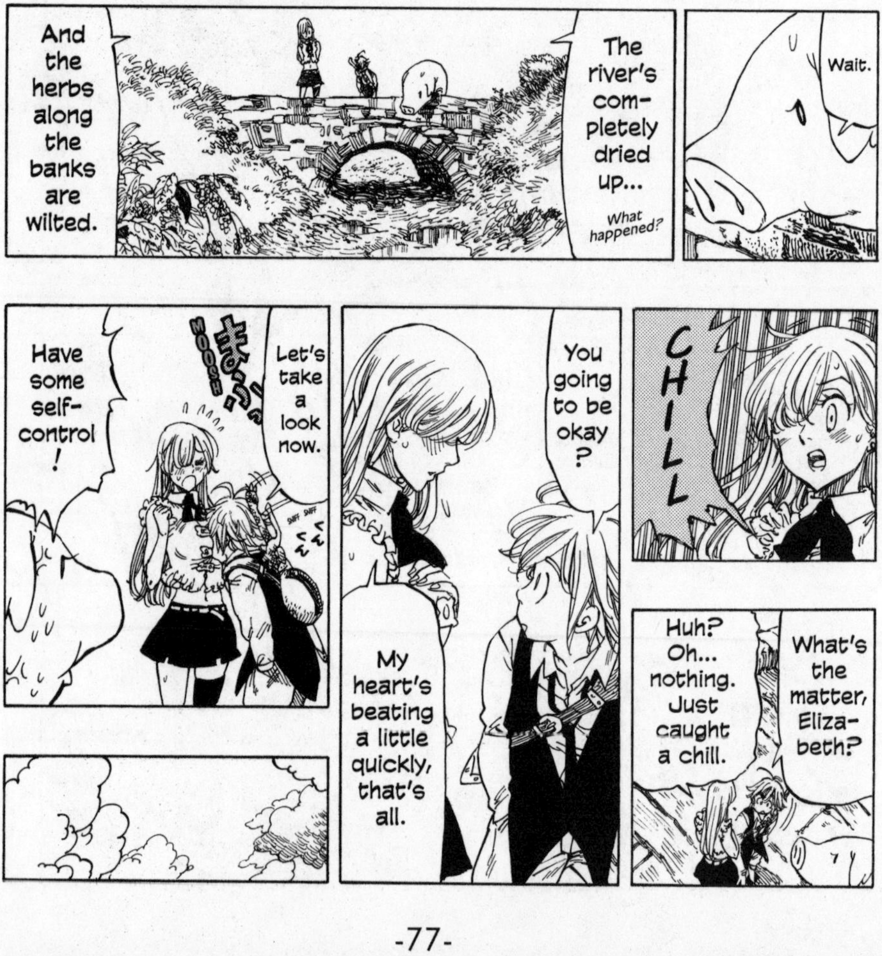
Wait.
The river's completely dried up...
What happened?
And the herbs along the banks are wilted.
CHILL
What's the matter, Elizabeth?
Huh? Oh... nothing. Just caught a chill.
You going to be okay?
My heart's beating a little quickly, that's all.
Let's take a look now.
MOOSH
SNIFF SNIFF
Have some self-control!

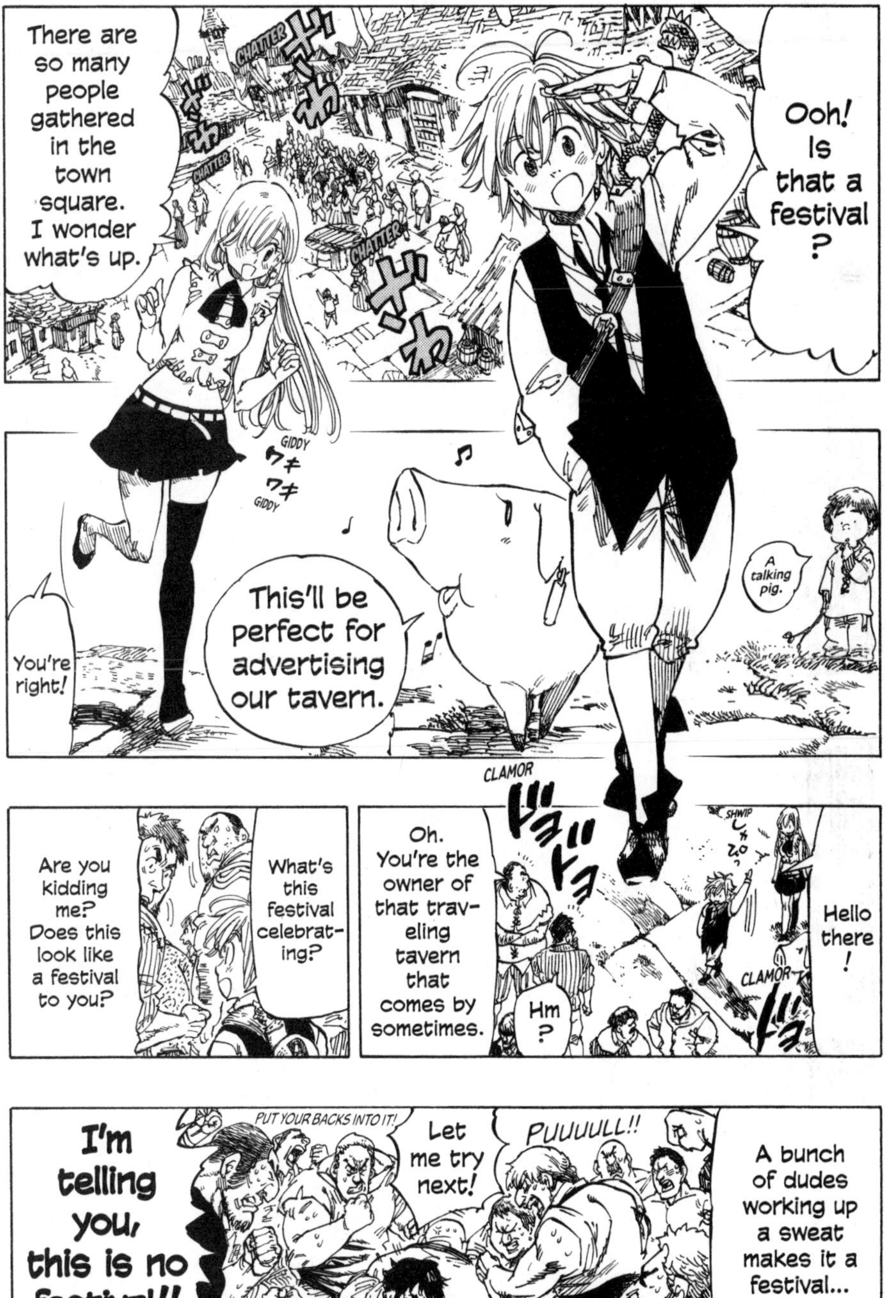
Ooh! Is that a festival?
There are so many people gathered in the town square. I wonder what's up.
CHATTER
CHATTER
CHATTER
A talking pig.
This'll be perfect for advertising our tavern.
GIDDY
GIDDY
You're right!
Hello there!
CLAMOR
SHWIP
CLAMOR
Oh. You're the owner of that trav-eling tavern that comes by sometimes.
Hm?
What's this festival celebrat-ing?
Are you kidding me? Does this look like a festival to you?
A bunch of dudes working up a sweat makes it a festival... doesn't it?
PUUUULL!!
Let me try next!
PUT YOUR BACKS INTO IT!
I'm telling you, this is no festival!!

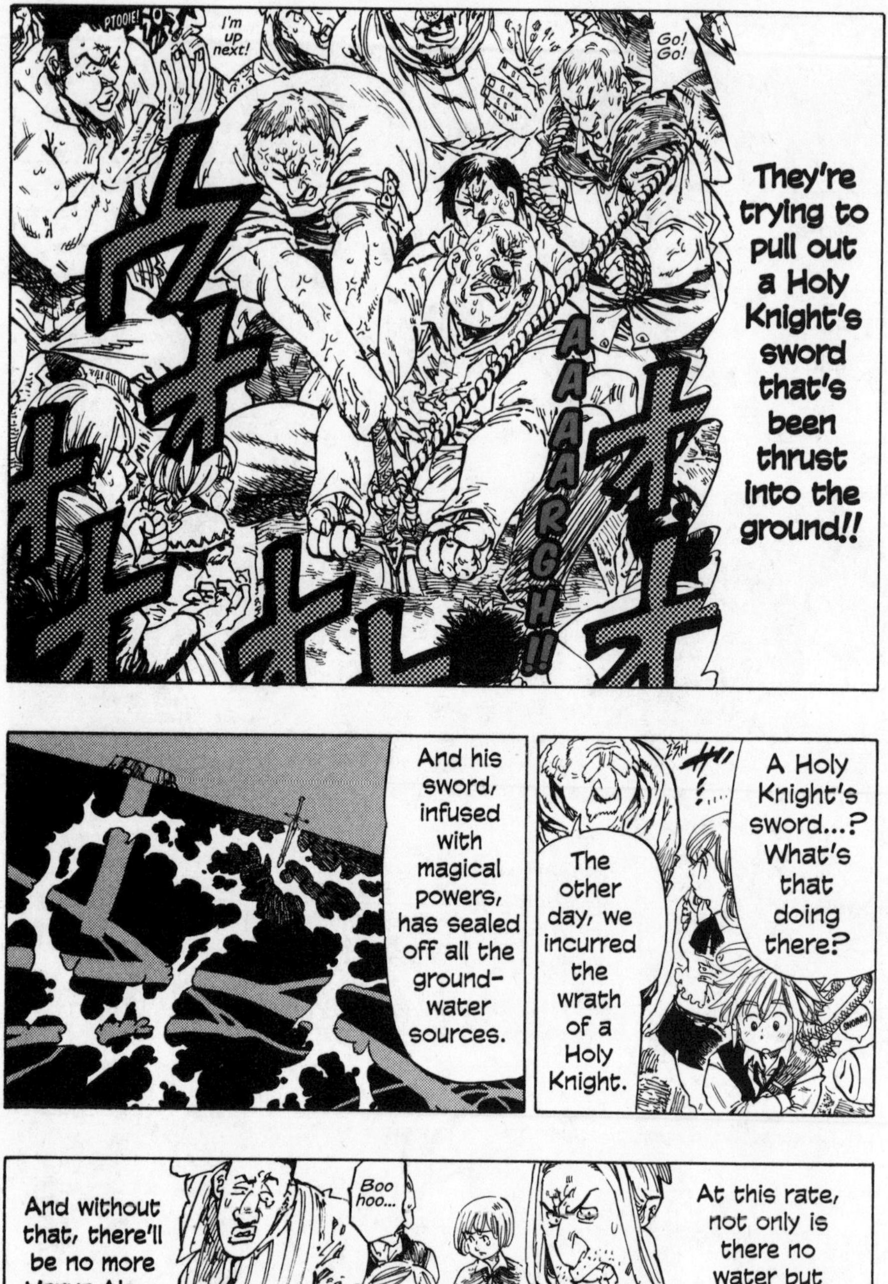
They're trying to pull out a Holy Knight's sword that's been thrust into the ground!!
Go! Go!
I'm up next!
PTOOIE!
AAAARGH!!
A Holy Knight's sword...? What's that doing there?
The other day, we incurred the wrath of a Holy Knight.
And his sword, infused with magical powers, has sealed off all the ground-water sources.
At this rate, not only is there no water but we'll lose all the grout!
Boo hoo...
And without that, there'll be no more Vanya Ale... Dammit!

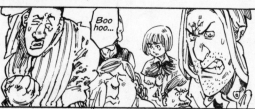

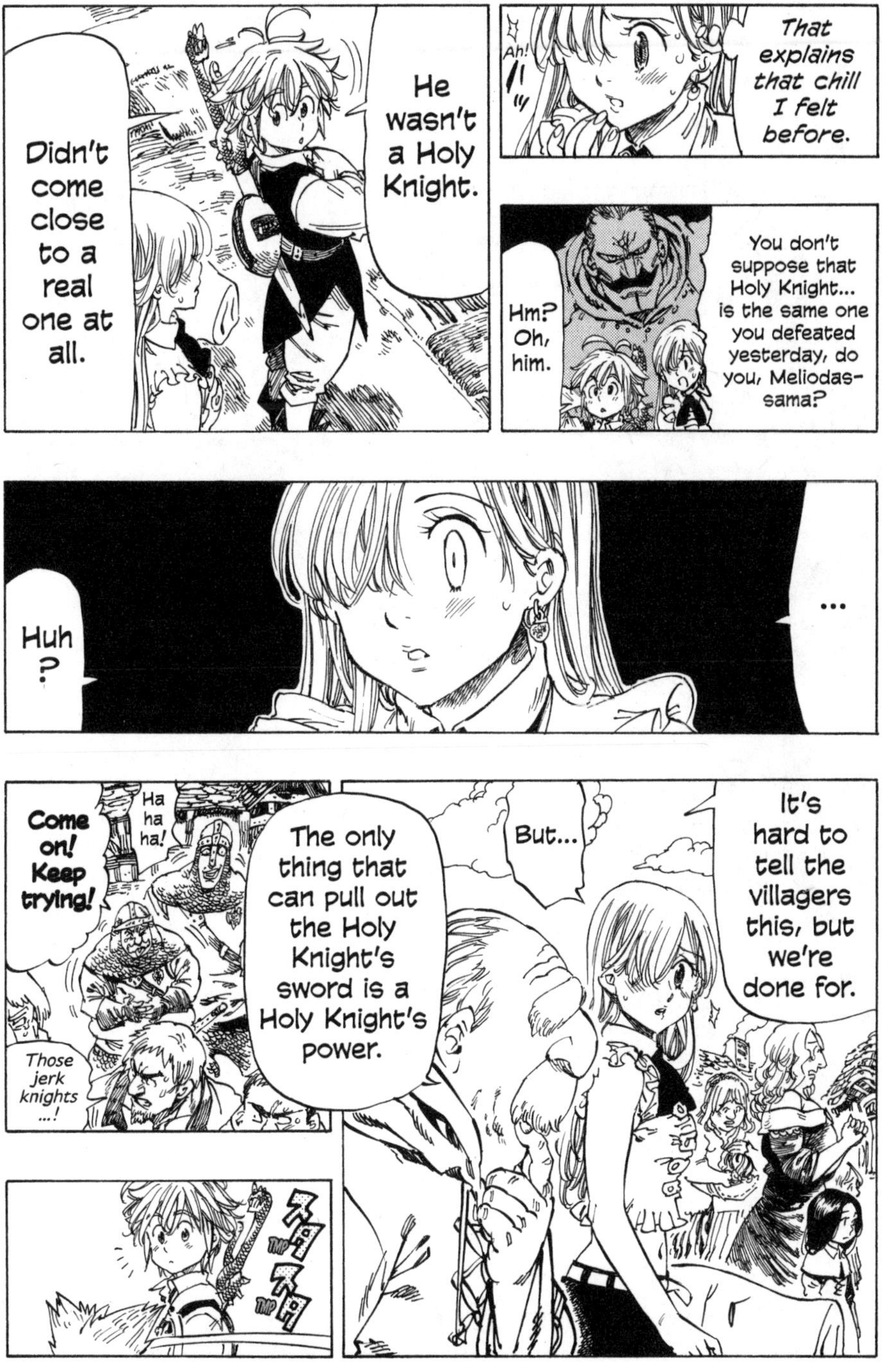

Ah!
That explains that chill I felt before.
You don't suppose that Holy Knight... is the same one you defeated yesterday, do you, Meliodas-sama?
Hm? Oh, him.
He wasn't a Holy Knight.
Didn't come close to a real one at all.
...
Huh?
It's hard to tell the villagers this, but we're done for.
But...
The only thing that can pull out the Holy Knight's sword is a Holy Knight's power.
Ha ha ha!
Come on! Keep trying!
Those jerk knights ...!
TMP
TMP

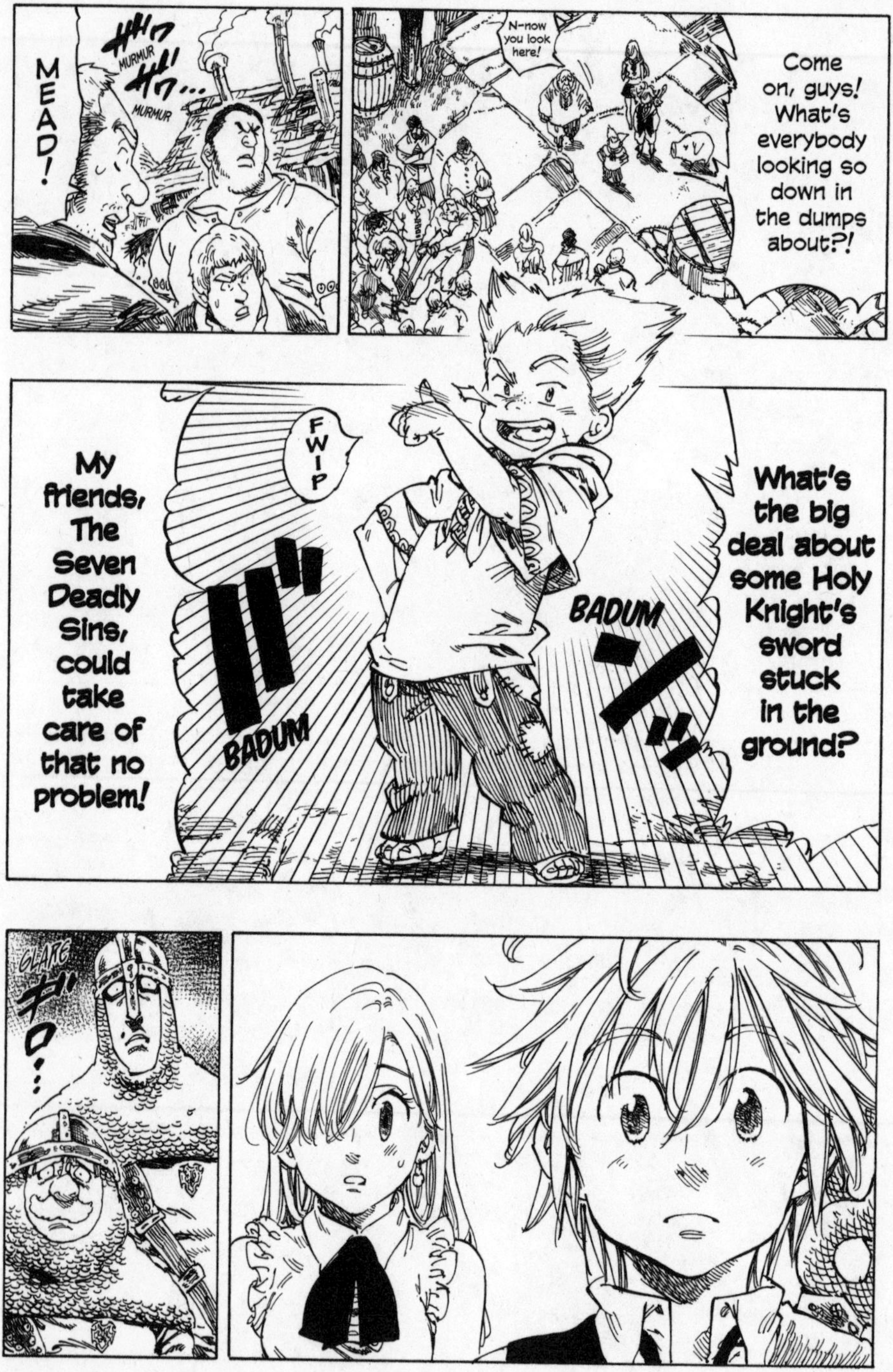
Come on, guys! What's everybody looking so down in the dumps about?!
N-now you look here!
MEAD!
MURMUR
MURMUR
What's the big deal about some Holy Knight's sword stuck in the ground?
BADUM
FWIP
My friends, The Seven Deadly Sins, could take care of that no problem!
BADUM
GLARE

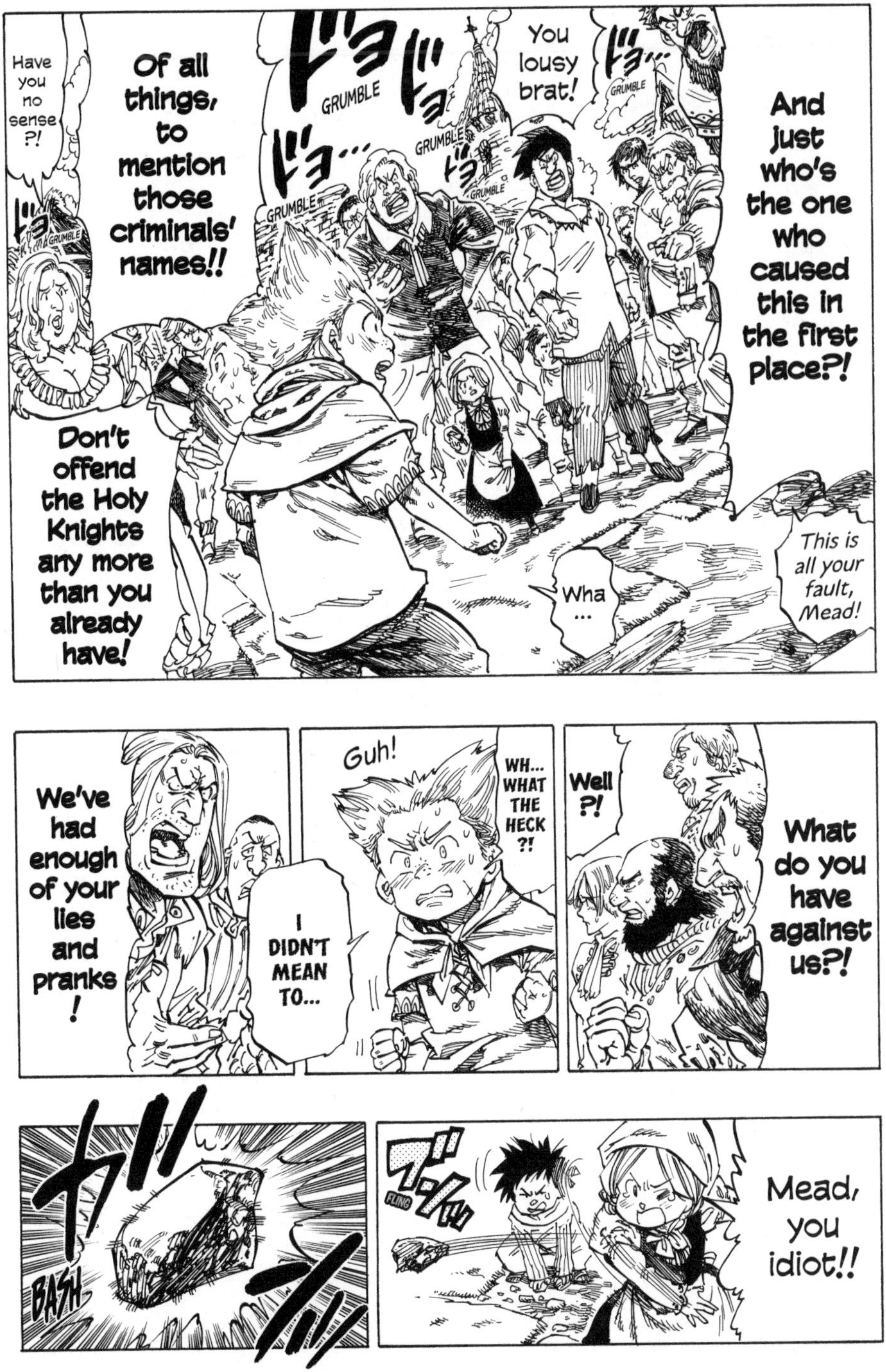
GRUMBLE
And just who's the one who caused this in the first place?!
You lousy brat!
GRUMBLE
GRUMBLE
GRUMBLE
GRUMBLE
Of all things, to mention those criminals' names!!
Have you no sense?!
GRUMBLE
This is all your fault, Mead!
Wha...
Don't offend the Holy Knights any more than you already have!
Well?!
What do you have against us?!
WH... WHAT THE HECK?!
Guh!
I DIDN'T MEAN TO...
We've had enough of your lies and pranks!
FLING
Mead, you idiot!!
BASH

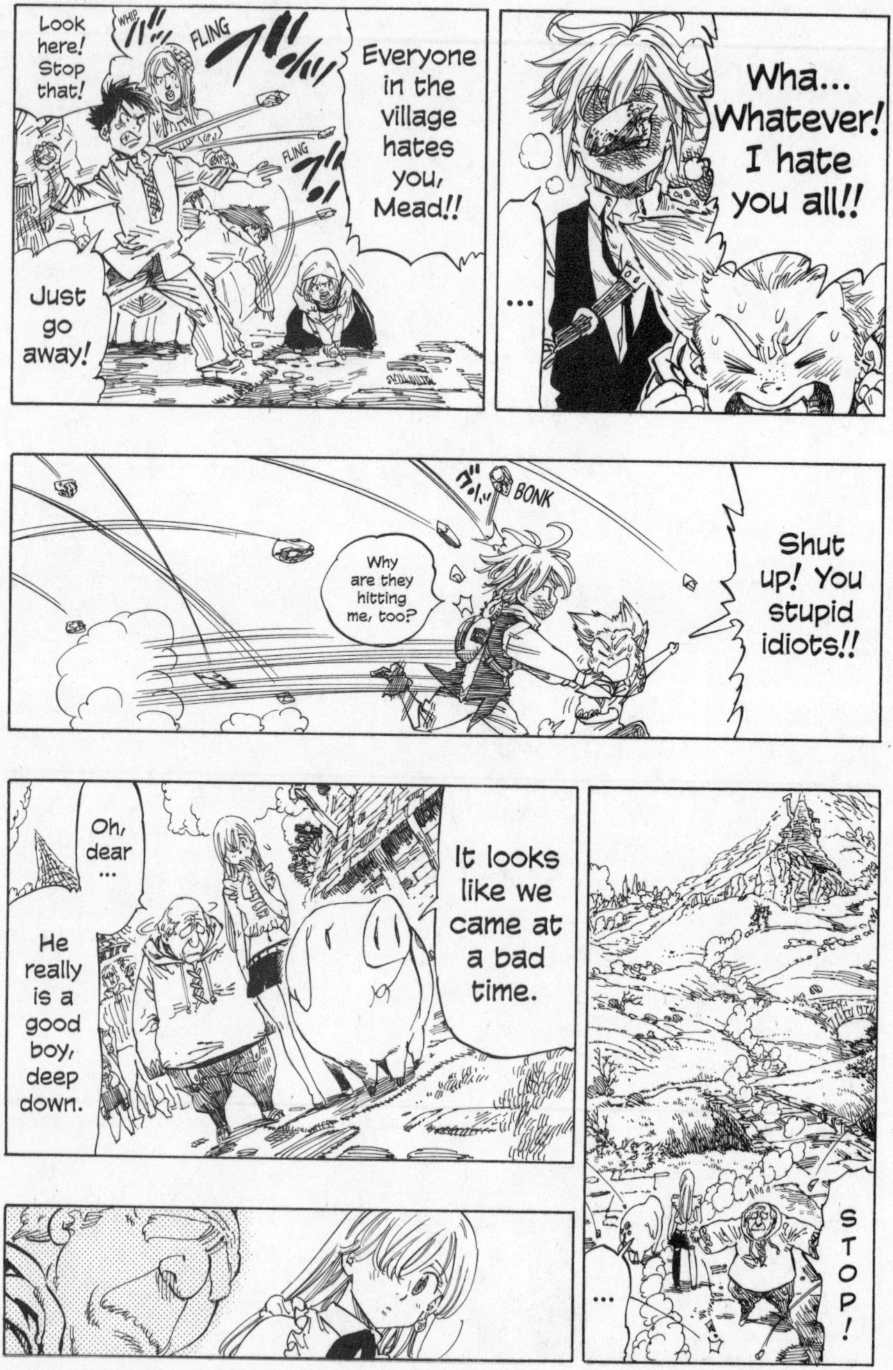
Wha... Whatever! I hate you all!!
...
Everyone in the village hates you, Mead!!
FLING
WHIP
Look here! Stop that!
FLING
Just go away!
BONK
Shut up! You stupid idiots!!
Why are they hitting me, too?
STOP!
...
It looks like we came at a bad time.
Oh, dear ...
He really is a good boy, deep down.

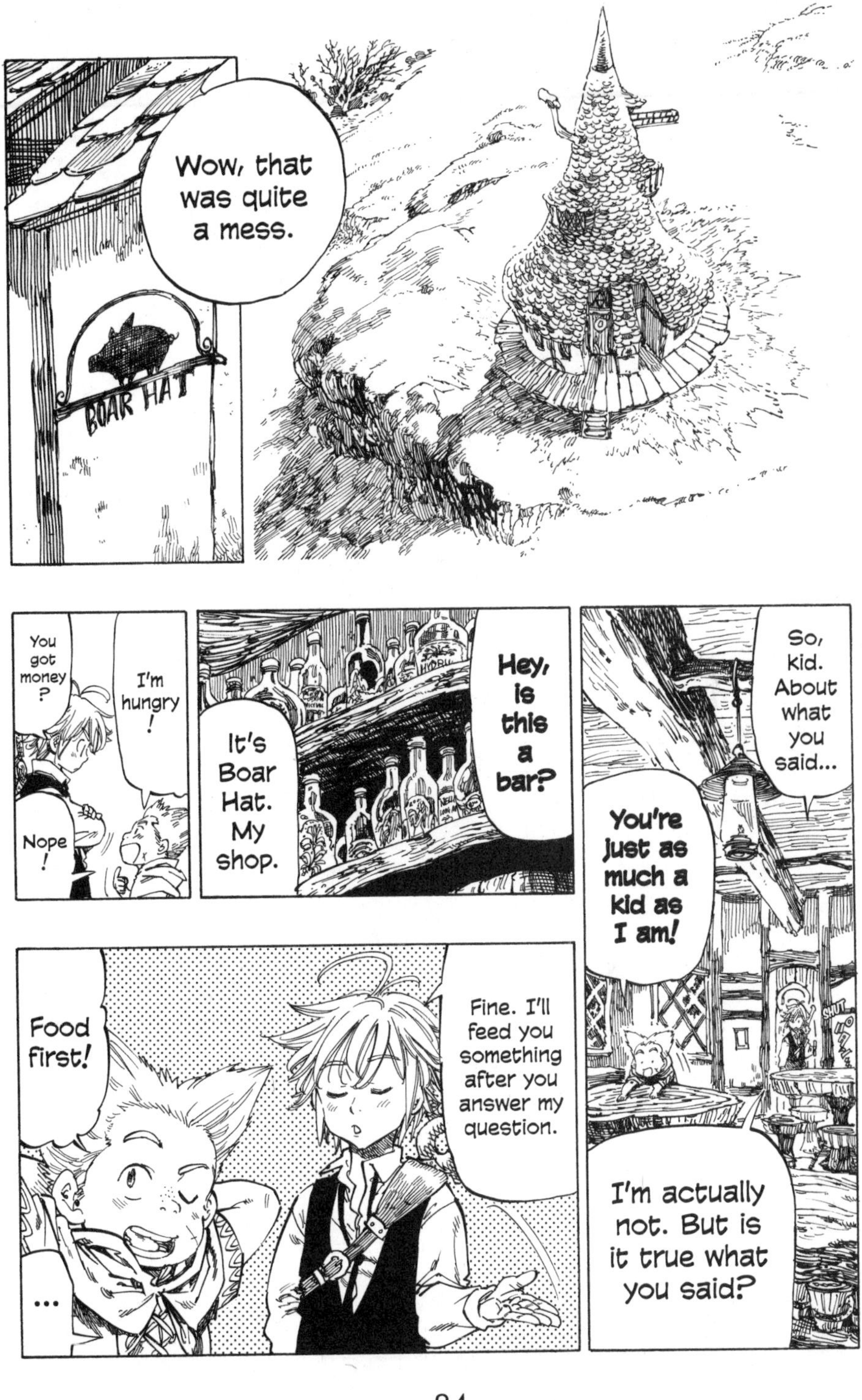

Wow, that was quite a mess.
BOAR HAT
So, kid. About what you said...
You're just as much a kid as I am!
SHUT
I'm actually not. But is it true what you said?
Hey, is this a bar?
It's Boar Hat. My shop.
I'm hungry!
You got money?
Nope!
Fine. I'll feed you something after you answer my question.
Food first!
...

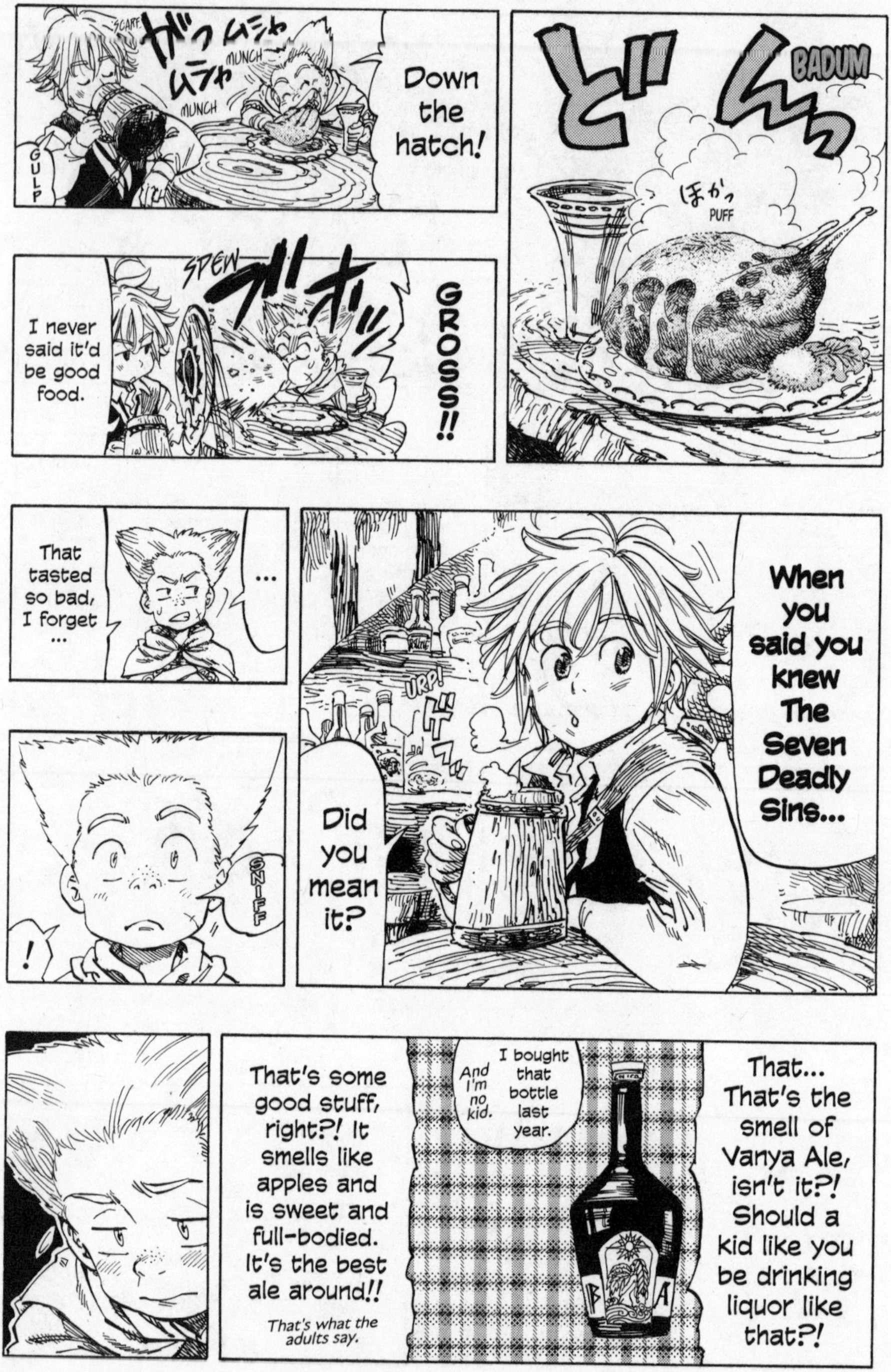
どん
BADUM
ほかっ
PUFF
Down the hatch!
ガッ ムシャ ムシャ
MUNCH
MUNCH
SCARF
GULP
GROSS!!
ブオッ
SPEW
I never said it'd be good food.
When you said you knew The Seven Deadly Sins...
Did you mean it?
ゲフッ
URP!
...
That tasted so bad, I forget ...
SNIFF
!
That... That's the smell of Vanya Ale, isn't it?! Should a kid like you be drinking liquor like that?!
I bought that bottle last year.
And I'm no kid.
That's some good stuff, right?! It smells like apples and is sweet and full-bodied. It's the best ale around!!
That's what the adults say.

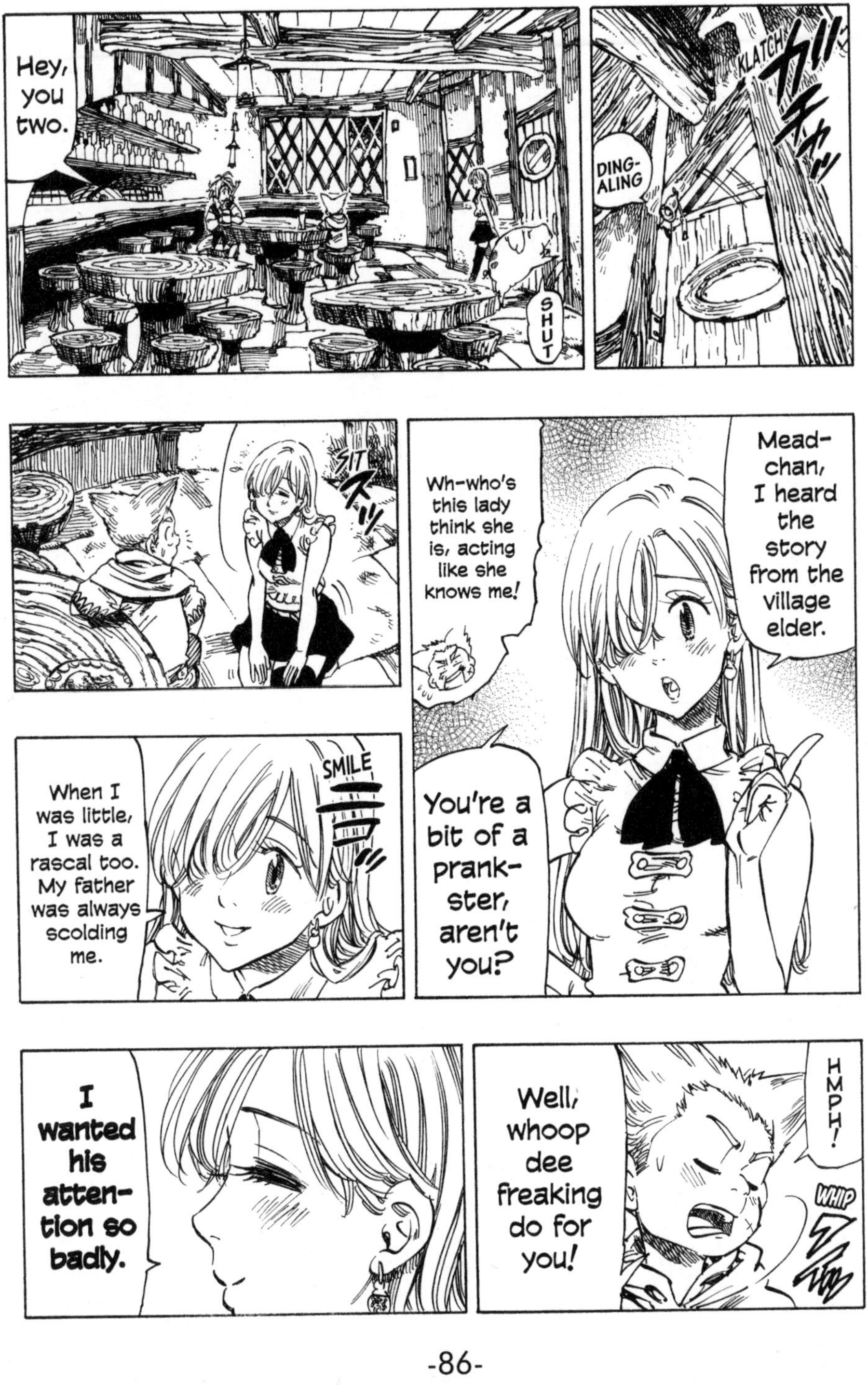
KLATCH
DING-ALING
Hey, you two.
SHUT
Mead-chan, I heard the story from the village elder.
Wh-who's this lady think she is, acting like she knows me!
You're a bit of a prank-ster, aren't you?
SIT
SMILE
When I was little, I was a rascal too. My father was always scolding me.
HMPH!
Well, whoop dee freaking do for you!
WHIP
I wanted his atten-tion so badly.

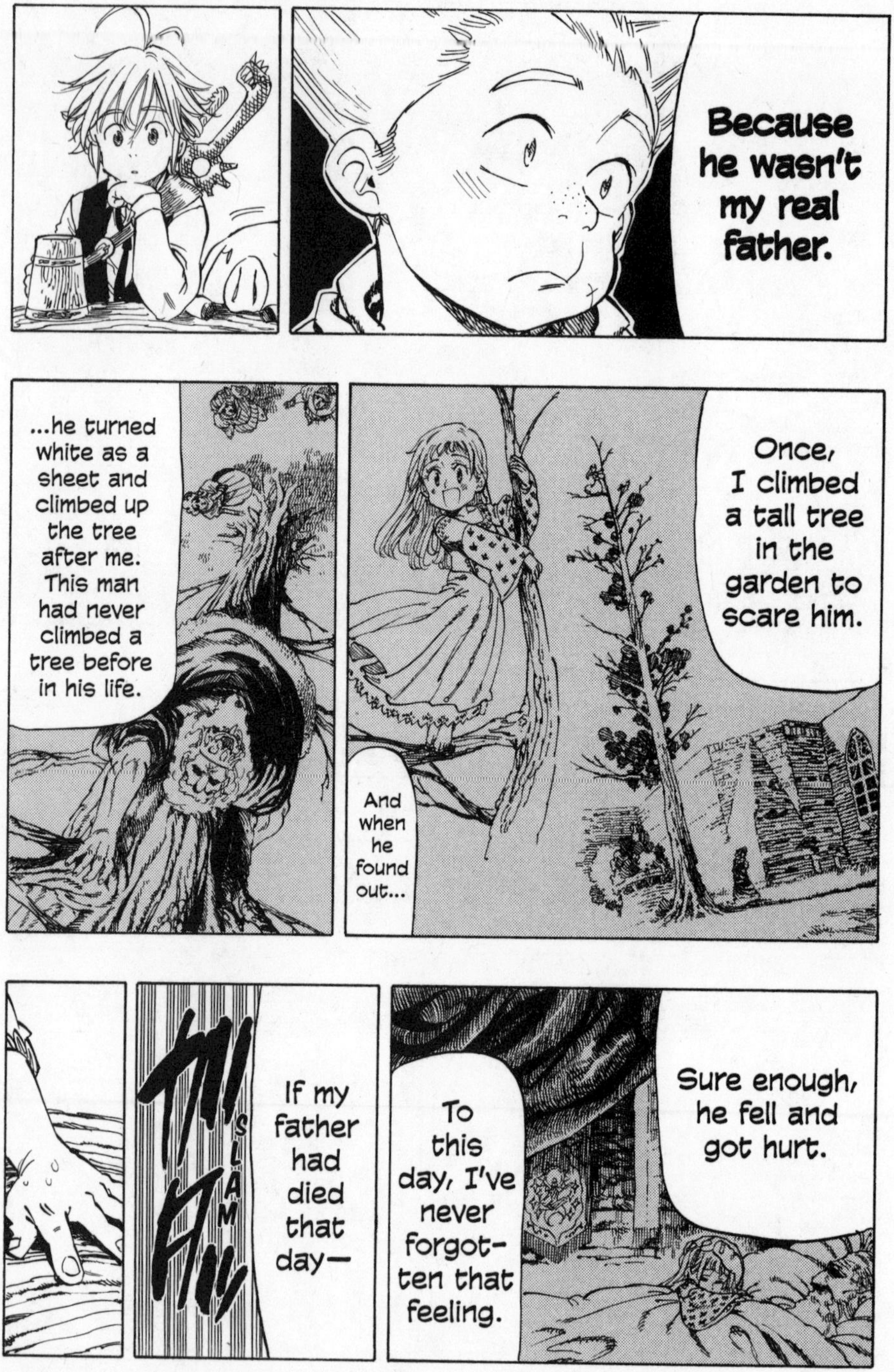
Because he wasn't my real father.
Once, I climbed a tall tree in the garden to scare him.
And when he found out...
...he turned white as a sheet and climbed up the tree after me. This man had never climbed a tree before in his life.
Sure enough, he fell and got hurt.
To this day, I've never forgotten that feeling.
If my father had died that day—
SLAM

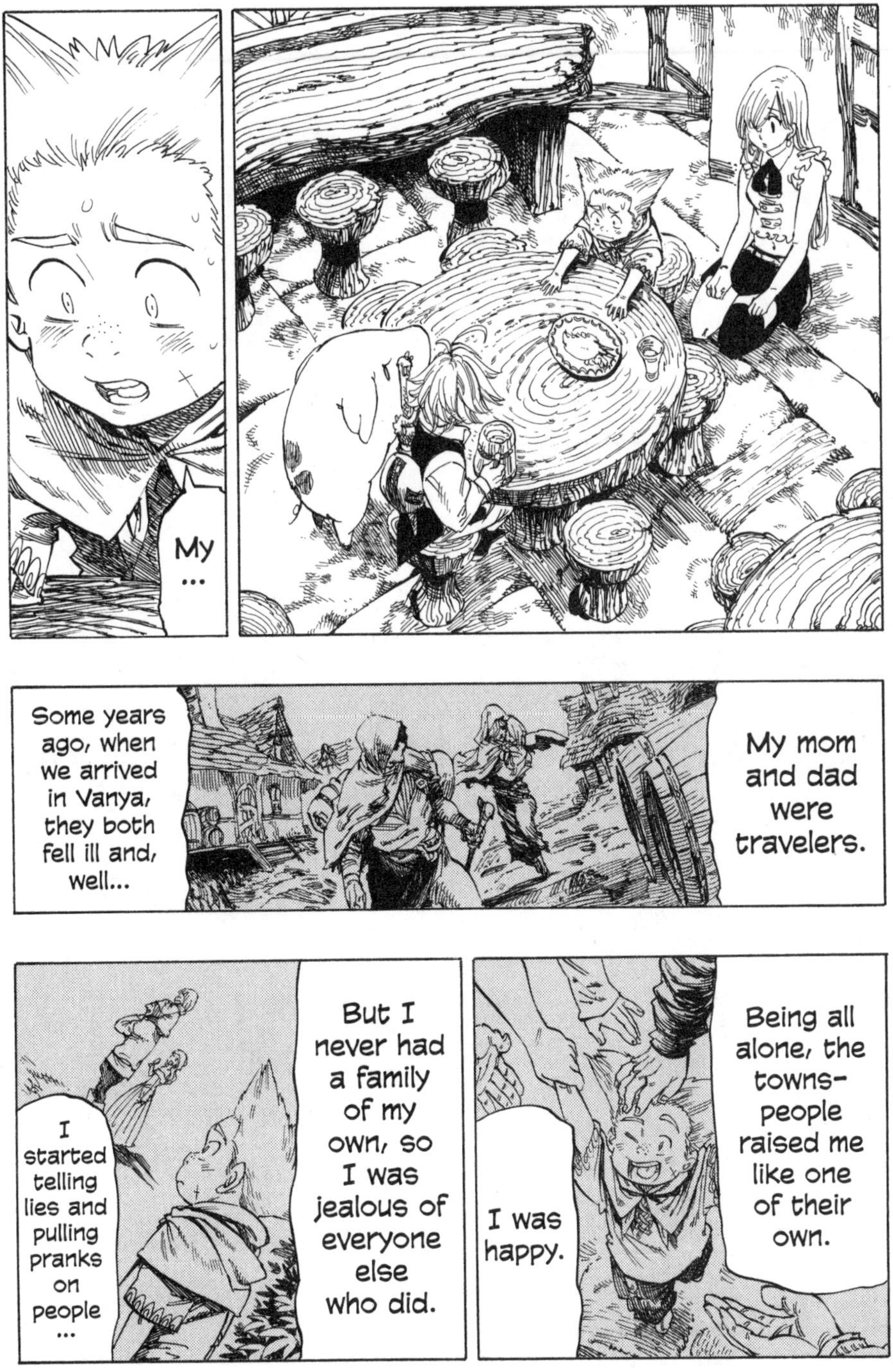
My ...
My mom and dad were travelers.
Some years ago, when we arrived in Vanya, they both fell ill and, well...
Being all alone, the towns-people raised me like one of their own.
I was happy.
But I never had a family of my own, so I was jealous of everyone else who did.
I started telling lies and pulling pranks on people ...

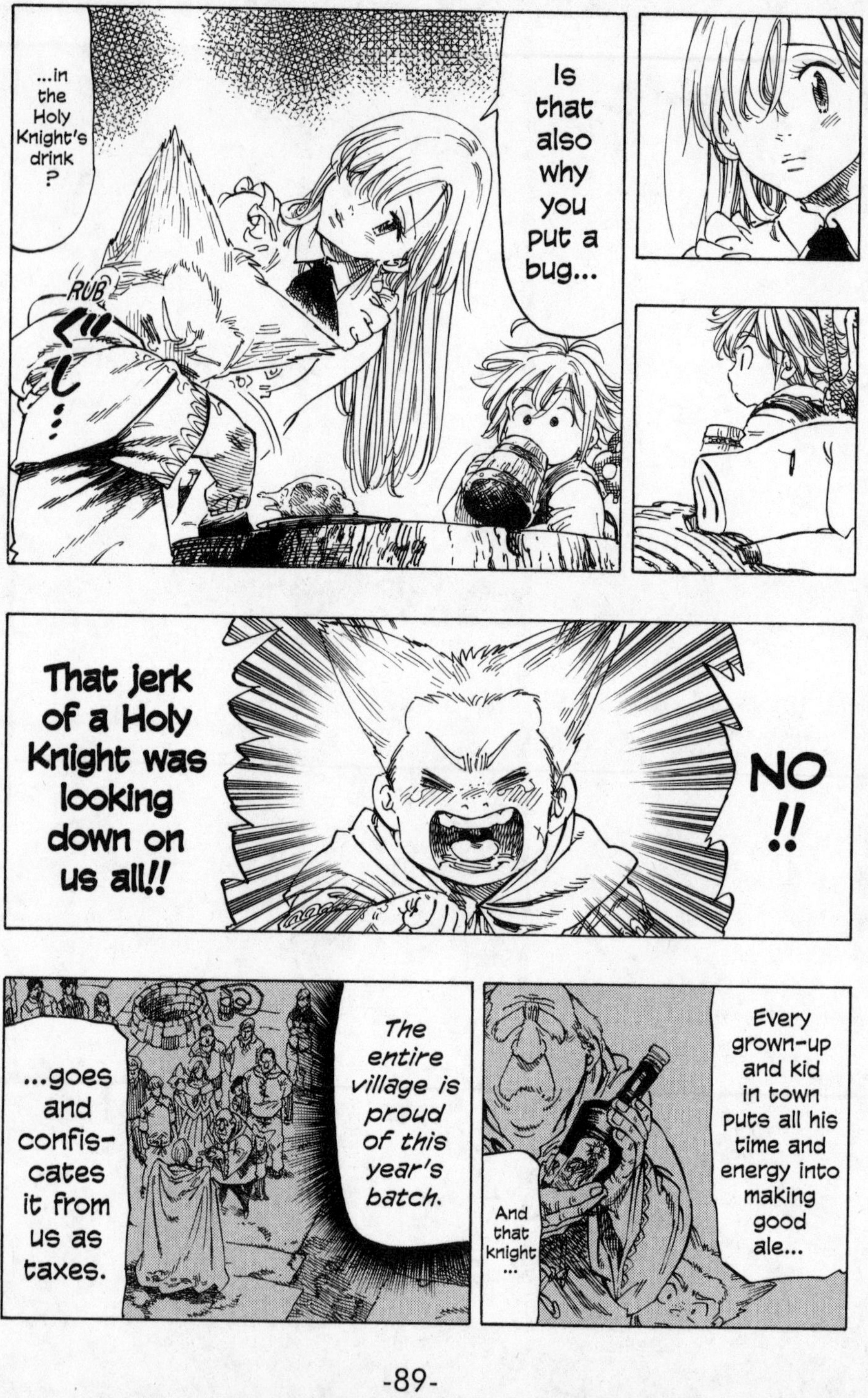
Is that also why you put a bug...
...in the Holy Knight's drink?
RUB
NO!!
That jerk of a Holy Knight was looking down on us all!!
Every grown-up and kid in town puts all his time and energy into making good ale...
And that knight...
The entire village is proud of this year's batch.
...goes and confiscates it from us as taxes.

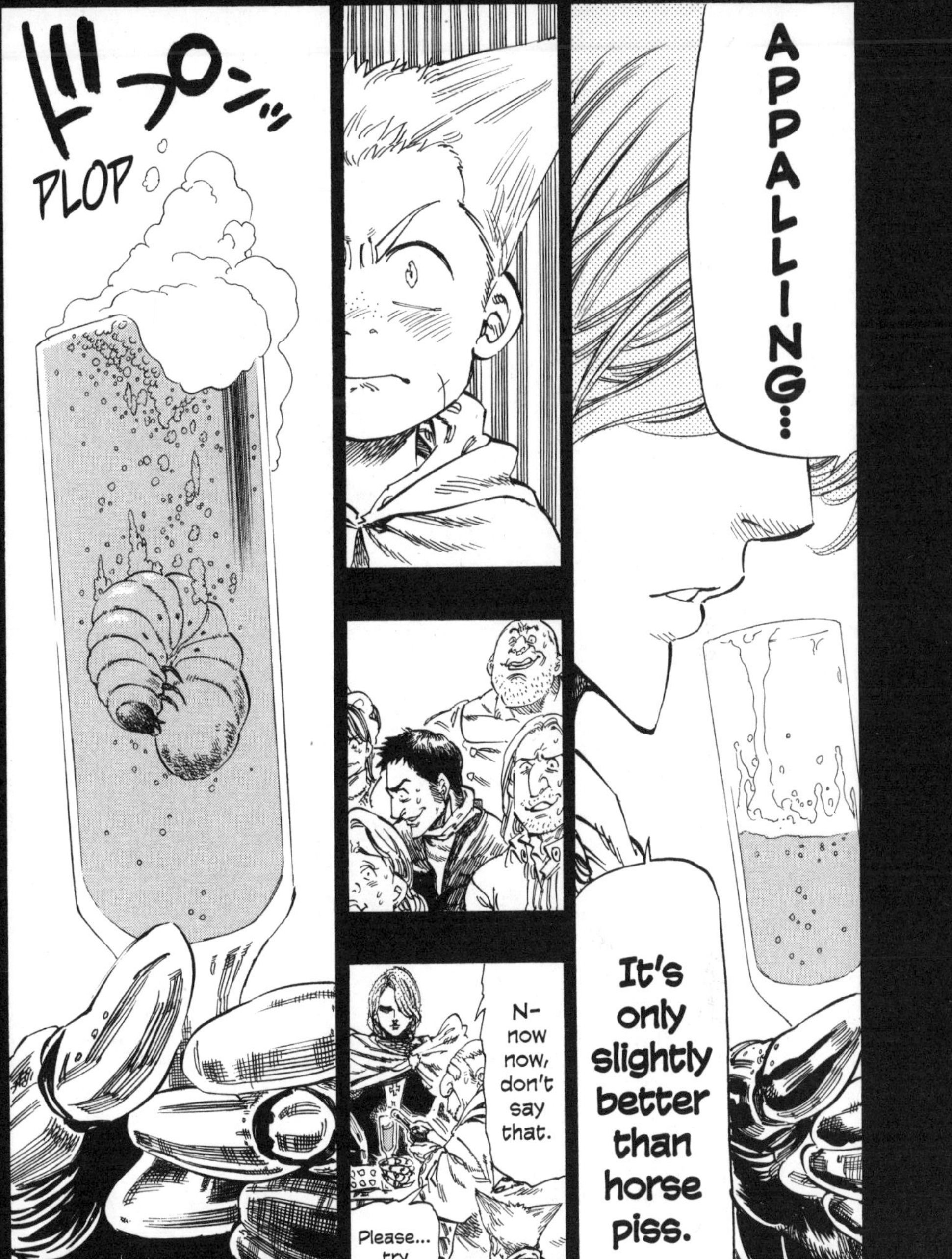
APPALLING...
It's only slightly better than horse piss.
N-now now, don't say that.
Please... try another glass.
ドプンッ
PLOP

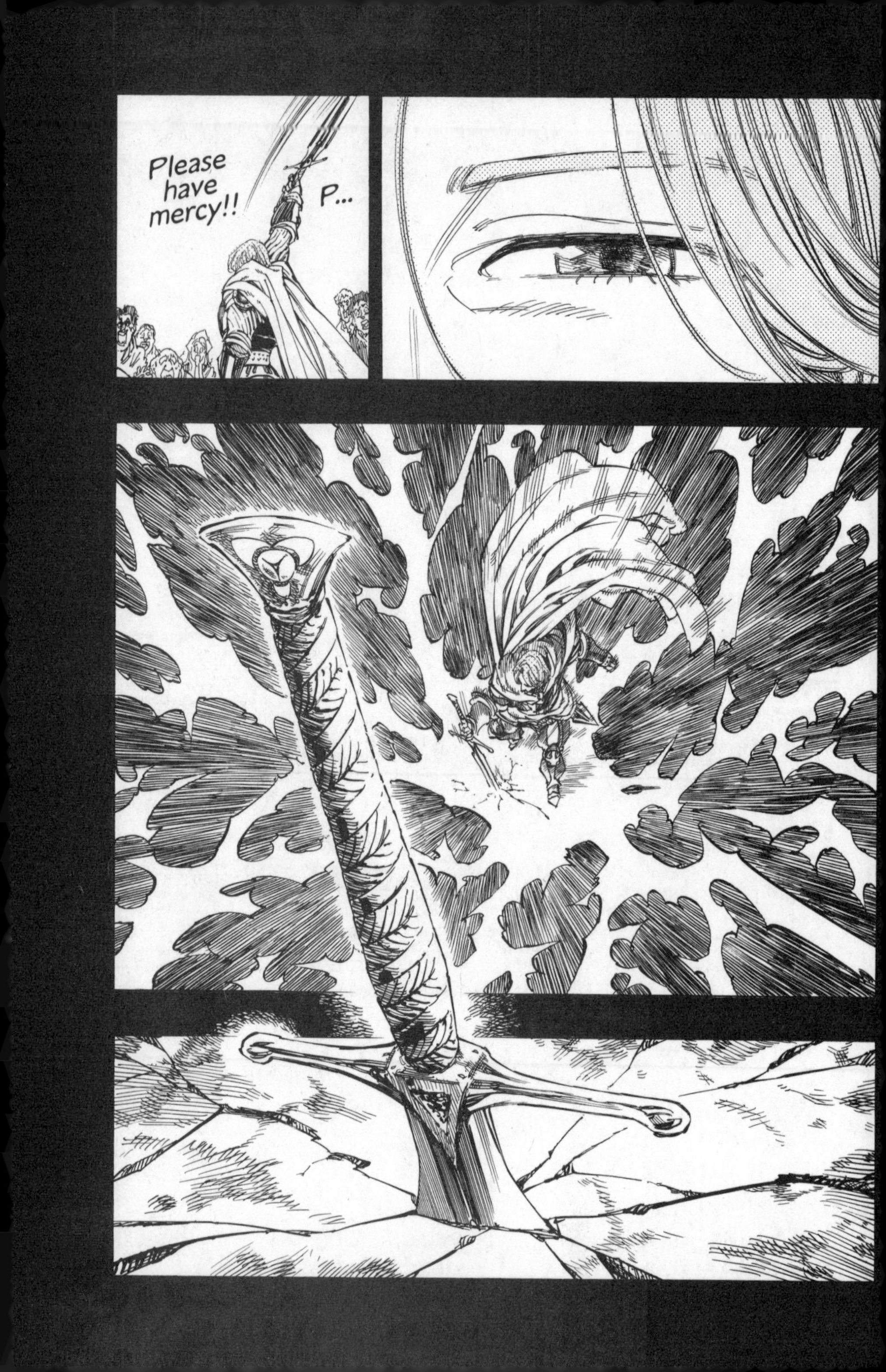
P...
Please have mercy!!

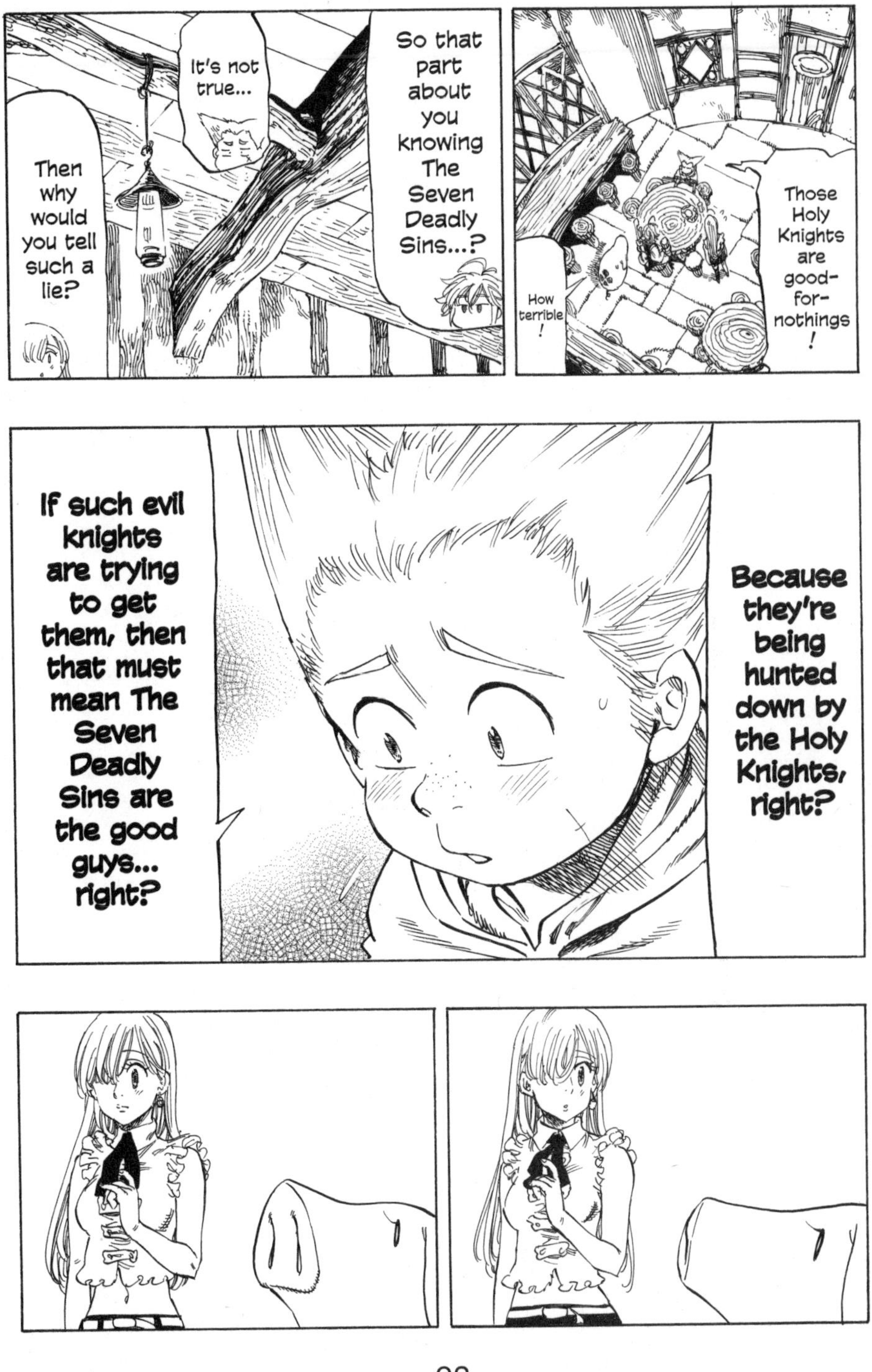
Those Holy Knights are good-for-nothings!
How terrible!
So that part about you knowing The Seven Deadly Sins...?
It's not true...
Then why would you tell such a lie?
Because they're being hunted down by the Holy Knights, right?
If such evil knights are trying to get them, then that must mean The Seven Deadly Sins are the good guys... right?

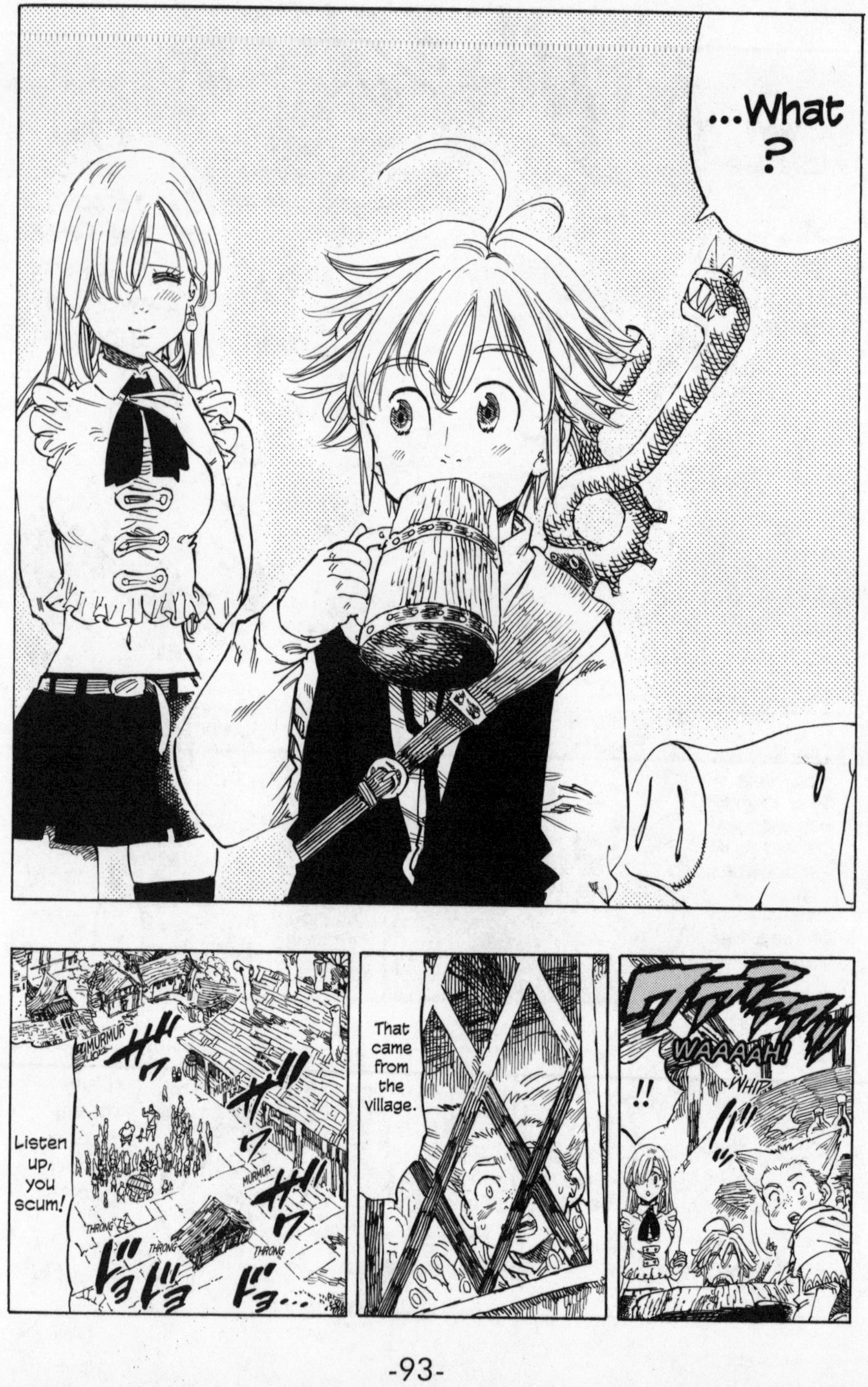
...What
?
WAAAAH!
WHIP
!!
That came from the village.
Listen up, you scum!
MURMUR
MURMUR
MURMUR
THRONG
THRONG
THRONG

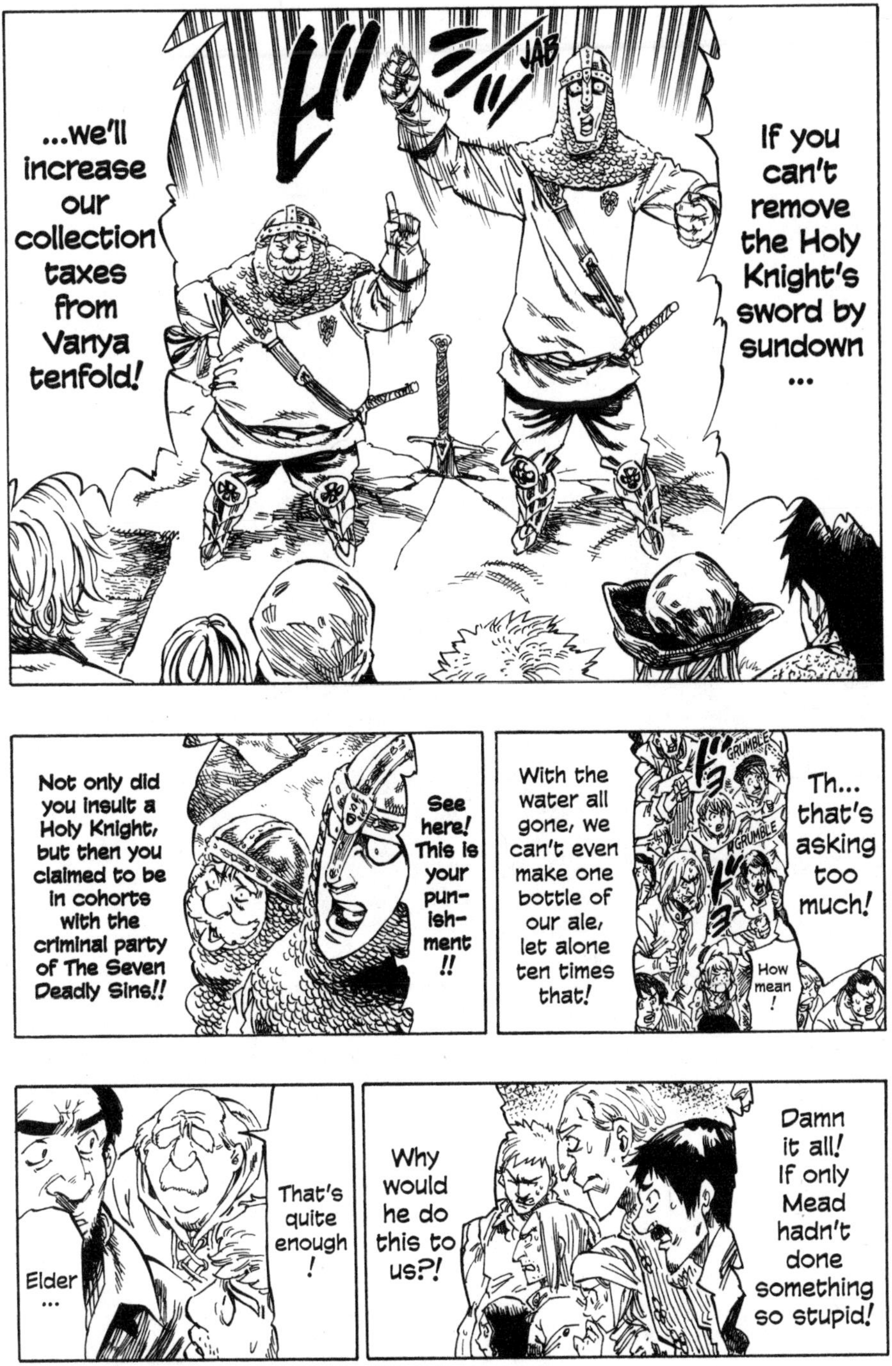
JAB
If you can't remove the Holy Knight's sword by sundown ...
...we'll increase our collection taxes from Vanya tenfold!
Th... that's asking too much!
GRUMBLE
GRUMBLE
How mean!
With the water all gone, we can't even make one bottle of our ale, let alone ten times that!
See here! This is your punishment!!
Not only did you insult a Holy Knight, but then you claimed to be in cohorts with the criminal party of The Seven Deadly Sins!!
Damn it all! If only Mead hadn't done something so stupid!
Why would he do this to us?!
That's quite enough!
Elder ...

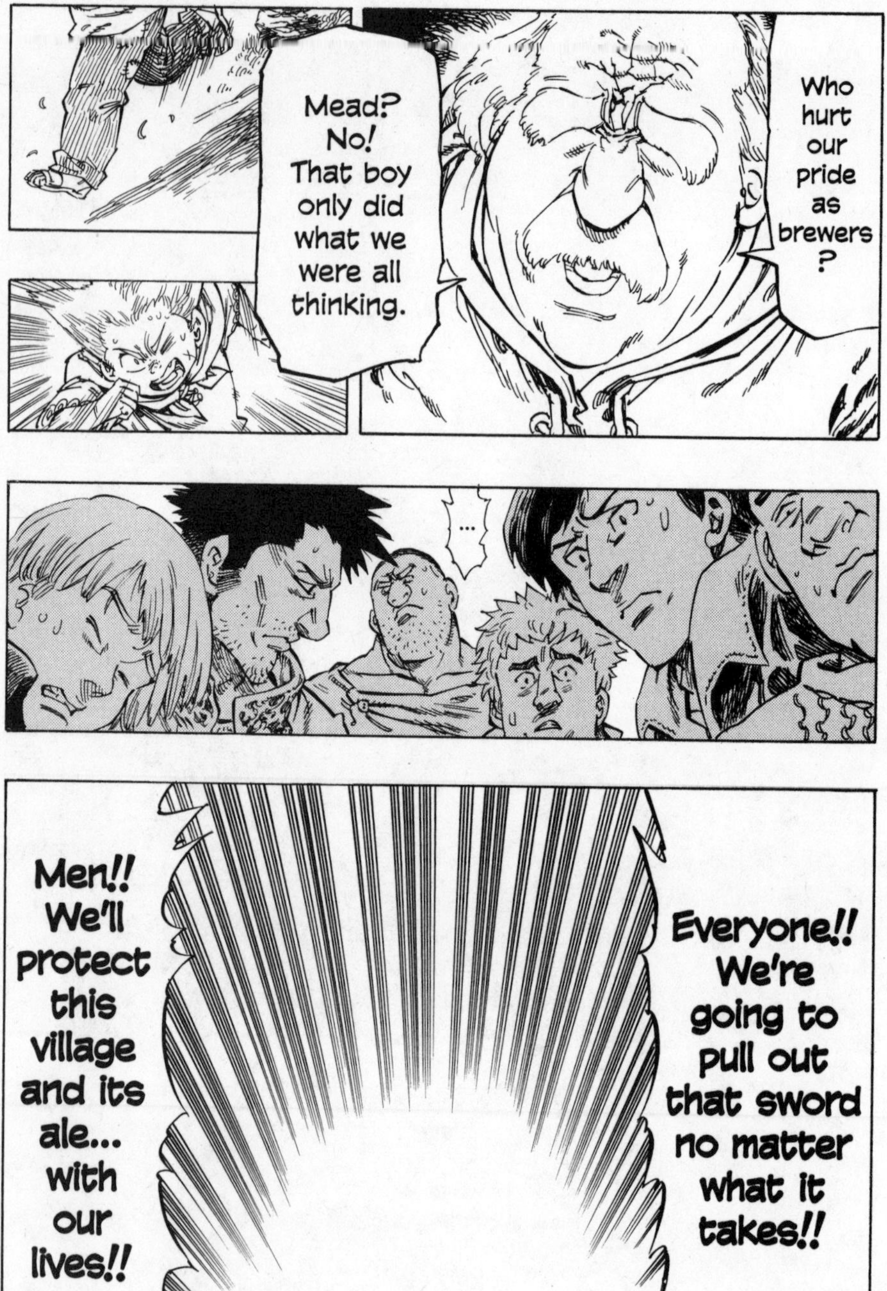
Who hurt our pride as brewers?
Mead? No! That boy only did what we were all thinking.
...
Everyone!! We're going to pull out that sword no matter what it takes!!
Men!! We'll protect this village and its ale... with our lives!!

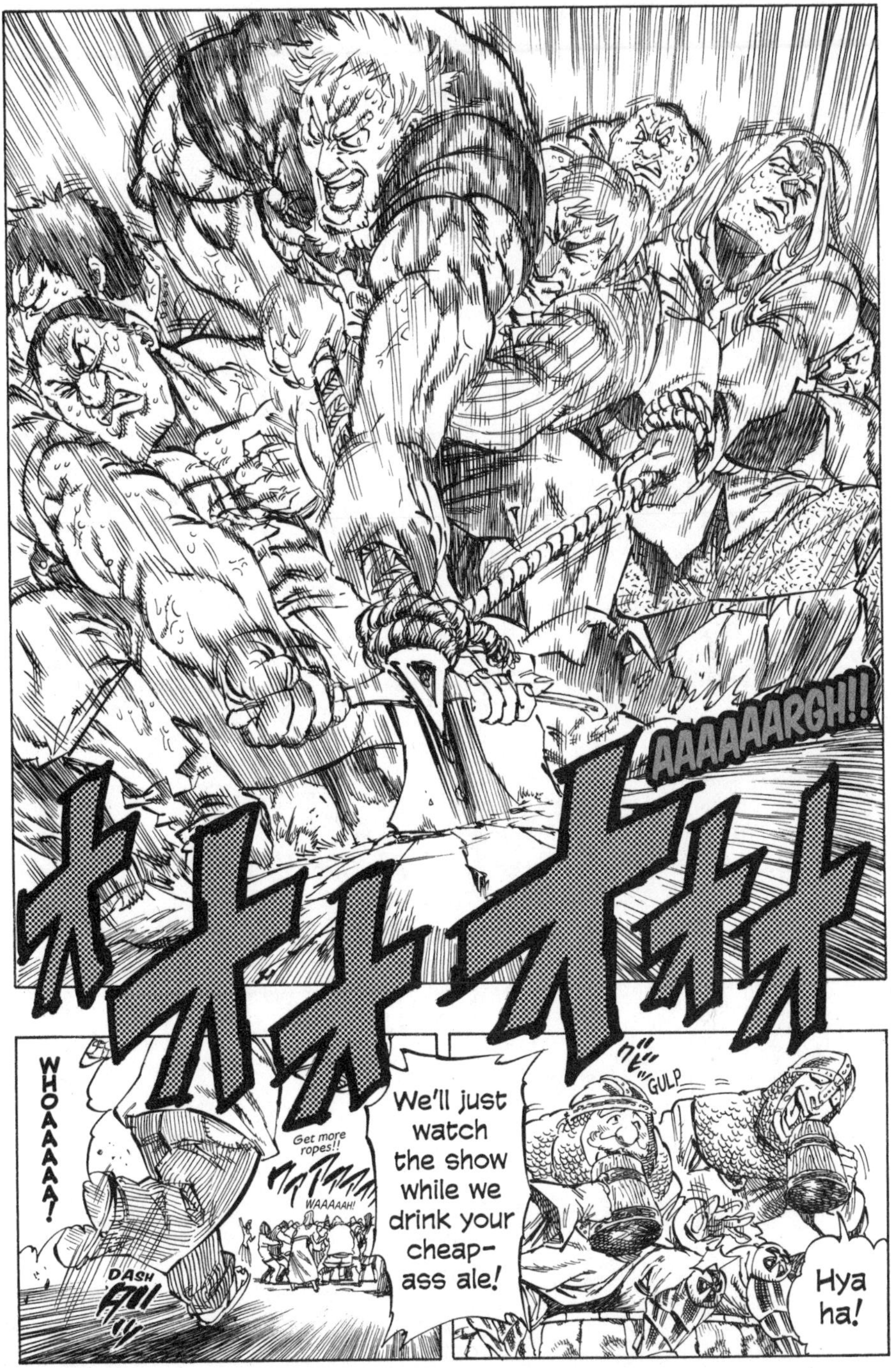

AAAAAARGH!!
オオオオォォ
Hya ha!
GULP
We'll just watch the show while we drink your cheap-ass ale!
Get more ropes!!
WAAAAAH!
WHOAAAAAA!
DASH

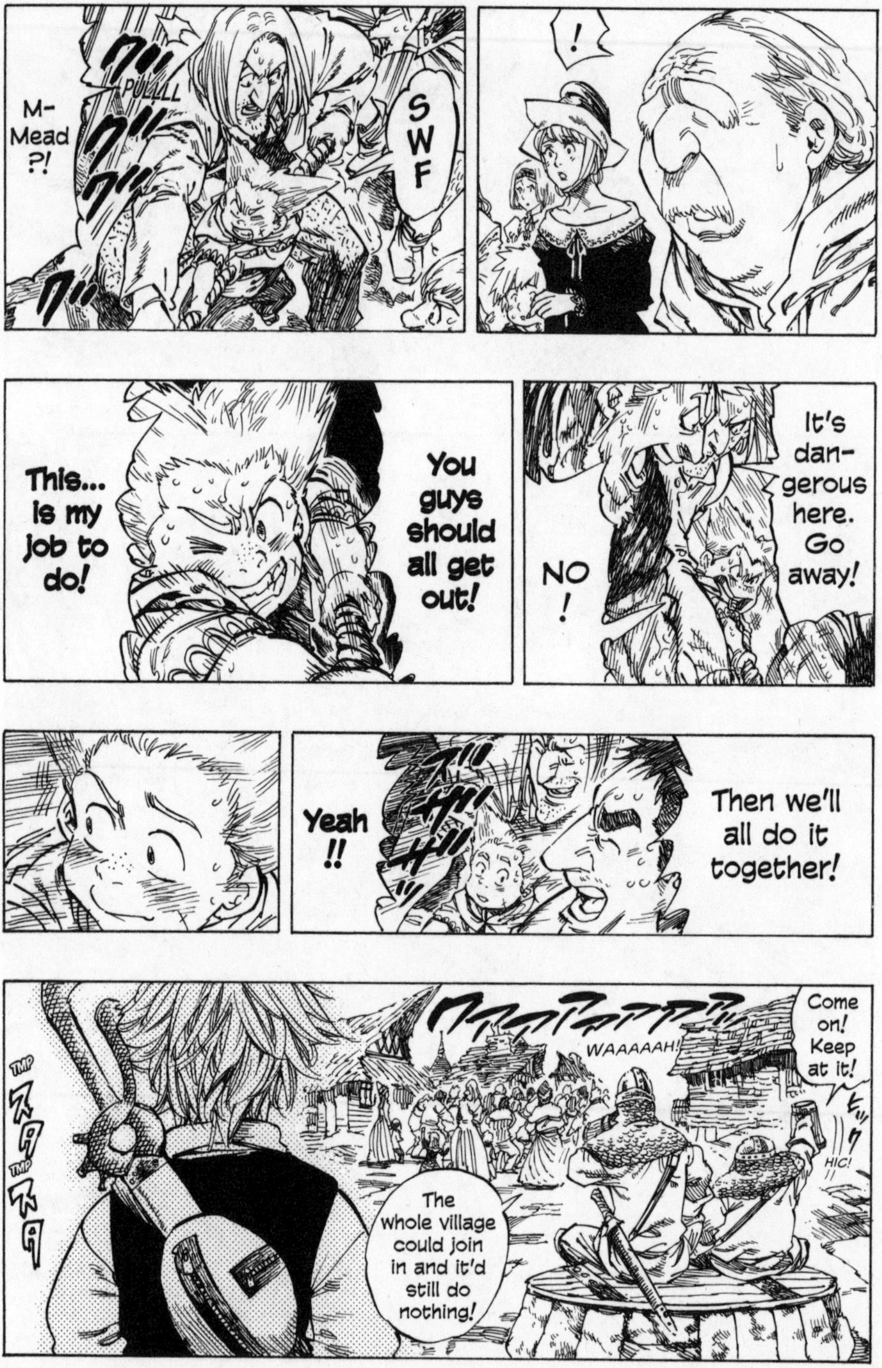
!
M-Mead ?!
PULLLL
SWF
It's dangerous here. Go away!
NO!
You guys should all get out!
This... is my job to do!
Then we'll all do it together!
Yeah!!
Come on! Keep at it!
HIC!
WAAAAAH!
TMP
TMP
The whole village could join in and it'd still do nothing!

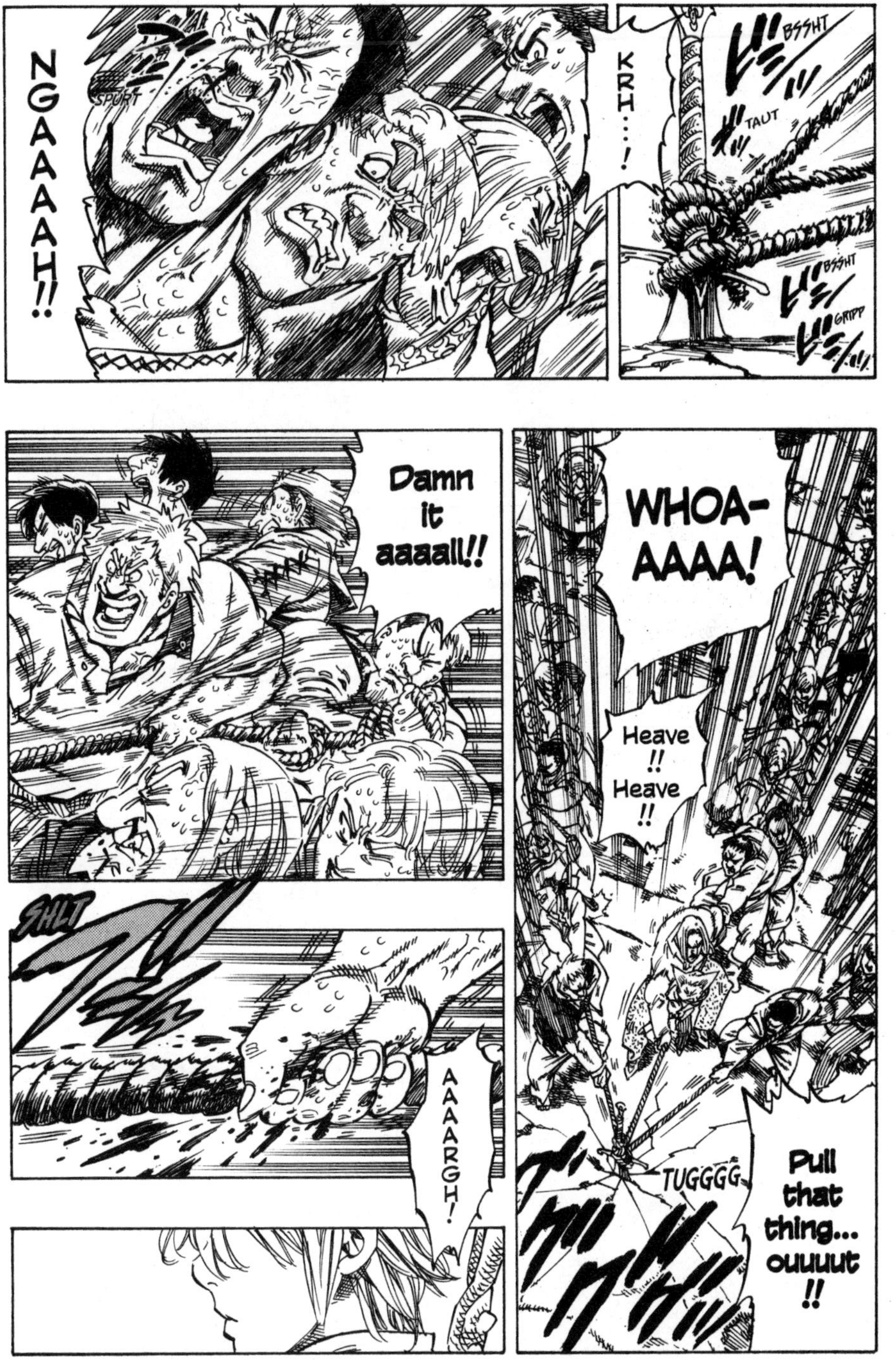
BSSHT
TAUT
KRH...!
BSSHT
GRIPP
NGAAAAAAH!!
SPURT
WHOA-AAAA!
Heave!! Heave!!
TUGGGG
Pull that thing... ouuuut!!
Damn it aaaall!!
SHLT
AAAARGH!

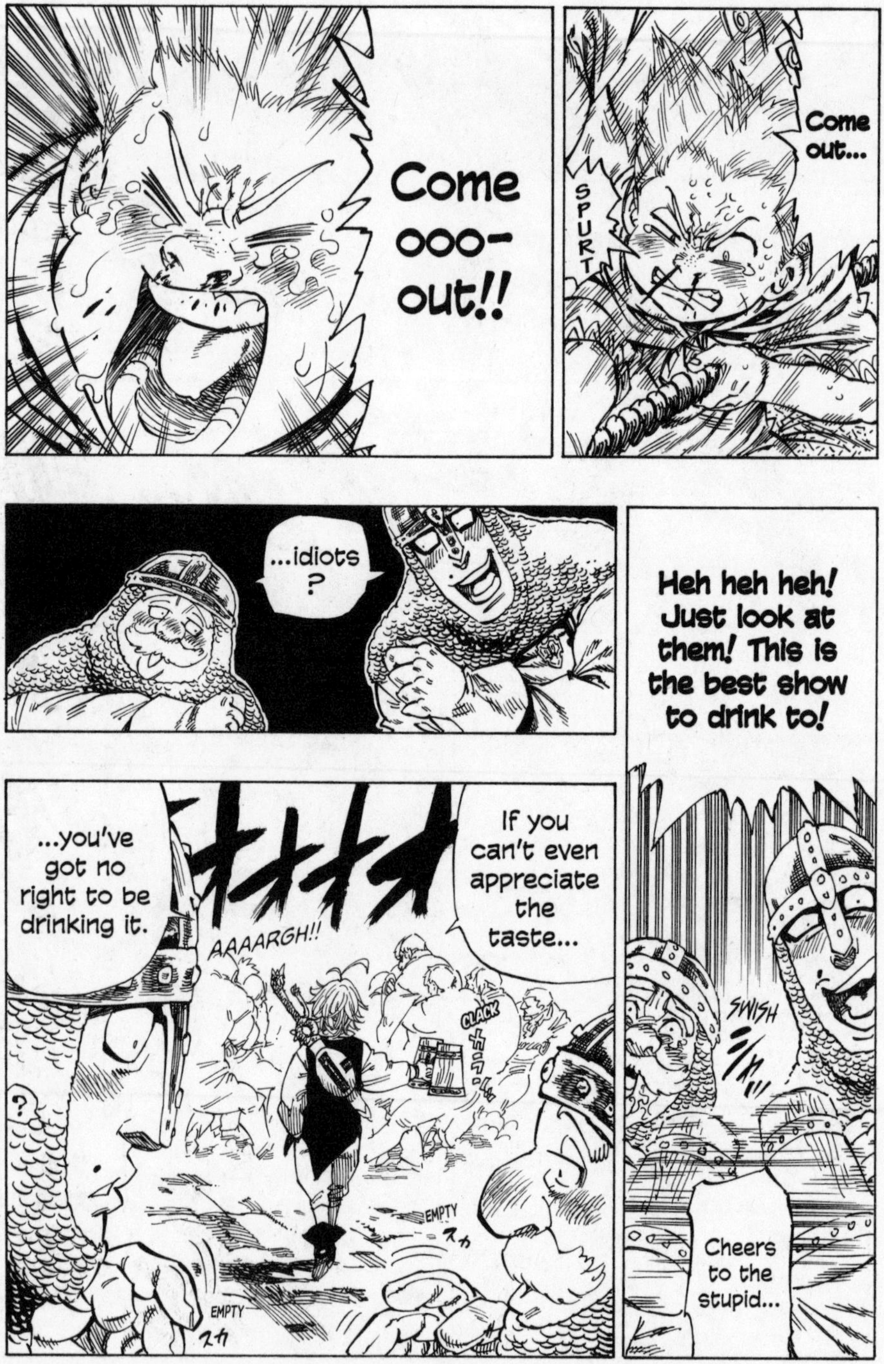

Come out...
SPURT
Come ooo-out!!
Heh heh heh! Just look at them! This is the best show to drink to!
SWISH
Cheers to the stupid...
...idiots?
If you can't even appreciate the taste...
...you've got no right to be drinking it.
AAAARGH!!
CLACK
EMPTY
スカ
EMPTY
スカ

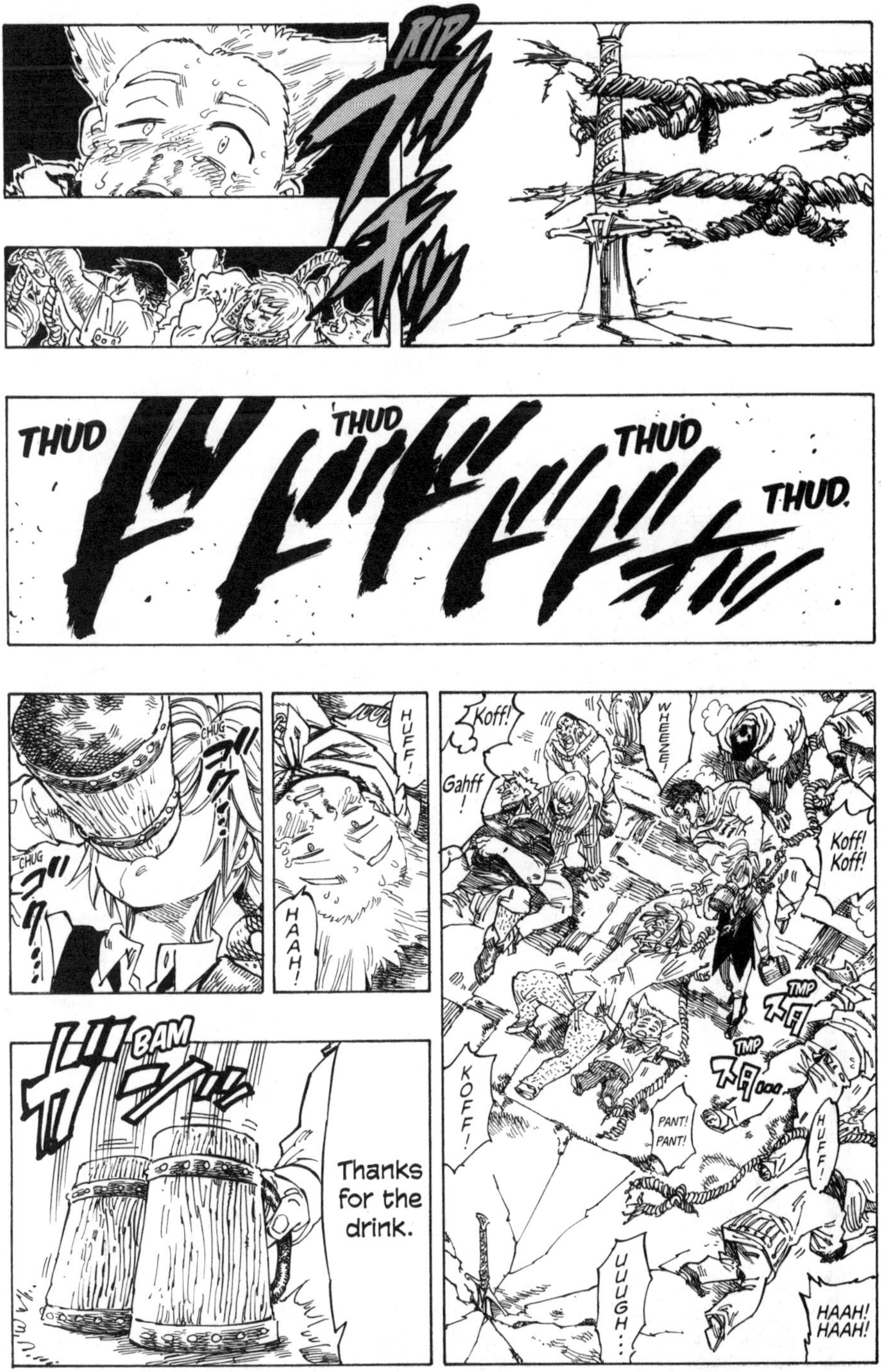
RIP
THUD
THUD
THUD
THUD.
WHEEZE!
Koff!
Koff! Koff!
Gahff!
TMP
TMP...
HUFF!
PANT! PANT!
KOFF!
HAAH! HAAH!
UUUGH...
HUFF!
HAAH!
CHUG
CHUG
BAM
Thanks for the drink.

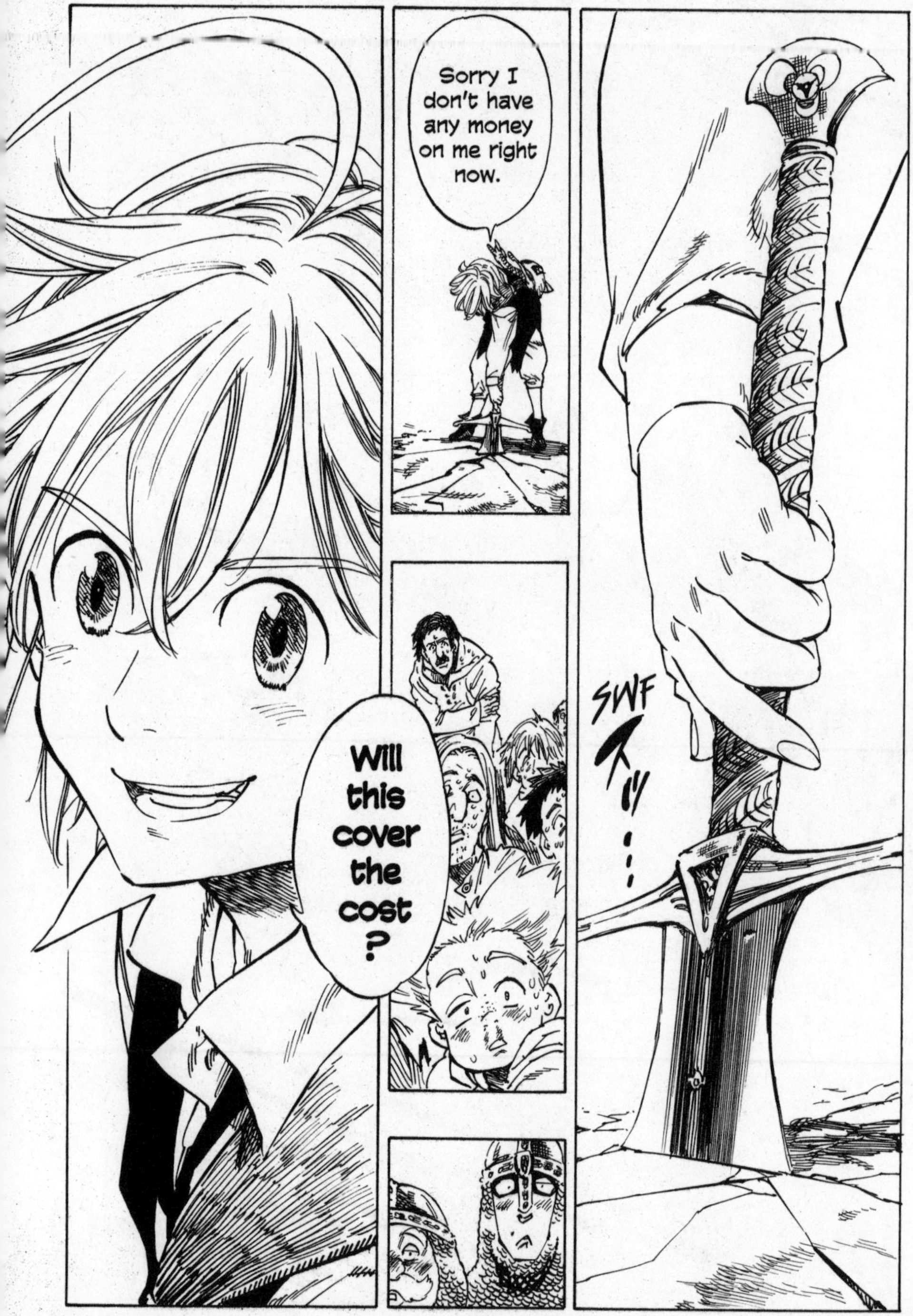
SWF
スッ・・・
Sorry I don't have any money on me right now.
Will this cover the cost?

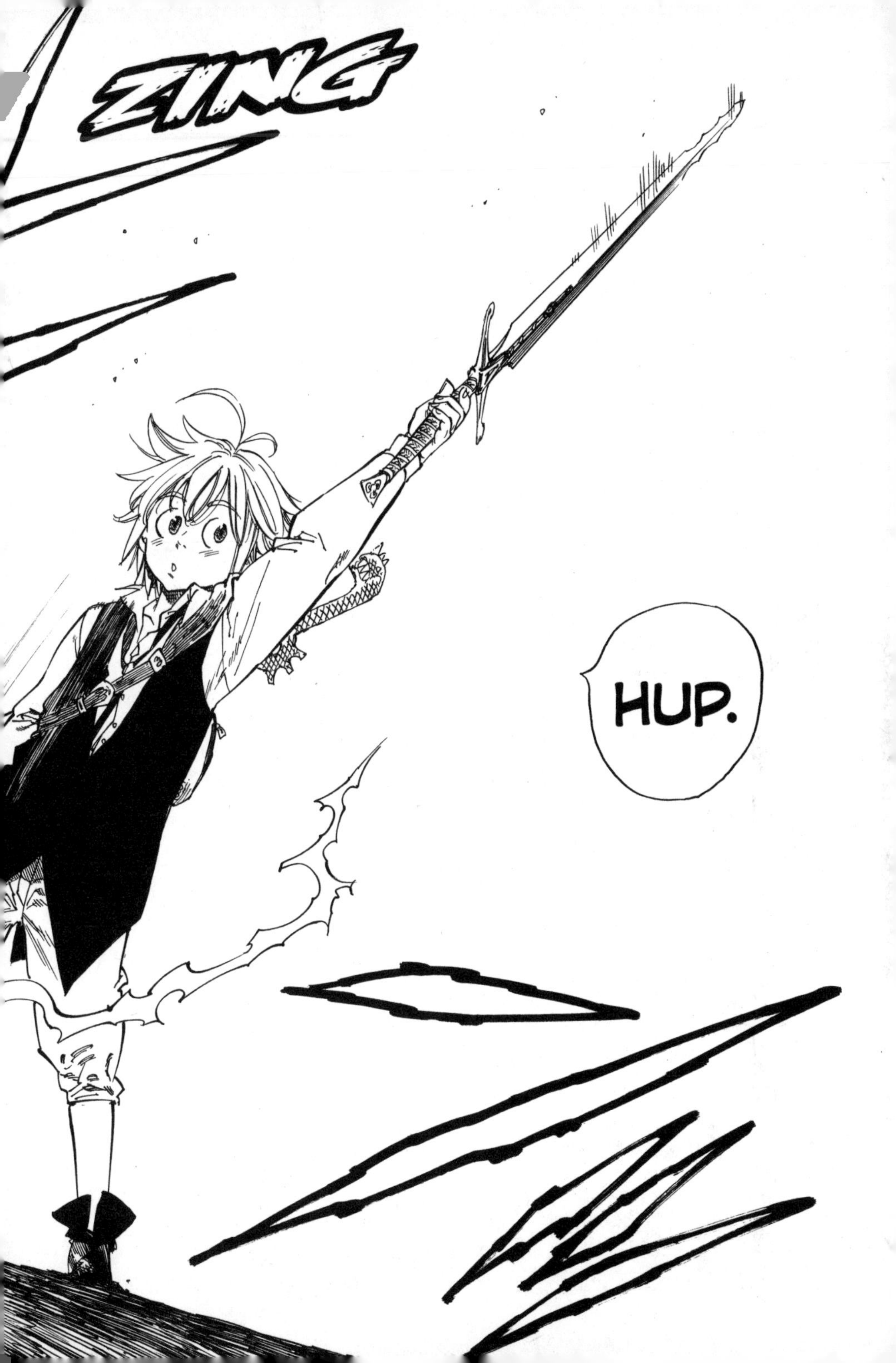
ZING
HUP.

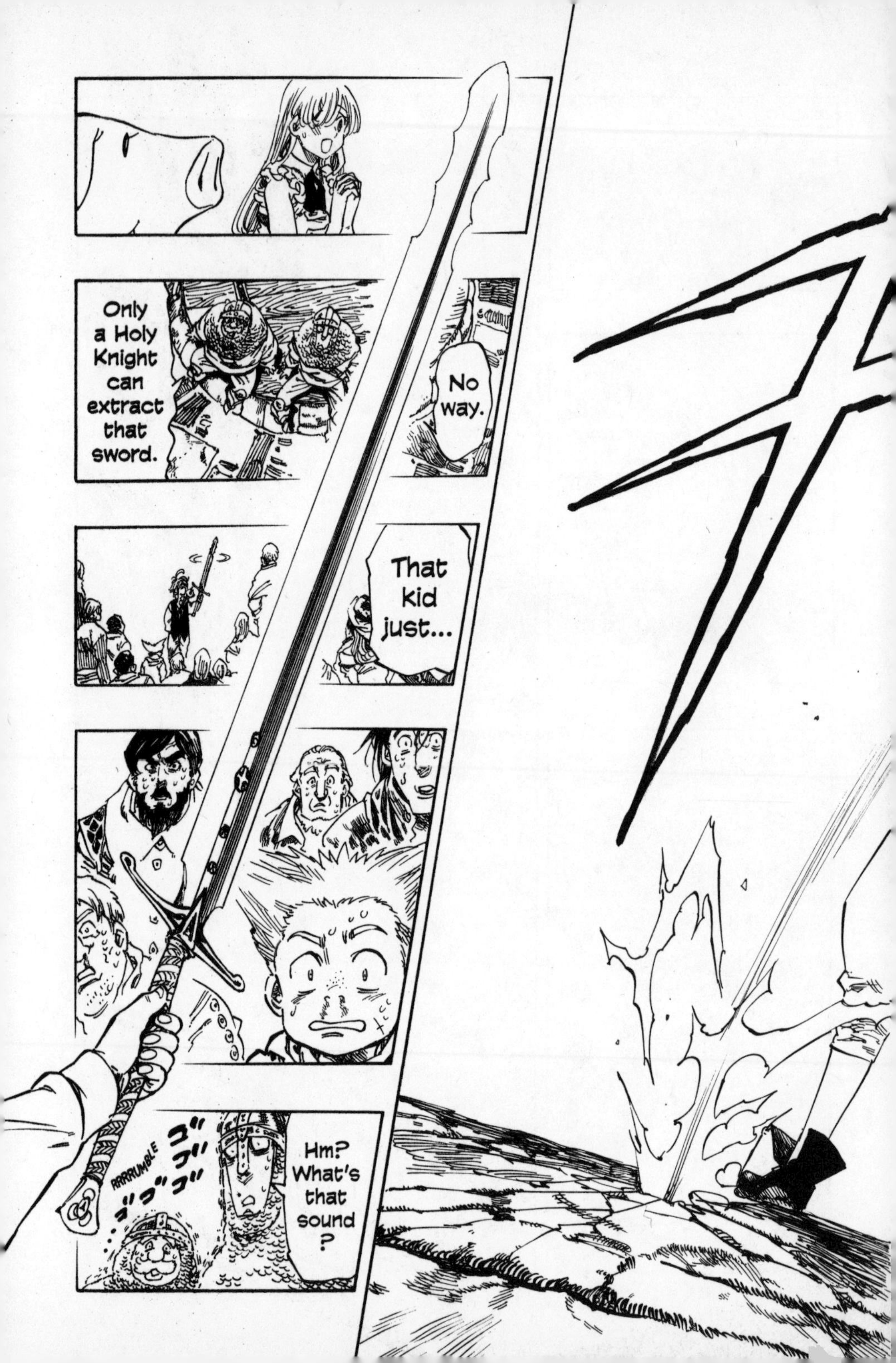
No way.
Only a Holy Knight can extract that sword.
That kid just...
Hm? What's that sound?
RRRRUMBLE
ゴゴゴゴ

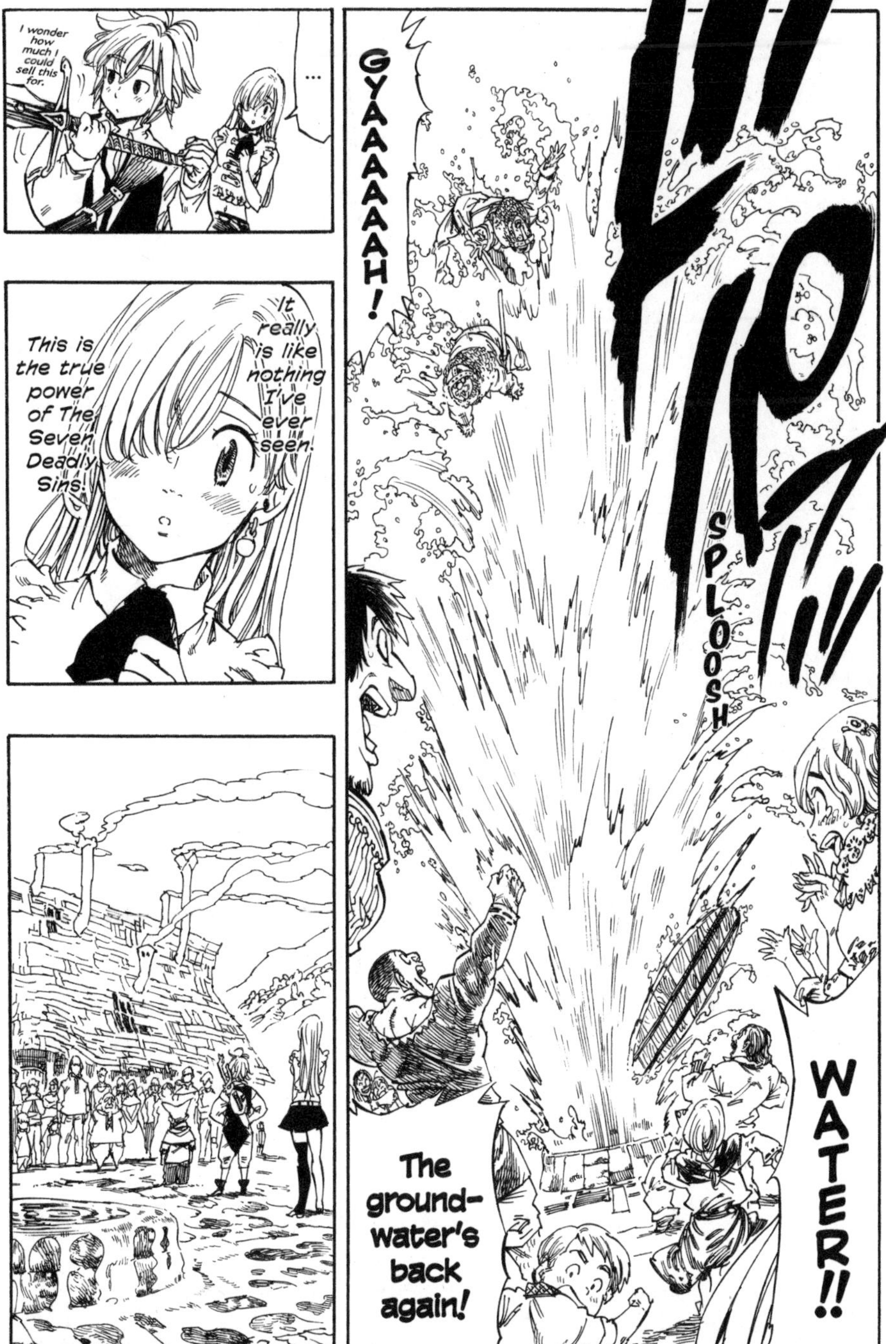
SPLOOSH
GYAAAAAAH!
WATER!!
The ground-water's back again!
...
I wonder how much I could sell this for.
It really is like nothing I've ever seen.
This is the true power of The Seven Deadly Sins.

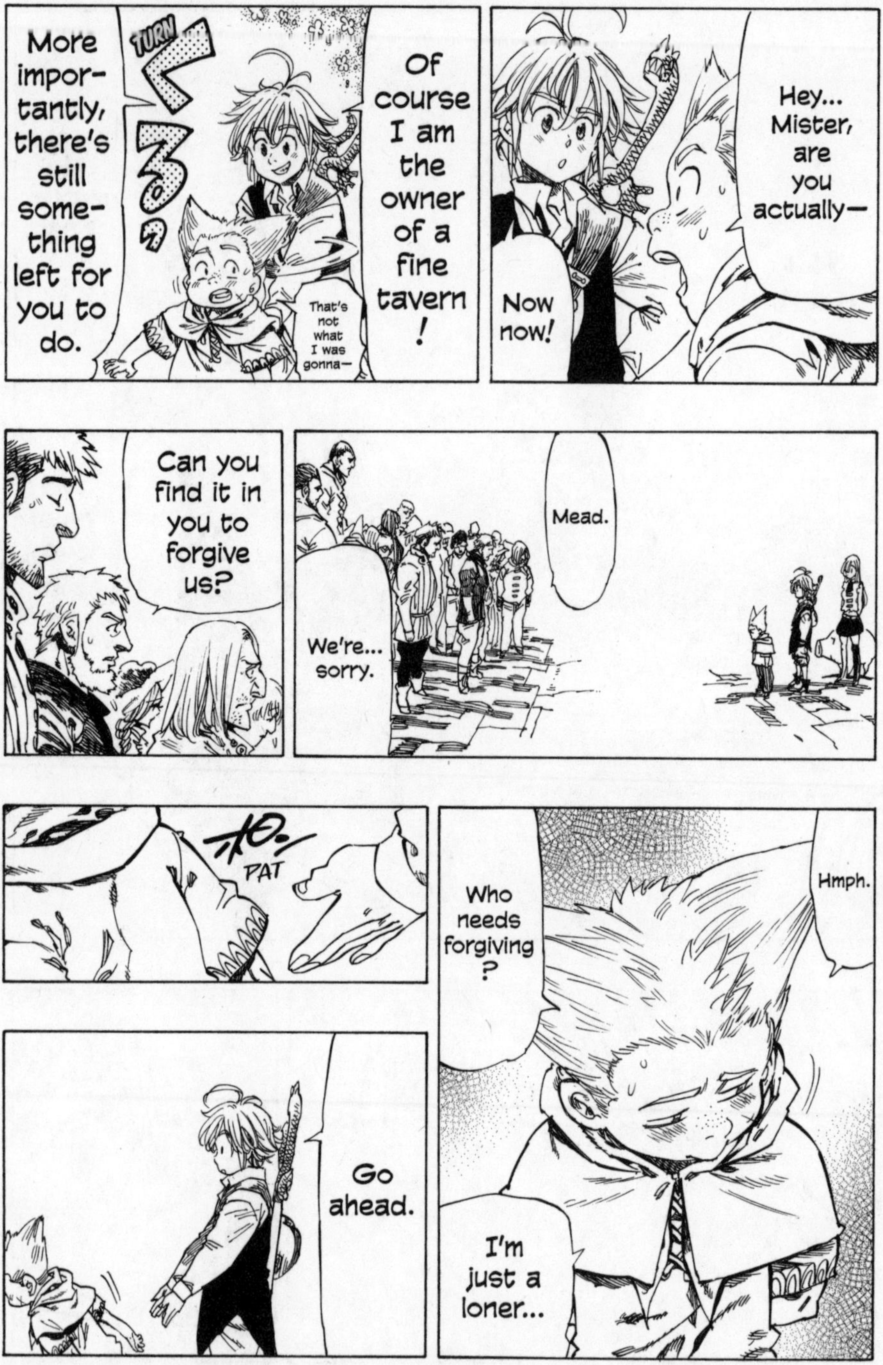
Hey... Mister, are you actually—
Now now!
Of course I am the owner of a fine tavern!
That's not what I was gonna—
TURN
More importantly, there's still something left for you to do.
Mead.
We're... sorry.
Can you find it in you to forgive us?
Hmph.
Who needs forgiving?
I'm just a loner...
PAT
Go ahead.

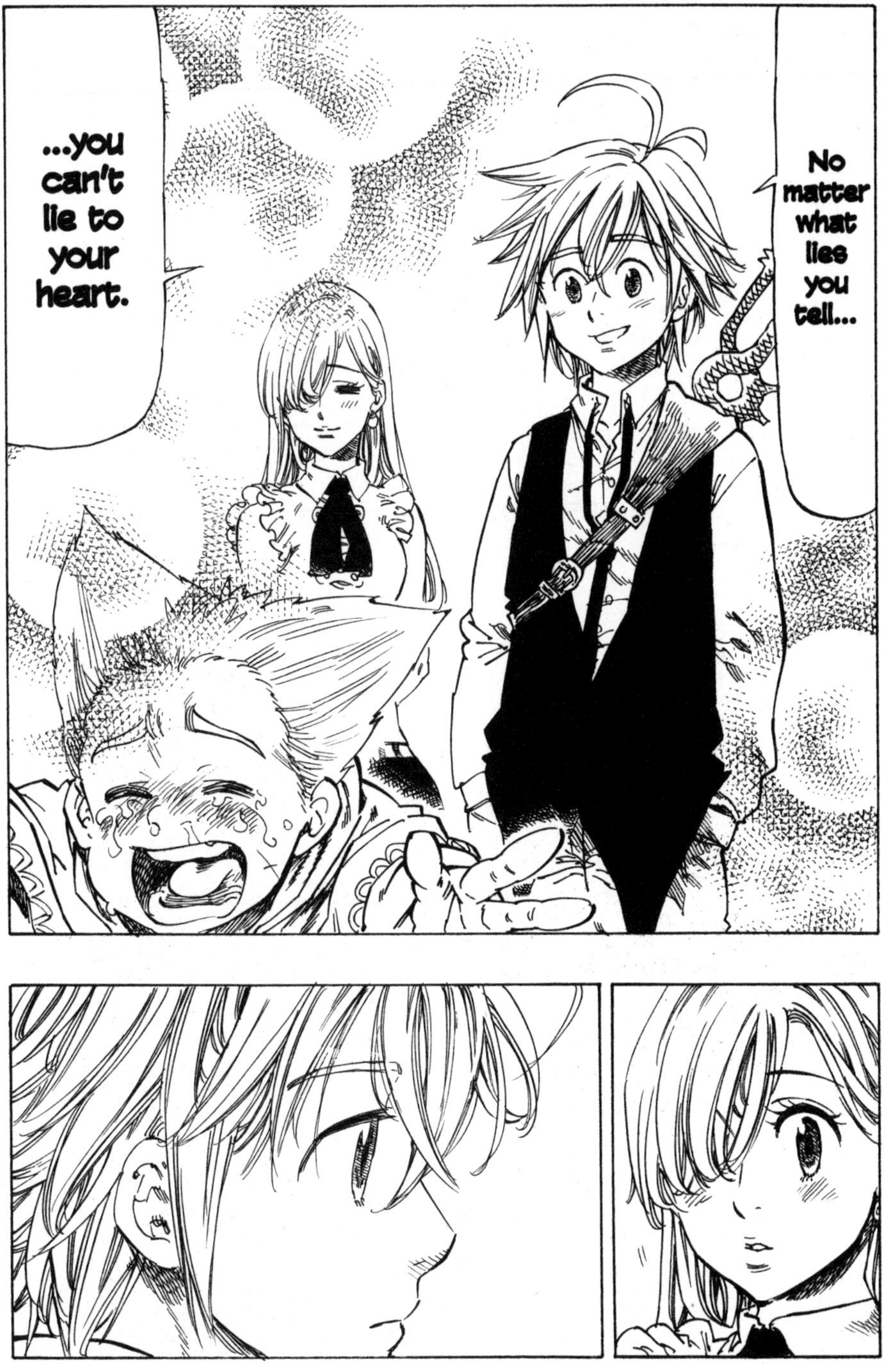
No matter what lies you tell...
...you can't lie to your heart.

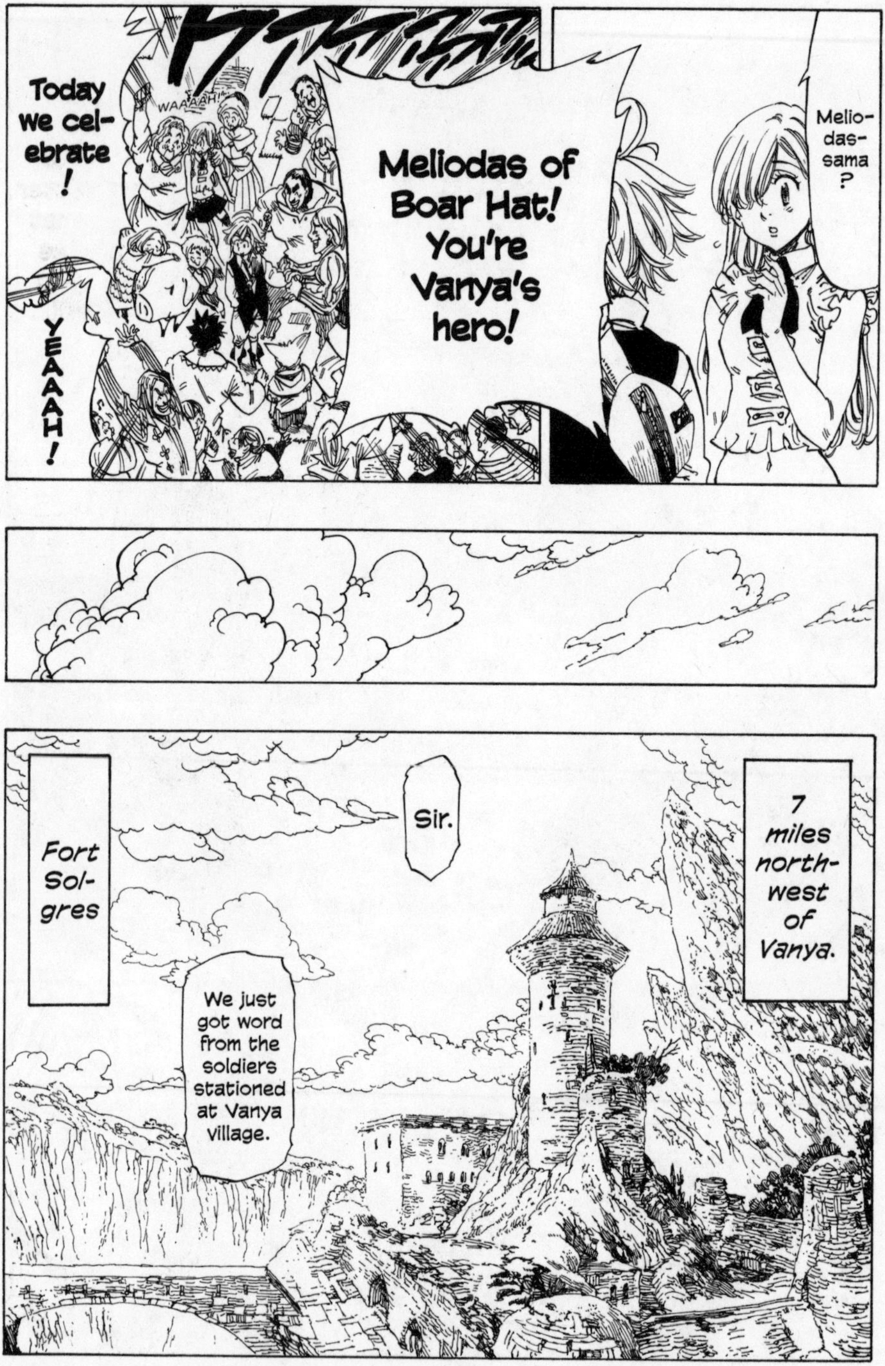
Meliodas-sama?
Meliodas of Boar Hat! You're Vanya's hero!
WAAAAH!
Today we celebrate!
YEAAAH!
7 miles northwest of Vanya.
Sir.
Fort Solgres
We just got word from the soldiers stationed at Vanya village.

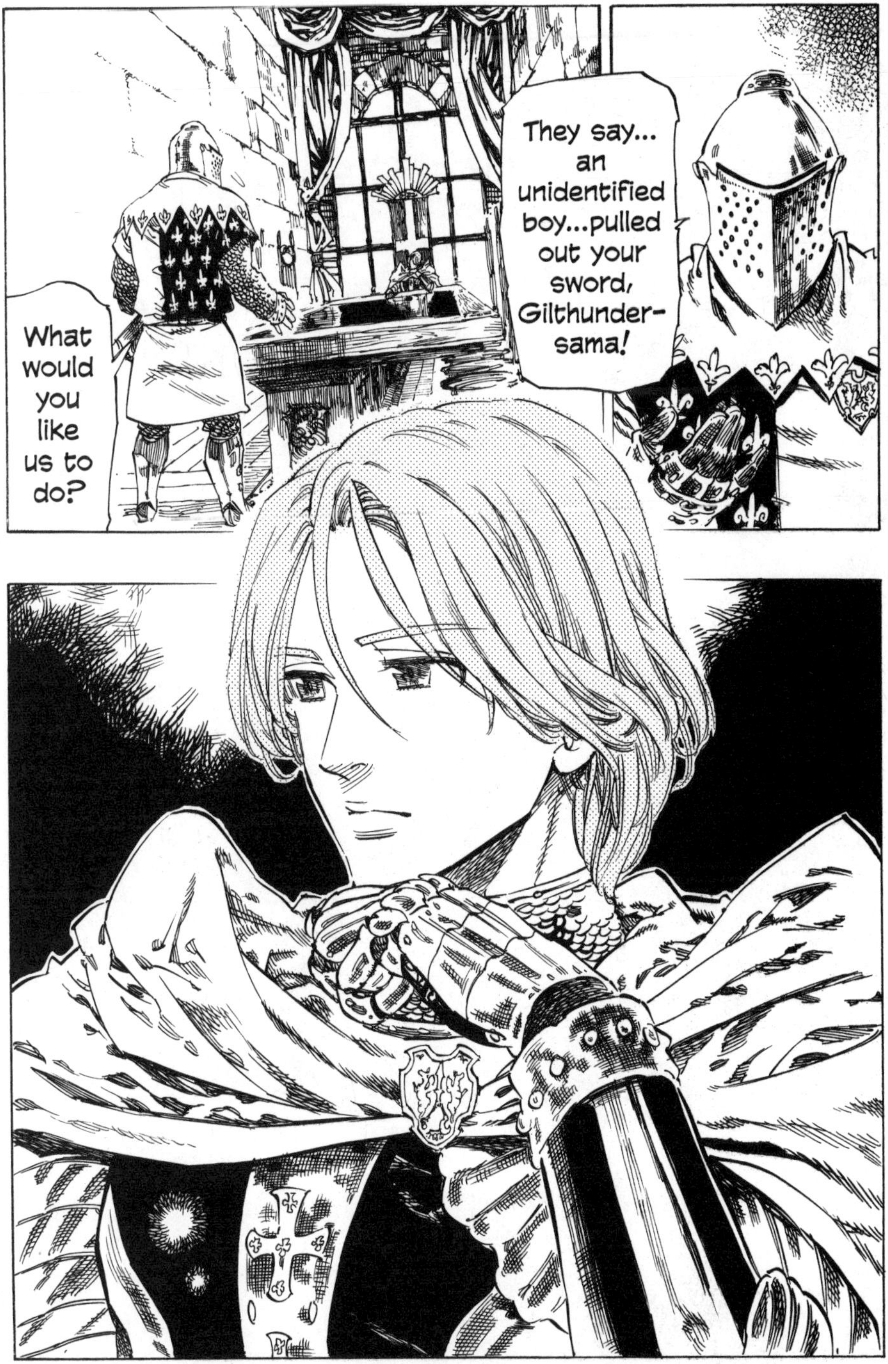
They say... an unidentified boy...pulled out your sword, Gilthunder-sama!
What would you like us to do?

Chapter 3 - What One Must Do

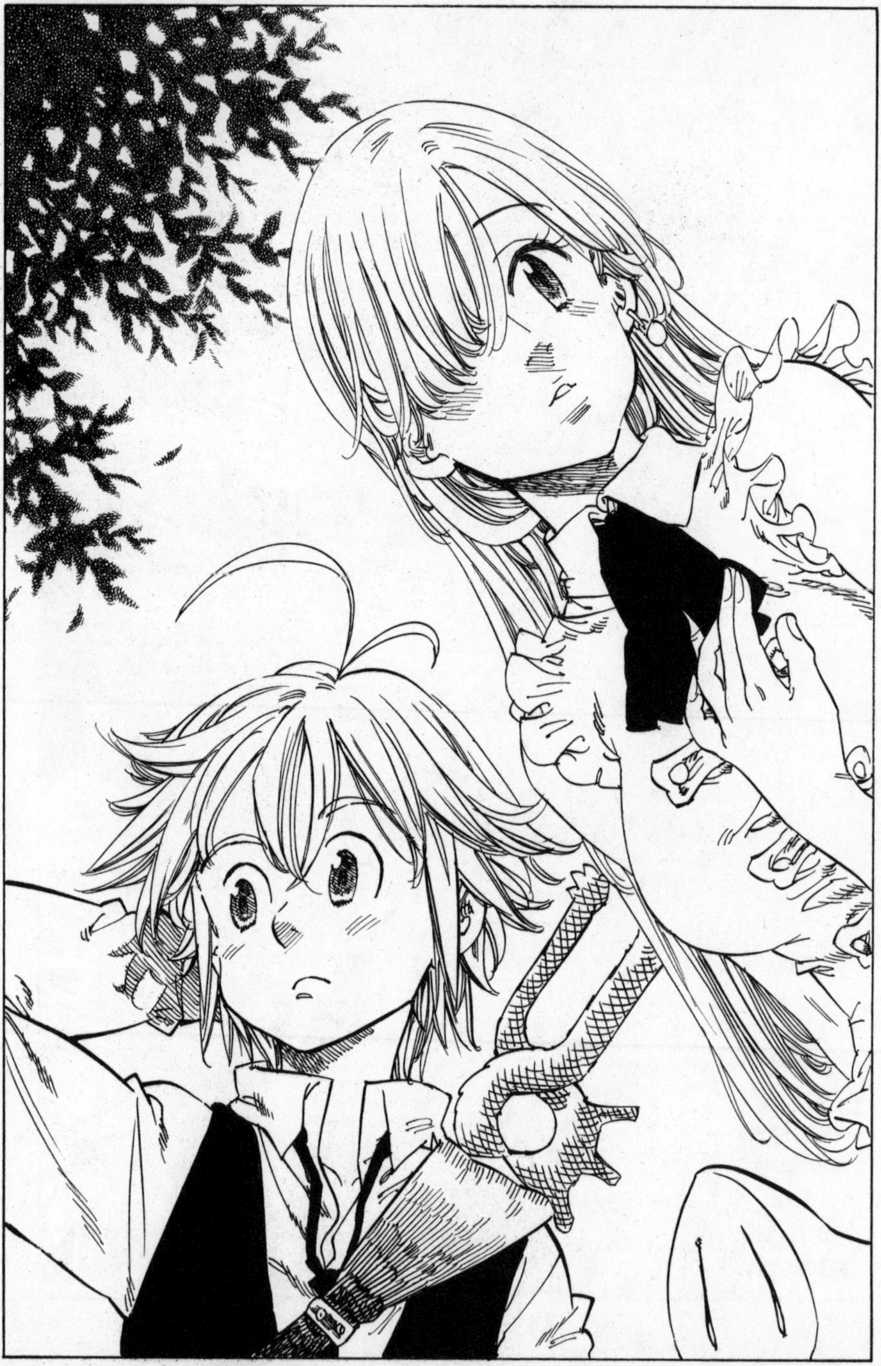

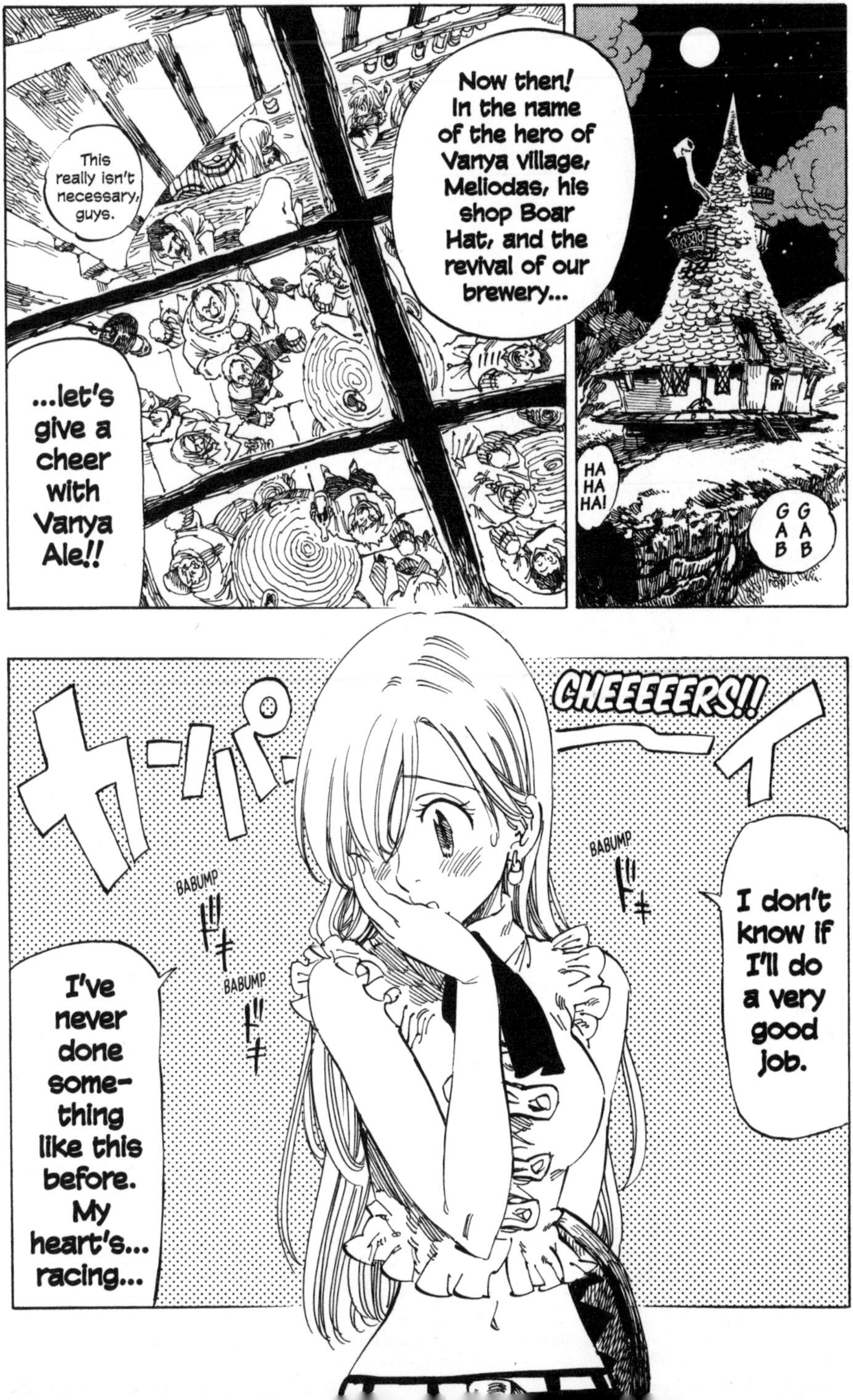
HA HA HA!
GAB GAB
Now then! In the name of the hero of Vanya village, Meliodas, his shop Boar Hat, and the revival of our brewery...
This really isn't necessary, guys.
...let's give a cheer with Vanya Ale!!
CHEEEEERS!!
BABUMP
I don't know if I'll do a very good job.
BABUMP
BABUMP
I've never done some-thing like this before. My heart's... racing...

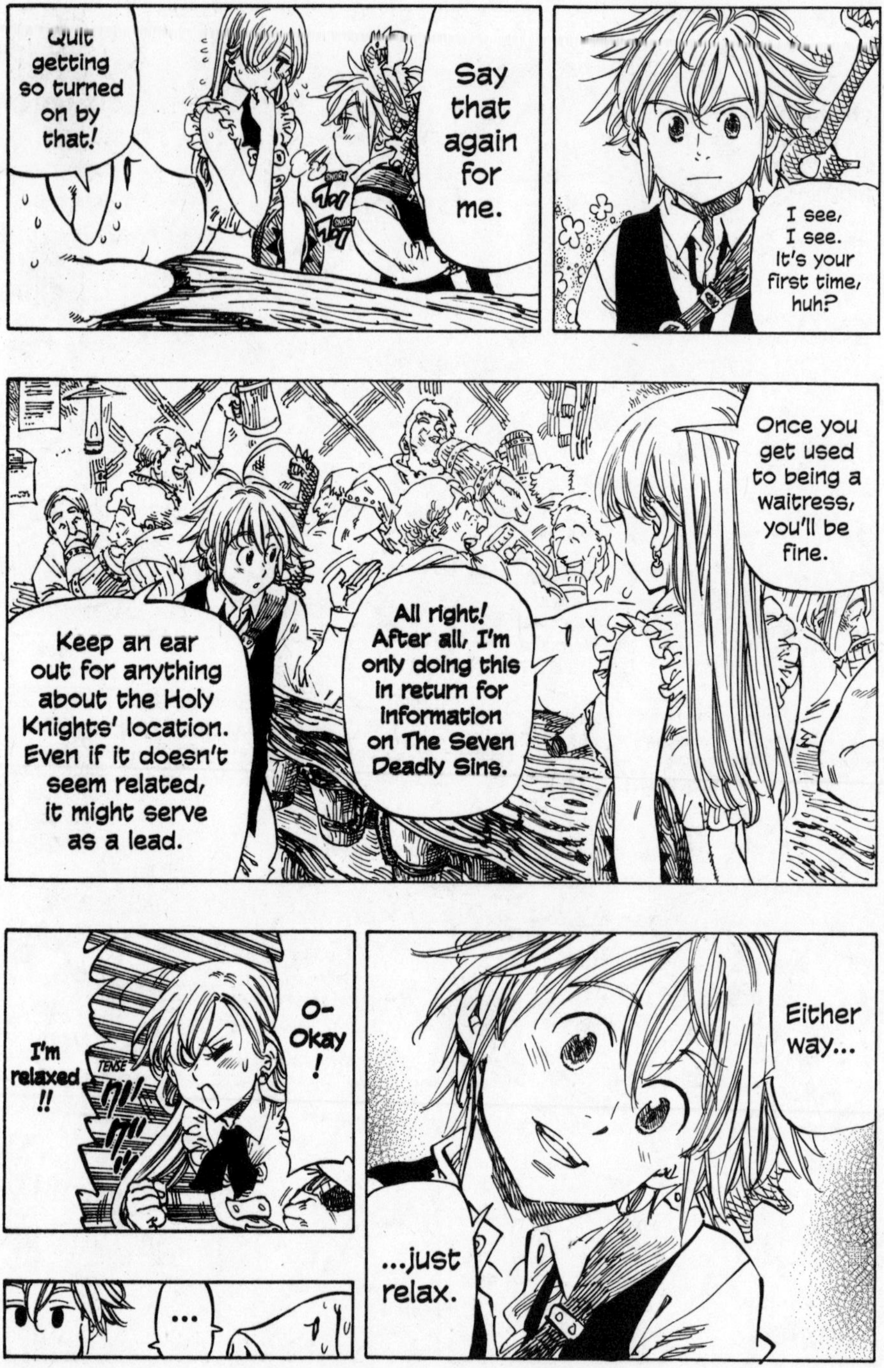
I see, I see. It's your first time, huh?
Say that again for me.
SNORT
SNORT
Quit getting so turned on by that!
Once you get used to being a waitress, you'll be fine.
All right! After all, I'm only doing this in return for information on The Seven Deadly Sins.
Keep an ear out for anything about the Holy Knights' location. Even if it doesn't seem related, it might serve as a lead.
Either way...
...just relax.
O-Okay!
TENSE
I'm relaxed!!
...

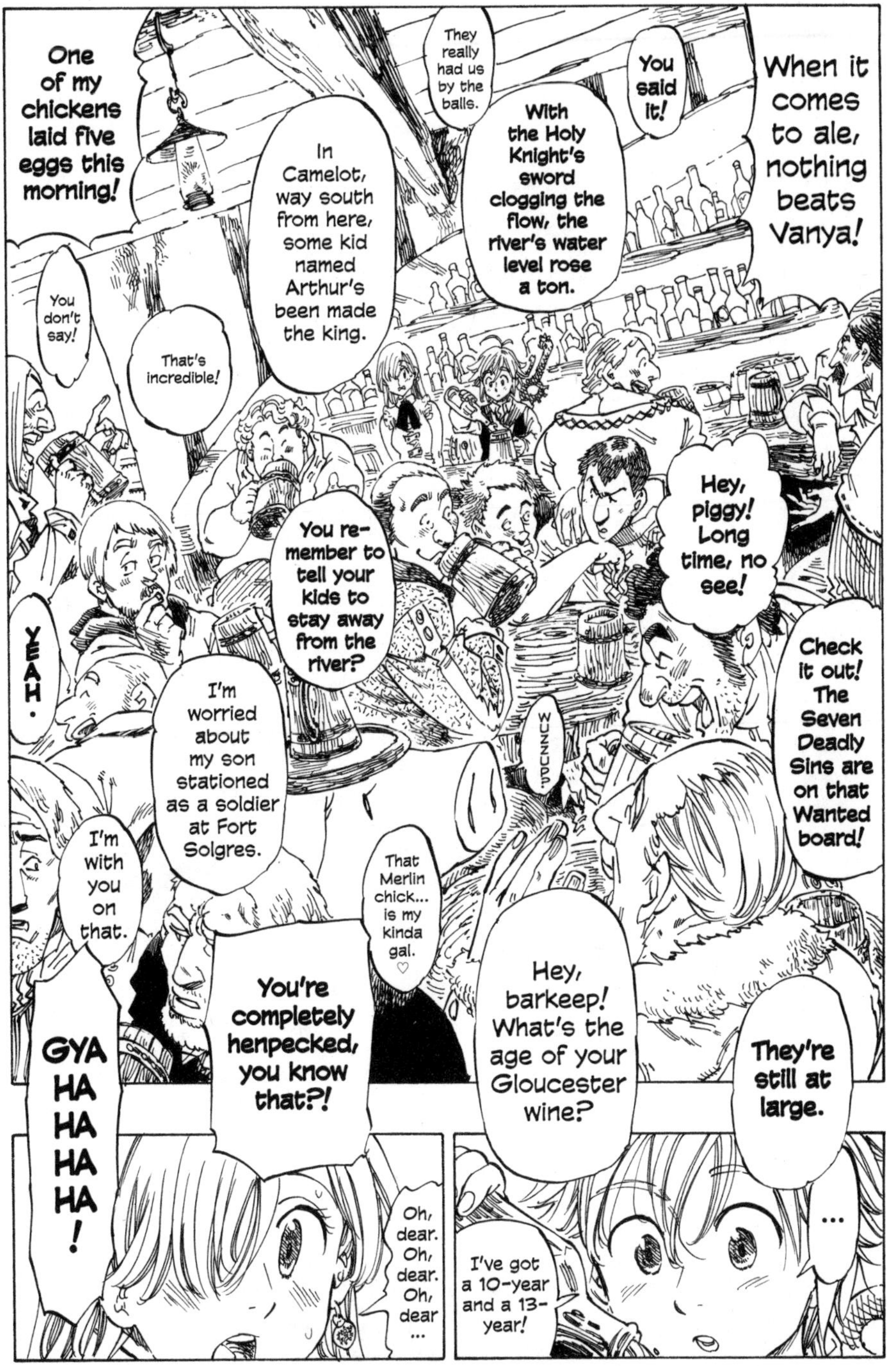
When it comes to ale, nothing beats Vanya!
You said it!
With the Holy Knight's sword clogging the flow, the river's water level rose a ton.
They really had us by the balls.
In Camelot, way south from here, some kid named Arthur's been made the king.
One of my chickens laid five eggs this morning!
That's incredible!
You don't say!
Hey, piggy! Long time, no see!
You re-member to tell your kids to stay away from the river?
YEAH.
Check it out! The Seven Deadly Sins are on that Wanted board!
WUZZUP?
I'm worried about my son stationed as a soldier at Fort Solgres.
That Merlin chick... is my kinda gal. ♡
I'm with you on that.
Hey, barkeep! What's the age of your Gloucester wine?
They're still at large.
You're completely henpecked, you know that?!
GYA HA HA HA HA!
...
I've got a 10-year and a 13-year!
Oh, dear. Oh, dear. Oh, dear...

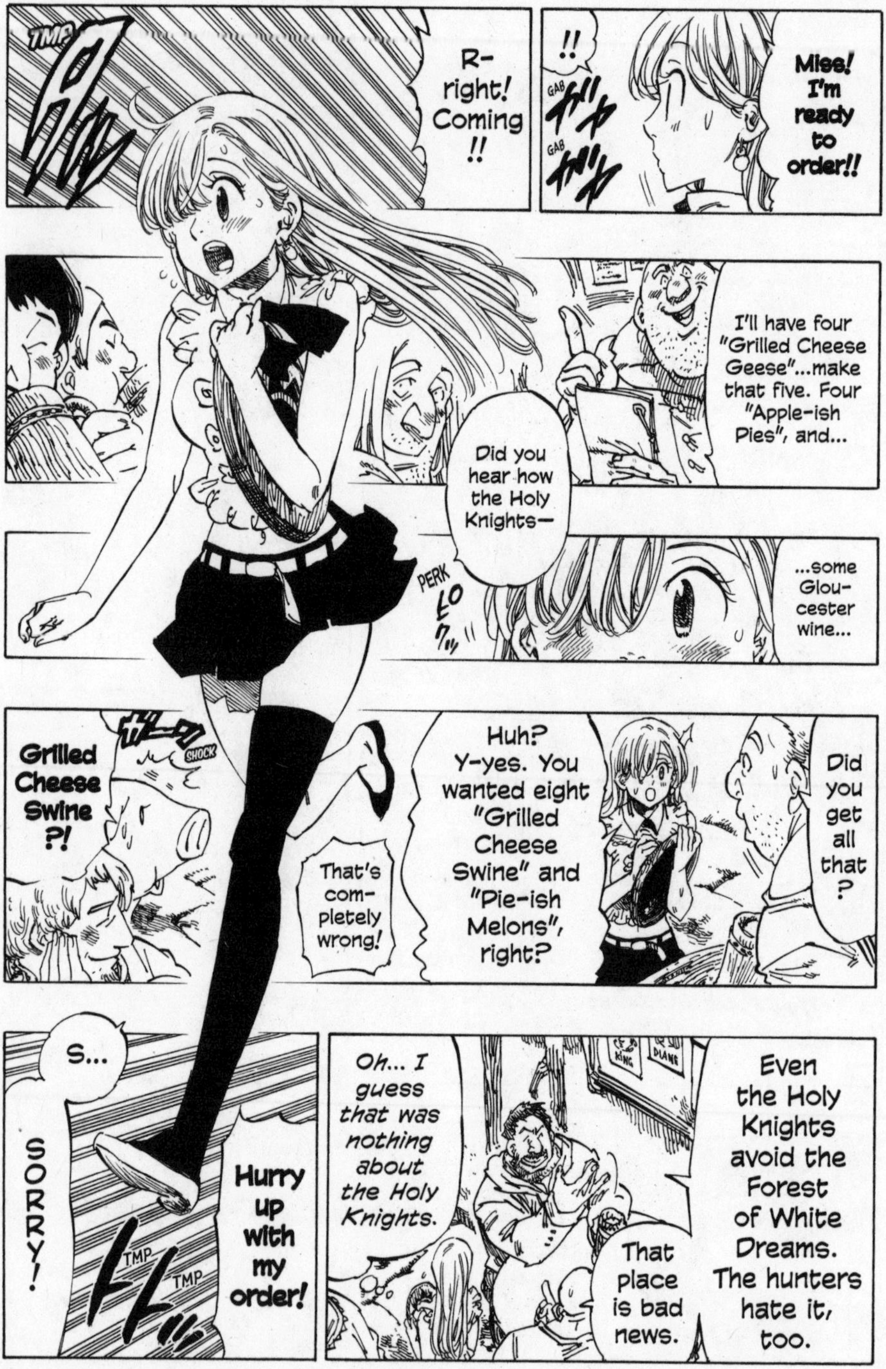
Miss! I'm ready to order!!
GAB
GAB
!!
R-right! Coming!!
TMP
I'll have four "Grilled Cheese Geese"...make that five. Four "Apple-ish Pies", and...
Did you hear how the Holy Knights—
...some Gloucester wine...
PERK
Did you get all that?
Huh? Y-yes. You wanted eight "Grilled Cheese Swine" and "Pie-ish Melons", right?
That's completely wrong!
SHOCK
Grilled Cheese Swine?!
Even the Holy Knights avoid the Forest of White Dreams. The hunters hate it, too.
That place is bad news.
Oh... I guess that was nothing about the Holy Knights.
Hurry up with my order!
S...
SORRY!
TMP
TMP

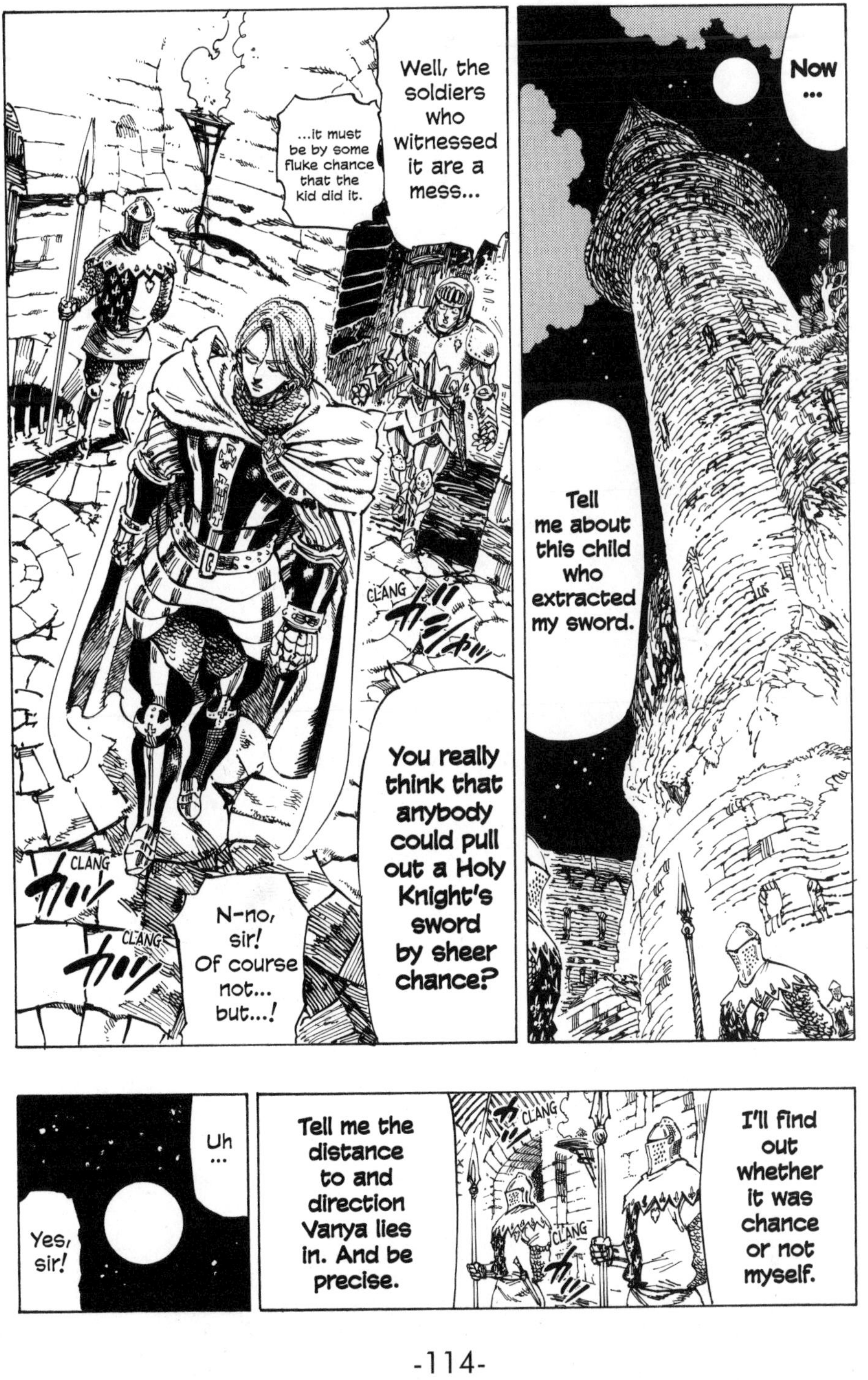
Now ...
Tell me about this child who extracted my sword.
Well, the soldiers who witnessed it are a mess...
...it must be by some fluke chance that the kid did it.
You really think that anybody could pull out a Holy Knight's sword by sheer chance?
CLANG
N-no, sir! Of course not... but...!
CLANG
CLANG
I'll find out whether it was chance or not myself.
CLANG
CLANG
Tell me the distance to and direction Vanya lies in. And be precise.
Uh ...
Yes, sir!

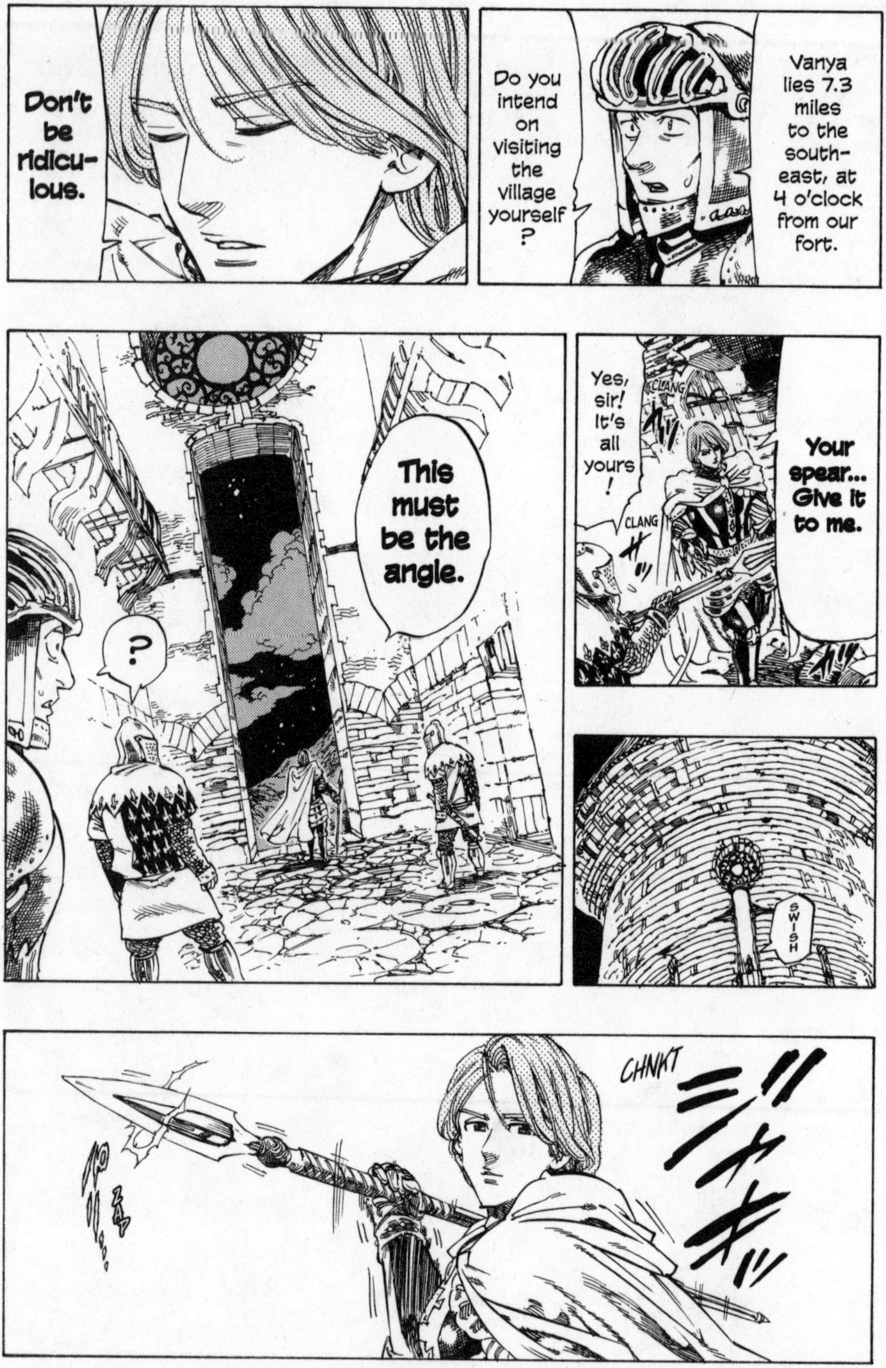

Vanya lies 7.3 miles to the south-east, at 4 o'clock from our fort.
Do you intend on visiting the village yourself?
Don't be ridicu-lous.
Your spear... Give it to me.
Yes, sir! It's all yours!
CLANG
CLANG
SWISH
This must be the angle.
?
CHNKT

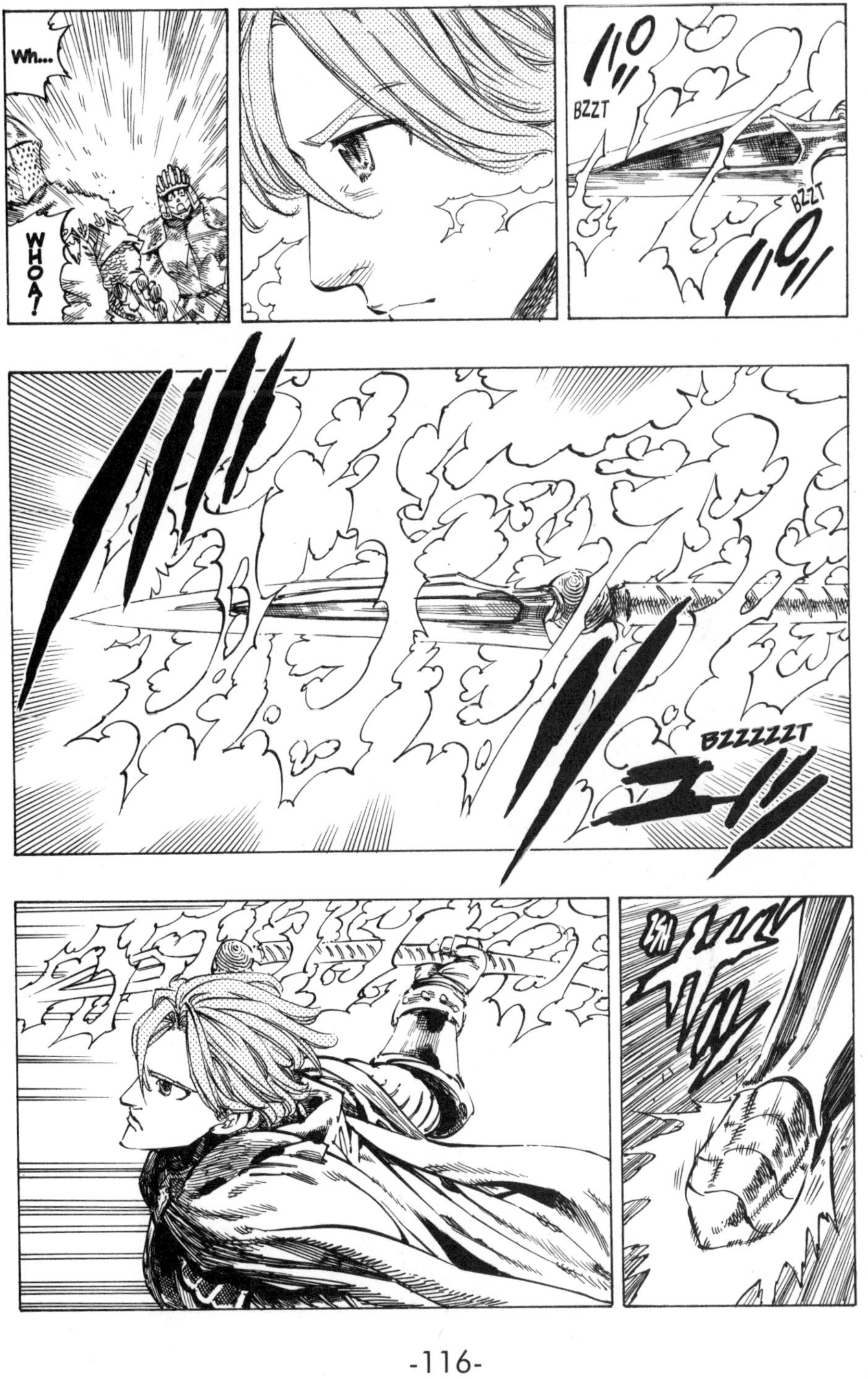
BZZT
BZZT
Wh...
WHOA!
BZZZZZT

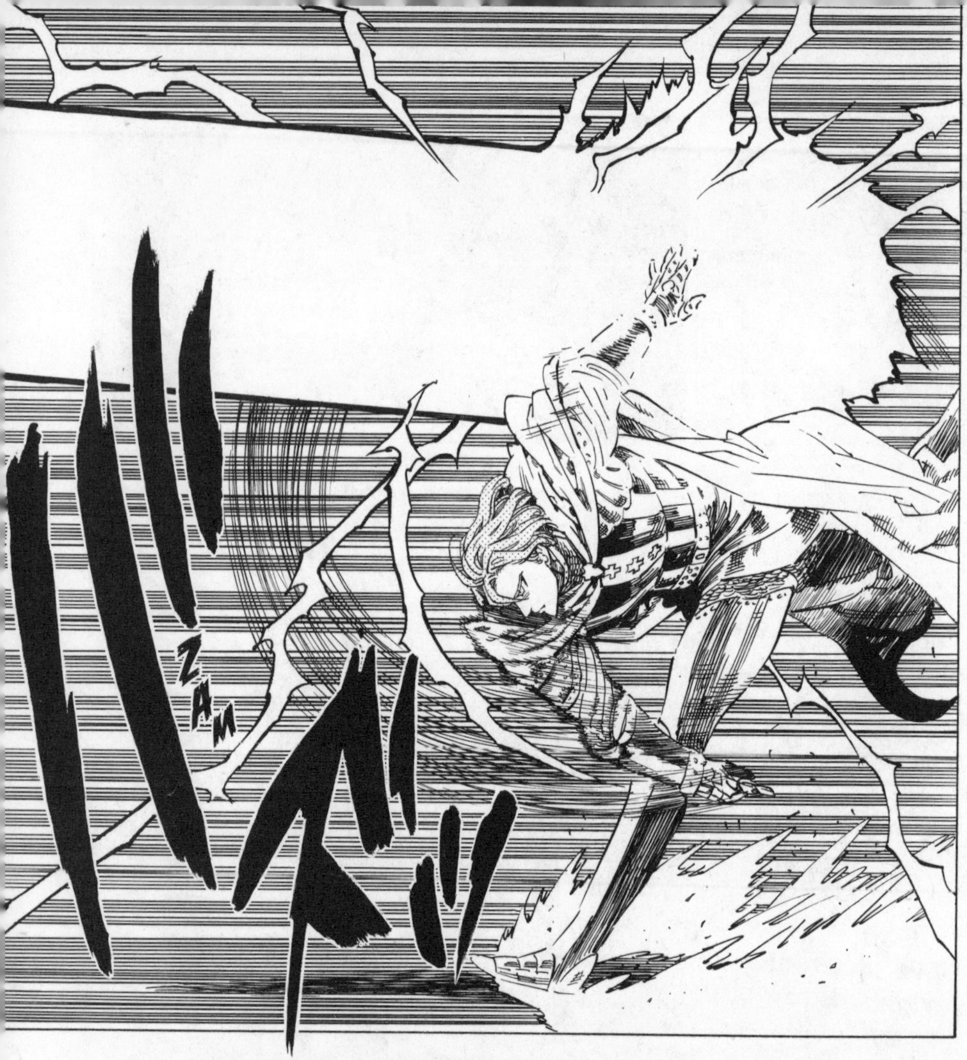
ZAM

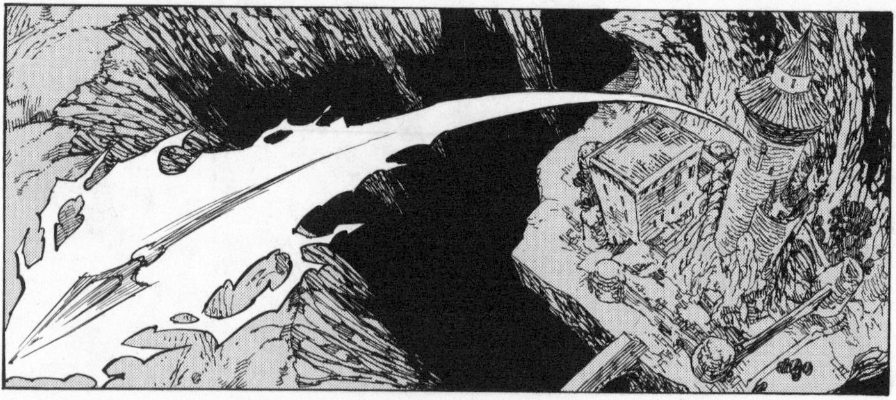

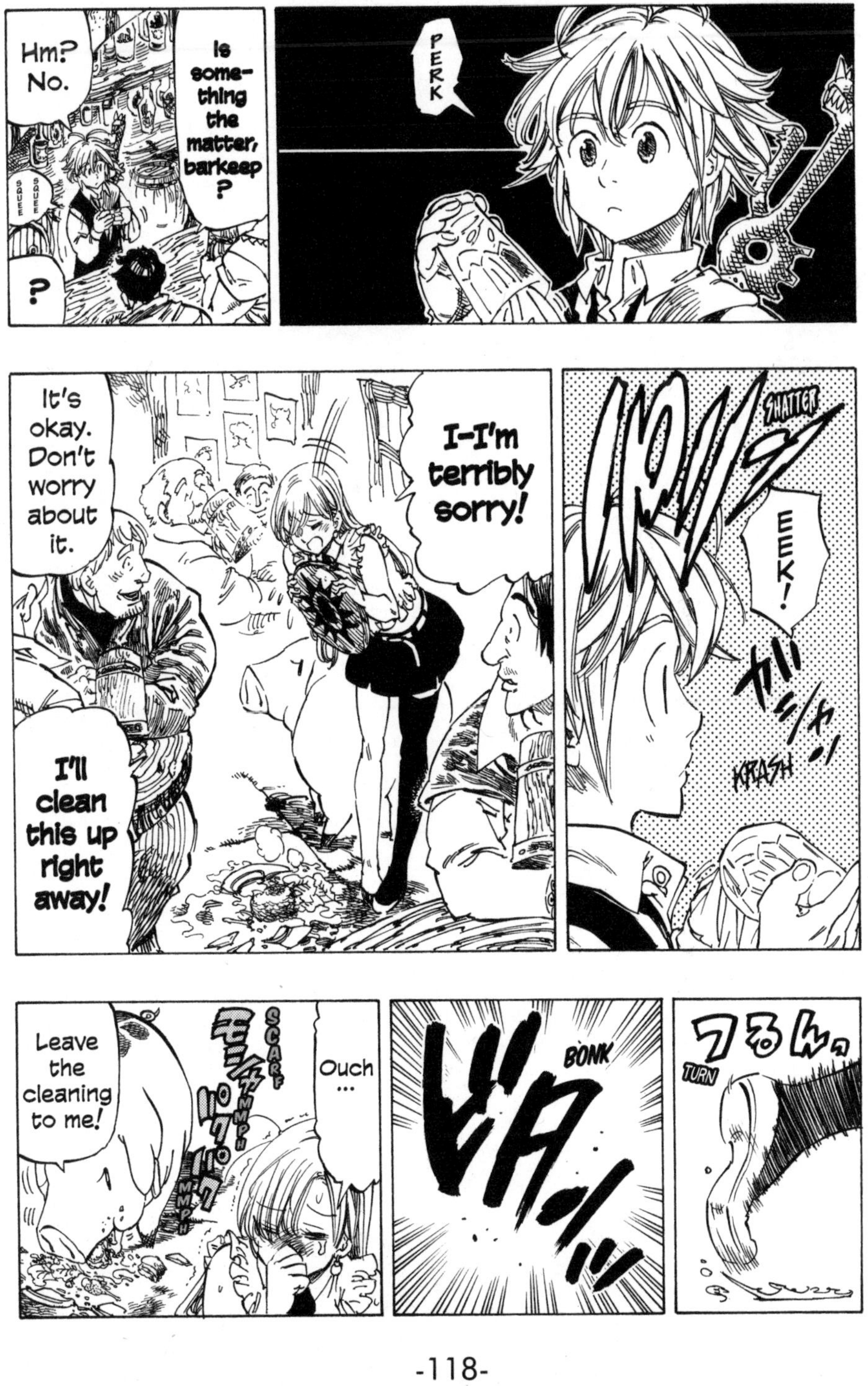
PERK
Is something the matter, barkeep?
Hm? No.
SQUEE SQUEE
?
SHATTER
EEK!
KRASH
I-I'm terribly sorry!
It's okay. Don't worry about it.
I'll clean this up right away!
TURN
BONK
Ouch ...
SCARF
MMPH
MMPH
Leave the cleaning to me!

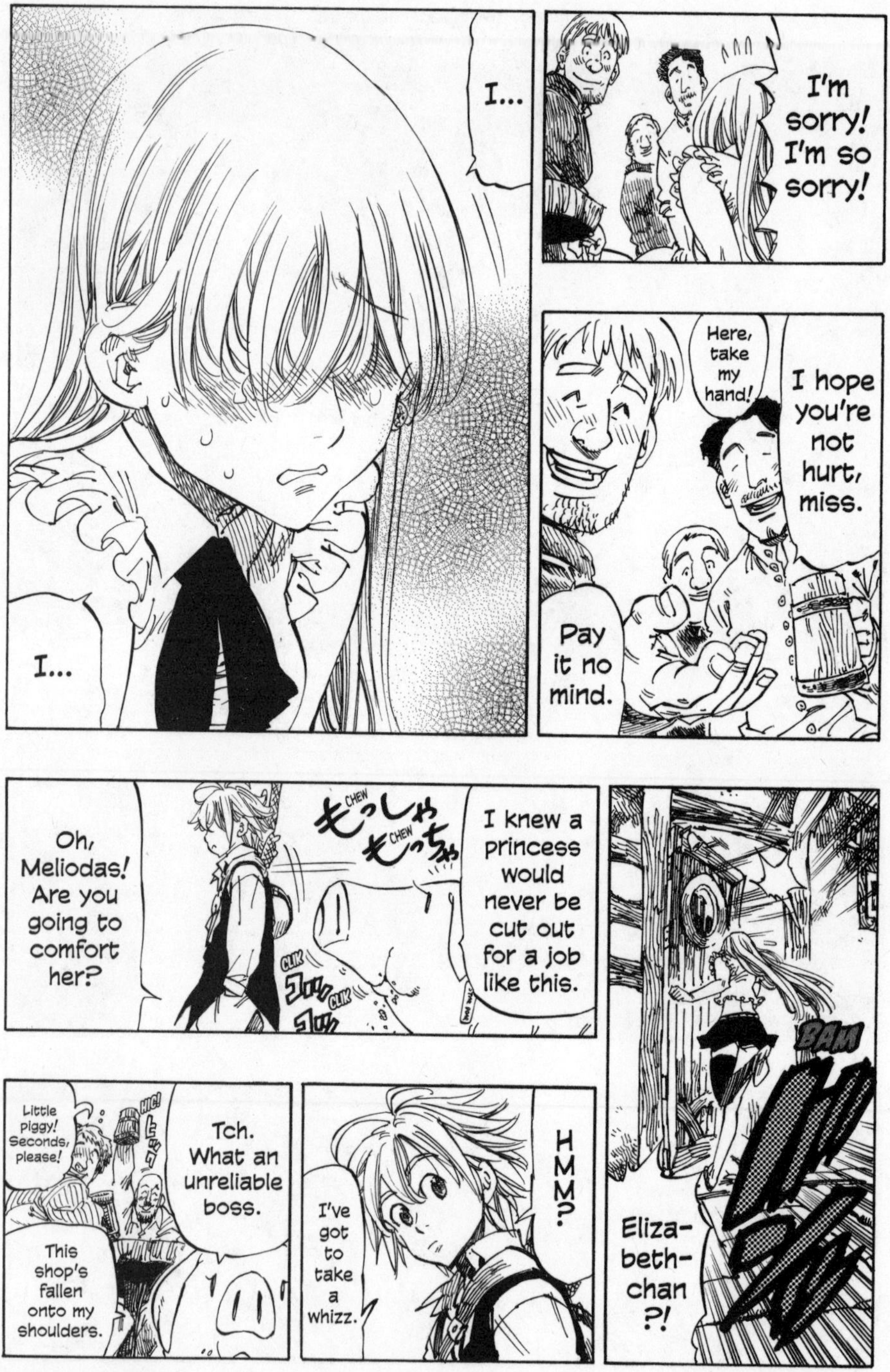
I'm sorry! I'm so sorry!
Here, take my hand!
I hope you're not hurt, miss.
Pay it no mind.
I...
I...
BAM
Eliza-beth-chan?!
I knew a princess would never be cut out for a job like this.
CHEW CHEW
もっしゃ もっちゃ
CLIK CLIK
Oh, Meliodas! Are you going to comfort her?
HMM?
I've got to take a whizz.
Tch. What an unreliable boss.
HIC!
Little piggy! Seconds, please!
This shop's fallen onto my shoulders.

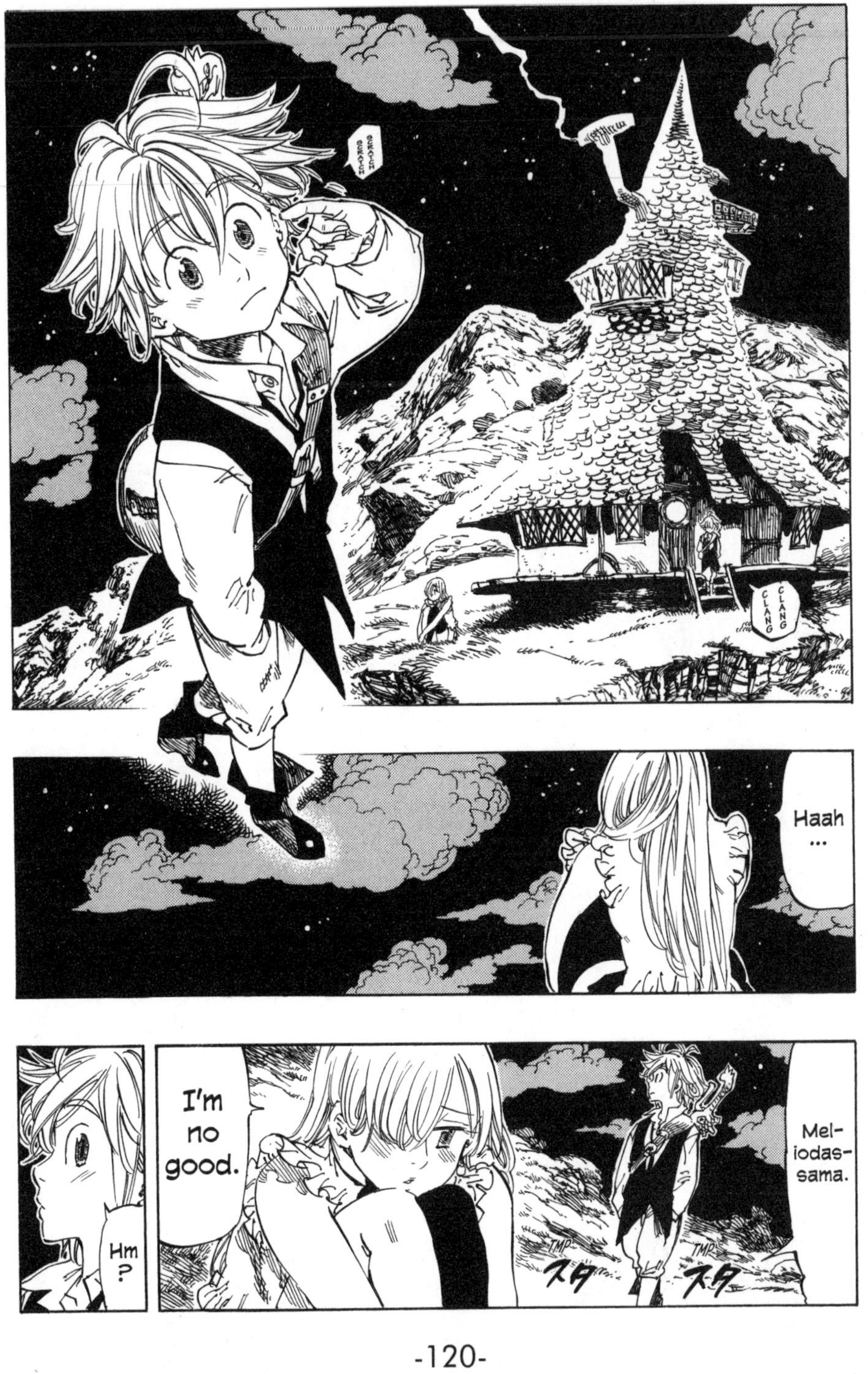
CLANG CLANG
SCRATCH SCRATCH
Haah ...
Mel- iodas- sama.
TMP スタ
TMP スタ
I'm no good.
Hm ?

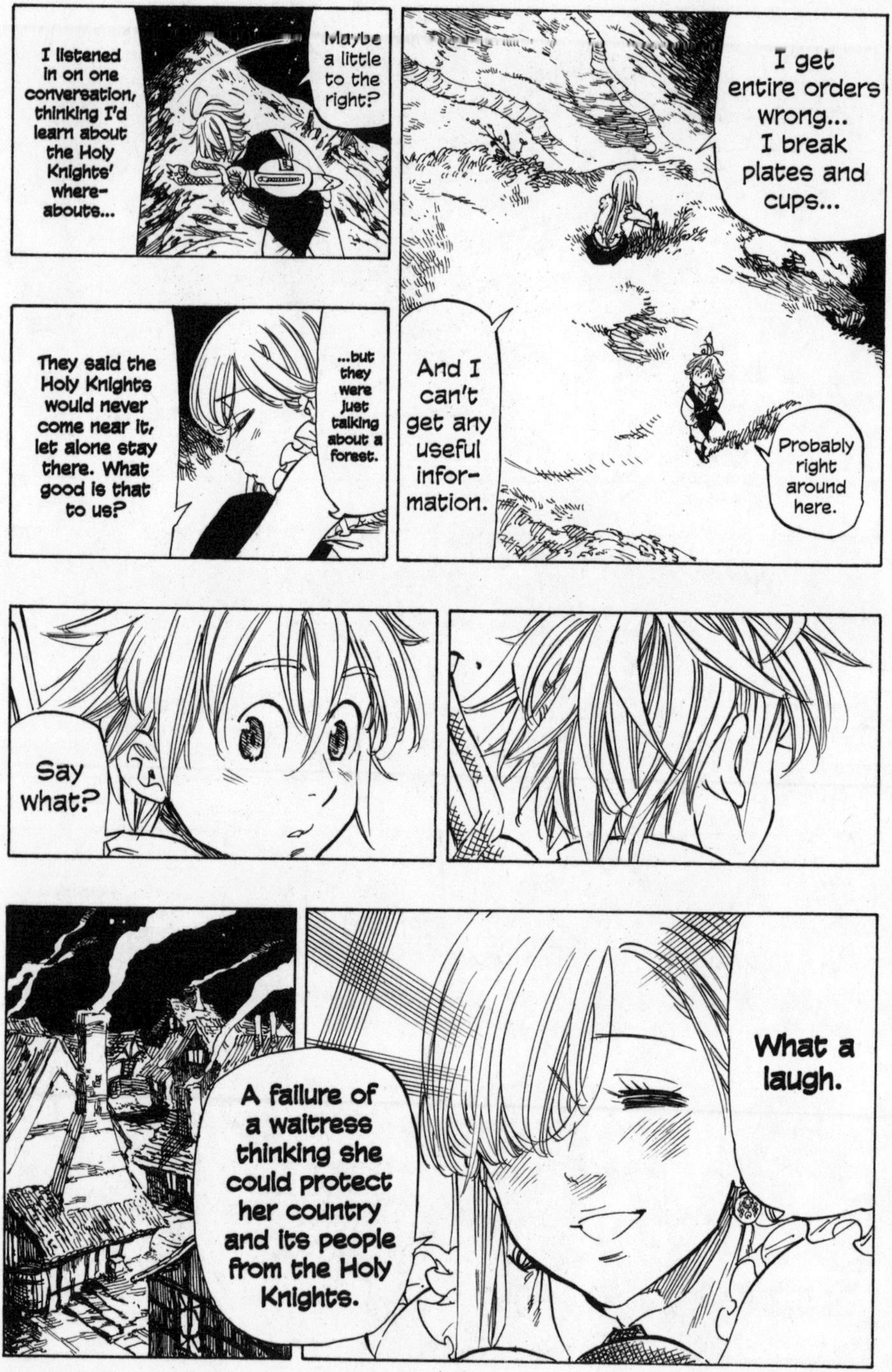
I get entire orders wrong... I break plates and cups...
And I can't get any useful infor-mation.
Probably right around here.
Maybe a little to the right?
I listened in on one conversation, thinking I'd learn about the Holy Knights' where-abouts...
...but they were just talking about a forest.
They said the Holy Knights would never come near it, let alone stay there. What good is that to us?
Say what?
What a laugh.
A failure of a waitress thinking she could protect her country and its people from the Holy Knights.

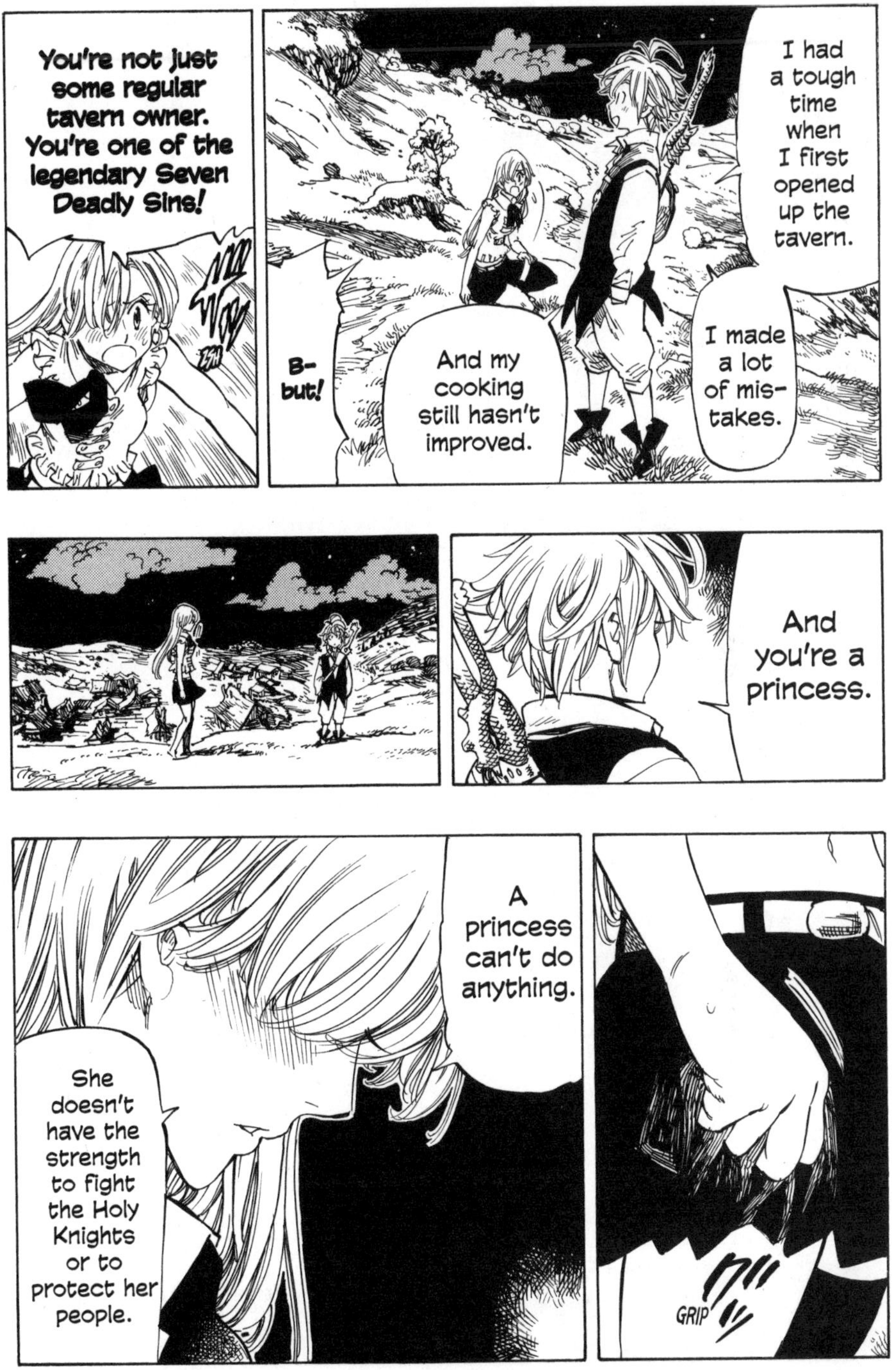
I had a tough time when I first opened up the tavern.
I made a lot of mistakes.
And my cooking still hasn't improved.
B-but!
You're not just some regular tavern owner. You're one of the legendary Seven Deadly Sins!
And you're a princess.
GRIP
A princess can't do anything.
She doesn't have the strength to fight the Holy Knights or to protect her people.

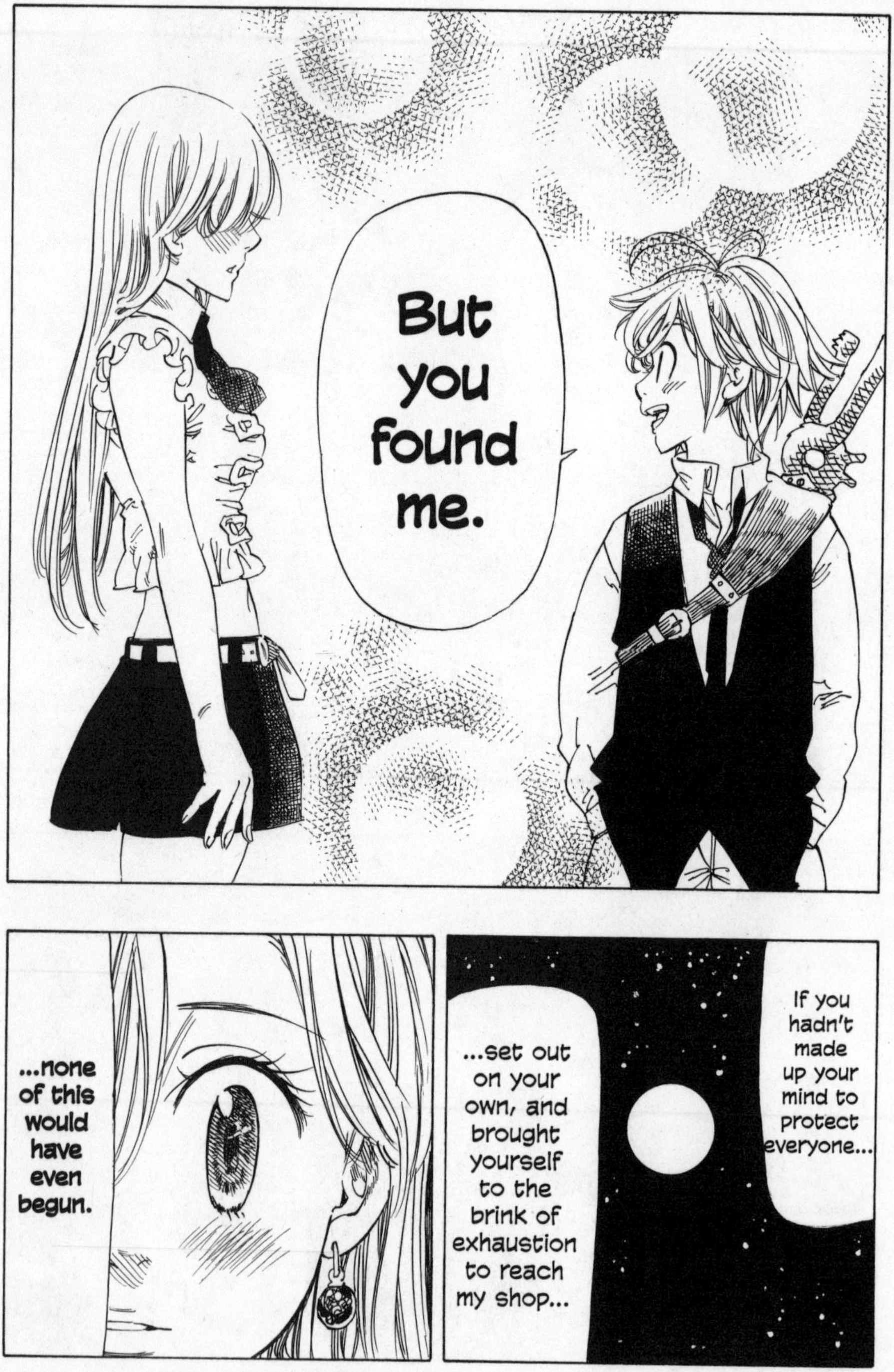
But you found me.
If you hadn't made up your mind to protect everyone...
...set out on your own, and brought yourself to the brink of exhaustion to reach my shop...
...none of this would have even begun.

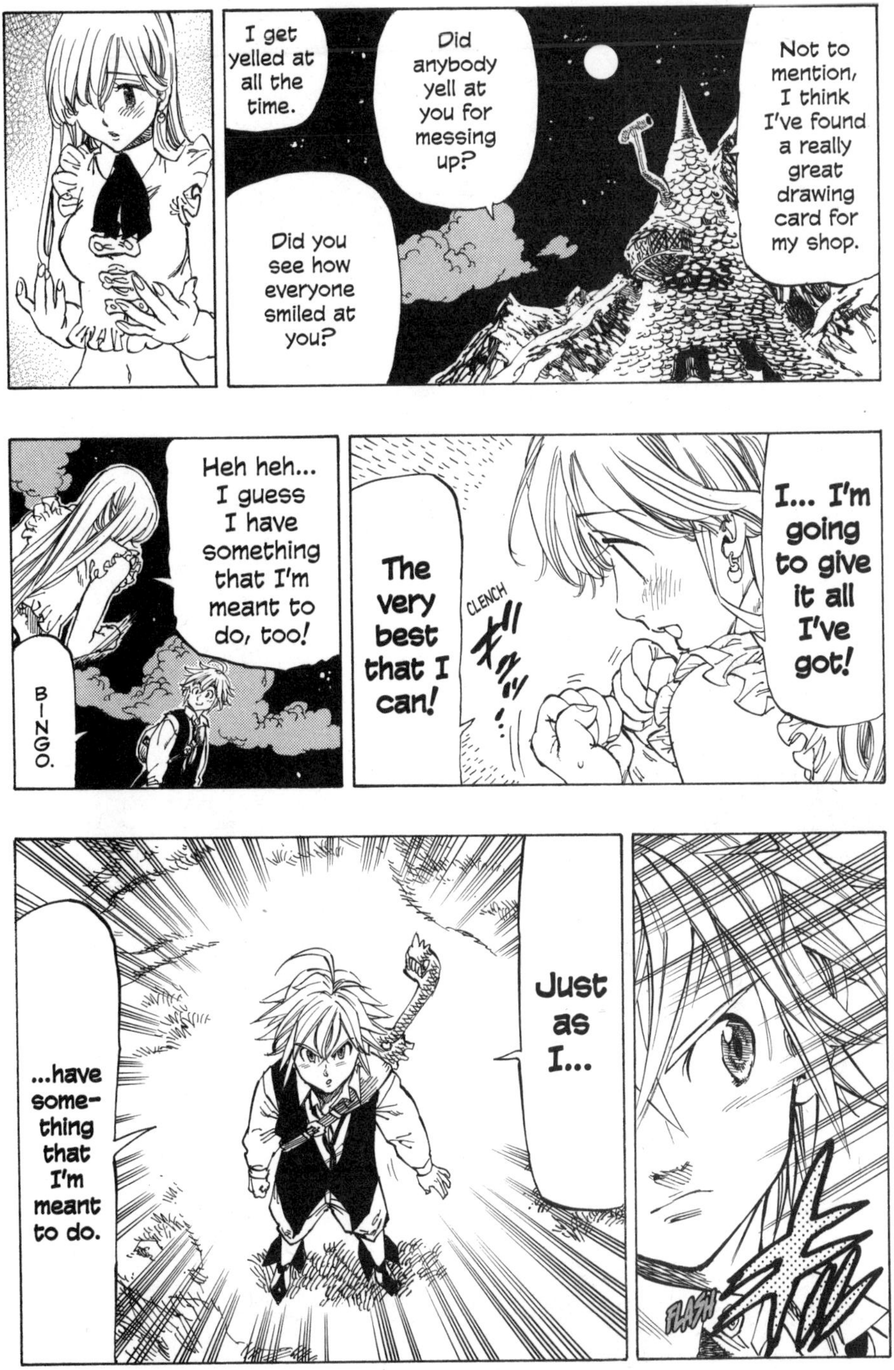

Not to mention, I think I've found a really great drawing card for my shop.
Did anybody yell at you for messing up?
I get yelled at all the time.
Did you see how everyone smiled at you?
I... I'm going to give it all I've got!
CLENCH
The very best that I can!
Heh heh... I guess I have something that I'm meant to do, too!
BINGO.
FLASH
Just as I...
...have something that I'm meant to do.

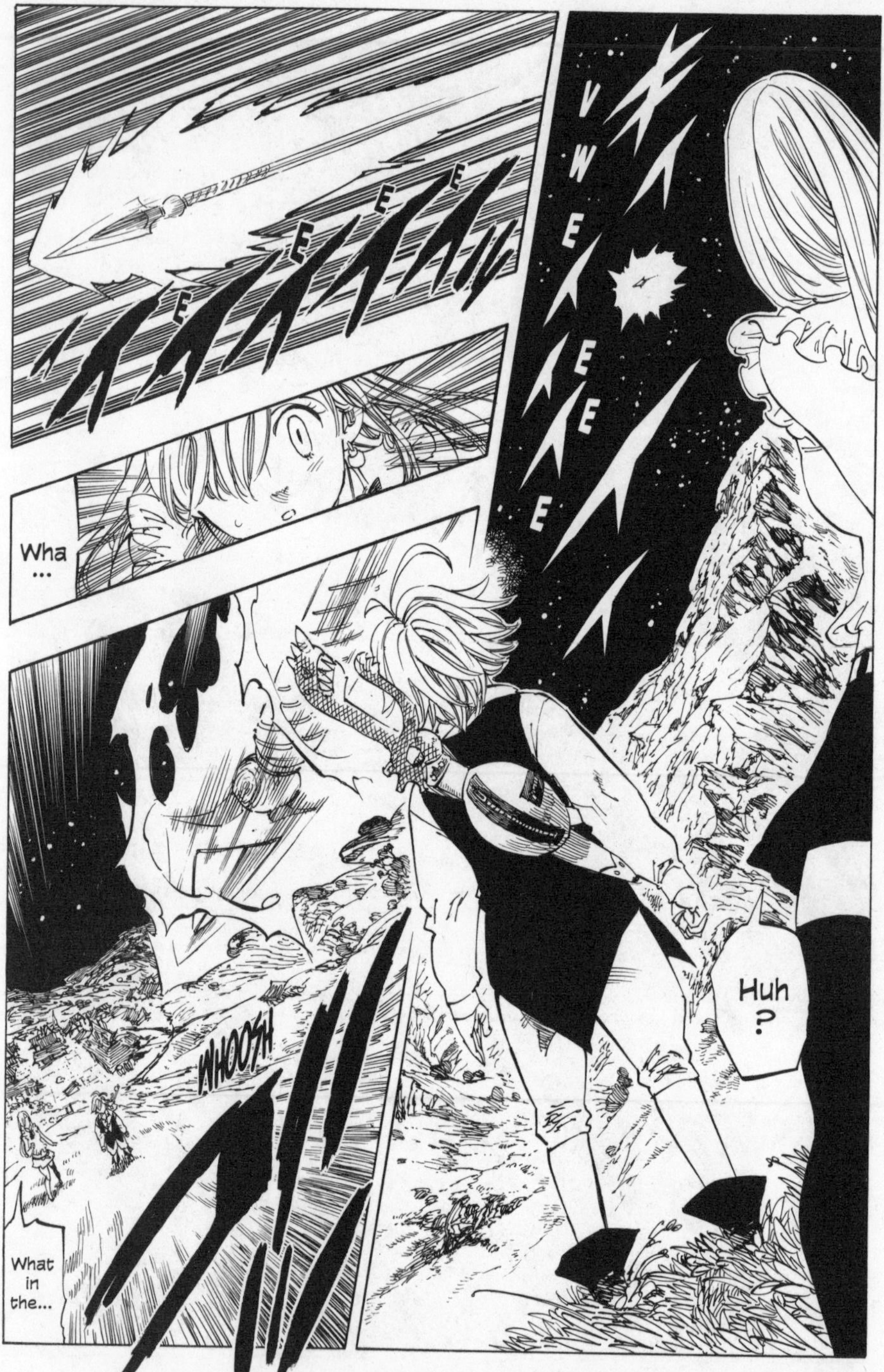
VWEEEEE
EEEE
Wha...
Huh?
WHOOSH
What in the...

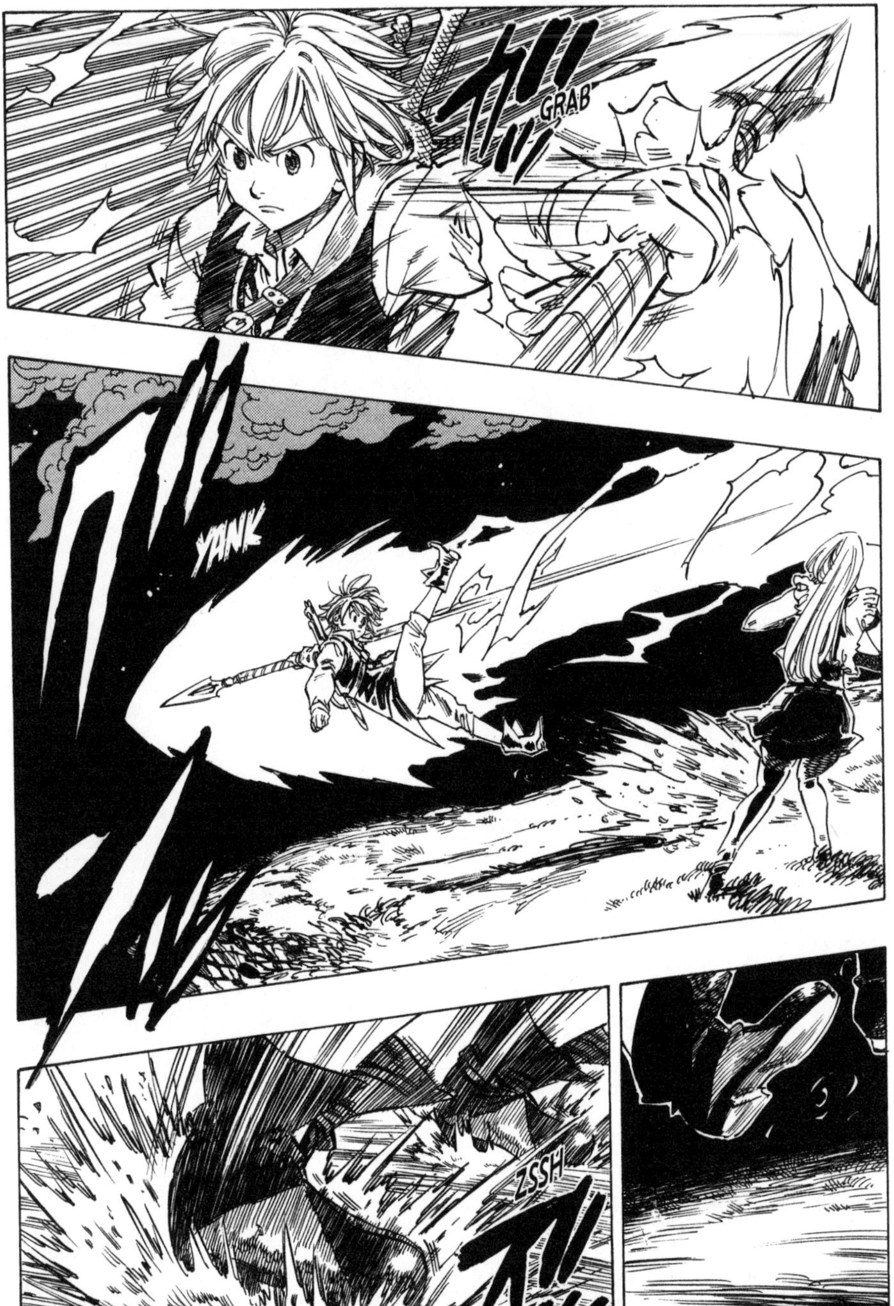
GRAB
YANK
ZSSH

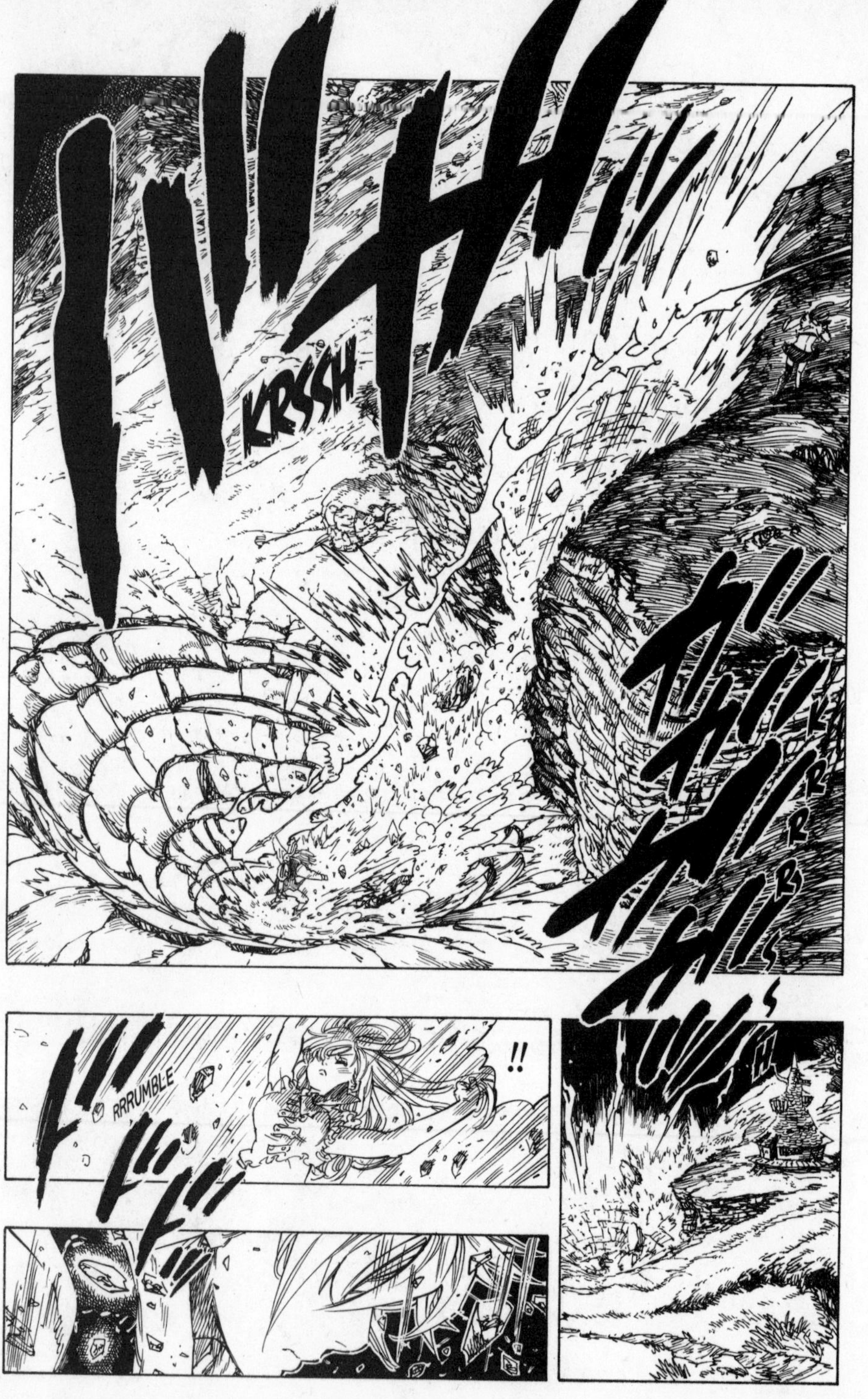
KRSSH
KRRRSSH
!!
RRRUMBLE

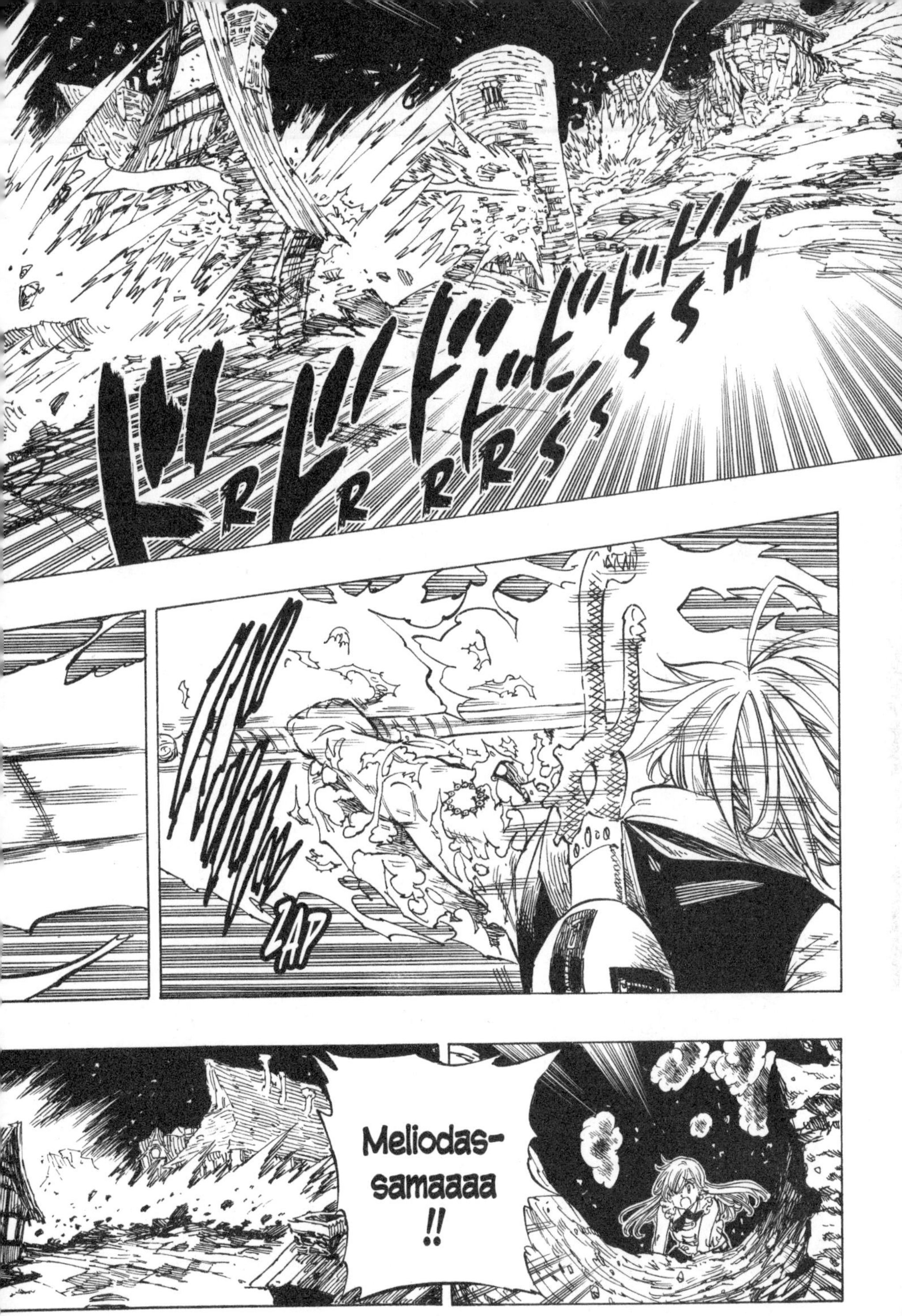
RRRRSSSSSH
ZAP
Meliodas-samaaaa!!

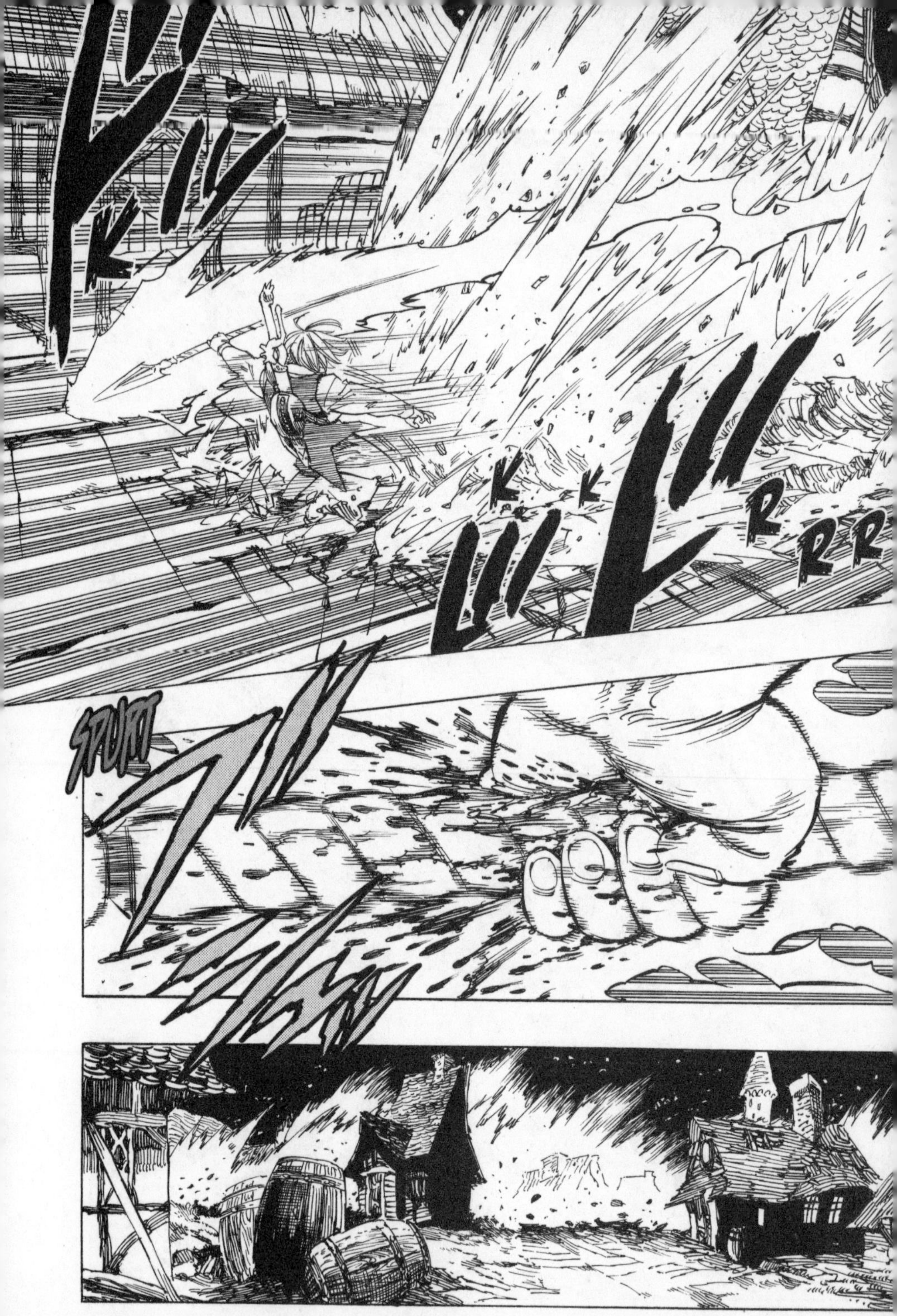
KKRRRR
SPURT

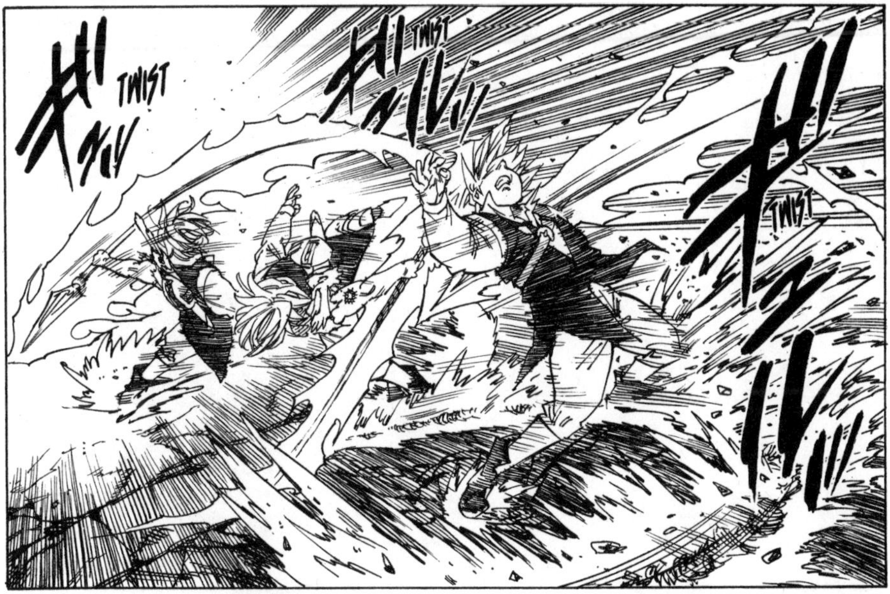
TWIST
TWIST
TWIST

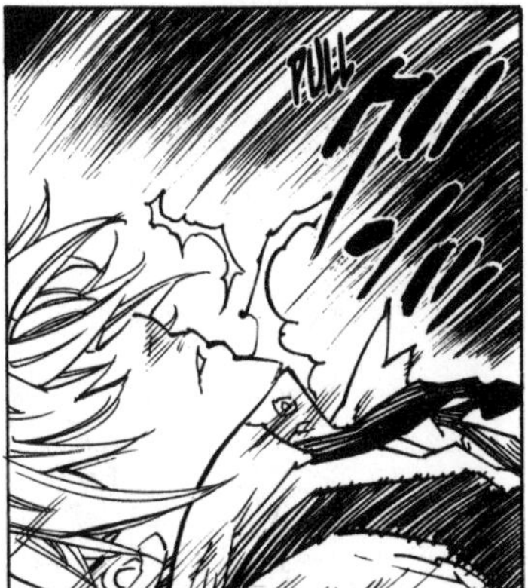
PULL

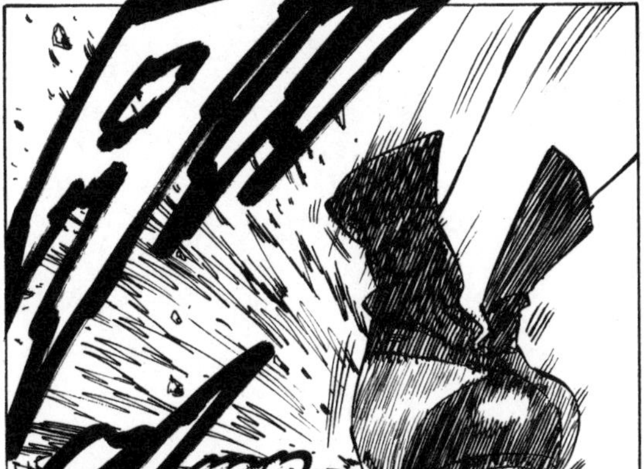
STOMP

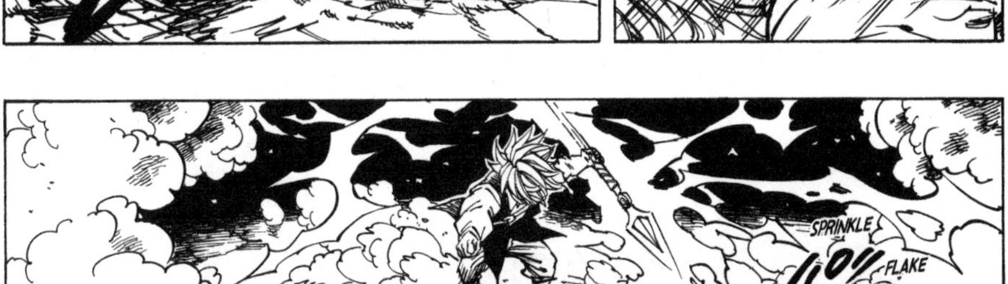
SPRINKLE
FLAKE

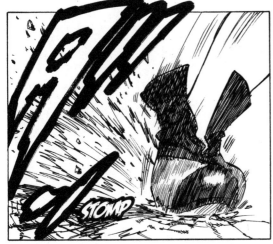

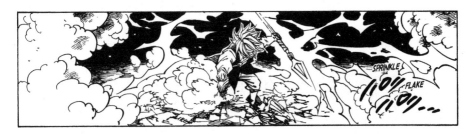

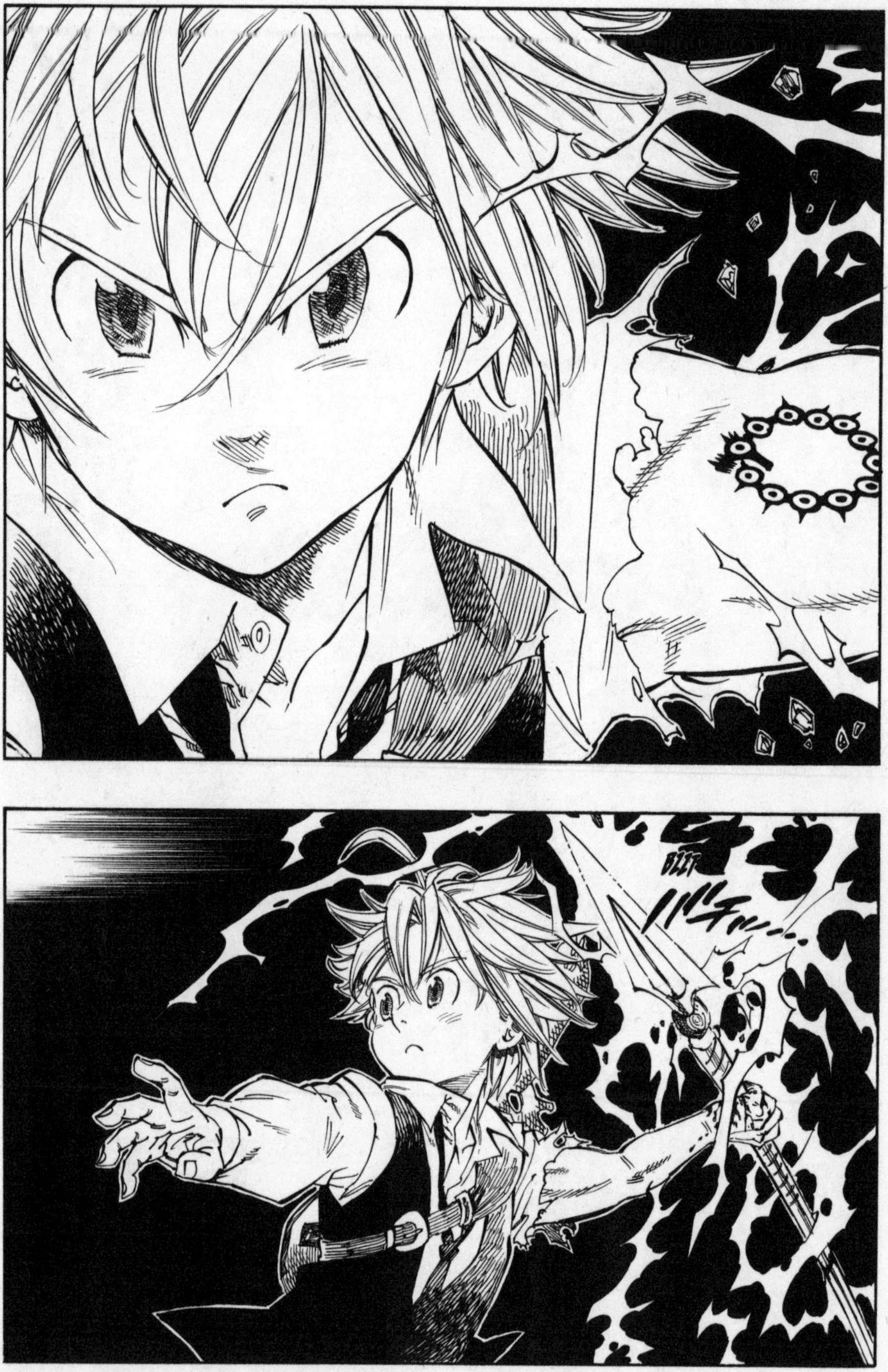
BZZT

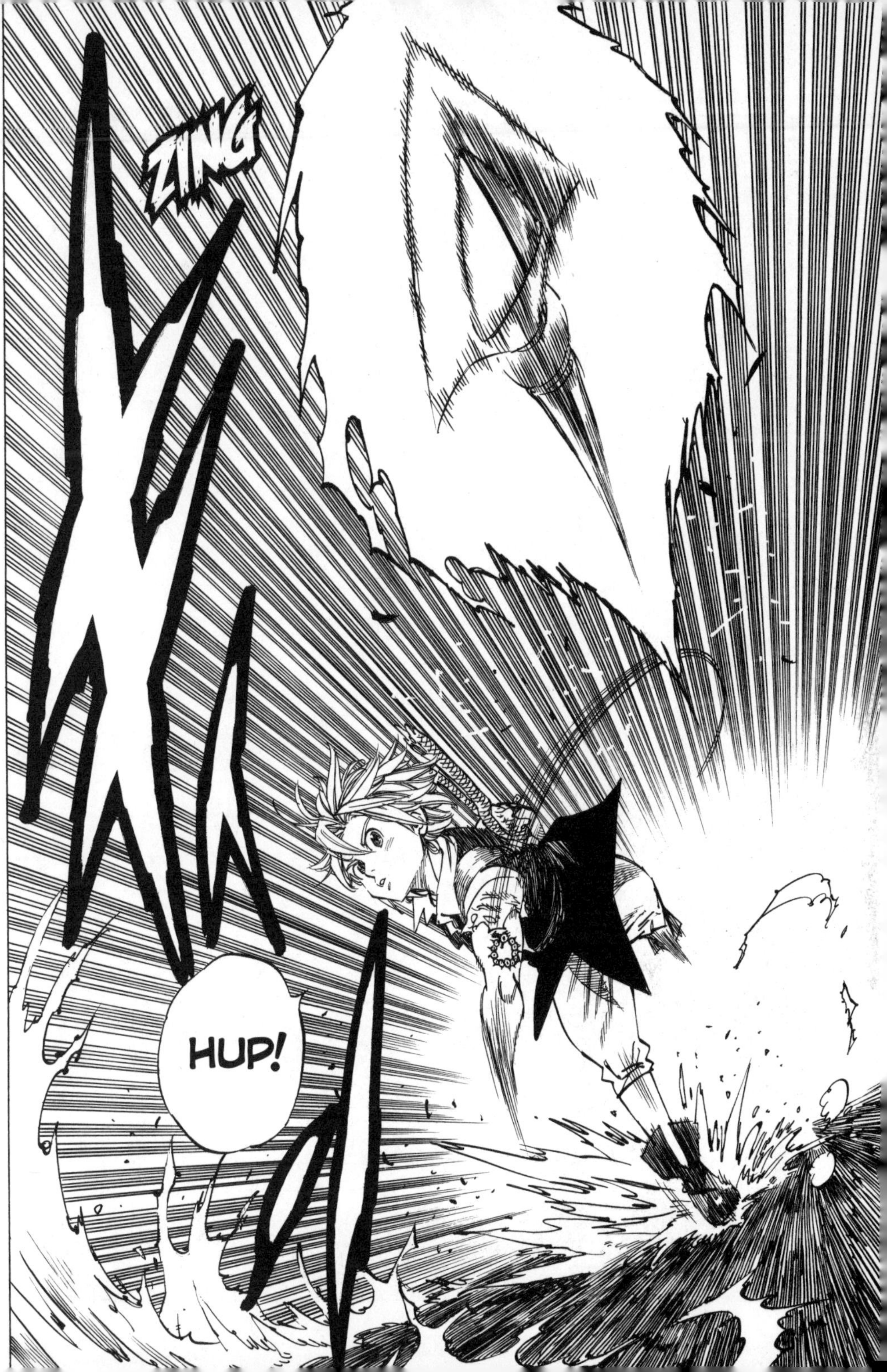
ZING
HUP!

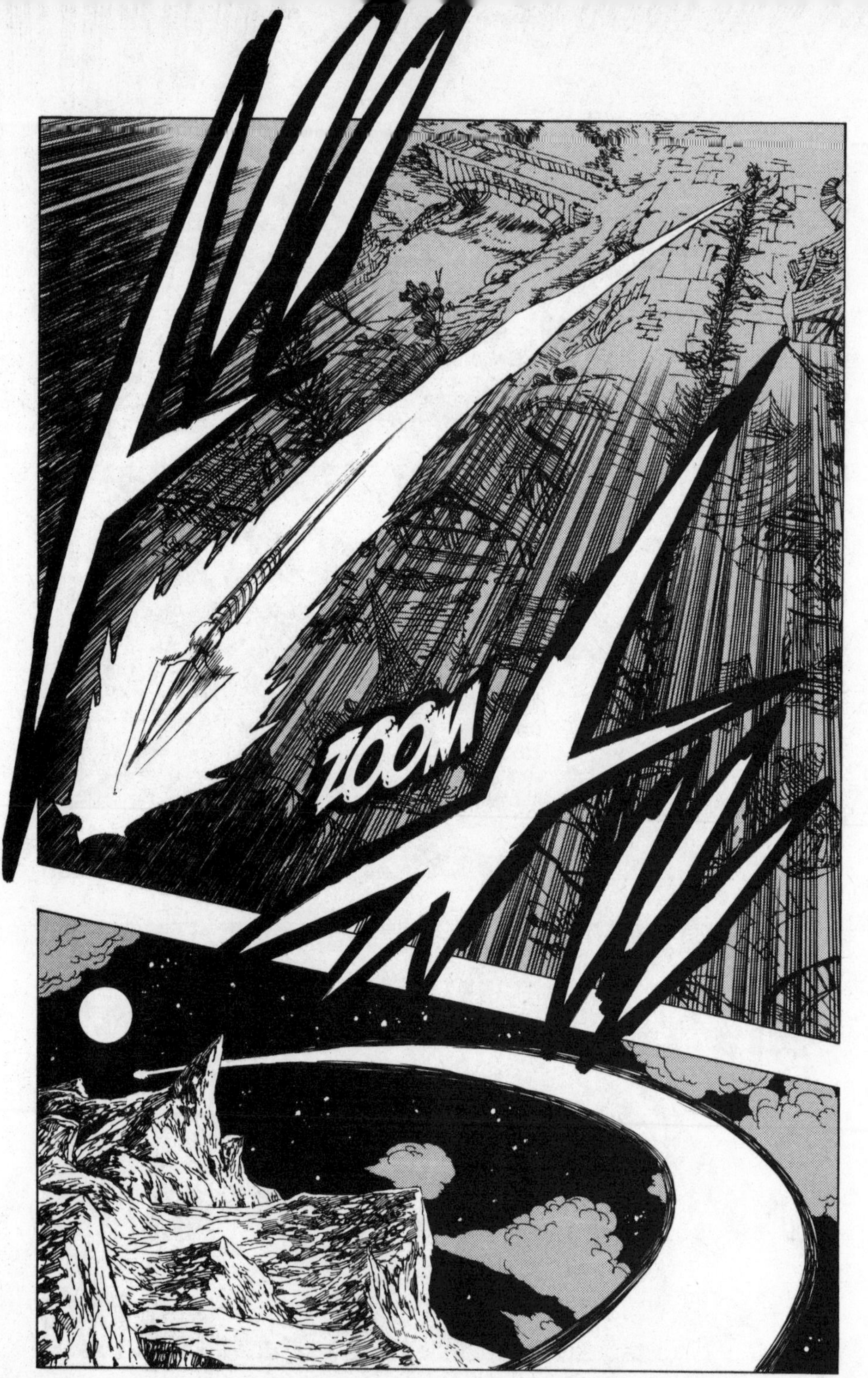
ZOOM

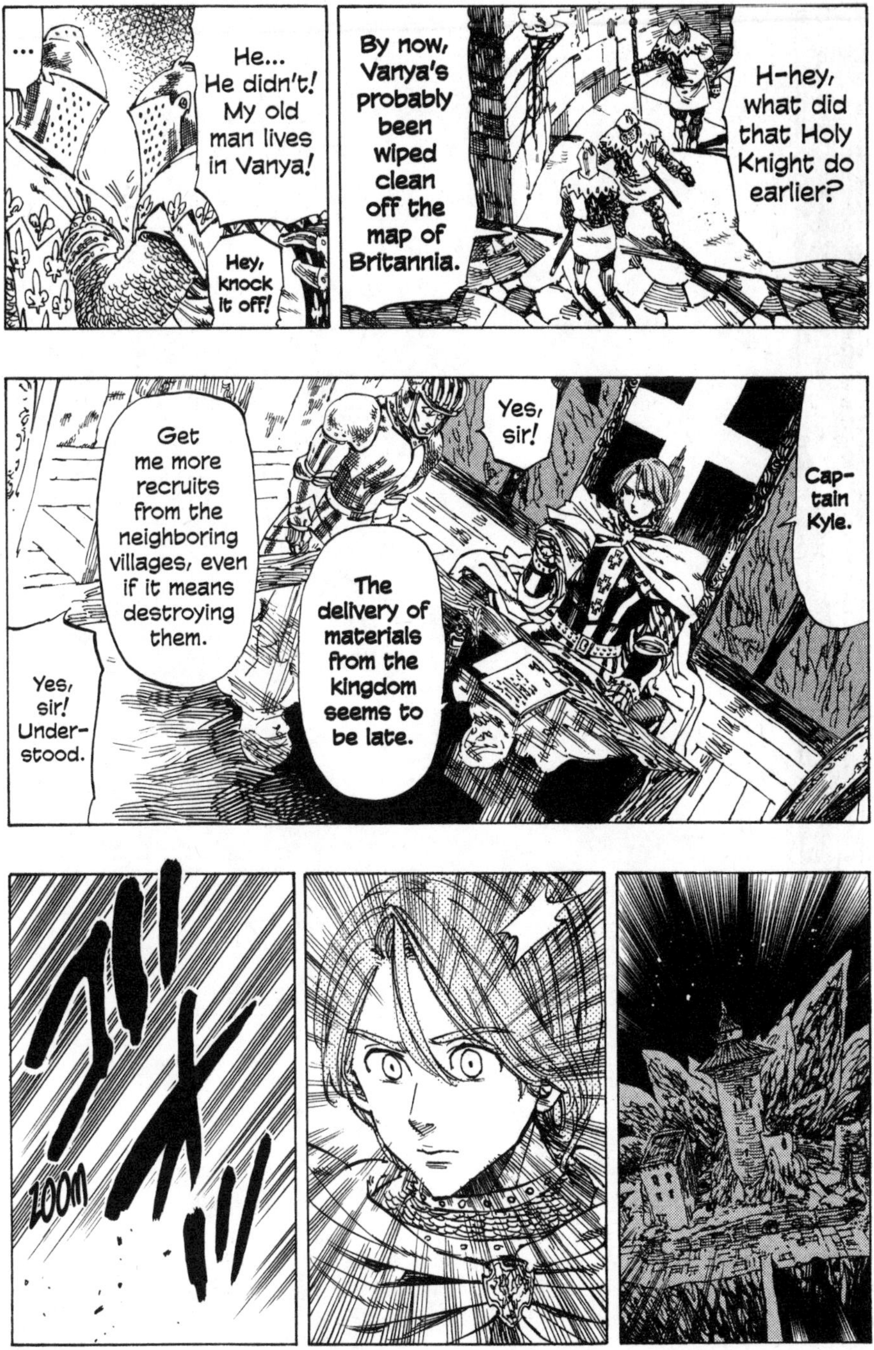
H-hey, what did that Holy Knight do earlier?
By now, Vanya's probably been wiped clean off the map of Britannia.
He... He didn't! My old man lives in Vanya!
Hey, knock it off!
...
Captain Kyle.
Yes, sir!
The delivery of materials from the kingdom seems to be late.
Get me more recruits from the neighboring villages, even if it means destroying them.
Yes, sir! Understood.
ZOOM

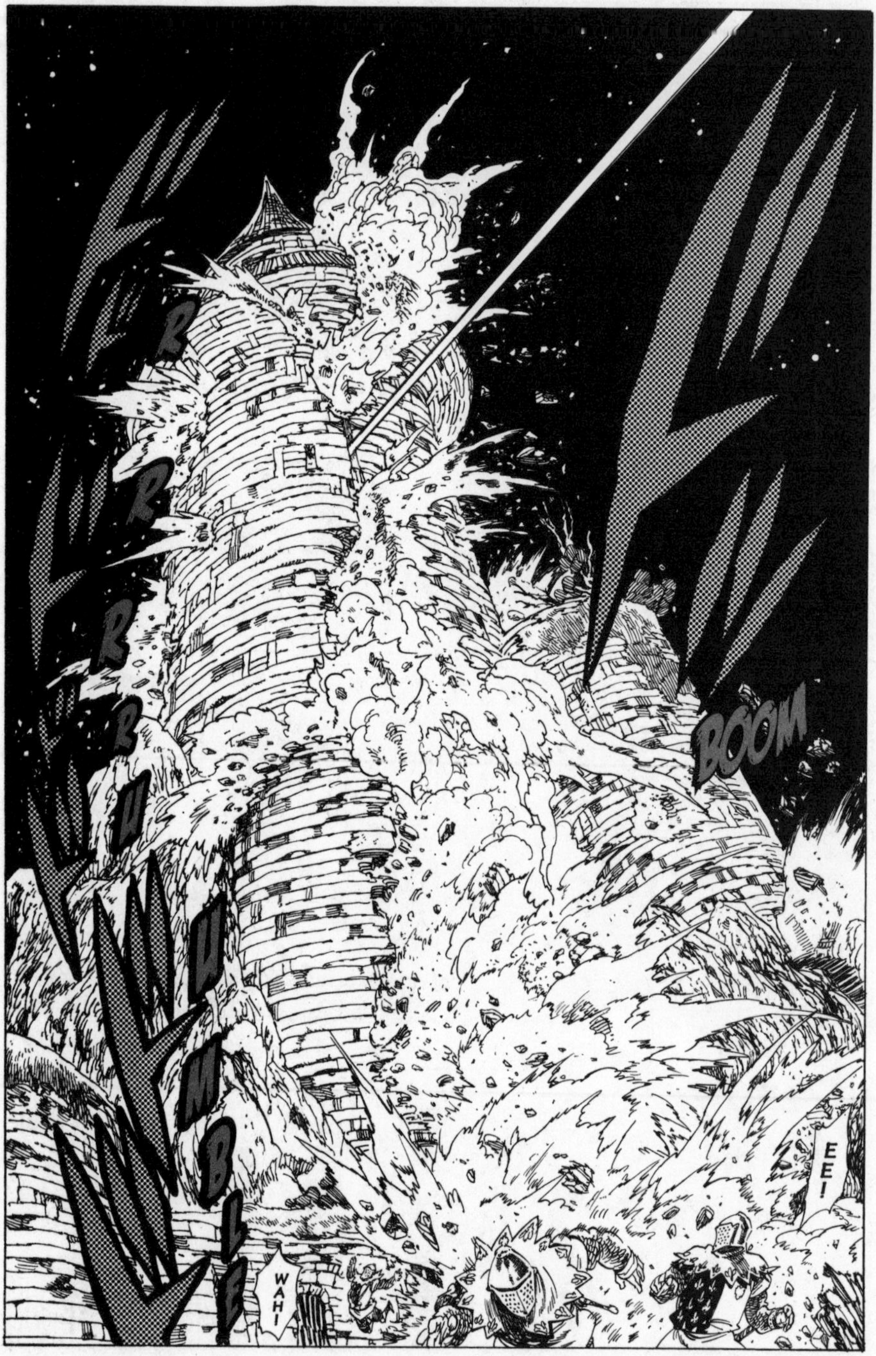
BOOM
EEI
RRRRRUUMBLE
WAHI

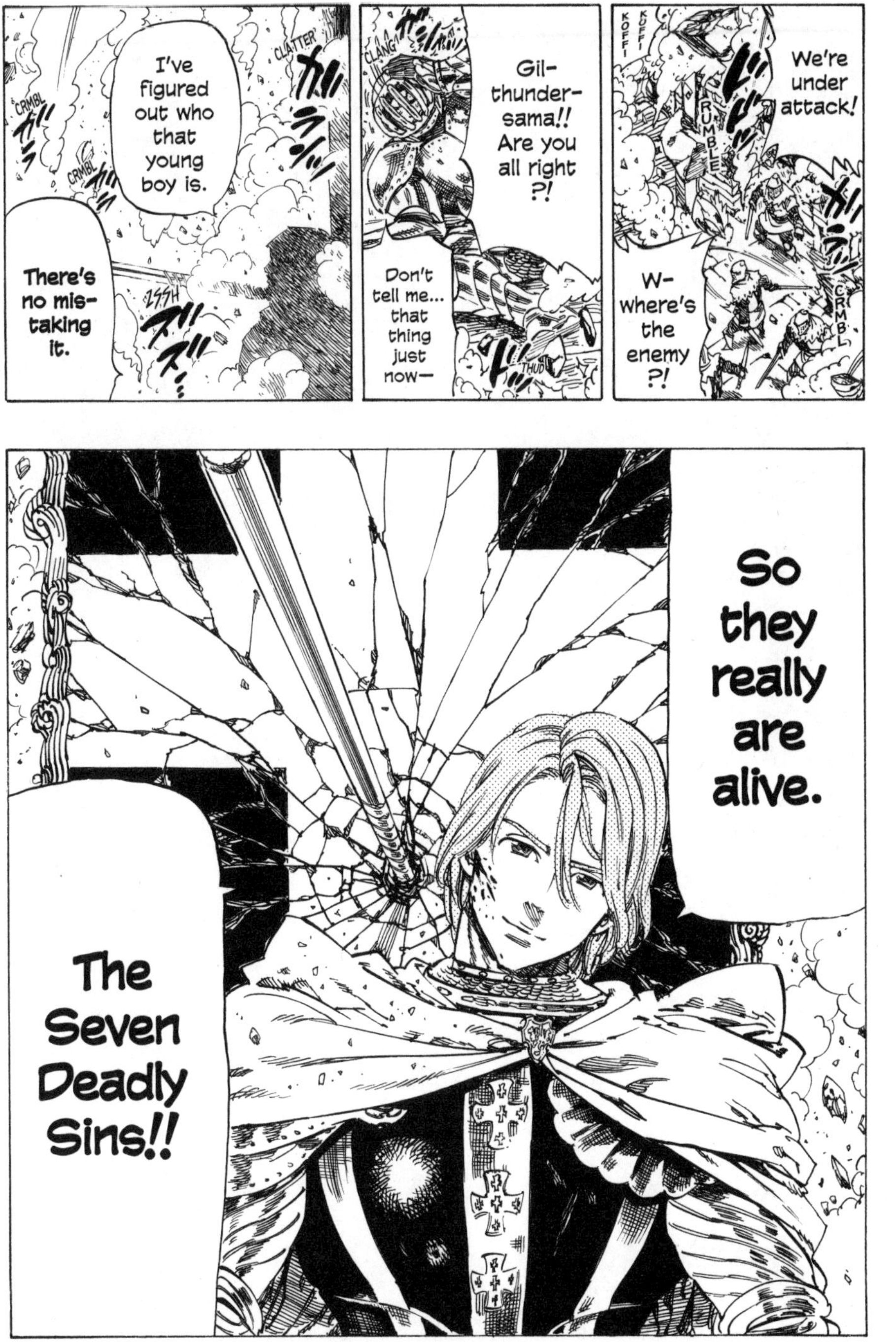
KOFFI
KOFFI
We're under attack!
RUMBLE
CRMBL
W-where's the enemy?!
CLANG
Gil-thunder-sama!! Are you all right?!
Don't tell me... that thing just now—
THUD
CLATTER
I've figured out who that young boy is.
CRMBL
CRMBL
There's no mistaking it.
ZSSH
So they really are alive.
The Seven Deadly Sins!!

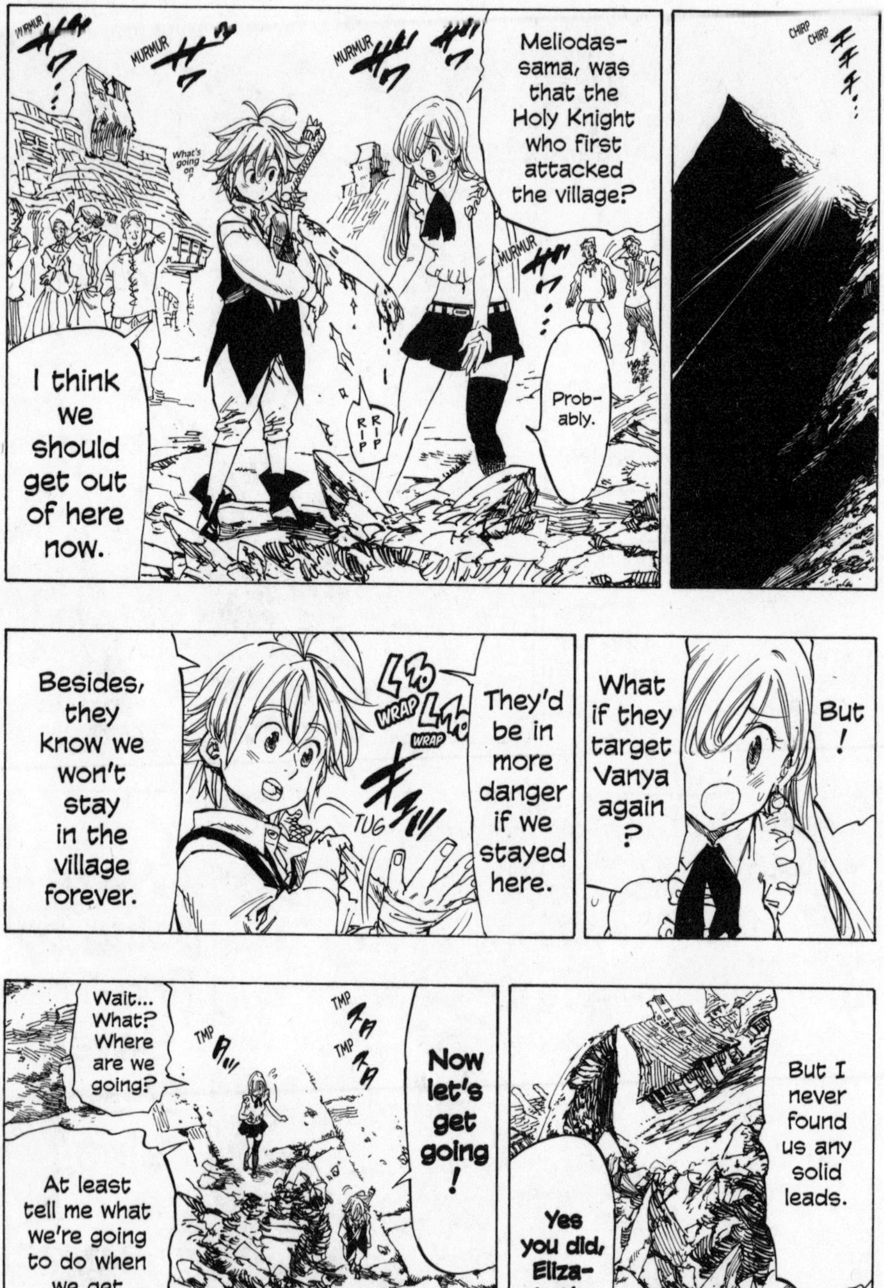
CHIRP CHIRP
Meliodas-sama, was that the Holy Knight who first attacked the village?
MURMUR
MURMUR
MURMUR
MURMUR
What's going on?
Prob-ably.
RIP RIP
I think we should get out of here now.
But!
What if they target Vanya again?
They'd be in more danger if we stayed here.
WRAP
WRAP
TUG
Besides, they know we won't stay in the village forever.
But I never found us any solid leads.
Yes you did, Eliza-beth.
Now let's get going!
TMP
TMP
TMP
Wait... What? Where are we going?
At least tell me what we're going to do when we get there.

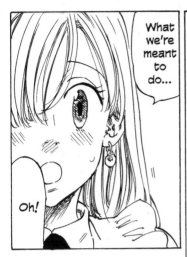

What we're meant to do...

Oh!

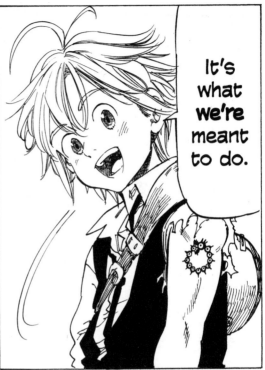

It's what we're meant to do.

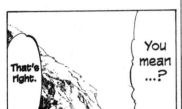

You mean ...?

That's right.

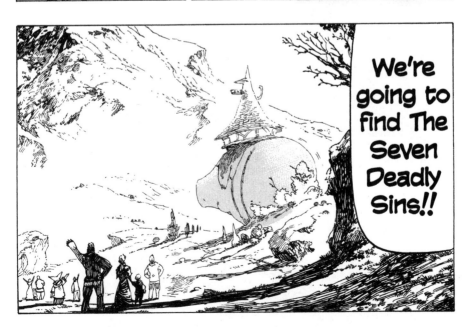

We're going to find The Seven Deadly Sins!!

Chapter 4 - The Sin in the Sleeping Forest

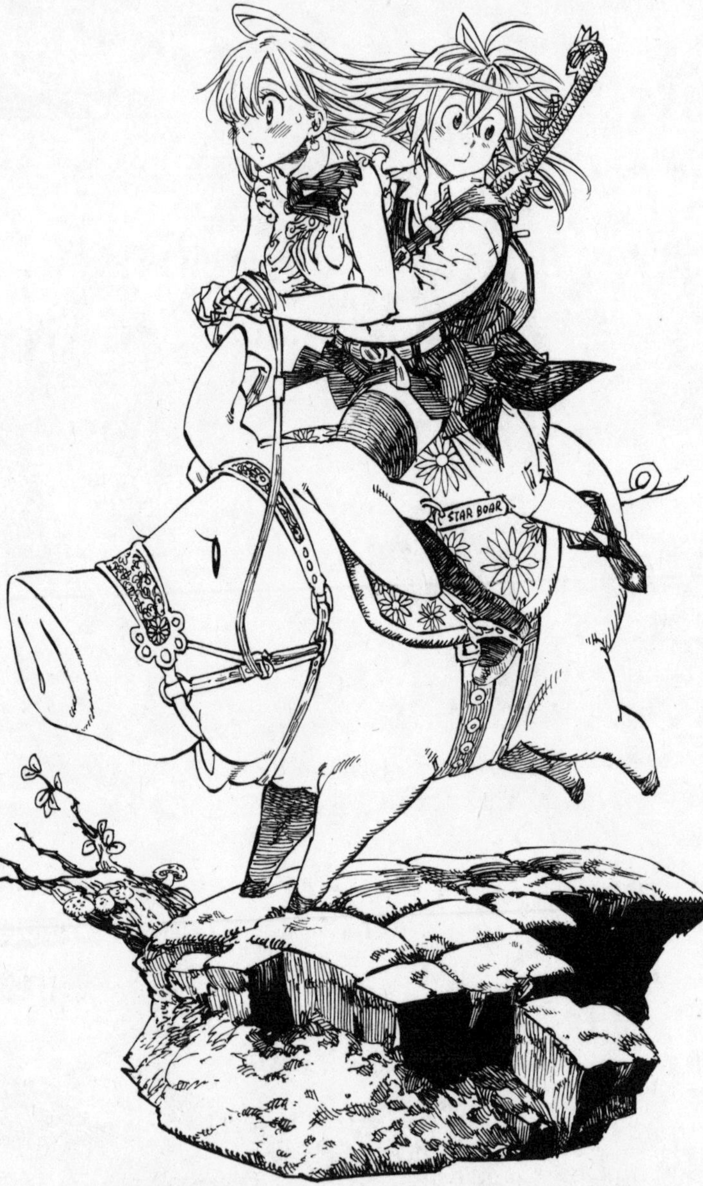
STAR BOAR

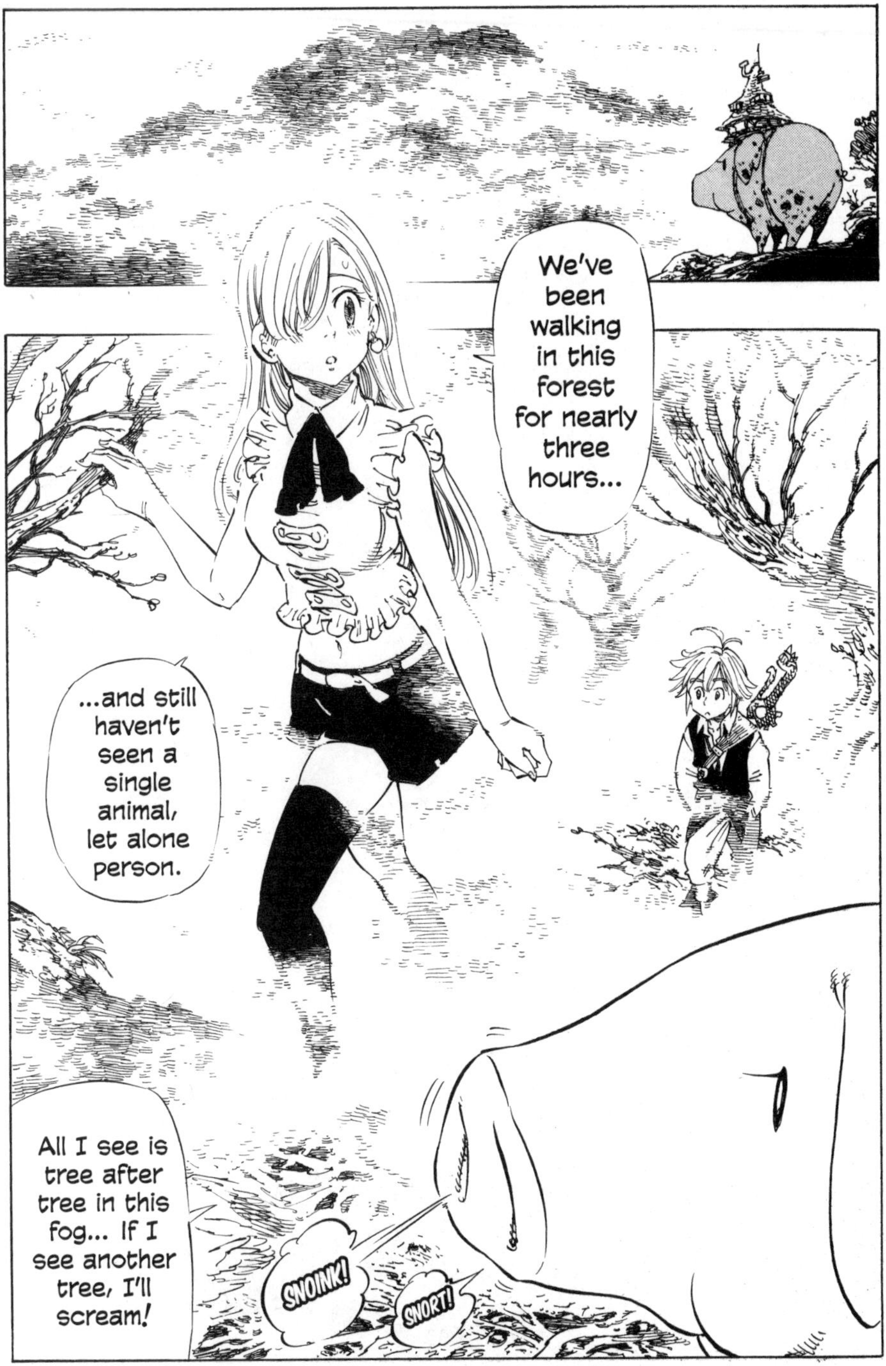
We've been walking in this forest for nearly three hours...
...and still haven't seen a single animal, let alone person.
All I see is tree after tree in this fog... If I see another tree, I'll scream!
SNORT!
SNOINK!

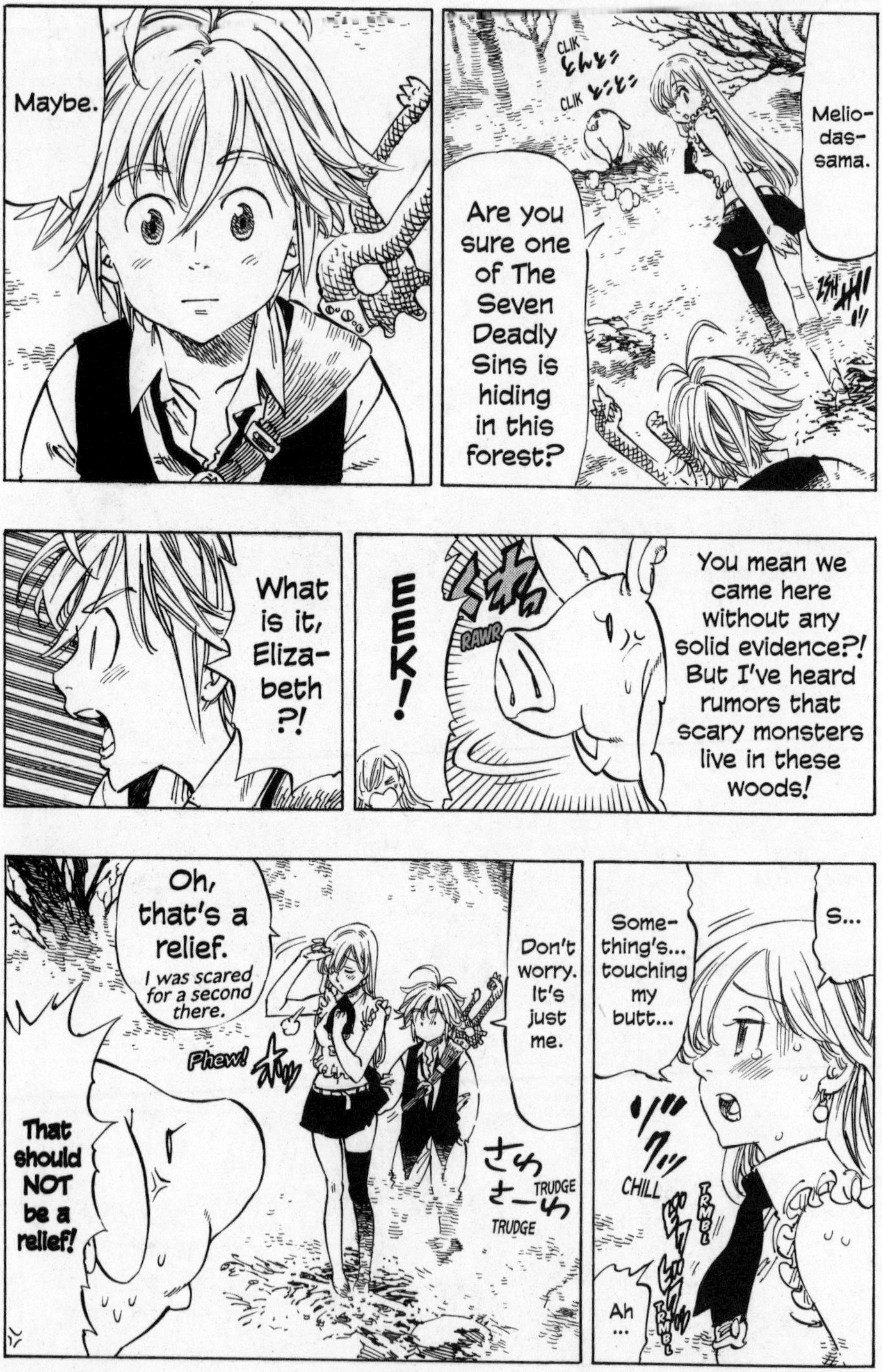
CLIK
CLIK
Melio-das-sama.
Are you sure one of The Seven Deadly Sins is hiding in this forest?
Maybe.
You mean we came here without any solid evidence?! But I've heard rumors that scary monsters live in these woods!
EEK!
RAWR
What is it, Eliza-beth?!
S...
Some-thing's... touching my butt...
CHILL
TRMBL
TRMBL
Ah...
Don't worry. It's just me.
Oh, that's a relief. I was scared for a second there.
Phew!
TRUDGE
TRUDGE
That should NOT be a relief!

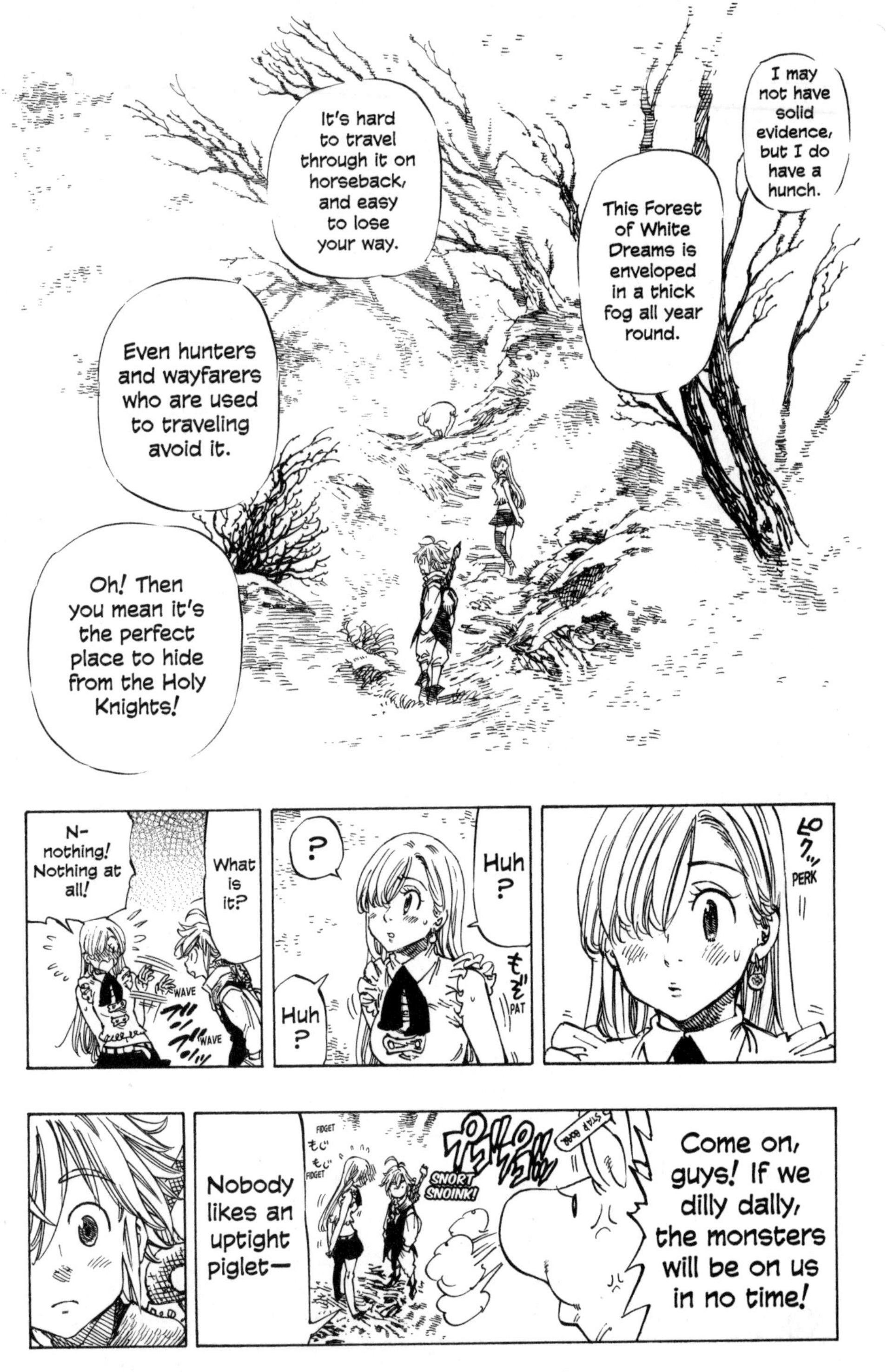

I may not have solid evidence, but I do have a hunch.
This Forest of White Dreams is enveloped in a thick fog all year round.
It's hard to travel through it on horseback, and easy to lose your way.
Even hunters and wayfarers who are used to traveling avoid it.
Oh! Then you mean it's the perfect place to hide from the Holy Knights!
PERK
Huh?
?
もぞ
PAT
Huh?
What is it?
N-nothing! Nothing at all!
WAVE
WAVE
Come on, guys! If we dilly dally, the monsters will be on us in no time!
SNORT SNOINK!
Nobody likes an uptight piglet—
FIDGET
もじ
もじ
FIDGET

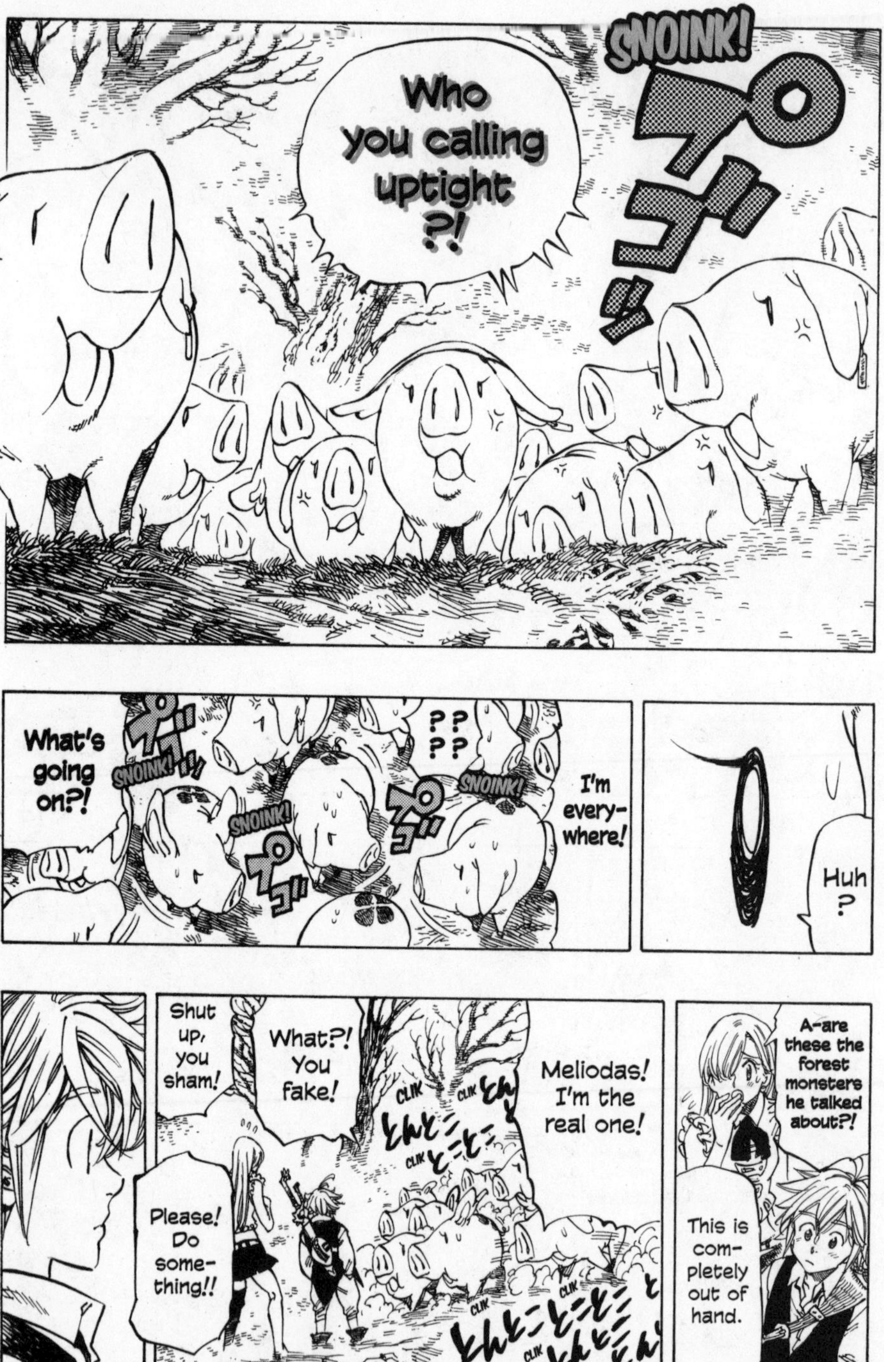
SNOINK!
Who you calling uptight ?!
Huh ?
I'm every-where!
? ? ? ?
SNOINK!
SNOINK!
SNOINK!
What's going on?!
A-are these the forest monsters he talked about?!
This is com-pletely out of hand.
Meliodas! I'm the real one!
CLIK
CLIK
CLIK
What?! You fake!
Shut up, you sham!
Please! Do some-thing!!
CLIK
CLIK
CLIK

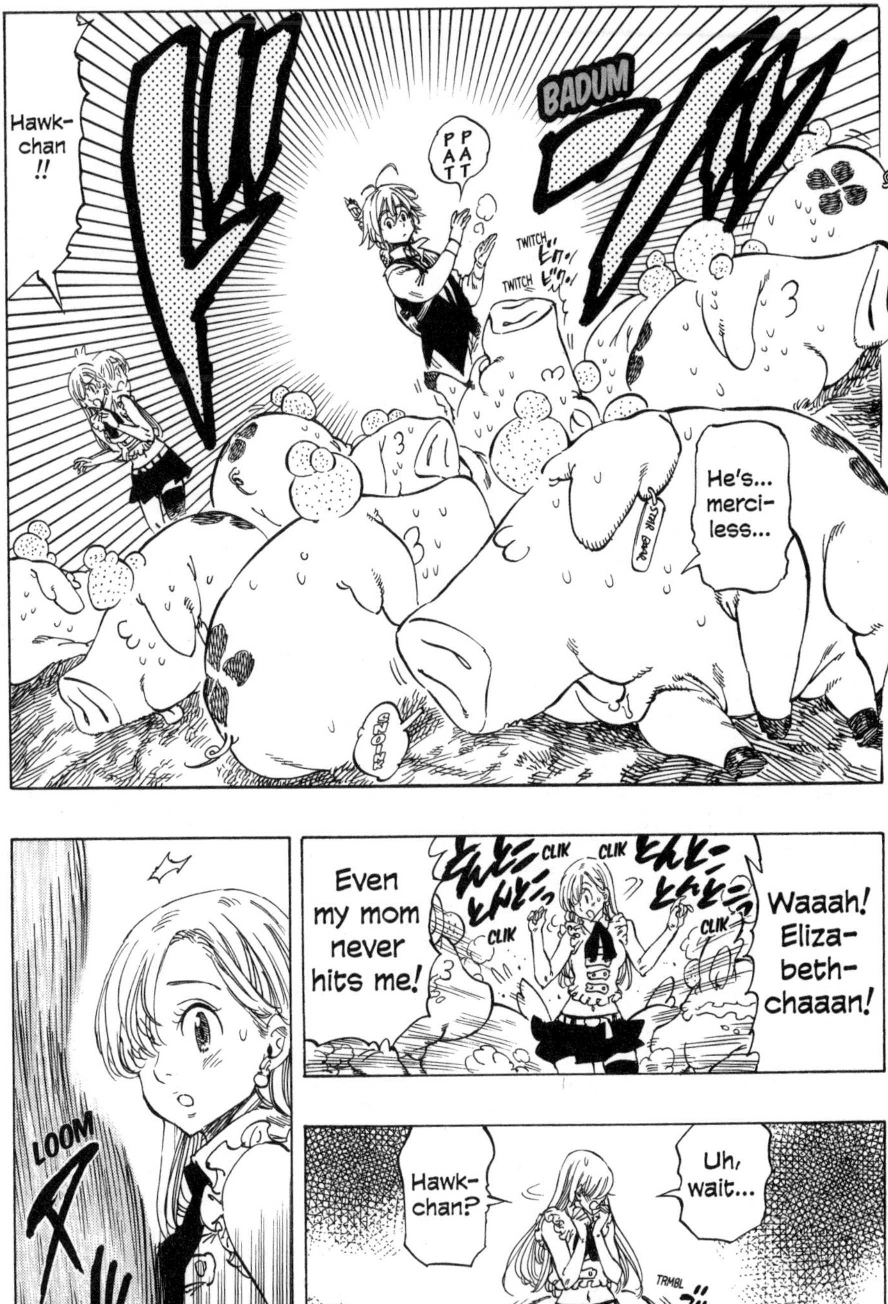
BADUM
PAT PAT
TWITCH
TWITCH
Hawk-chan!!
He's... merciless...
Waaah! Eliza-beth-chaaan!
CLIK
CLIK
CLIK
CLIK
Even my mom never hits me!
Uh, wait...
Hawk-chan?
TRMBL
TRMBL
TRMBL
LOOM

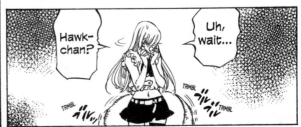

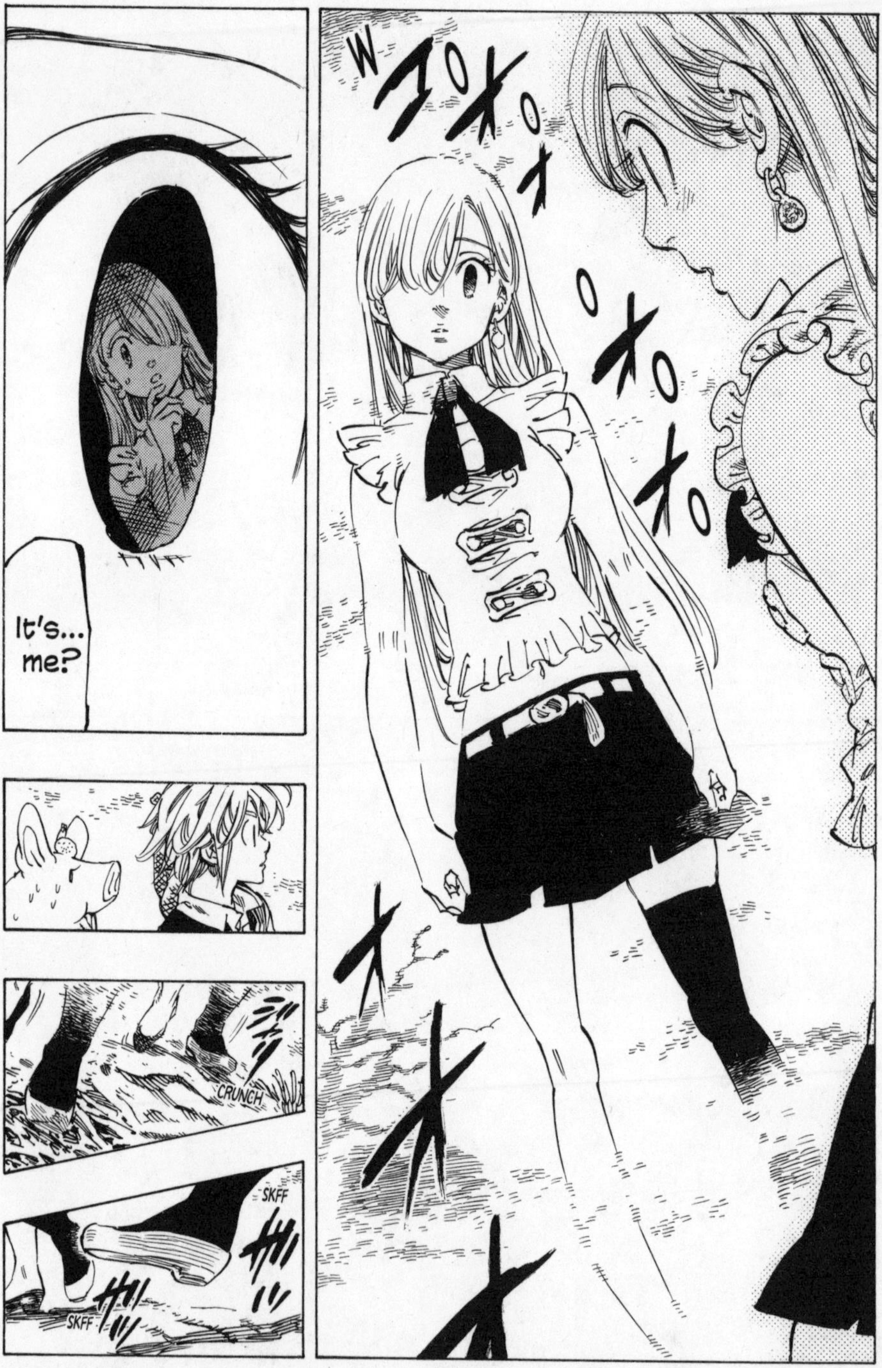
W
It's... me?
CRUNCH
SKFF
SKFF

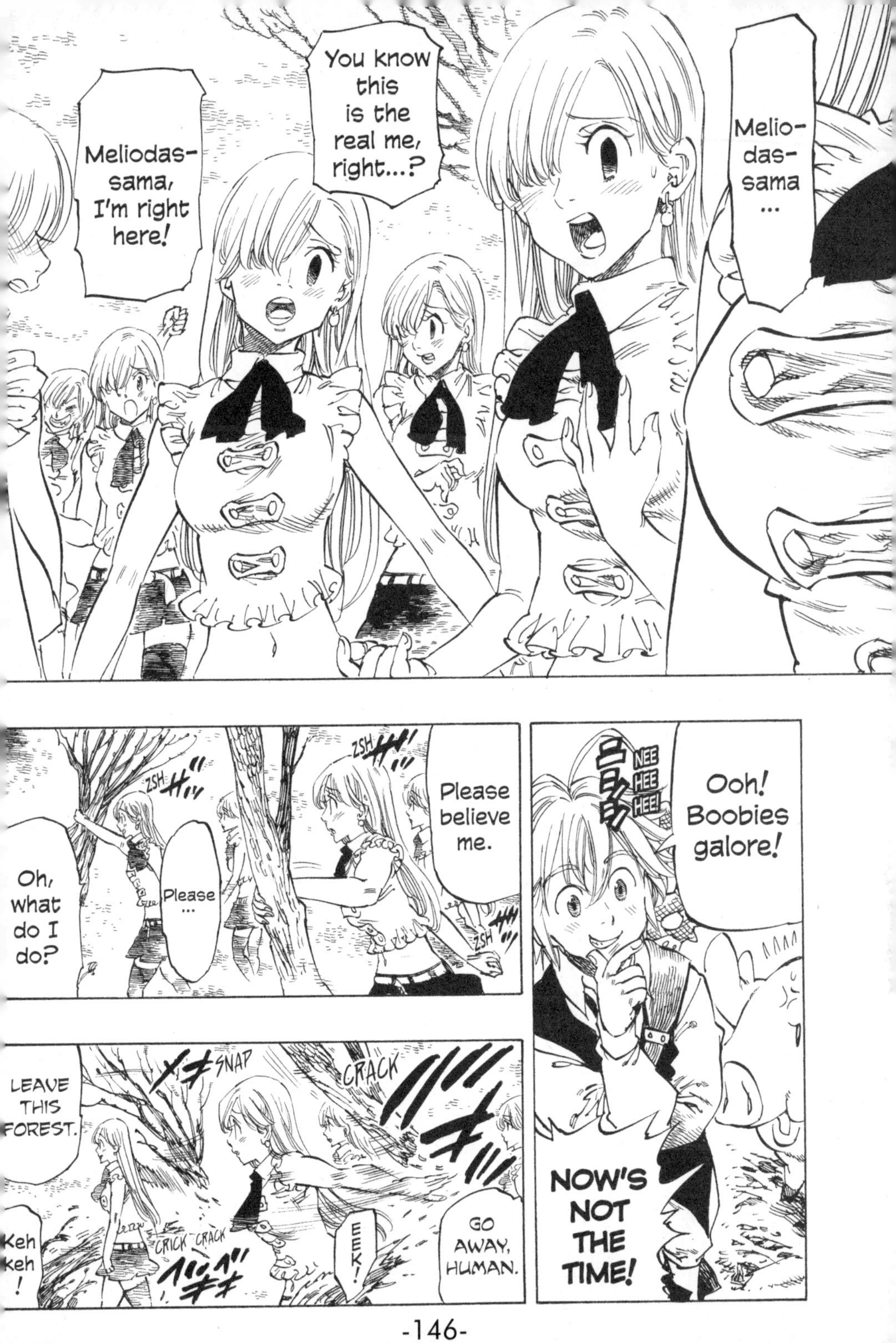
Melio-das-sama ...
You know this is the real me, right...?
Meliodas-sama, I'm right here!
NEE HEE HEE!
Ooh! Boobies galore!
NOW'S NOT THE TIME!
ZSH
Please believe me.
ZSH
ZSH
Please ...
Oh, what do I do?
CRACK
GO AWAY, HUMAN.
EEK!
SNAP
CRICK CRACK
LEAVE THIS FOREST.
Keh keh!

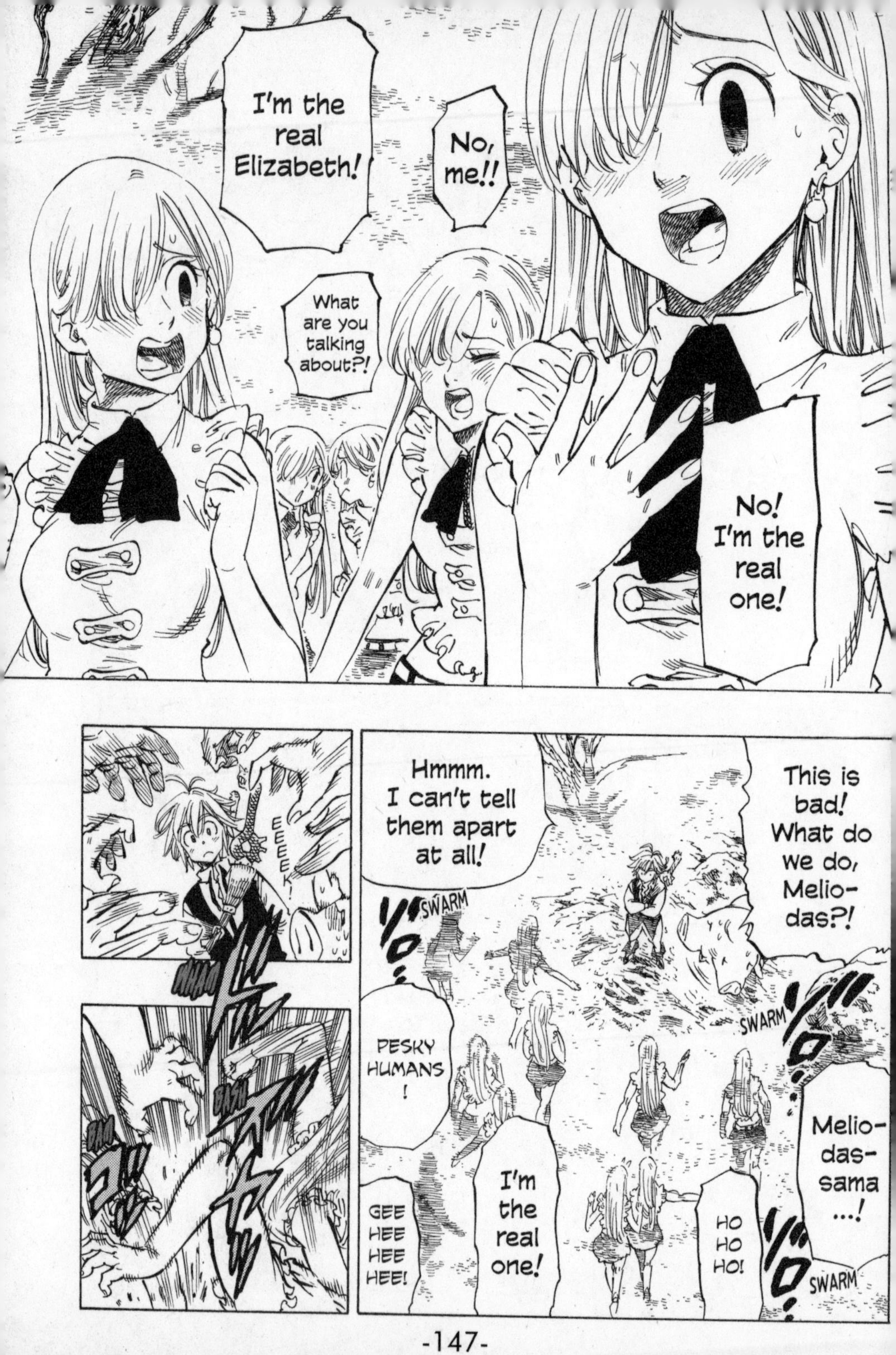
I'm the real Elizabeth!
No, me!!
What are you talking about?!
No! I'm the real one!
This is bad! What do we do, Melio-das?!
Hmmm. I can't tell them apart at all!
SWARM
SWARM
Melio-das-sama...!
PESKY HUMANS!
HO HO HO!
I'm the real one!
GEE HEE HEE HEE!
SWARM
EEEEK!
WHAM
BASH
BAM

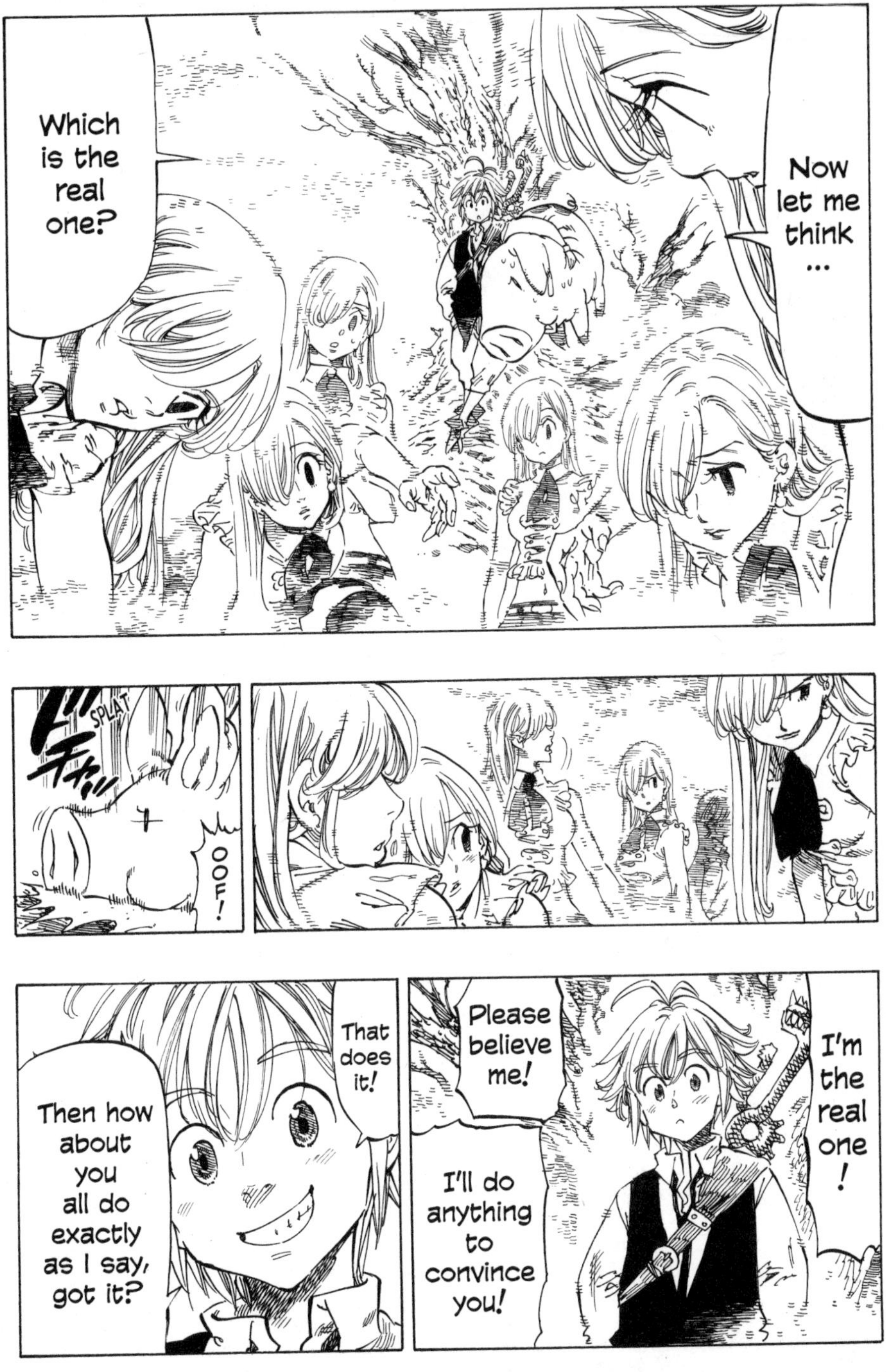
Now let me think ...
Which is the real one?
SPLAT
OOF!
I'm the real one!
Please believe me!
I'll do anything to convince you!
That does it!
Then how about you all do exactly as I say, got it?

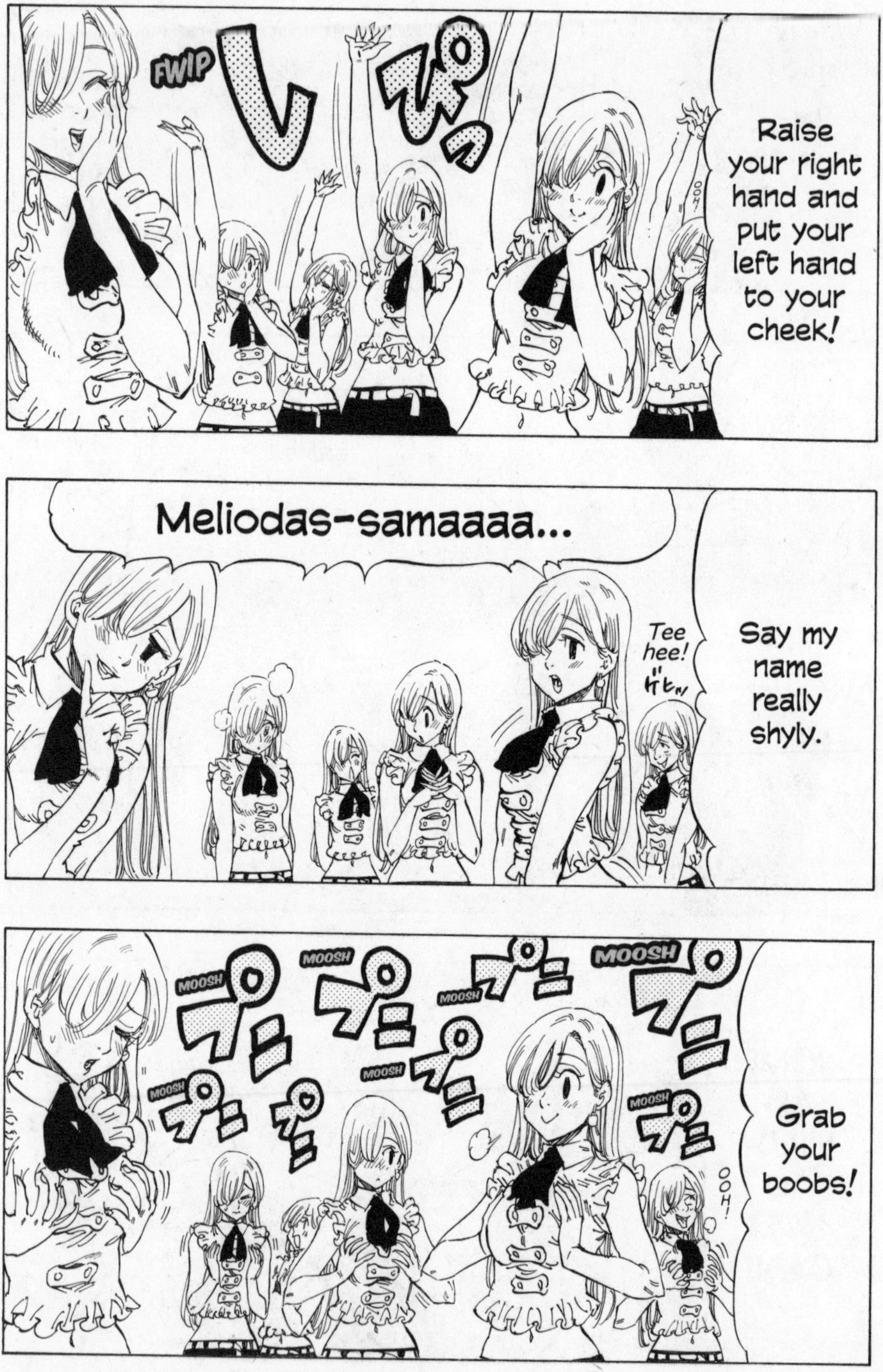
Raise your right hand and put your left hand to your cheek!
OOH!
FWIP
Say my name really shyly.
Tee hee!
Meliodas-samaaaa...
Grab your boobs!
OOH!
MOOSH
MOOSH
MOOSH
MOOSH
MOOSH
MOOSH
MOOSH

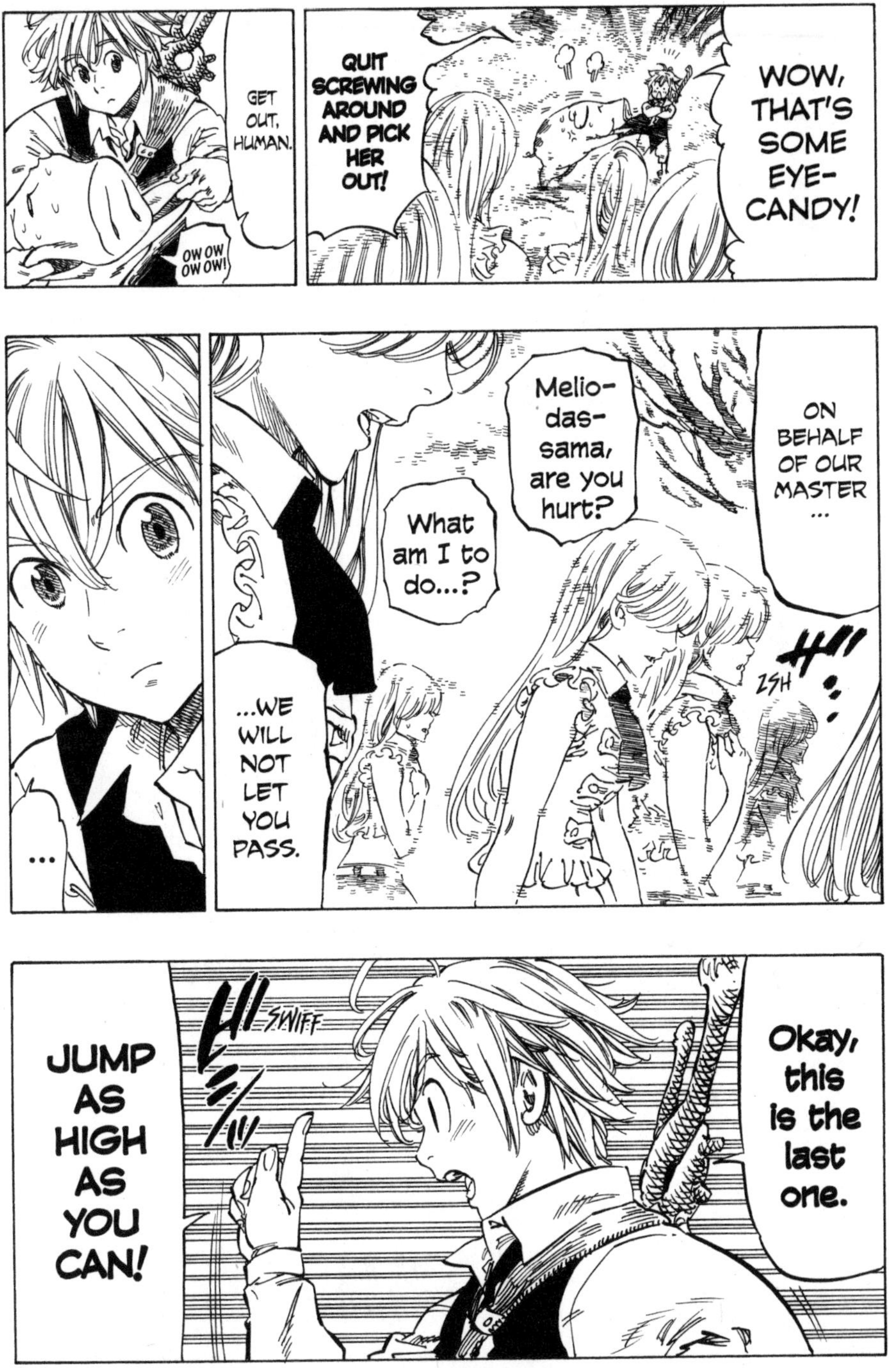
WOW, THAT'S SOME EYE-CANDY!
QUIT SCREWING AROUND AND PICK HER OUT!
GET OUT, HUMAN.
OW OW OW OW!
ON BEHALF OF OUR MASTER...
ZSH
Melio-das-sama, are you hurt?
What am I to do...?
...WE WILL NOT LET YOU PASS.
...
Okay, this is the last one.
SWIFF
JUMP AS HIGH AS YOU CAN!

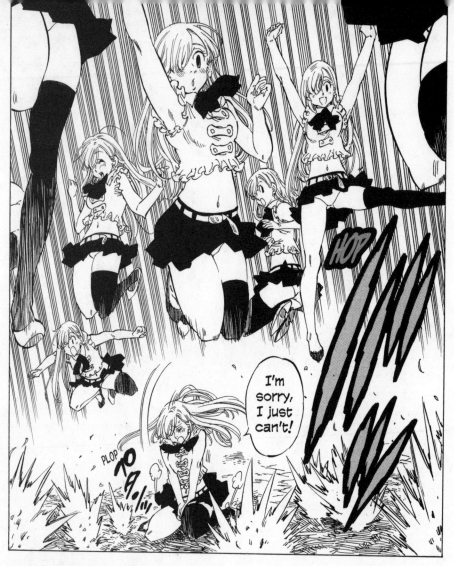

HOP

I'm sorry, I just can't!

PLOP

SHNKT

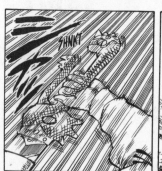

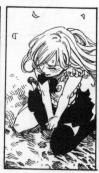

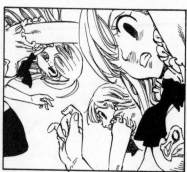

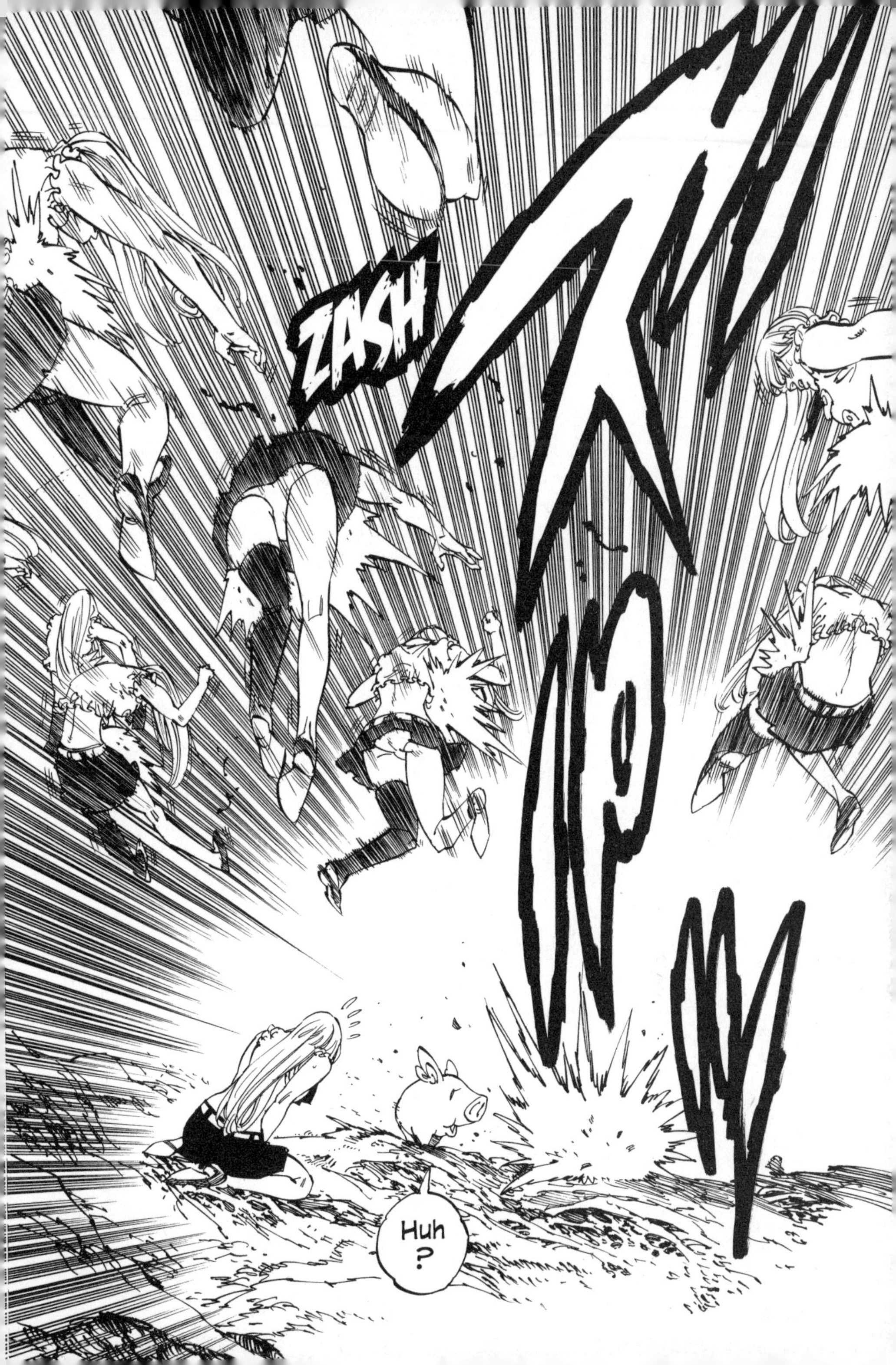
ZASH
Huh
?

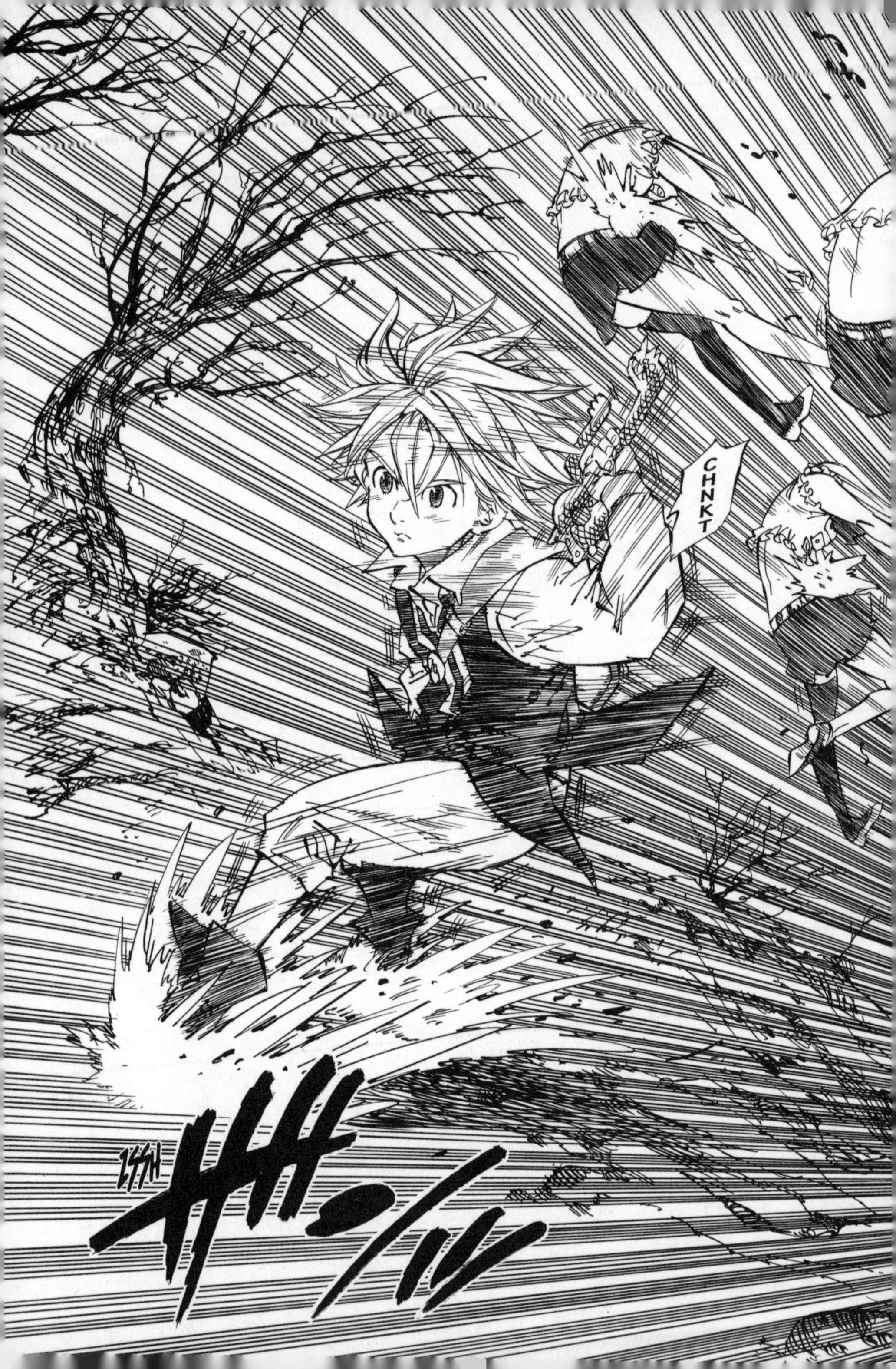
CHNKT
ZSSH

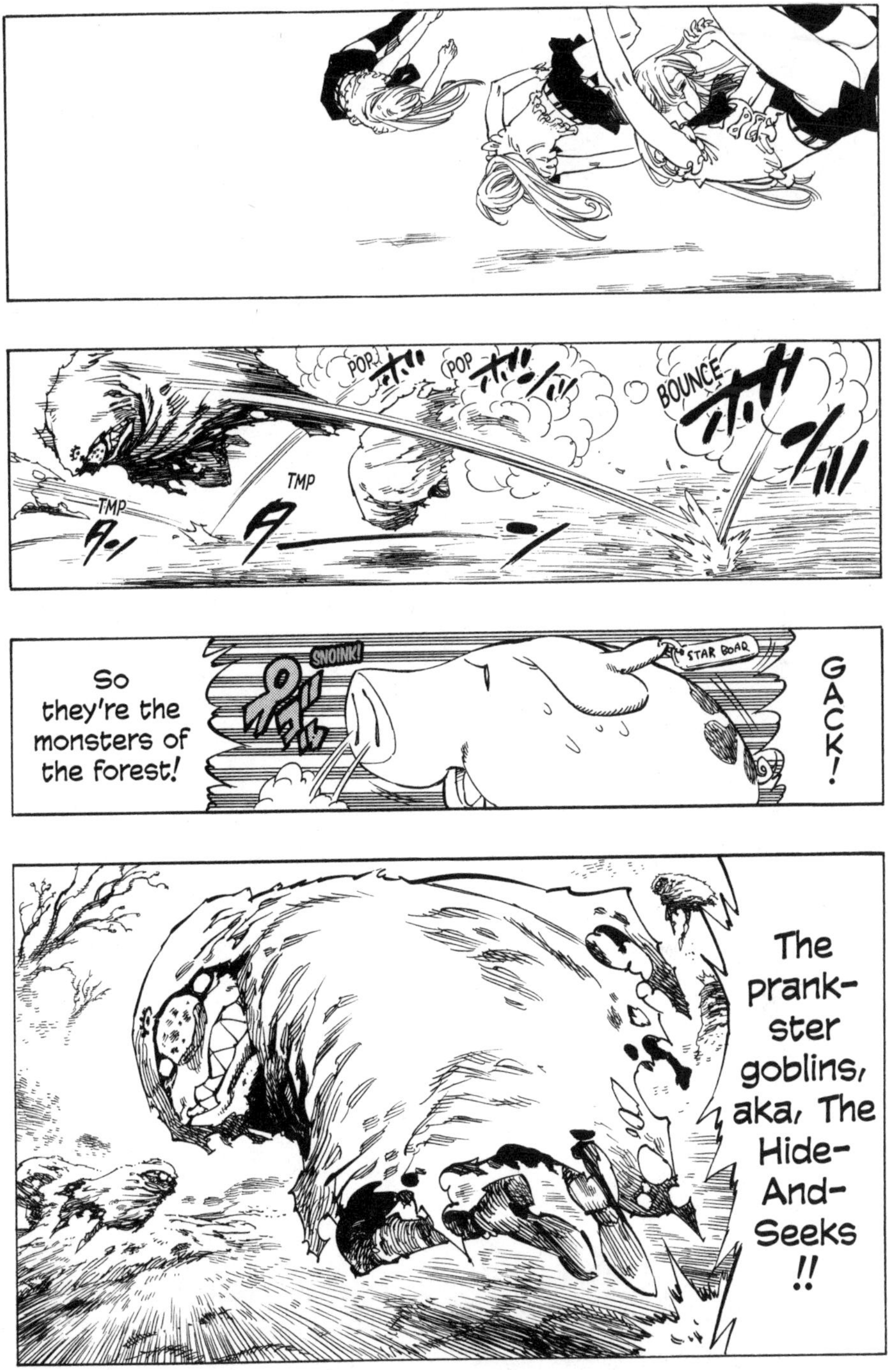
BOUNCE
POP
POP
TMP
TMP
GACK!
STAR BOAR
SNOINK!
So they're the monsters of the forest!
The prank-ster goblins, aka, The Hide-And-Seeks!!

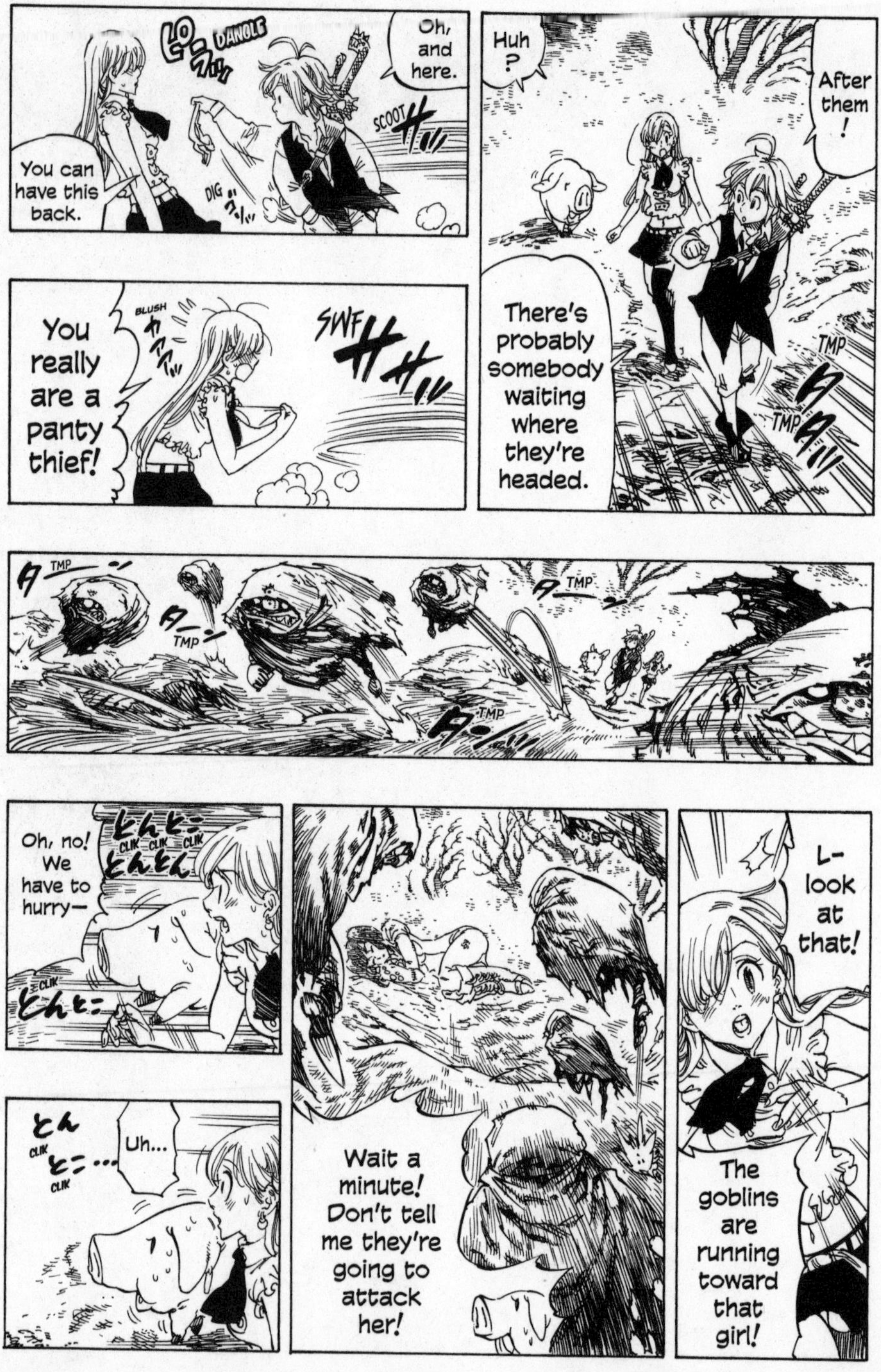
After them!
Huh?
TMP
TMP
There's probably somebody waiting where they're headed.
Oh, and here.
DANGLE
SCOOT
DIG
You can have this back.
SWF
BLUSH
You really are a panty thief!
TMP
TMP
TMP
TMP
L-look at that!
The goblins are running toward that girl!
Wait a minute! Don't tell me they're going to attack her!
CLIK CLIK CLIK
Oh, no! We have to hurry—
CLIK
Uh...
CLIK
CLIK

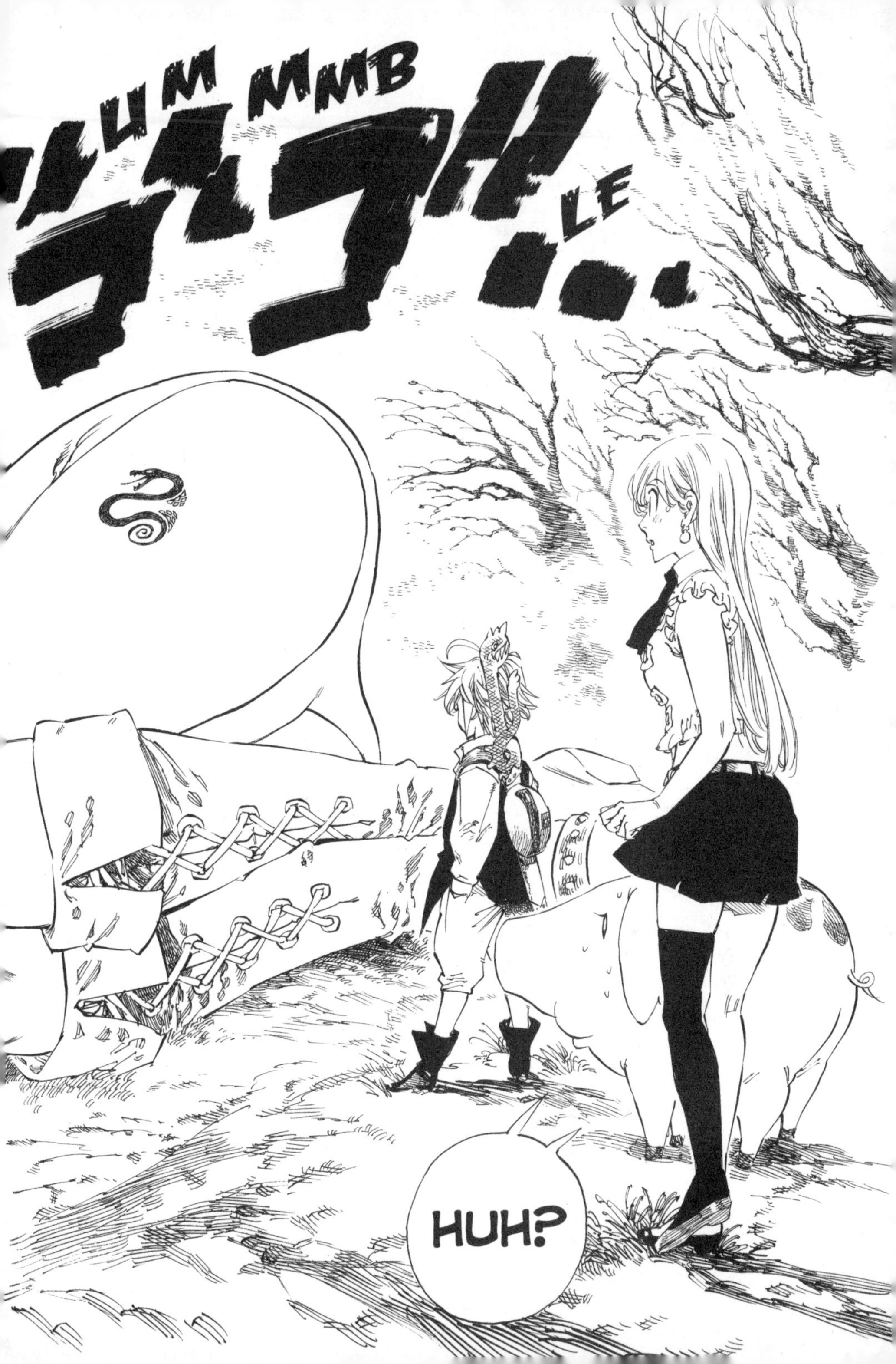
HUH?

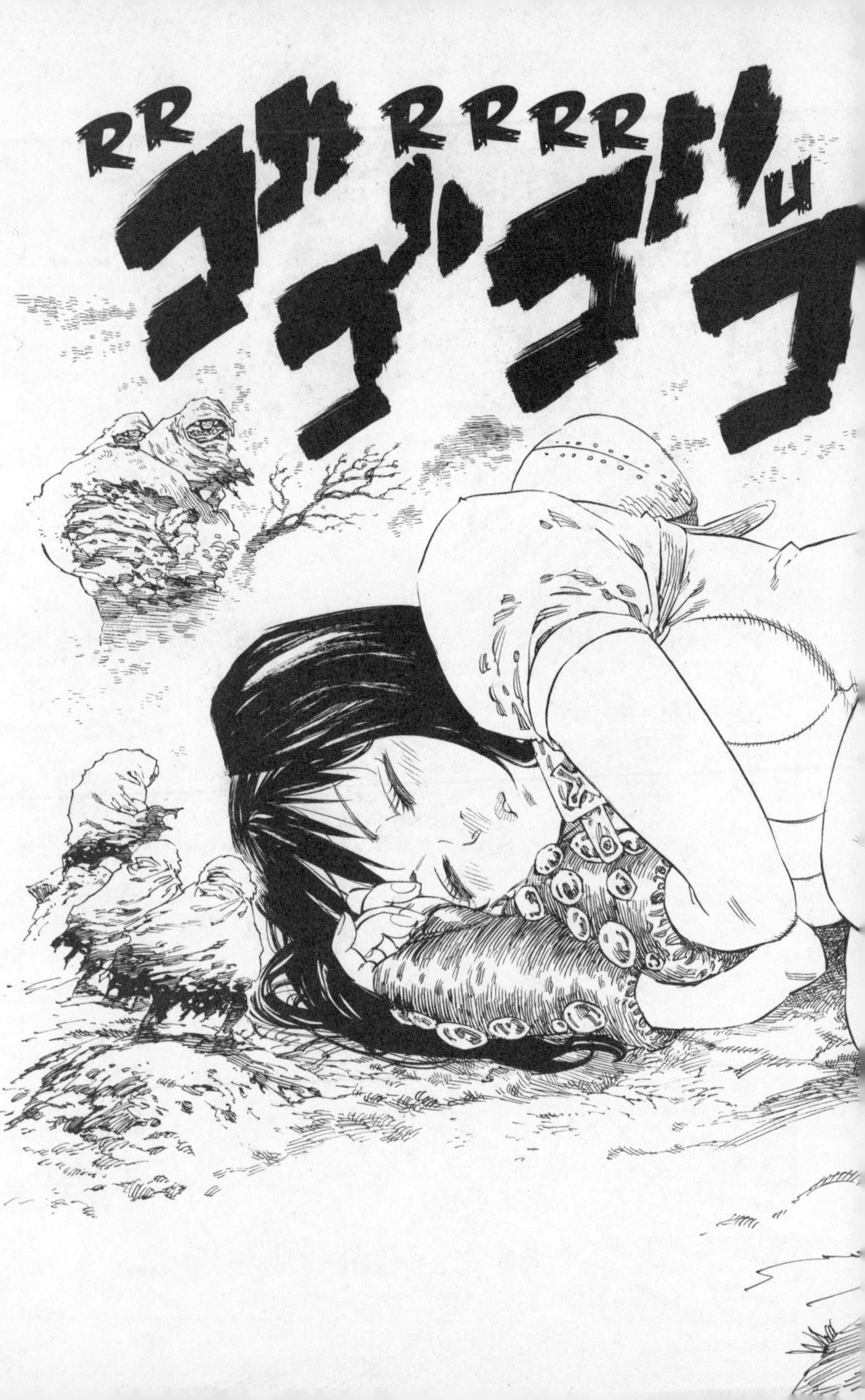
RRRRRRRU
ゴゴゴゴ

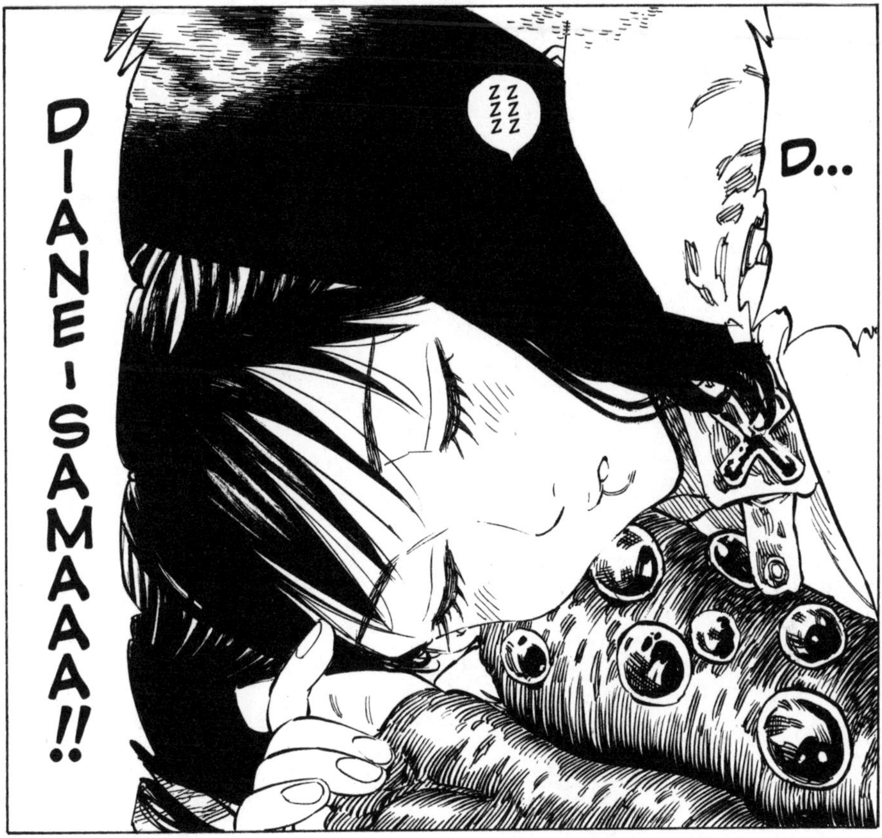
D...
Z Z Z Z Z Z
DIANE-SAMAAAA!!

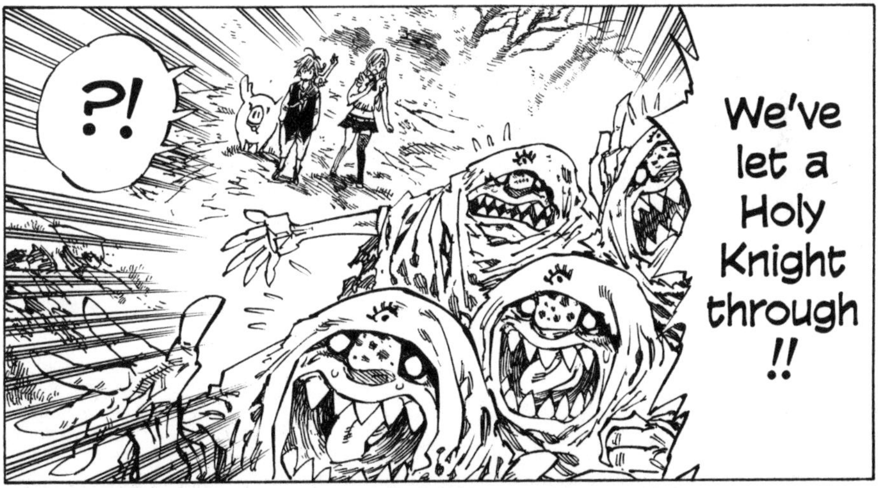
We've let a Holy Knight through!!
?!

Now Accepting Letters!

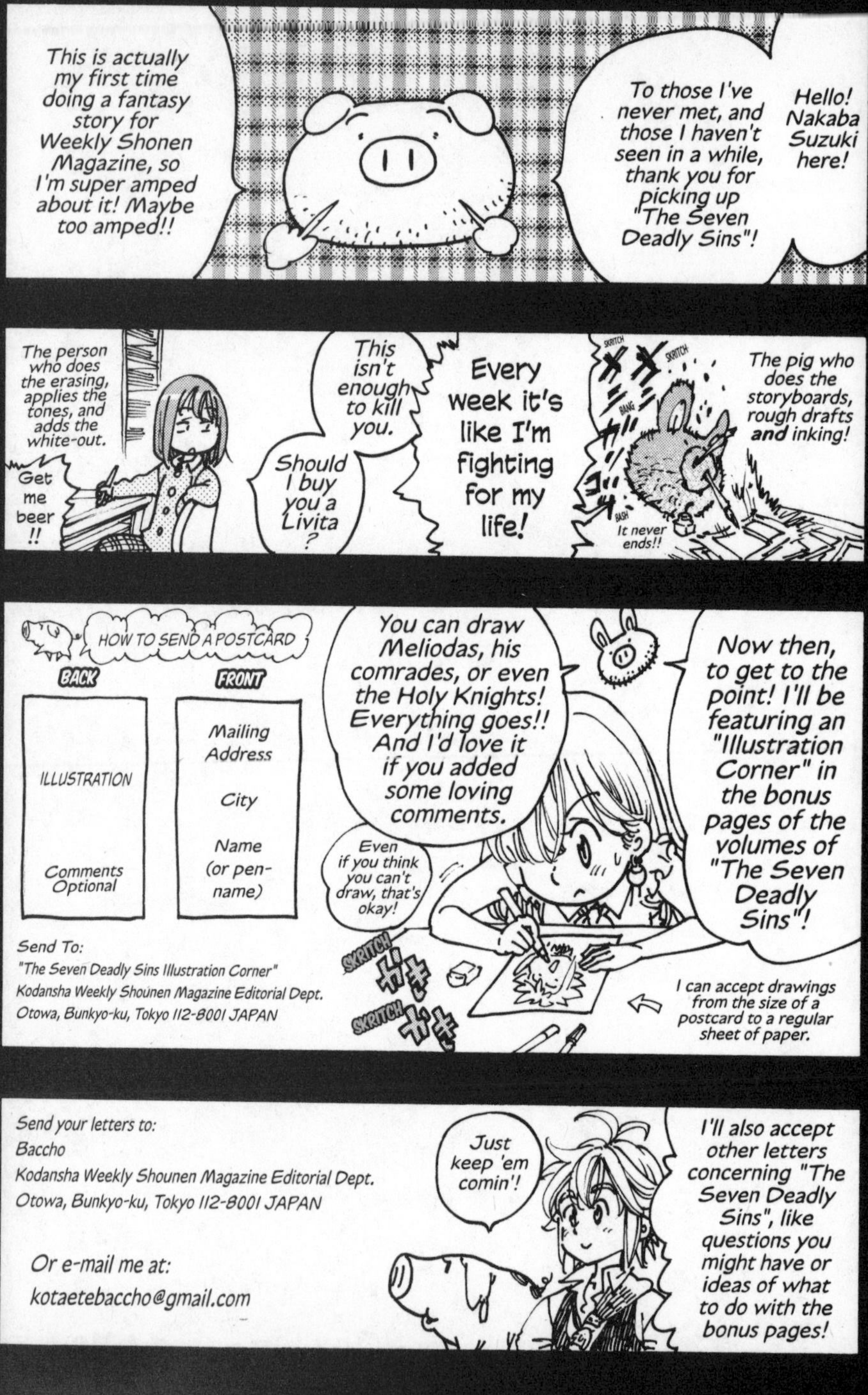

Hello! Nakaba Suzuki here!
To those I've never met, and those I haven't seen in a while, thank you for picking up "The Seven Deadly Sins"!
This is actually my first time doing a fantasy story for Weekly Shonen Magazine, so I'm super amped about it! Maybe too amped!!
The pig who does the storyboards, rough drafts **and** inking!
SKRITCH
SKRITCH
BANG
BASH
It never ends!!
Every week it's like I'm fighting for my life!
This isn't enough to kill you.
Should I buy you a Livita?
The person who does the erasing, applies the tones, and adds the white-out.
Get me beer!!
Now then, to get to the point! I'll be featuring an "Illustration Corner" in the bonus pages of the volumes of "The Seven Deadly Sins"!
You can draw Meliodas, his comrades, or even the Holy Knights! Everything goes!! And I'd love it if you added some loving comments.
Even if you think you can't draw, that's okay!
I can accept drawings from the size of a postcard to a regular sheet of paper.
SKRITCH
SKRITCH
HOW TO SEND A POSTCARD
BACK
ILLUSTRATION
Comments Optional
FRONT
Mailing Address
City
Name (or pen-name)
Send To:
"The Seven Deadly Sins Illustration Corner"
Kodansha Weekly Shounen Magazine Editorial Dept.
Otowa, Bunkyo-ku, Tokyo 112-8001 JAPAN
I'll also accept other letters concerning "The Seven Deadly Sins", like questions you might have or ideas of what to do with the bonus pages!
Just keep 'em comin'!
Send your letters to:
Baccho
Kodansha Weekly Shounen Magazine Editorial Dept.
Otowa, Bunkyo-ku, Tokyo 112-8001 JAPAN
Or e-mail me at:
kotaetebaccho@gmail.com

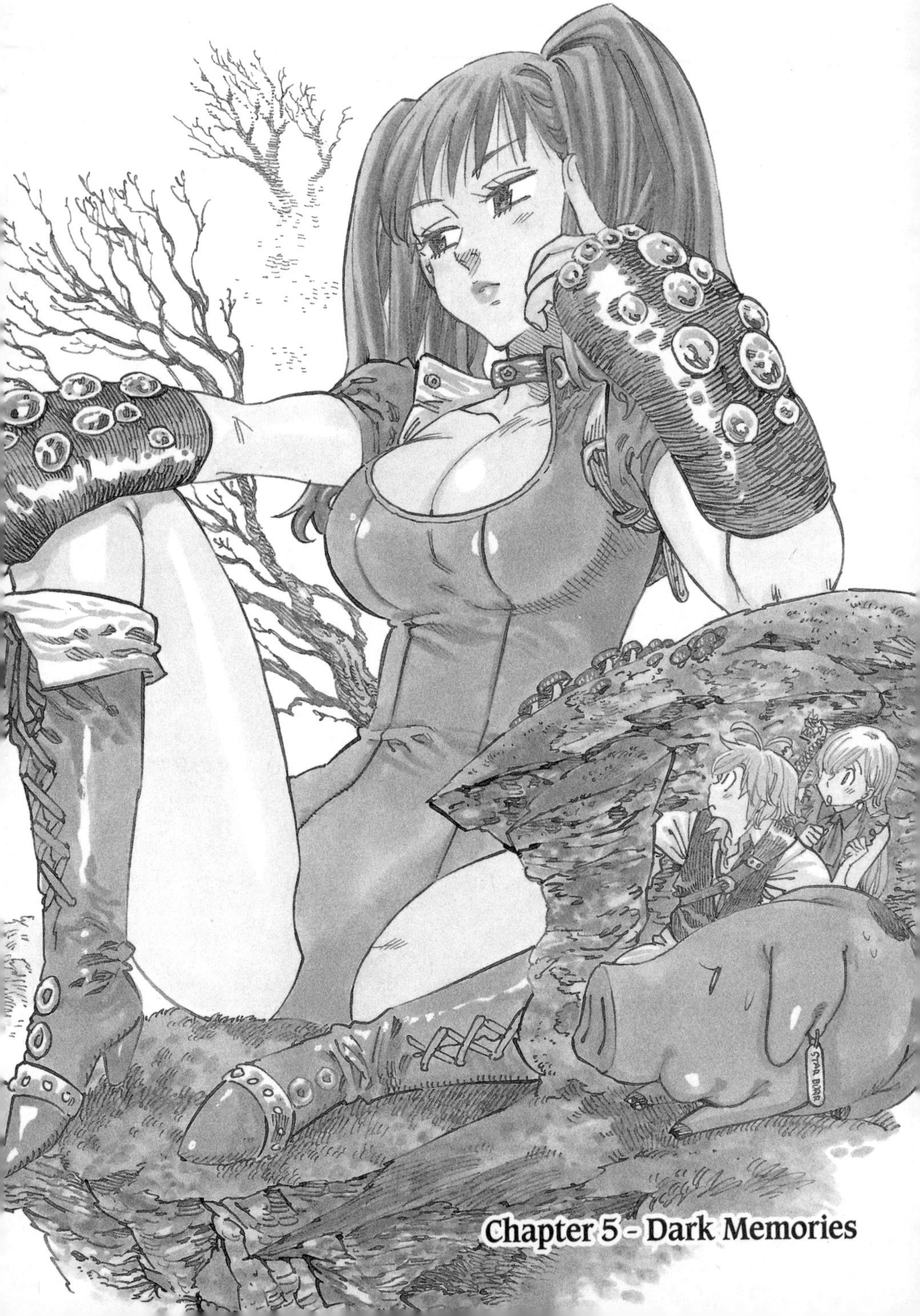

Chapter 5 - Dark Memories

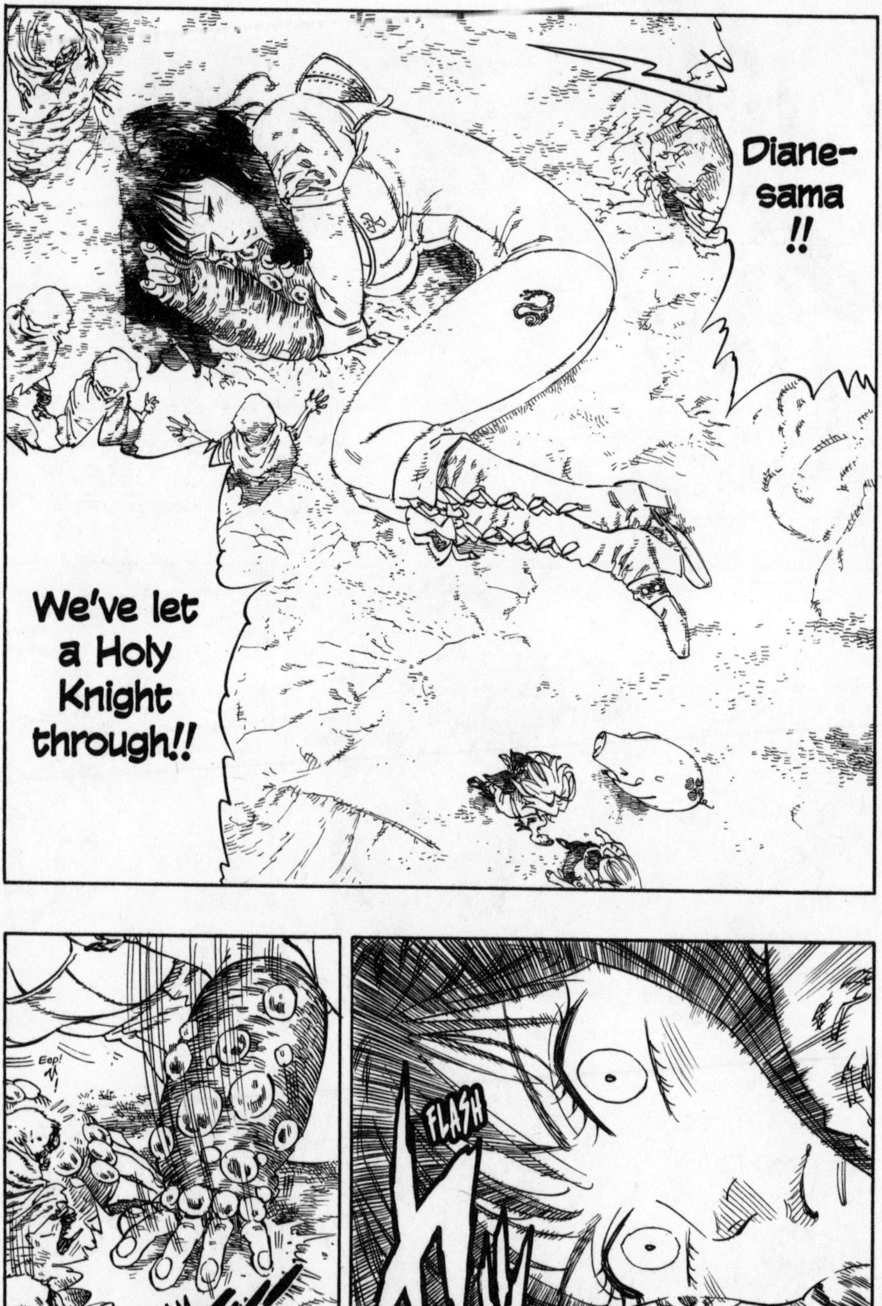
Diane-sama!!
We've let a Holy Knight through!!
FLASH
Eep!
BAM

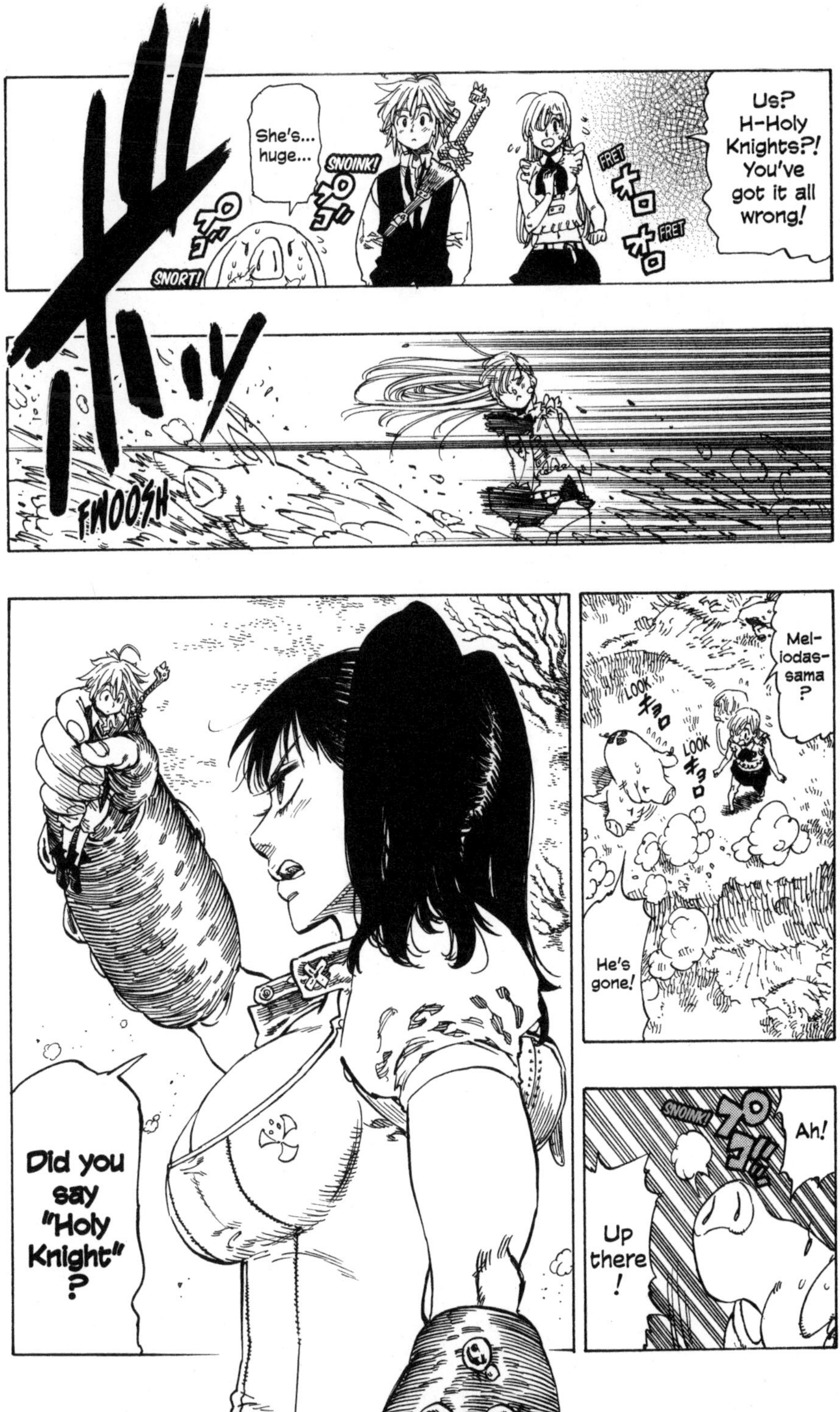
Us? H-Holy Knights?! You've got it all wrong!
FRET
FRET
She's... huge...
SNOINK!
SNORT!
FWOOSH
Mel-iodas-sama?
LOOK
LOOK
He's gone!
Ah!
SNOINK!
Up there!
Did you say "Holy Knight"?

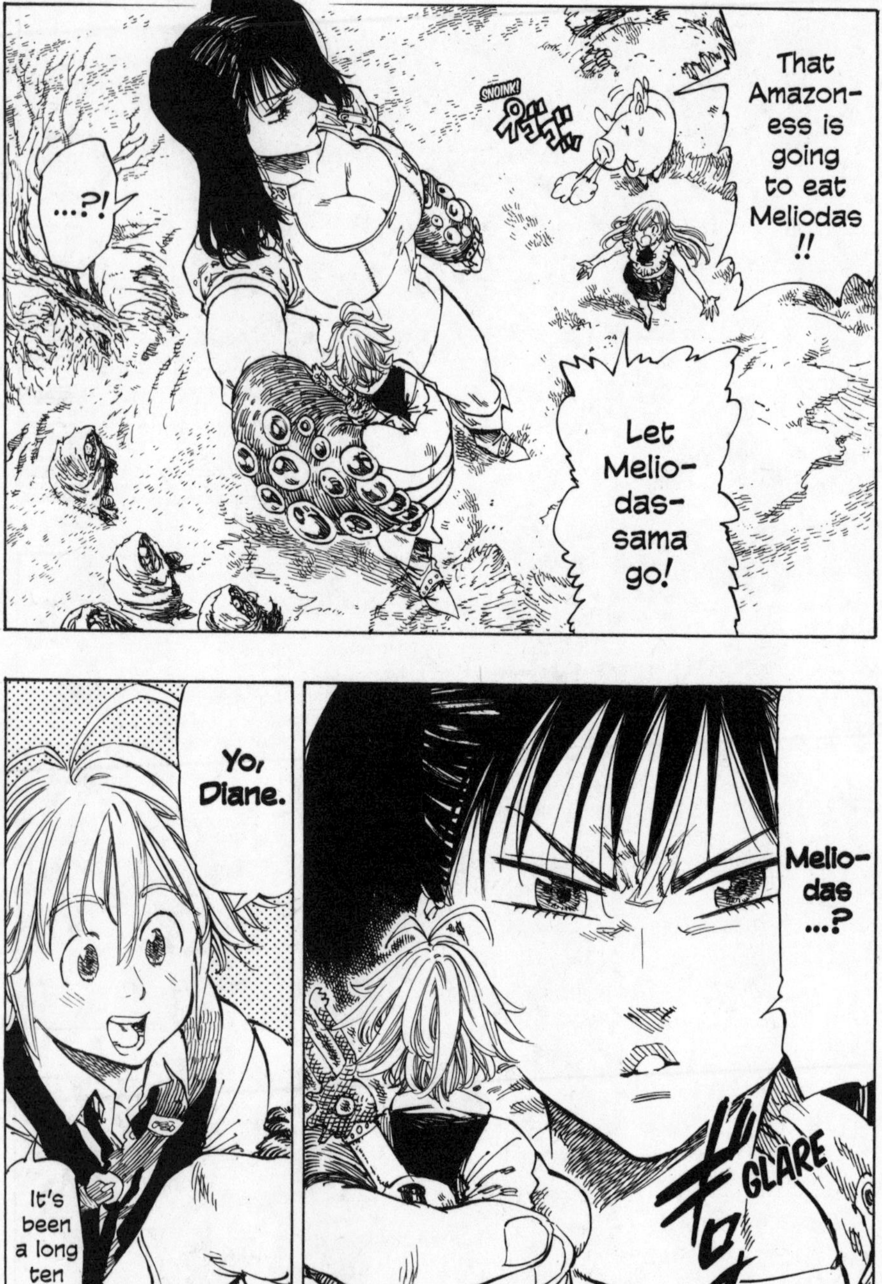

That Amazon-ess is going to eat Meliodas !!
SNOINK!
Let Melio-das-sama go!
...?!
Melio-das ...?
GLARE
Yo, Diane.
It's been a long ten years.

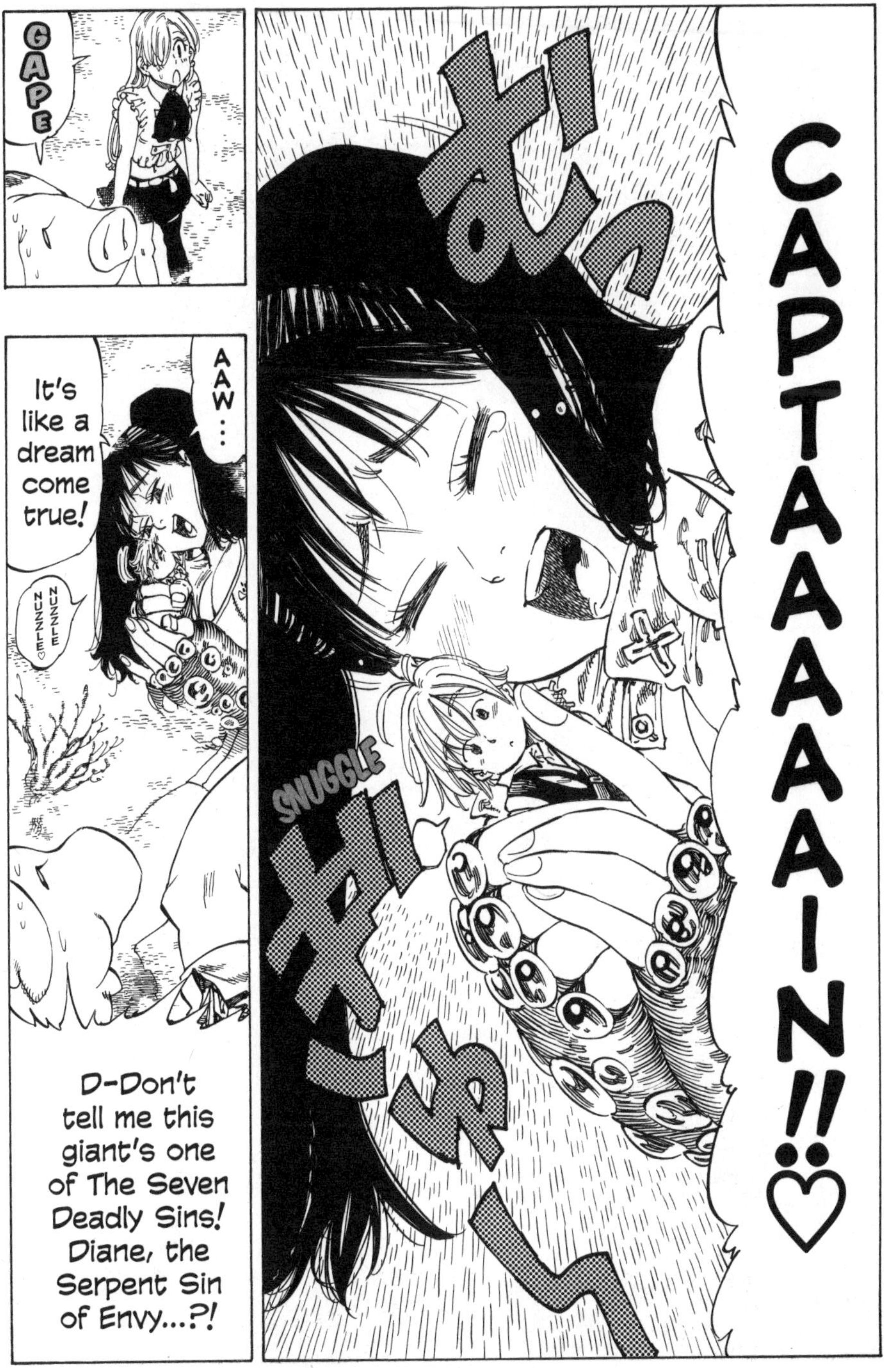
CAPTAAAAAIN!!♥
SNUGGLE
GAPE
AAW...
It's like a dream come true!
NUZZLE NUZZLE♡
D-Don't tell me this giant's one of The Seven Deadly Sins! Diane, the Serpent Sin of Envy...?!

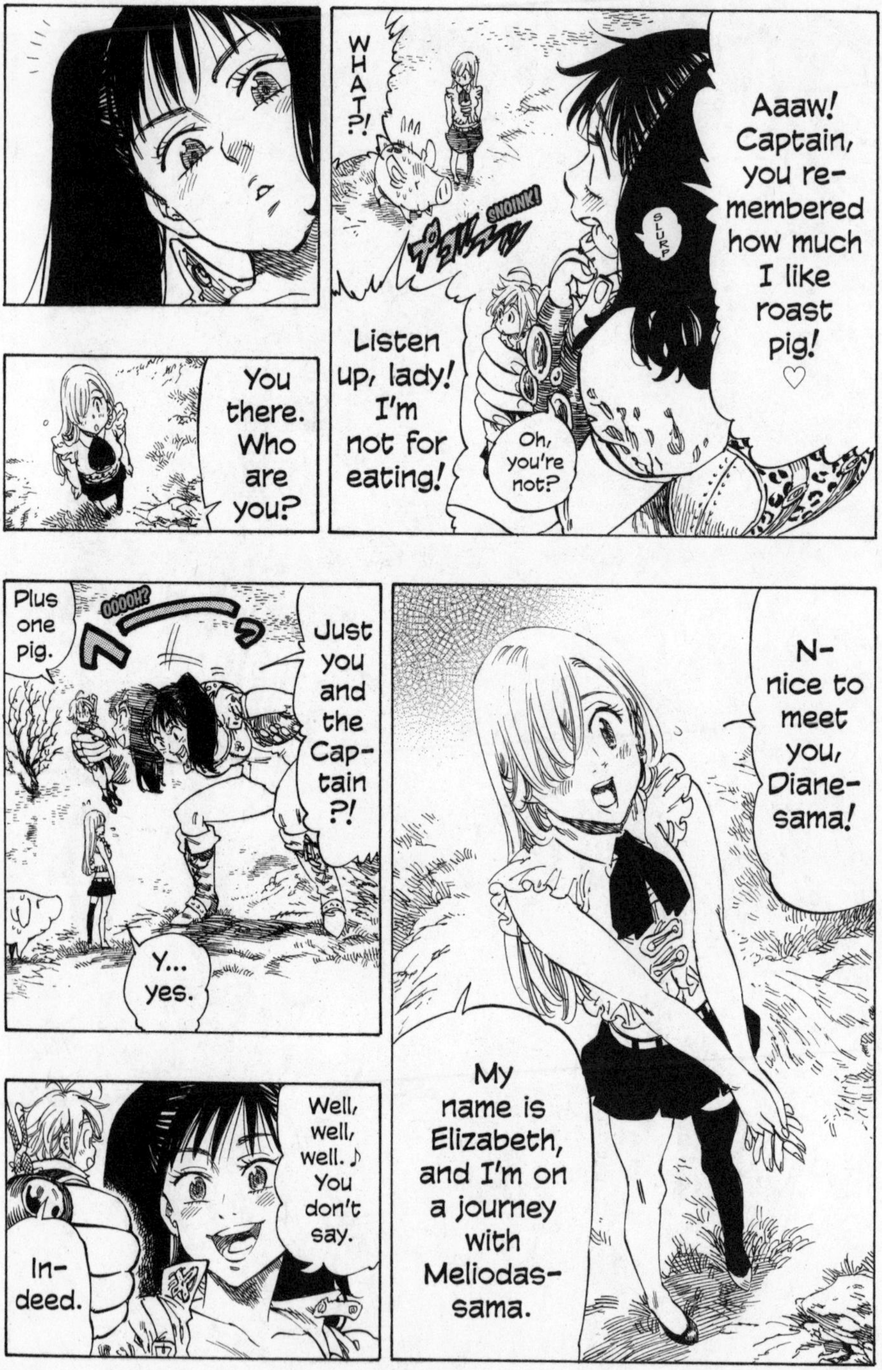
Aaaw! Captain, you re- membered how much I like roast pig! ♡
SLURP
WHAT?!
SNOINK!
Oh, you're not?
Listen up, lady! I'm not for eating!
You there. Who are you?
N- nice to meet you, Diane-sama!
My name is Elizabeth, and I'm on a journey with Meliodas-sama.
Just you and the Cap- tain?!
OOOOH?
Plus one pig.
Y... yes.
Well, well, well. ♪ You don't say.
In- deed.

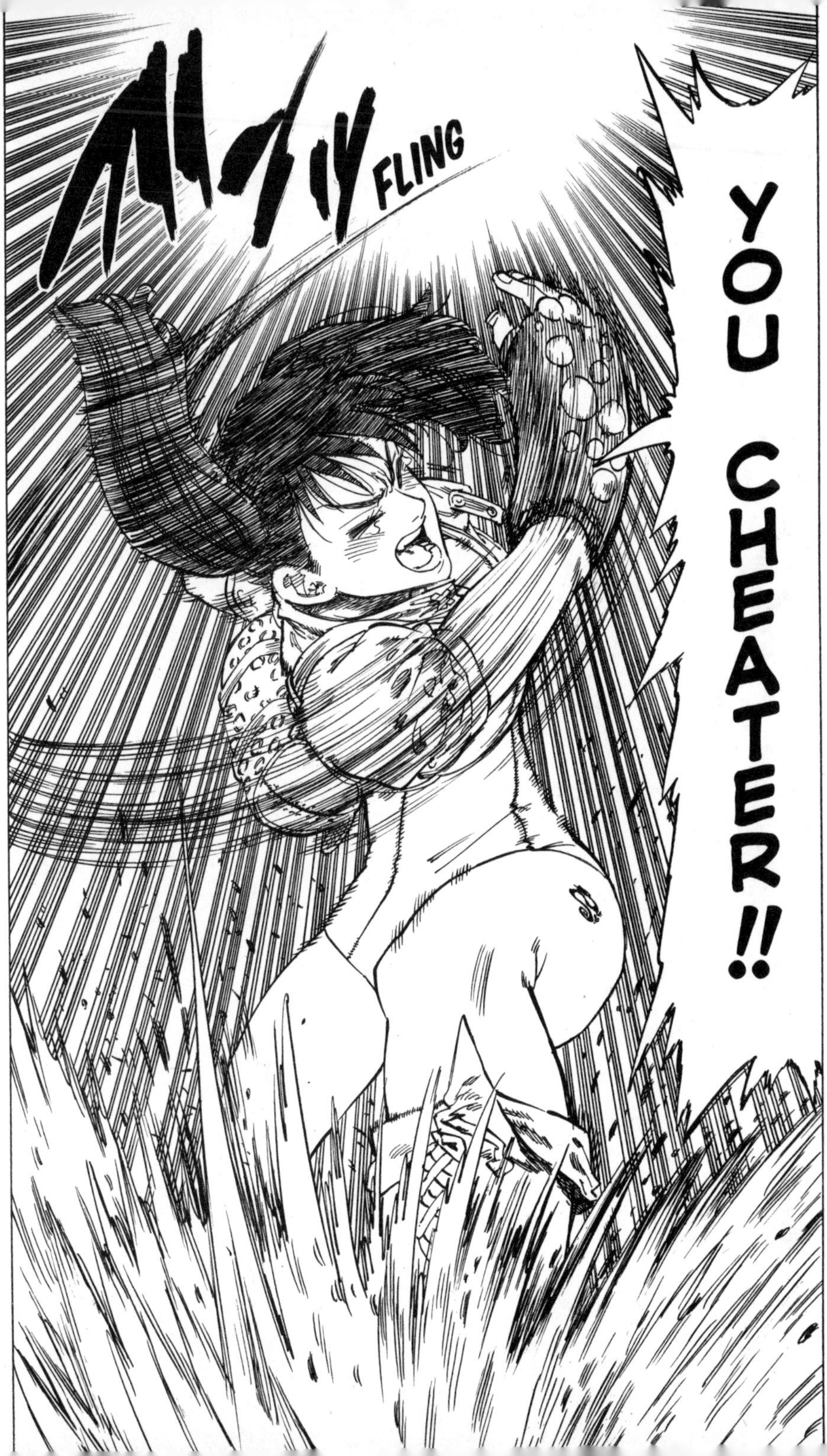
YOU CHEATER!!
FLING

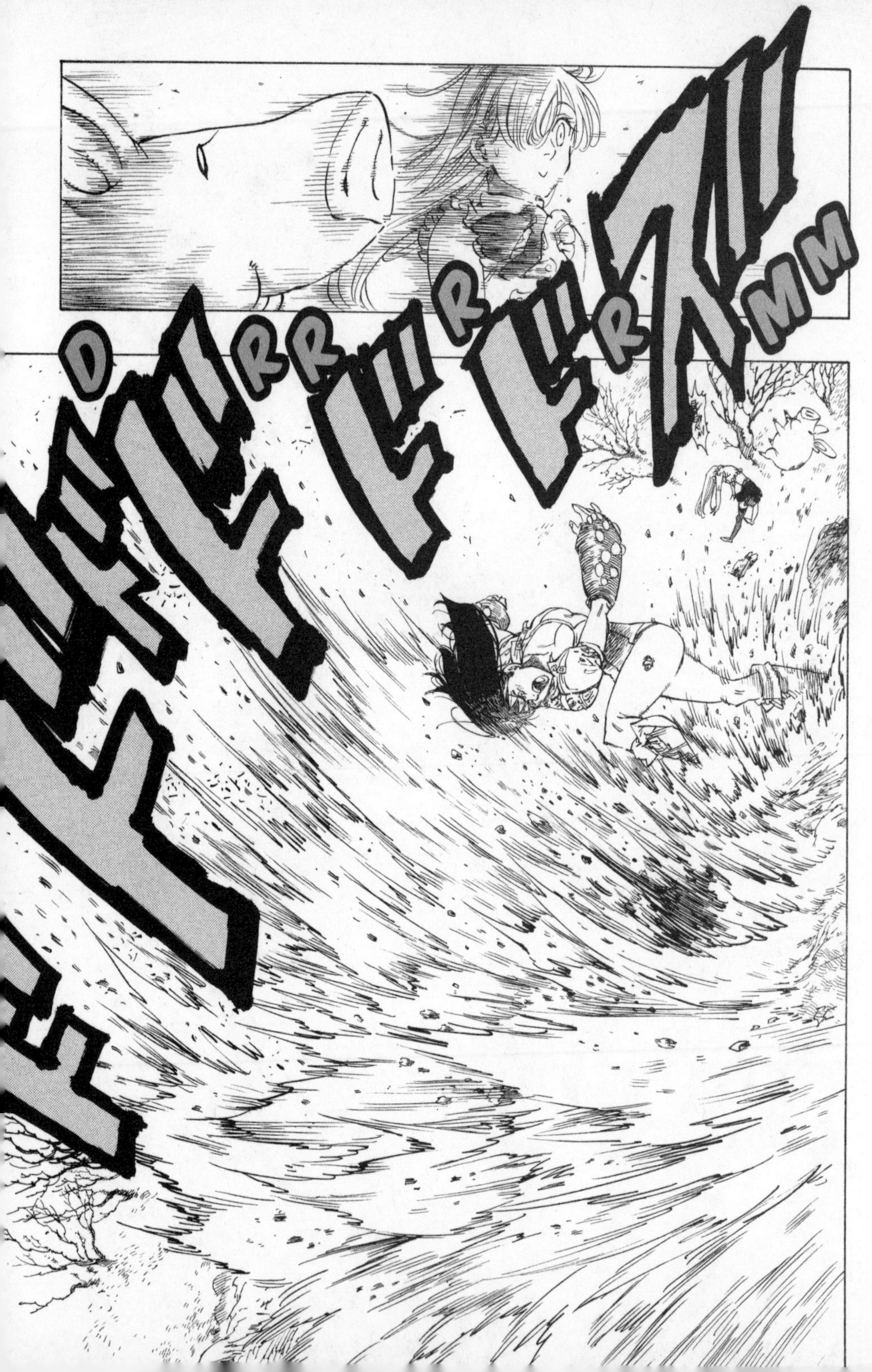
DRRRRMM

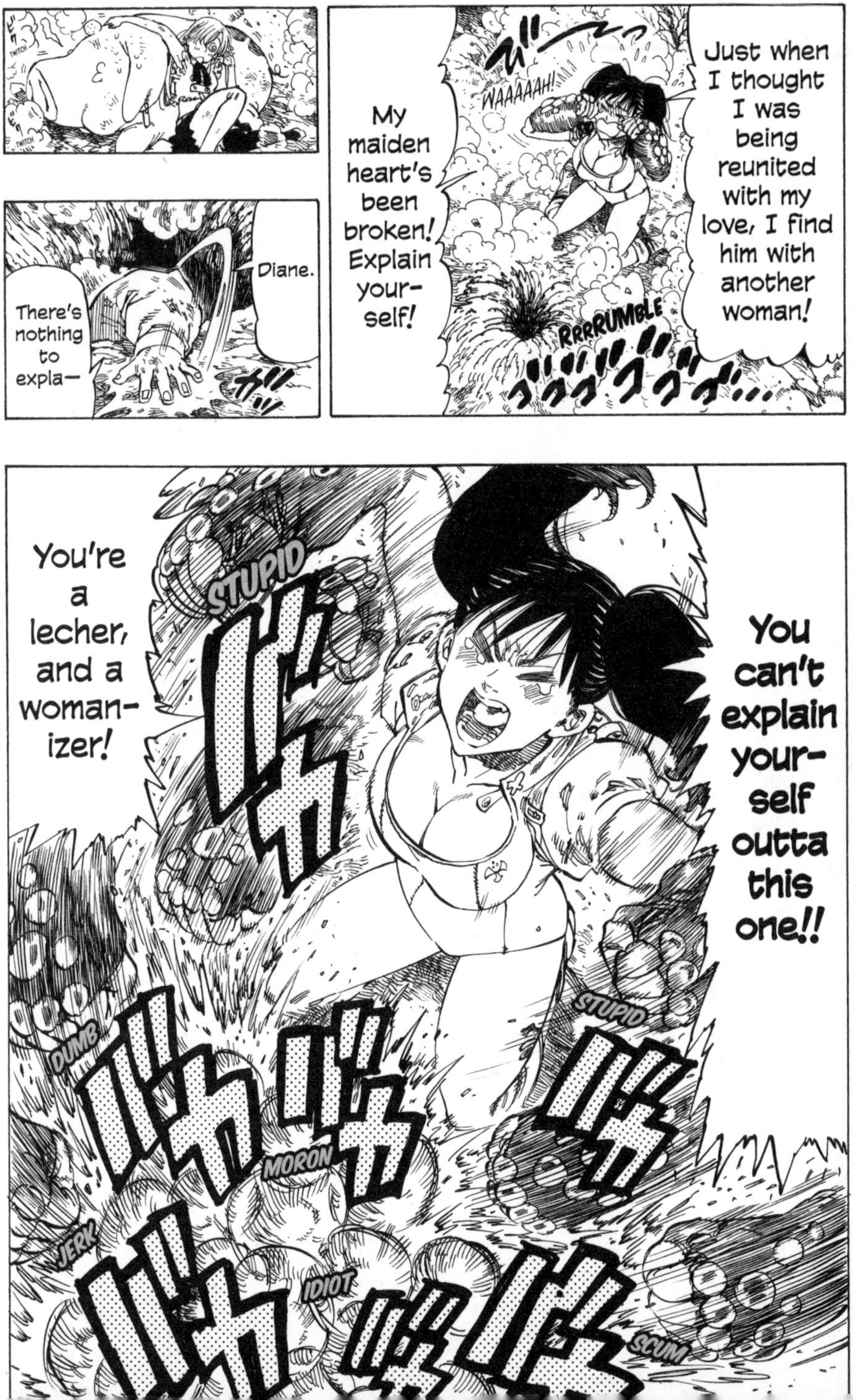
Just when I thought I was being reunited with my love, I find him with another woman!
WAAAAAH!
My maiden heart's been broken! Explain your-self!
RRRRUMBLE
TWITCH
TWITCH
Diane.
There's nothing to expla—
You can't explain your-self outta this one!!
You're a lecher, and a woman-izer!
STUPID
STUPID
DUMB
MORON
JERK
IDIOT
SCUM

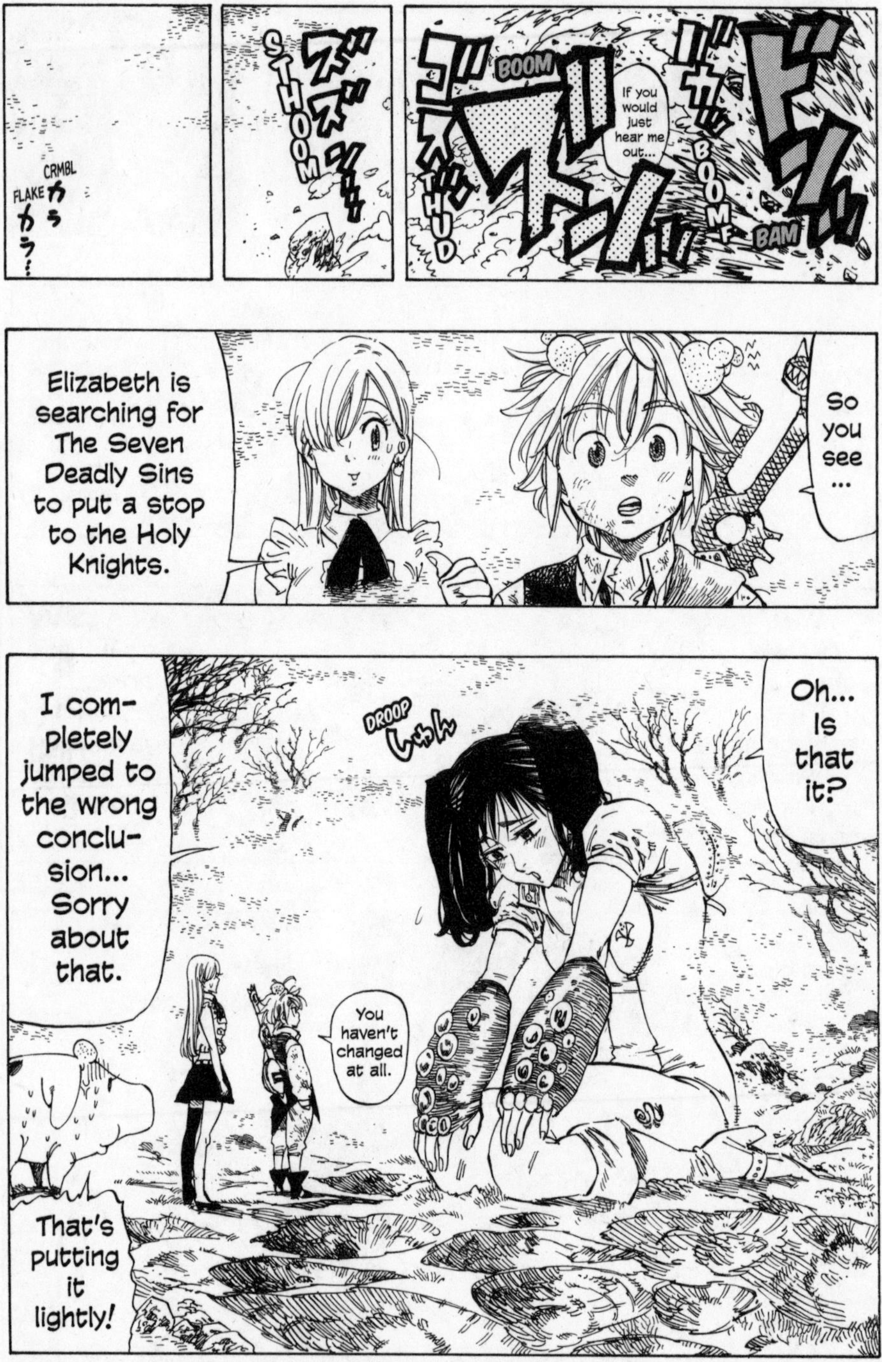
BAM
BOOMF
If you would just hear me out...
BOOM
THUD
STHOOM
CRMBL
FLAKE
カラカラ...
So you see...
Elizabeth is searching for The Seven Deadly Sins to put a stop to the Holy Knights.
Oh... Is that it?
DROOP
しゅん
I com-pletely jumped to the wrong conclu-sion... Sorry about that.
You haven't changed at all.
That's putting it lightly!

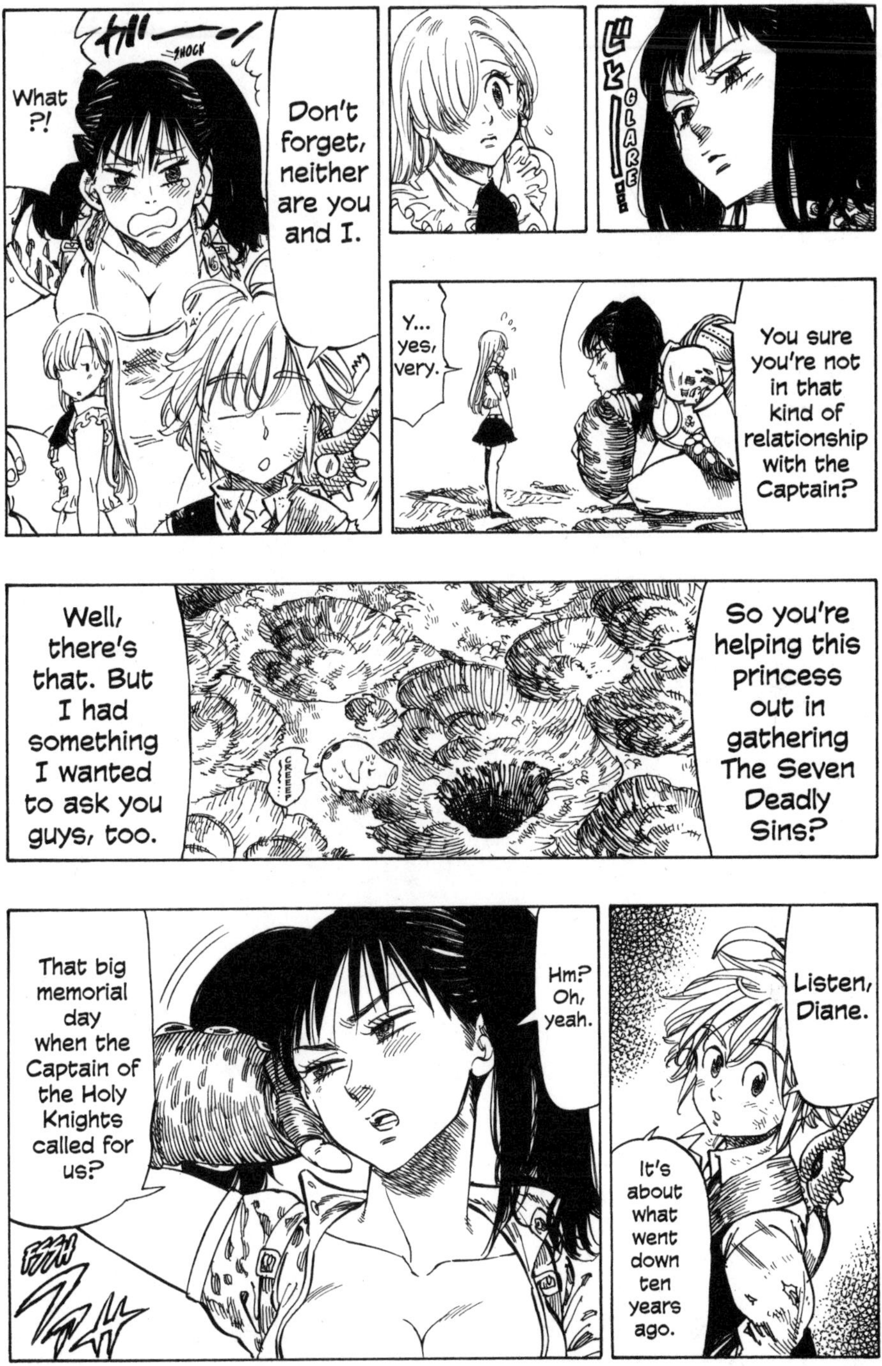

GLARE
You sure you're not in that kind of relationship with the Captain?
Y... yes, very.
Don't forget, neither are you and I.
SHOCK
What?!
So you're helping this princess out in gathering The Seven Deadly Sins?
CREEEP
Well, there's that. But I had something I wanted to ask you guys, too.
Listen, Diane.
It's about what went down ten years ago.
Hm? Oh, yeah.
That big memorial day when the Captain of the Holy Knights called for us?
FSSH

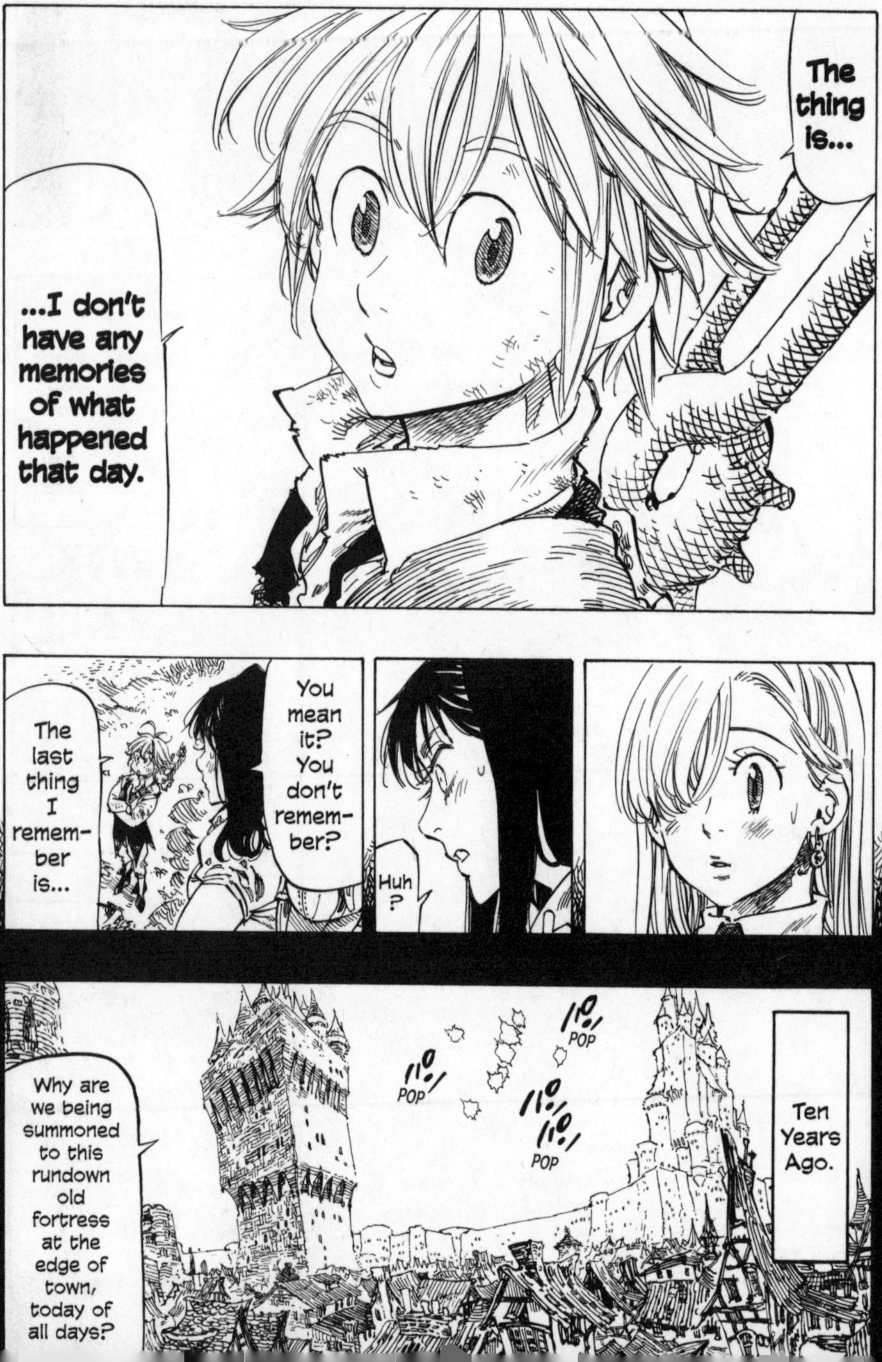
The thing is...
...I don't have any memories of what happened that day.
Huh?
You mean it? You don't remember?
The last thing I remember is...
Ten Years Ago.
POP
POP
POP
Why are we being summoned to this rundown old fortress at the edge of town, today of all days?

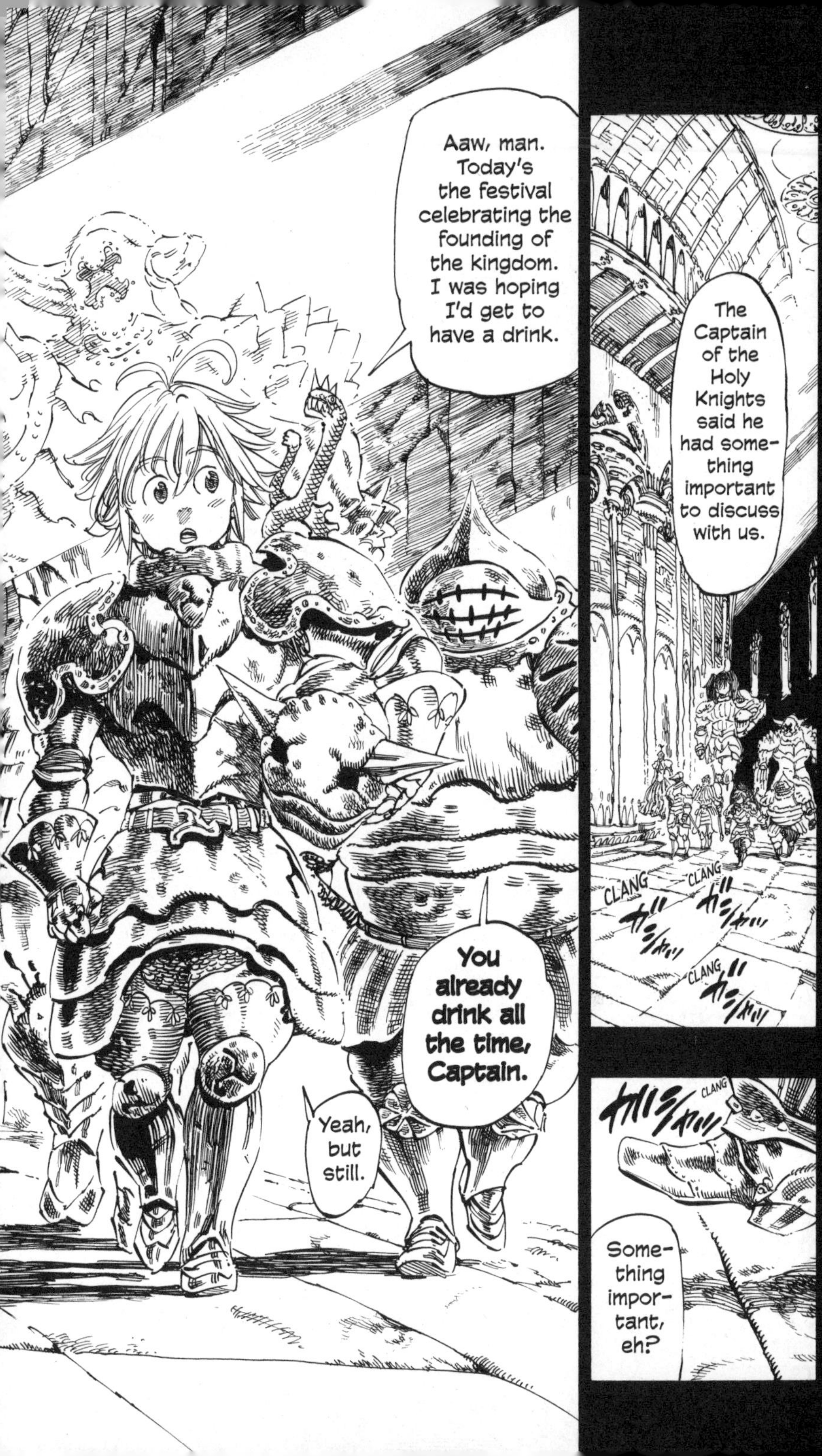
The Captain of the Holy Knights said he had some-thing important to discuss with us.
CLANG
CLANG
CLANG
CLANG
Some-thing impor-tant, eh?
Aaw, man. Today's the festival celebrating the founding of the kingdom. I was hoping I'd get to have a drink.
You already drink all the time, Captain.
Yeah, but still.

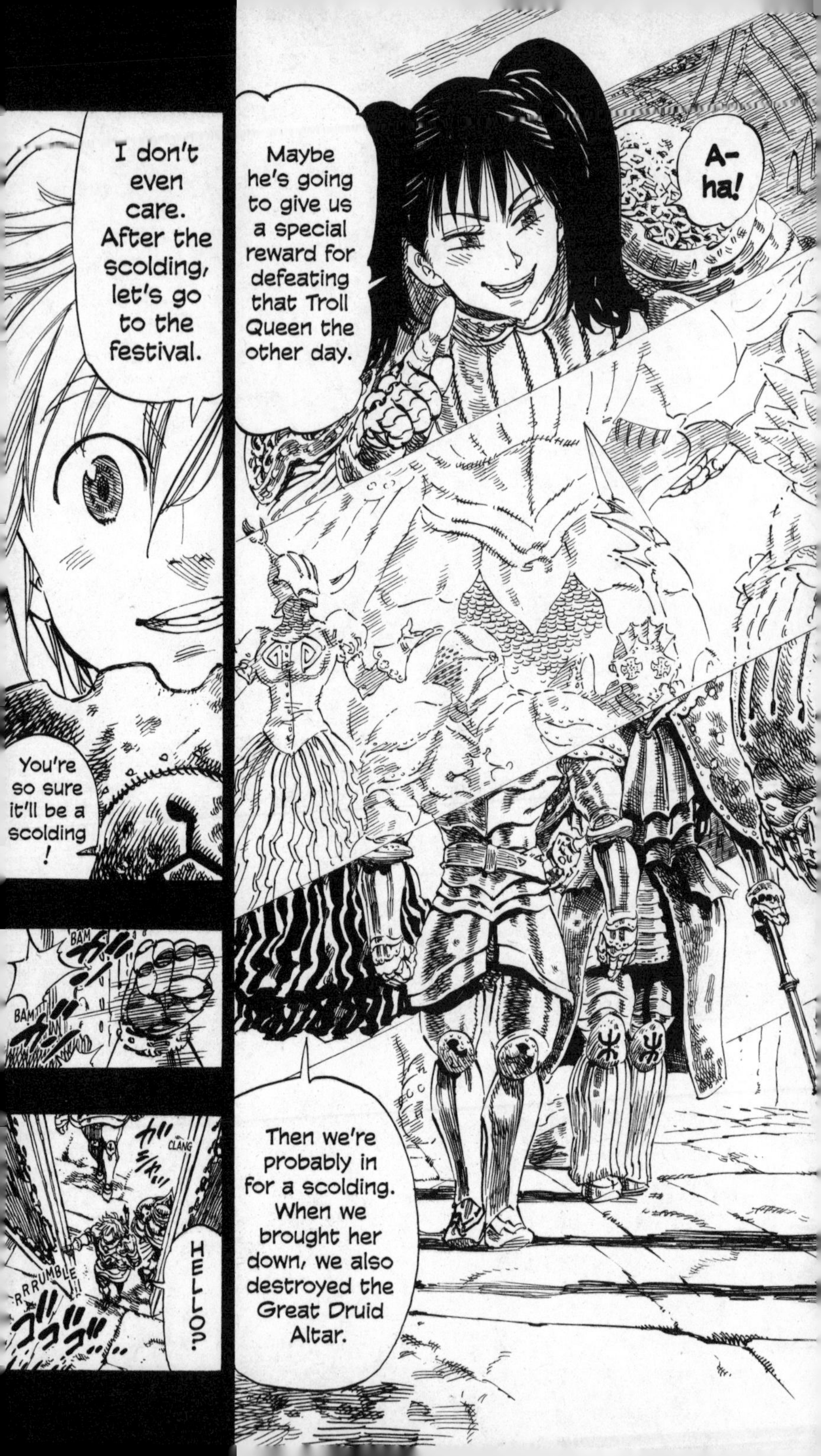

A-ha!
Maybe he's going to give us a special reward for defeating that Troll Queen the other day.
Then we're probably in for a scolding. When we brought her down, we also destroyed the Great Druid Altar.
I don't even care. After the scolding, let's go to the festival.
You're so sure it'll be a scolding!
BAM
BAM
CLANG
HELLO?
RRRUMBLE

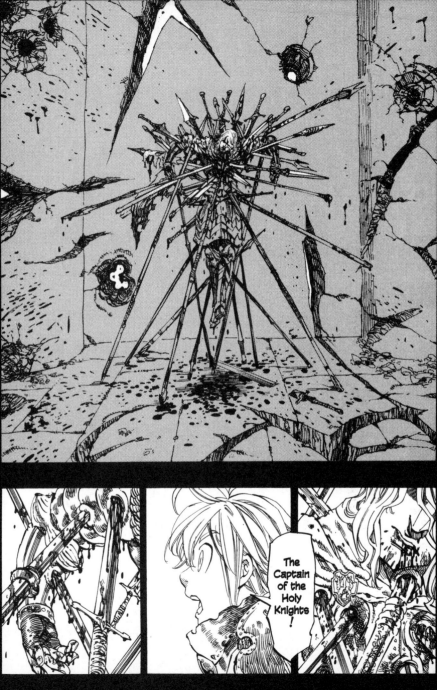

The Captain of the Holy Knights!

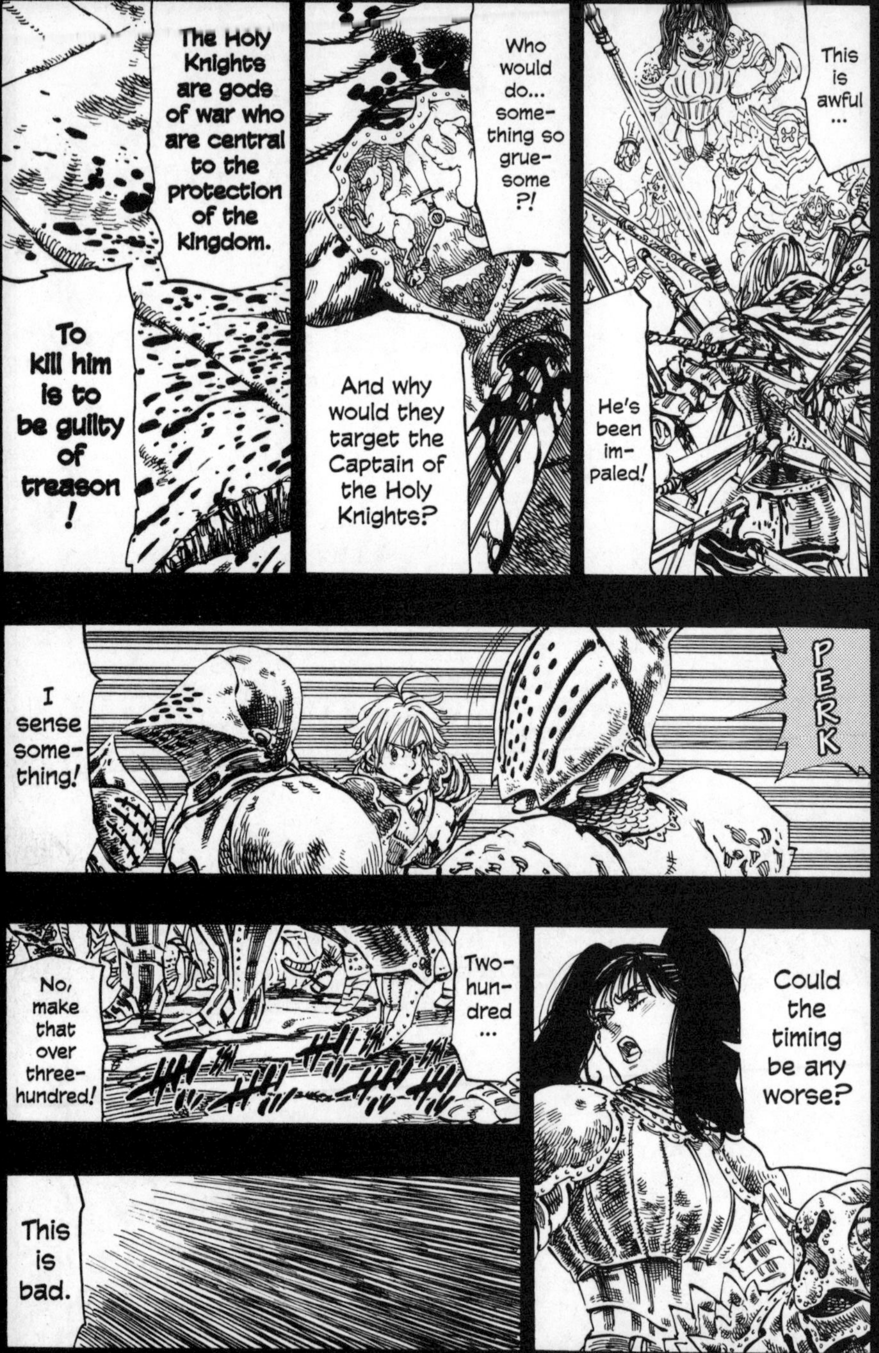
This is awful ...
He's been impaled!
Who would do... something so gruesome?!
And why would they target the Captain of the Holy Knights?
The Holy Knights are gods of war who are central to the protection of the kingdom.
To kill him is to be guilty of treason!
PERK
I sense something!
Could the timing be any worse?
Two-hundred ...
No, make that over three-hundred!
This is bad.

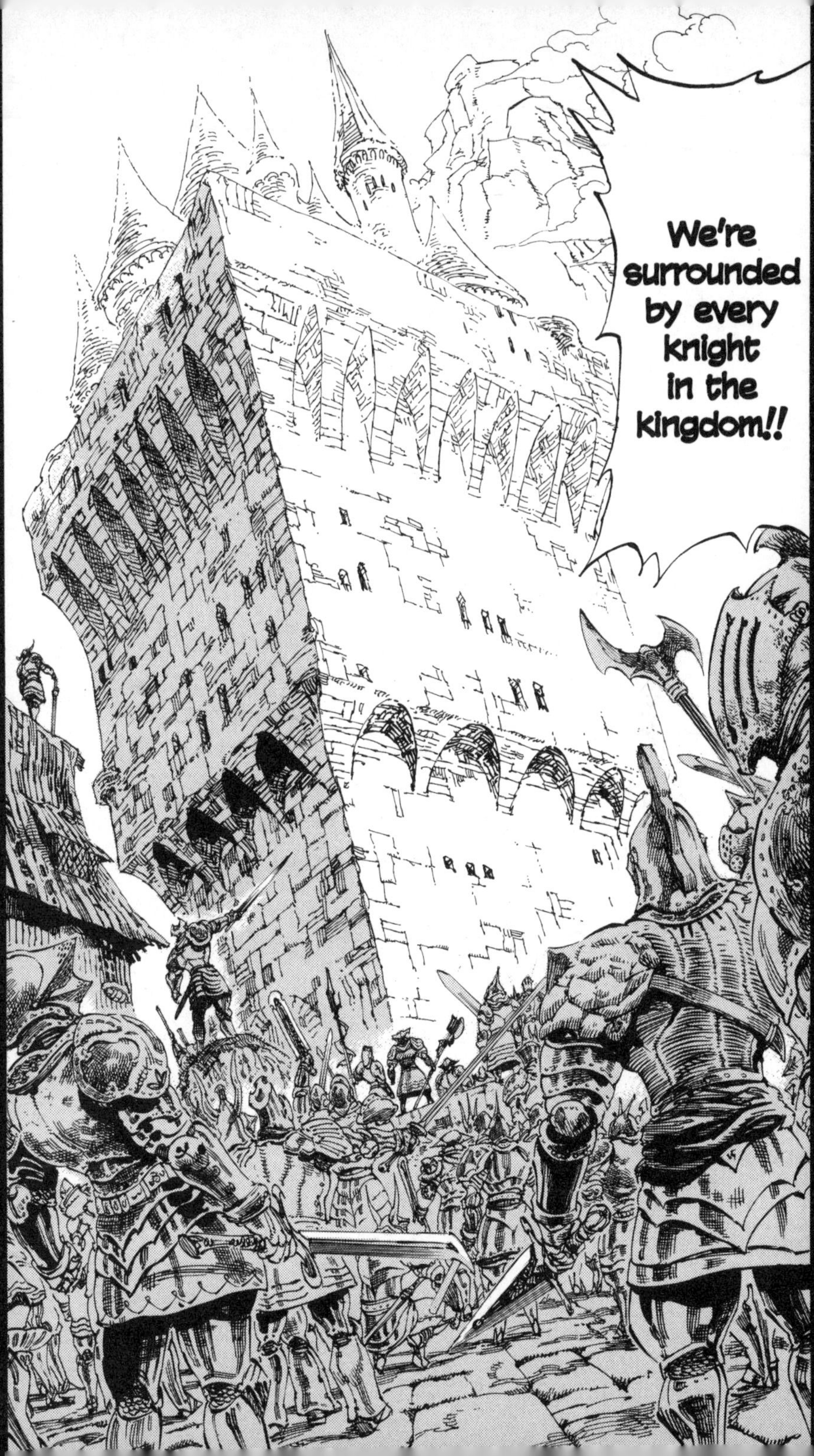
We're surrounded by every knight in the kingdom!!

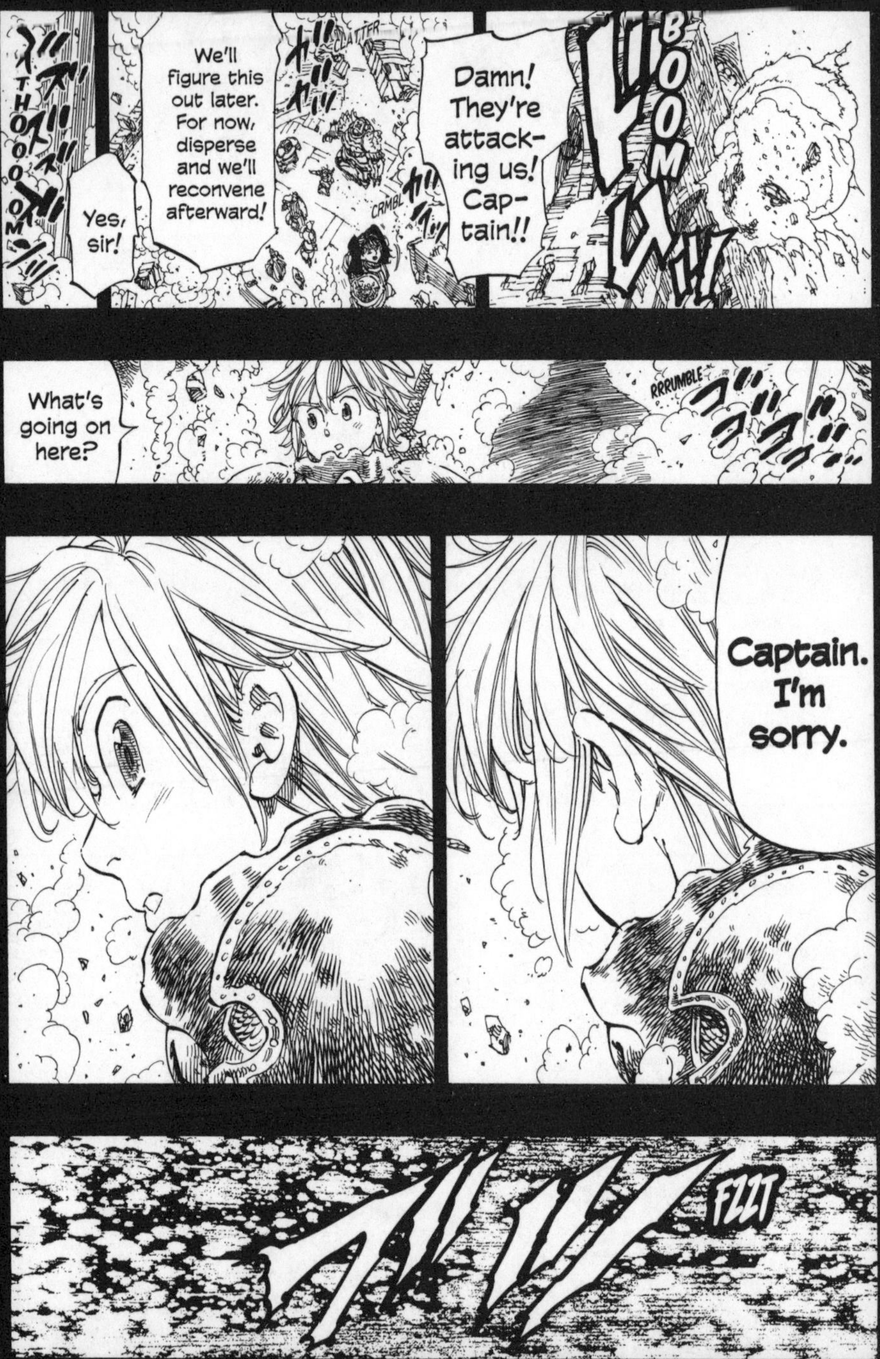
BOOM
Damn! They're attack-ing us! Cap-tain!!
We'll figure this out later. For now, disperse and we'll reconvene afterward!
CLATTER
CRMBL
Yes, sir!
THOOOOOM
RRRUMBLE
What's going on here?
Captain. I'm sorry.
FZZT

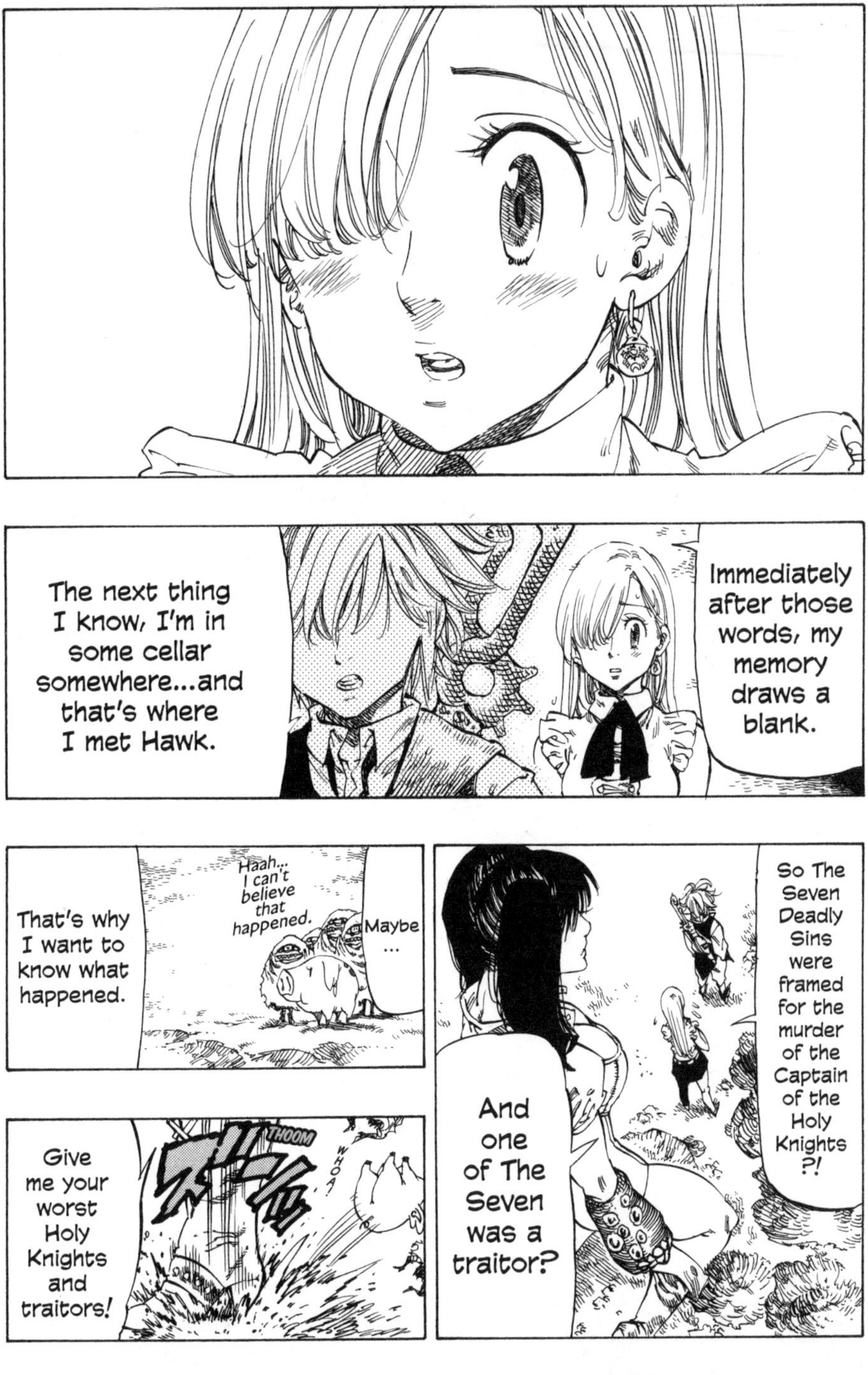

Immediately after those words, my memory draws a blank.
The next thing I know, I'm in some cellar somewhere...and that's where I met Hawk.
So The Seven Deadly Sins were framed for the murder of the Captain of the Holy Knights?!
And one of The Seven was a traitor?
Maybe...
Haah... I can't believe that happened.
That's why I want to know what happened.
WHOA
THOOM
Give me your worst Holy Knights and traitors!

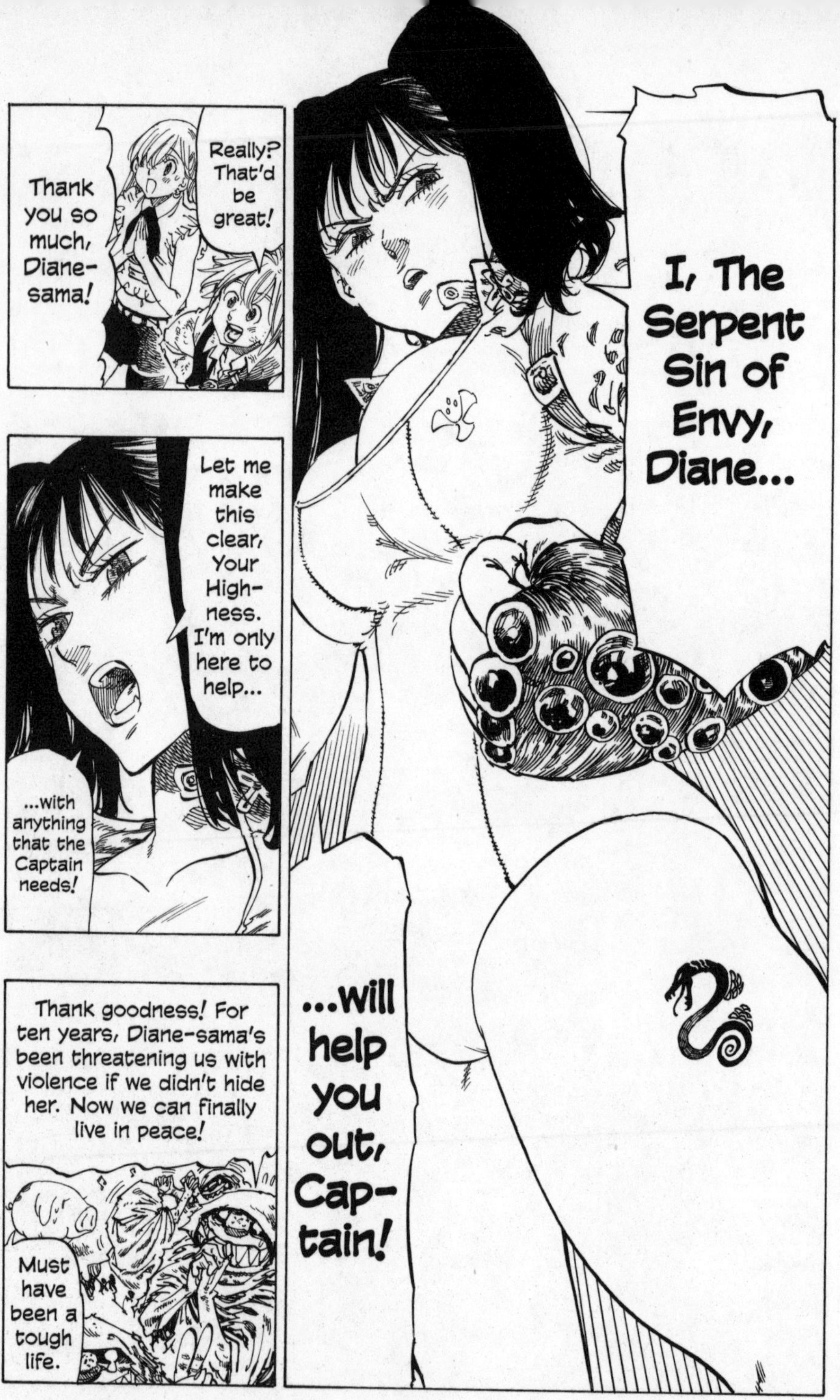
I, The Serpent Sin of Envy, Diane...
...will help you out, Captain!
Really? That'd be great!
Thank you so much, Diane-sama!
Let me make this clear, Your Highness. I'm only here to help...
...with anything that the Captain needs!
Thank goodness! For ten years, Diane-sama's been threatening us with violence if we didn't hide her. Now we can finally live in peace!
Must have been a tough life.

RUSTLE
RUSTLE
SNOINK
SNOINK
I smell rain.
GACK!
Guys, look up there!
RRRUMBLE
It's a giant thunder-cloud!
CRACK

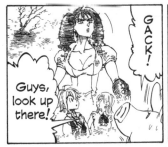

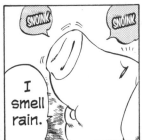

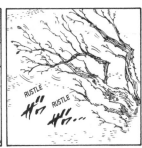

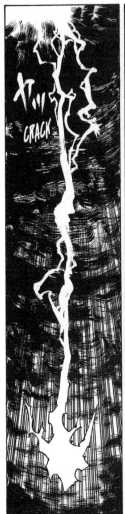

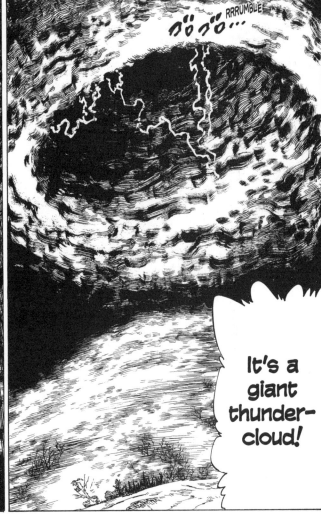

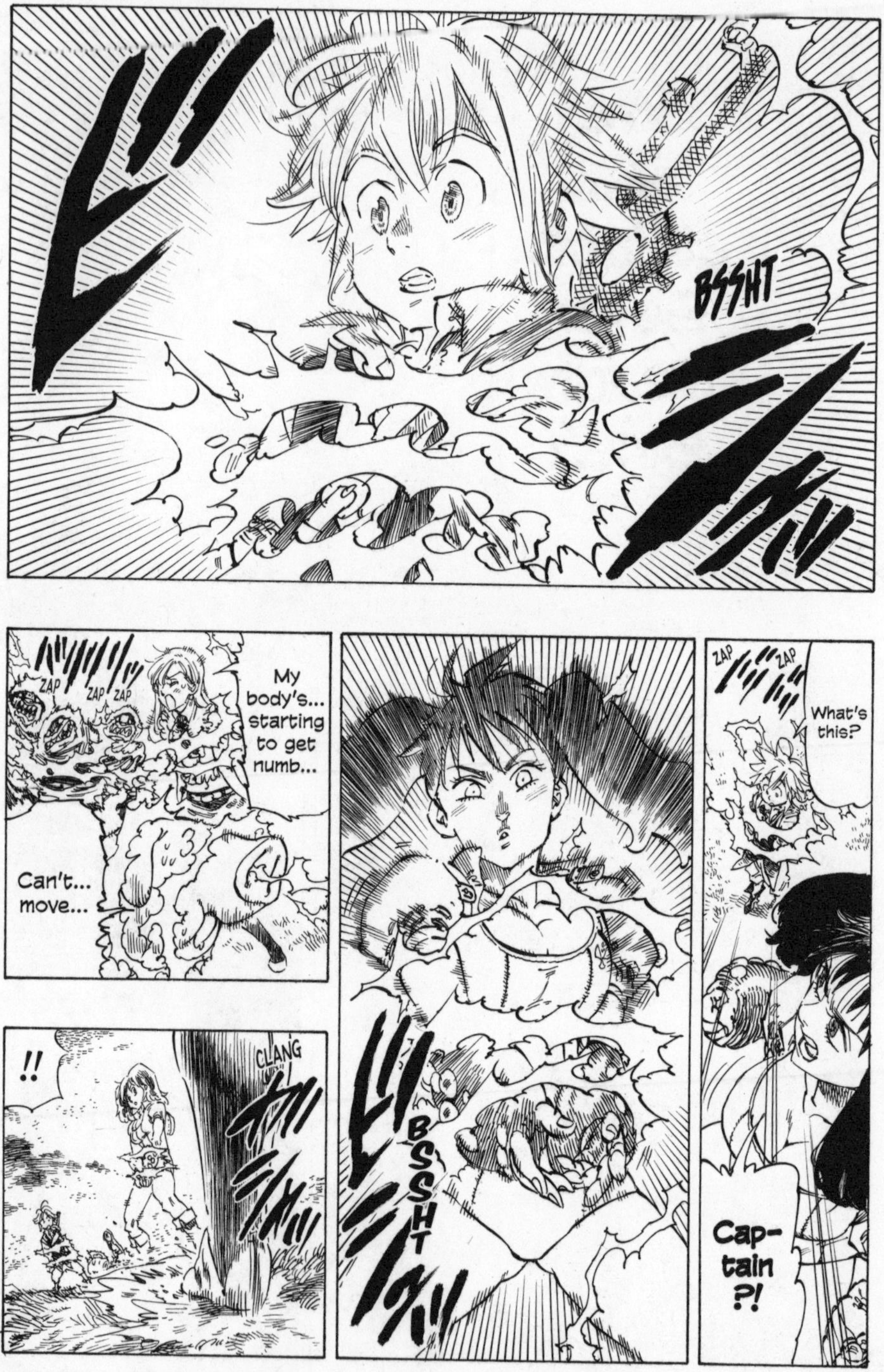
BSSHT
ZAP
ZAP
What's this?
Cap-tain?!
BSSHT
ZAP
ZAP
ZAP
My body's... starting to get numb...
Can't... move...
!!
CLANG

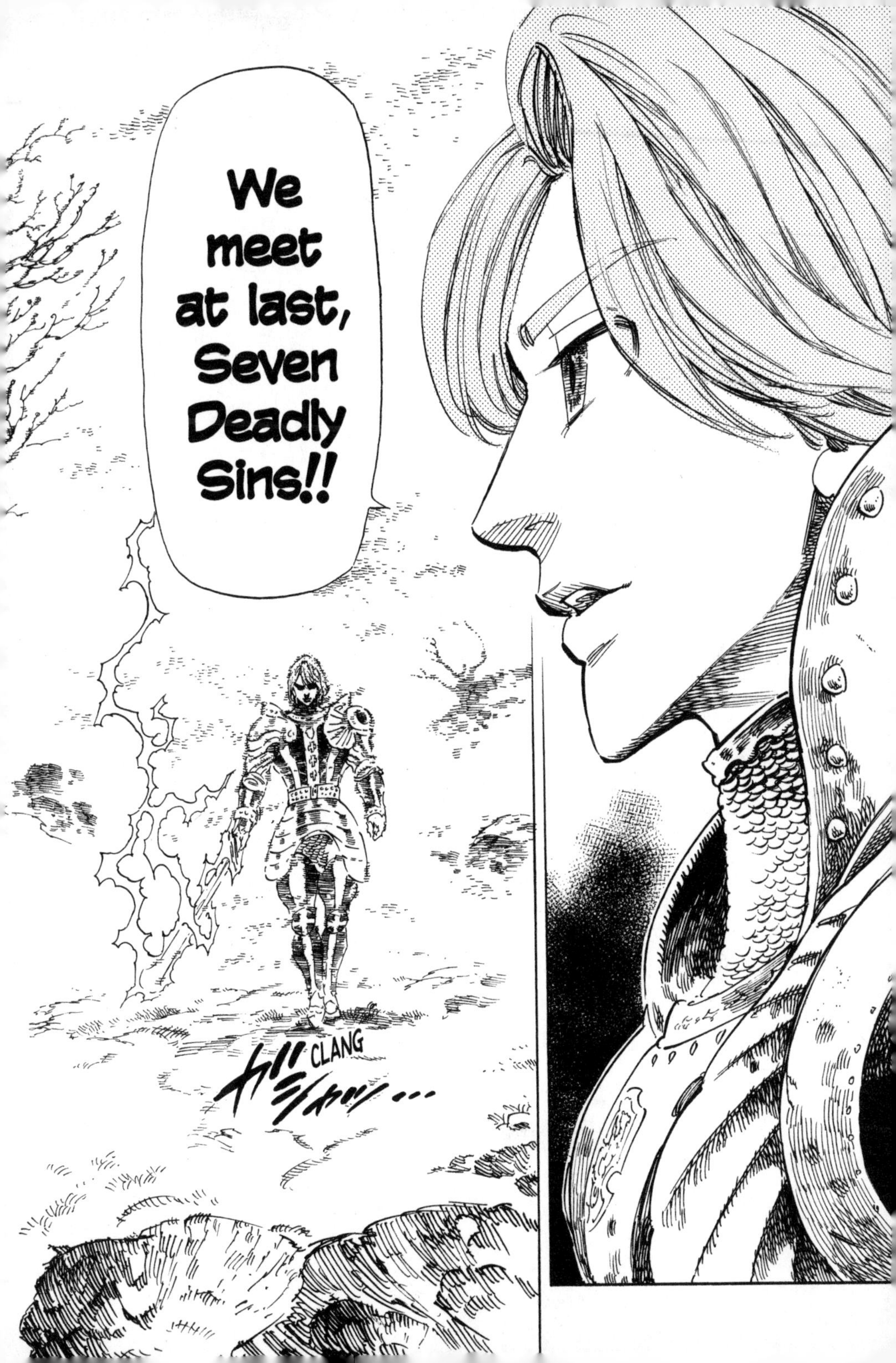
We meet at last, Seven Deadly Sins!!
CLANG

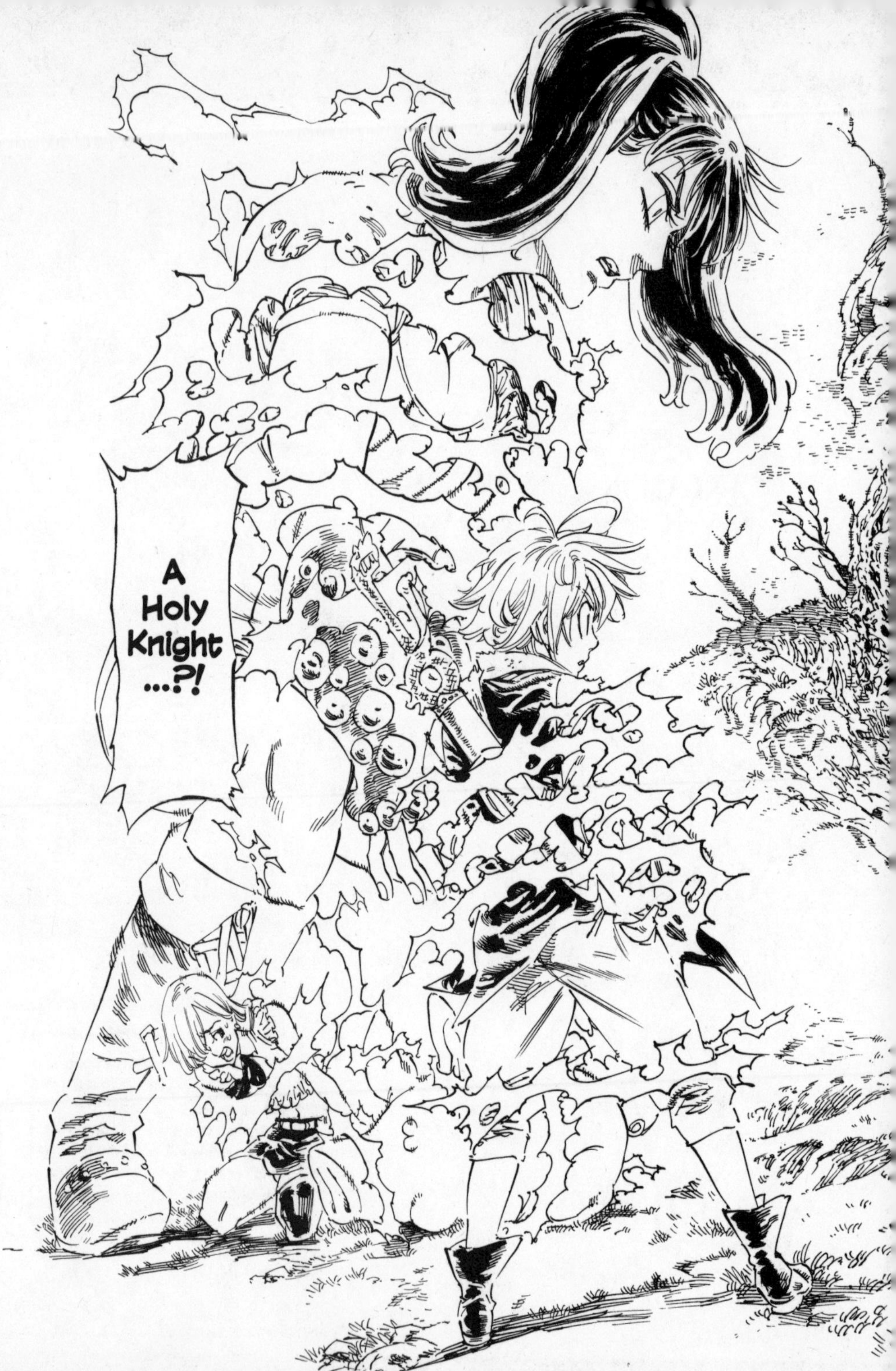
A Holy Knight ...?!

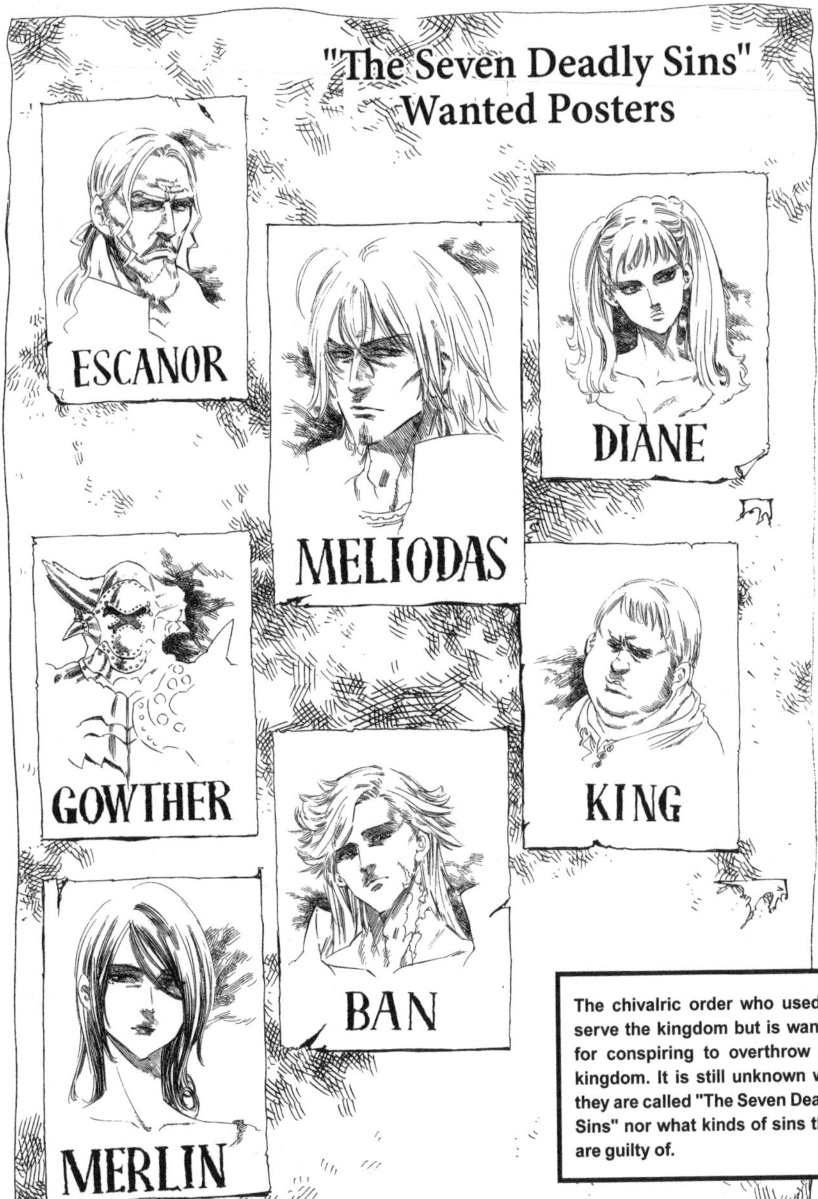
"The Seven Deadly Sins"
Wanted Posters
ESCANOR
DIANE
MELIODAS
KING
GOWTHER
BAN
MERLIN

The chivalric order who used to serve the kingdom but is wanted for conspiring to overthrow the kingdom. It is still unknown why they are called "The Seven Deadly Sins" nor what kinds of sins they are guilty of.

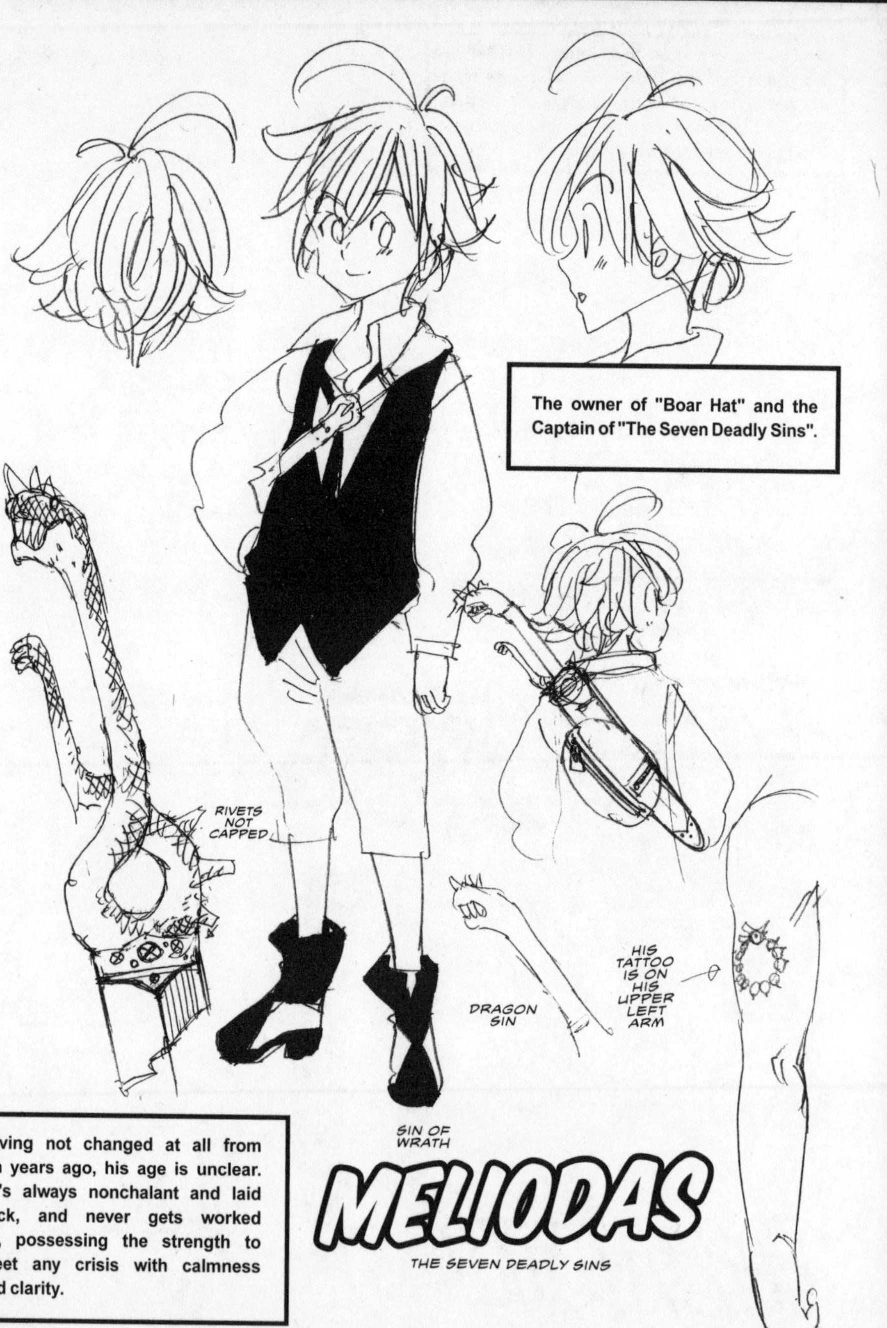
RIVETS NOT CAPPED
HIS TATTOO IS ON HIS UPPER LEFT ARM
DRAGON SIN
SIN OF WRATH
MELIODAS
THE SEVEN DEADLY SINS

The owner of "Boar Hat" and the Captain of "The Seven Deadly Sins".

Having not changed at all from ten years ago, his age is unclear. He's always nonchalant and laid back, and never gets worked up, possessing the strength to greet any crisis with calmness and clarity.

The third princess of the Liones royal family who rules the land of Britannia. She goes on a journey to find "The Seven Deadly Sins" in order to save her country and its people who have been taken over by the Holy Knights.

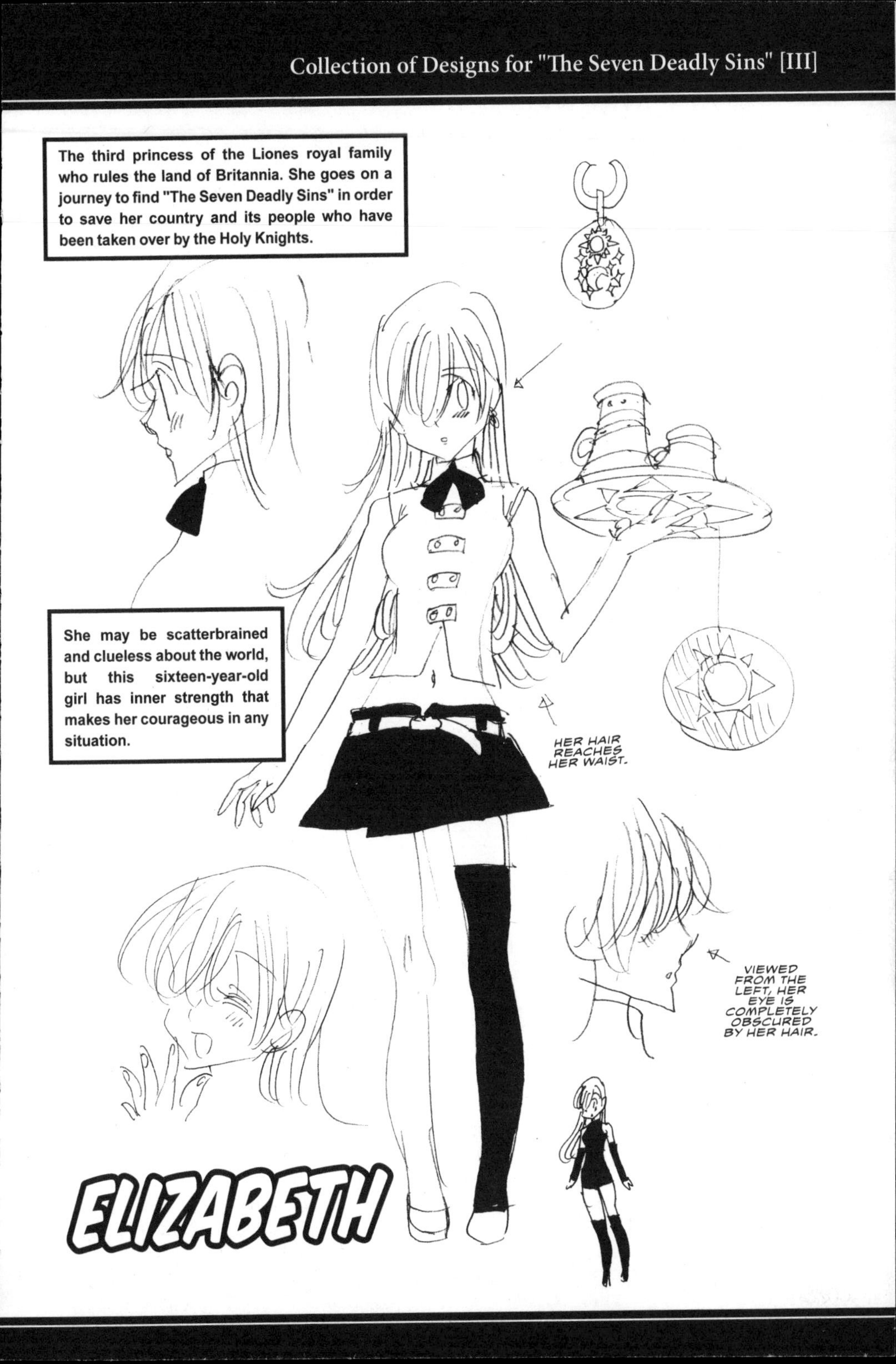
HER HAIR REACHES HER WAIST.
VIEWED FROM THE LEFT, HER EYE IS COMPLETELY OBSCURED BY HER HAIR.
ELIZABETH

She may be scatterbrained and clueless about the world, but this sixteen-year-old girl has inner strength that makes her courageous in any situation.

HAWK

The main attraction at "Boar Hat". For unexplained reasons, he can speak and understand human speech. His favorite thing to eat is leftovers and his nose can detect food scraps up to one mile away.

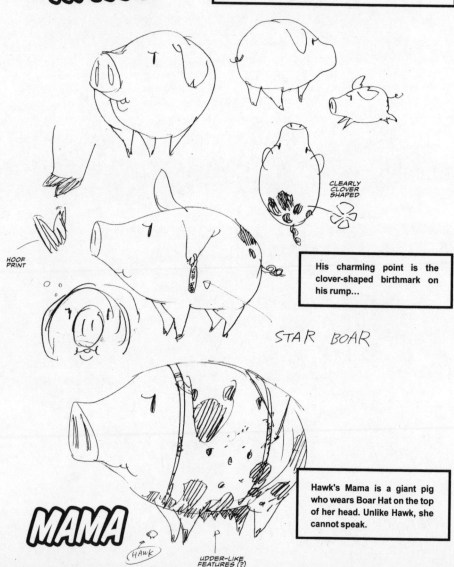

CLEARLY
CLOVER
SHAPED

HOOF
PRINT

His charming point is the clover-shaped birthmark on his rump...

STAR BOAR

Hawk's Mama is a giant pig who wears Boar Hat on the top of her head. Unlike Hawk, she cannot speak.

MAMA

HAWK

UDDER-LIKE
FEATURES (?)

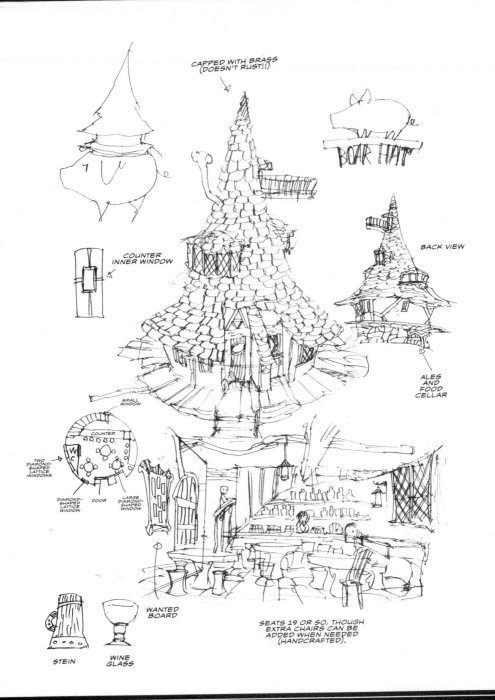

CAPPED WITH BRASS
(DOESN'T RUST!!)

BOAR HAT

BACK VIEW

COUNTER
INNER WINDOW

ALES
AND
FOOD
CELLAR

SMALL
WINDOW

COUNTER

TWO
DIAMOND-
SHAPED
LATTICE
WINDOWS

DIAMOND-
SHAPED
LATTICE
WINDOW

DOOR

LARGE
DIAMOND-
SHAPED
WINDOW

WANTED
BOARD

SEATS 19 OR SO, THOUGH
EXTRA CHAIRS CAN BE
ADDED WHEN NEEDED
(HANDCRAFTED).

STEIN

WINE
GLASS

Actually an Apprentice Holy Knight. His sword attacks can produce a powerful blast of wind, but he is not yet regarded worthy of Holy Knight status.

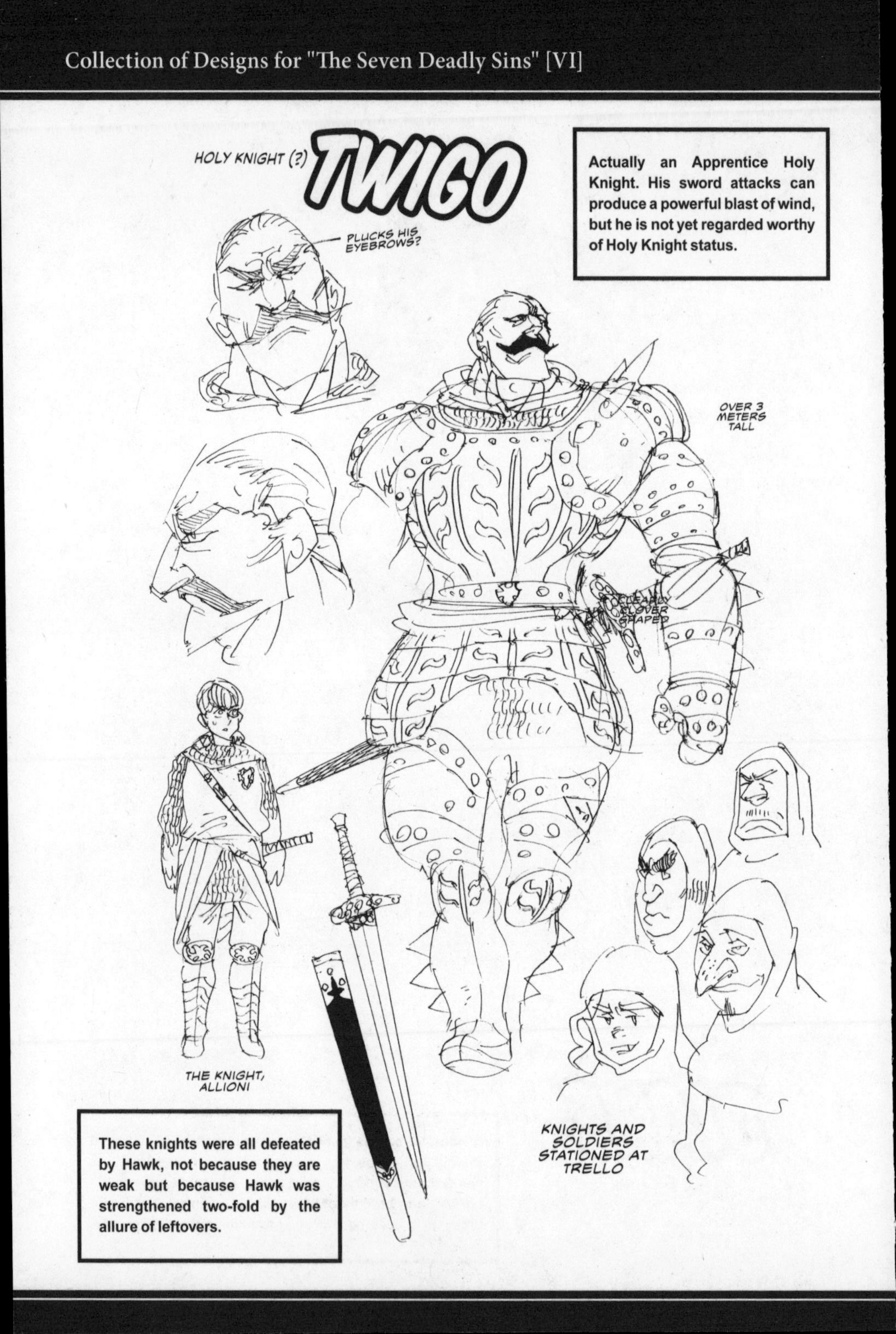
HOLY KNIGHT (?)
TWIGO
PLUCKS HIS EYEBROWS?
OVER 3 METERS TALL
CLEARLY CLOVER SHAPED
THE KNIGHT, ALLIONI
KNIGHTS AND SOLDIERS STATIONED AT TRELLO

These knights were all defeated by Hawk, not because they are weak but because Hawk was strengthened two-fold by the allure of leftovers.

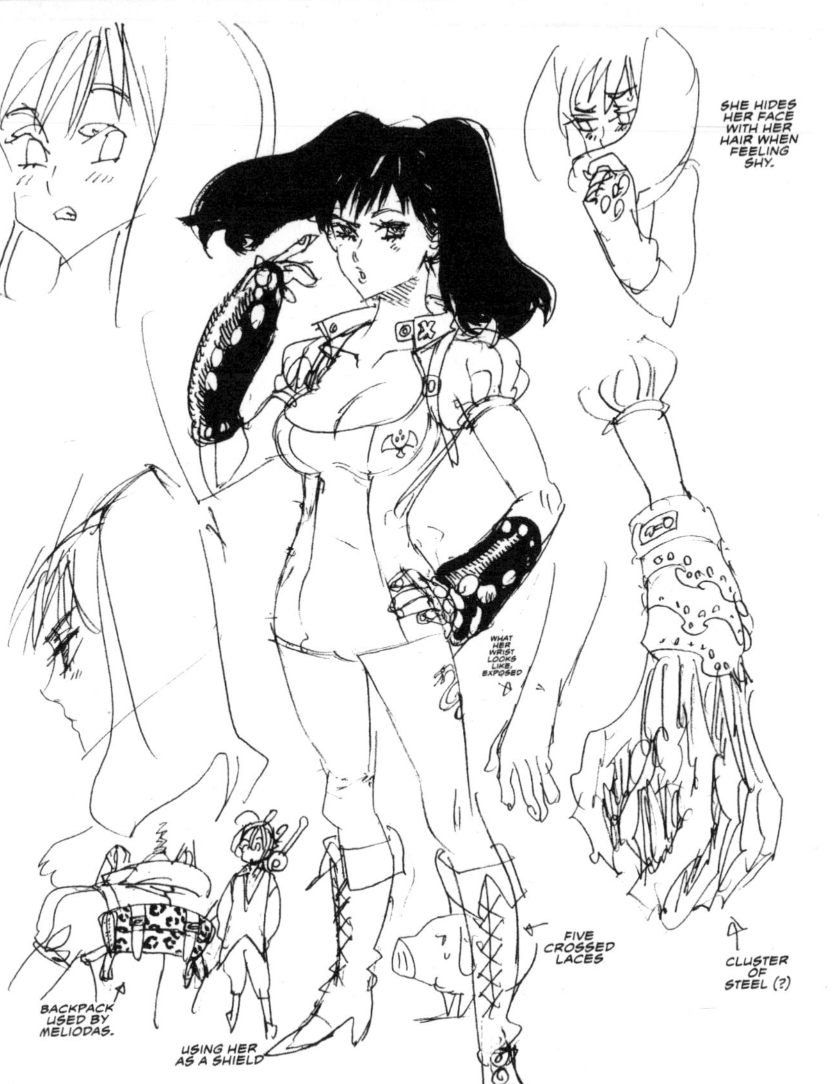
SHE HIDES HER FACE WITH HER HAIR WHEN FEELING SHY.
WHAT HER WRIST LOOKS LIKE, EXPOSED
FIVE CROSSED LACES
CLUSTER OF STEEL (?)
BACKPACK USED BY MELIODAS.
USING HER AS A SHIELD

THE SEVEN DEADLY SINS' SERPENT SIN

DIANE

SIN OF ENVY

A woman from the giant clan and a member of The Seven Deadly Sins. She has a huge crush on Meliodas and can become jealous very quickly. But that's apparently unrelated to her title of "Serpent Sin of Envy". Her future dream is to become little and have children with Meliodas.

Design Sketches for the One-Shot of "The Seven Deadly Sins"

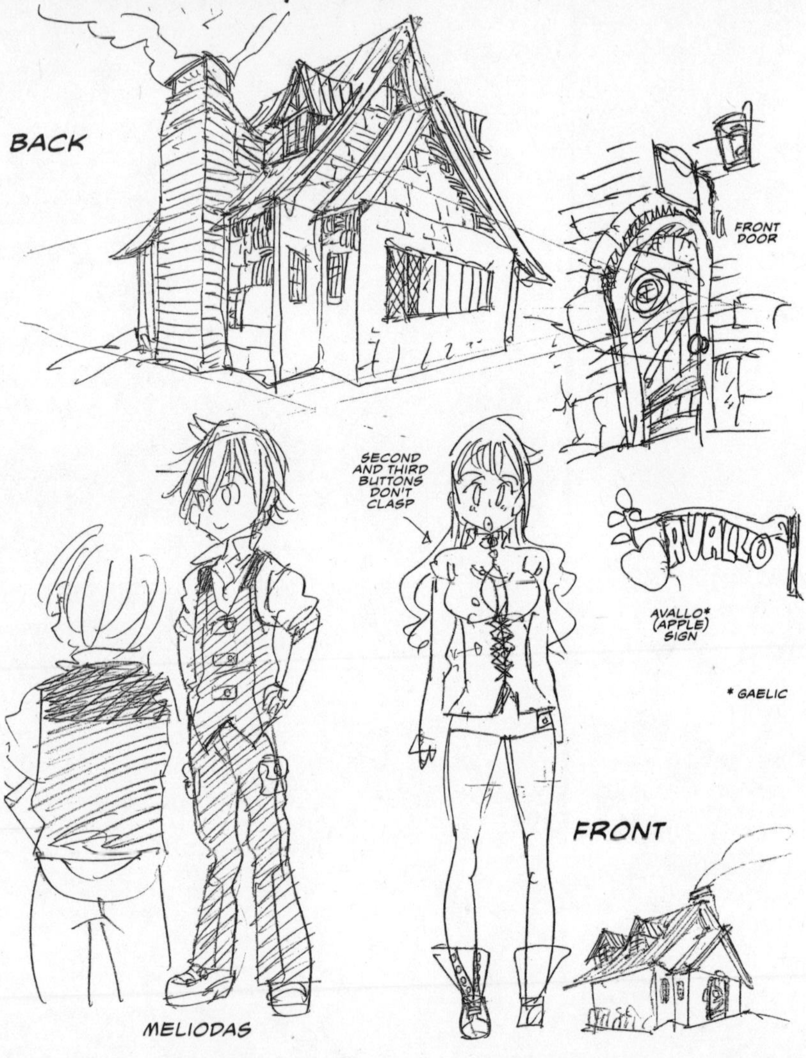
BACK
FRONT DOOR
SECOND AND THIRD BUTTONS DON'T CLASP
AVALLO
AVALLO* (APPLE) SIGN
* GAELIC
FRONT
MELIODAS

The tavern in the one-shot version was called Apple. The appearance is completely different, and only the feature of it being a mobile tavern is a shared point. But what the tavern was riding on was a giant spider-shaped mechanism. Meliodas' and Elizabeth's appearances, clothes and personalities are pretty identical to the serialized version, and the cast was a little simpler in that there was no mascot-like character. Also, the enemy Holy Knight is Allioni who showed up in chapter one of the serialized version.

THE SEVEN DEADLY SINS

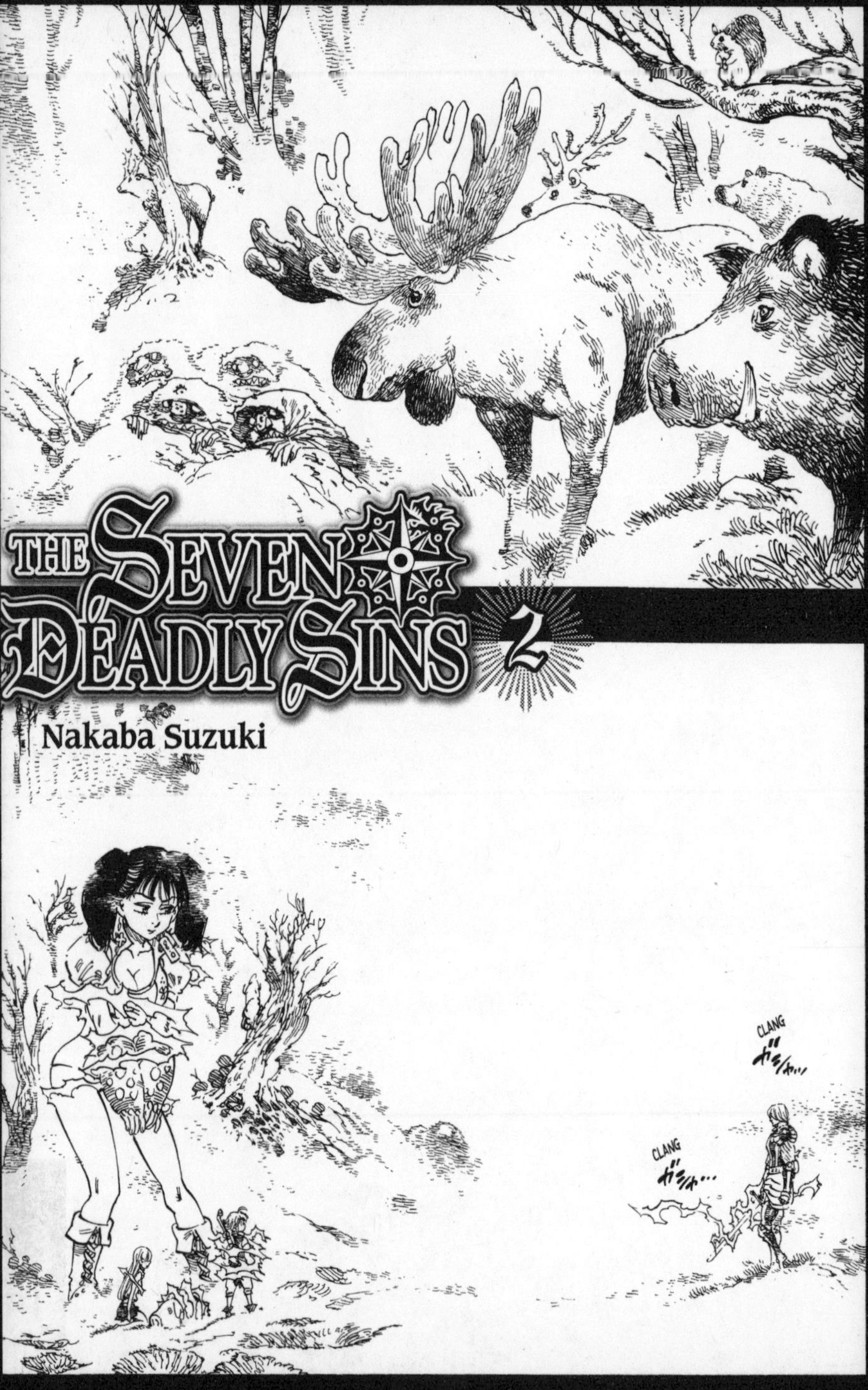
THE SEVEN DEADLY SINS
2
Nakaba Suzuki
CLANG
CLANG

nakaba suzuki presents

THE SEVEN
DEADLY SINS

Chapter 6 - The Holy Knight Gilthunder

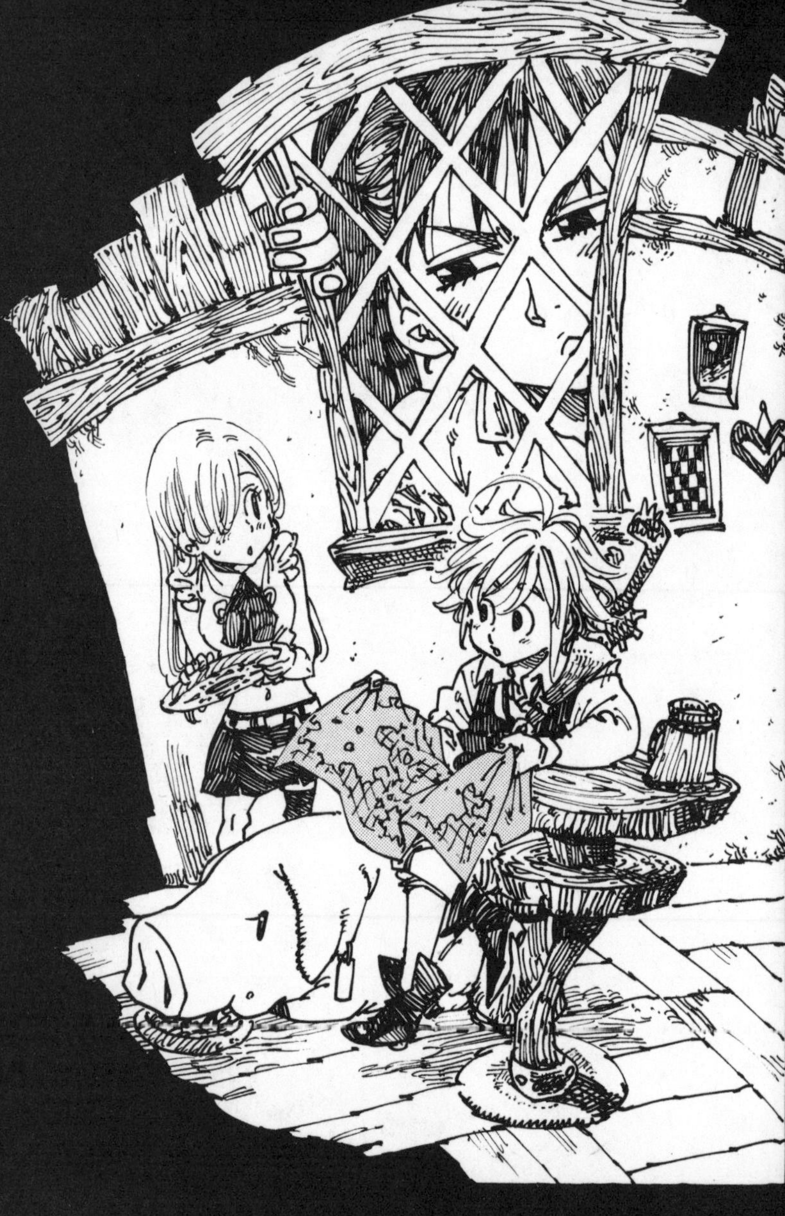

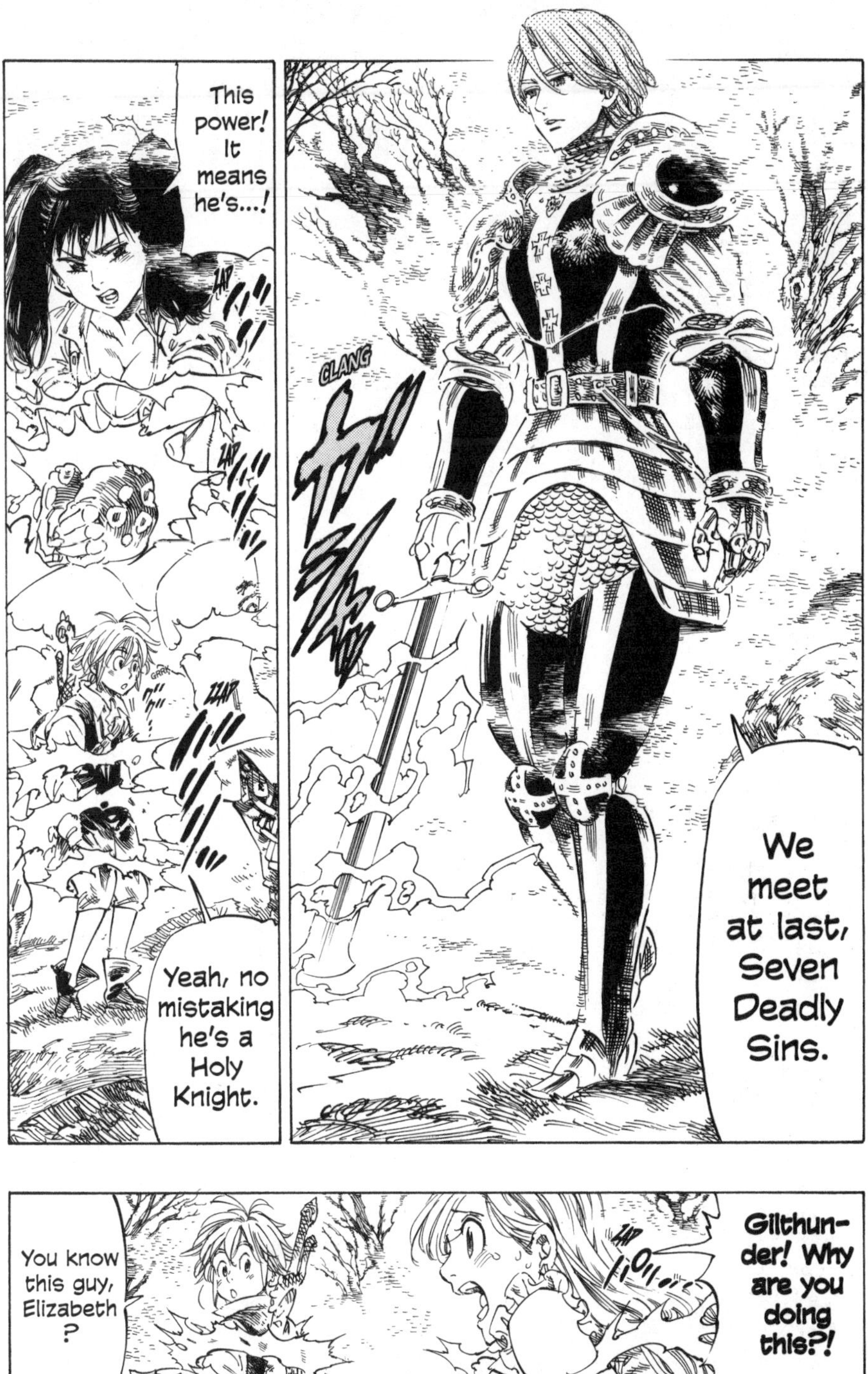
CLANG
We meet at last, Seven Deadly Sins.
This power! It means he's...!
ZAP
ZAP
GRRK
ZZAP
Yeah, no mistaking he's a Holy Knight.
Gilthun-der! Why are you doing this?!
ZAP
You know this guy, Elizabeth?

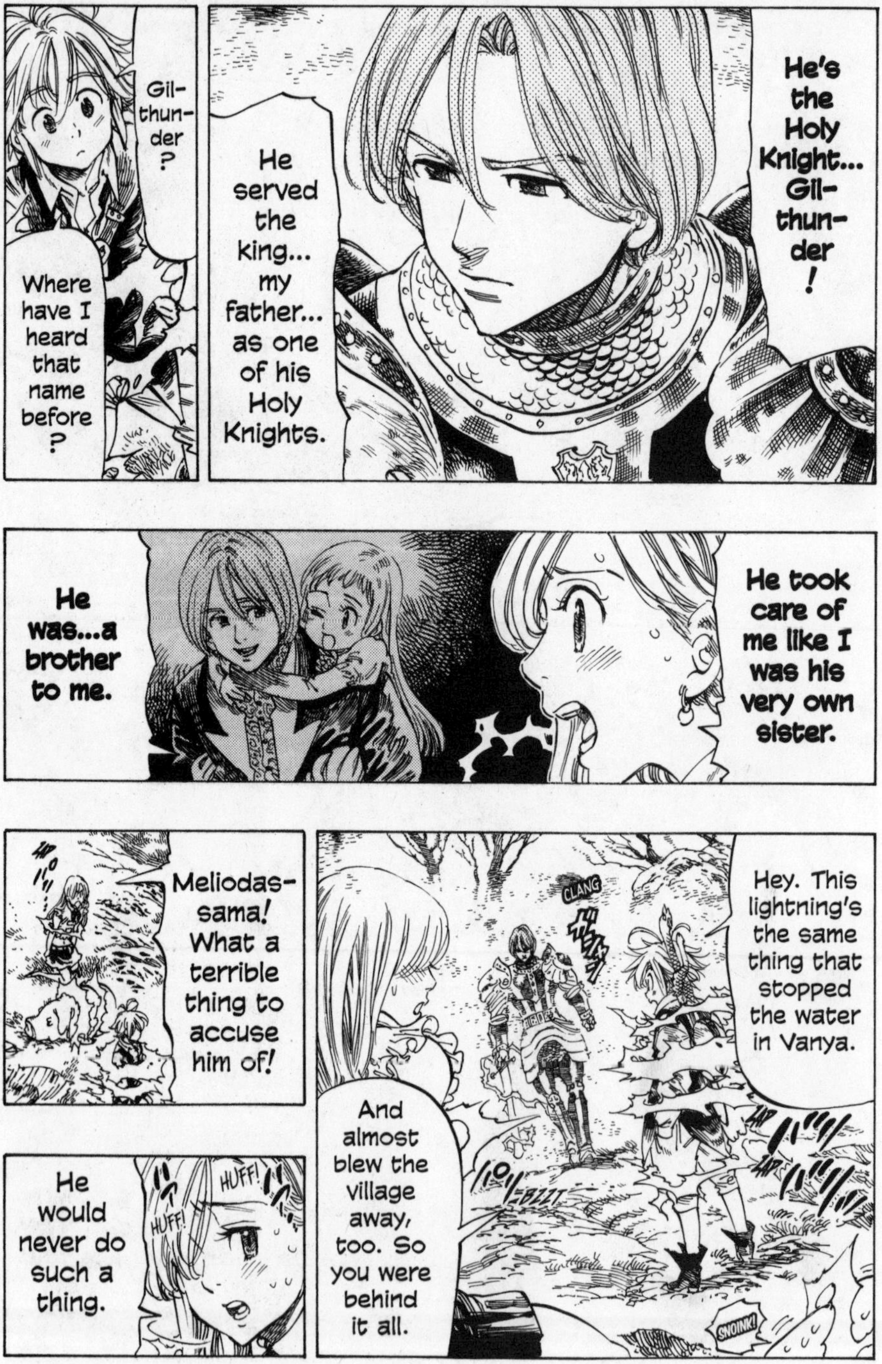
He's the Holy Knight... Gilthunder!
He served the king... my father... as one of his Holy Knights.
Gil-thun-der?
Where have I heard that name before?
He took care of me like I was his very own sister.
He was...a brother to me.
Hey. This lightning's the same thing that stopped the water in Vanya.
CLANG
BZZT
SNOINK!
And almost blew the village away, too. So you were behind it all.
Meliodas-sama! What a terrible thing to accuse him of!
HUFF!
HUFF!
He would never do such a thing.

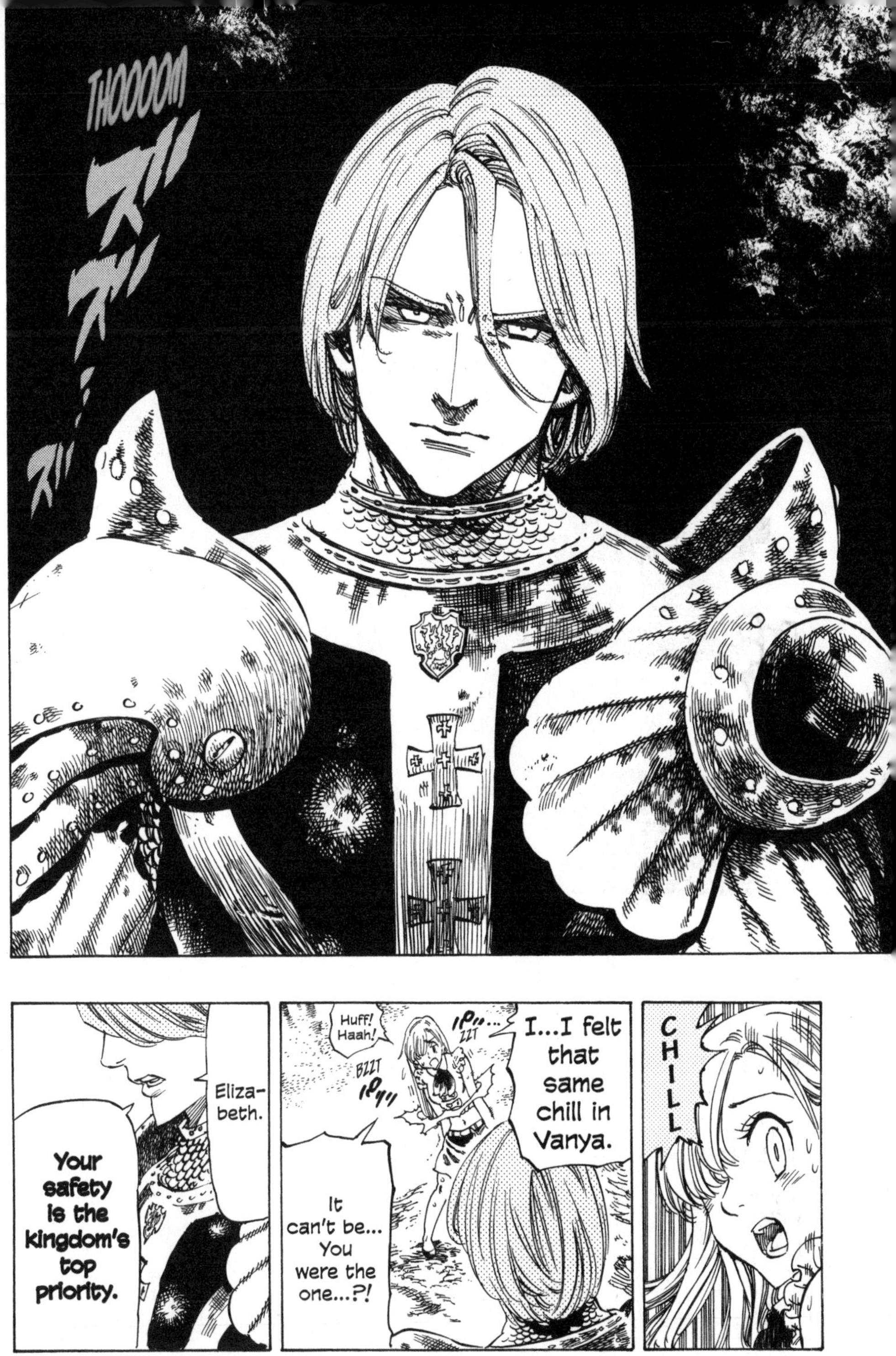
THOOOOM
CHILL
I...I felt that same chill in Vanya.
Huff! Haah!
ZZT
BZZT
It can't be... You were the one...?!
Eliza-beth.
Your safety is the kingdom's top priority.

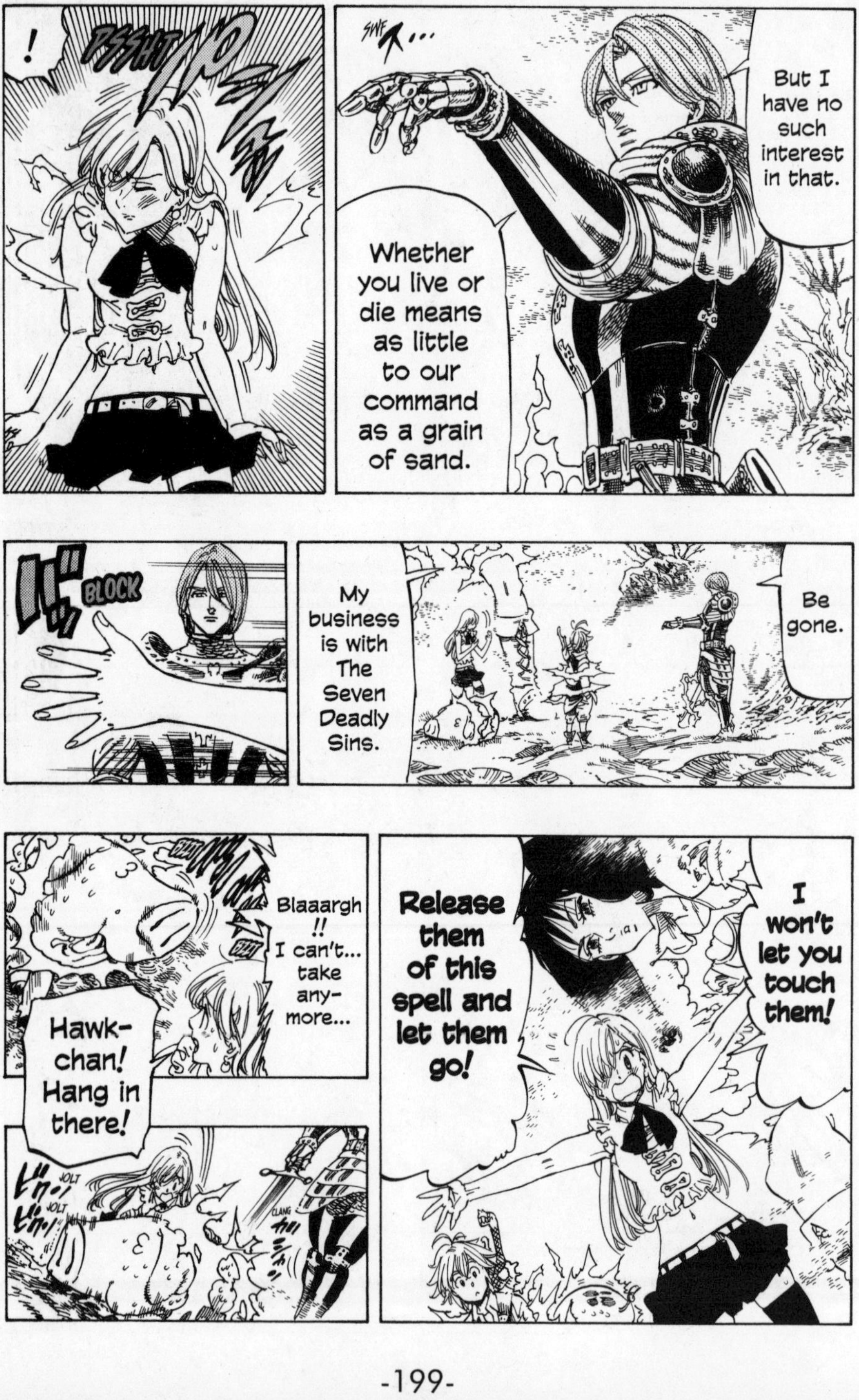
SWF
But I have no such interest in that.
Whether you live or die means as little to our command as a grain of sand.
PSSHT
!
Be gone.
My business is with The Seven Deadly Sins.
BLOCK
I won't let you touch them!
Release them of this spell and let them go!
Blaaargh!! I can't... take any-more...
Hawk-chan! Hang in there!
JOLT
JOLT
CLANG

PUNT
SNOINK
Hawk-chan!!
BOING
TMP
HOGYAAAAAH!
AAAAAH...
SHNNT

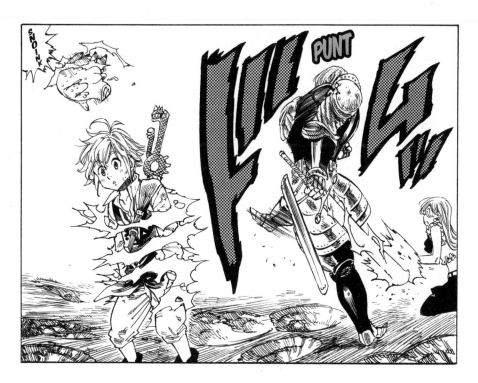

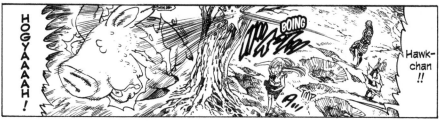

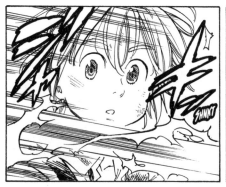

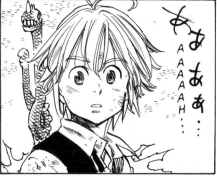

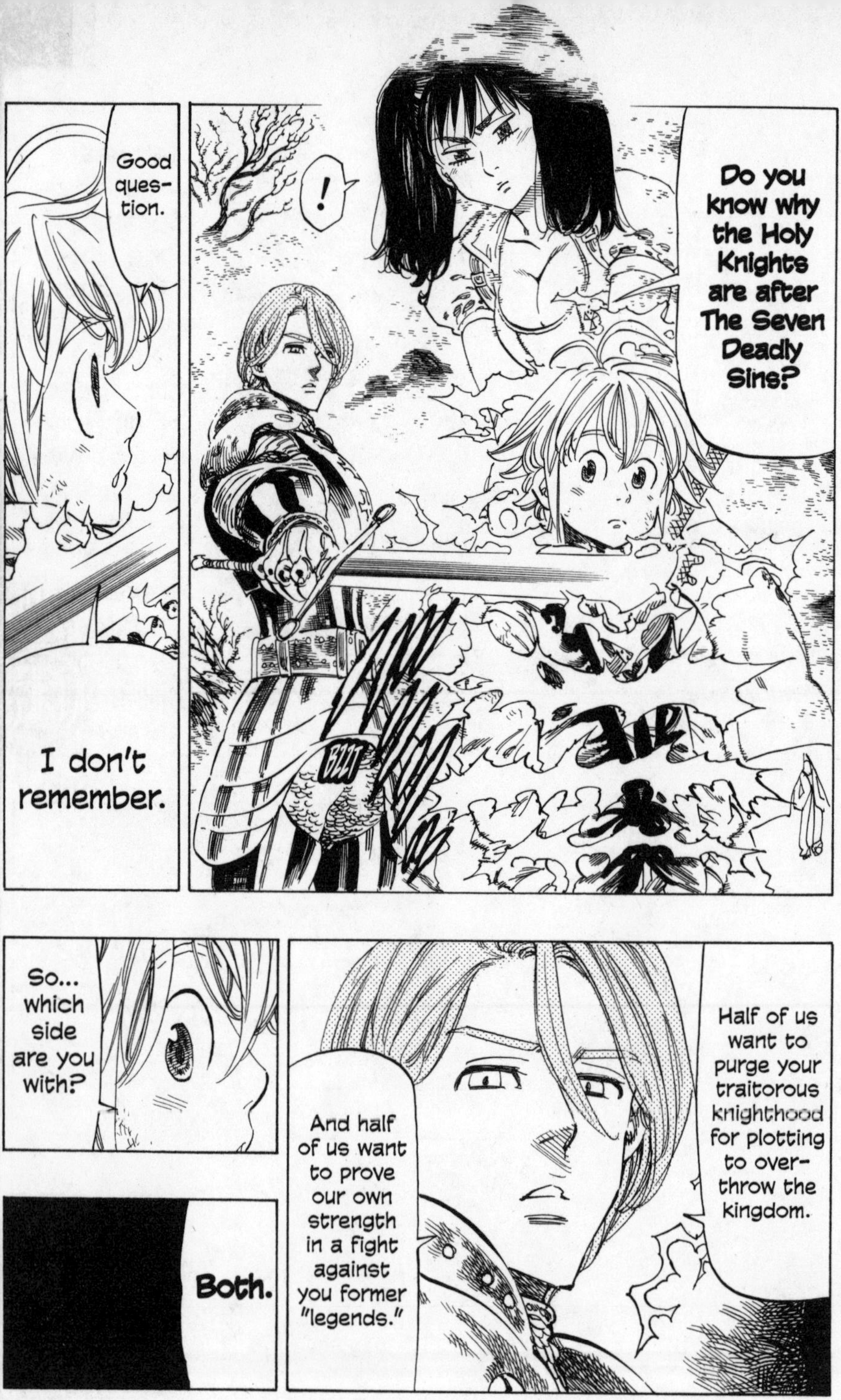
Do you know why the Holy Knights are after The Seven Deadly Sins?
!
BZZT
Good question.
I don't remember.
Half of us want to purge your traitorous knighthood for plotting to overthrow the kingdom.
And half of us want to prove our own strength in a fight against you former "legends."
So... which side are you with?
Both.

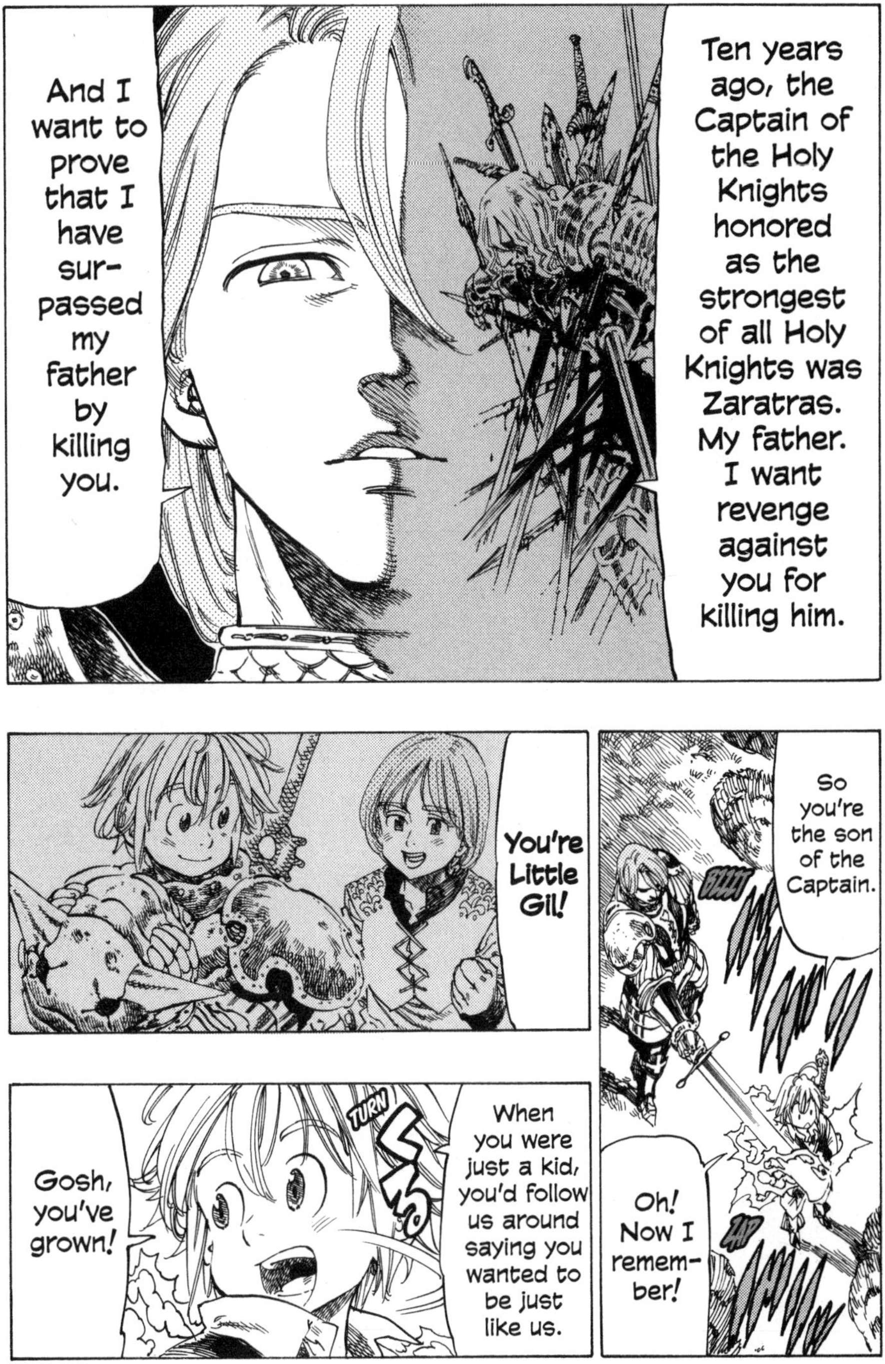
Ten years ago, the Captain of the Holy Knights honored as the strongest of all Holy Knights was Zaratras. My father. I want revenge against you for killing him.
And I want to prove that I have surpassed my father by killing you.
So you're the son of the Captain.
Oh! Now I remember!
ZAP
You're Little Gil!
When you were just a kid, you'd follow us around saying you wanted to be just like us.
TURN
Gosh, you've grown!

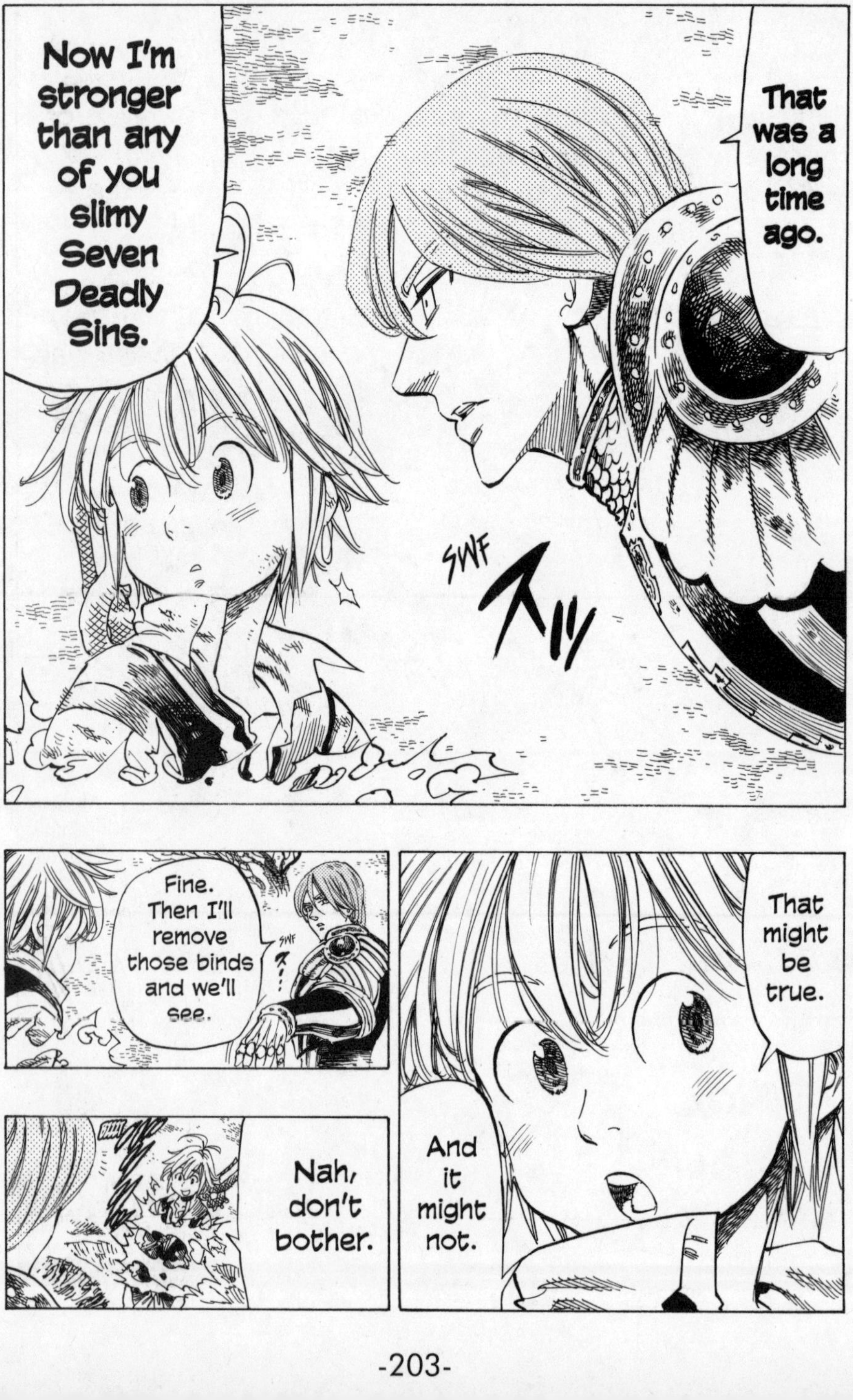
That was a long time ago.
Now I'm stronger than any of you slimy Seven Deadly Sins.
SWF
スッ
That might be true.
And it might not.
Fine. Then I'll remove those binds and we'll see.
SWF
スッ
Nah, don't bother.

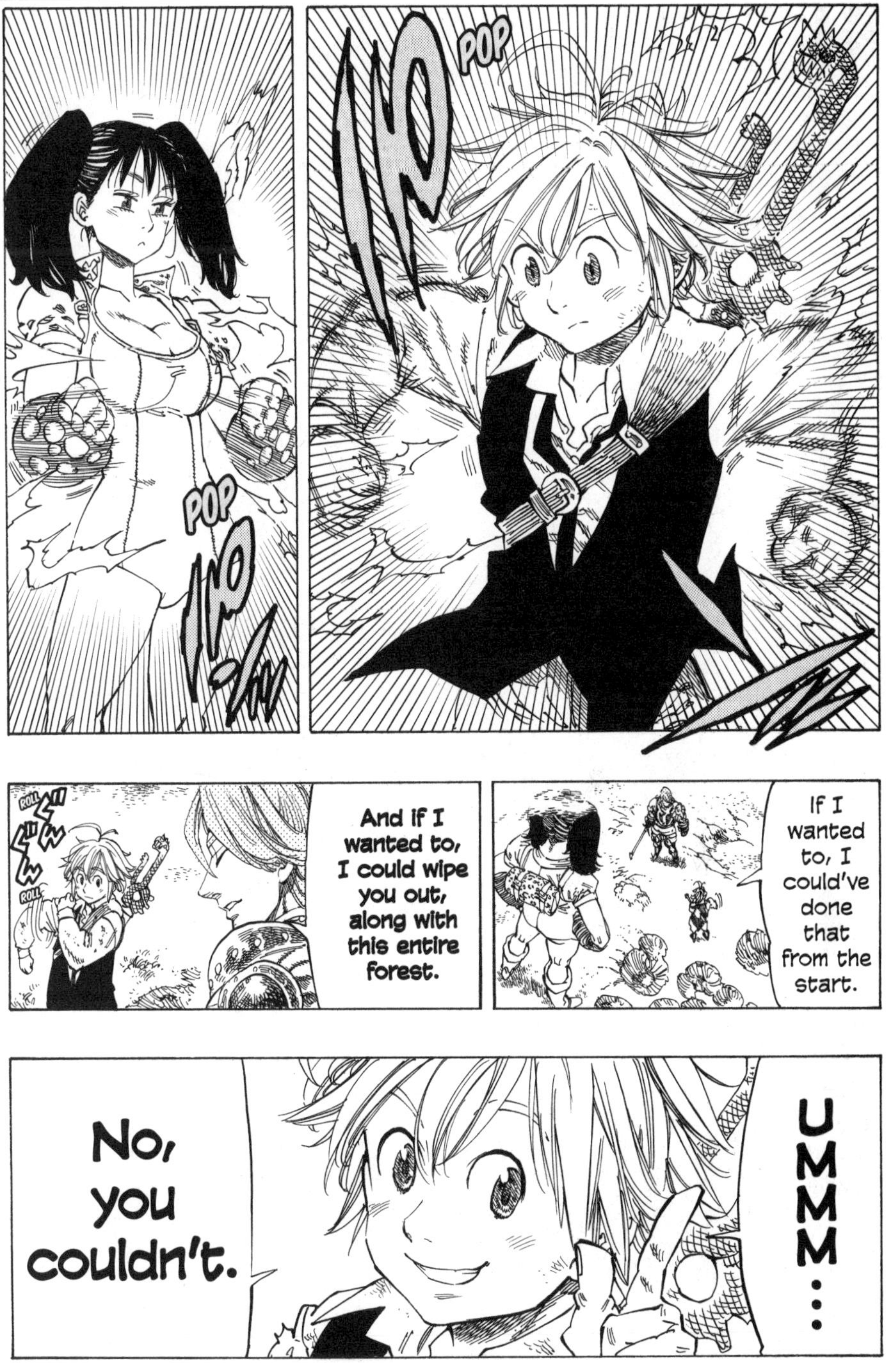
POP
POP
If I wanted to, I could've done that from the start.
ROLL
ROLL
And if I wanted to, I could wipe you out, along with this entire forest.
UMMM...
No, you couldn't.

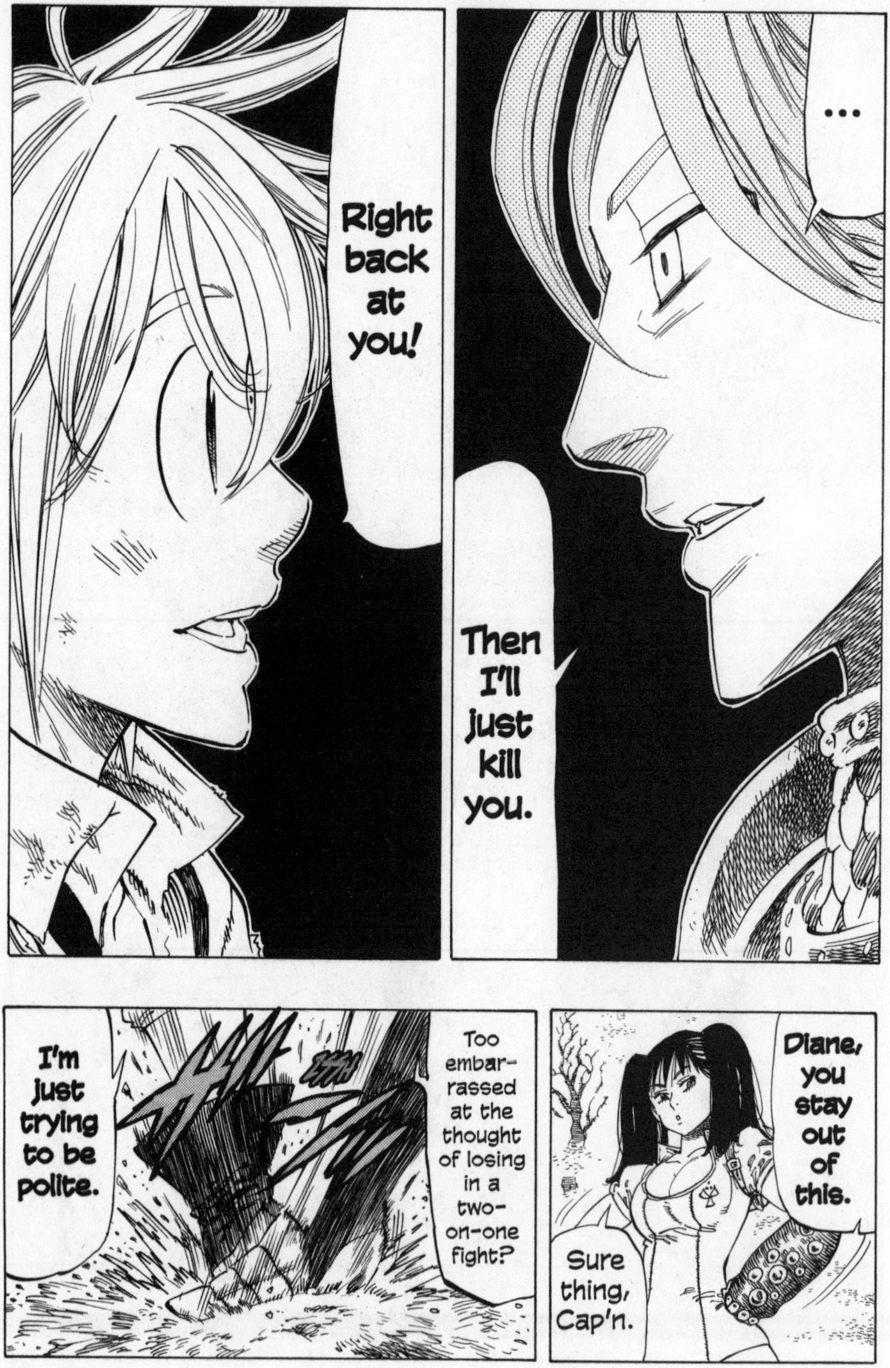
...
Then I'll just kill you.
Right back at you!
Diane, you stay out of this.
Sure thing, Cap'n.
Too embarrassed at the thought of losing in a two-on-one fight?
I'm just trying to be polite.

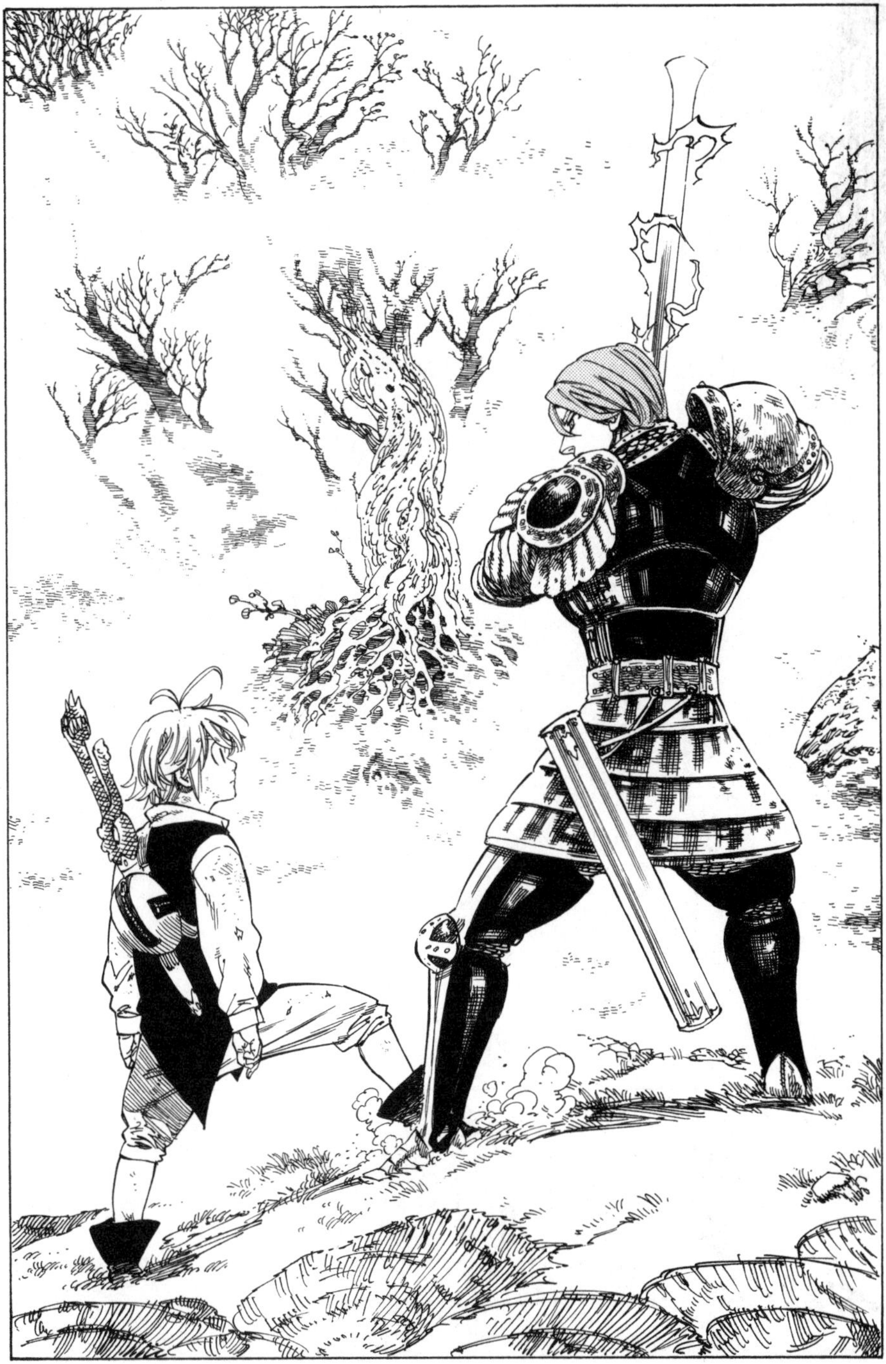

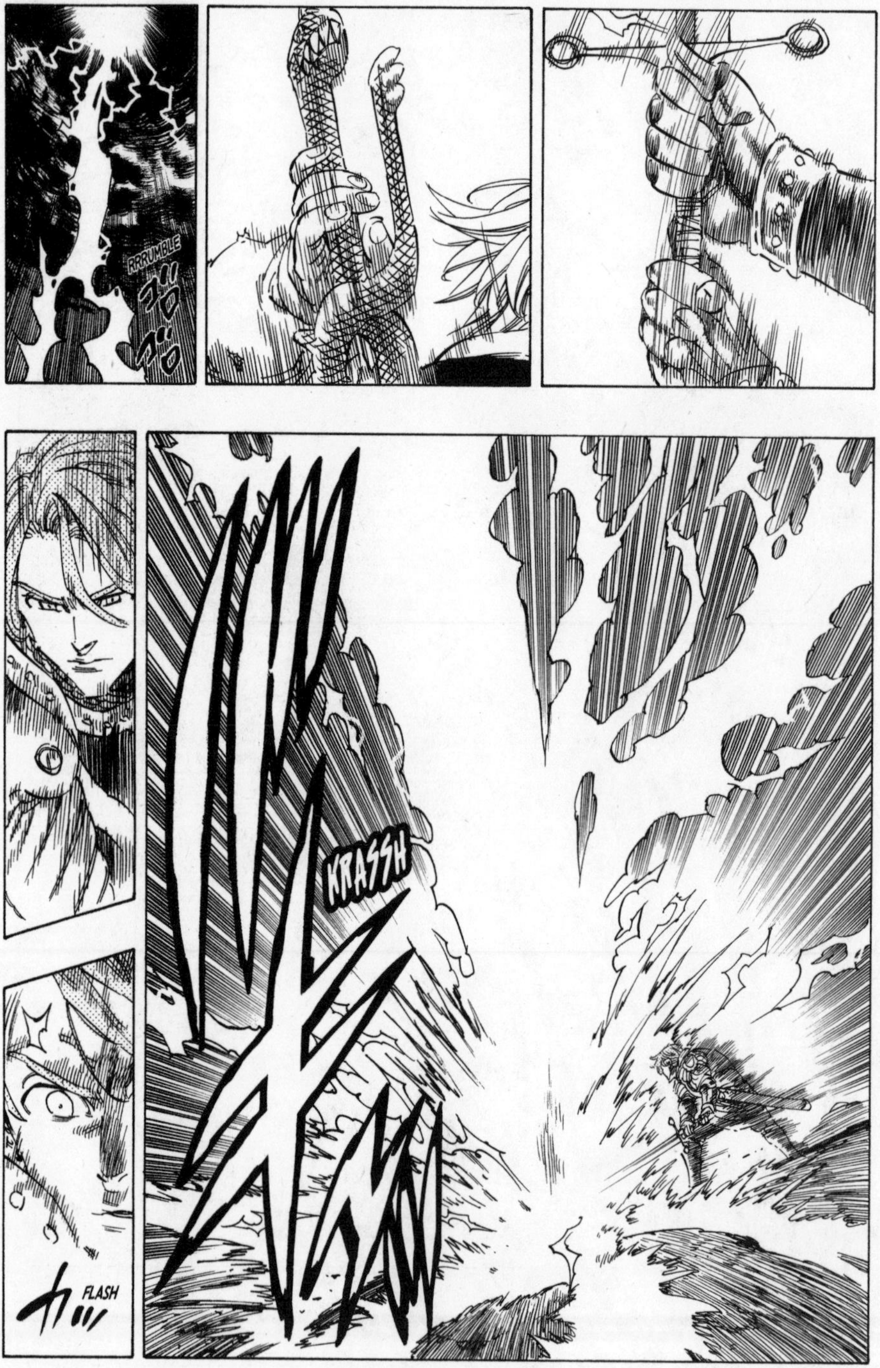
RRRUMBLE
ゴロゴロ
KRASSH
FLASH
カッ

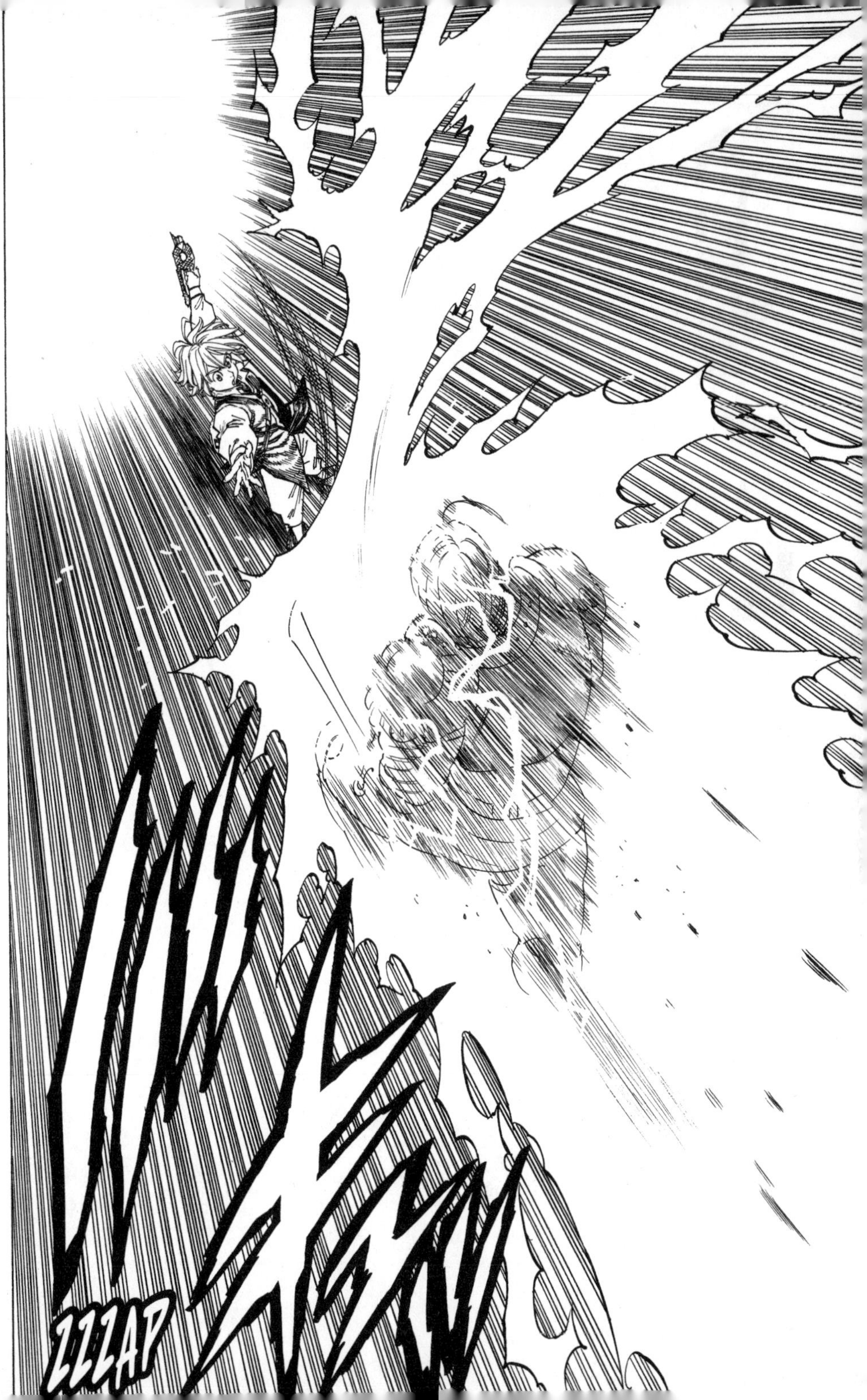
ZZZAP

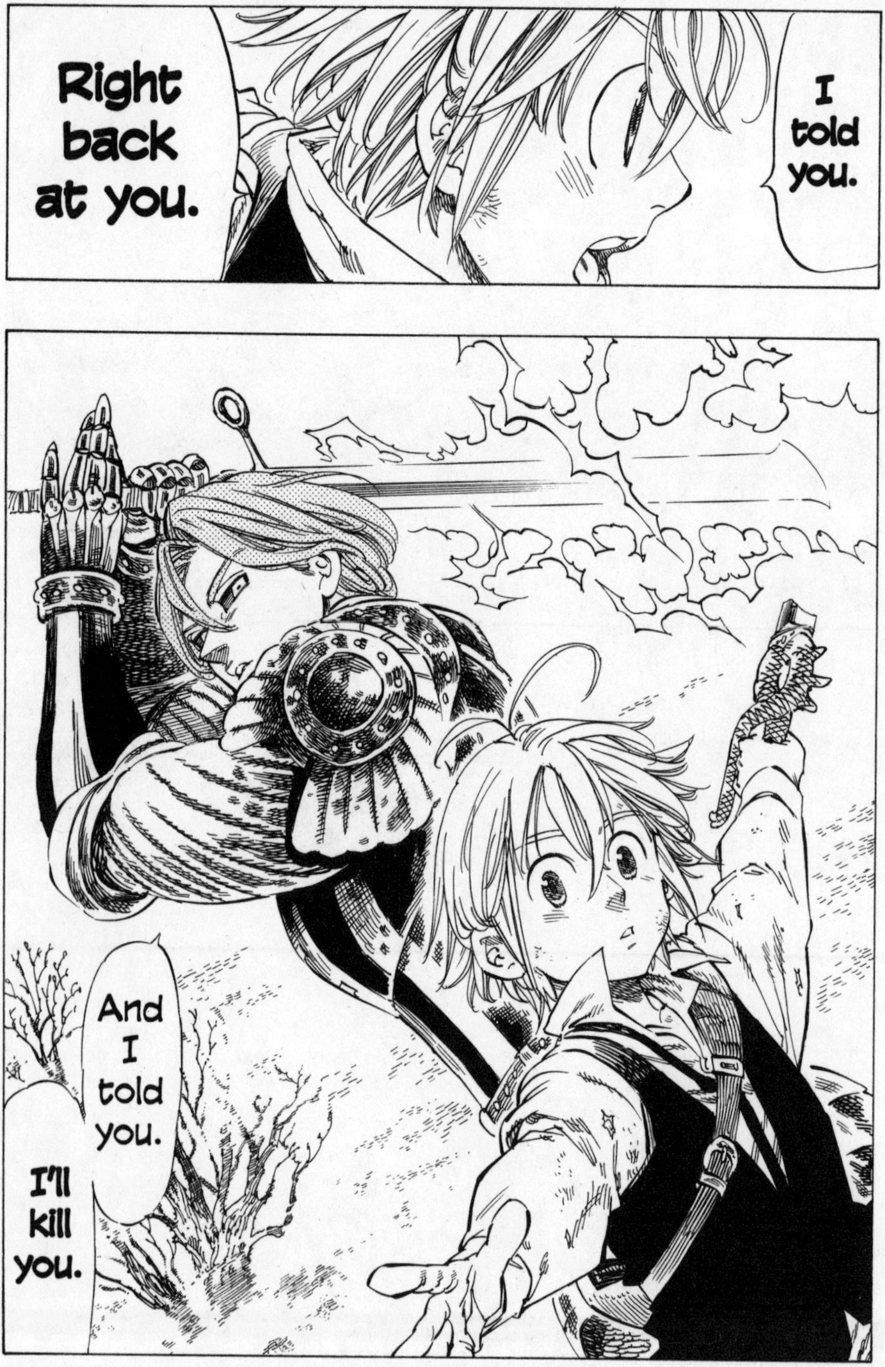
I told you.
Right back at you.
And I told you.
I'll kill you.

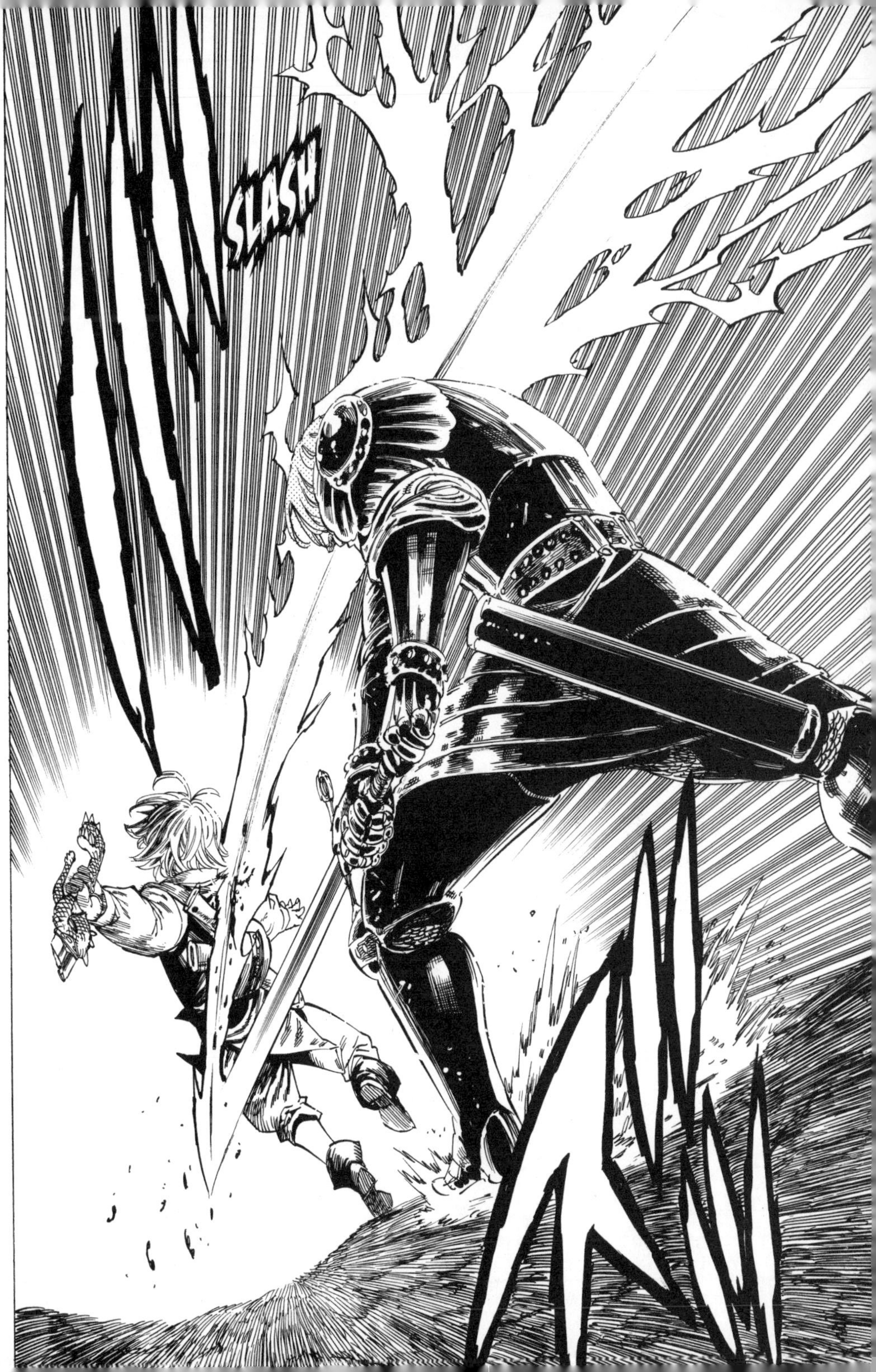
SLASH

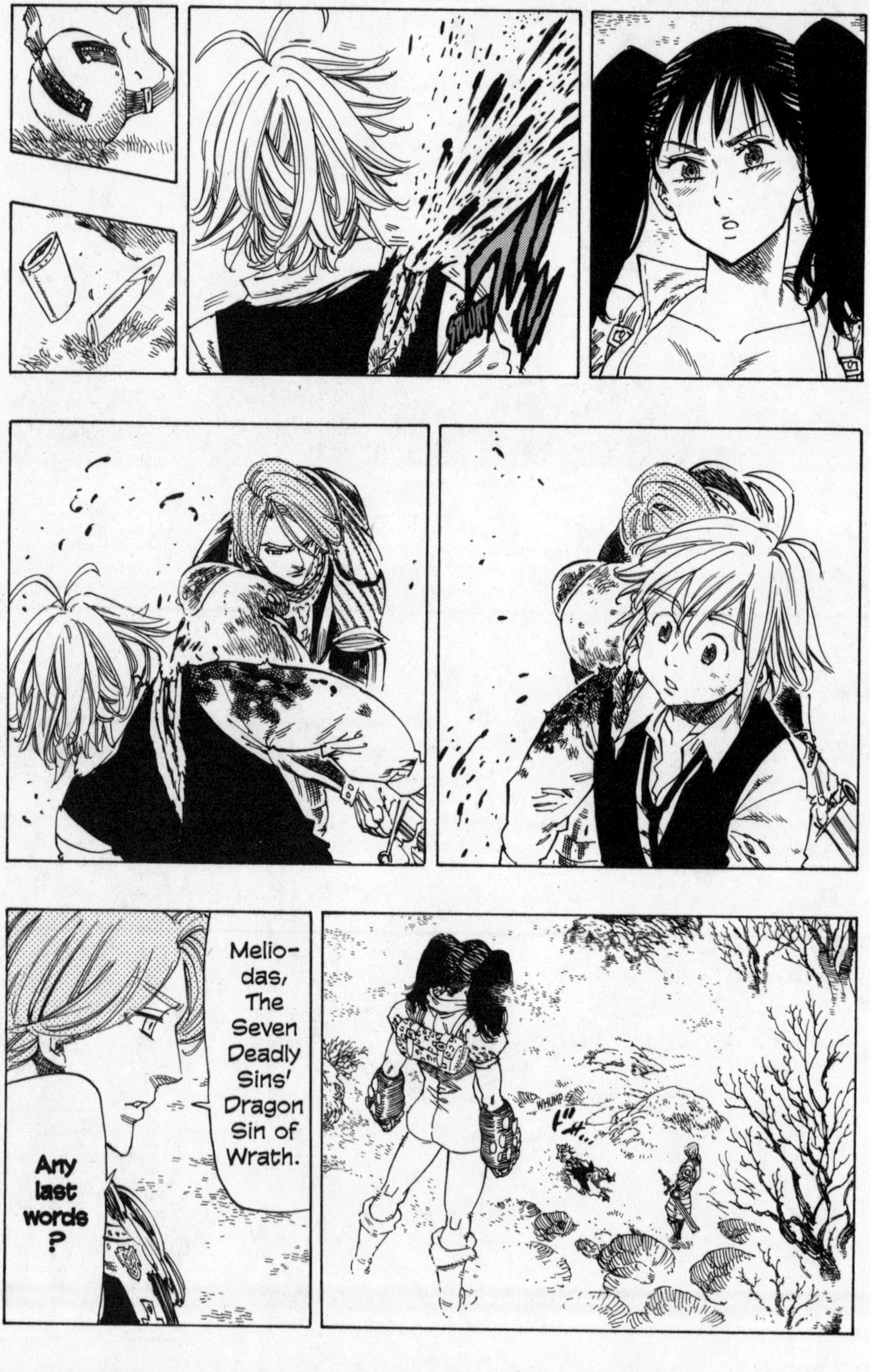

SPLURT
WHUMP
Melio-
das,
The
Seven
Deadly
Sins'
Dragon
Sin of
Wrath.
Any
last
words
?

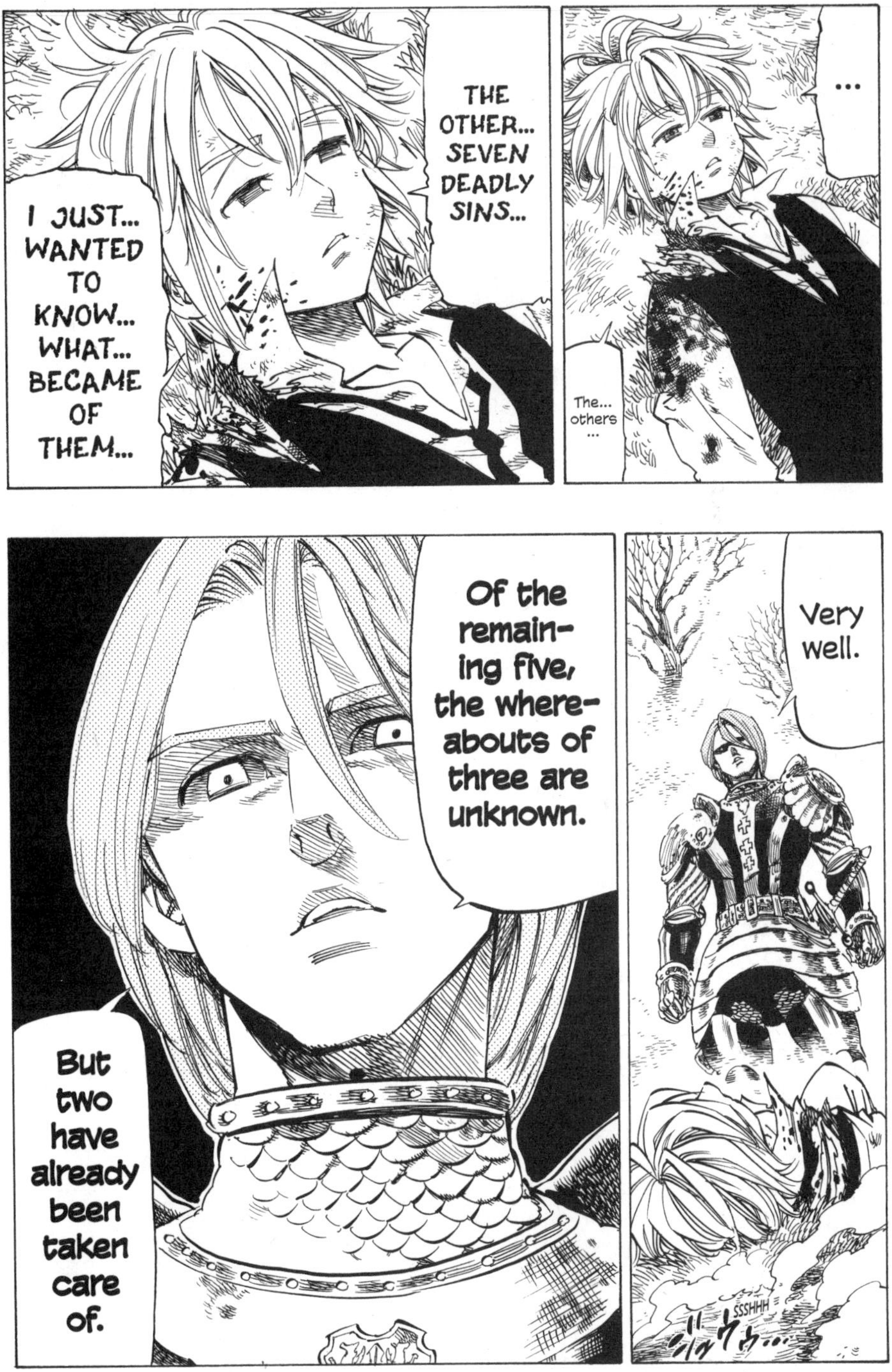
...
The... others...
THE OTHER... SEVEN DEADLY SINS...
I JUST... WANTED TO KNOW... WHAT... BECAME OF THEM...
Very well.
SSSHHH
Of the remaining five, the whereabouts of three are unknown.
But two have already been taken care of.

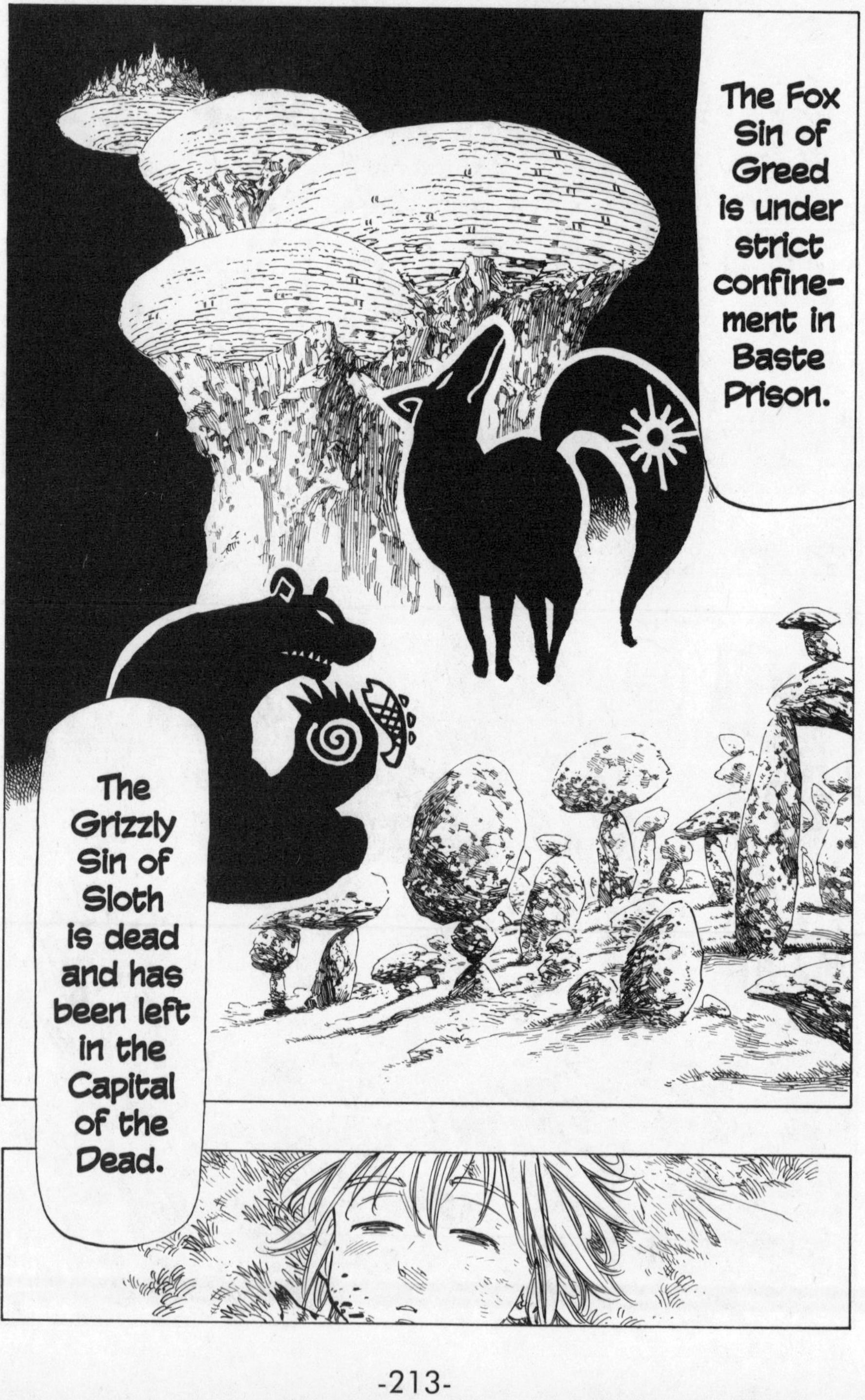
The Fox Sin of Greed is under strict confinement in Baste Prison.
The Grizzly Sin of Sloth is dead and has been left in the Capital of the Dead.

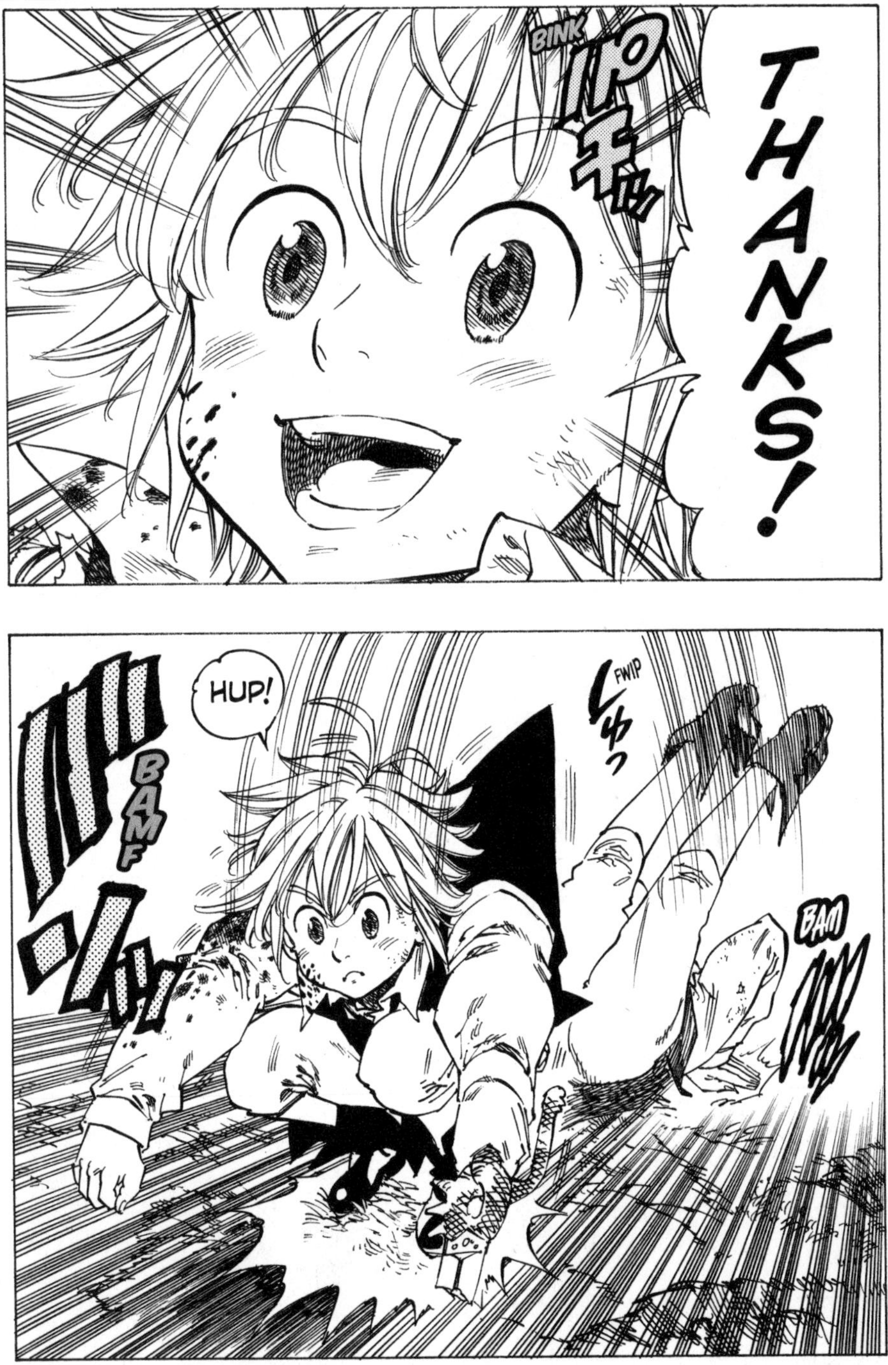
THANKS!
BINK
FWIP
BAM
HUP!
BAMF

Chapter 7 - Dark Prisoner

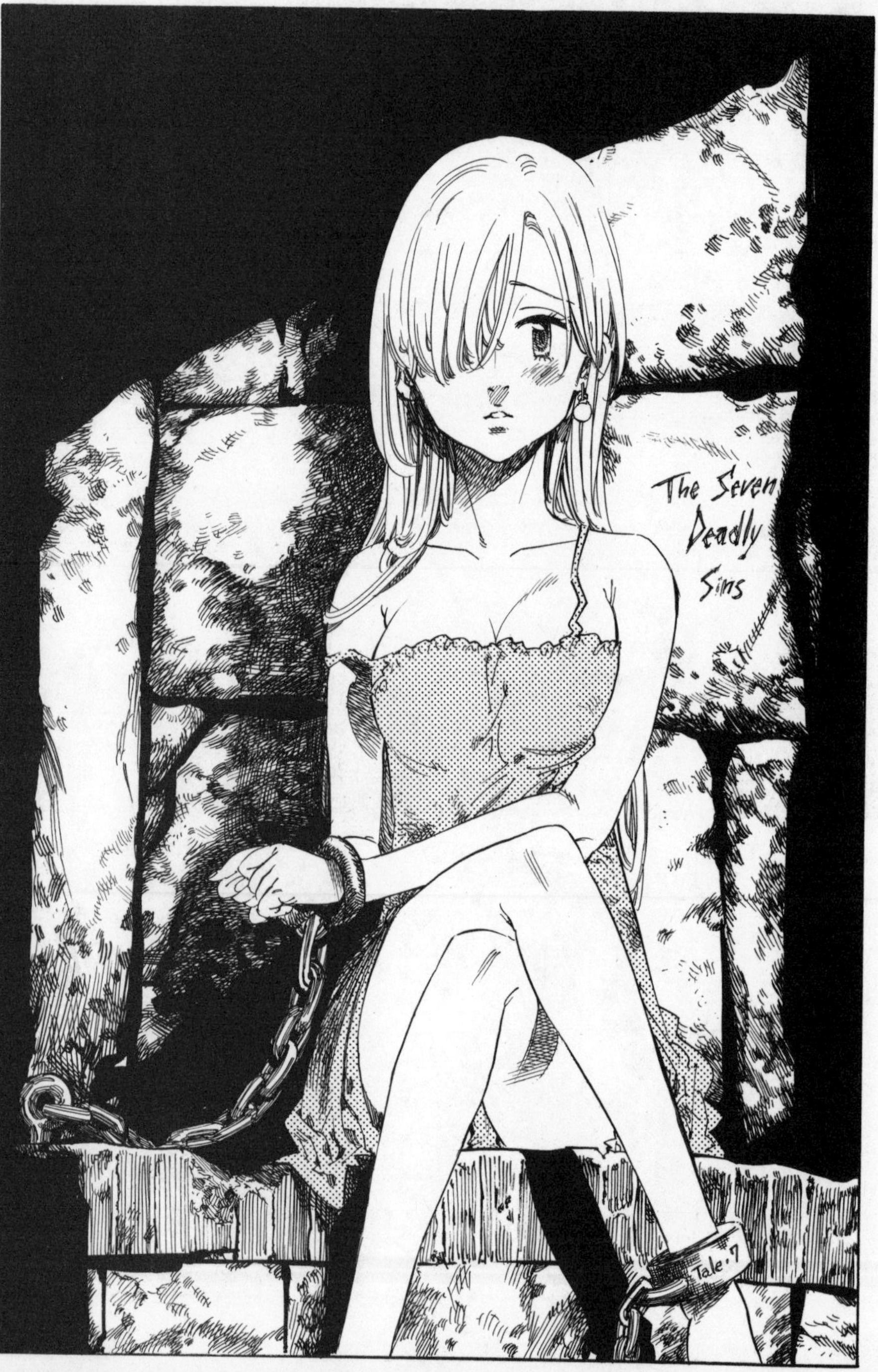
The Seven Deadly Sins
Tale.7

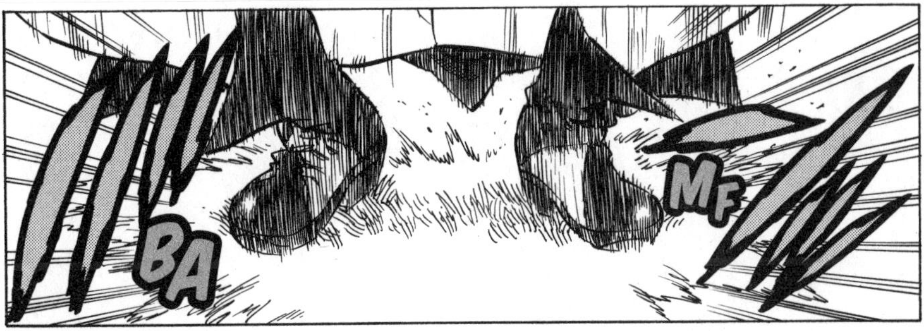
BA
MF

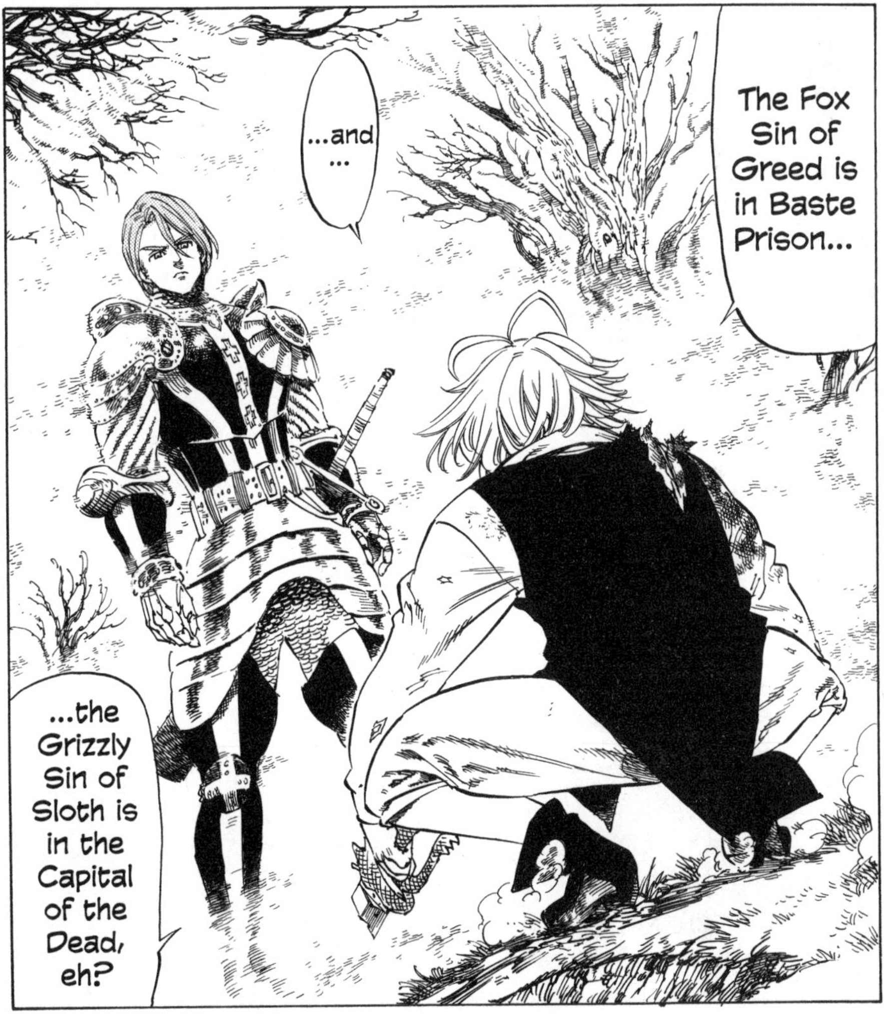
The Fox Sin of Greed is in Baste Prison...
...and ...
...the Grizzly Sin of Sloth is in the Capital of the Dead, eh?

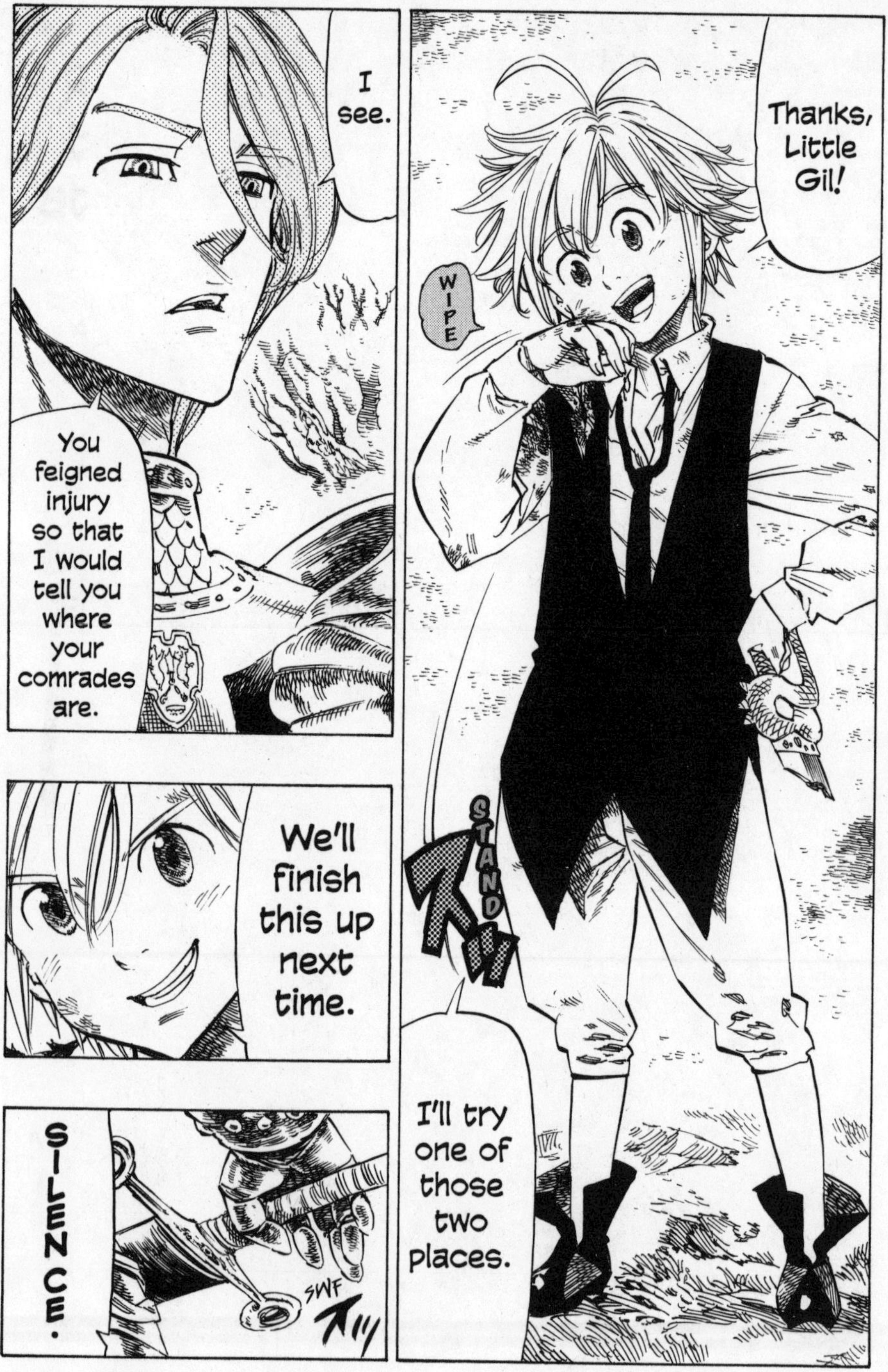
Thanks, Little Gil!
WIPE
STAND
I'll try one of those two places.
I see.
You feigned injury so that I would tell you where your comrades are.
We'll finish this up next time.
SILENCE.
SWF

SWISH
TMP
HOP
HOP
HOP

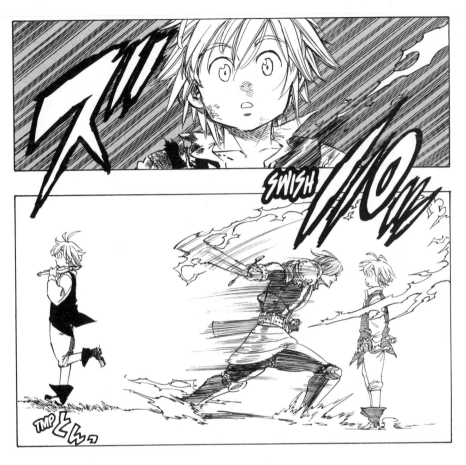

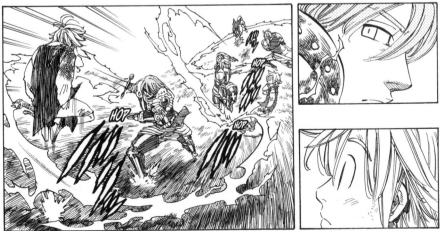

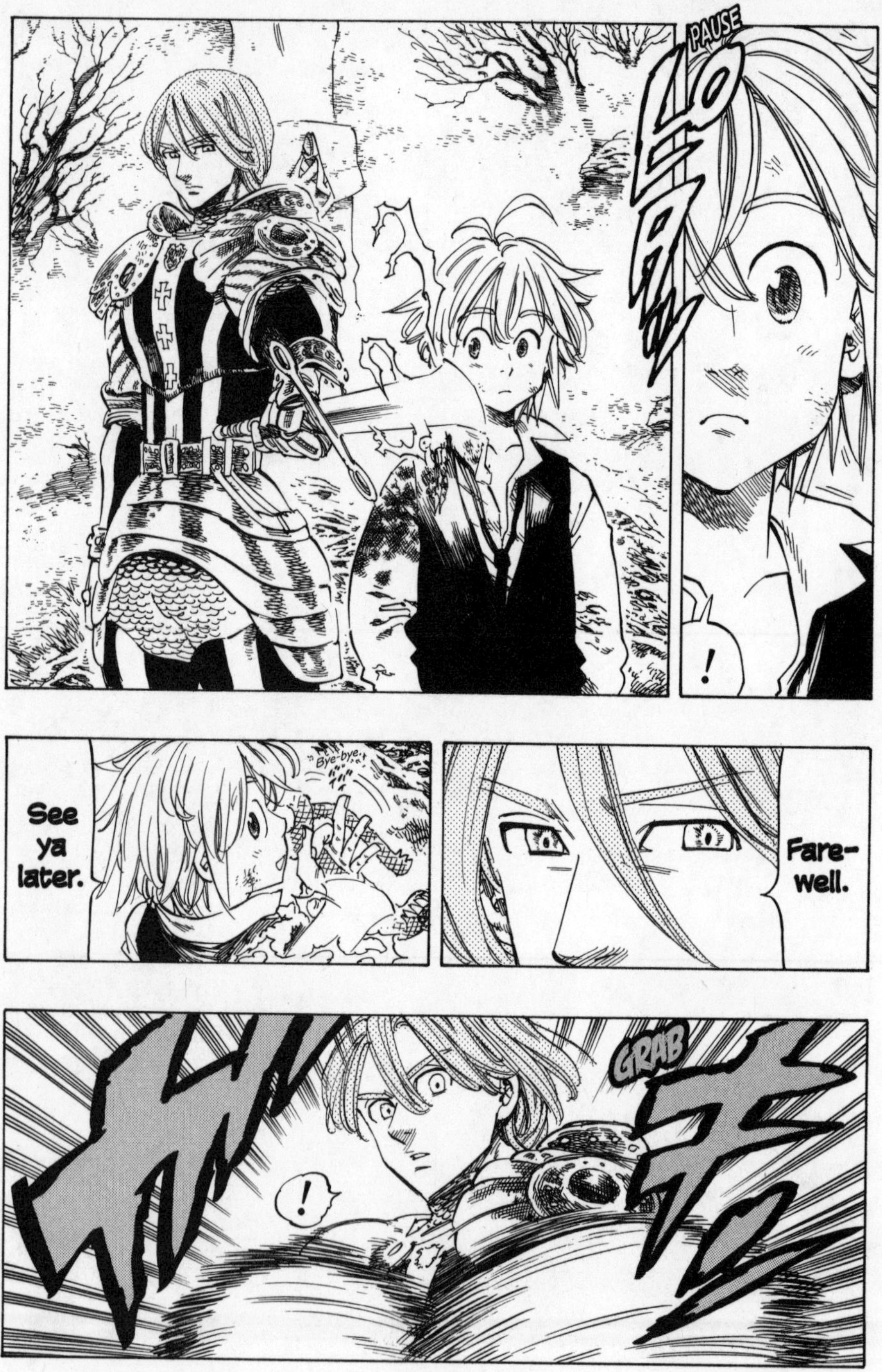

PAUSE
!
Fare-well.
See ya later.
Bye-bye
GRAB
!

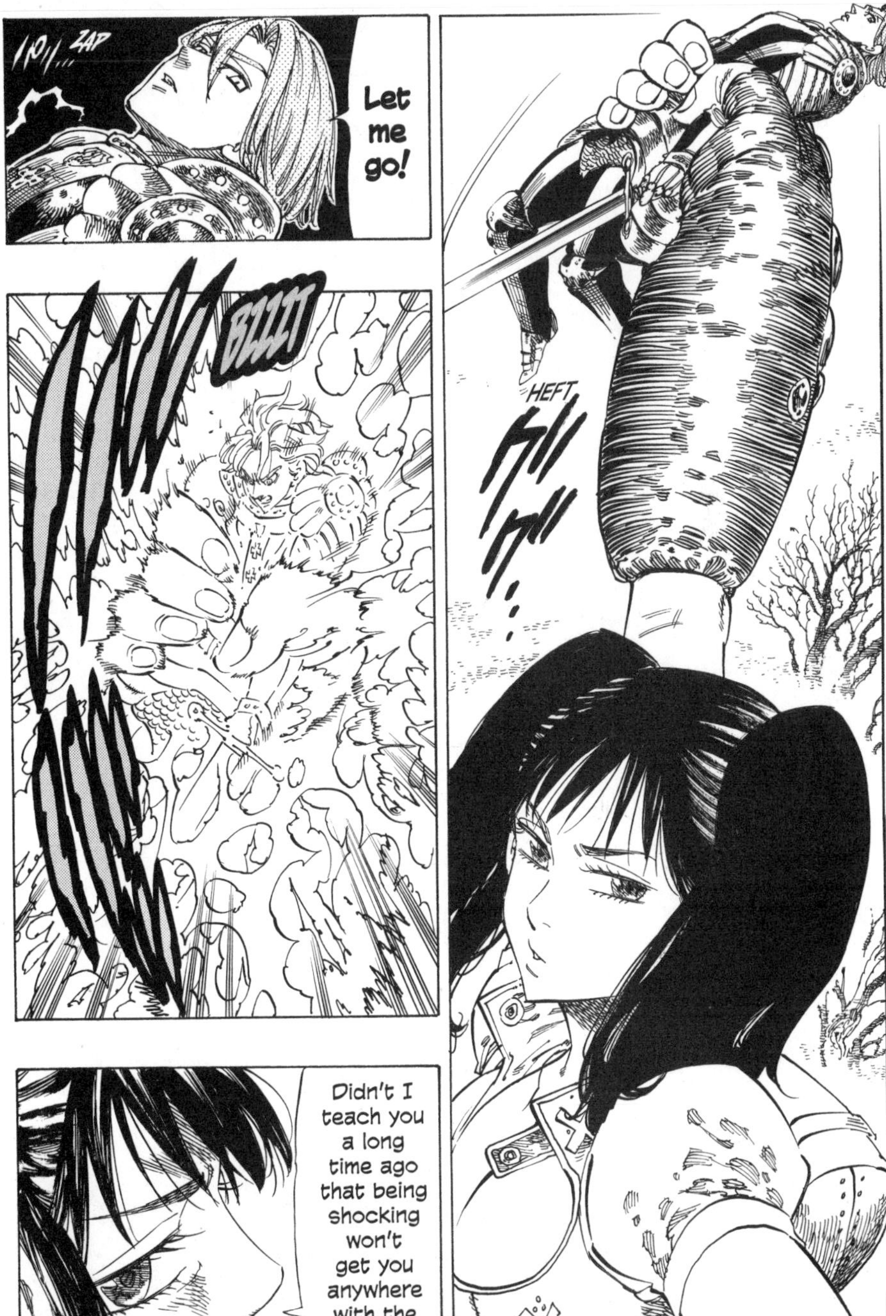
HEFT
ZAP
Let me go!
BZZZT
Didn't I teach you a long time ago that being shocking won't get you anywhere with the girls?

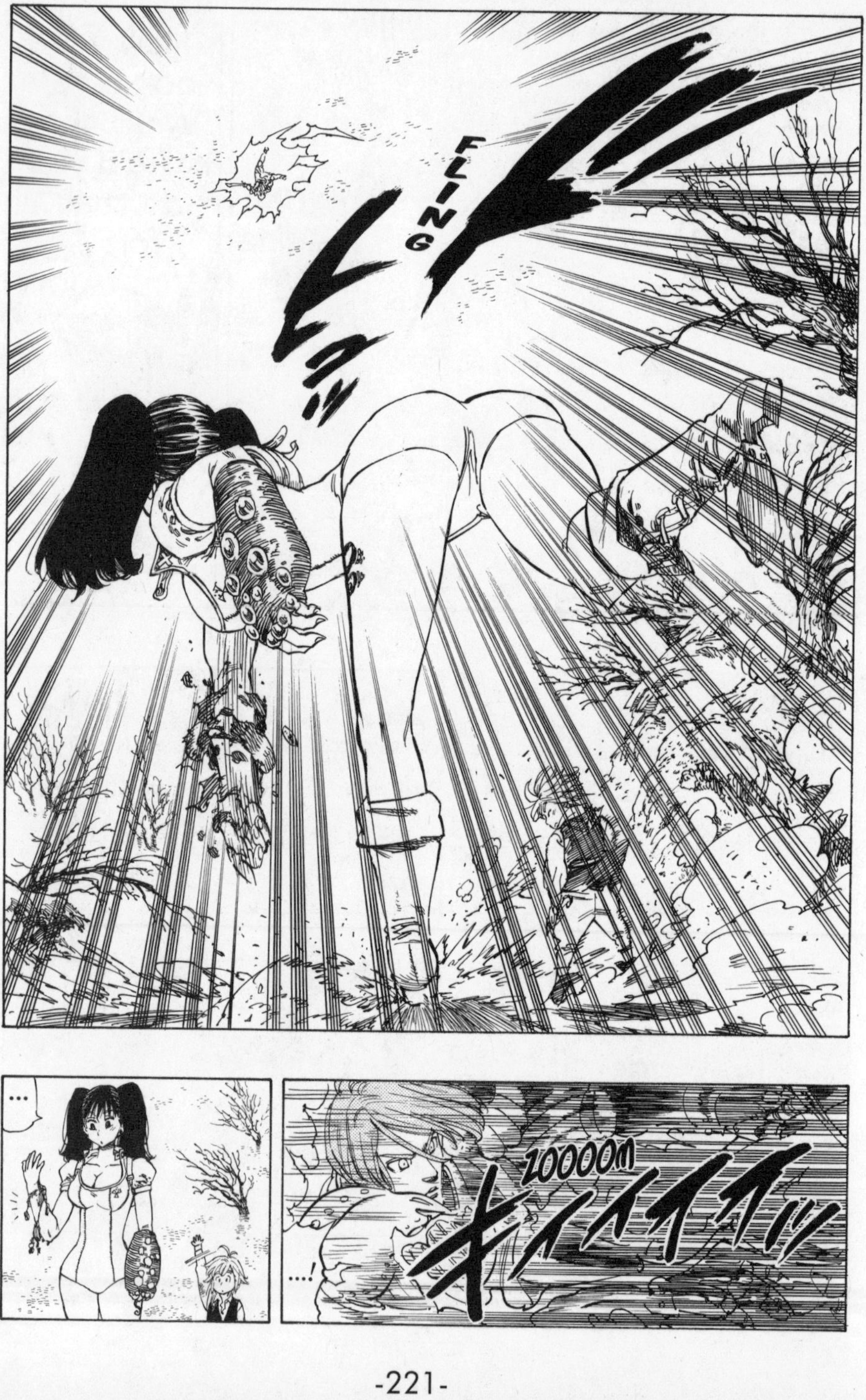
FLING
ZOOOOM
....!
...

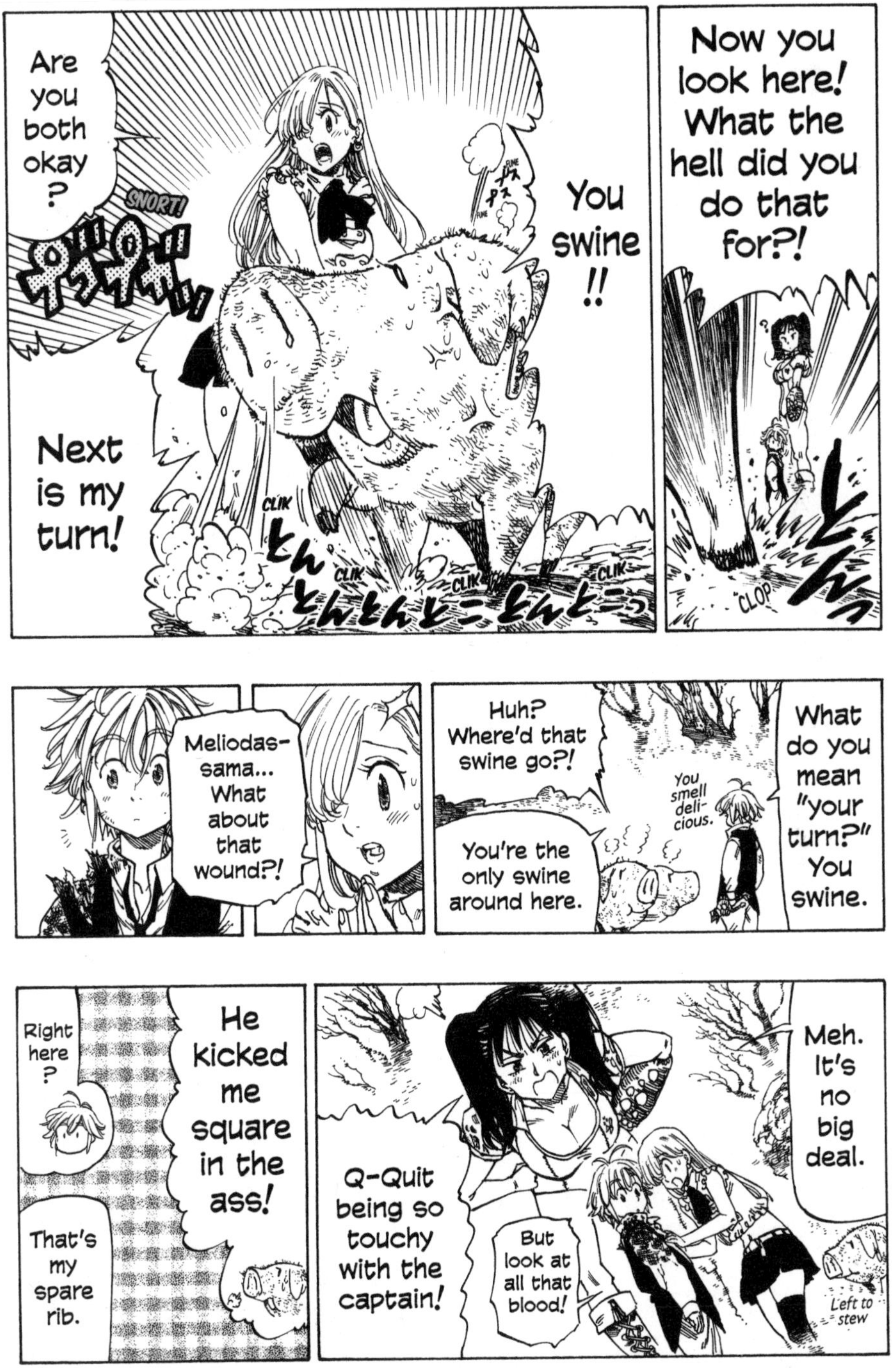

Now you look here! What the hell did you do that for?!
CLOP
You swine!!
Are you both okay?
SNORT!
Next is my turn!
CLIK
CLIK
CLIK
CLIK
What do you mean "your turn?" You swine.
You smell delicious.
Huh? Where'd that swine go?!
You're the only swine around here.
Meliodas-sama... What about that wound?!
Meh. It's no big deal.
Q-Quit being so touchy with the captain!
But look at all that blood!
Left to stew
He kicked me square in the ass!
Right here?
That's my spare rib.

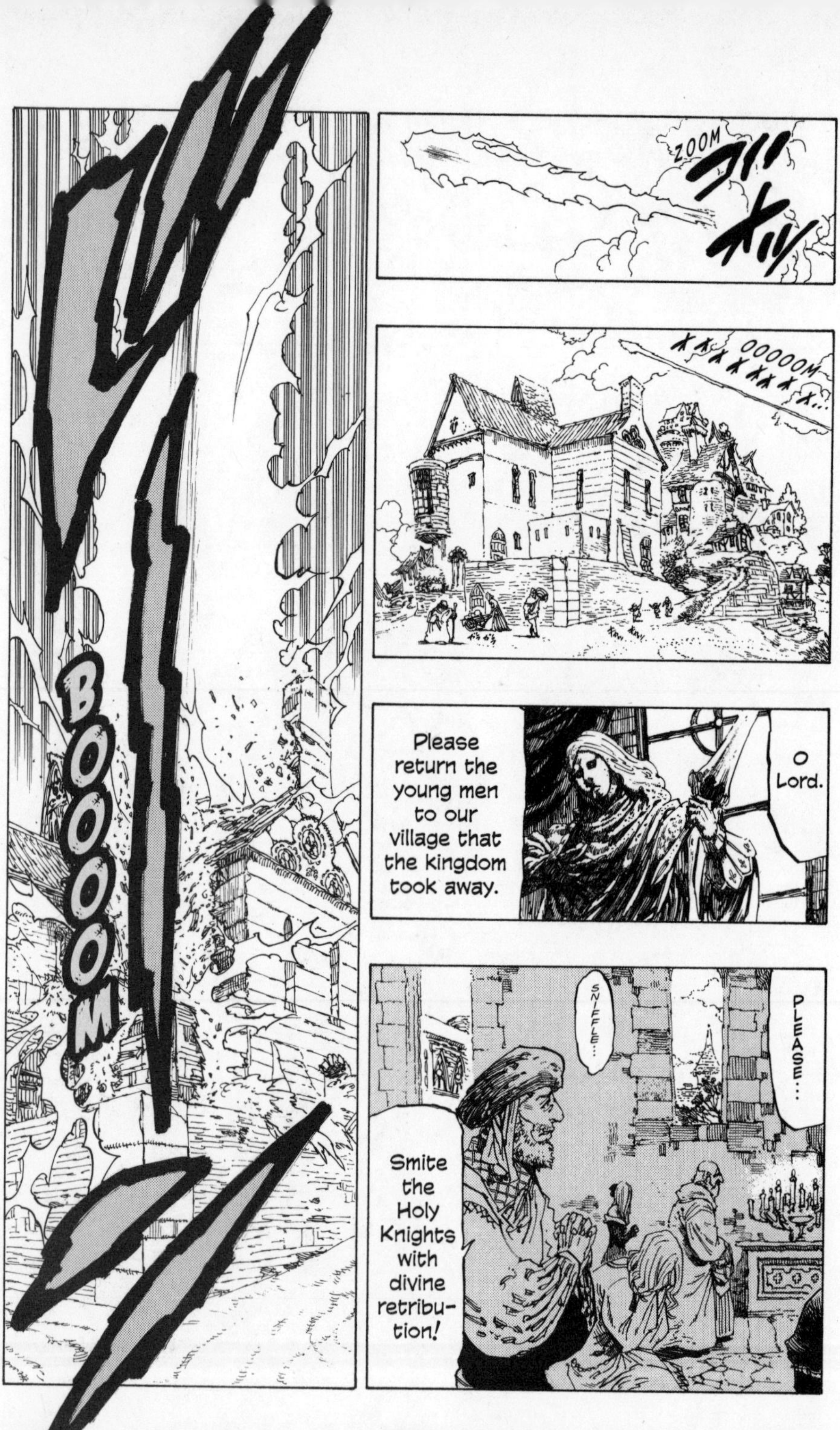
ZOOM
OOOOOM...
O Lord.
Please return the young men to our village that the kingdom took away.
PLEASE...
SNIFFLE...
Smite the Holy Knights with divine retribution!
BOOOOOM

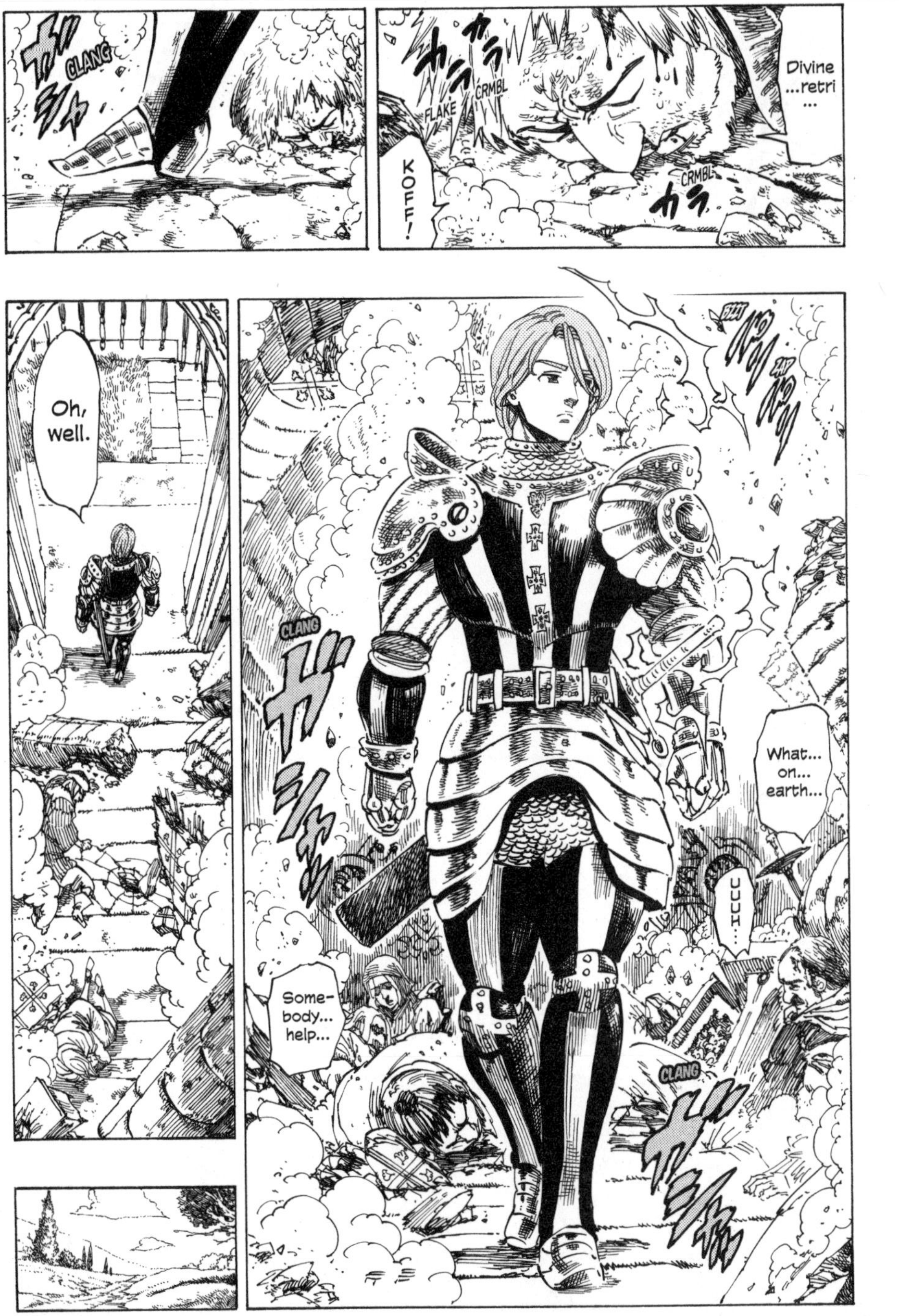
Divine ...retri ...
CRMBL
FLAKE
KOFF!
CRMBL
CLANG
CLANG
What... on... earth...
UUUH...
Some-body... help...
CLANG
Oh, well.

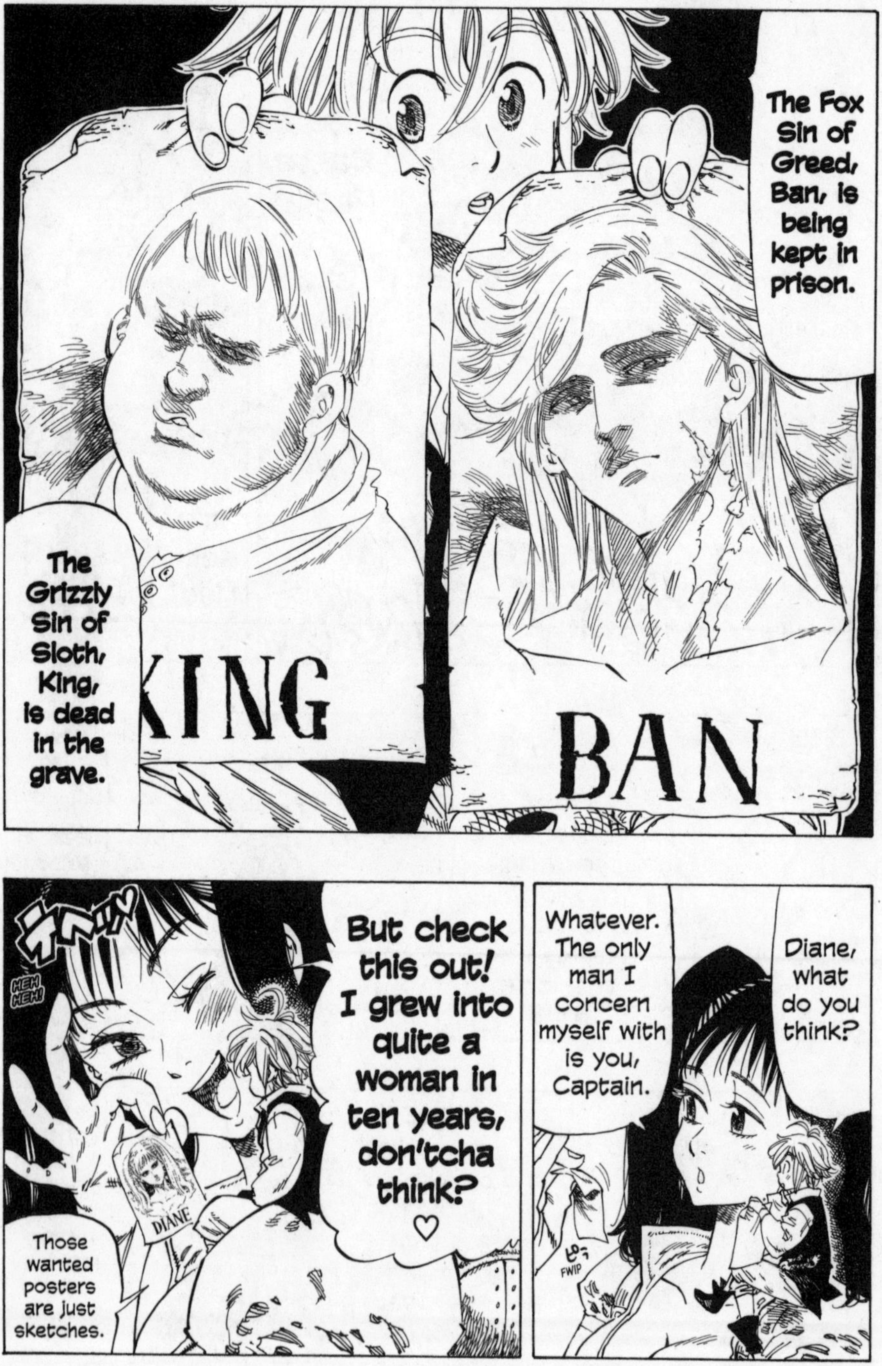
The Fox Sin of Greed, Ban, is being kept in prison.
BAN
KING
The Grizzly Sin of Sloth, King, is dead in the grave.
Diane, what do you think?
Whatever. The only man I concern myself with is you, Captain.
FWIP
But check this out! I grew into quite a woman in ten years, don'tcha think? ♡
HEH HEH!
DIANE
Those wanted posters are just sketches.

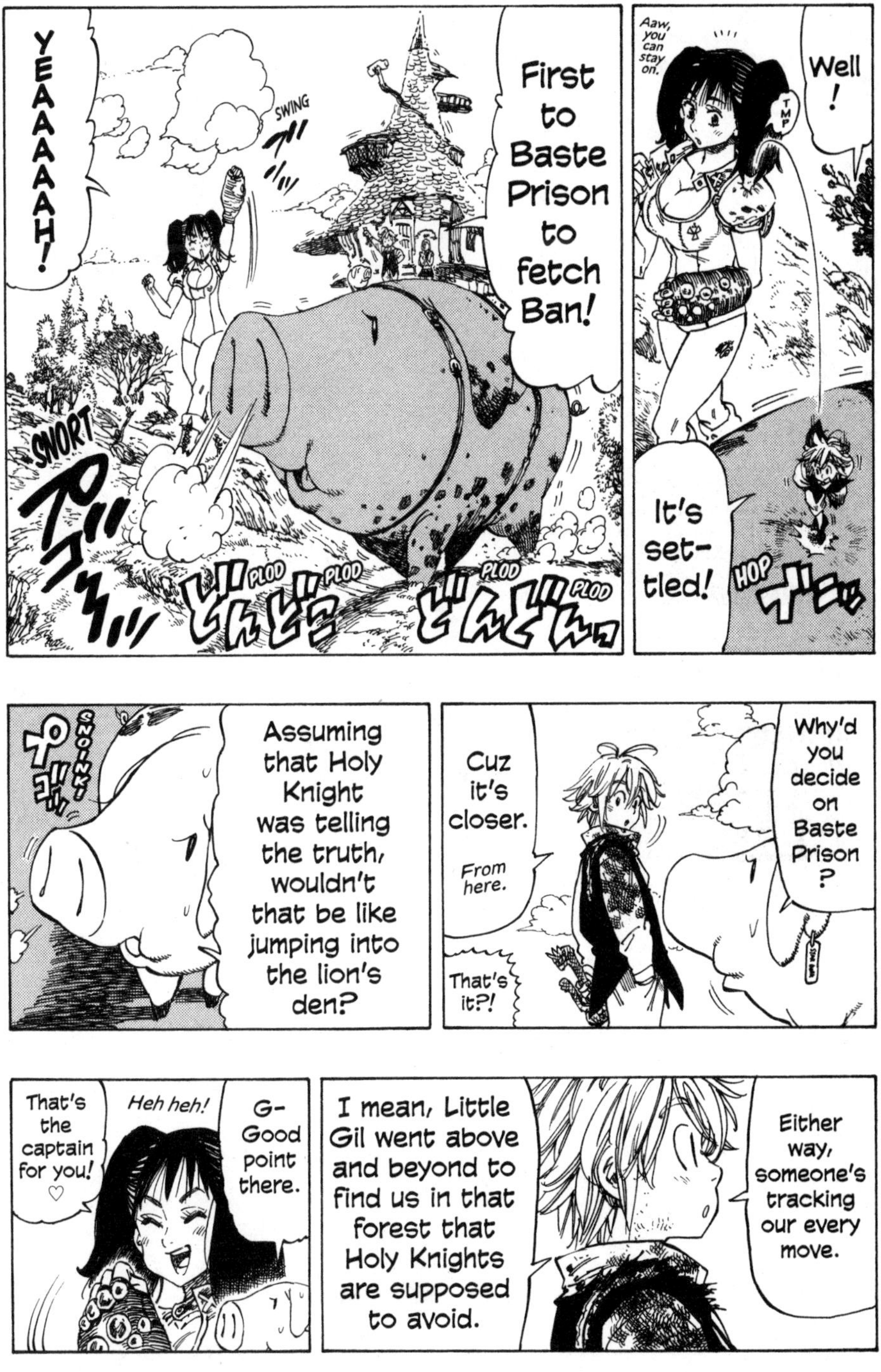

Well!
TMP
Aaw, you can stay on.
It's set-tled!
HOP
First to Baste Prison to fetch Ban!
SWING
YEAAAAAH!
SNORT
PLOD PLOD
PLOD PLOD
Why'd you decide on Baste Prison?
Cuz it's closer.
From here.
That's it?!
Assuming that Holy Knight was telling the truth, wouldn't that be like jumping into the lion's den?
SNOINK!
Either way, someone's tracking our every move.
I mean, Little Gil went above and beyond to find us in that forest that Holy Knights are supposed to avoid.
G-Good point there.
Heh heh!
That's the captain for you! ♡

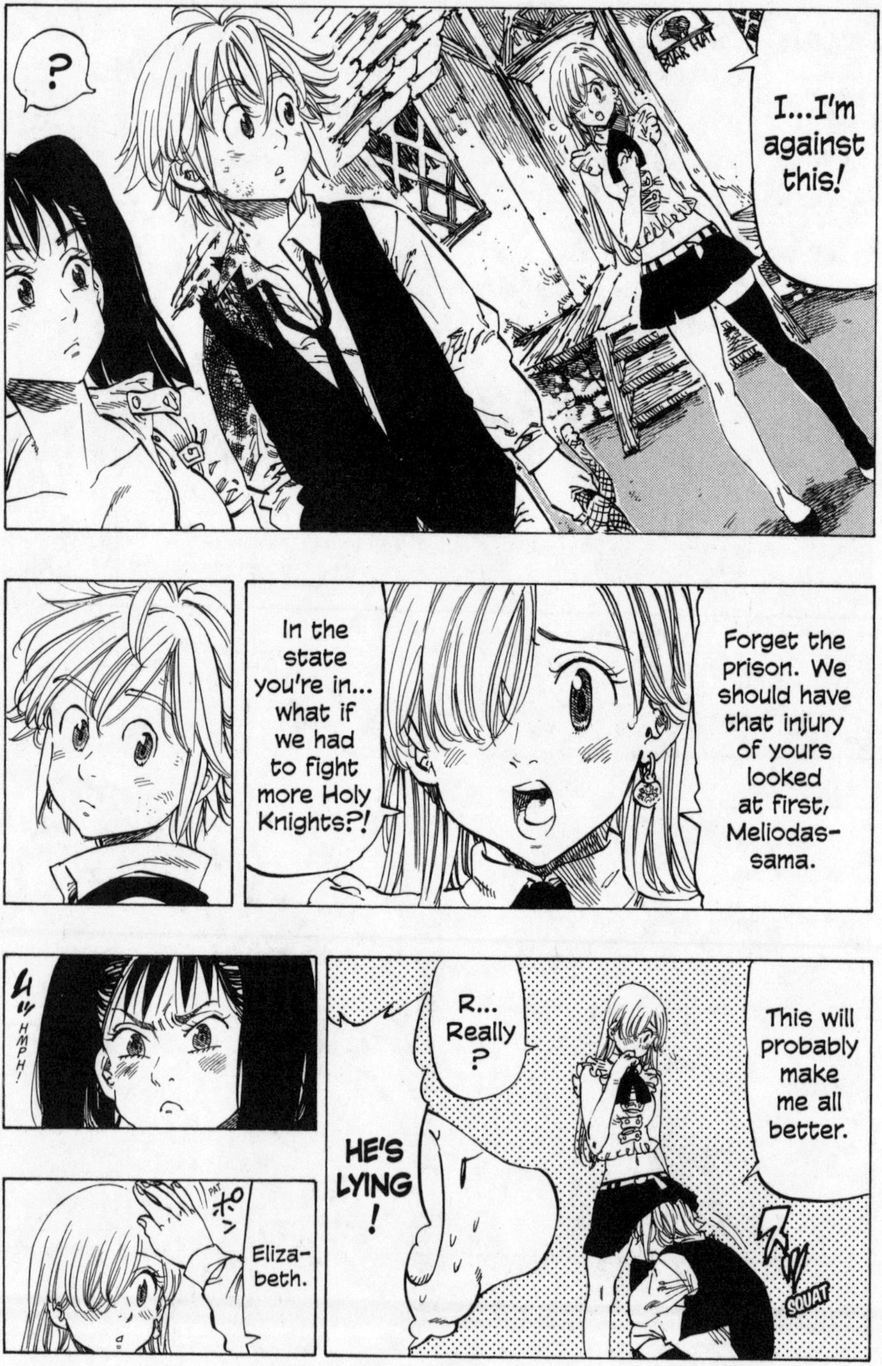
BOAR HAT
I...I'm against this!
?
Forget the prison. We should have that injury of yours looked at first, Meliodas-sama.
In the state you're in... what if we had to fight more Holy Knights?!
This will probably make me all better.
R... Really?
HE'S LYING!
SQUAT
ムッ
HMPH!
ポン
PAT
Eliza-beth.

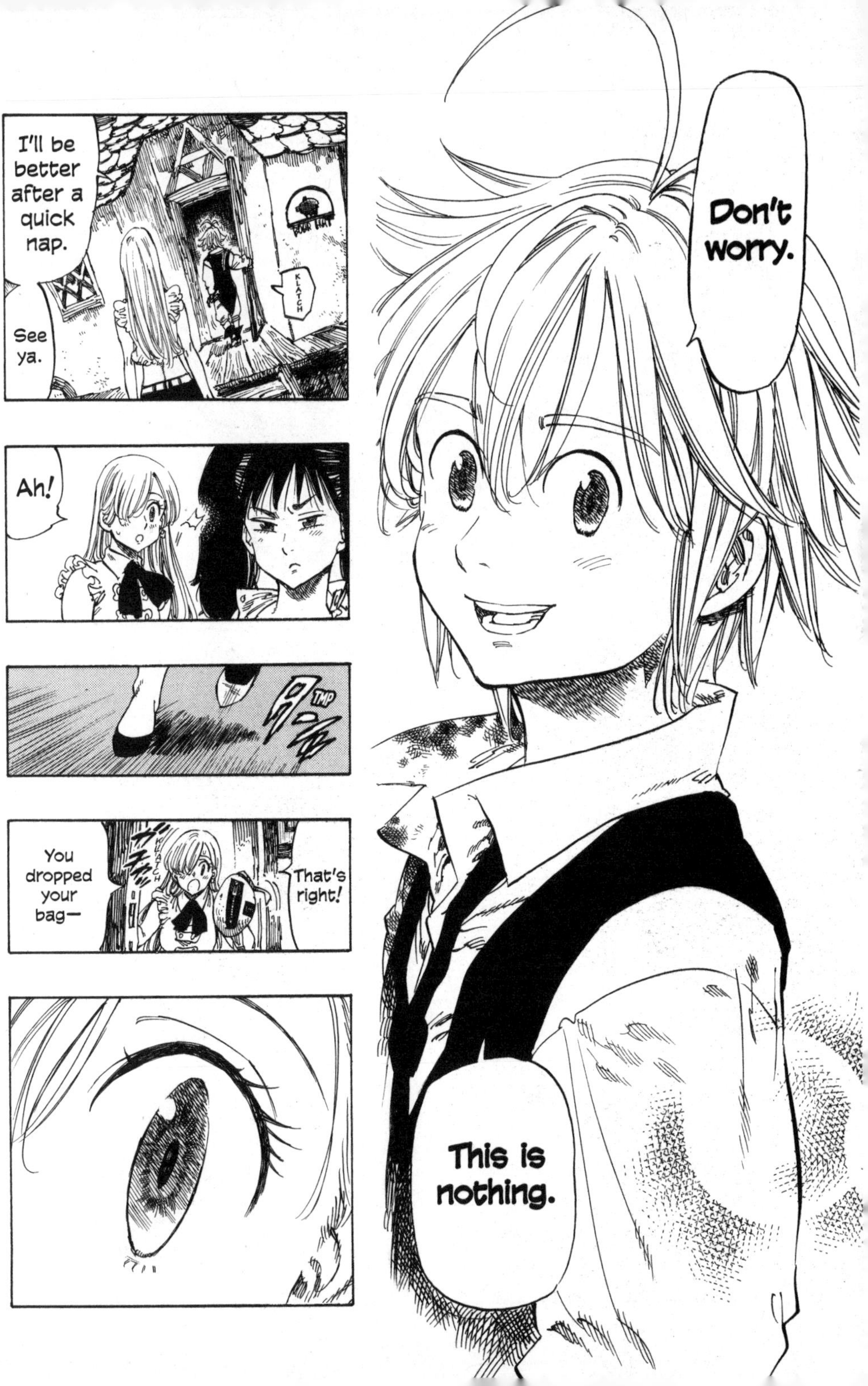
Don't worry.
This is nothing.
I'll be better after a quick nap.
KLATCH
See ya.
Ah!
TMP
That's right!
KLATCH
You dropped your bag—

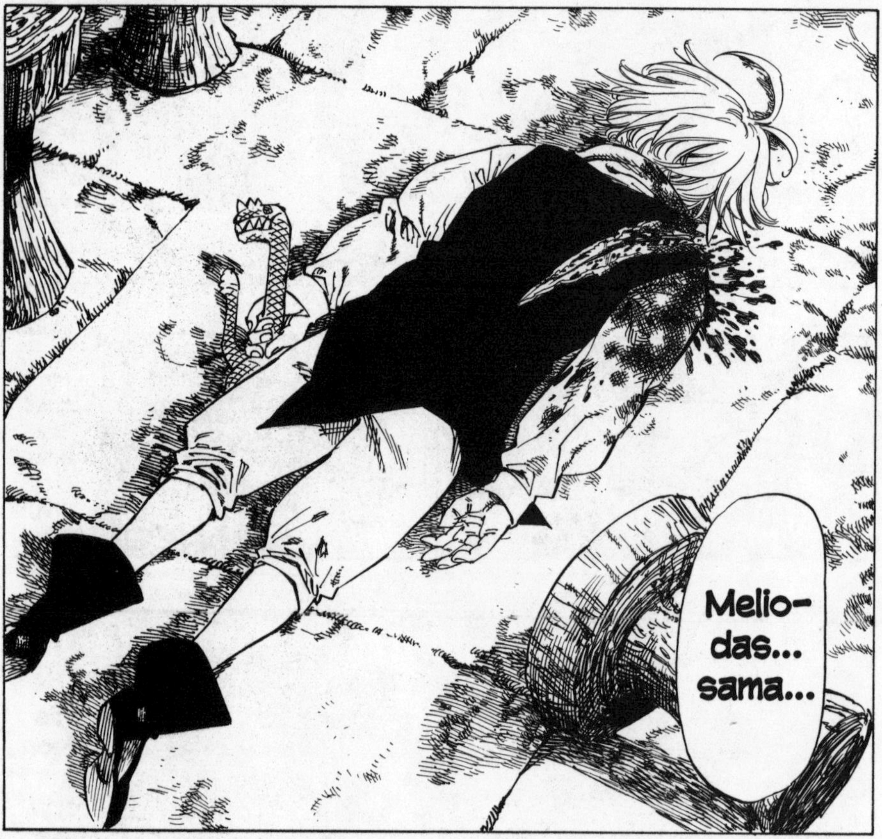
Melio-
das...
sama...

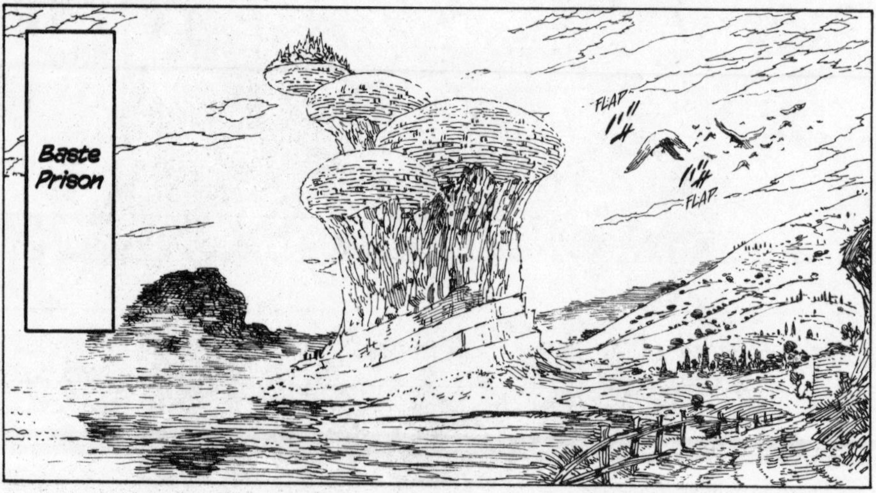
Baste
Prison
FLAP
FLAP

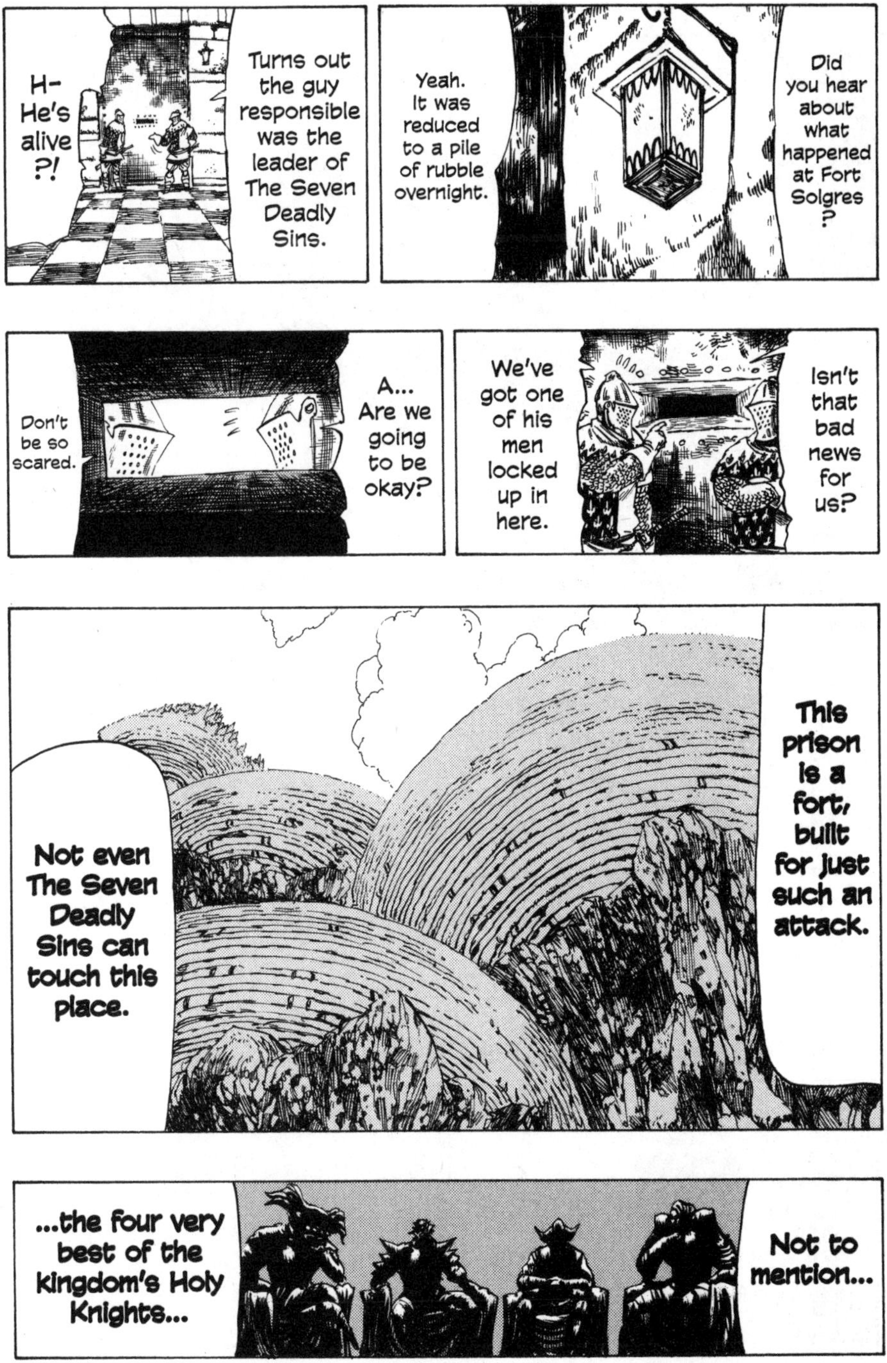
Did you hear about what happened at Fort Solgres?
Yeah. It was reduced to a pile of rubble overnight.
Turns out the guy responsible was the leader of The Seven Deadly Sins.
H- He's alive?!
Isn't that bad news for us?
We've got one of his men locked up in here.
A... Are we going to be okay?
Don't be so scared.
This prison is a fort, built for just such an attack.
Not even The Seven Deadly Sins can touch this place.
Not to mention...
...the four very best of the kingdom's Holy Knights...

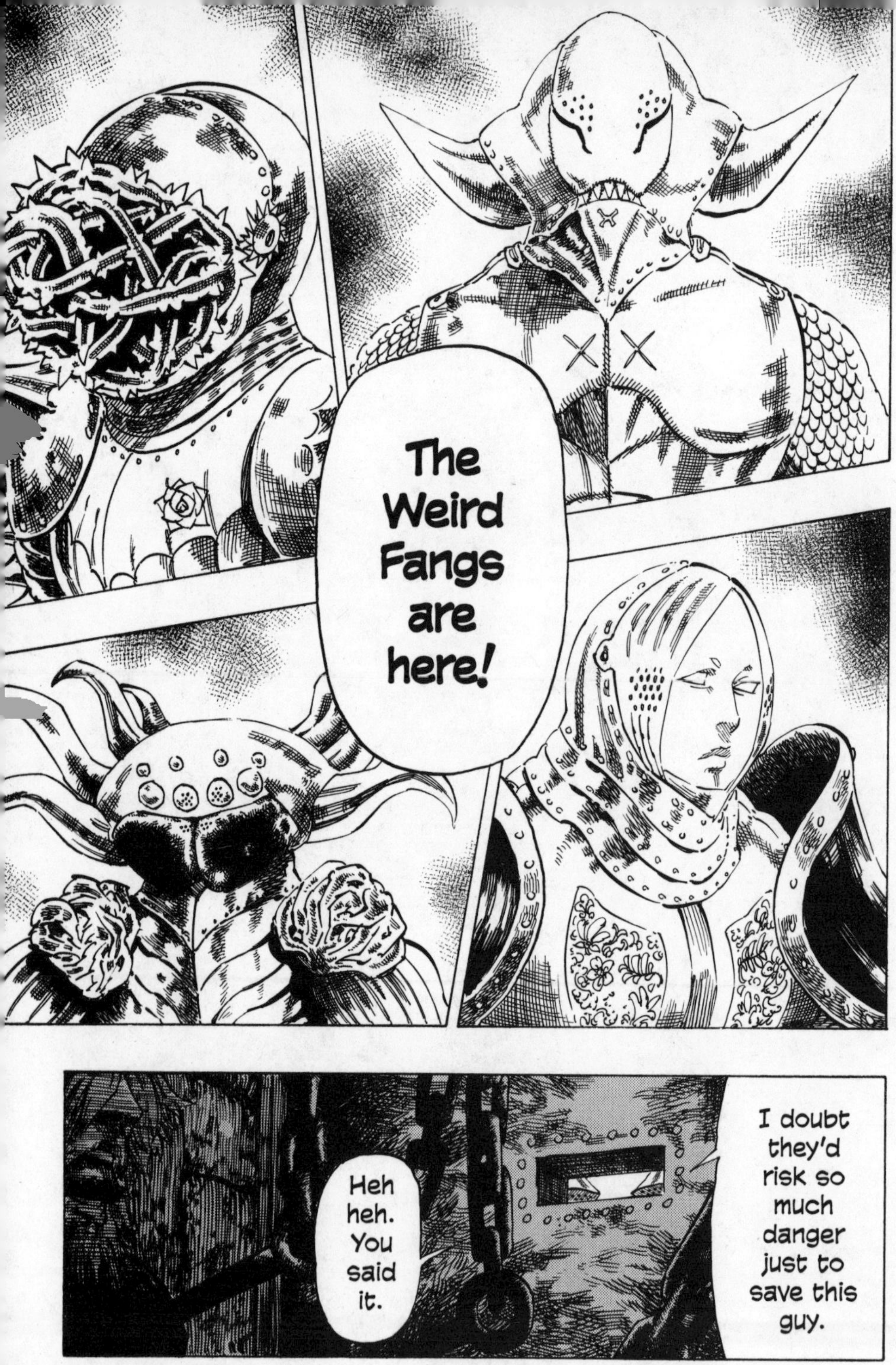
The Weird Fangs are here!
I doubt they'd risk so much danger just to save this guy.
Heh heh. You said it.

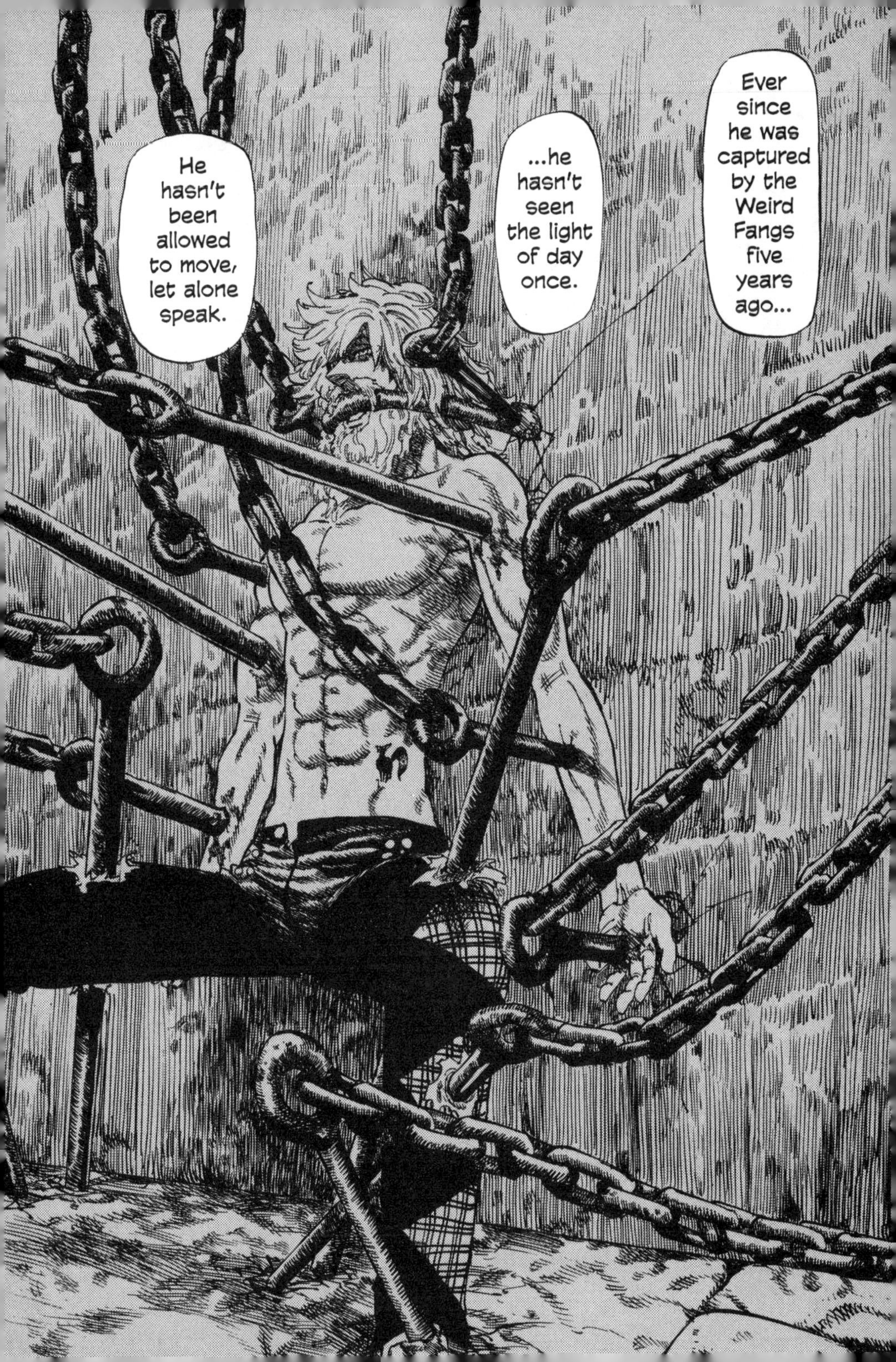
Ever since he was captured by the Weird Fangs five years ago...
...he hasn't seen the light of day once.
He hasn't been allowed to move, let alone speak.

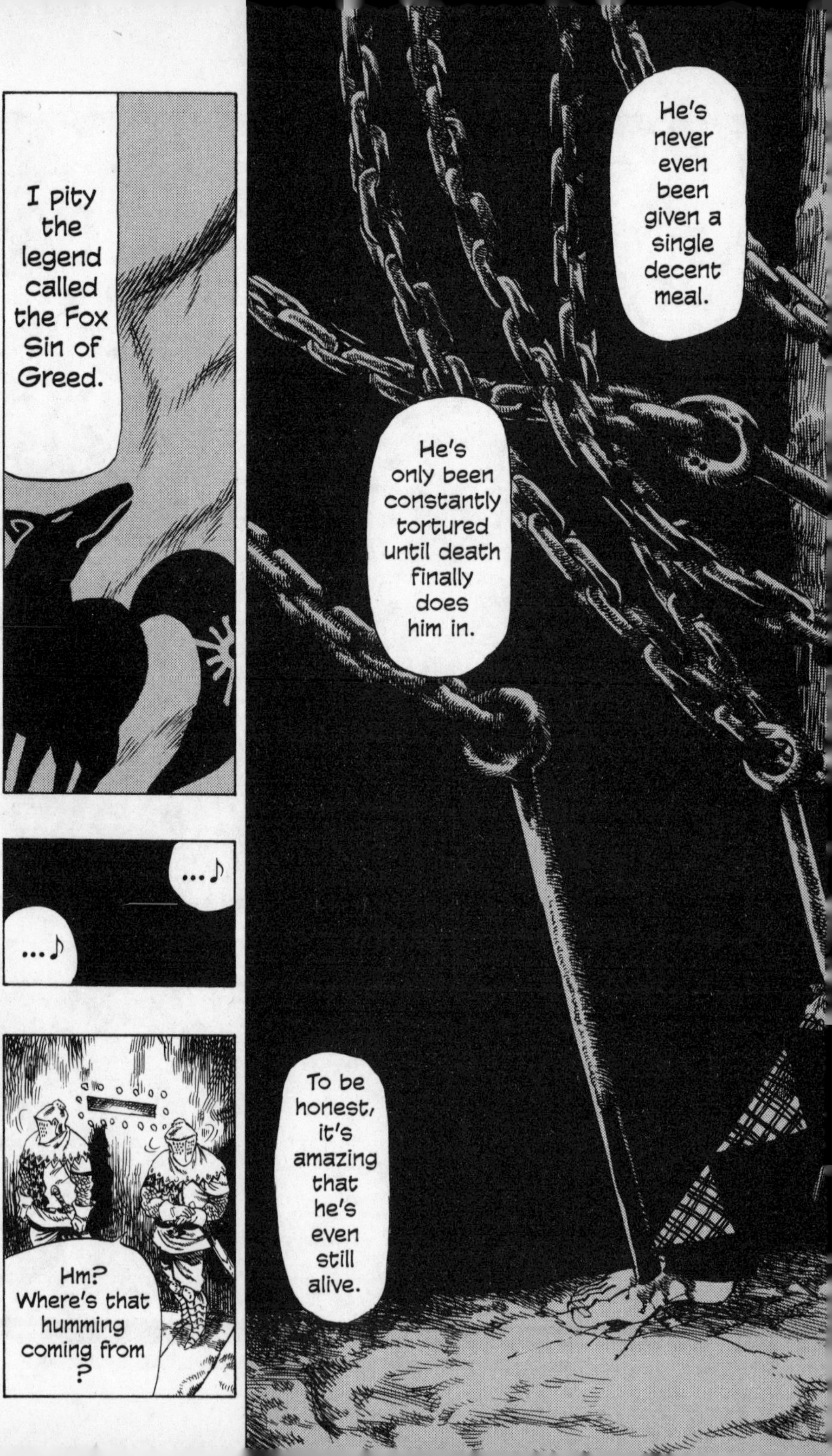
He's never even been given a single decent meal.
He's only been constantly tortured until death finally does him in.
To be honest, it's amazing that he's even still alive.
I pity the legend called the Fox Sin of Greed.
...♪
...♪
Hm? Where's that humming coming from?

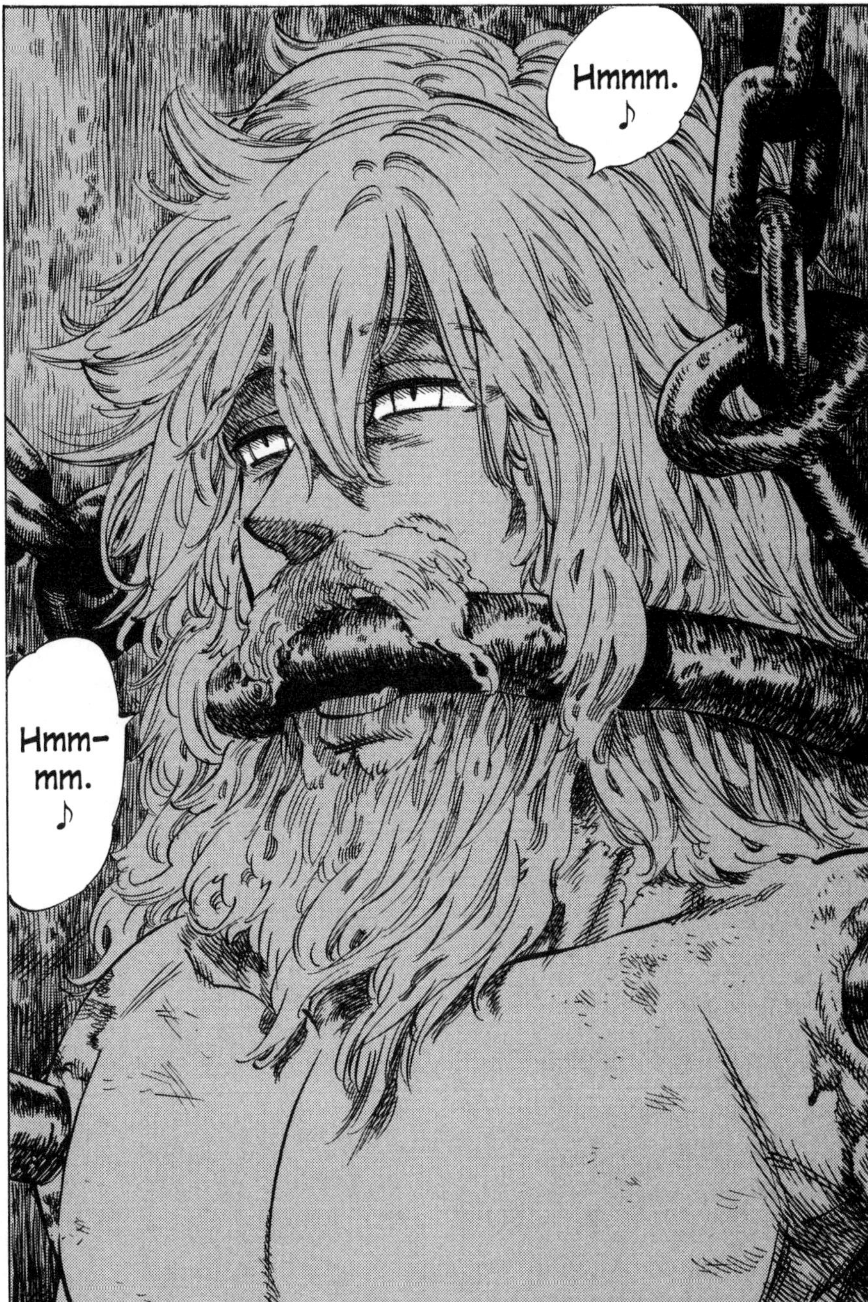
Hmmm. ♪
Hmm-mm. ♪

Chapter 8 - A Girl's Dream

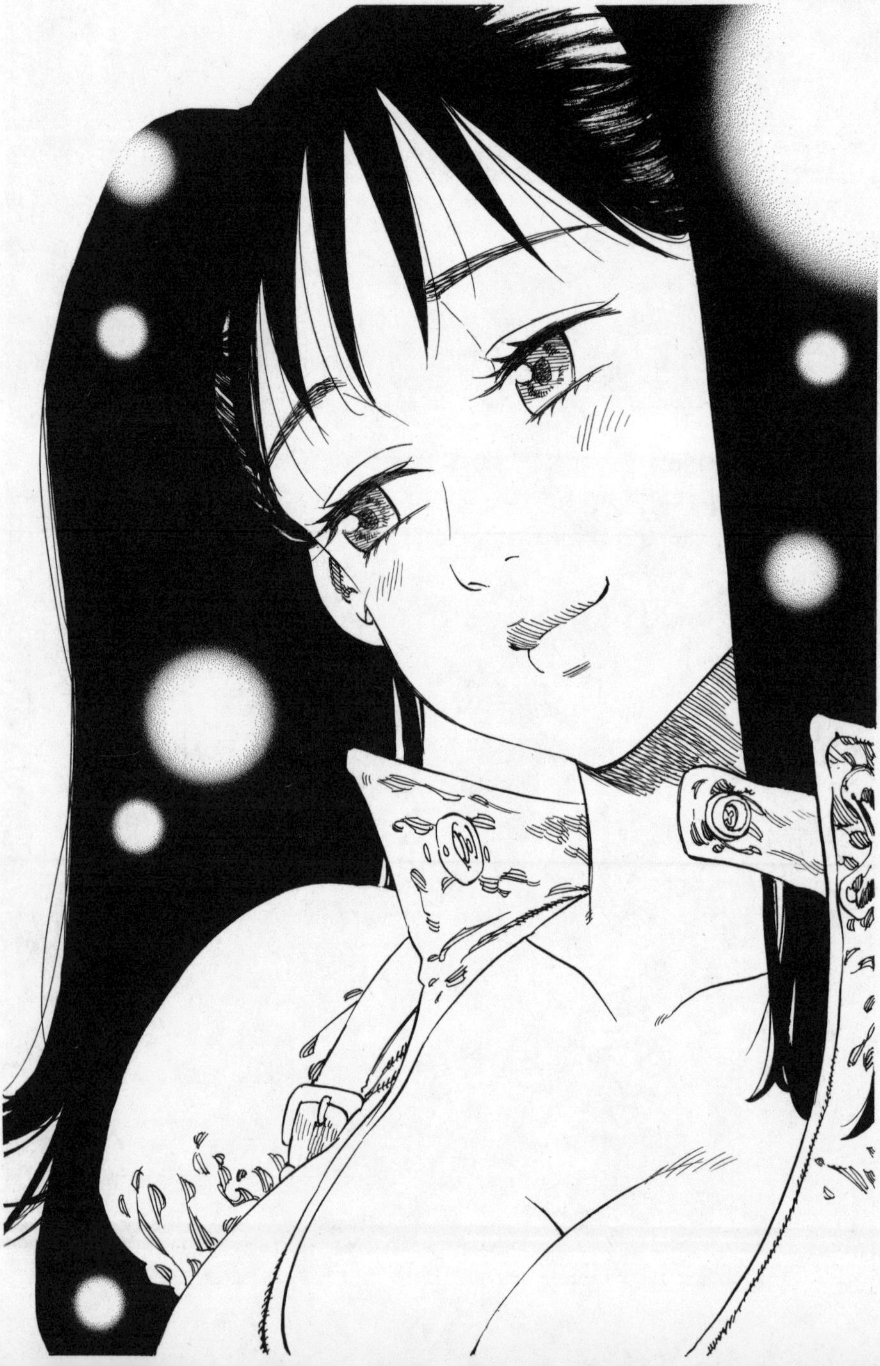

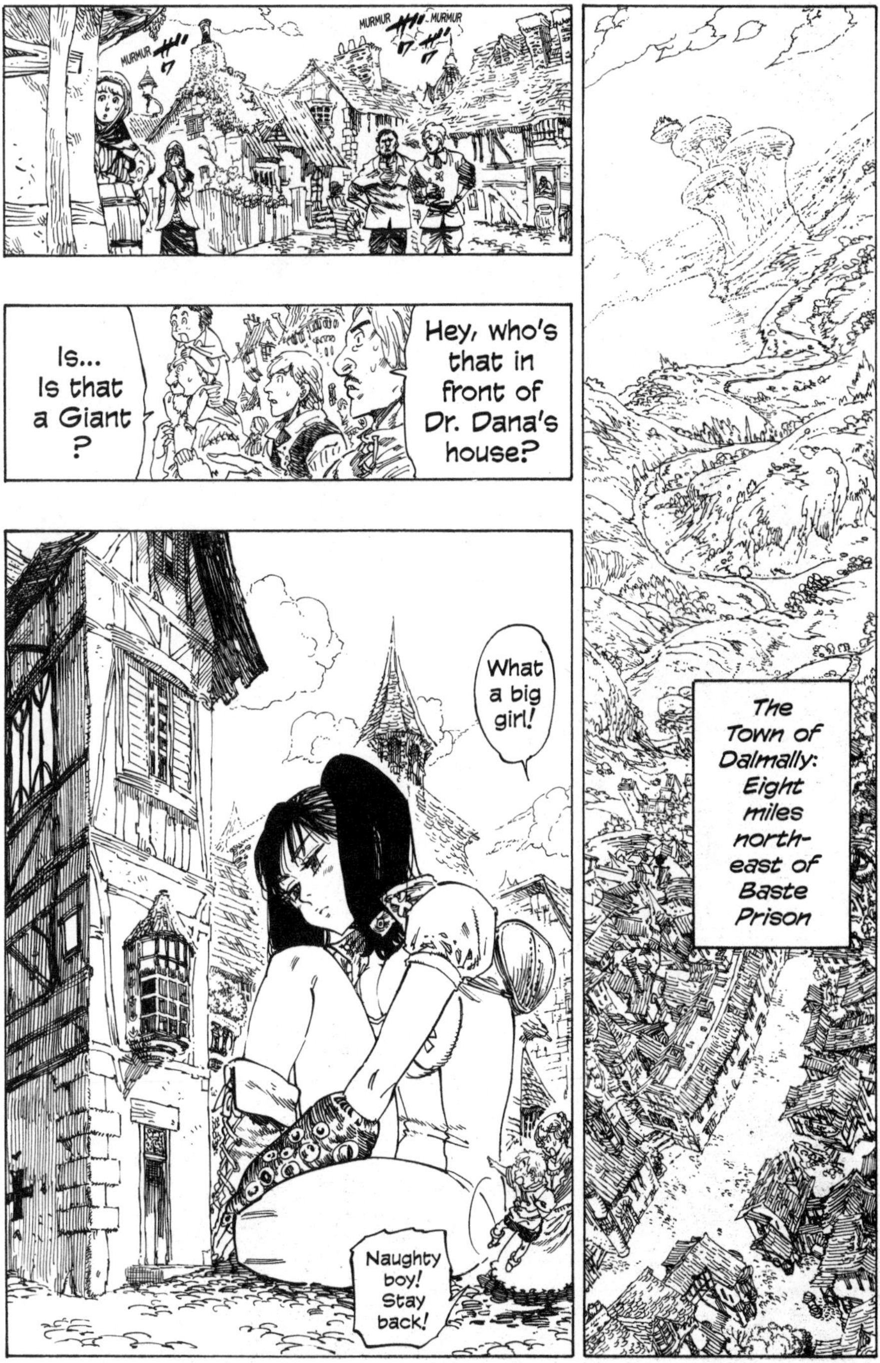
The Town of Dalmally: Eight miles north-east of Baste Prison
MURMUR MURMUR
MURMUR
Hey, who's that in front of Dr. Dana's house?
Is... Is that a Giant?
What a big girl!
Naughty boy! Stay back!

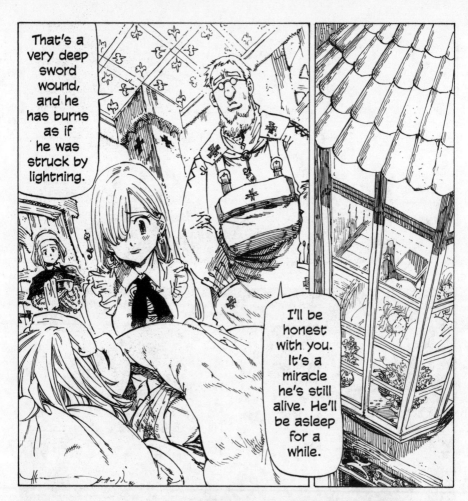

That's a very deep sword wound, and he has burns as if he was struck by lightning.

I'll be honest with you. It's a miracle he's still alive. He'll be asleep for a while.

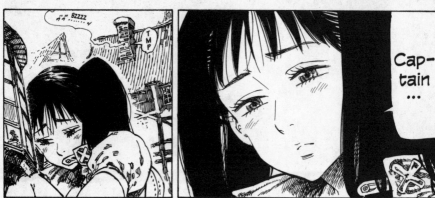

BZZZZ

TMP

Cap-tain...

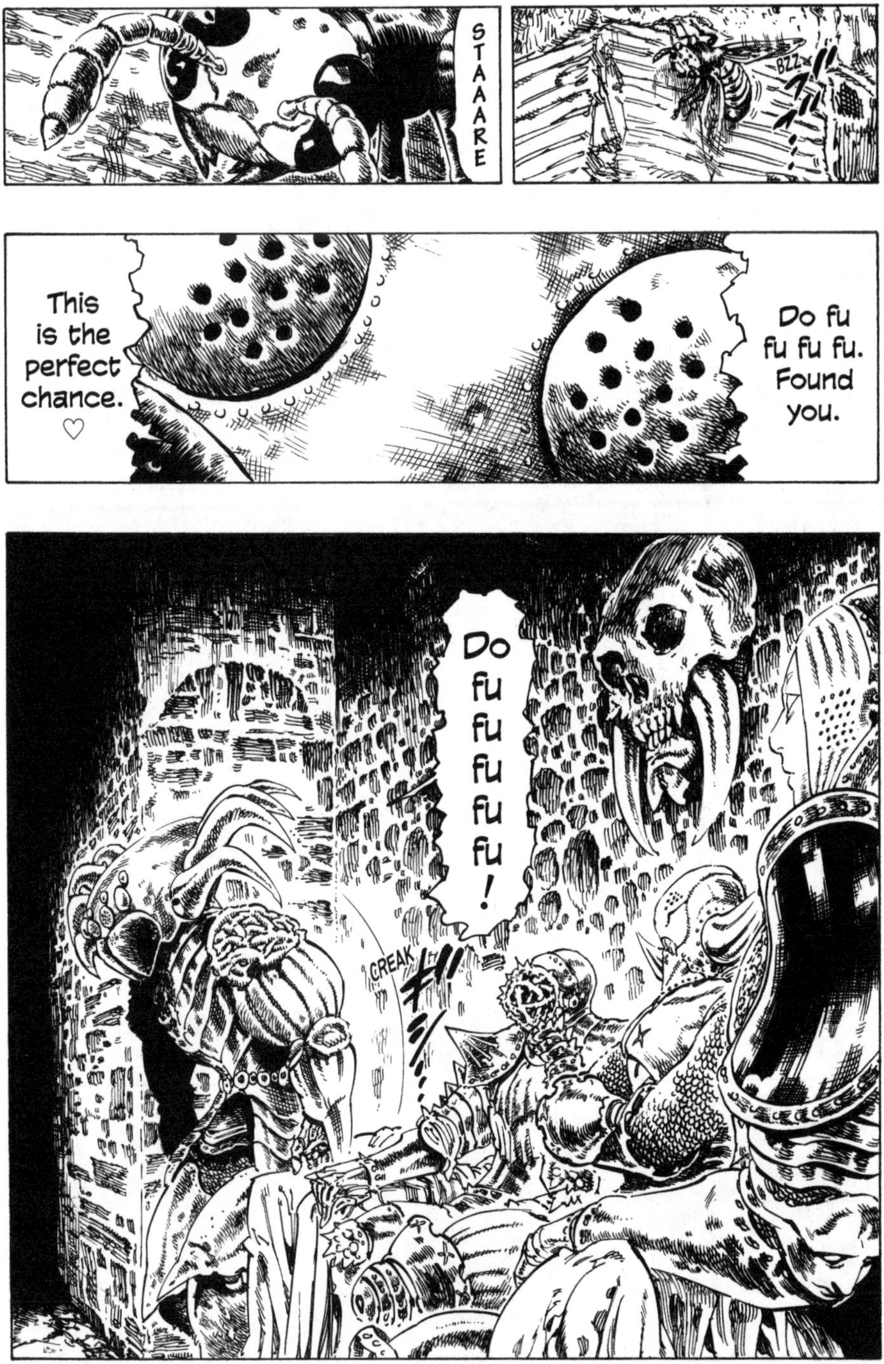
BZZ
STAAARE
Do fu fu fu fu. Found you.
This is the perfect chance. ♡
Do fu fu fu fu fu!
CREAK

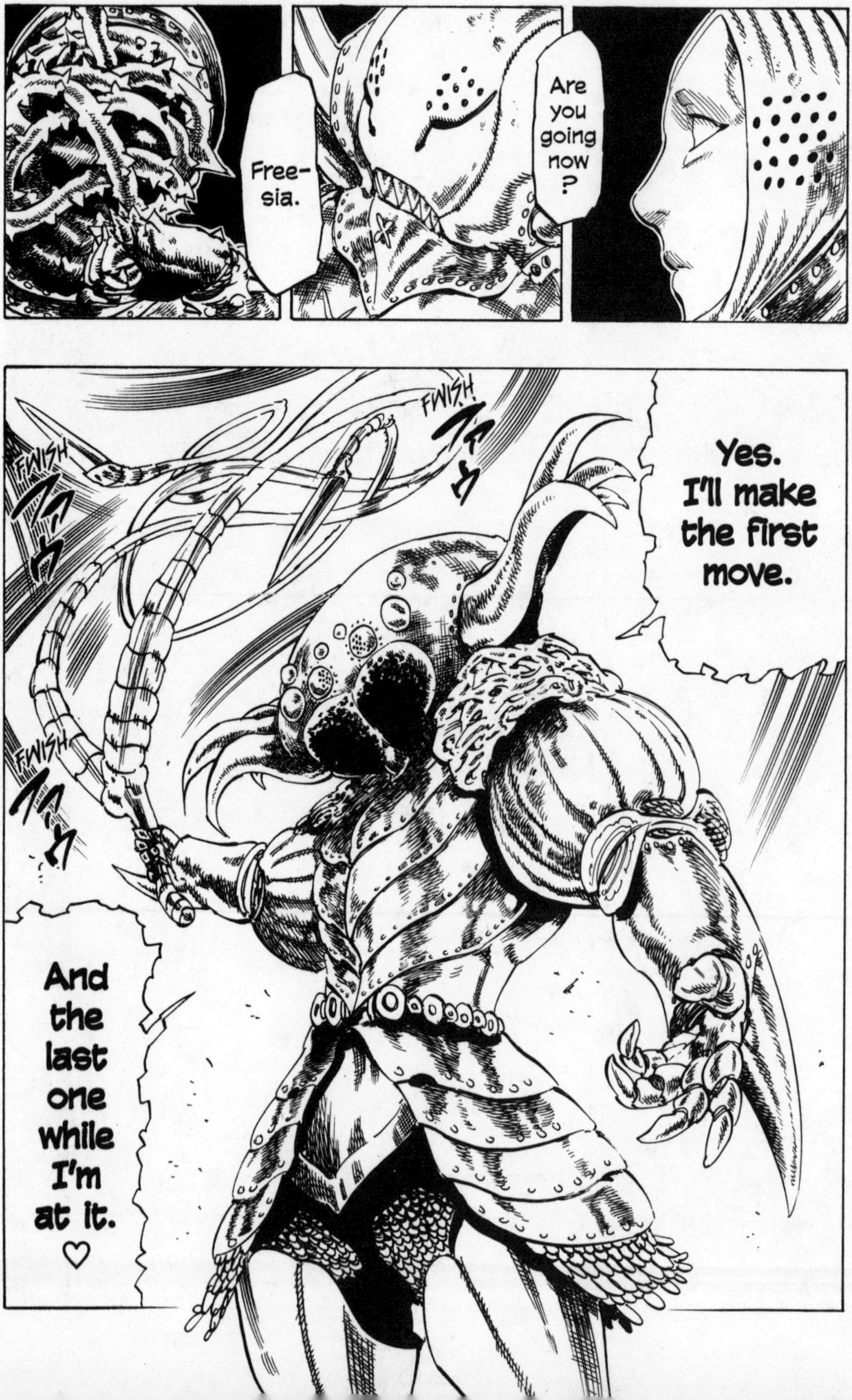
Are you going now?
Free-sia.
Yes. I'll make the first move.
FWISH
FWISH
FWISH
And the last one while I'm at it. ♡

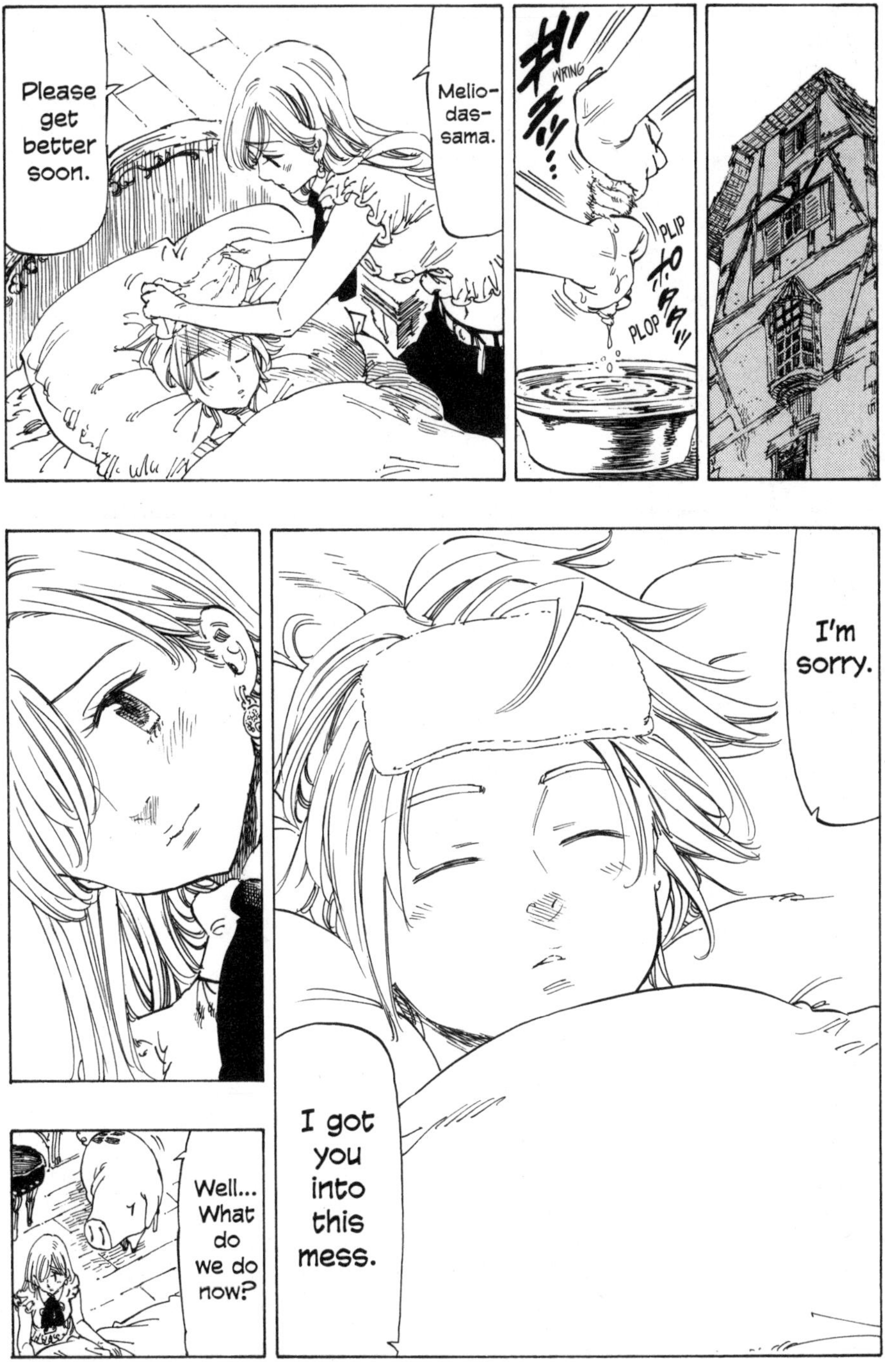
WRING
PLIP
PLOP
Melio-dassama.
Please get better soon.
I'm sorry.
I got you into this mess.
Well... What do we do now?

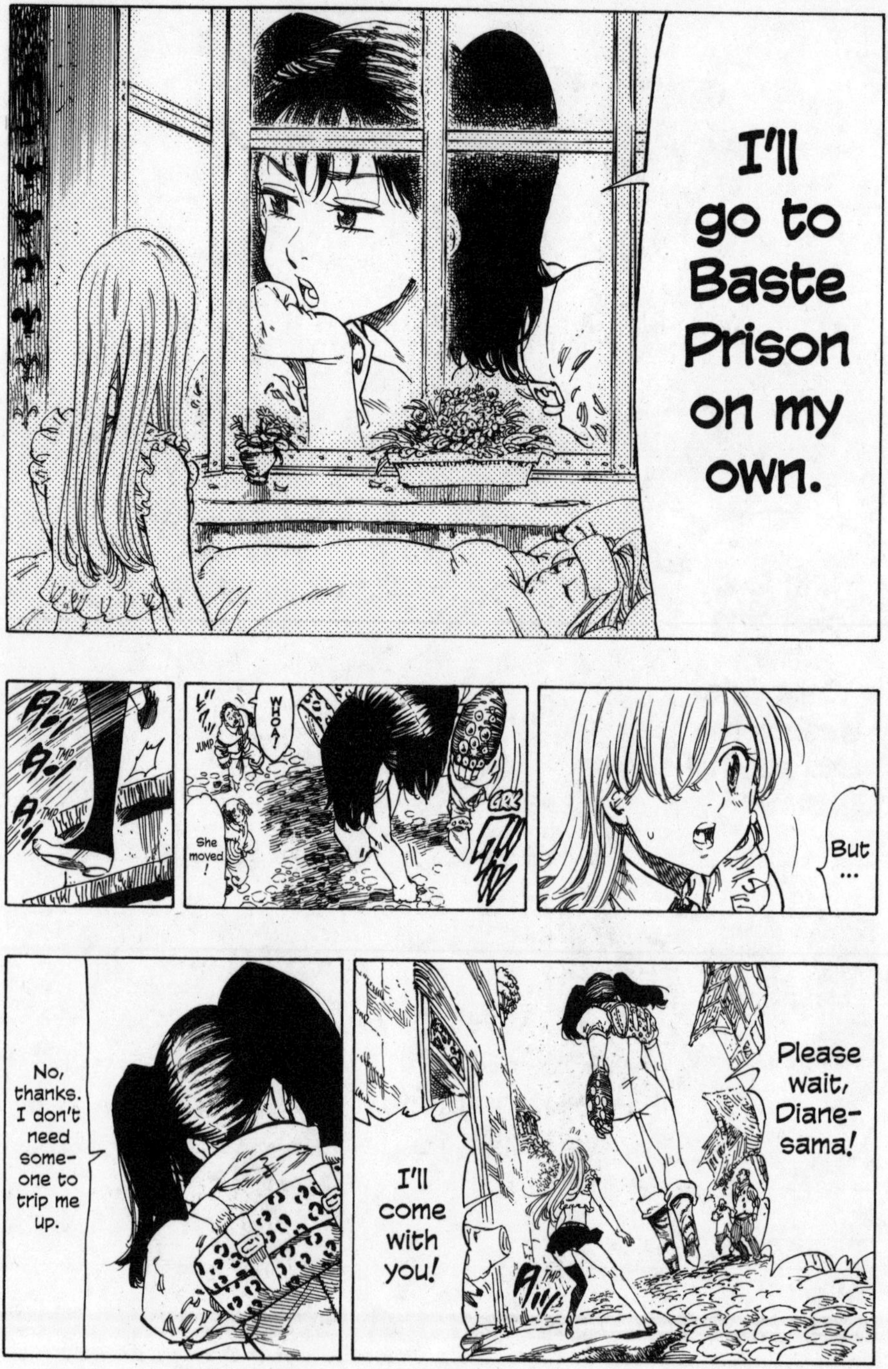
I'll go to Baste Prison on my own.
But ...
WHOA!
JUMP
She moved!
GRK
TMP
TMP
TMP
Please wait, Diane-sama!
I'll come with you!
TMP
No, thanks. I don't need someone to trip me up.

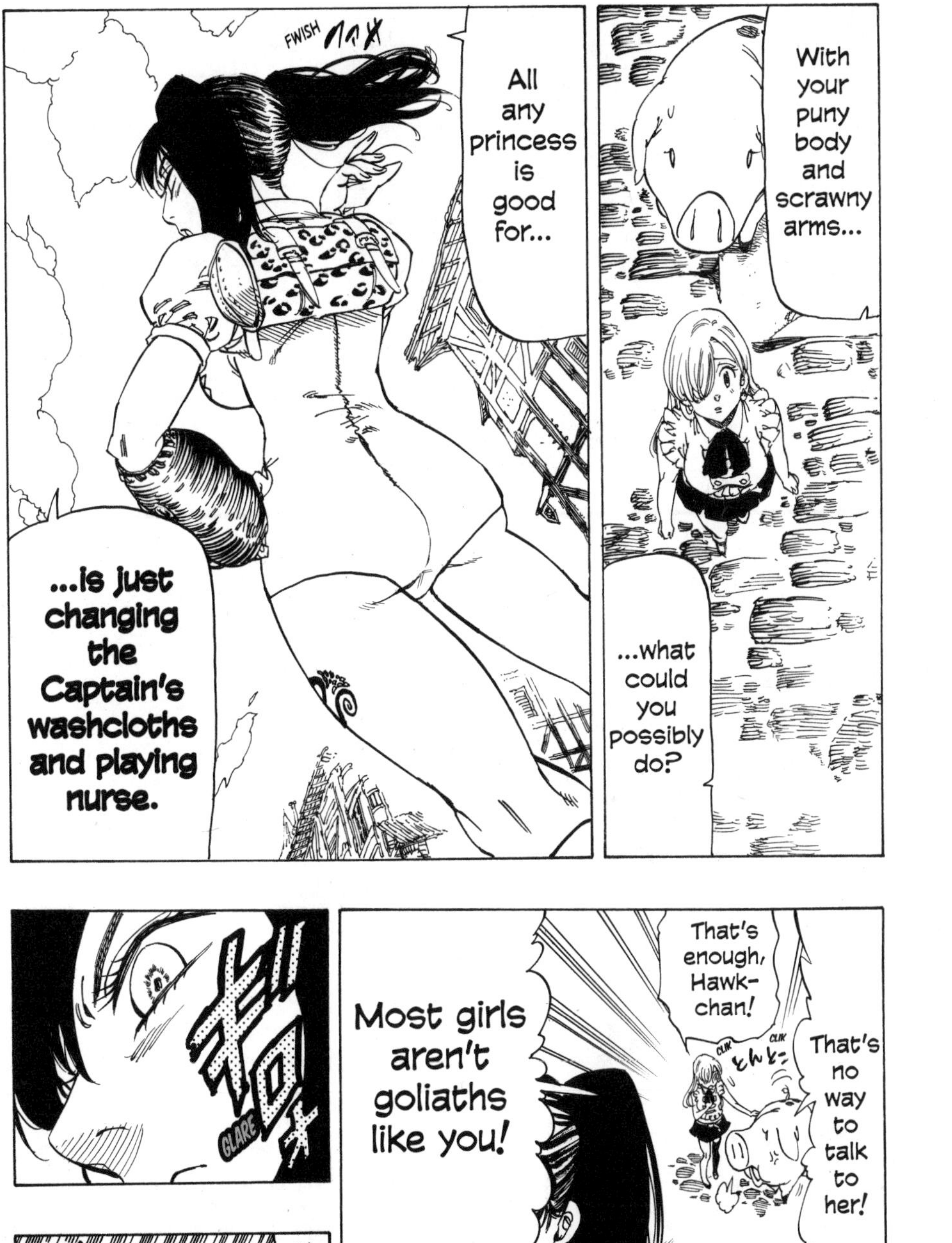
With your puny body and scrawny arms...
...what could you possibly do?
FWISH
All any princess is good for...
...is just changing the Captain's washcloths and playing nurse.
That's enough, Hawk-chan!
That's no way to talk to her!
CLIK CLIK
Most girls aren't goliaths like you!
GLARE
JUMP
YIPE!

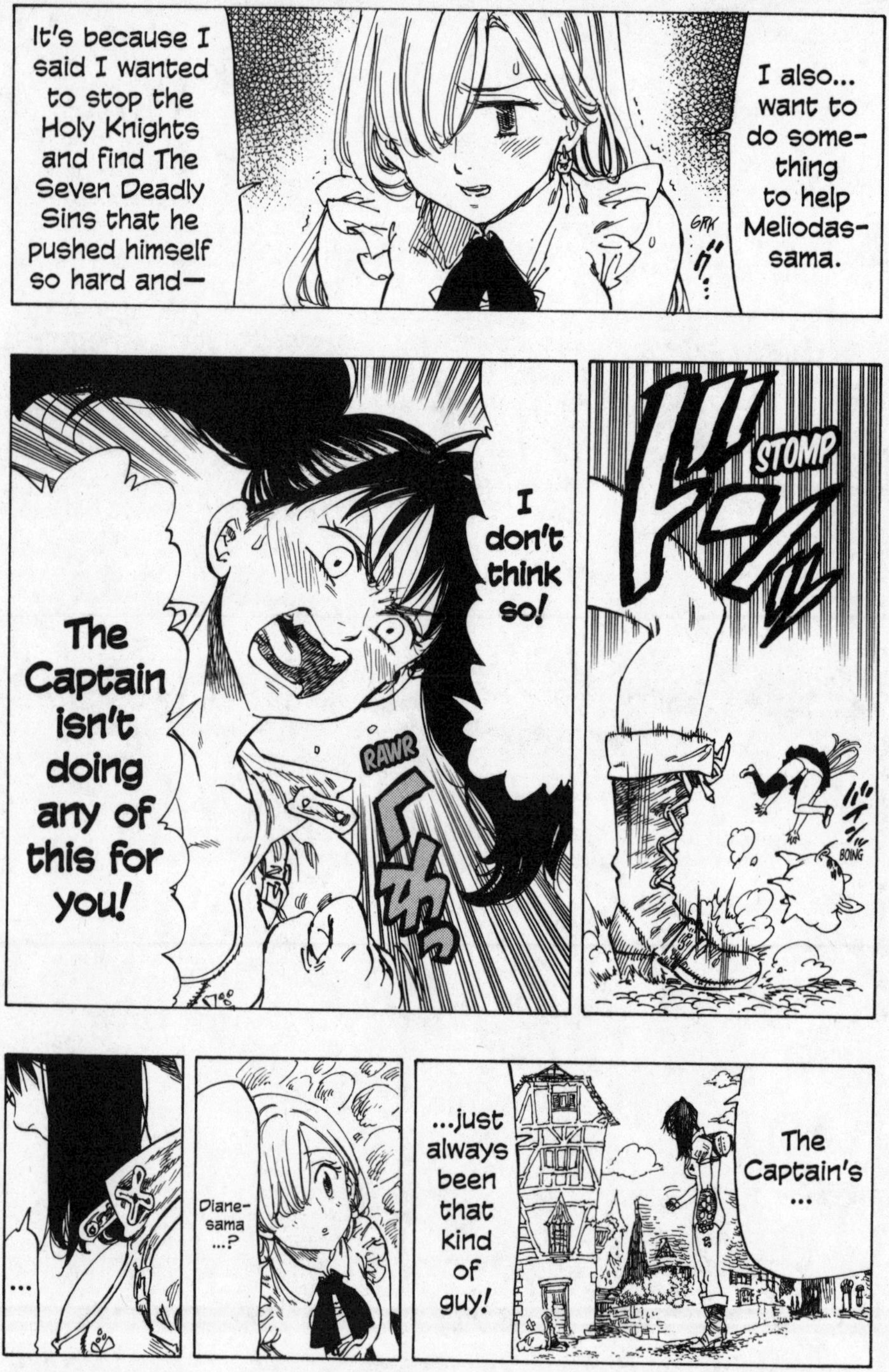
I also... want to do some-thing to help Meliodas-sama.
GRK
It's because I said I wanted to stop the Holy Knights and find The Seven Deadly Sins that he pushed himself so hard and—
STOMP
BOING
I don't think so!
RAWR
The Captain isn't doing any of this for you!
The Captain's...
...just always been that kind of guy!
Diane-sama ...?
...

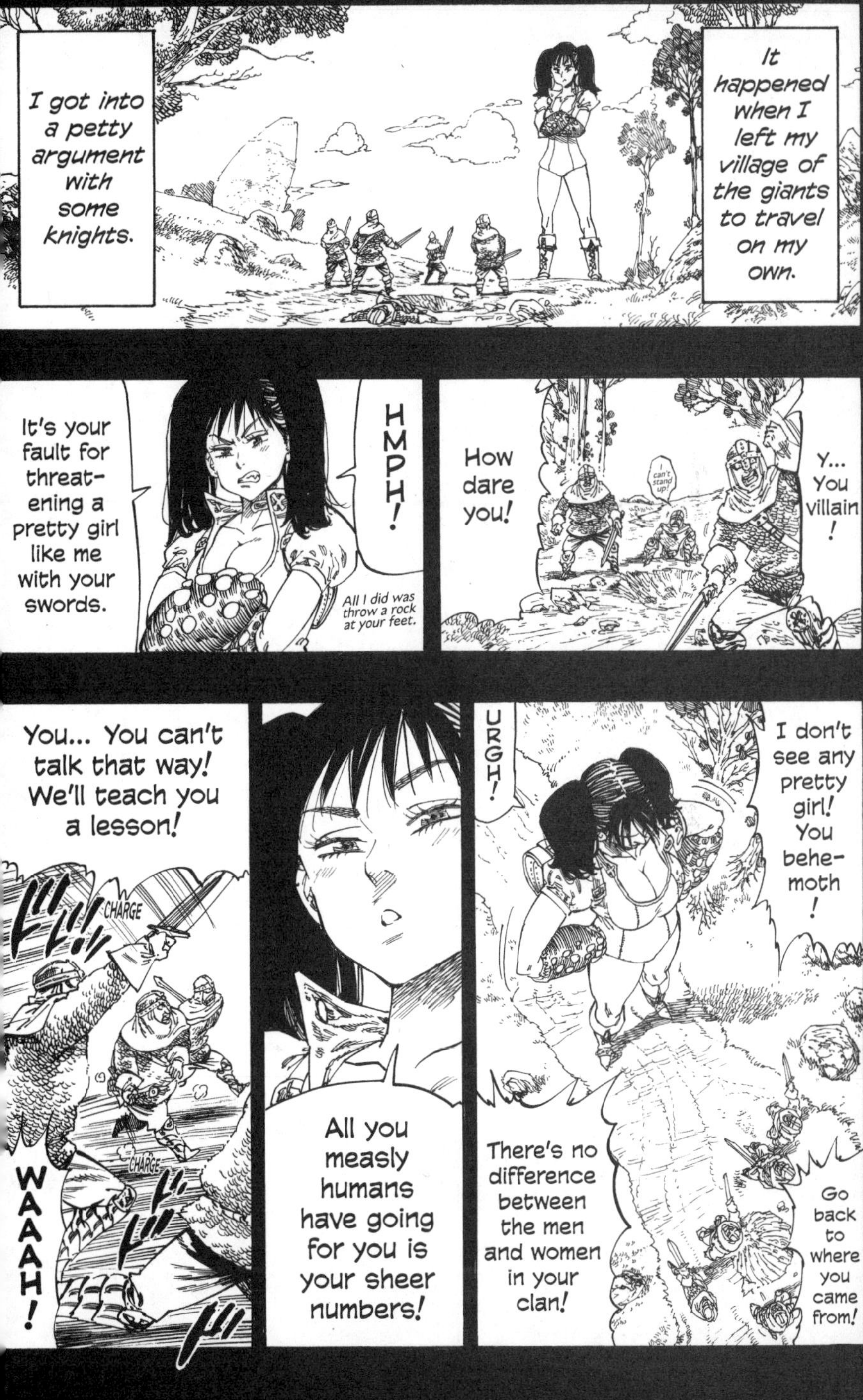
It happened when I left my village of the giants to travel on my own.
I got into a petty argument with some knights.
Y... You villain!
I can't stand up!
How dare you!
HMPH!
It's your fault for threatening a pretty girl like me with your swords.
All I did was throw a rock at your feet.
URGH!
I don't see any pretty girl! You behemoth!
Go back to where you came from!
There's no difference between the men and women in your clan!
All you measly humans have going for you is your sheer numbers!
You... You can't talk that way! We'll teach you a lesson!
CHARGE
CHARGE
WAAAAH!

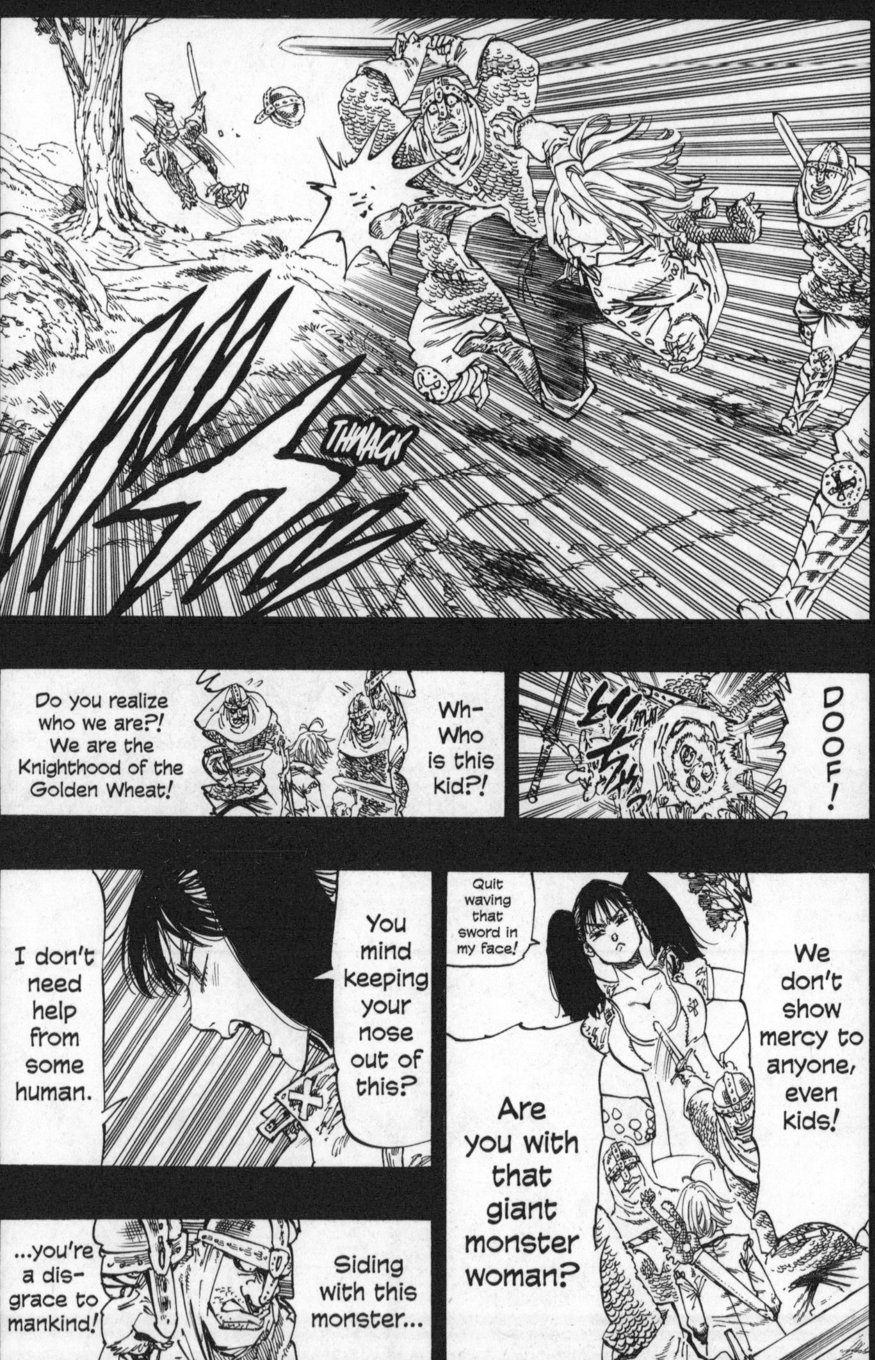

THWACK
DOOF!
Wh- Who is this kid?!
Do you realize who we are?! We are the Knighthood of the Golden Wheat!
We don't show mercy to anyone, even kids!
Are you with that giant monster woman?
Quit waving that sword in my face!
You mind keeping your nose out of this?
I don't need help from some human.
Siding with this monster...
...you're a disgrace to mankind!

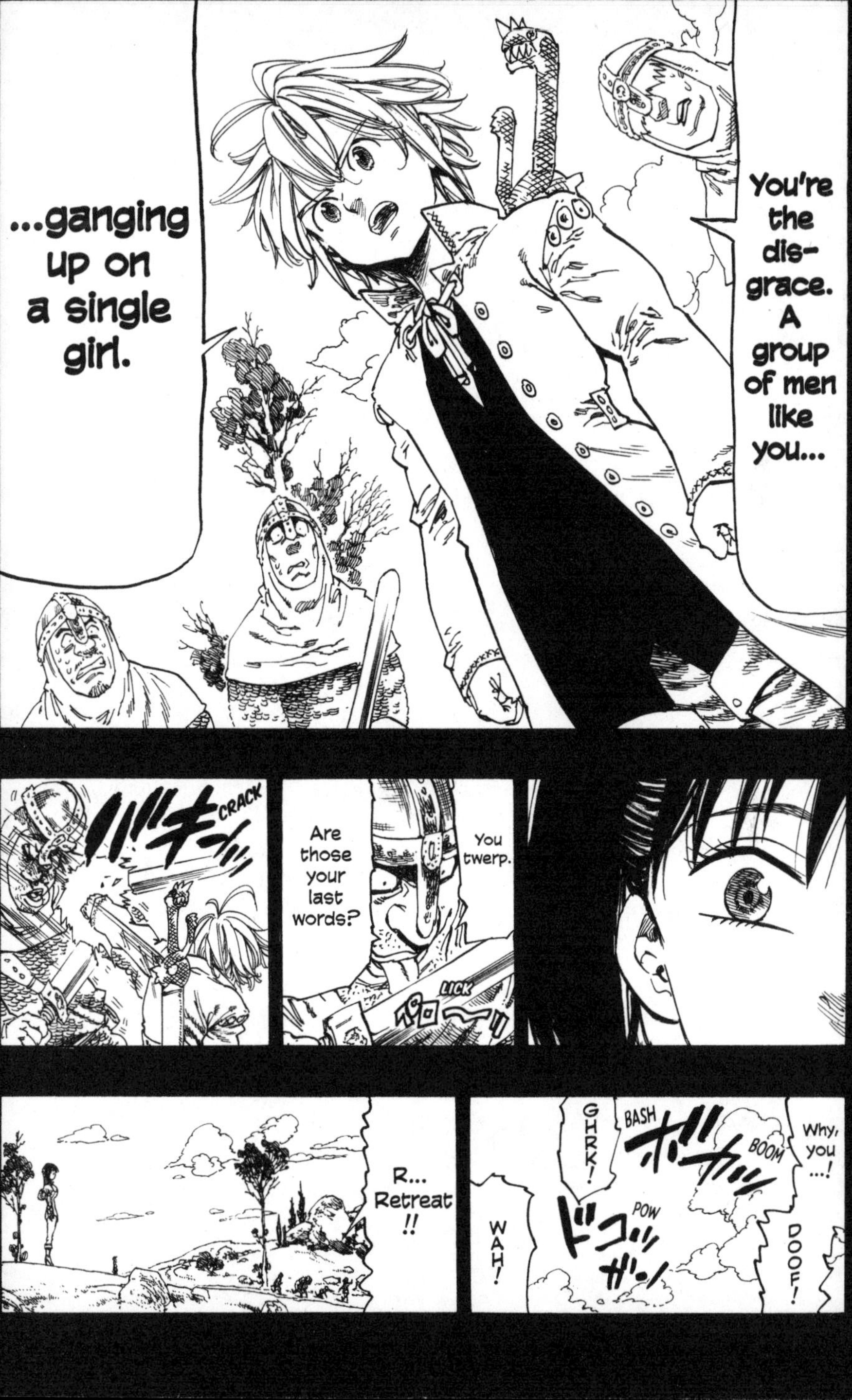
You're the dis-grace. A group of men like you...
...ganging up on a single girl.
You twerp.
Are those your last words?
ペロ～ッ
LICK
バキッ
CRACK
Why, you ...!
BASH
ボカッ
BOOM
GHRK!
DOOF!
POW
ドゴッ
ガッ
WAH!
R... Retreat!!

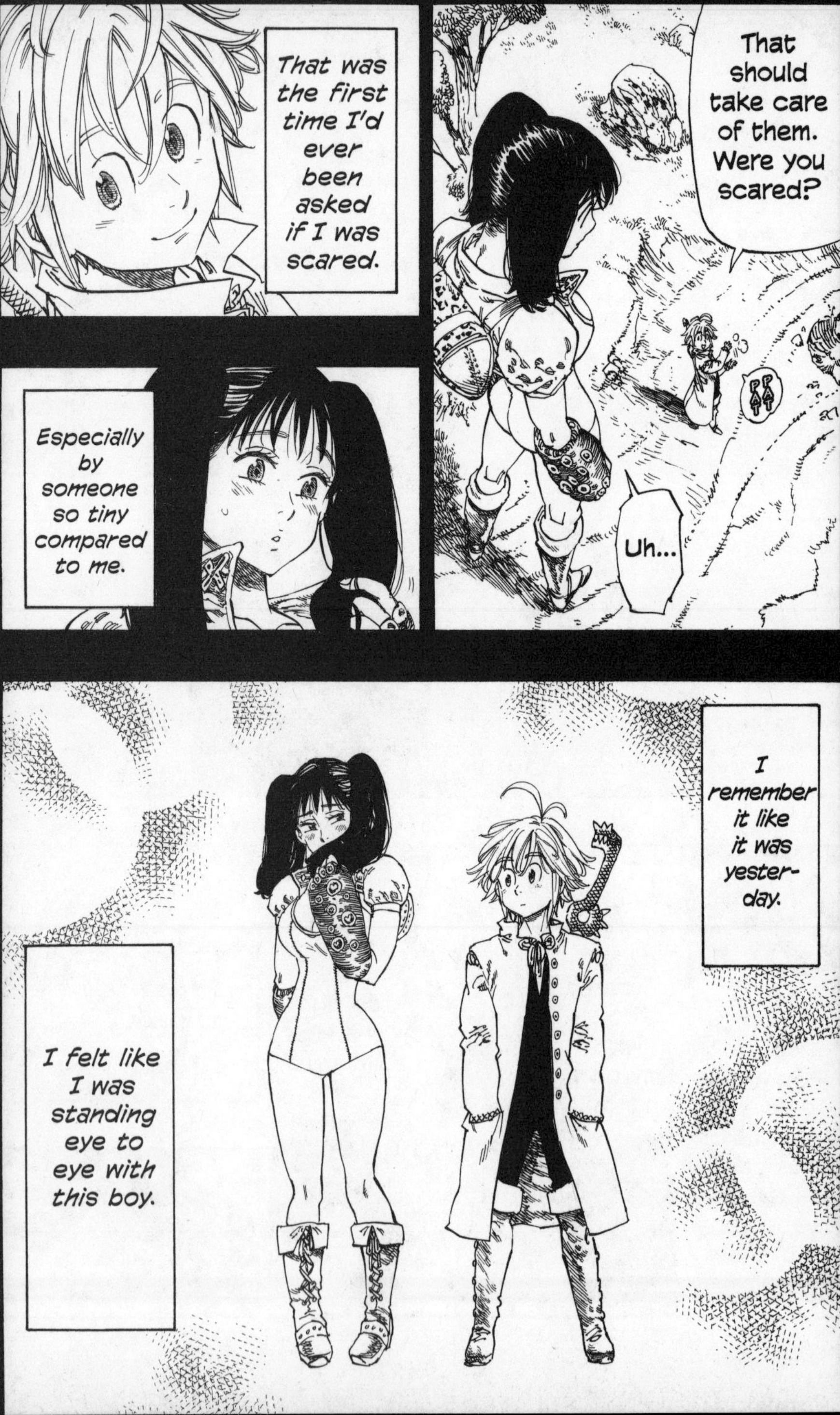
That should take care of them. Were you scared?
Uh...
That was the first time I'd ever been asked if I was scared.
Especially by someone so tiny compared to me.
I remember it like it was yesterday.
I felt like I was standing eye to eye with this boy.

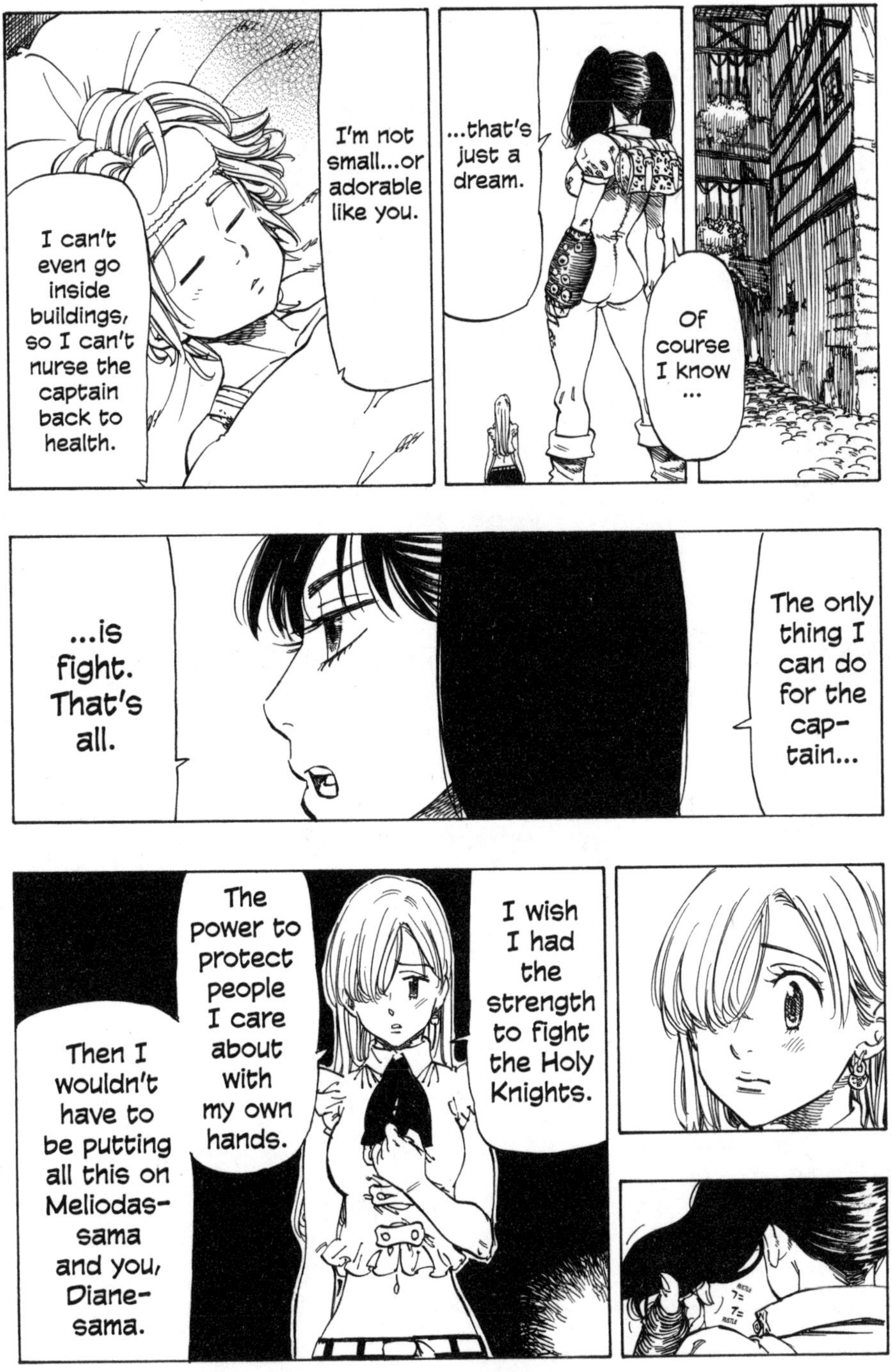
Of course I know ...
...that's just a dream.
I'm not small...or adorable like you.
I can't even go inside buildings, so I can't nurse the captain back to health.
The only thing I can do for the captain...
...is fight. That's all.
I wish I had the strength to fight the Holy Knights.
The power to protect people I care about with my own hands.
Then I wouldn't have to be putting all this on Meliodas-sama and you, Diane-sama.

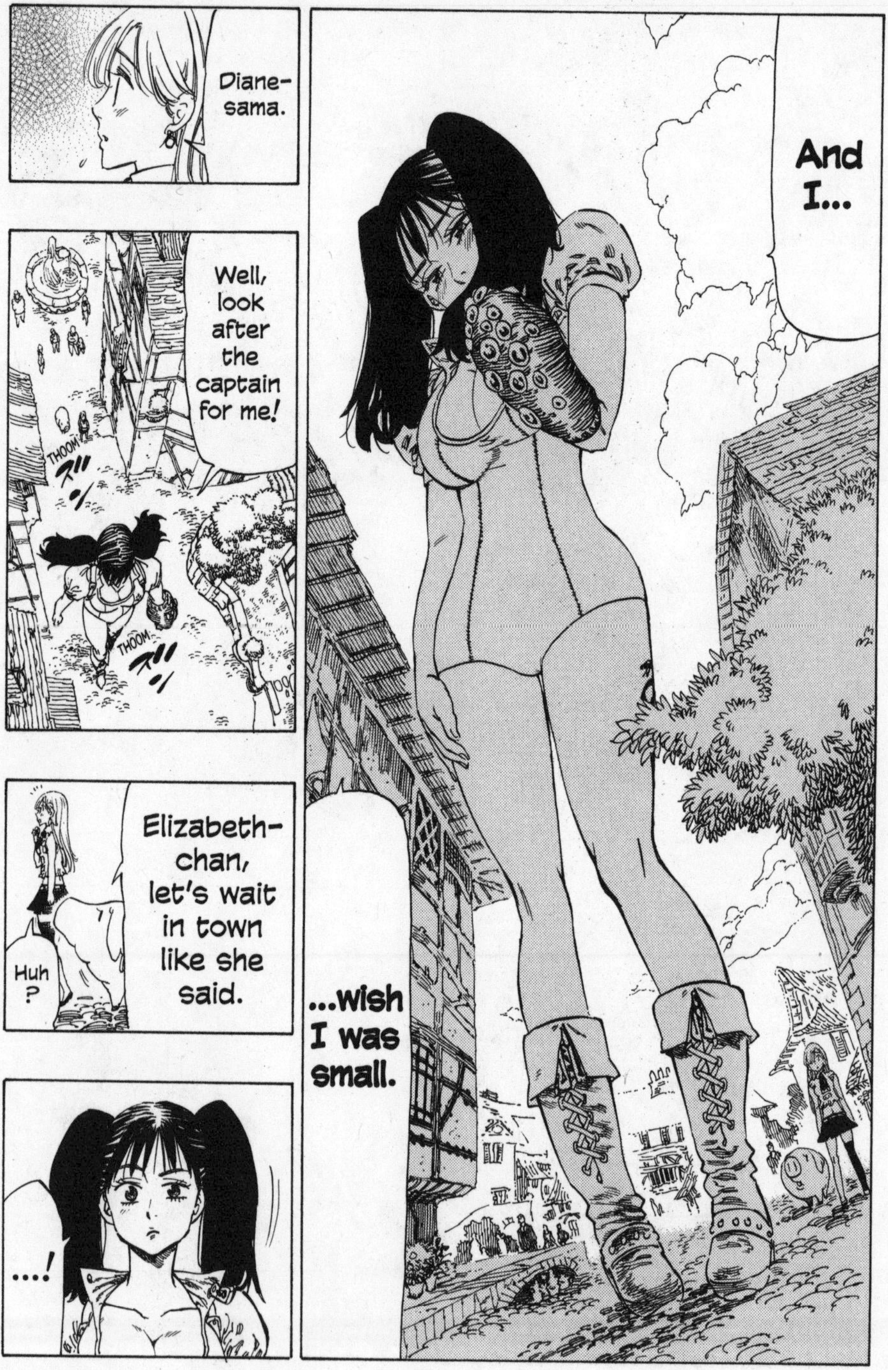
And I...
...wish I was small.
Diane-sama.
Well, look after the captain for me!
THOOM
THOOM
Elizabeth-chan, let's wait in town like she said.
Huh?
....!

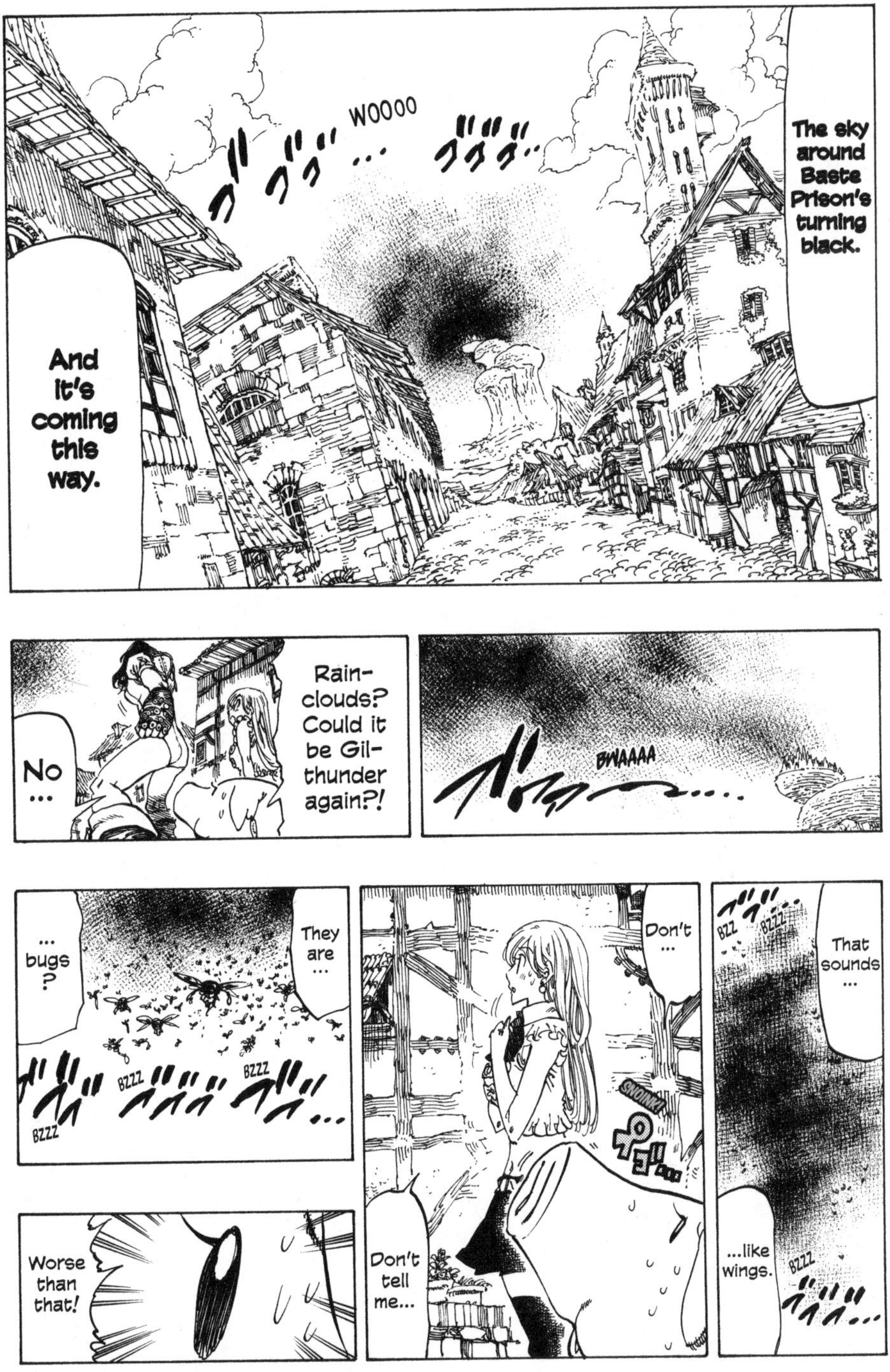

The sky around Baste Prison's turning black.
WOOOO
And it's coming this way.
BWAAAA
Rain-clouds? Could it be Gil-thunder again?!
No ...
BZZZ
That sounds ...
...like wings.
BZZZ
Don't ...
SNOINK!
Don't tell me...
They are ...
... bugs ?
BZZZ
BZZZ
BZZZ
Worse than that!

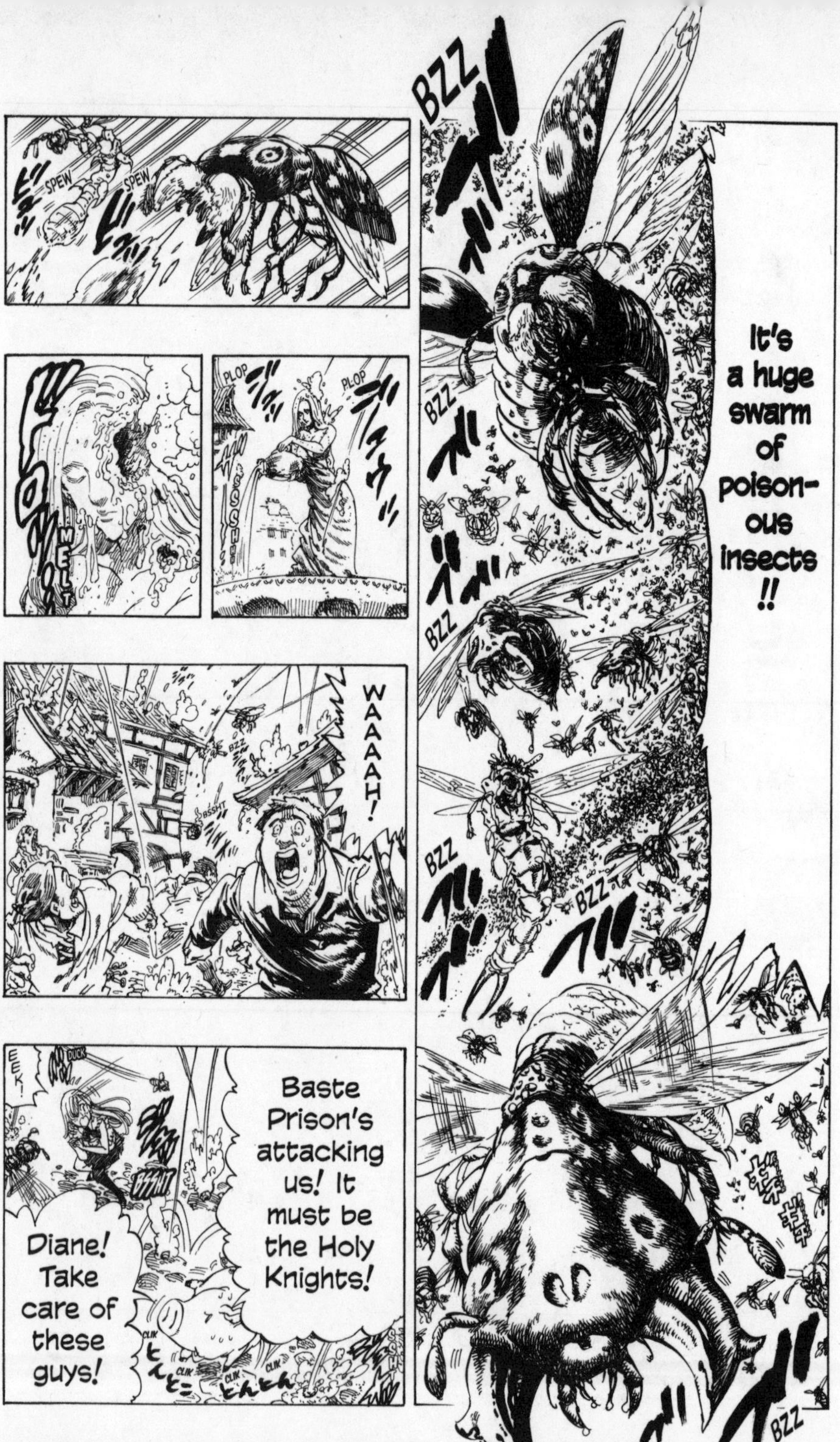
BZZ
BZZ
BZZ
It's a huge swarm of poison-ous insects!!
BZZ
BZZ
BZZ
SPEW
SPEW
PLOP
PLOP
SSSH
MELT
WAAAAH!
BZZ
BSSHT
Baste Prison's attacking us! It must be the Holy Knights!
EEK!
DUCK
Diane! Take care of these guys!
CLIK
CLIK
CLIK

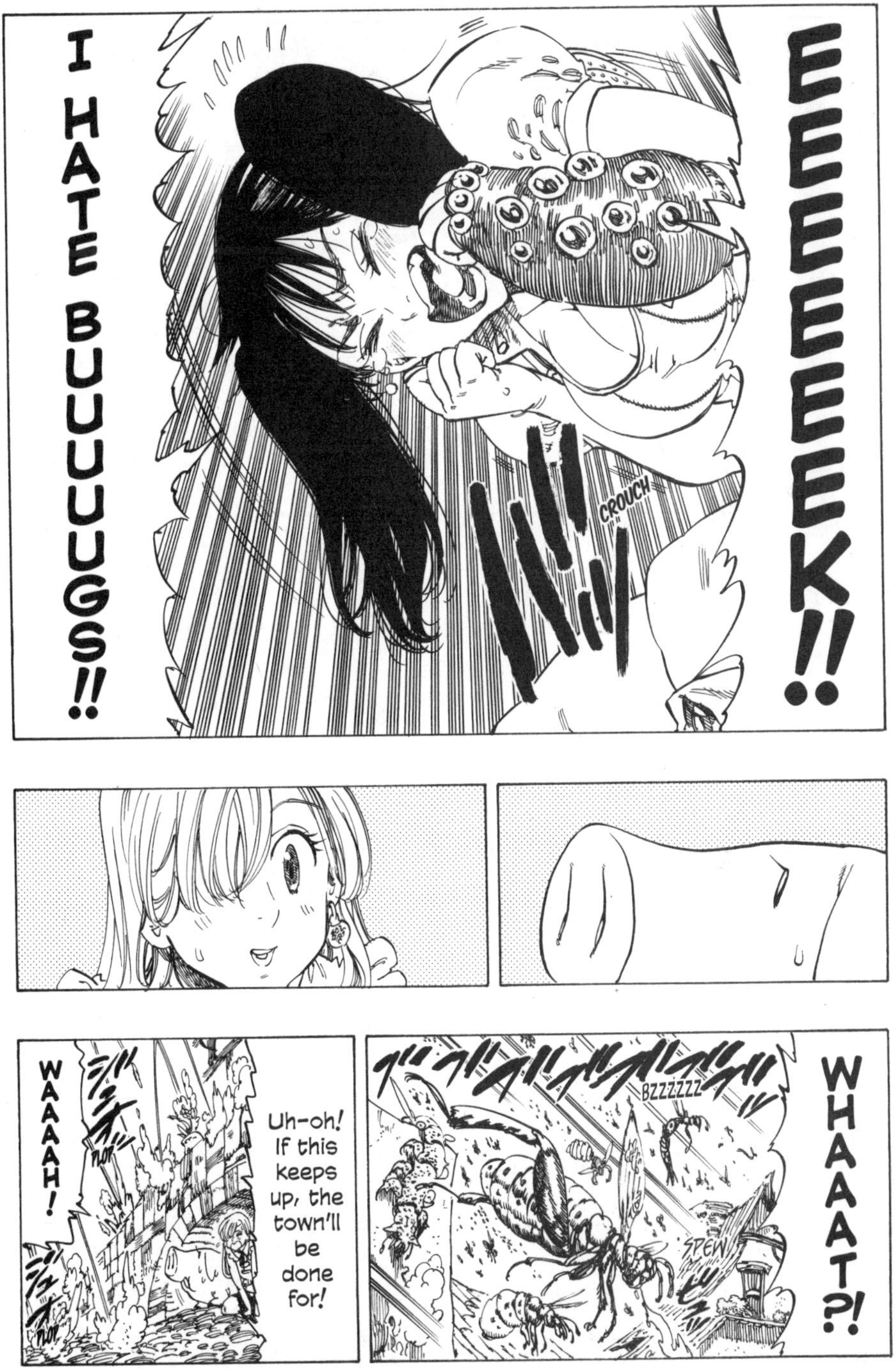
EEEEEEEK!!
CROUCH
I HATE BUUUUUGS!!
WHAAAT?!
BZZZZZZ
SPEW
Uh-oh! If this keeps up, the town'll be done for!
WAAAAH!
PLOP
PLOP

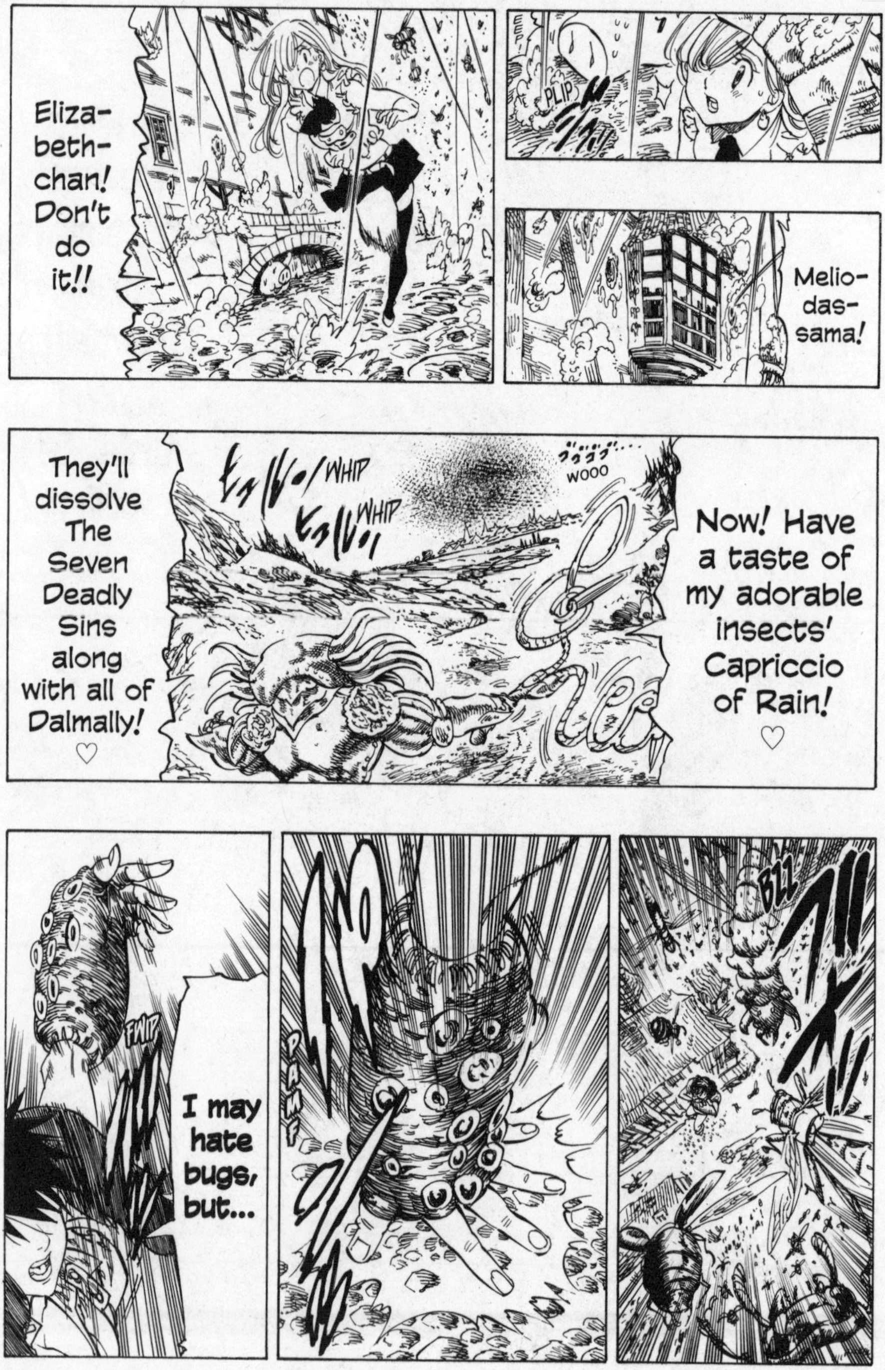
EEP!
PLIP
Melio-das-sama!
Eliza-beth-chan! Don't do it!!
Now! Have a taste of my adorable insects' Capriccio of Rain! ♡
WOOO
WHIP
WHIP
They'll dissolve The Seven Deadly Sins along with all of Dalmally! ♡
BZZ
PAMF
FWIP
I may hate bugs, but...

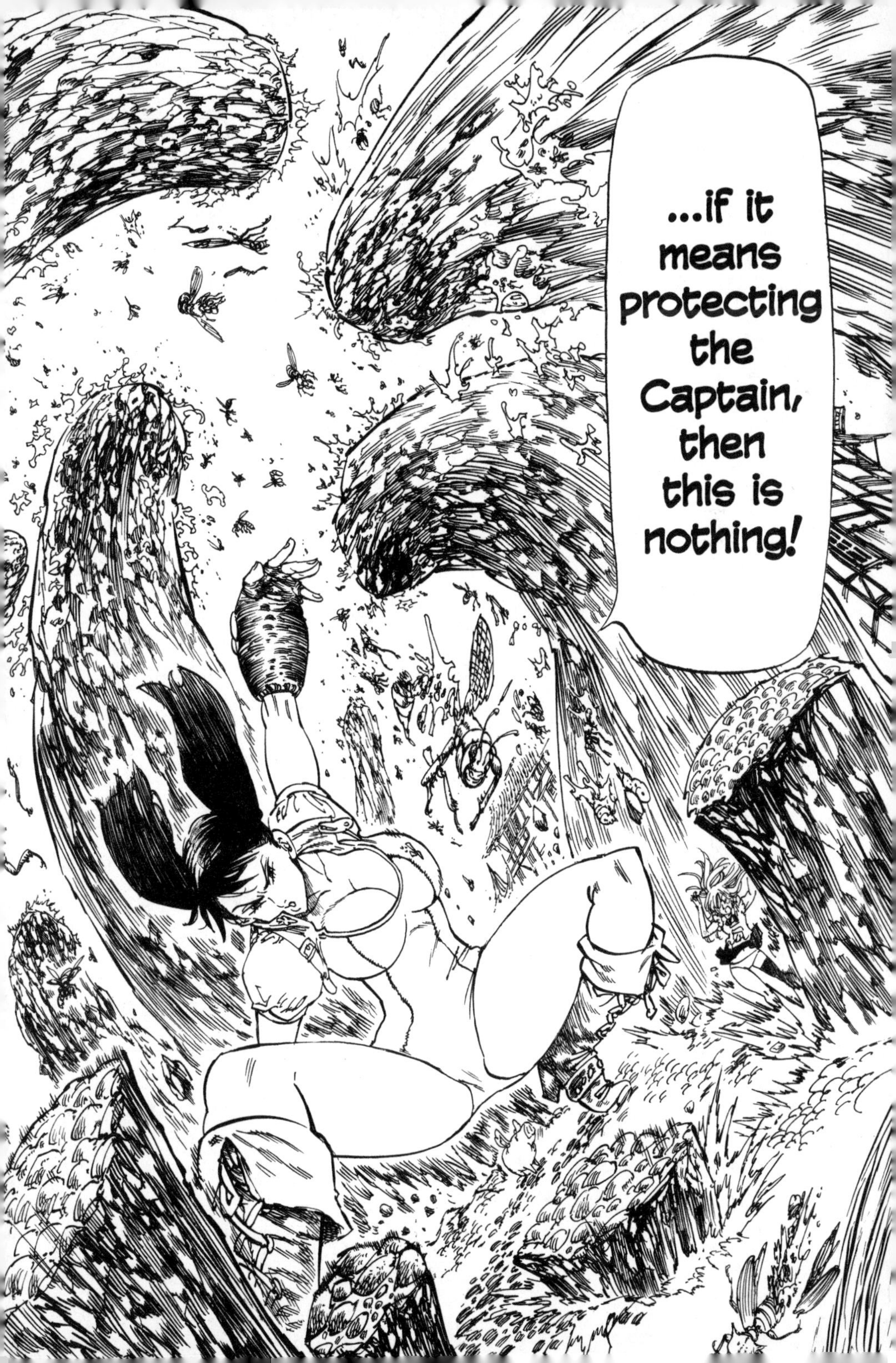
...if it means protecting the Captain, then this is nothing!

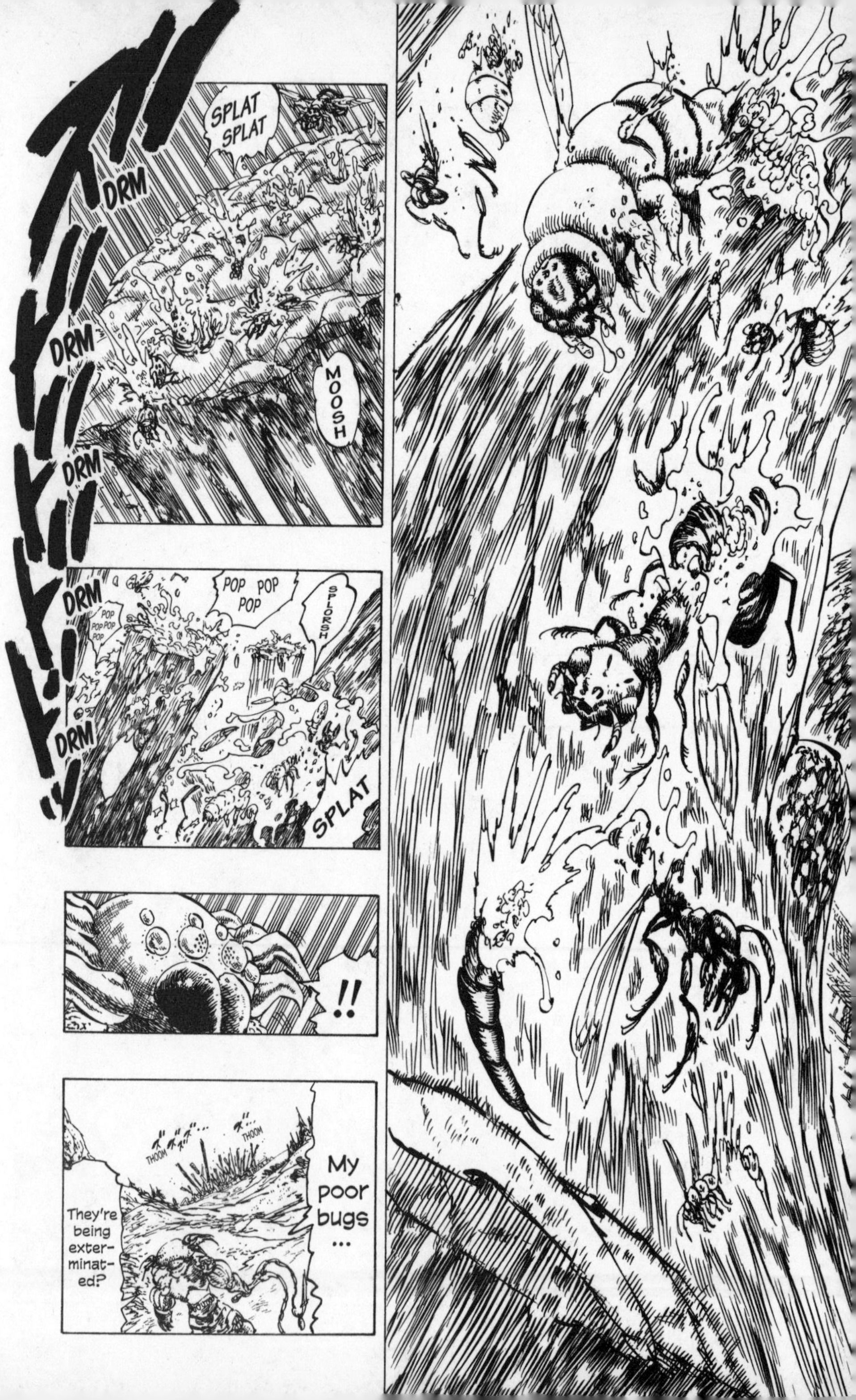
SPLAT SPLAT
MOOSH
DRM DRM DRM DRM DRM
POP POP POP
SPLORSH
POP POP POP POP
SPLAT
!!
THOOM
THOOM
My poor bugs...
They're being exter-minat-ed?

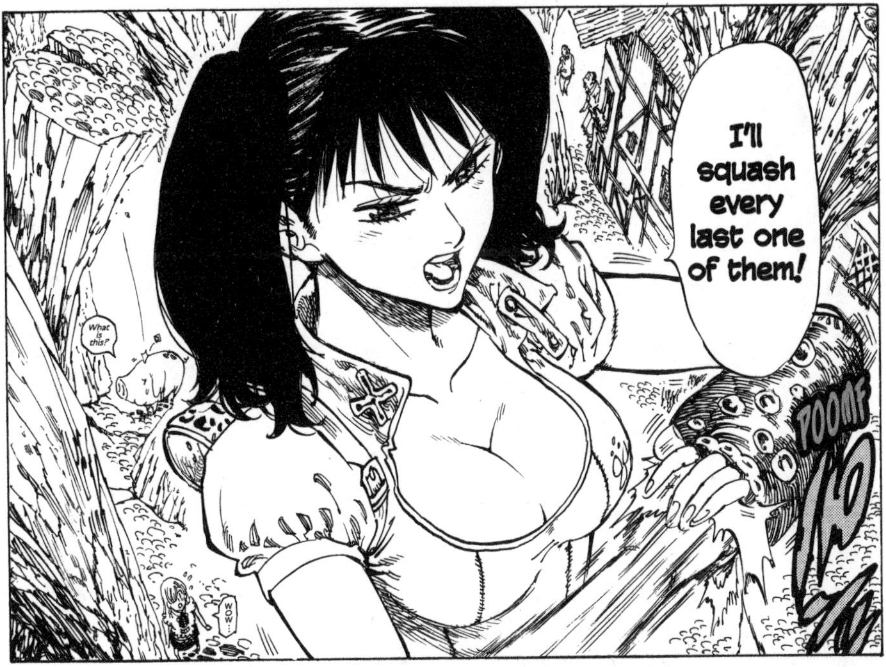
I'll squash every last one of them!
POOMF
What is this?
Wow...

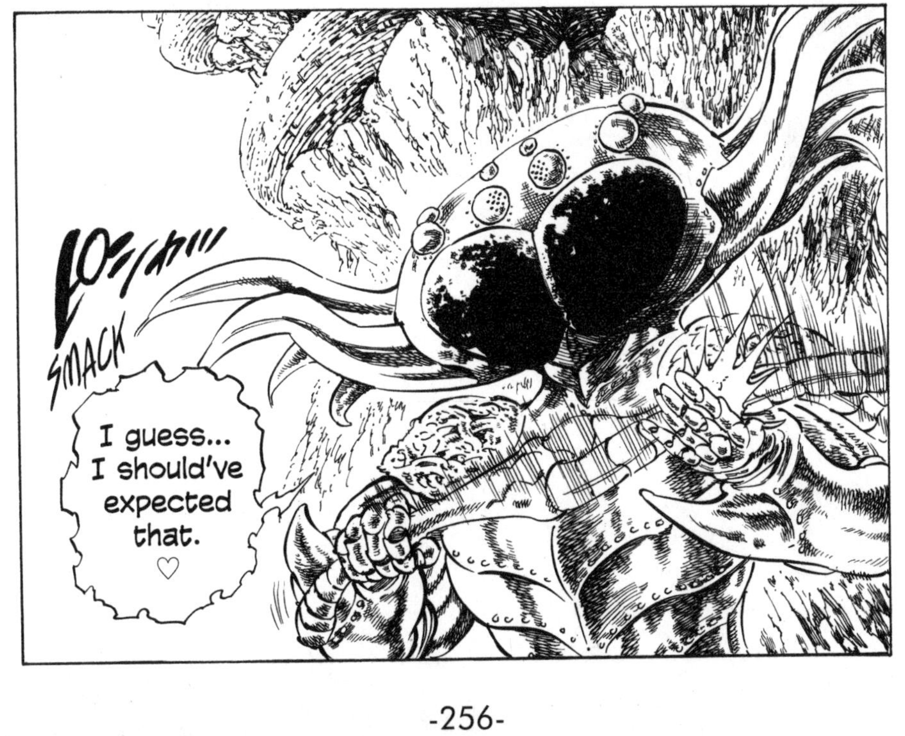
SMACK
I guess... I should've expected that. ♡

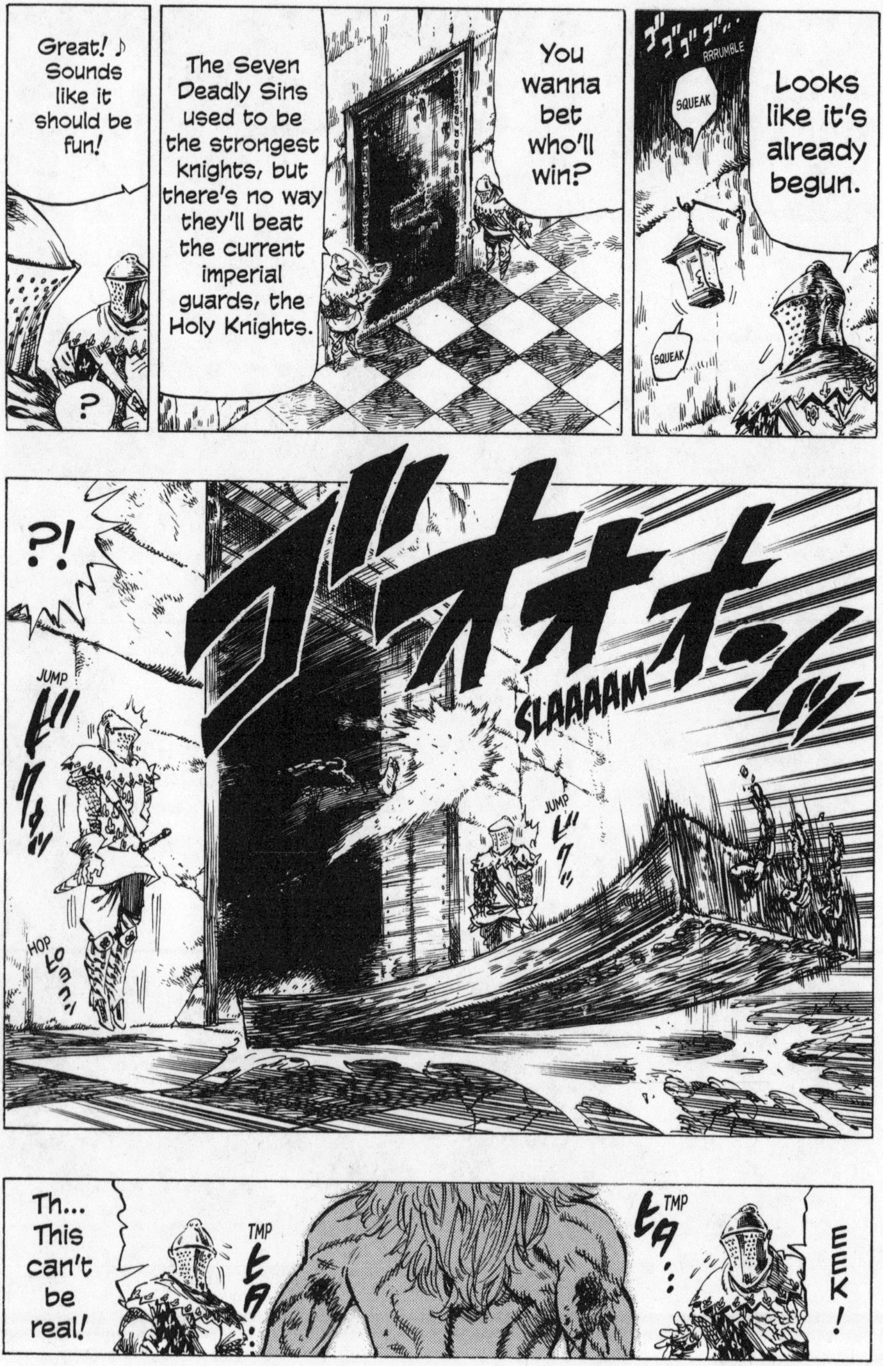
RRRUMBLE
Looks like it's already begun.
SQUEAK
SQUEAK
You wanna bet who'll win?
The Seven Deadly Sins used to be the strongest knights, but there's no way they'll beat the current imperial guards, the Holy Knights.
Great! ♪ Sounds like it should be fun!
?
SLAAAAM
JUMP
?!
JUMP
HOP
EEK!
TMP
TMP
Th... This can't be real!

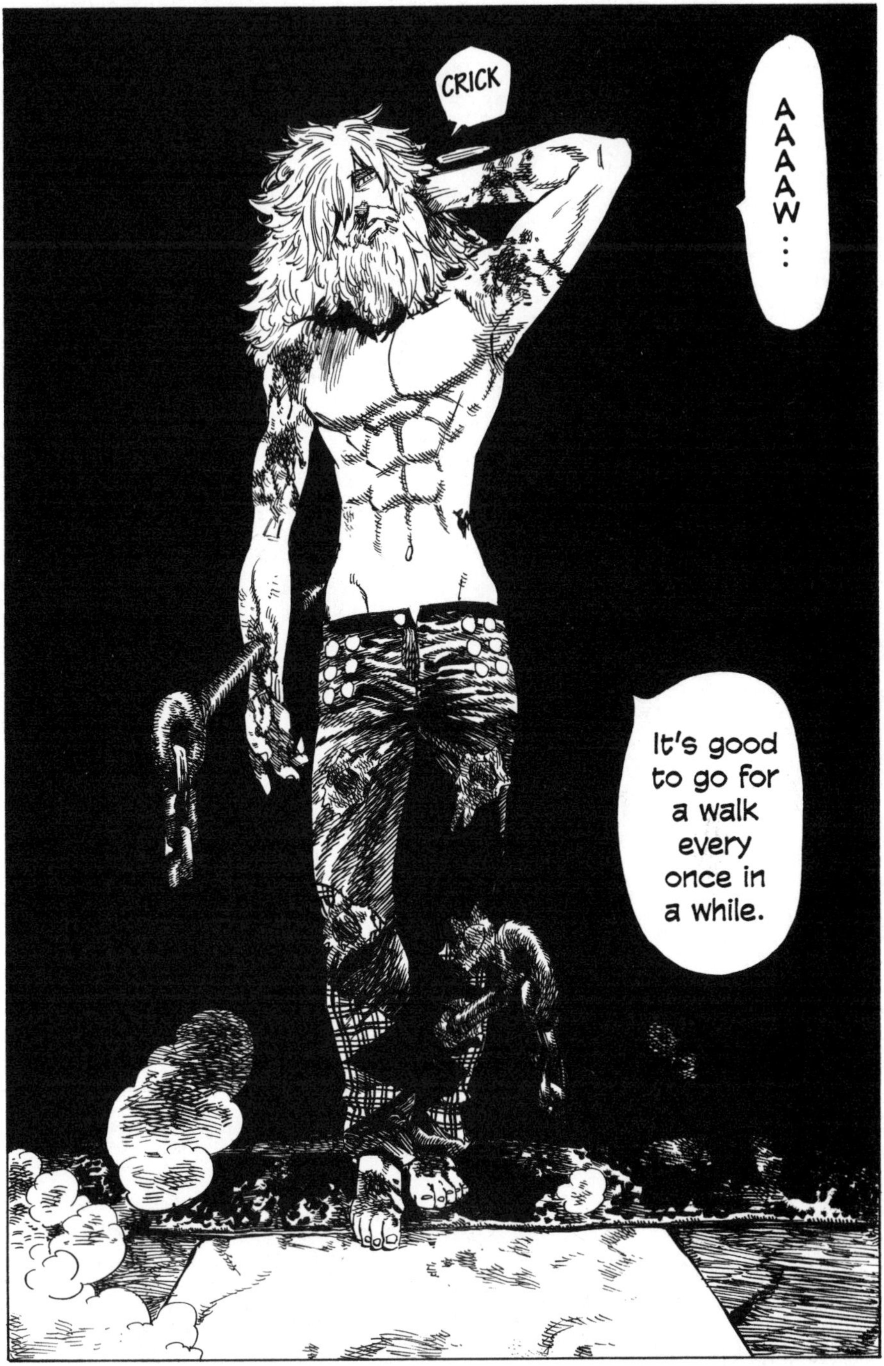
AAAAW...
CRICK
It's good to go for a walk every once in a while.

Illustration Corner Present Announcement

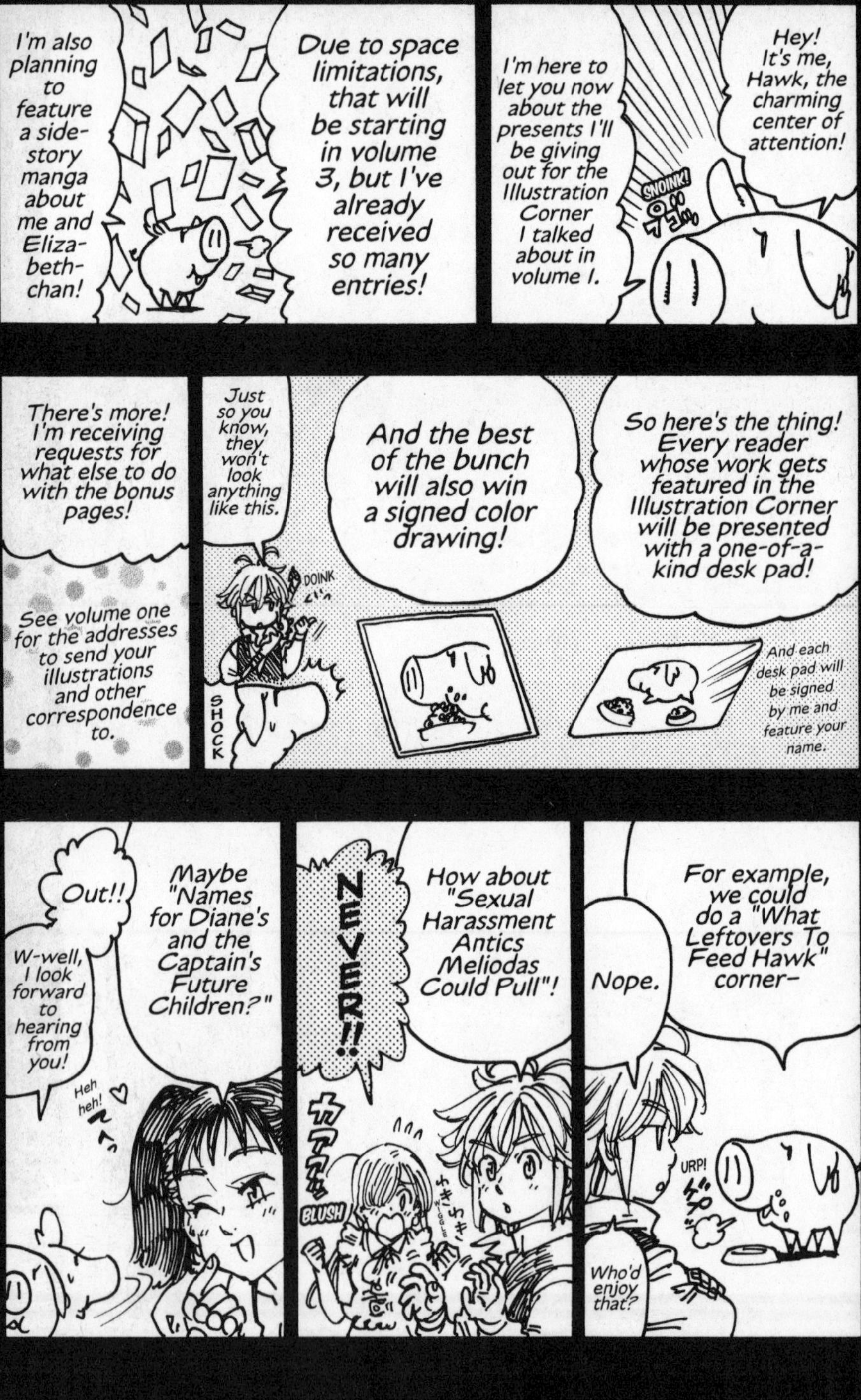
Hey! It's me, Hawk, the charming center of attention!
SNOINK!
I'm here to let you now about the presents I'll be giving out for the Illustration Corner I talked about in volume 1.
Due to space limitations, that will be starting in volume 3, but I've already received so many entries!
I'm also planning to feature a side-story manga about me and Eliza-beth-chan!
So here's the thing! Every reader whose work gets featured in the Illustration Corner will be presented with a one-of-a-kind desk pad!
And the best of the bunch will also win a signed color drawing!
And each desk pad will be signed by me and feature your name.
Just so you know, they won't look anything like this.
DOINK
SHOCK
There's more! I'm receiving requests for what else to do with the bonus pages!
See volume one for the addresses to send your illustrations and other correspondence to.
For example, we could do a "What Leftovers To Feed Hawk" corner–
Nope.
URP!
Who'd enjoy that?
How about "Sexual Harassment Antics Meliodas Could Pull"!
NEVER!!
BLUSH
WIGGLE
Maybe "Names for Diane's and the Captain's Future Children?"
Out!!
W-well, I look forward to hearing from you!
Heh heh!

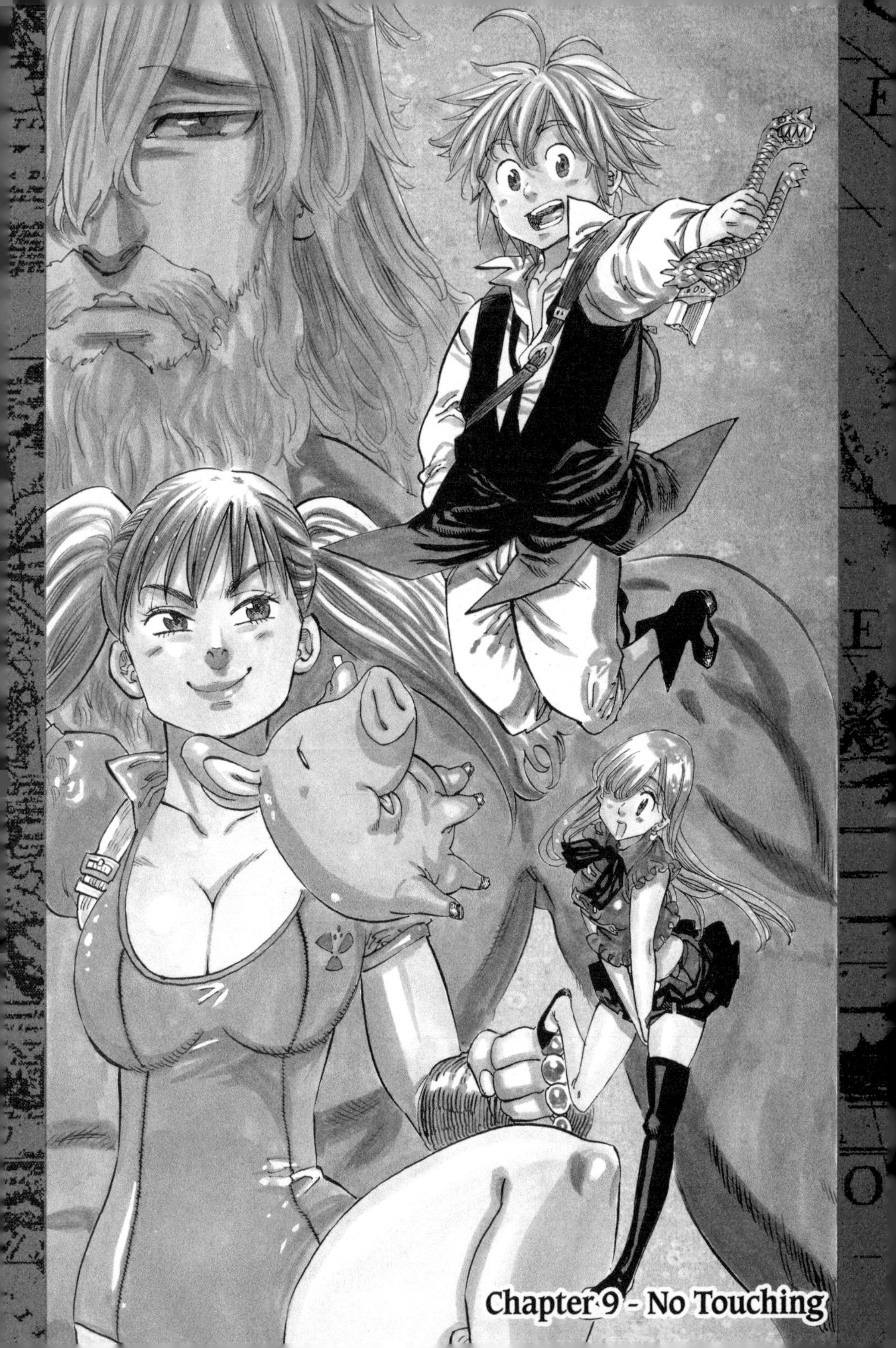
Chapter 9 - No Touching

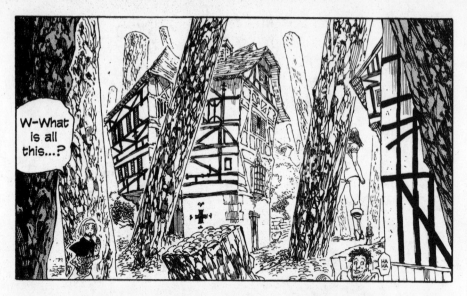

W-What is all this...?
HA HA
Dr. Dana! It's chaos out there!
BAM
Dr. Dana?
I know! But what matters most right now is the patient!
Y... Yes, doctor.
Oh, what's that medicine?
It's a special formula I concocted.
SIP
This will make all the pain go away.

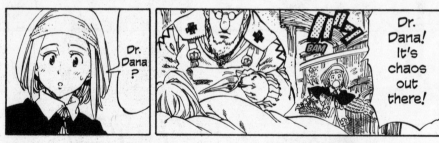

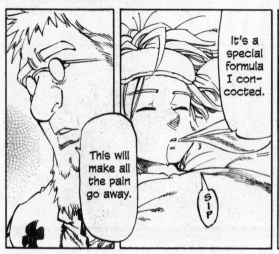

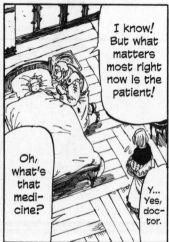

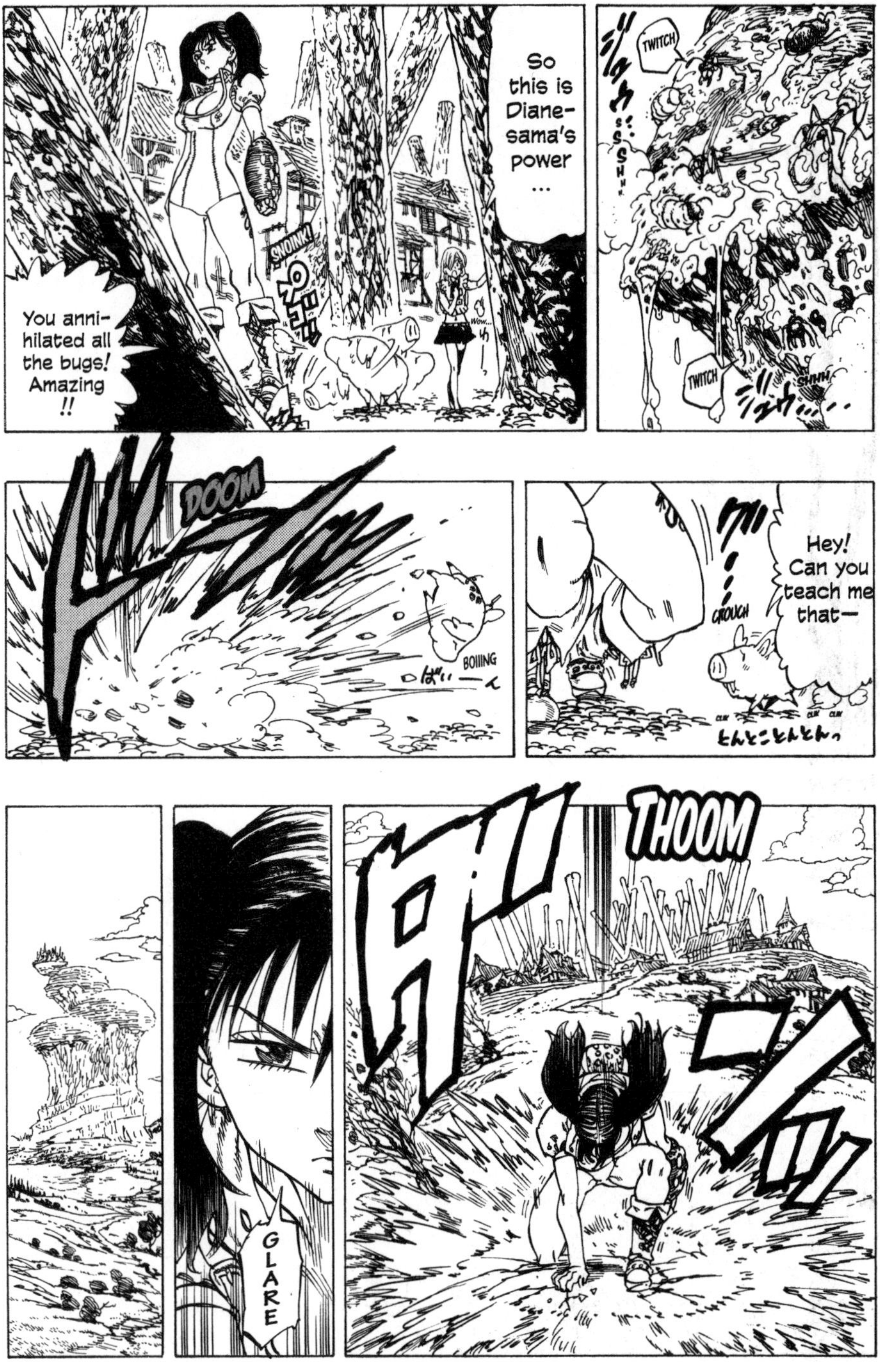
TWITCH
SSSHHH
TWITCH
SHHH
So this is Diane-sama's power ...
You annihilated all the bugs! Amazing !!
SNOINK!
Wow...
Hey! Can you teach me that—
CROUCH
CLIK CLIK CLIK
とんとことんとんっ
DOOM
BOIIING
ばいーん
THOOM
GLARE

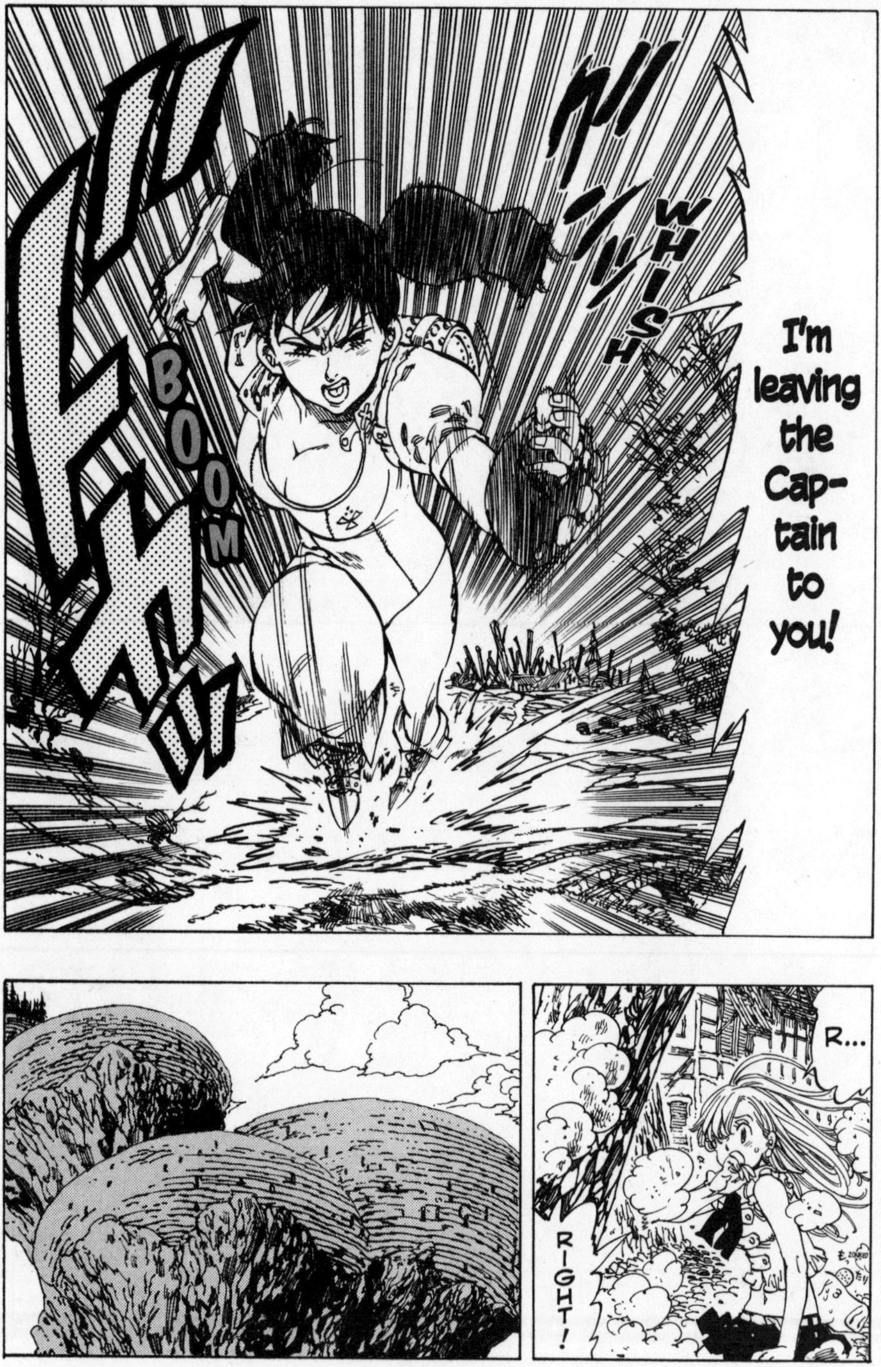
WHISH
I'm leaving the Captain to you!
BOOM
R...
RIGHT!

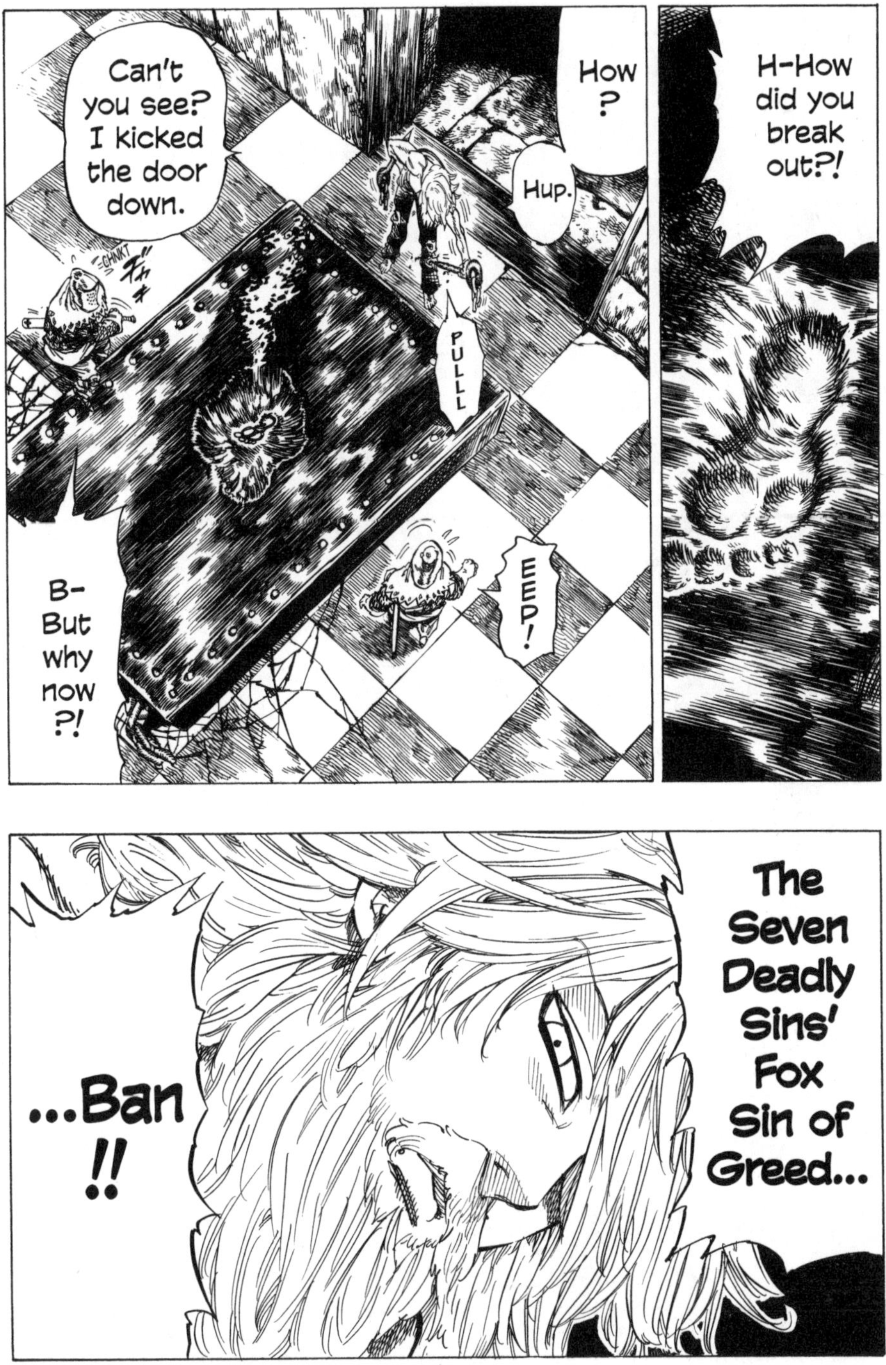
H-How did you break out?!
How?
Hup.
Can't you see? I kicked the door down.
GHNKT
PULLL
EEP!
B-But why now?!
The Seven Deadly Sins' Fox Sin of Greed...
...Ban!!

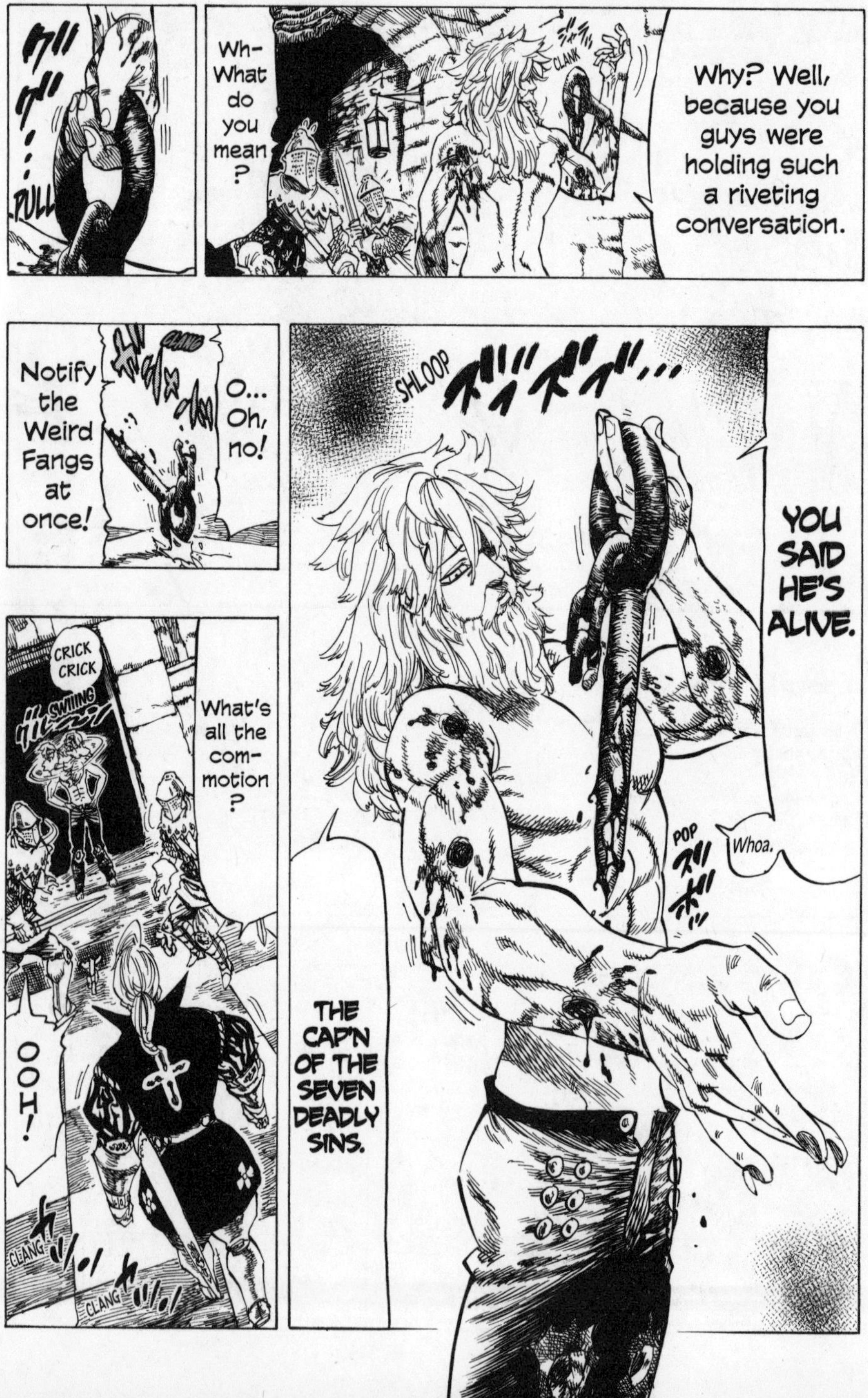
CLANK
Why? Well, because you guys were holding such a riveting conversation.
Wh- What do you mean?
PULL
SHLOOP
YOU SAID HE'S ALIVE.
Whoa.
POP
THE CAP'N OF THE SEVEN DEADLY SINS.
O... Oh, no!
Notify the Weird Fangs at once!
What's all the commotion?
CRICK CRICK
SWIIING
OOH!
CLANG
CLANG

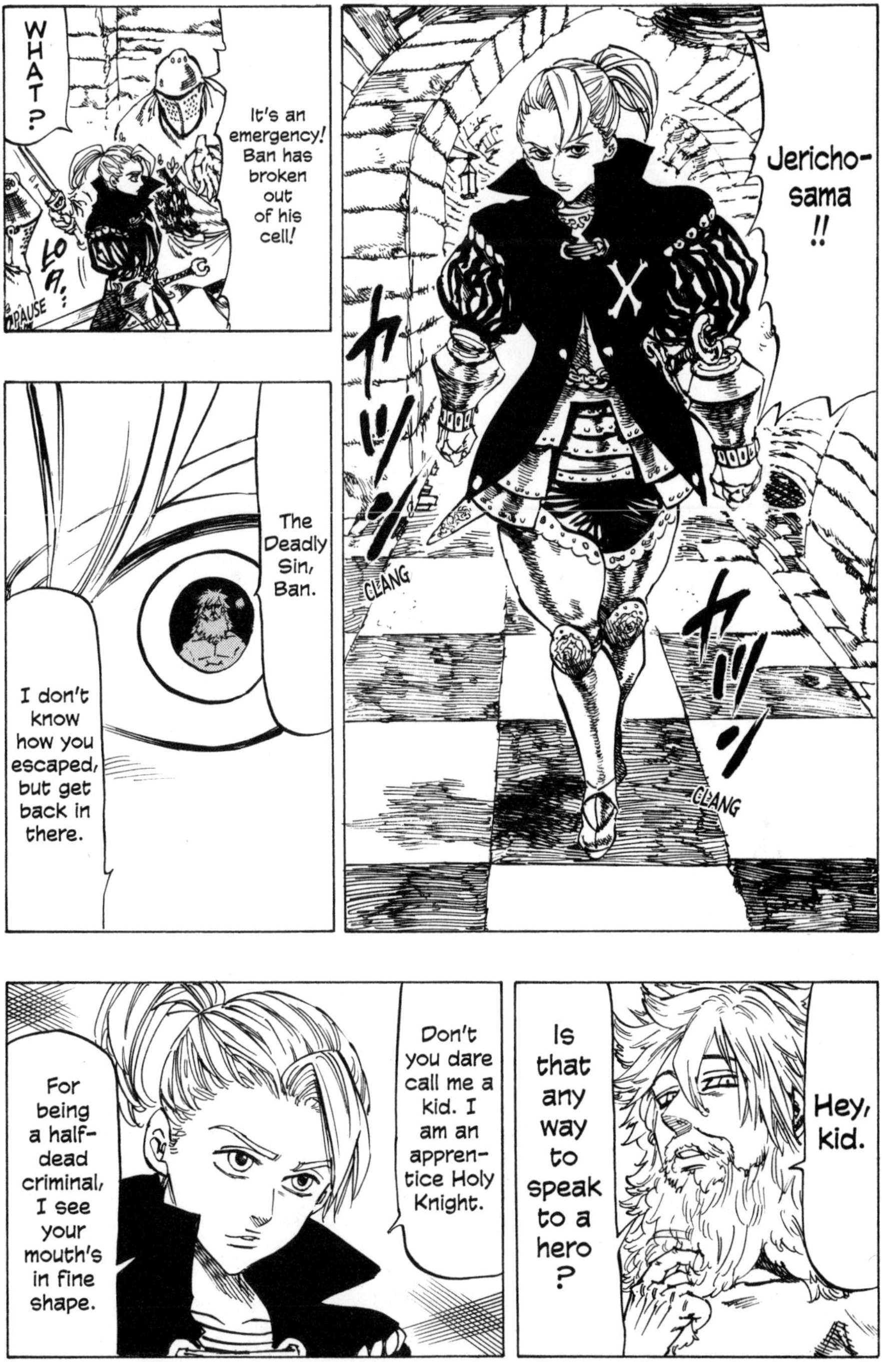
Jericho-sama!!
CLANG
CLANG
It's an emergency! Ban has broken out of his cell!
WHAT?
PAUSE
The Deadly Sin, Ban.
I don't know how you escaped, but get back in there.
Hey, kid.
Is that any way to speak to a hero?
Don't you dare call me a kid. I am an apprentice Holy Knight.
For being a half-dead criminal, I see your mouth's in fine shape.

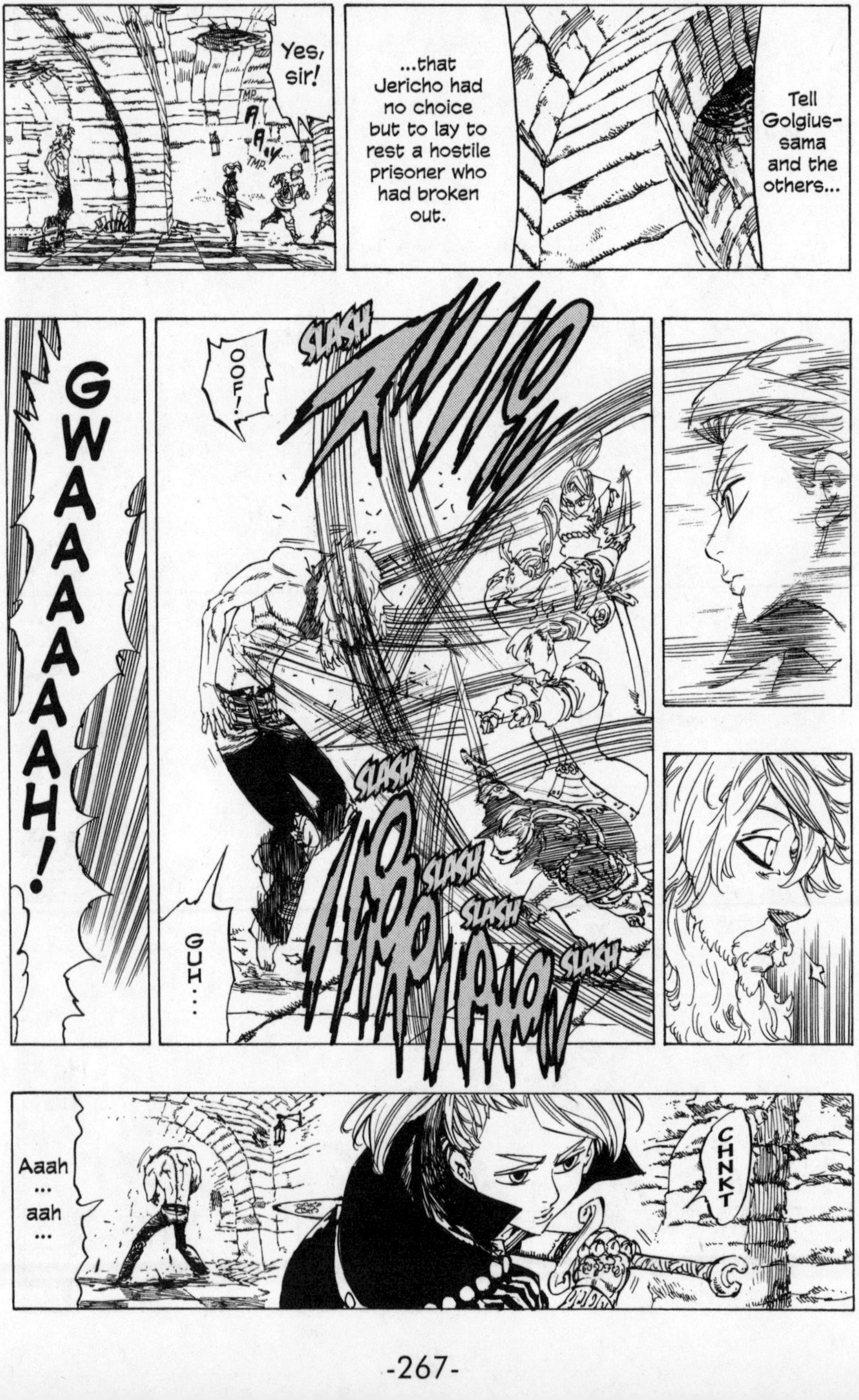
Tell Golgius-sama and the others...
...that Jericho had no choice but to lay to rest a hostile prisoner who had broken out.
Yes, sir!
TMP
TMP
SLASH
OOF!
SLASH
SLASH
SLASH
SLASH
GUH...
GWAAAAAAAH!
CHNKT
Aaah... aah...

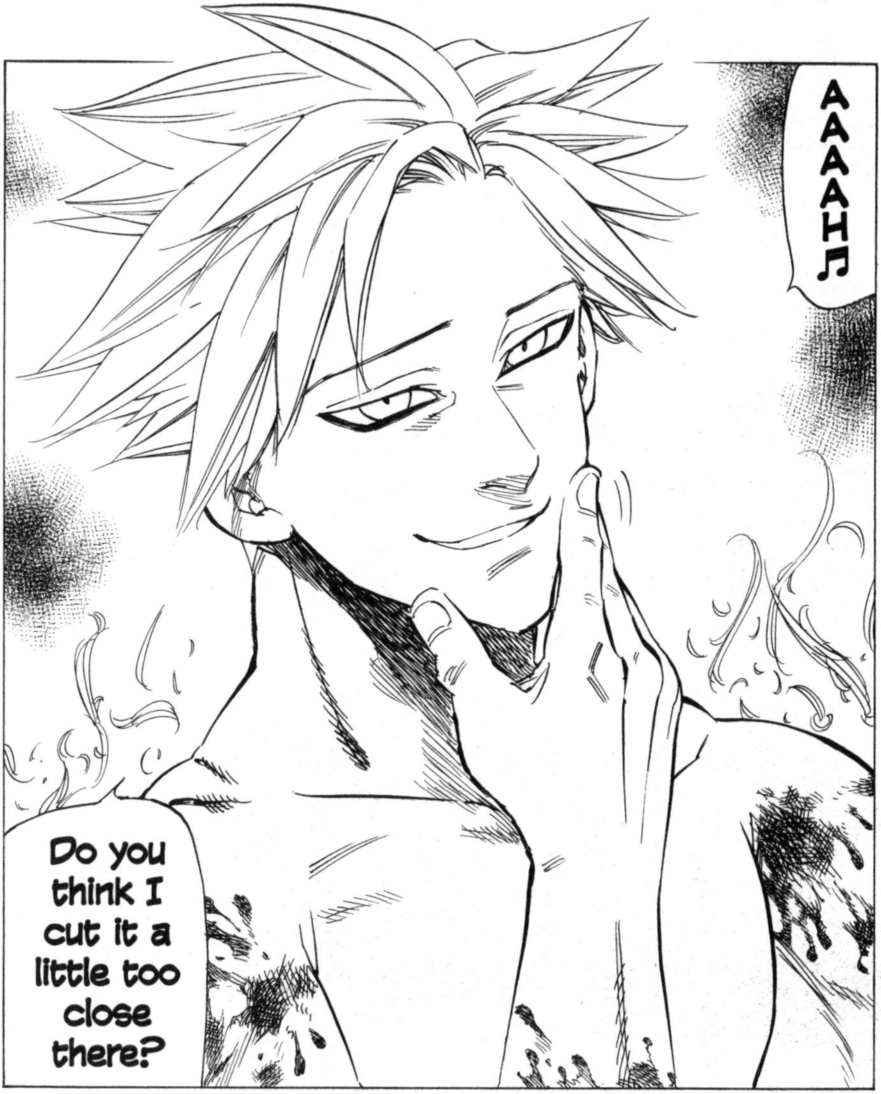
AAAAH♫
Do you think I cut it a little too close there?

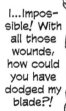

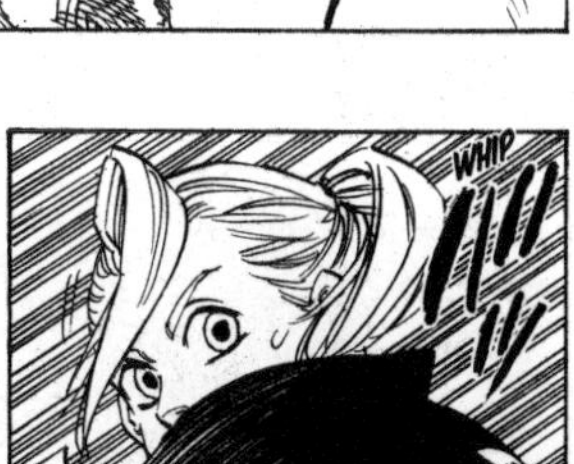
WHIP
...?!

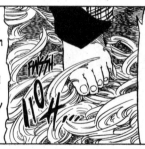

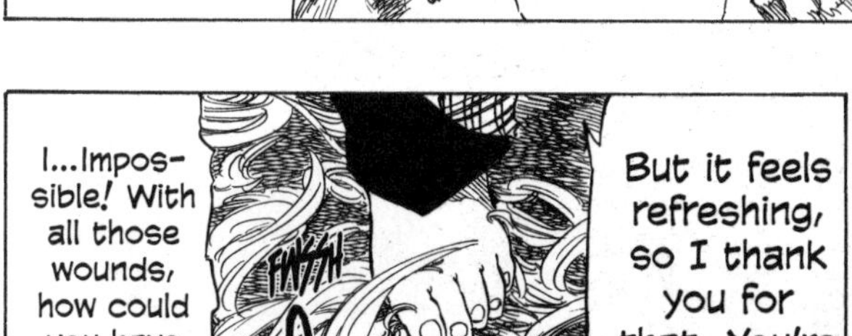
But it feels refreshing, so I thank you for that. You're a talented barber. ♪
FWSSH
I...Impossible! With all those wounds, how could you have dodged my blade?!

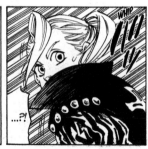

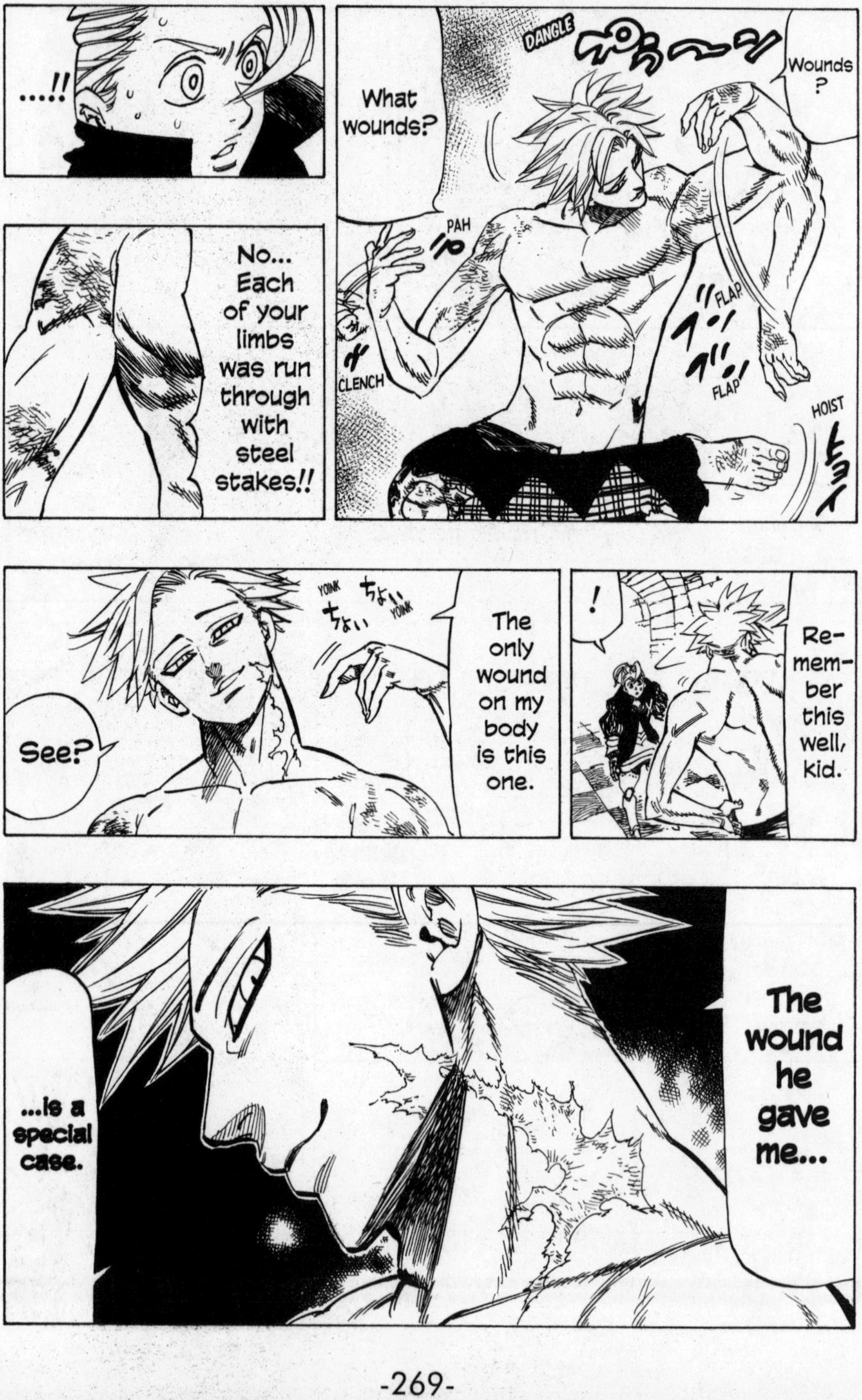
DANGLE
Wounds ?
What wounds?
PAH
CLENCH
FLAP
FLAP
HOIST
...!!
No... Each of your limbs was run through with steel stakes!!
!
Re-mem-ber this well, kid.
YOINK
YOINK
The only wound on my body is this one.
See?
The wound he gave me...
...is a special case.

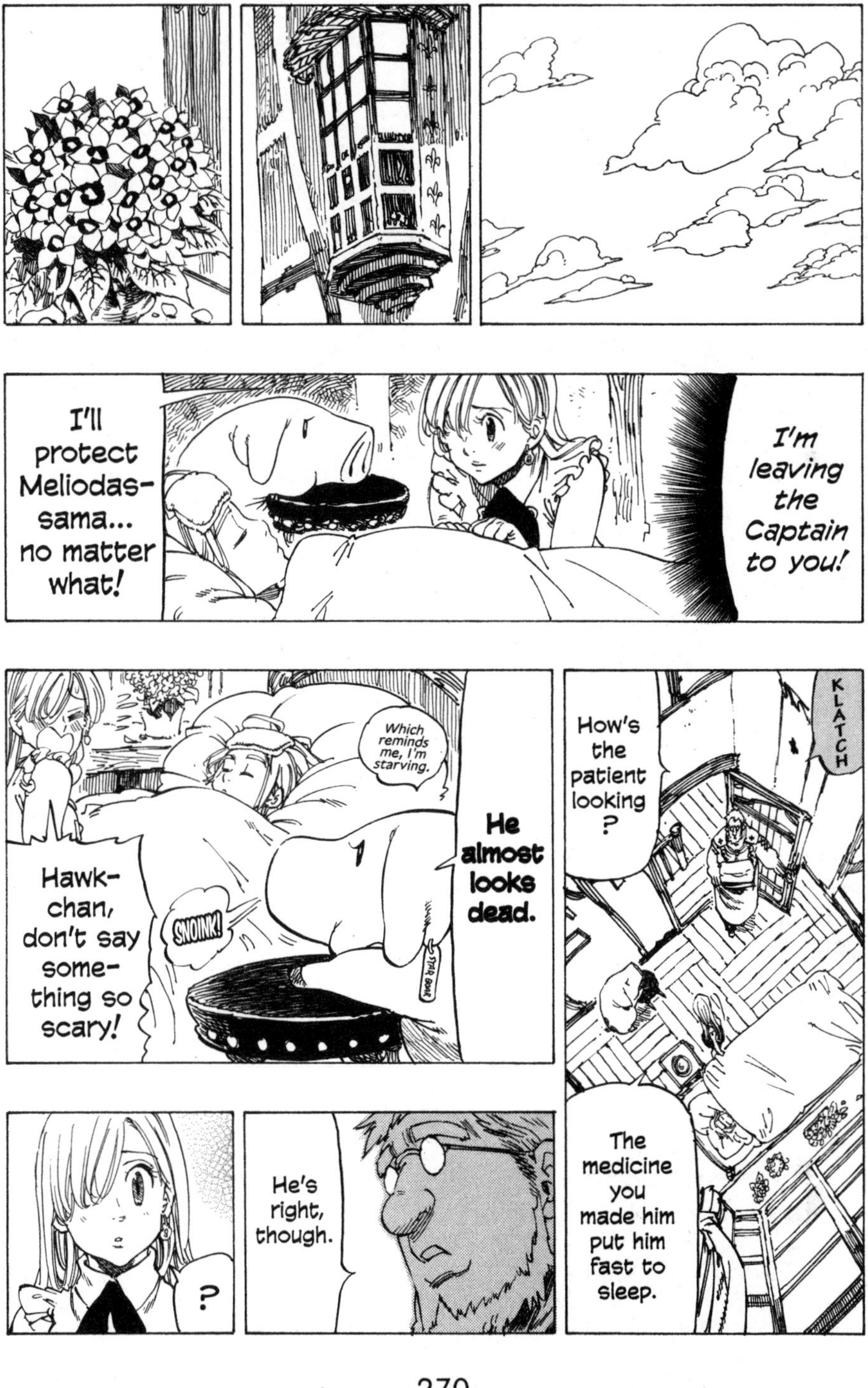

I'm leaving the Captain to you!
I'll protect Meliodas-sama... no matter what!
KLATCH
How's the patient looking?
The medicine you made him put him fast to sleep.
He almost looks dead.
Which reminds me, I'm starving.
SNOINK!
Hawk-chan, don't say something so scary!
He's right, though.
?

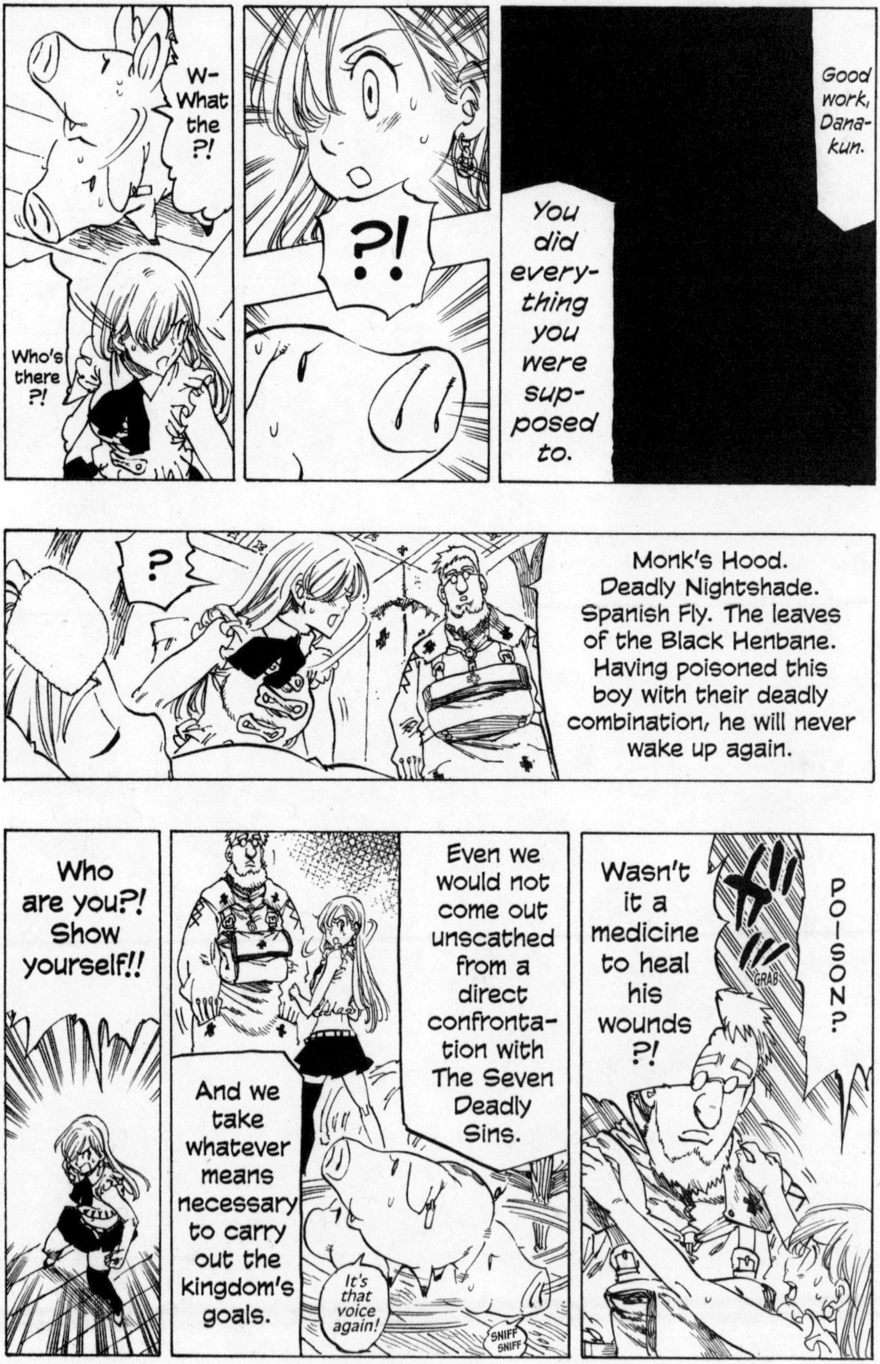

Good work, Dana-kun.
You did everything you were supposed to.
?!
W-What the ?!
Who's there ?!
Monk's Hood. Deadly Nightshade. Spanish Fly. The leaves of the Black Henbane. Having poisoned this boy with their deadly combination, he will never wake up again.
?
POISON?
Wasn't it a medicine to heal his wounds ?!
GRAB
Even we would not come out unscathed from a direct confrontation with The Seven Deadly Sins.
And we take whatever means necessary to carry out the kingdom's goals.
It's that voice again!
SNIFF SNIFF
Who are you?! Show yourself!!

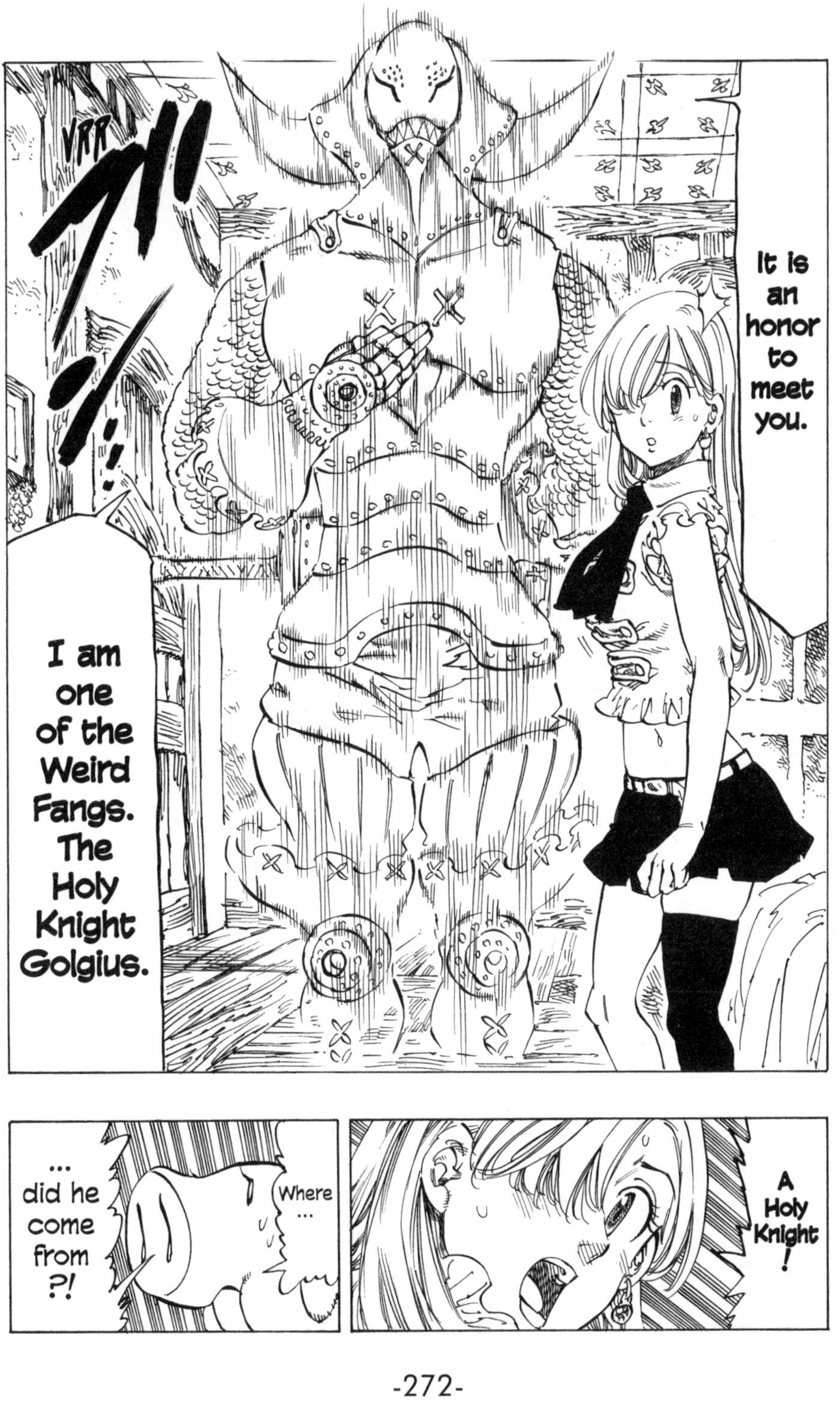
It is an honor to meet you.
VRR
I am one of the Weird Fangs. The Holy Knight Golgius.
A Holy Knight!
Where...
...did he come from?!

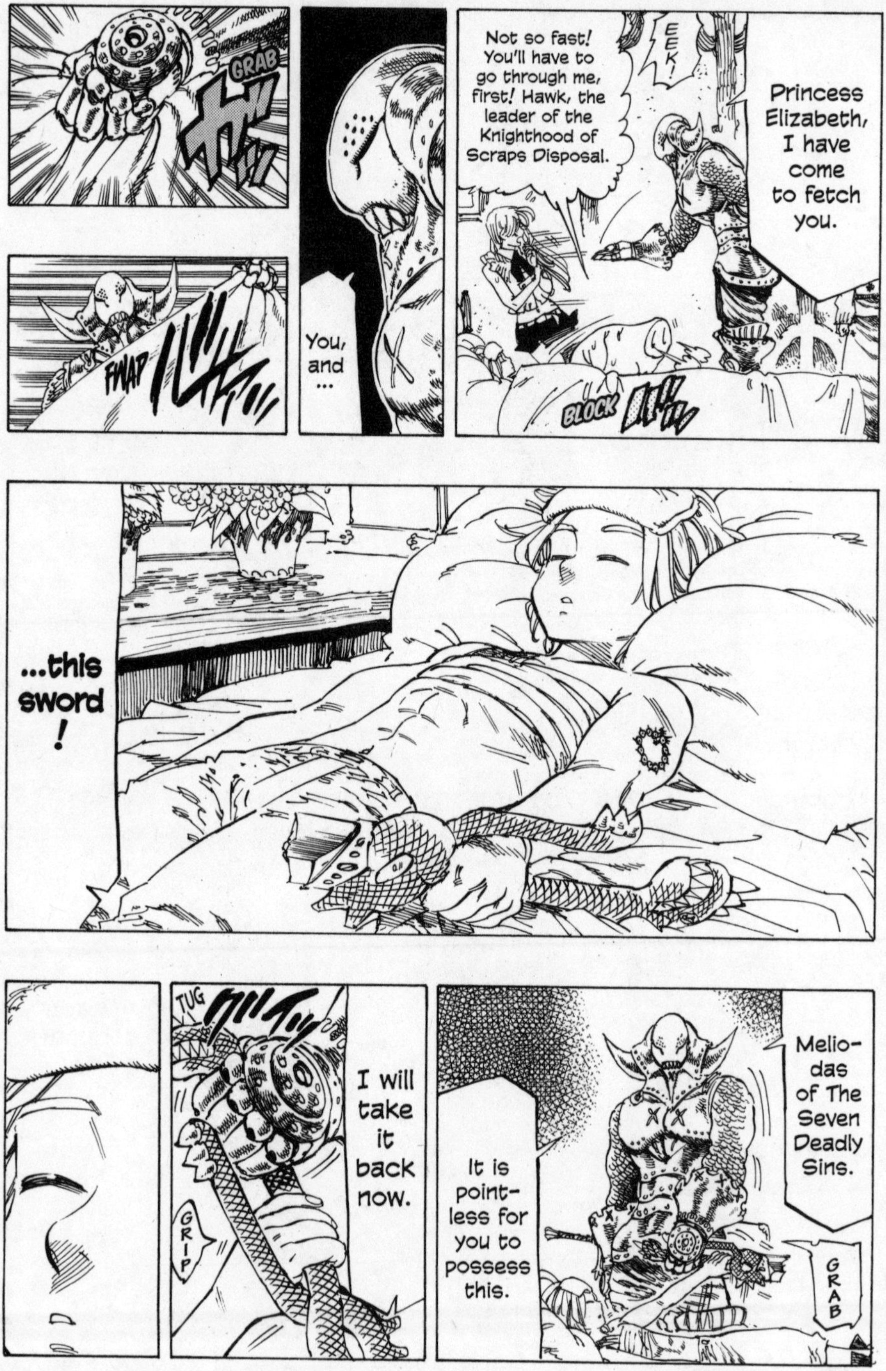
Princess Elizabeth, I have come to fetch you.
EEK!
Not so fast! You'll have to go through me, first! Hawk, the leader of the Knighthood of Scraps Disposal.
BLOCK
You, and ...
GRAB
FWAP
...this sword!
Melio-das of The Seven Deadly Sins.
GRAB
It is point-less for you to possess this.
I will take it back now.
TUG
GRIP

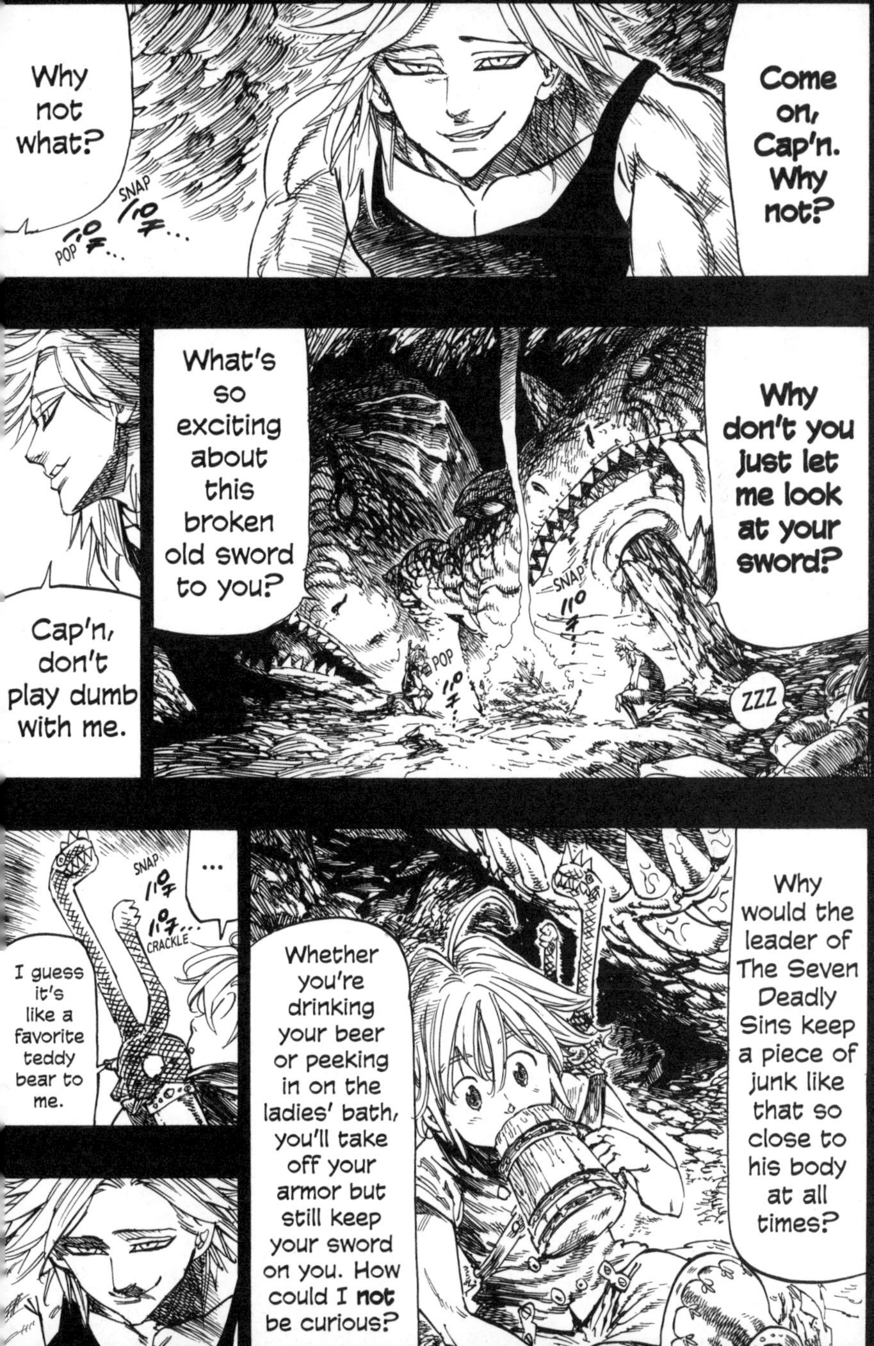
Come on, Cap'n. Why not?
Why not what?
SNAP
POP
Why don't you just let me look at your sword?
What's so exciting about this broken old sword to you?
SNAP
POP
ZZZ
Cap'n, don't play dumb with me.
Why would the leader of The Seven Deadly Sins keep a piece of junk like that so close to his body at all times?
Whether you're drinking your beer or peeking in on the ladies' bath, you'll take off your armor but still keep your sword on you. How could I **not** be curious?
...
SNAP
CRACKLE
I guess it's like a favorite teddy bear to me.

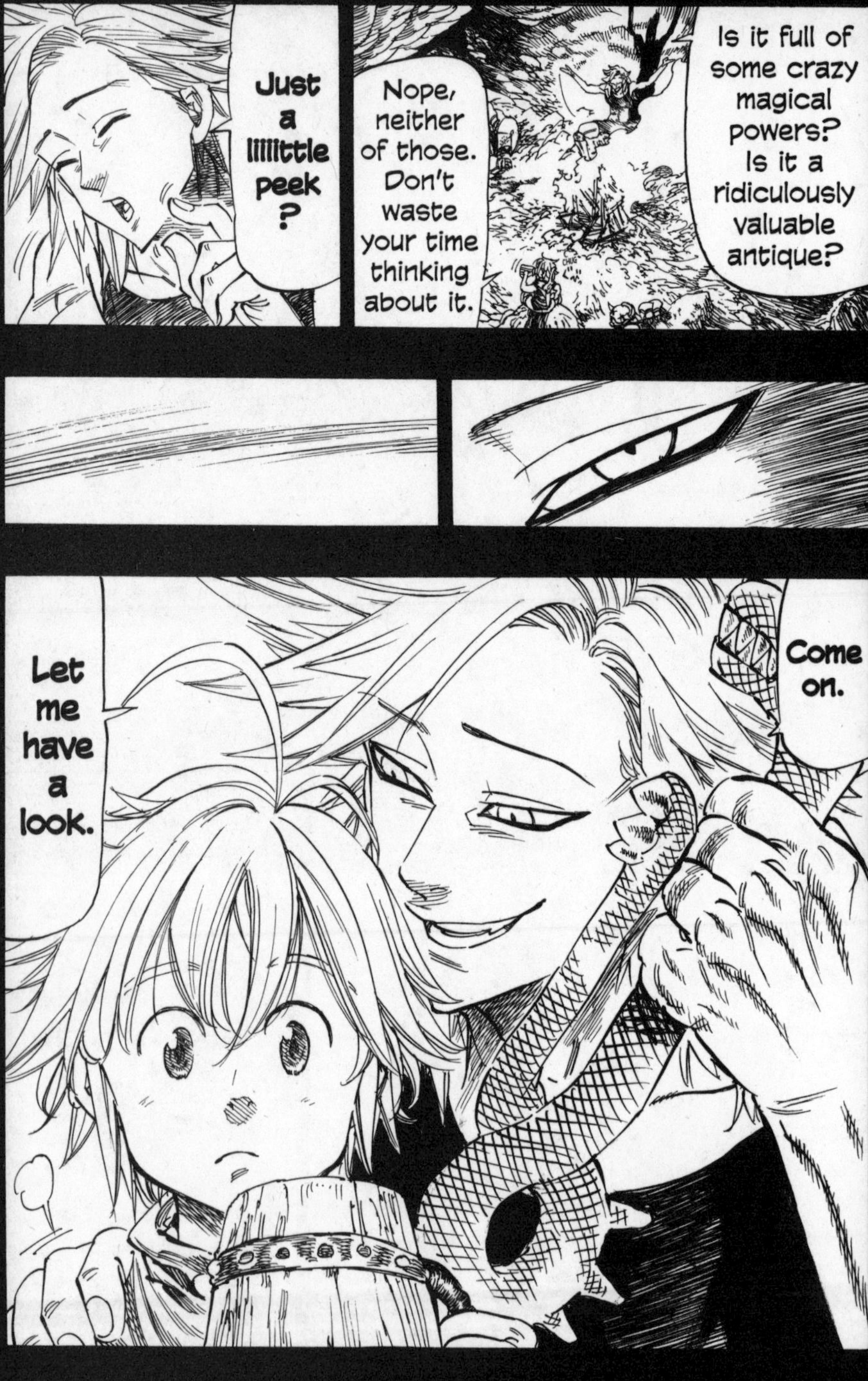
Is it full of some crazy magical powers? Is it a ridiculously valuable antique?
Nope, neither of those. Don't waste your time thinking about it.
Just a lillittle peek?
Come on.
Let me have a look.

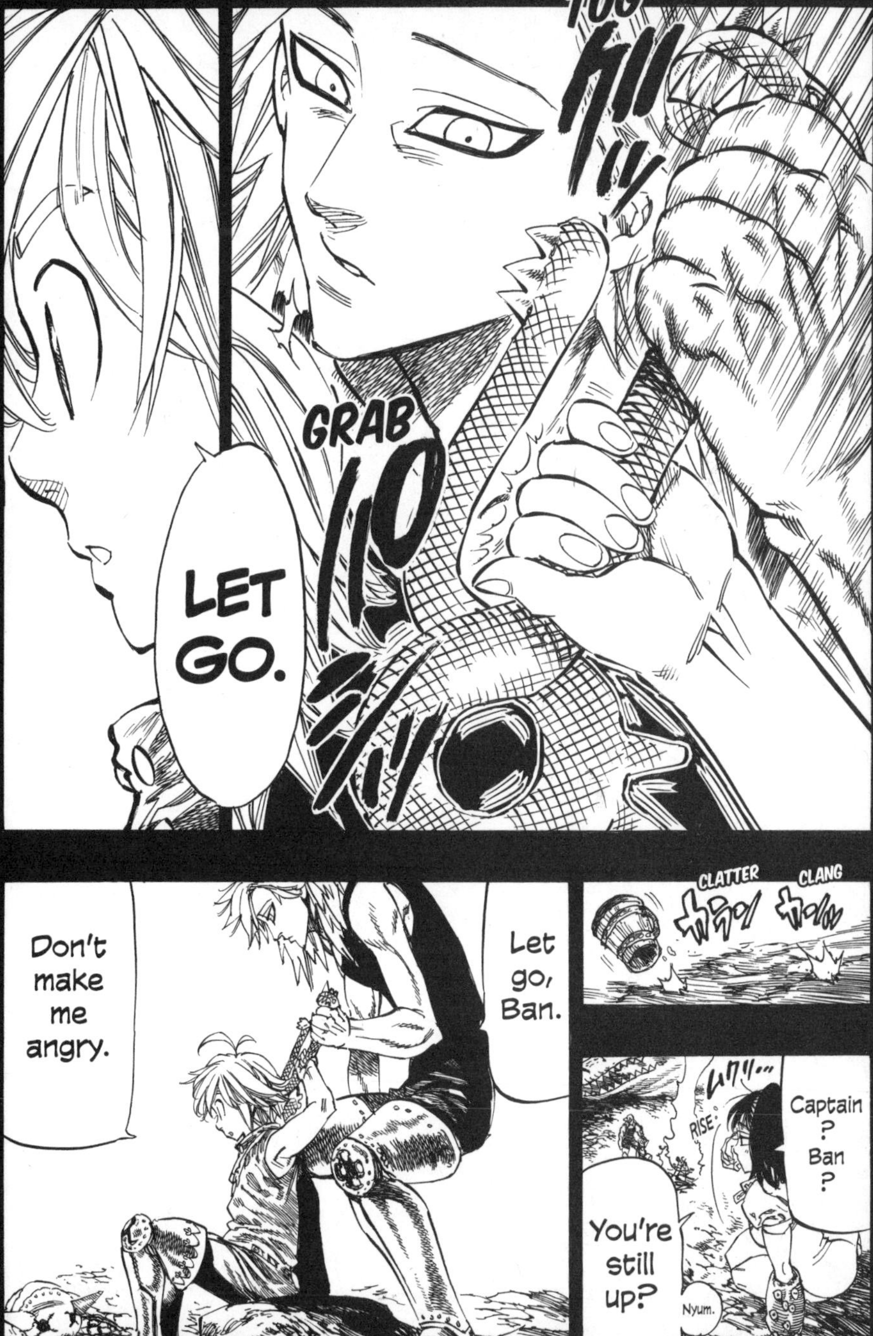
TUG
GRAB
LET GO.
CLATTER
CLANG
Captain? Ban?
RISE
You're still up?
Nyum.
Let go, Ban.
Don't make me angry.

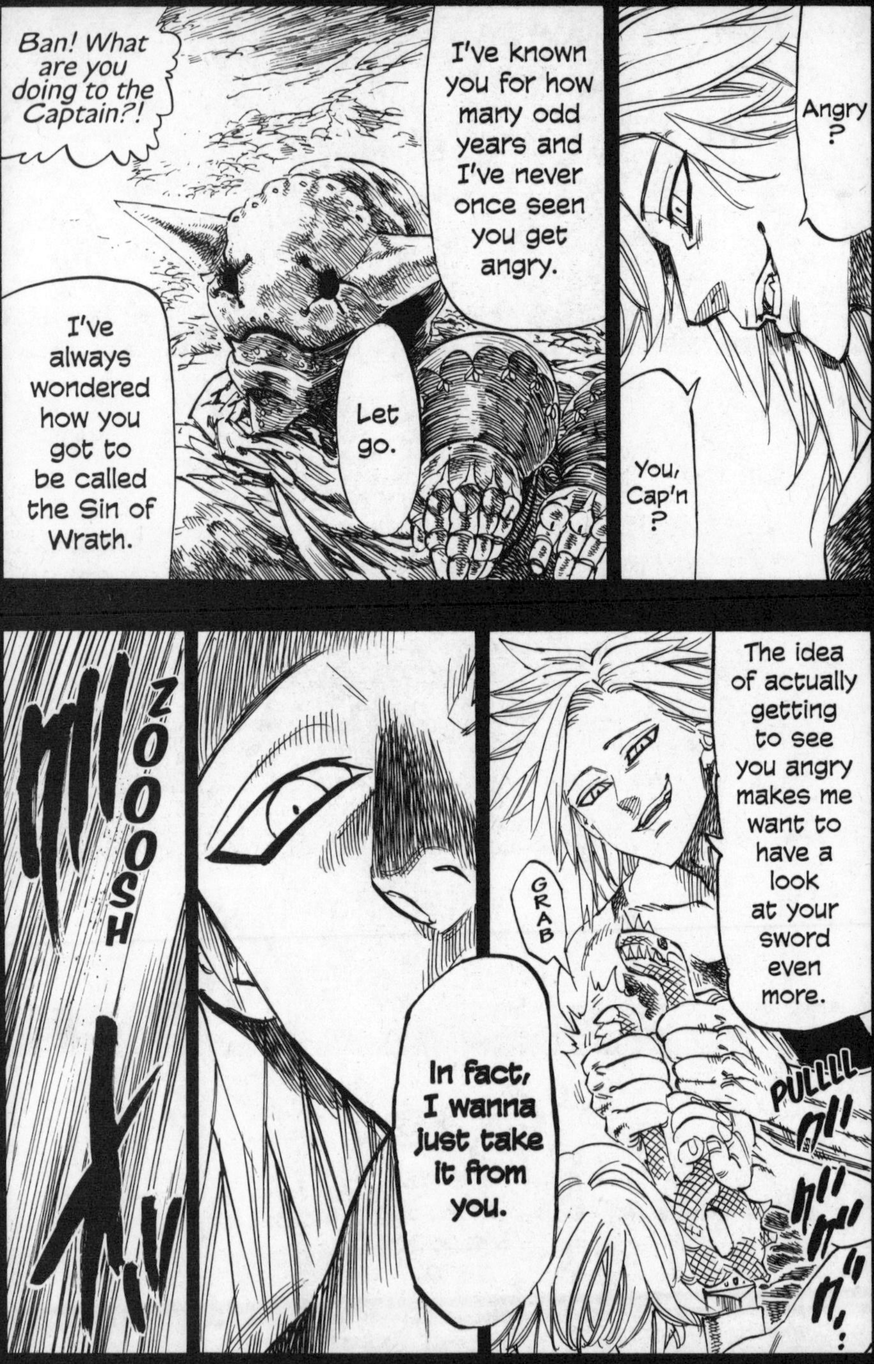
Ban! What are you doing to the Captain?!
Let go.
I've always wondered how you got to be called the Sin of Wrath.
I've known you for how many odd years and I've never once seen you get angry.
Angry?
You, Cap'n?
The idea of actually getting to see you angry makes me want to have a look at your sword even more.
GRAB
PULLLL
In fact, I wanna just take it from you.
ZOOOOSH

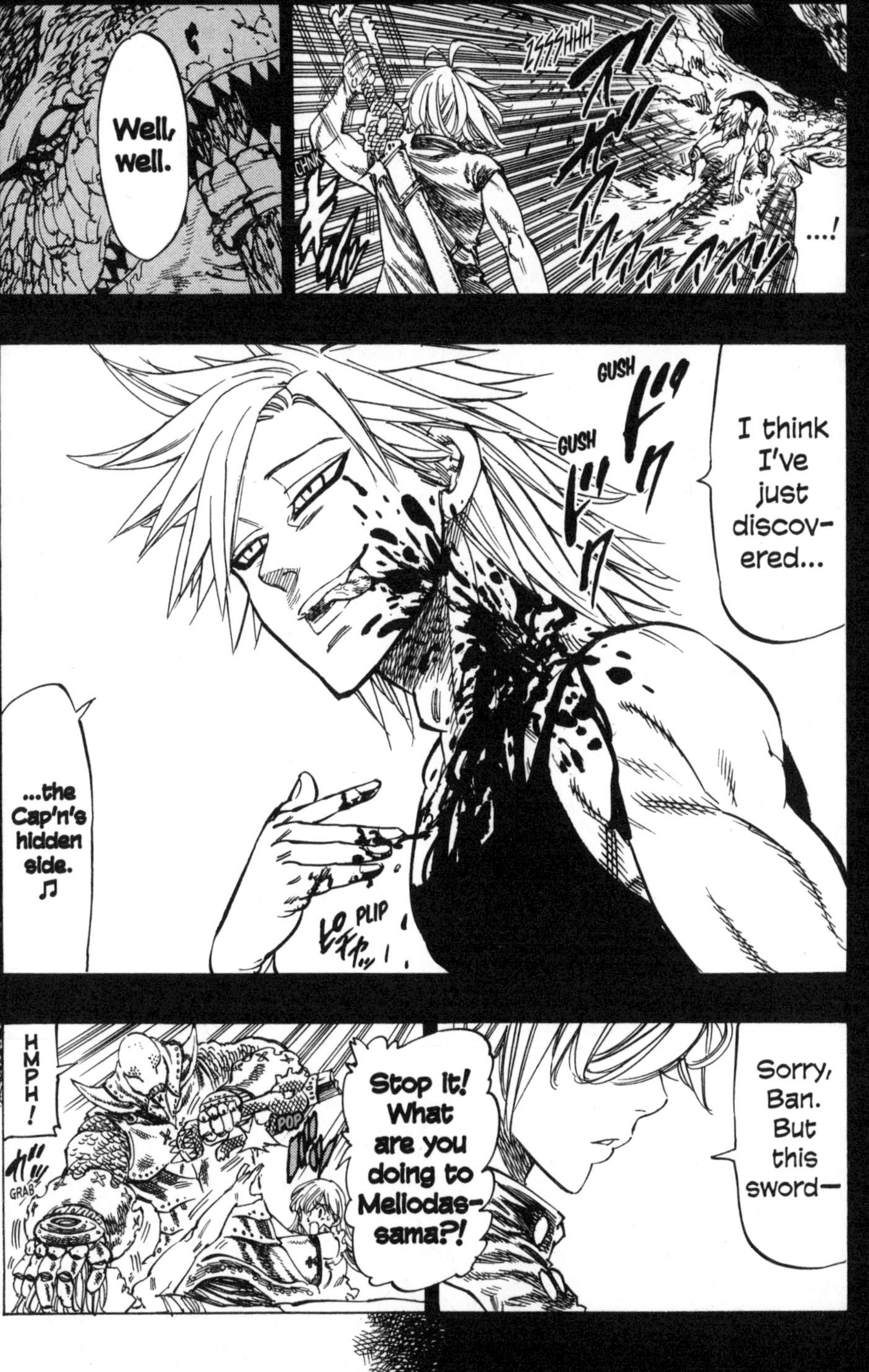
ZSSSHHH
CHINK
...!
Well, well.
GUSH
GUSH
I think I've just discovered...
...the Cap'n's hidden side. ♫
PLIP
Sorry, Ban. But this sword—
Stop it! What are you doing to Meliodas-sama?!
POP
HMPH!
GRAB

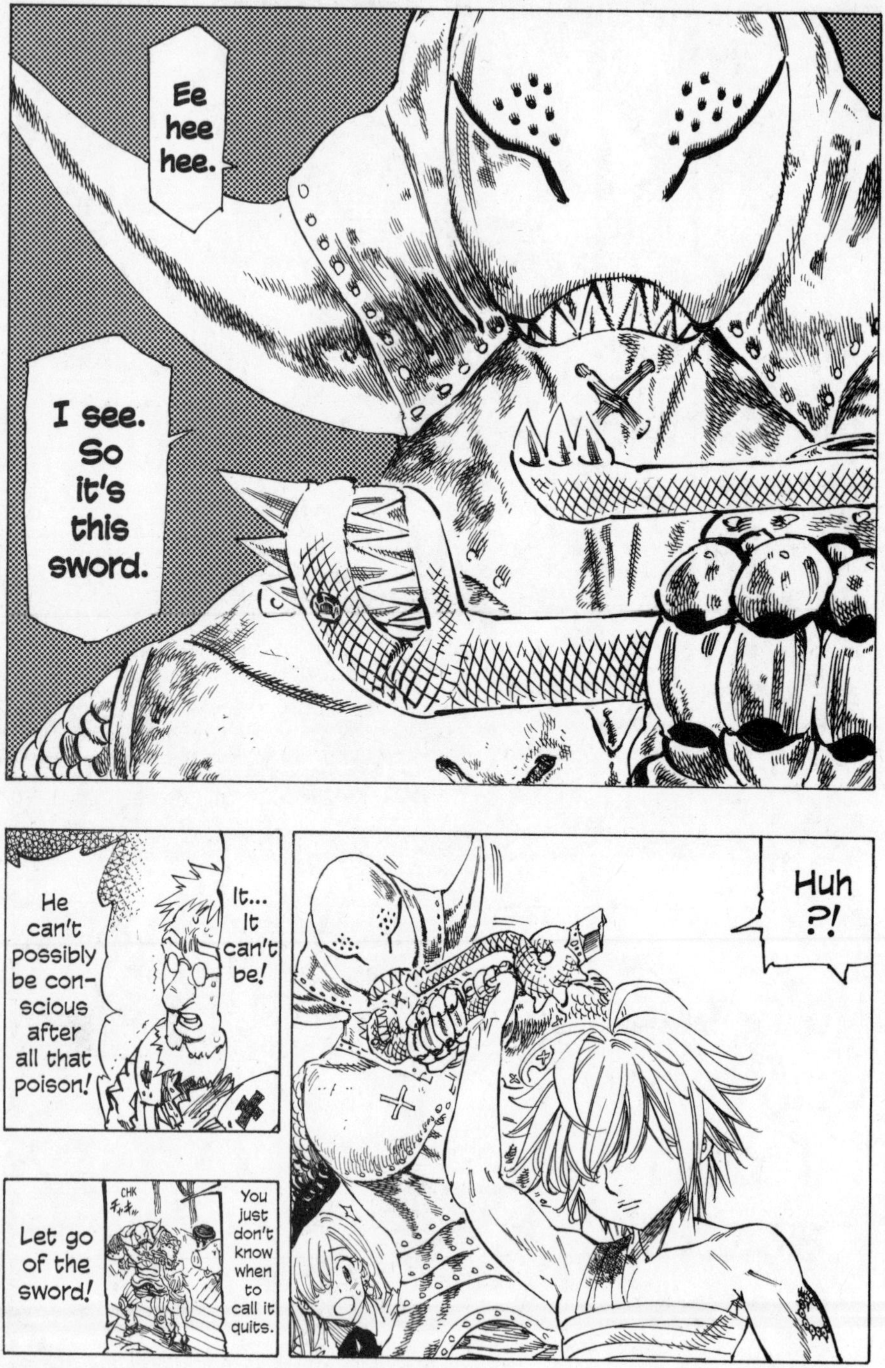

Ee hee hee.
I see. So it's this sword.
Huh?!
It... It can't be!
He can't possibly be conscious after all that poison!
You just don't know when to call it quits.
CHK
Let go of the sword!

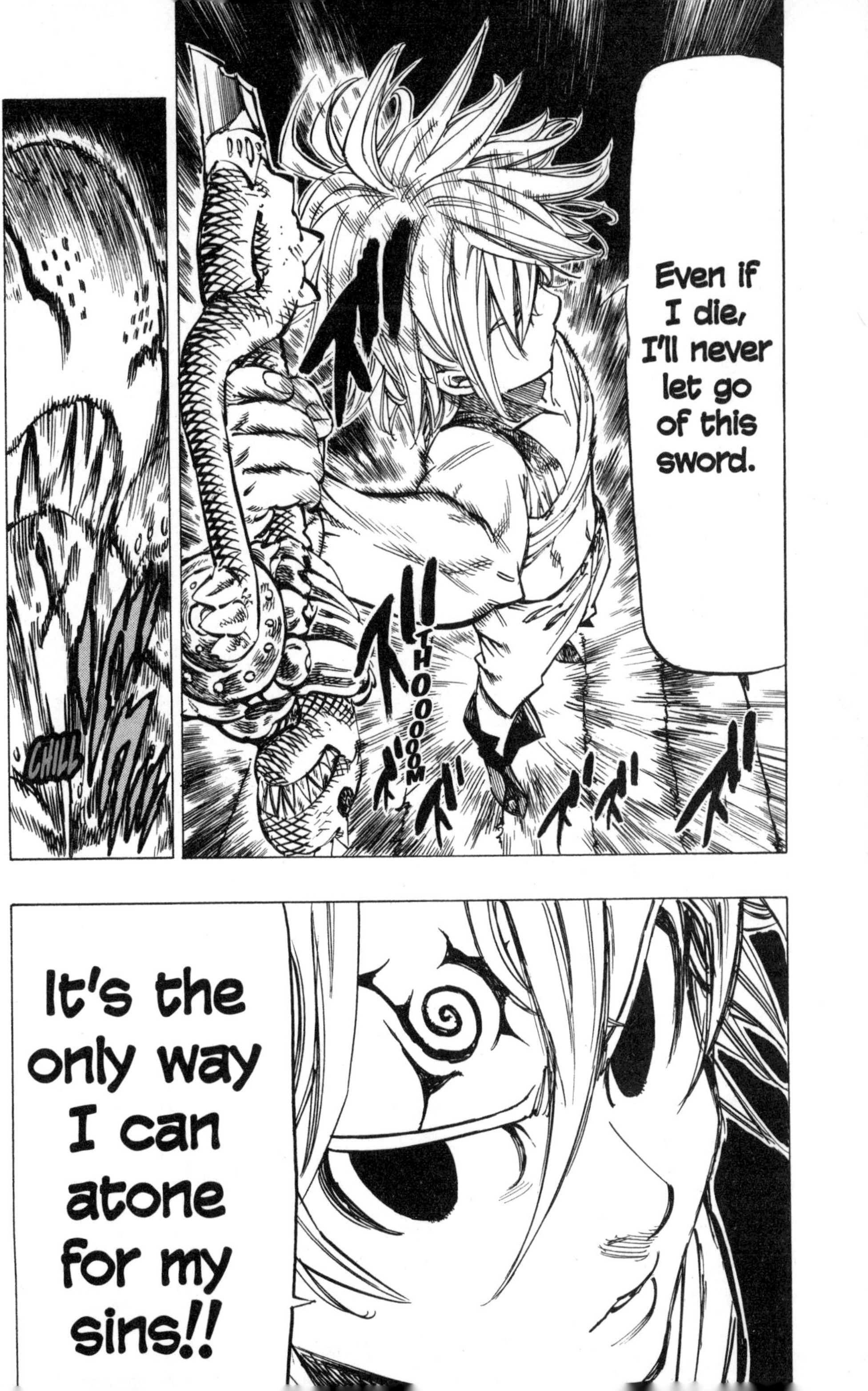
Even if I die, I'll never let go of this sword.
THOOOOOM
CHILL
It's the only way I can atone for my sins!!

Chapter 10 - An Unseen Malice

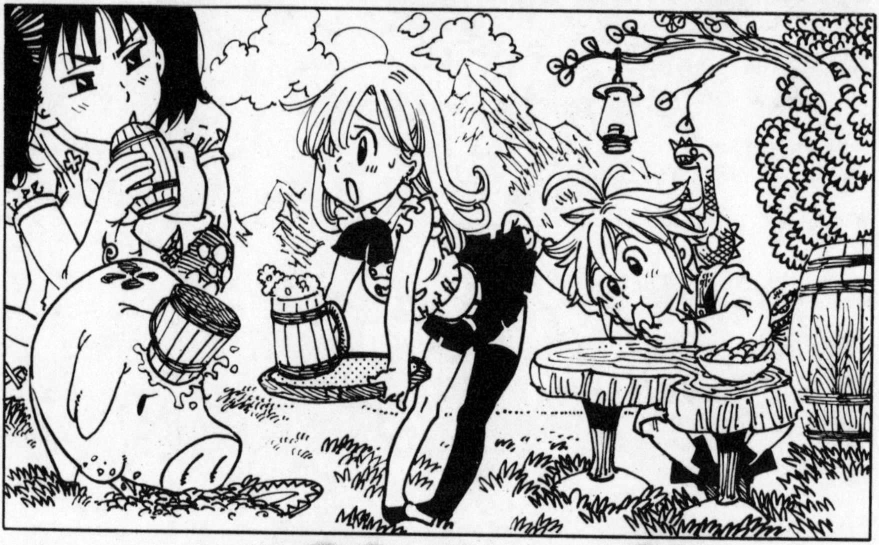

THE SEVEN DEADLY SINS

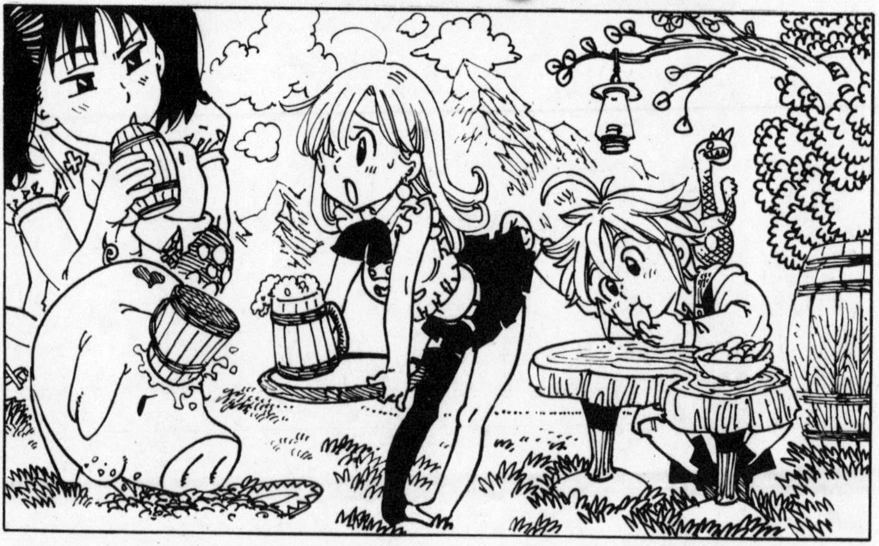

★ **There are nine things different between these two images! Can you find them all?**

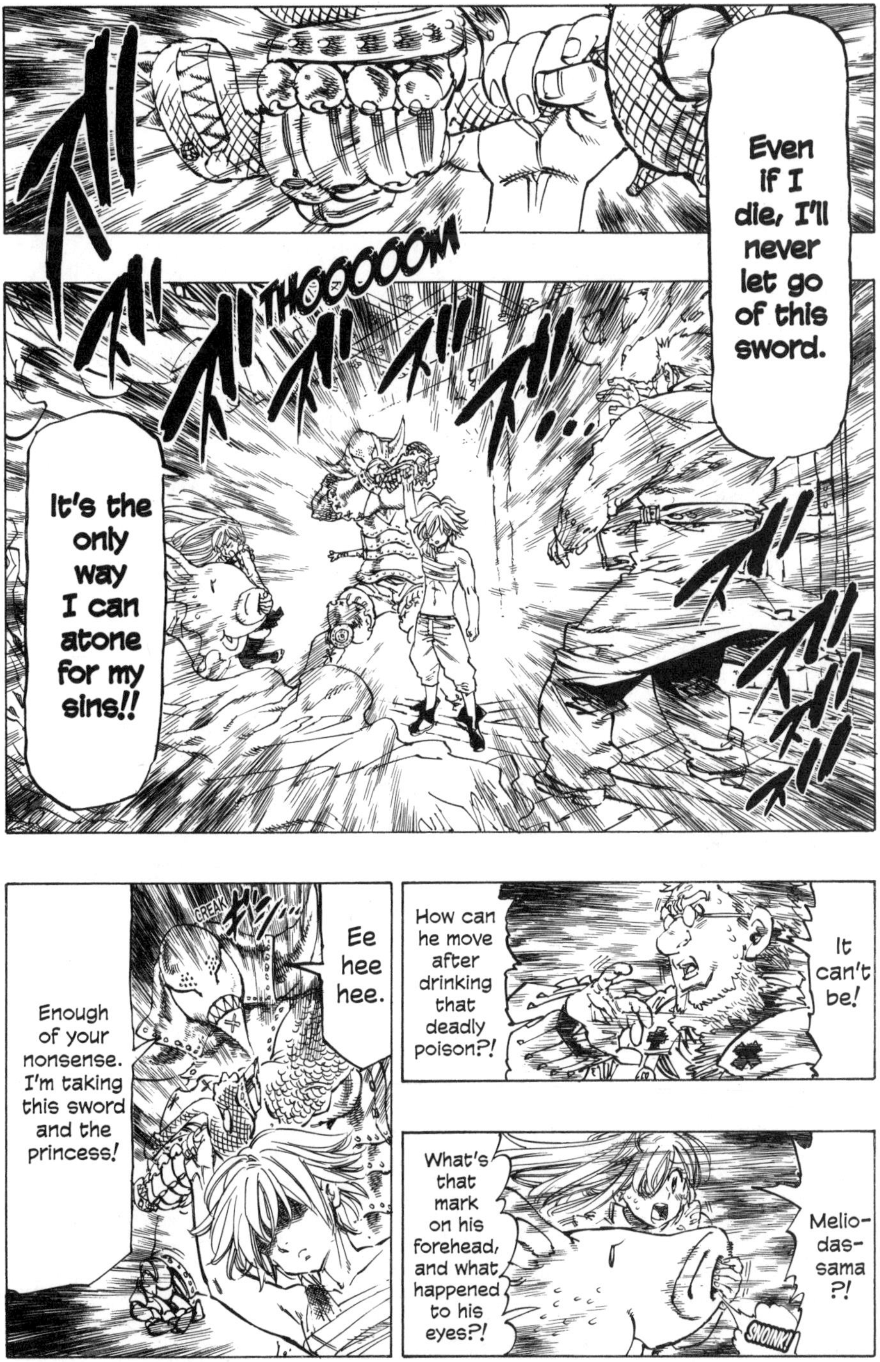
Even if I die, I'll never let go of this sword.
THOOOOOM
It's the only way I can atone for my sins!!
It can't be!
How can he move after drinking that deadly poison?!
Melio-das-sama?!
What's that mark on his forehead, and what happened to his eyes?!
SNOINK!
CREAK
Ee hee hee.
Enough of your nonsense. I'm taking this sword and the princess!

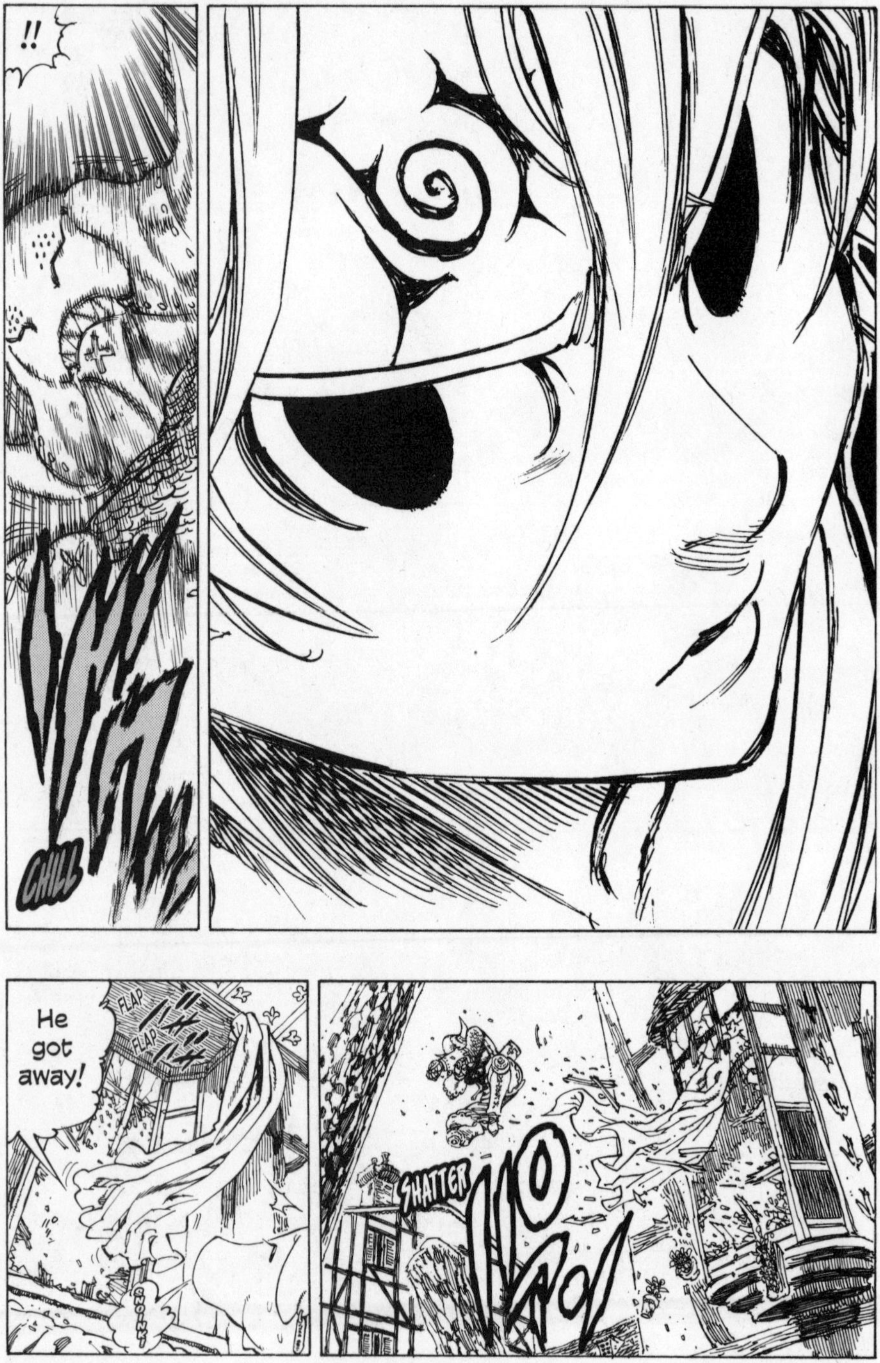
!!
CHILL
SHATTER
He got away!
FLAP
FLAP
SNOINK!

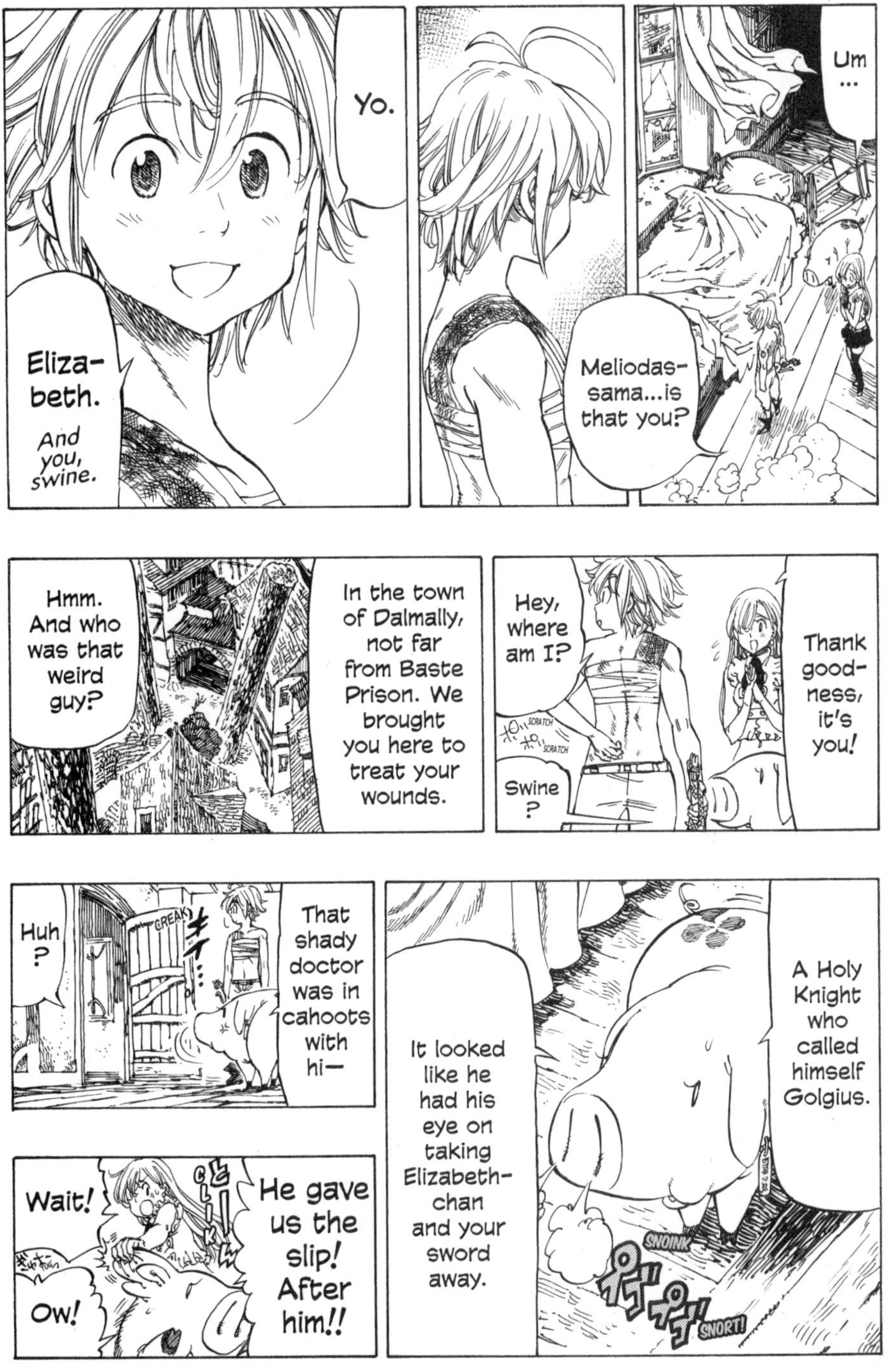
Um ...
Meliodas-sama...is that you?
Yo.
Eliza-beth.
And you, swine.
Thank good-ness, it's you!
Hey, where am I?
SCRATCH
SCRATCH
Swine?
In the town of Dalmally, not far from Baste Prison. We brought you here to treat your wounds.
Hmm. And who was that weird guy?
A Holy Knight who called himself Golgius.
It looked like he had his eye on taking Elizabeth-chan and your sword away.
SNOINK
SNORT!
That shady doctor was in cahoots with hi—
CREAK
Huh?
He gave us the slip! After him!!
Wait!
Ow!

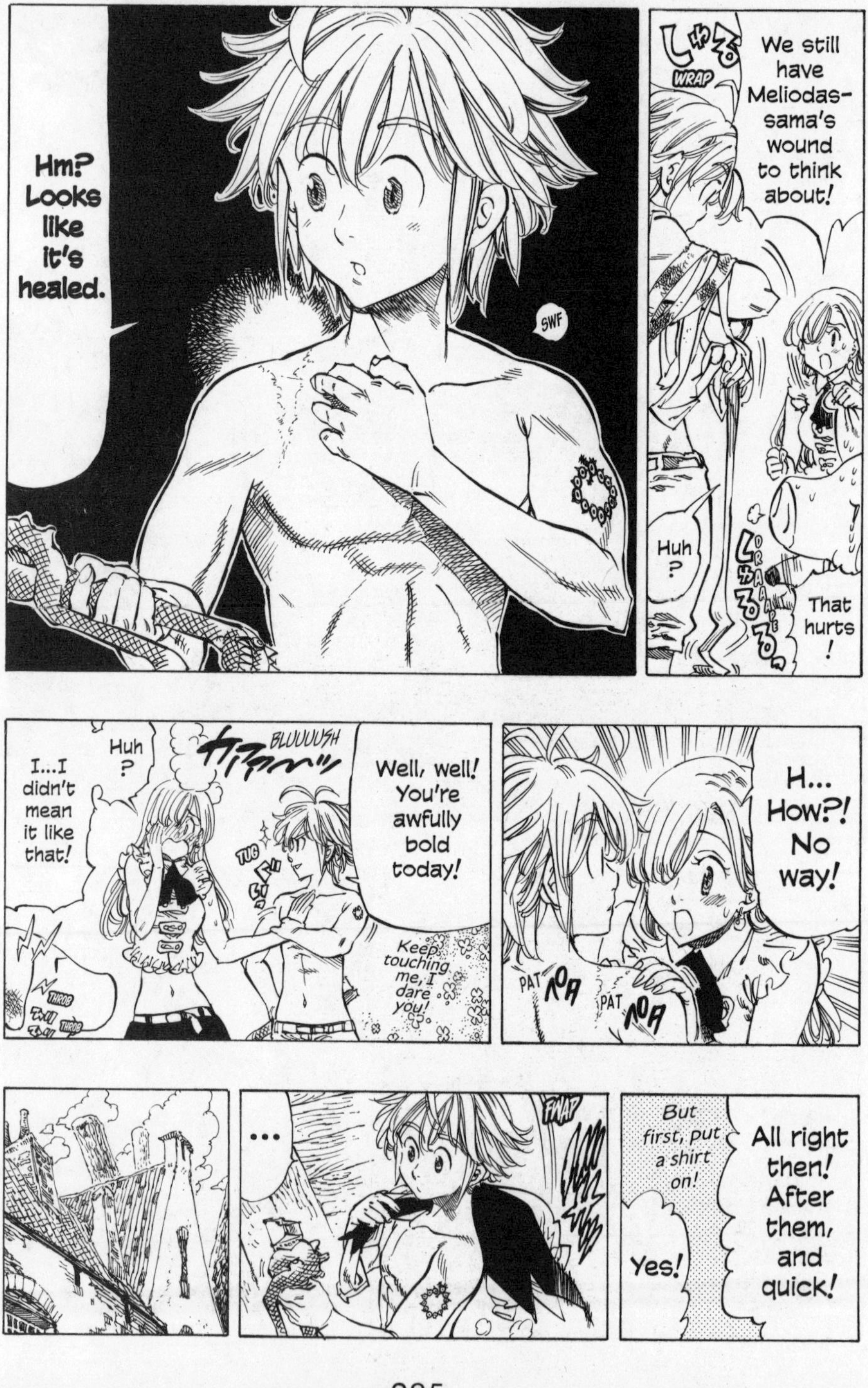
WRAP
We still have Meliodas-sama's wound to think about!
Huh?
That hurts!
Hm? Looks like it's healed.
SWF
H... How?! No way!
PAT
PAT
Well, well! You're awfully bold today!
BLUUUUSH
Huh?
I...I didn't mean it like that!
TUG
Keep touching me, I dare you!
THROB
THROB
All right then! After them, and quick!
But first, put a shirt on!
Yes!
FWAP
...

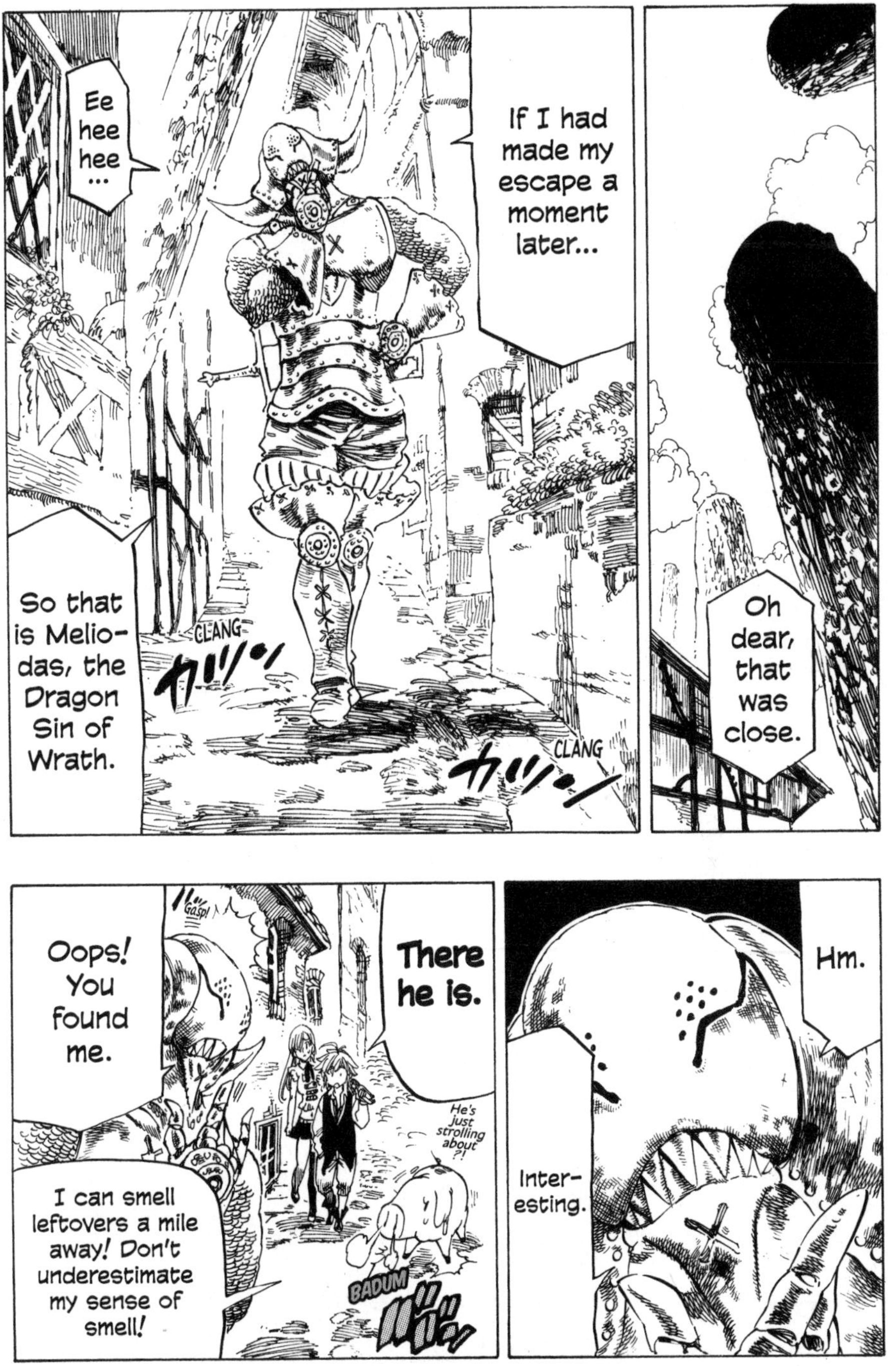

Oh dear, that was close.
If I had made my escape a moment later...
Ee hee hee...
CLANG
CLANG
So that is Meliodas, the Dragon Sin of Wrath.
Hm.
Inter-esting.
There he is.
Gasp!
Oops! You found me.
He's just strolling about?!
BADUM
I can smell leftovers a mile away! Don't underestimate my sense of smell!

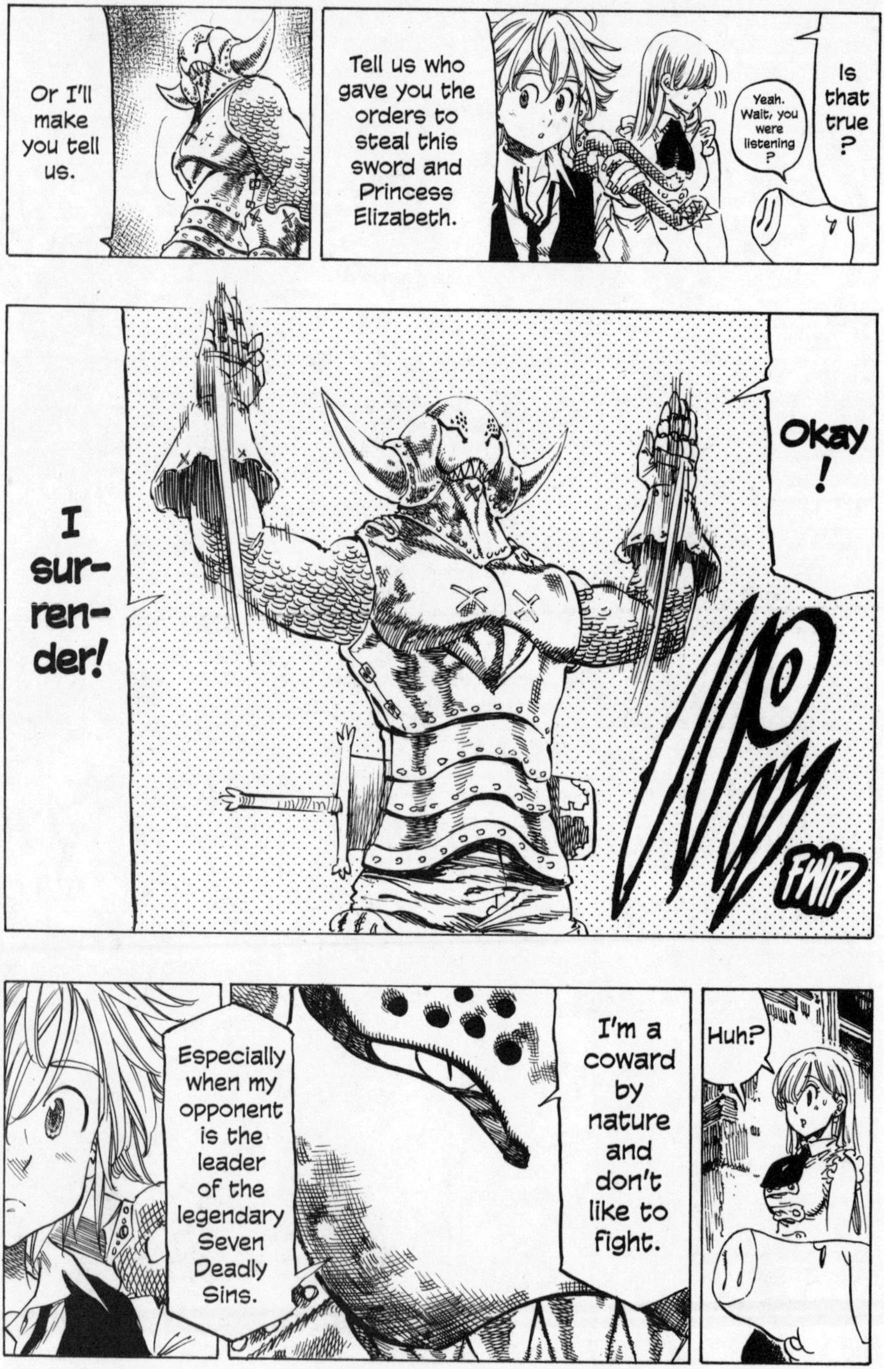
Is that true?
Yeah. Wait, you were listening?
Tell us who gave you the orders to steal this sword and Princess Elizabeth.
Or I'll make you tell us.
Okay!
FWIP
I surrender!
Huh?
I'm a coward by nature and don't like to fight.
Especially when my opponent is the leader of the legendary Seven Deadly Sins.

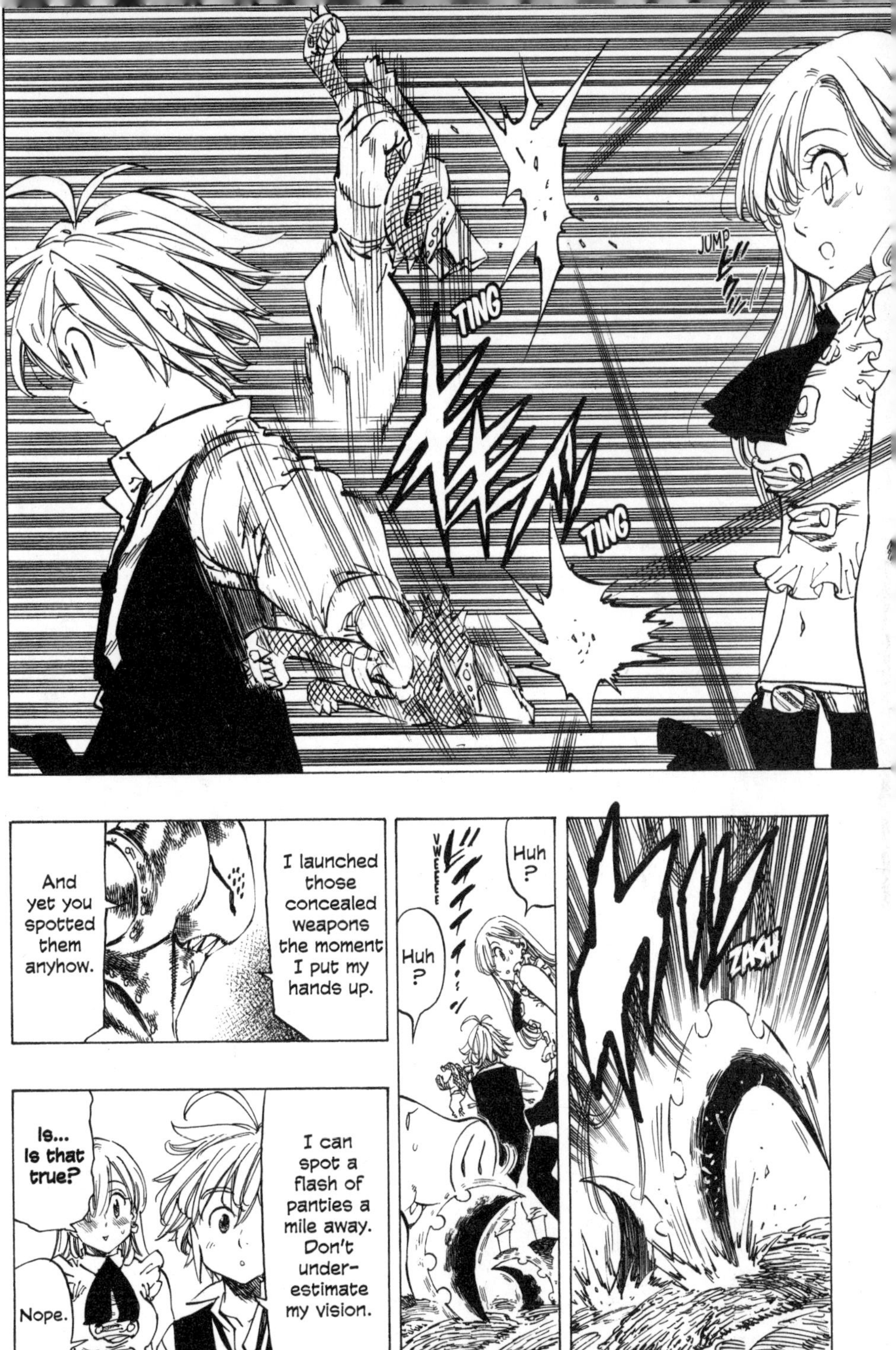

JUMP
TING
TING
ZASH
Huh?
VWEEEE
Huh?
I launched those concealed weapons the moment I put my hands up.
And yet you spotted them anyhow.
I can spot a flash of panties a mile away. Don't under-estimate my vision.
Is... Is that true?
Nope.

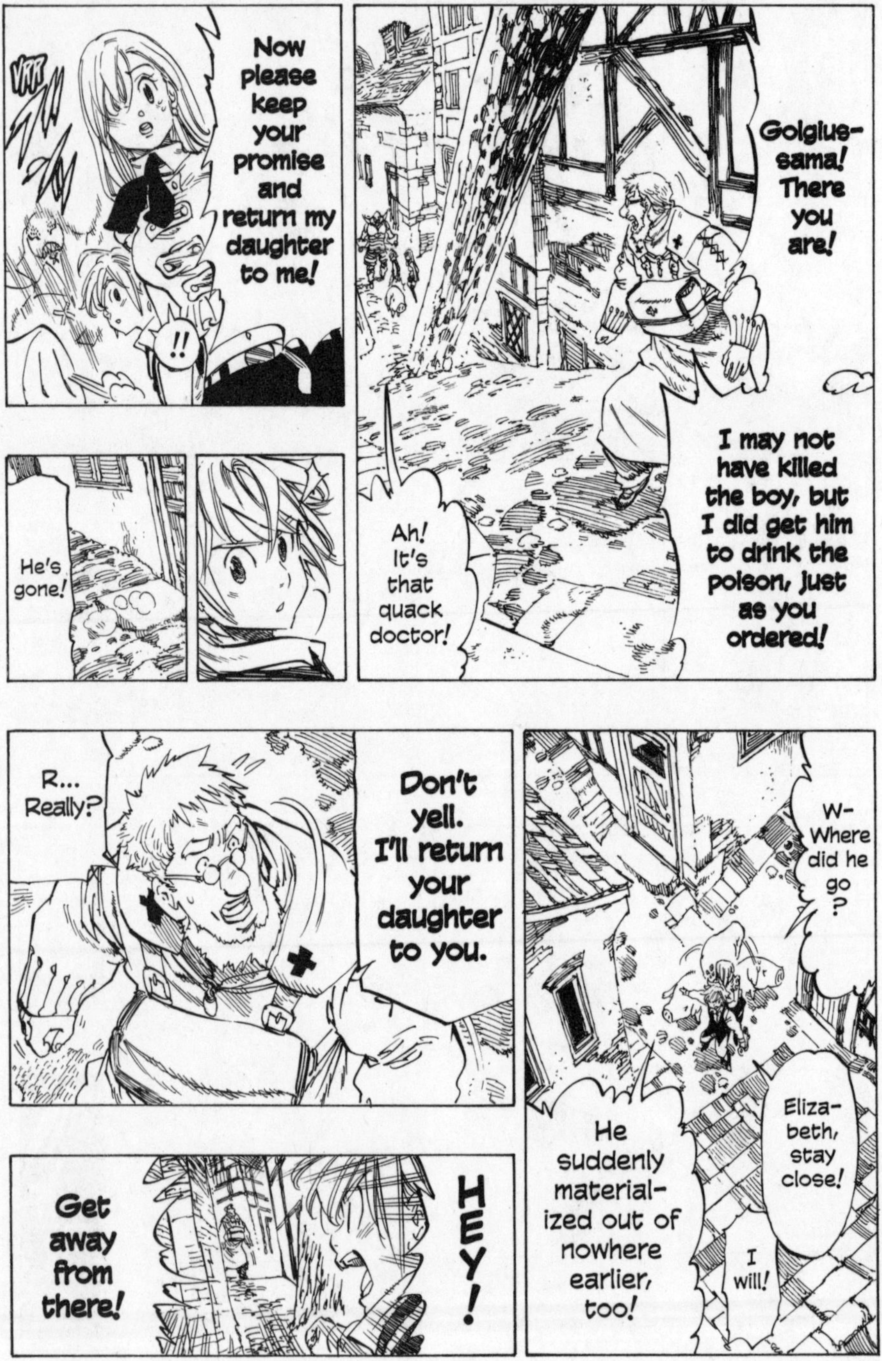
Golgius-sama! There you are!
I may not have killed the boy, but I did get him to drink the poison, just as you ordered!
Ah! It's that quack doctor!
Now please keep your promise and return my daughter to me!
VRR
!!
He's gone!
W-Where did he go?
Eliza-beth, stay close!
He suddenly material-ized out of nowhere earlier, too!
I will!
Don't yell. I'll return your daughter to you.
R... Really?
HEY!
Get away from there!

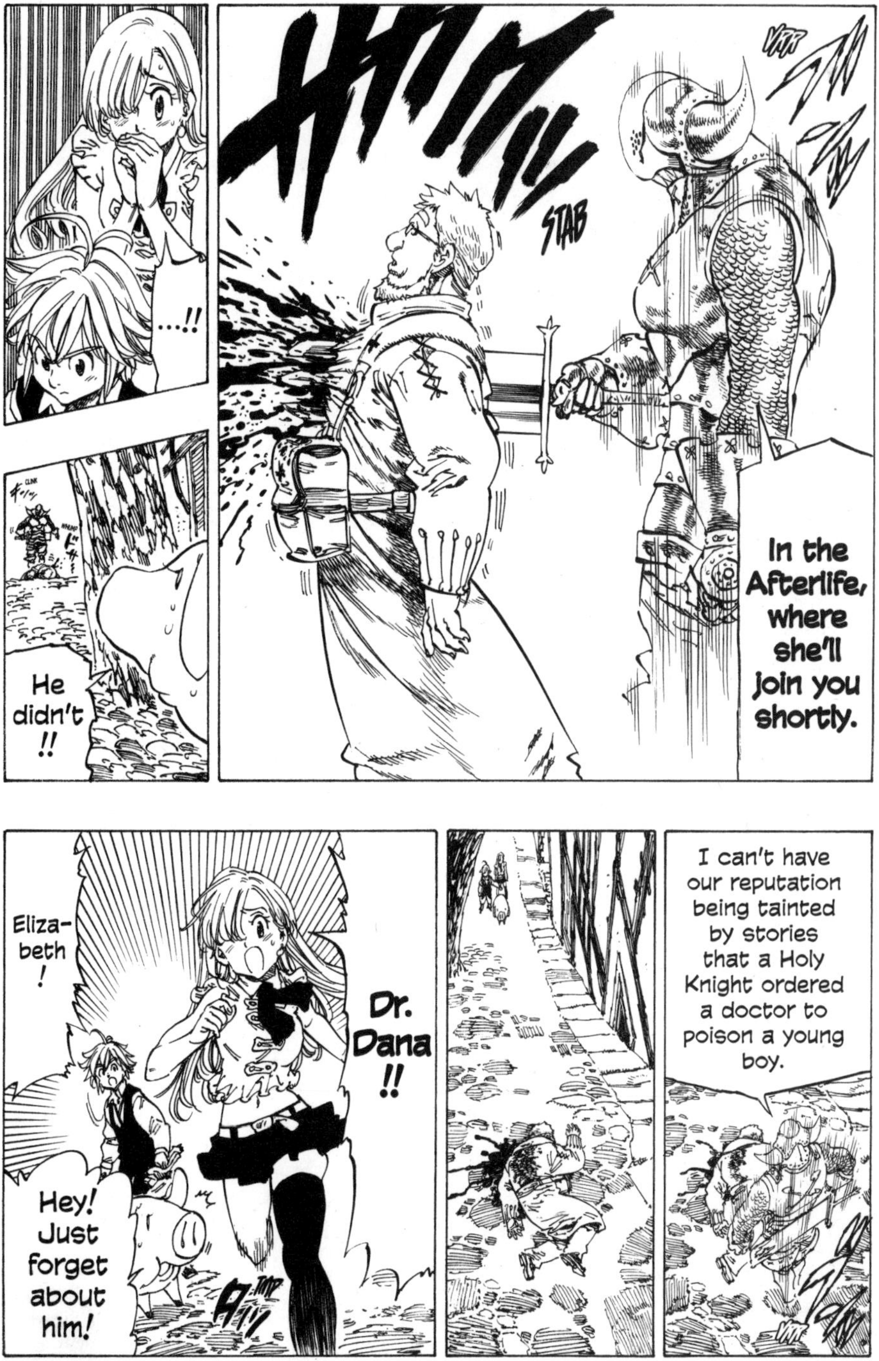
VRR
STAB
In the Afterlife, where she'll join you shortly.
...!!
He didn't !!
I can't have our reputation being tainted by stories that a Holy Knight ordered a doctor to poison a young boy.
Dr. Dana !!
Eliza-beth !
Hey! Just forget about him!

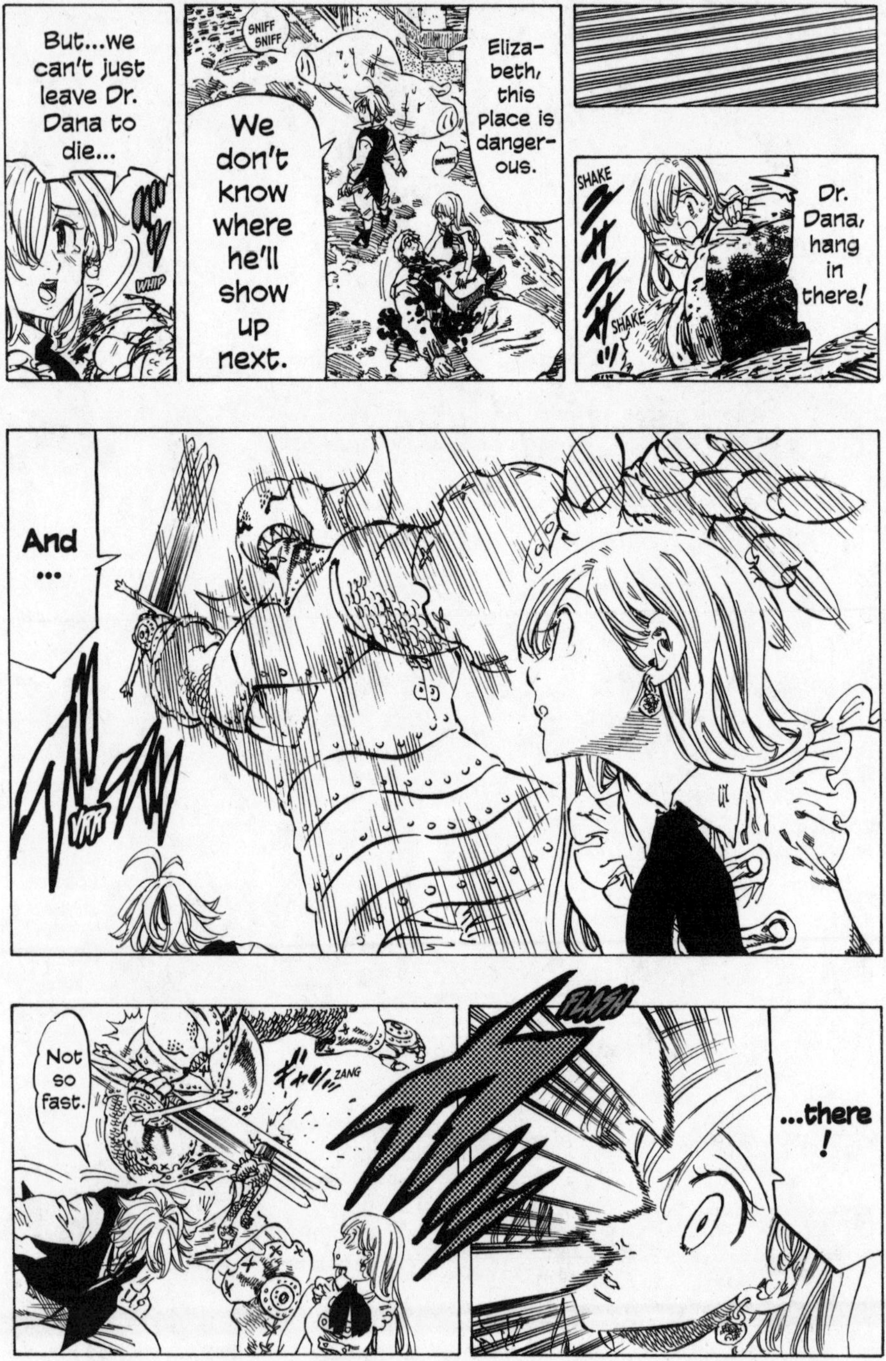
SHAKE
SHAKE
Dr. Dana, hang in there!
Eliza-beth, this place is danger-ous.
SNIFF SNIFF
We don't know where he'll show up next.
But...we can't just leave Dr. Dana to die...
WHIP
And ...
VRR
FLASH
...there!
ZANG
Not so fast.

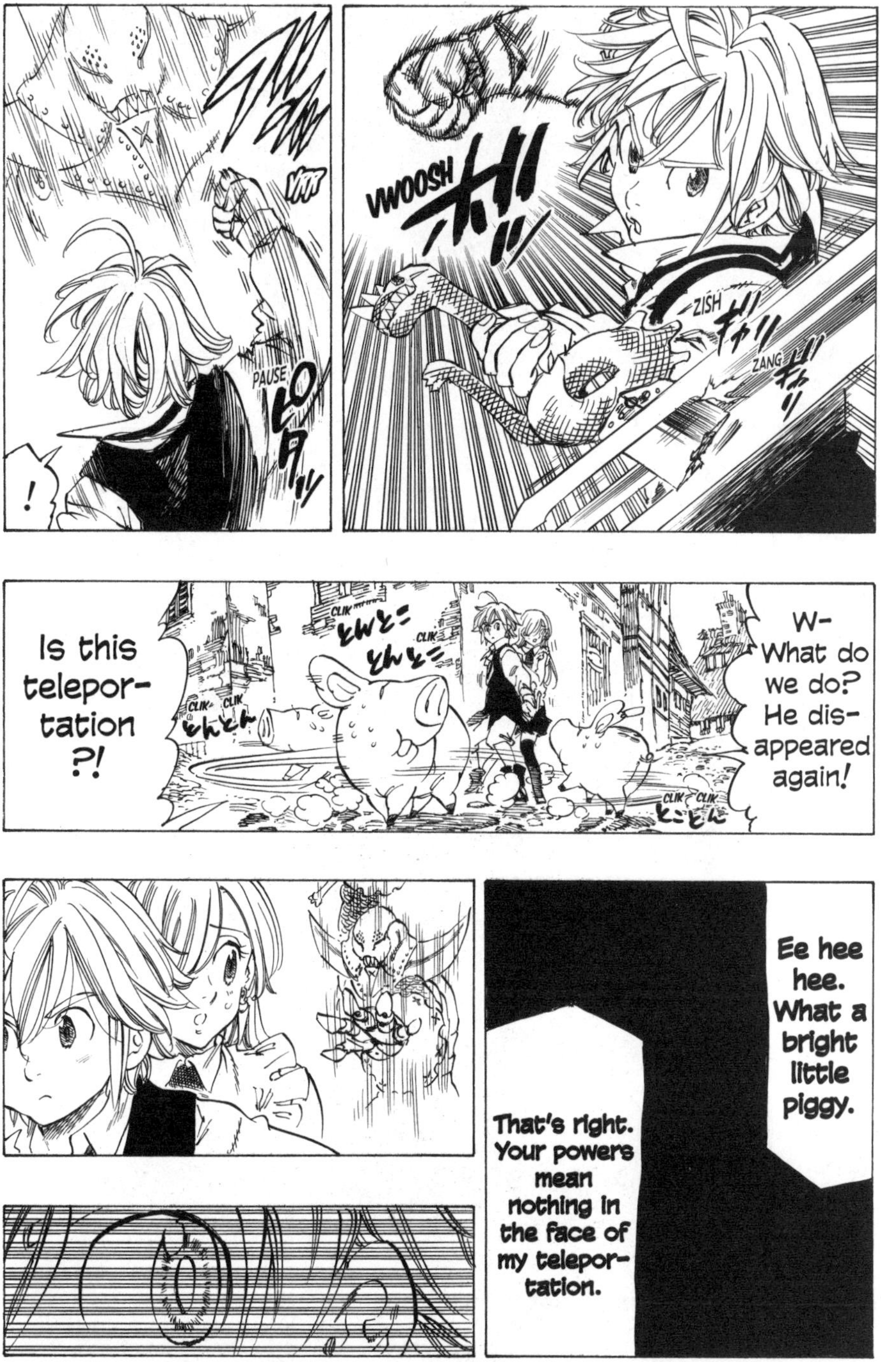

VWOOSH
ZISH
ZANG
VRR
PAUSE
!
W- What do we do? He dis-appeared again!
CLIK
CLIK
CLIK
CLIK
CLIK CLIK
Is this telepor-tation ?!
Ee hee hee. What a bright little piggy.
That's right. Your powers mean nothing in the face of my telepor-tation.

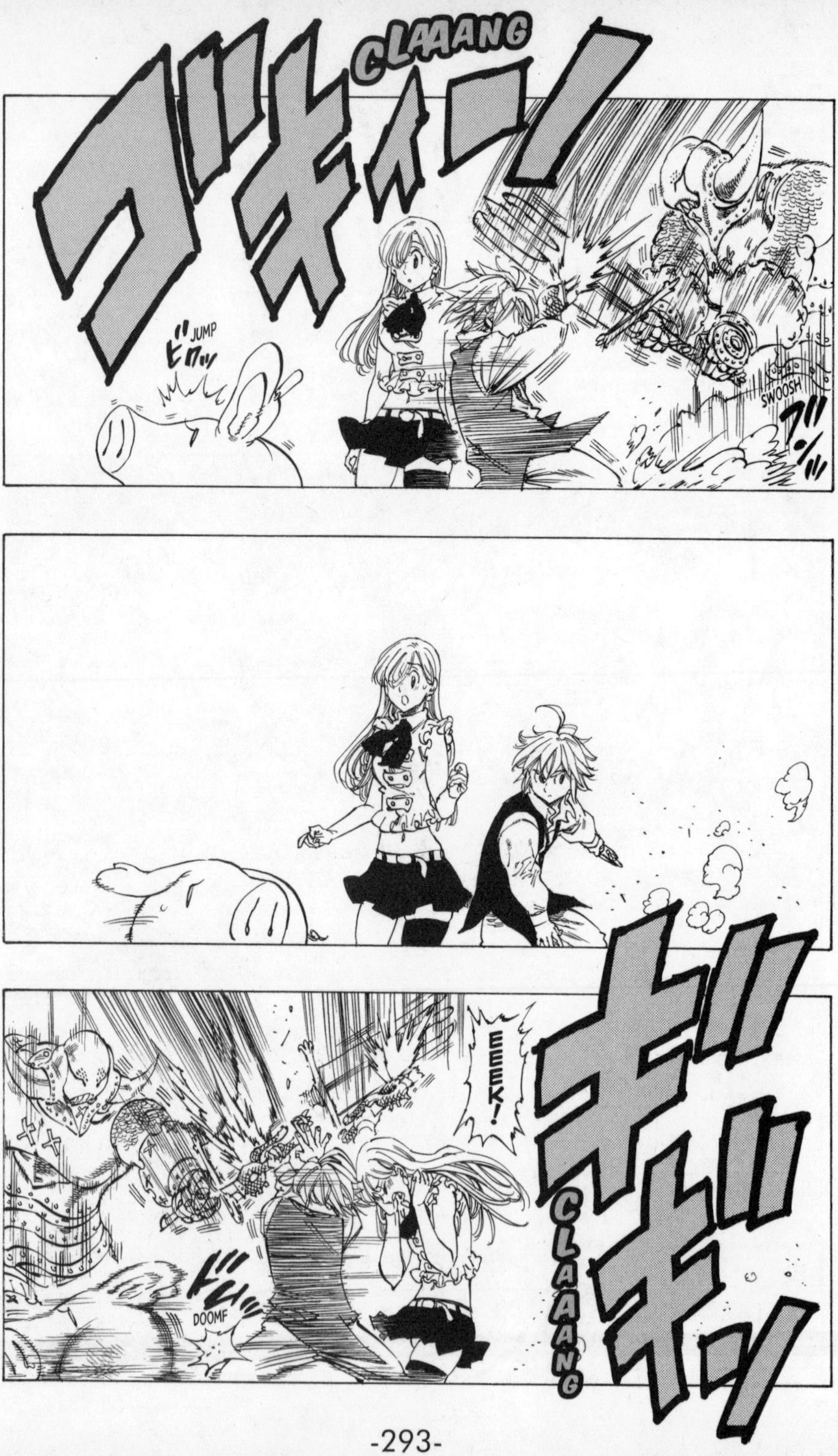
ゴギィーン!
CLAAANG
ブンッ
SWOOSH
ビクッ
JUMP
ギギギッ
CLAAANG
EEEK!
ドムッ
DOOMF

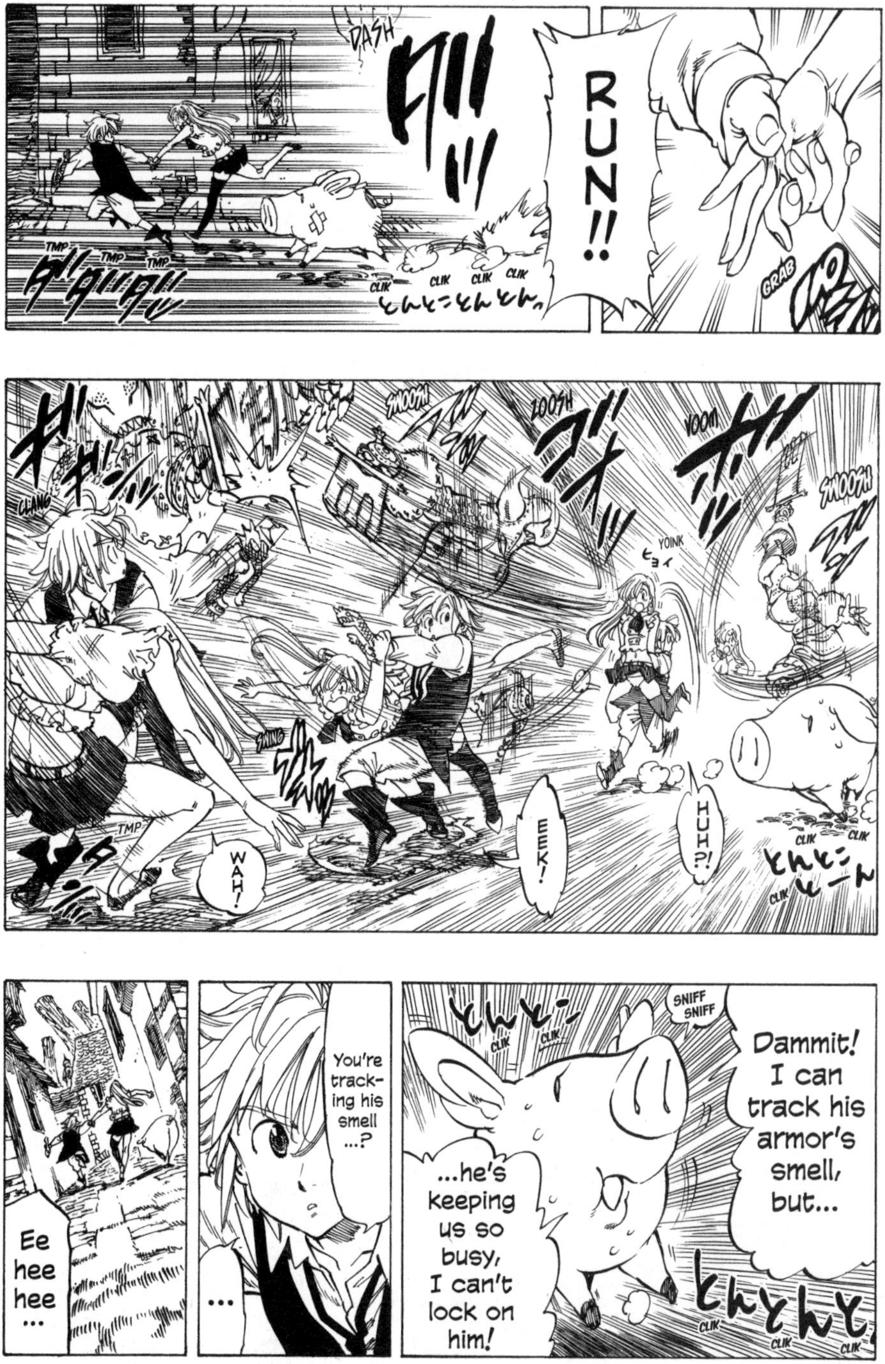

GRAB
RUN!!
DASH
TMP TMP TMP
CLIK CLIK CLIK CLIK
SWOOSH
VOOM
LOOSH
SWOOSH
CLANG
YOINK
HUH?!
EEK!
SWING
WAH!
TMP
CLIK CLIK CLIK
SNIFF SNIFF
Dammit! I can track his armor's smell, but...
...he's keeping us so busy, I can't lock on him!
CLIK CLIK CLIK CLIK CLIK
You're tracking his smell ...?
...
Ee hee hee ...

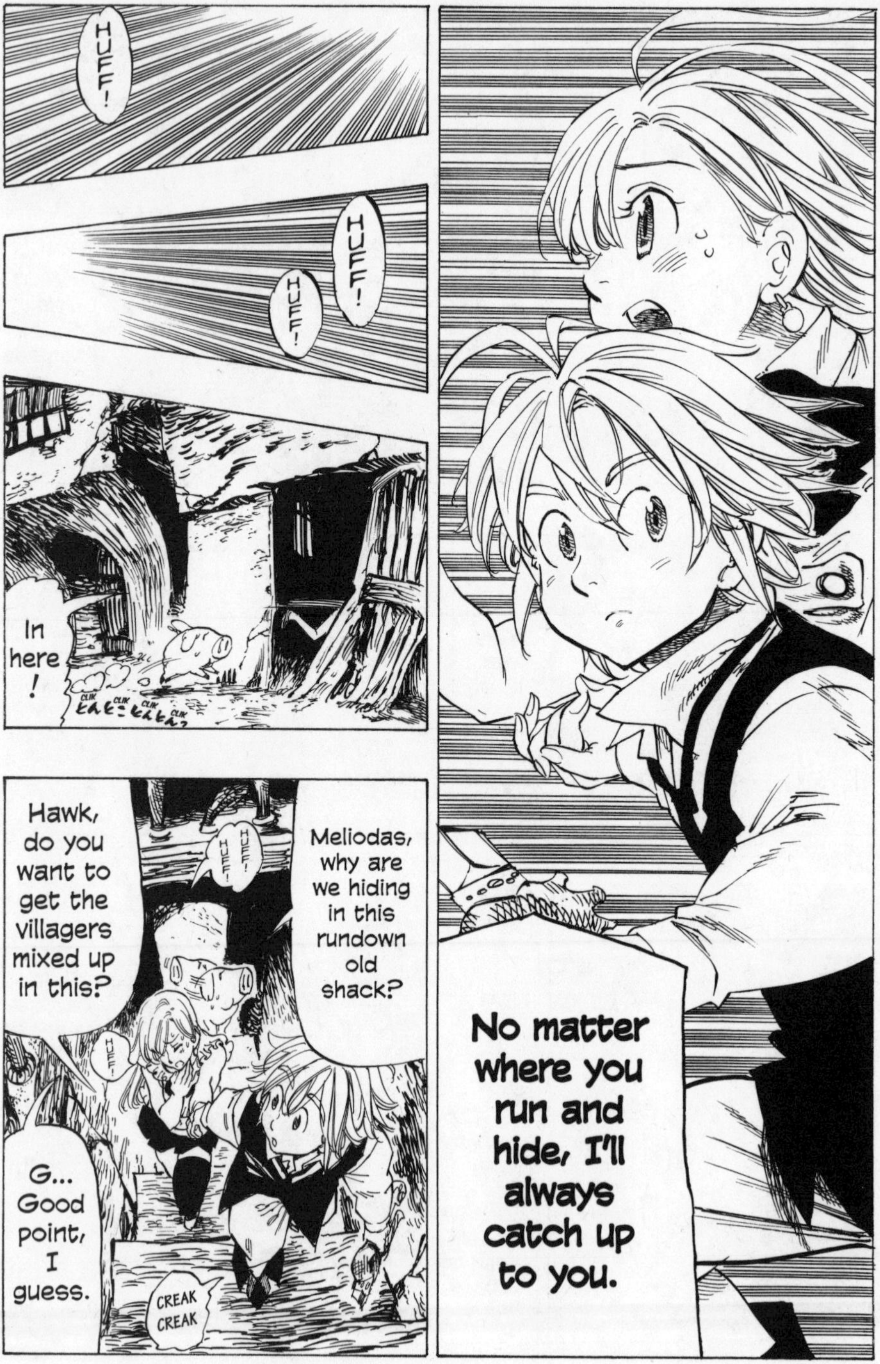
No matter where you run and hide, I'll always catch up to you.
HUFF!
HUFF!
HUFF!
In here!
CLIK CLIK CLIK CLIK
Meliodas, why are we hiding in this rundown old shack?
HUFF! HUFF!
Hawk, do you want to get the villagers mixed up in this?
HUFF!
G... Good point, I guess.
CREAK CREAK

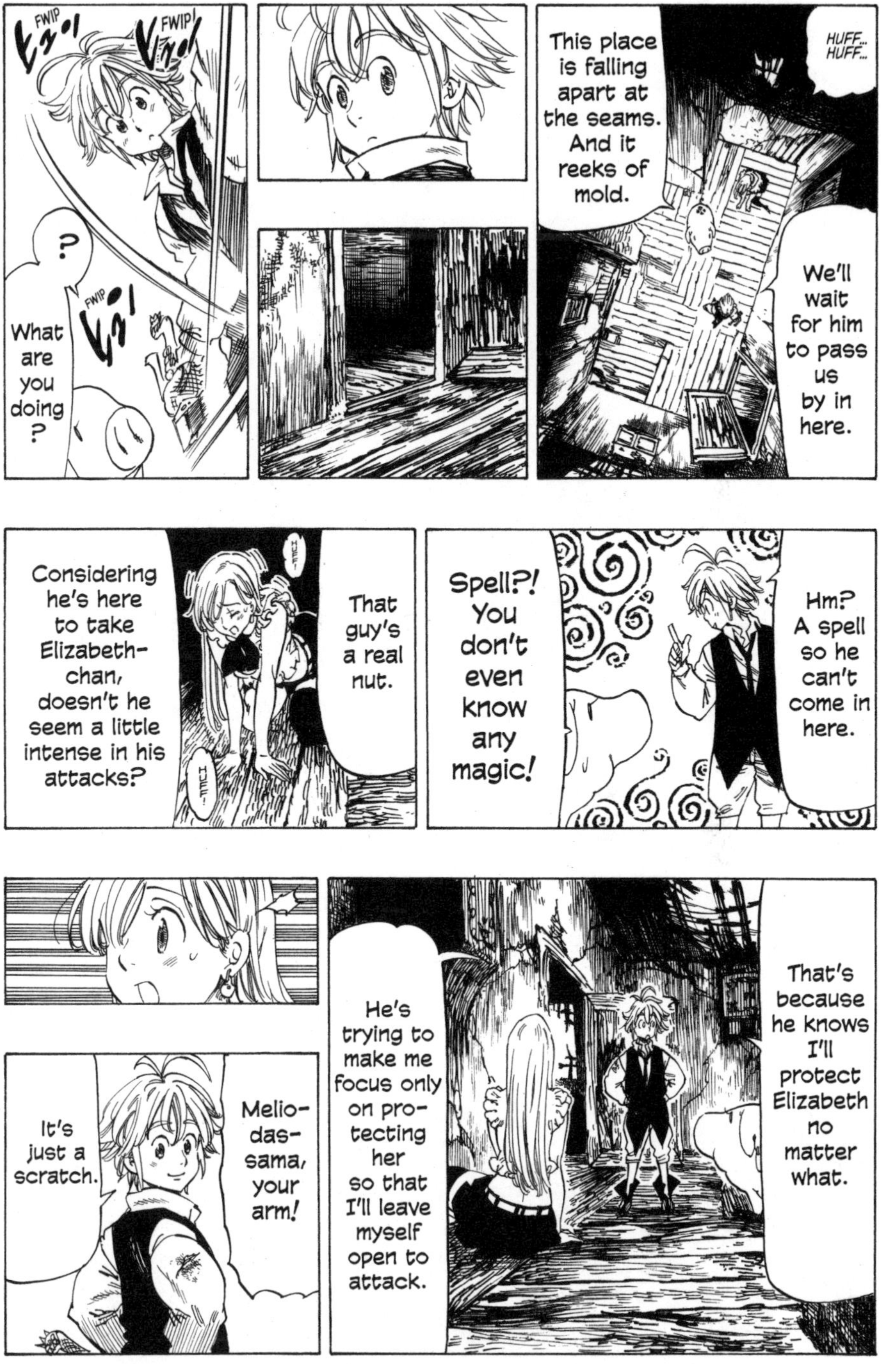
HUFF... HUFF...
This place is falling apart at the seams. And it reeks of mold.
We'll wait for him to pass us by in here.
FWIP!
FWIP
?
FWIP
What are you doing?
Hm? A spell so he can't come in here.
Spell?! You don't even know any magic!
That guy's a real nut.
HUFF
Considering he's here to take Elizabeth-chan, doesn't he seem a little intense in his attacks?
HUFF
That's because he knows I'll protect Elizabeth no matter what.
He's trying to make me focus only on protecting her so that I'll leave myself open to attack.
Melio-das-sama, your arm!
It's just a scratch.

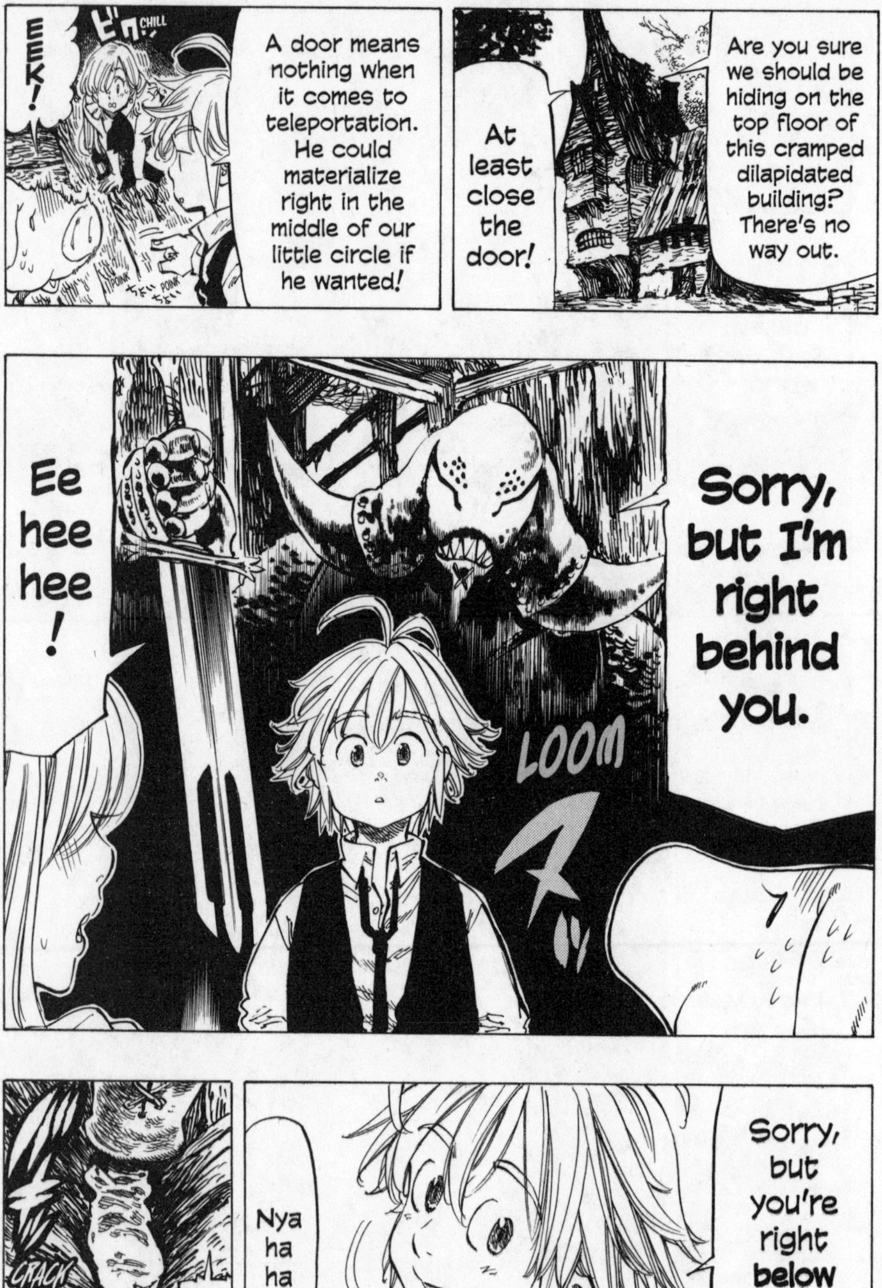
Are you sure we should be hiding on the top floor of this cramped dilapidated building? There's no way out.
At least close the door!
A door means nothing when it comes to teleportation. He could materialize right in the middle of our little circle if he wanted!
EEK!
CHILL
POINK
POINK
Sorry, but I'm right behind you.
LOOM
Ee hee hee!
Sorry, but you're right below us.
Nya ha ha!
CRACK
?!

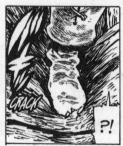

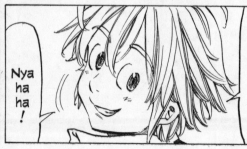

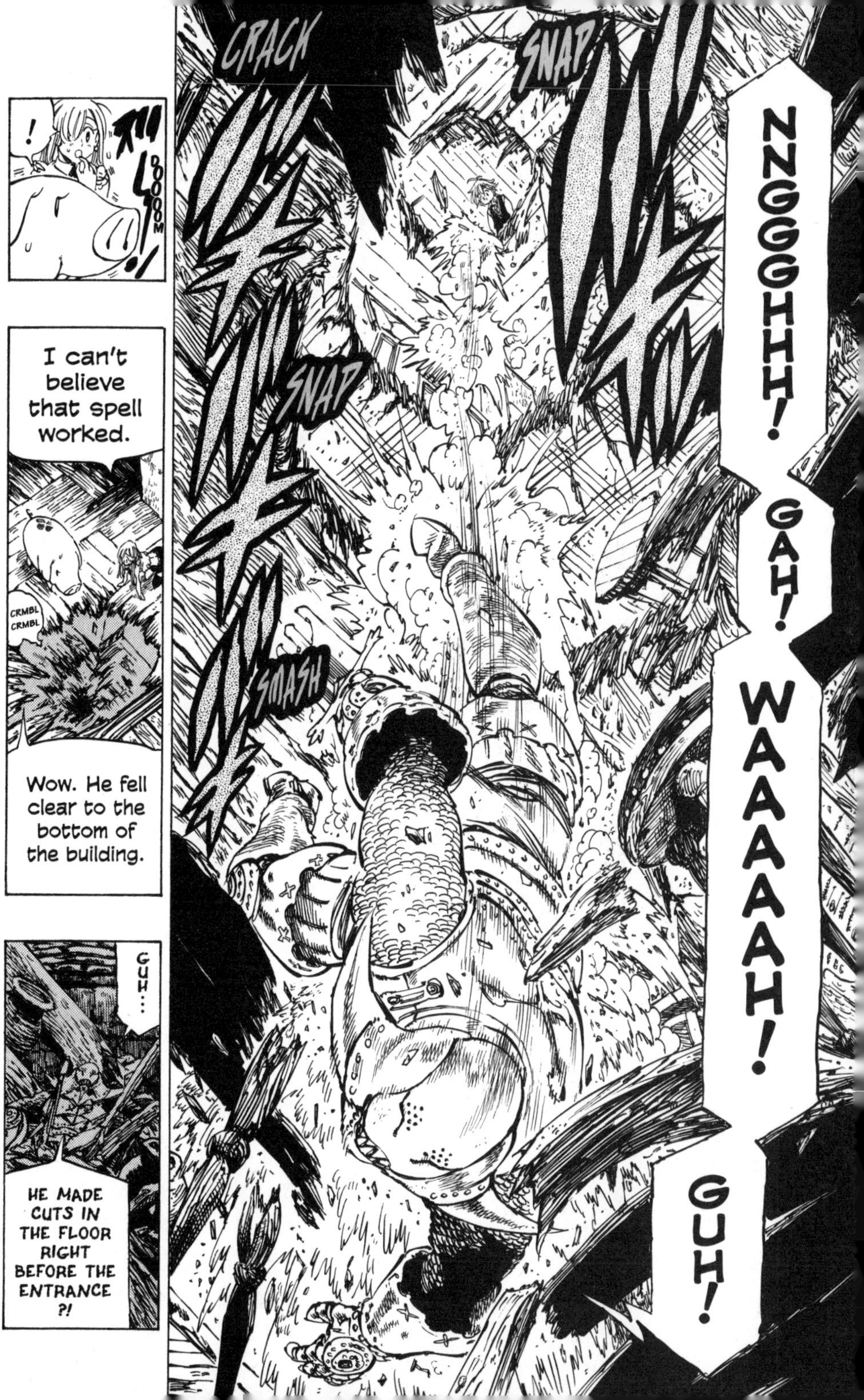
SNAP
CRACK
NNGGGHHH!
GAH!
WAAAAAAH!
SNAP
SMASH
GUH!
!
DOOOOOM!
I can't believe that spell worked.
CRMBL CRMBL
Wow. He fell clear to the bottom of the building.
GUH...
HE MADE CUTS IN THE FLOOR RIGHT BEFORE THE ENTRANCE ?!

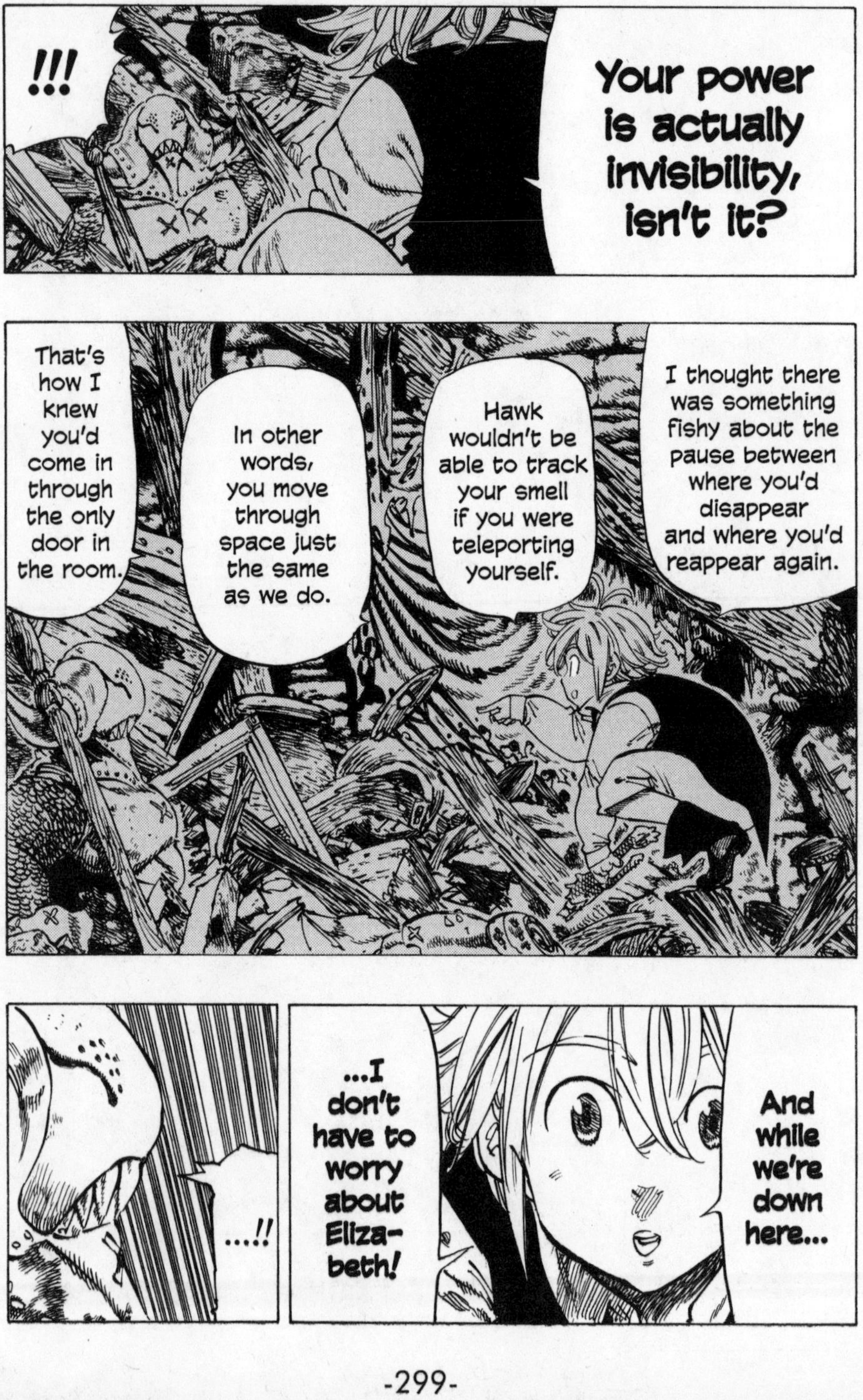
Your power is actually invisibility, isn't it?
!!!
I thought there was something fishy about the pause between where you'd disappear and where you'd reappear again.
Hawk wouldn't be able to track your smell if you were teleporting yourself.
In other words, you move through space just the same as we do.
That's how I knew you'd come in through the only door in the room.
And while we're down here...
...I don't have to worry about Eliza-beth!
...!!

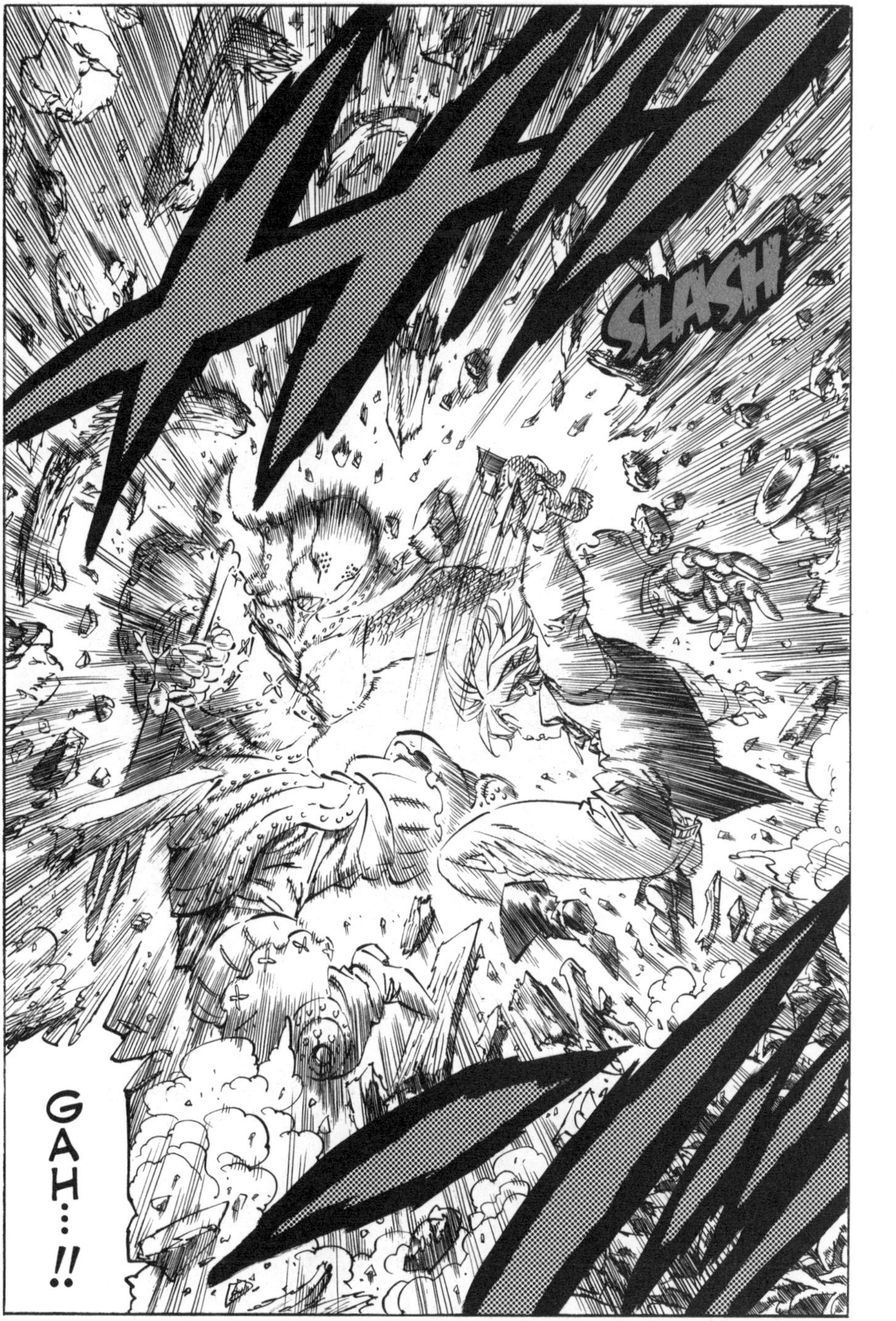
SLASH
GAH...!!

Chapter 11 - Even If You Died

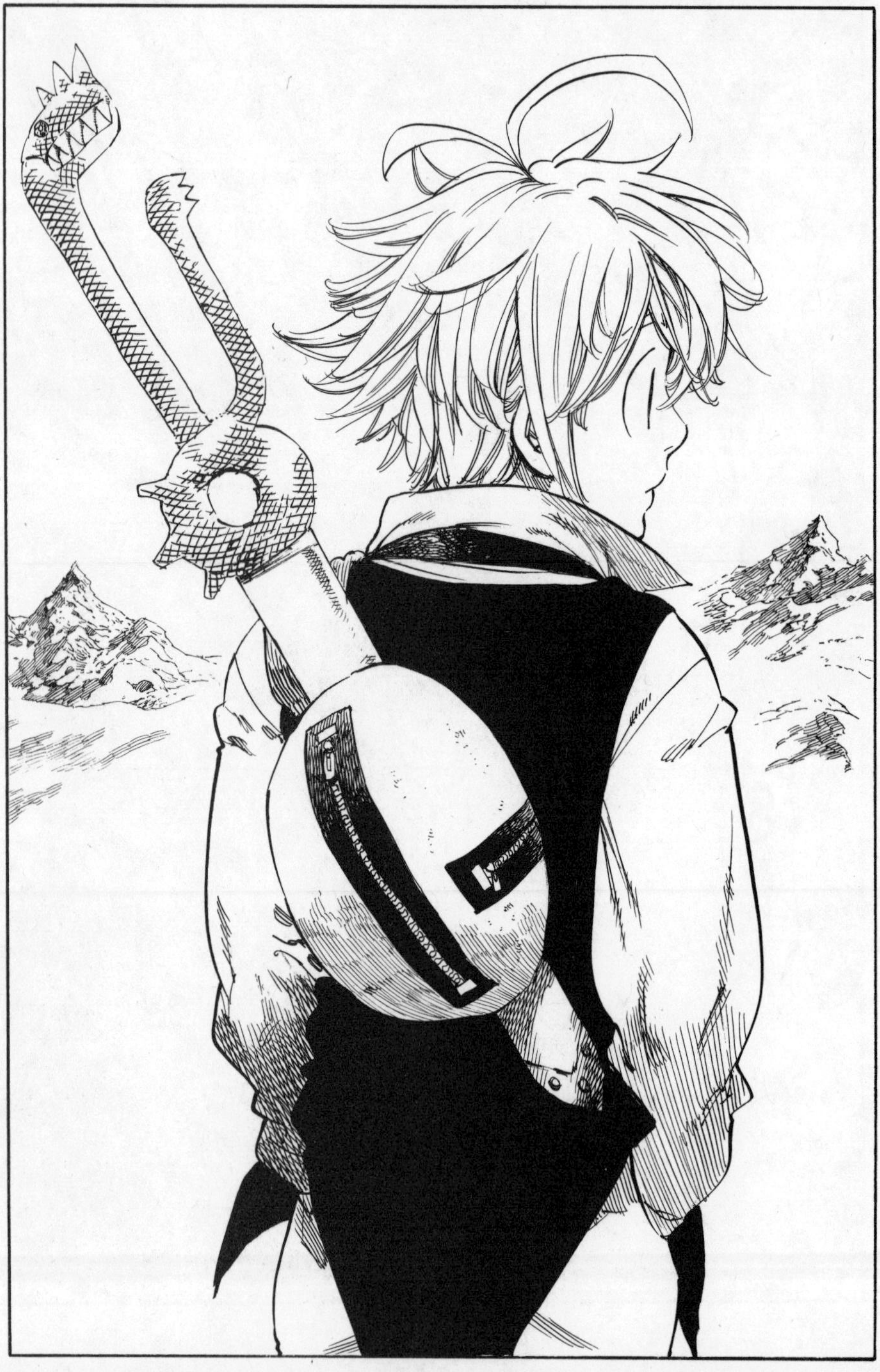

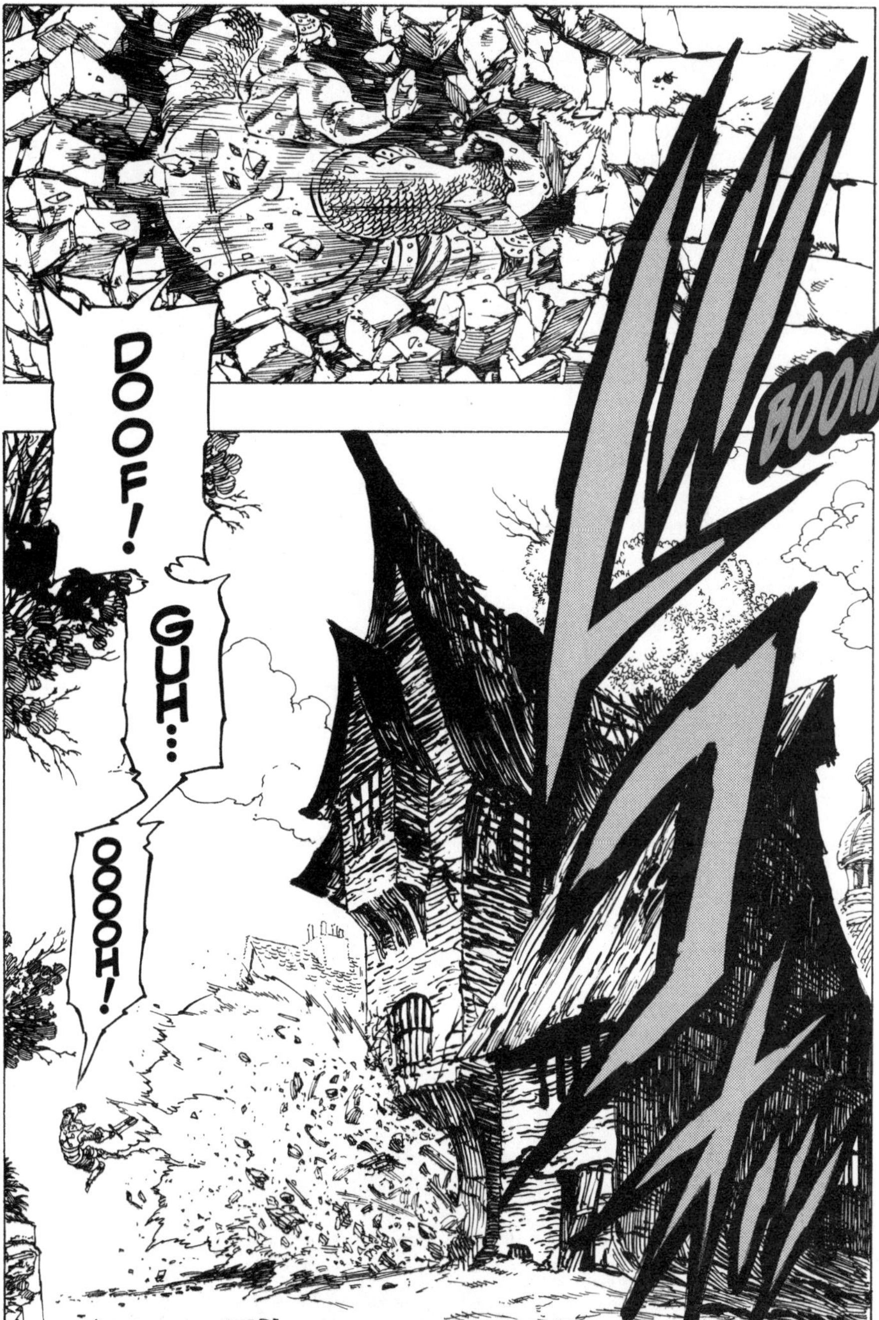
DOOF! GUH... OOOOH!
BOOM

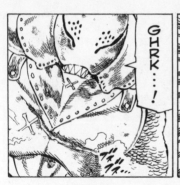

BOOM
GHRK...!
SSSHHH
Now then. I hope you'll answer my questions, Golgius-chan.
CRMBL
SLUMP
Why are you after my sword and the princess? And who ordered you on this mission?
TAP TAP
CRMBL
CRMBL
FLAKE
Melio-das-sama!
We didn't know what happened to you for a moment there!
TMP
TMP
CLIK
CLIK
Ah!

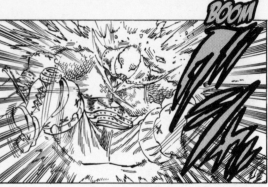

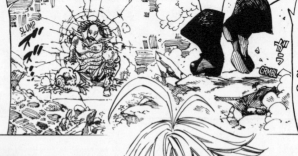

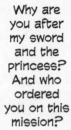

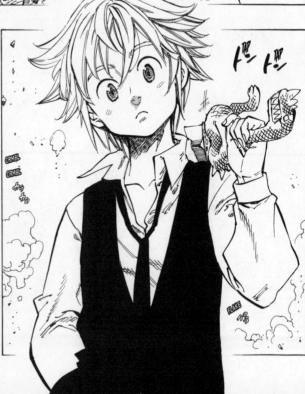

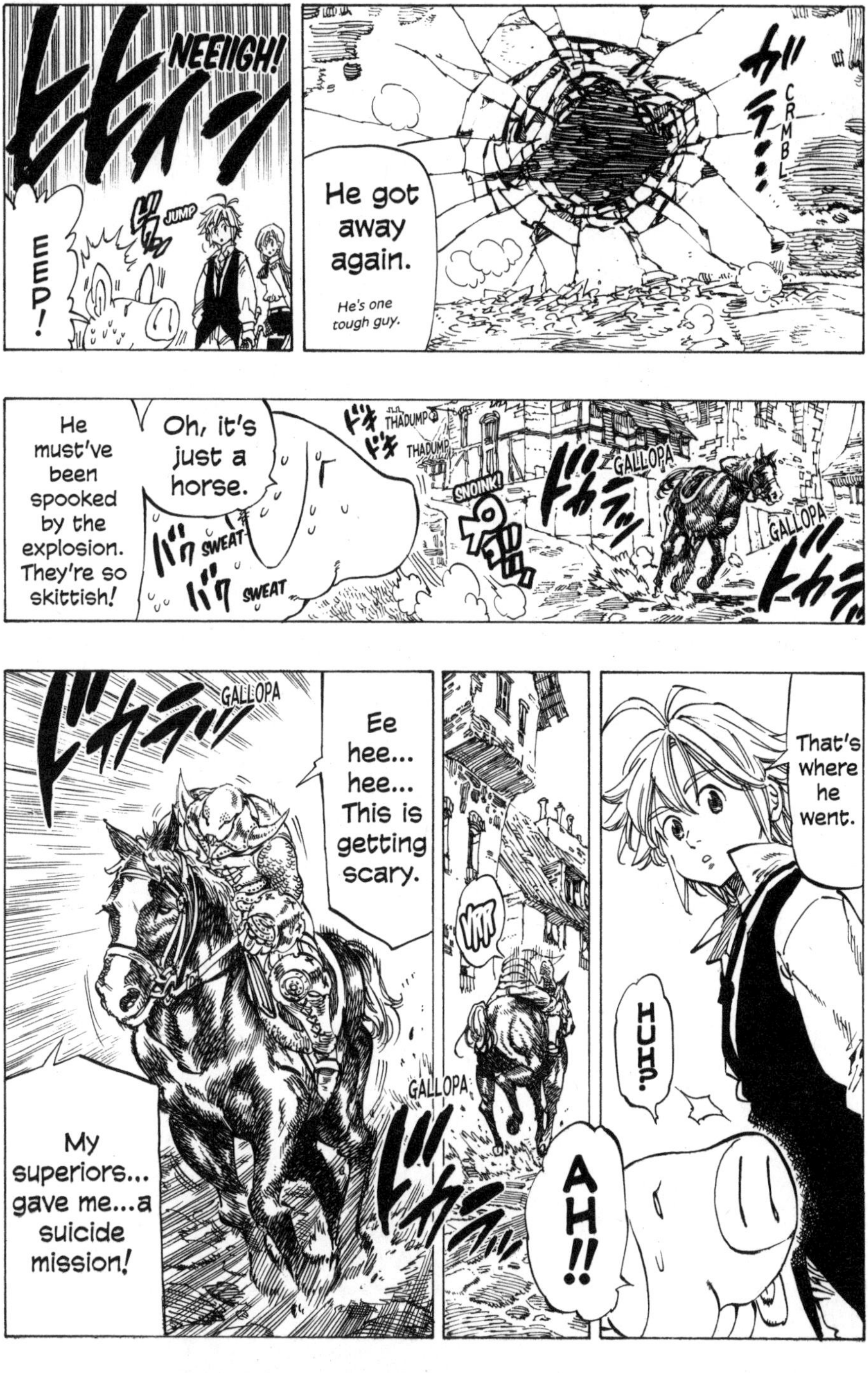

CRMBL
He got away again.
He's one tough guy.
NEEIIGH!
JUMP
EEP!
GALLOPA
GALLOPA
SNOINK!
THADUMP
THADUMP
Oh, it's just a horse.
SWEAT
SWEAT
He must've been spooked by the explosion. They're so skittish!
That's where he went.
HUH?
AH!!
VRRR
GALLOPA
GALLOPA
Ee hee... hee... This is getting scary.
My superiors... gave me...a suicide mission!

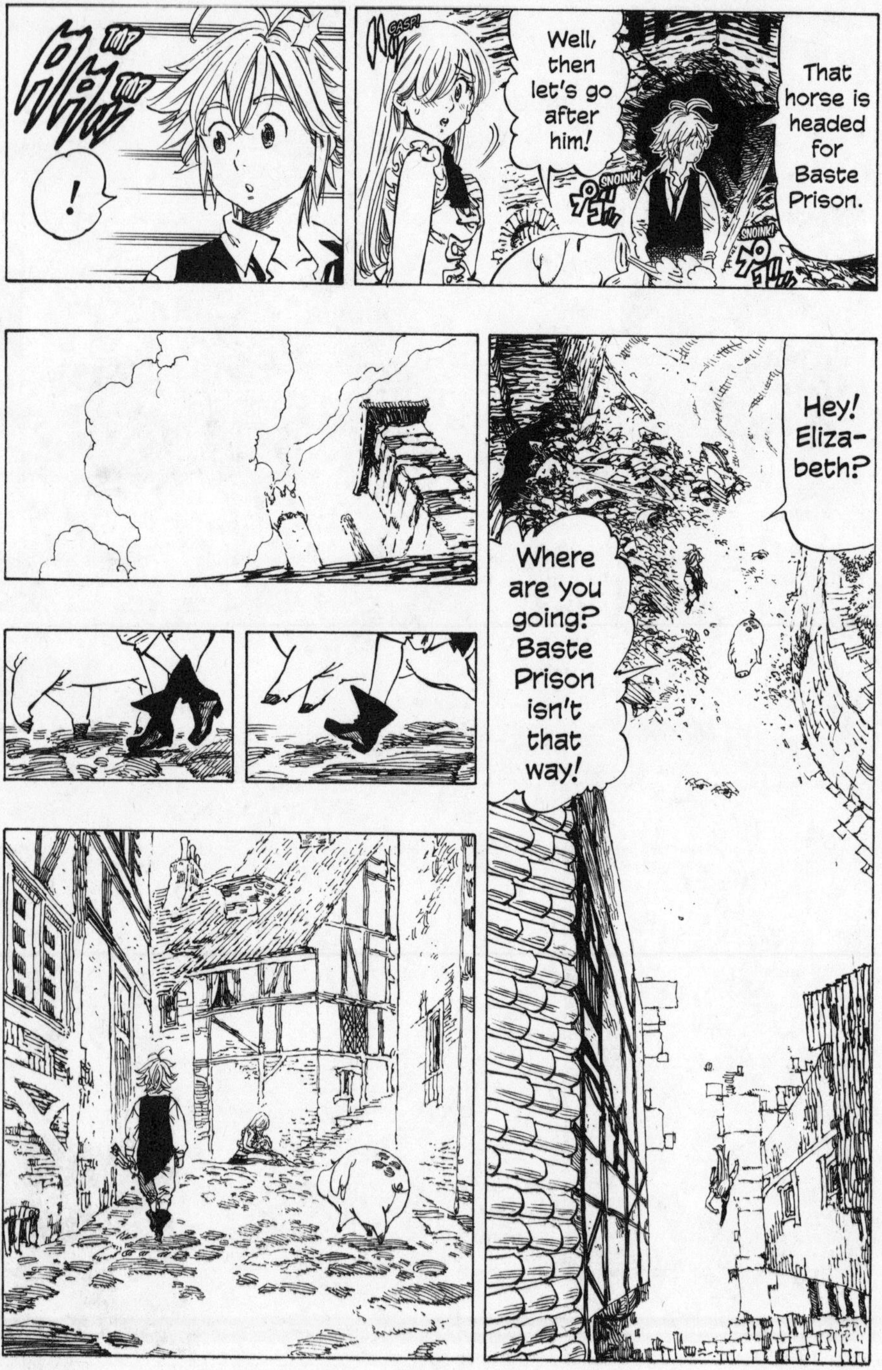
That horse is headed for Baste Prison.
SNOINK!
SNOINK!
Well, then let's go after him!
GASP!
TMP
TMP
!
Hey! Elizabeth?
Where are you going? Baste Prison isn't that way!

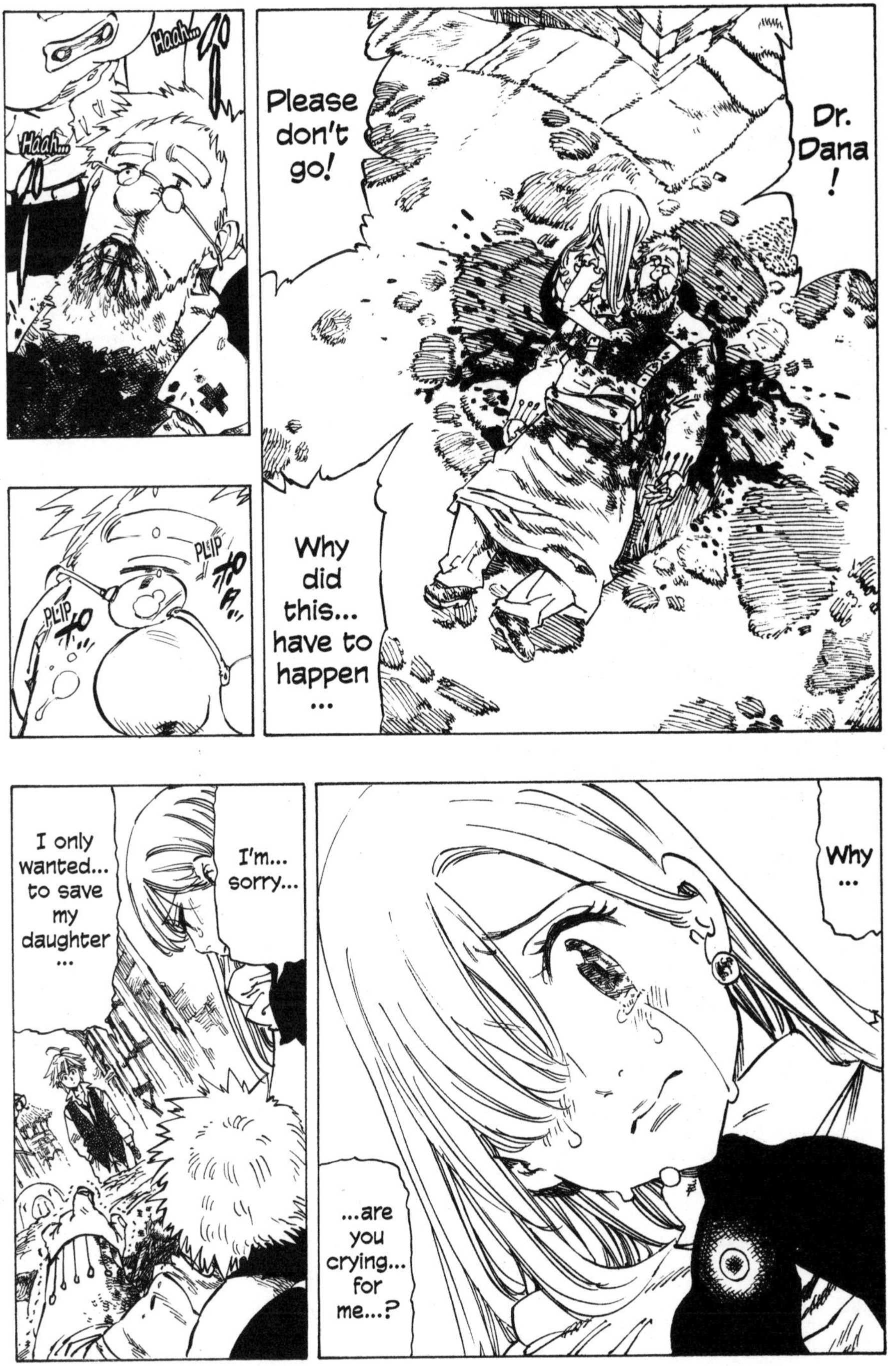
Dr. Dana!
Please don't go!
Why did this... have to happen...
Haah...
Haah...
PLIP
PLIP
Why...
...are you crying... for me...?
I'm... sorry...
I only wanted... to save my daughter...

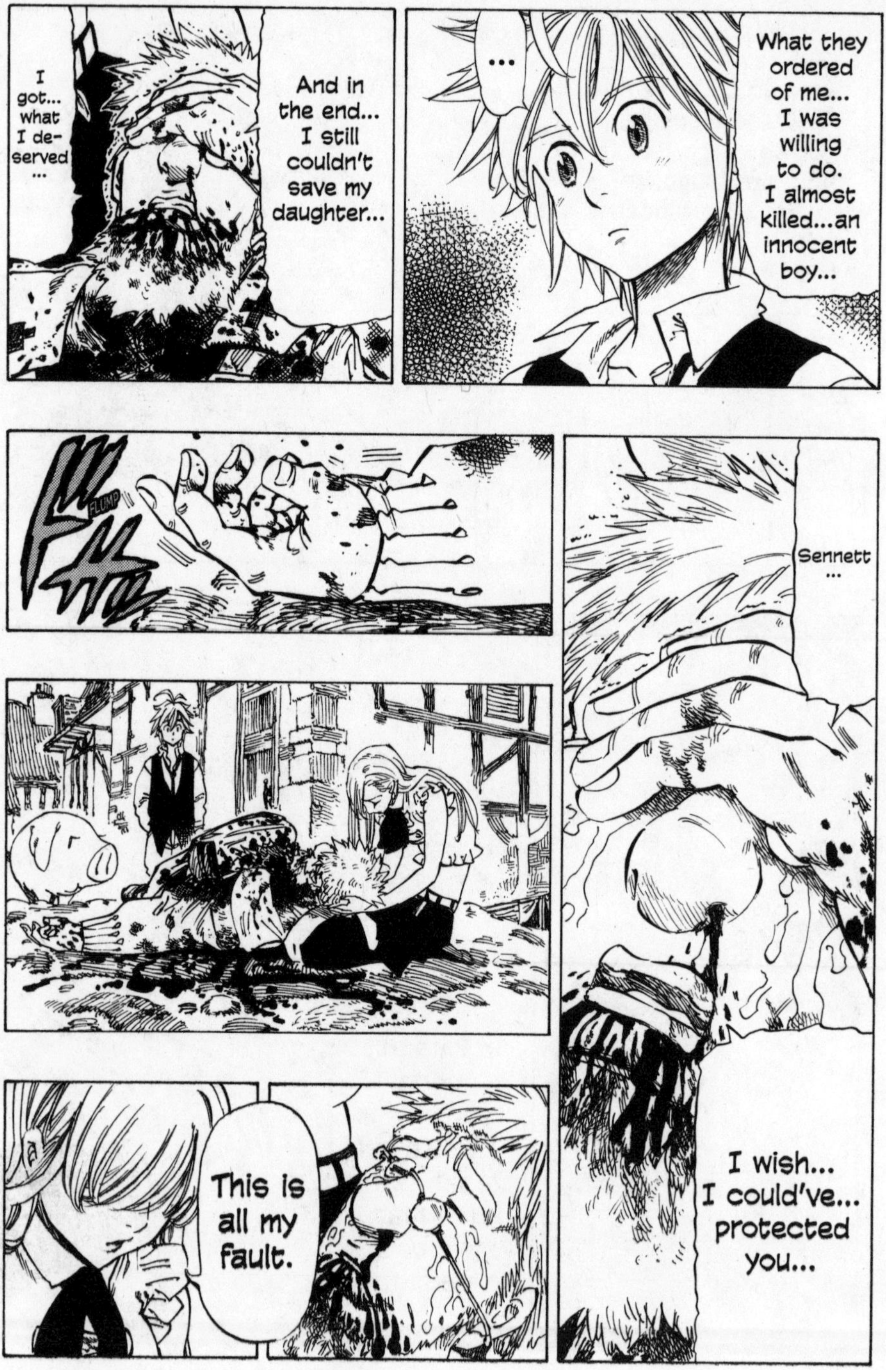
What they ordered of me... I was willing to do. I almost killed...an innocent boy...
...
And in the end... I still couldn't save my daughter...
I got... what I deserved...
Sennett...
I wish... I could've... protected you...
FLUMP
This is all my fault.

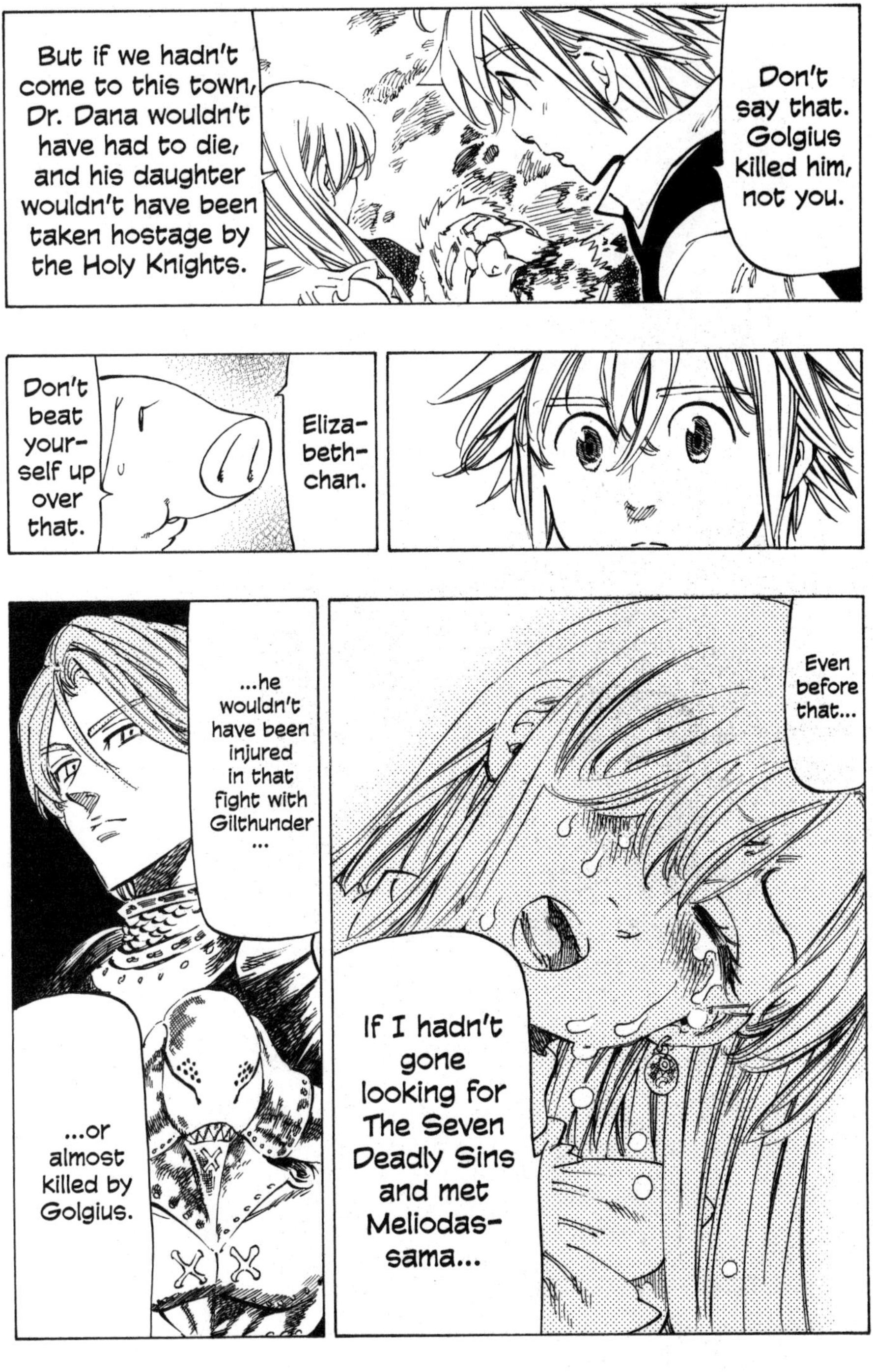
Don't say that. Golgius killed him, not you.
But if we hadn't come to this town, Dr. Dana wouldn't have had to die, and his daughter wouldn't have been taken hostage by the Holy Knights.
Eliza-beth-chan.
Don't beat your-self up over that.
Even before that...
If I hadn't gone looking for The Seven Deadly Sins and met Meliodas-sama...
...he wouldn't have been injured in that fight with Gilthunder...
...or almost killed by Golgius.

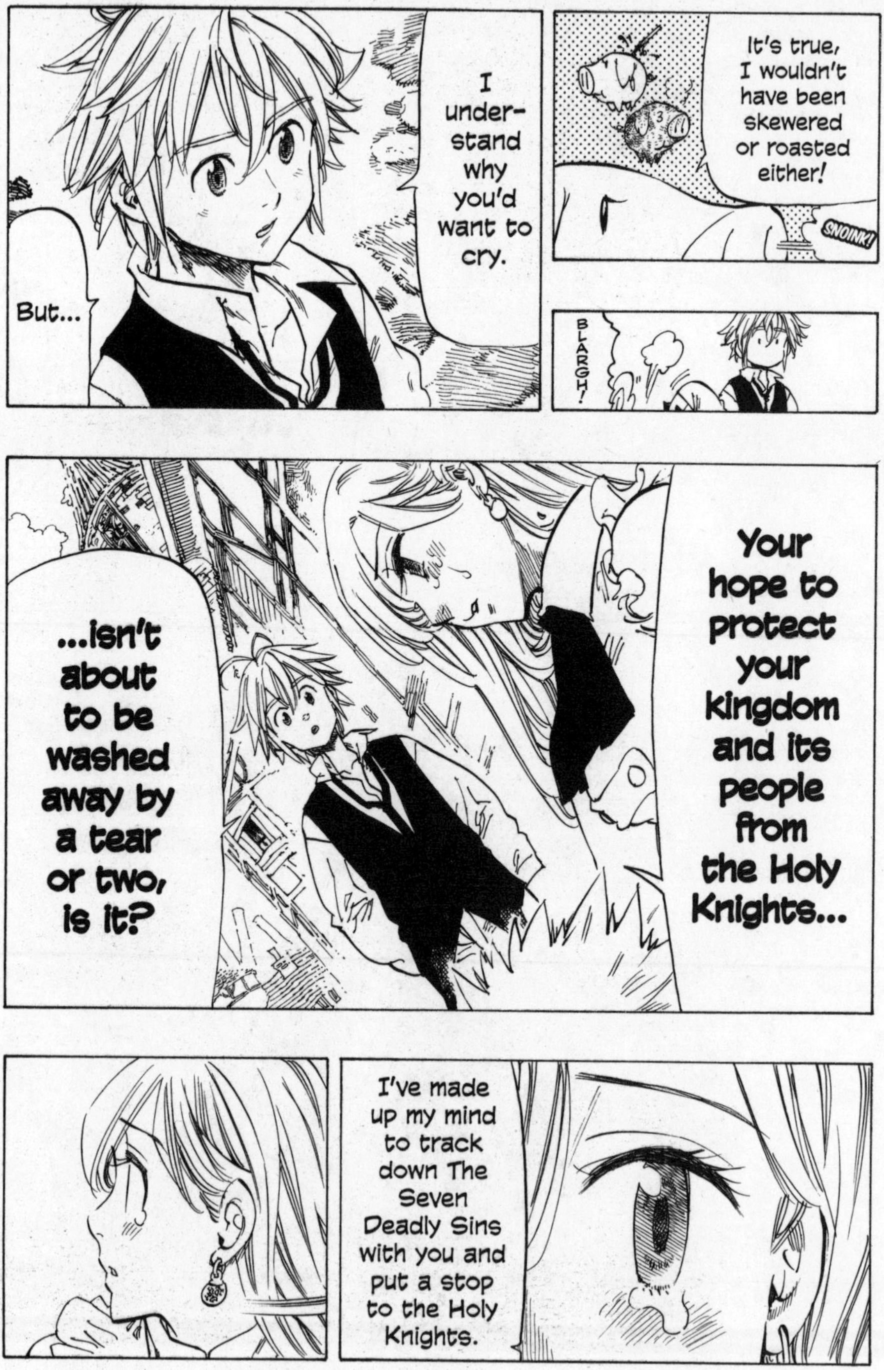
It's true, I wouldn't have been skewered or roasted either!
SNOINK!
BLARGH!
I understand why you'd want to cry.
But...
Your hope to protect your kingdom and its people from the Holy Knights...
...isn't about to be washed away by a tear or two, is it?
I've made up my mind to track down The Seven Deadly Sins with you and put a stop to the Holy Knights.

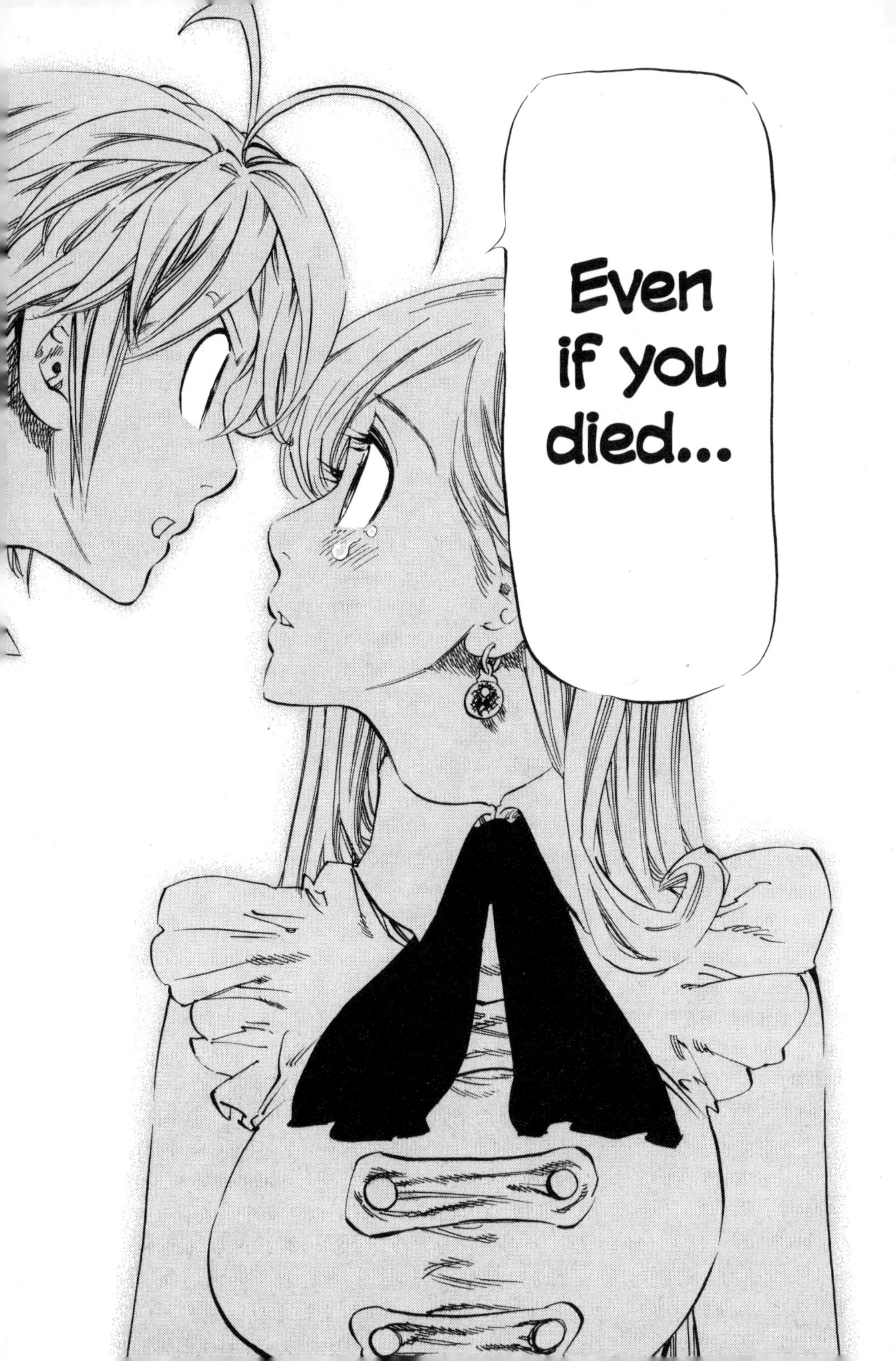
Even if you died...

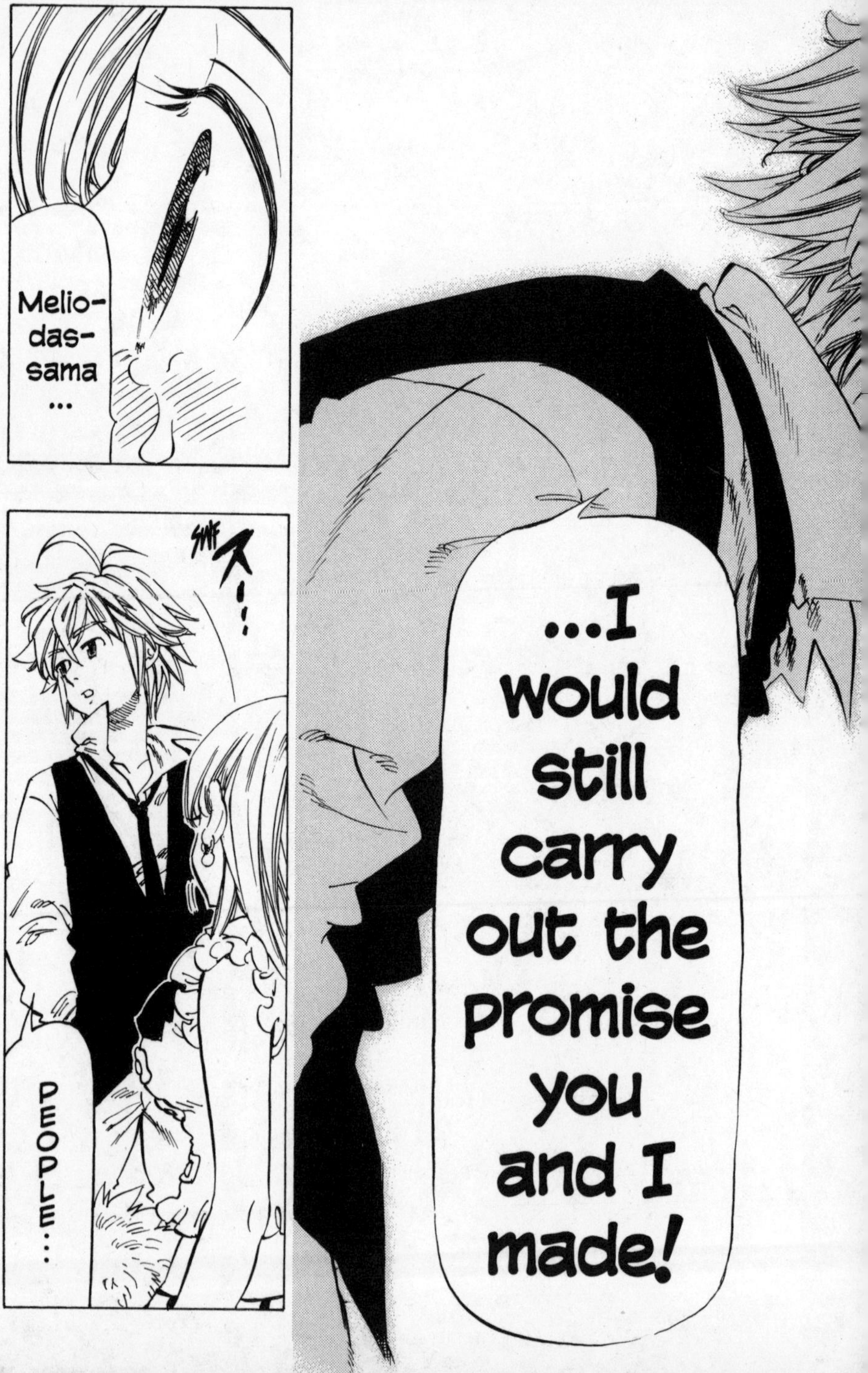
...I would still carry out the promise you and I made!
Melio-das-sama...
SNIF
ス!!
PEOPLE...

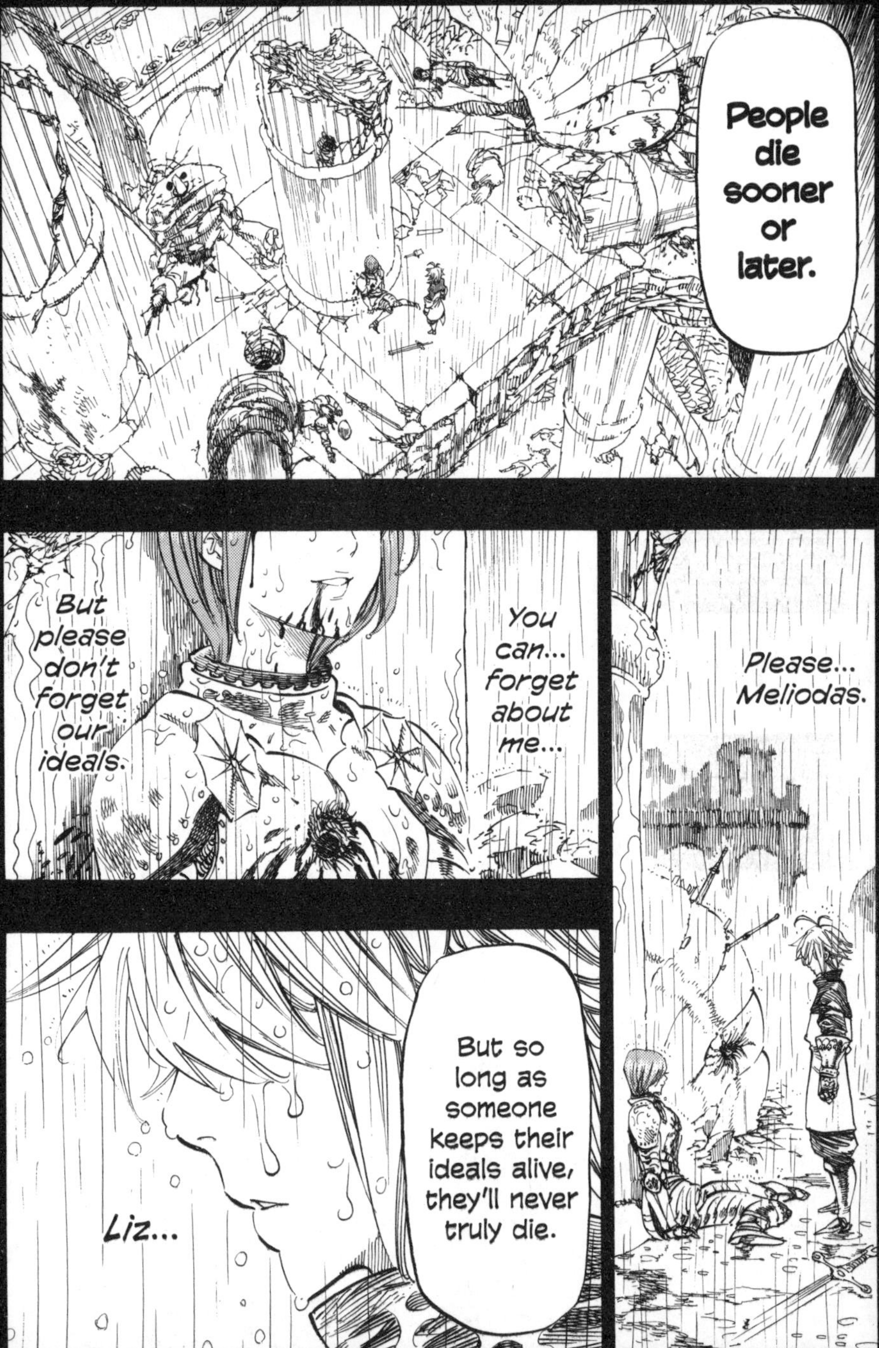
People die sooner or later.
Please... Meliodas.
You can... forget about me...
But please don't forget our ideals.
But so long as someone keeps their ideals alive, they'll never truly die.
Liz...

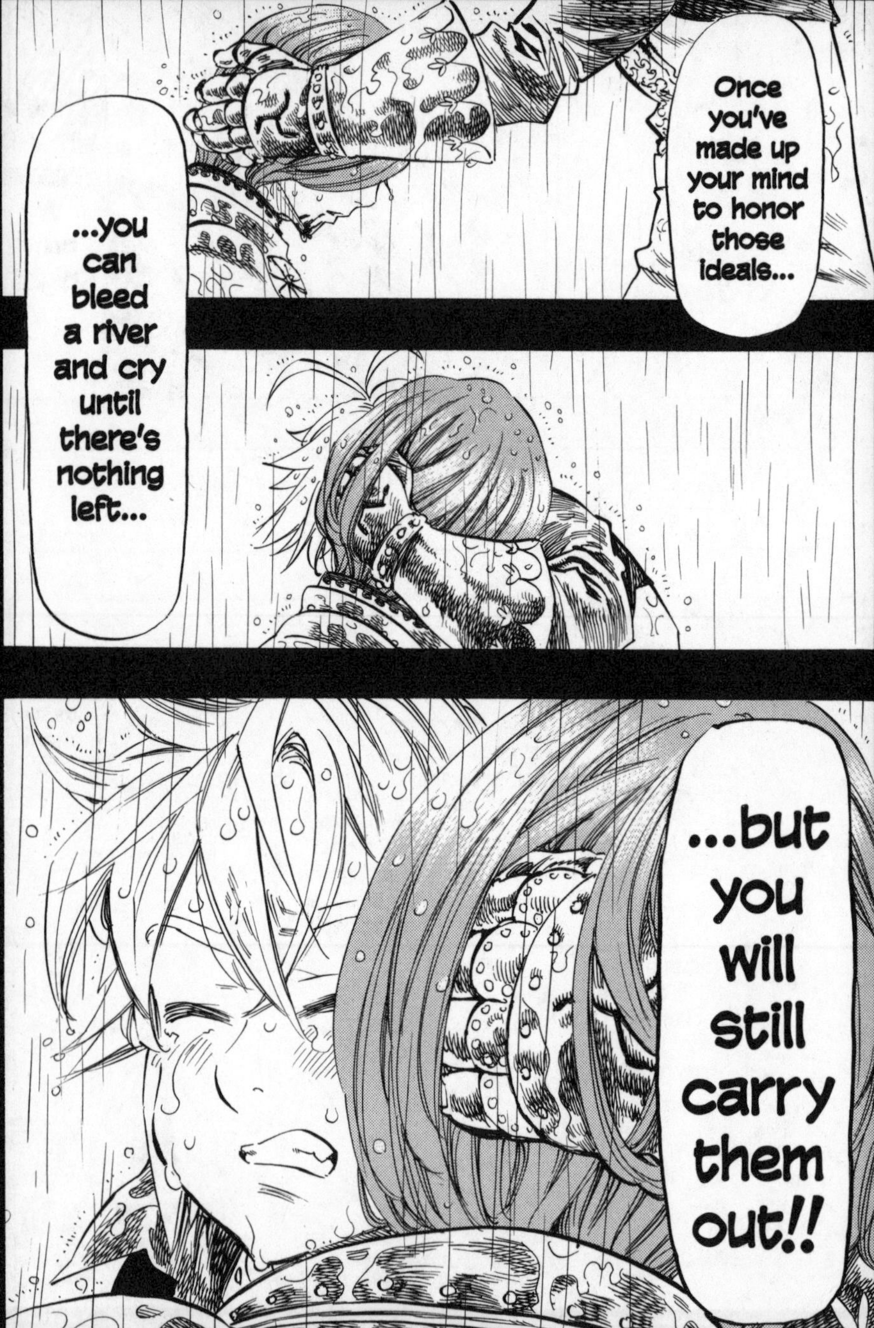
Once you've made up your mind to honor those ideals...
...you can bleed a river and cry until there's nothing left...
...but you will still carry them out!!

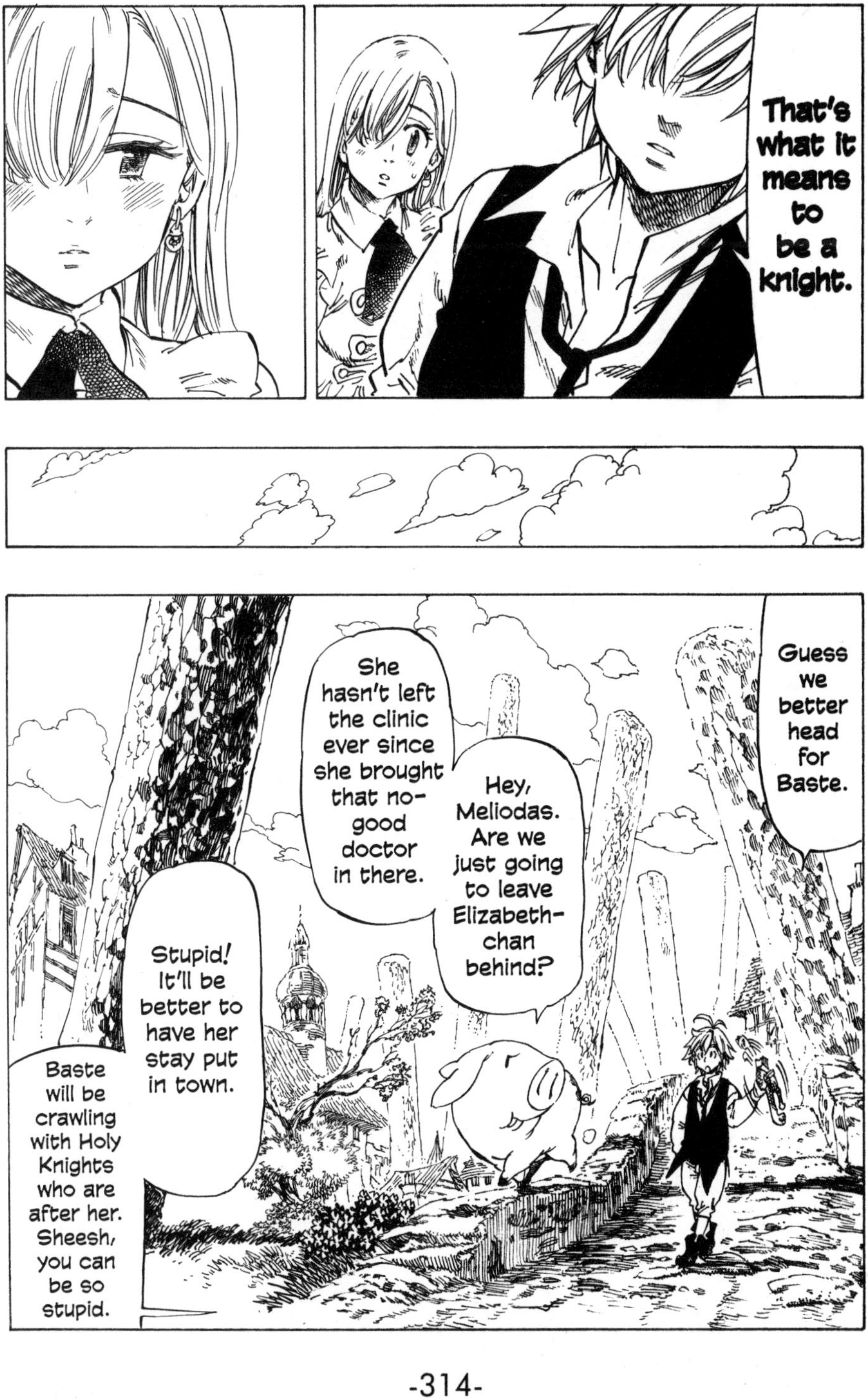
That's what it means to be a knight.
Guess we better head for Baste.
Hey, Meliodas. Are we just going to leave Elizabeth-chan behind?
She hasn't left the clinic ever since she brought that no-good doctor in there.
Stupid! It'll be better to have her stay put in town.
Baste will be crawling with Holy Knights who are after her. Sheesh, you can be so stupid.

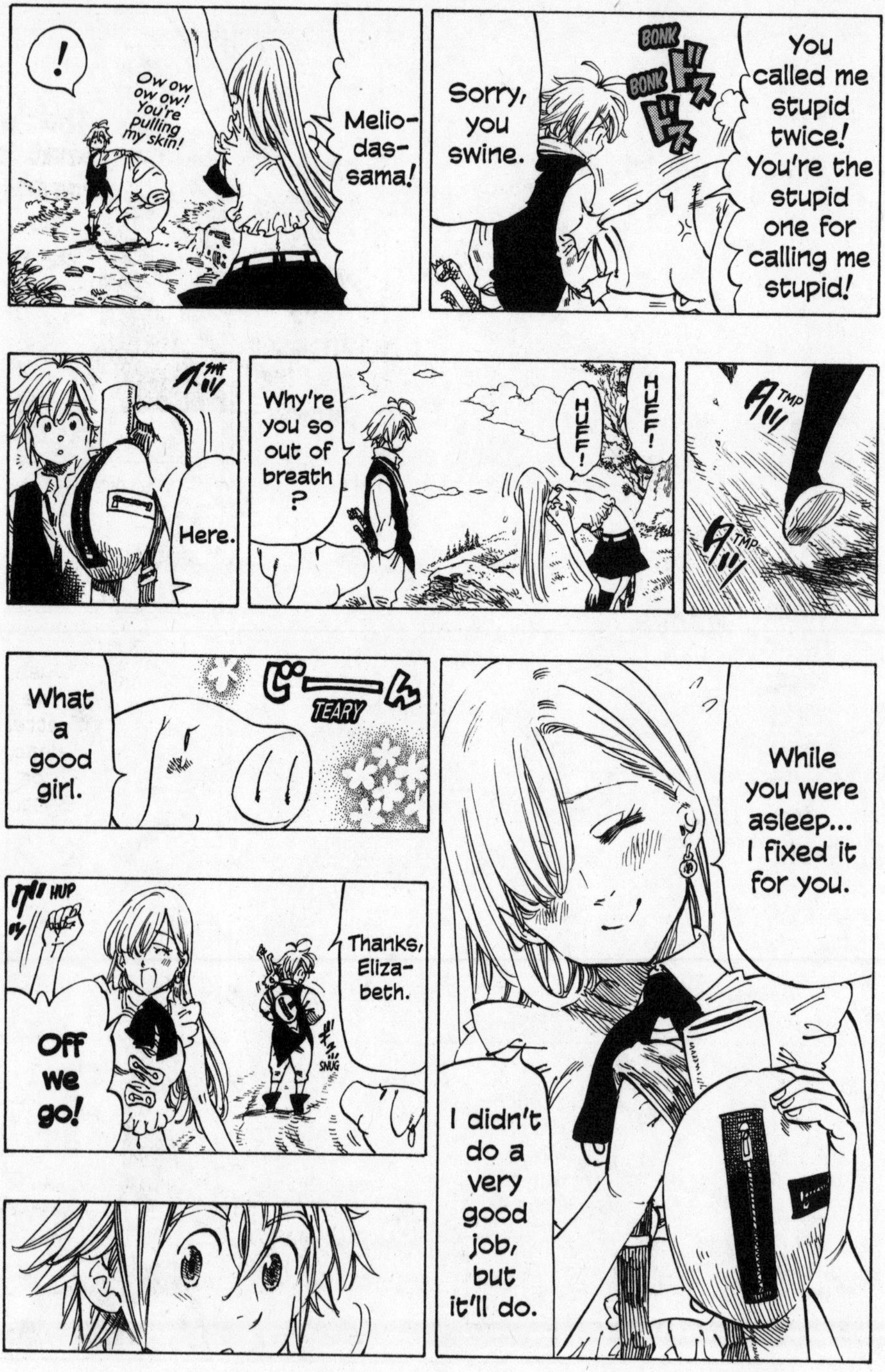

You called me stupid twice! You're the stupid one for calling me stupid!
BONK
BONK
Sorry, you swine.
Melio-das-sama!
!
Ow ow ow ow! You're pulling my skin!
TMP
TMP
HUFF!
HUFF!
Why're you so out of breath?
SWF
Here.
While you were asleep... I fixed it for you.
I didn't do a very good job, but it'll do.
TEARY
What a good girl.
Thanks, Eliza-beth.
SNUG
HUP
Off we go!

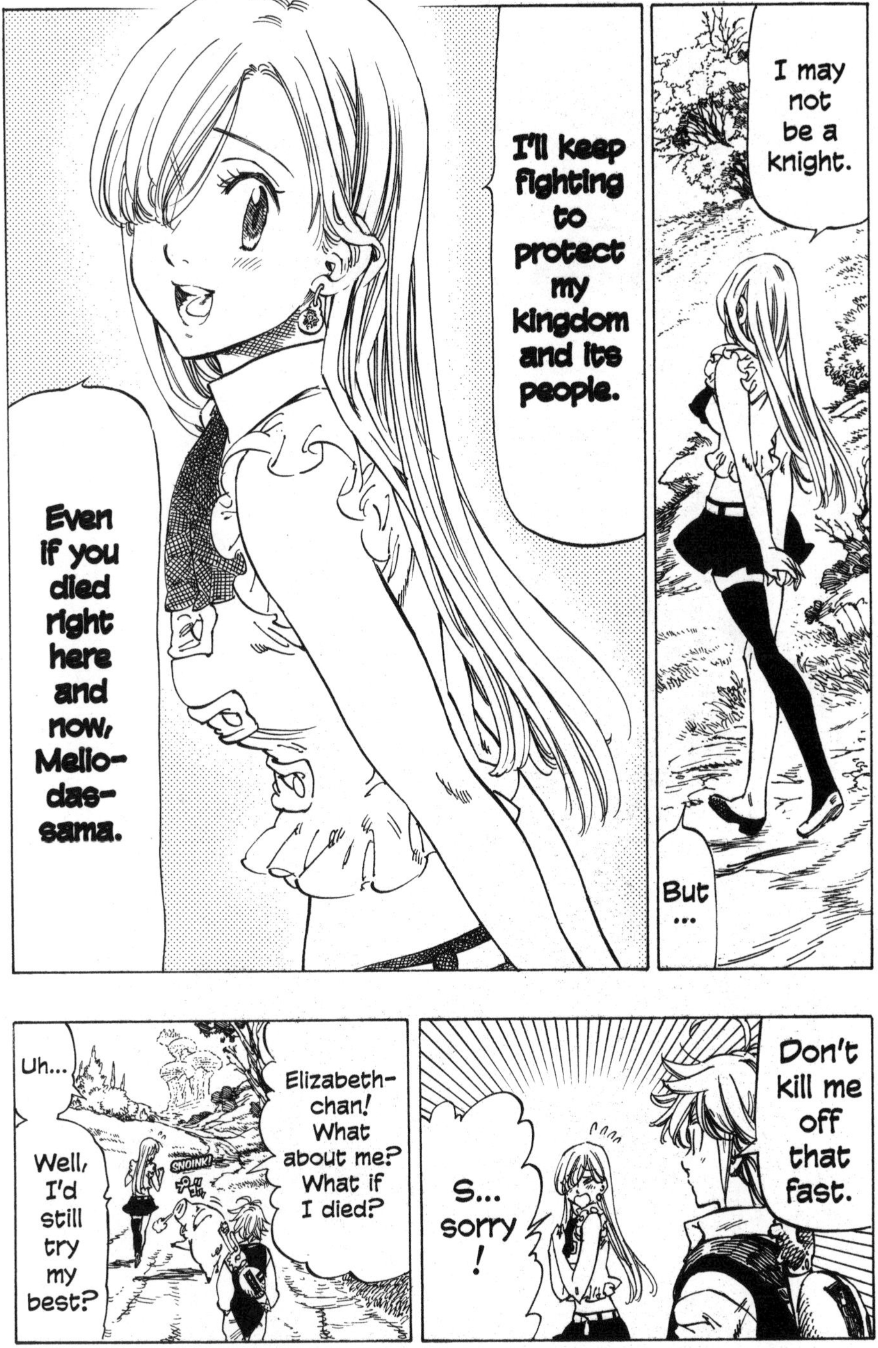
I may not be a knight.
But...
I'll keep fighting to protect my kingdom and its people.
Even if you died right here and now, Meliodas-sama.
Don't kill me off that fast.
S... sorry!
Elizabeth-chan! What about me? What if I died?
SNOINK!
Uh...
Well, I'd still try my best?

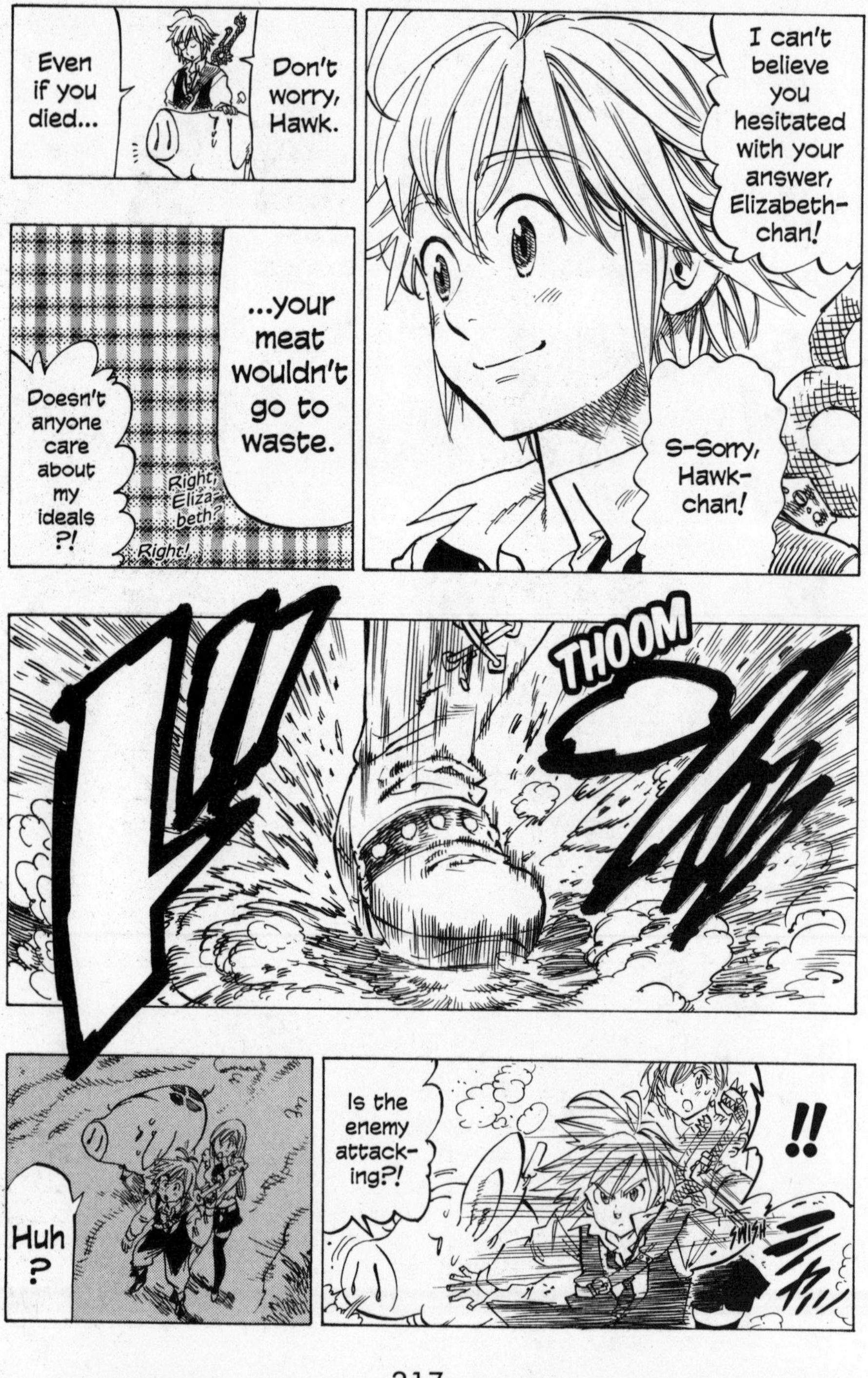

I can't believe you hesitated with your answer, Elizabeth-chan!
S-Sorry, Hawk-chan!
Don't worry, Hawk.
Even if you died...
...your meat wouldn't go to waste.
Right, Eliza-beth?
Right!
Doesn't anyone care about my ideals?!
THOOM
!!
Is the enemy attacking?!
SWISH
Huh?

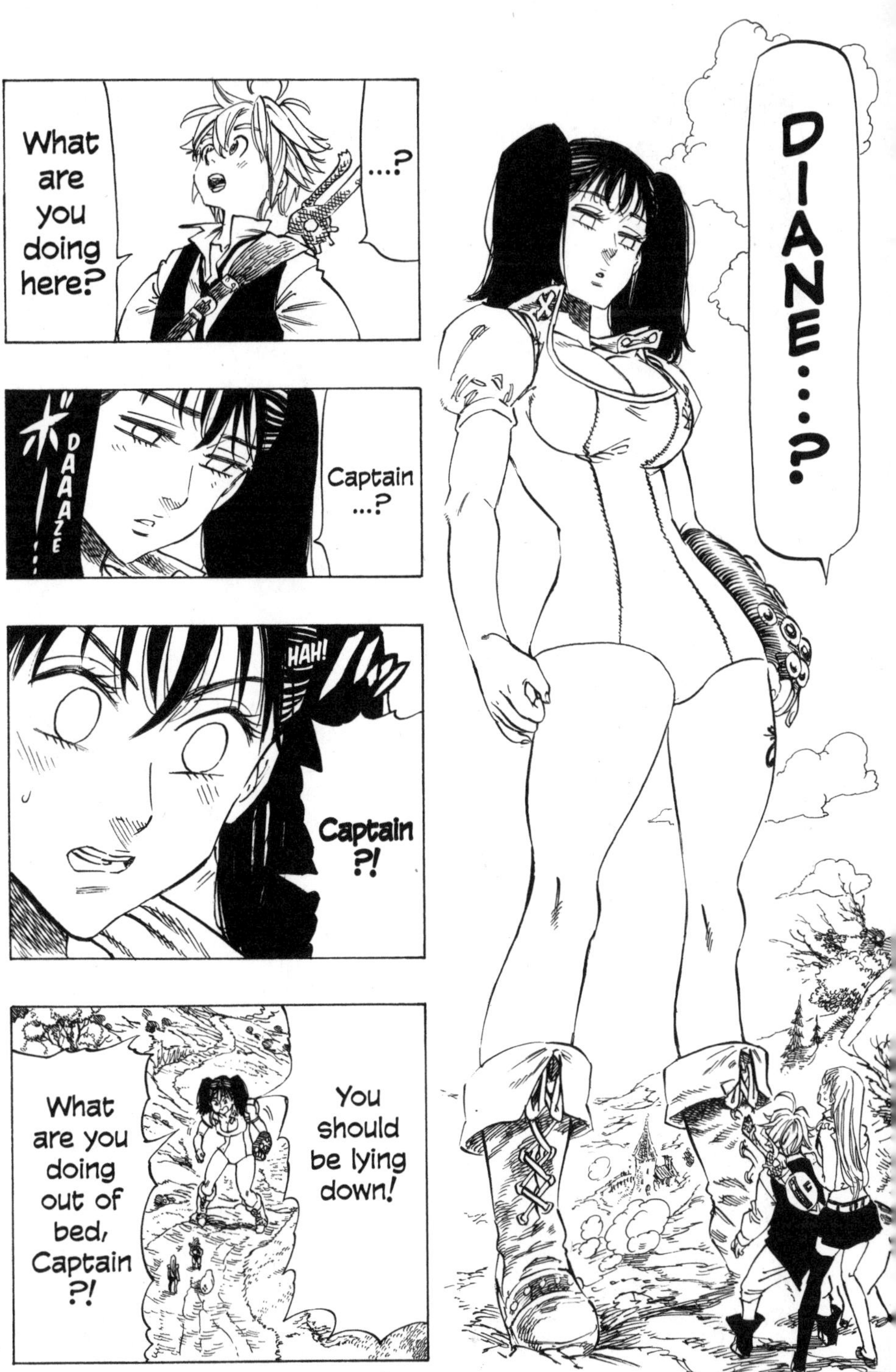
DIANE...?
...?
What are you doing here?
Captain ...?
DAAAAZE
HAH!
Captain ?!
You should be lying down!
What are you doing out of bed, Captain ?!

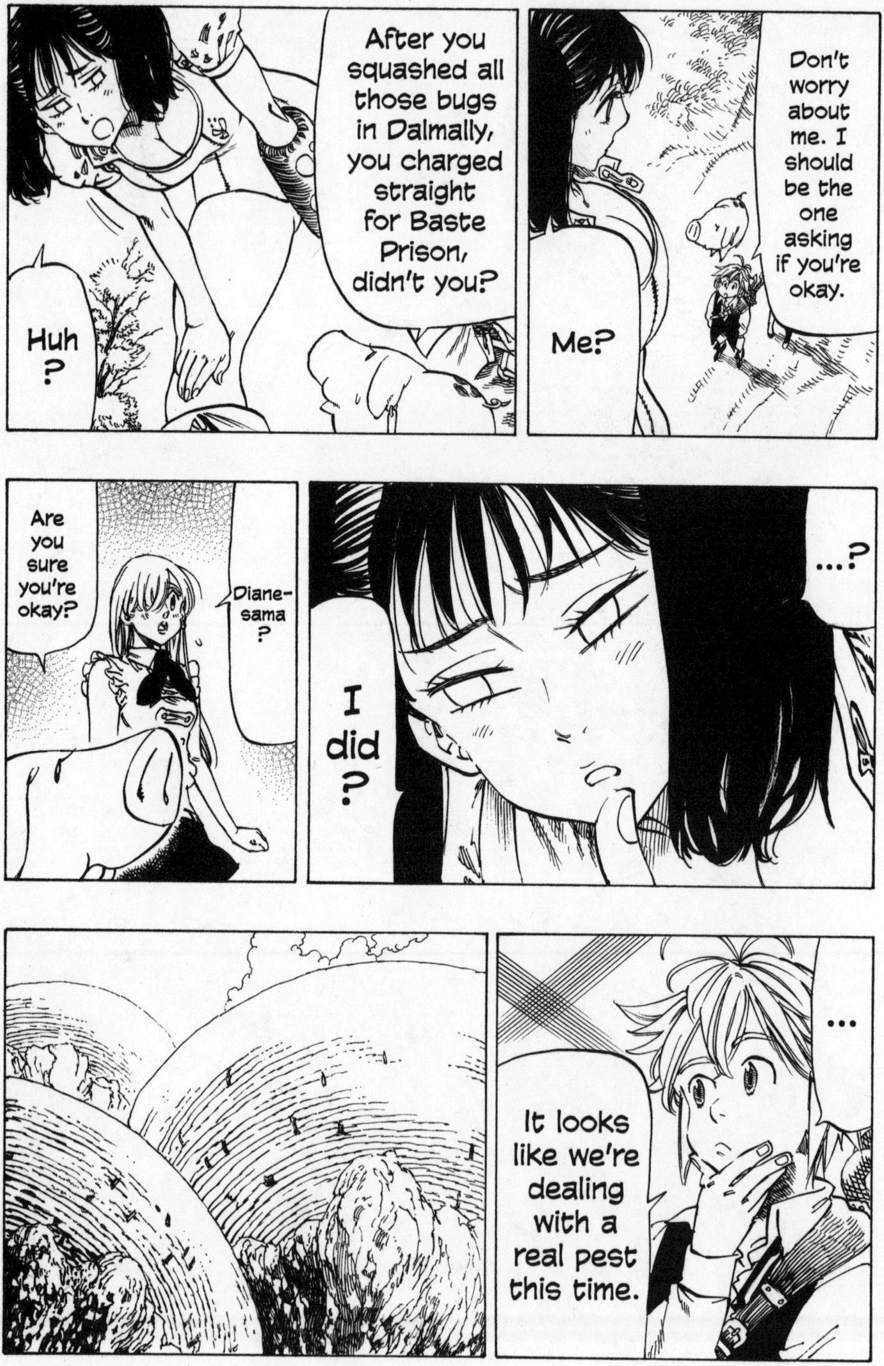
Don't worry about me. I should be the one asking if you're okay.
Me?
After you squashed all those bugs in Dalmally, you charged straight for Baste Prison, didn't you?
Huh?
...?
I did?
Diane-sama?
Are you sure you're okay?
...
It looks like we're dealing with a real pest this time.

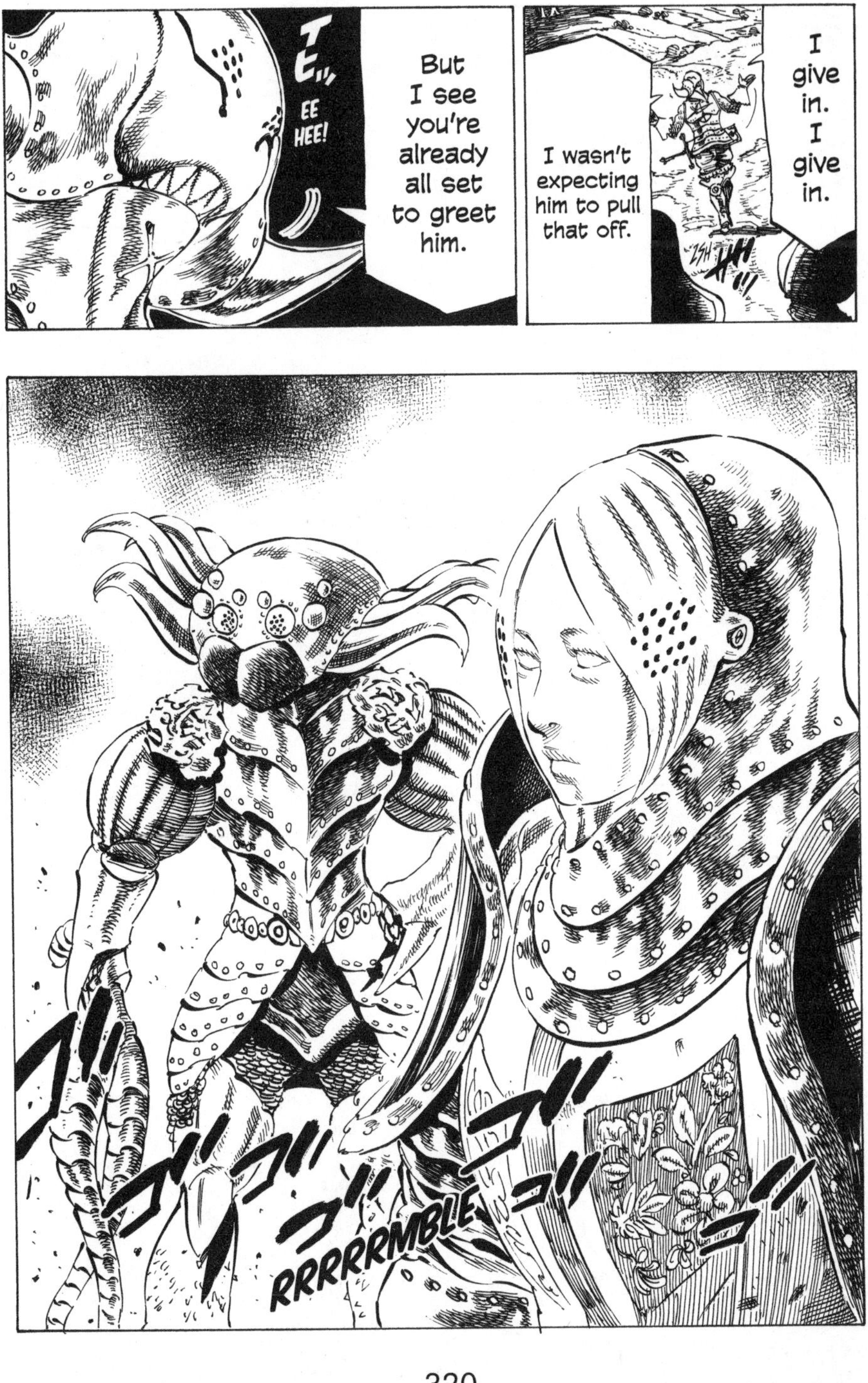
I give in. I give in.
I wasn't expecting him to pull that off.
ZSH
EE HEE!
But I see you're already all set to greet him.
RRRRRMBLE

Chapter 12 - A Chaotic Party

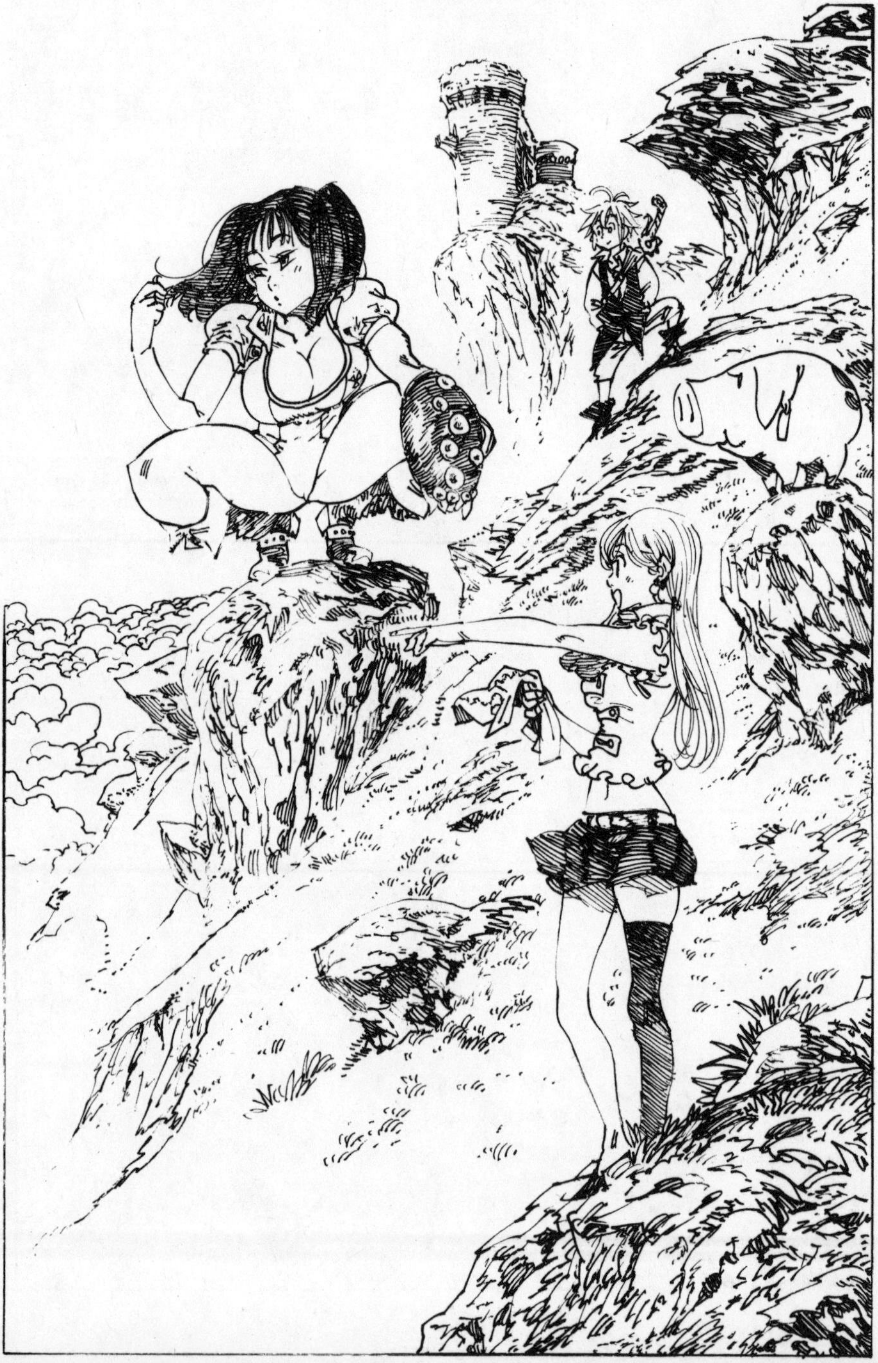

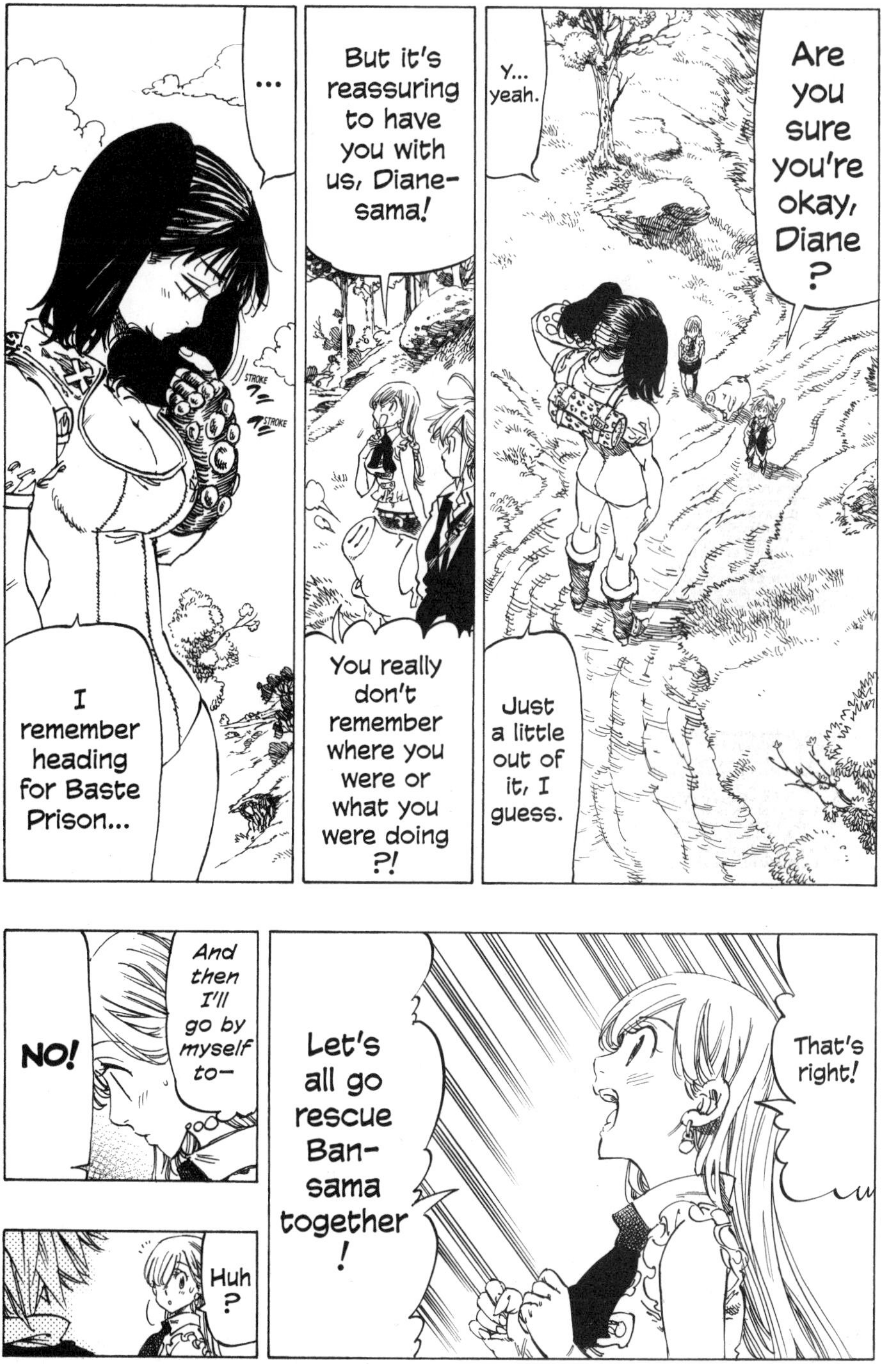

Are you sure you're okay, Diane?
Y... yeah.
Just a little out of it, I guess.
But it's reassuring to have you with us, Diane-sama!
You really don't remember where you were or what you were doing?!
...
STROKE
STROKE
I remember heading for Baste Prison...
That's right!
Let's all go rescue Ban-sama together!
And then I'll go by myself to—
NO!
Huh?

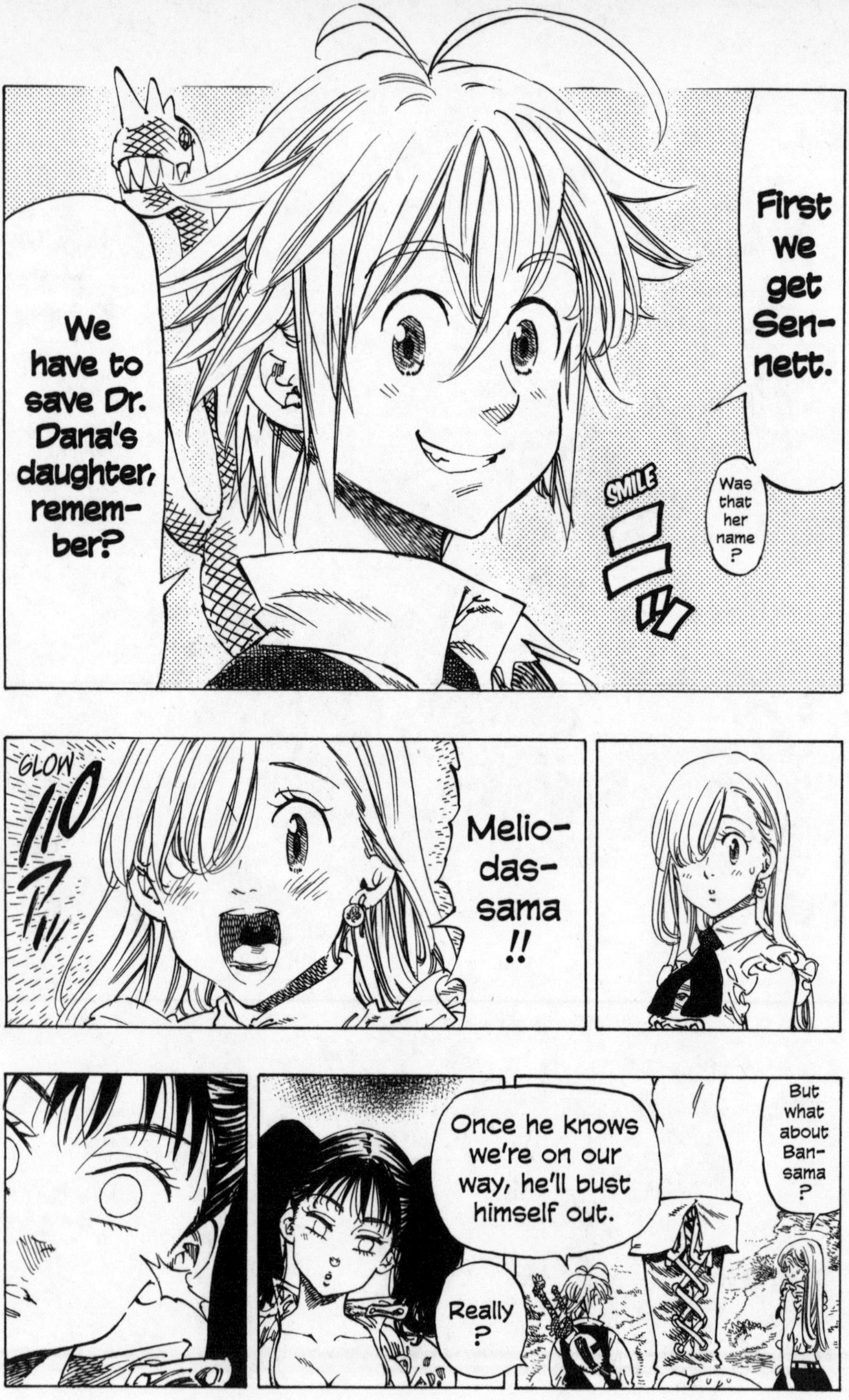
First we get Sen-nett.
Was that her name?
SMILE
We have to save Dr. Dana's daughter, remember?
Melio-das-sama!!
GLOW
But what about Ban-sama?
Once he knows we're on our way, he'll bust himself out.
Really?

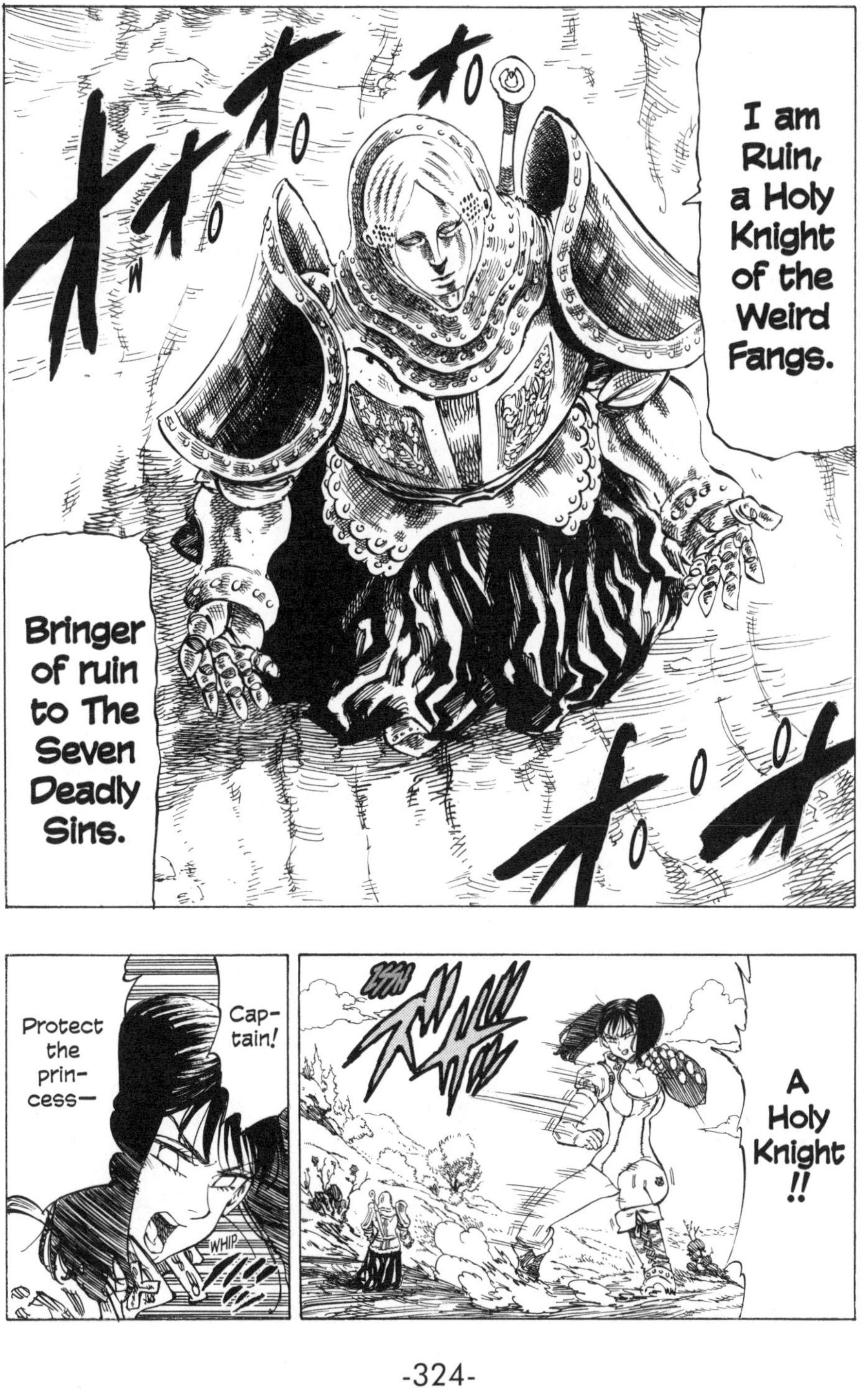
I am Ruin, a Holy Knight of the Weird Fangs.
Bringer of ruin to The Seven Deadly Sins.
A Holy Knight!!
Cap-tain!
Protect the prin-cess—
WHIP

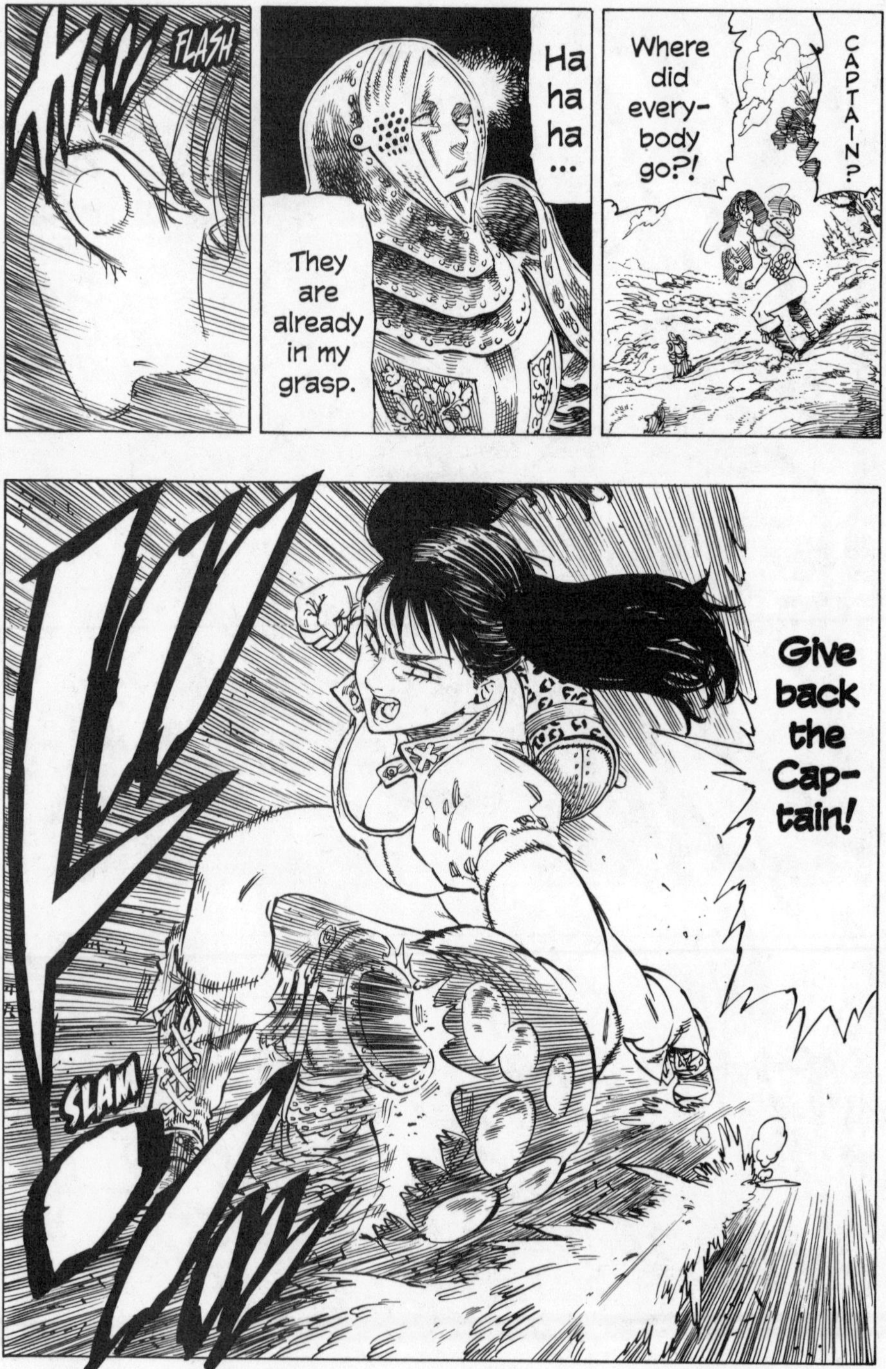
CAPTAIN?
Where did every-body go?!
Ha ha ha...
They are already in my grasp.
FLASH
Give back the Cap-tain!
SLAM

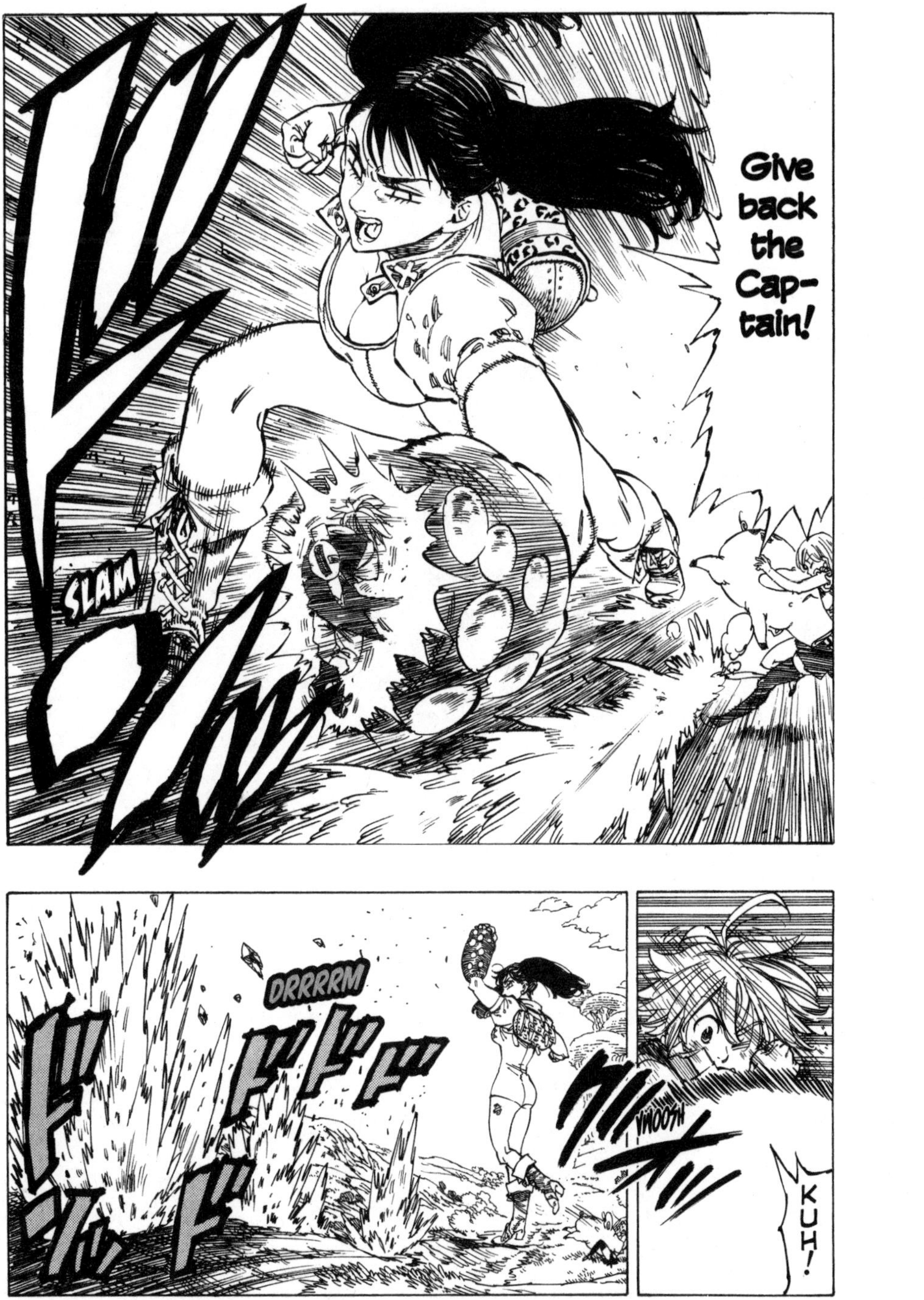
Give back the Cap-tain!
SLAM
KUH!
DRRRRM
VMOOSH

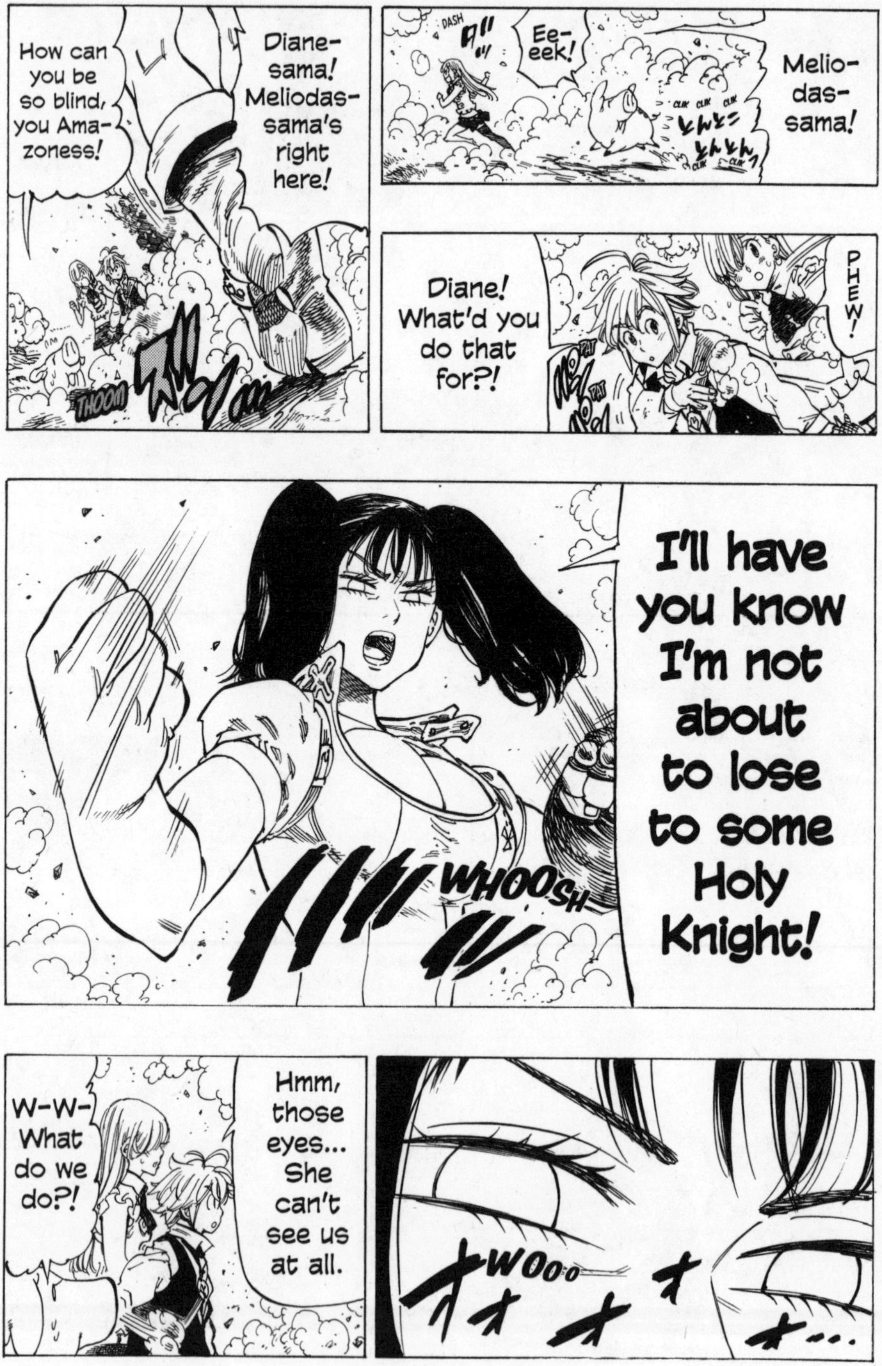
Melio-das-sama!
Eeeek!
DASH
CLIK CLIK CLIK
CLIK CLIK
PHEW!
Diane! What'd you do that for?!
PAT PAT
Diane-sama! Meliodas-sama's right here!
How can you be so blind, you Amazoness!
THOOM
I'll have you know I'm not about to lose to some Holy Knight!
WHOOSH
WOOoo
Hmm, those eyes... She can't see us at all.
W-W-What do we do?!

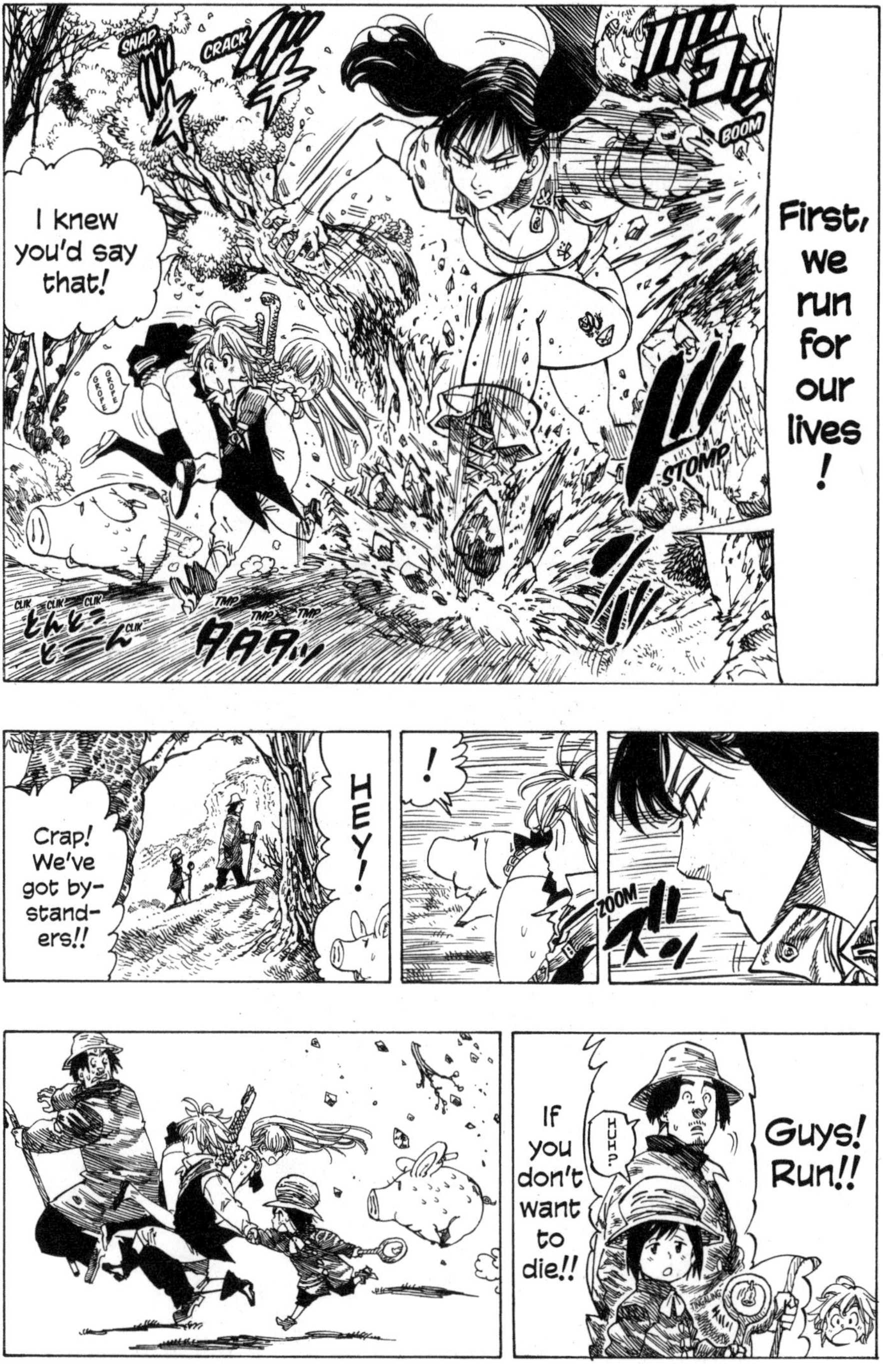
First, we run for our lives!
BOOM
STOMP
CRACK
SNAP
I knew you'd say that!
GROPE GROPE
TMP TMP TMP
CLIK CLIK CLIK CLIK
ZOOM
!
HEY!
Crap! We've got by-standers!!
Guys! Run!!
If you don't want to die!!
HUH?

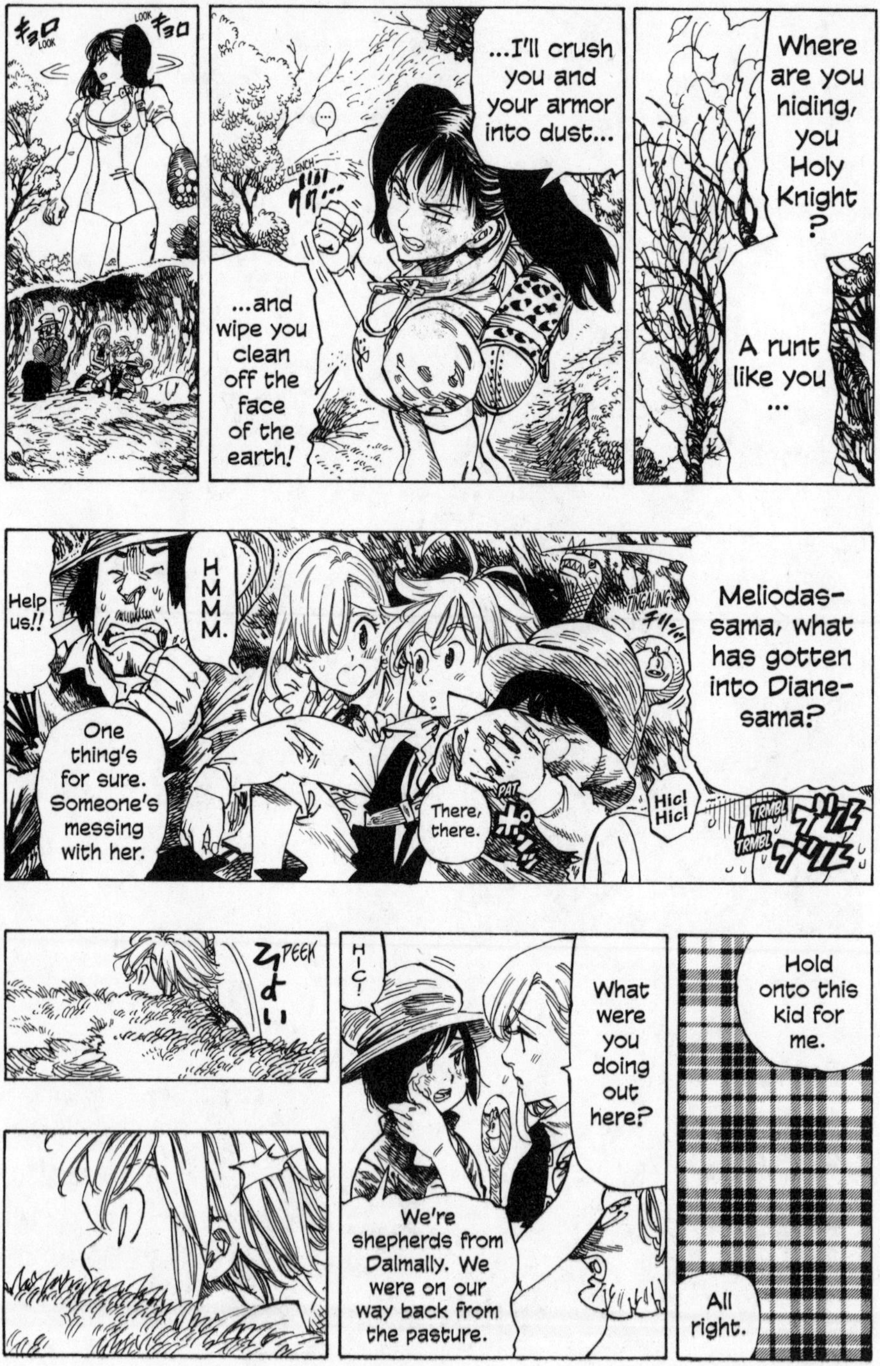
Where are you hiding, you Holy Knight?
A runt like you...
...I'll crush you and your armor into dust...
CLENCH
...and wipe you clean off the face of the earth!
LOOK
LOOK
Meliodas-sama, what has gotten into Diane-sama?
TINGALING
TRMBL
TRMBL
Hic! Hic!
PAT
There, there.
HMMM.
Help us!!
One thing's for sure. Someone's messing with her.
Hold onto this kid for me.
All right.
What were you doing out here?
HIC!
We're shepherds from Dalmally. We were on our way back from the pasture.
PEEK

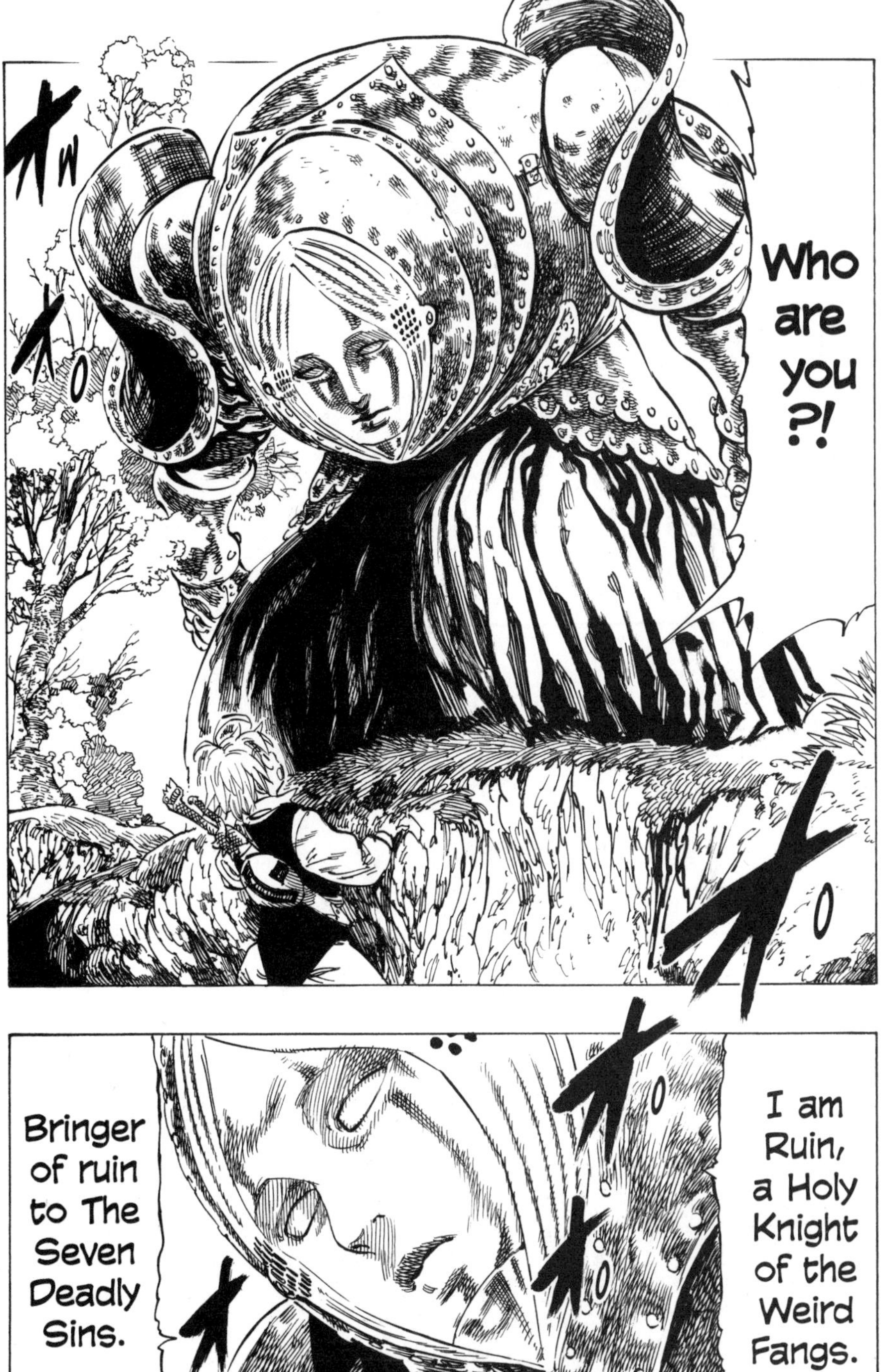
Who are you ?!
I am Ruin, a Holy Knight of the Weird Fangs.
Bringer of ruin to The Seven Deadly Sins.

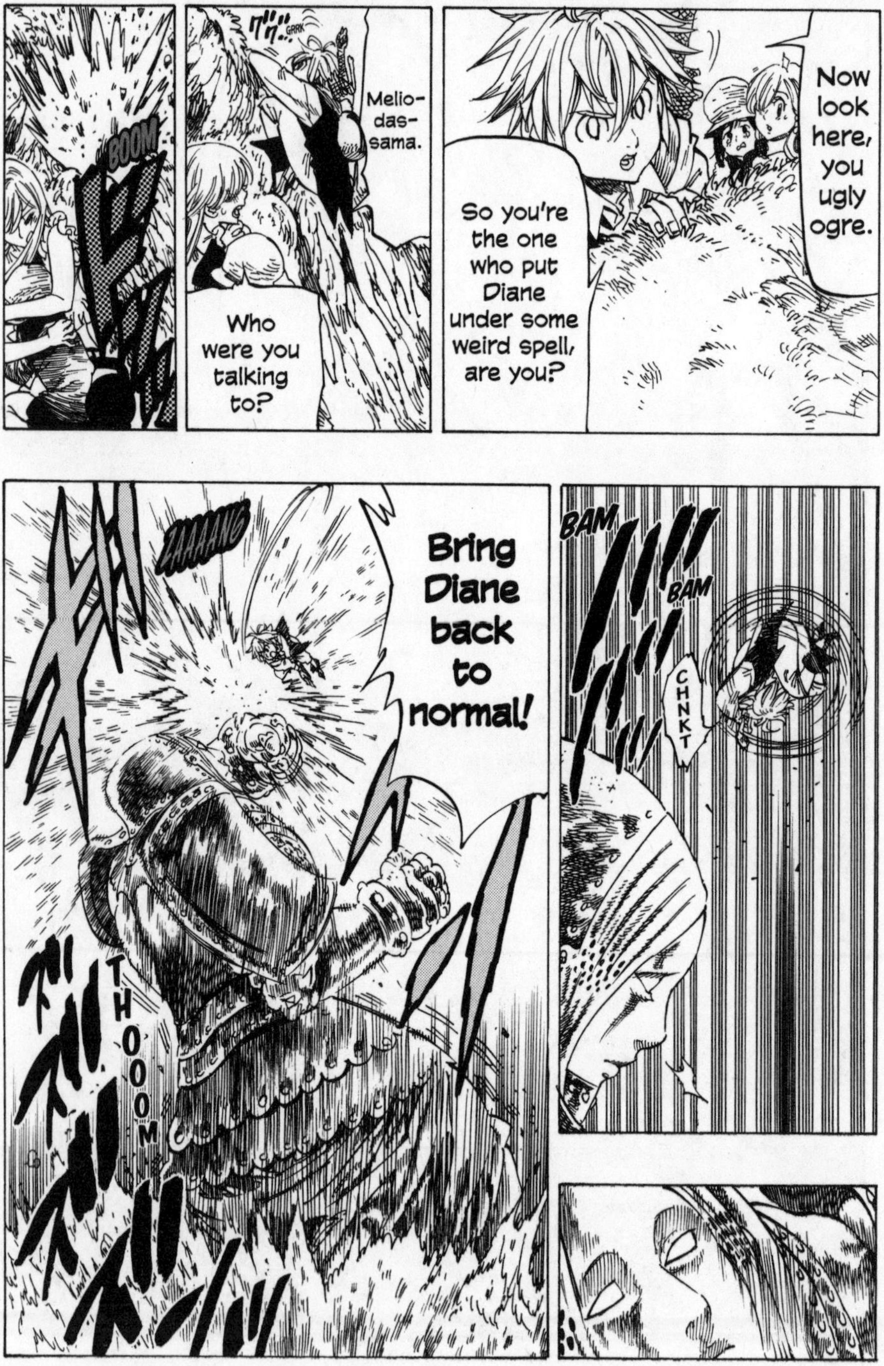
Now look here, you ugly ogre.
So you're the one who put Diane under some weird spell, are you?
GRRK
Melio-das-sama.
Who were you talking to?
BOOM
BAM
BAM
CHNKT
ZAAAANG
Bring Diane back to normal!
THOOOOM

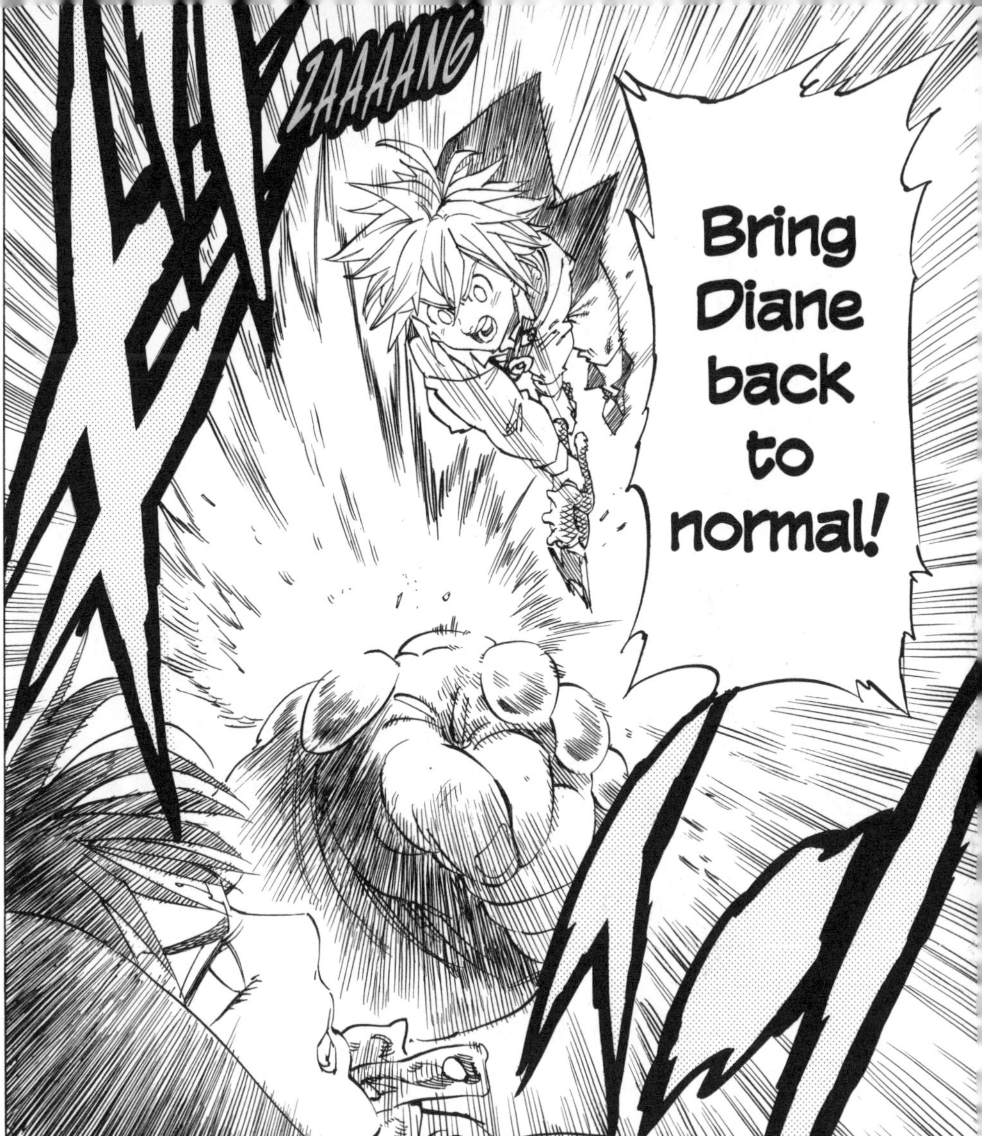
ZAAAANG
Bring Diane back to normal!

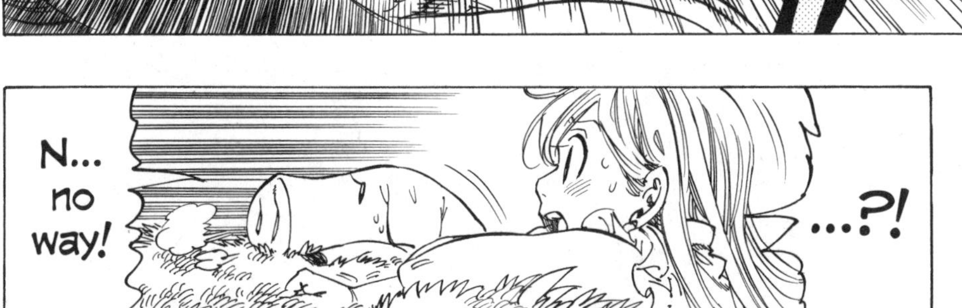
...?!
N... no way!

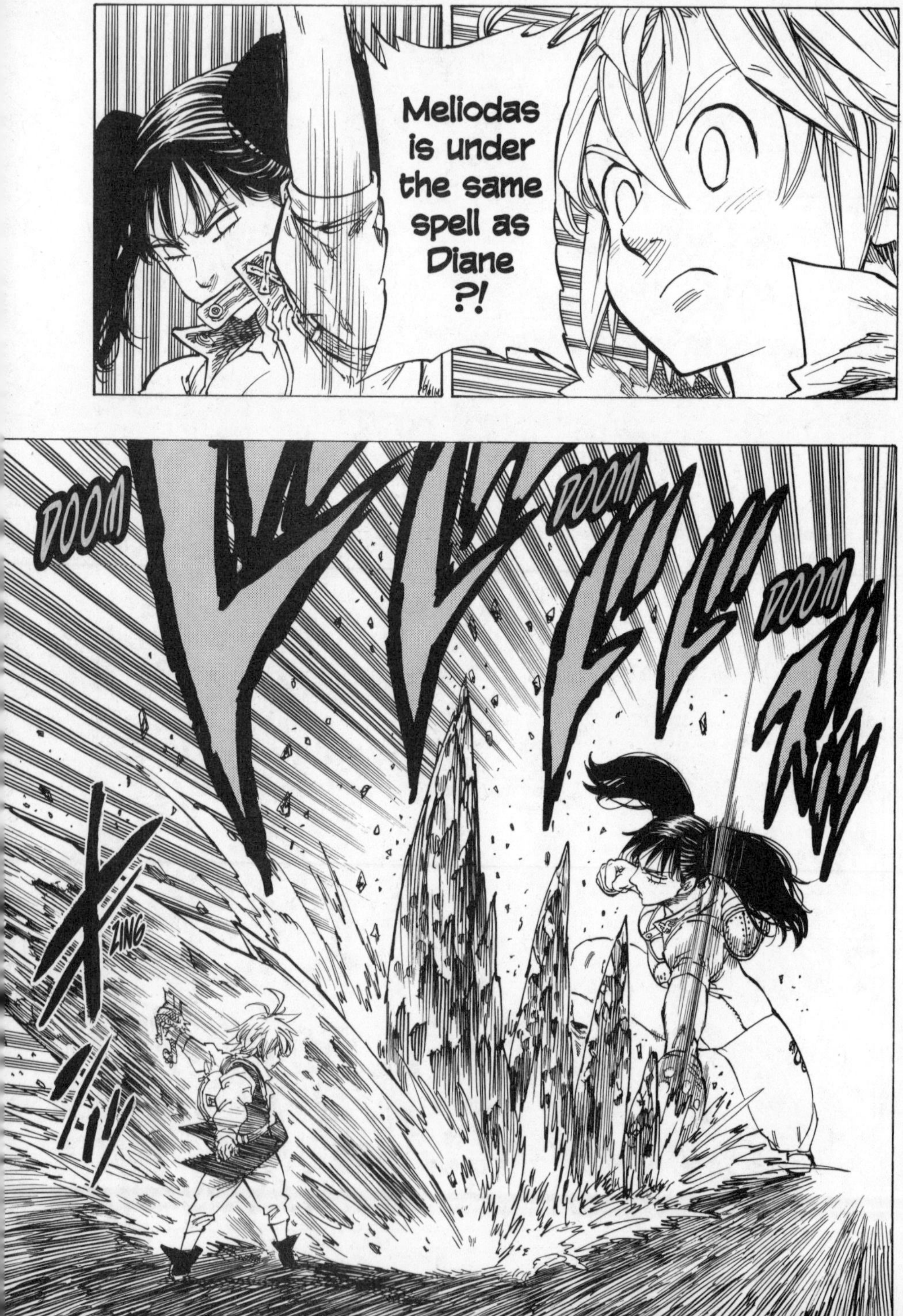
Meliodas is under the same spell as Diane ?!
DOOM
DOOM
DOOM
ZING

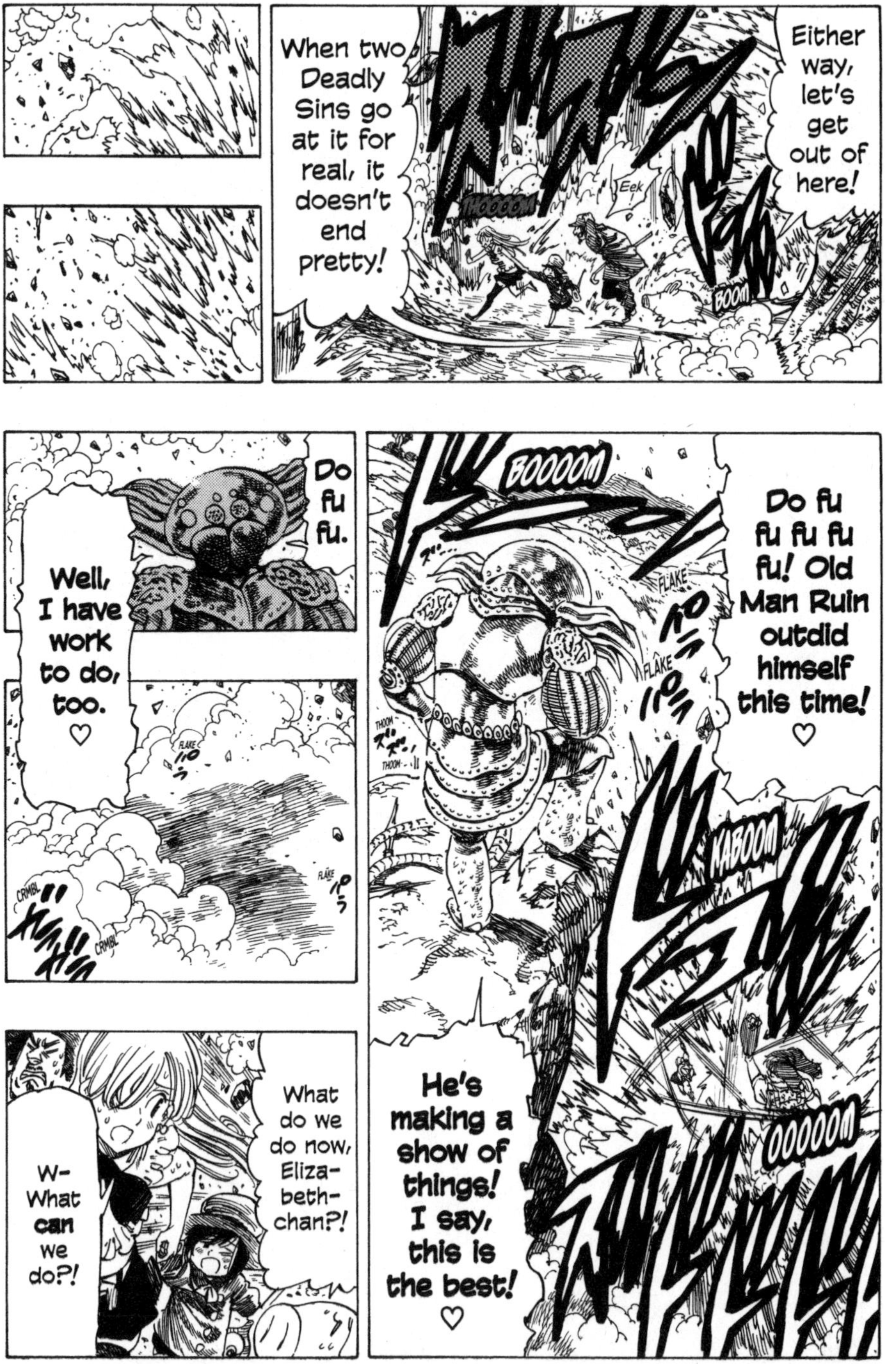
Either way, let's get out of here!
BOOM
Eek
THOOOOM
When two Deadly Sins go at it for real, it doesn't end pretty!
Do fu fu fu fu fu! Old Man Ruin outdid himself this time! ♡
BOOOOM
FLAKE
FLAKE
THOOM
THOOM
KABOOM
OOOOOM
He's making a show of things! I say, this is the best! ♡
Do fu fu.
Well, I have work to do, too. ♡
FLAKE
FLAKE
CRMBL
CRMBL
What do we do now, Eliza-beth-chan?!
W-What can we do?!

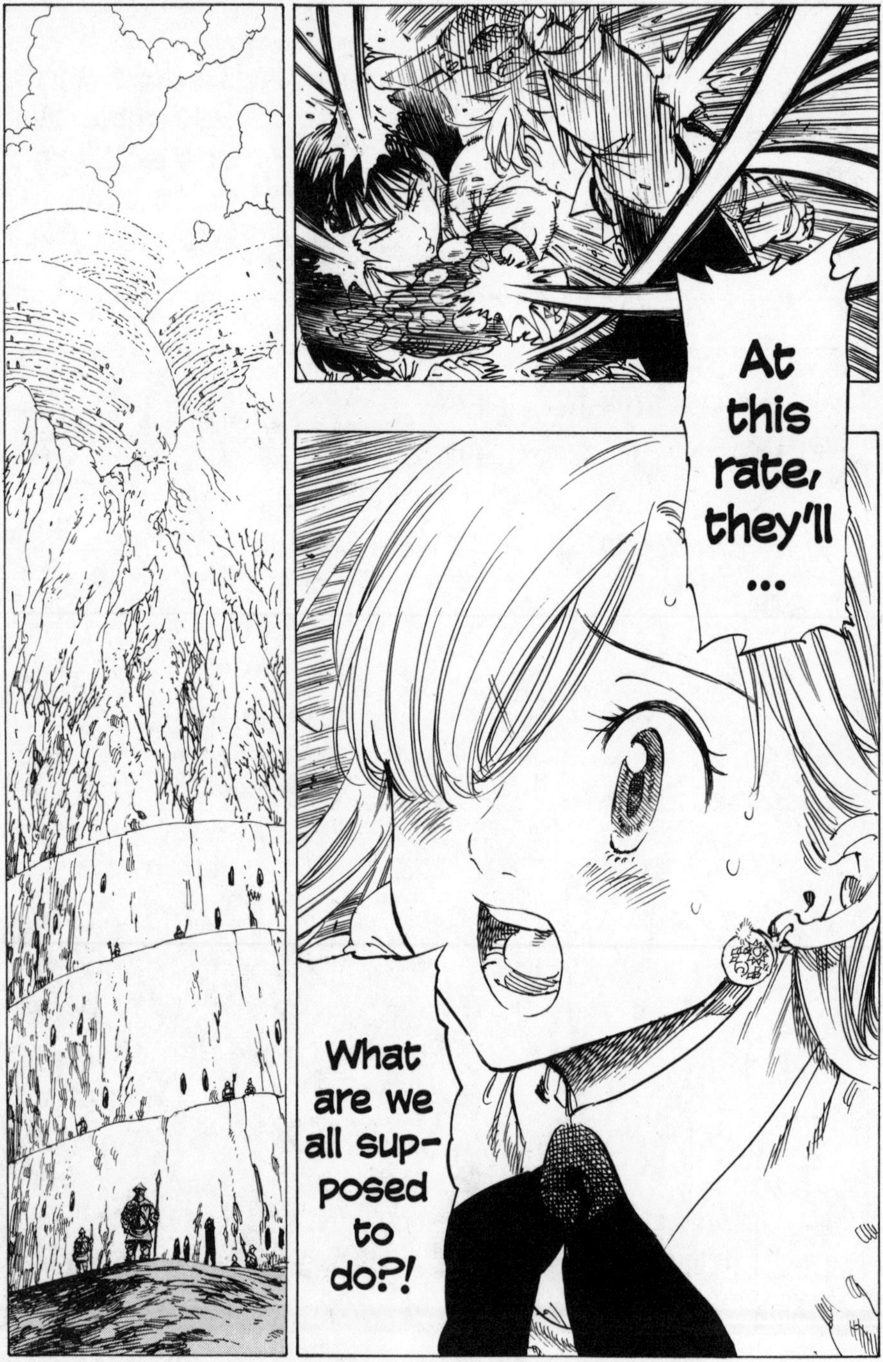
At this rate, they'll ...
What are we all sup-posed to do?!

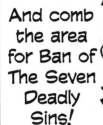

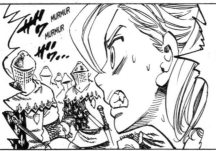

G...Go and assemble all the soldiers in the prison!!
MURMUR
MURMUR
And comb the area for Ban of The Seven Deadly Sins!
B-But Jericho-sama...
What are you wearing that for?
Who cares?! Just bring me a change of clothes and armor!
RIGHT NOW!
Y... yes, ma'am!
PLIP
CLANK
HMMM...
I knew it. Too small.
CLANK

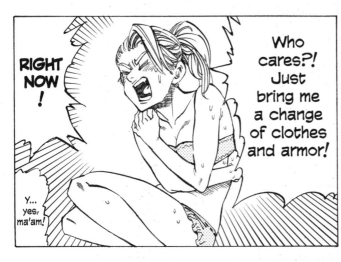

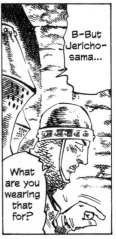

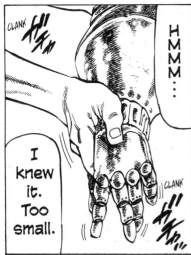

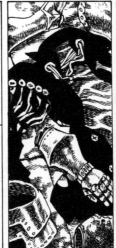

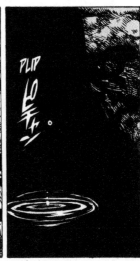

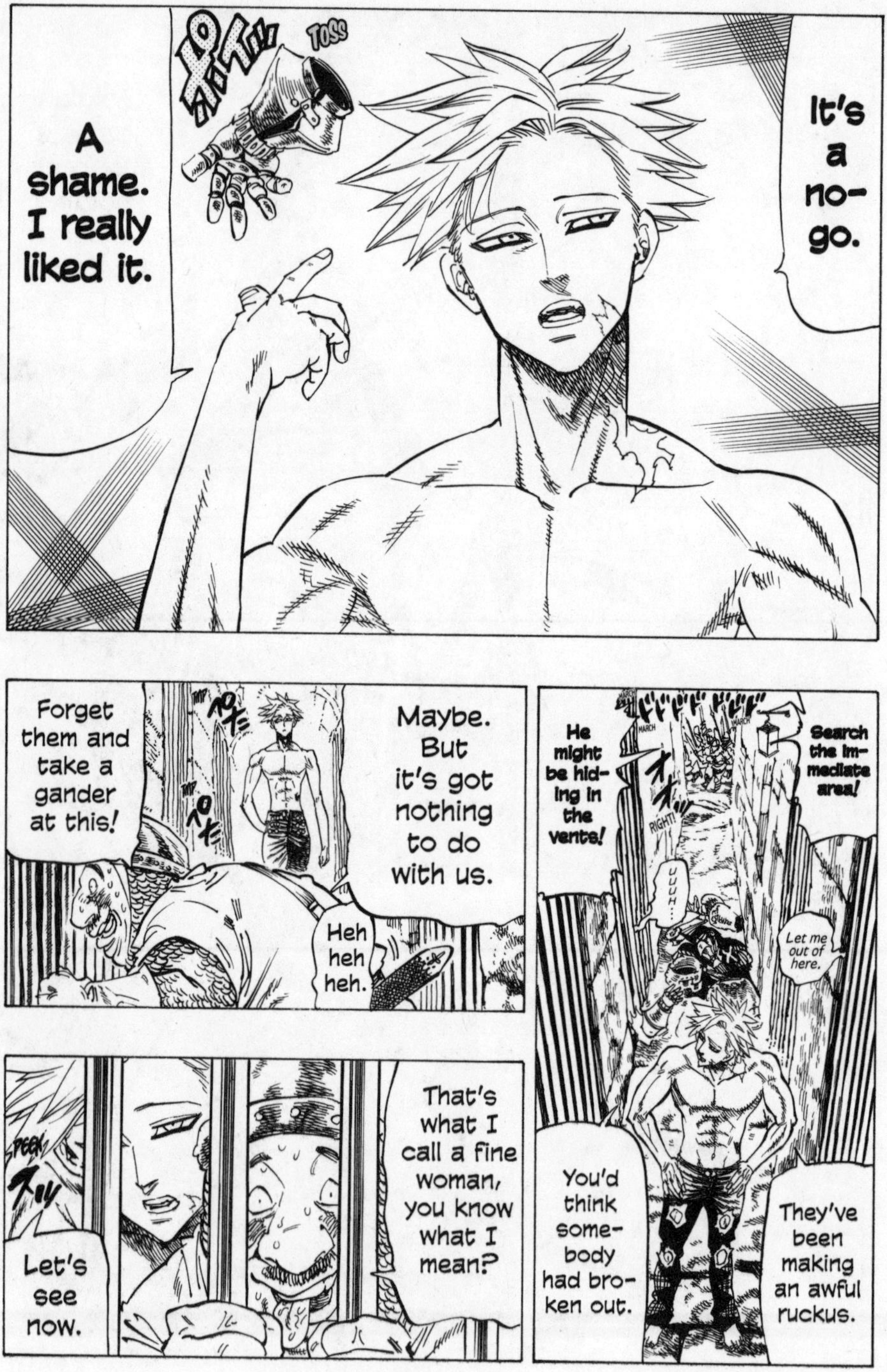
TOSS
It's a no-go.
A shame. I really liked it.
MARCH
Search the immediate area!
He might be hiding in the vents!
RIGHT!
UUUH...
Let me out of here.
They've been making an awful ruckus.
You'd think somebody had broken out.
TAP
Maybe. But it's got nothing to do with us.
Forget them and take a gander at this!
Heh heh heh.
That's what I call a fine woman, you know what I mean?
Let's see now.

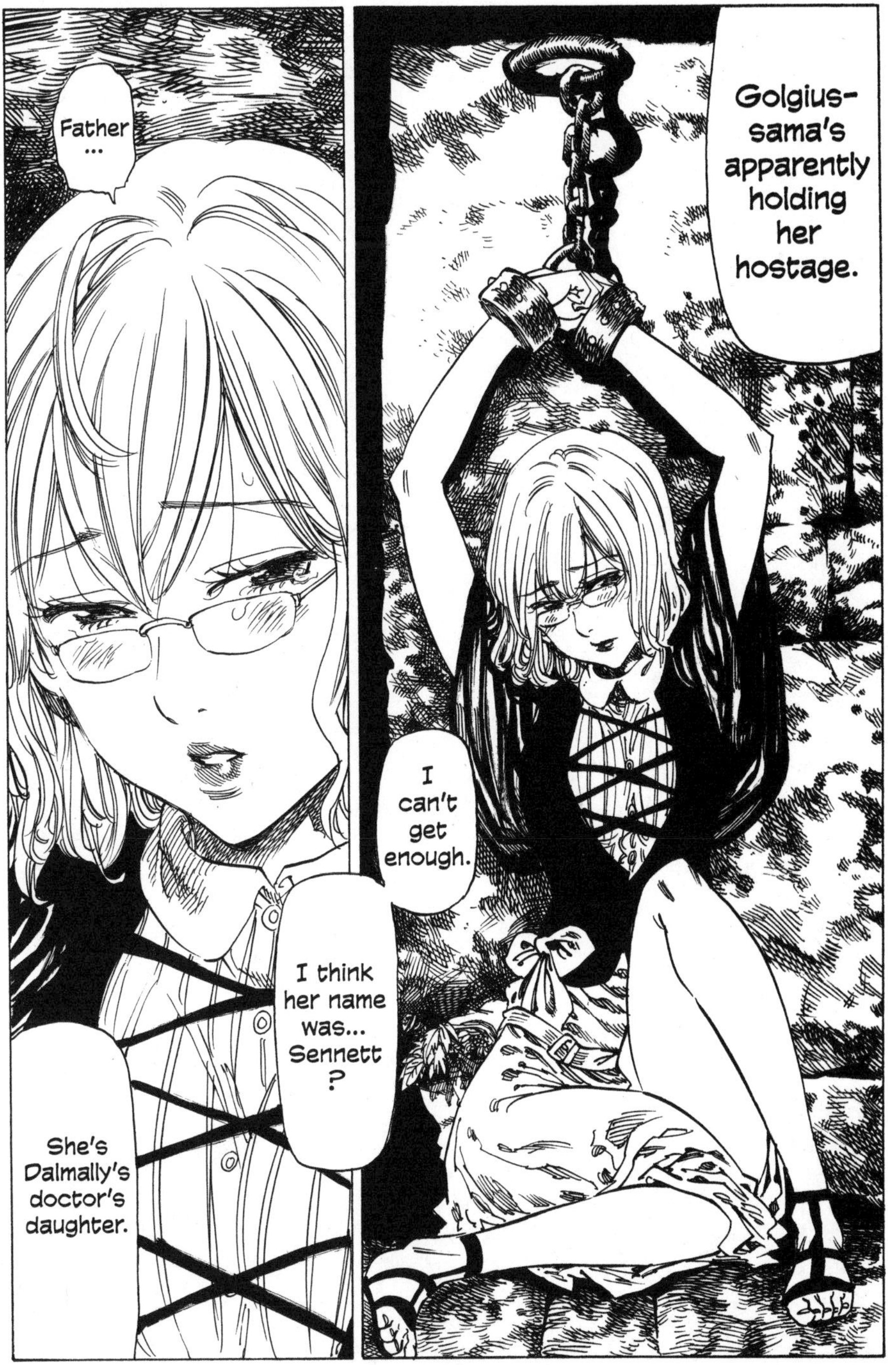
Golgius-sama's apparently holding her hostage.
I can't get enough.
Father ...
I think her name was... Sennett ?
She's Dalmally's doctor's daughter.

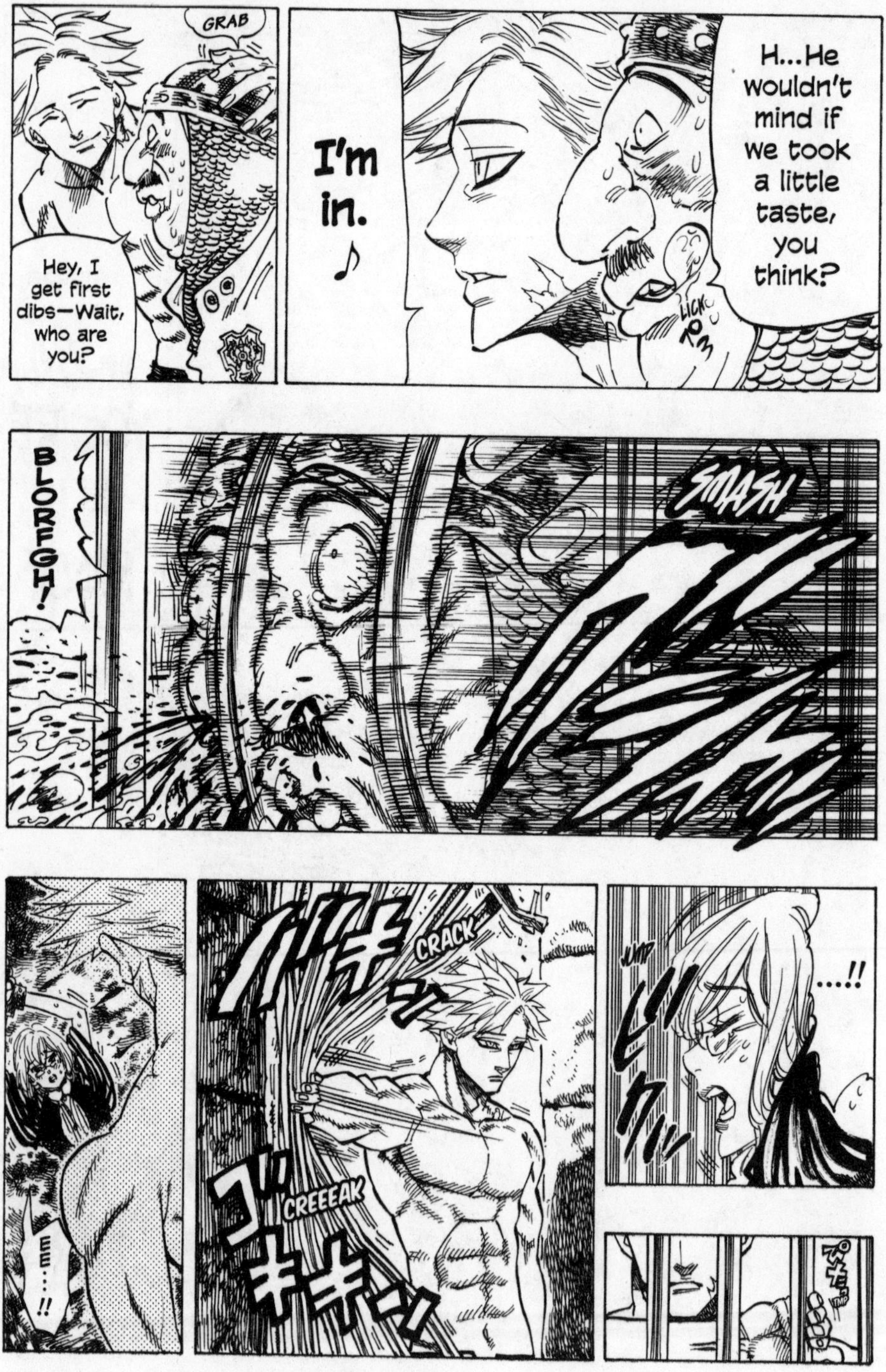
H...He wouldn't mind if we took a little taste, you think?
LICK
I'm in. ♪
GRAB
Hey, I get first dibs—Wait, who are you?
SMASH
BLORFGH!
...!!
CRACK
CREEEAK
EE...!!

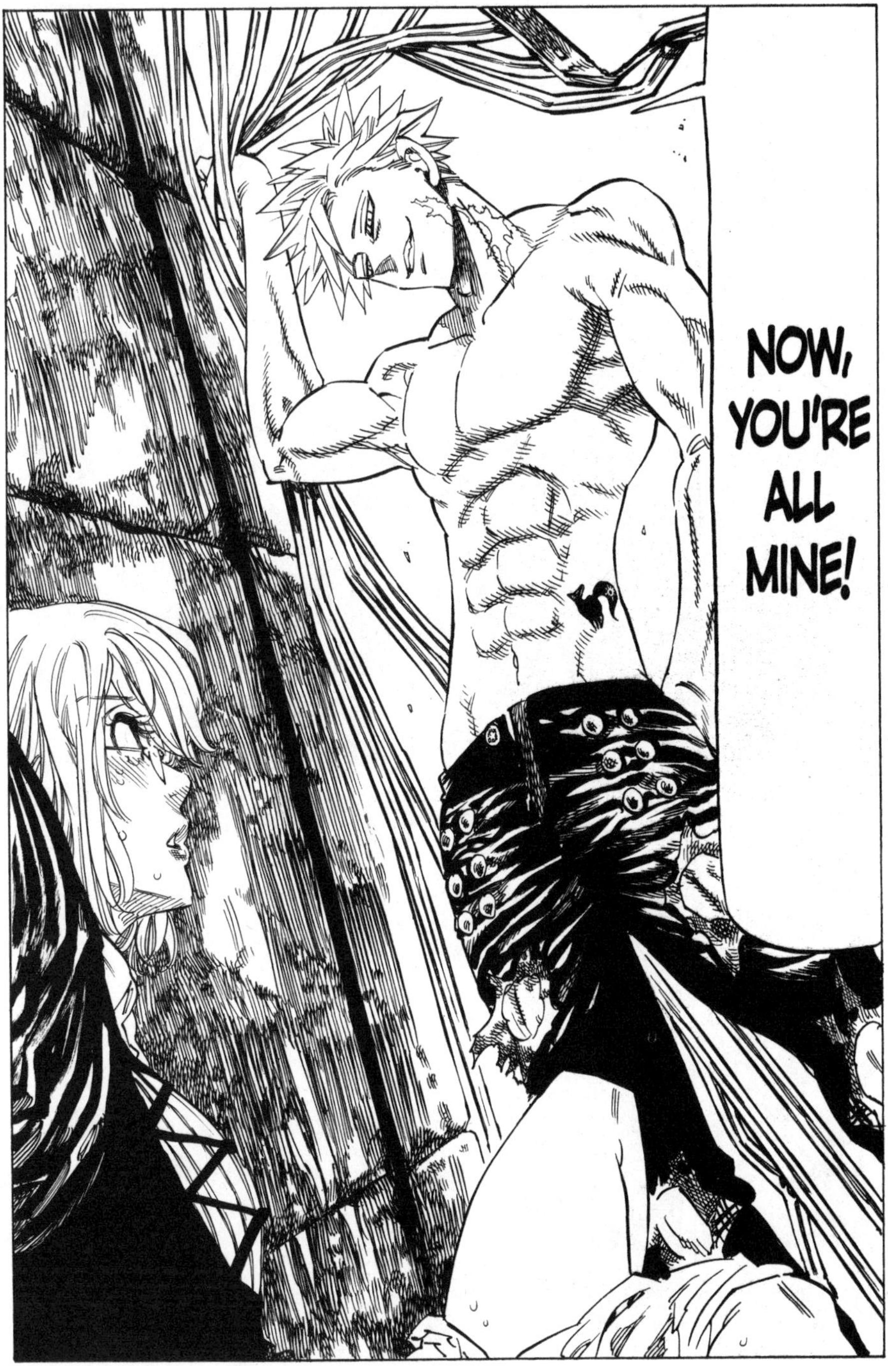
NOW, YOU'RE ALL MINE!

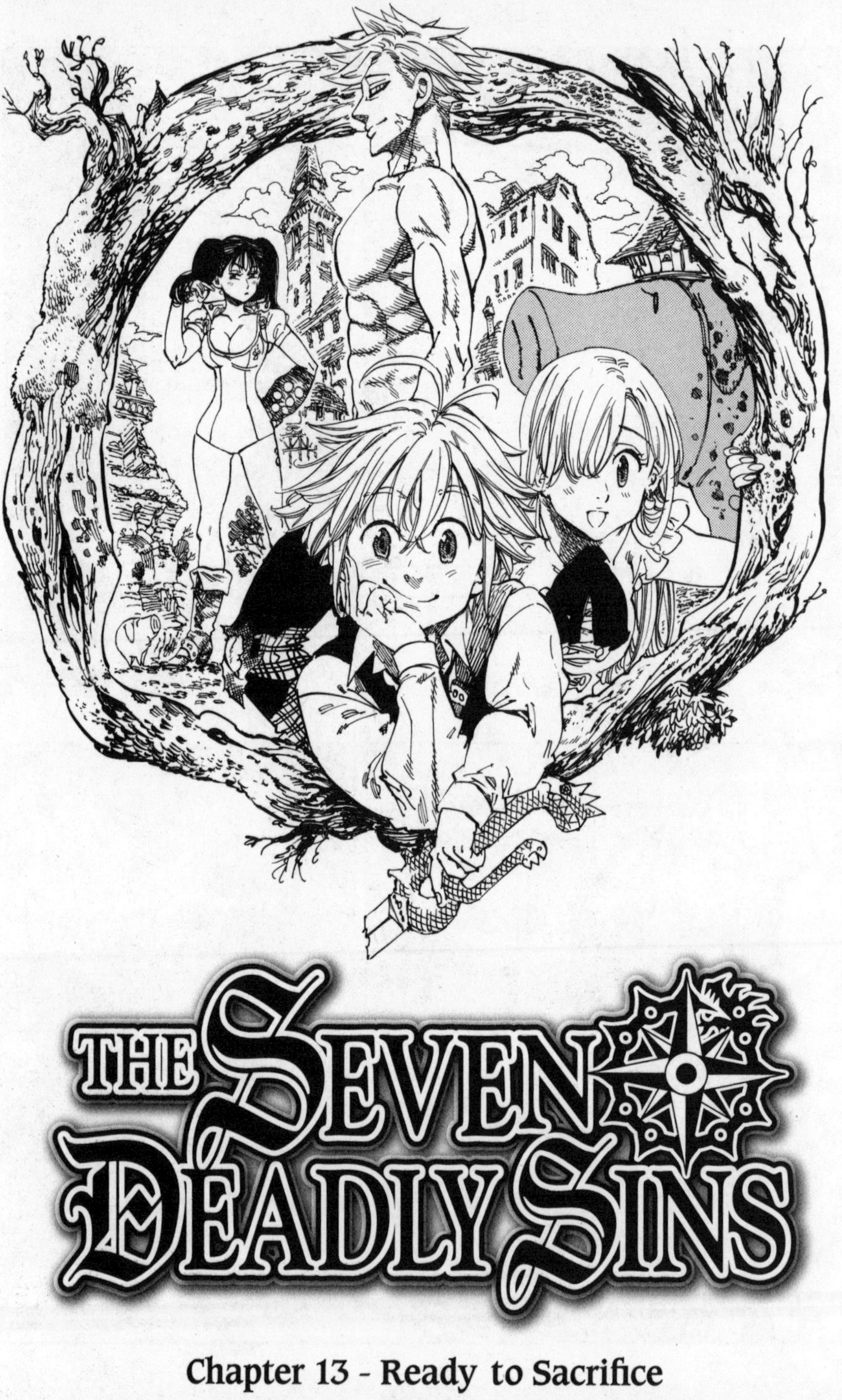

THE SEVEN DEADLY SINS

Chapter 13 - Ready to Sacrifice

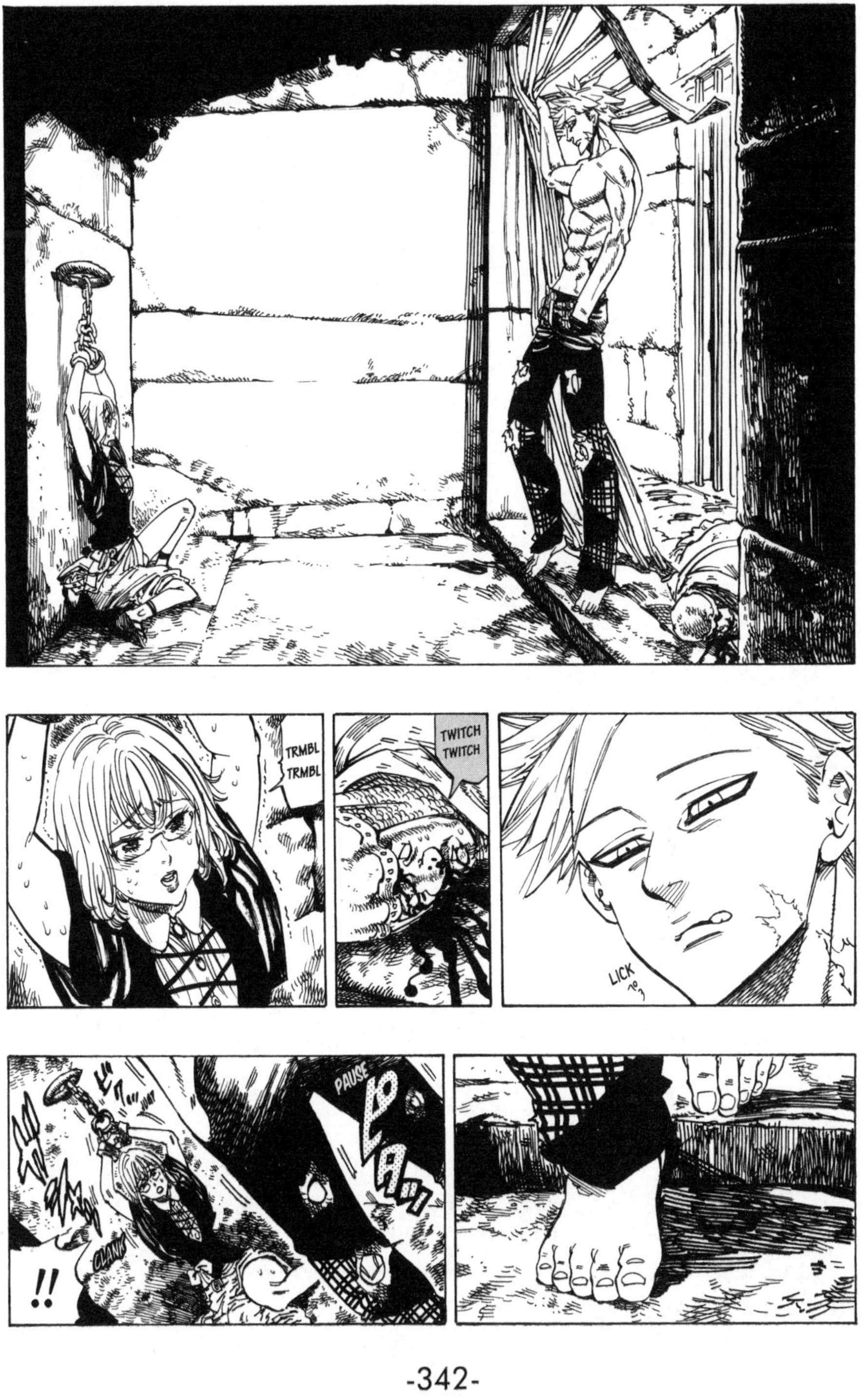
LICK
TWITCH TWITCH
TRMBL TRMBL
PAUSE
CLANK
!!

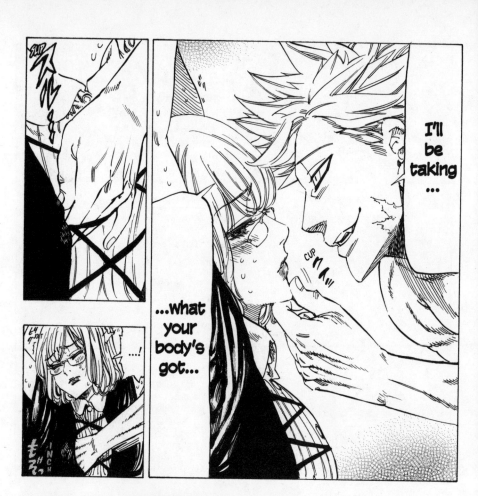

I'll be taking...

...what your body's got...

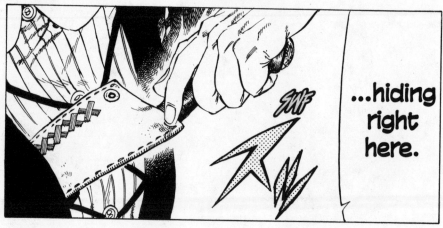

...hiding right here.

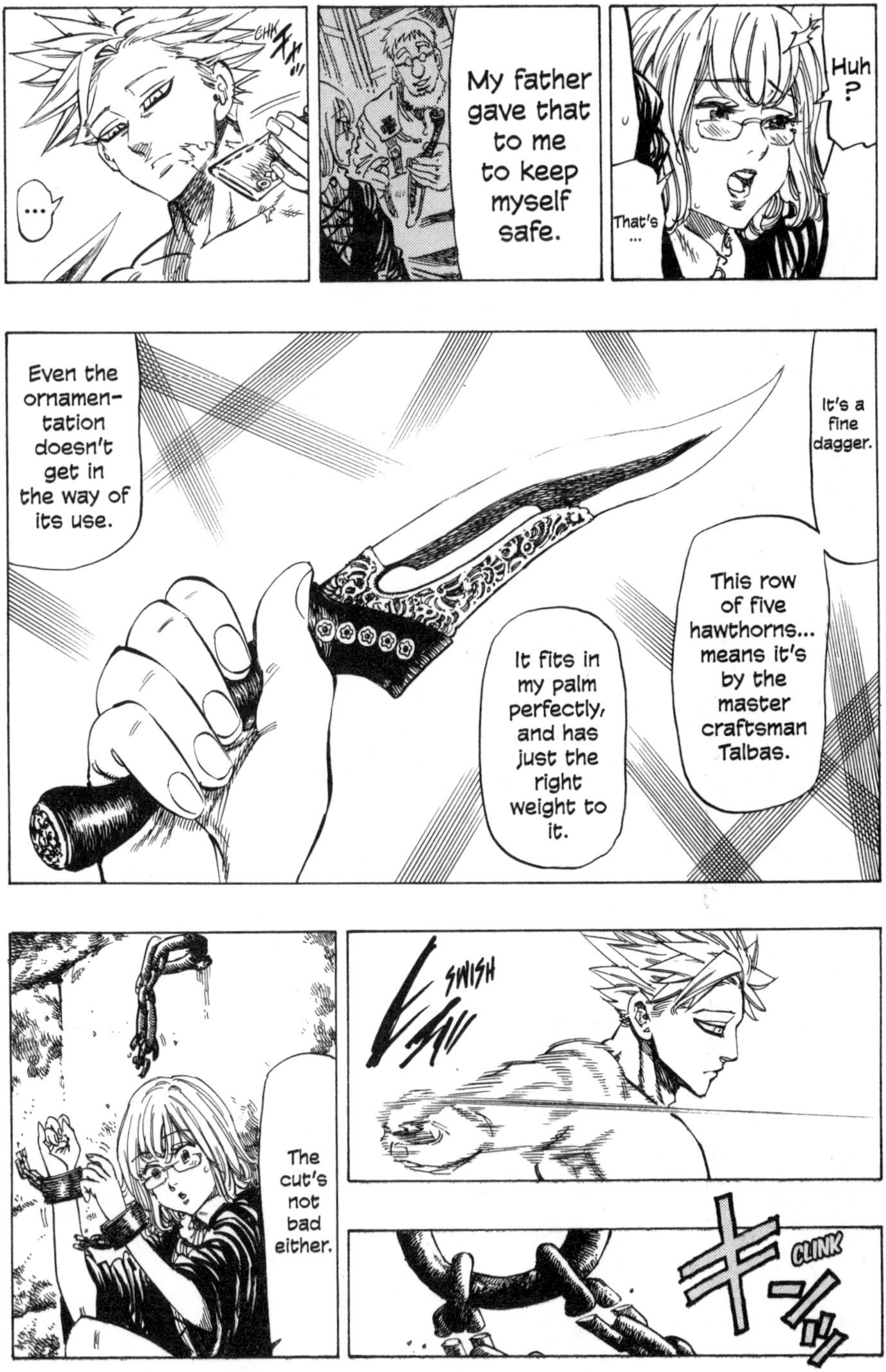
Huh?
That's...
My father gave that to me to keep myself safe.
CHK
...
It's a fine dagger.
This row of five hawthorns... means it's by the master craftsman Talbas.
It fits in my palm perfectly, and has just the right weight to it.
Even the ornamentation doesn't get in the way of its use.
SWISH
CLINK
The cut's not bad either.

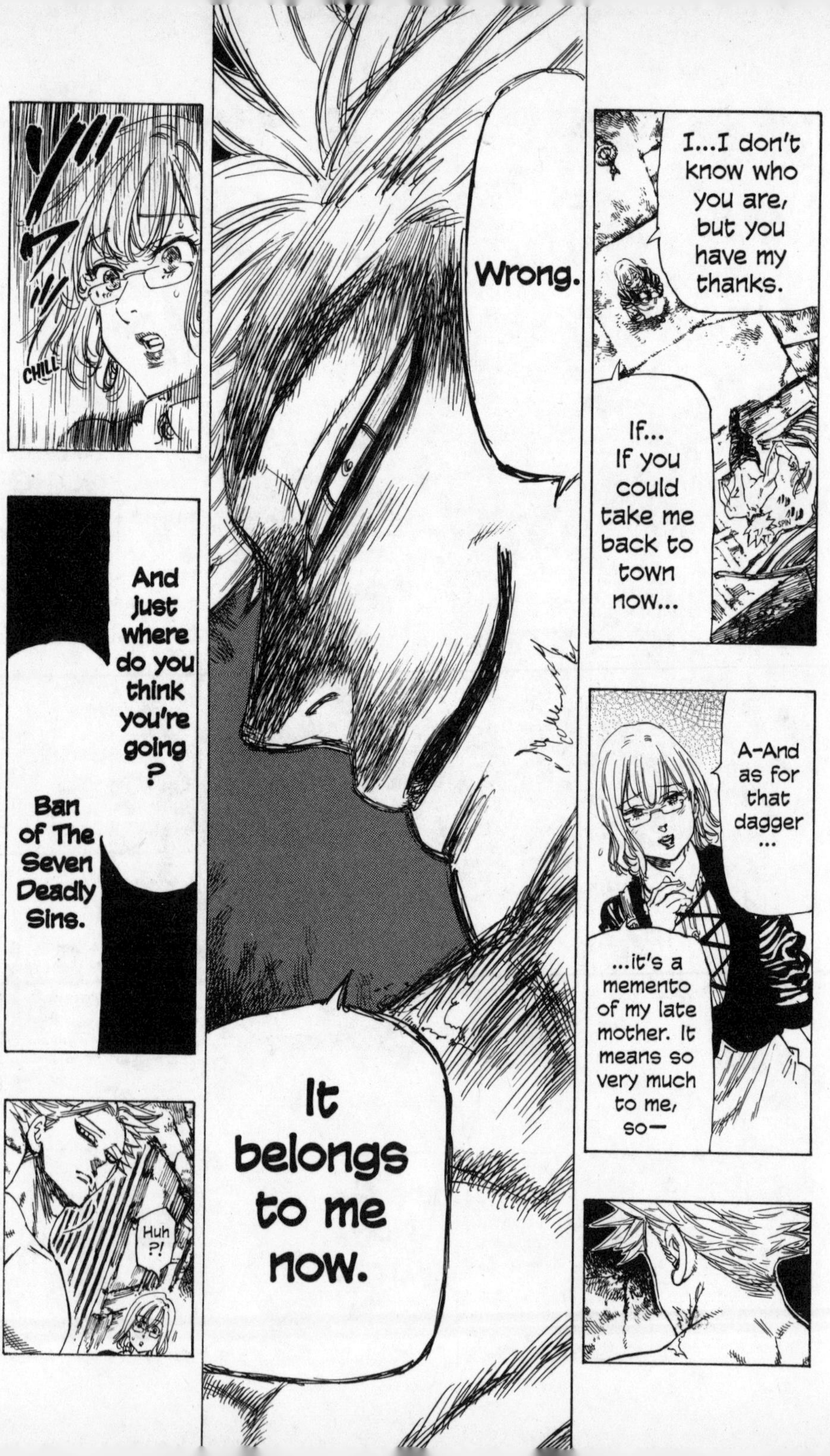

I...I don't know who you are, but you have my thanks.
If... If you could take me back to town now...
SPIN
A-And as for that dagger...
...it's a memento of my late mother. It means so very much to me, so—
Wrong.
It belongs to me now.
CHILL
And just where do you think you're going?
Ban of The Seven Deadly Sins.
Huh?!

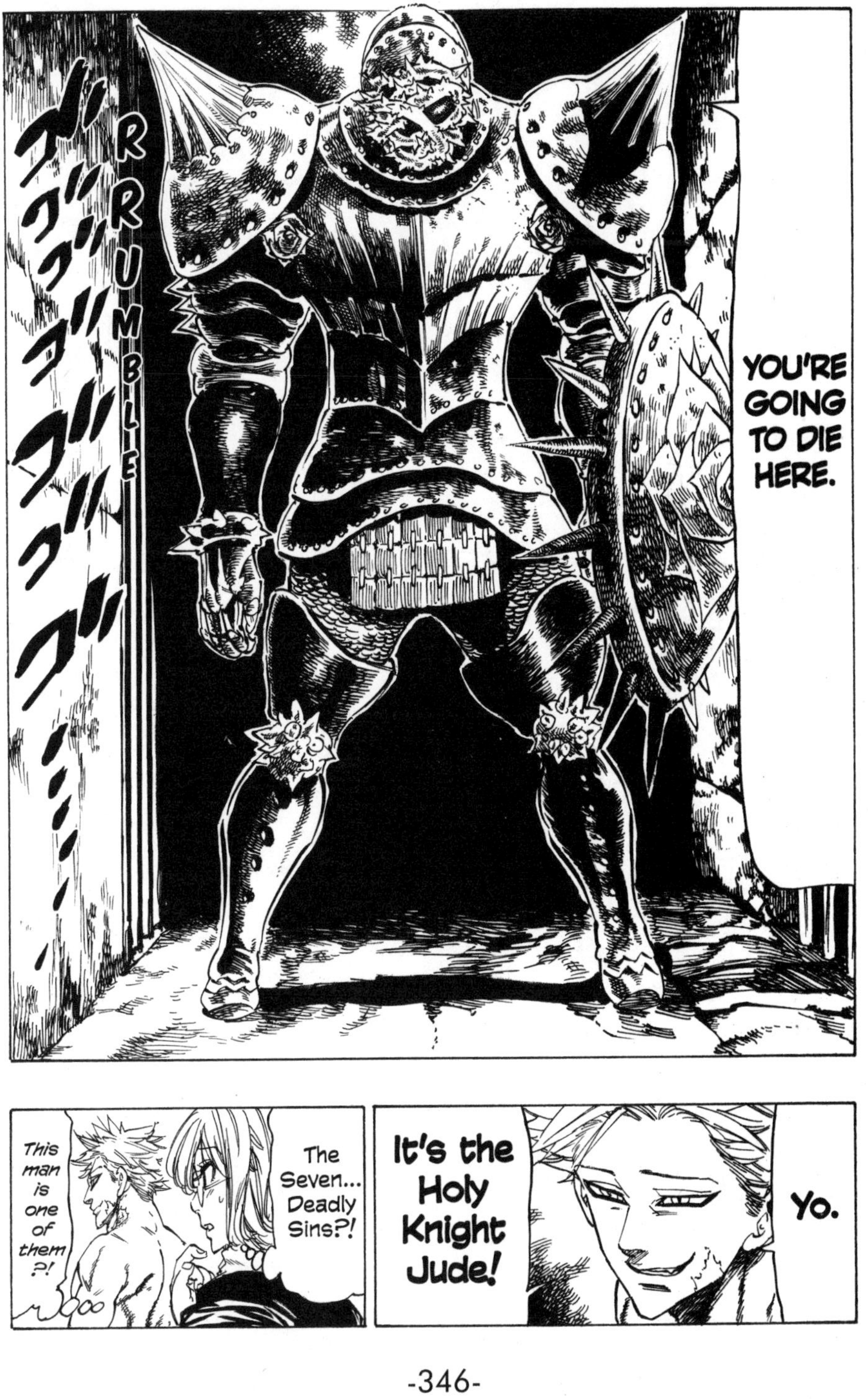
YOU'RE GOING TO DIE HERE.
RRUMBLE
Yo.
It's the Holy Knight Jude!
The Seven... Deadly Sins?!
This man is one of them?!

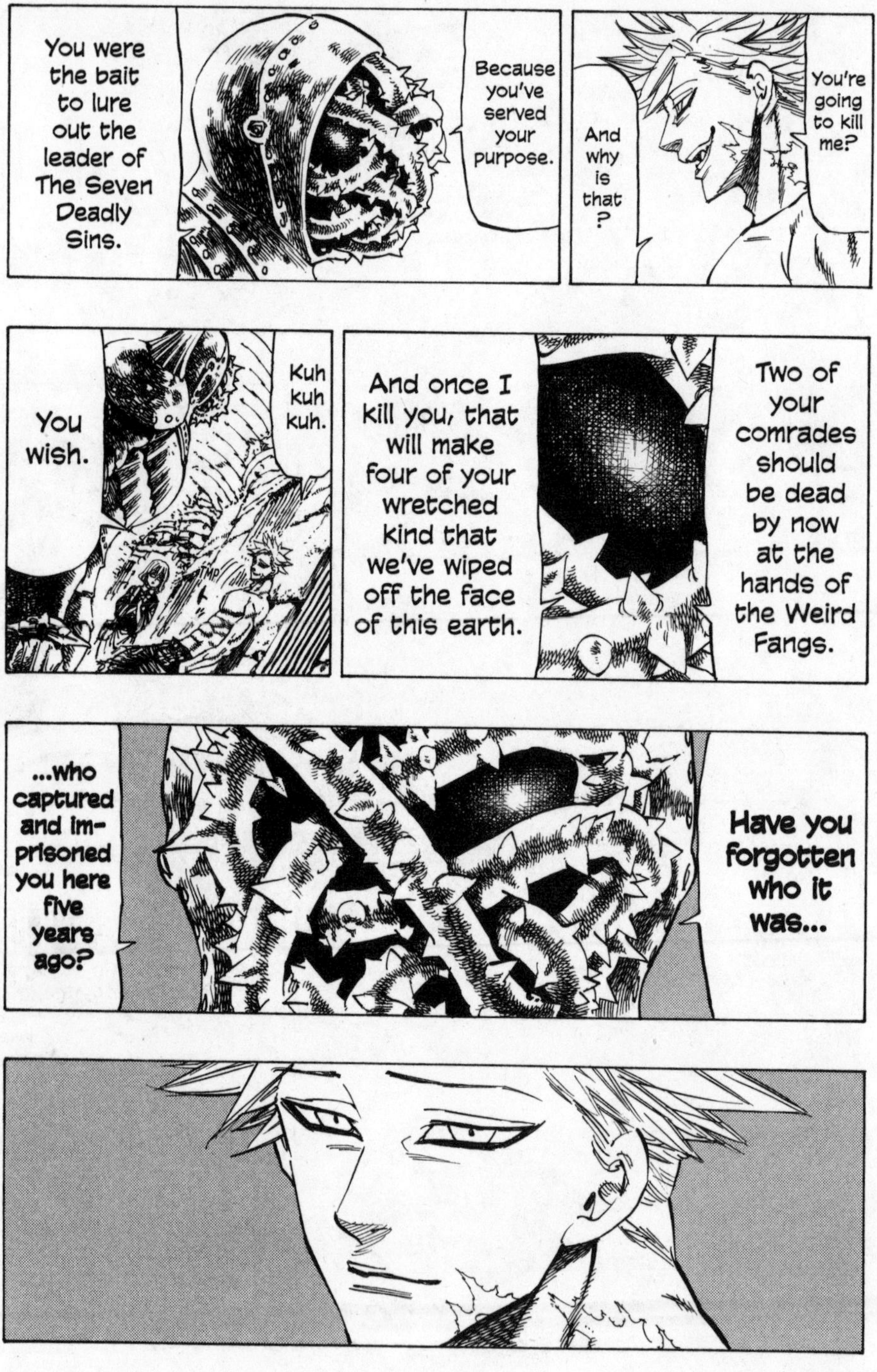
You're going to kill me?
And why is that?
Because you've served your purpose.
You were the bait to lure out the leader of The Seven Deadly Sins.
Two of your comrades should be dead by now at the hands of the Weird Fangs.
And once I kill you, that will make four of your wretched kind that we've wiped off the face of this earth.
Kuh kuh kuh.
You wish.
Have you forgotten who it was...
...who captured and imprisoned you here five years ago?

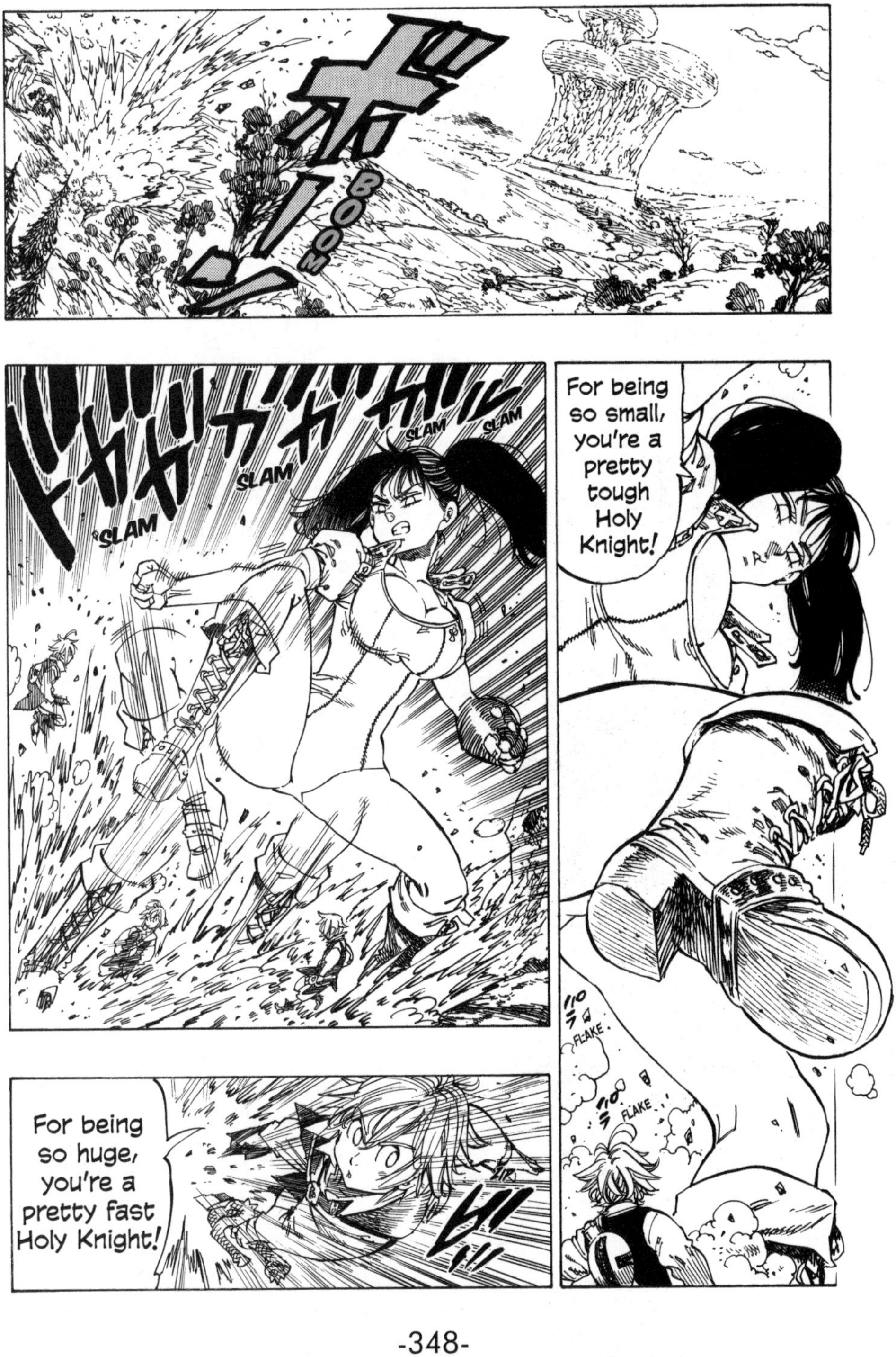
BOOM
For being so small, you're a pretty tough Holy Knight!
FLAKE
FLAKE
SLAM
SLAM
SLAM
SLAM
For being so huge, you're a pretty fast Holy Knight!

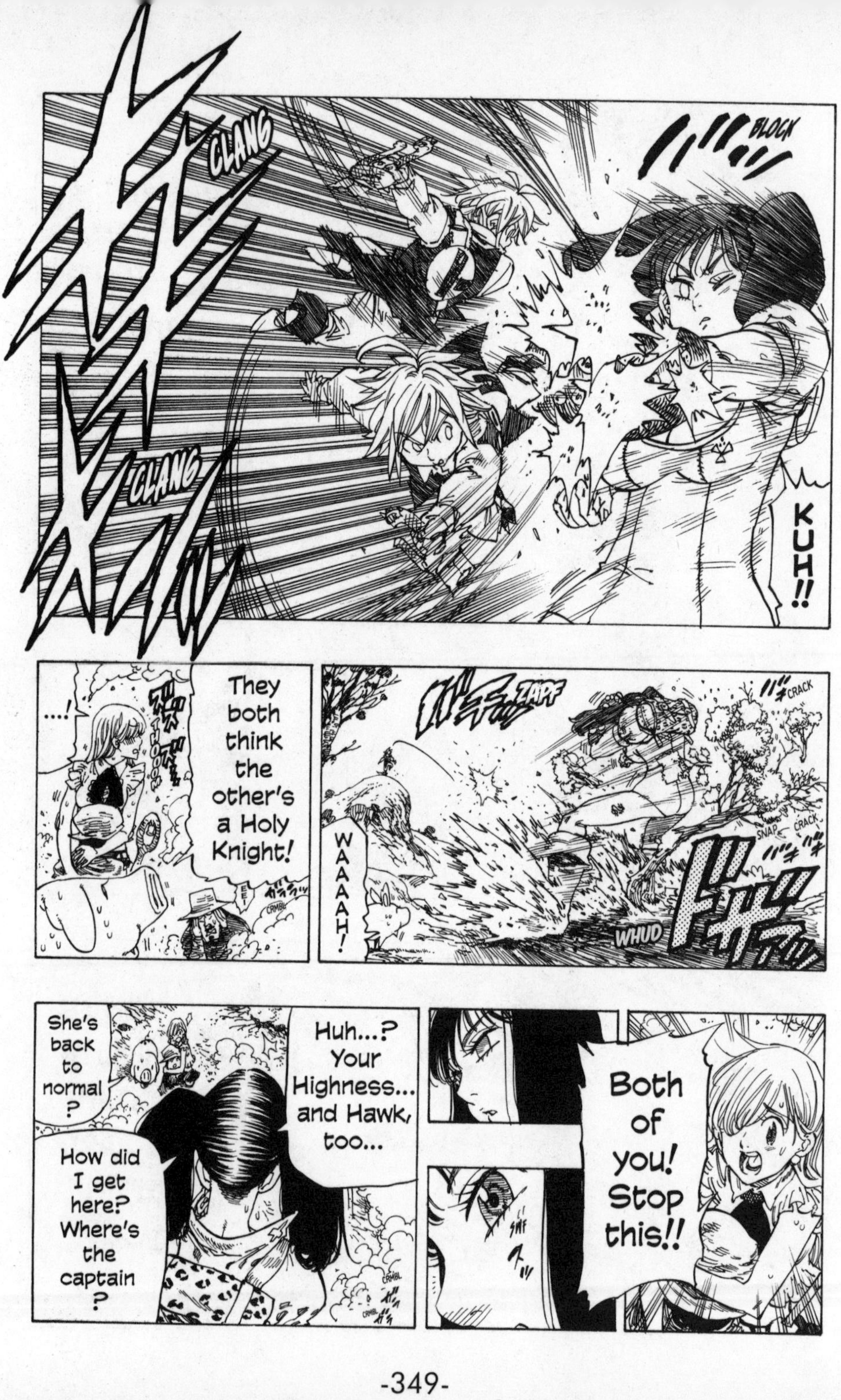
BLOCK
KUH!!
CLANG
CLANG
ZAPF
CRACK
SNAP
CRACK
WHUD
WAAAAAH!
They both think the other's a Holy Knight!
....!
CRMBL
Both of you! Stop this!!
SNF
Huh...? Your Highness... and Hawk, too...
She's back to normal?
How did I get here? Where's the captain?
CRMBL
CRMBL

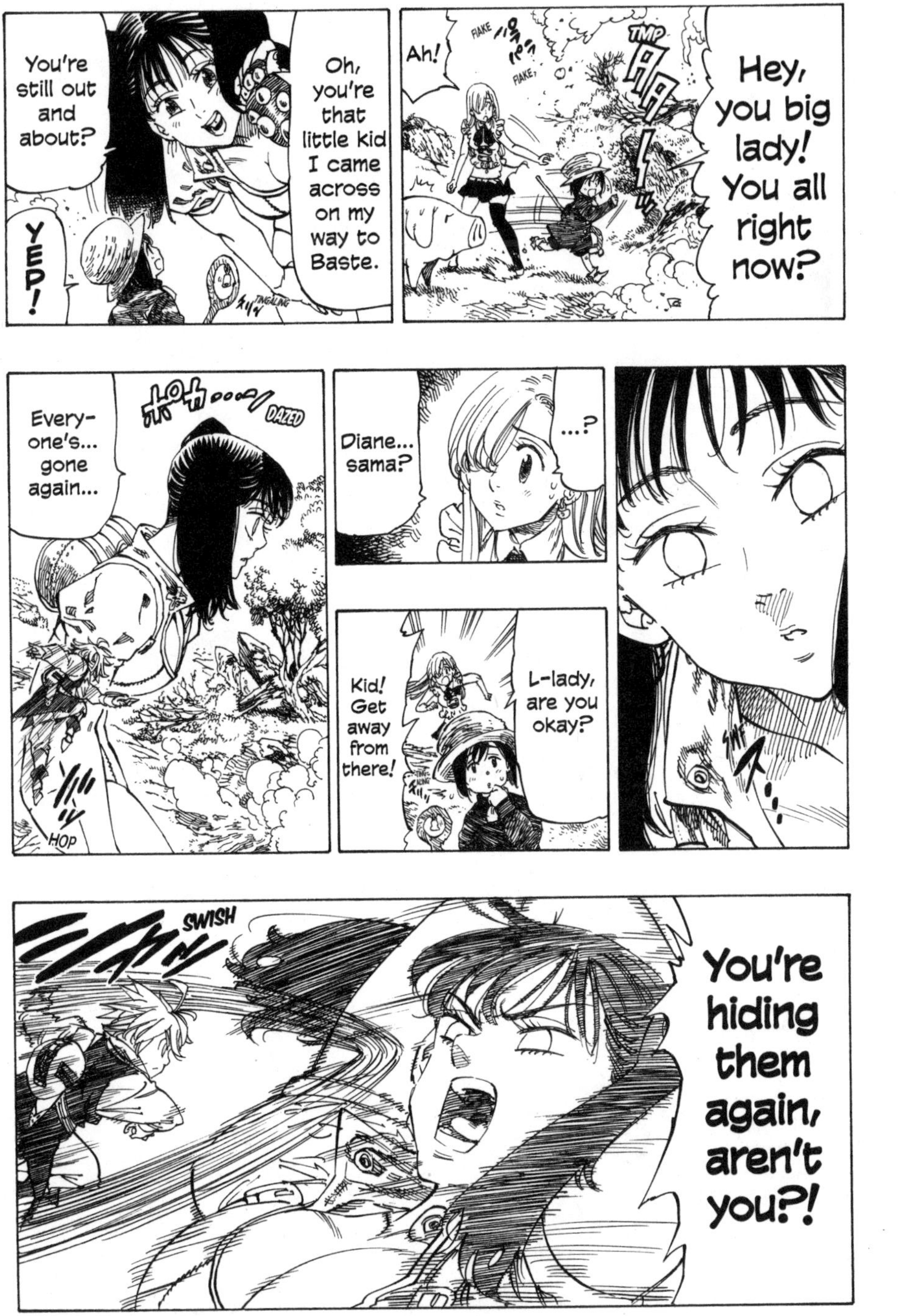

Hey, you big lady! You all right now?
TMP
Ah!
FLAKE
FLAKE
Oh, you're that little kid I came across on my way to Baste.
You're still out and about?
YEP!
TINGALING
SWF
...?
Diane... sama?
L-lady, are you okay?
Kid! Get away from there!
TINGALING
DAZED
Every-one's... gone again...
HOP
You're hiding them again, aren't you?!
SWISH

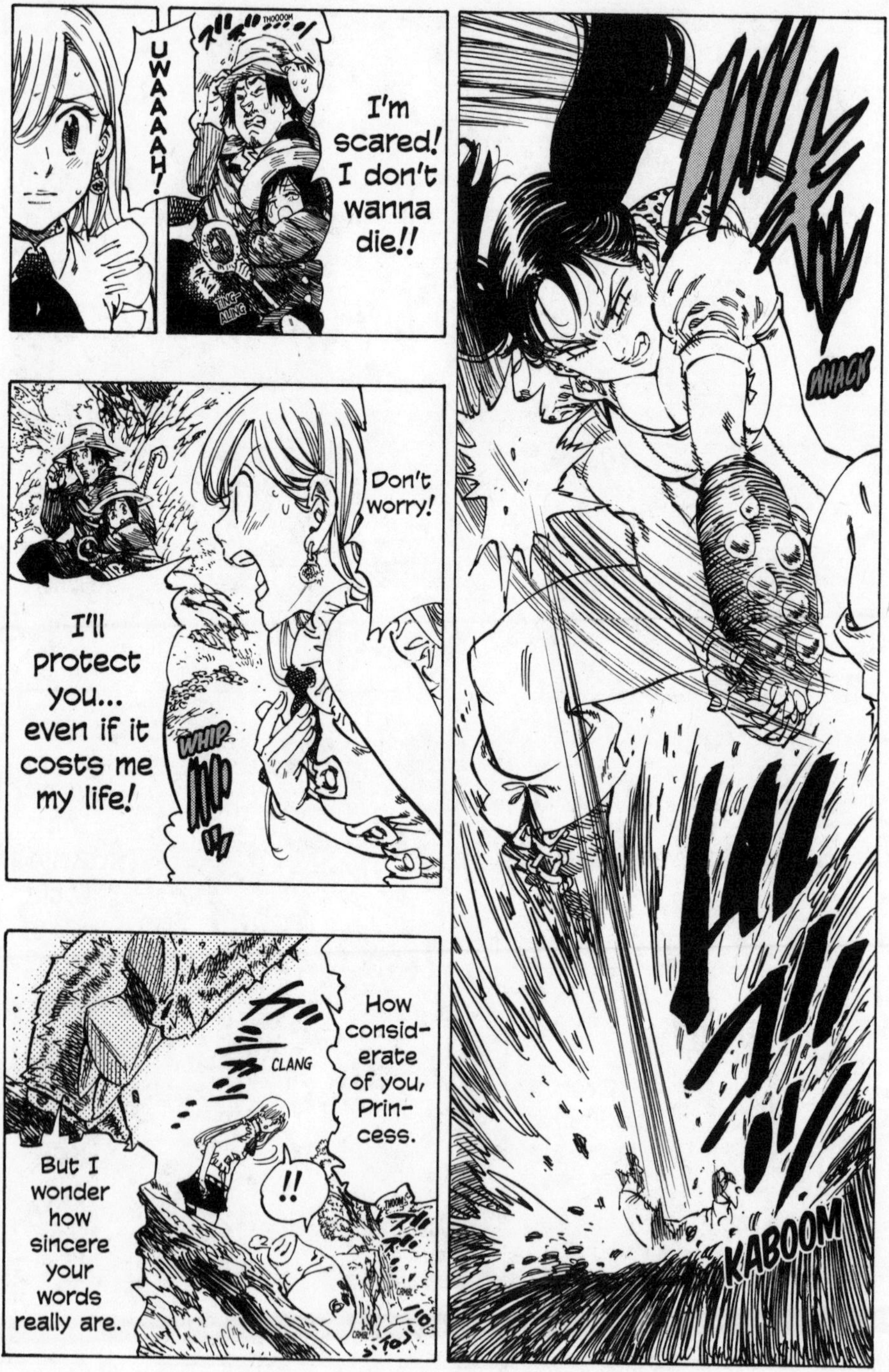
WHACK
KABOOM
THOOOOM
UWAAAAH!
I'm scared! I don't wanna die!!
TING-ALING
Don't worry!
I'll protect you... even if it costs me my life!
WHIP
How considerate of you, Princess.
CLANG
!!
But I wonder how sincere your words really are.
THOOM

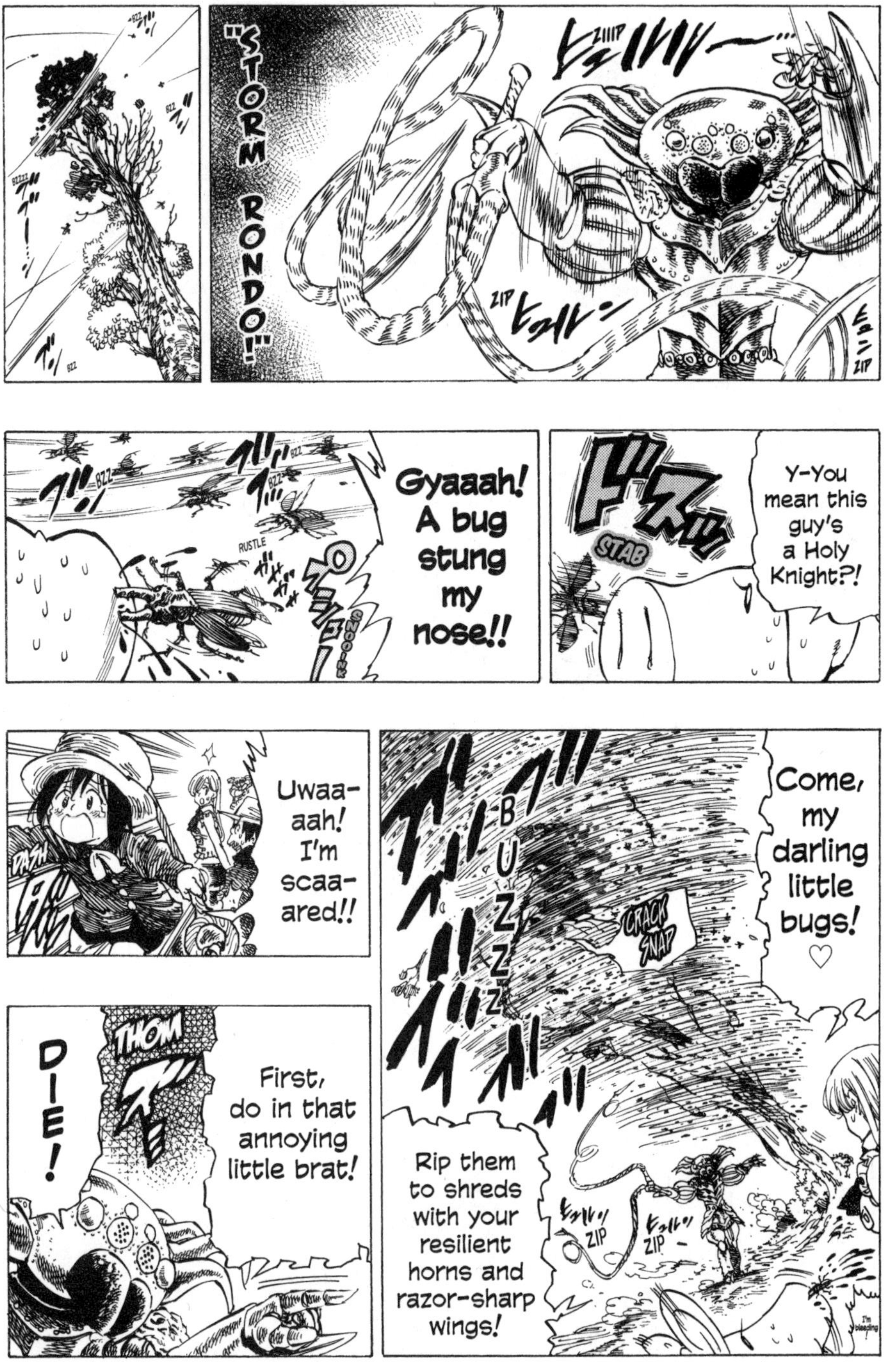
"STORM RONDO!!"
ZIIIP
ZIP
ZIP
BZZZ
BZZ
BZZ
Y-You mean this guy's a Holy Knight?!
STAB
Gyaaah! A bug stung my nose!!
BZZ
RUSTLE
Come, my darling little bugs! ♡
BUZZZ
CRACK SNAP
Rip them to shreds with your resilient horns and razor-sharp wings!
ZIP
ZIP
I'm bleeding!
Uwaa-aah! I'm scaa-ared!!
DASH
First, do in that annoying little brat!
DIE!
THOM

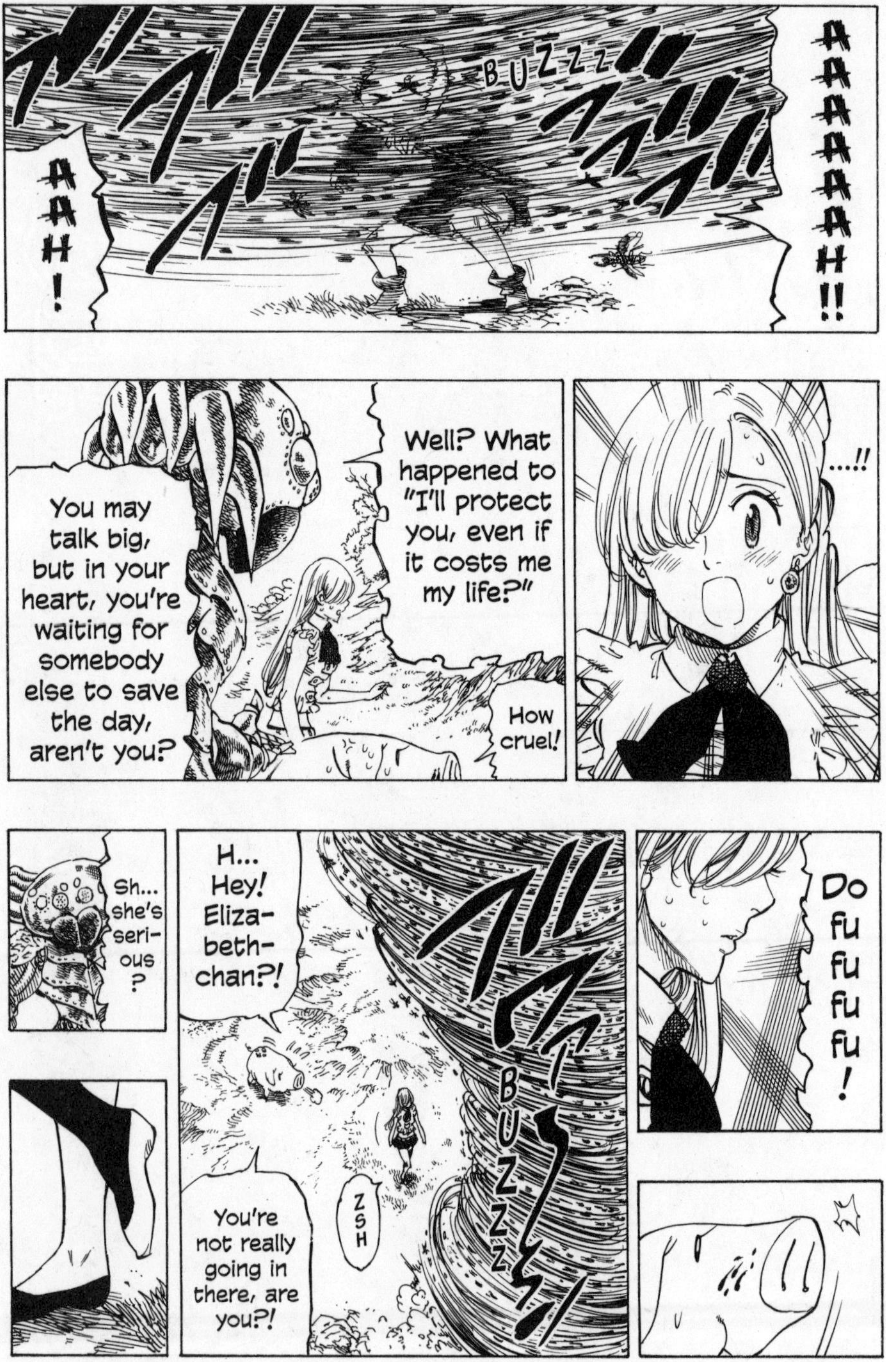
AAAAAAAH!!
BUZzzz
AAH!
...!!
Well? What happened to "I'll protect you, even if it costs me my life?"
How cruel!
You may talk big, but in your heart, you're waiting for somebody else to save the day, aren't you?
Do fu fu fu fu!
H... Hey! Eliza-beth-chan?!
BUZZZ
ZSH
You're not really going in there, are you?!
Sh... she's seri-ous?

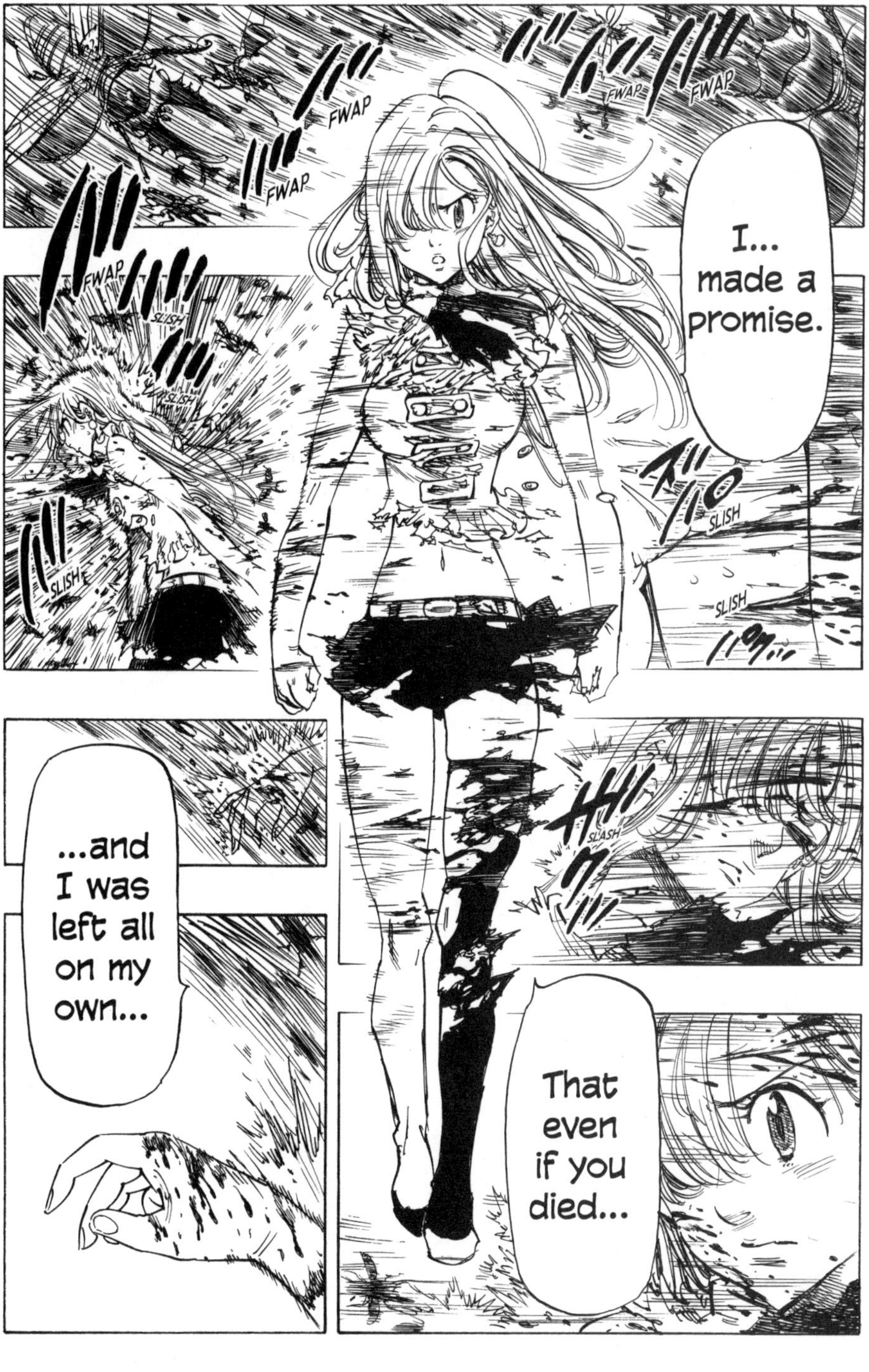

FWAP
FWAP
FWAP
FWAP
I... made a promise.
SLISH
SLISH
FWAP
SLISH
SLISH
SLISH
SLASH
That even if you died...
...and I was left all on my own...

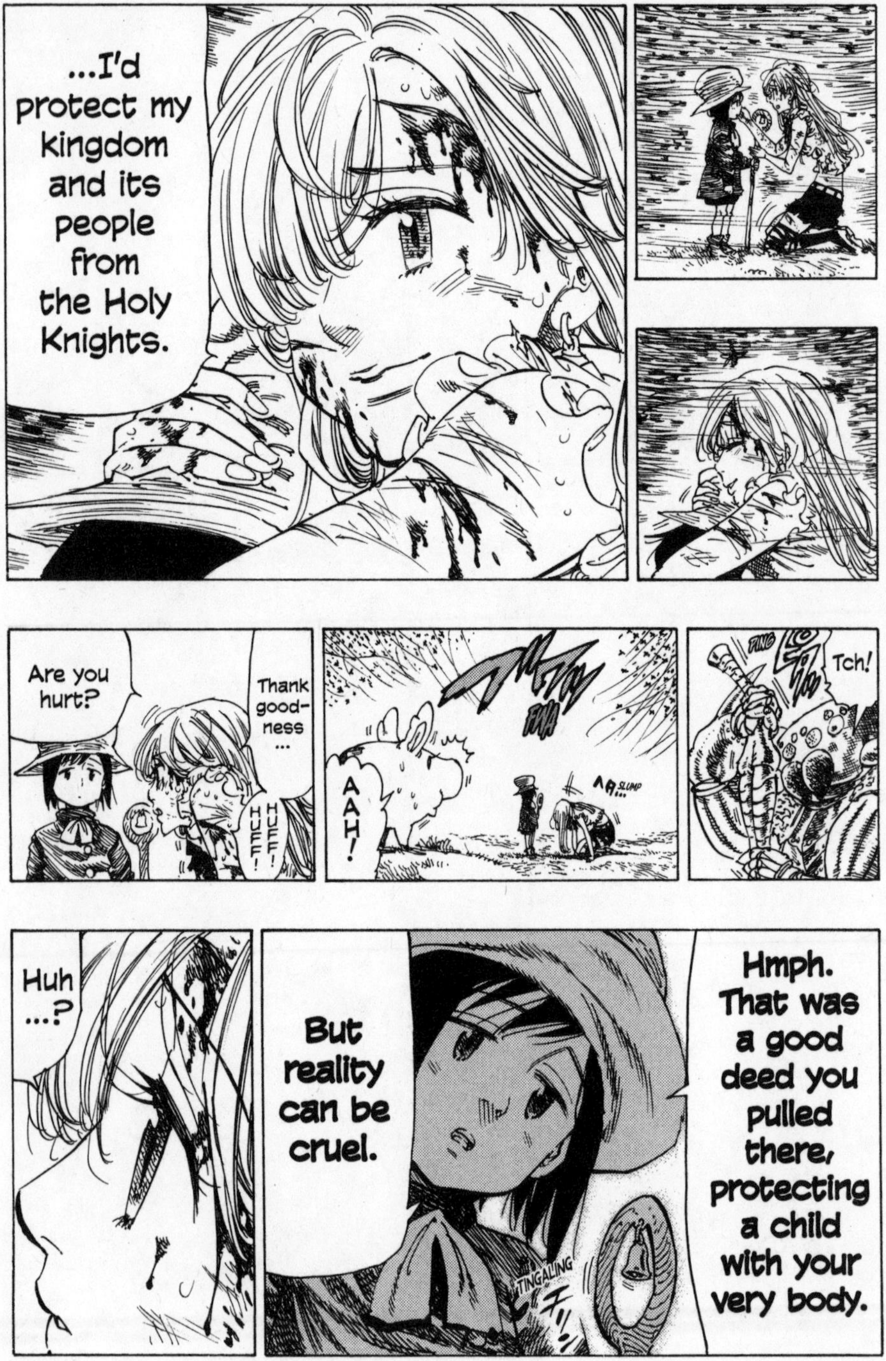
...I'd protect my kingdom and its people from the Holy Knights.
TING
Tch!
FWA
AAH!
SLUMP
Thank goodness ...
HUFF! HUFF!
Are you hurt?
Hmph. That was a good deed you pulled there, protecting a child with your very body.
But reality can be cruel.
TINGALING
Huh ...?

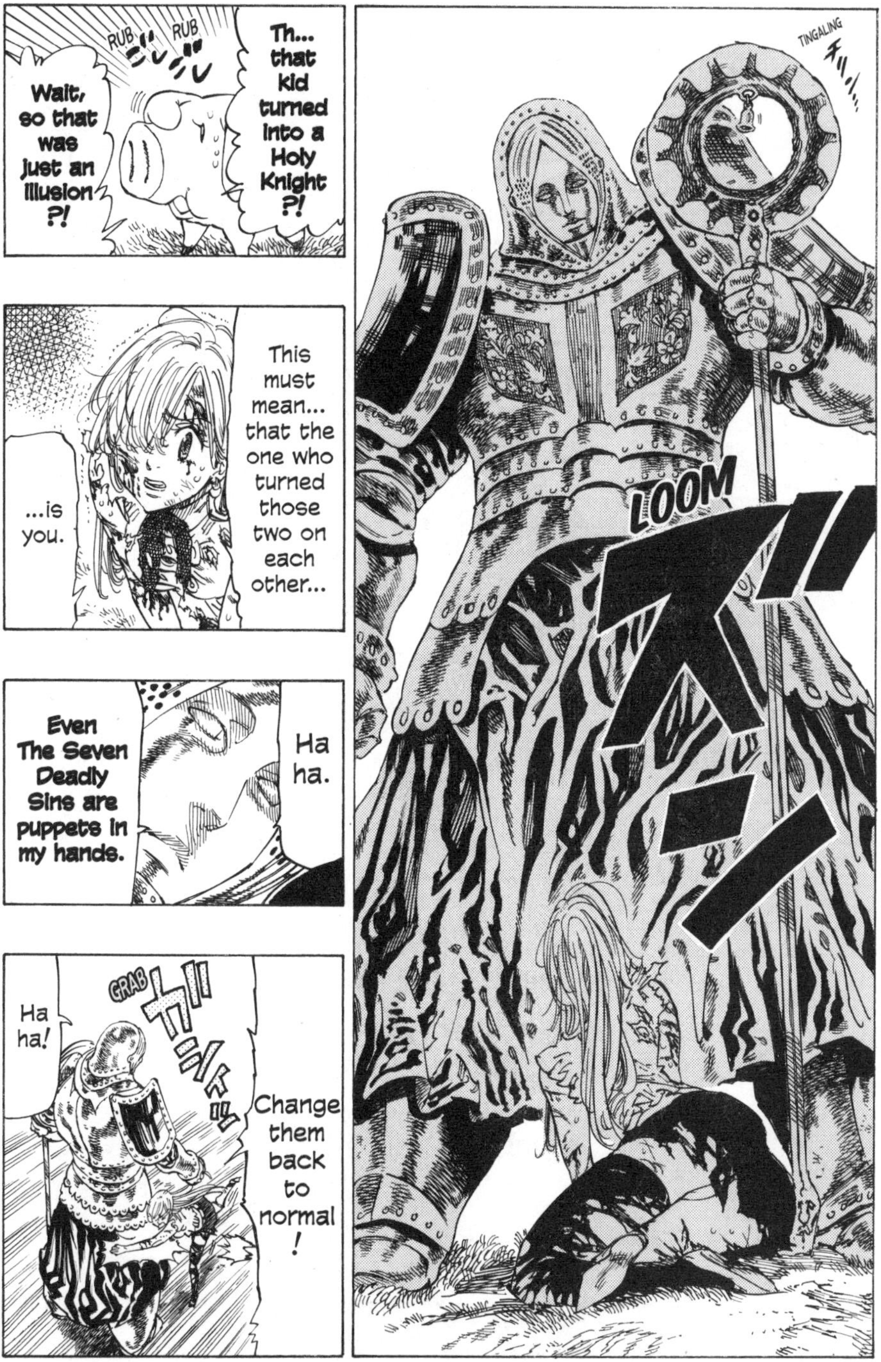
TINGALING
LOOM
Th... that kid turned into a Holy Knight?!
RUB RUB
Wait, so that was just an illusion?!
This must mean... that the one who turned those two on each other...
...is you.
Ha ha.
Even The Seven Deadly Sins are puppets in my hands.
Change them back to normal!
GRAB
Ha ha!

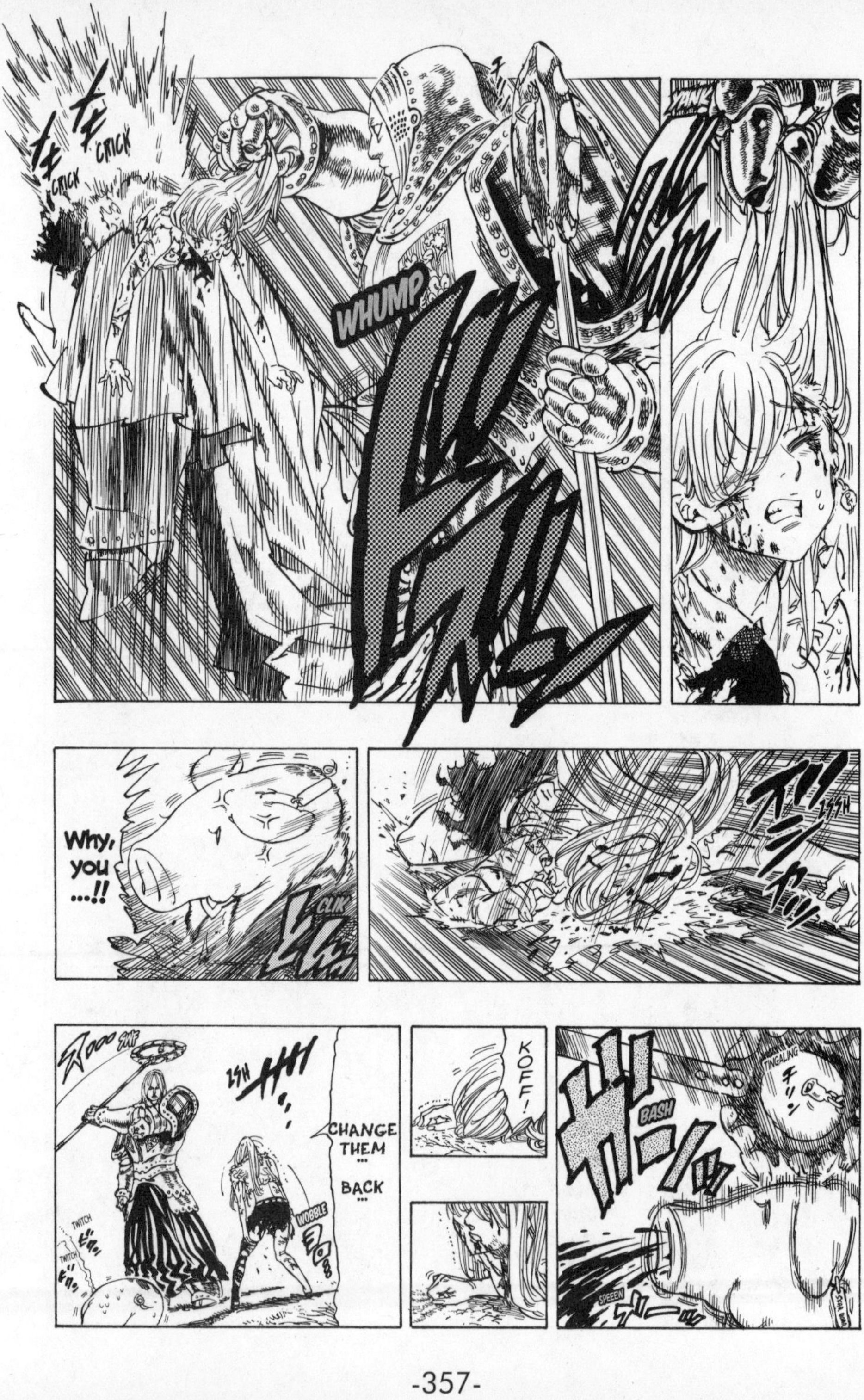

YANK
CRICK
CRICK
WHUMP
ISSH
Why, you ...!!
CLIK
TINGALING
チリン
BASH
SPEEEN
KOFF!
SHF
ZSH
CHANGE THEM ... BACK ...
WOBBLE
TWITCH
TWITCH

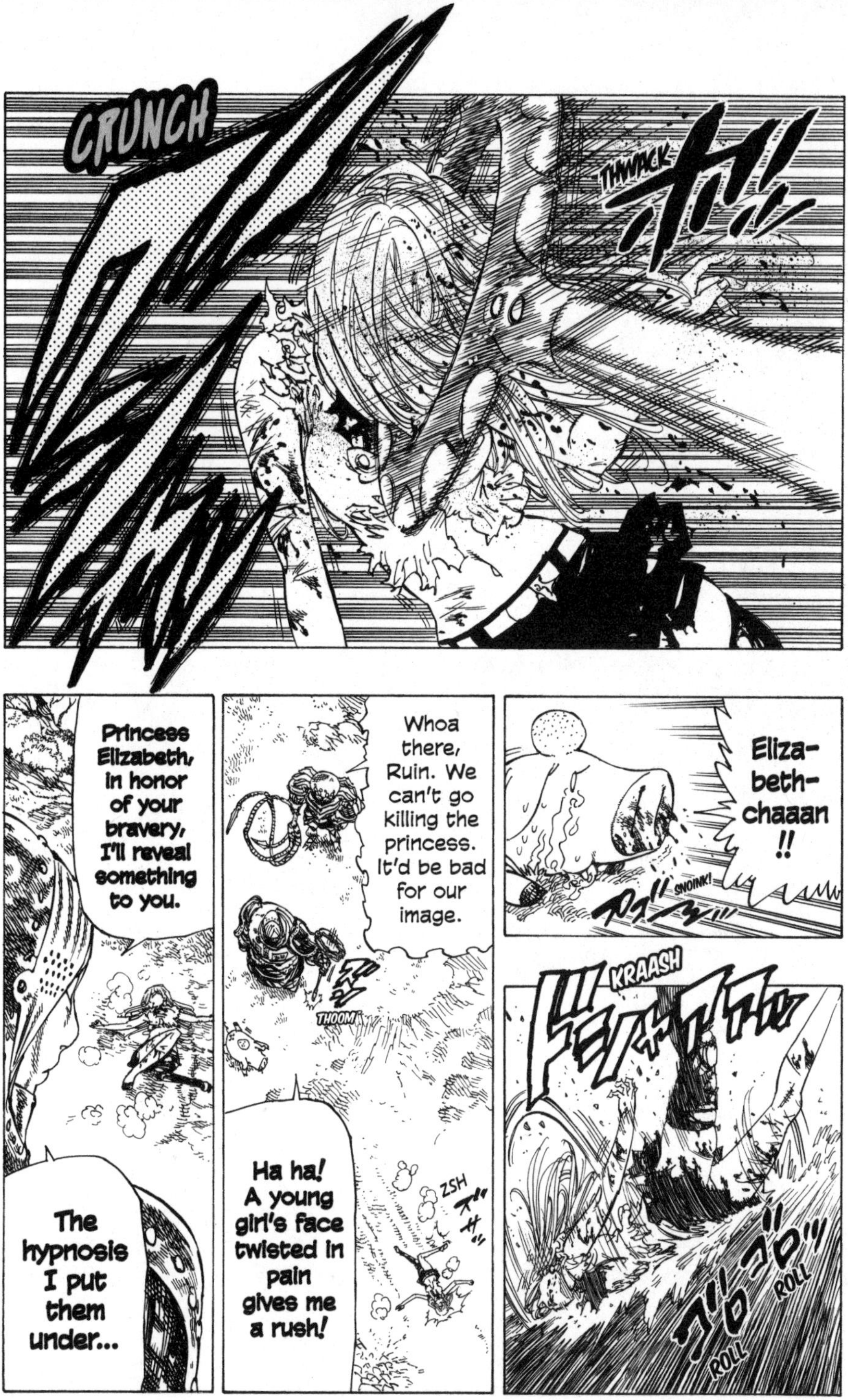
THWACK
CRUNCH
Eliza-beth-chaaan!!
SNOINK!
KRAASH
ROLL
ROLL
Whoa there, Ruin. We can't go killing the princess. It'd be bad for our image.
THOOM
Ha ha! A young girl's face twisted in pain gives me a rush!
ZSH
Princess Elizabeth, in honor of your bravery, I'll reveal something to you.
The hypnosis I put them under...

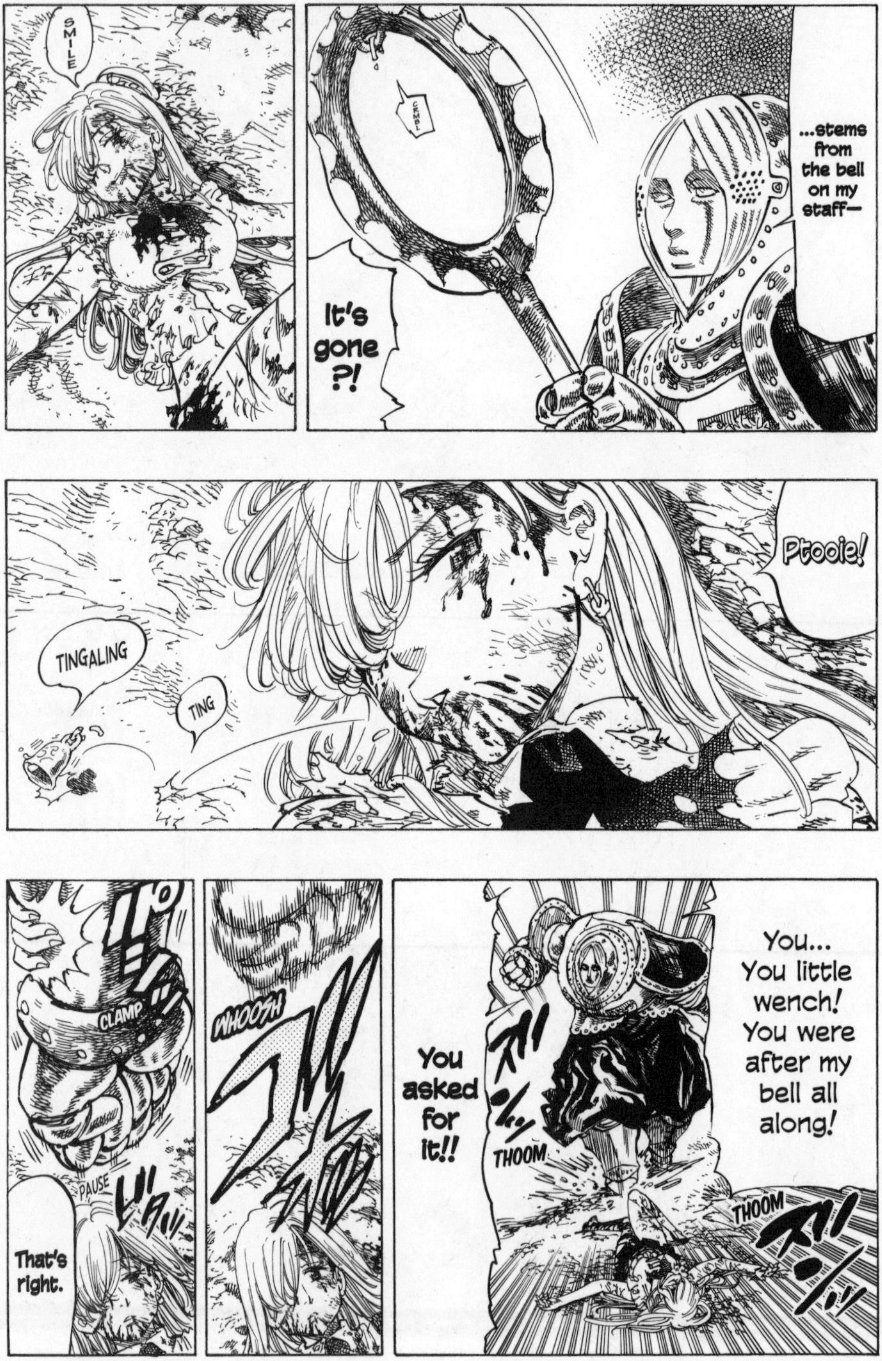
...stems from the bell on my staff—
It's gone?!
SMILE
Ptooie!
TINGALING
TING
You... You little wench! You were after my bell all along!
You asked for it!!
THOOM
THOOM
WHOOSH
CLAMP
PAUSE
That's right.

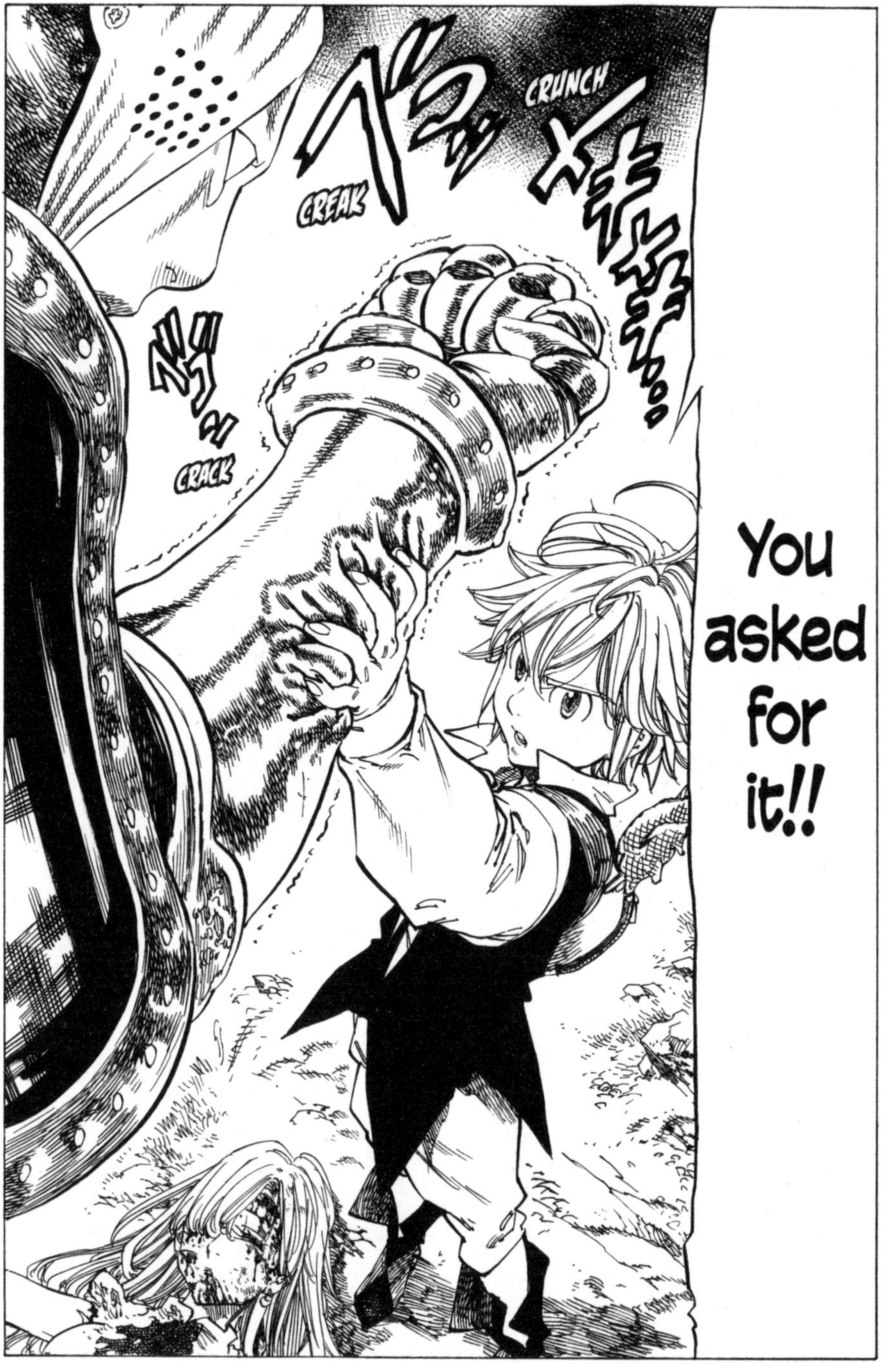
You asked for it!!
CRUNCH
CREAK
CRACK

THE SEVEN DEADLY SINS

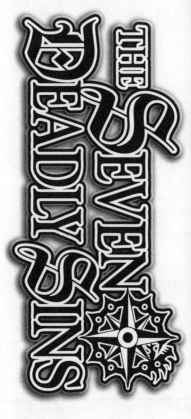

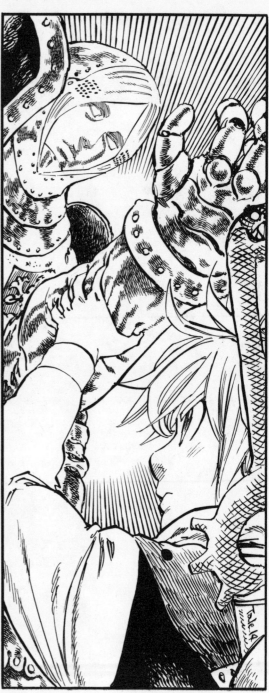

Chapter 14 - Explosion

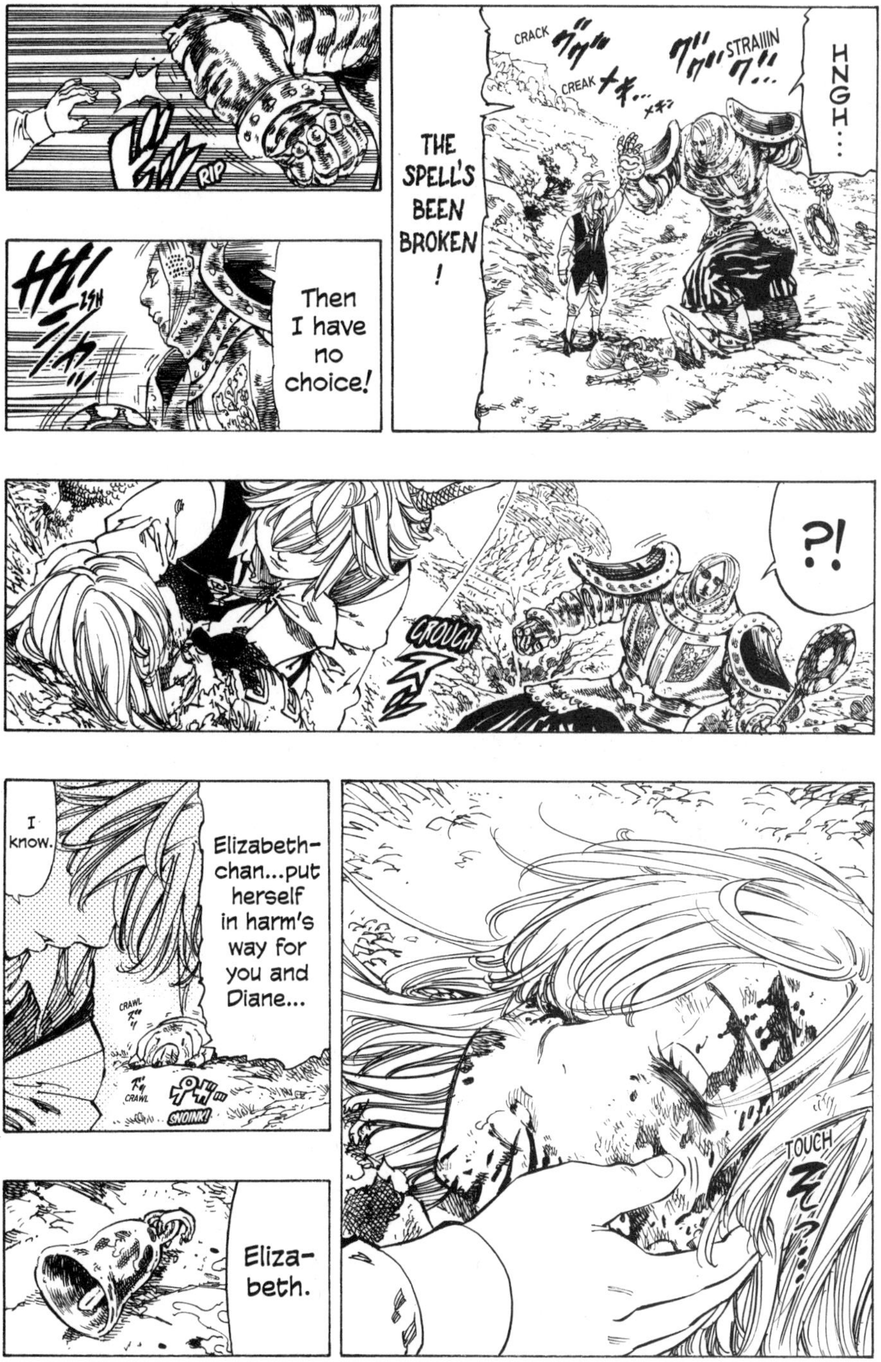
HNGH...
STRAIIIN
CRACK
CREAK
THE SPELL'S BEEN BROKEN!
RIP
Then I have no choice!
?!
CROUCH
TOUCH
Elizabeth-chan...put herself in harm's way for you and Diane...
I know.
CRAWL
CRAWL
SNOINK!
Eliza-beth.

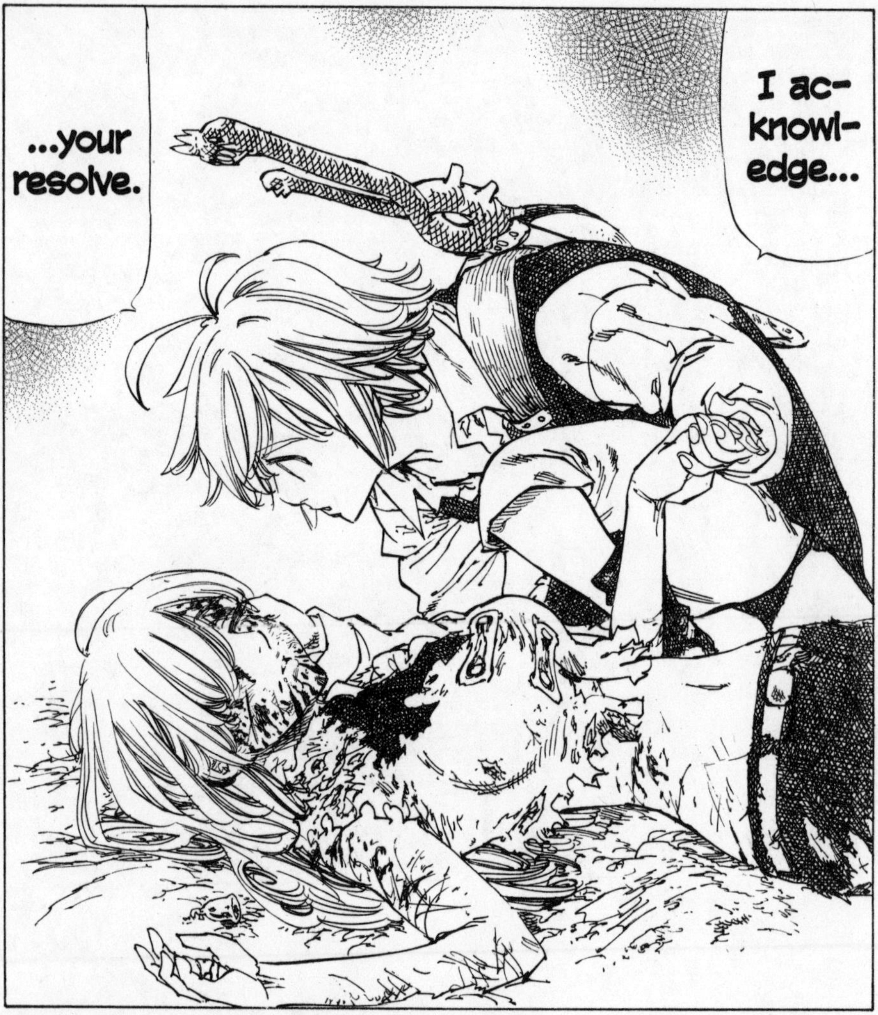
I ac-
knowl-
edge...
...your
resolve.

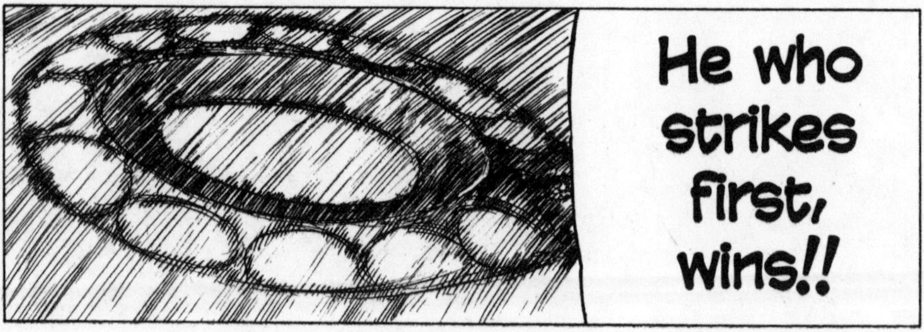
He who
strikes
first,
wins!!

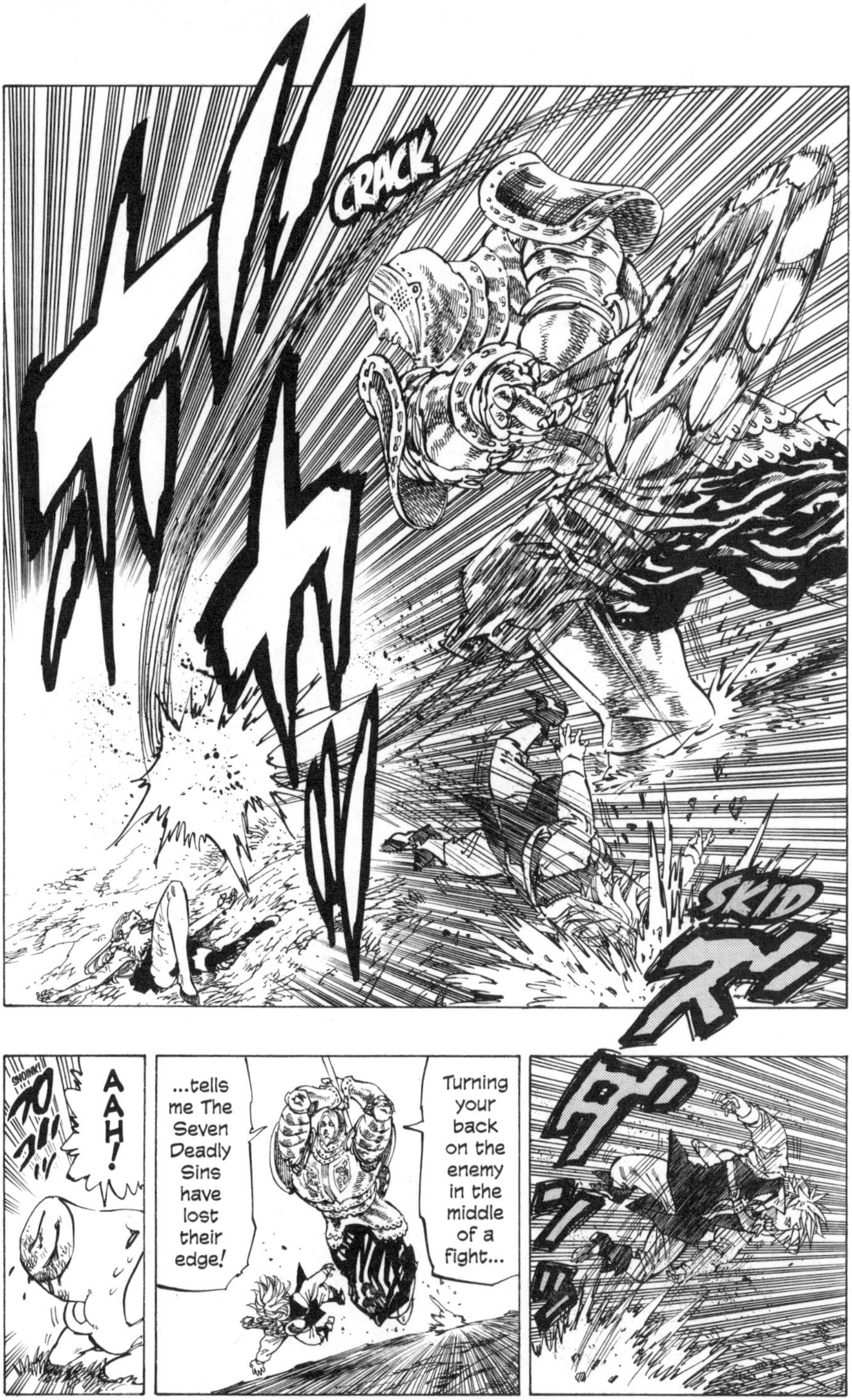
CRACK
SKID
Turning your back on the enemy in the middle of a fight...
...tells me The Seven Deadly Sins have lost their edge!
SNOINK!
AAH!

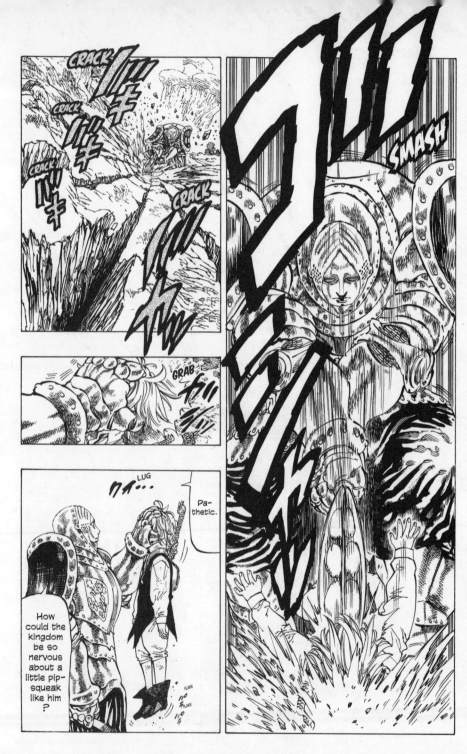

CRACK!

CRACK

CRACK

CRACK

SMASH

GRAB

LUG

フラ...

Pa-thetic.

How could the kingdom be so nervous about a little pip-squeak like him?

FLAKE
フラ
FLAKE
フラ

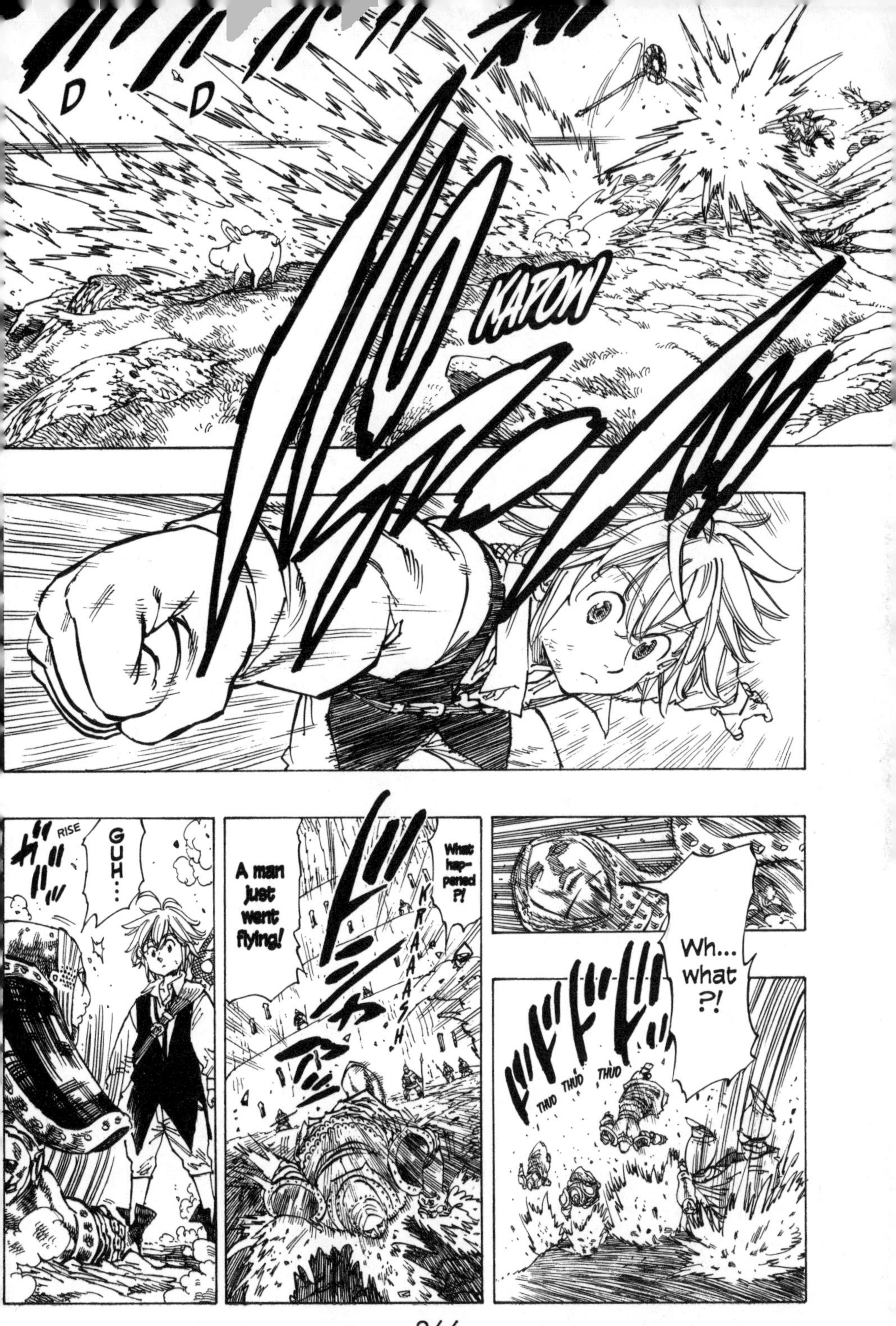

D
D
KAPOW
Wh... what?!
THUD THUD THUD
What hap-pened?!
A man just went flying!
KRAASH
GUH...
RISE

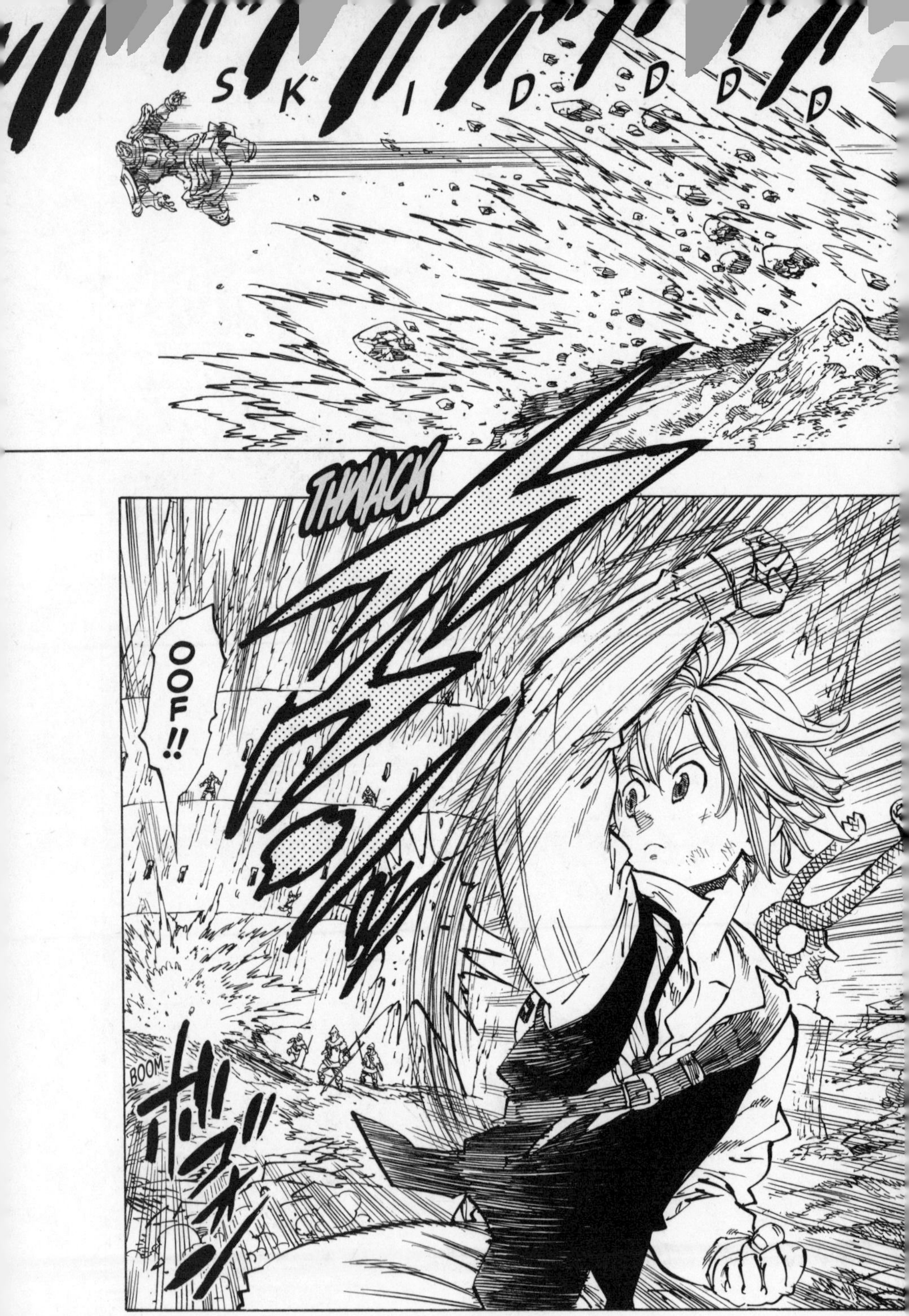

SKIDDDD
THWACK
OOF!!
BOOM

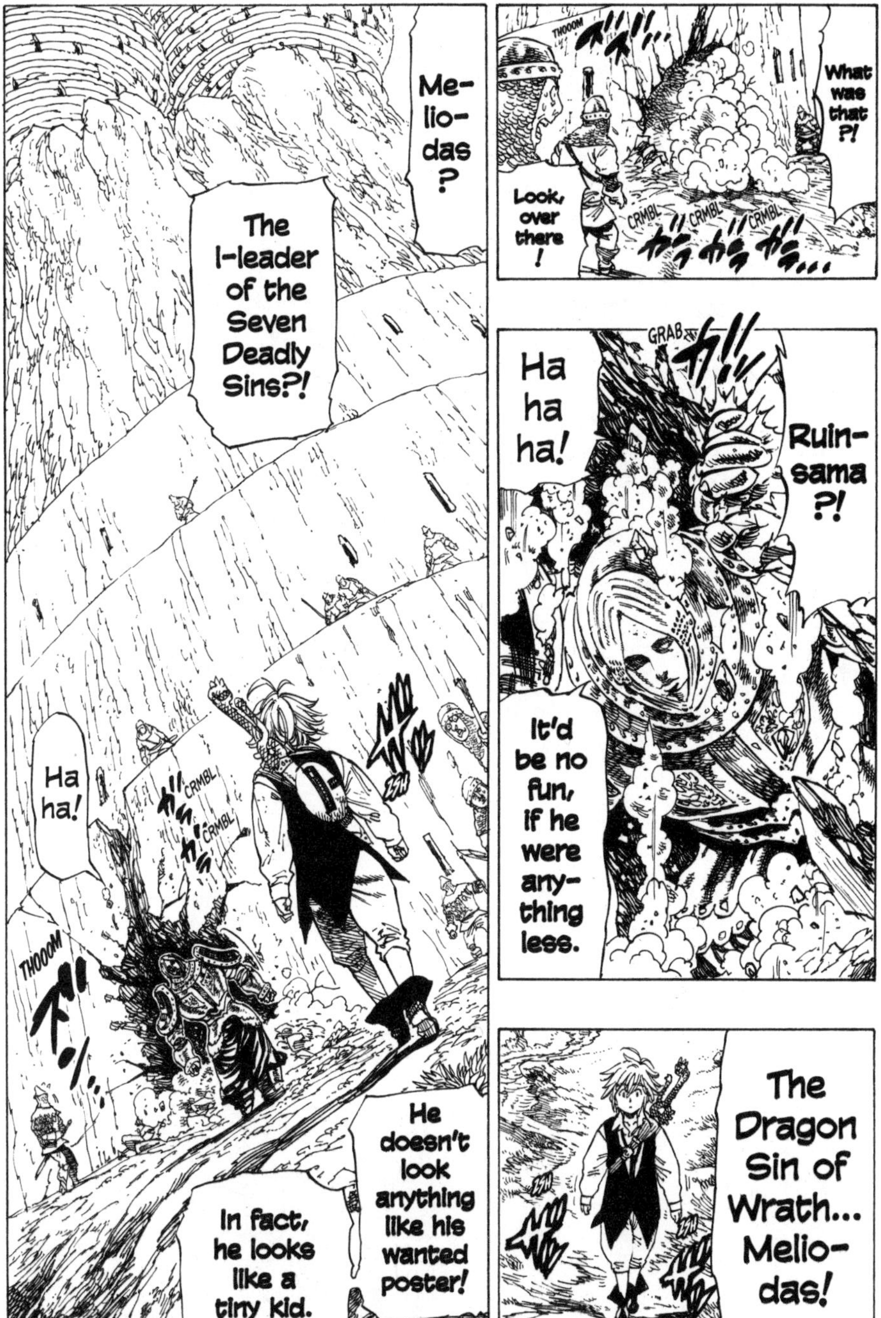
What was that?!
THOOOM
Look, over there!
CRMBL CRMBL CRMBL
Ruin-sama?!
GRAB
Ha ha ha!
It'd be no fun, if he were anything less.
The Dragon Sin of Wrath... Meliodas!
ZSH
Me-lio-das?
The l-leader of the Seven Deadly Sins?!
ZSH
Ha ha!
CRMBL
CRMBL
THOOOM
He doesn't look anything like his wanted poster!
In fact, he looks like a tiny kid.

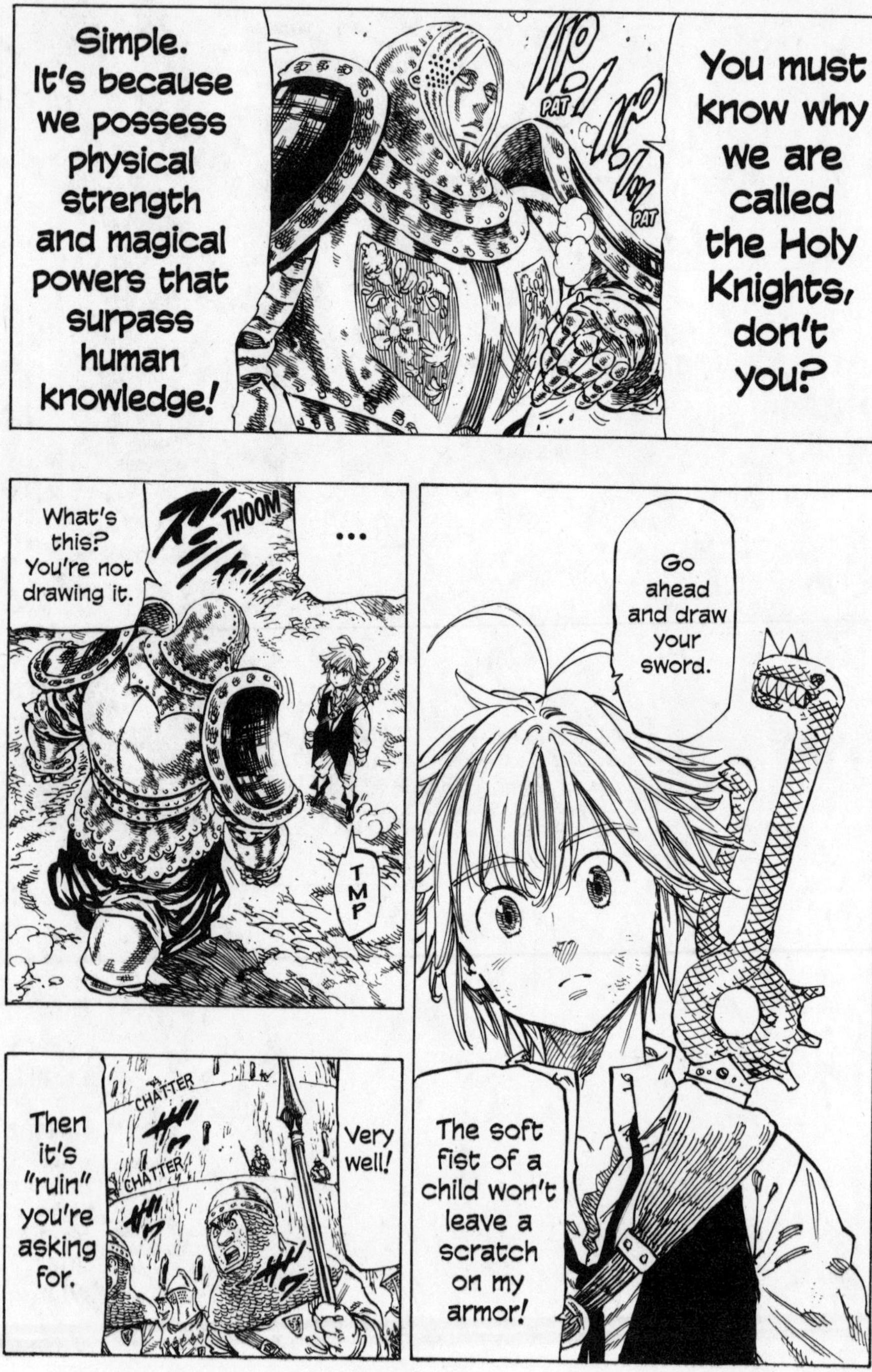
You must know why we are called the Holy Knights, don't you?
PAT
PAT
Simple. It's because we possess physical strength and magical powers that surpass human knowledge!
Go ahead and draw your sword.
The soft fist of a child won't leave a scratch on my armor!
...
THOOM
What's this? You're not drawing it.
TMP
Very well!
CHATTER
CHATTER
Then it's "ruin" you're asking for.

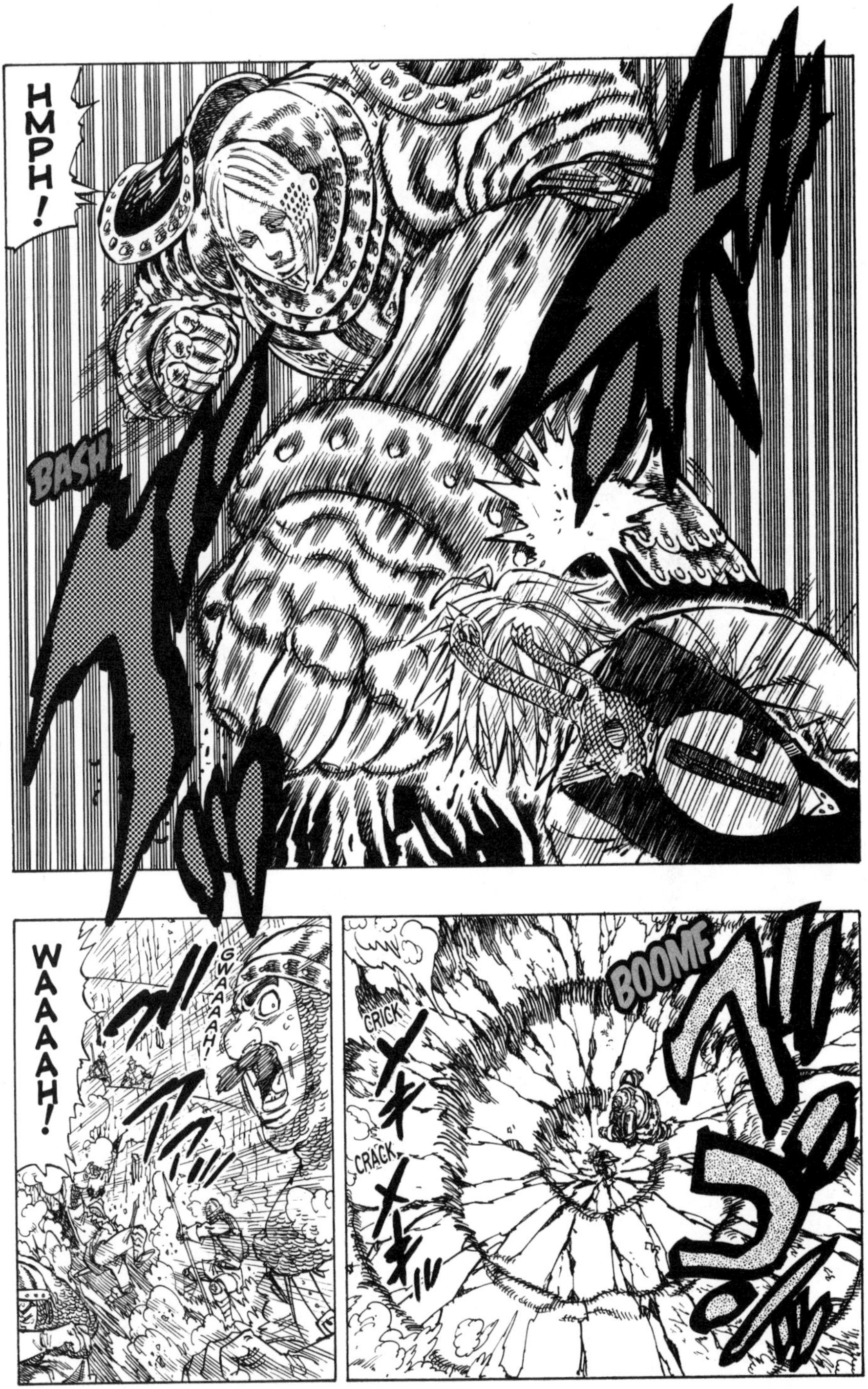
HMPH!
BASH
BOOMF
GRICK
CRACK
GWAAAAAH!
WAAAAAH!

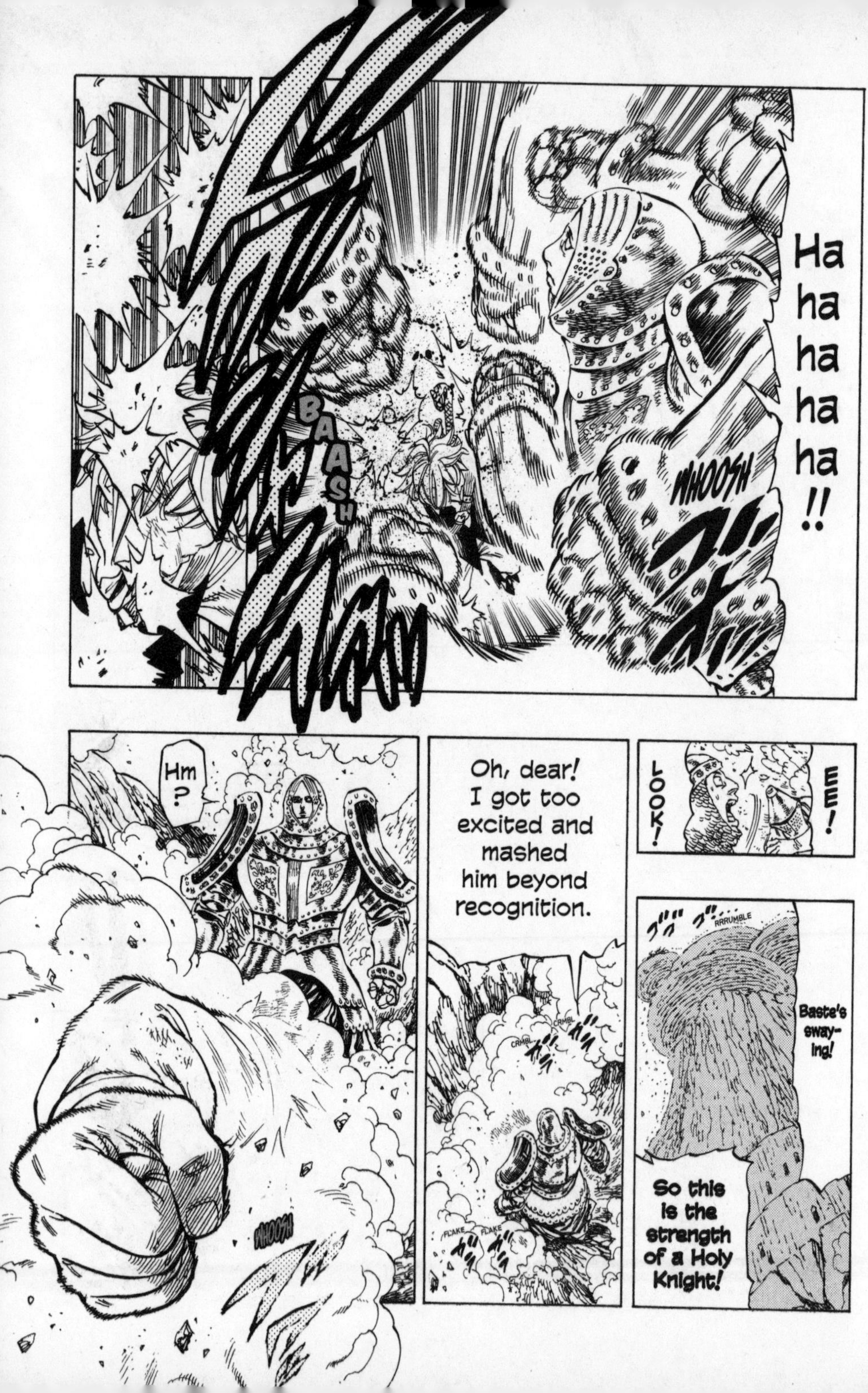
Ha ha ha ha ha!!
WHOOSH
BAASH
LOOK!
EE!
RRRUMBLE
Baste's sway-ing!
So this is the strength of a Holy Knight!
Oh, dear! I got too excited and mashed him beyond recognition.
CRMBL
CRMBL
FLAKE
FLAKE
Hm?
WHOOSH

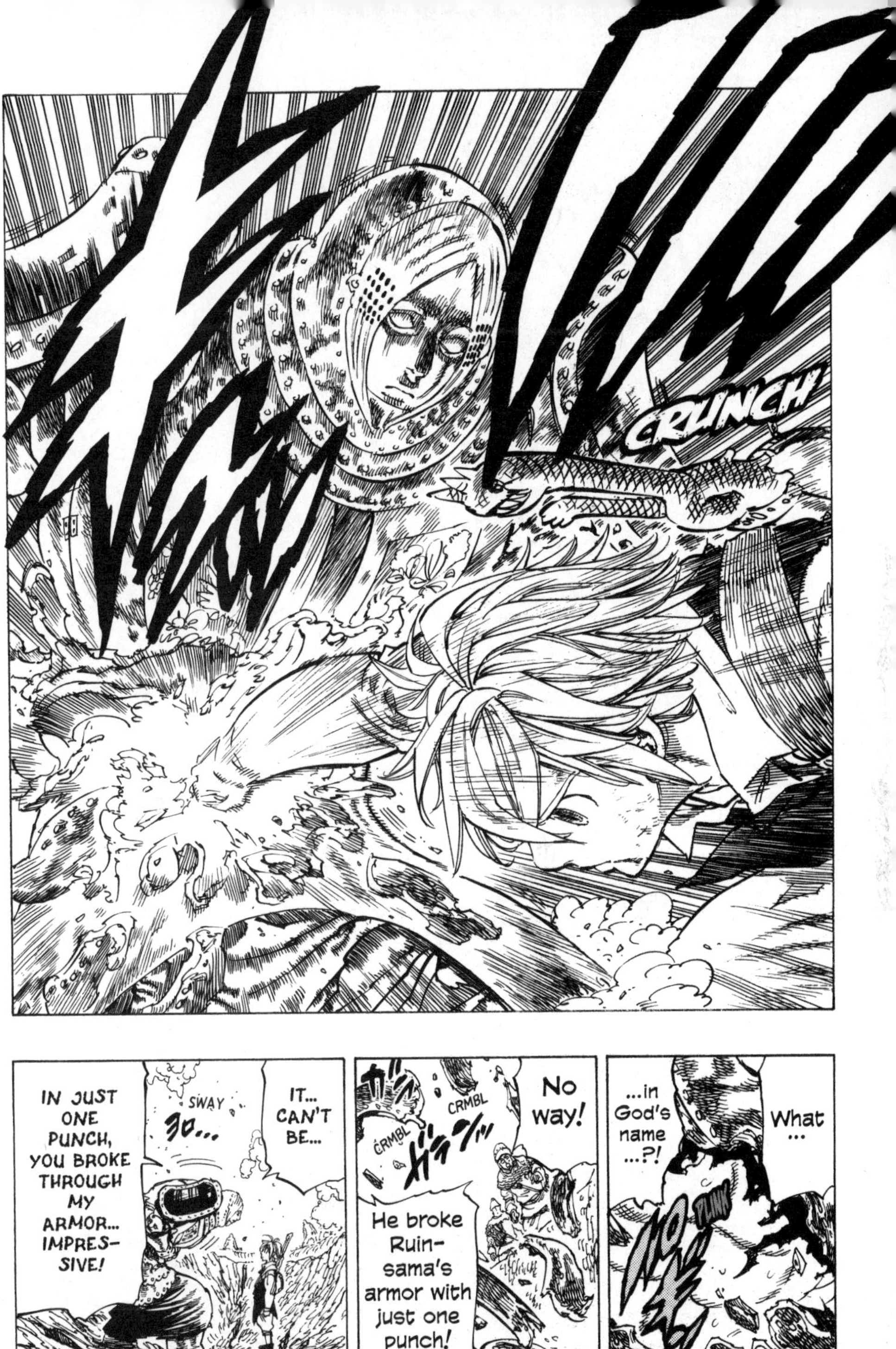
CRUNCH
What ...
...in God's name ...?!
PLINK
No way!
CRMBL
CRMBL
He broke Ruin-sama's armor with just one punch!
IT... CAN'T BE...
SWAY
IN JUST ONE PUNCH, YOU BROKE THROUGH MY ARMOR... IMPRESSIVE!

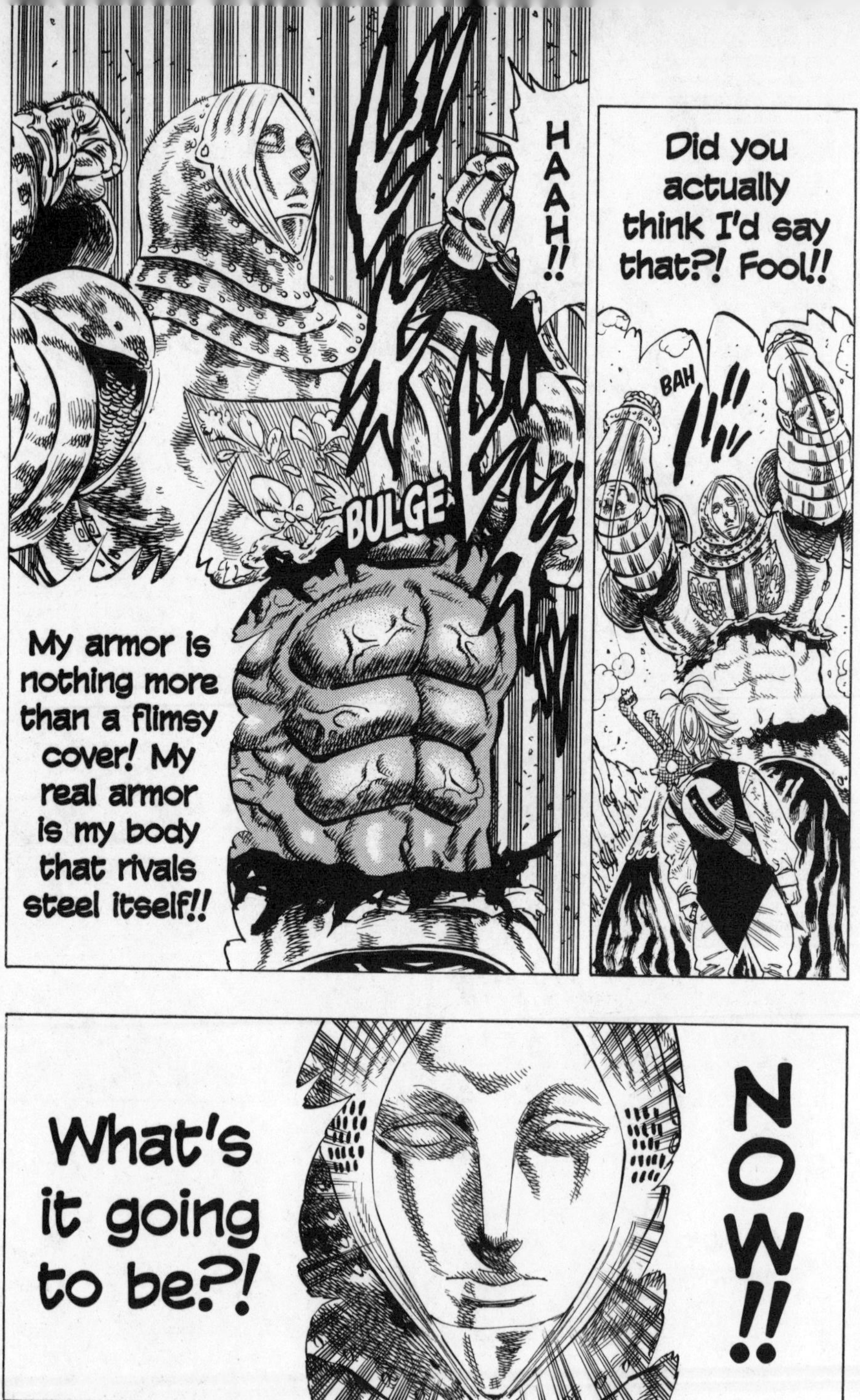
Did you actually think I'd say that?! Fool!!
BAH
HAAH!!
BULGE
My armor is nothing more than a flimsy cover! My real armor is my body that rivals steel itself!!
NOW!!
What's it going to be?!

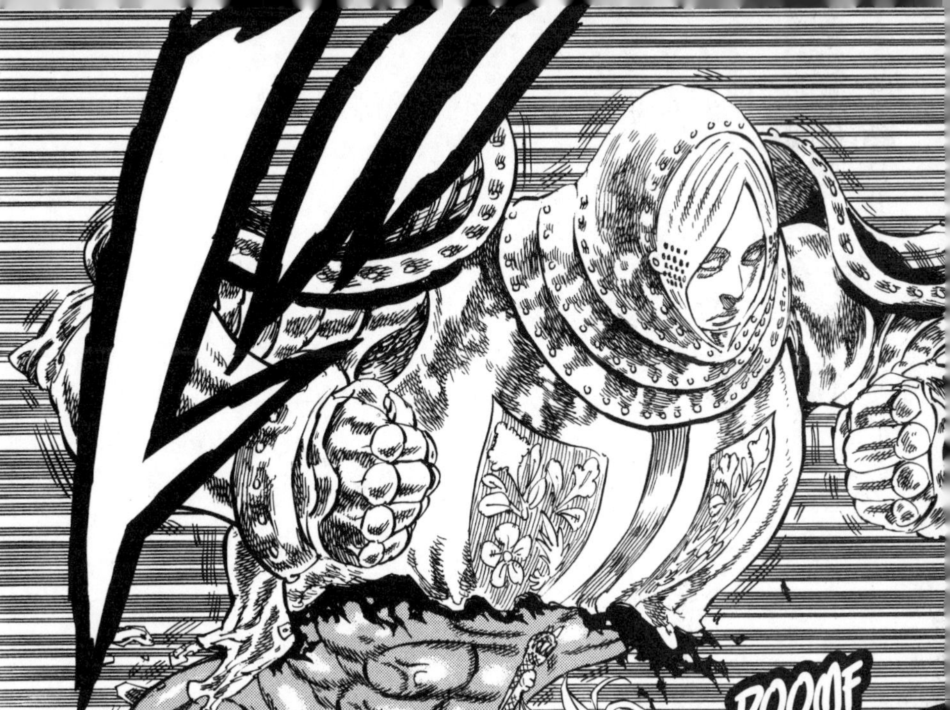
DOOMF
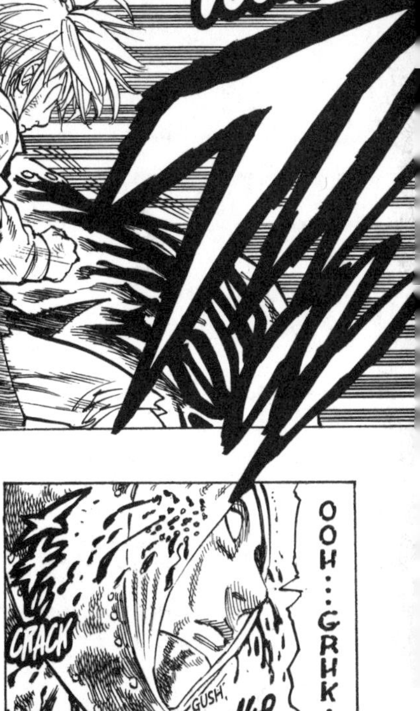
OOH...GRHK...
CRACK
GUSH
GUSH
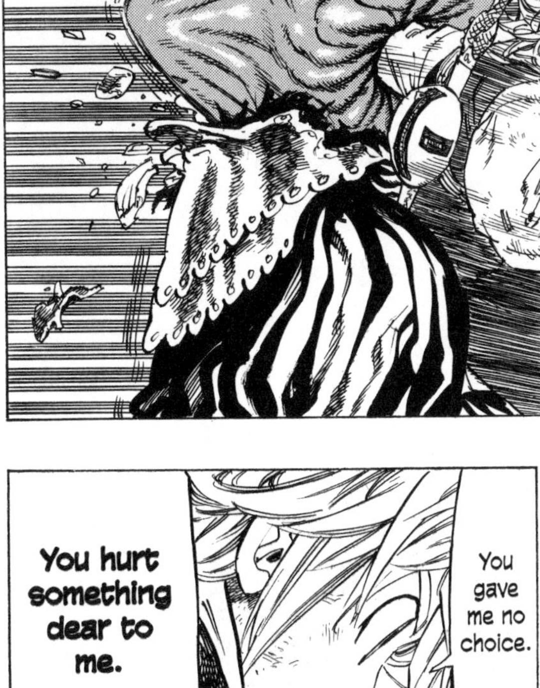
You gave me no choice.
You hurt something dear to me.

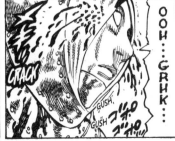

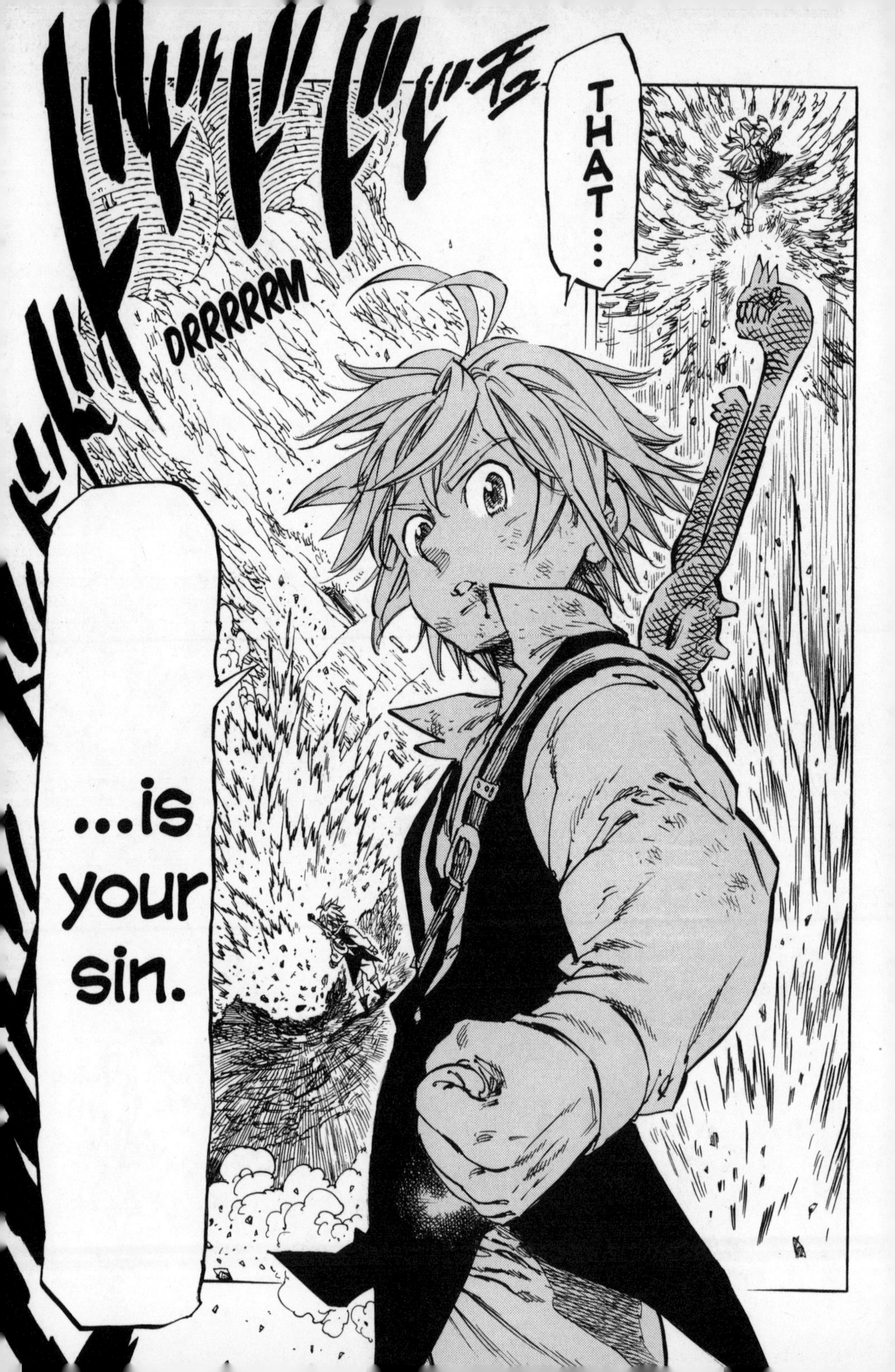
THAT...
DRRRRRM
...is your sin.

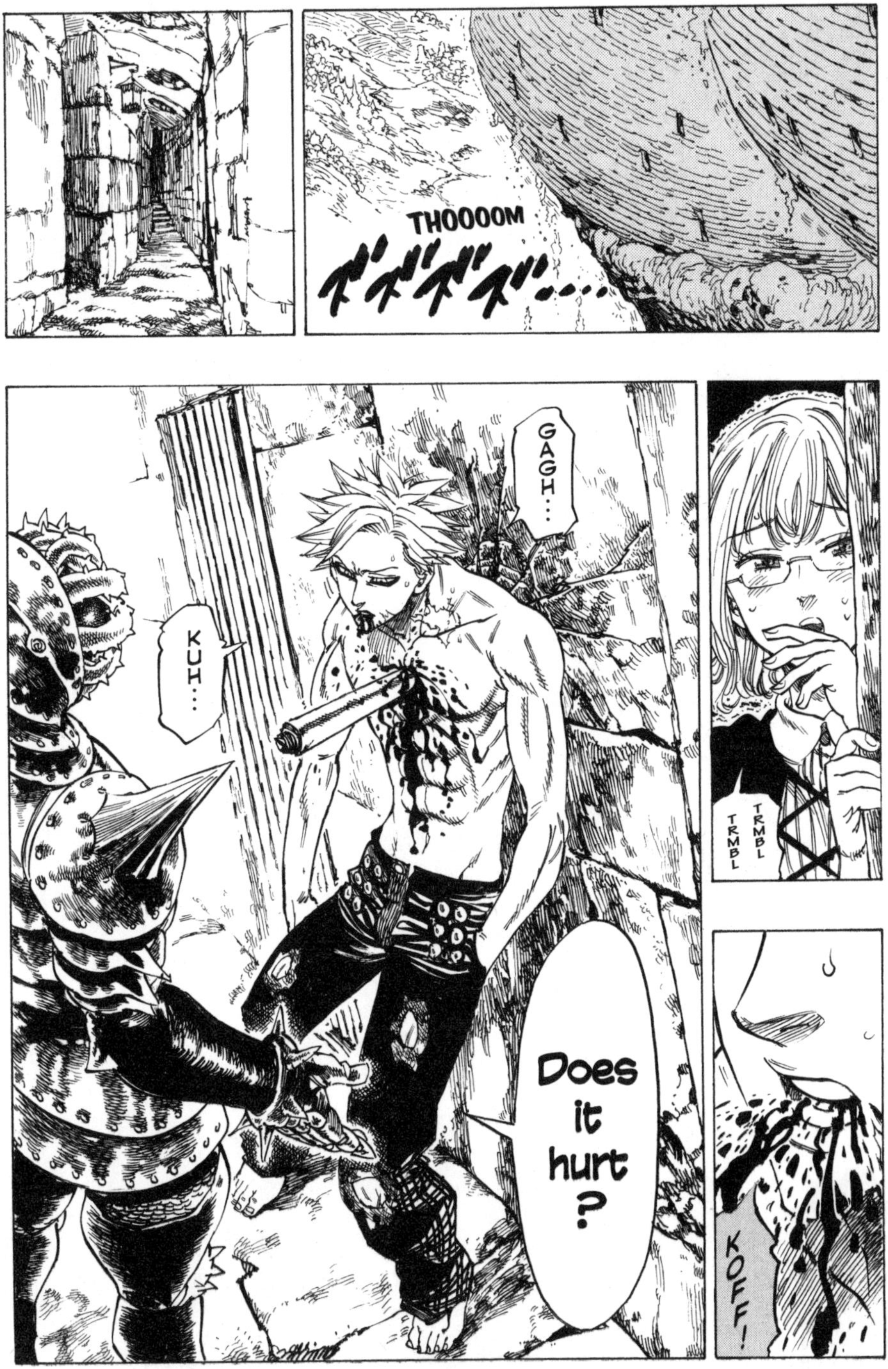
THOOOOM
ズズズズ....
TRMBL TRMBL
KOFF!
GAGH...
KUH...
Does it hurt?

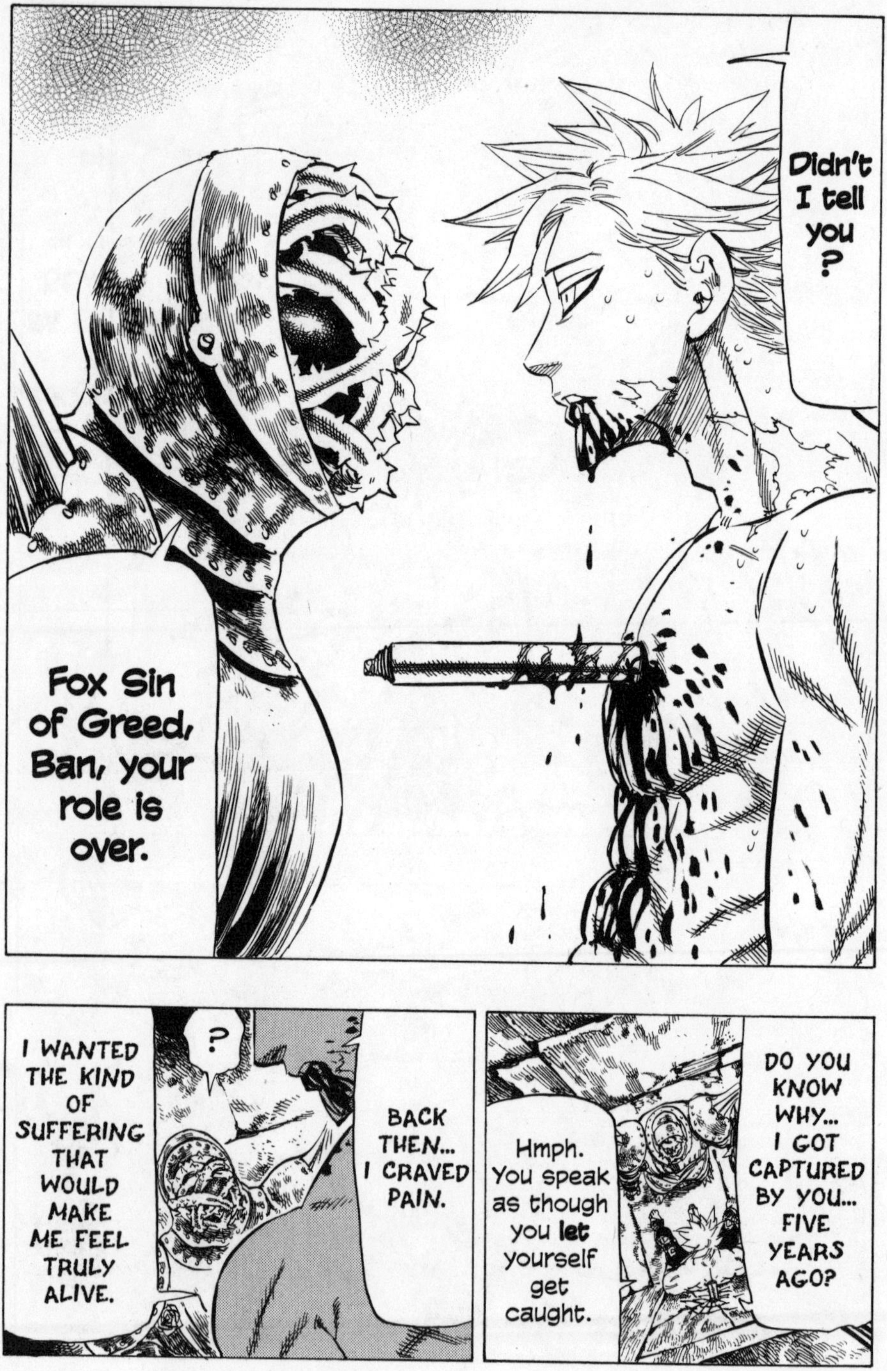
Didn't I tell you?
Fox Sin of Greed, Ban, your role is over.
DO YOU KNOW WHY... I GOT CAPTURED BY YOU... FIVE YEARS AGO?
Hmph. You speak as though you **let** yourself get caught.
?
BACK THEN... I CRAVED PAIN.
I WANTED THE KIND OF SUFFERING THAT WOULD MAKE ME FEEL TRULY ALIVE.

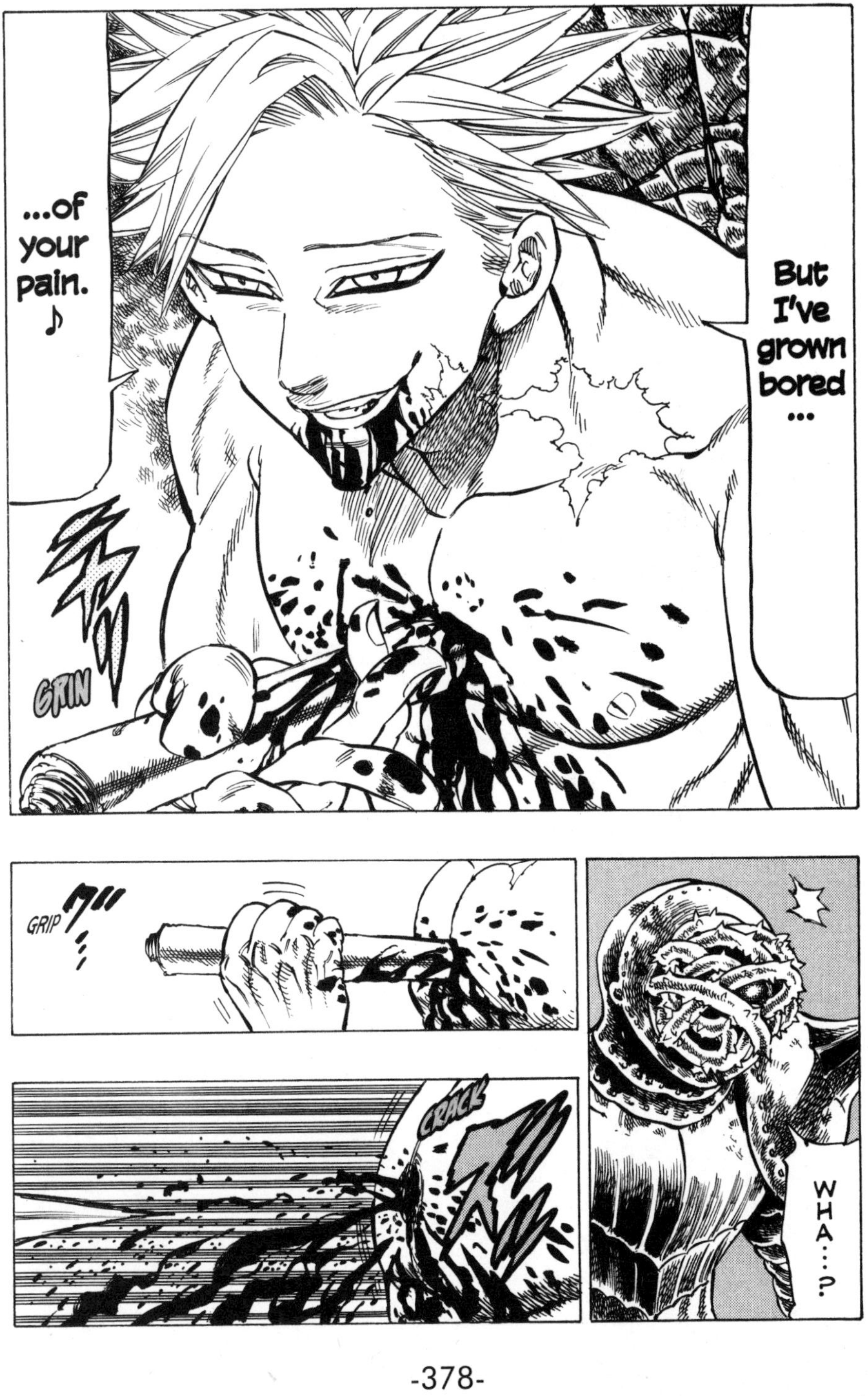
But I've grown bored...
...of your pain. ♪
GRIN
WHA...?
GRIP
CRACK

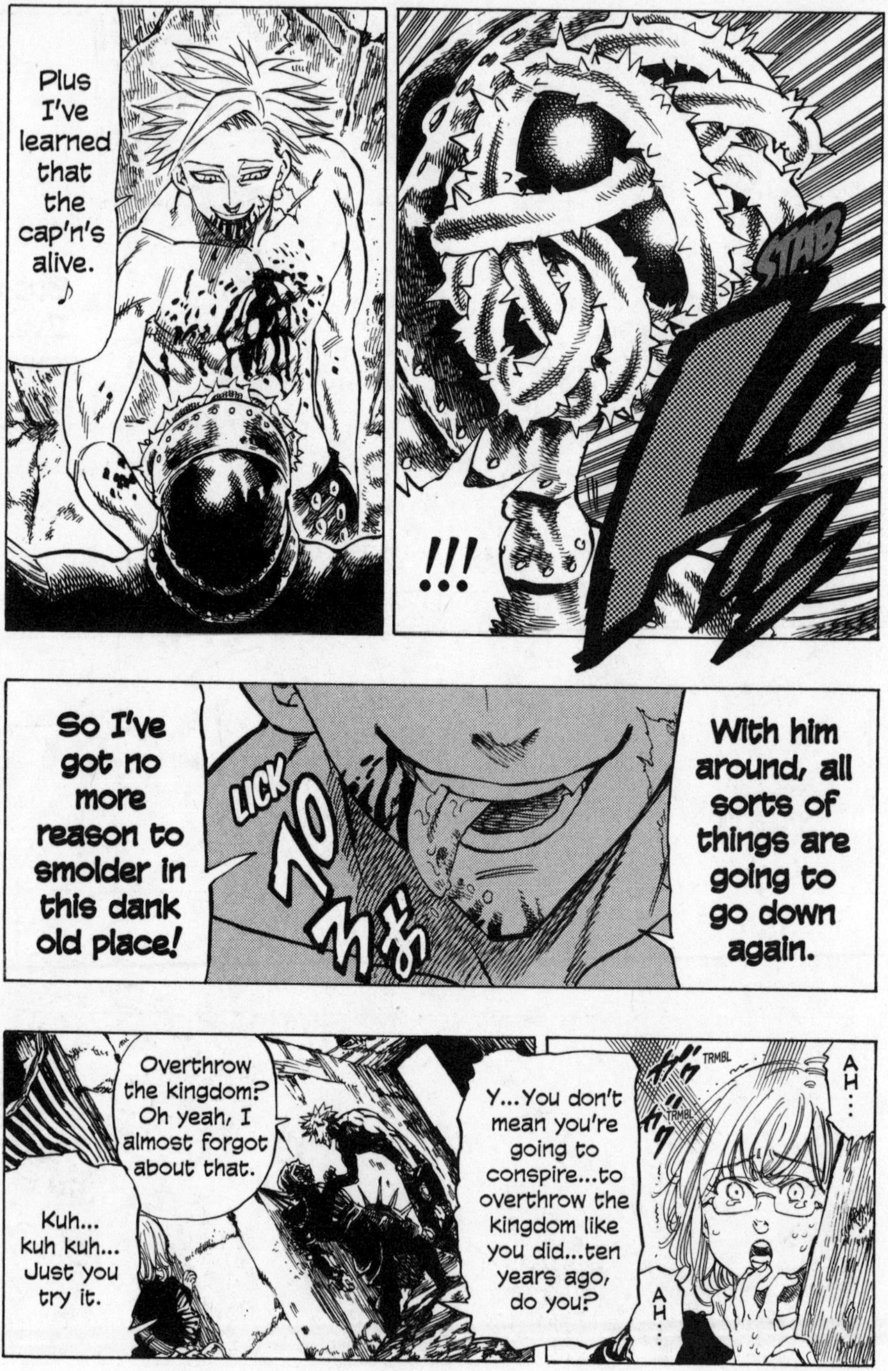
STAB
!!!
Plus I've learned that the cap'n's alive. ♪
With him around, all sorts of things are going to go down again.
LICK
So I've got no more reason to smolder in this dank old place!
AH...
TRMBL
TRMBL
Y...You don't mean you're going to conspire...to overthrow the kingdom like you did...ten years ago, do you?
AH...
Overthrow the kingdom? Oh yeah, I almost forgot about that.
Kuh... kuh kuh... Just you try it.

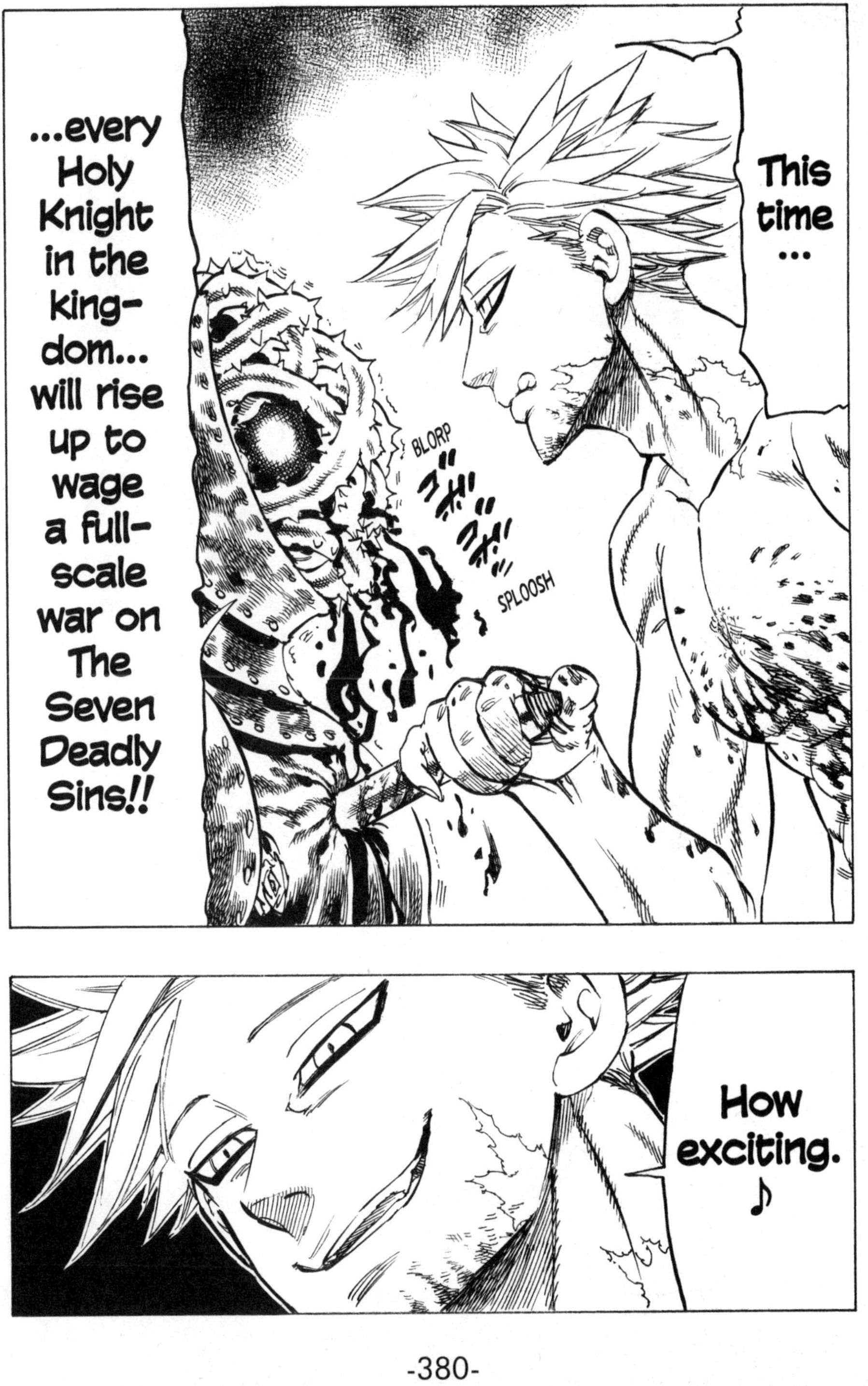
This time...
...every Holy Knight in the kingdom... will rise up to wage a full-scale war on The Seven Deadly Sins!!
BLORP
SPLOOSH
How exciting. ♪

Interview with a Pig

Q: Can you really smell leftovers one mile away?

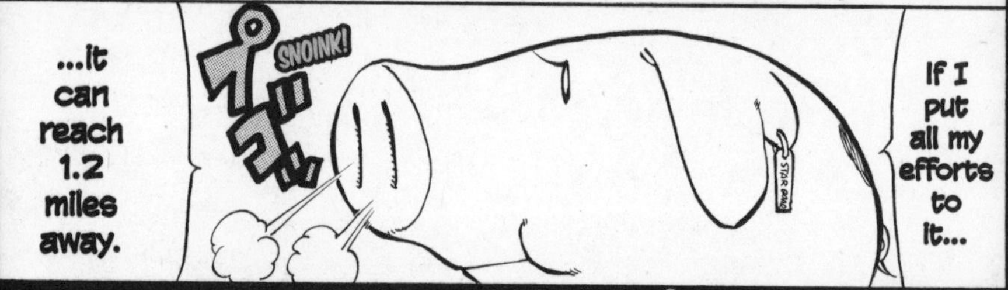
If I put all my efforts to it...
SNOINK!
...it can reach 1.2 miles away.

Q: What count as leftovers to you?

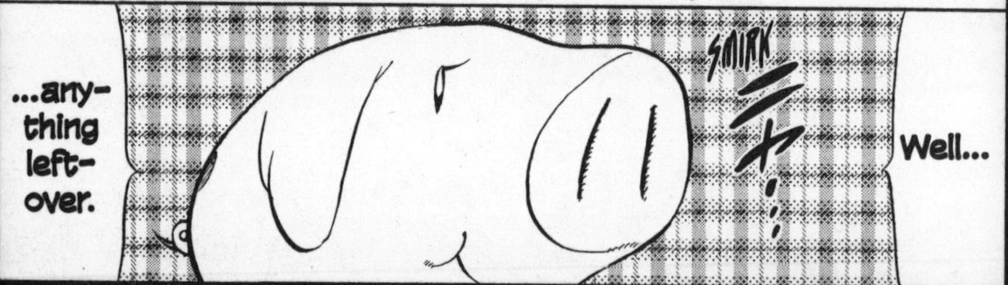
Well...
SMIRK
...anything left-over.

Q: How is it you can speak? You're just a pig.

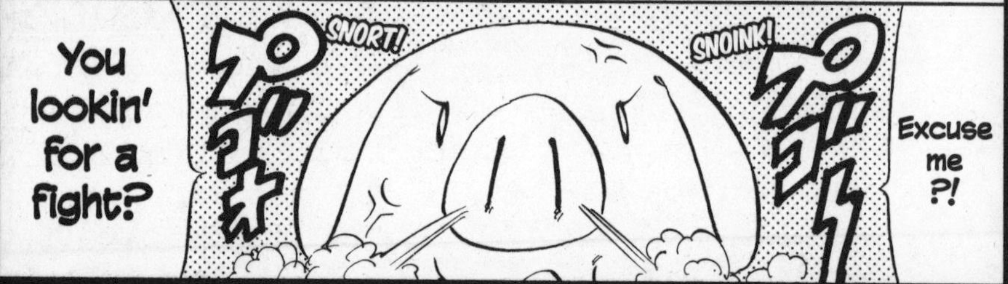
Excuse me?!
SNOINK!
SNORT!
You lookin' for a fight?

Q: What's one thing you'd ask of your partner, Meliodas?

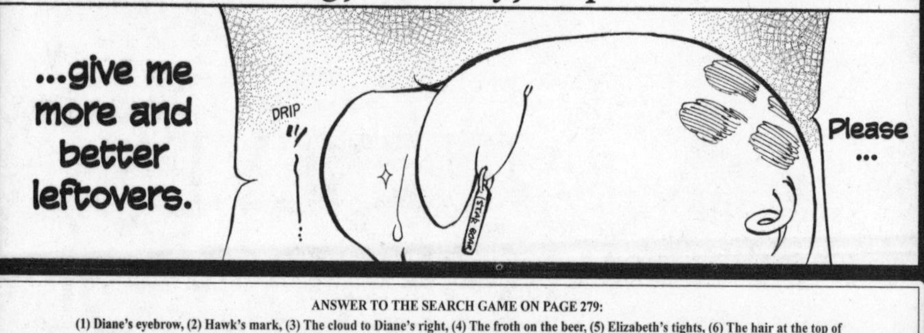
Please...
DRIP
...give me more and better leftovers.

ANSWER TO THE SEARCH GAME ON PAGE 279:

(1) Diane's eyebrow, (2) Hawk's mark, (3) The cloud to Diane's right, (4) The froth on the beer, (5) Elizabeth's tights, (6) The hair at the top of Meliodas' head, (7) The orientation of the hilt of Meliodas' sword, (8) The shape of the tree branch above Meliodas, (9) The little creature next to Meliodas

THE SEVEN
DEADLY SINS

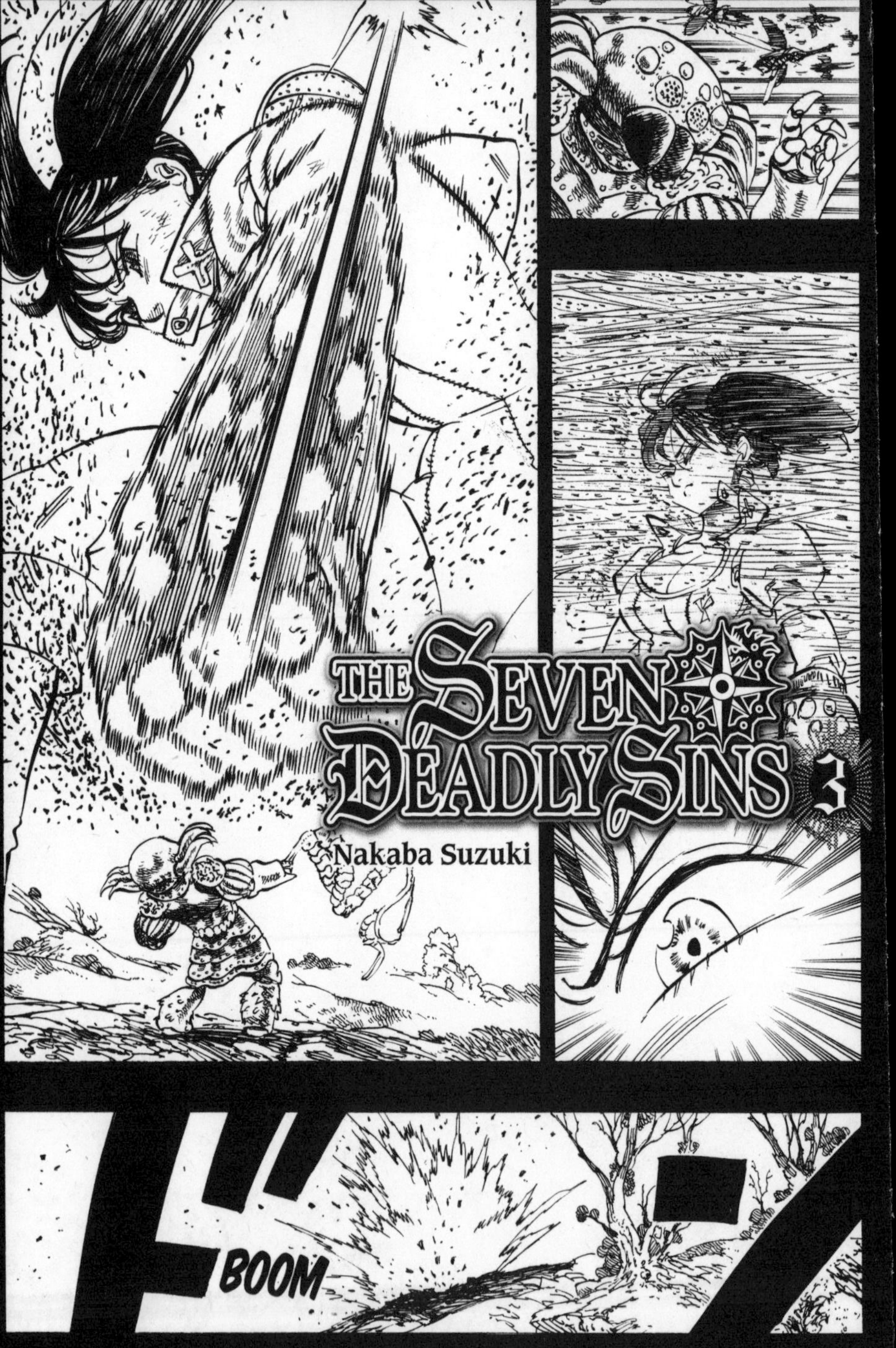
THE SEVEN DEADLY SINS
3
Nakaba Suzuki
BOOM

nakaba suzuki presents

THE SEVEN DEADLY SINS

THE SEVEN DEADLY SINS

STAR BOAR

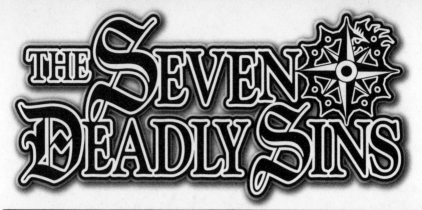

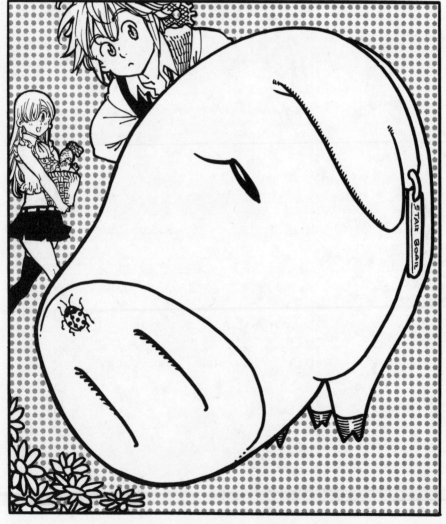

Chapter 15 - Caught in the Reunion

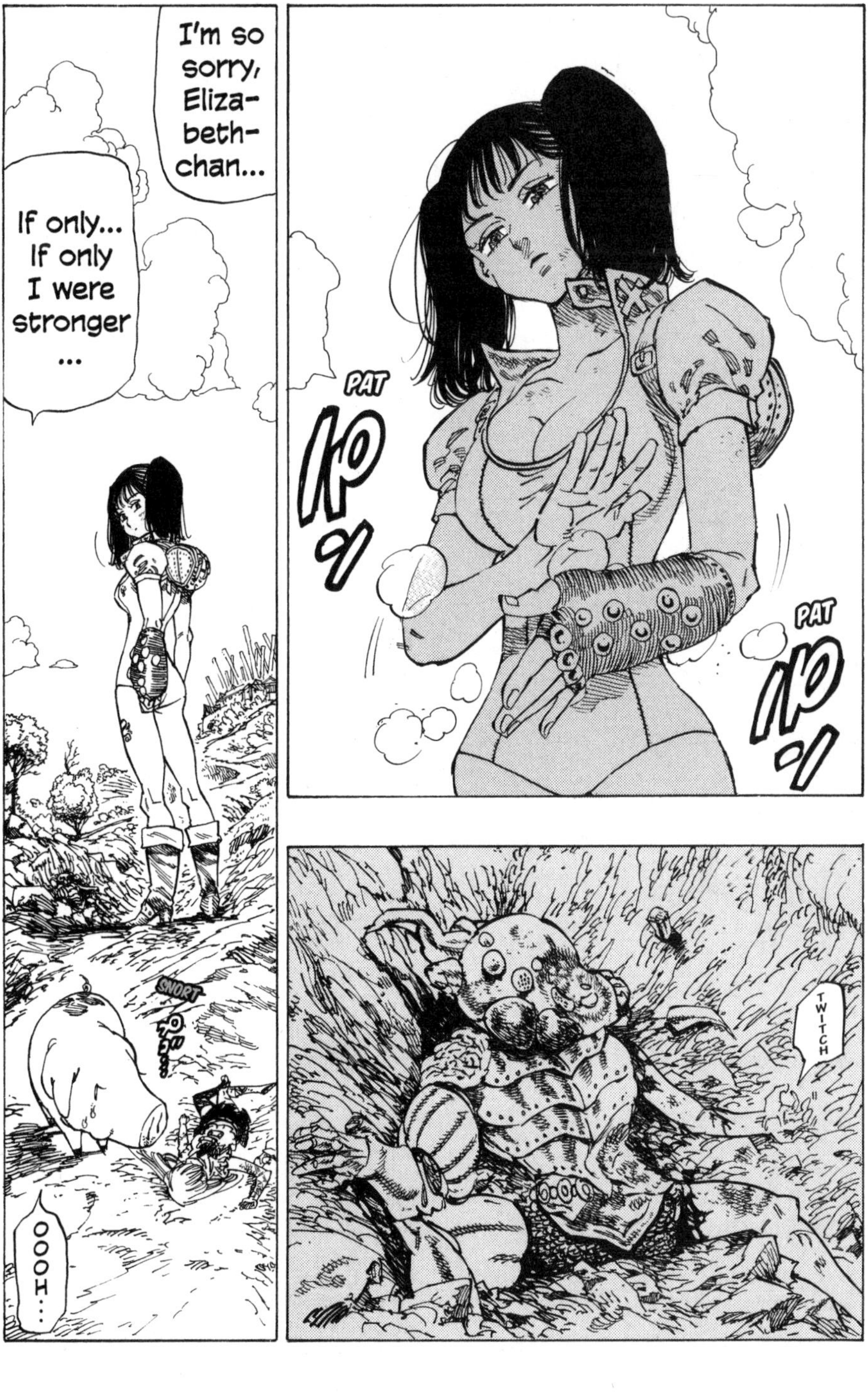
PAT
PAT
TWITCH
I'm so sorry, Eliza-beth-chan...
If only... If only I were stronger ...
SNORT
OOOH...

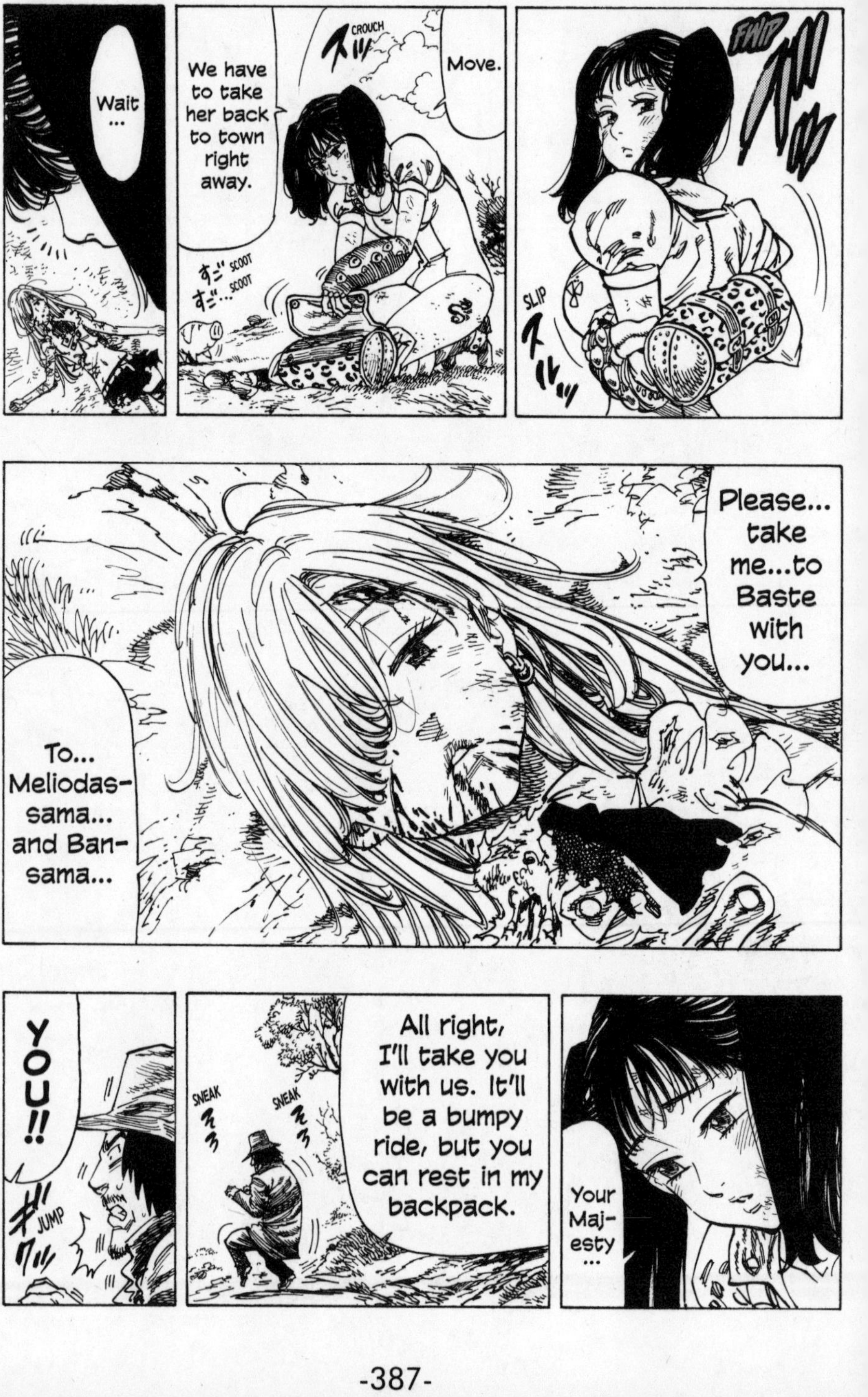
FWIP
SLIP
Move.
CROUCH
We have to take her back to town right away.
SCOOT
SCOOT
Wait...
Please... take me...to Baste with you...
To... Meliodas-sama... and Ban-sama...
Your Majesty...
All right, I'll take you with us. It'll be a bumpy ride, but you can rest in my backpack.
SNEAK
SNEAK
YOU!!
JUMP

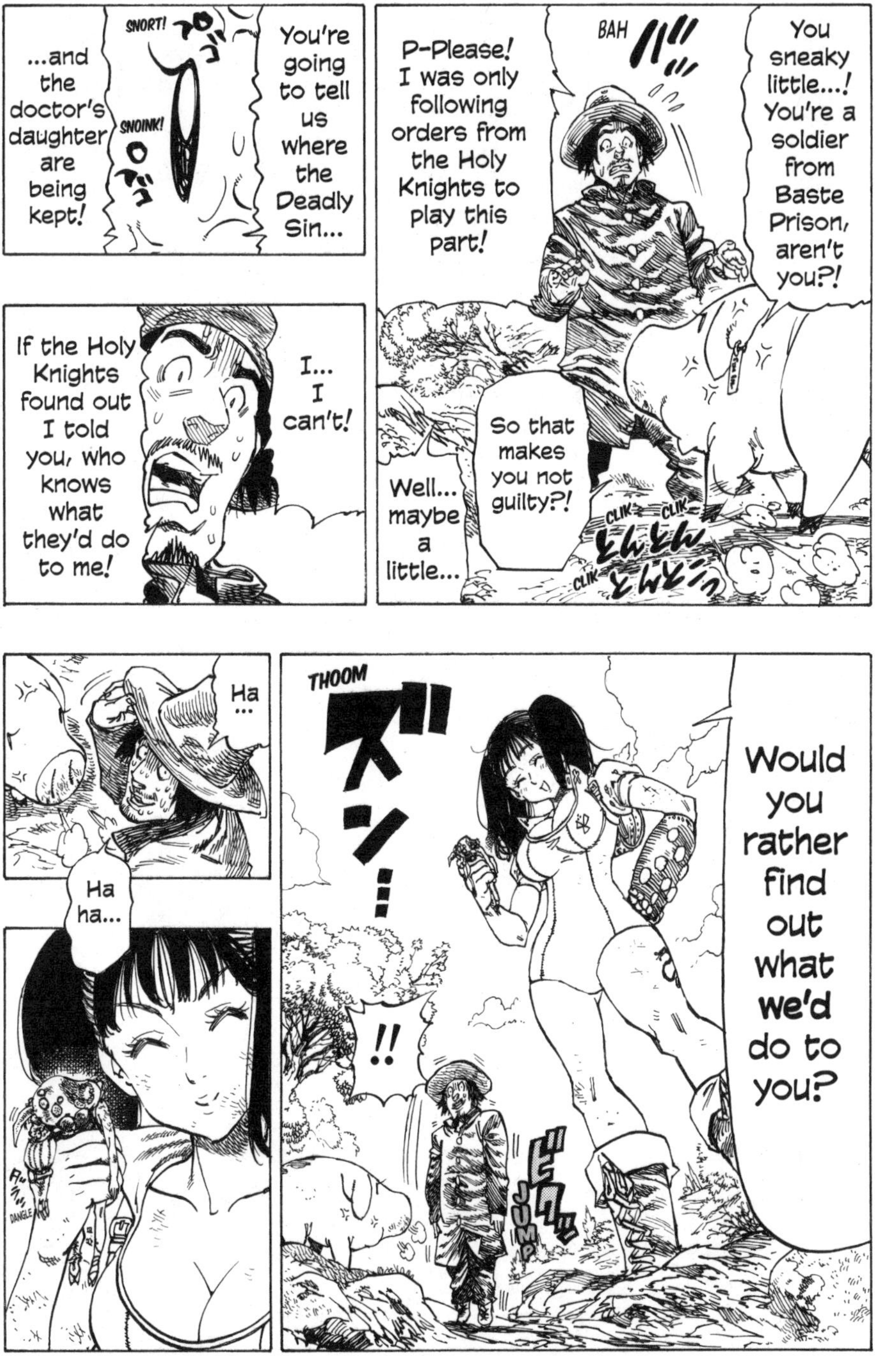

You sneaky little...! You're a soldier from Baste Prison, aren't you?!
BAH
P-Please! I was only following orders from the Holy Knights to play this part!
So that makes you not guilty?!
CLIK
CLIK
CLIK
Well... maybe a little...
You're going to tell us where the Deadly Sin...
SNORT!
SNOINK!
...and the doctor's daughter are being kept!
I... I can't!
If the Holy Knights found out I told you, who knows what they'd do to me!
THOOM
Would you rather find out what we'd do to you?
!!
JUMP
Ha ...
Ha ha...
DANGLE

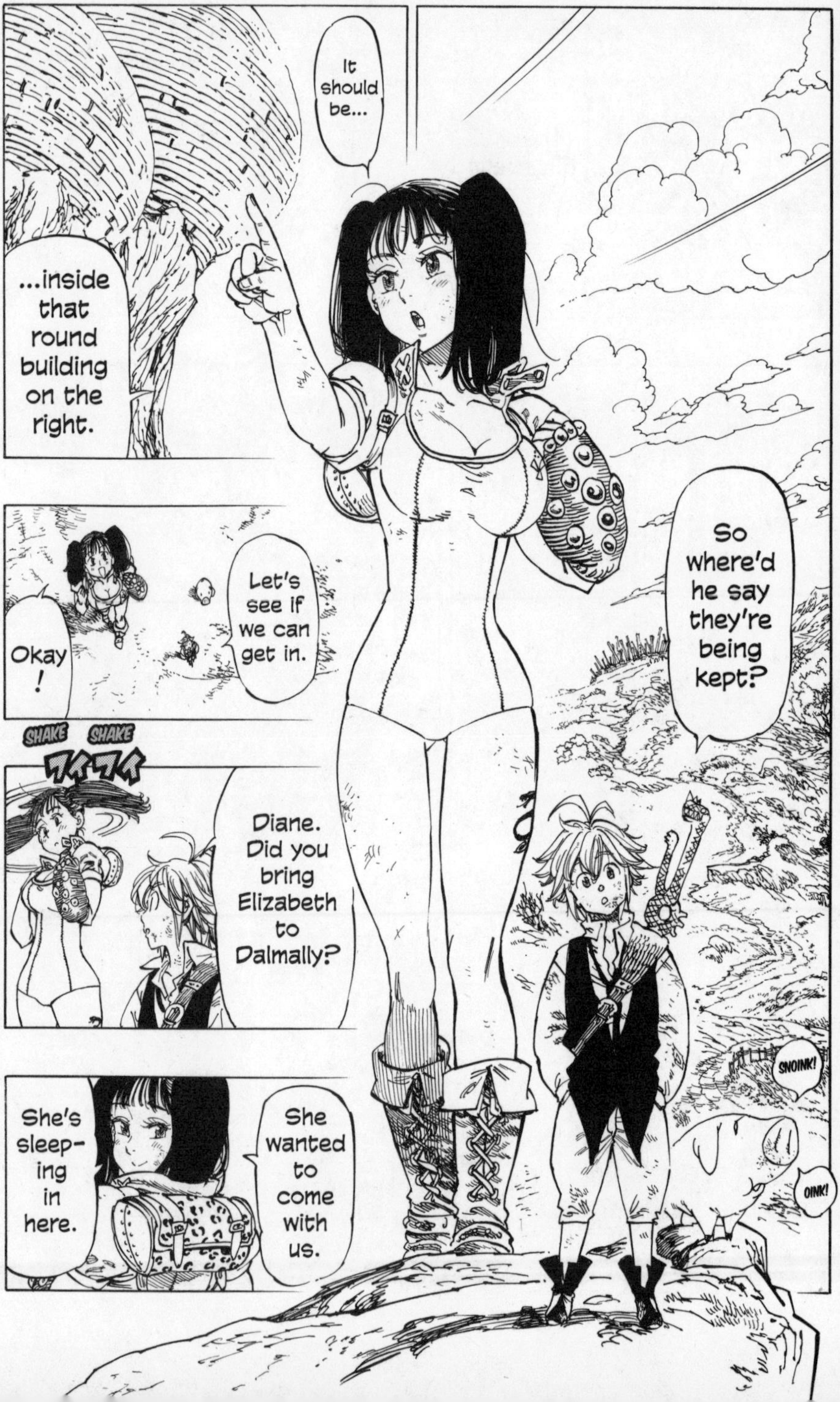
So where'd he say they're being kept?
It should be...
SNOINK!
OINK!
...inside that round building on the right.
Let's see if we can get in.
Okay!
SHAKE SHAKE
Diane. Did you bring Elizabeth to Dalmally?
She wanted to come with us.
She's sleep-ing in here.

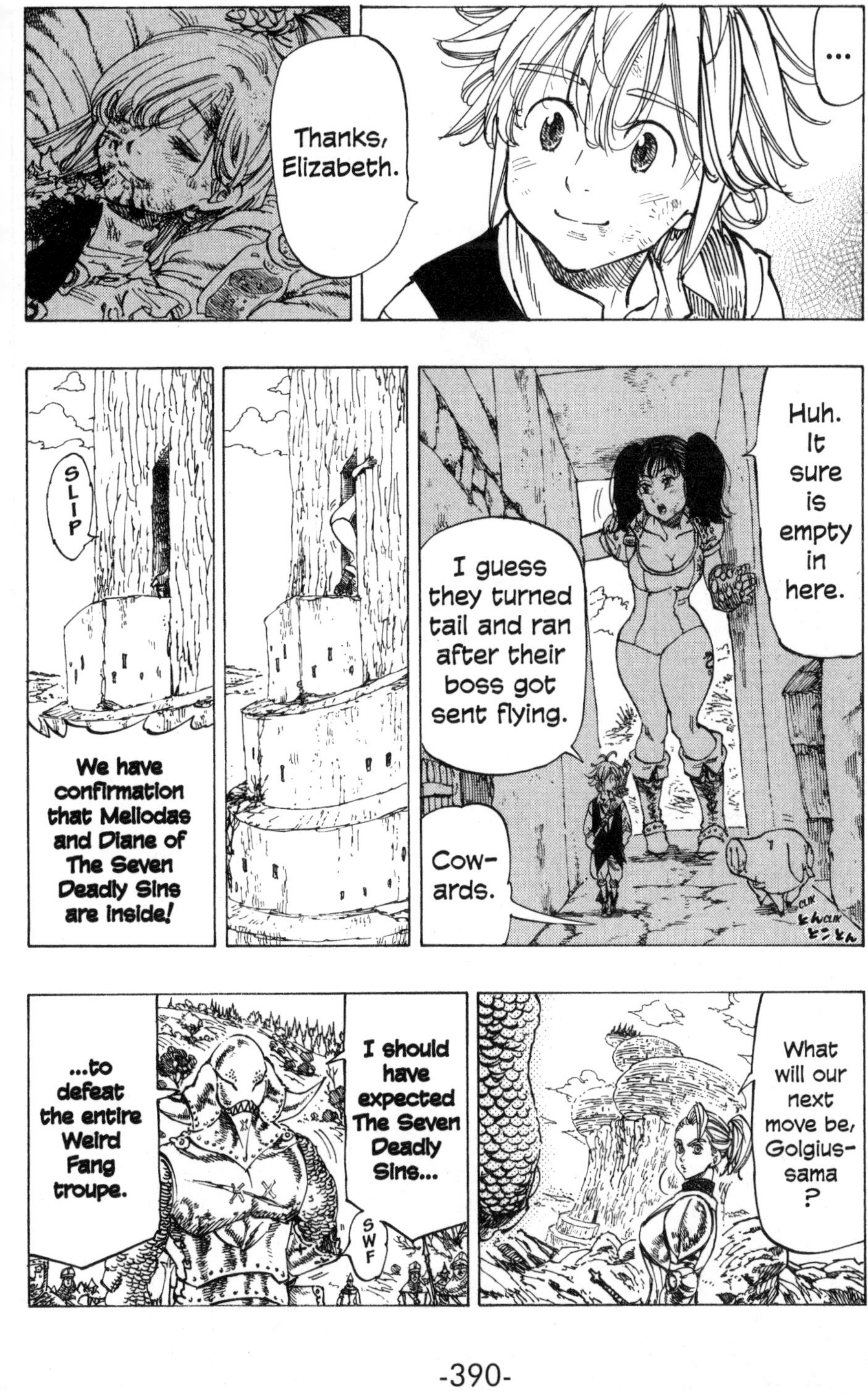
...
Thanks, Elizabeth.
Huh. It sure is empty in here.
I guess they turned tail and ran after their boss got sent flying.
Cow-ards.
CLIK
SLIP
We have confirmation that Meliodas and Diane of The Seven Deadly Sins are inside!
What will our next move be, Golgius-sama?
I should have expected The Seven Deadly Sins...
SWF
...to defeat the entire Weird Fang troupe.

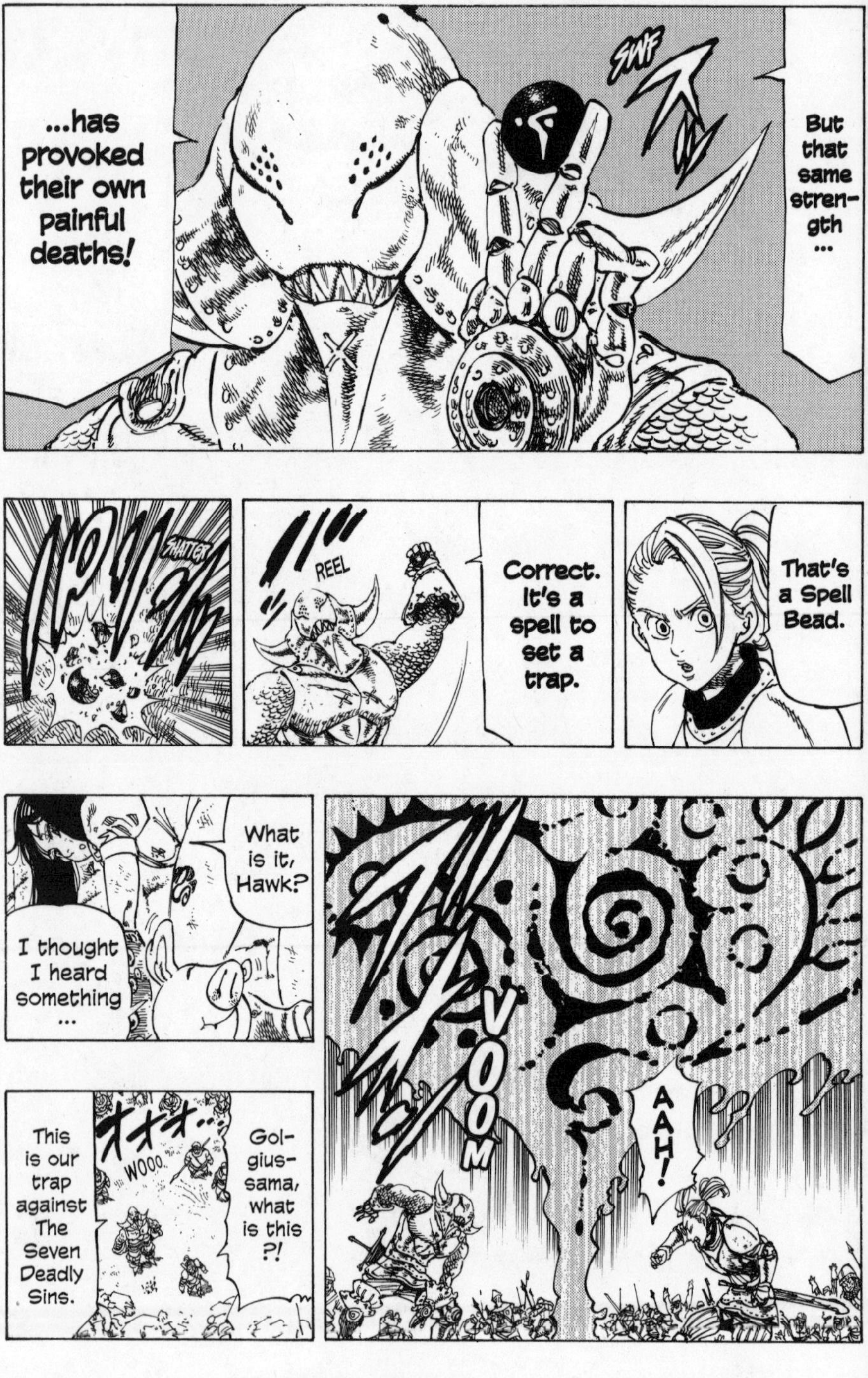
SWF
But that same strength...
...has provoked their own painful deaths!
That's a Spell Bead.
Correct. It's a spell to set a trap.
REEL
SHATTER
VOOM
AAH!
What is it, Hawk?
I thought I heard something...
Golgius-sama, what is this?!
オオオ…
WOOO
This is our trap against The Seven Deadly Sins.

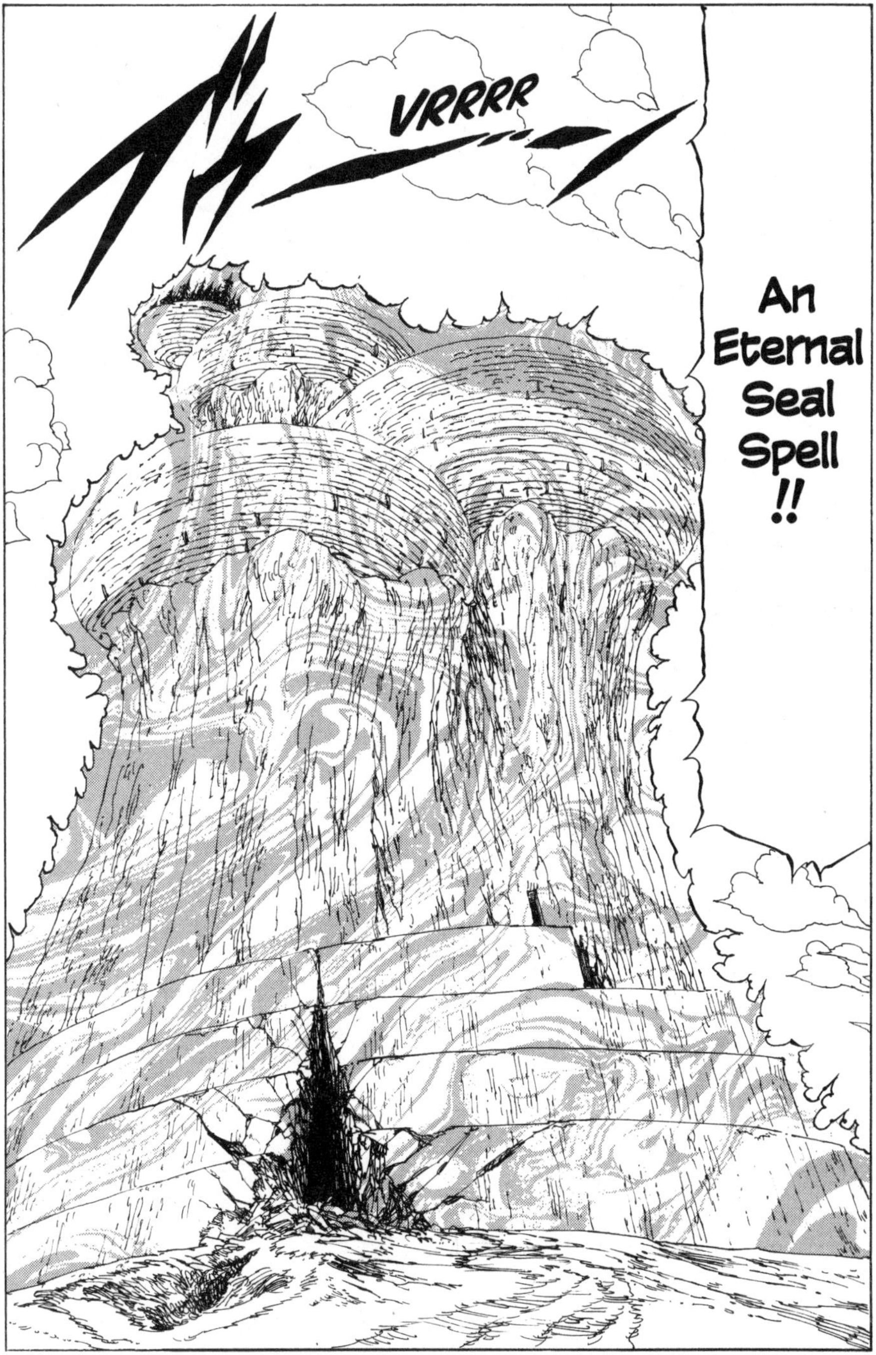
VRRRR
An Eternal Seal Spell !!

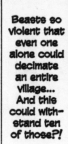

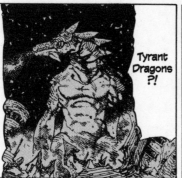

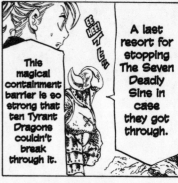

A last resort for stopping The Seven Deadly Sins in case they got through.
EE HEE!
This magical containment barrier is so strong that ten Tyrant Dragons couldn't break through it.
Tyrant Dragons ?!
Beasts so violent that even one alone could decimate an entire village... And this could withstand ten of those?!
In other words, the one path left for our sorry friends in there...
...is to die an agonizing death as they rot away within their cage!
It's too small for me to go any farther.
S... Save me !!
?!
What's a girl doing in here?
TMP
TMP
I... I'm the daughter of Dalmally's doctor, and I've been taken here against my will!
Oh! Then you're ...
Who ?
TMP
TMP
B-But first! There's a legendary criminal in there who just killed a Holy Knight!

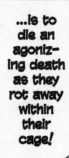

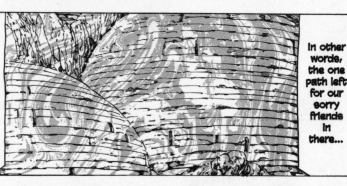

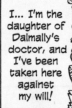

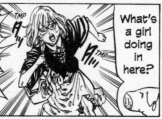

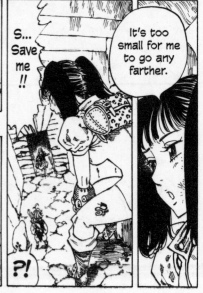

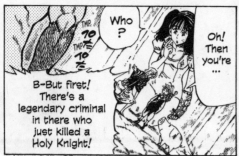

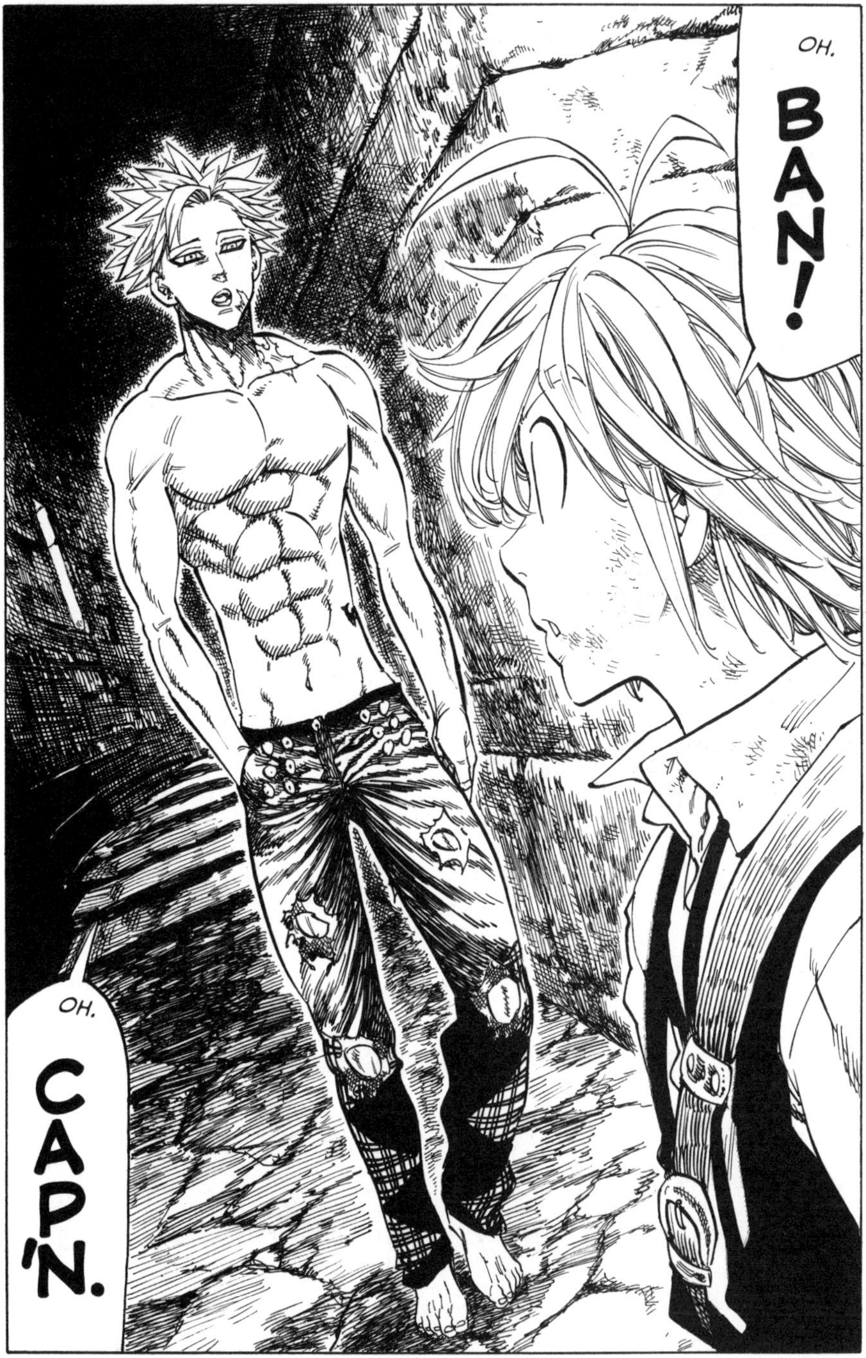
OH. BAN!
OH. CAP'N.

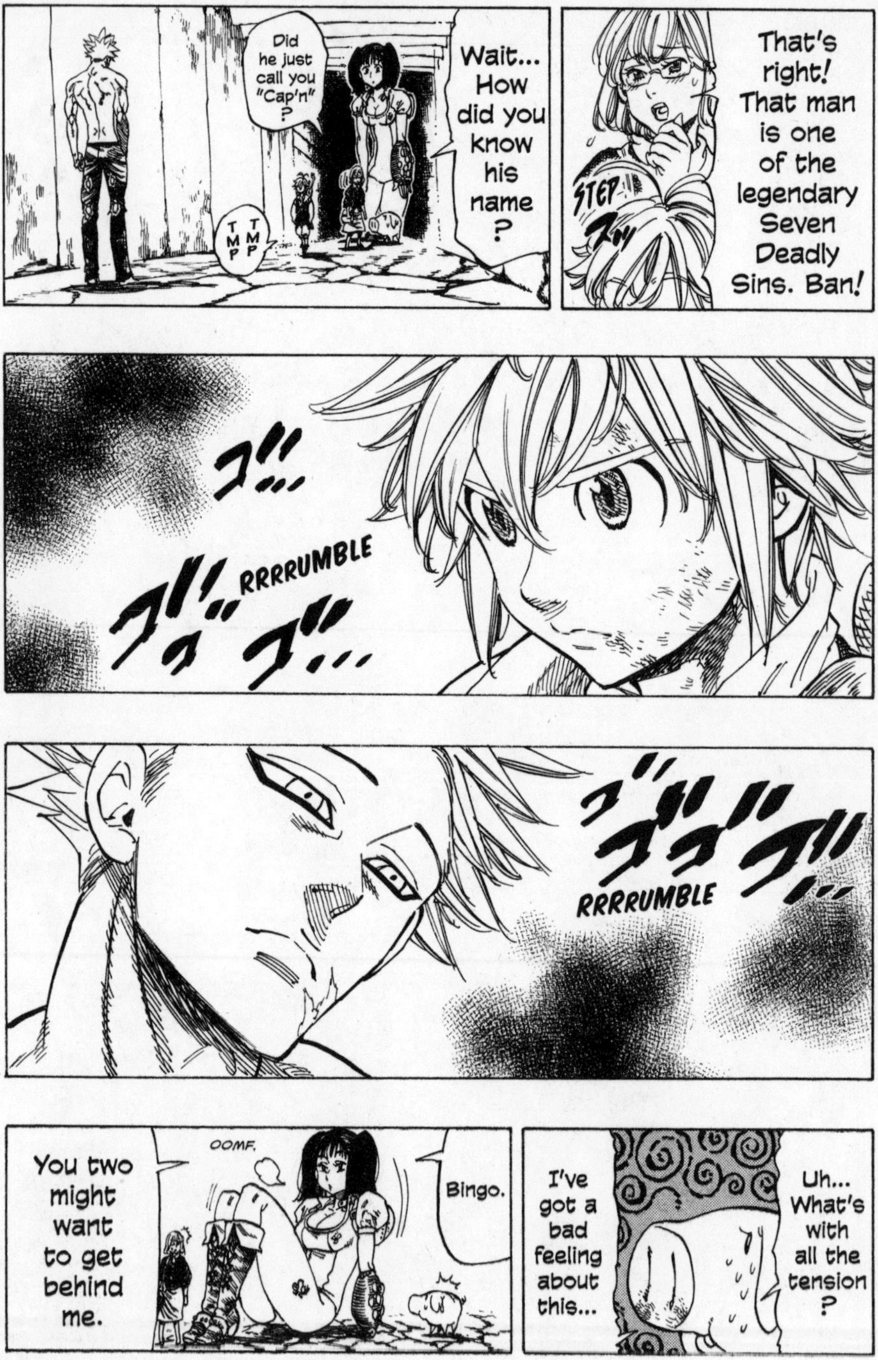
STEP
That's right! That man is one of the legendary Seven Deadly Sins. Ban!
Wait... How did you know his name?
Did he just call you "Cap'n"?
TMP TMP
RRRRUMBLE
RRRRUMBLE
Uh... What's with all the tension?
I've got a bad feeling about this...
Bingo.
OOMF.
You two might want to get behind me.

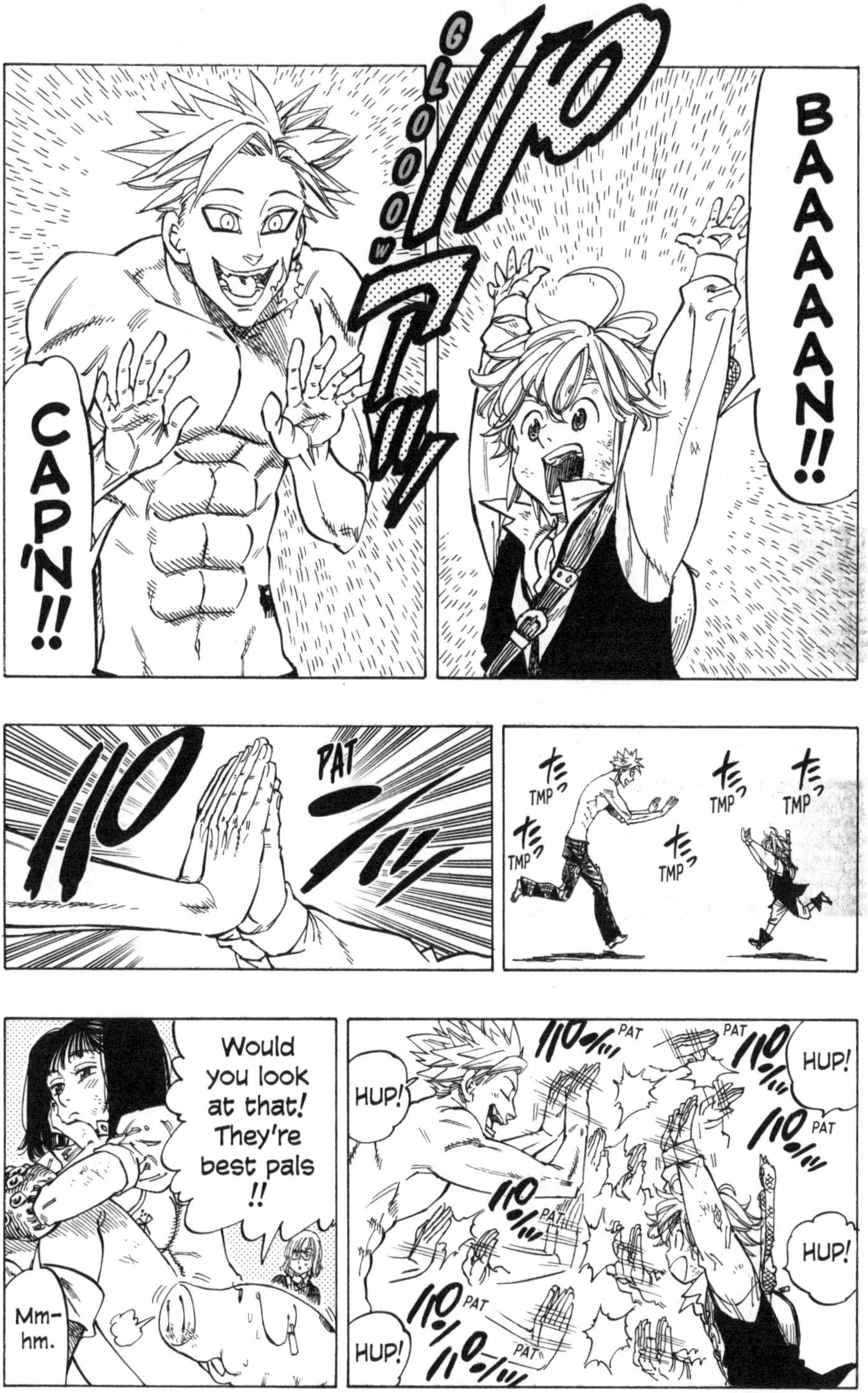
BAAAAAAN!!
GLOOOOW
CAP'N!!
TMP
TMP
TMP
TMP
TMP
PAT
PAT
PAT
HUP!
PAT
HUP!
HUP!
PAT
PAT
PAT
HUP!
Would you look at that! They're best pals!!
Mm-hm.

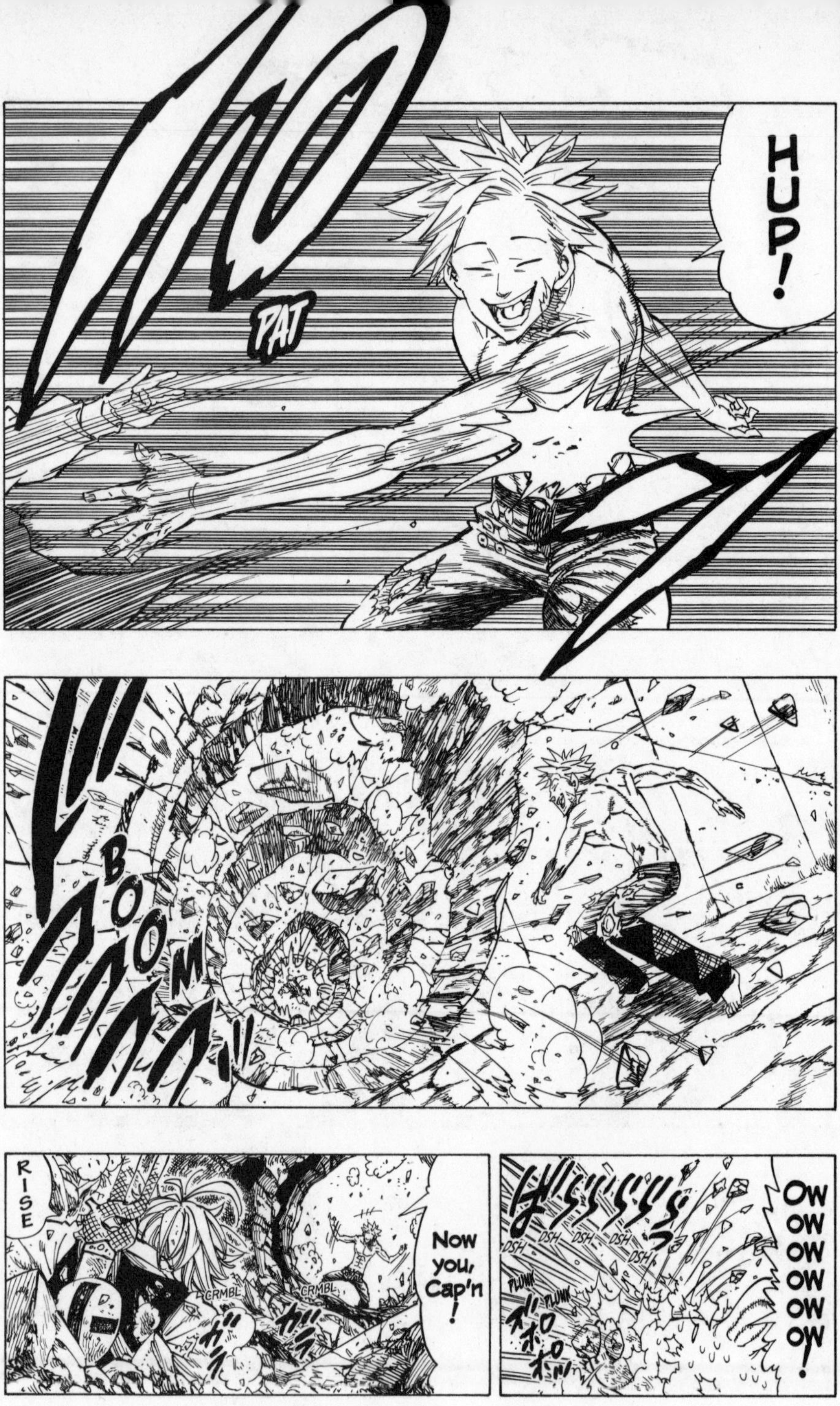
HUP!
PAT
BOOM!!
OW OW OW OW OW OW!
DSH DSH DSH DSH
PLUNK PLUNK
Now you, Cap'n!
RISE
CRMBL CRMBL

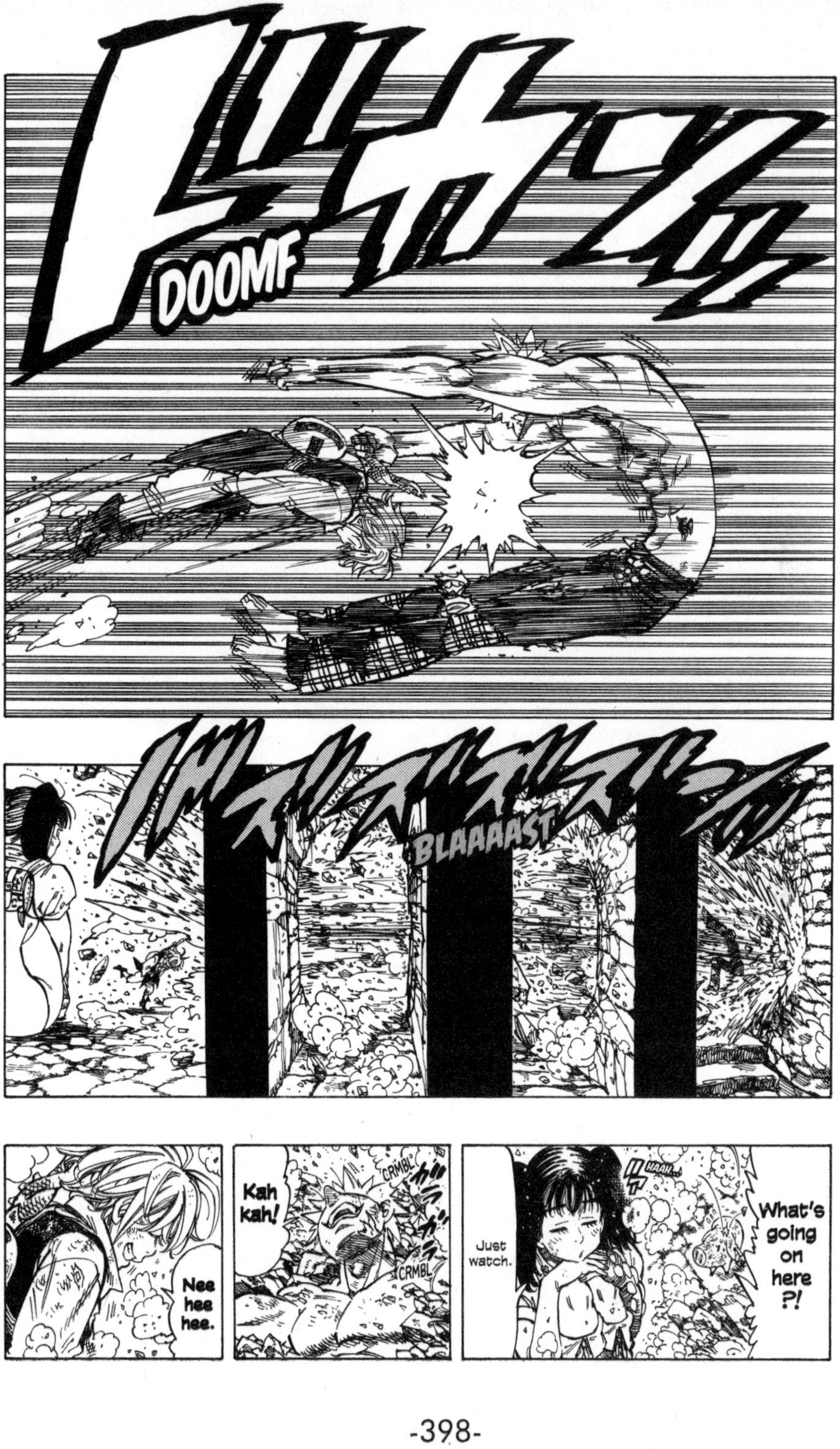
DOOMF
BLAAAAST
HAAH...
What's going on here?!
Just watch.
CRMBL
Kah kah!
CRMBL
Nee hee hee.

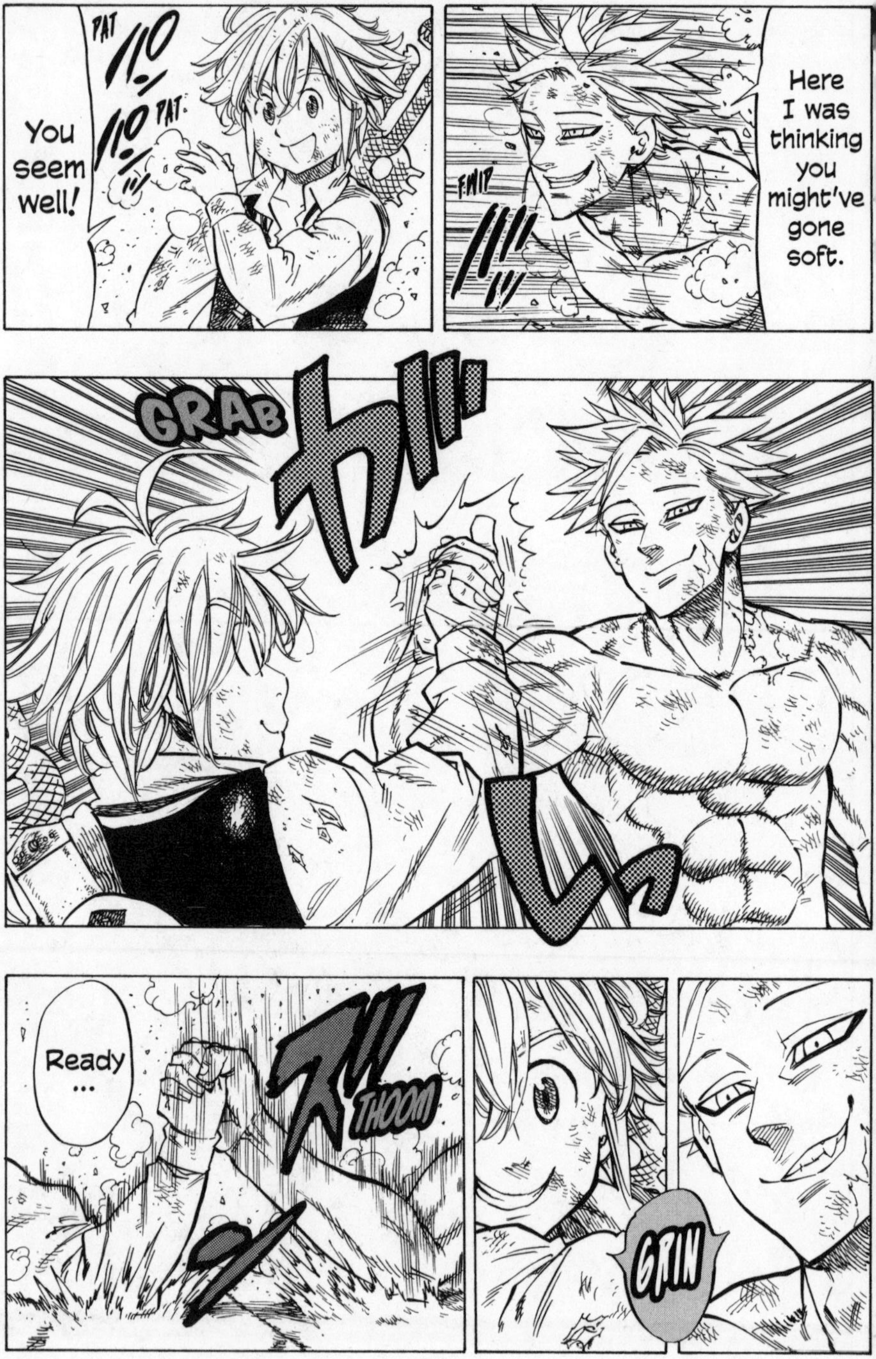
FWIP
Here I was thinking you might've gone soft.
PAT
PAT
You seem well!
GRAB
GRIN
Ready ...
THOOM

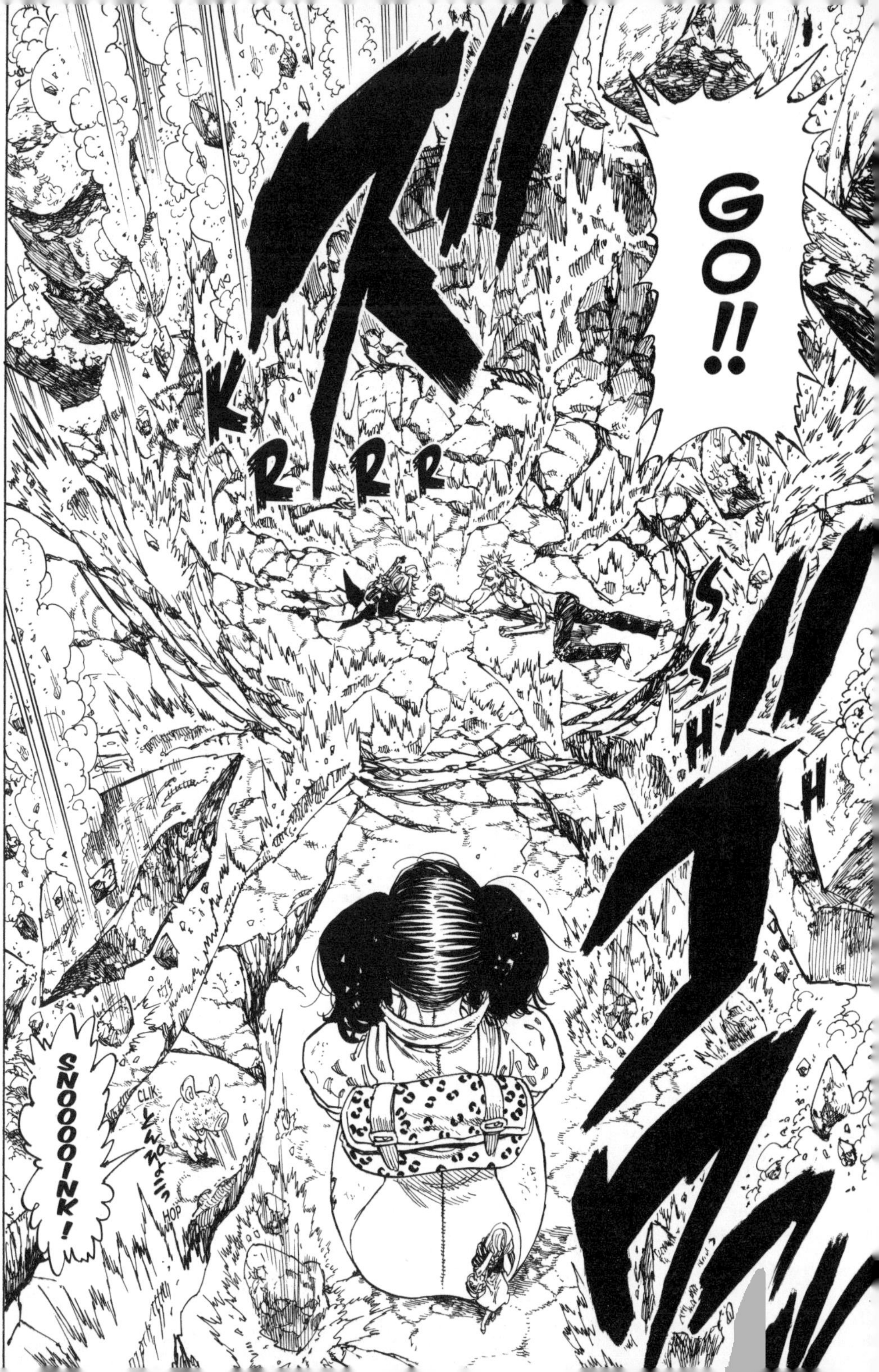
GO!!
KRRRR
SSHH
SNOOOOINK!
CLIK
HOP

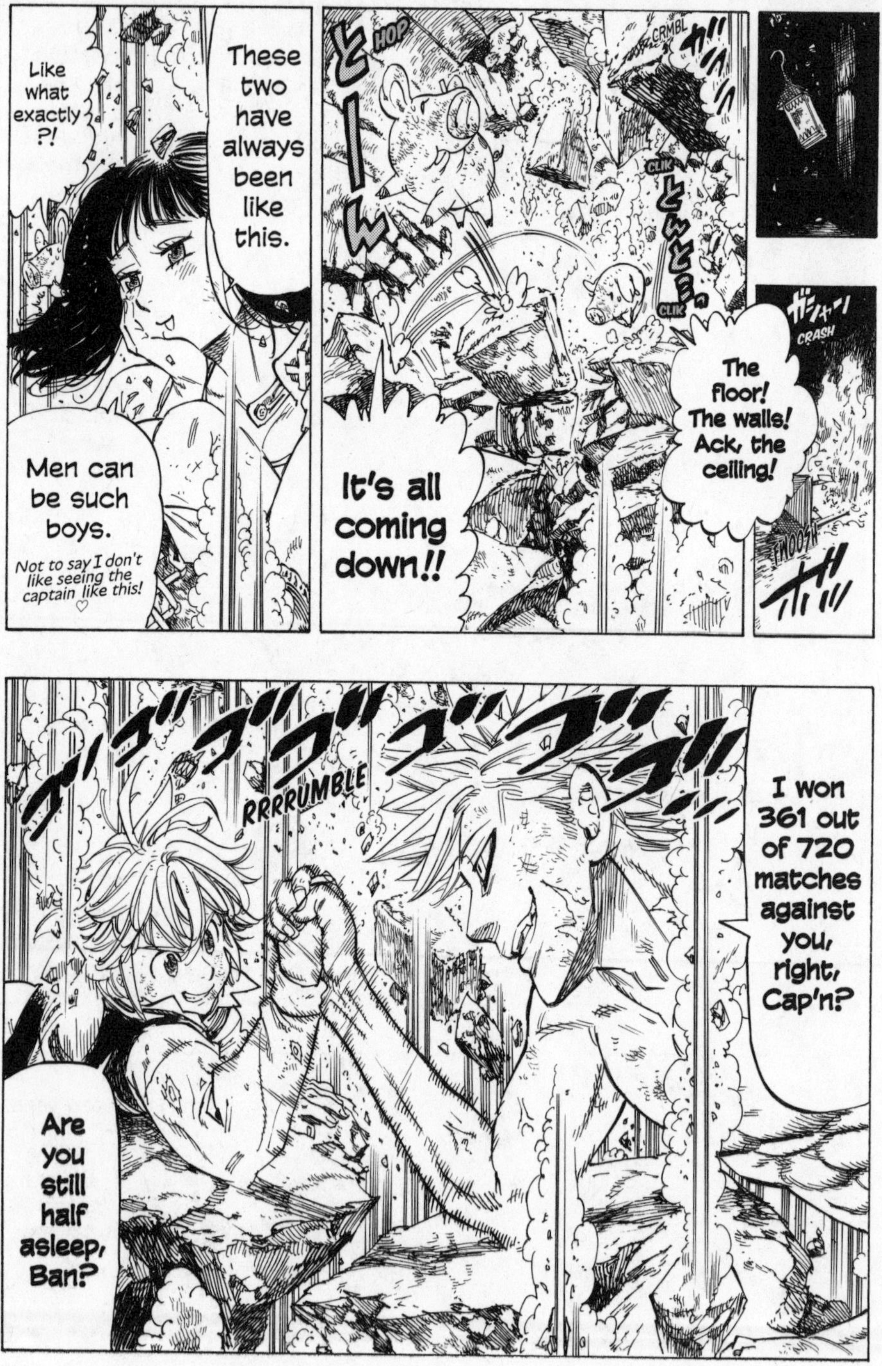
CRASH
FWOOSH
HOP
CRMBL
CLIK
CLIK
The floor! The walls! Ack, the ceiling!
It's all coming down!!
These two have always been like this.
Like what exactly?!
Men can be such boys.
Not to say I don't like seeing the captain like this! ♡
RRRUMBLE
I won 361 out of 720 matches against you, right, Cap'n?
Are you still half asleep, Ban?

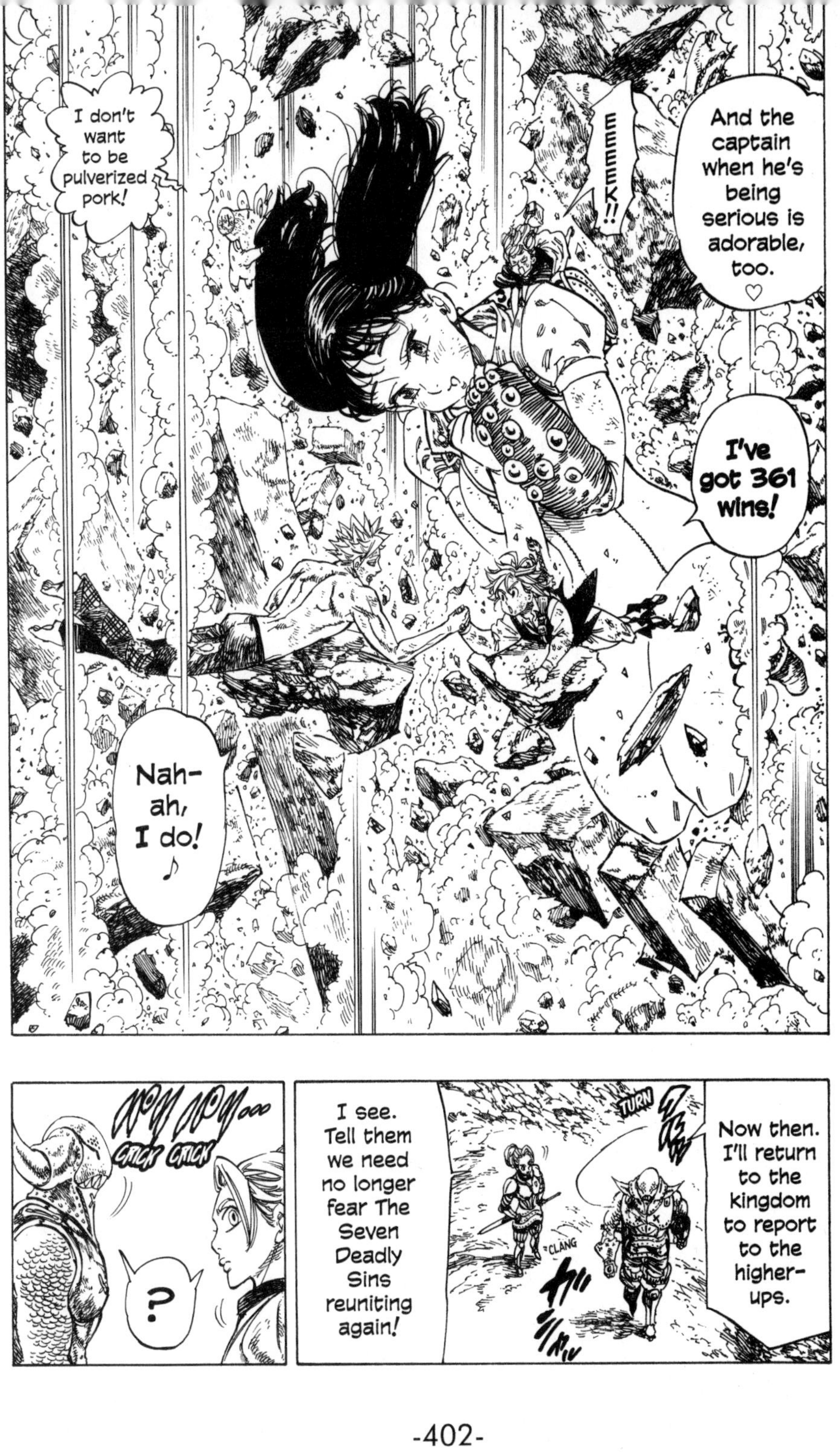
And the captain when he's being serious is adorable, too. ♡
EEEEK!!
I don't want to be pulverized pork!
I've got 361 wins!
Nah-ah, I do! ♪
Now then. I'll return to the kingdom to report to the higher-ups.
TURN
CLANG
I see. Tell them we need no longer fear The Seven Deadly Sins reuniting again!
CRICK CRICK
?

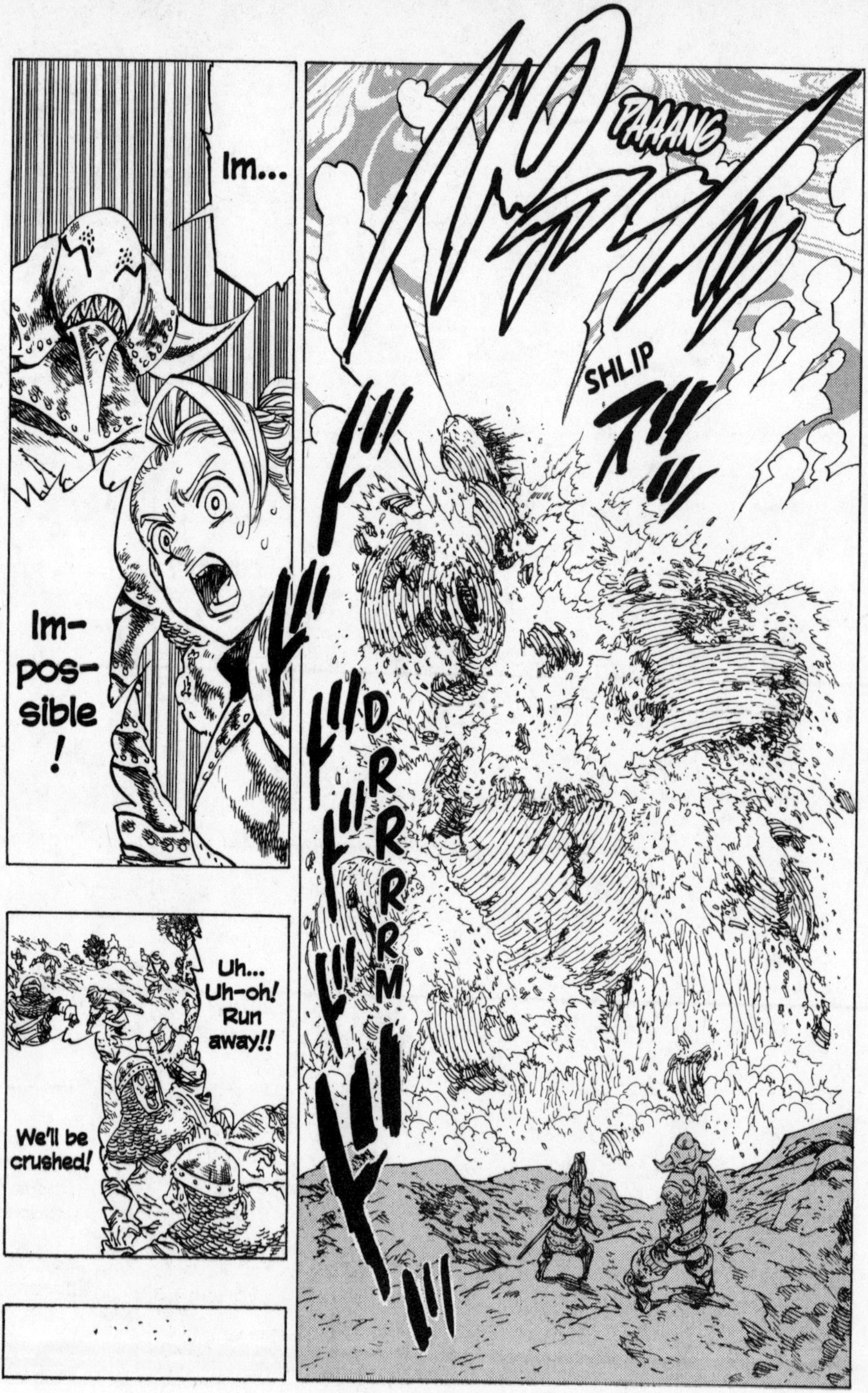
PAAANG
SHLIP
DRRRRM
Im...
Im-possible!
Uh... Uh-oh! Run away!!
We'll be crushed!
. . . :

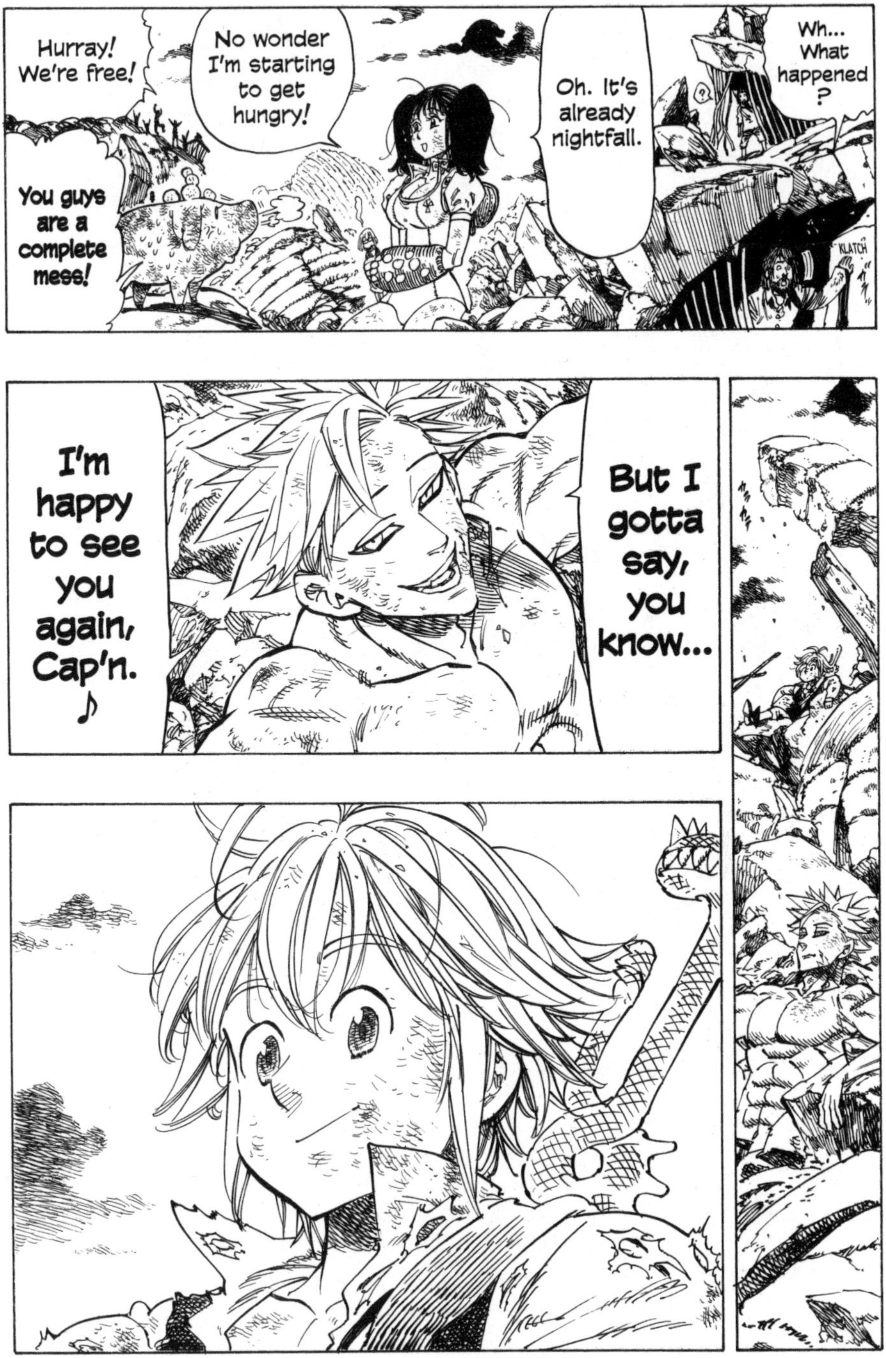

Wh... What happened?
KLATCH
Oh. It's already nightfall.
No wonder I'm starting to get hungry!
Hurray! We're free!
You guys are a complete mess!
But I gotta say, you know...
I'm happy to see you again, Cap'n. ♪

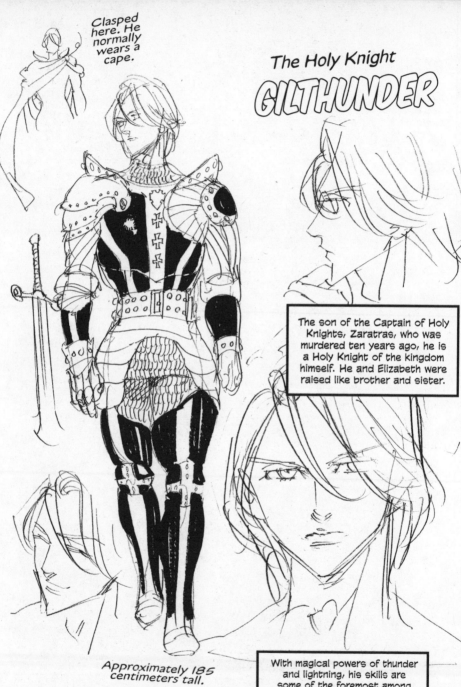

Clasped here. He normally wears a cape.

The Holy Knight

GILTHUNDER

The son of the Captain of Holy Knights, Zaratras, who was murdered ten years ago, he is a Holy Knight of the kingdom himself. He and Elizabeth were raised like brother and sister.

Approximately 185 centimeters tall.

With magical powers of thunder and lightning, his skills are some of the foremost among the Holy Knights.

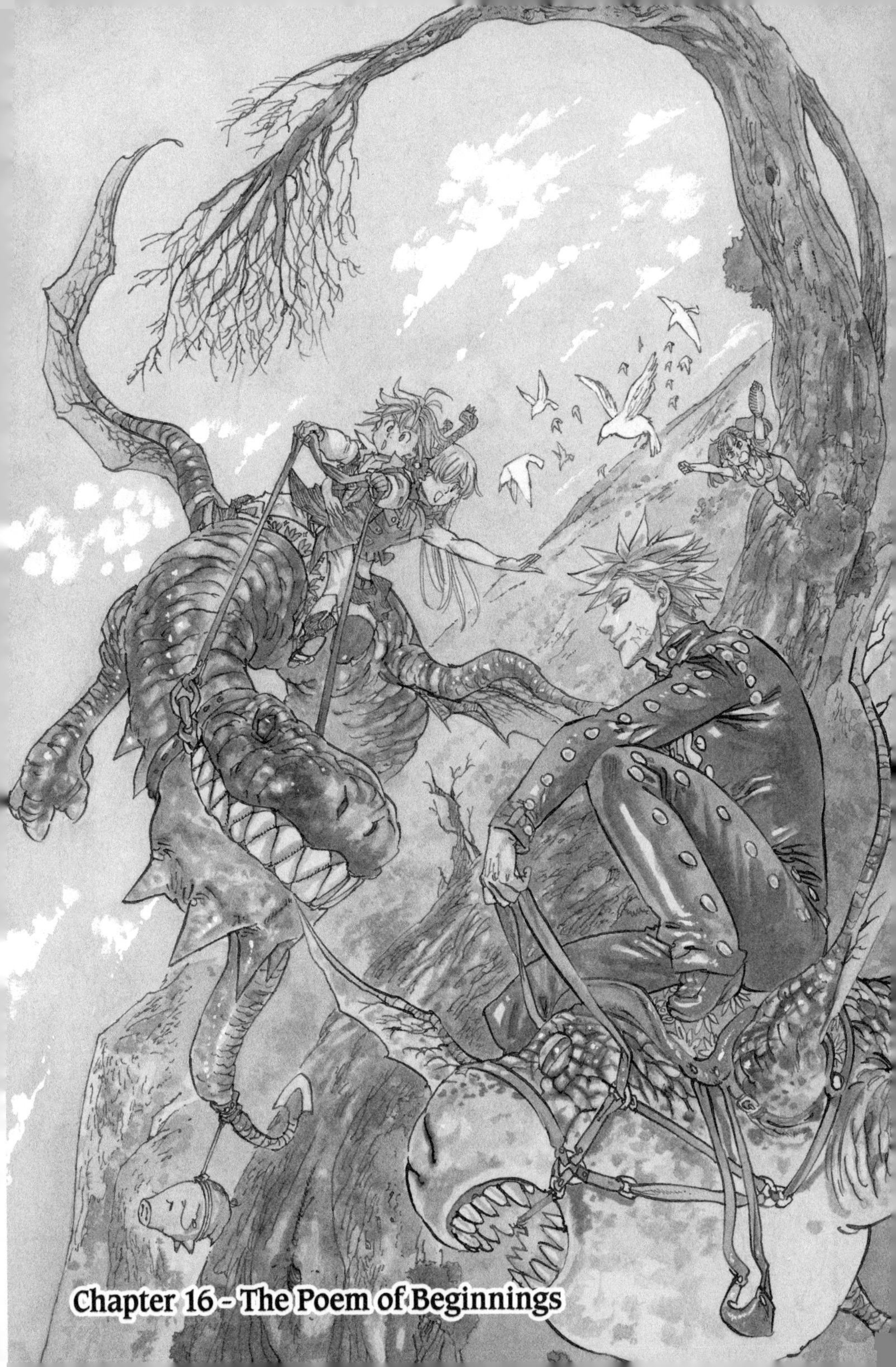
Chapter 16 - The Poem of Beginnings

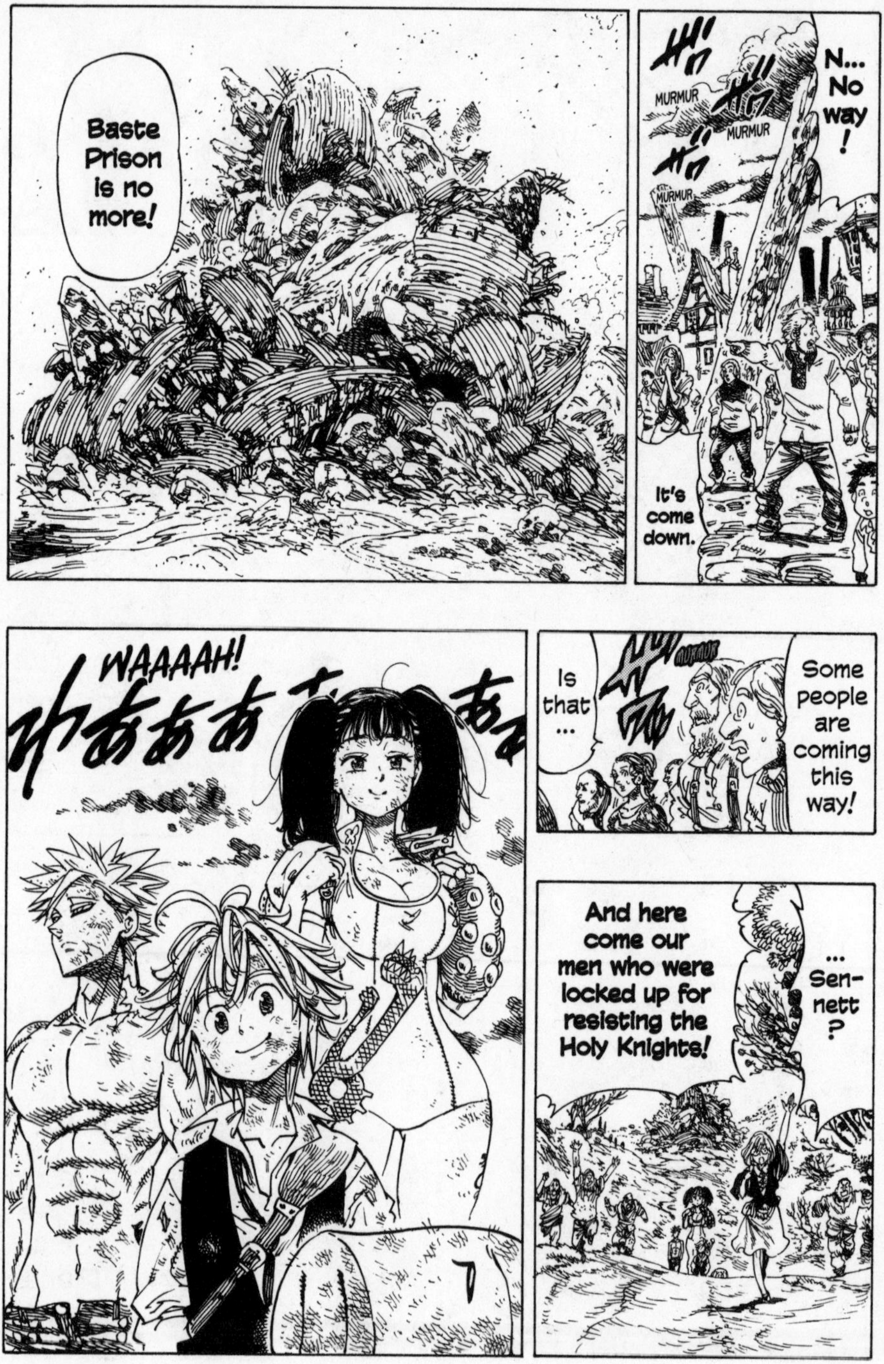

N... No way!
MURMUR
MURMUR
MURMUR
It's come down.
Baste Prison is no more!
Some people are coming this way!
MURMUR
Is that...
...Sen-nett?
And here come our men who were locked up for resisting the Holy Knights!
WAAAAH!

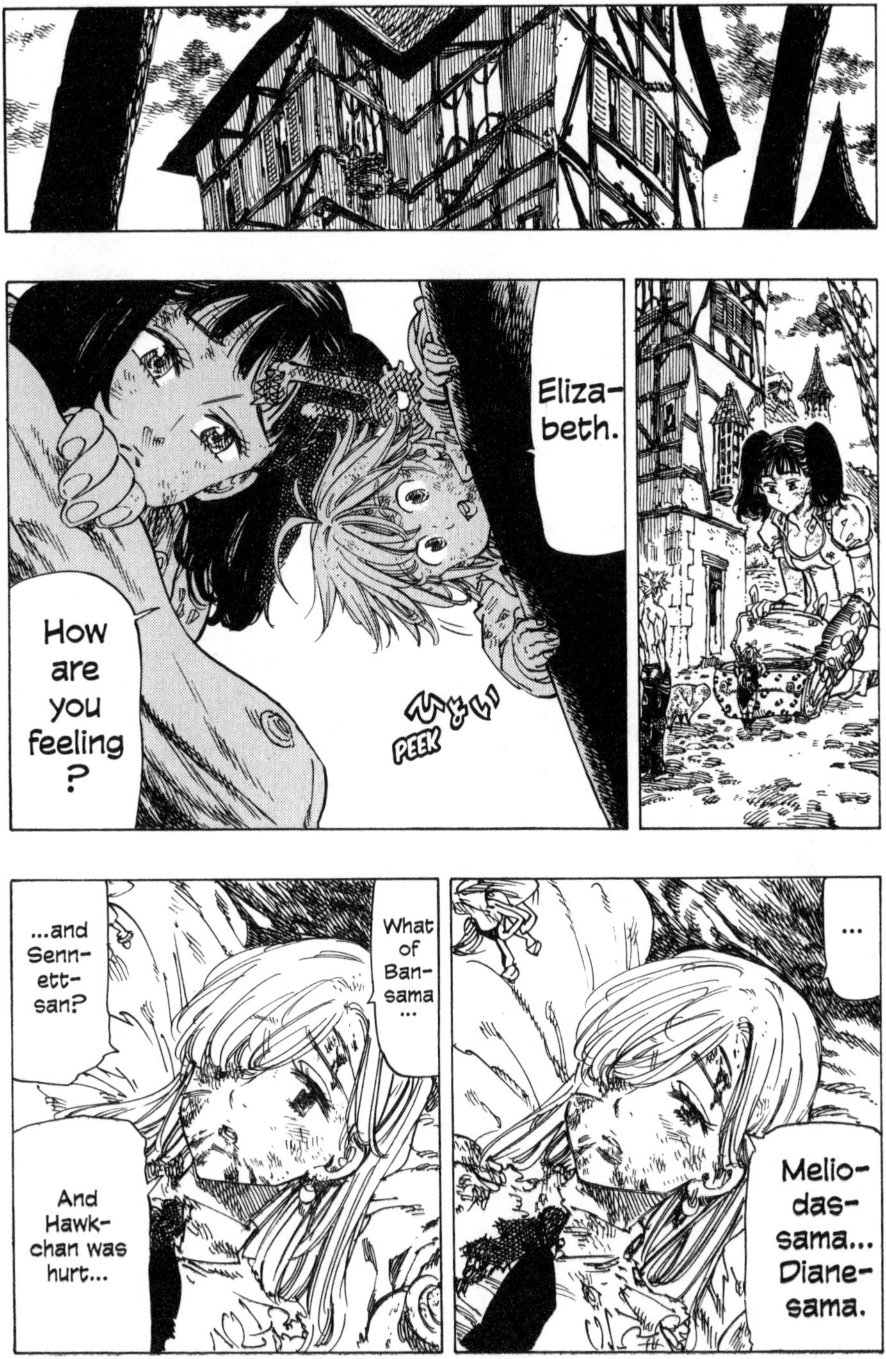
Eliza-beth.
PEEK
How are you feeling?
...
Melio-das-sama... Diane-sama.
What of Ban-sama...
...and Senn-ett-san?
And Hawk-chan was hurt...

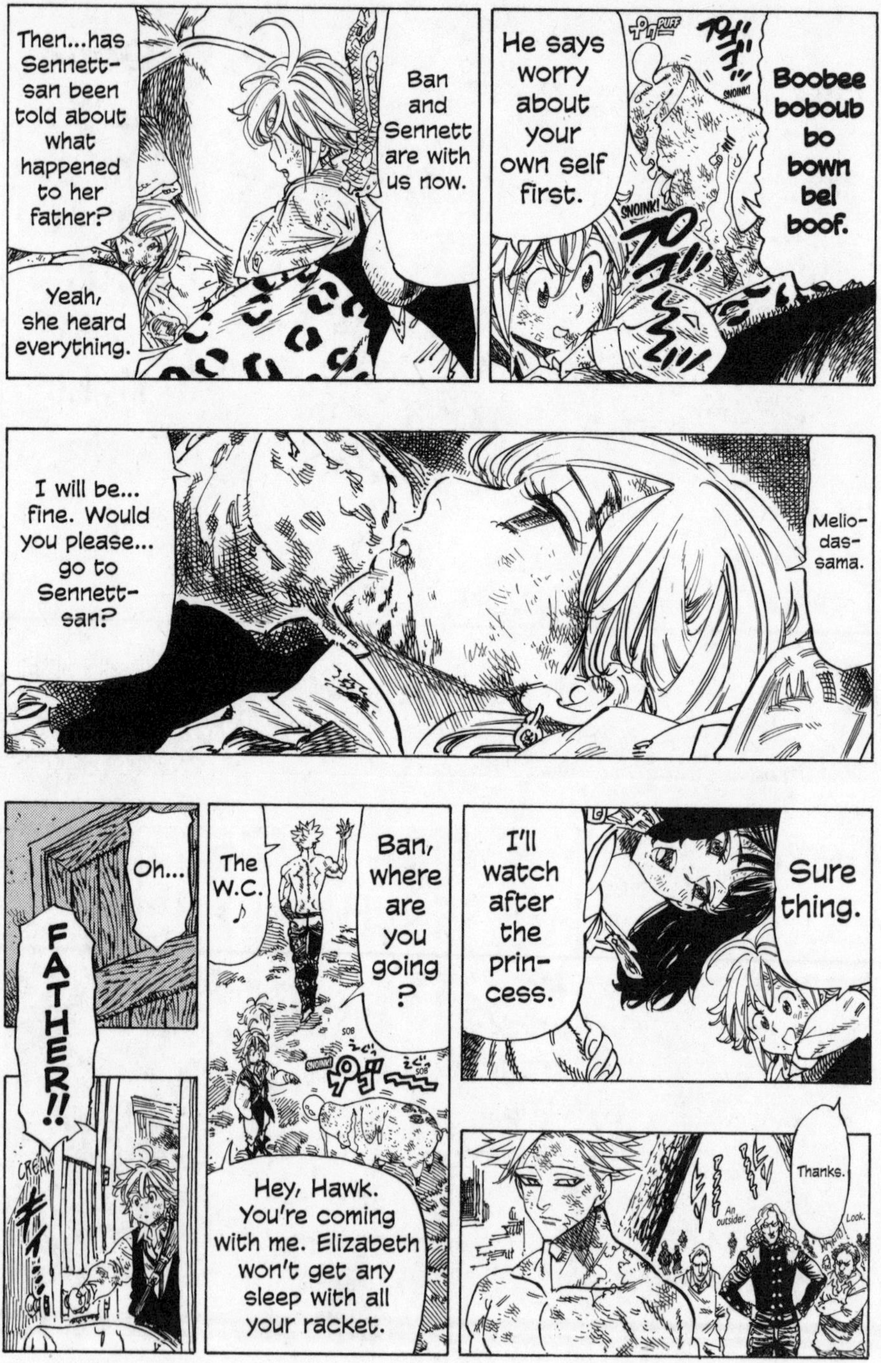
Boobee boboub bo bown bel boof.
SNOINK!
PUFF
He says worry about your own self first.
SNOINK!
Ban and Sennett are with us now.
Then...has Sennett-san been told about what happened to her father?
Yeah, she heard everything.
Melio-das-sama.
I will be... fine. Would you please... go to Sennett-san?
Sure thing.
I'll watch after the princess.
Thanks.
Look.
An outsider.
Ban, where are you going?
The W.C. ♪
SOB
SNOINK!
SOB
Hey, Hawk. You're coming with me. Elizabeth won't get any sleep with all your racket.
Oh...
FATHER!!
CREAK

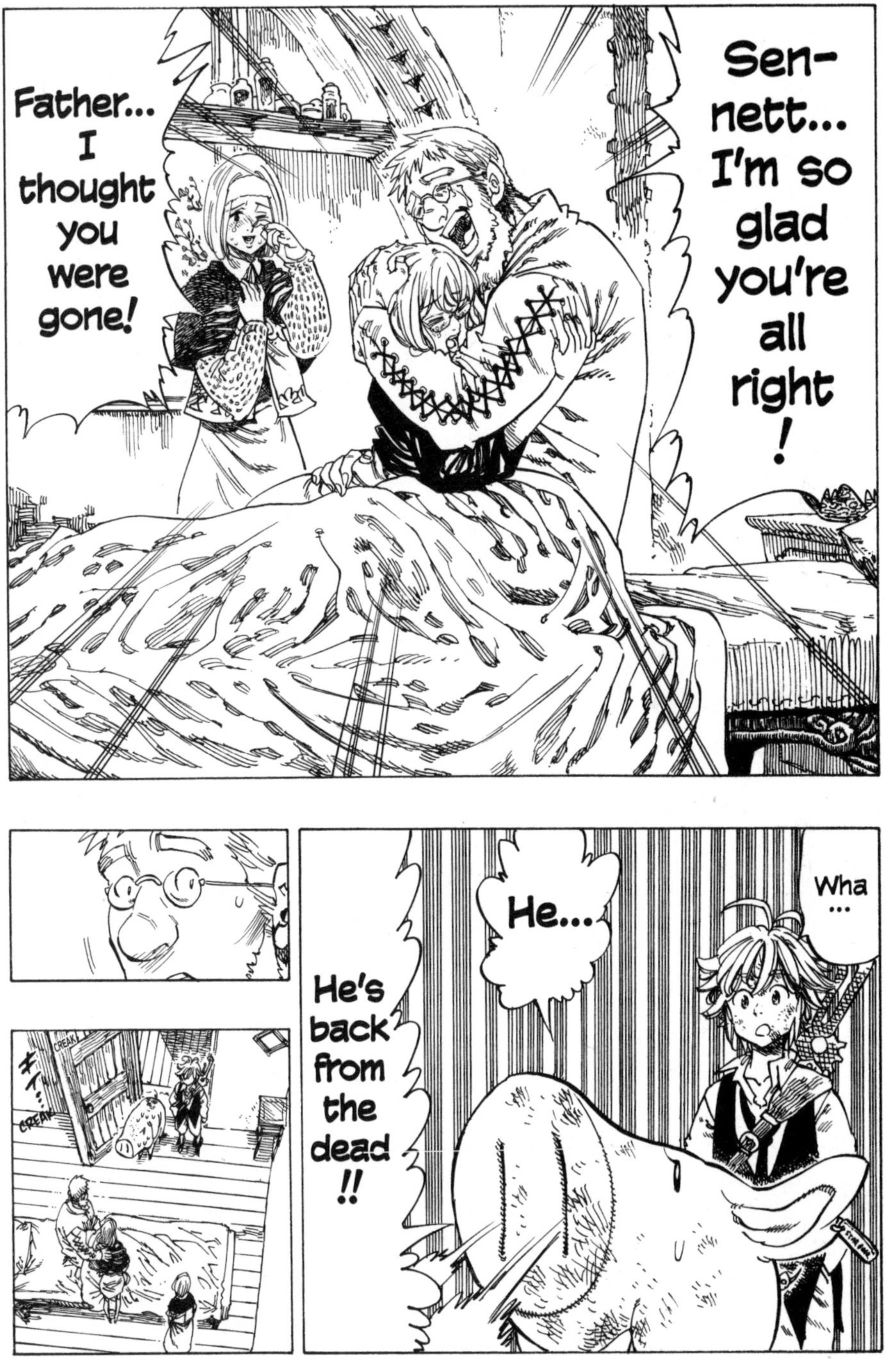
Sen-nett... I'm so glad you're all right!
Father... I thought you were gone!
Wha...
He...
He's back from the dead!!
CREAK
キイ…
CREAK

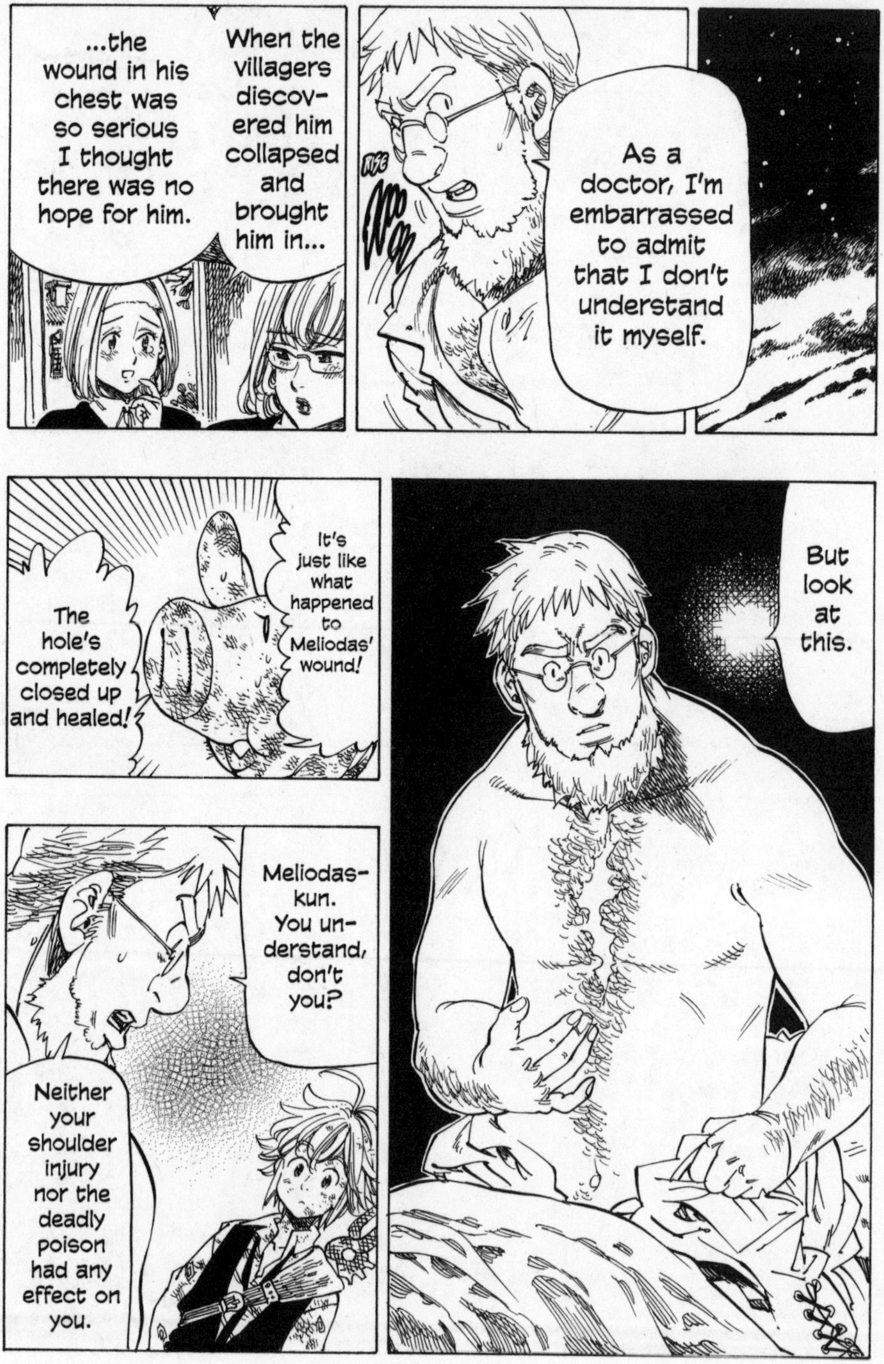
As a doctor, I'm embarrassed to admit that I don't understand it myself.
When the villagers discovered him collapsed and brought him in...
...the wound in his chest was so serious I thought there was no hope for him.
But look at this.
It's just like what happened to Meliodas' wound!
The hole's completely closed up and healed!
Meliodas-kun. You understand, don't you?
Neither your shoulder injury nor the deadly poison had any effect on you.

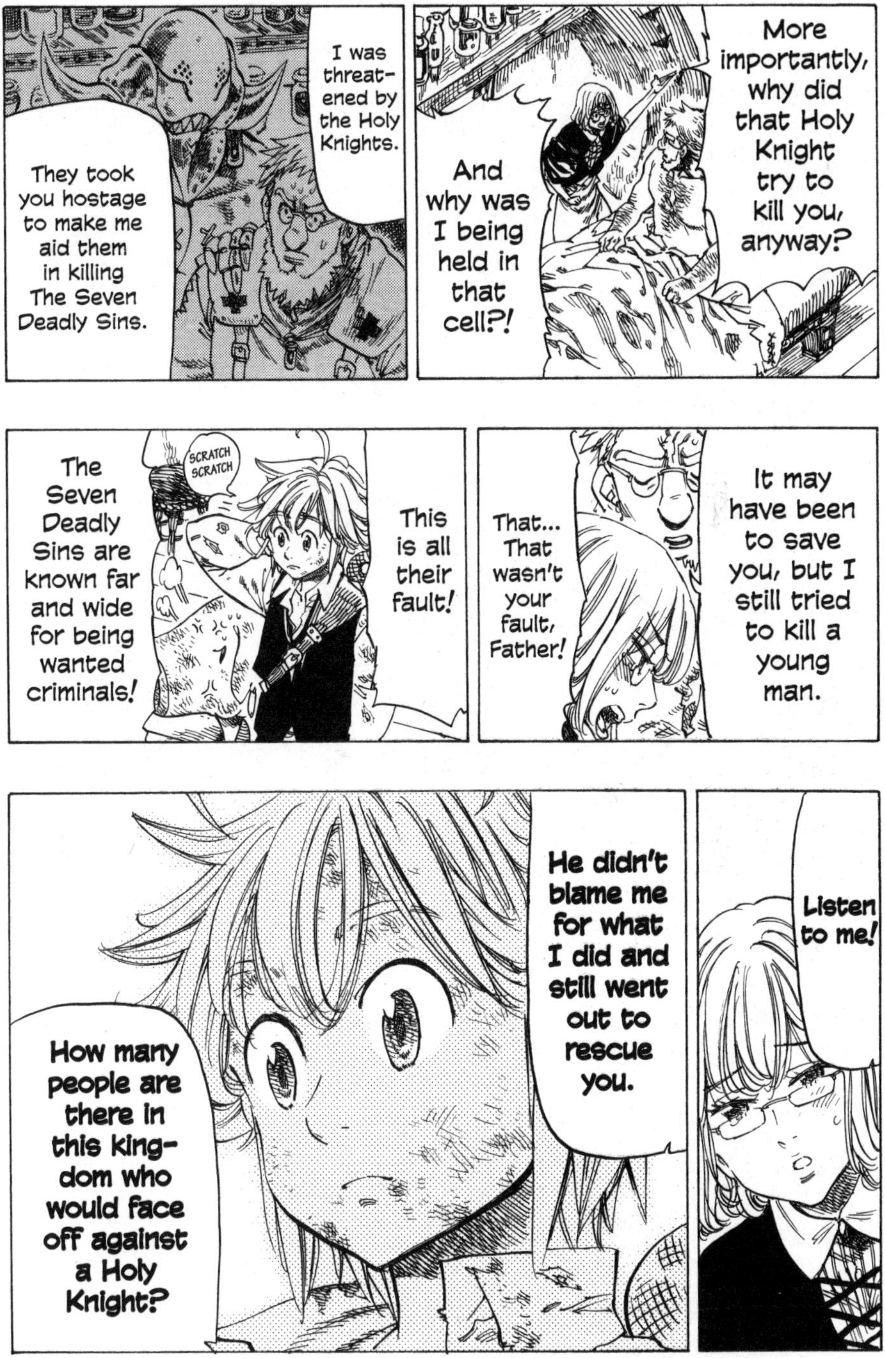
More importantly, why did that Holy Knight try to kill you, anyway?
And why was I being held in that cell?!
I was threatened by the Holy Knights.
They took you hostage to make me aid them in killing The Seven Deadly Sins.
It may have been to save you, but I still tried to kill a young man.
That... That wasn't your fault, Father!
This is all their fault!
SCRATCH SCRATCH
The Seven Deadly Sins are known far and wide for being wanted criminals!
Listen to me!
He didn't blame me for what I did and still went out to rescue you.
How many people are there in this kingdom who would face off against a Holy Knight?

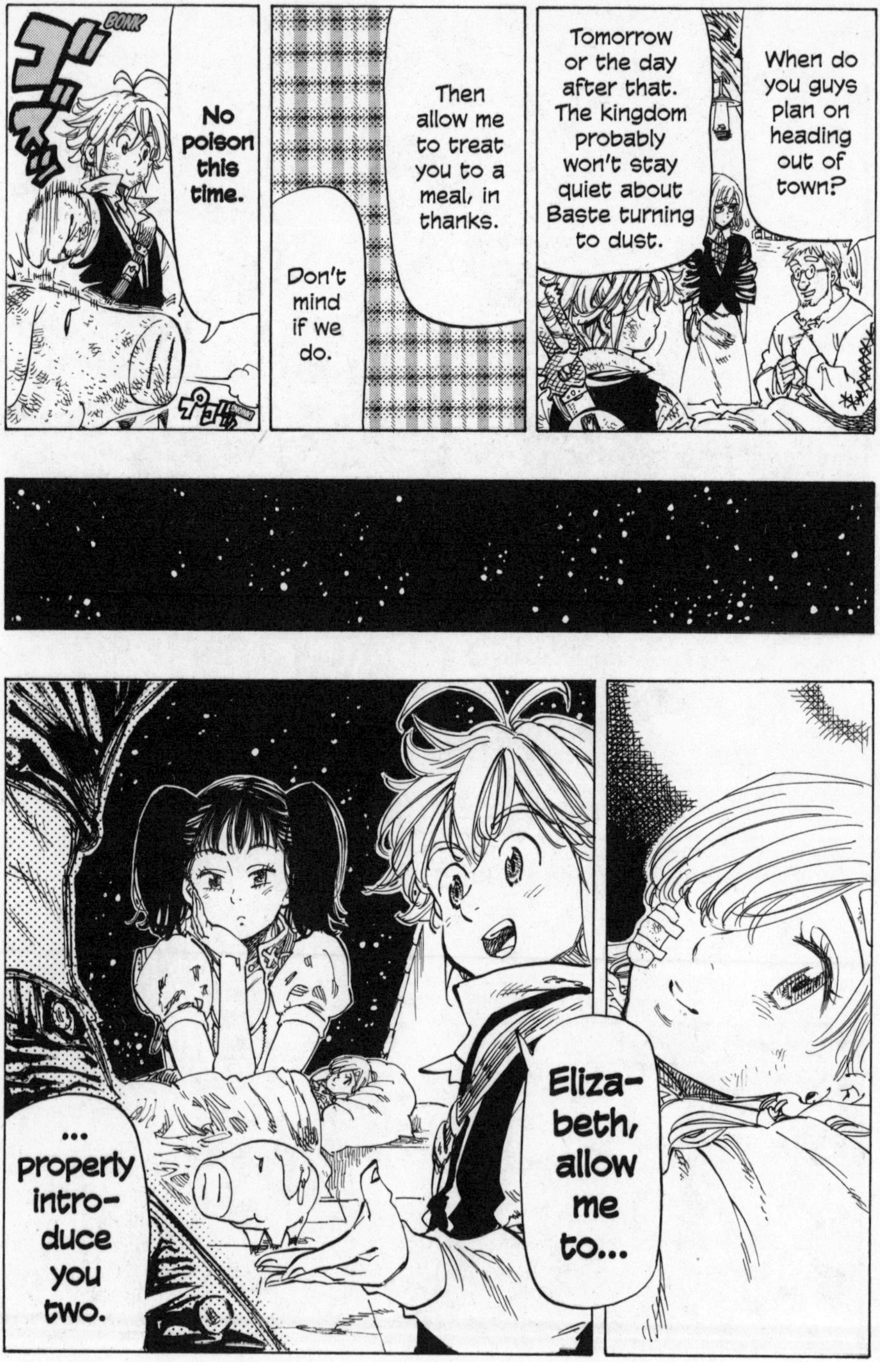
When do you guys plan on heading out of town?
Tomorrow or the day after that. The kingdom probably won't stay quiet about Baste turning to dust.
Then allow me to treat you to a meal, in thanks.
Don't mind if we do.
BONK
No poison this time.
Eliza-beth, allow me to...
...properly intro-duce you two.

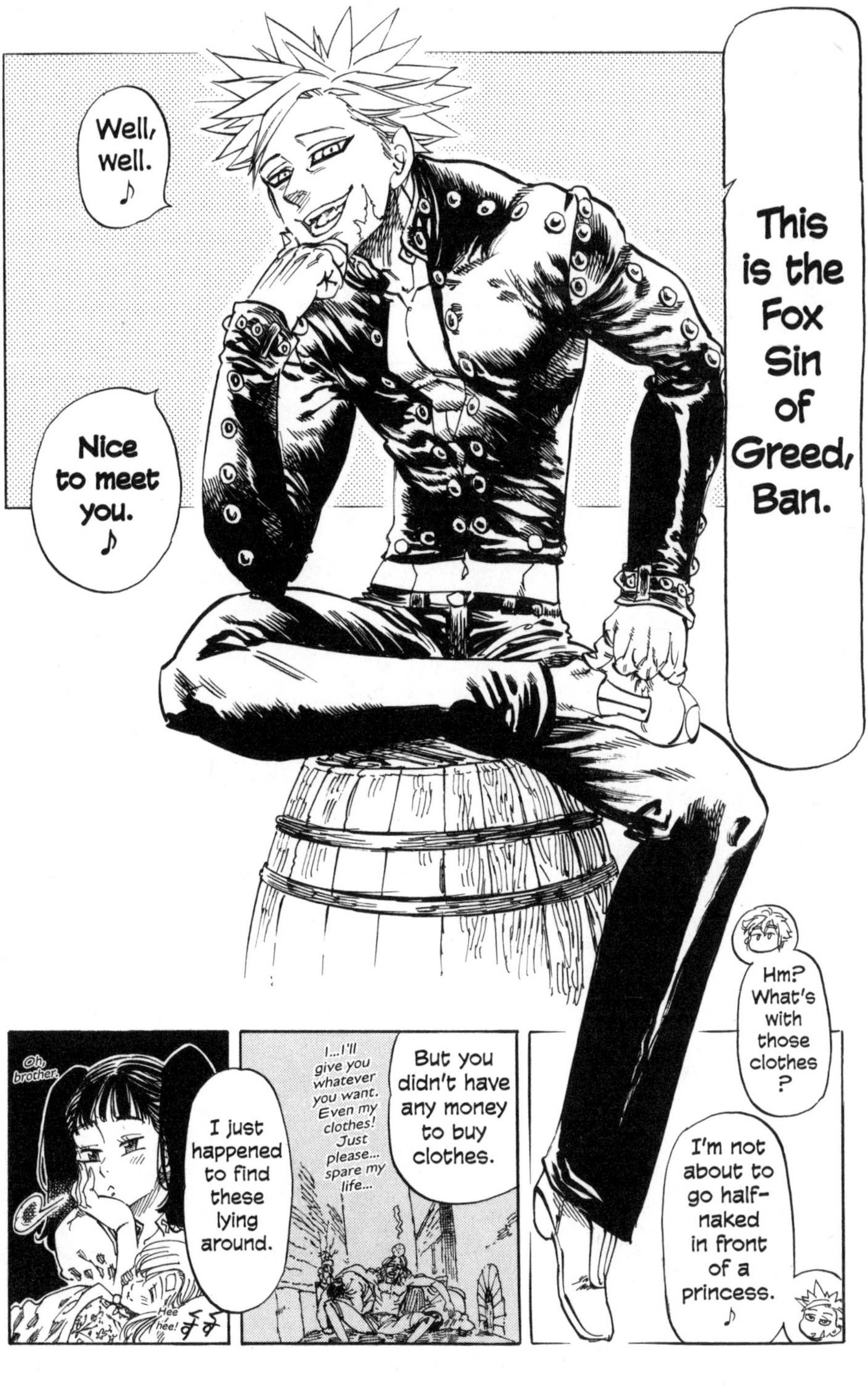
This is the Fox Sin of Greed, Ban.
Well, well. ♪
Nice to meet you. ♪
Hm? What's with those clothes?
I'm not about to go half-naked in front of a princess. ♪
But you didn't have any money to buy clothes.
I...I'll give you whatever you want. Even my clothes! Just please... spare my life...
I just happened to find these lying around.
Oh, brother.
Hee hee!

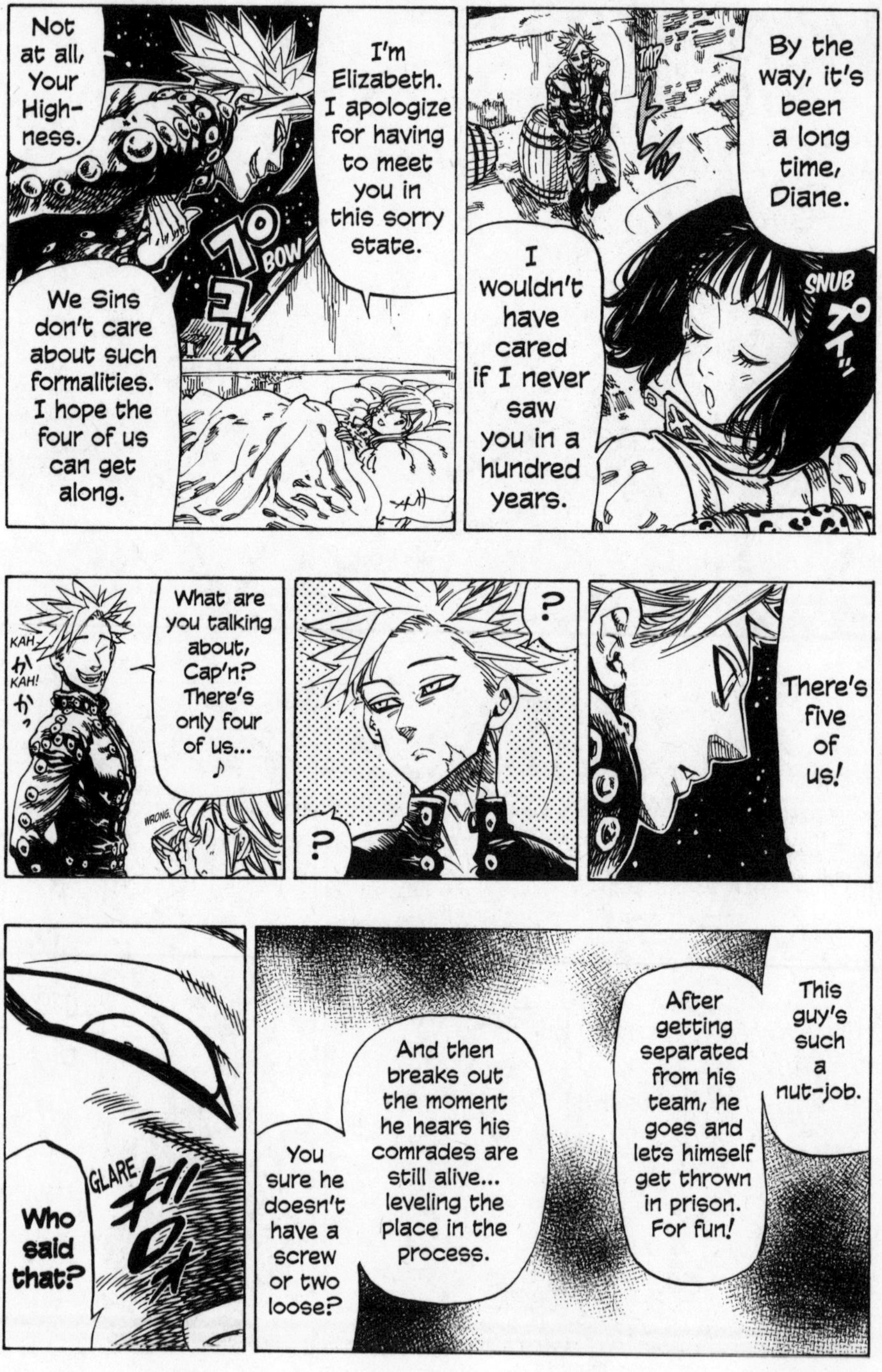
By the way, it's been a long time, Diane.
SNUB
I wouldn't have cared if I never saw you in a hundred years.
I'm Elizabeth. I apologize for having to meet you in this sorry state.
Not at all, Your Highness.
BOW
We Sins don't care about such formalities. I hope the four of us can get along.
There's five of us!
?
?
What are you talking about, Cap'n? There's only four of us... ♪
KAH
KAH!
WRONG.
This guy's such a nut-job.
After getting separated from his team, he goes and lets himself get thrown in prison. For fun!
And then breaks out the moment he hears his comrades are still alive... leveling the place in the process.
You sure he doesn't have a screw or two loose?
GLARE
Who said that?

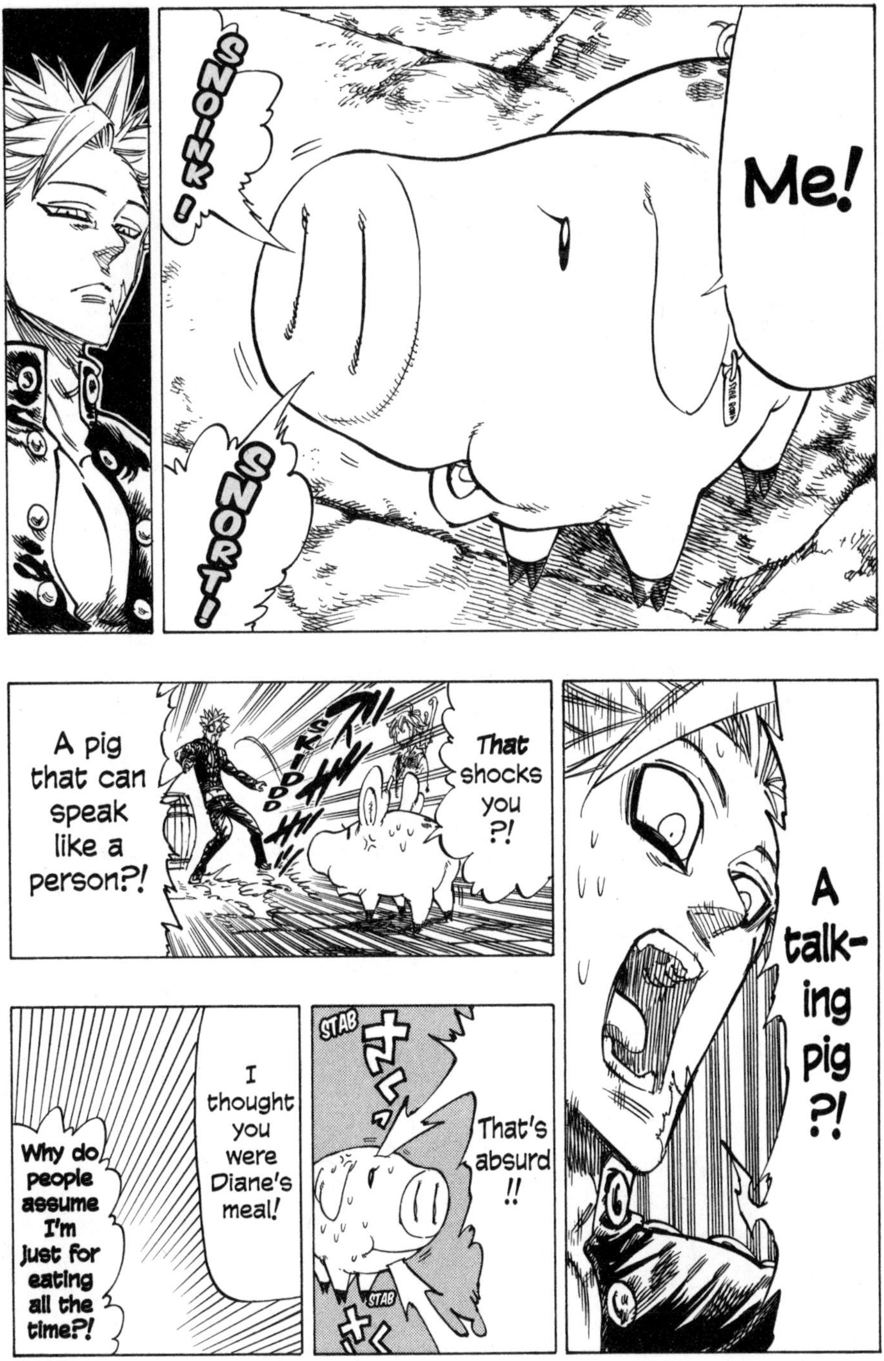
Me!
SNOINK!
SNORT!
A talking-pig?!
That shocks you?!
SKIDDD
A pig that can speak like a person?!
That's absurd!!
STAB
STAB
I thought you were Diane's meal!
Why do people assume I'm just for eating all the time?!

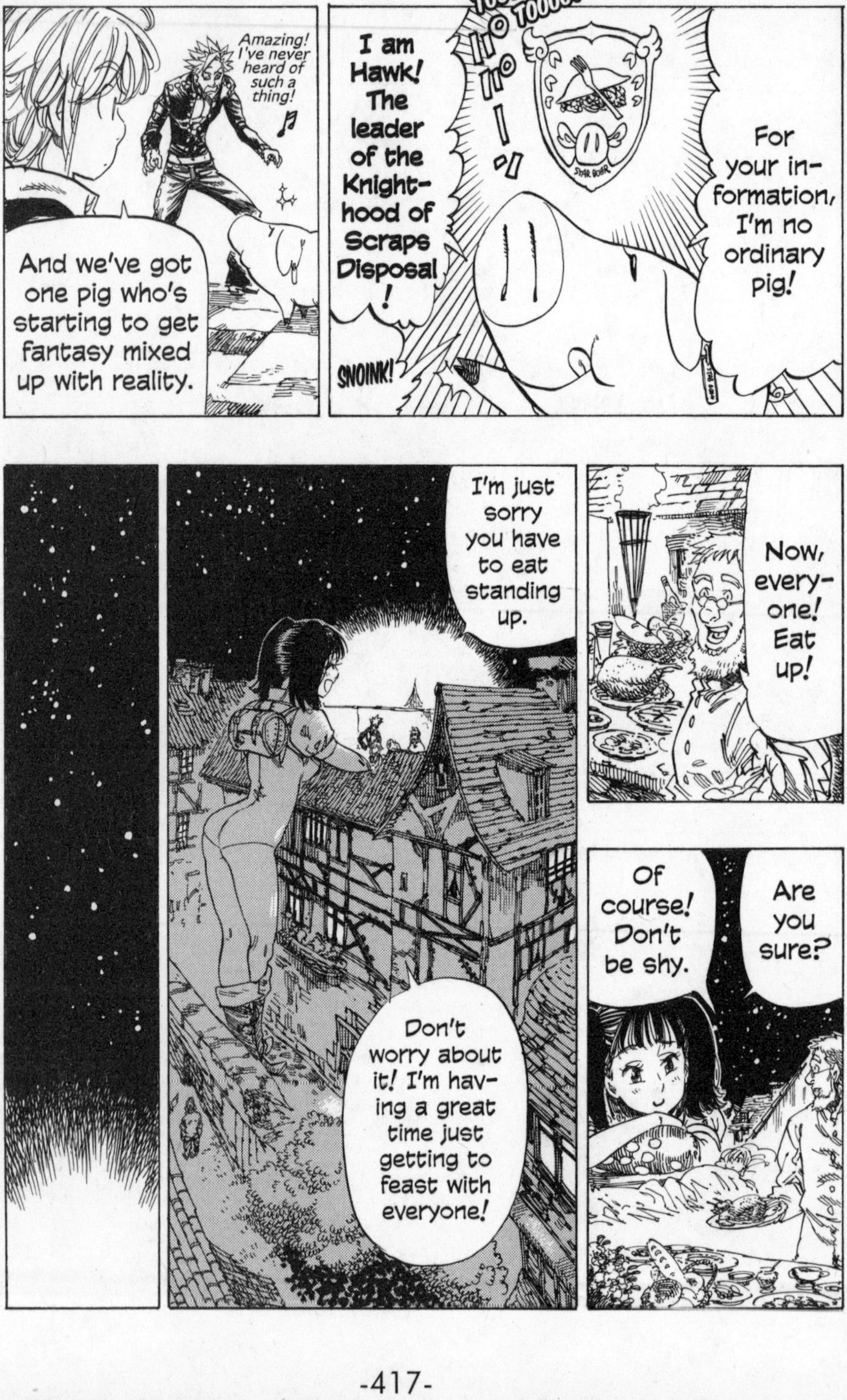
TOOT
TOOOOT
For your information, I'm no ordinary pig!
I am Hawk! The leader of the Knighthood of Scraps Disposal!
SNOINK!
Amazing! I've never heard of such a thing!
And we've got one pig who's starting to get fantasy mixed up with reality.
Now, everyone! Eat up!
Are you sure?
Of course! Don't be shy.
I'm just sorry you have to eat standing up.
Don't worry about it! I'm having a great time just getting to feast with everyone!

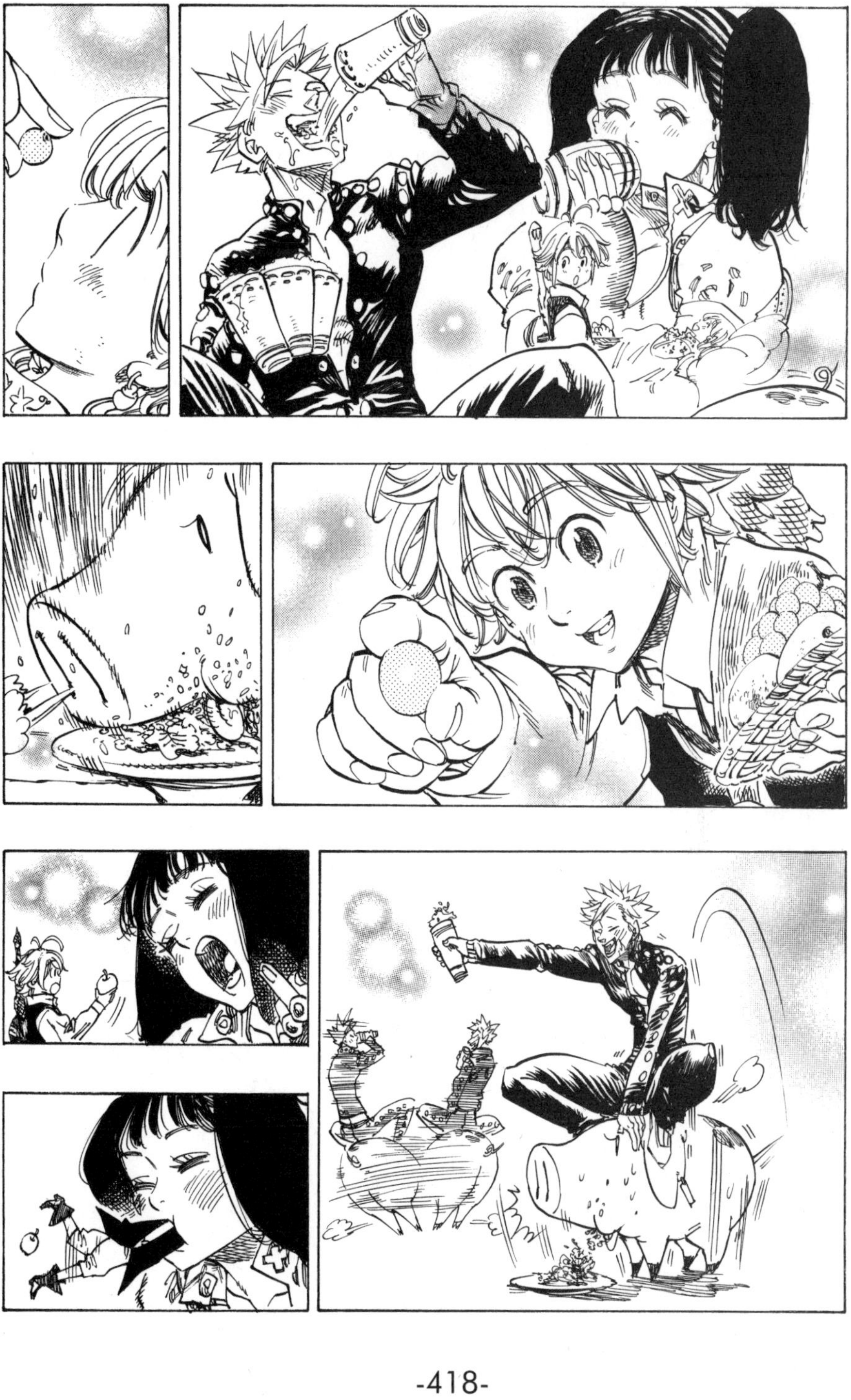

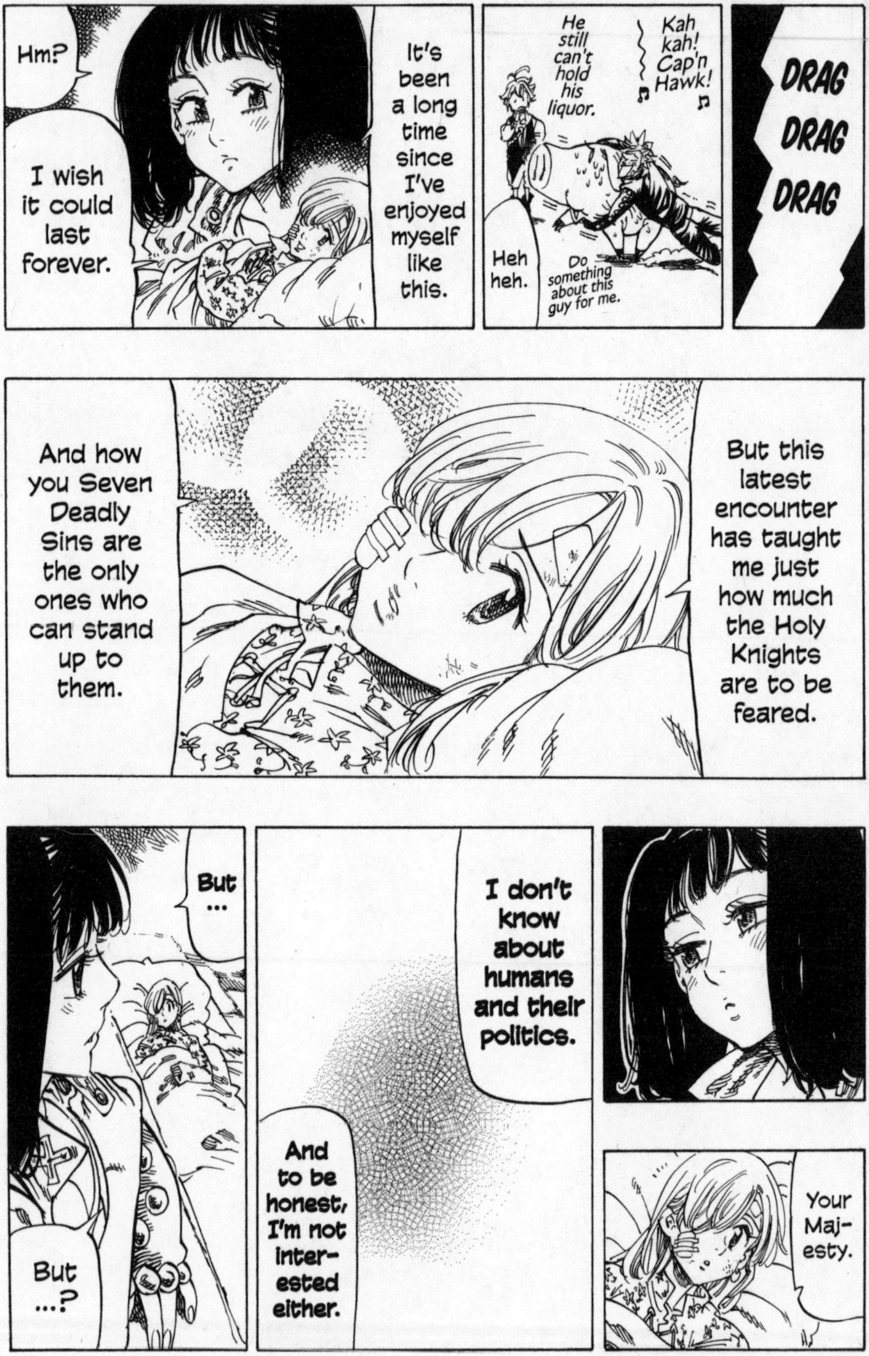

DRAG
DRAG
DRAG
Kah kah! Cap'n Hawk! ♫ ♫
He still can't hold his liquor.
Do something about this guy for me.
Heh heh.
It's been a long time since I've enjoyed myself like this.
Hm?
I wish it could last forever.
But this latest encounter has taught me just how much the Holy Knights are to be feared.
And how you Seven Deadly Sins are the only ones who can stand up to them.
Your Maj-esty.
I don't know about humans and their politics.
And to be honest, I'm not inter-ested either.
But ...
But ...?

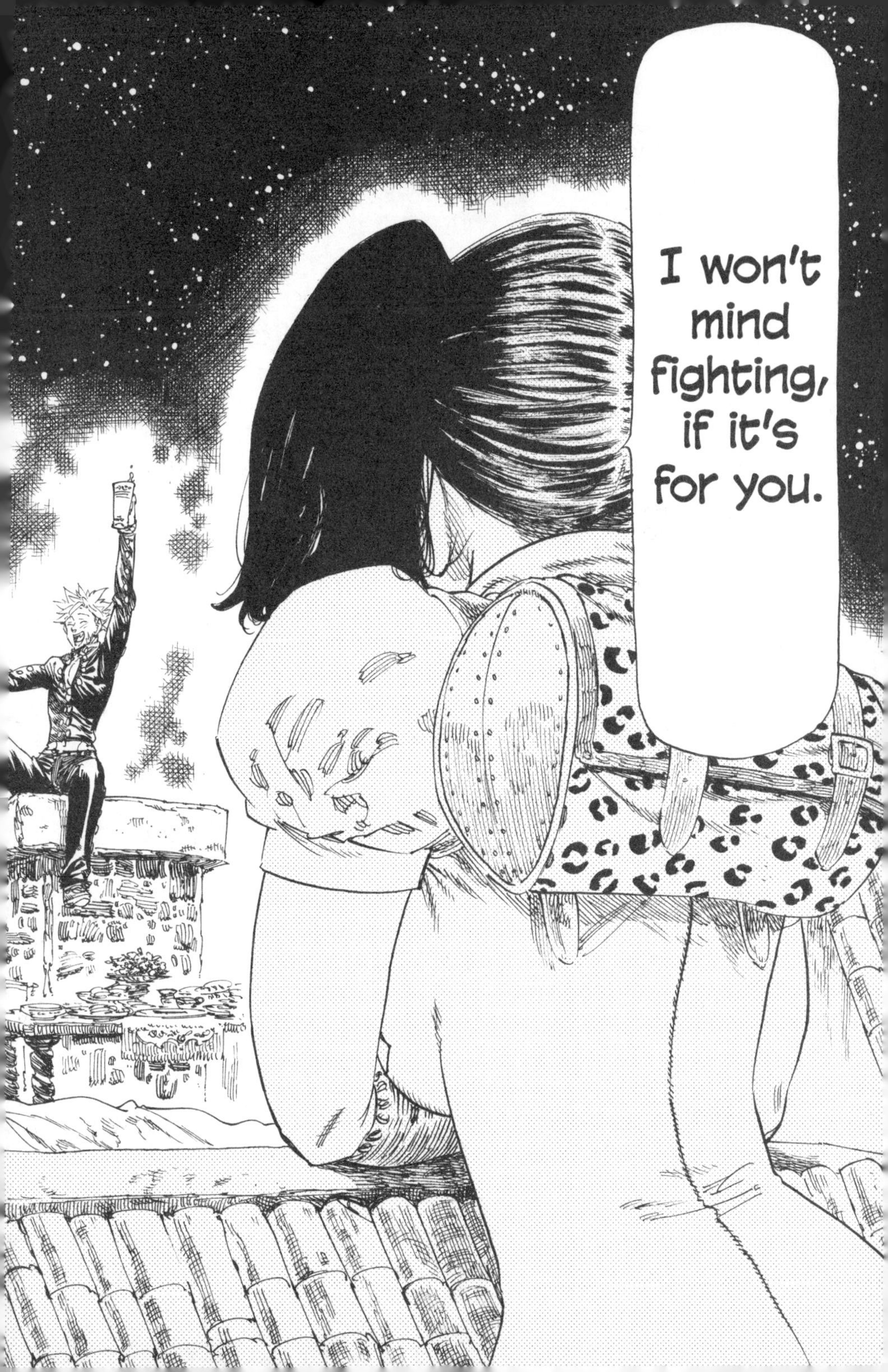
I won't mind fighting, if it's for you.

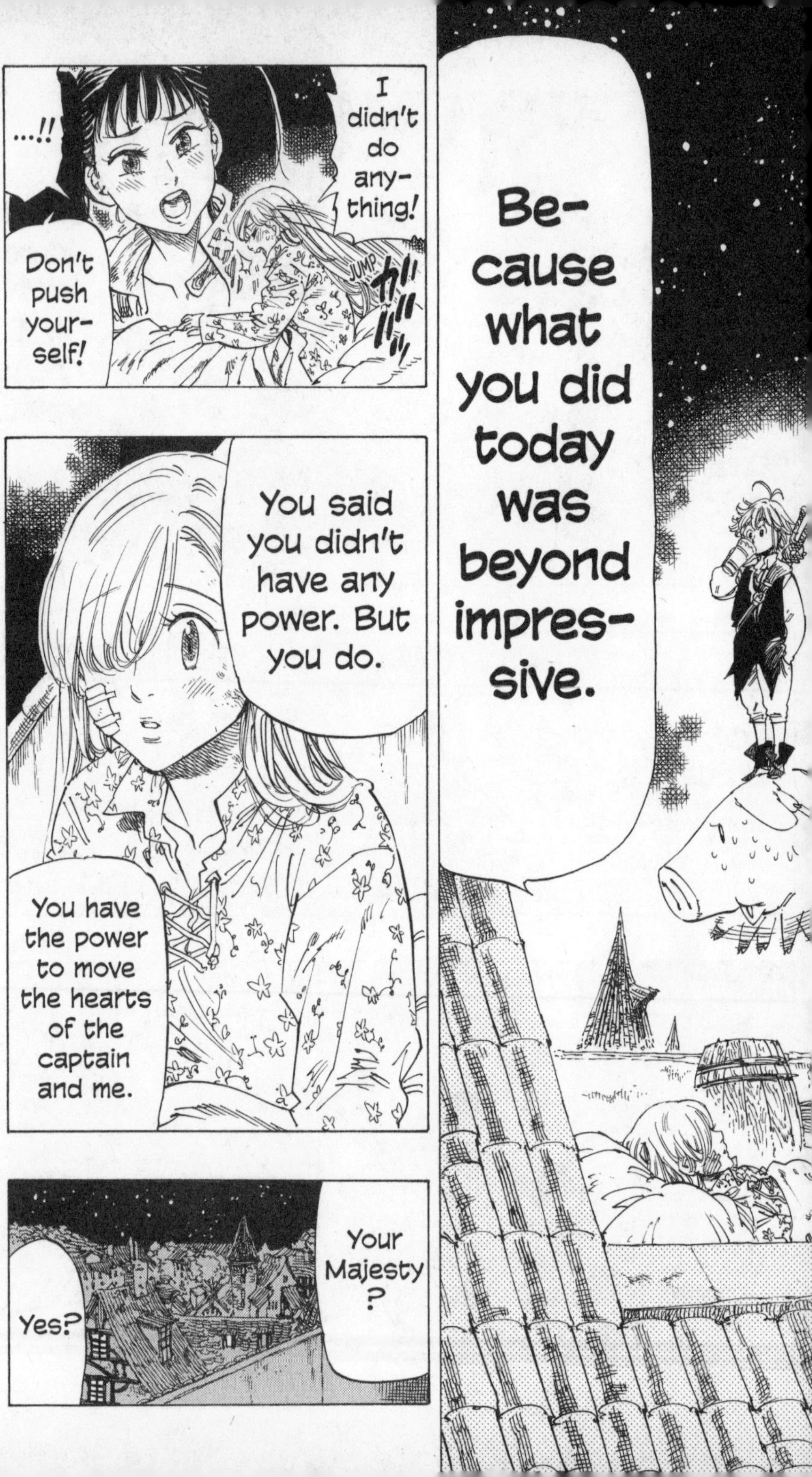
Be-cause what you did today was beyond impres-sive.
I didn't do any-thing!
...!!
Don't push your-self!
JUMP
You said you didn't have any power. But you do.
You have the power to move the hearts of the captain and me.
Your Majesty?
Yes?

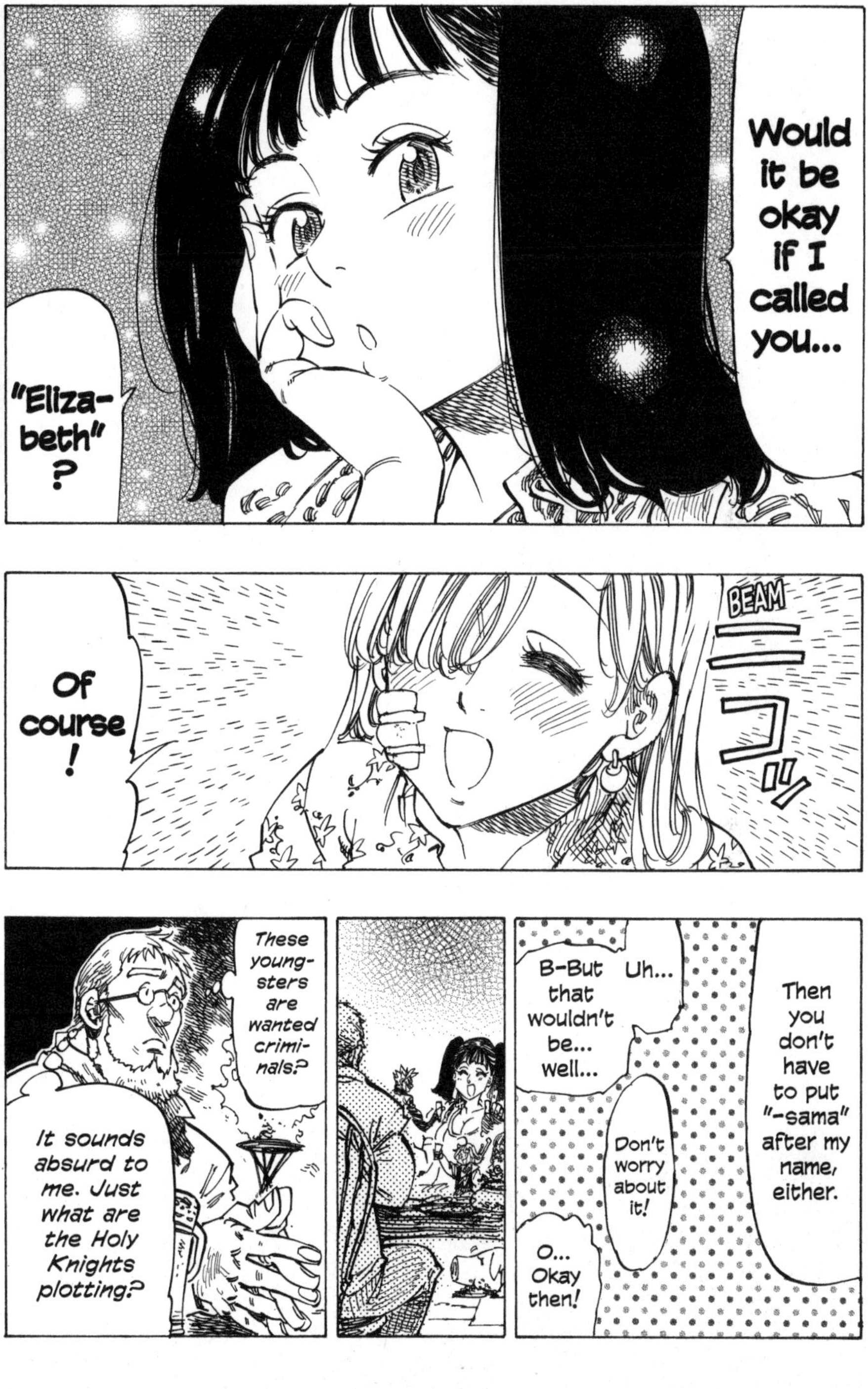
Would it be okay if I called you...
"Eliza-beth"?
BEAM
Of course!
Then you don't have to put "-sama" after my name, either.
Uh...
B-But that wouldn't be... well...
Don't worry about it!
O... Okay then!
These youngsters are wanted criminals?
It sounds absurd to me. Just what are the Holy Knights plotting?

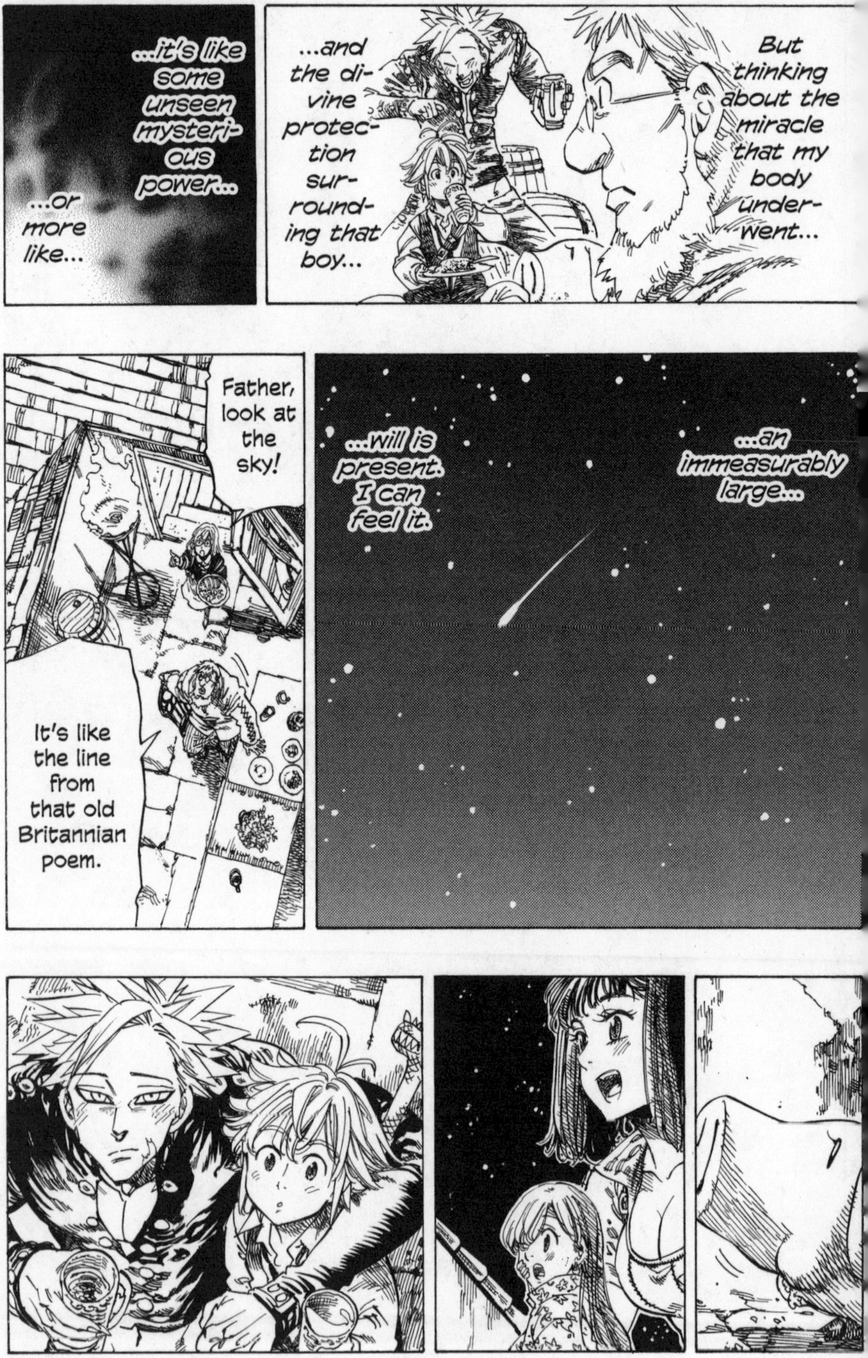
But thinking about the miracle that my body underwent...
...and the divine protection surrounding that boy...
...it's like some unseen mysterious power...
...or more like...
...an immeasurably large...
...will is present. I can feel it.
Father, look at the sky!
It's like the line from that old Britannian poem.

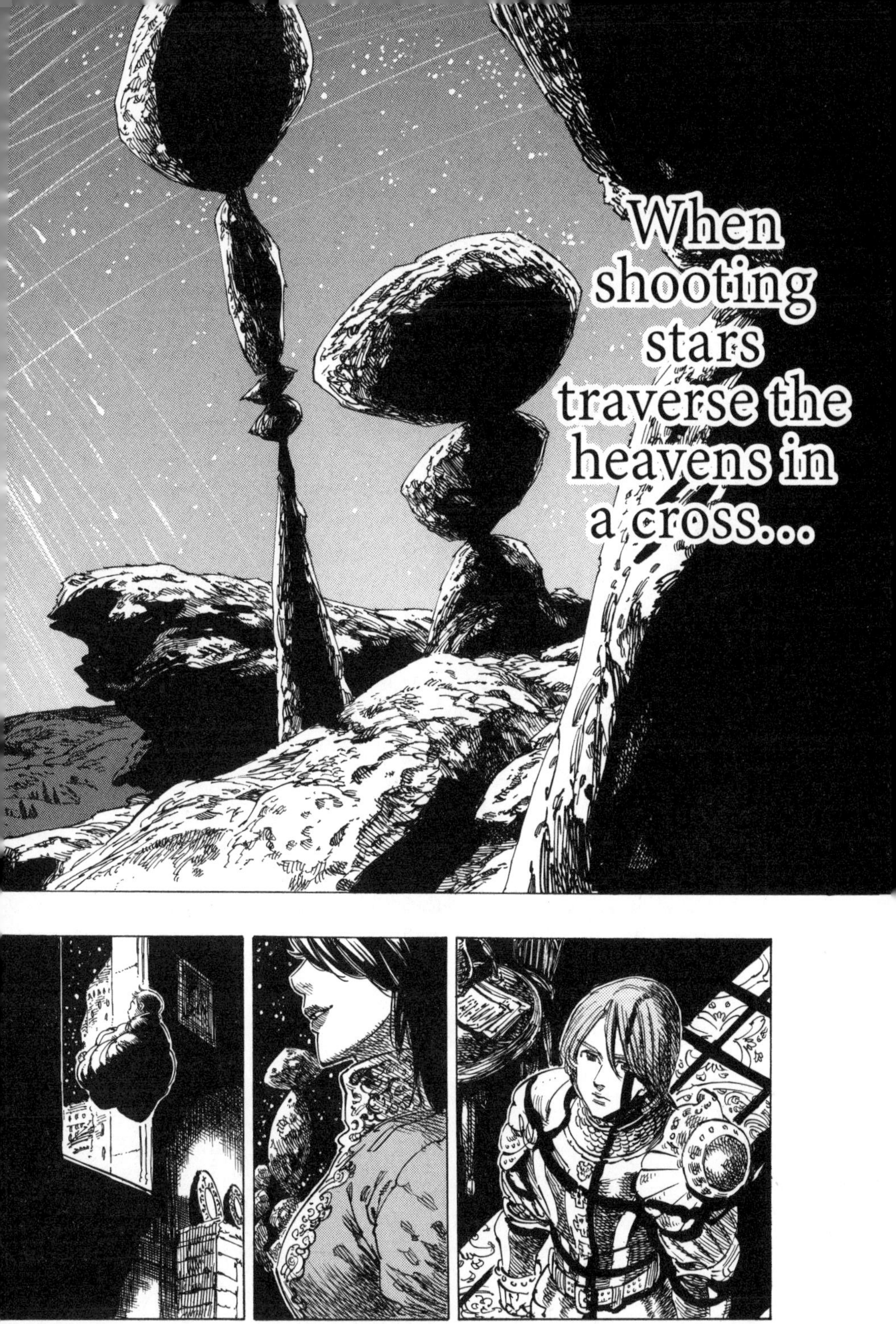
When shooting stars traverse the heavens in a cross...

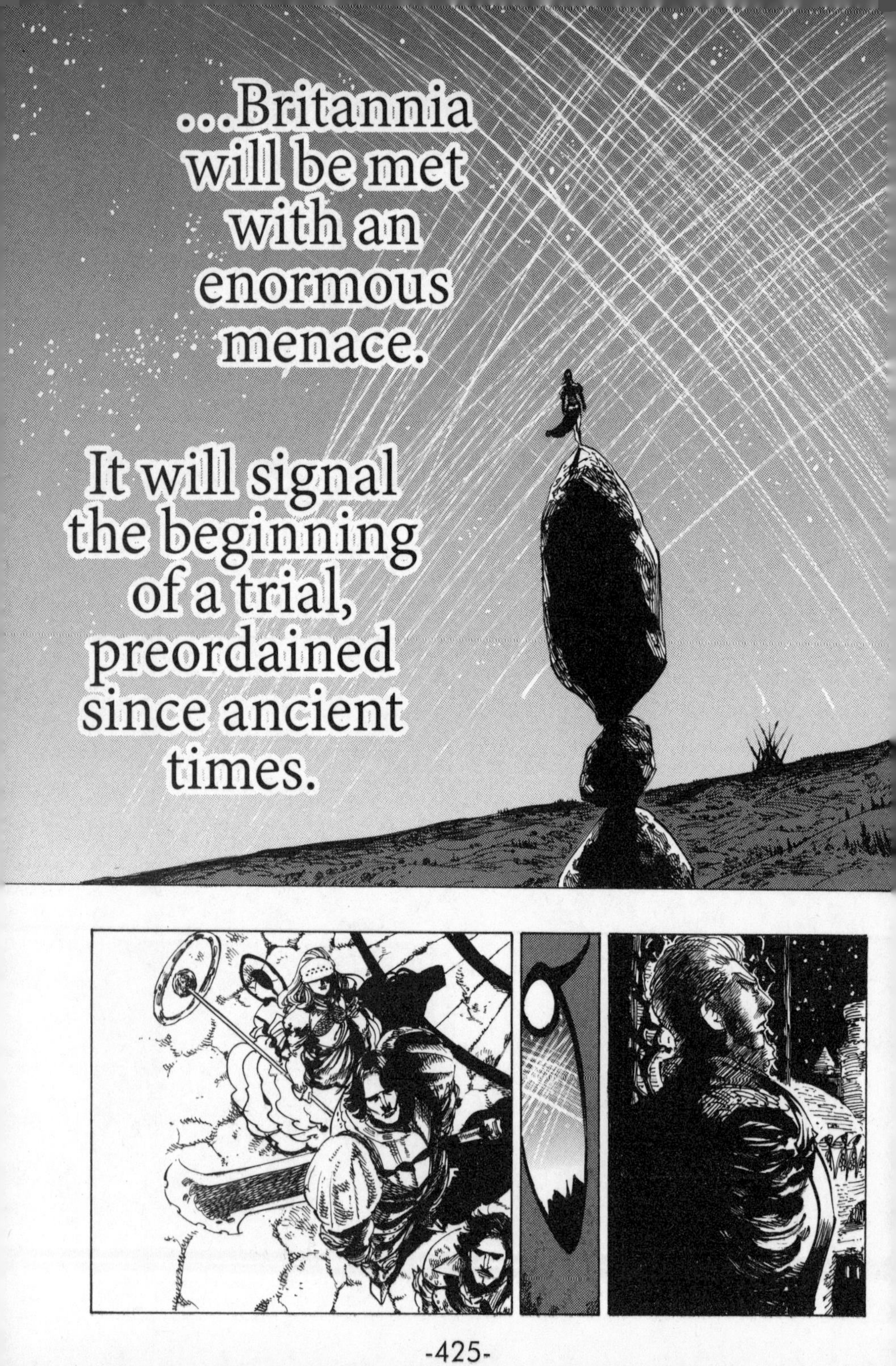
...Britannia will be met with an enormous menace.
It will signal the beginning of a trial, preordained since ancient times.

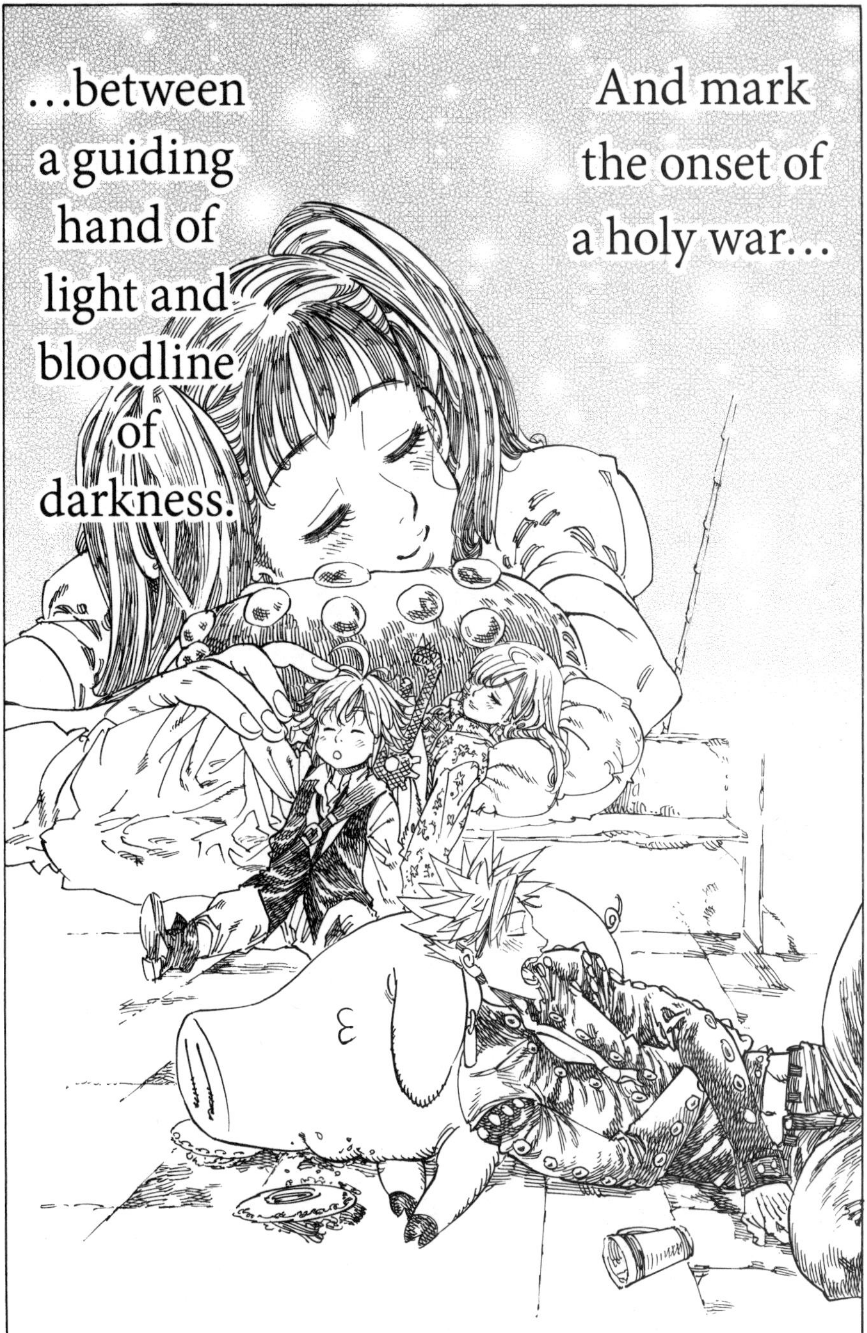
And mark the onset of a holy war…
…between a guiding hand of light and bloodline of darkness.

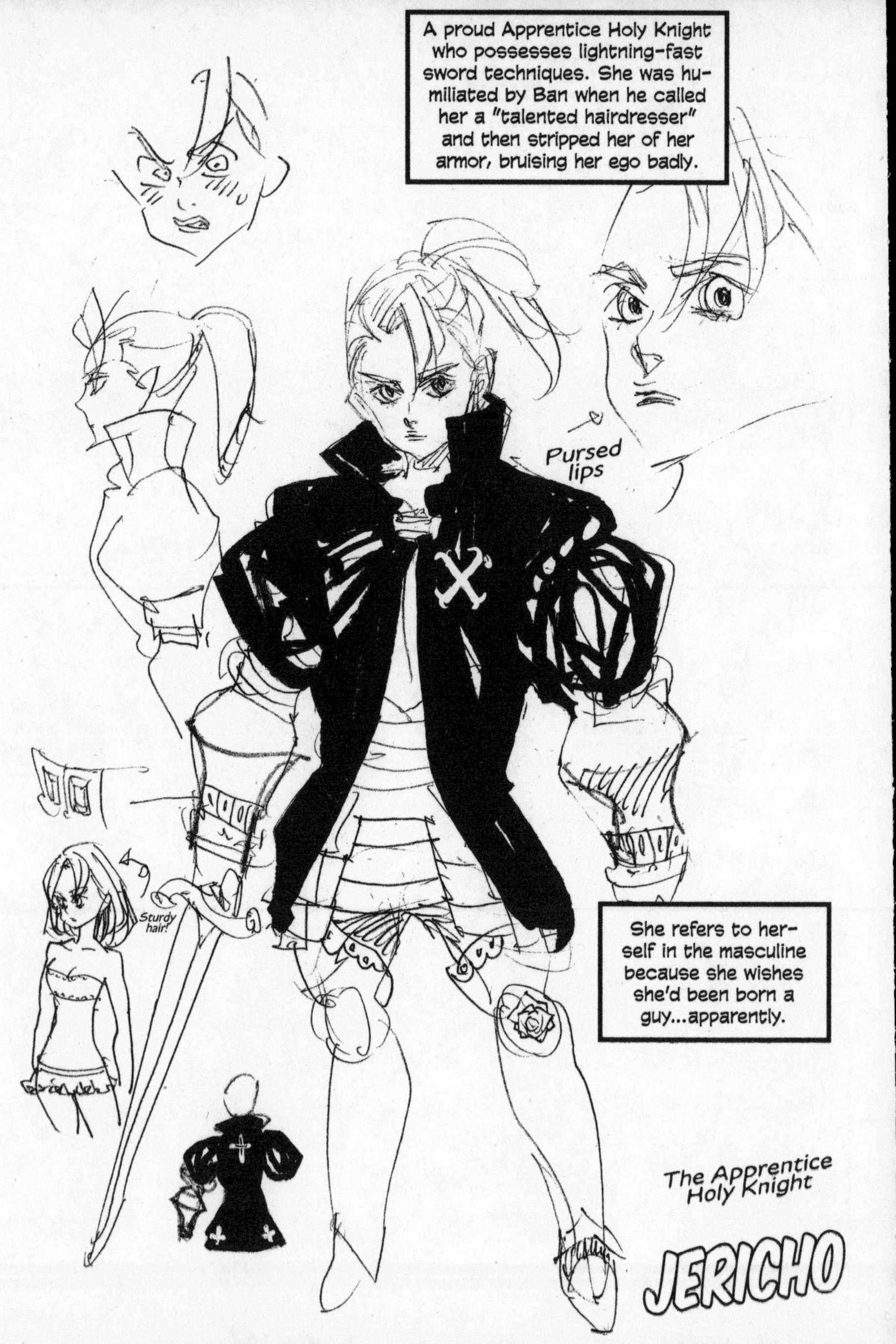
A proud Apprentice Holy Knight who possesses lightning-fast sword techniques. She was humiliated by Ban when he called her a "talented hairdresser" and then stripped her of her armor, bruising her ego badly.
Pursed lips
Sturdy hair!
She refers to herself in the masculine because she wishes she'd been born a guy...apparently.
The Apprentice Holy Knight
JERICHO

THE SEVEN DEADLY SINS

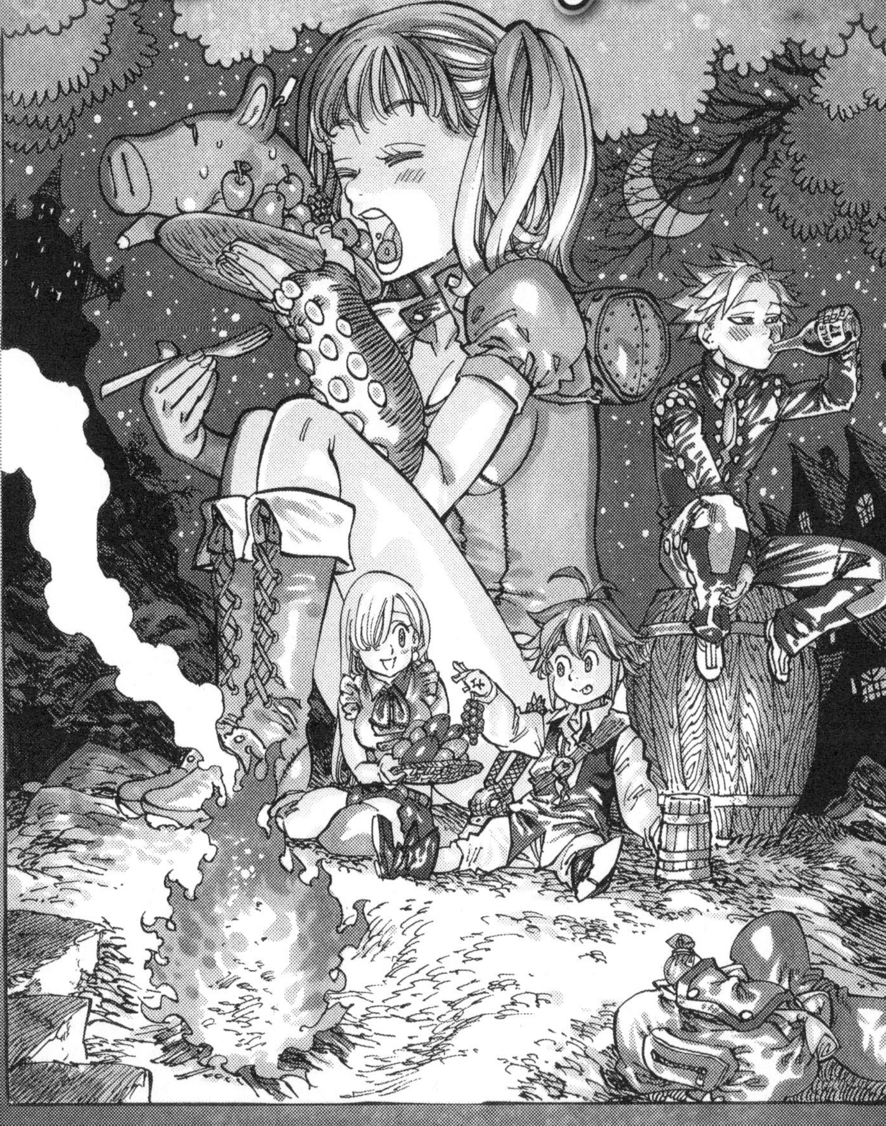

Chapter 17 - Storm's Brewing

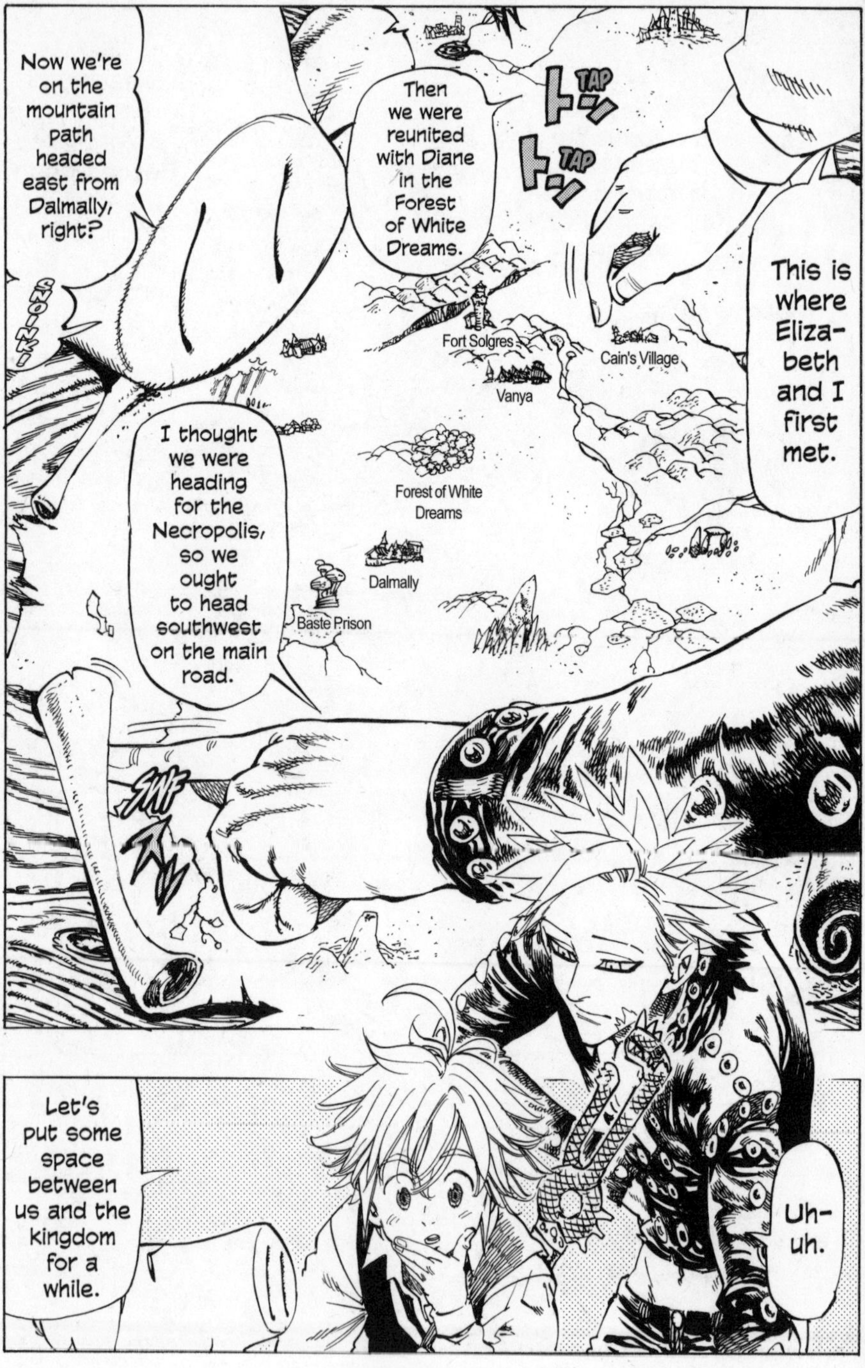
This is where Eliza-beth and I first met.
TAP
TAP
Then we were reunited with Diane in the Forest of White Dreams.
Now we're on the mountain path headed east from Dalmally, right?
SNOINK!
Fort Solgres
Cain's Village
Vanya
Forest of White Dreams
Dalmally
Baste Prison
I thought we were heading for the Necropolis, so we ought to head southwest on the main road.
SWF
Uh-uh.
Let's put some space between us and the kingdom for a while.

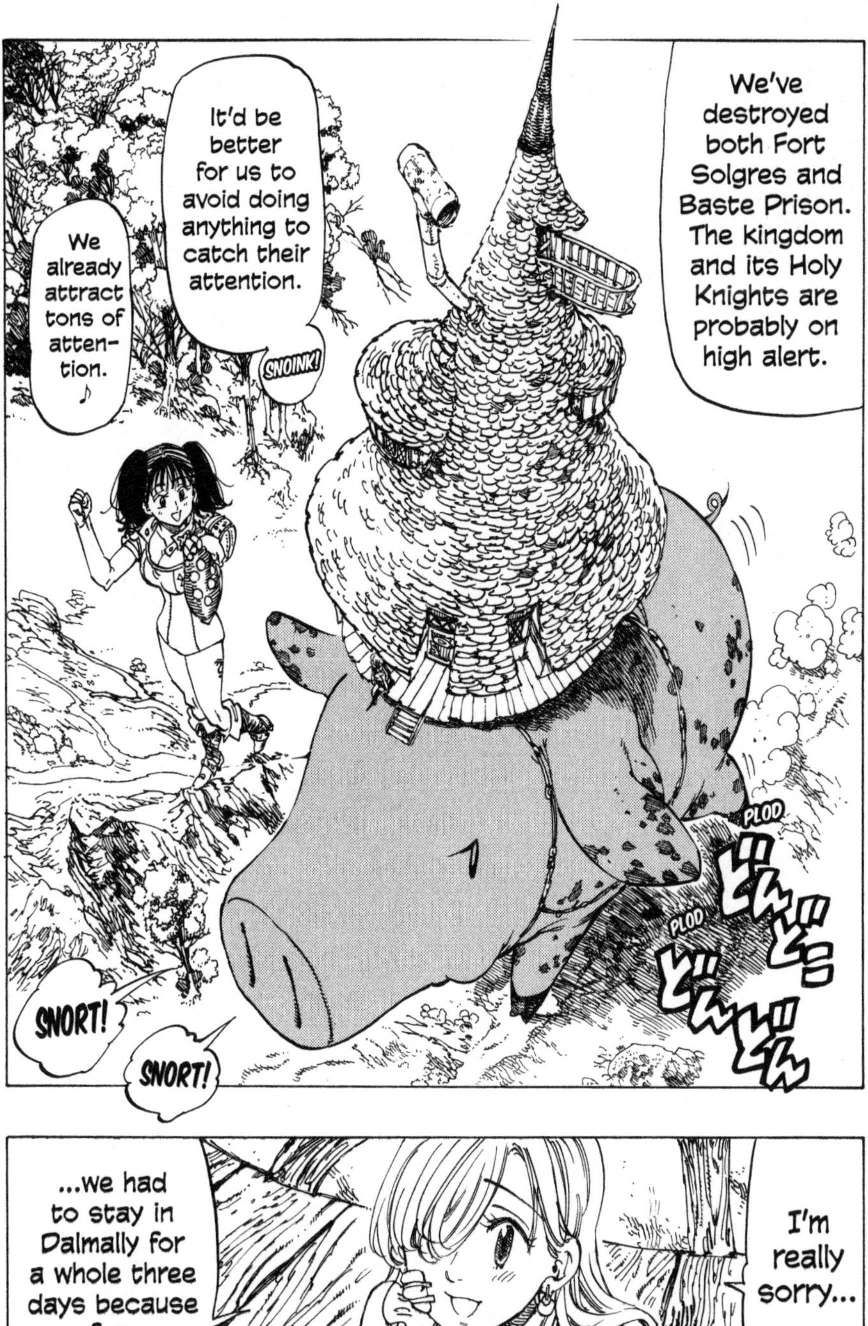
We've destroyed both Fort Solgres and Baste Prison. The kingdom and its Holy Knights are probably on high alert.
It'd be better for us to avoid doing anything to catch their attention.
SNOINK!
We already attract tons of atten-tion. ♪
PLOD
PLOD
SNORT!
SNORT!
I'm really sorry...
...we had to stay in Dalmally for a whole three days because of me.

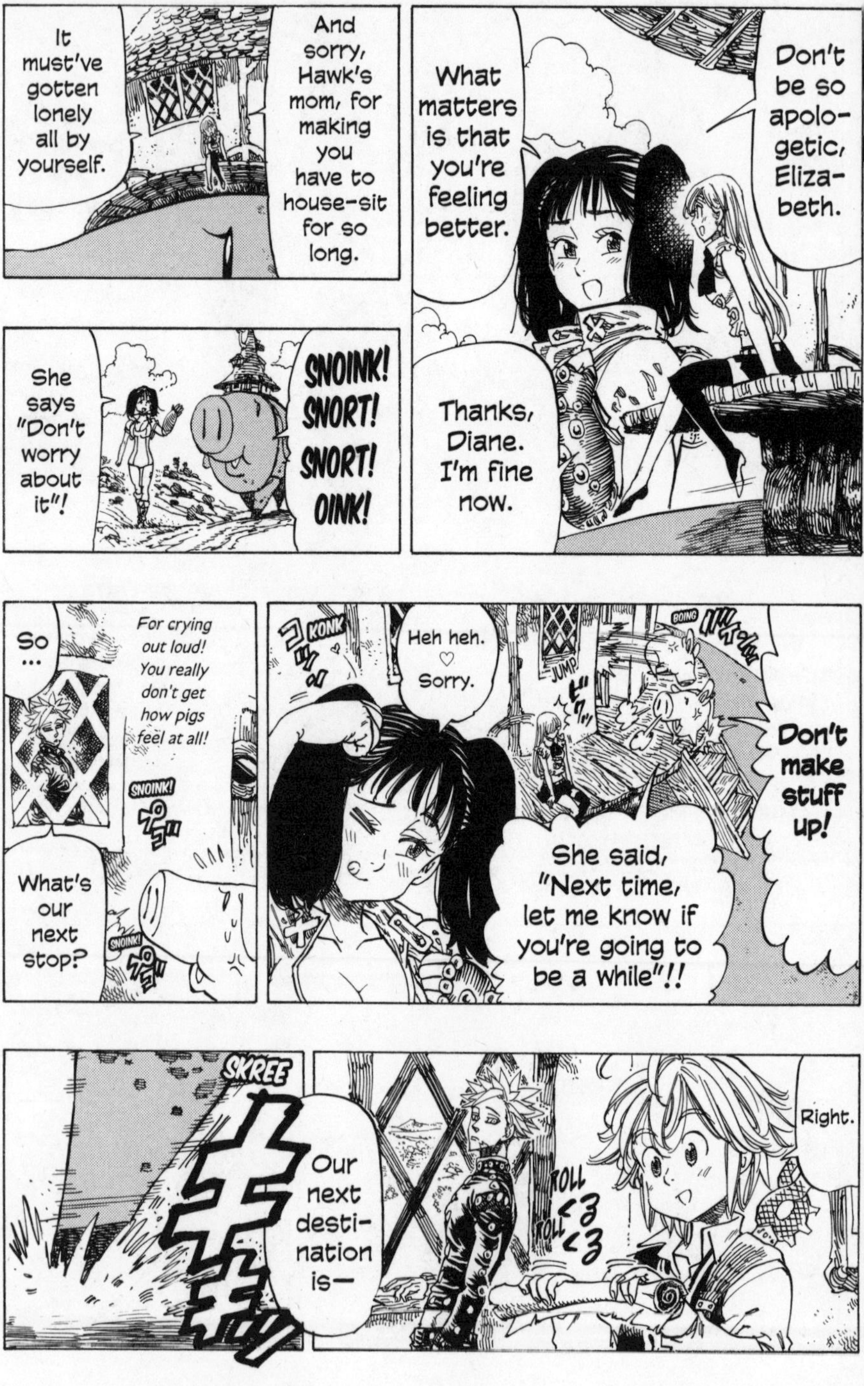
Don't be so apologetic, Elizabeth.
What matters is that you're feeling better.
Thanks, Diane. I'm fine now.
And sorry, Hawk's mom, for making you have to house-sit for so long.
It must've gotten lonely all by yourself.
SNOINK! SNORT! SNORT! OINK!
She says "Don't worry about it"!
Don't make stuff up!
BOING
JUMP
Heh heh. ♡ Sorry.
KONK
She said, "Next time, let me know if you're going to be a while"!!
So ...
For crying out loud! You really don't get how pigs feel at all!
SNOINK!
What's our next stop?
SNOINK!
Right.
ROLL
ROLL
SKREE
Our next destination is—

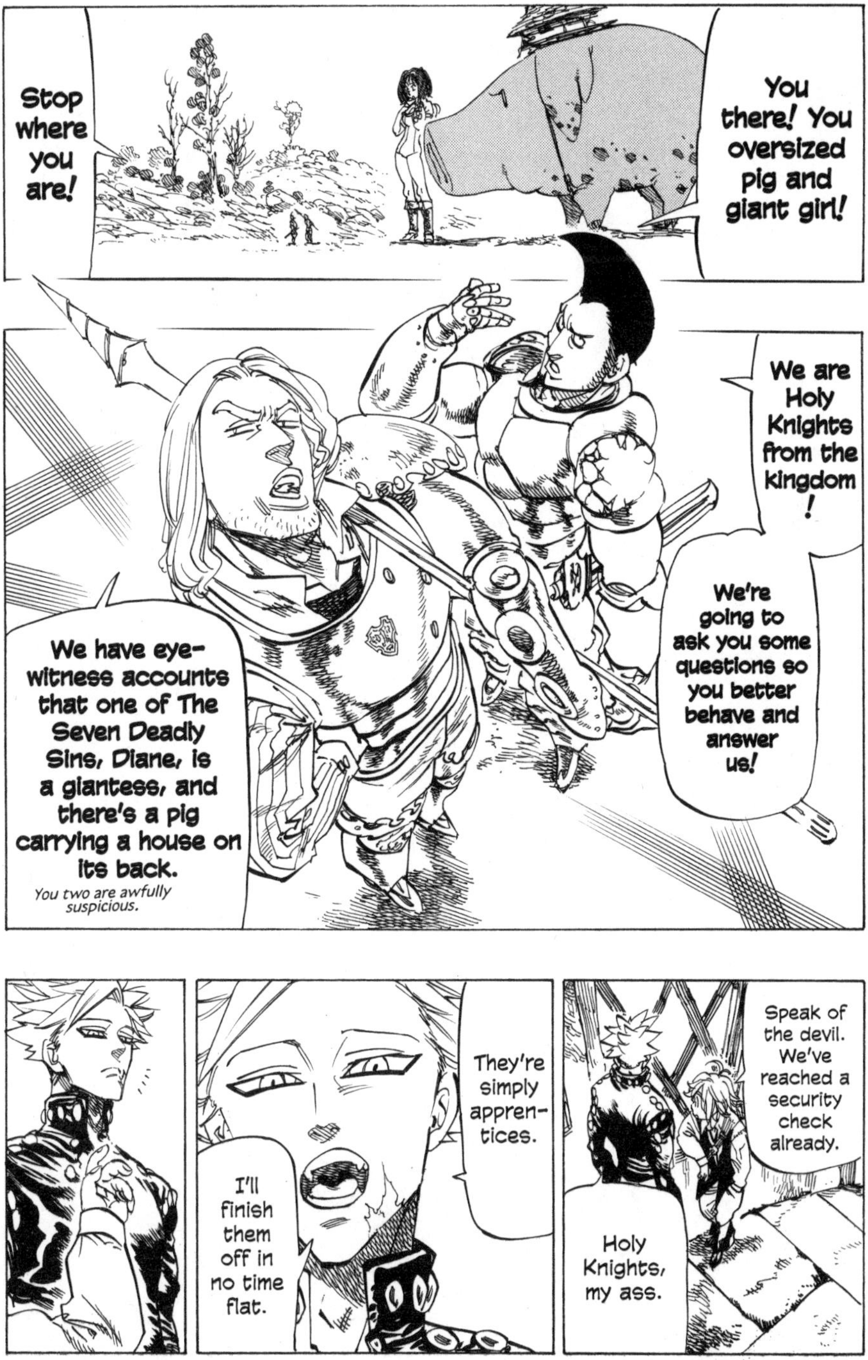
You there! You oversized pig and giant girl!
Stop where you are!
We are Holy Knights from the kingdom!
We're going to ask you some questions so you better behave and answer us!
We have eye-witness accounts that one of The Seven Deadly Sins, Diane, is a giantess, and there's a pig carrying a house on its back.
You two are awfully suspicious.
Speak of the devil. We've reached a security check already.
Holy Knights, my ass.
They're simply apprentices.
I'll finish them off in no time flat.

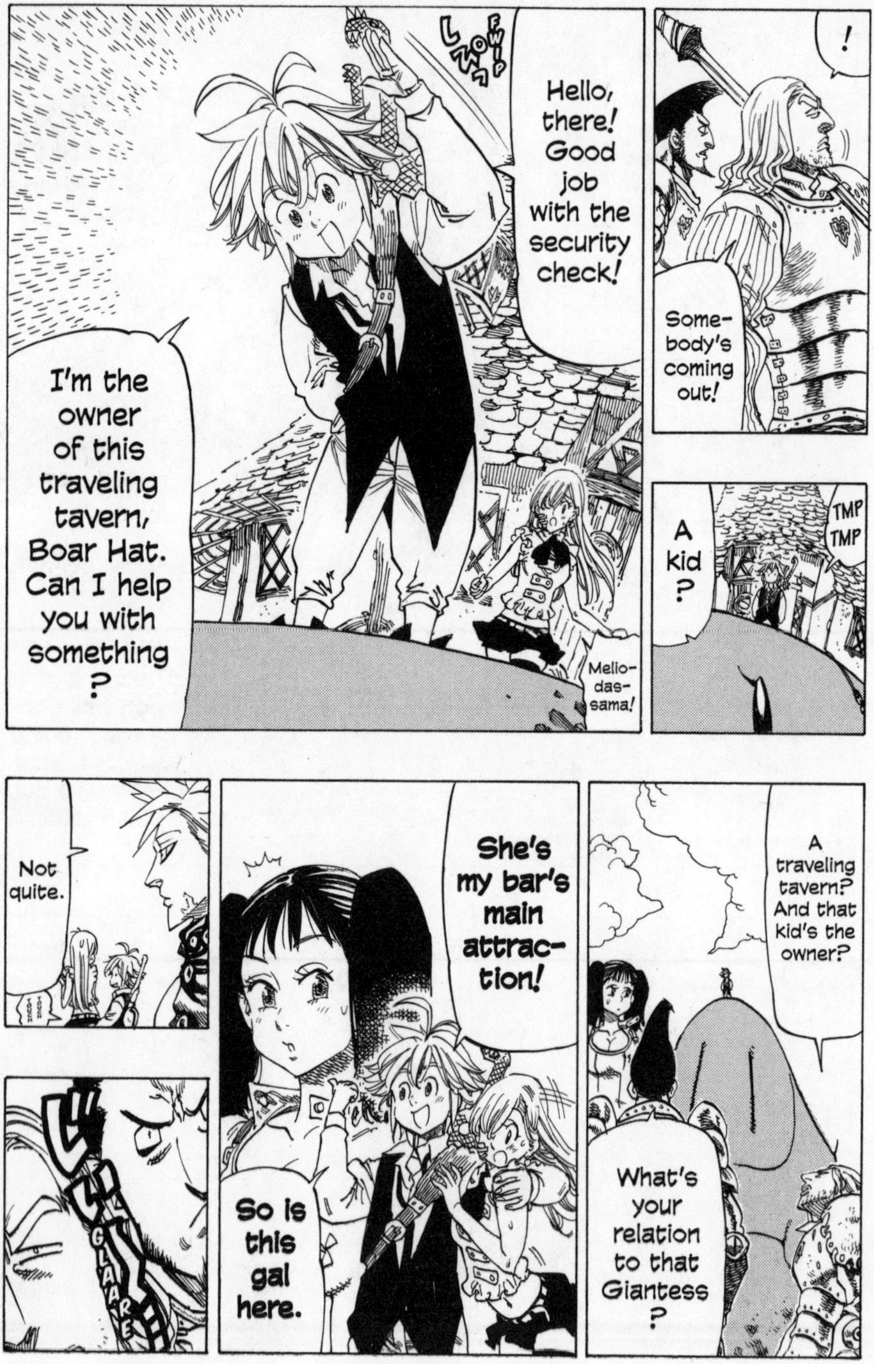
!
Some-body's coming out!
TMP TMP
A kid?
FWIP
Hello, there! Good job with the security check!
I'm the owner of this traveling tavern, Boar Hat. Can I help you with something?
Melio-das-sama!
A traveling tavern? And that kid's the owner?
What's your relation to that Giantess?
She's my bar's main attrac-tion!
So is this gal here.
Not quite.
TOUCH TOUCH
GLAARE

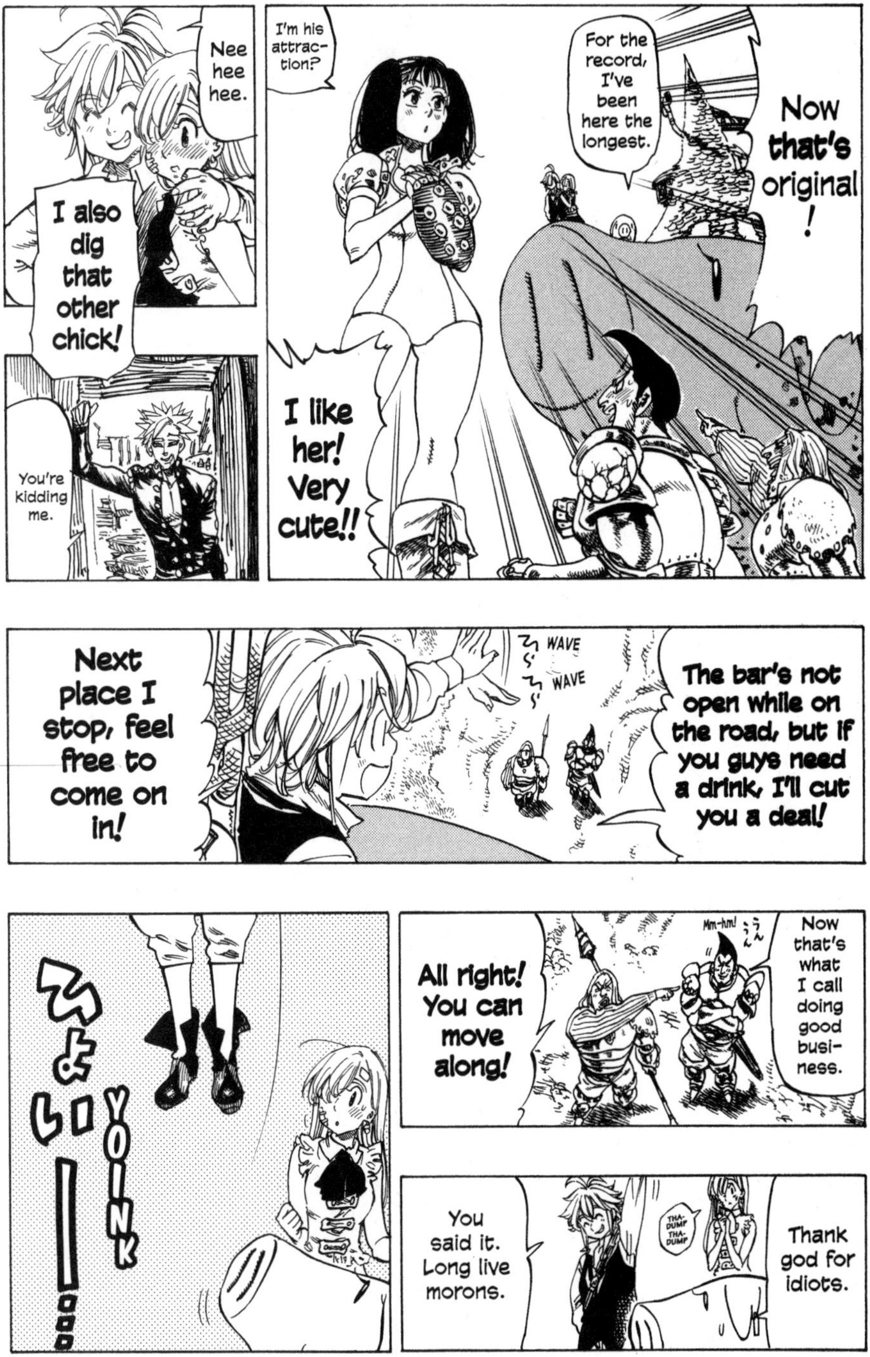
For the record, I've been here the longest.
Now that's original!
I'm his attraction?
I like her! Very cute!!
Nee hee hee.
I also dig that other chick!
You're kidding me.
The bar's not open while on the road, but if you guys need a drink, I'll cut you a deal!
WAVE
WAVE
Next place I stop, feel free to come on in!
Now that's what I call doing good business.
Mm-hm!
All right! You can move along!
Thank god for idiots.
THA-DUMP THA-DUMP
You said it. Long live morons.
YOINK

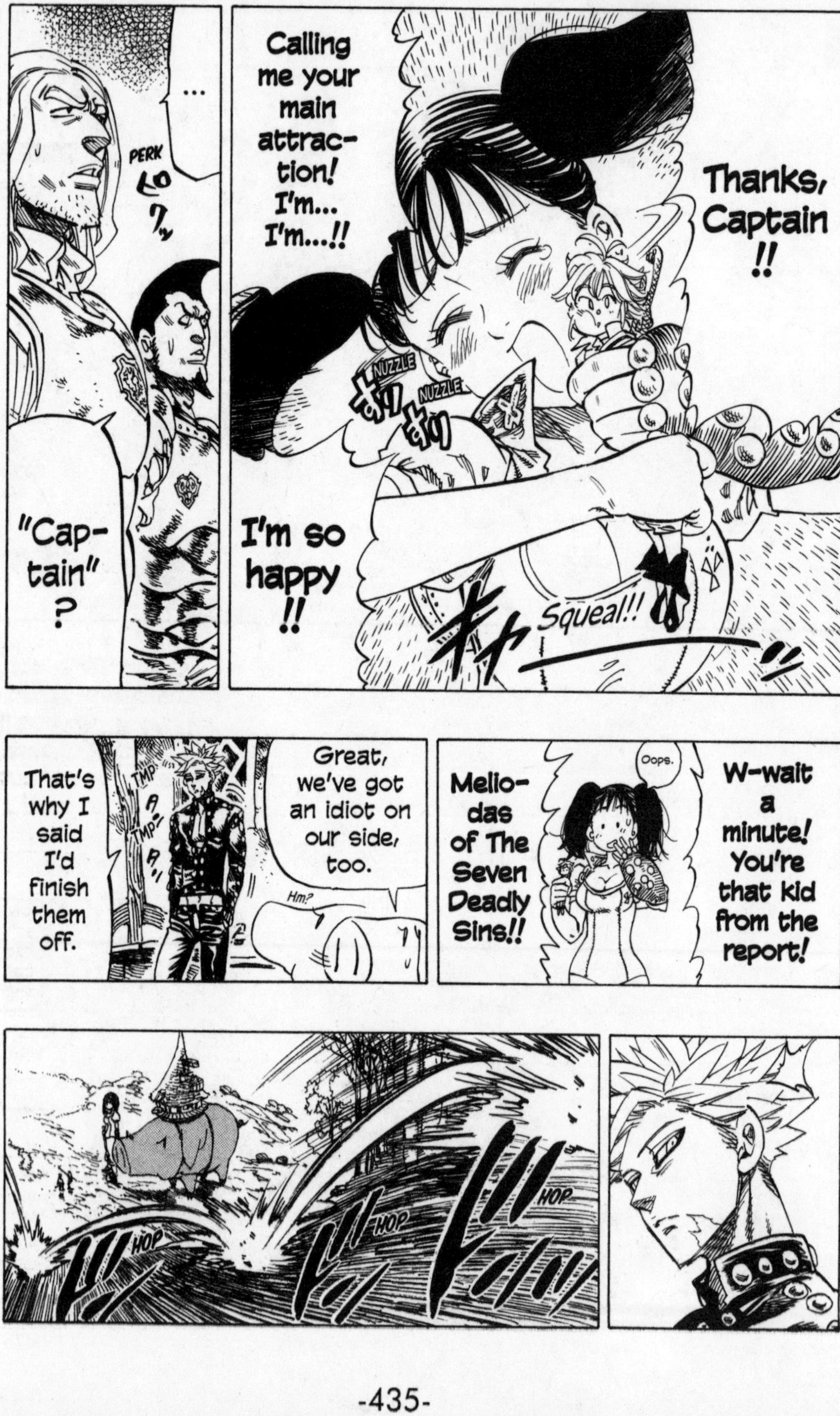

Thanks, Captain!!
Calling me your main attraction! I'm... I'm...!!
NUZZLE
NUZZLE
I'm so happy!!
Squeal!!
...
PERK
"Captain"?
W-wait a minute! You're that kid from the report!
Oops.
Meliodas of The Seven Deadly Sins!!
Great, we've got an idiot on our side, too.
Hm?
That's why I said I'd finish them off.
TMP
TMP
HOP
HOP
HOP

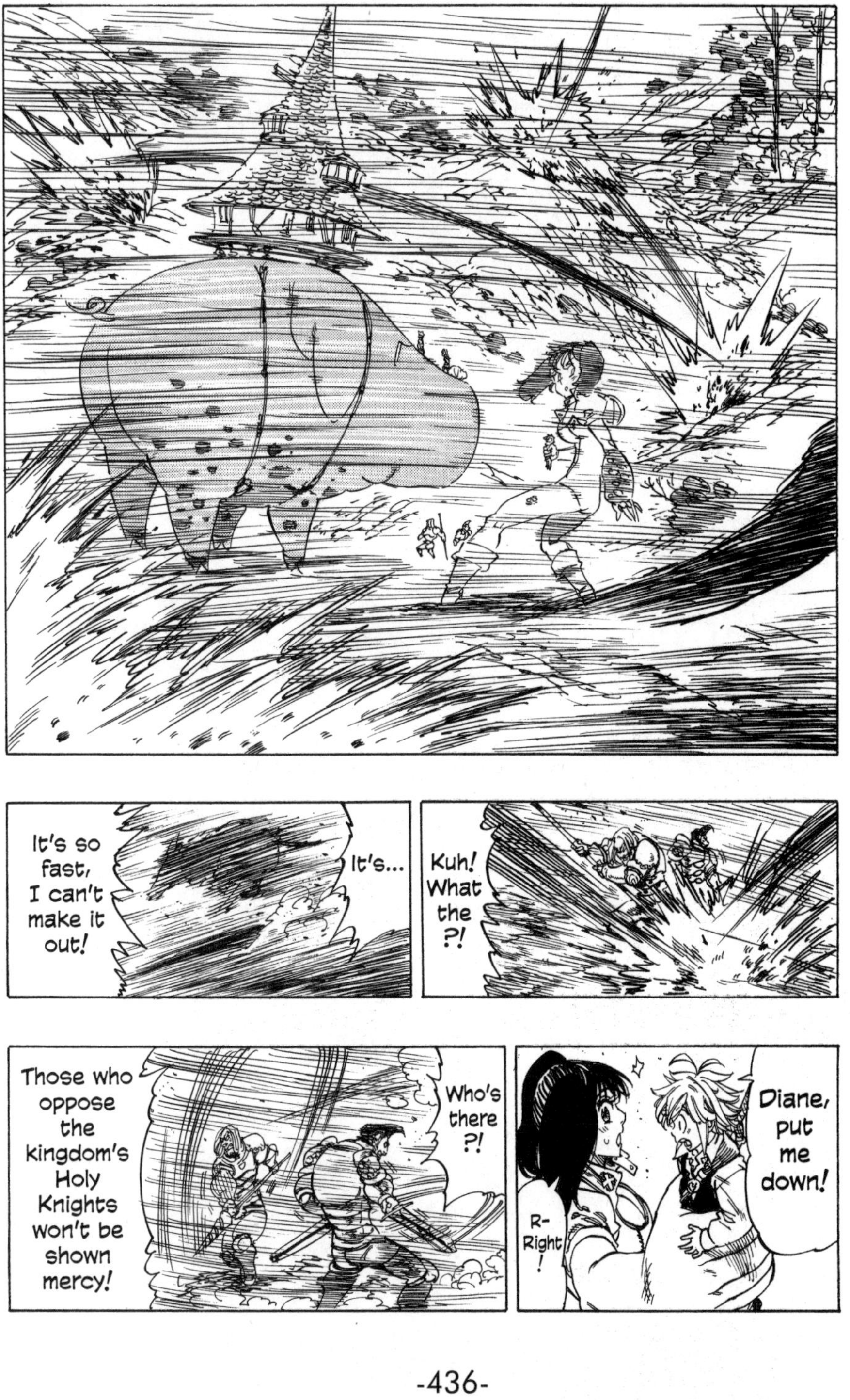
Kuh! What the ?!
It's...
It's so fast, I can't make it out!
Diane, put me down!
R-Right!
Who's there ?!
Those who oppose the kingdom's Holy Knights won't be shown mercy!

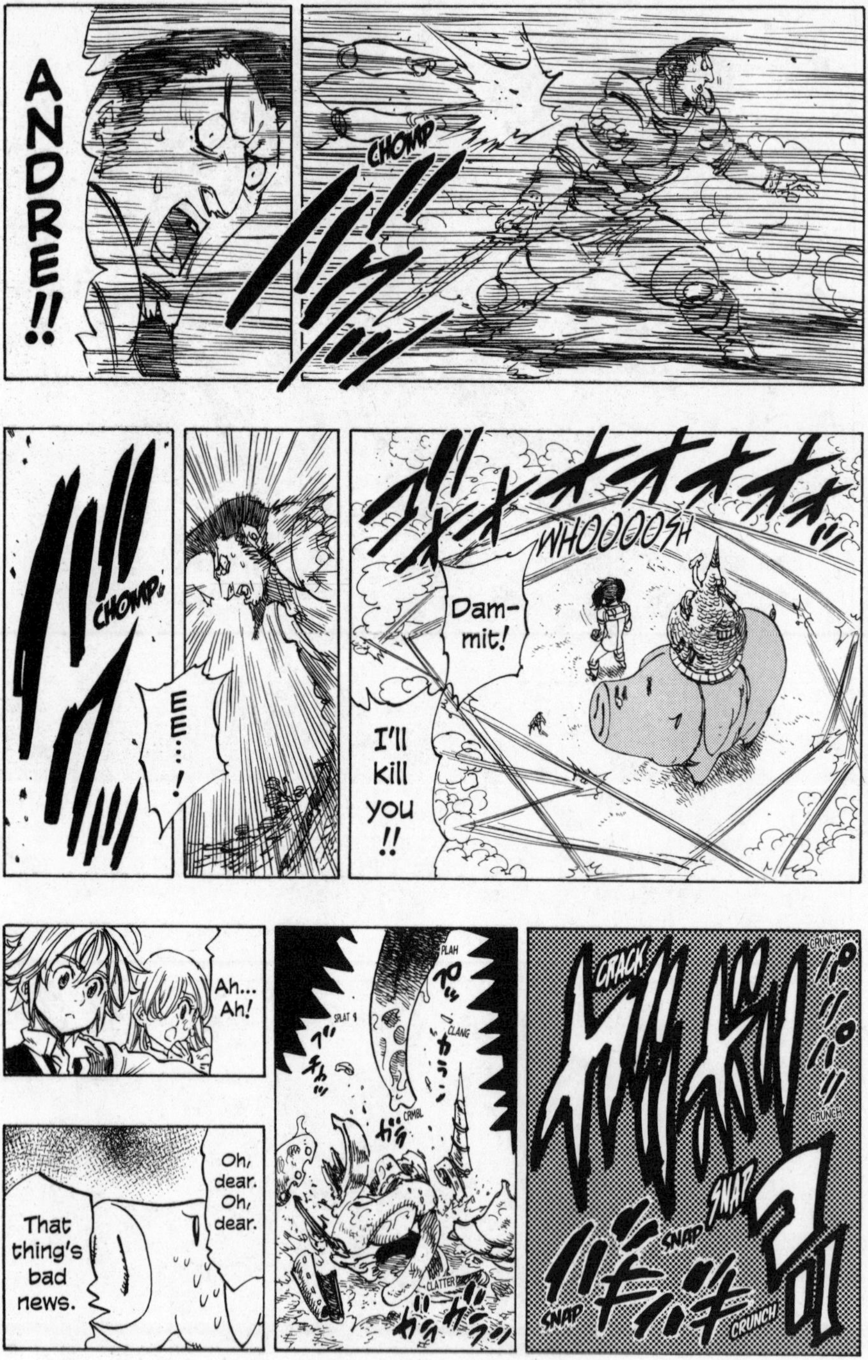
CHOMP
ANDRE!!
WHOOOOSH
Dam-mit!
I'll kill you!!
EE...!
CHOMP
CRACK
CRUNCH
CRUNCH
SNAP
SNAP
SNAP
CRUNCH
PLAH
SPLAT
CLANG
CRMBL
CLATTER
Ah... Ah!
Oh, dear. Oh, dear.
That thing's bad news.

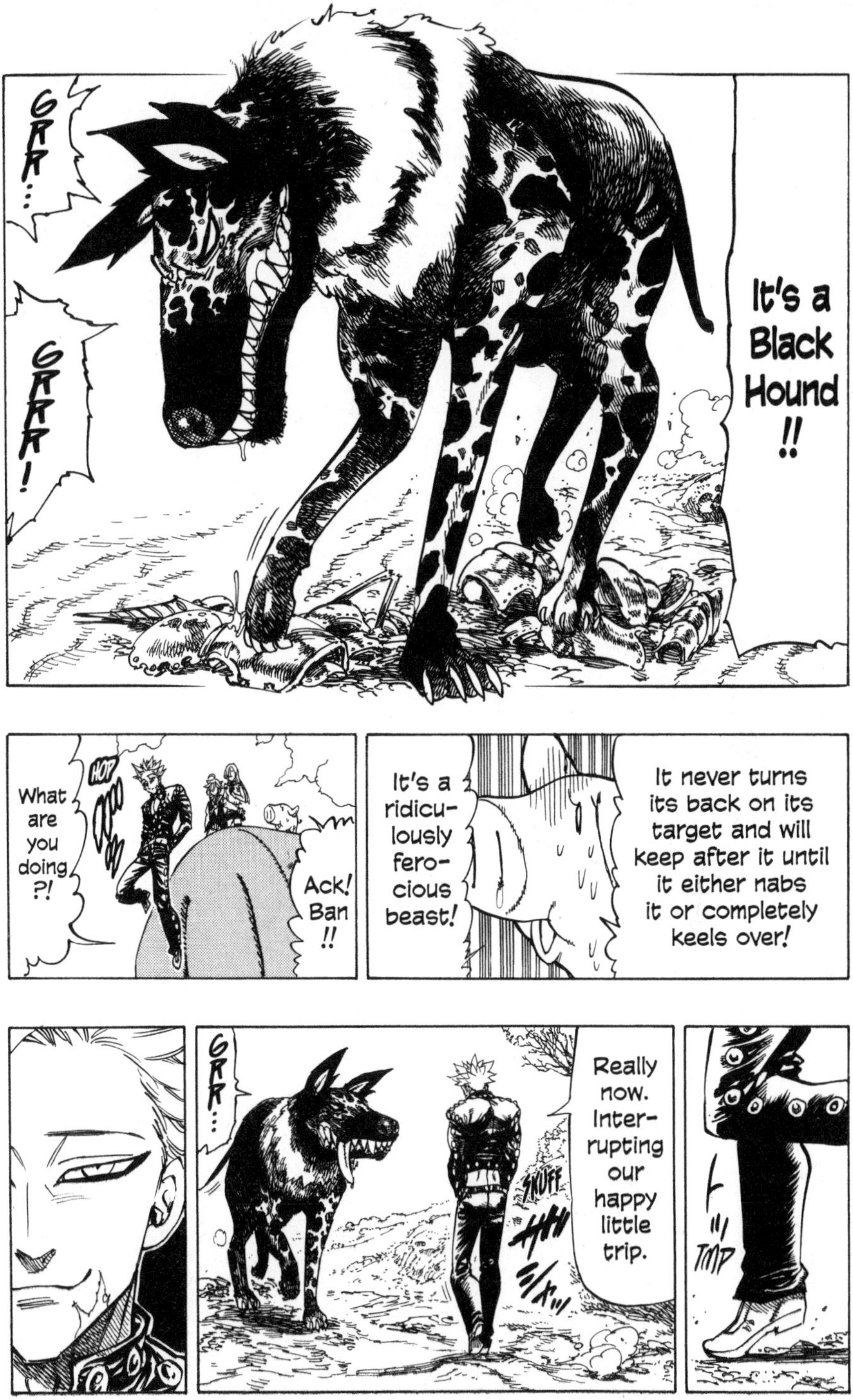
It's a Black Hound!!
GRR...
GRRR!
It never turns its back on its target and will keep after it until it either nabs it or completely keels over!
It's a ridiculously ferocious beast!
Ack! Ban!!
HOP
What are you doing?!
TMP
Really now. Interrupting our happy little trip.
SNUFF
GRR...

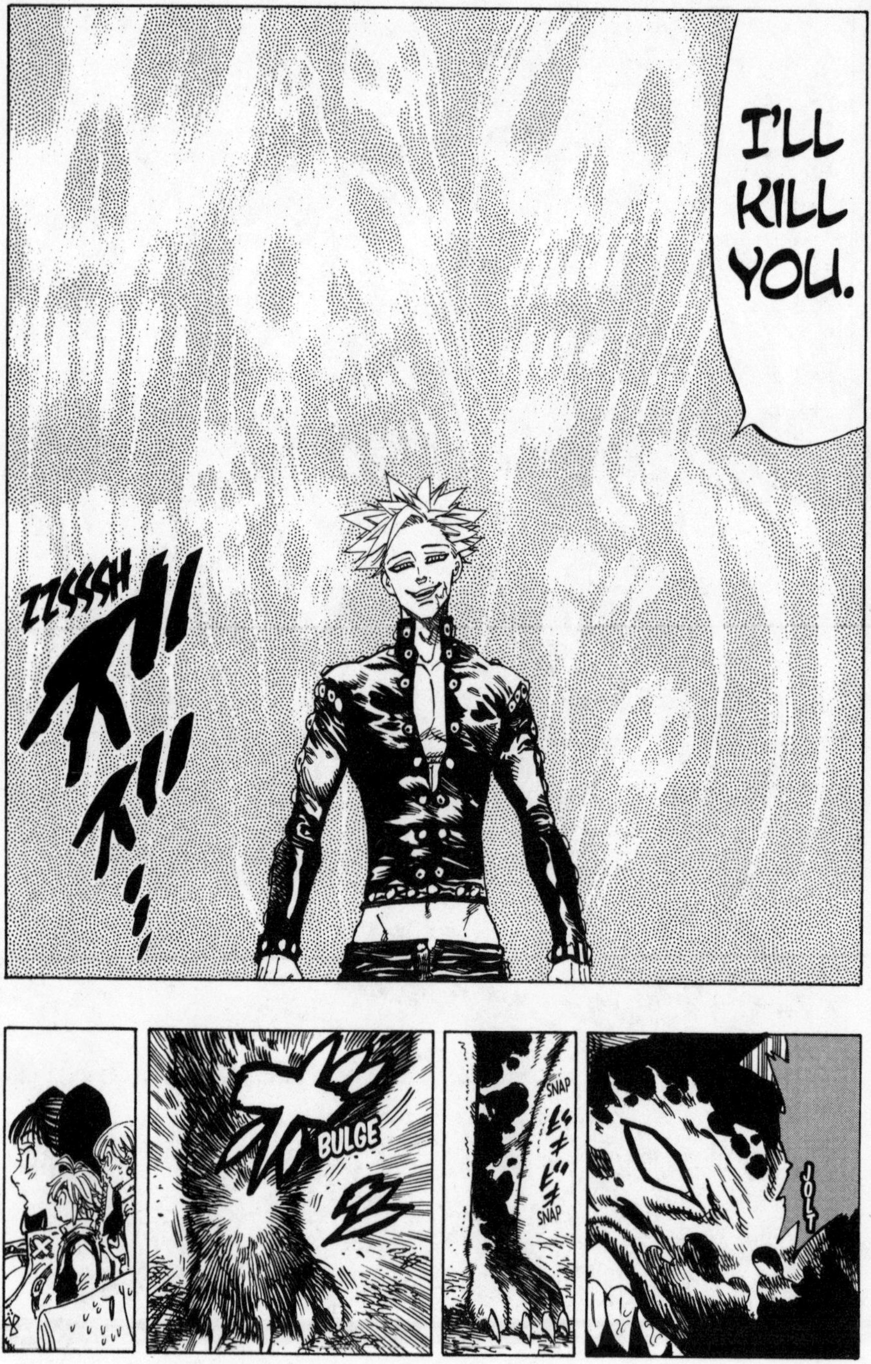
I'LL KILL YOU.
ZZSSSH
JOLT
SNAP
SNAP
BULGE

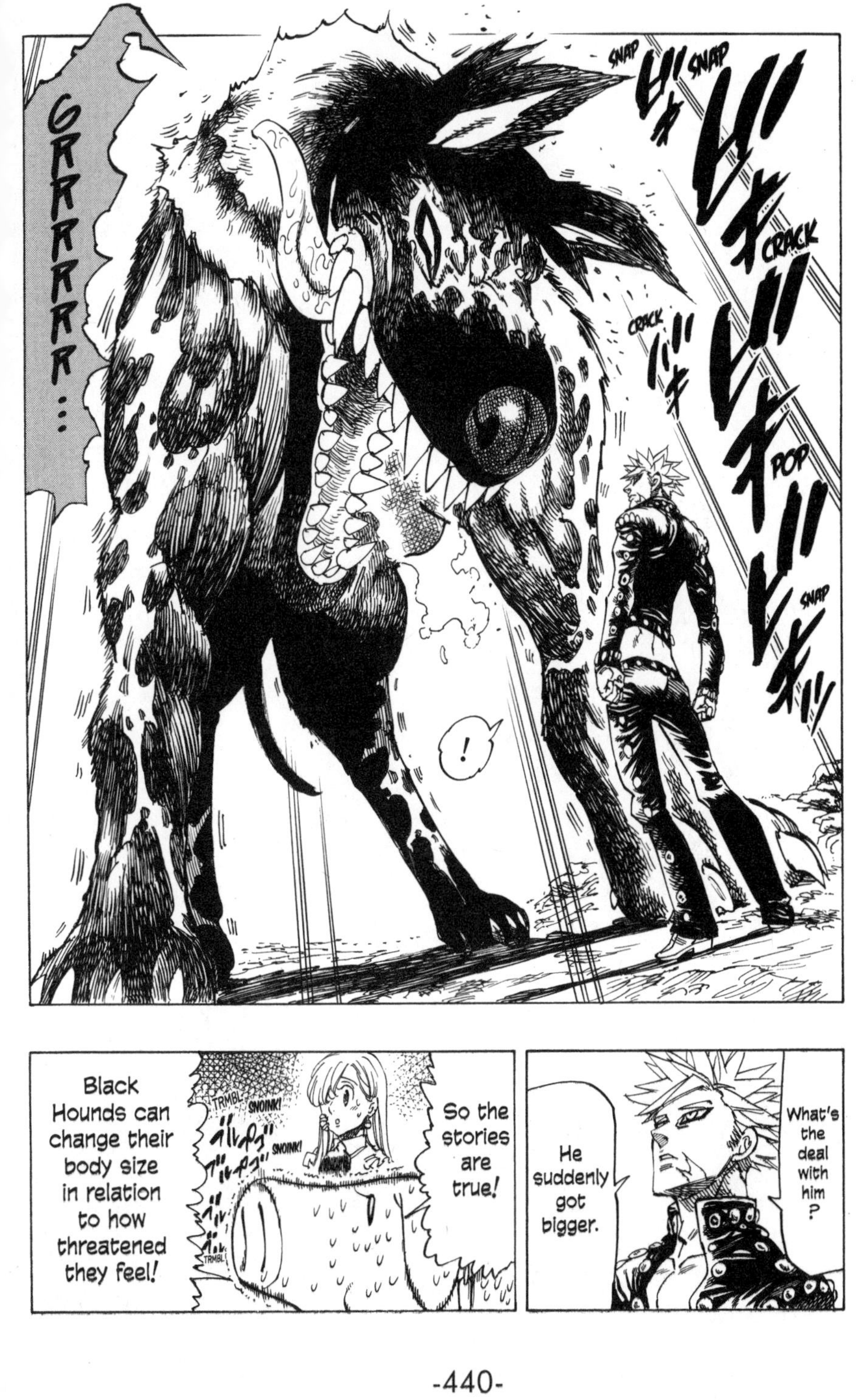
SNAP
SNAP
CRACK
CRACK
POP
SNAP
GRRRRRRR...
!
What's the deal with him?
He suddenly got bigger.
So the stories are true!
TRMBL
SNOINK!
SNOINK!
TRMBL
Black Hounds can change their body size in relation to how threatened they feel!

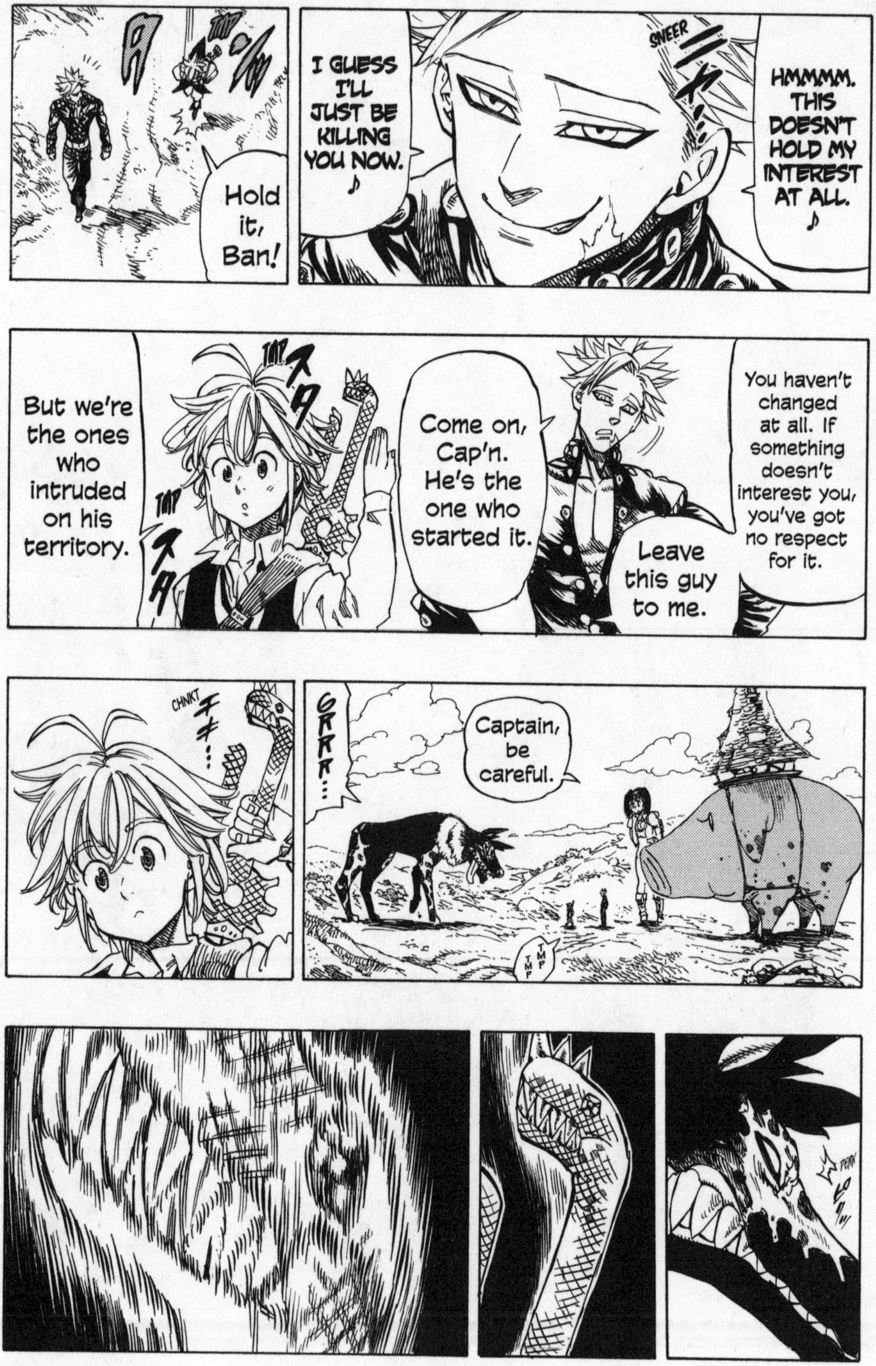
SWEER
HMMMM. THIS DOESN'T HOLD MY INTEREST AT ALL. ♪
I GUESS I'LL JUST BE KILLING YOU NOW. ♪
Hold it, Ban!
TAP
You haven't changed at all. If something doesn't interest you, you've got no respect for it.
Leave this guy to me.
Come on, Cap'n. He's the one who started it.
TAP
TAP
But we're the ones who intruded on his territory.
Captain, be careful.
TMP TMP
CHNKT
PERK

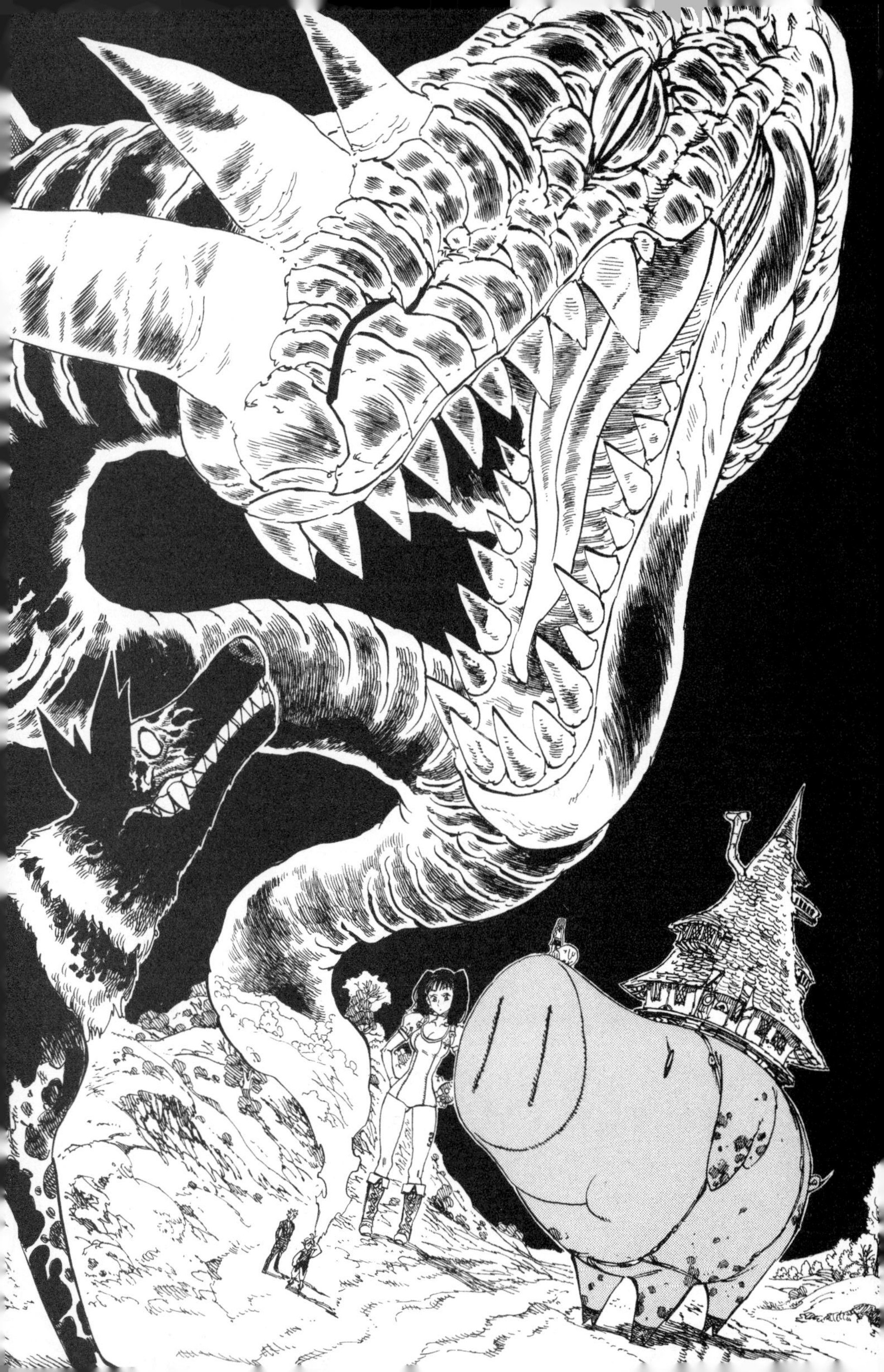

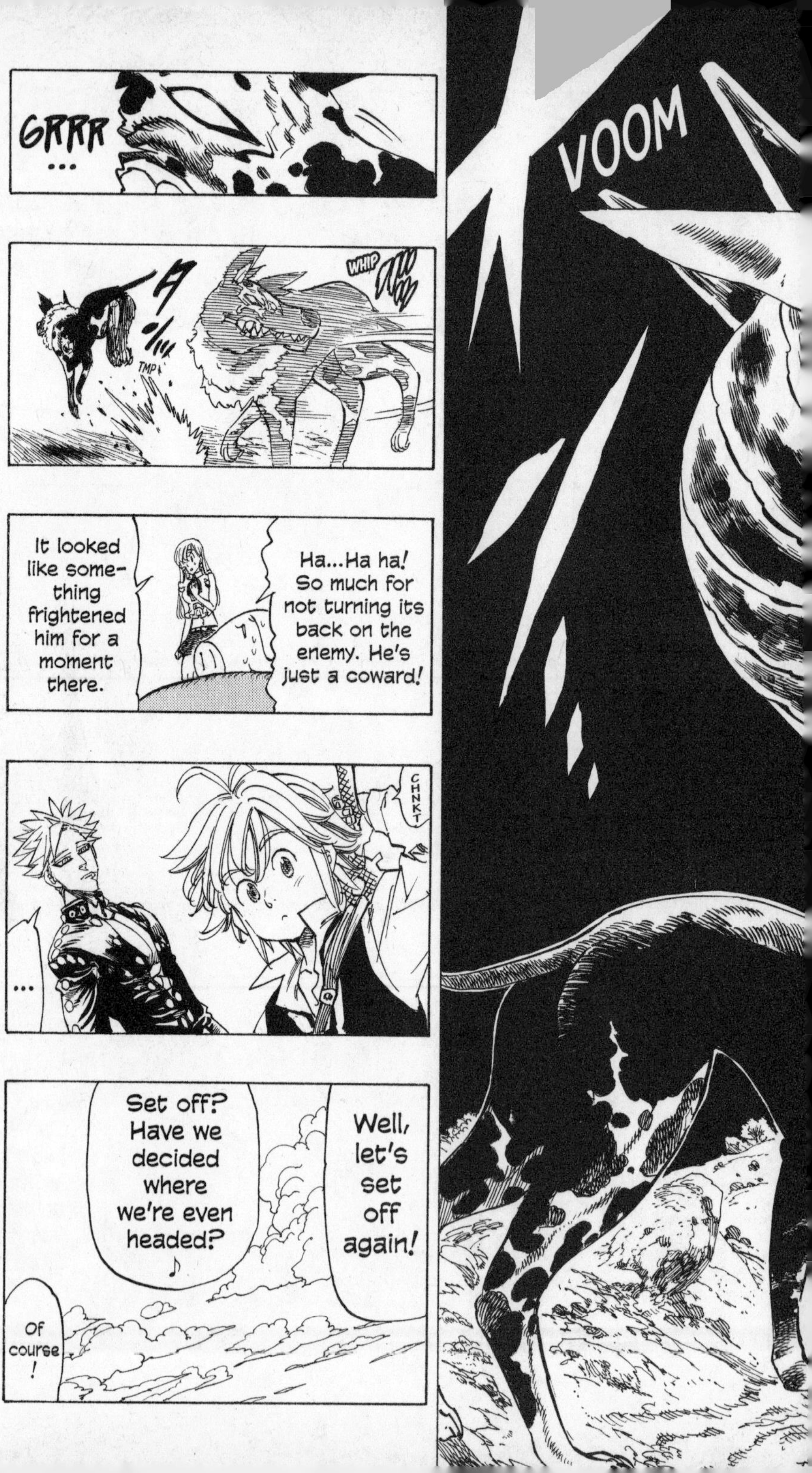
VOOM
GRRR...
WHIP
TMP
Ha...Ha ha! So much for not turning its back on the enemy. He's just a coward!
It looked like something frightened him for a moment there.
CHNKT
...
Well, let's set off again!
Set off? Have we decided where we're even headed? ♪
Of course!

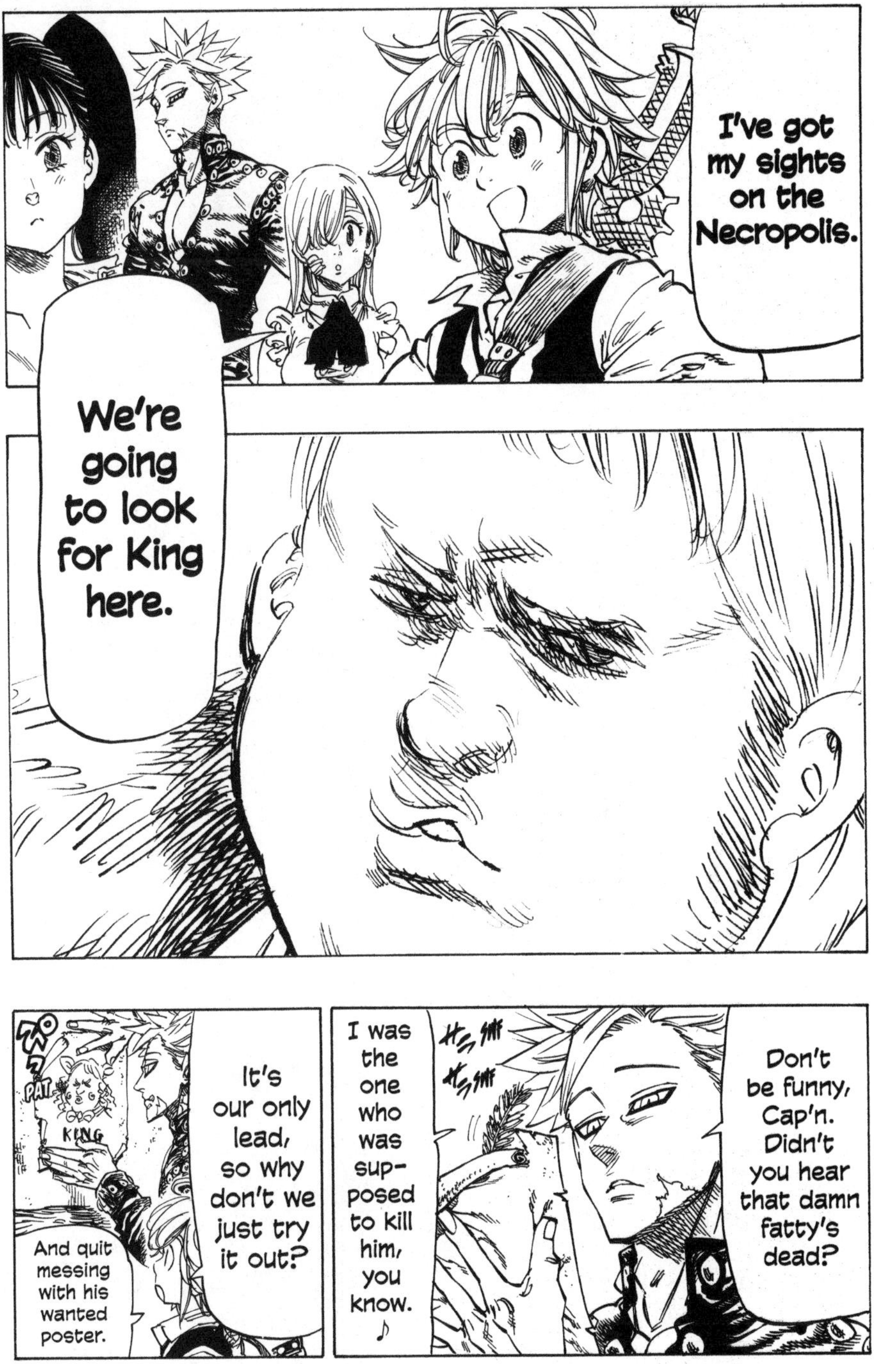
I've got my sights on the Necropolis.
We're going to look for King here.
Don't be funny, Cap'n. Didn't you hear that damn fatty's dead?
SNF SNF
I was the one who was sup-posed to kill him, you know. ♪
It's our only lead, so why don't we just try it out?
PAT
KING
And quit messing with his wanted poster.

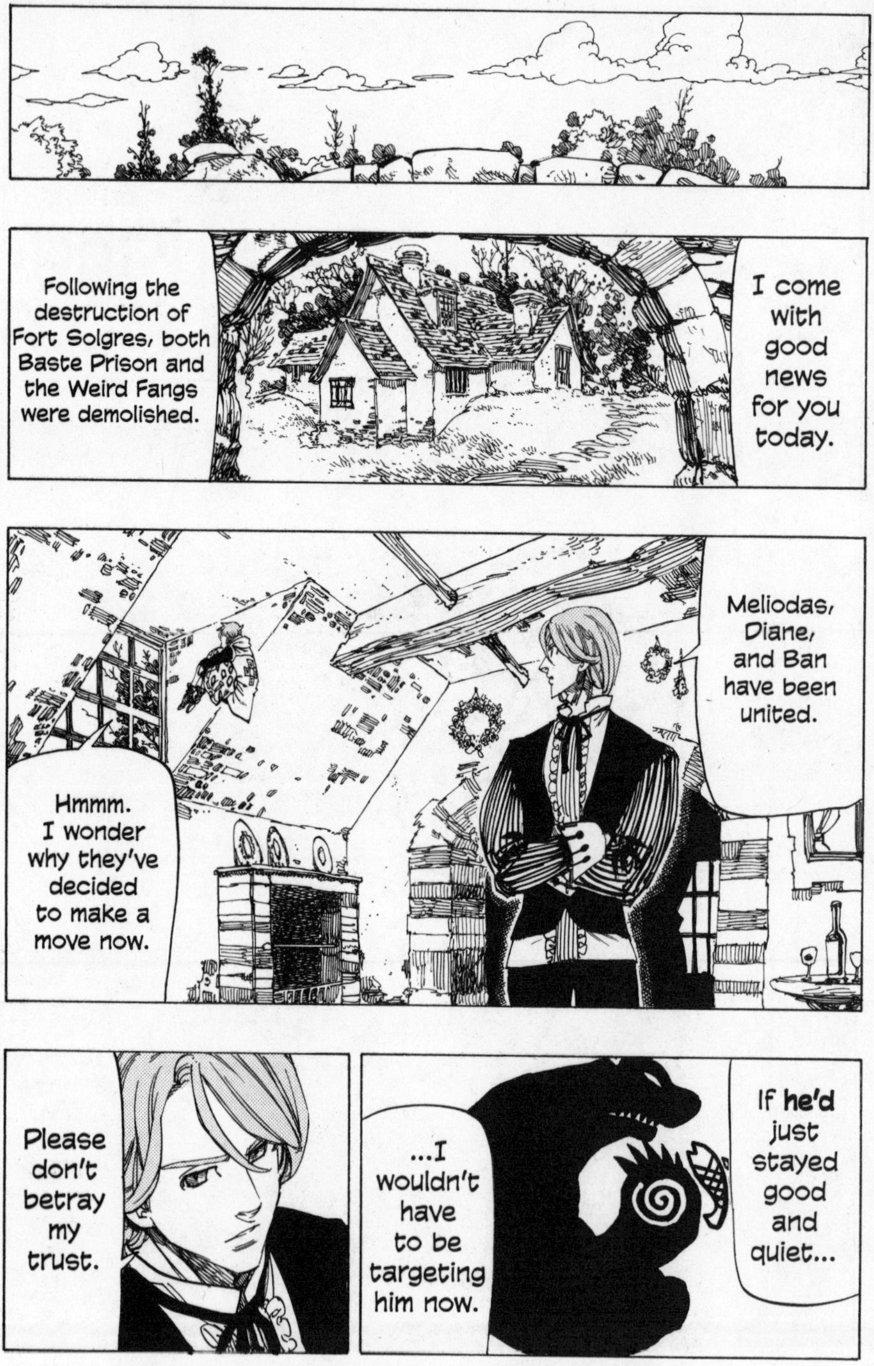
I come with good news for you today.
Following the destruction of Fort Solgres, both Baste Prison and the Weird Fangs were demolished.
Meliodas, Diane, and Ban have been united.
Hmmm. I wonder why they've decided to make a move now.
If **he'd** just stayed good and quiet...
...I wouldn't have to be targeting him now.
Please don't betray my trust.

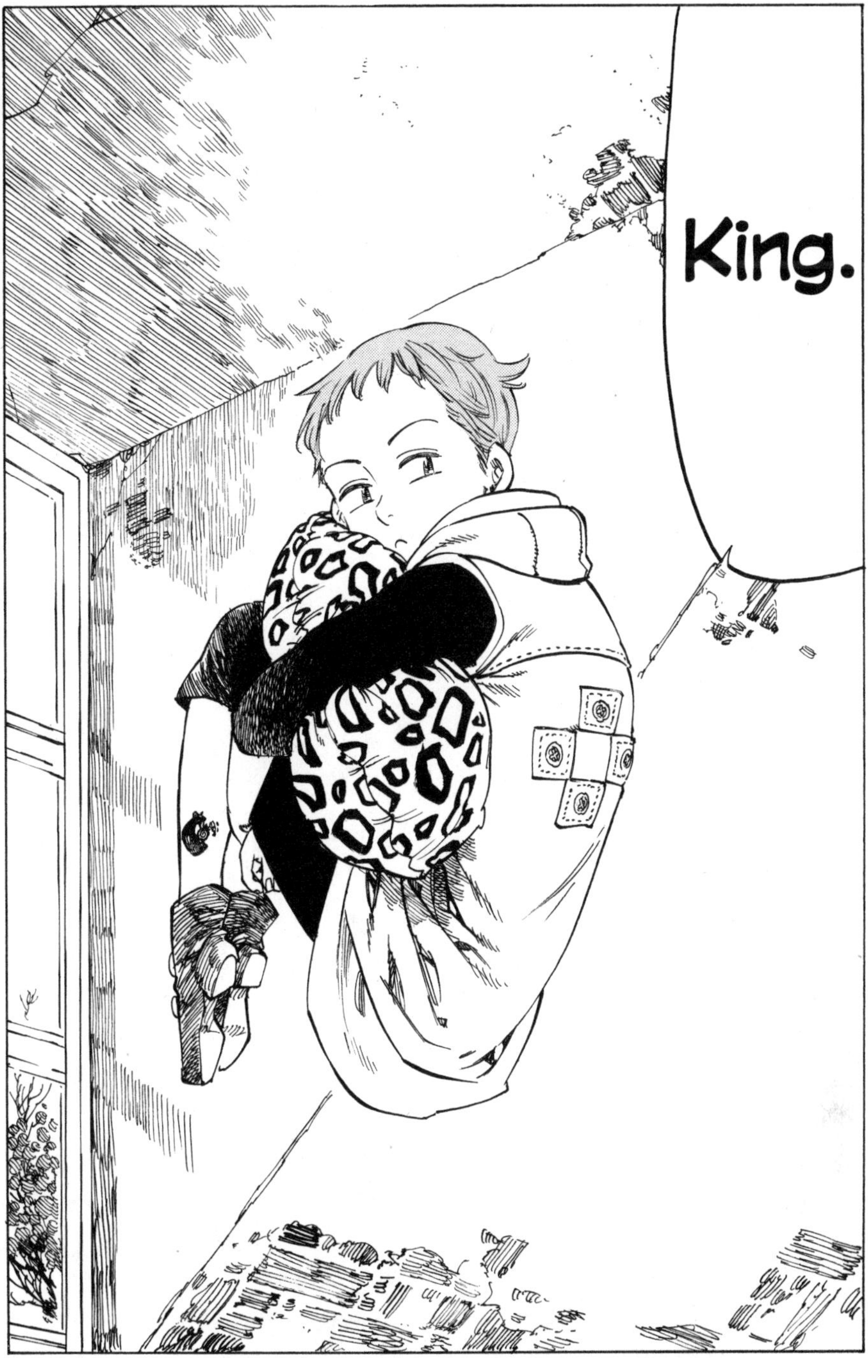
King.

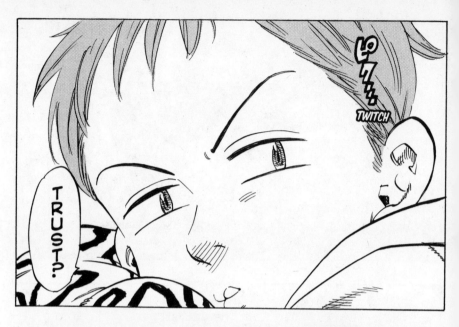

ピクッ
TWITCH
TRUST?
Sorry, but keep that between you Humans.
FLOAT
ふよ…
ふよ ふよ ふよ ふよ
BOB BOB BOB BOB
Yaaawn.
Won't that be more convenient for you guys anyway?
I'll do what I want to do.
Sure.
Who's there?
TRUDGE
のし

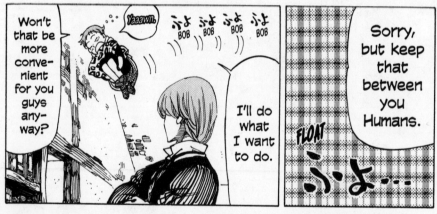

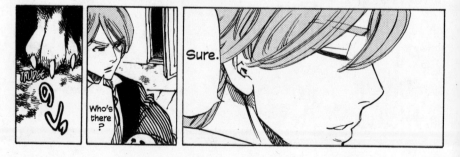

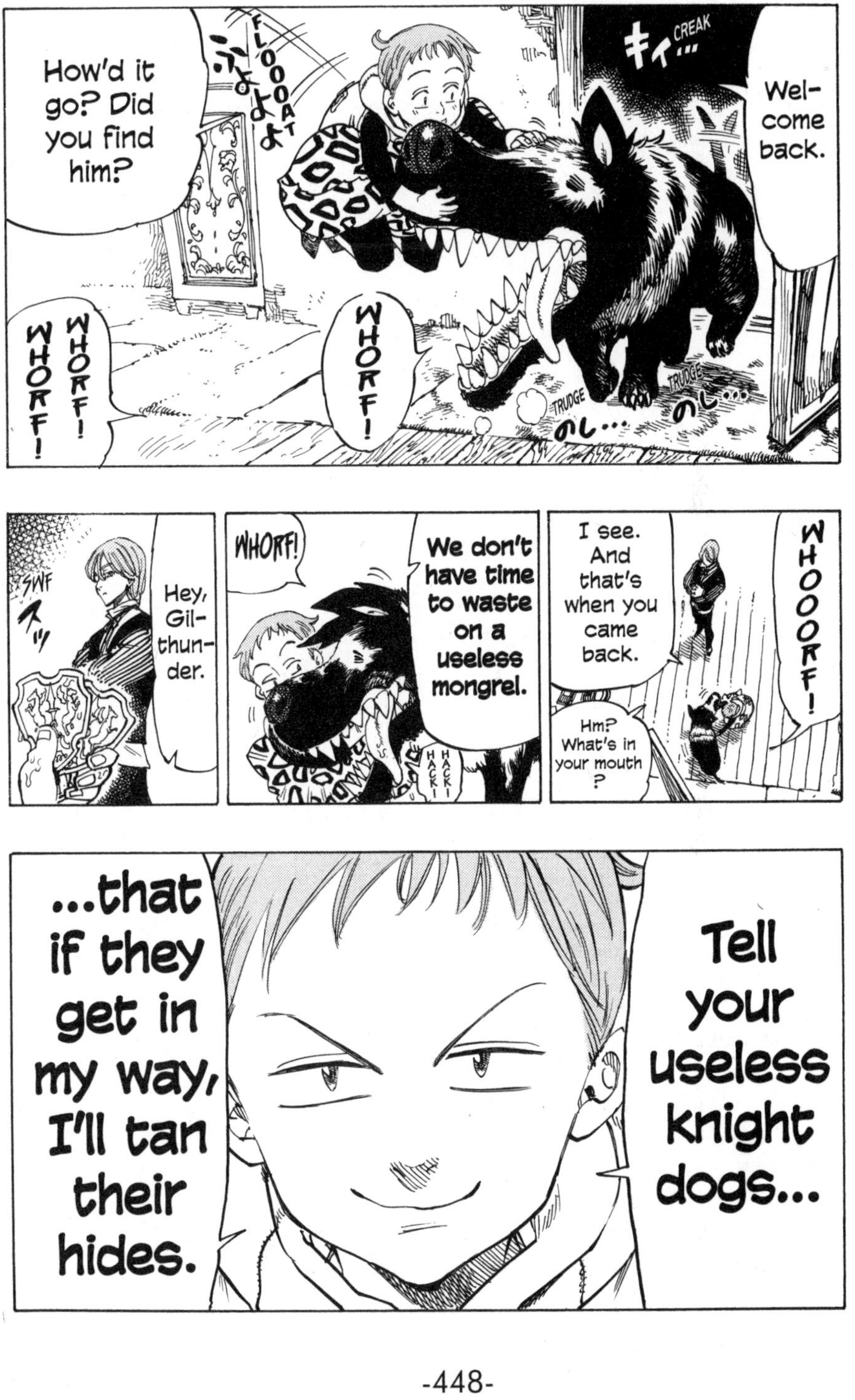
キィ… CREAK
Welcome back.
ふよよよ FLOOOOAT
How'd it go? Did you find him?
WHORF!
のし… TRUDGE
のし… TRUDGE
WHORF! WHORF!
WHOOOORF!
I see. And that's when you came back.
Hm? What's in your mouth?
We don't have time to waste on a useless mongrel.
WHORF!
HACK! HACK!
Hey, Gilthunder.
SWF スッ
Tell your useless knight dogs...
...that if they get in my way, I'll tan their hides.

Chapter 18 - A Touching Reunion

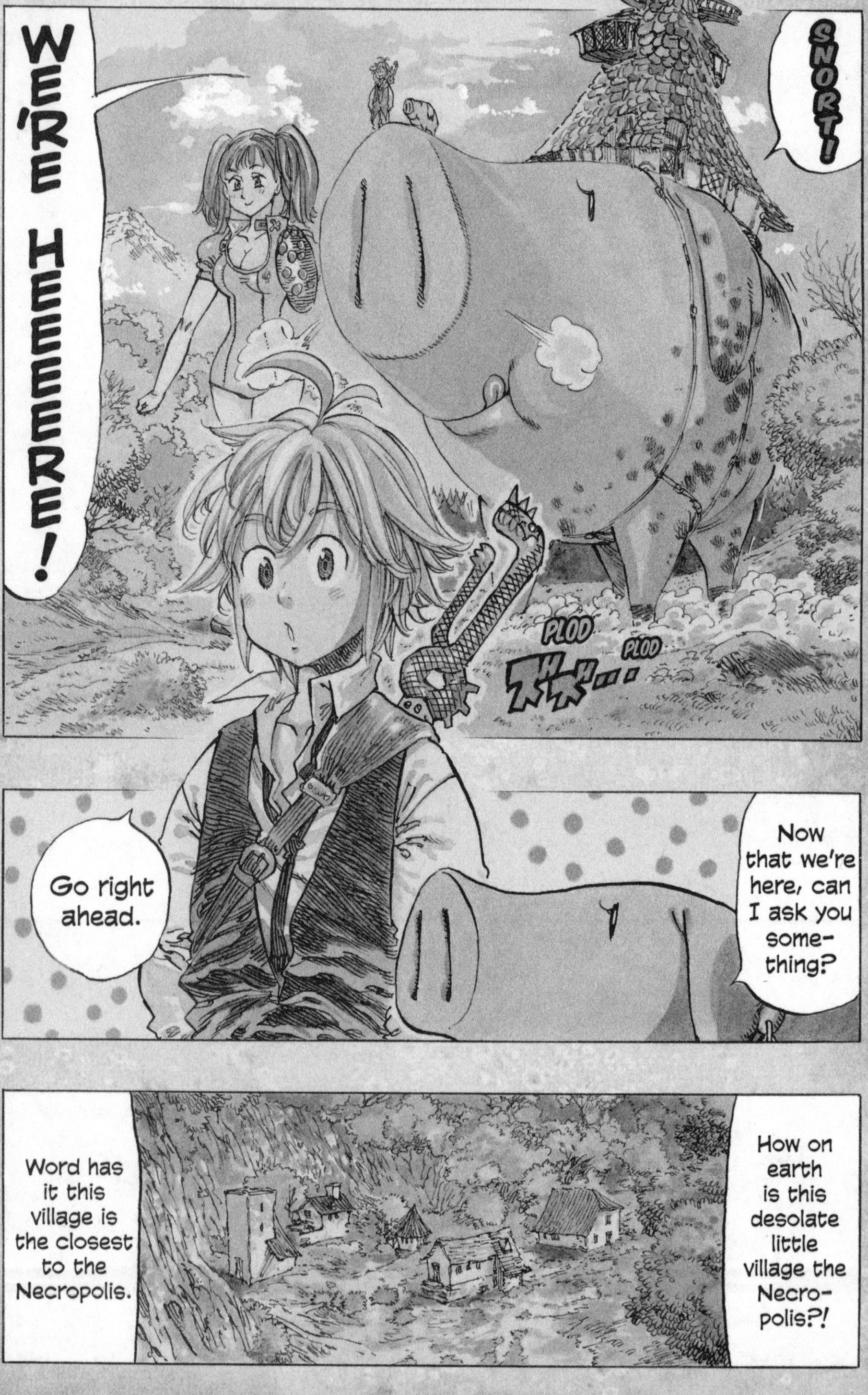
SNORT!
WE'RE HEEEEERE!
PLOD
PLOD
Now that we're here, can I ask you some-thing?
Go right ahead.
How on earth is this desolate little village the Necro-polis?!
Word has it this village is the closest to the Necropolis.

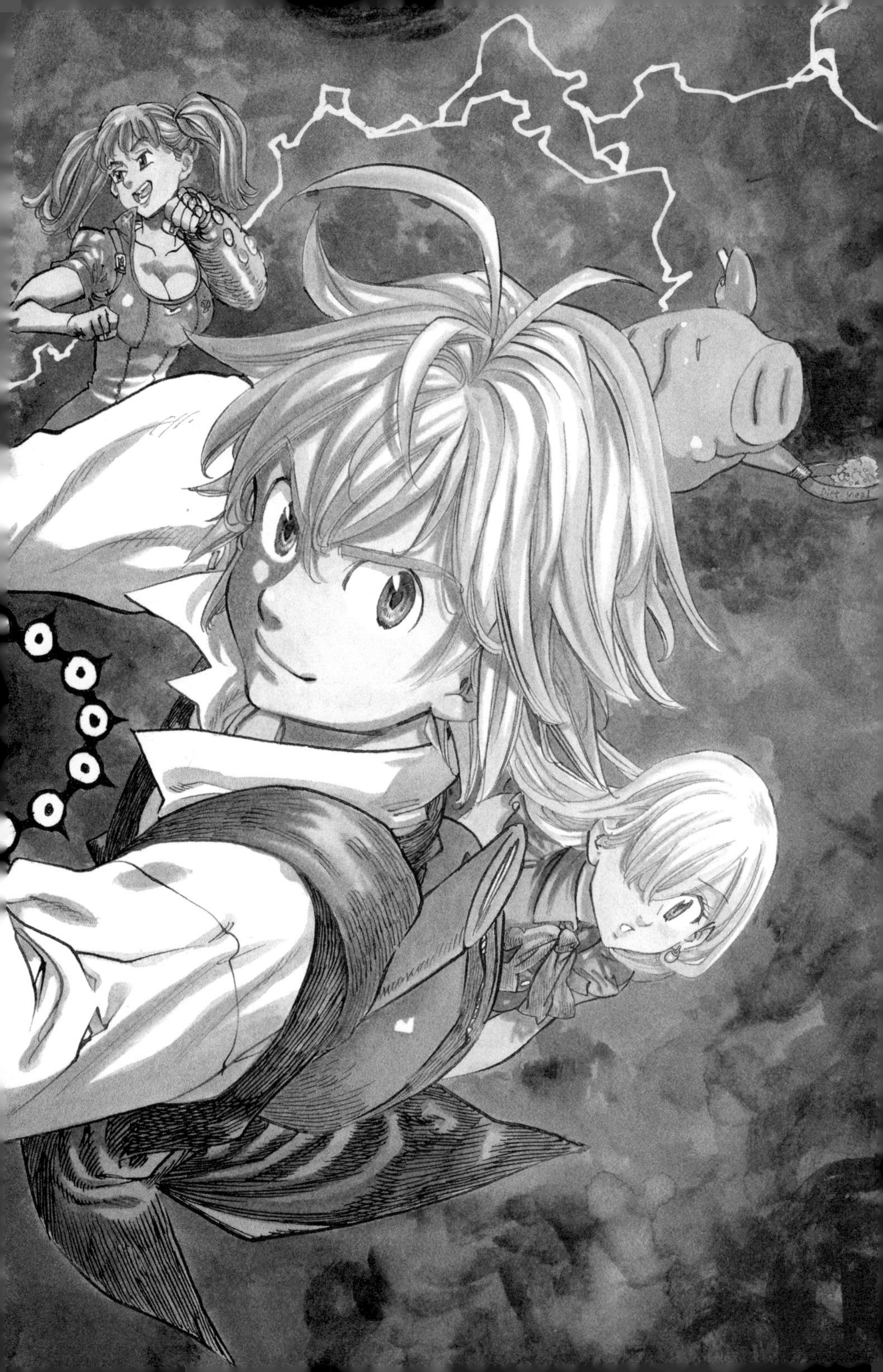
Diet meal

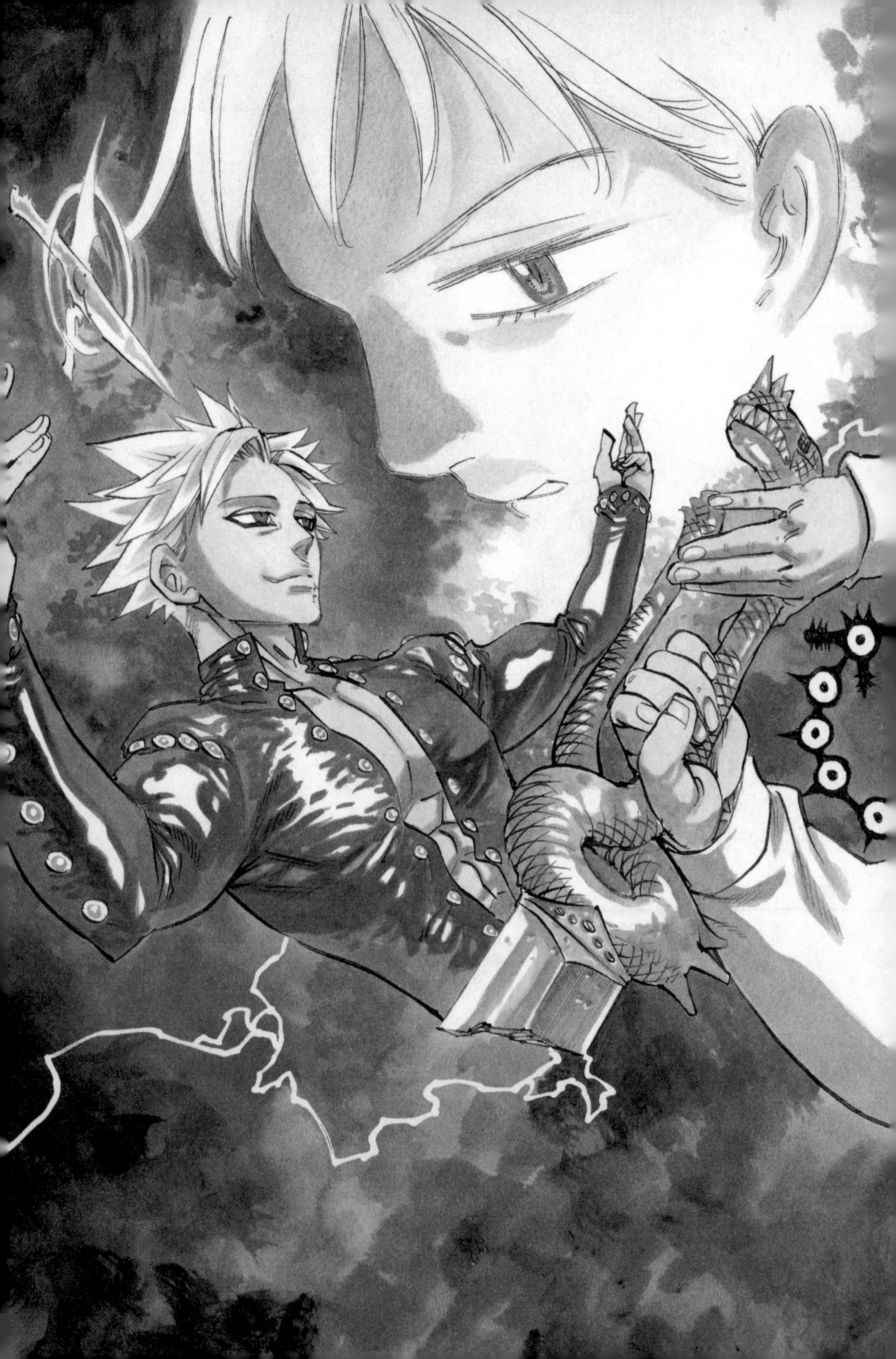

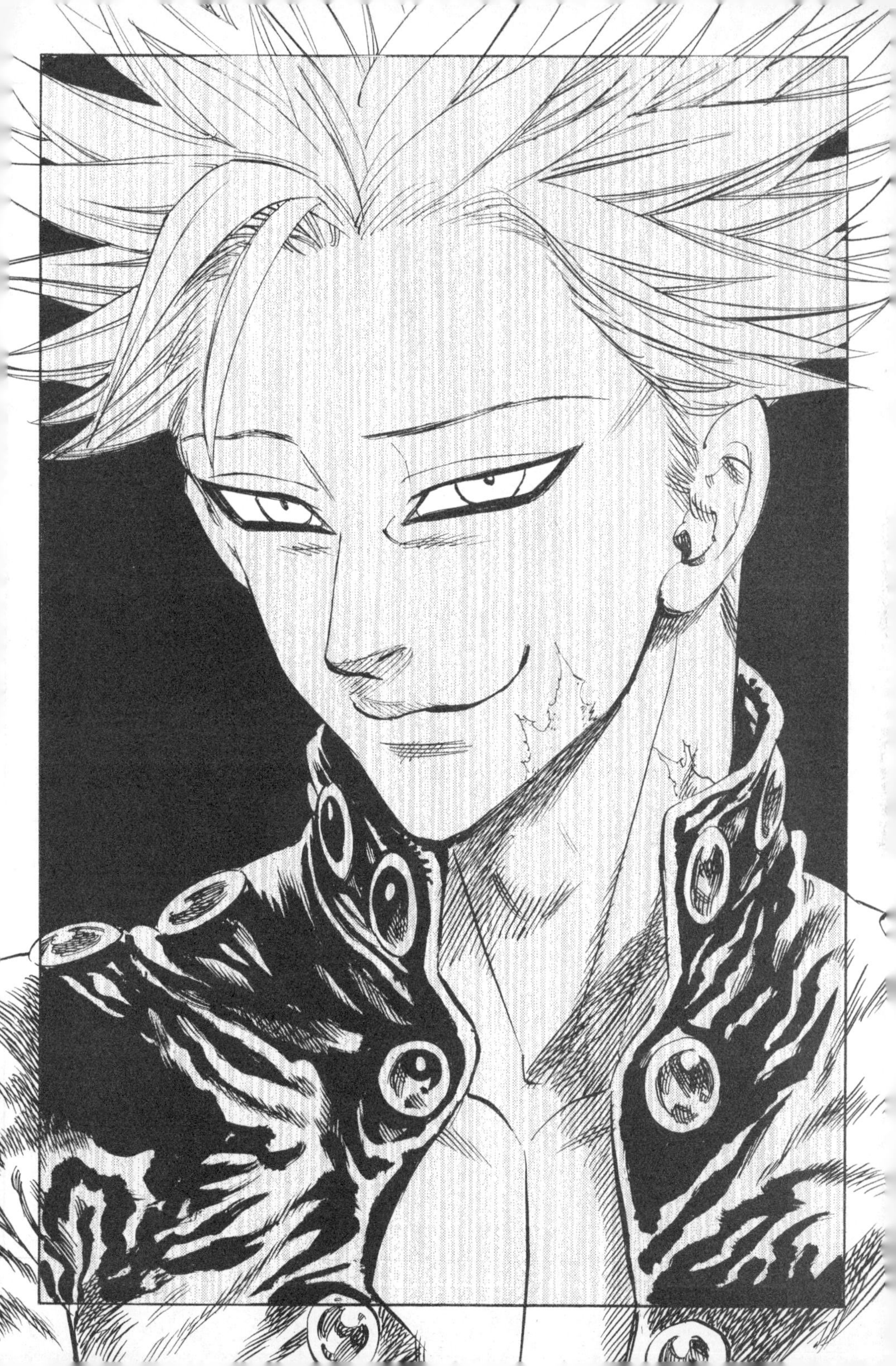

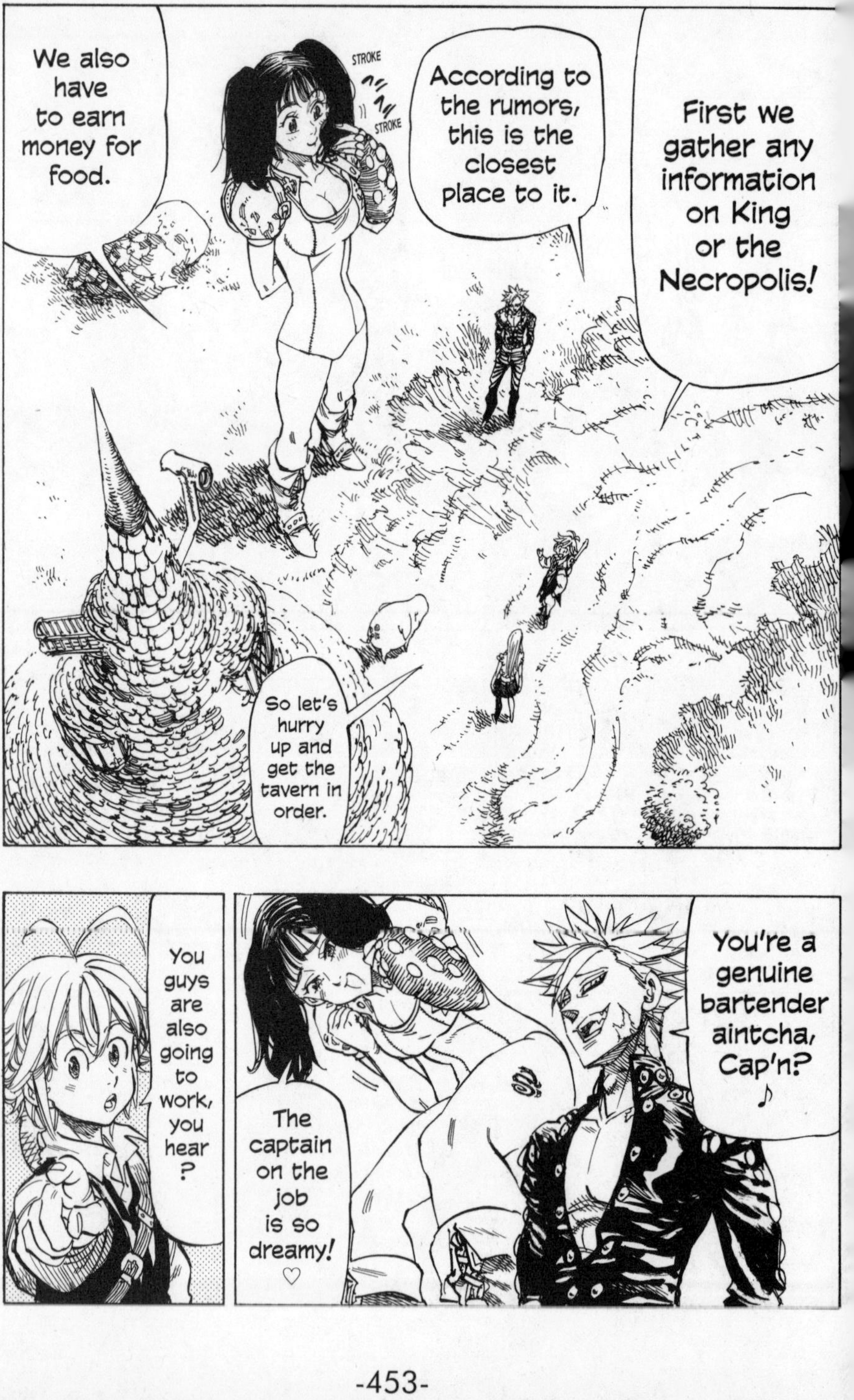
First we gather any information on King or the Necropolis!
According to the rumors, this is the closest place to it.
STROKE
STROKE
We also have to earn money for food.
So let's hurry up and get the tavern in order.
You're a genuine bartender aintcha, Cap'n? ♪
The captain on the job is so dreamy! ♡
You guys are also going to work, you hear?

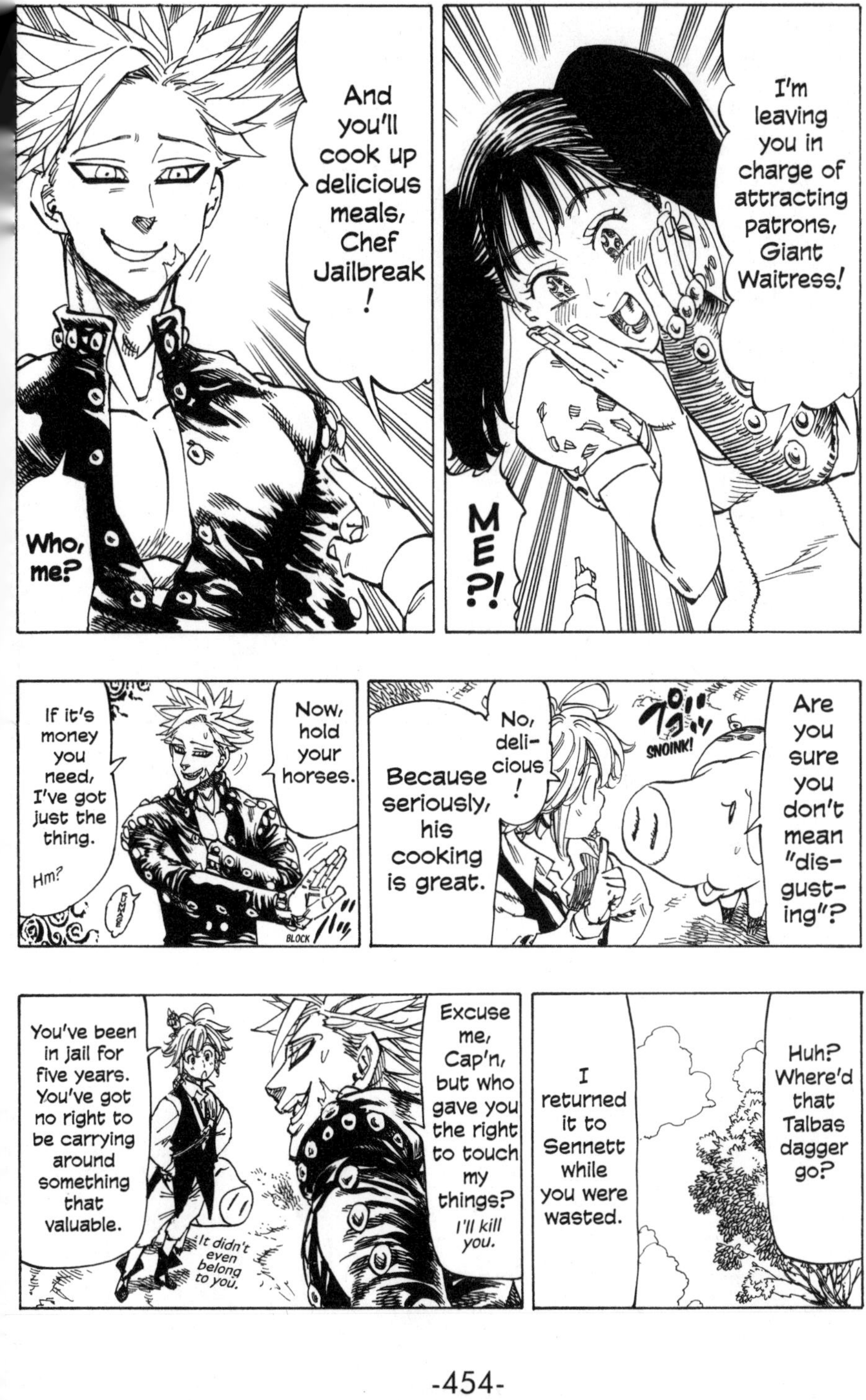

I'm leaving you in charge of attracting patrons, Giant Waitress!
ME?!
And you'll cook up delicious meals, Chef Jailbreak!
Who, me?
Are you sure you don't mean "dis-gust-ing"?
SNOINK!
No, deli-cious!
Because seriously, his cooking is great.
Now, hold your horses.
If it's money you need, I've got just the thing.
Hm?
BLOCK
Huh? Where'd that Talbas dagger go?
I returned it to Sennett while you were wasted.
Excuse me, Cap'n, but who gave you the right to touch my things?
I'll kill you.
You've been in jail for five years. You've got no right to be carrying around something that valuable.
It didn't even belong to you.

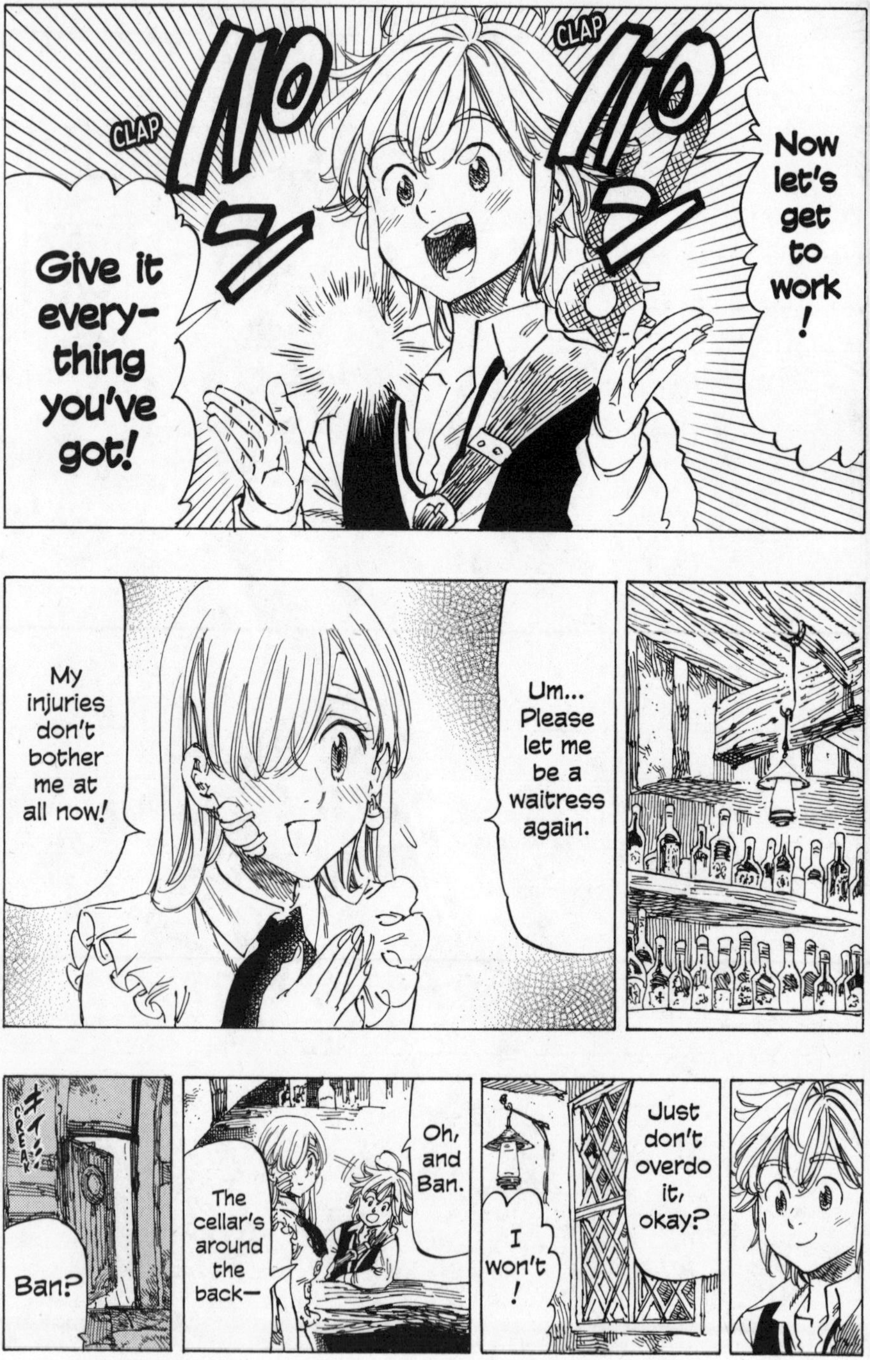
CLAP
Now let's get to work!
CLAP
Give it everything you've got!
Um... Please let me be a waitress again.
My injuries don't bother me at all now!
Just don't overdo it, okay?
I won't!
Oh, and Ban.
The cellar's around the back—
CREAK
Ban?

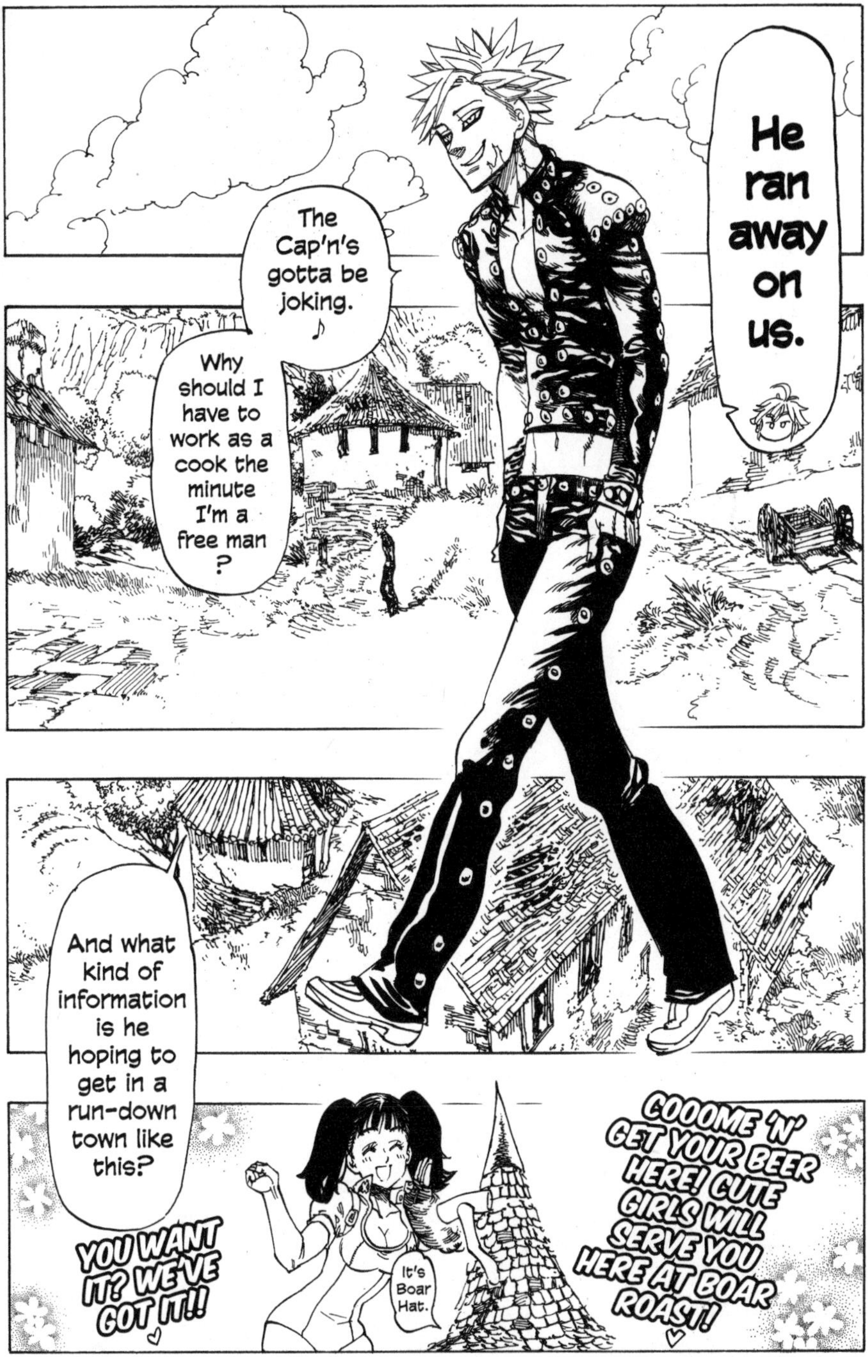
He ran away on us.
The Cap'n's gotta be joking. ♪
Why should I have to work as a cook the minute I'm a free man?
And what kind of information is he hoping to get in a run-down town like this?
COOOME 'N' GET YOUR BEER HERE! CUTE GIRLS WILL SERVE YOU HERE AT BOAR ROAST! ♡
It's Boar Hat.
YOU WANT IT? WE'VE GOT IT!! ♡

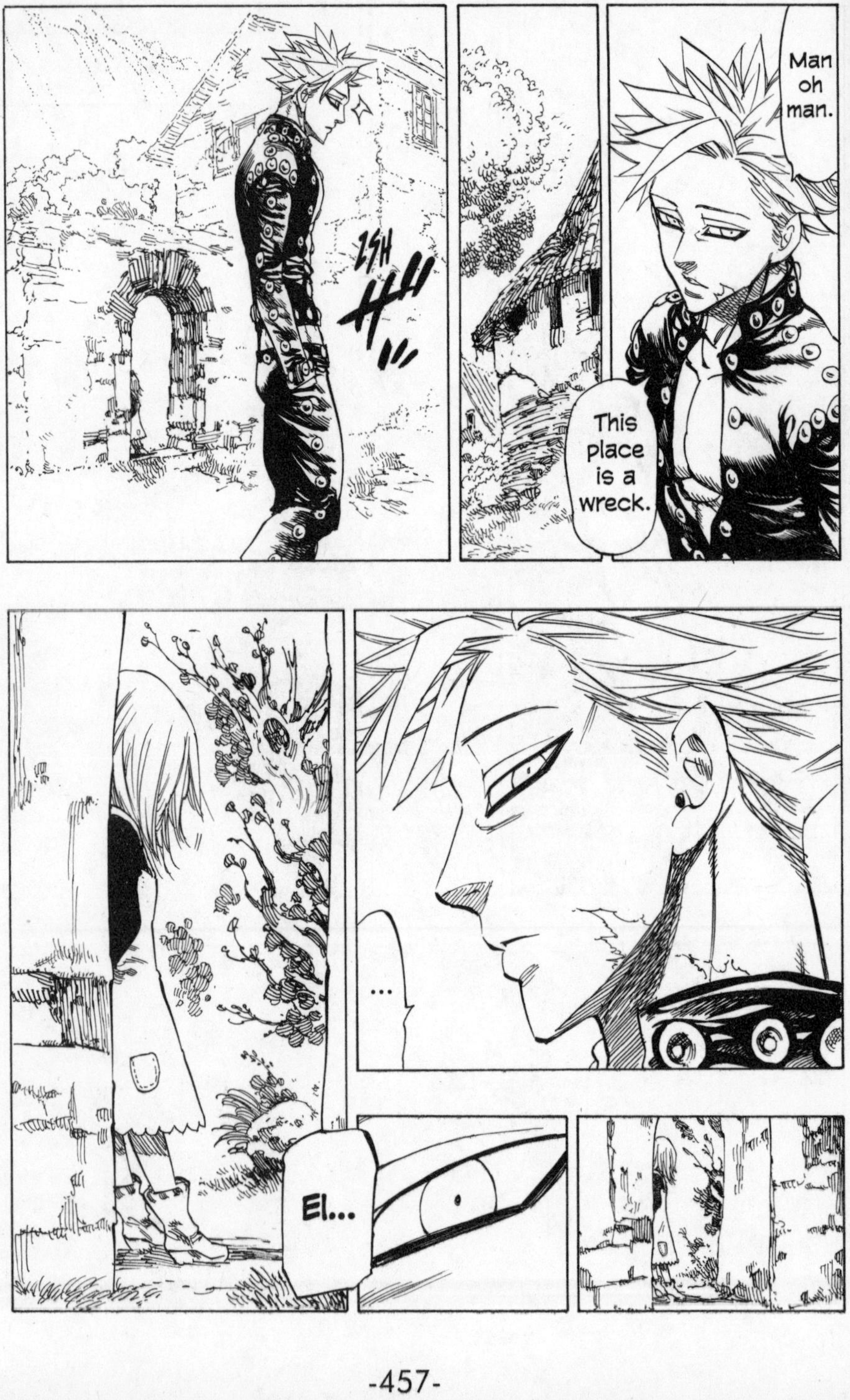
Man oh man.
This place is a wreck.
ZSH
...
El...

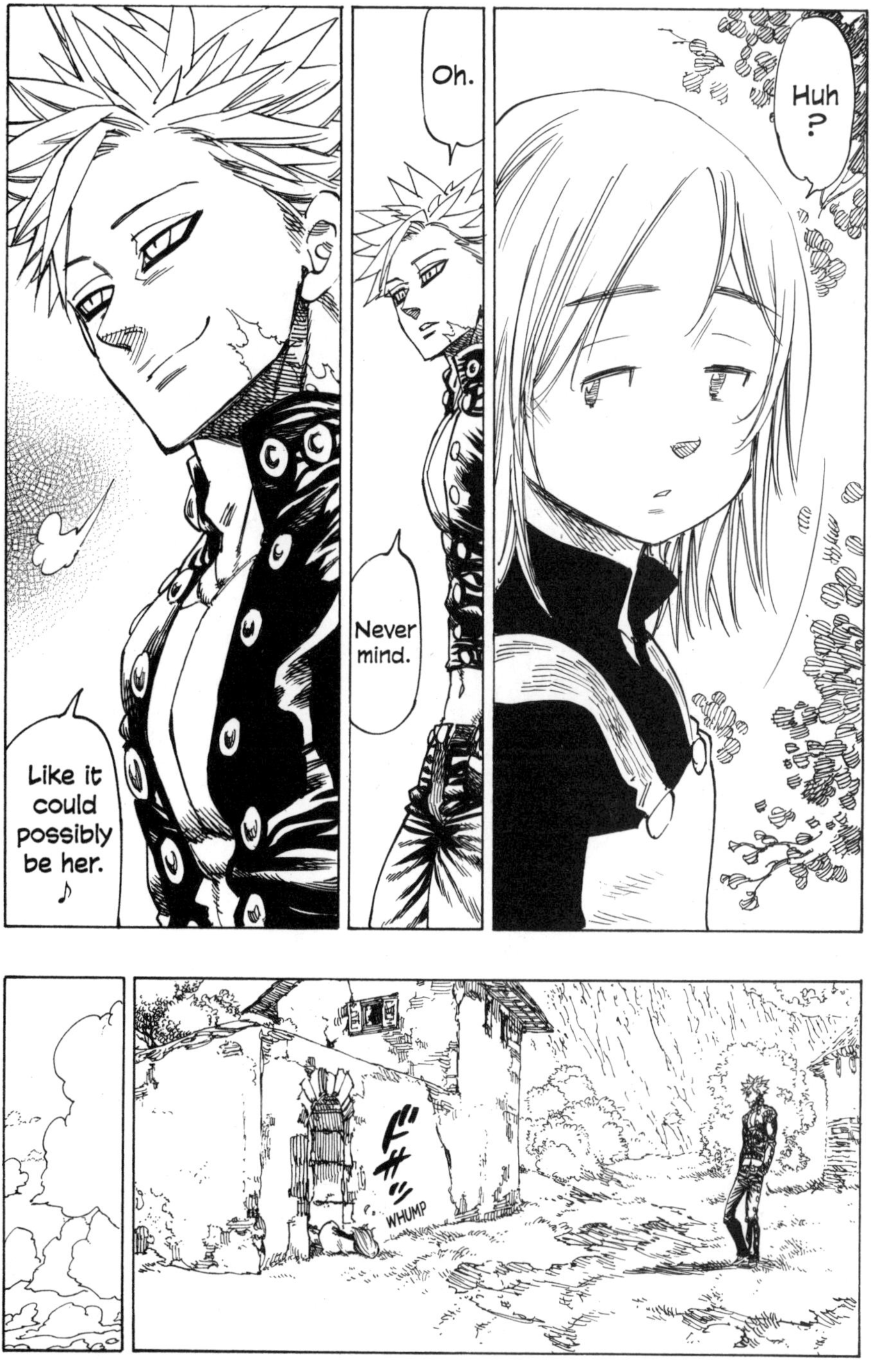
Huh ?
Oh.
Never mind.
Like it could possibly be her. ♪
ドサッ
WHUMP

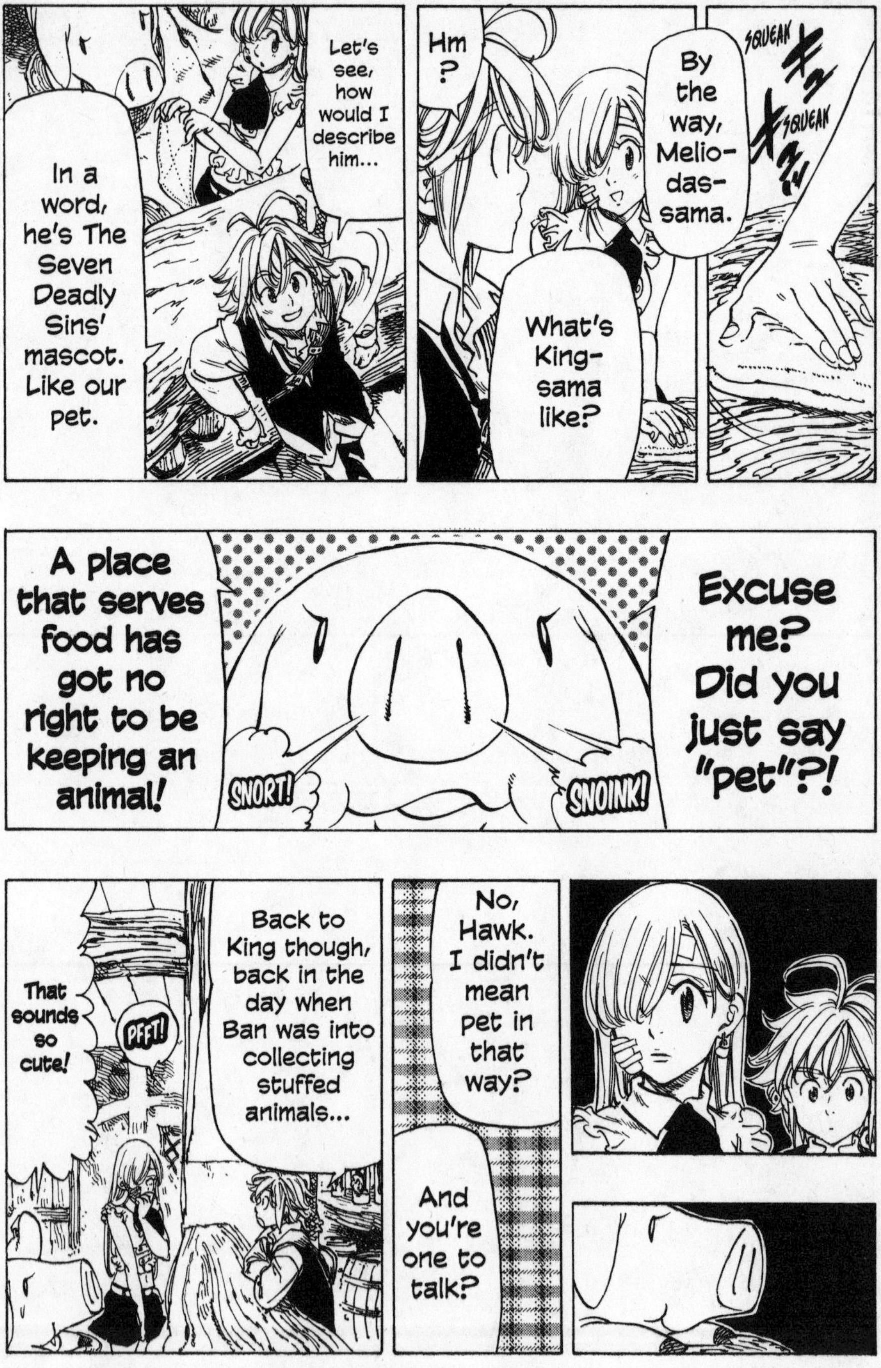
SQUEAK
SQUEAK
By the way, Melio-das-sama.
Hm?
What's King-sama like?
Let's see, how would I describe him...
In a word, he's The Seven Deadly Sins' mascot. Like our pet.
Excuse me? Did you just say "pet"?!
SNOINK!
SNORT!
A place that serves food has got no right to be keeping an animal!
No, Hawk. I didn't mean pet in that way?
And you're one to talk?
Back to King though, back in the day when Ban was into collecting stuffed animals...
PFFT!
That sounds so cute!

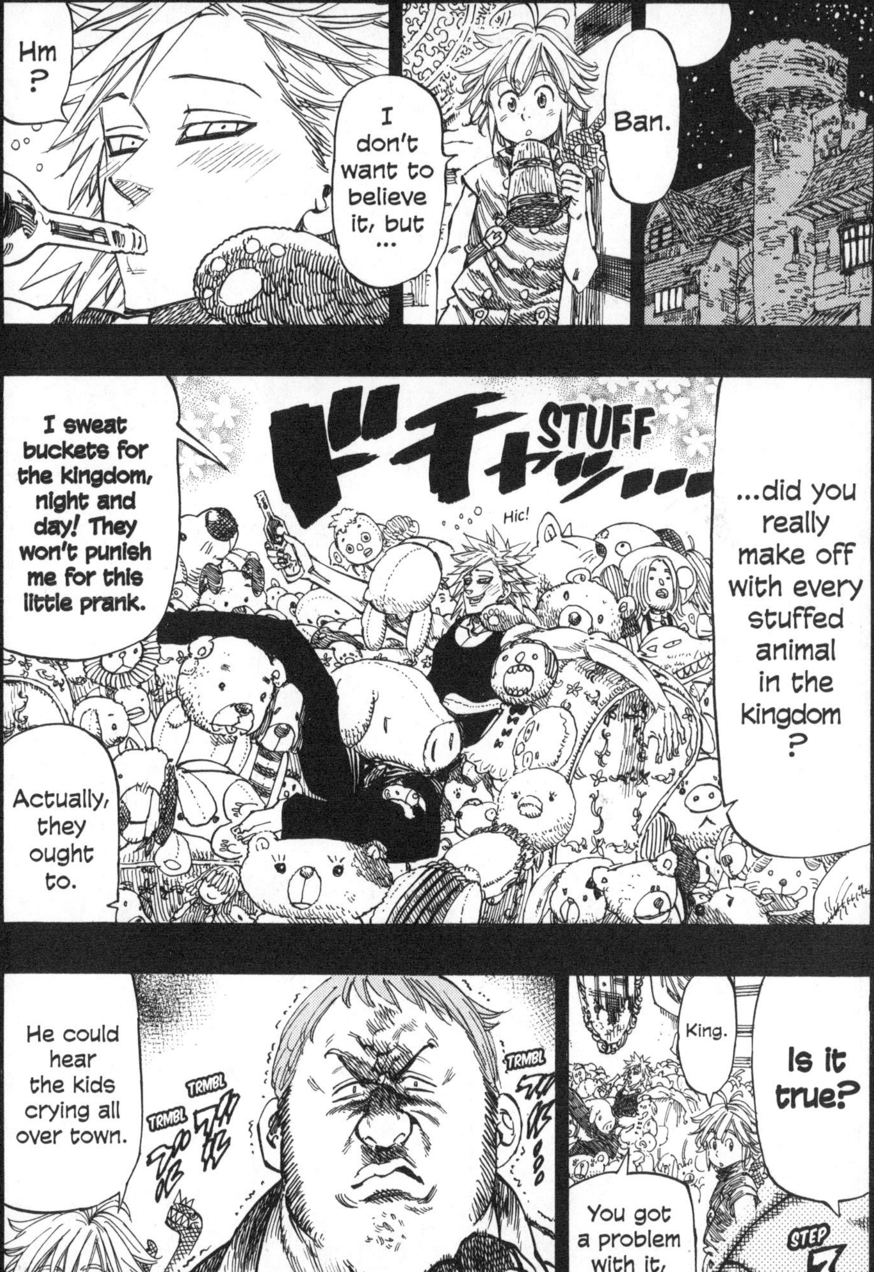
Ban.
I don't want to believe it, but ...
Hm ?
...did you really make off with every stuffed animal in the kingdom ?
STUFF
Hic!
I sweat buckets for the kingdom, night and day! They won't punish me for this little prank.
Actually, they ought to.
King.
Is it true?
You got a problem with it, you damn fatty?
STEP
TRMBL
TRMBL
TRMBL
He could hear the kids crying all over town.

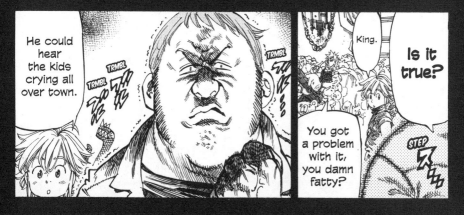

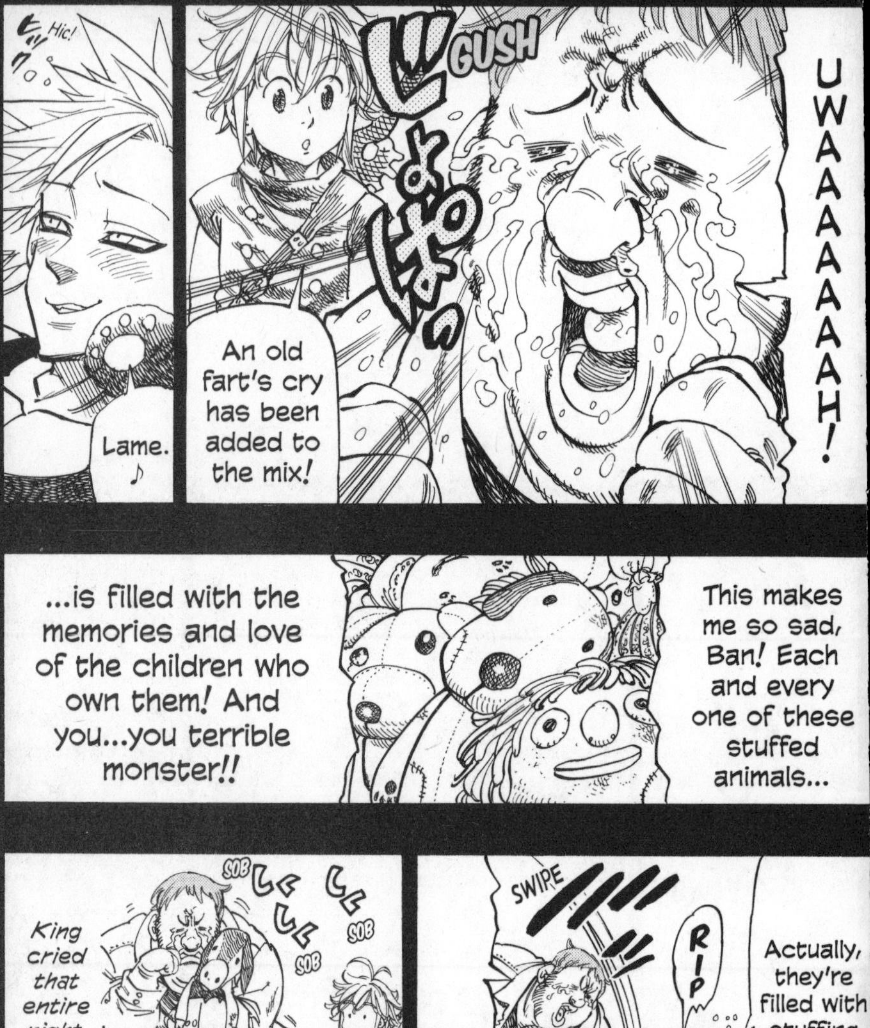
UWAAAAAAAH!
GUSH
An old fart's cry has been added to the mix!
Hic!
Lame. ♪
This makes me so sad, Ban! Each and every one of these stuffed animals...
...is filled with the memories and love of the children who own them! And you...you terrible monster!!
Actually, they're filled with stuffing and old rags.
RIP
SWIPE
Stop that!!
SOB
SOB
SOB
King cried that entire night.
There, there.
But at sunrise, when Ban was satisfied and snoring away...

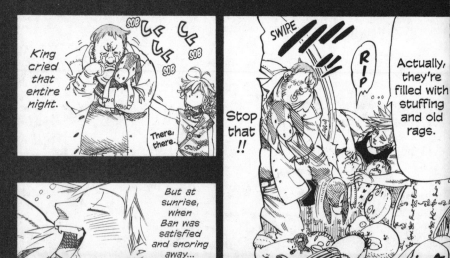

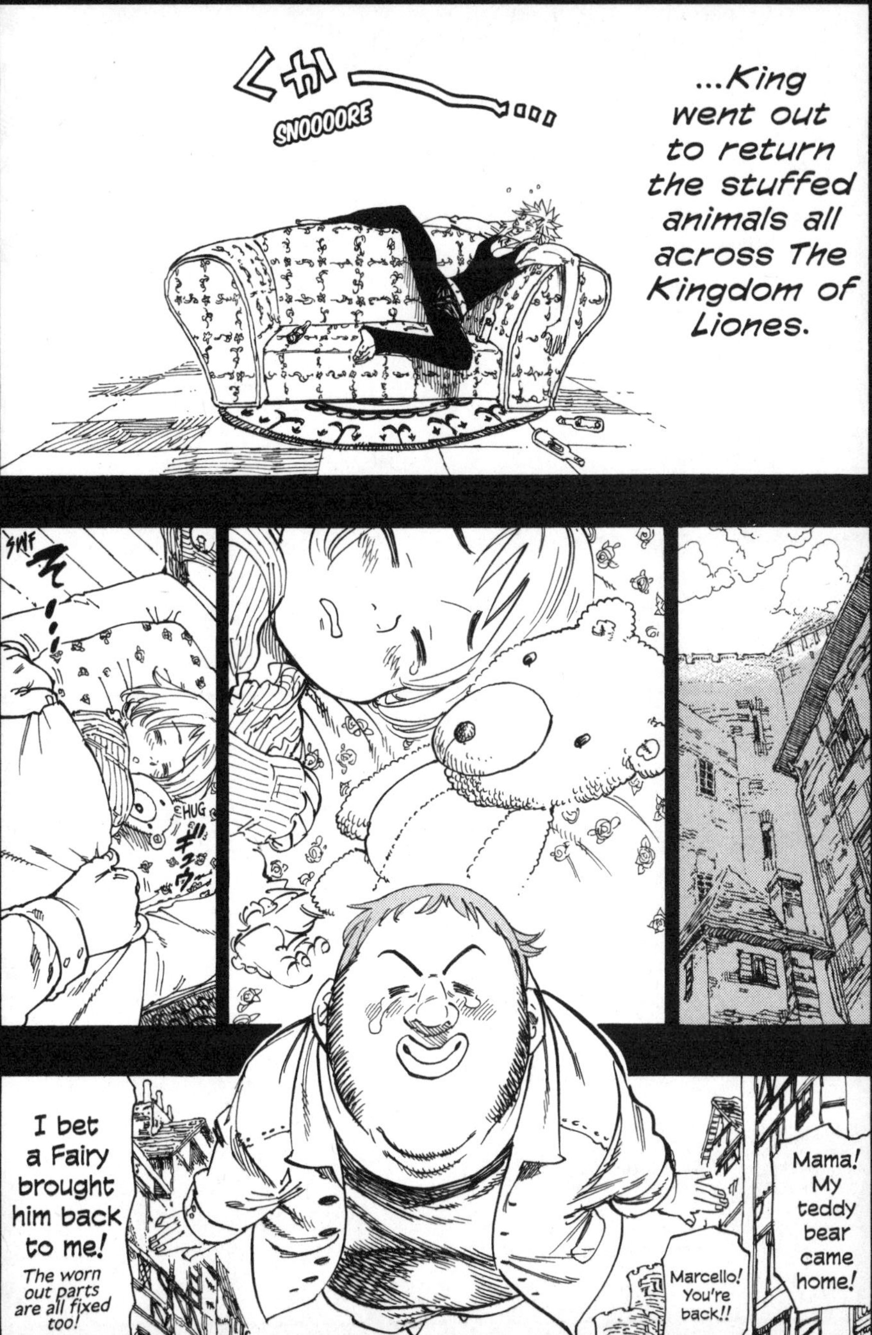
...King went out to return the stuffed animals all across The Kingdom of Liones.
SNOOOORE
SNF
HUG
Mama! My teddy bear came home!
Marcello! You're back!!
I bet a Fairy brought him back to me!
The worn out parts are all fixed too!

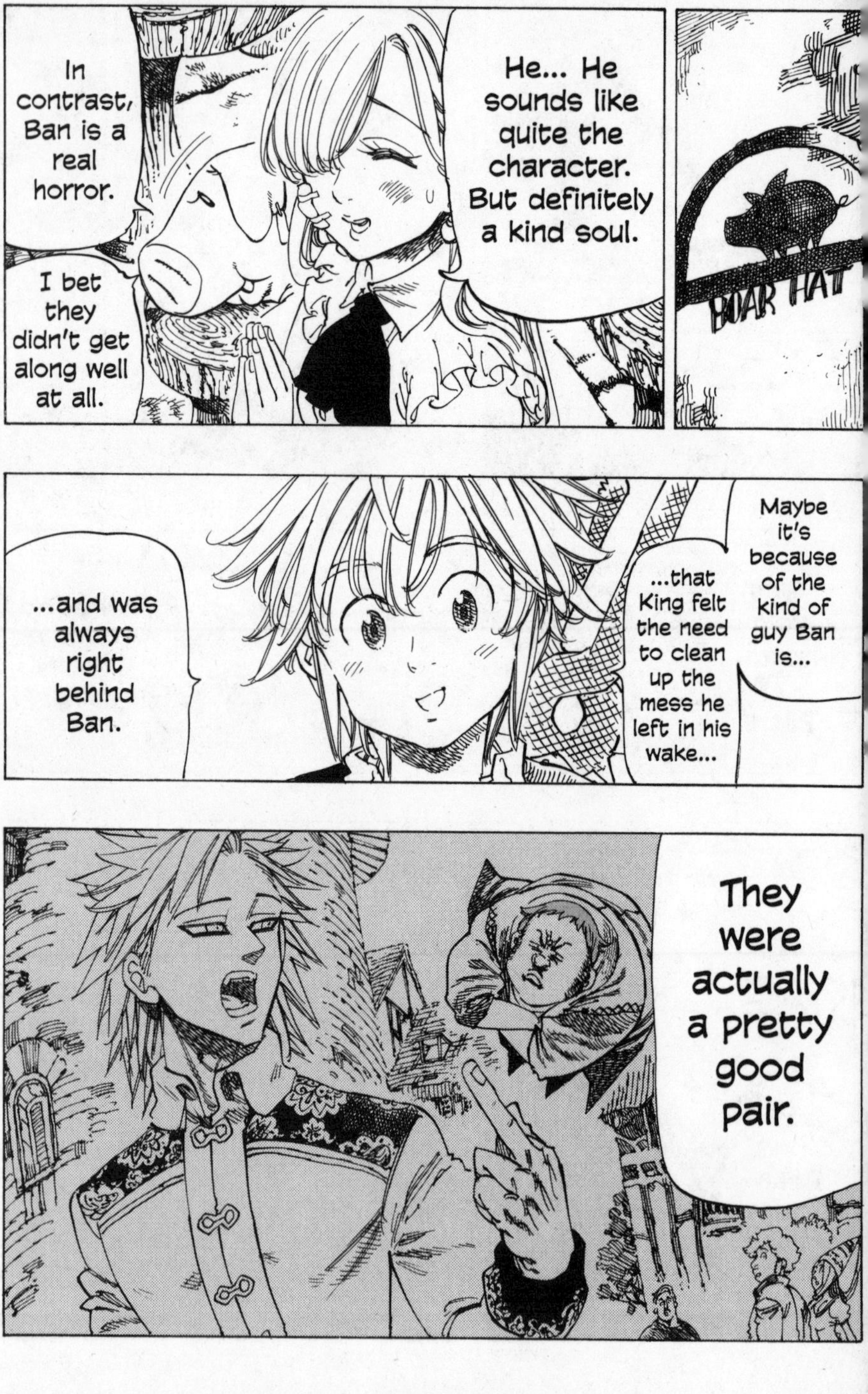
BOAR HAT
He... He sounds like quite the character. But definitely a kind soul.
In contrast, Ban is a real horror.
I bet they didn't get along well at all.
Maybe it's because of the kind of guy Ban is...
...that King felt the need to clean up the mess he left in his wake...
...and was always right behind Ban.
They were actually a pretty good pair.

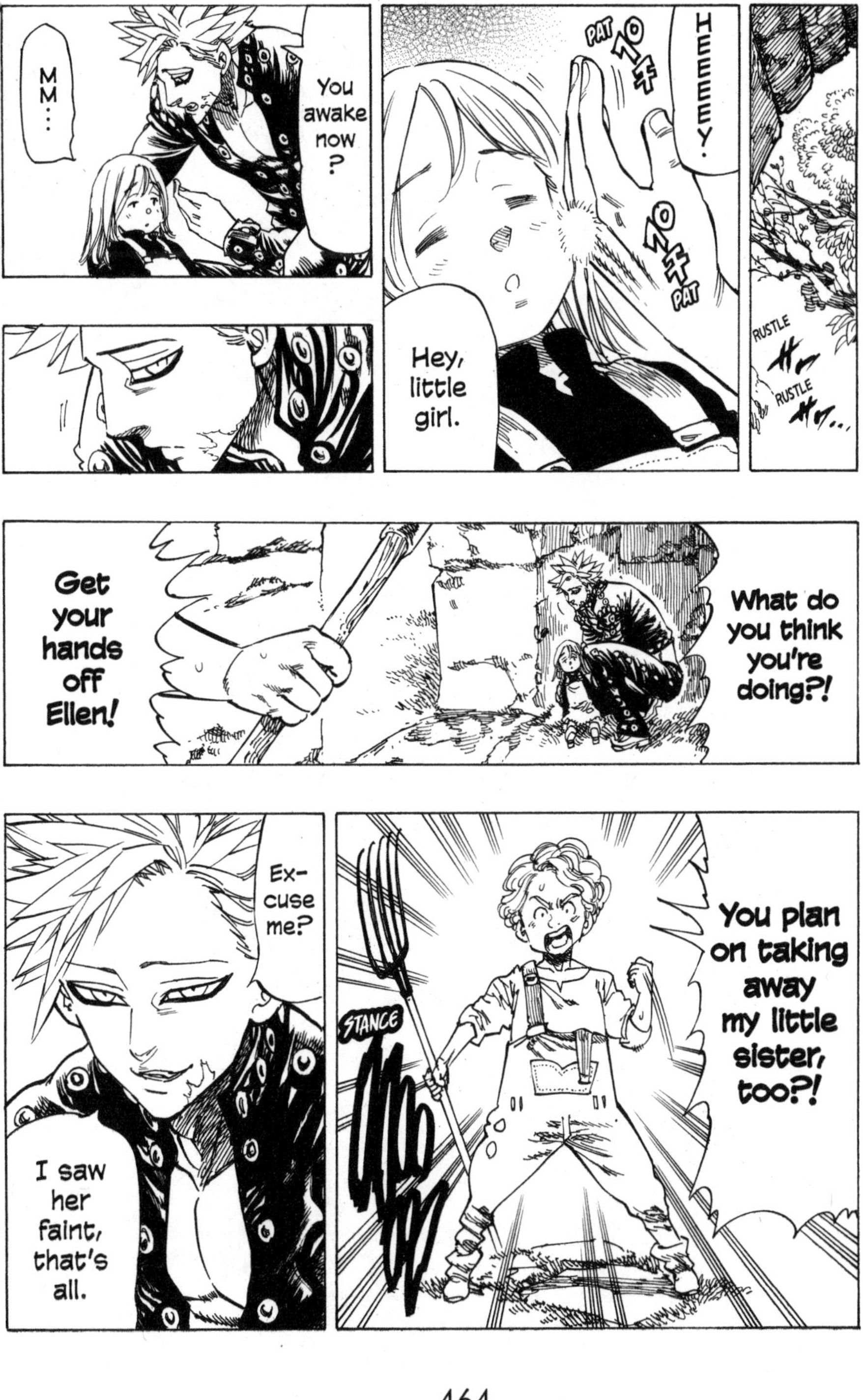
RUSTLE
RUSTLE
HEEEEEY.
PAT
PAT
Hey, little girl.
You awake now?
MM...
What do you think you're doing?!
Get your hands off Ellen!
You plan on taking away my little sister, too?!
STANCE
Ex-cuse me?
I saw her faint, that's all.

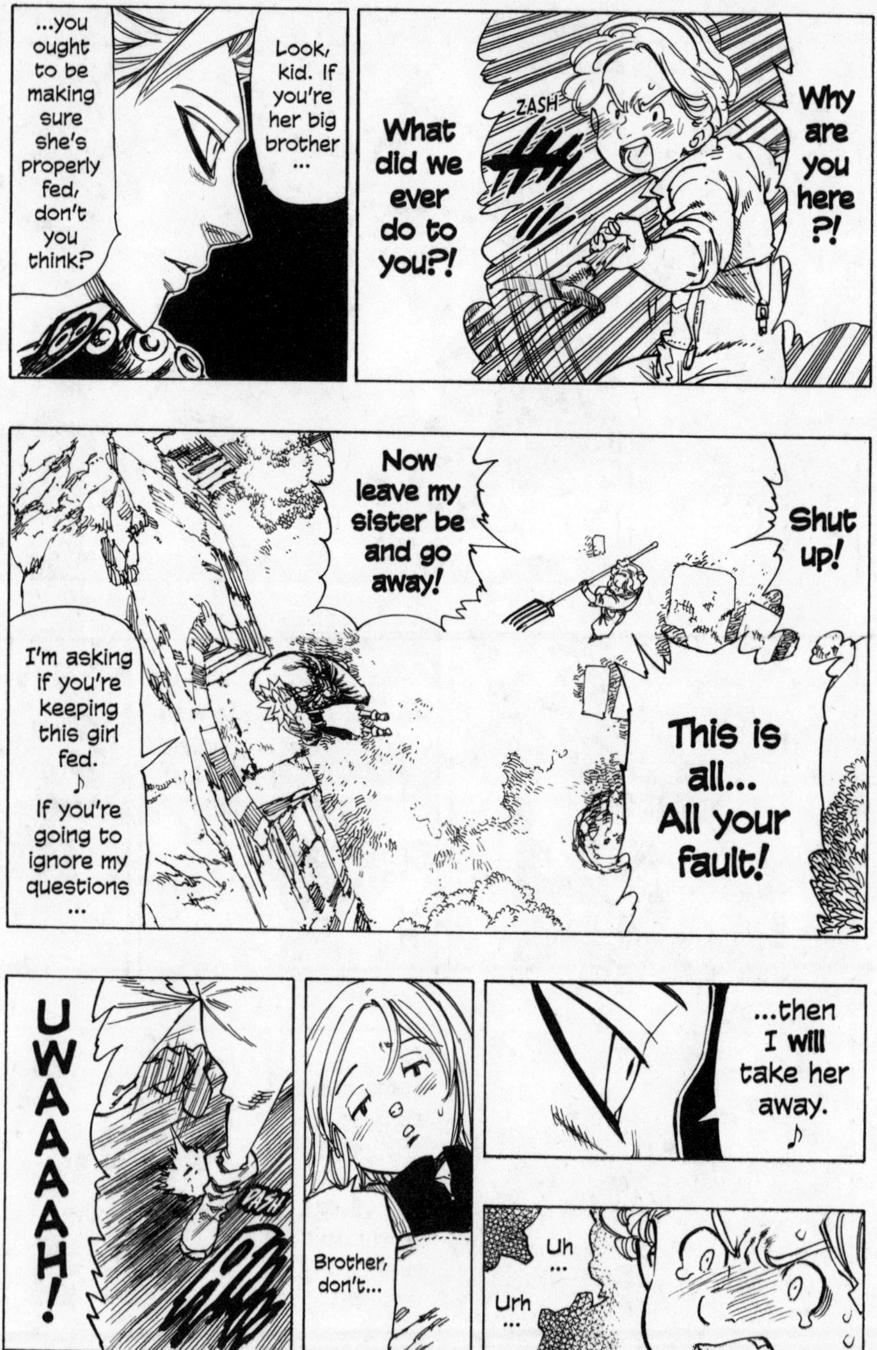

Why are you here?!
ZASH
What did we ever do to you?!
Look, kid. If you're her big brother...
...you ought to be making sure she's properly fed, don't you think?
Shut up!
Now leave my sister be and go away!
This is all... All your fault!
I'm asking if you're keeping this girl fed. ♪
If you're going to ignore my questions...
...then I will take her away. ♪
Uh...
Urh...
Brother, don't...
UWAAAAAH!
PASH

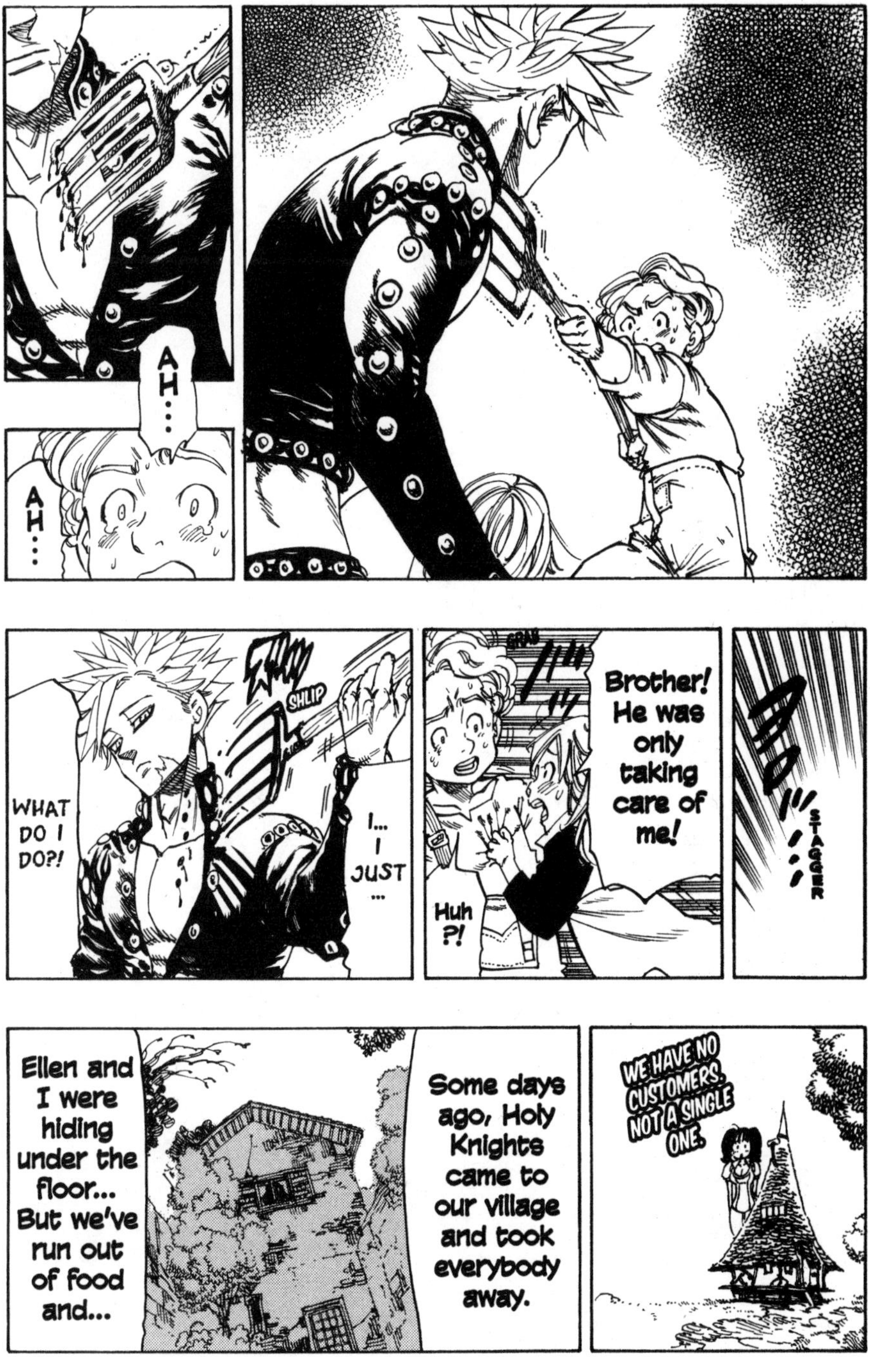
AH...
AH...
STAGGER
Brother! He was only taking care of me!
Huh ?!
SHLIP
I... I JUST ...
WHAT DO I DO?!
WE HAVE NO CUSTOMERS. NOT A SINGLE ONE.
Some days ago, Holy Knights came to our village and took everybody away.
Ellen and I were hiding under the floor... But we've run out of food and...

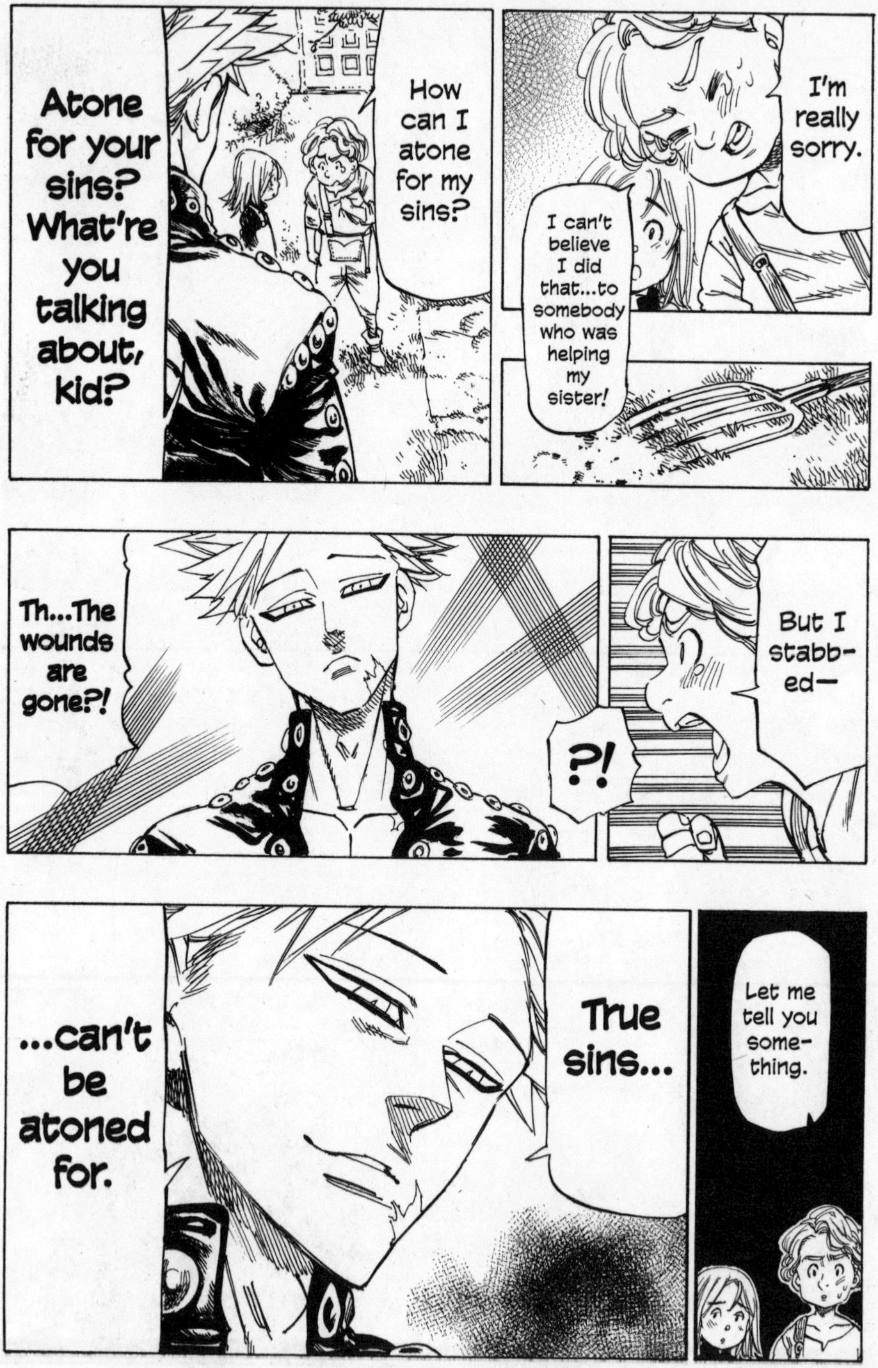
I'm really sorry.
I can't believe I did that...to somebody who was helping my sister!
How can I atone for my sins?
Atone for your sins? What're you talking about, kid?
But I stabb-ed—
?!
Th...The wounds are gone?!
Let me tell you some-thing.
True sins...
...can't be atoned for.

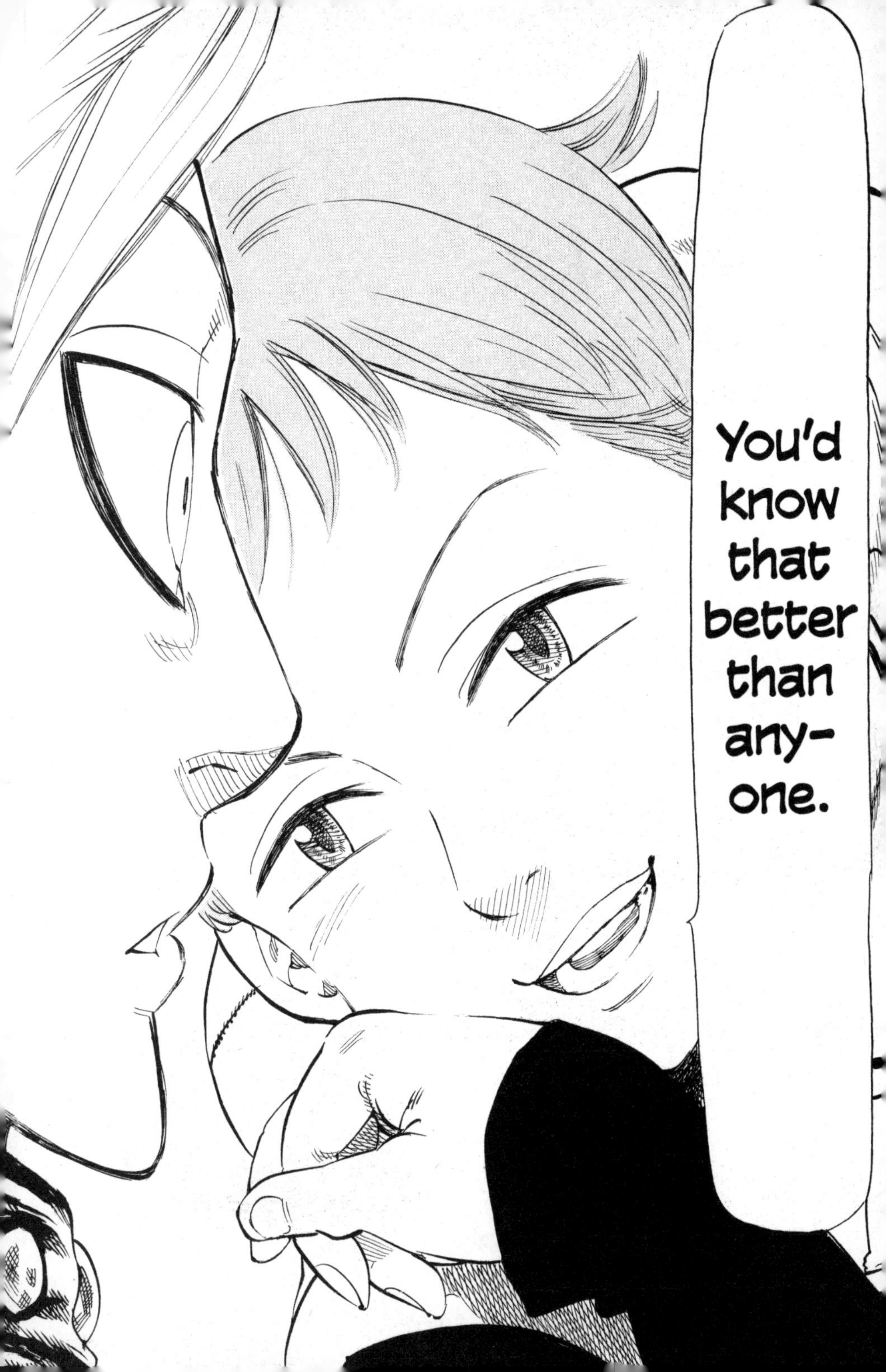
You'd know that better than any-one.

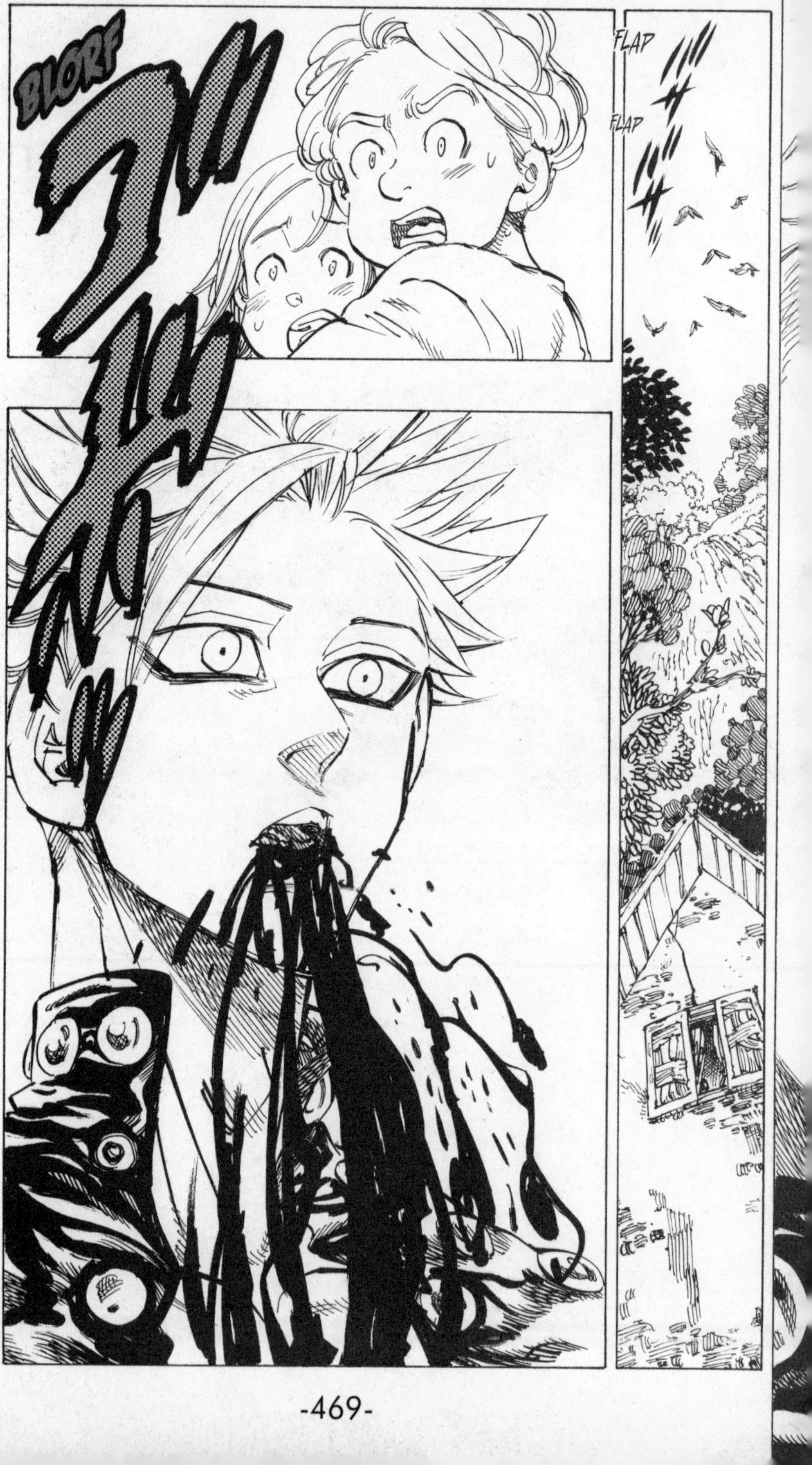
FLAP
FLAP
BLORF

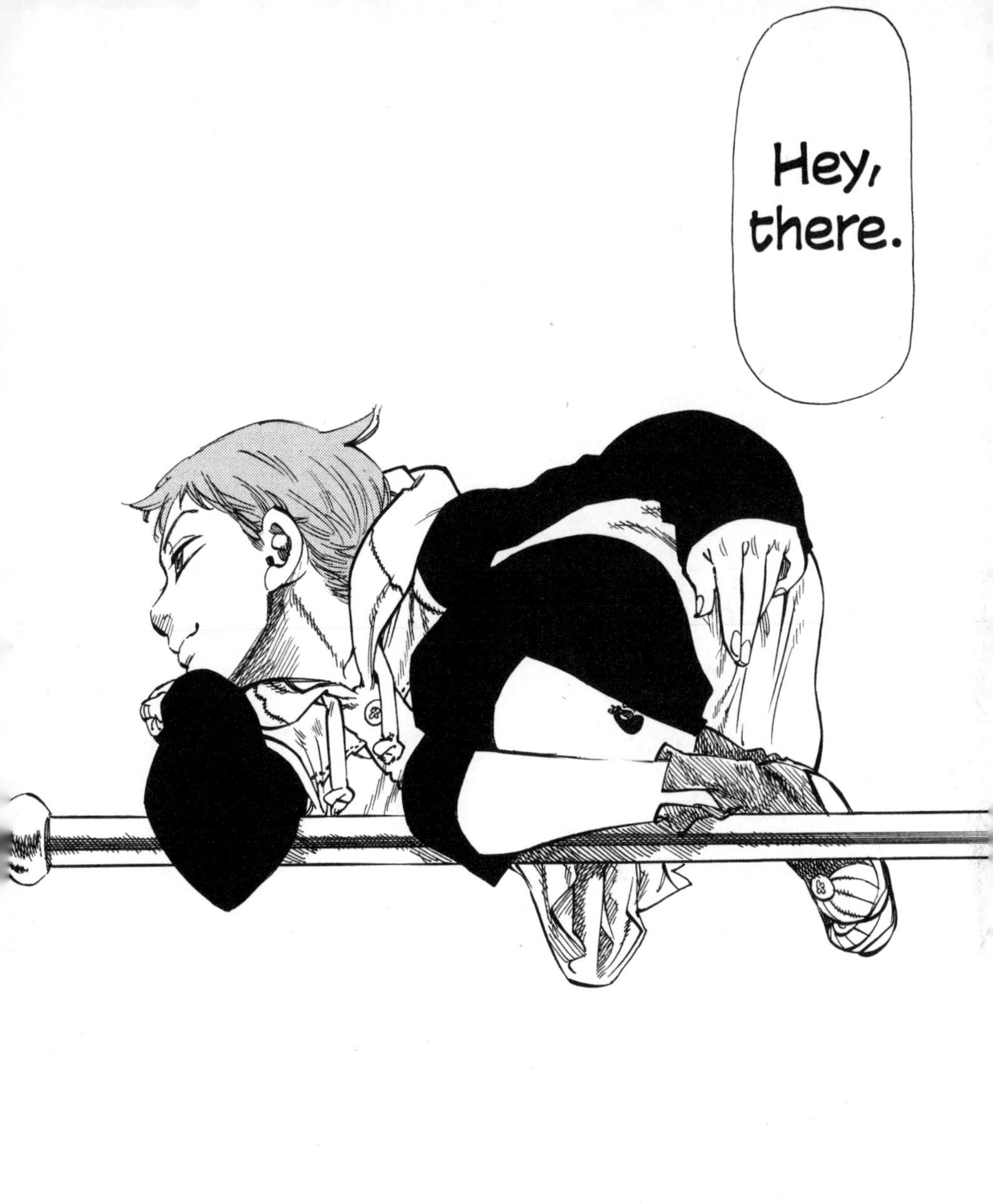
Hey, there.

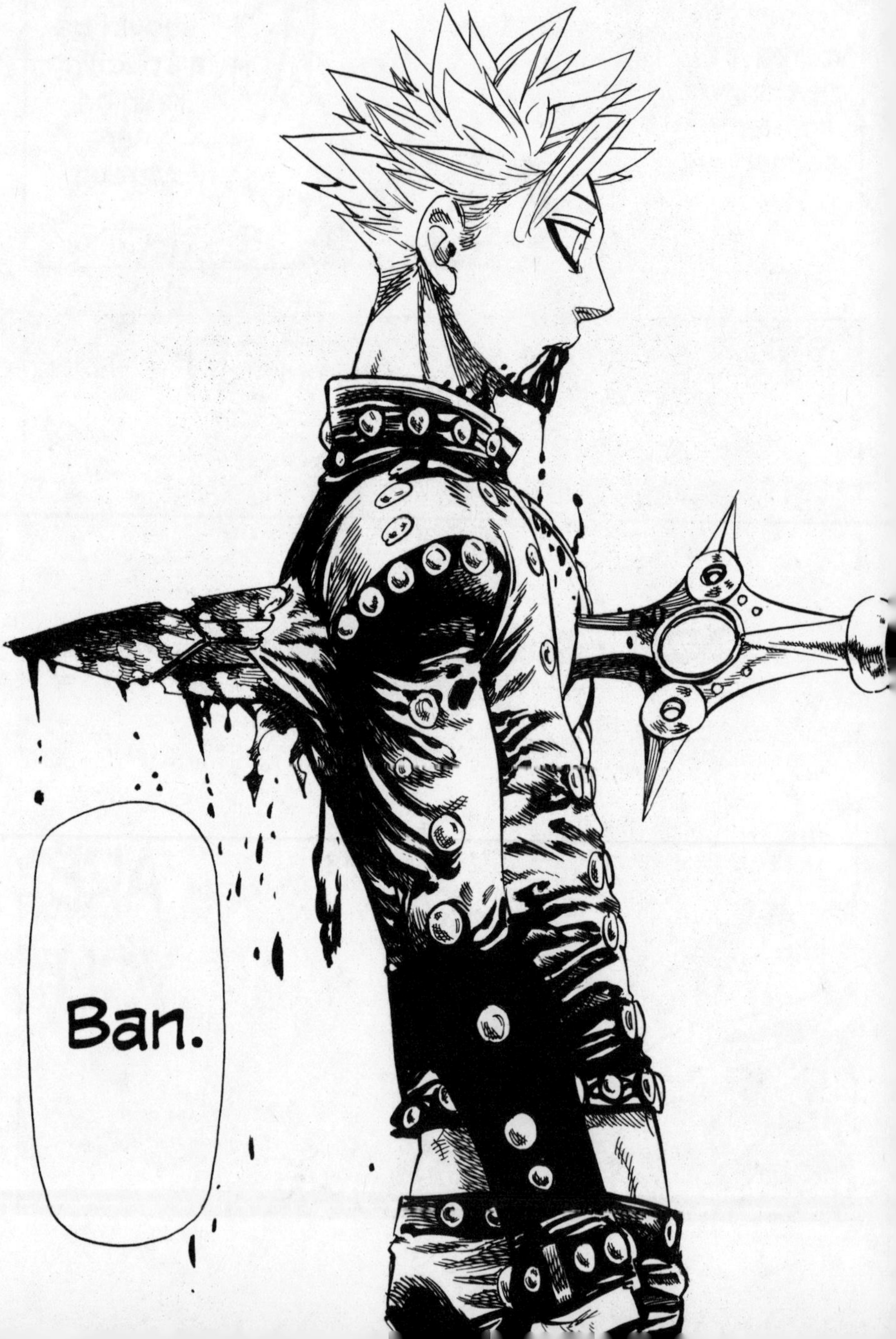
Ban.

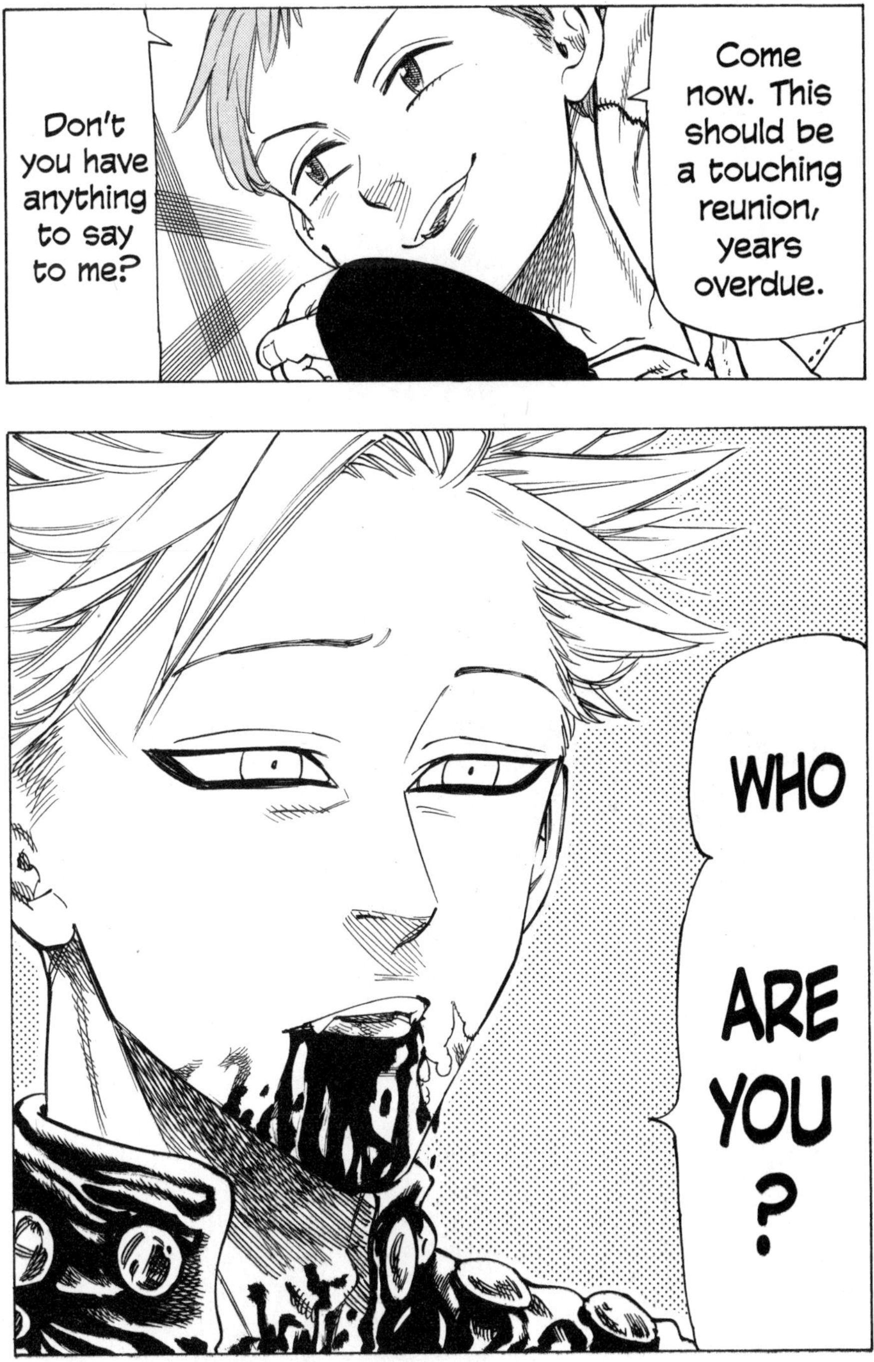
Come now. This should be a touching reunion, years overdue.
Don't you have anything to say to me?
WHO ARE YOU?

Chapter 19 - The Sin of Greed

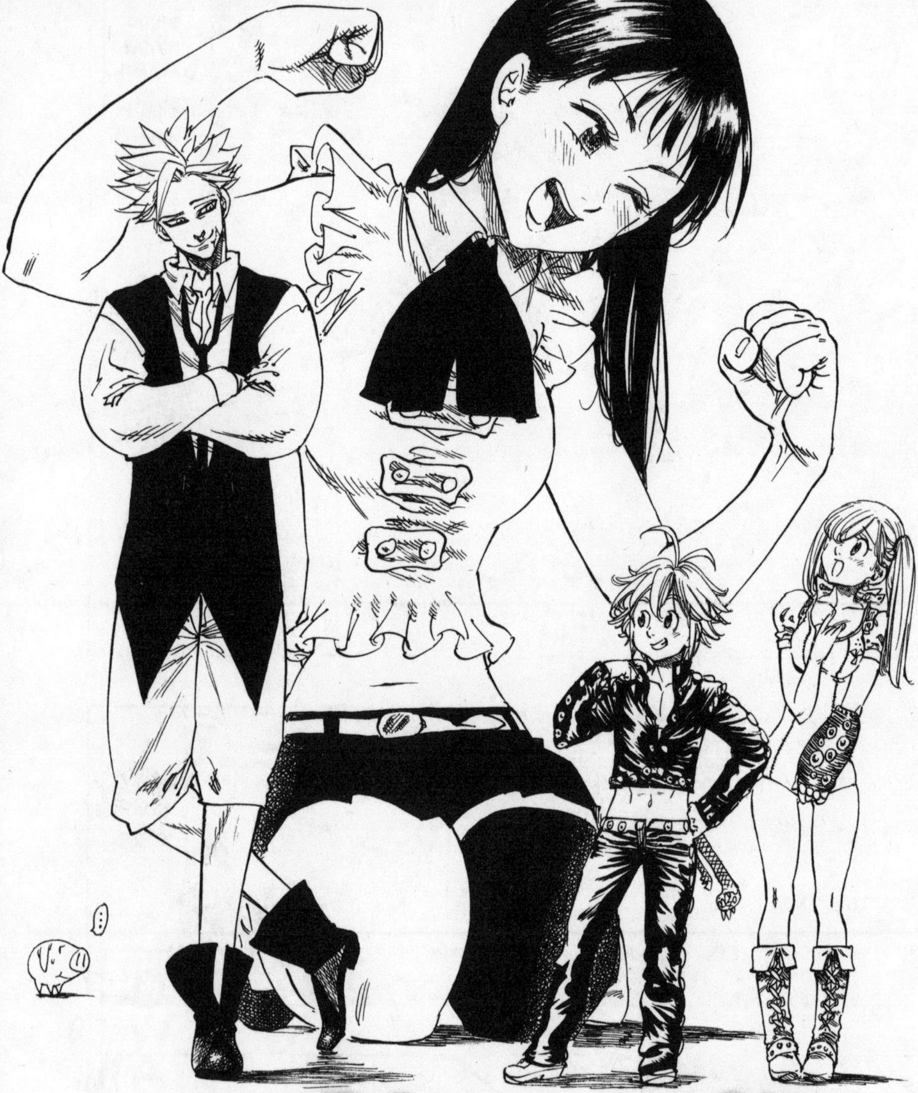

THE SEVEN DEADLY SINS

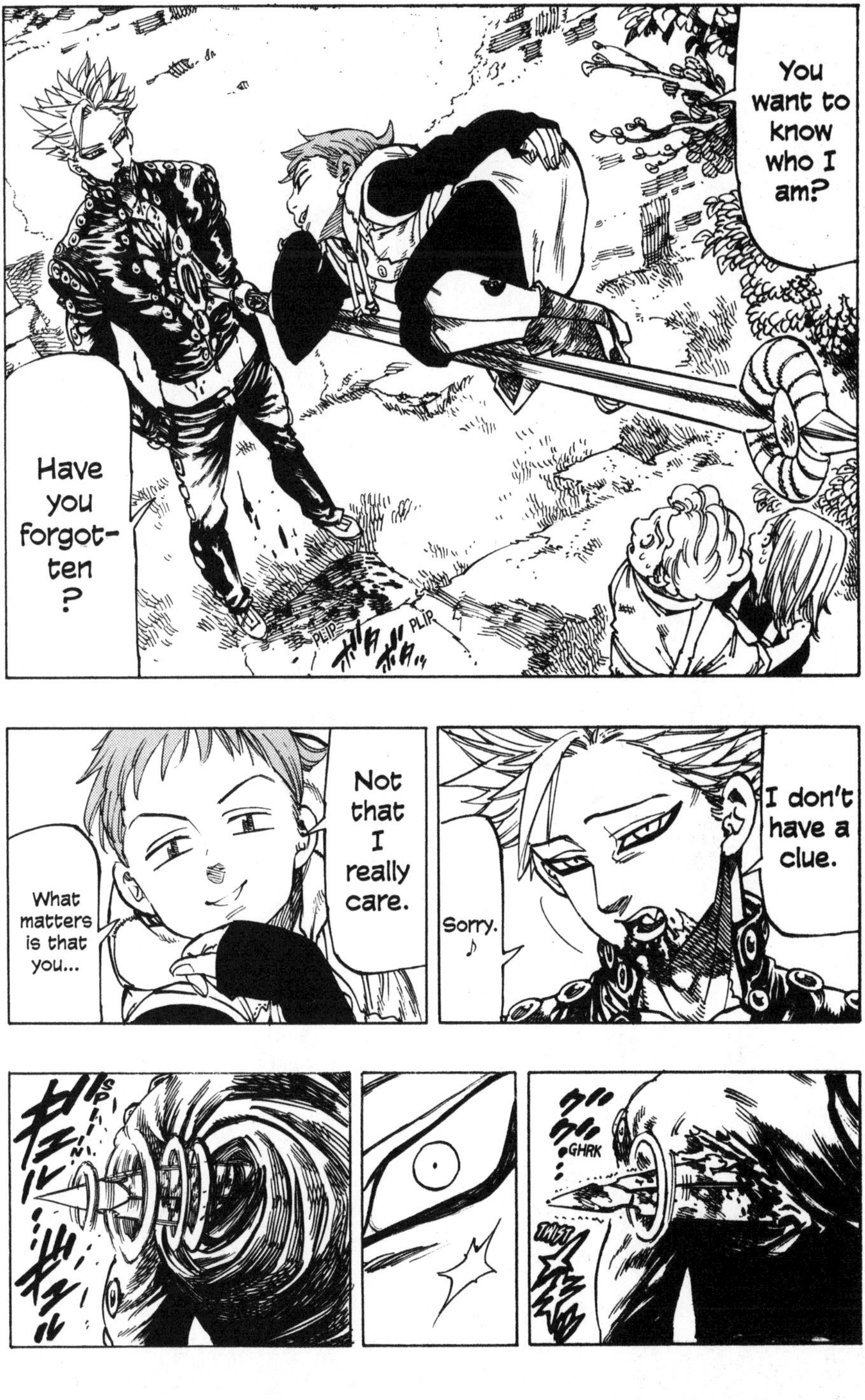
You want to know who I am?
Have you forgotten?
PLIP
PLIP
I don't have a clue.
Sorry. ♪
Not that I really care.
What matters is that you...
GHRK
TWIST
SPIIIN

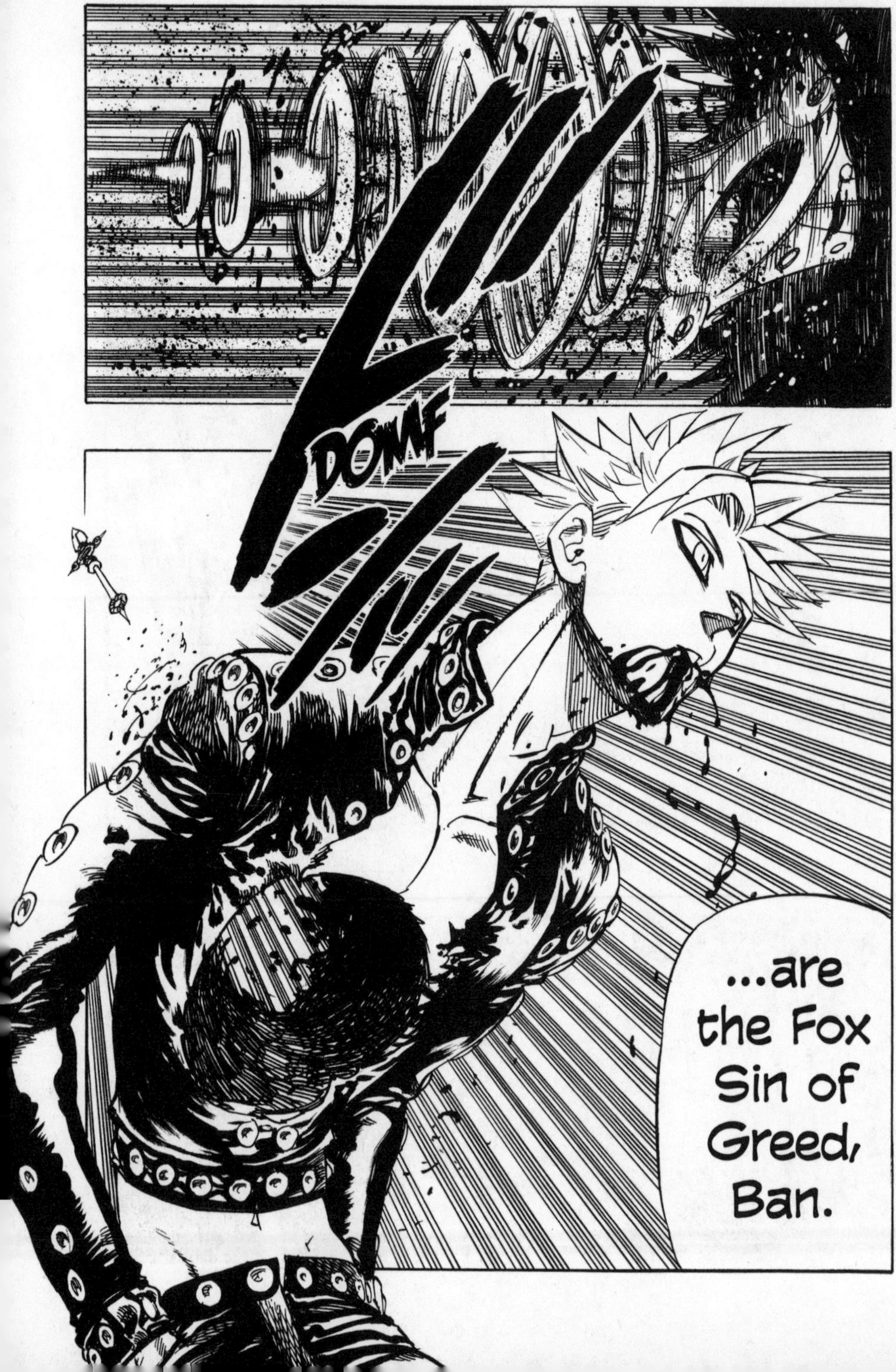
DOMF
...are the Fox Sin of Greed, Ban.

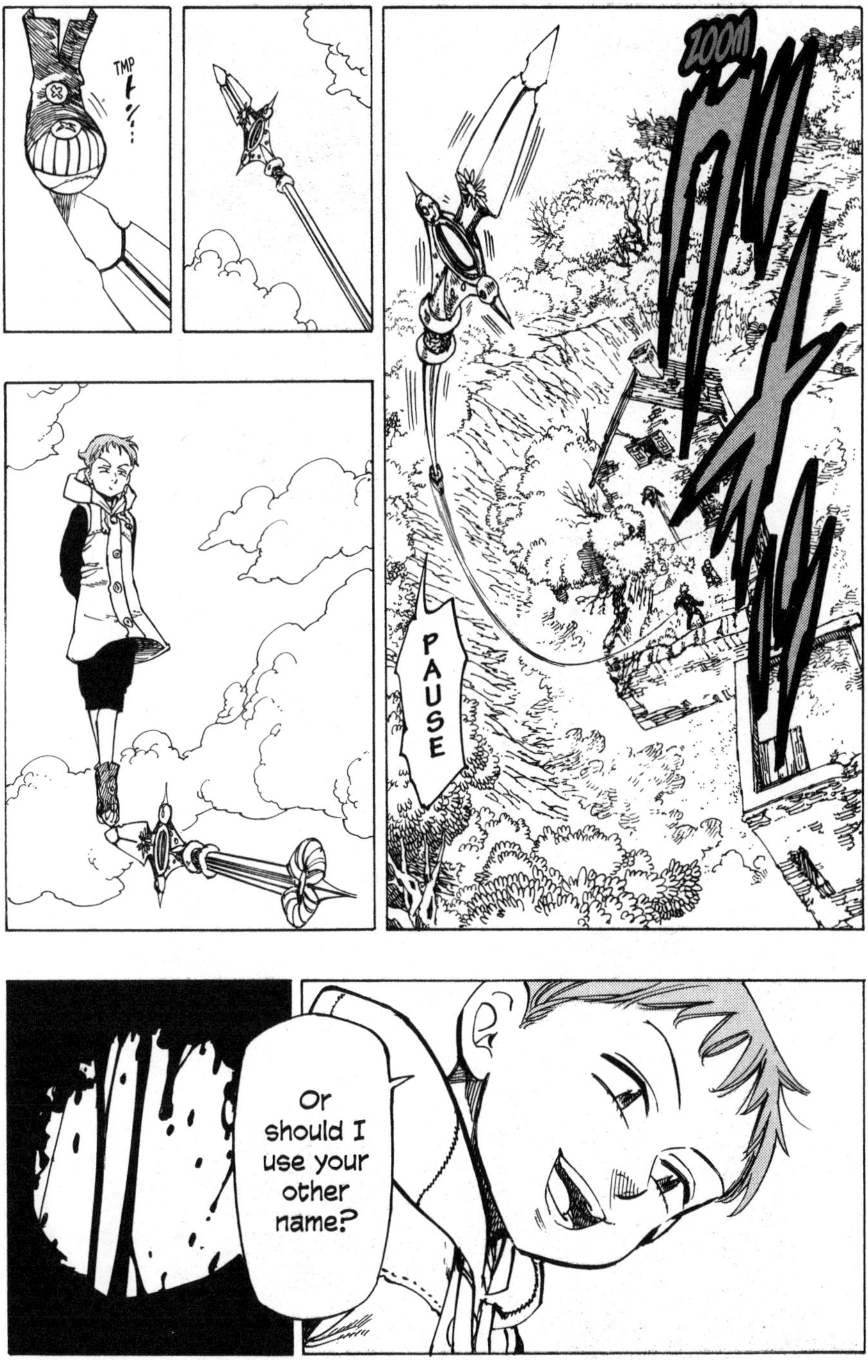
ZOOM
PAUSE
TMP
Or should I use your other name?

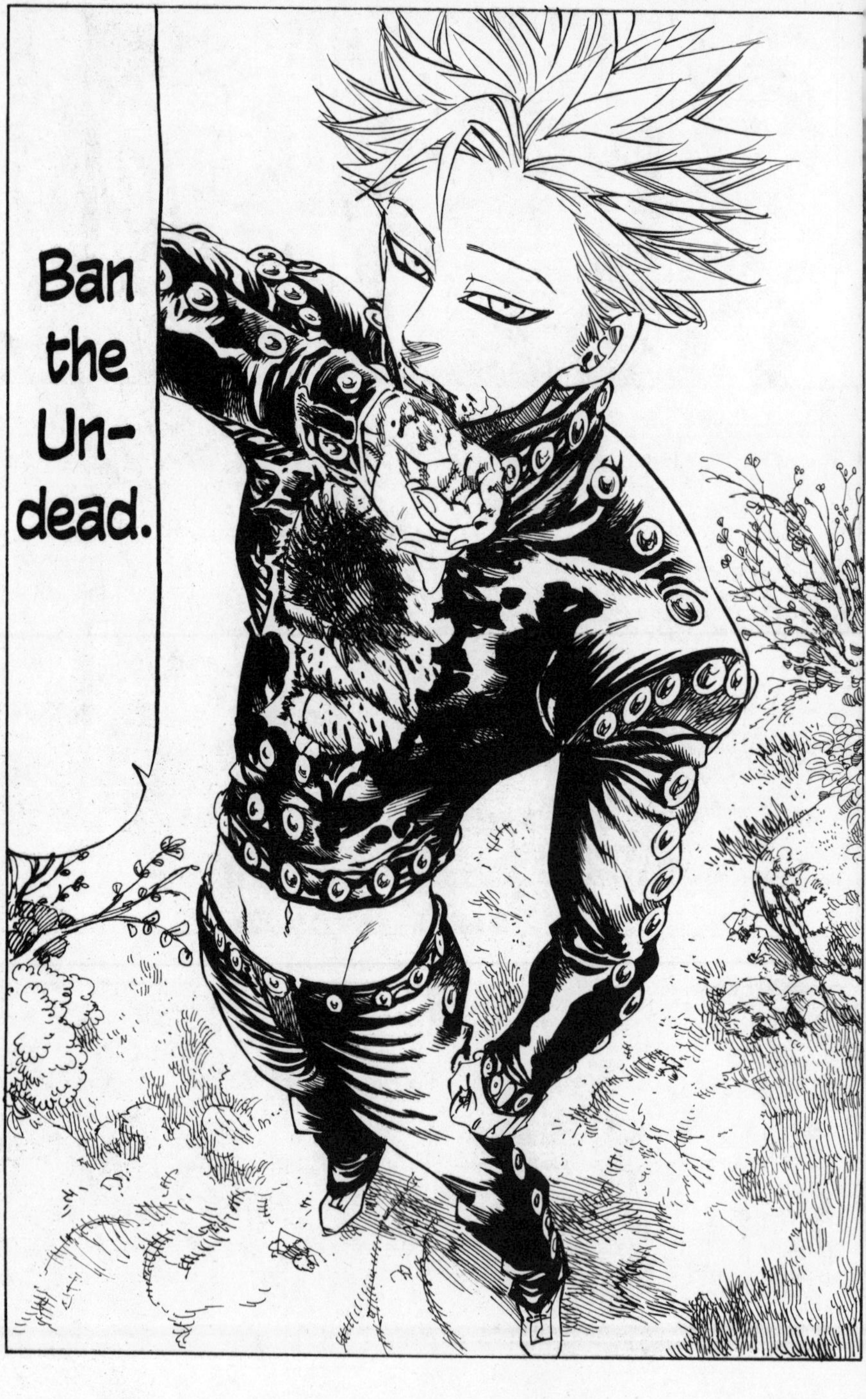
Ban the Un-dead.

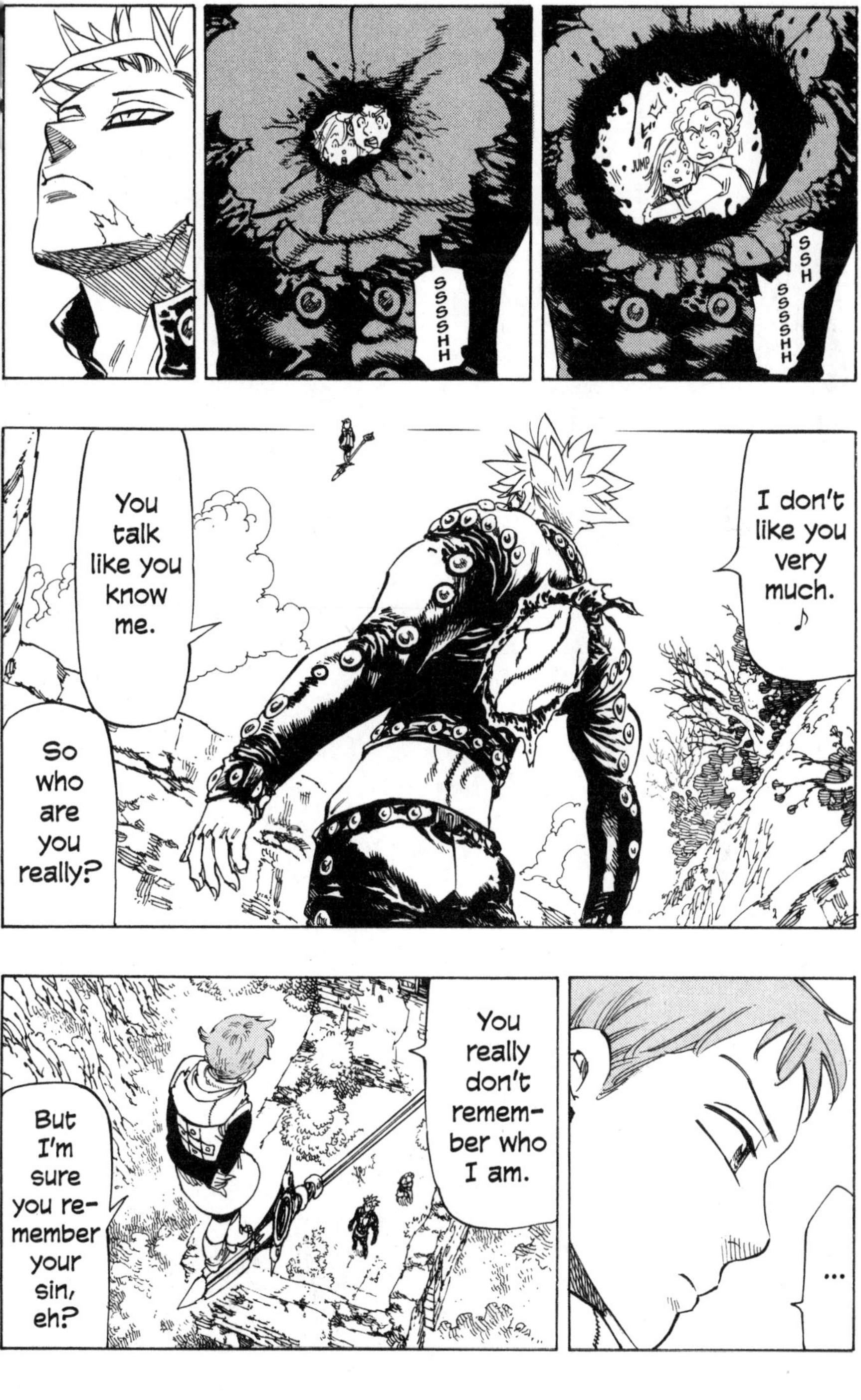
JUMP
SSH
SSSSHH
SSSSHH
I don't like you very much. ♪
You talk like you know me.
So who are you really?
...
You really don't remem-ber who I am.
But I'm sure you re-member your sin, eh?

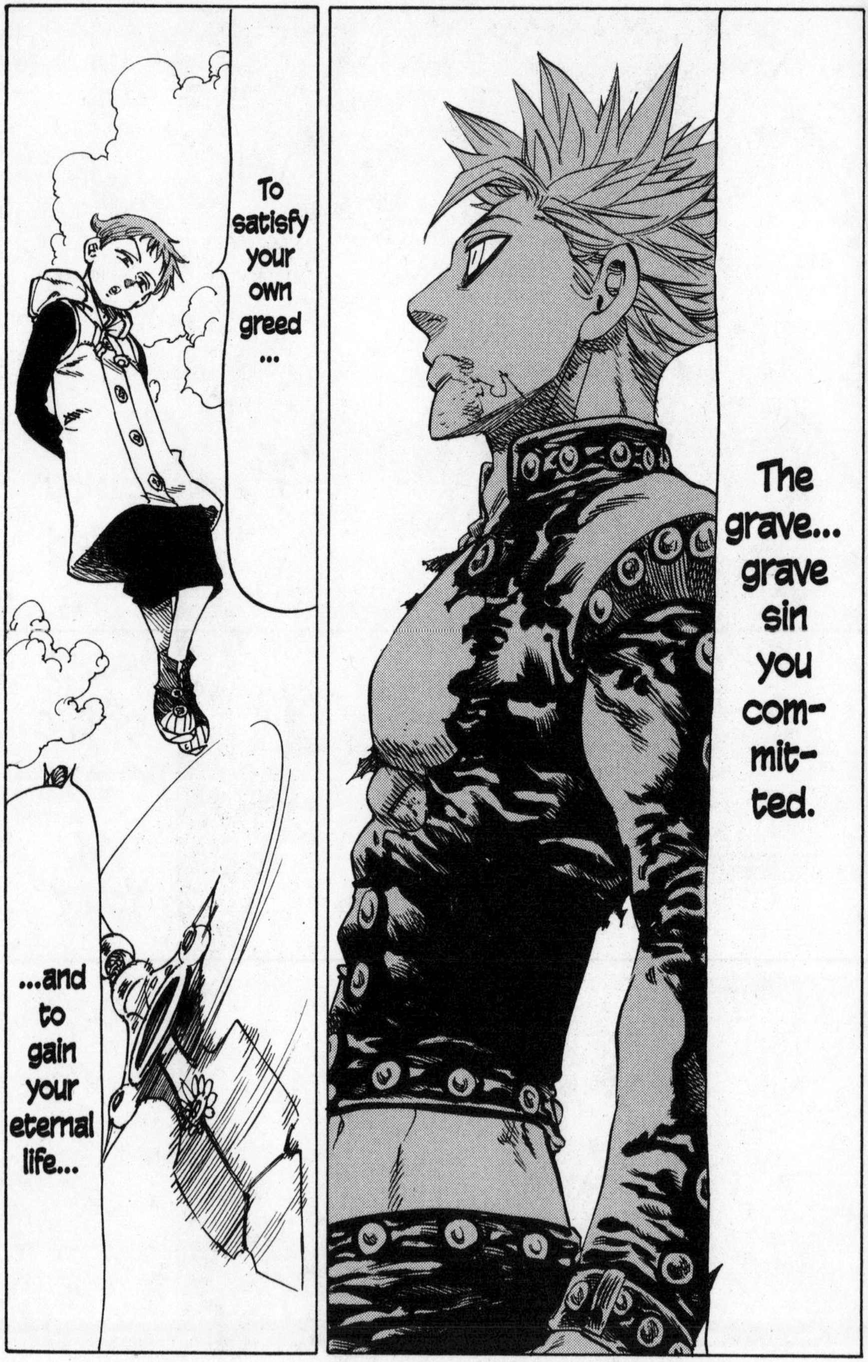
The grave... grave sin you com-mit-ted.
To satisfy your own greed ...
...and to gain your eternal life...

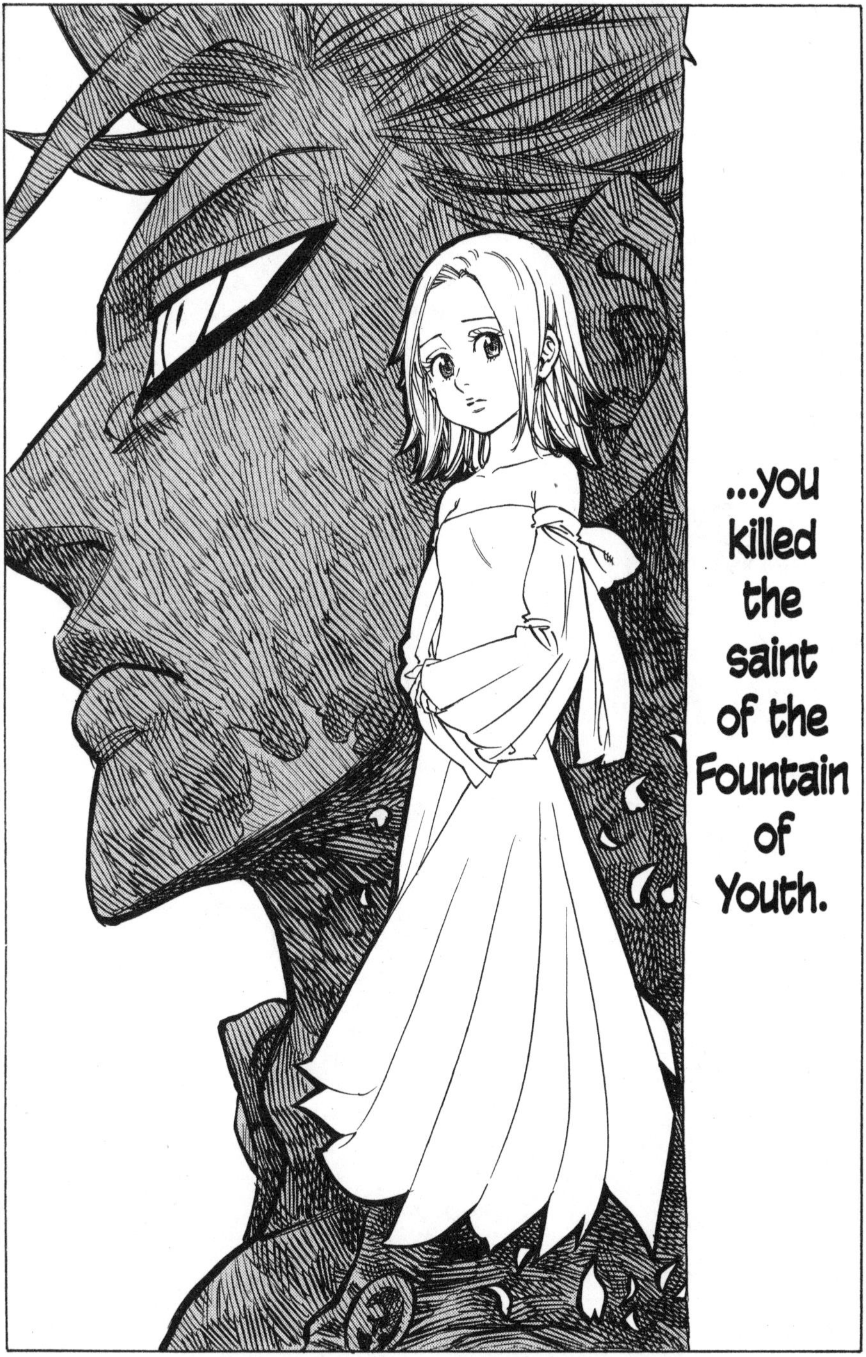
...you killed the saint of the Fountain of Youth.

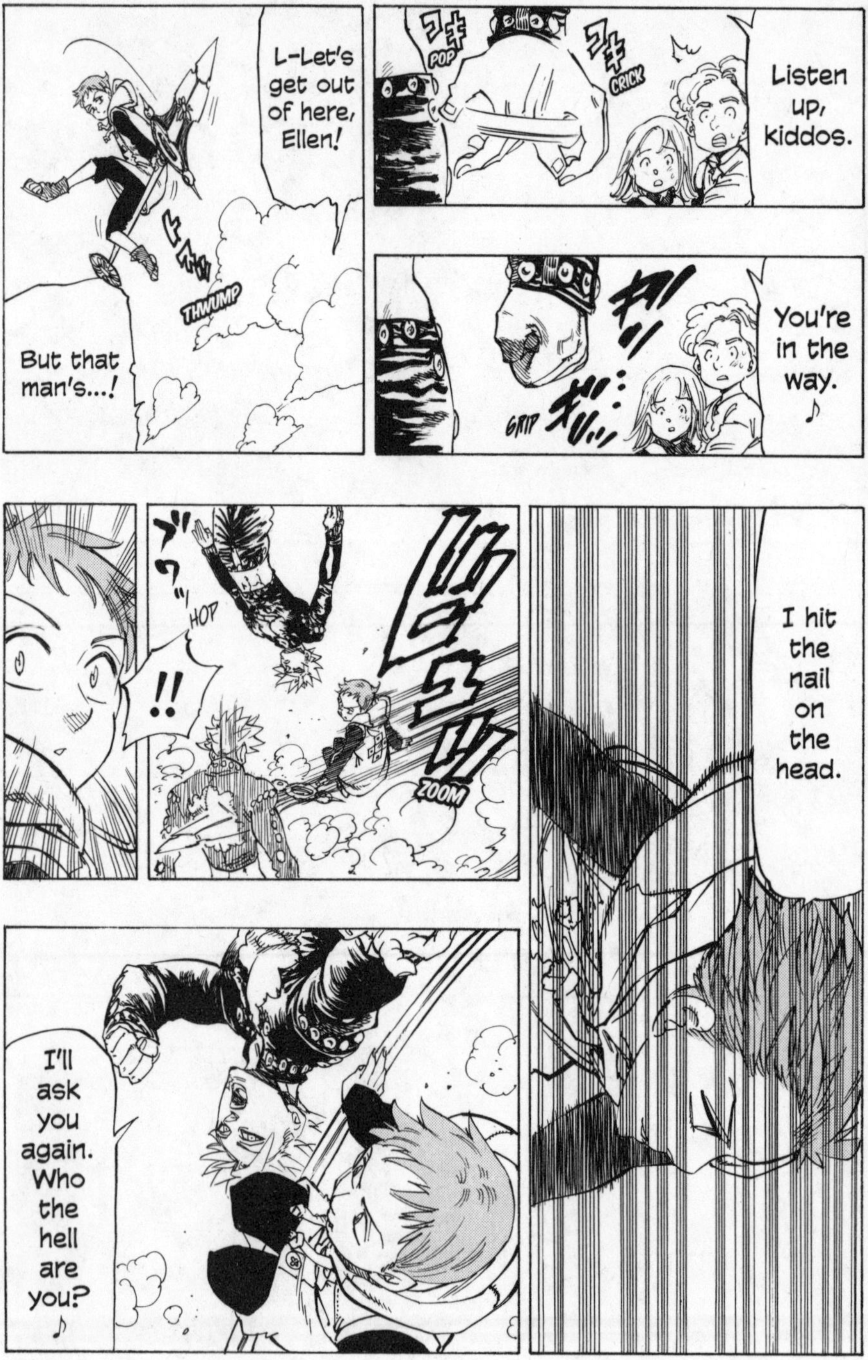
POP
CRICK
Listen up, kiddos.
GRIP
You're in the way. ♪
L-Let's get out of here, Ellen!
THWUMP
But that man's...!
I hit the nail on the head.
ZOOM
HOP
!!
I'll ask you again. Who the hell are you? ♪

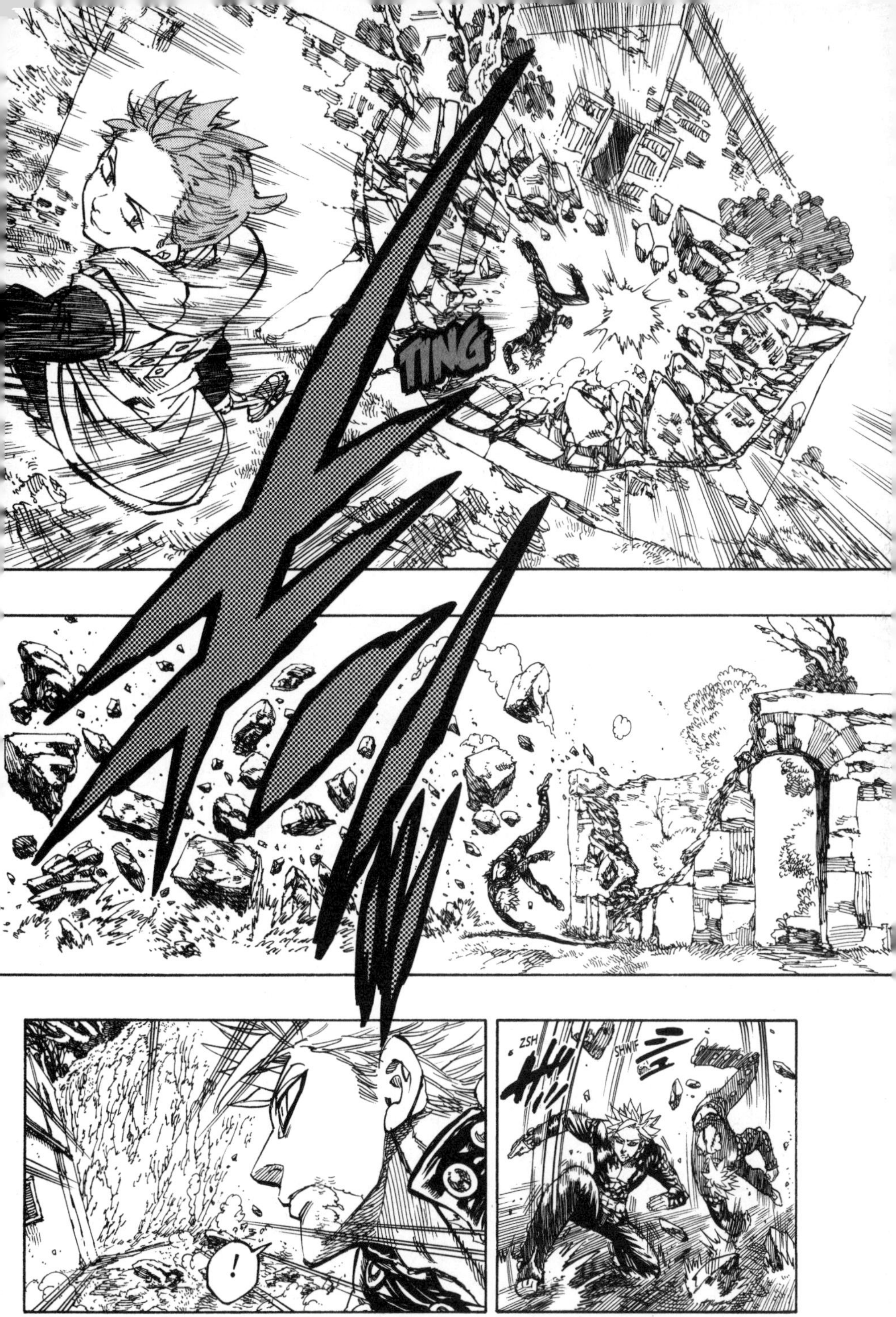
TING
ZSH
SHWIF
!

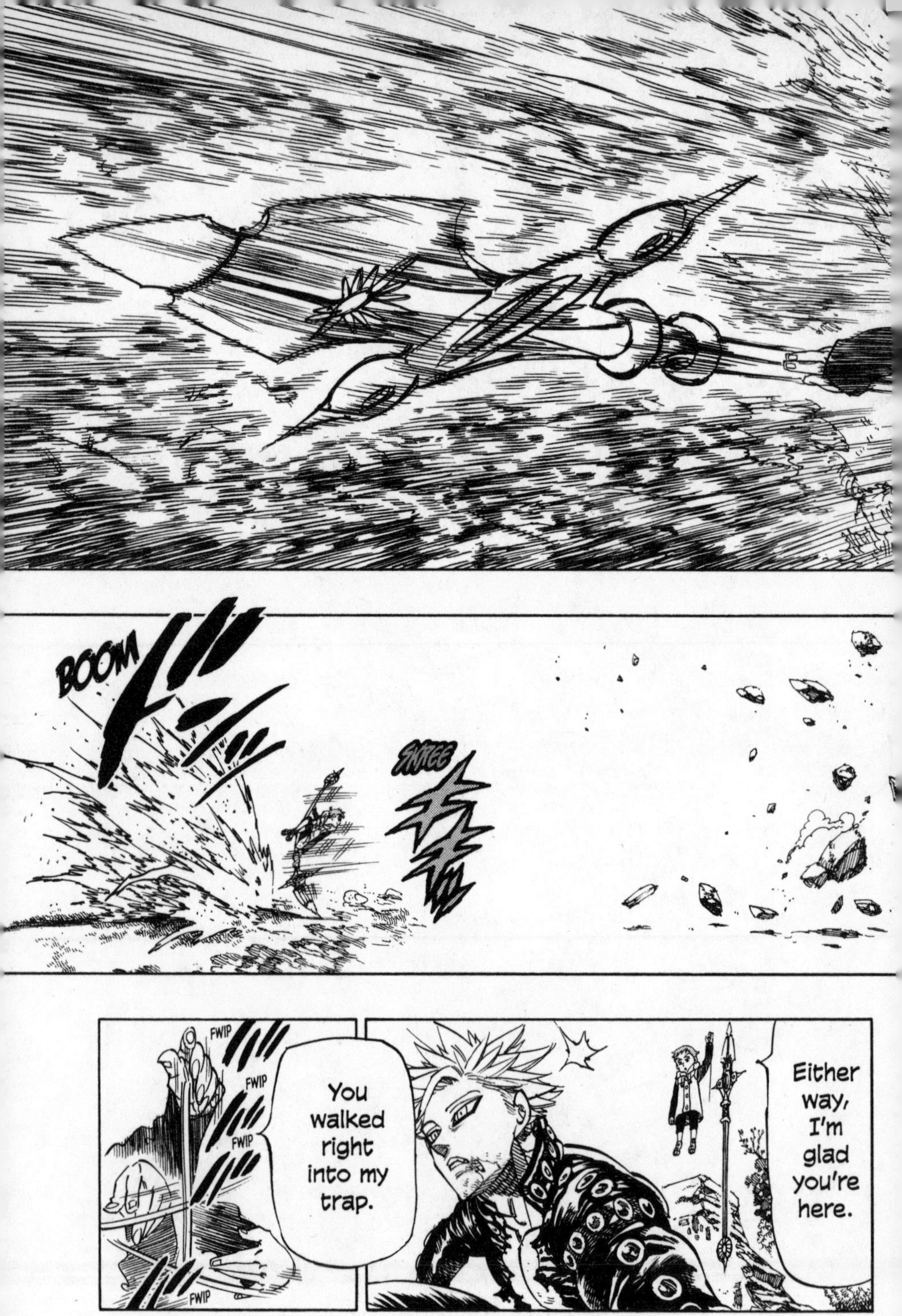
SKREE
BOOM
Either way, I'm glad you're here.
You walked right into my trap.
FWIP
FWIP
FWIP
FWIP

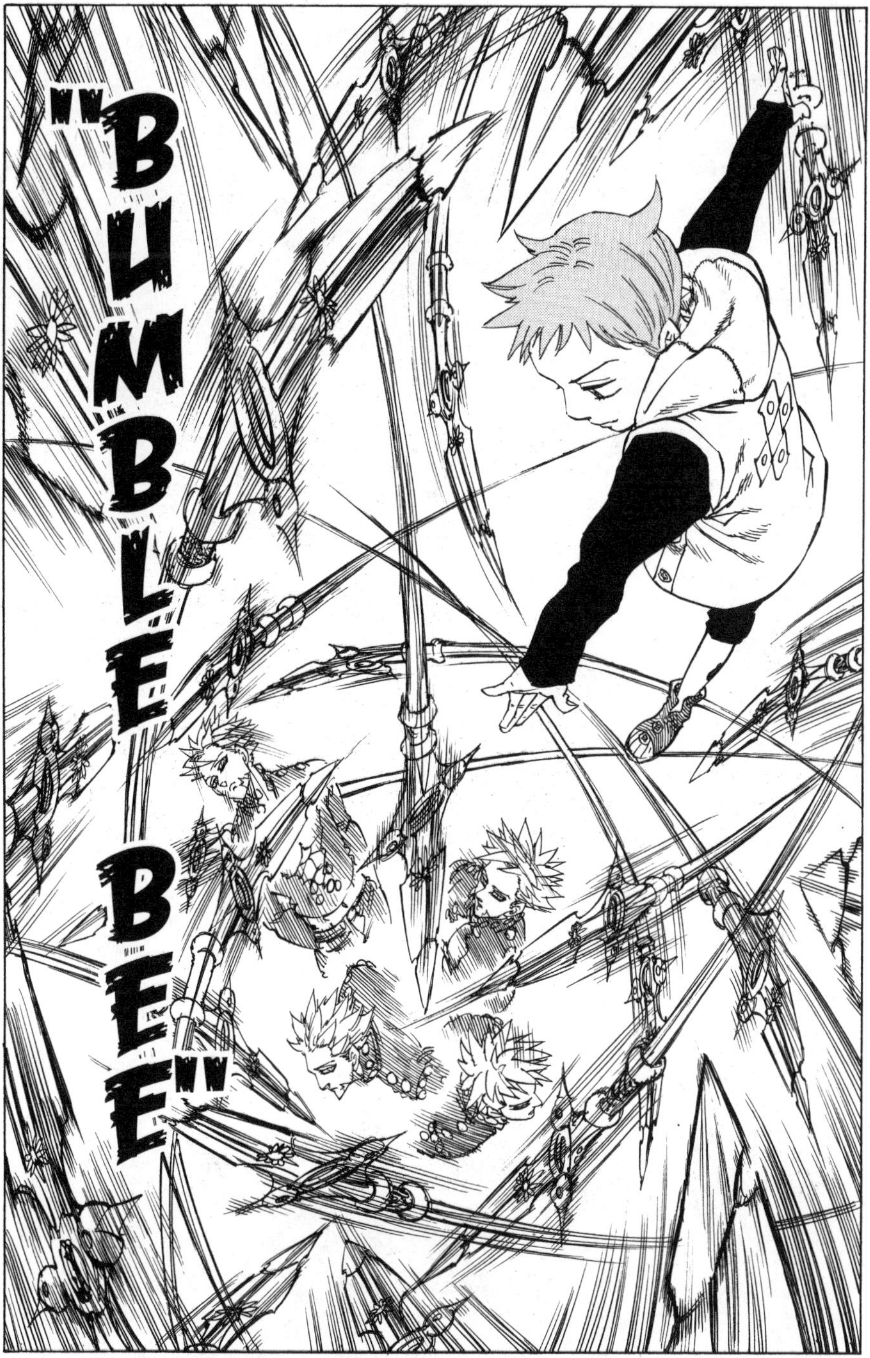
"BUMBLE BEE"

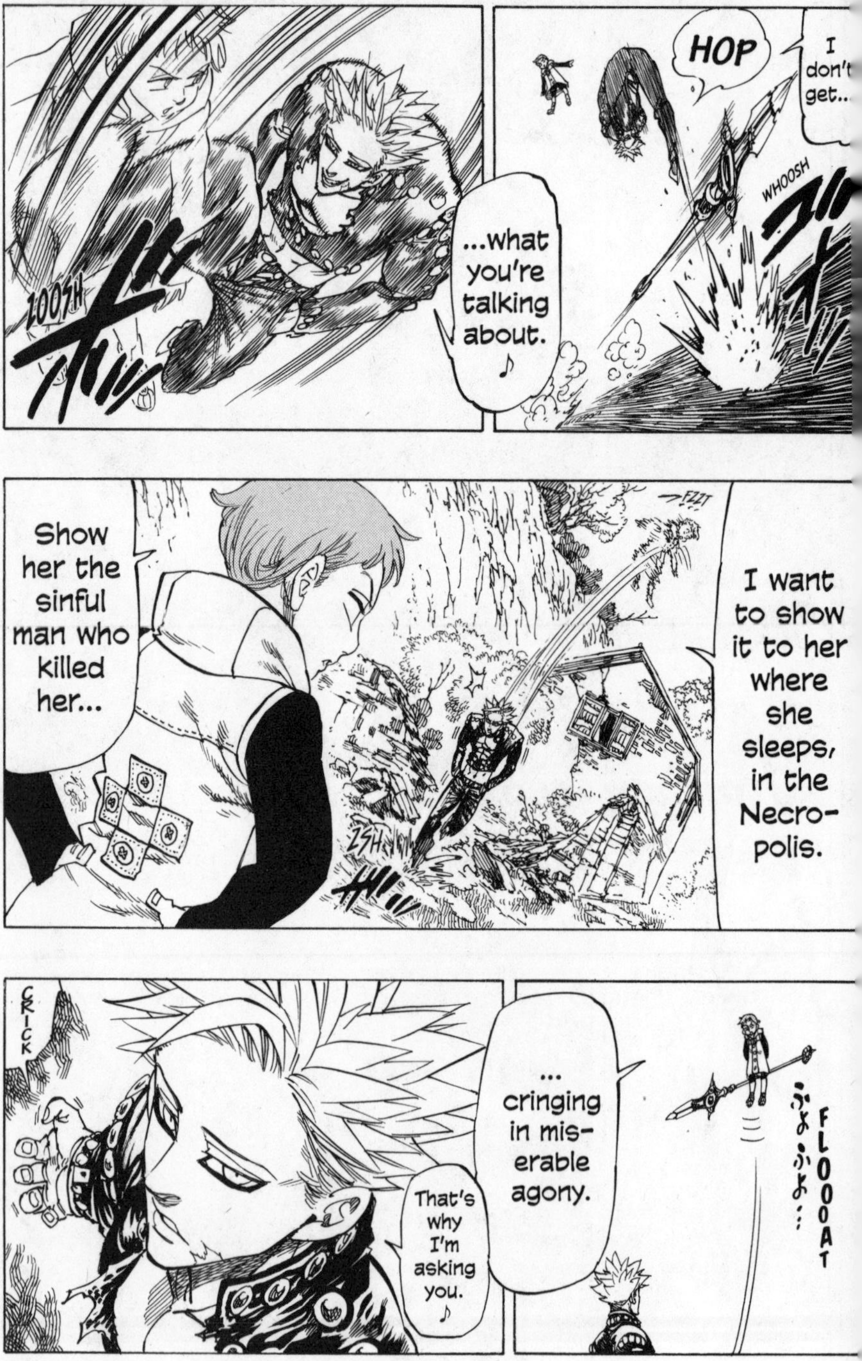
HOP
I don't get...
WHOOSH
...what you're talking about. ♪
ZOOSH
I want to show it to her where she sleeps, in the Necropolis.
FZZT
ZSH
Show her the sinful man who killed her...
ふよふよ…
FLOOOAT
...cringing in miserable agony.
That's why I'm asking you. ♪
CRICK

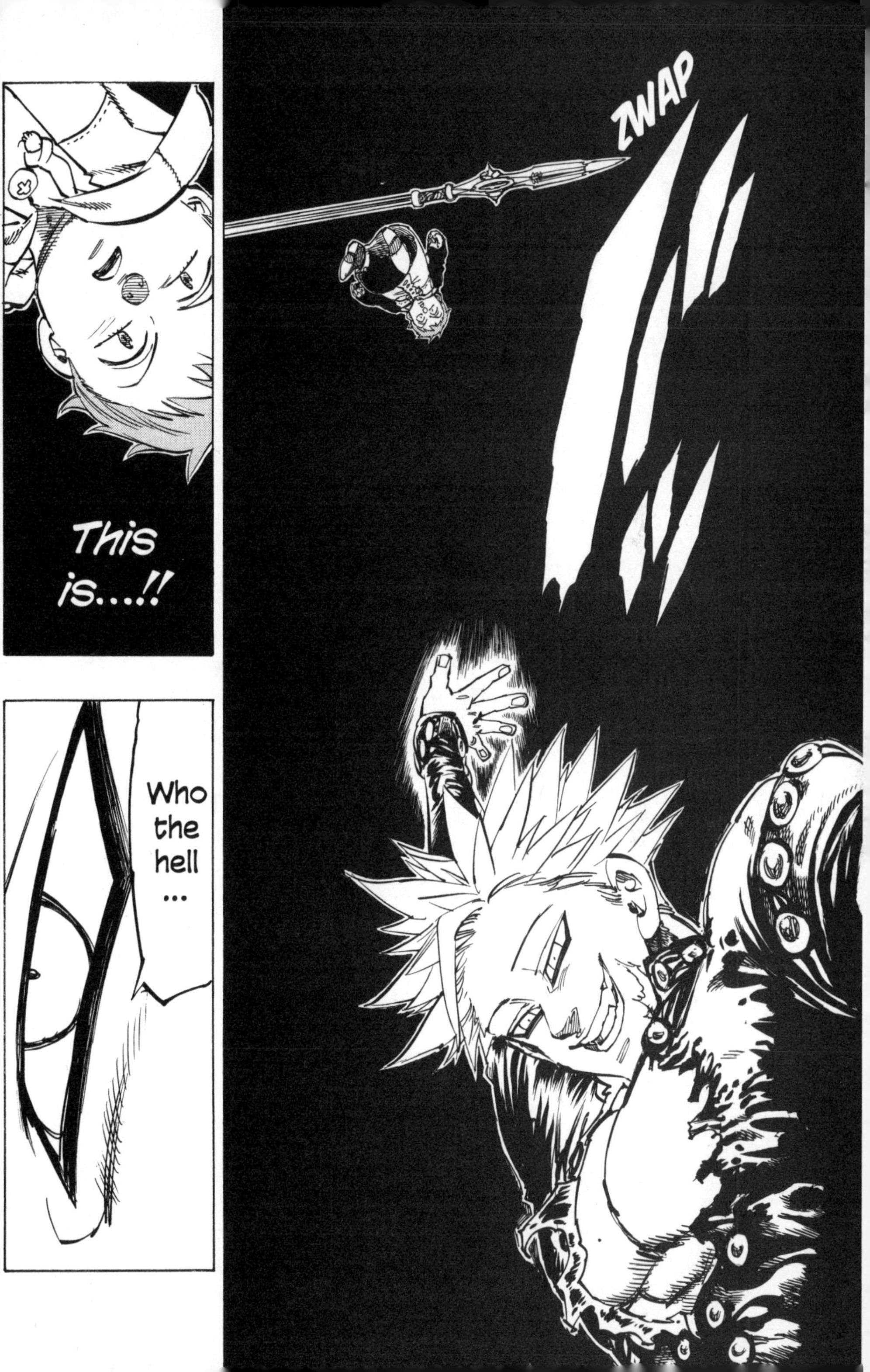
ZWAP
This is...!!
Who the hell ...

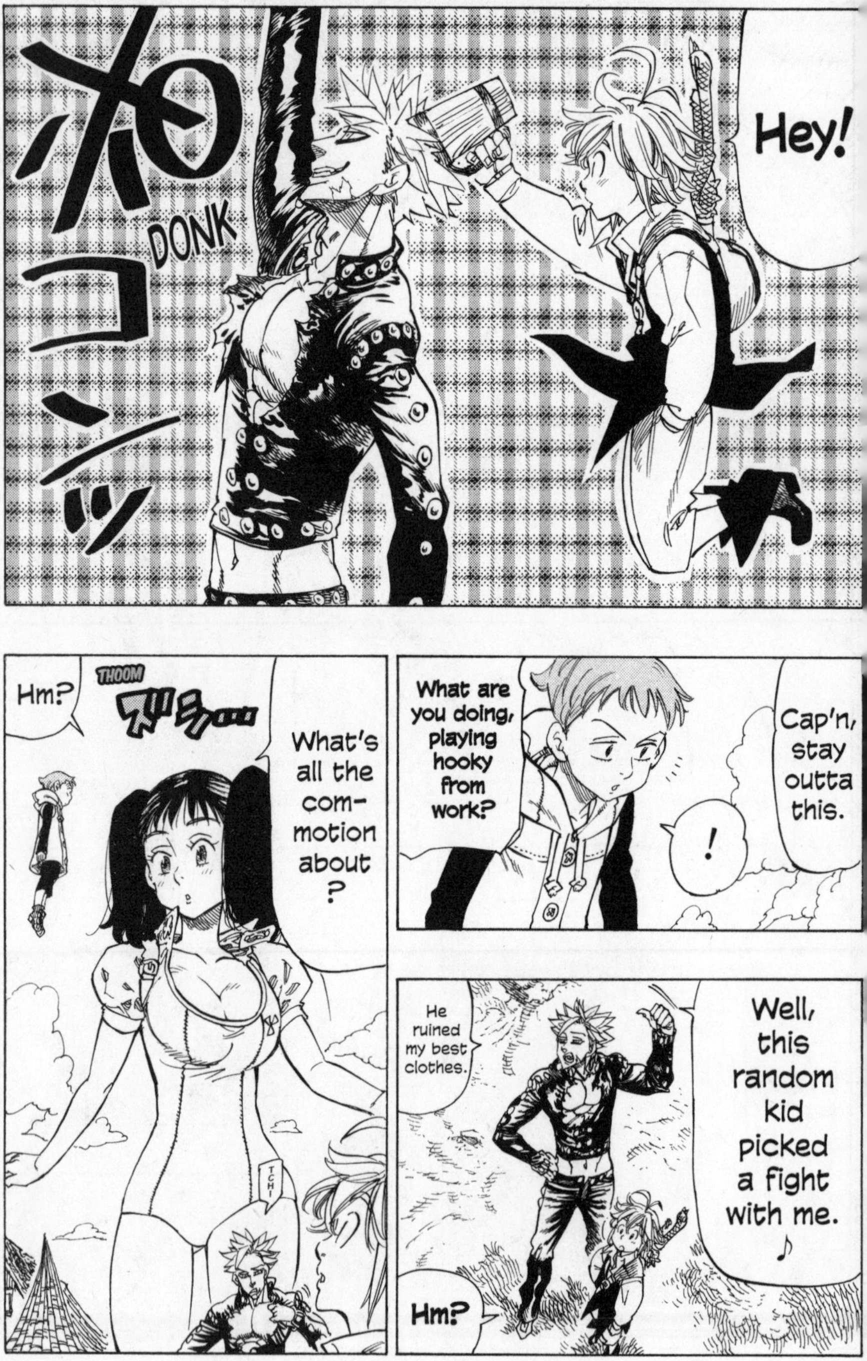
Hey!
DONK
Cap'n, stay outta this.
!
What are you doing, playing hooky from work?
Well, this random kid picked a fight with me. ♪
He ruined my best clothes.
Hm?
What's all the com-motion about?
THOOM
Hm?
TCHI

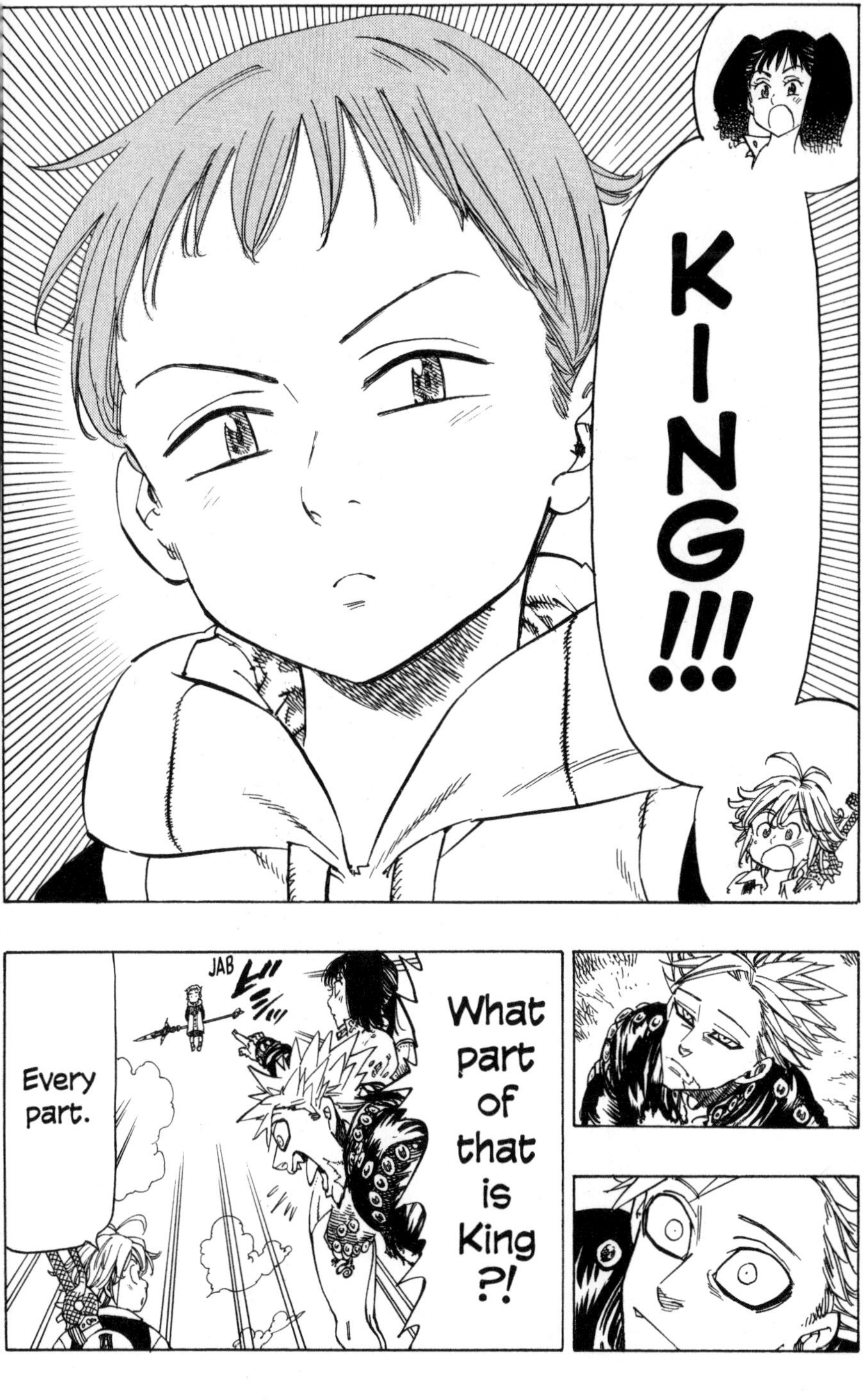
KING!!!
What part of that is King?!
JAB
Every part.

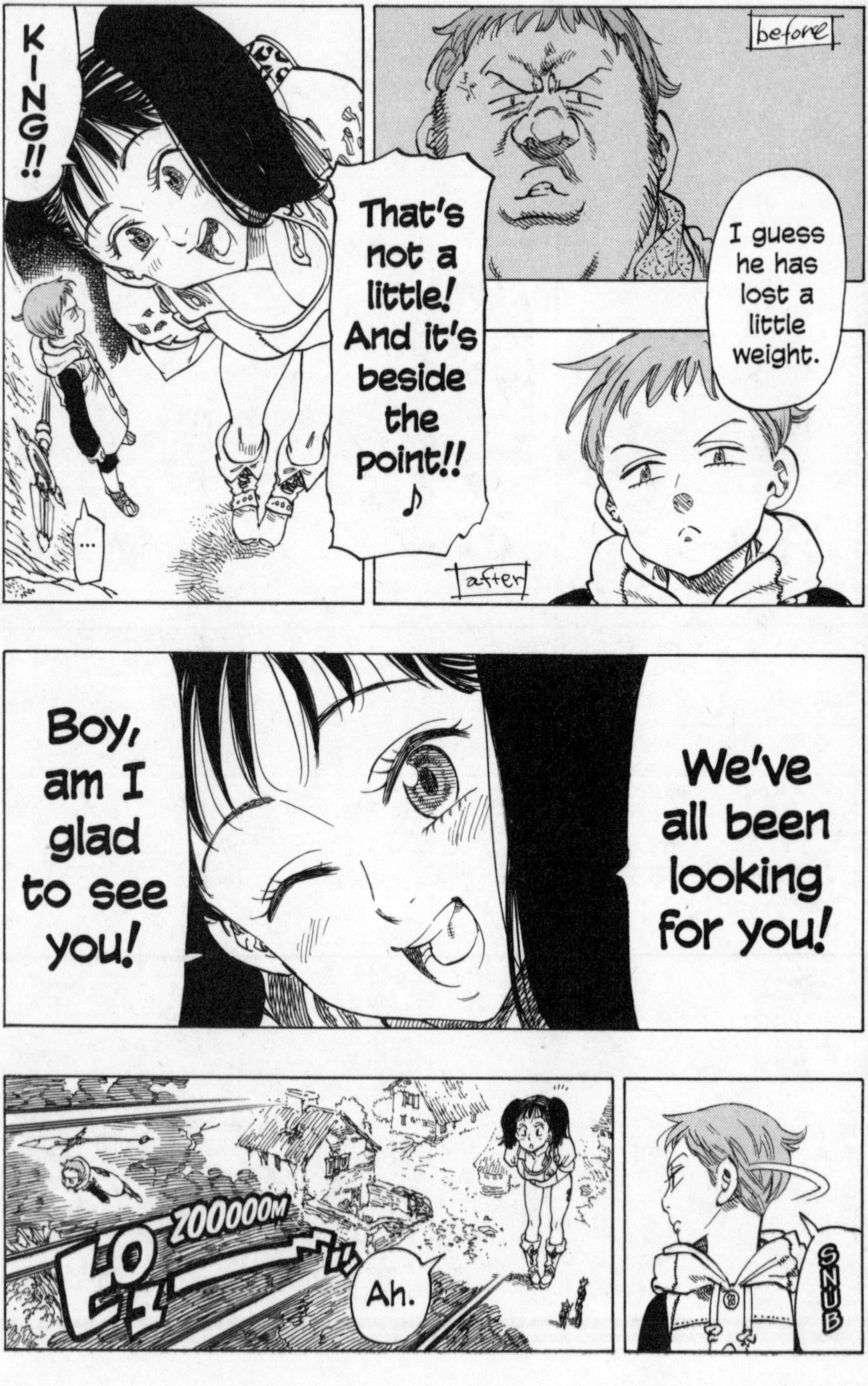

before
I guess he has lost a little weight.
after
KING!!
That's not a little! And it's beside the point!! ♪
...
We've all been looking for you!
Boy, am I glad to see you!
SNUB
ZOOOOOM
Ah.

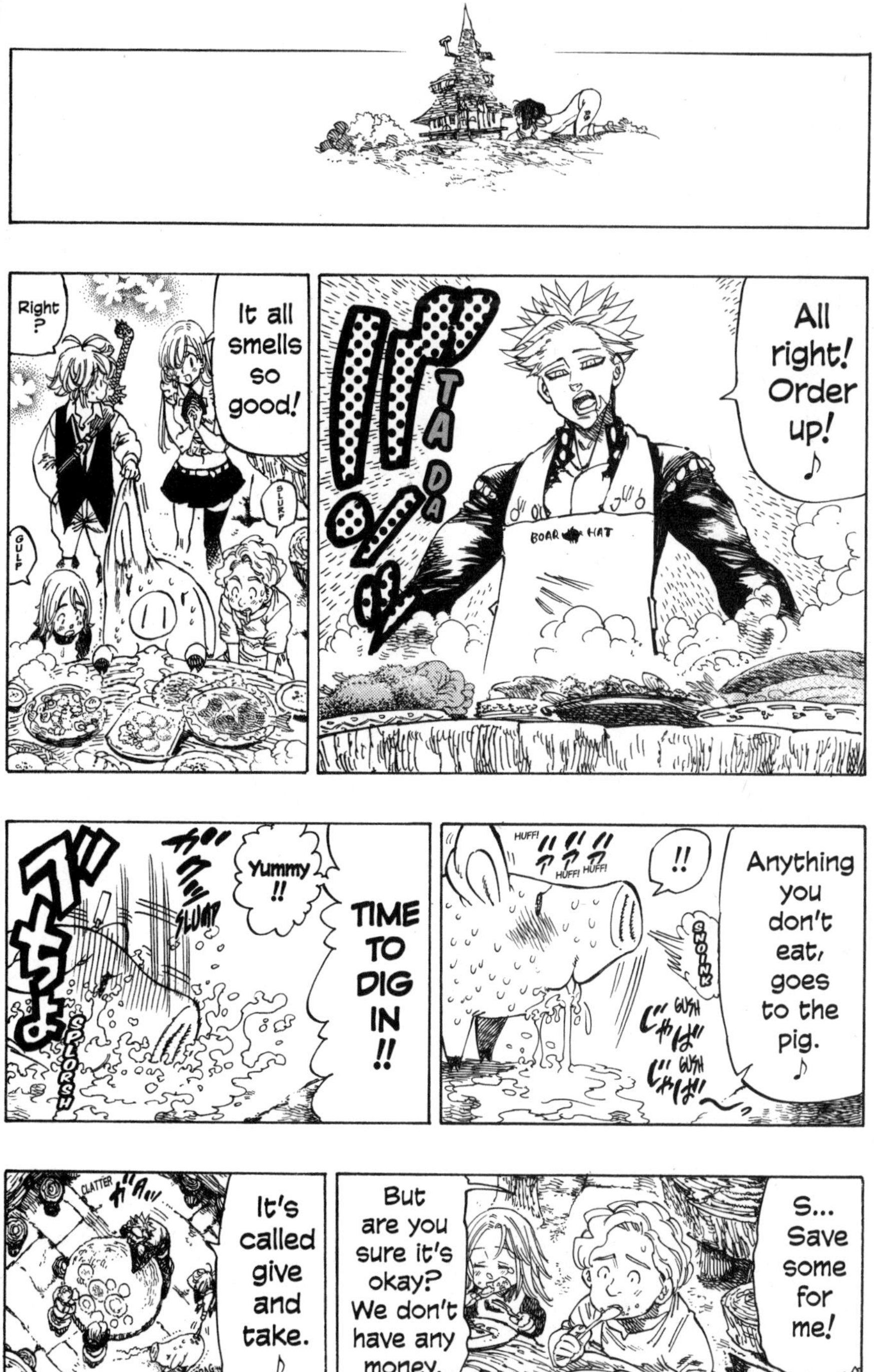
All right! Order up! ♪
TA DA
It all smells so good!
Right?
SLURP
GULP
Anything you don't eat, goes to the pig. ♪
!!
HUFF! HUFF! HUFF!
GUSH
GUSH
TIME TO DIG IN!!
Yummy!!
SLURP
SPLORSH
S... Save some for me!
But are you sure it's okay? We don't have any money.
It's called give and take. ♪
CLATTER
DRAG DRAG

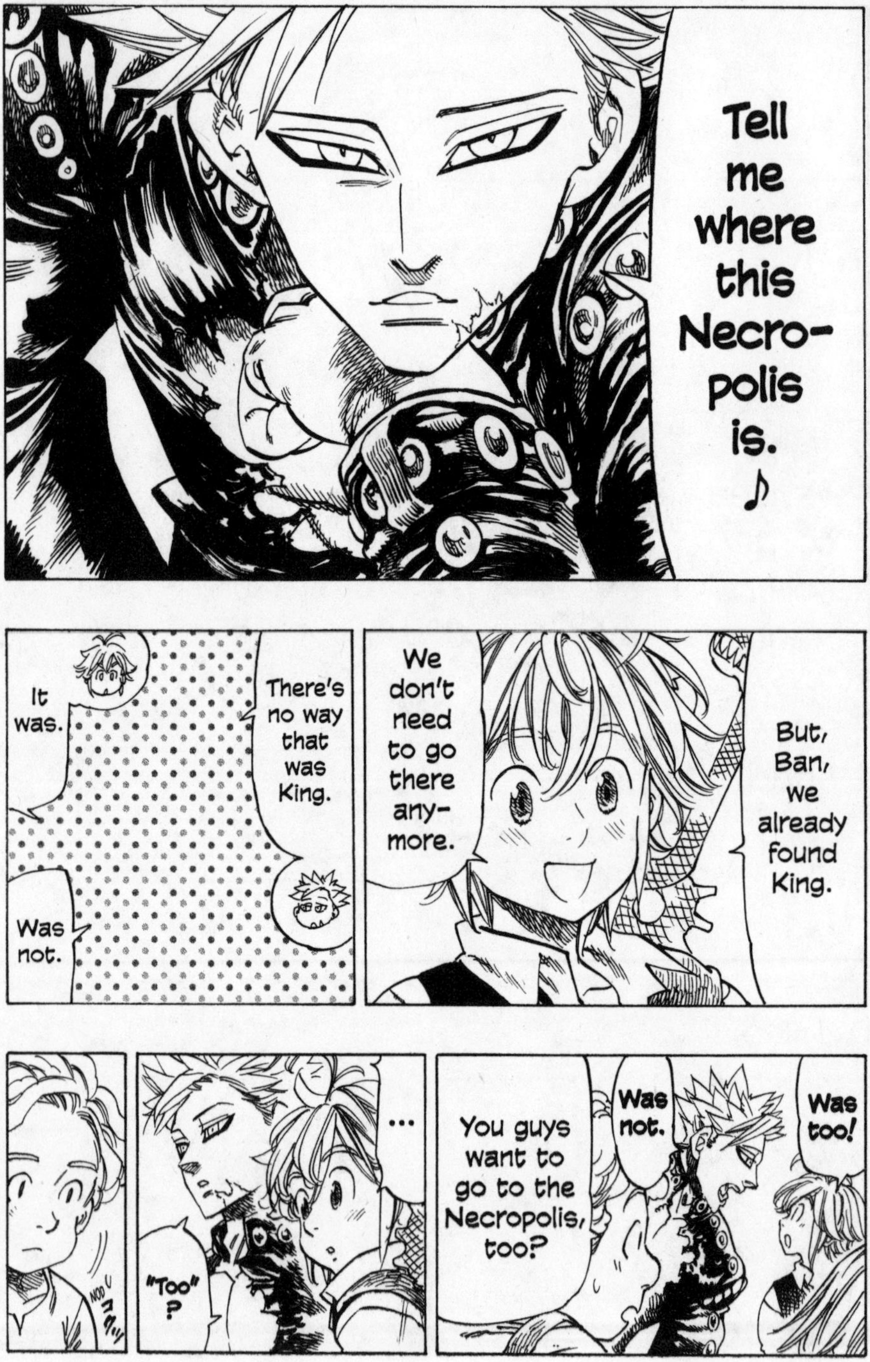
Tell me where this Necropolis is. ♪
But, Ban, we already found King.
We don't need to go there anymore.
There's no way that was King.
It was.
Was not.
Was too!
Was not.
You guys want to go to the Necropolis, too?
...
"Too"?
NOD

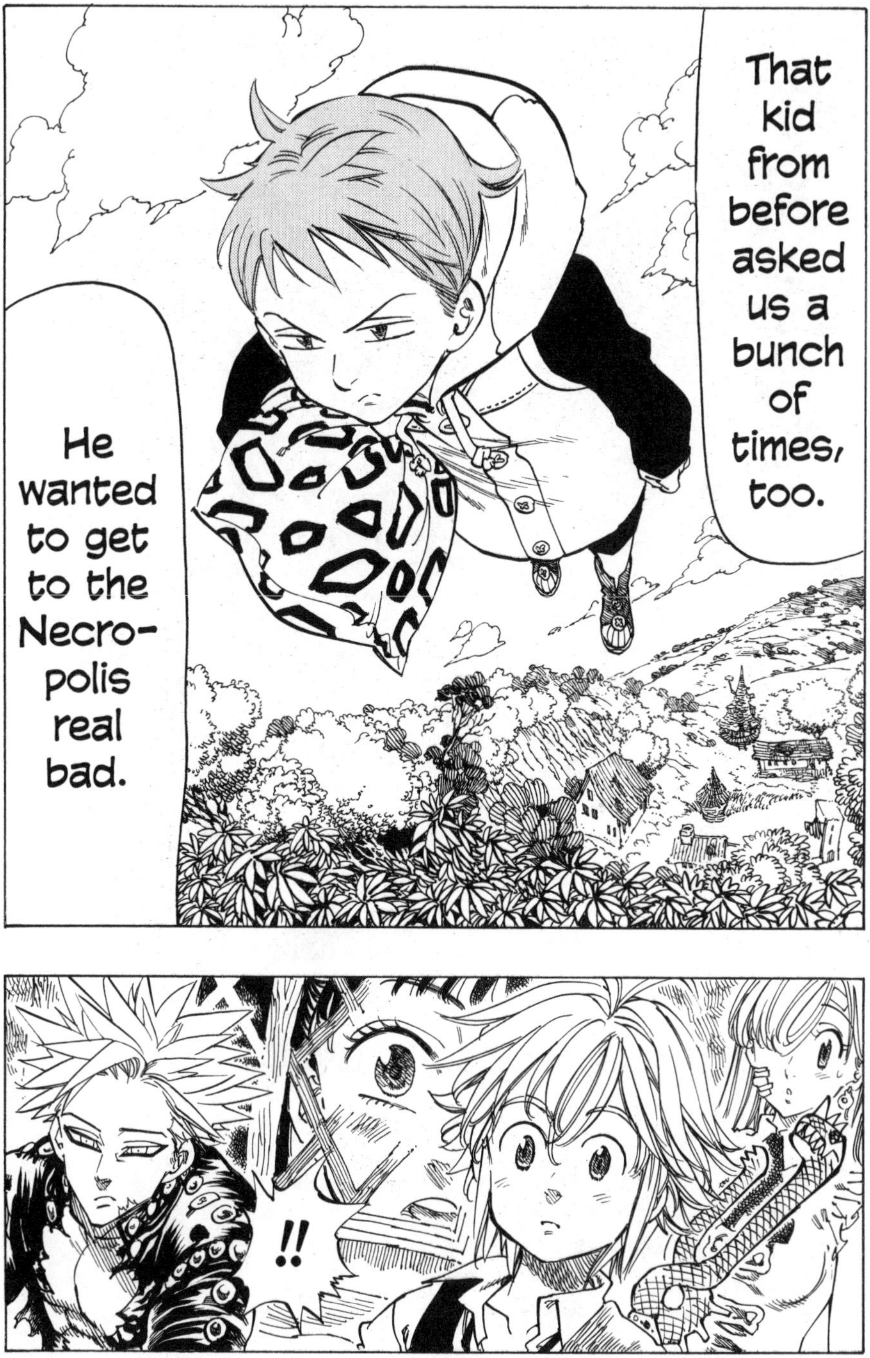
That kid from before asked us a bunch of times, too.
He wanted to get to the Necropolis real bad.
!!

Chapter 20 - Two Paths

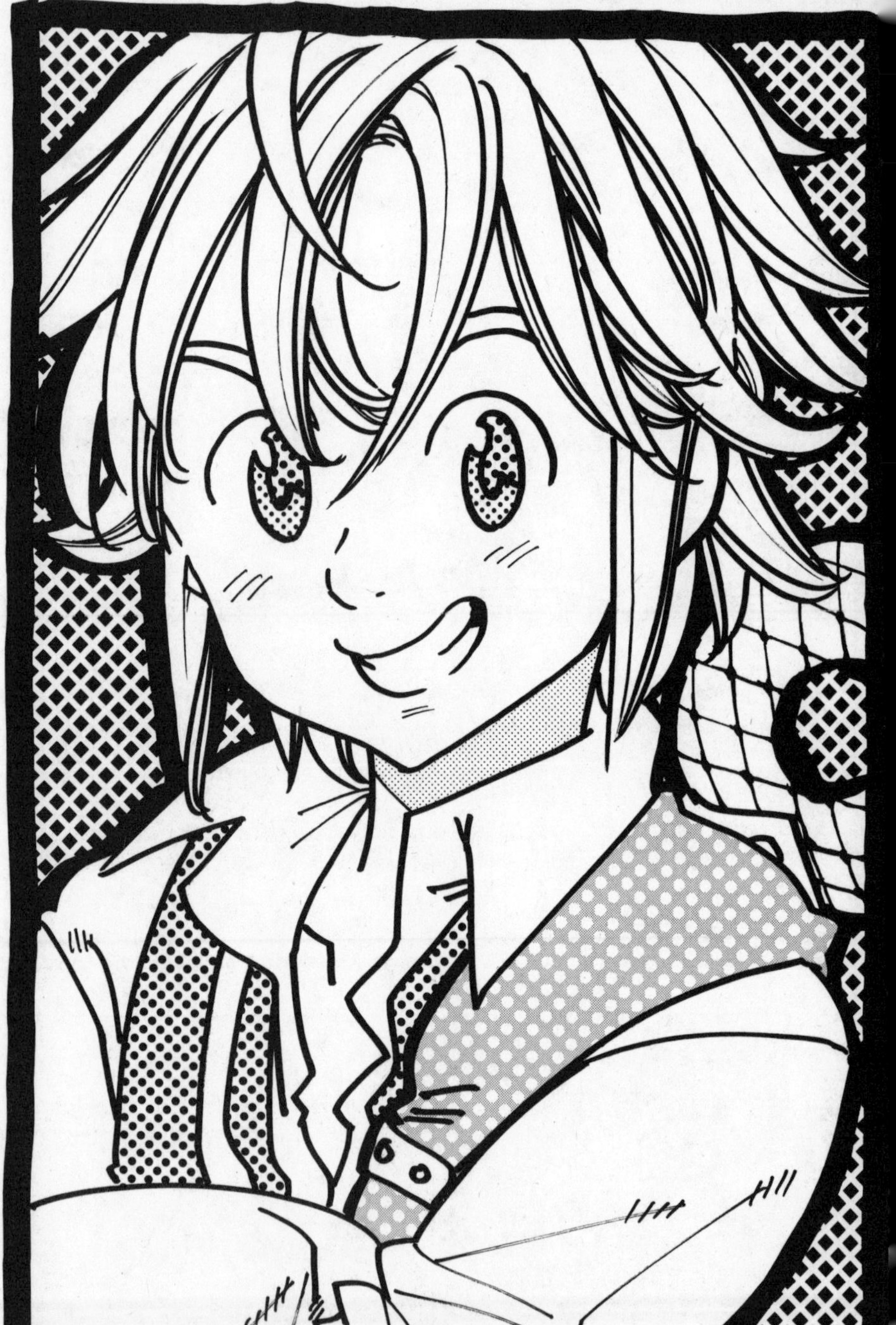

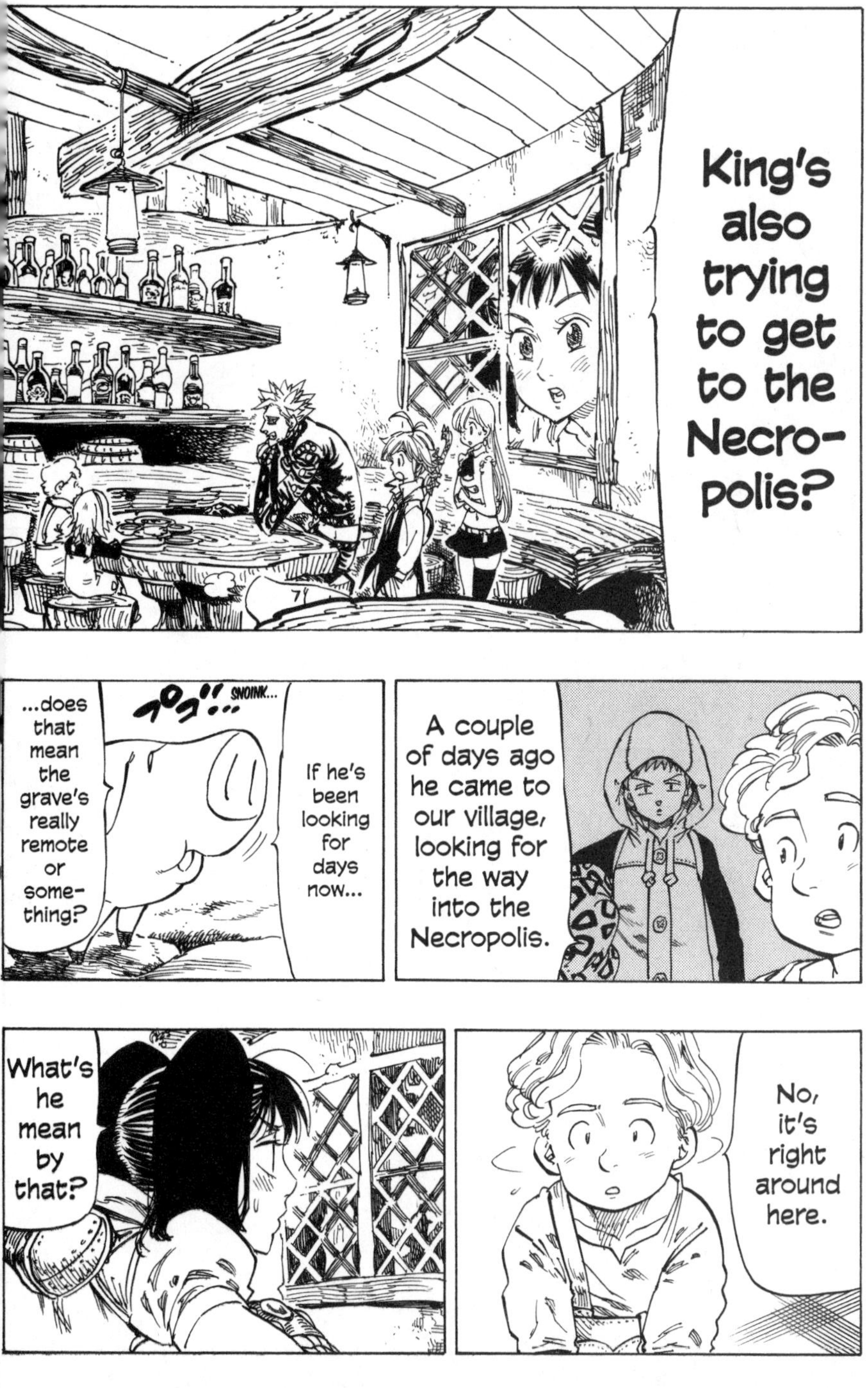
King's also trying to get to the Necropolis?
A couple of days ago he came to our village, looking for the way into the Necropolis.
If he's been looking for days now...
SNOINK...
...does that mean the grave's really remote or something?
No, it's right around here.
What's he mean by that?

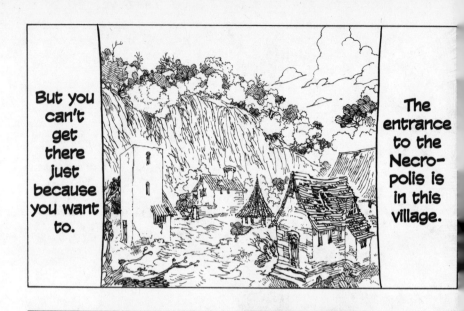

The entrance to the Necropolis is in this village.
But you can't get there just because you want to.
?
I've got no interest in riddles.
I get it. In other words ...
TUG
It's something like this!
TADAAA
SNOINK!
I don't think that's quite it...

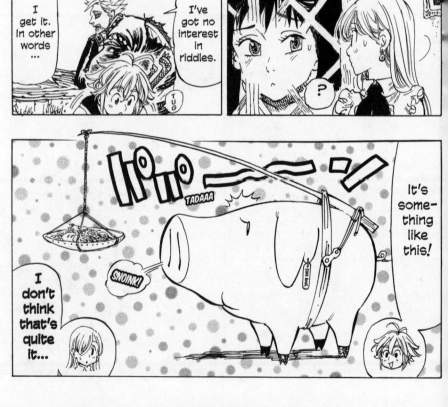

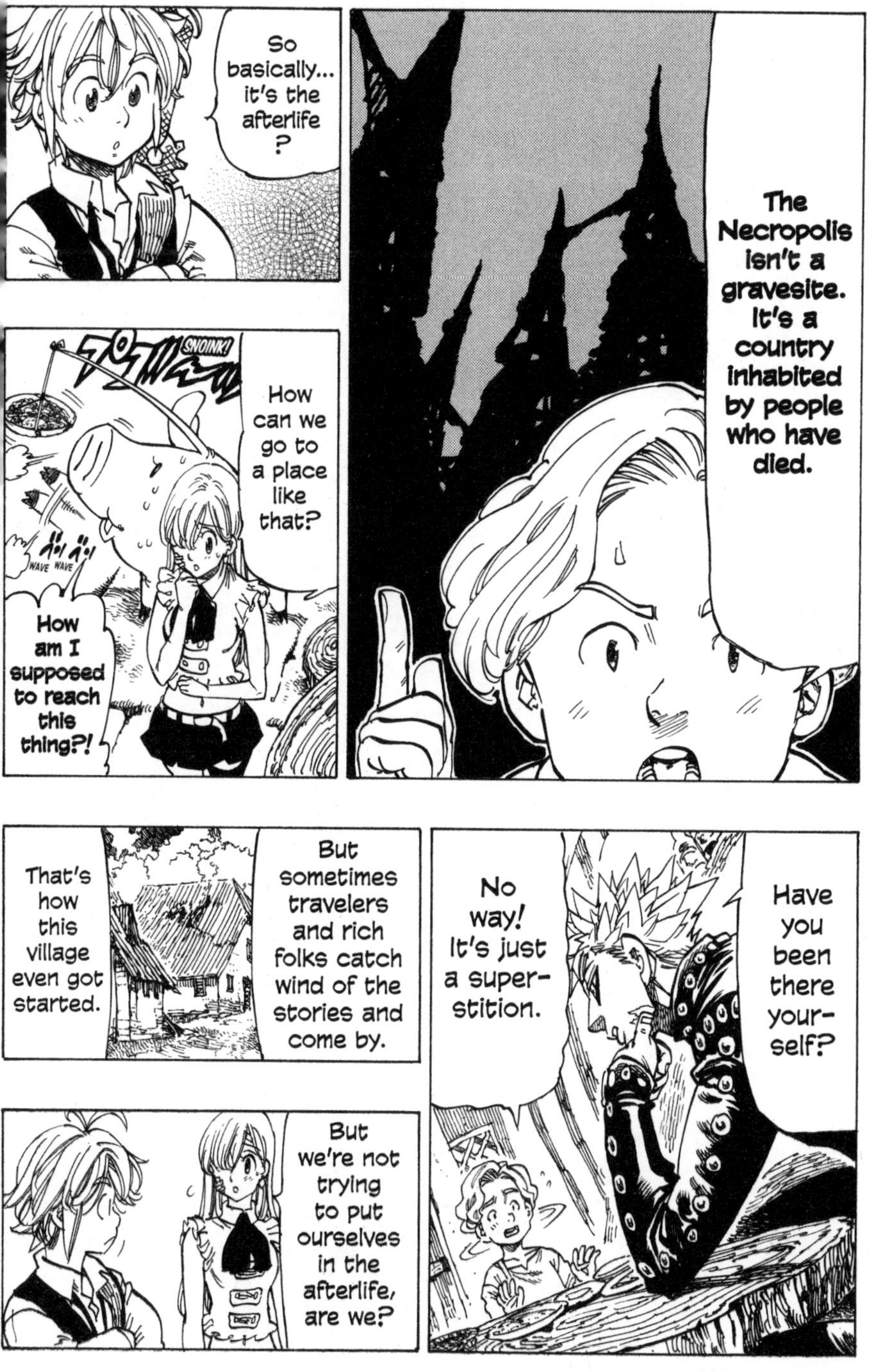
The Necropolis isn't a gravesite. It's a country inhabited by people who have died.
So basically... it's the afterlife?
SNOINK!
How can we go to a place like that?
WAVE WAVE
How am I supposed to reach this thing?!
Have you been there yourself?
No way! It's just a superstition.
But sometimes travelers and rich folks catch wind of the stories and come by.
That's how this village even got started.
But we're not trying to put ourselves in the afterlife, are we?

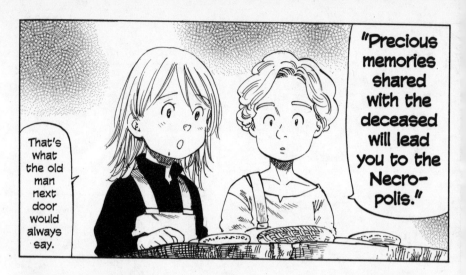

"Precious memories shared with the deceased will lead you to the Necro-polis."
That's what the old man next door would always say.
I'm sorry...but that's all we know.
PAT
Thanks, Elaine. ♪
That information was more than enough to cover your meal.
But there's still some on your plate.
RUSTLE
...
Um... My name's Ellen.
Oops, my bad. Ellen, it is! ♪

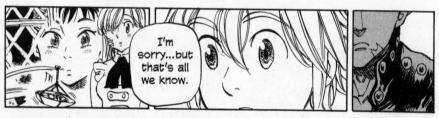

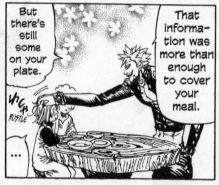

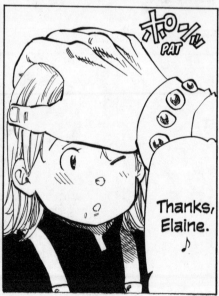

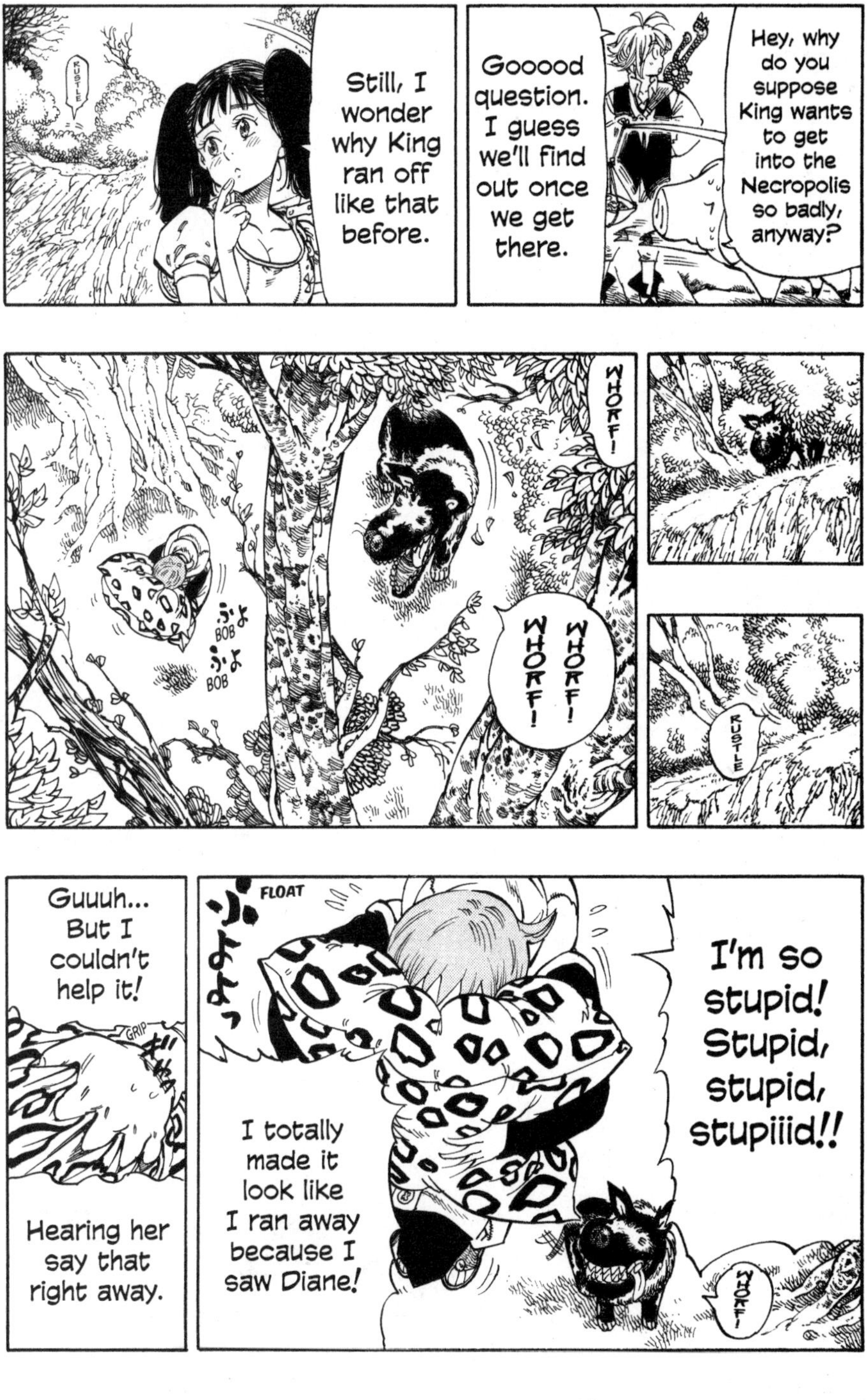

Hey, why do you suppose King wants to get into the Necropolis so badly, anyway?
Gooood question. I guess we'll find out once we get there.
RUSTLE
Still, I wonder why King ran off like that before.
RUSTLE
WHORF!
WHORF! WHORF!
ふよ BOB
ふよ BOB
FLOAT
I'm so stupid! Stupid, stupid, stupiiid!!
I totally made it look like I ran away because I saw Diane!
WHORF!
Guuuh... But I couldn't help it!
GRIP
Hearing her say that right away.

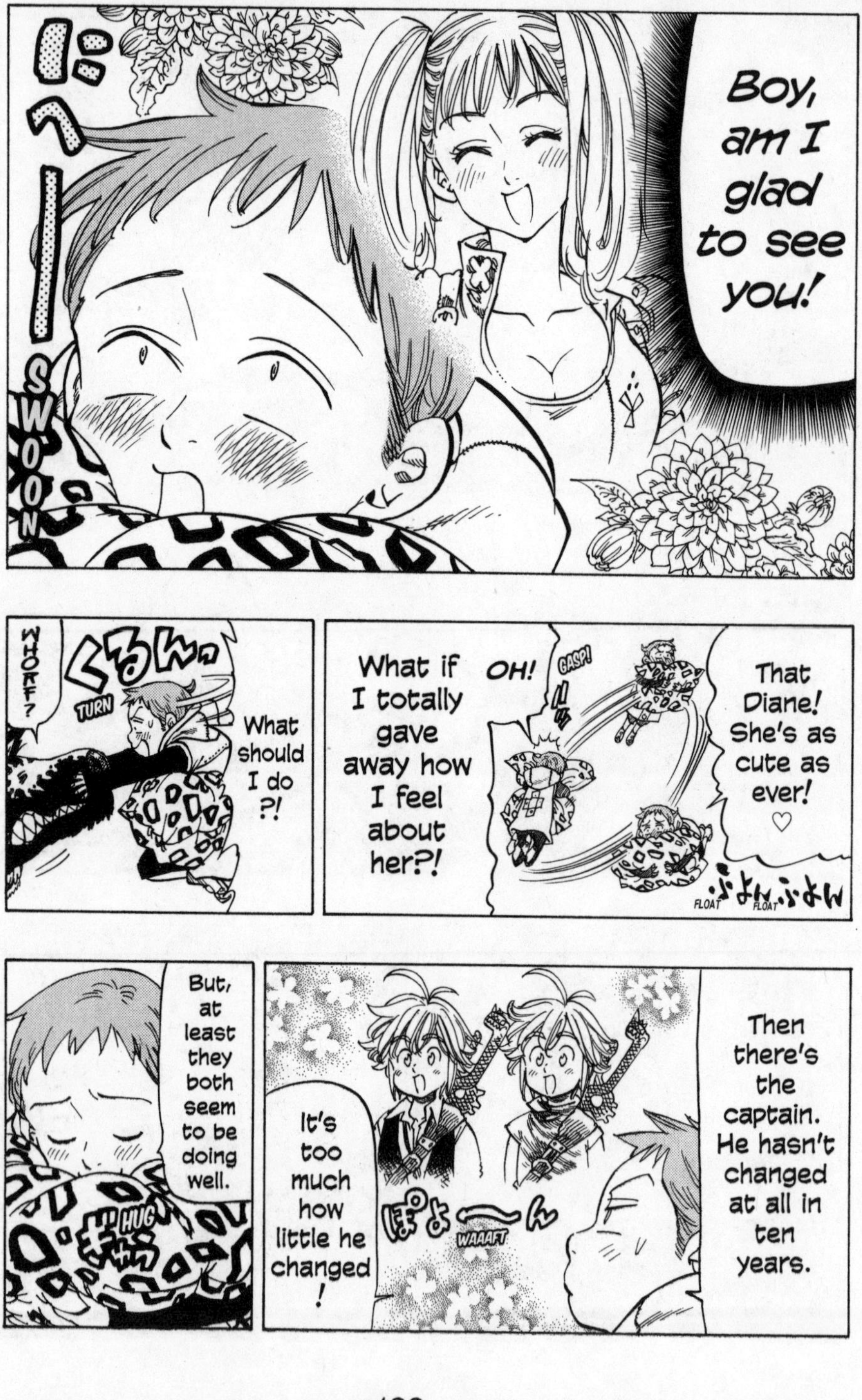
Boy, am I glad to see you!
にへーー
SWOON
That Diane! She's as cute as ever! ♡
GASP!
OH!
What if I totally gave away how I feel about her?!
ぷよんぷよん
FLOAT FLOAT
What should I do?!
WHORF?
くるんっ
TURN
Then there's the captain. He hasn't changed at all in ten years.
It's too much how little he changed!
ぽよーん
WAAAFT
But, at least they both seem to be doing well.
HUG

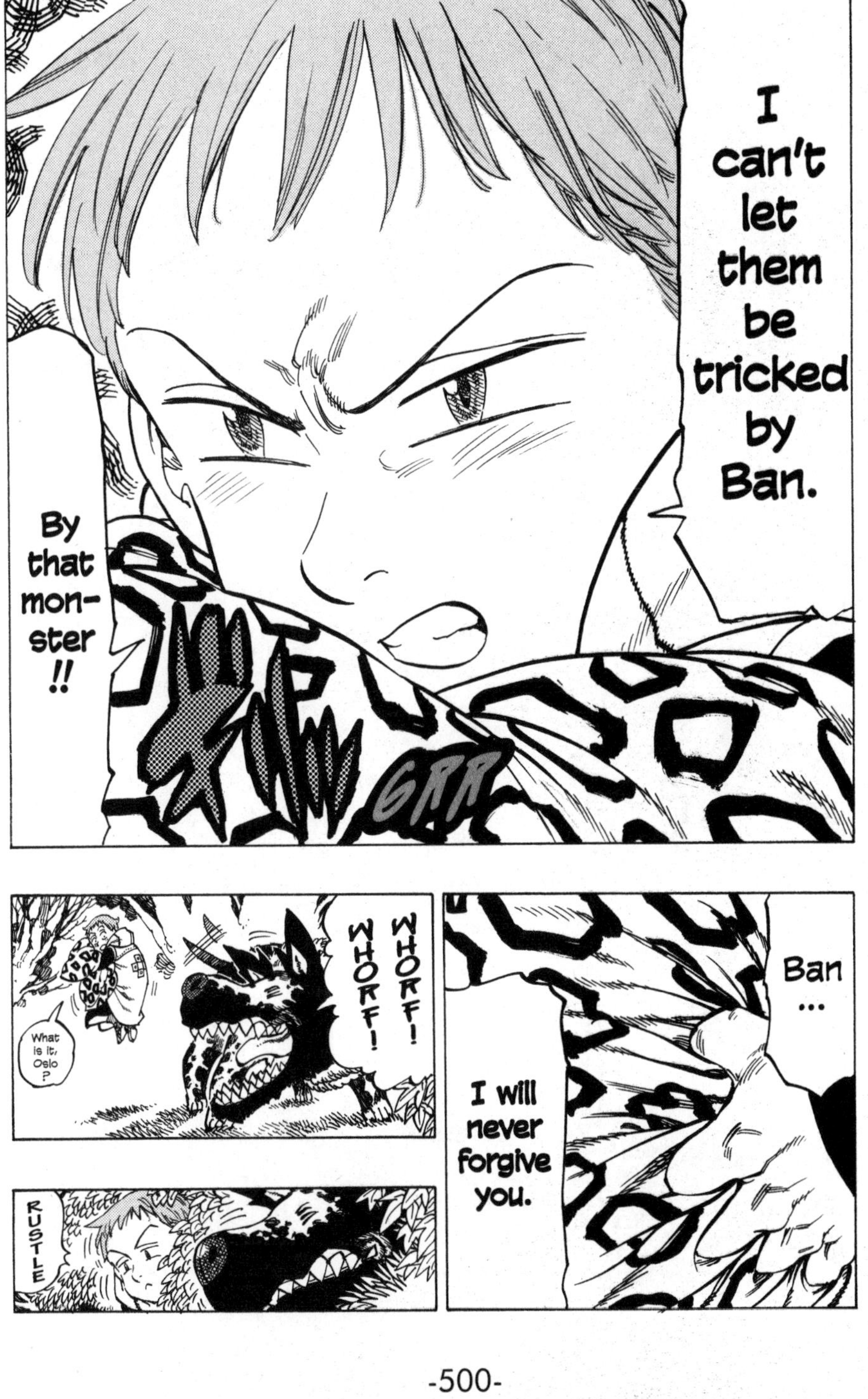
I can't let them be tricked by Ban.
By that mon-ster!!
GRR
Ban...
I will never forgive you.
WHORF! WHORF!
What is it, Oslo?
RUSTLE

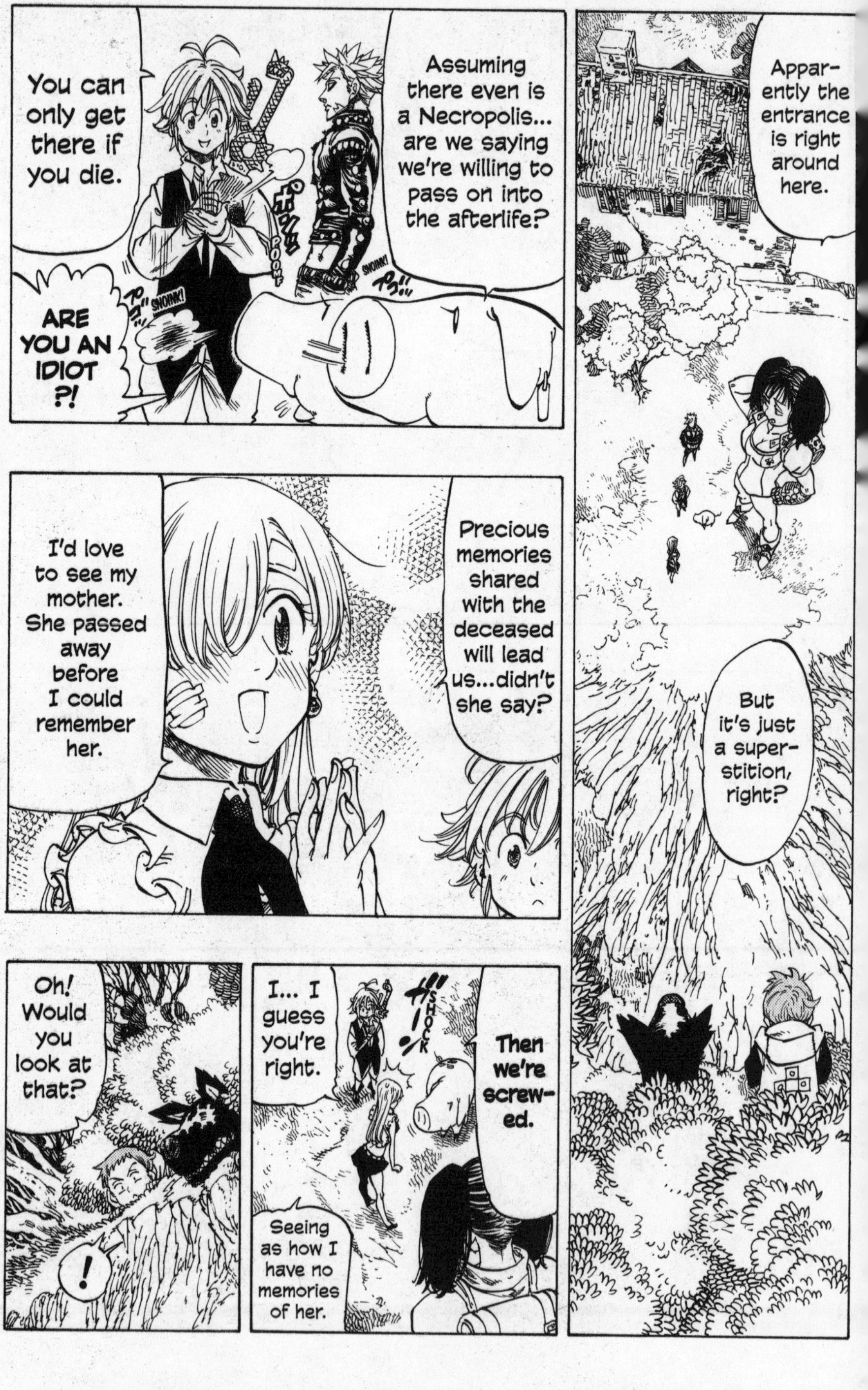
Apparently the entrance is right around here.
But it's just a superstition, right?
Assuming there even is a Necropolis... are we saying we're willing to pass on into the afterlife?
POOMF
You can only get there if you die.
SNOINK!
SNOINK!
ARE YOU AN IDIOT ?!
Precious memories shared with the deceased will lead us...didn't she say?
I'd love to see my mother. She passed away before I could remember her.
Then we're screwed.
SHOCK
I... I guess you're right.
Seeing as how I have no memories of her.
Oh! Would you look at that?
!

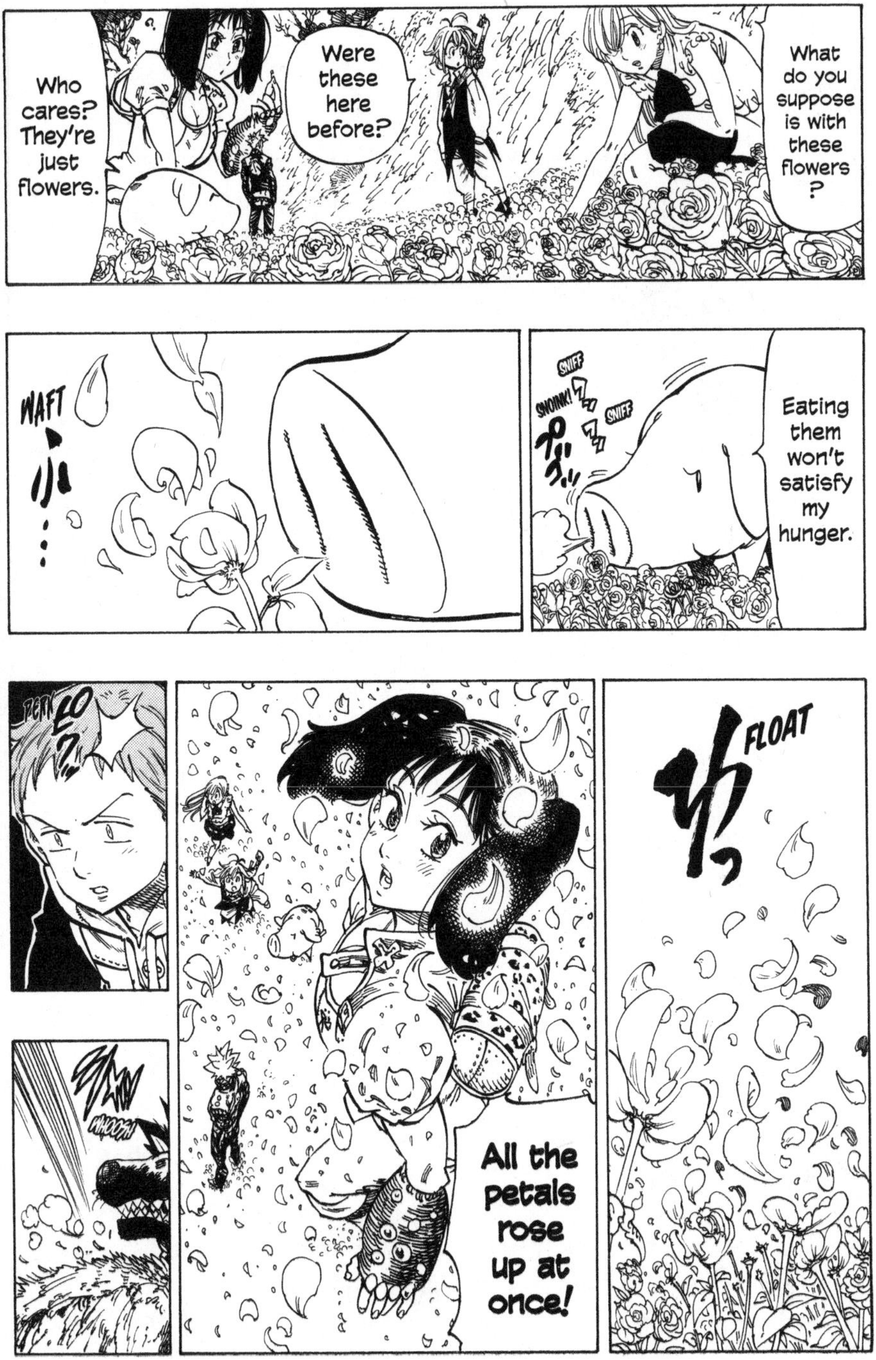
What do you suppose is with these flowers?
Were these here before?
Who cares? They're just flowers.
SNIFF
SNOINK!
SNIFF
Eating them won't satisfy my hunger.
WAFT
FLOAT
All the petals rose up at once!
PERK
WHOOSH

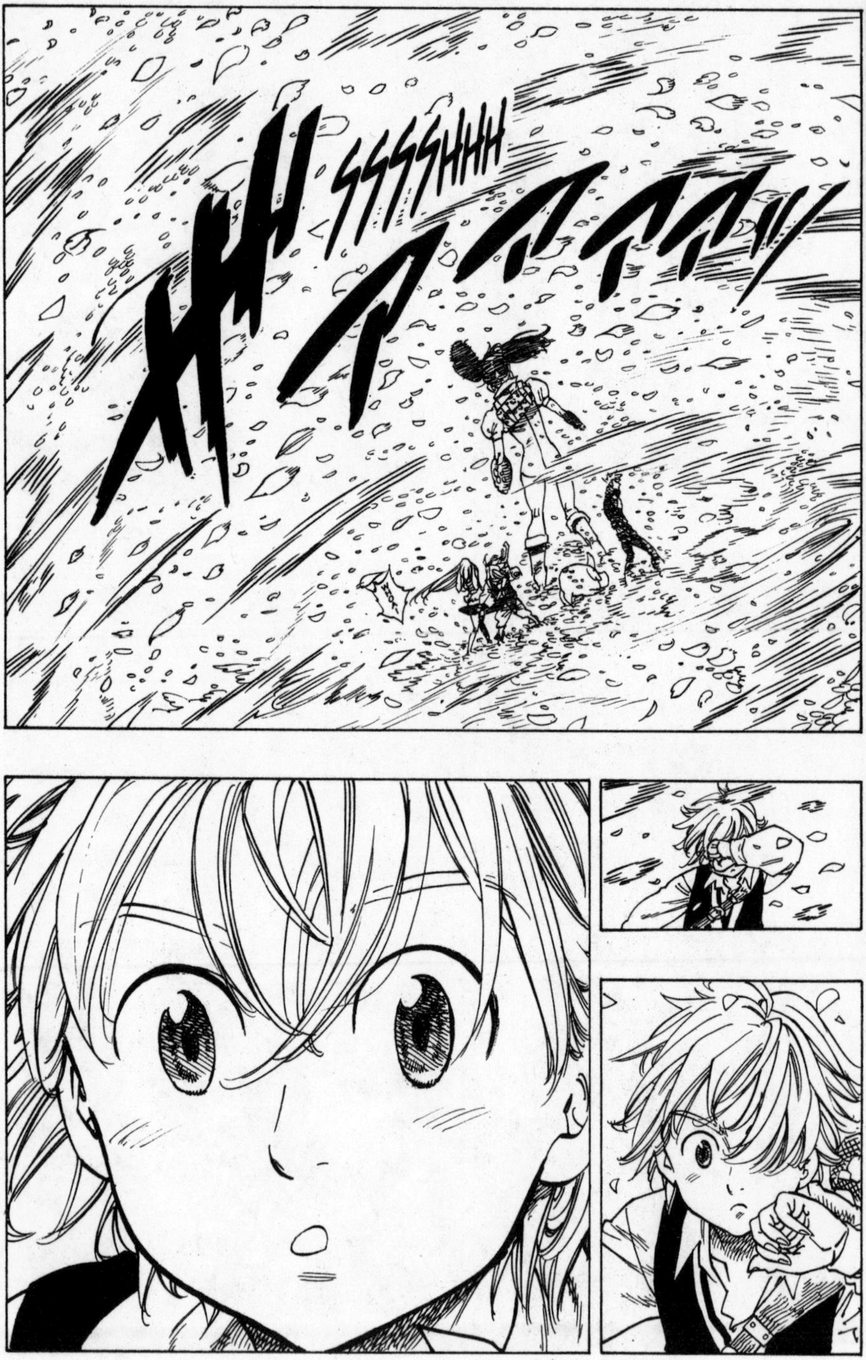
SSSSHHH
WHOK!

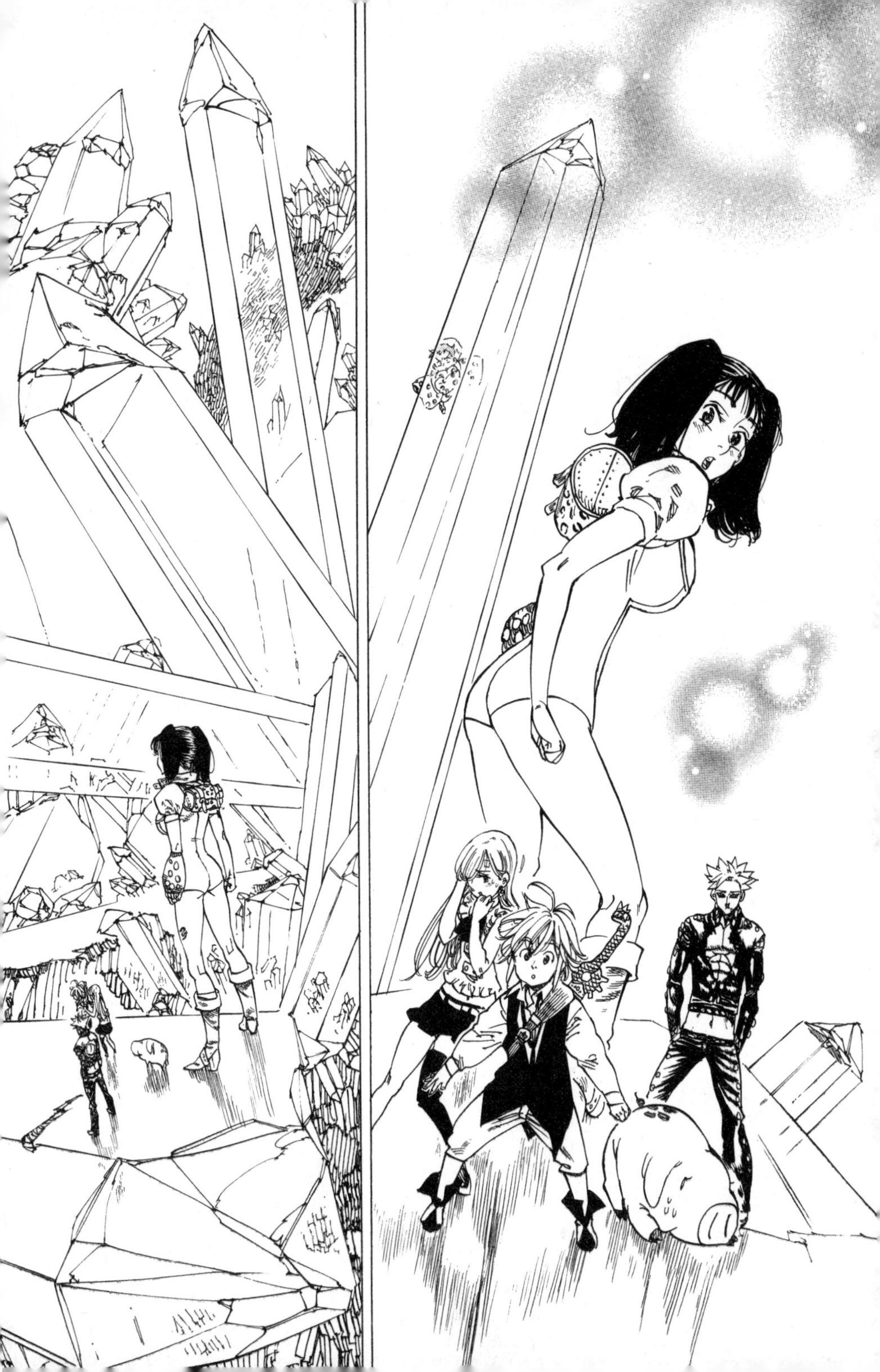

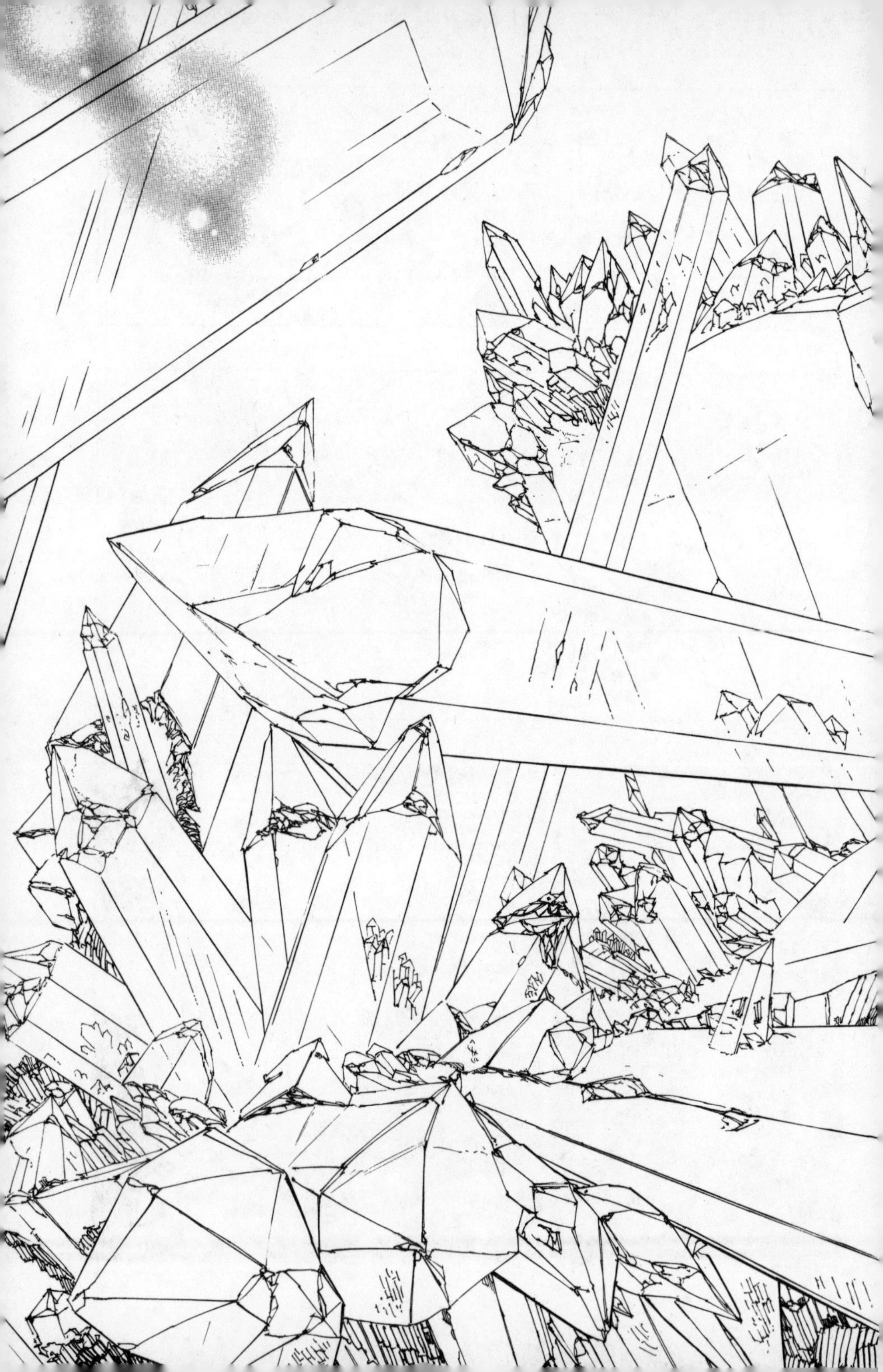

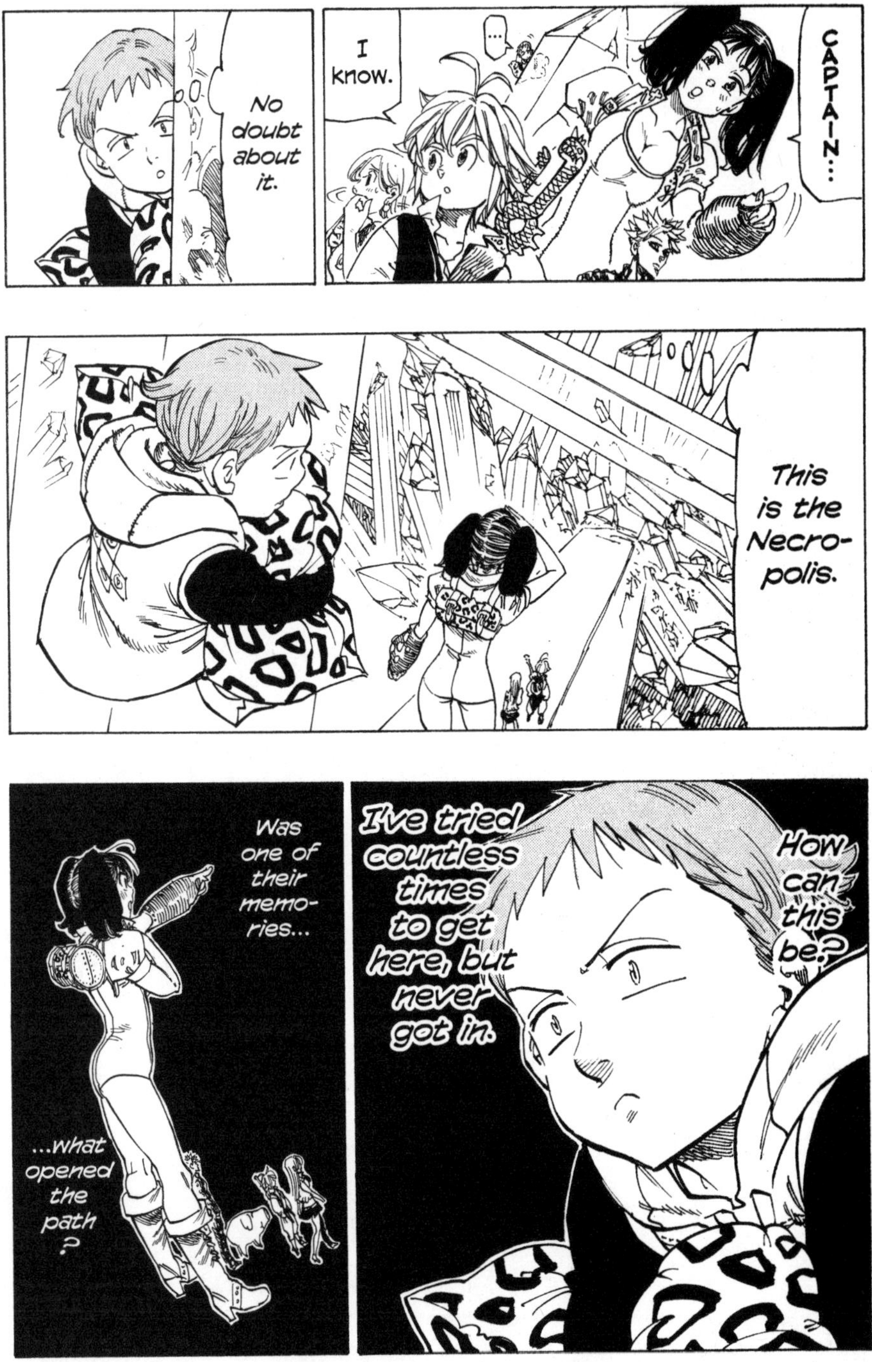
CAPTAIN...
...
I know.
No doubt about it.
This is the Necropolis.
How can this be?
I've tried countless times to get here, but never got in.
Was one of their memories...
...what opened the path?

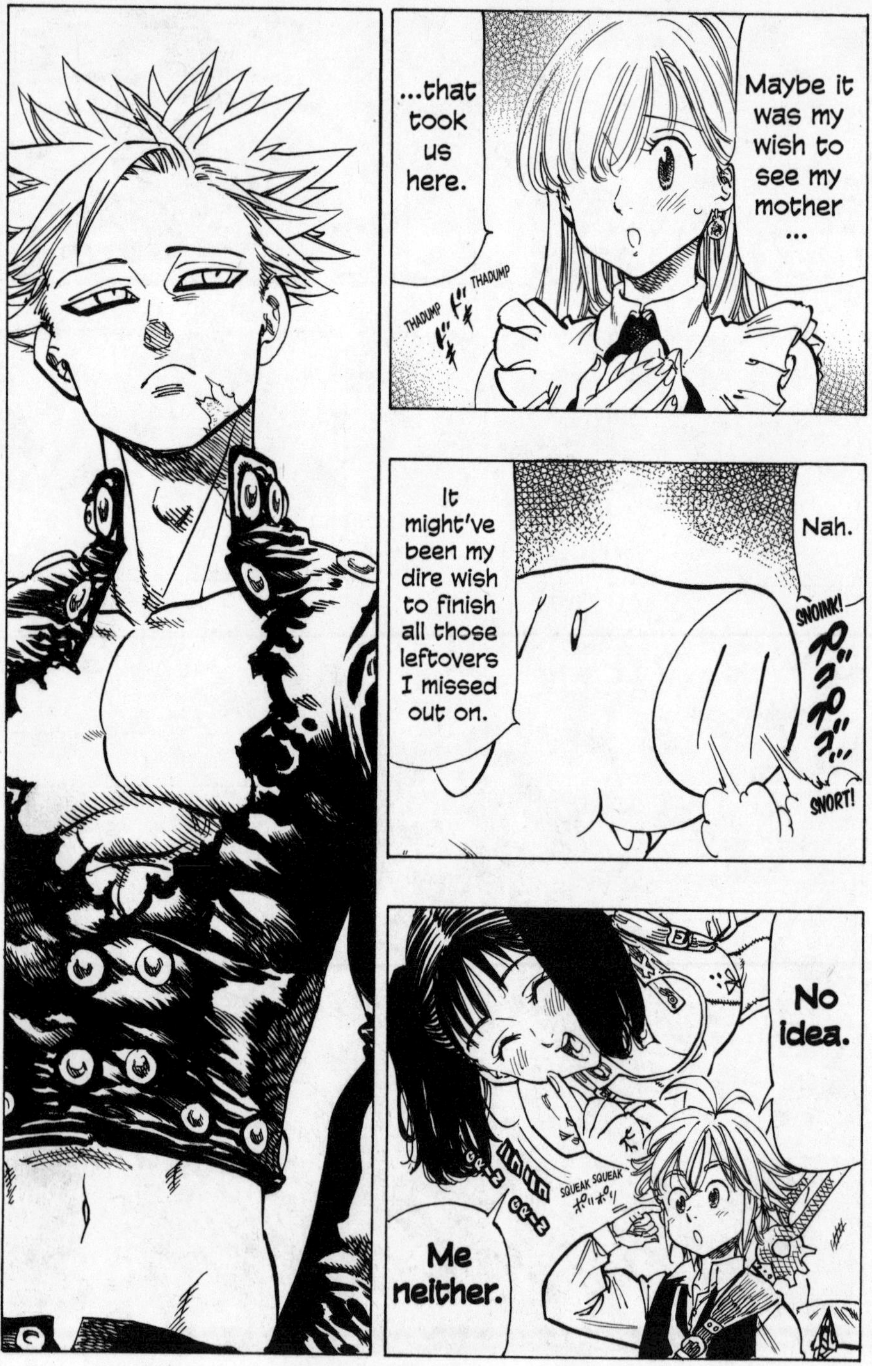
Maybe it was my wish to see my mother ...
...that took us here.
THADUMP THADUMP
Nah.
SNOINK! SNORT!
It might've been my dire wish to finish all those leftovers I missed out on.
No idea.
SQUEAK SQUEAK
Me neither.

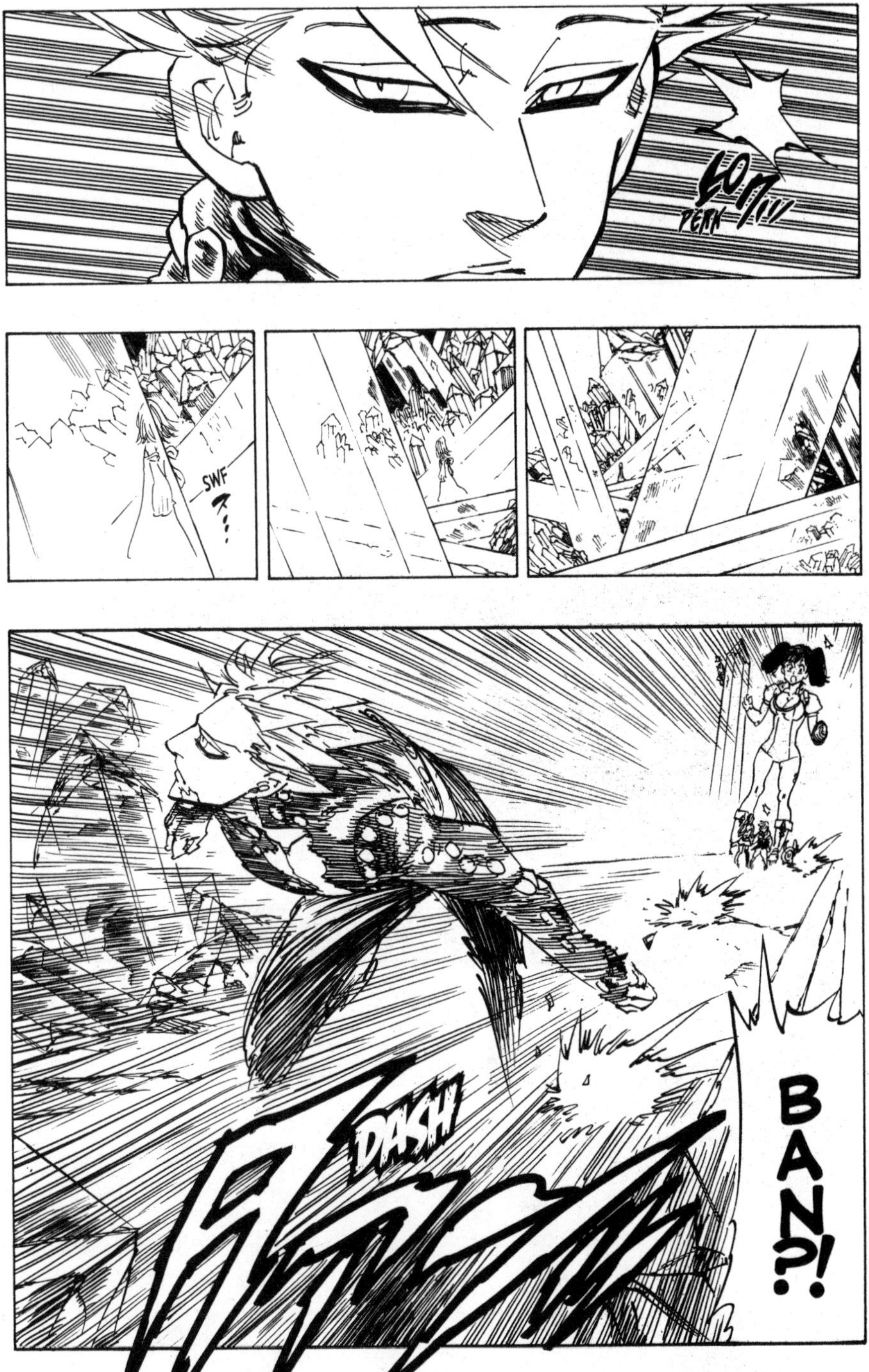
PERK
SWF
BAN?!
DASH!

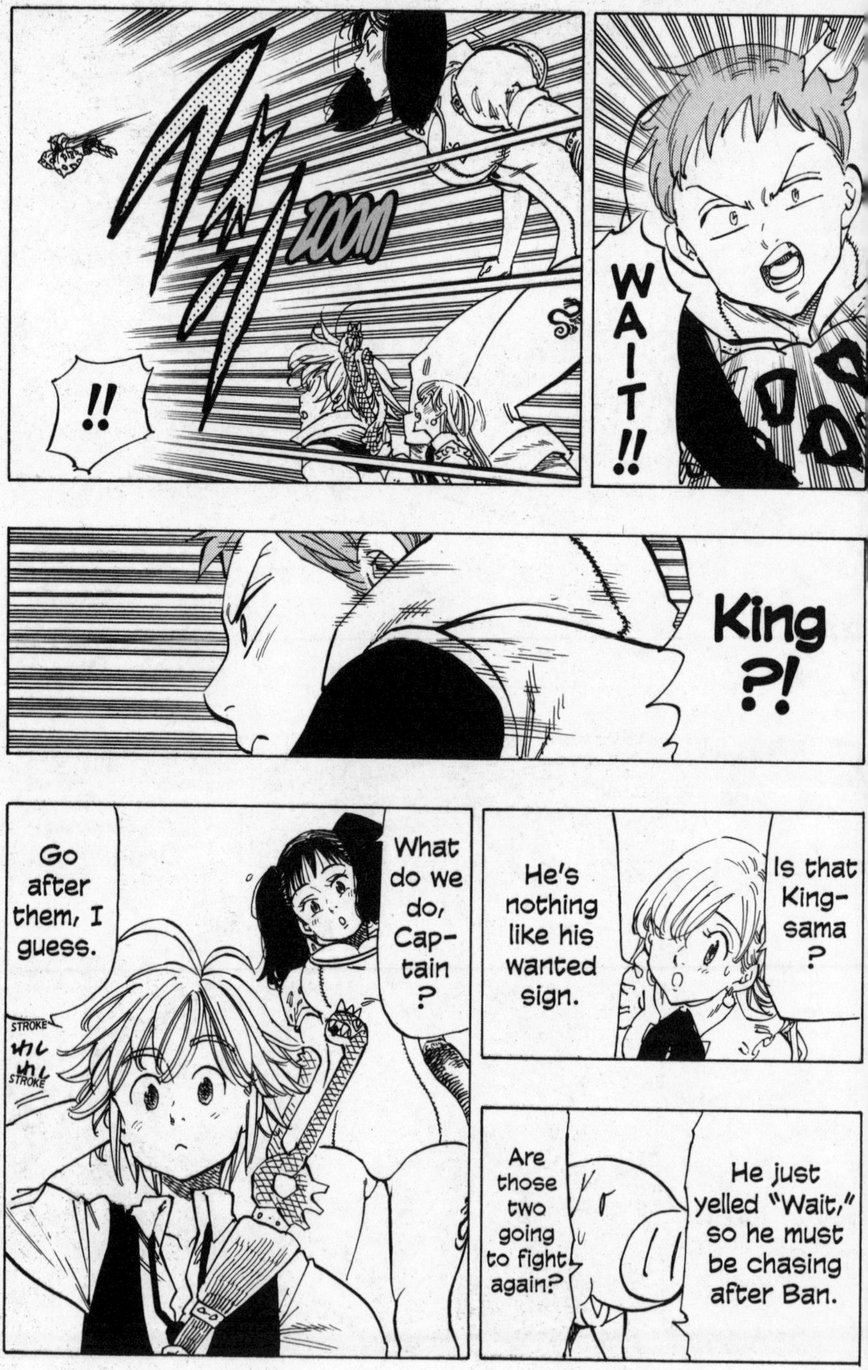
WAIT!!
ZOOM
!!
King ?!
Is that King-sama ?
He's nothing like his wanted sign.
He just yelled "Wait," so he must be chasing after Ban.
Are those two going to fight again?
What do we do, Captain ?
Go after them, I guess.
STROKE
STROKE

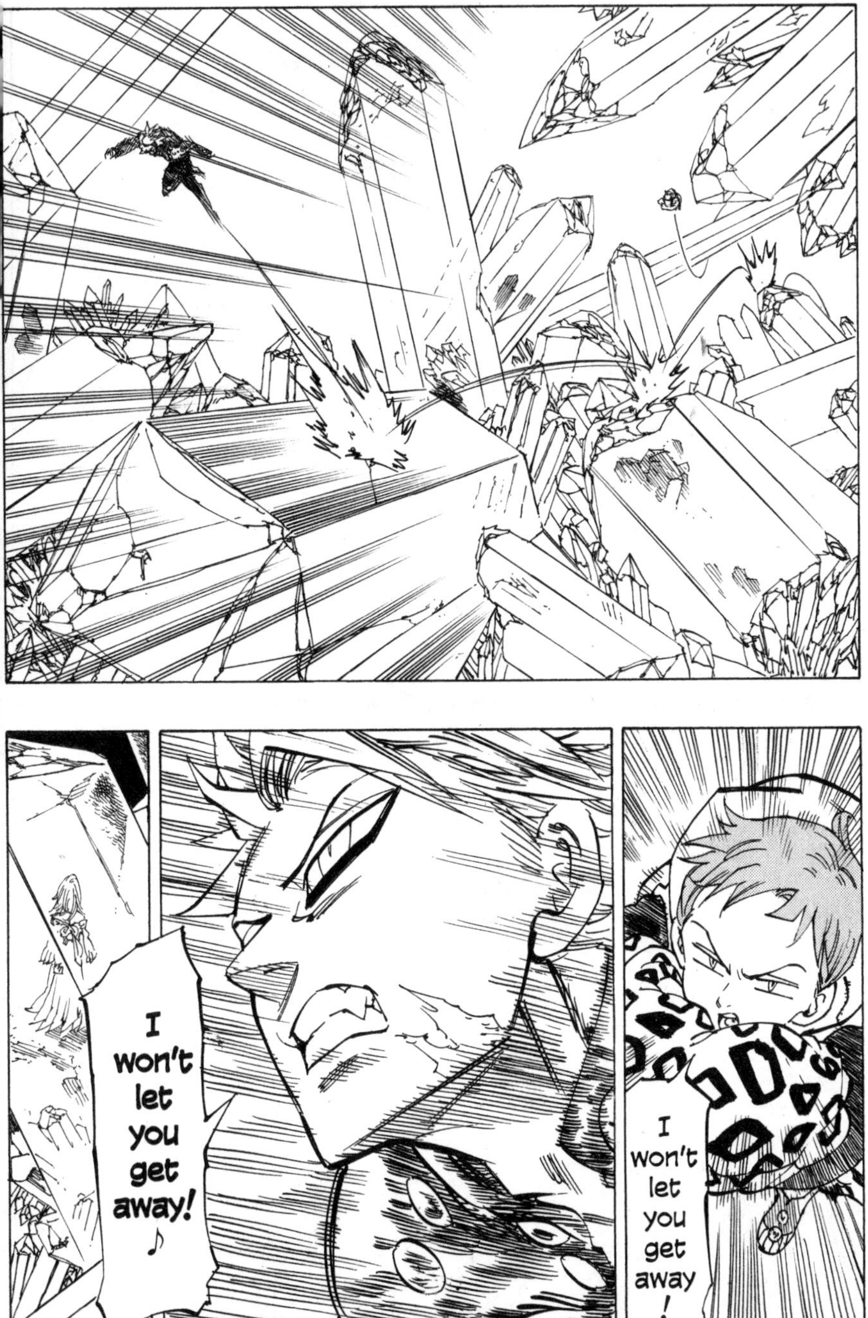
I won't let you get away!
I won't let you get away! ♪

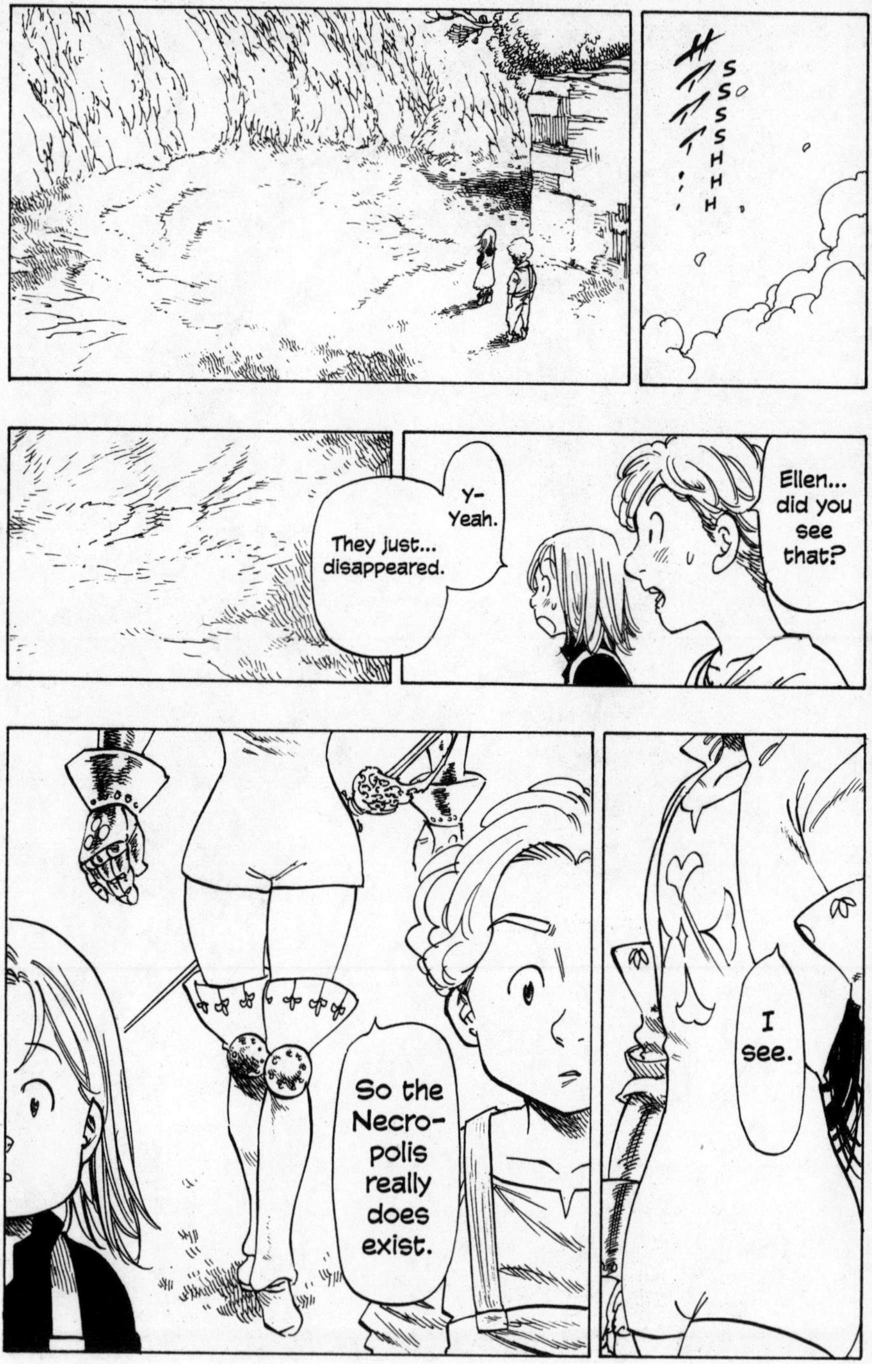
SSSSHHH
Ellen... did you see that?
Y- Yeah.
They just... disappeared.
I see.
So the Necropolis really does exist.

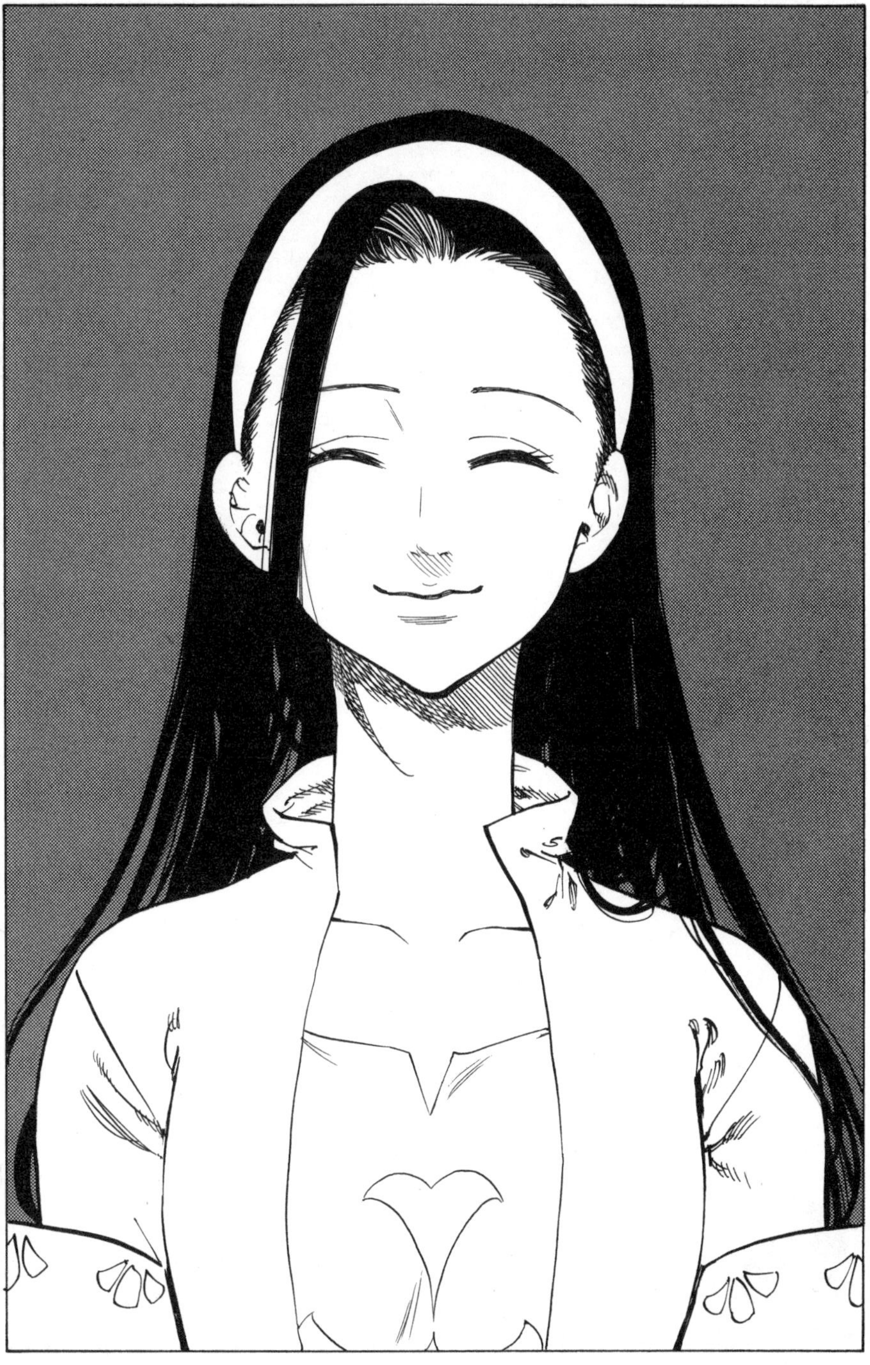

Chapter 21 - Revenge Knight

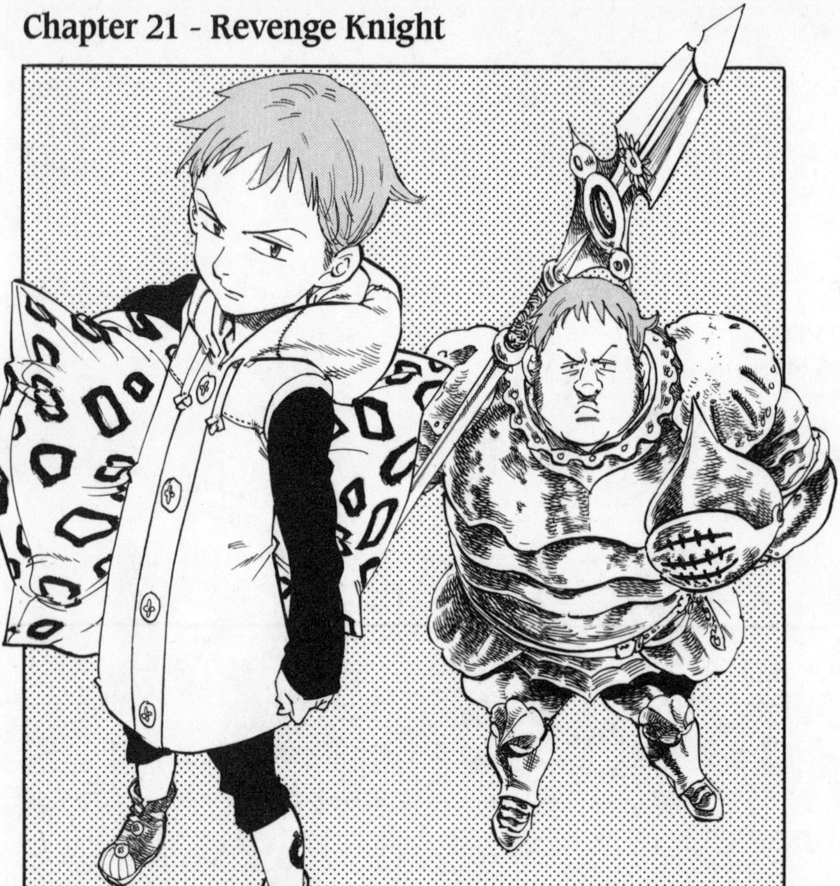

THE SEVEN DEADLY SINS

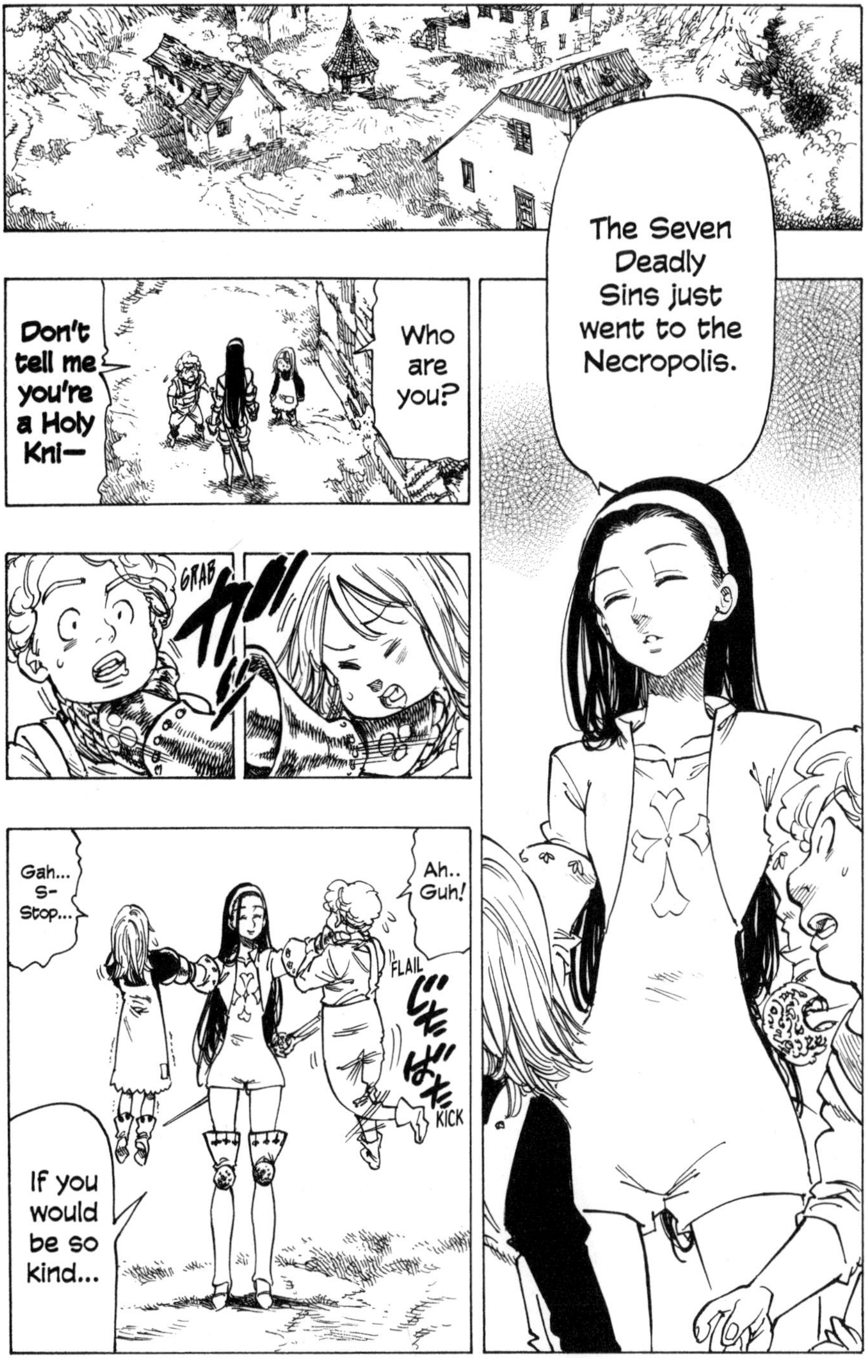
The Seven Deadly Sins just went to the Necropolis.
Who are you?
Don't tell me you're a Holy Kni—
GRAB
Ah.. Guh!
FLAIL
KICK
Gah... S- Stop...
If you would be so kind...

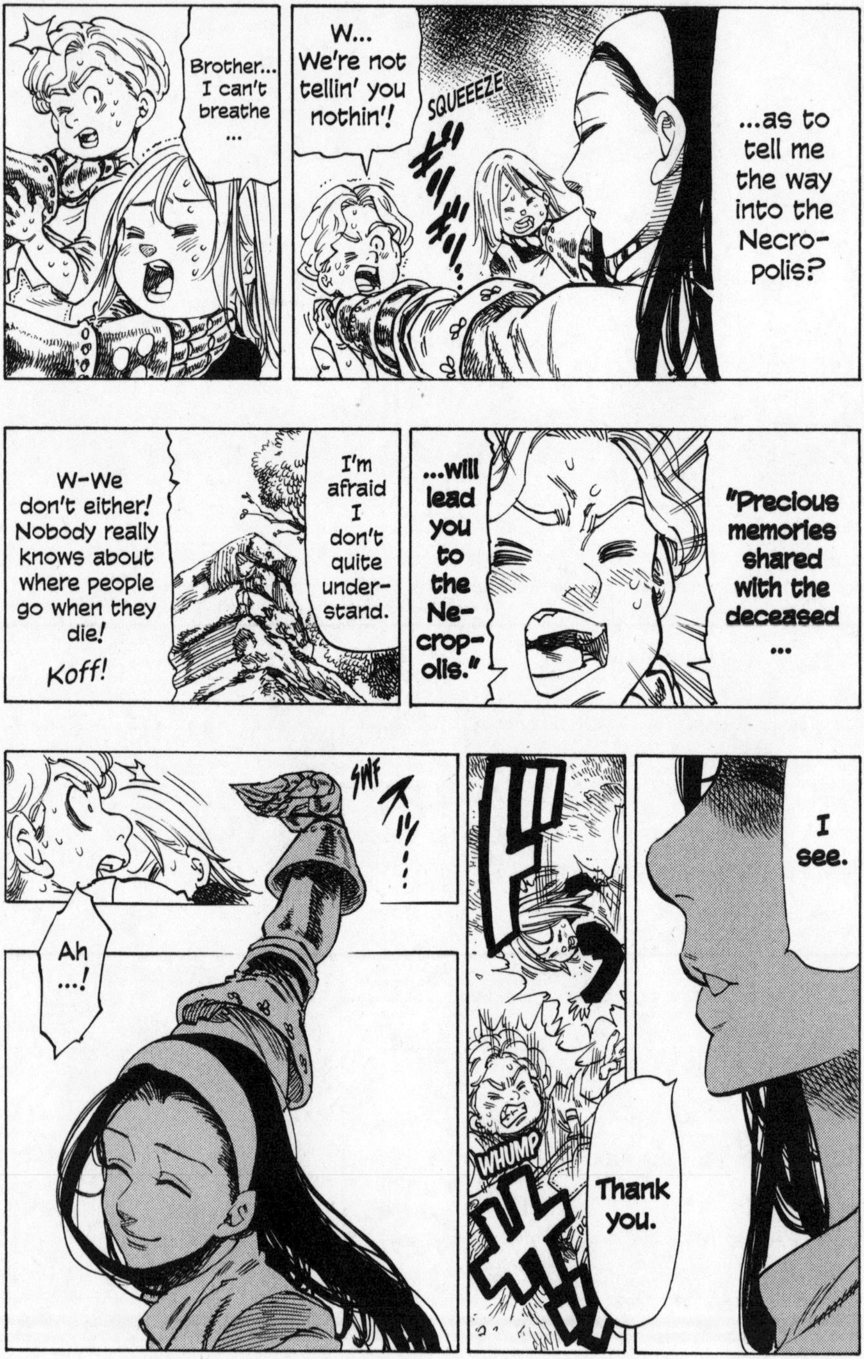
...as to tell me the way into the Necropolis?
W... We're not tellin' you nothin'!
SQUEEEZE
Brother... I can't breathe ...
"Precious memories shared with the deceased ...
...will lead you to the Necropolis."
I'm afraid I don't quite understand.
W-We don't either! Nobody really knows about where people go when they die!
Koff!
I see.
Thank you.
WHUMP
SWF
Ah ...!

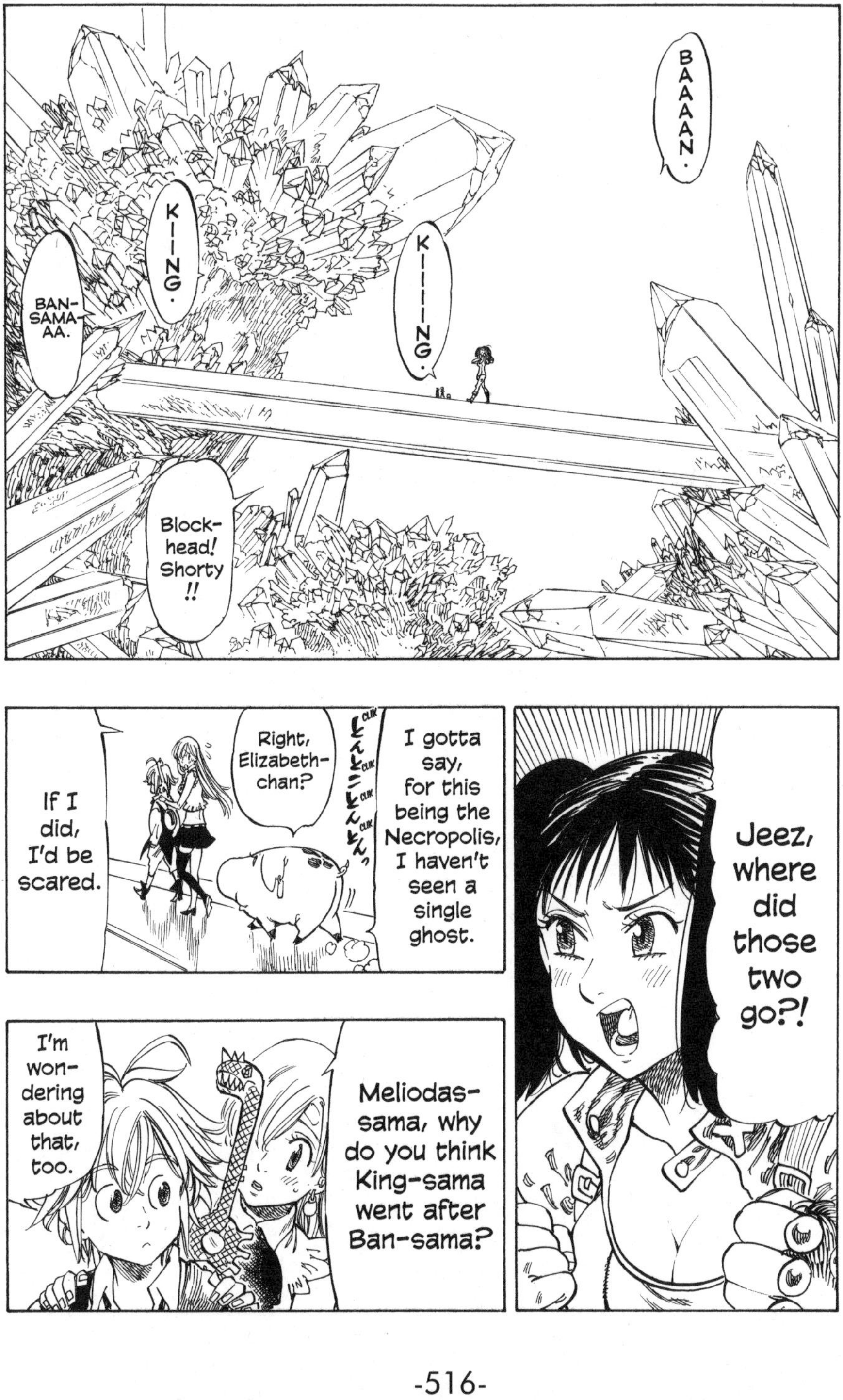
BAAAAN.
KIIIING.
KIING.
BAN-SAMAAA.
Blockhead! Shorty!!
Jeez, where did those two go?!
I gotta say, for this being the Necropolis, I haven't seen a single ghost.
CLIK CLIK CLIK CLIK
Right, Elizabeth-chan?
If I did, I'd be scared.
Meliodas-sama, why do you think King-sama went after Ban-sama?
I'm wondering about that, too.

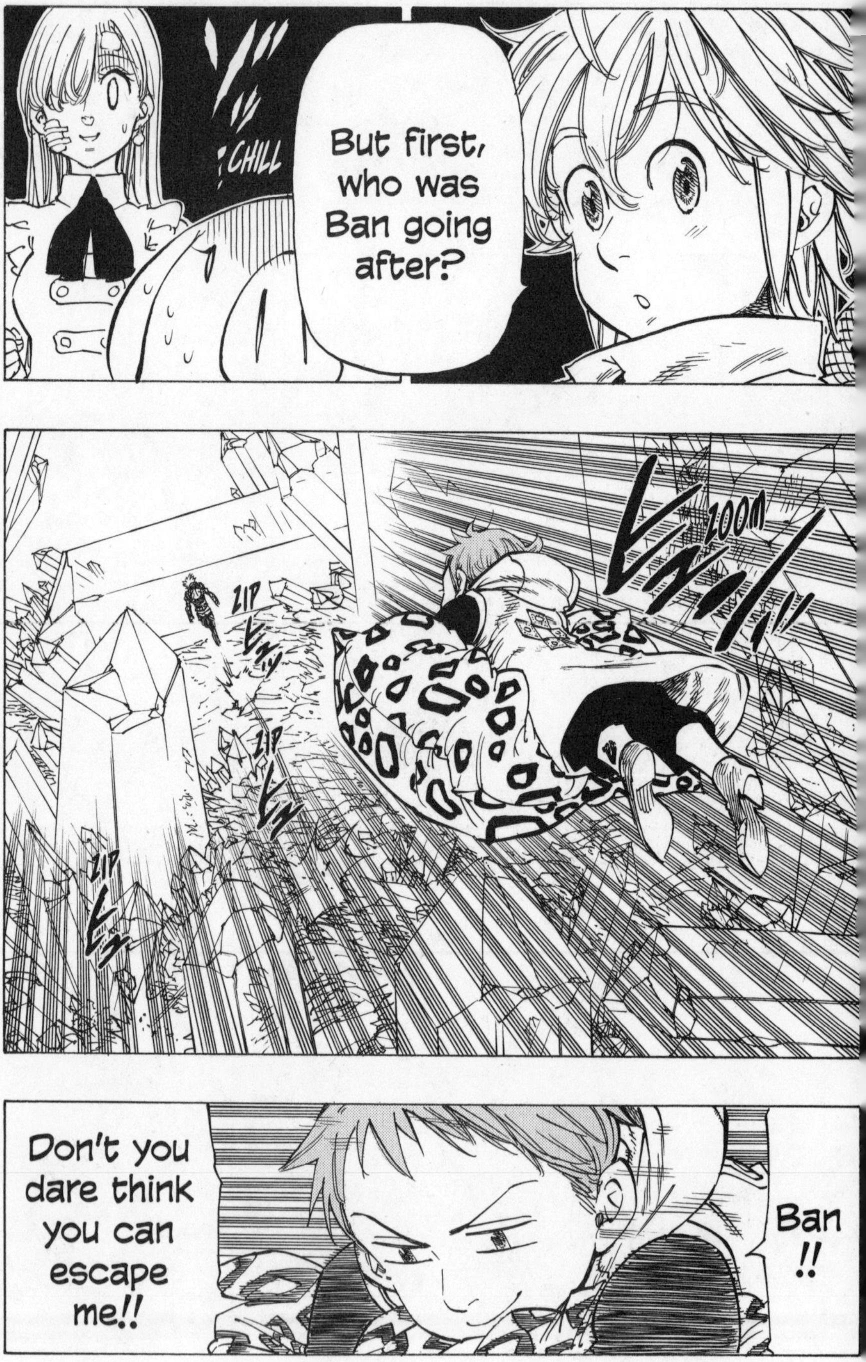
But first, who was Ban going after?
CHILL
ZOOM
ZIP
ZIP
ZIP
Ban!!
Don't you dare think you can escape me!!

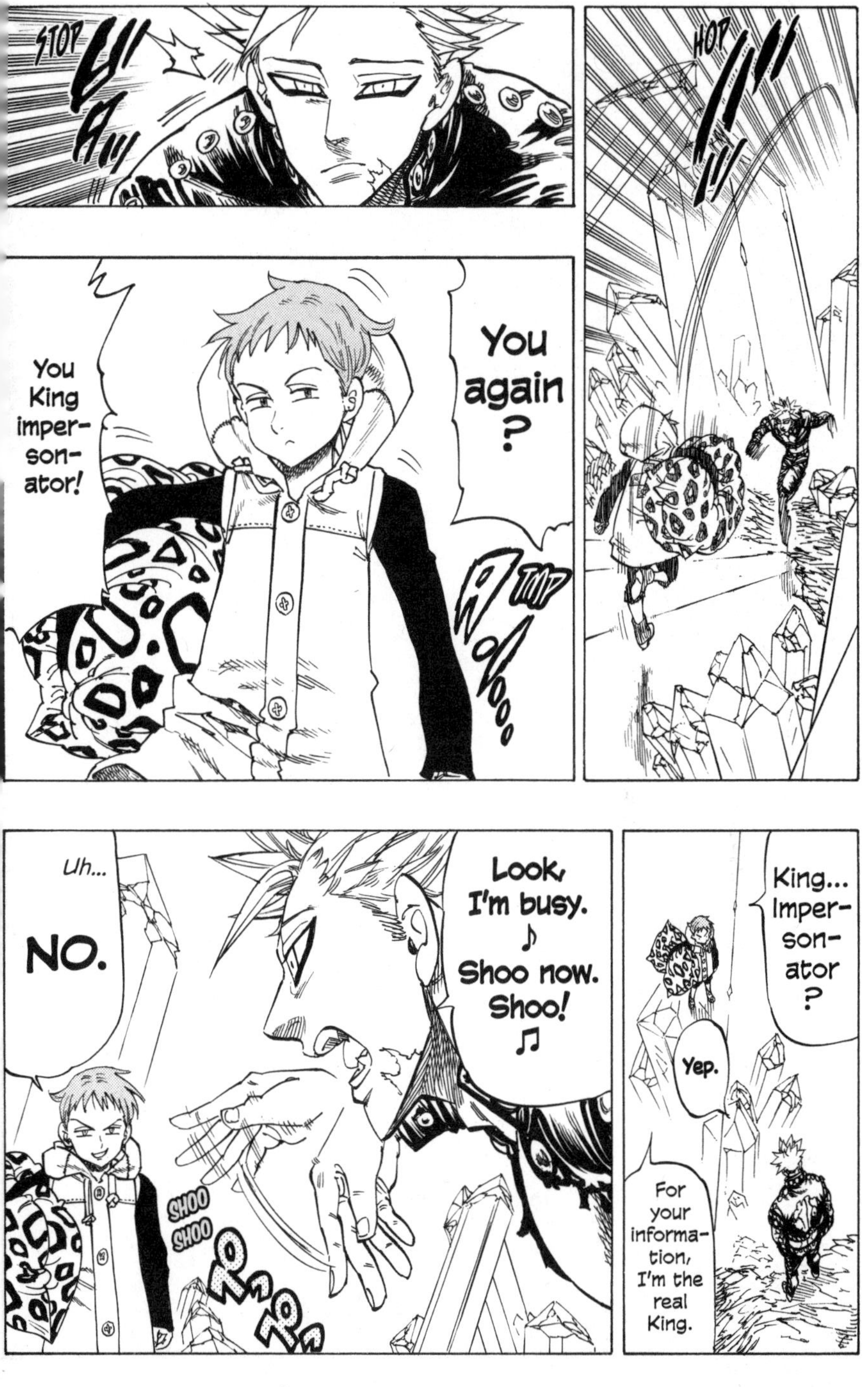
HOP
STOP
You again?
You King imper-son-ator!
TOP
King... Imper-son-ator?
Yep.
For your information, I'm the real King.
Look, I'm busy. ♪ Shoo now. Shoo! ♫
Uh...
NO.
SHOO SHOO

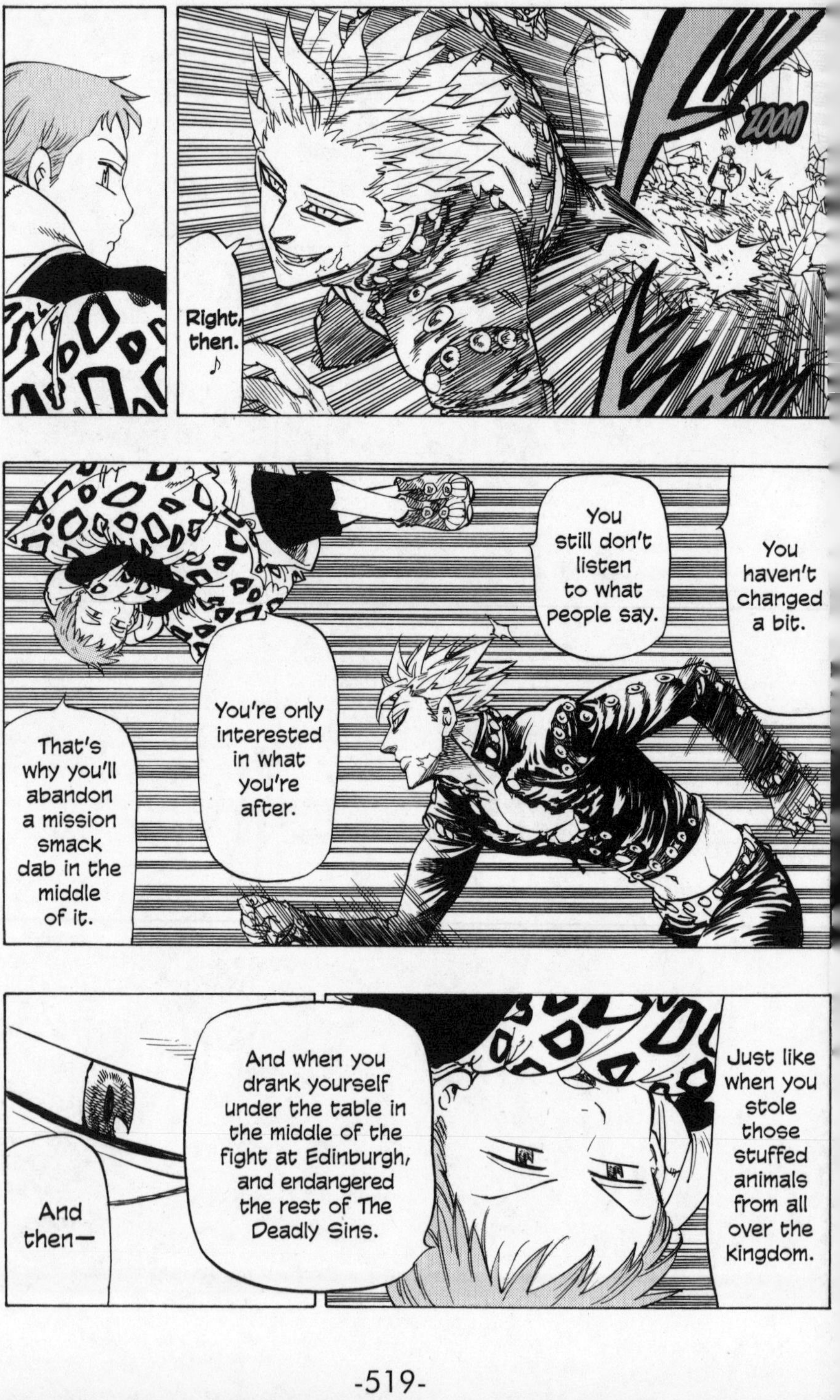
ZOOM
Right, then. ♪
You haven't changed a bit.
You still don't listen to what people say.
You're only interested in what you're after.
That's why you'll abandon a mission smack dab in the middle of it.
Just like when you stole those stuffed animals from all over the kingdom.
And when you drank yourself under the table in the middle of the fight at Edinburgh, and endangered the rest of The Deadly Sins.
And then—

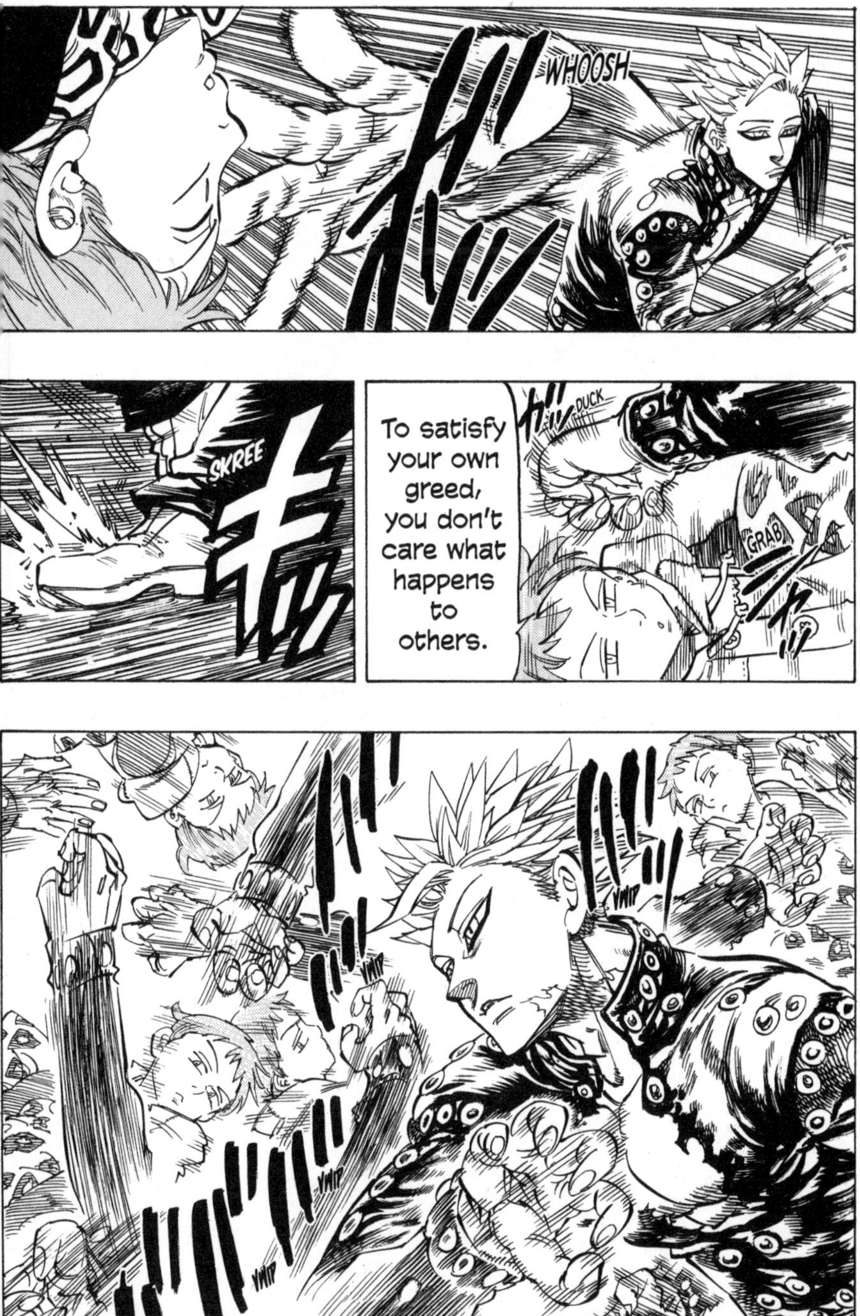
WHOOSH
DUCK
To satisfy your own greed, you don't care what happens to others.
GRAB
SKREE
VWIP
VWIP
VWIP
VWIP

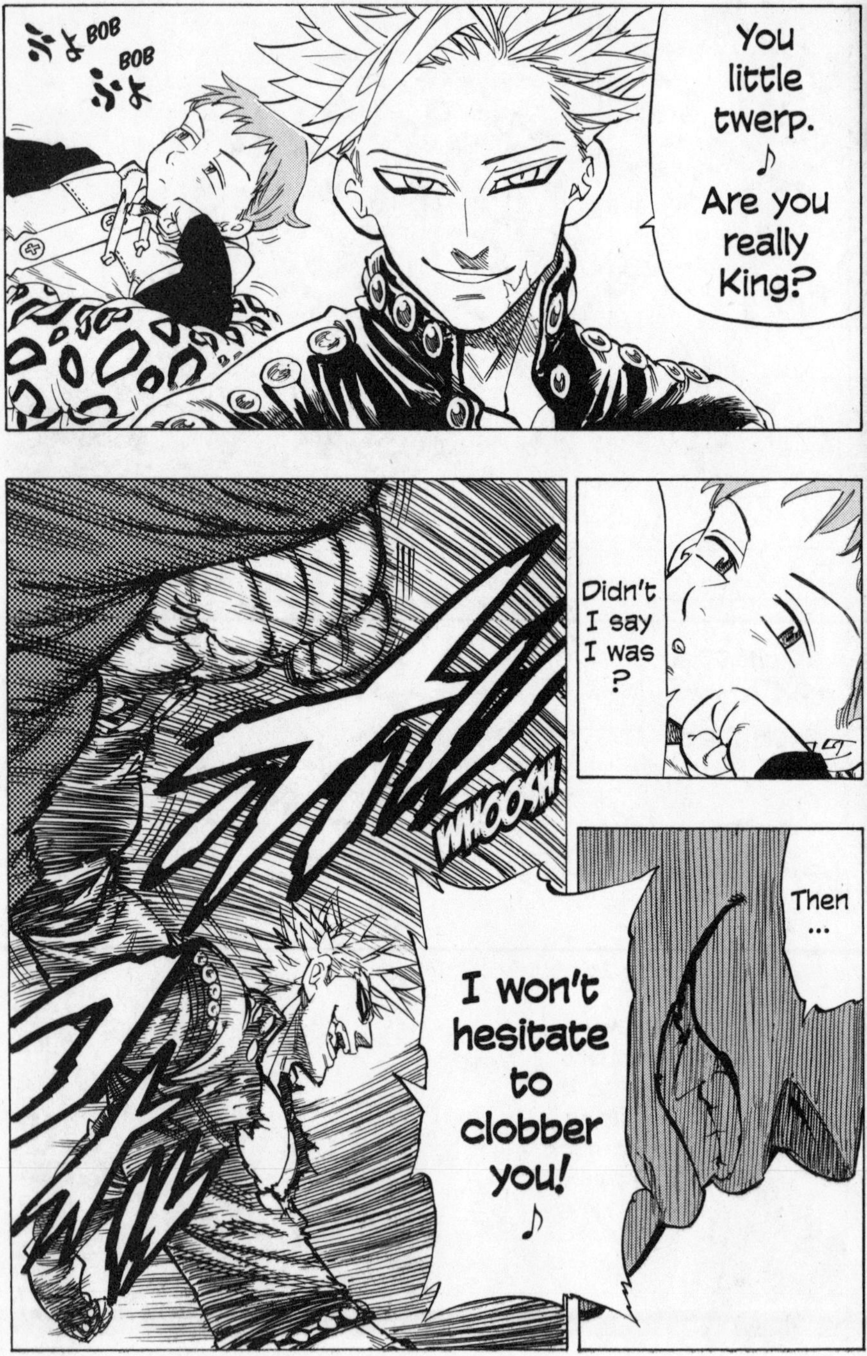
You little twerp. ♪ Are you really King?
ぷよ BOB
ぷよ BOB
Didn't I say I was?
Then...
I won't hesitate to clobber you! ♪
WHOOSH

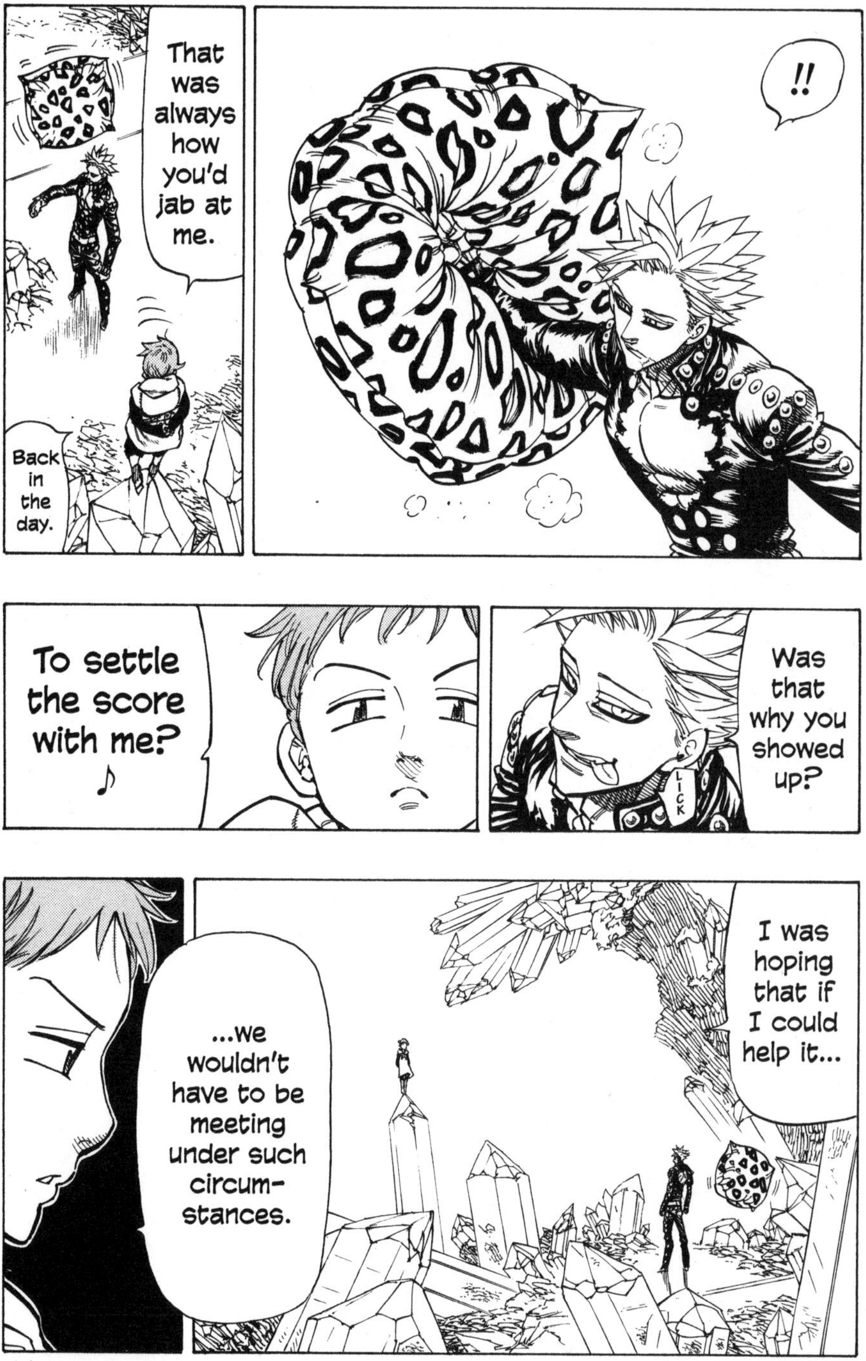
!!
That was always how you'd jab at me.
Back in the day.
Was that why you showed up?
LICK
To settle the score with me? ♪
I was hoping that if I could help it...
...we wouldn't have to be meeting under such circumstances.

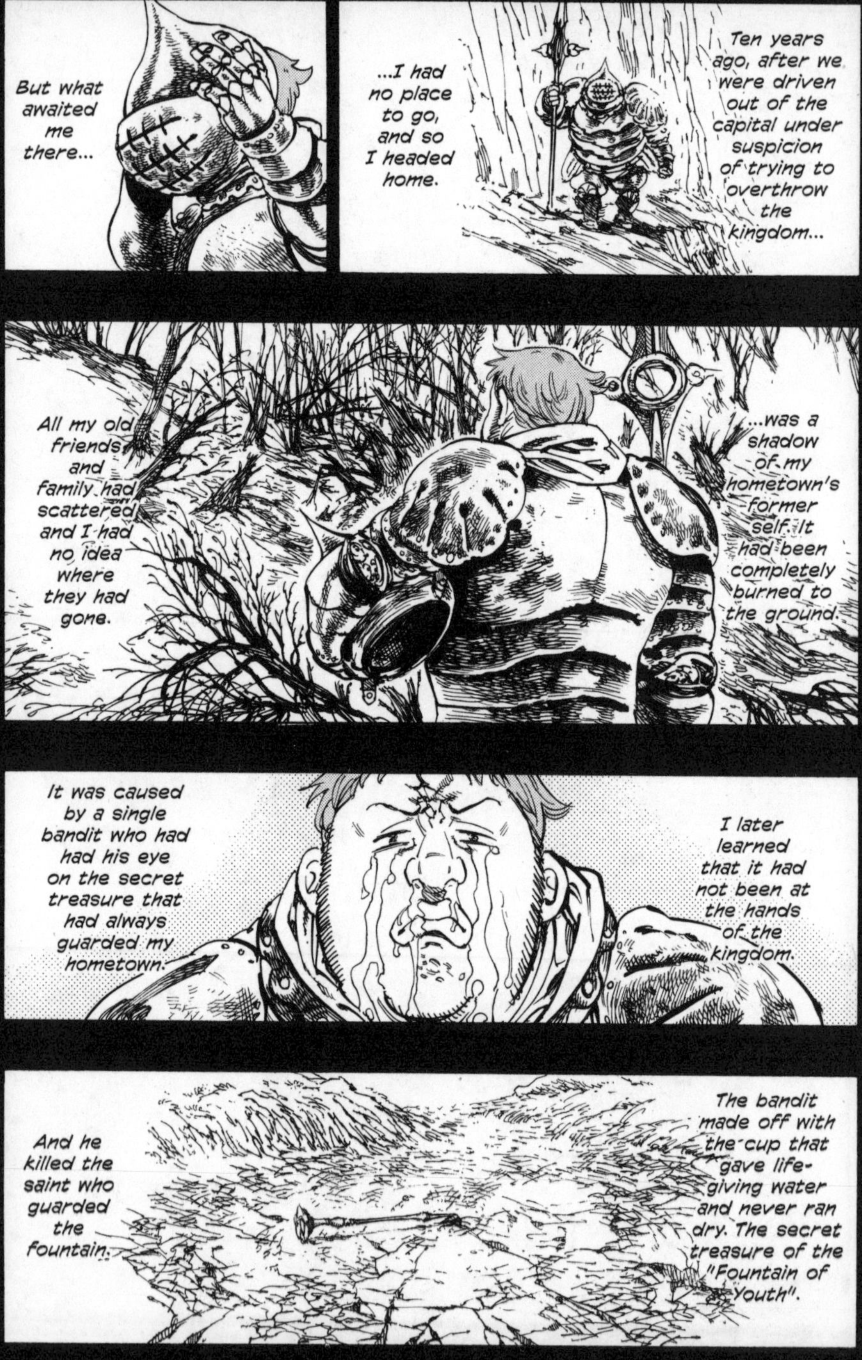
Ten years ago, after we were driven out of the capital under suspicion of trying to overthrow the kingdom...
...I had no place to go, and so I headed home.
But what awaited me there...
...was a shadow of my hometown's former self. It had been completely burned to the ground.
All my old friends and family had scattered and I had no idea where they had gone.
I later learned that it had not been at the hands of the kingdom.
It was caused by a single bandit who had had his eye on the secret treasure that had always guarded my hometown.
The bandit made off with the cup that gave life-giving water and never ran dry. The secret treasure of the "Fountain of Youth".
And he killed the saint who guarded the fountain.

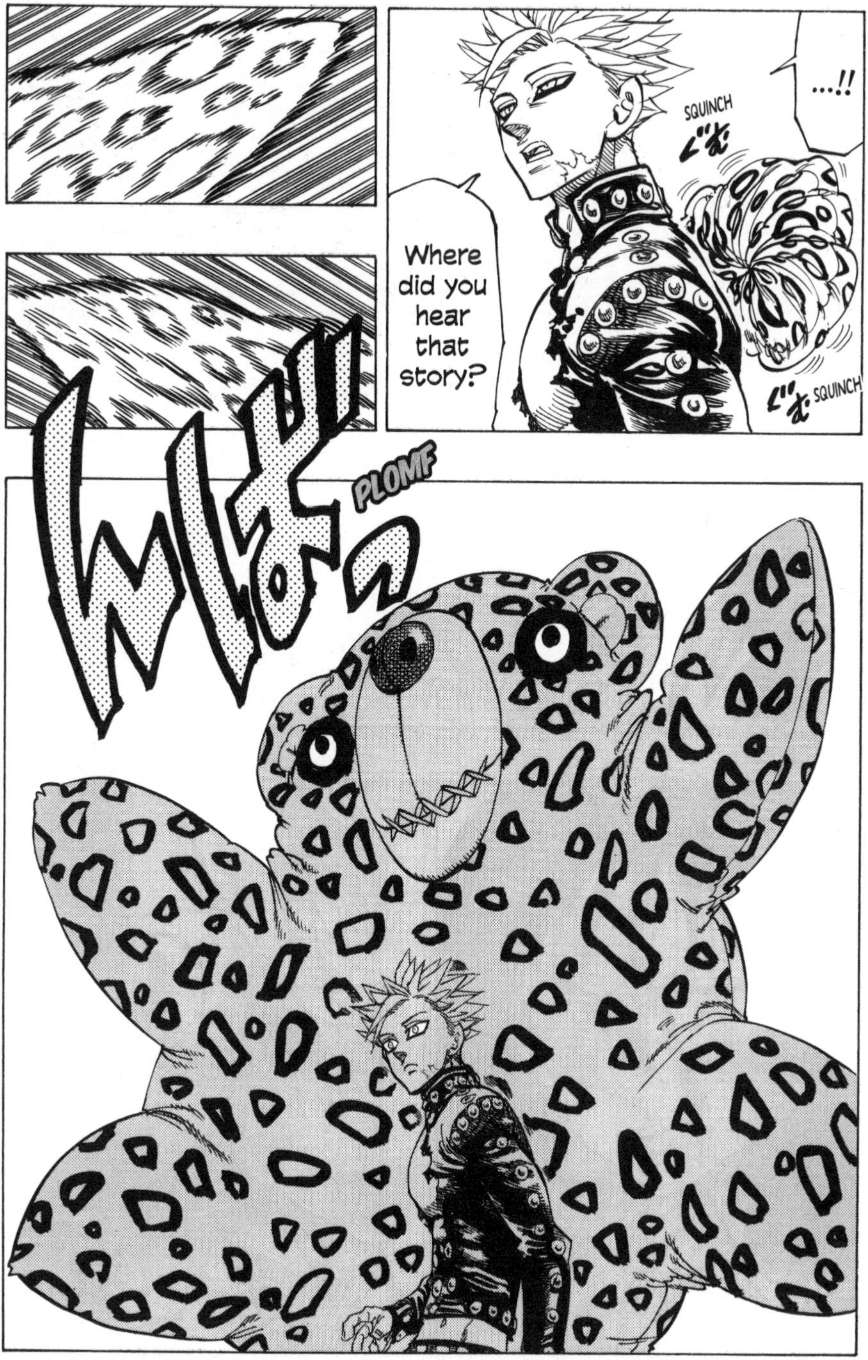
...!!
SQUINCH
Where did you hear that story?
SQUINCH
PLOMF

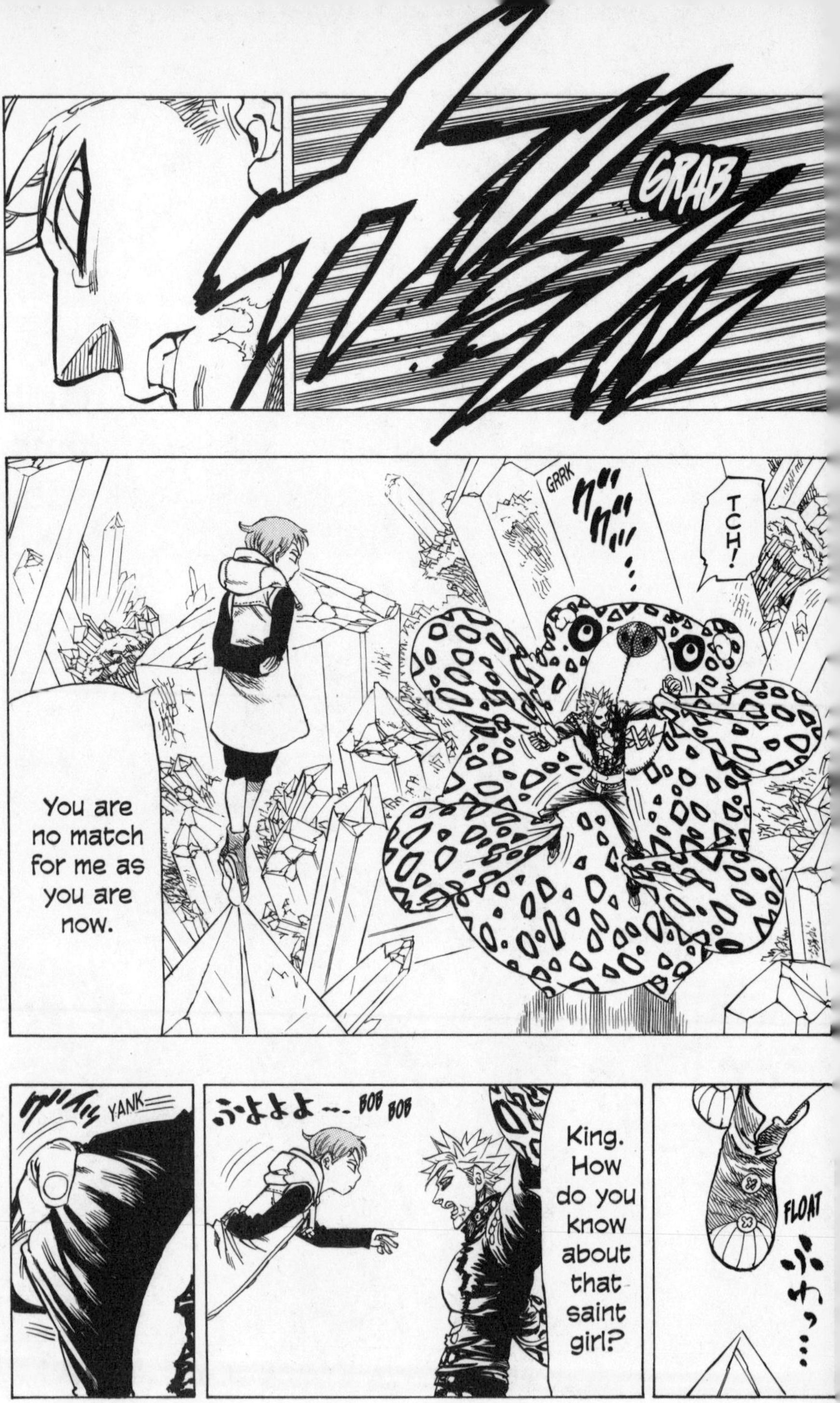
GRAB
GRRK
TCH!
You are no match for me as you are now.
FLOAT
ふわっ…
ふよよよ…
BOB BOB
King. How do you know about that saint girl?
YANK

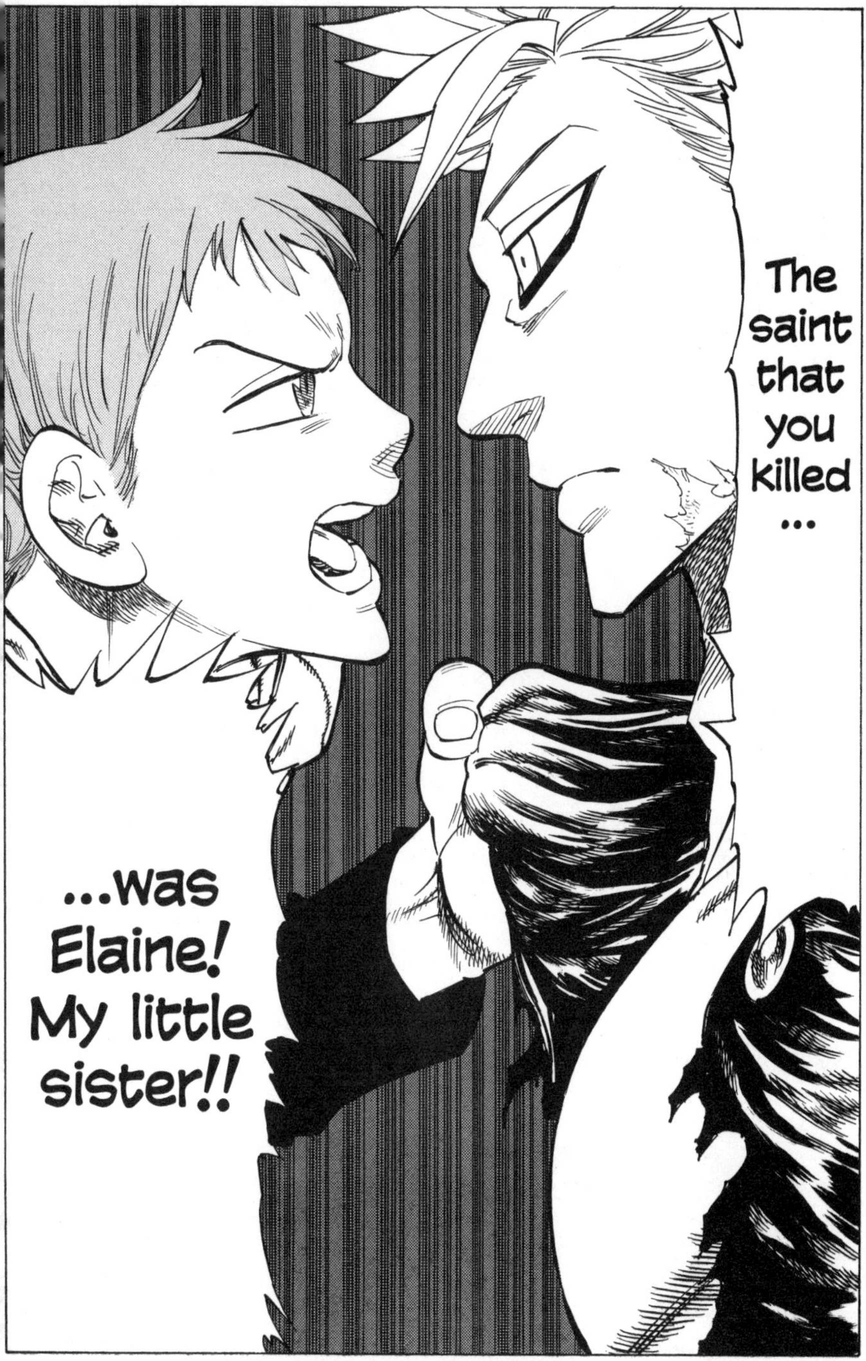
The saint that you killed ...
...was Elaine! My little sister!!

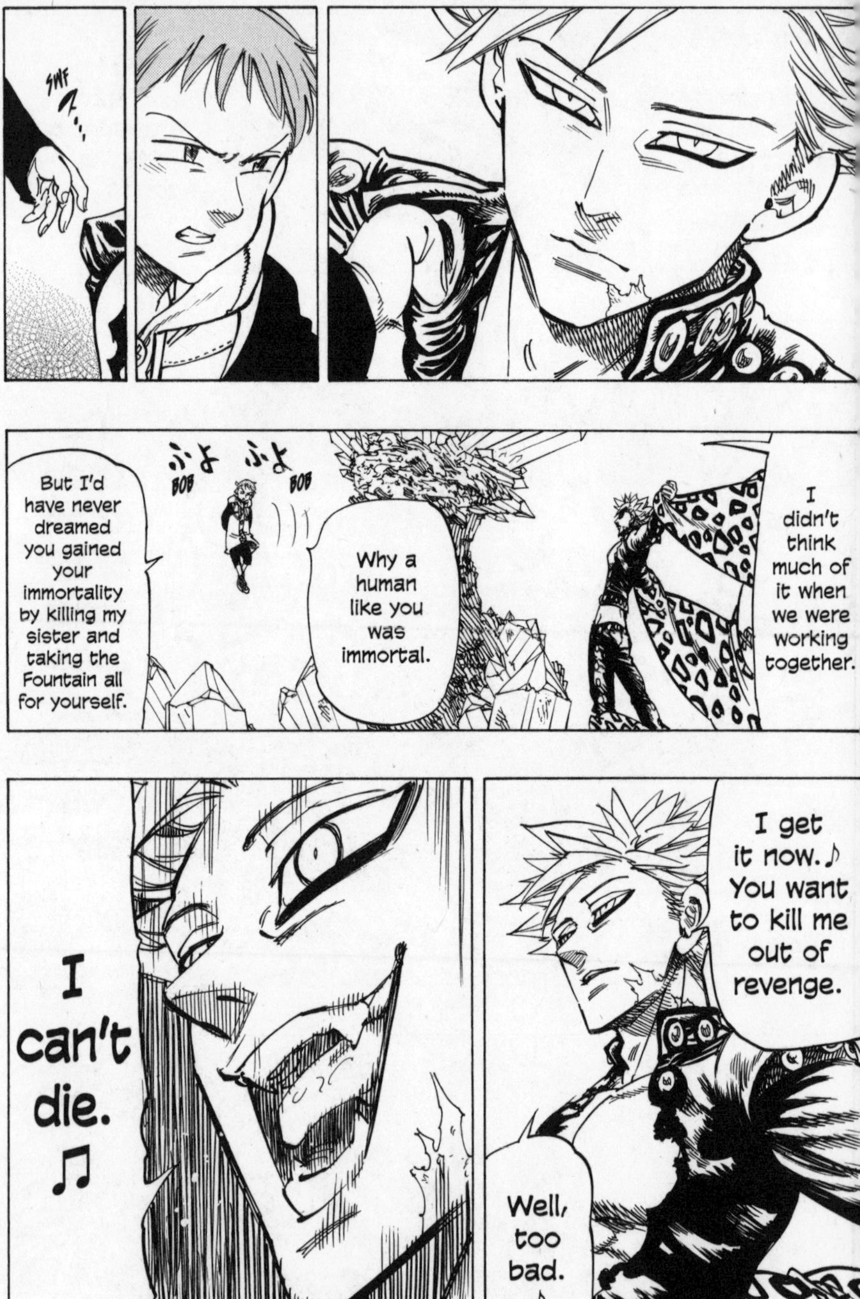
SWF
I didn't think much of it when we were working together.
Why a human like you was immortal.
ふよ ふよ
BOB BOB
But I'd have never dreamed you gained your immortality by killing my sister and taking the Fountain all for yourself.
I get it now.♪ You want to kill me out of revenge.
Well, too bad. ♪
I can't die. ♫

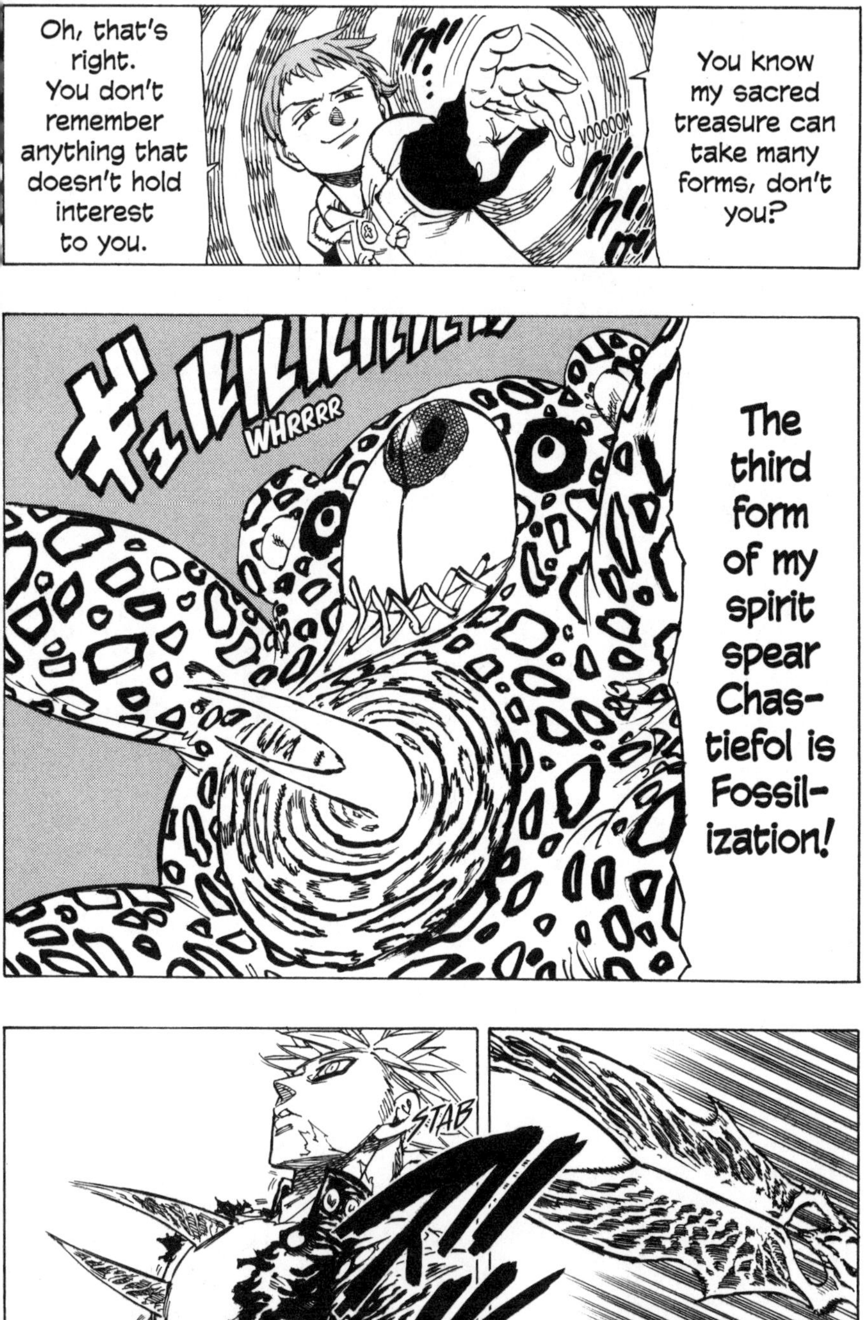
You know my sacred treasure can take many forms, don't you?
VOOOOOM
Oh, that's right. You don't remember anything that doesn't hold interest to you.
The third form of my spirit spear Chastiefol is Fossilization!
WHRRRR
STAB

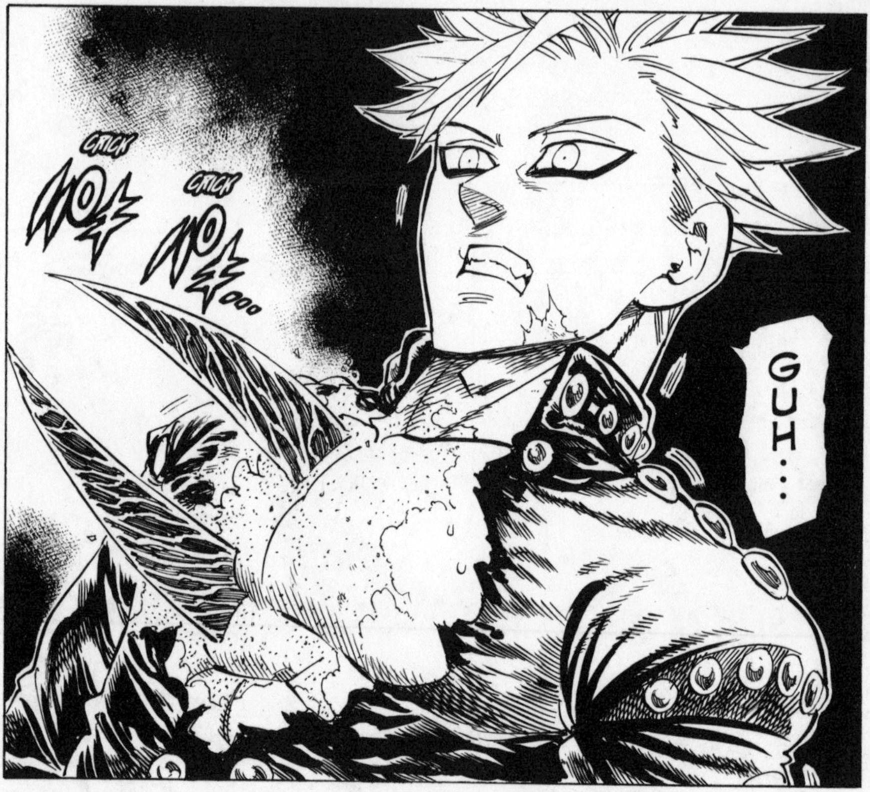
GUH...
CRICK
CRICK

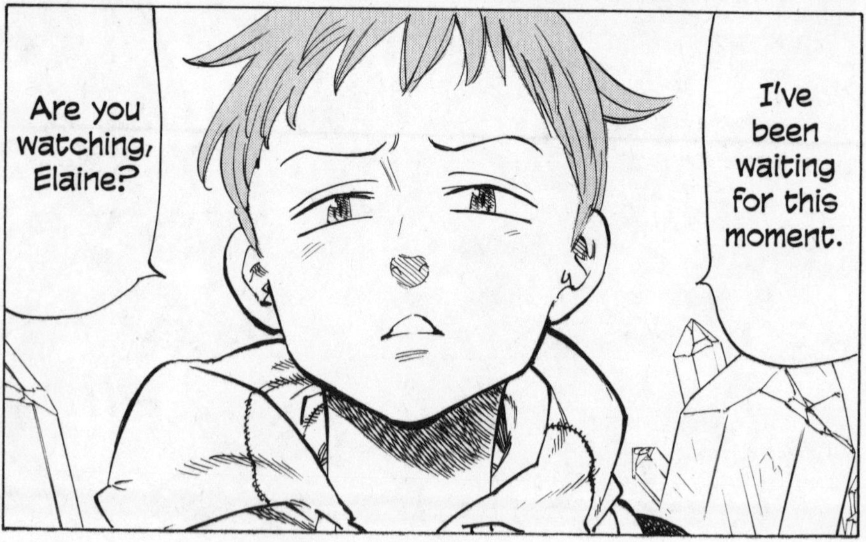
I've been waiting for this moment.
Are you watching, Elaine?

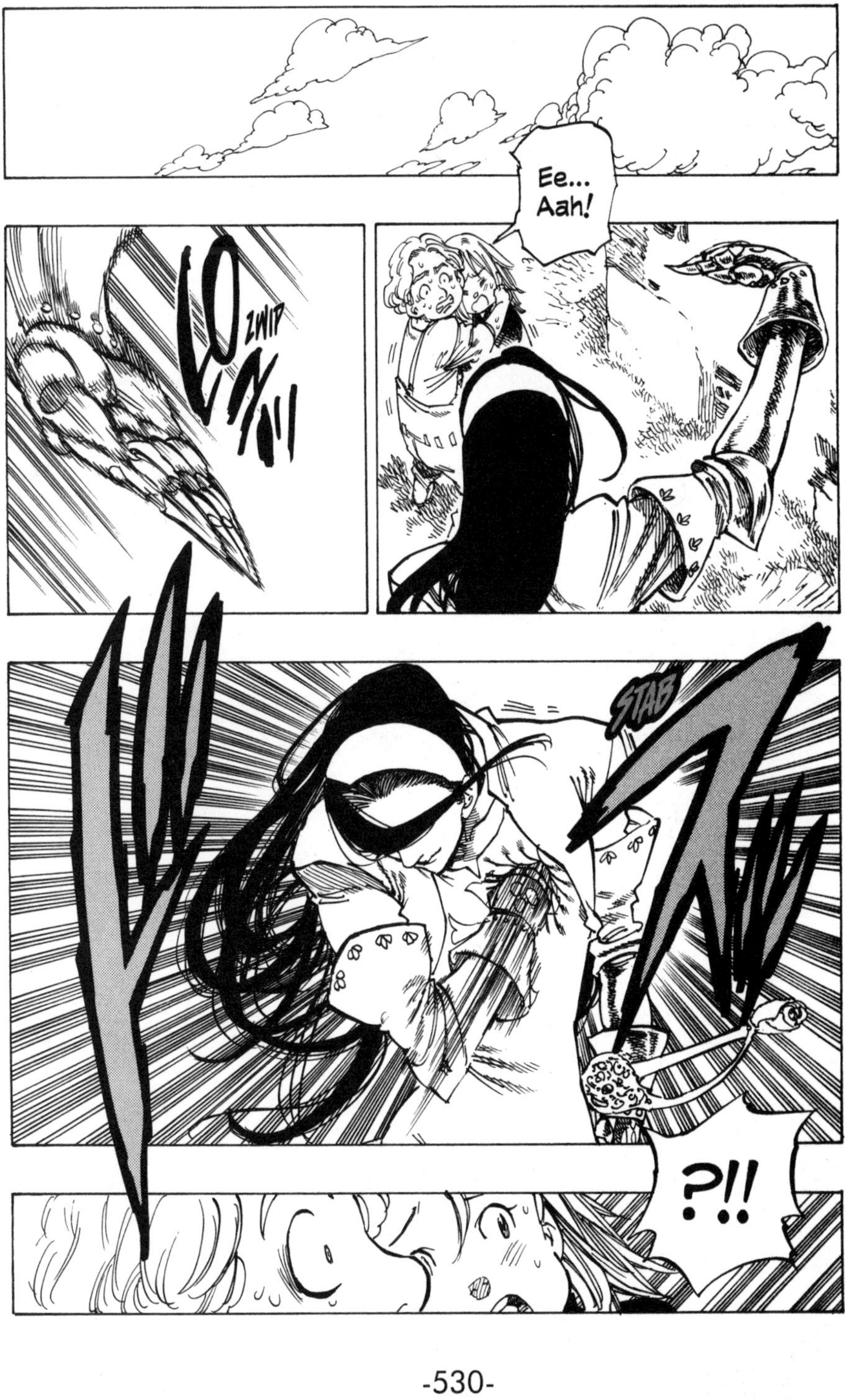
Ee... Aah!
ZWIP
STAB
?!!

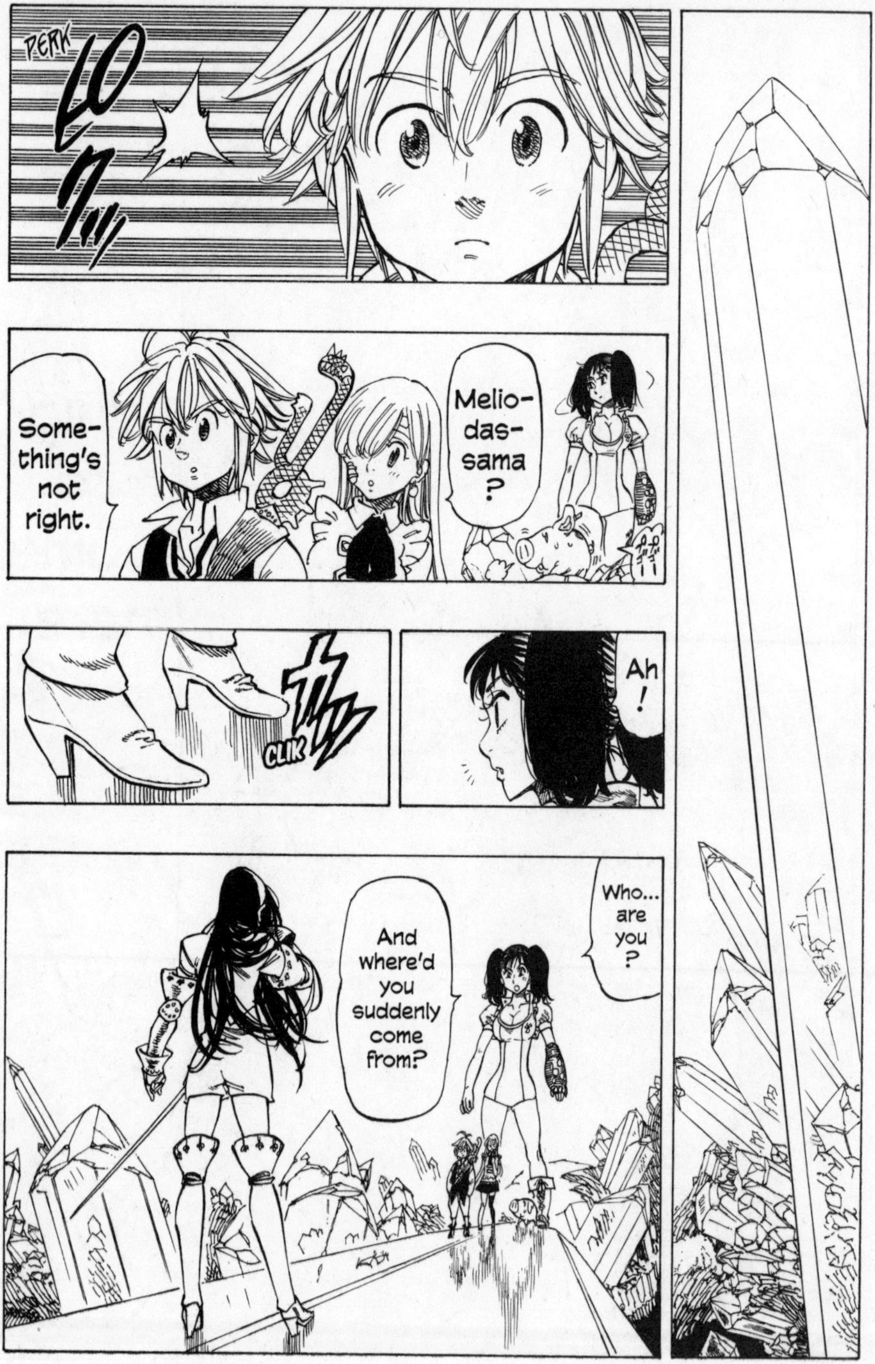
PERK
Melio-das-sama?
Something's not right.
Ah!
CLIK
Who... are you?
And where'd you suddenly come from?

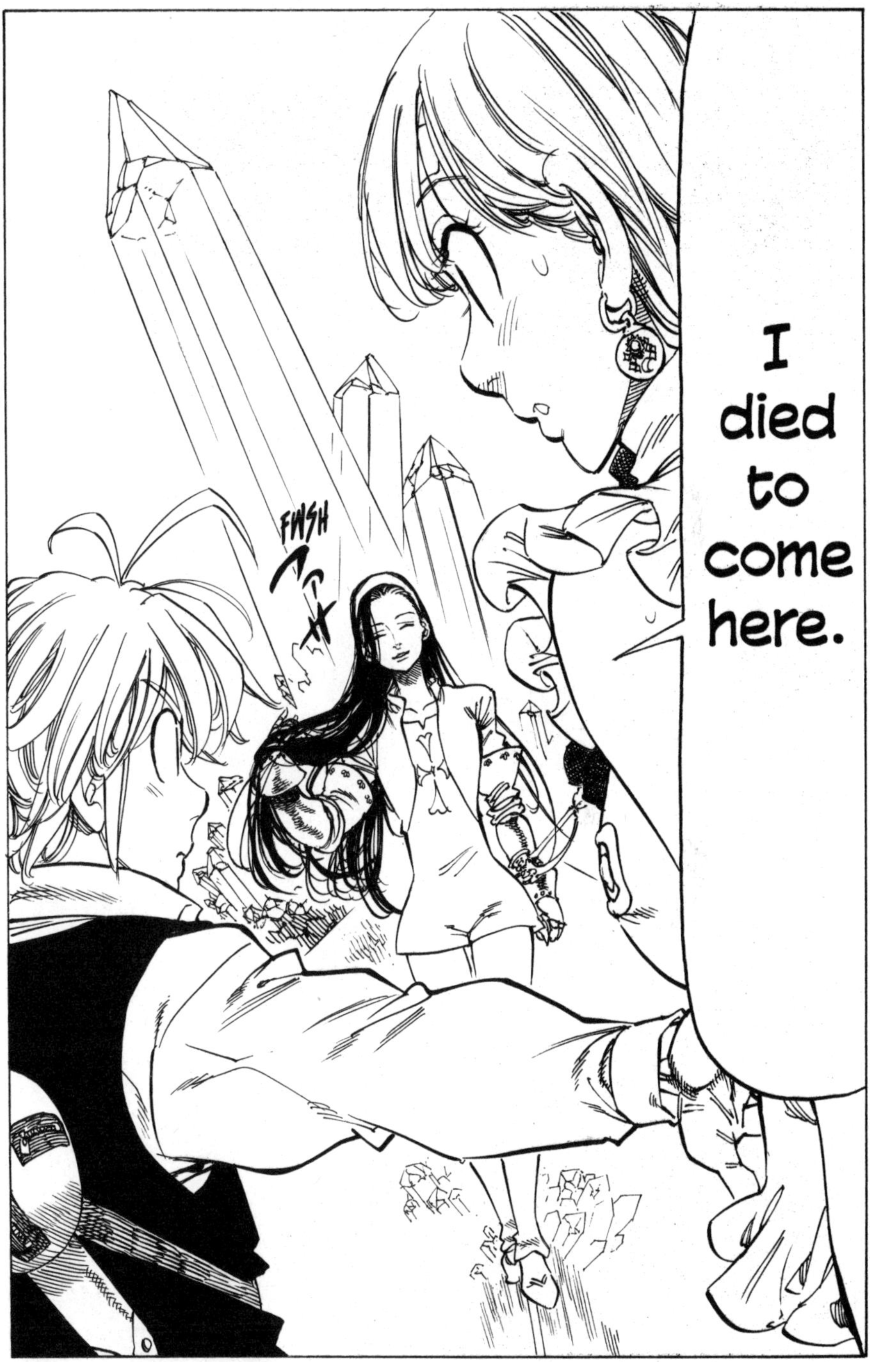
I died to come here.
FWSH

Chapter 22 - A Pursuer to Fear

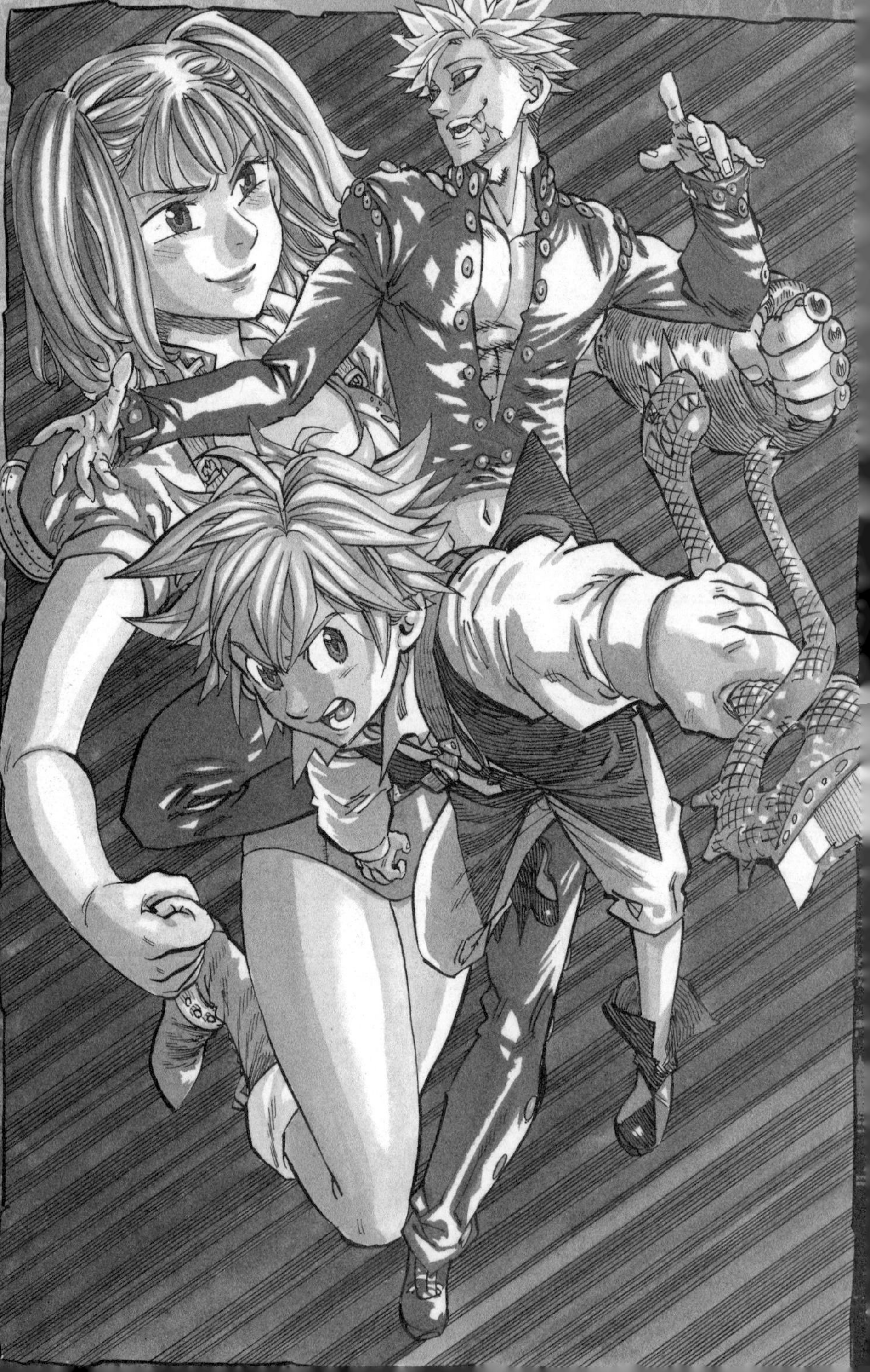

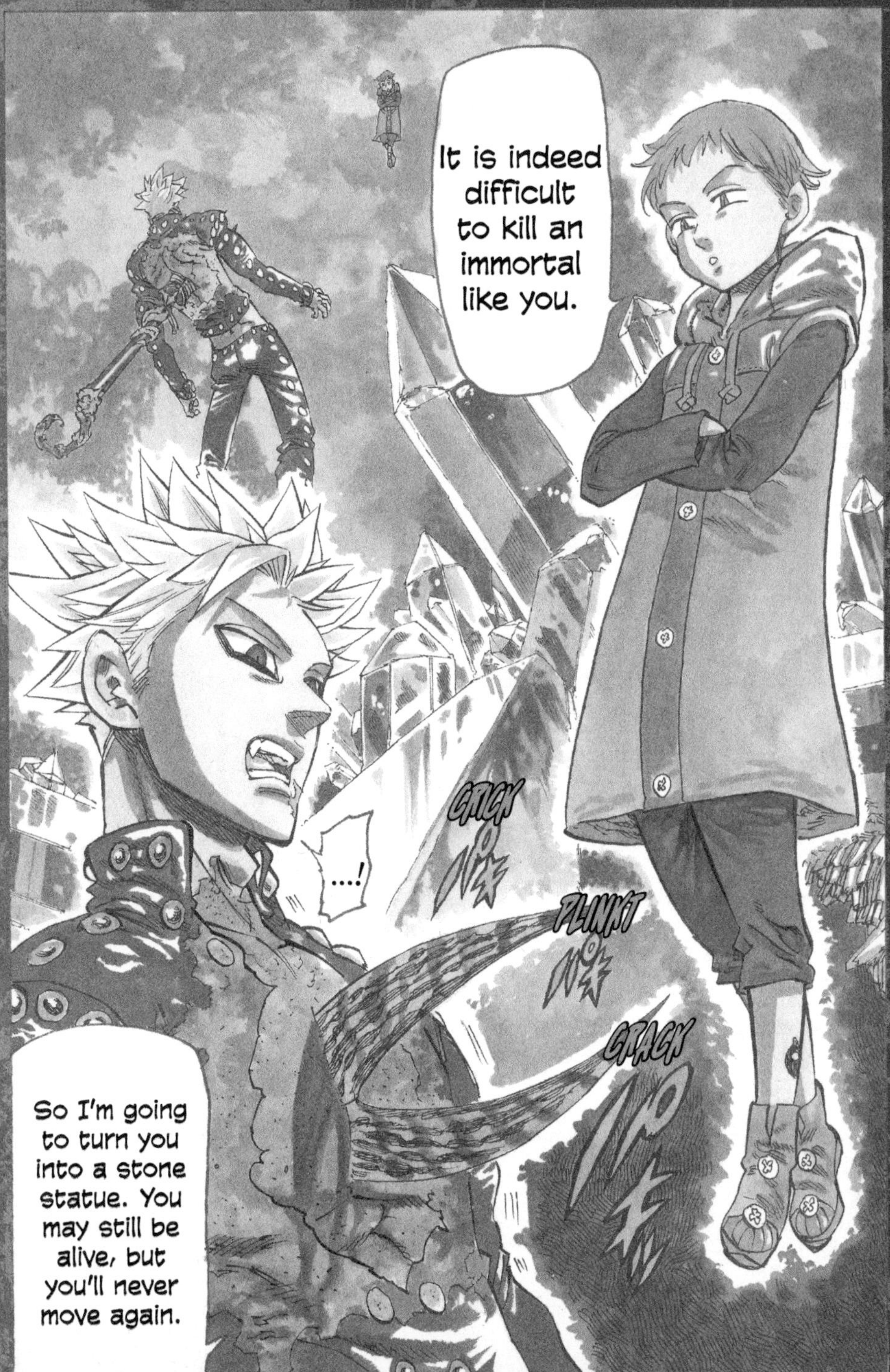
It is indeed difficult to kill an immortal like you.
CRICK
...!
PLINK
CRACK
So I'm going to turn you into a stone statue. You may still be alive, but you'll never move again.

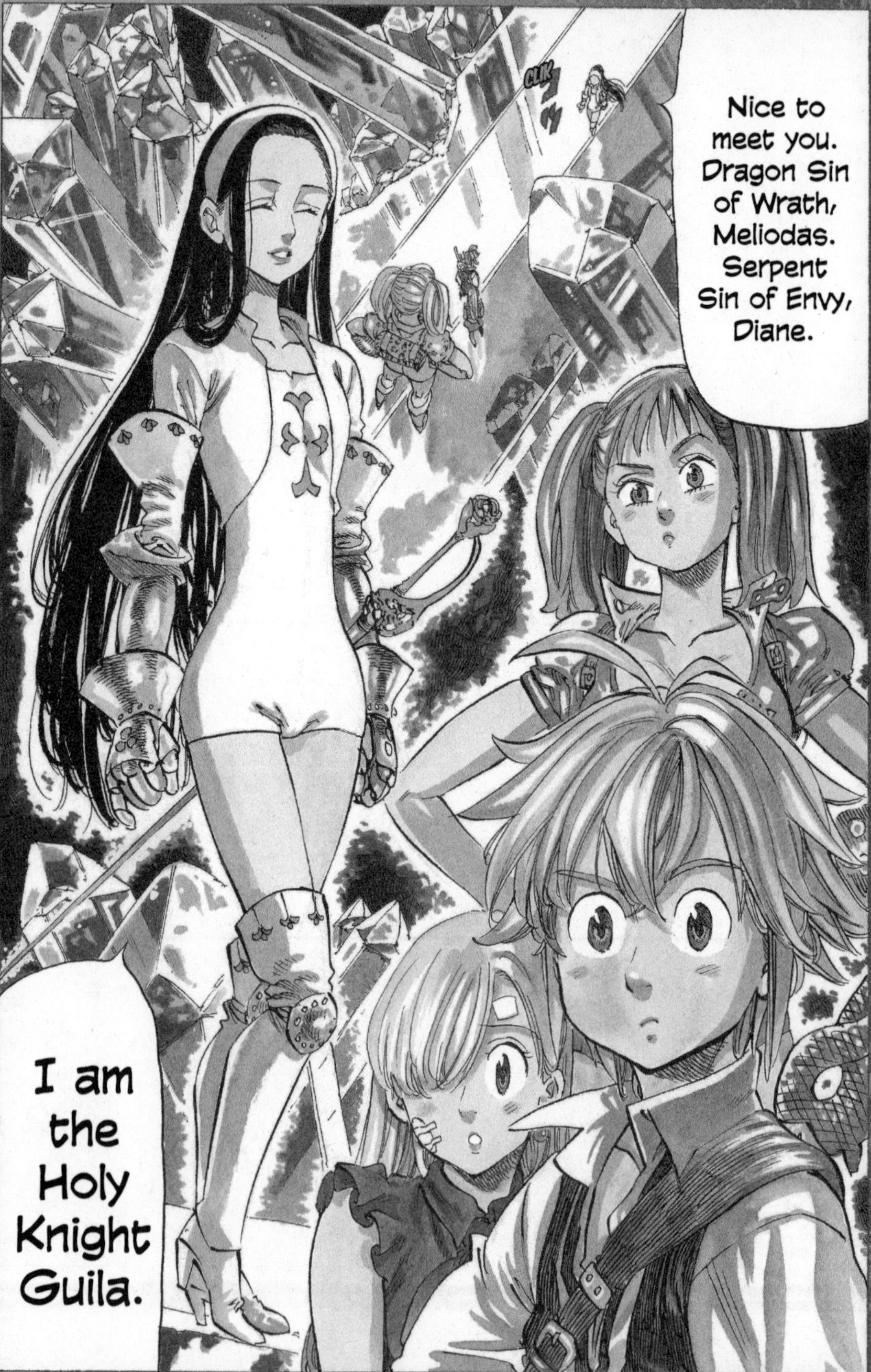
Nice to meet you. Dragon Sin of Wrath, Meliodas. Serpent Sin of Envy, Diane.
CLIK
I am the Holy Knight Guila.

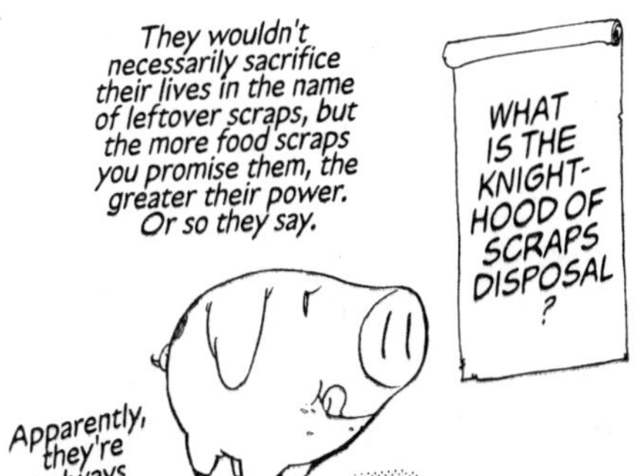
They wouldn't necessarily sacrifice their lives in the name of leftover scraps, but the more food scraps you promise them, the greater their power. Or so they say.
WHAT IS THE KNIGHT-HOOD OF SCRAPS DISPOSAL ?
Apparently, they're always looking for new members.

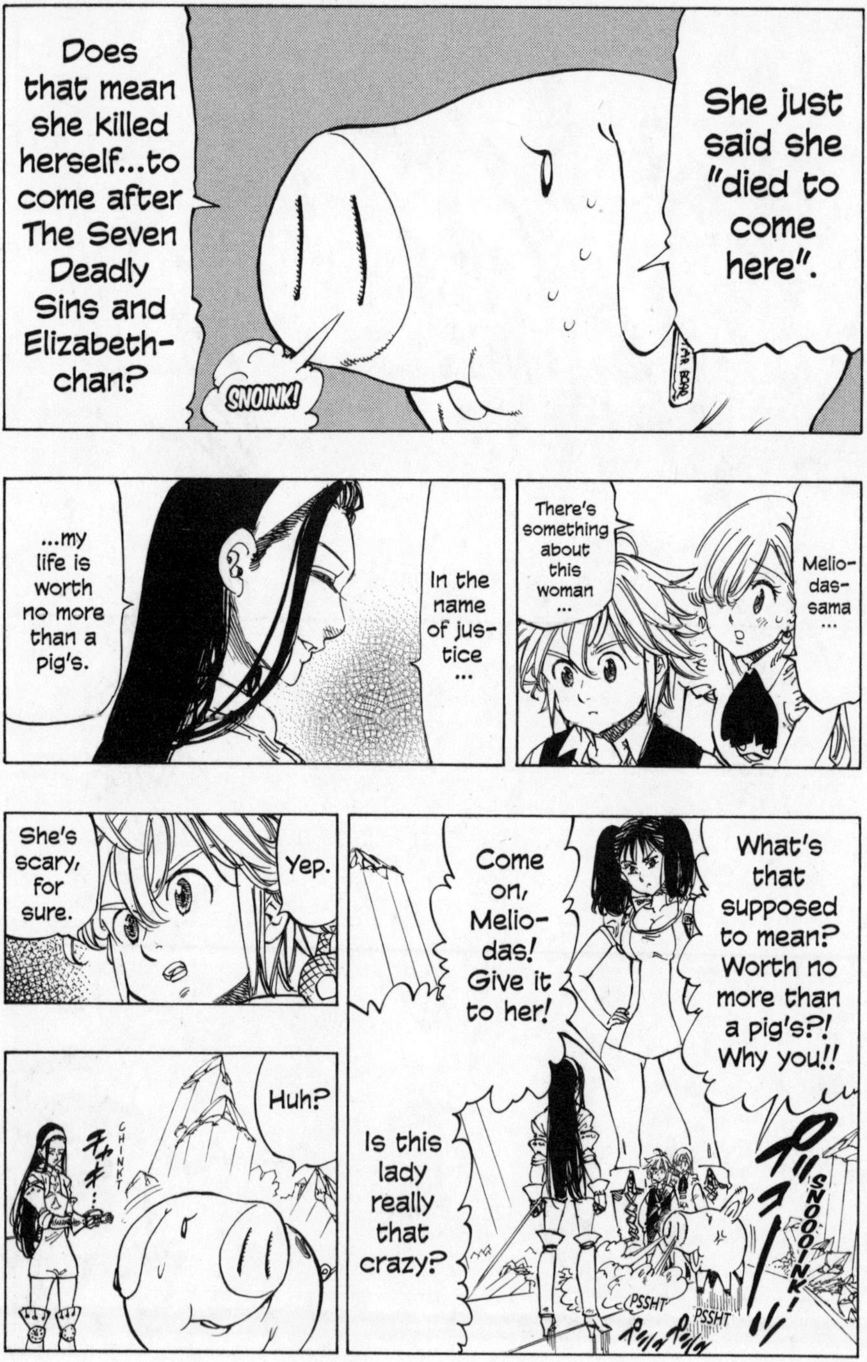
She just said she "died to come here".
Does that mean she killed herself...to come after The Seven Deadly Sins and Elizabeth-chan?
SNOINK!
Melio-das-sama ...
There's something about this woman ...
In the name of jus-tice ...
...my life is worth no more than a pig's.
What's that supposed to mean? Worth no more than a pig's?! Why you!!
Come on, Melio-das! Give it to her!
SNOOOINK!
Is this lady really that crazy?
PSSHT
PSSHT
Yep.
She's scary, for sure.
Huh?
CHINK

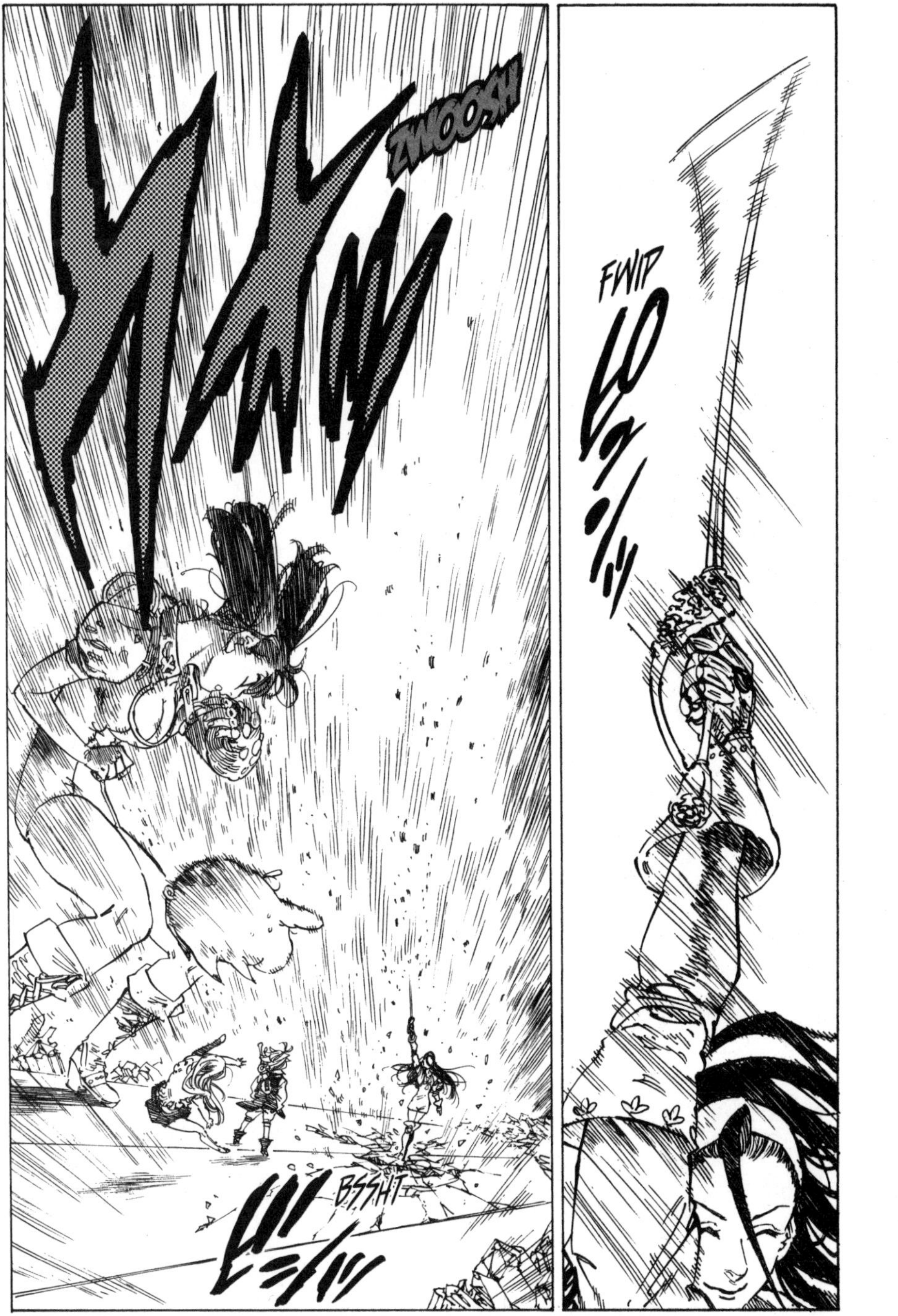
FWIP
ZWOOSH
BSSHT

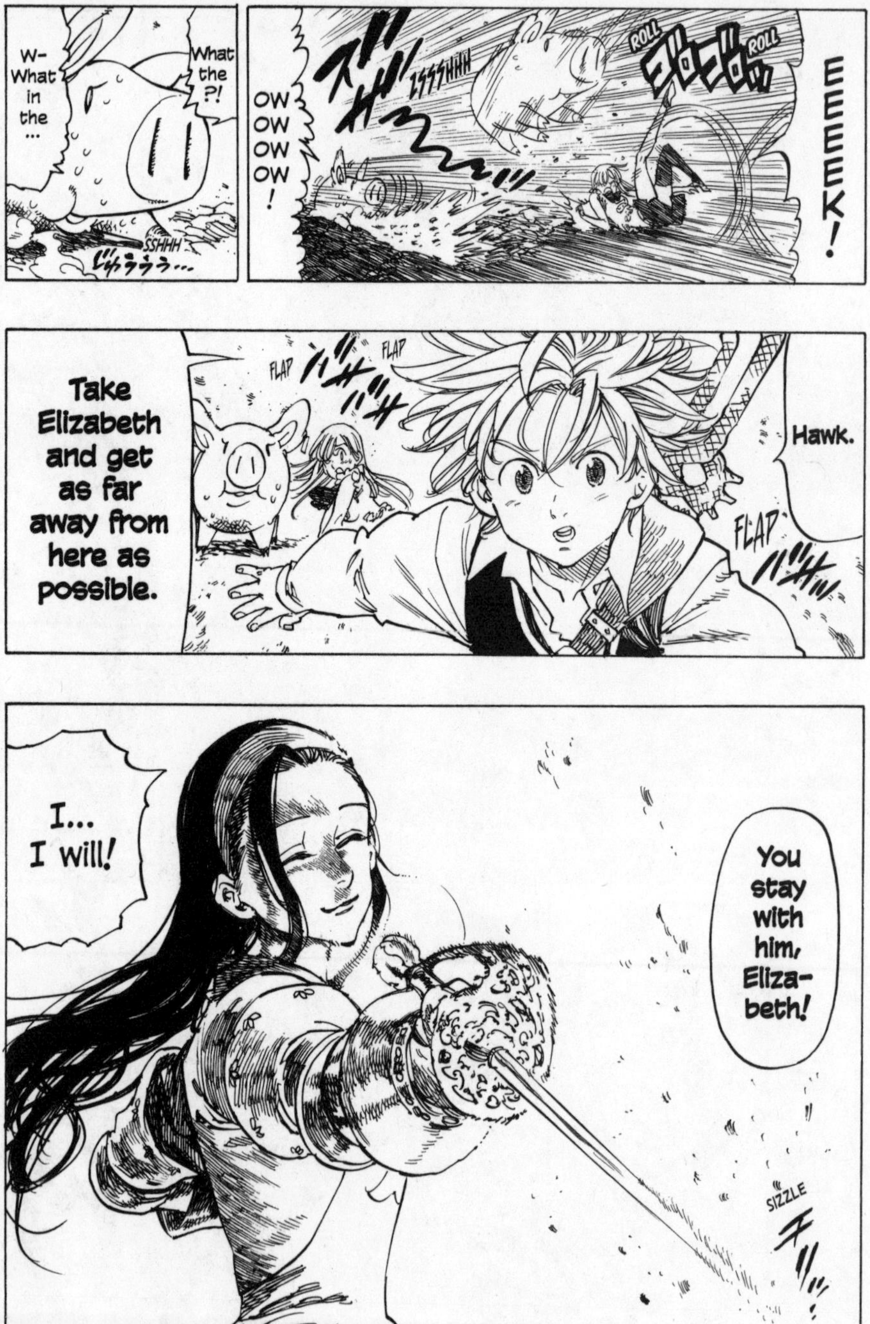
EEEEEK!
ROLL
ROLL
ZSSSHHH
OW OW OW OW!
What the ?!
W- What in the ...
SSHHH
Hawk.
FLAP
FLAP
FLAP
Take Elizabeth and get as far away from here as possible.
You stay with him, Eliza-beth!
I... I will!
SIZZLE

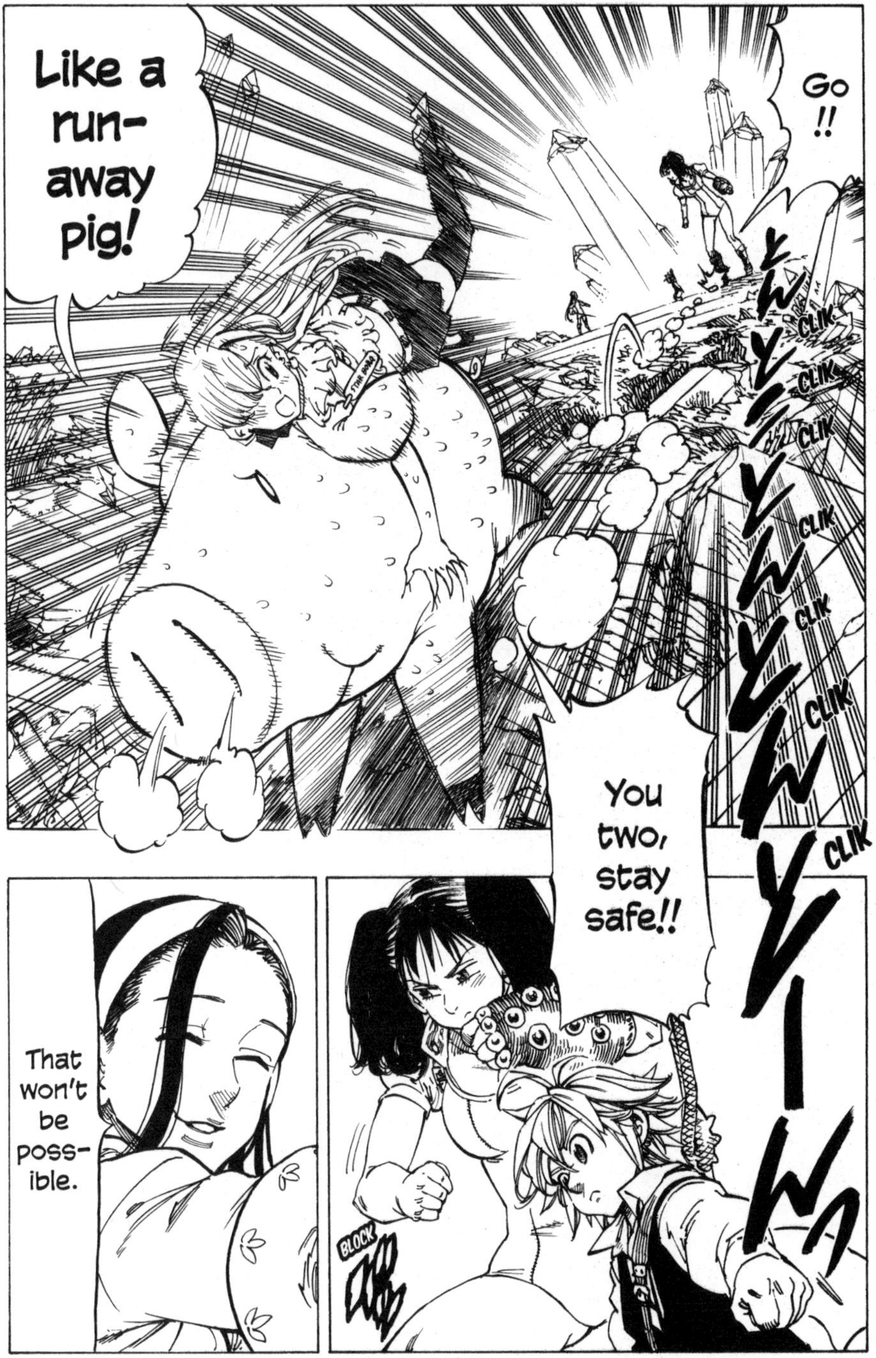
Go!!
Like a run-away pig!
CLIK
CLIK
CLIK
CLIK
CLIK
CLIK
CLIK
You two, stay safe!!
BLOCK
That won't be poss-ible.

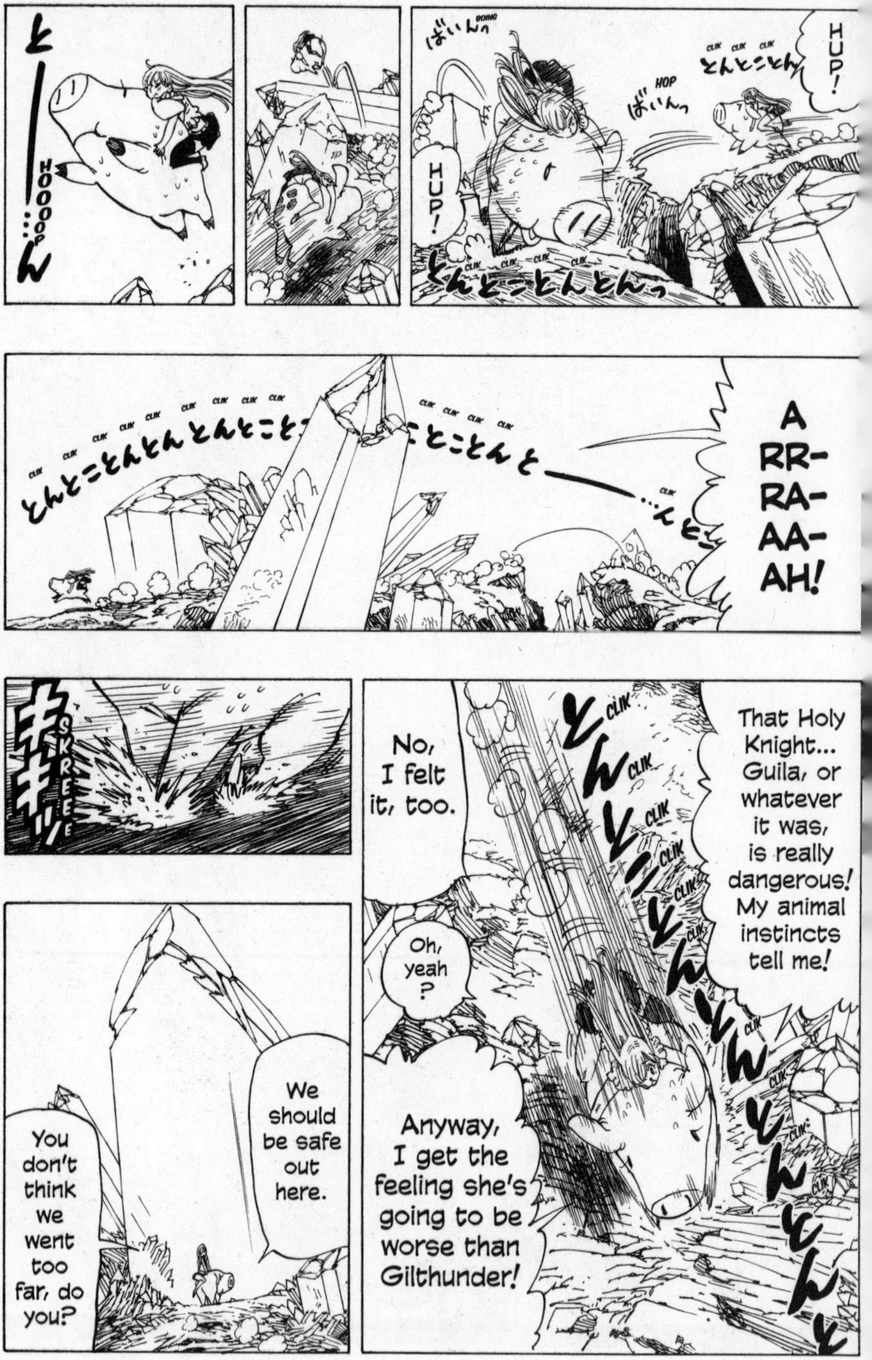
HUP!
CLIK CLIK CLIK
とんとことん
HOP
ばいんっ
BOING
ばいんっ
HUP!
CLIK CLIK CLIK CLIK
とんとことんとんっ
と――…ん
HOOOOOP
A RR-RA-AA-AH!
CLIK
とんとことんとん とんとこと
ことことんと――…
That Holy Knight... Guila, or whatever it was, is really dangerous! My animal instincts tell me!
No, I felt it, too.
Oh, yeah?
Anyway, I get the feeling she's going to be worse than Gilthunder!
CLIK
キキッ
SKREEE
We should be safe out here.
You don't think we went too far, do you?

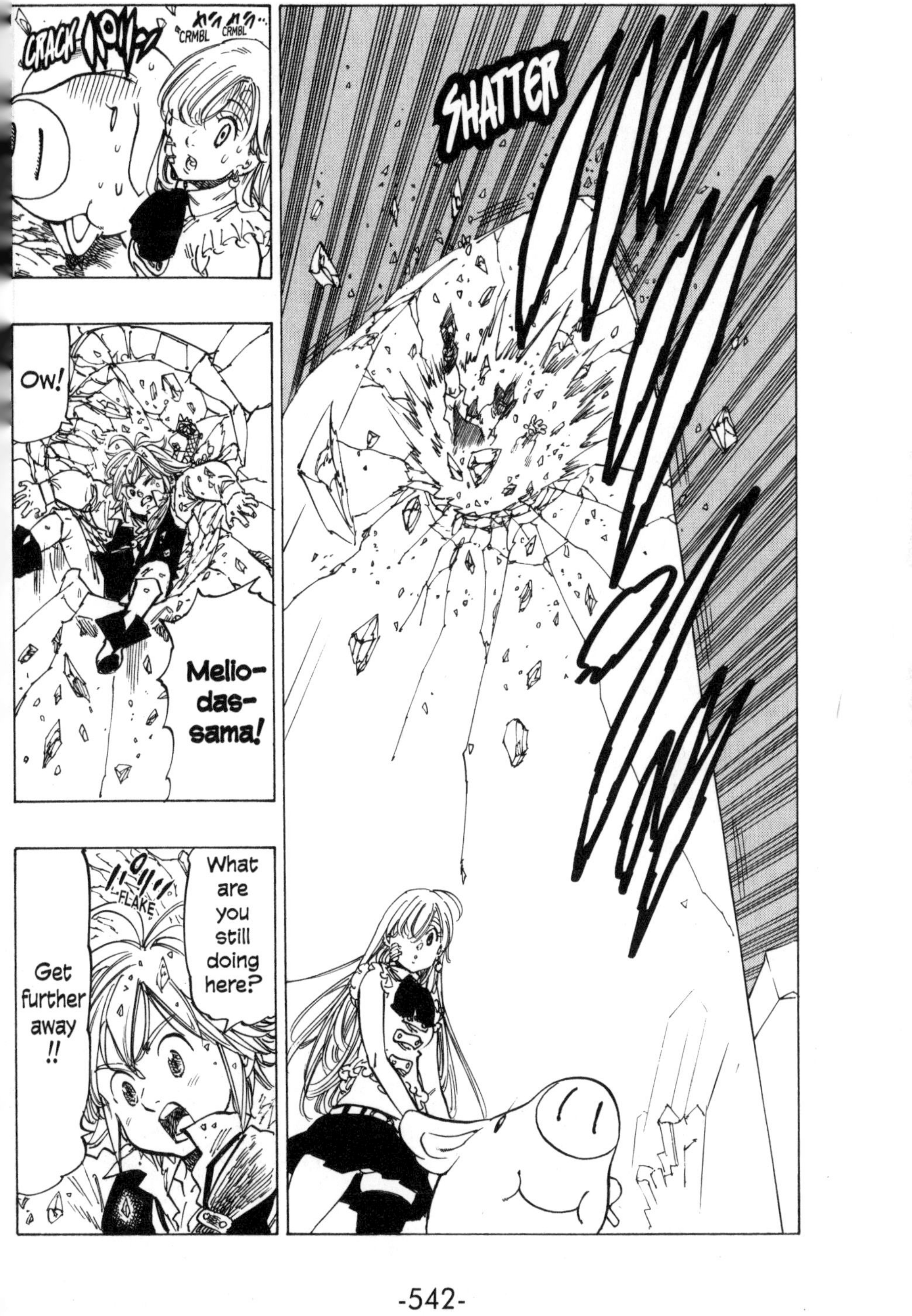
SHATTER
CRACK
CRMBL CRMBL
Ow!
Melio-das-sama!
FLAKE
What are you still doing here?
Get further away !!

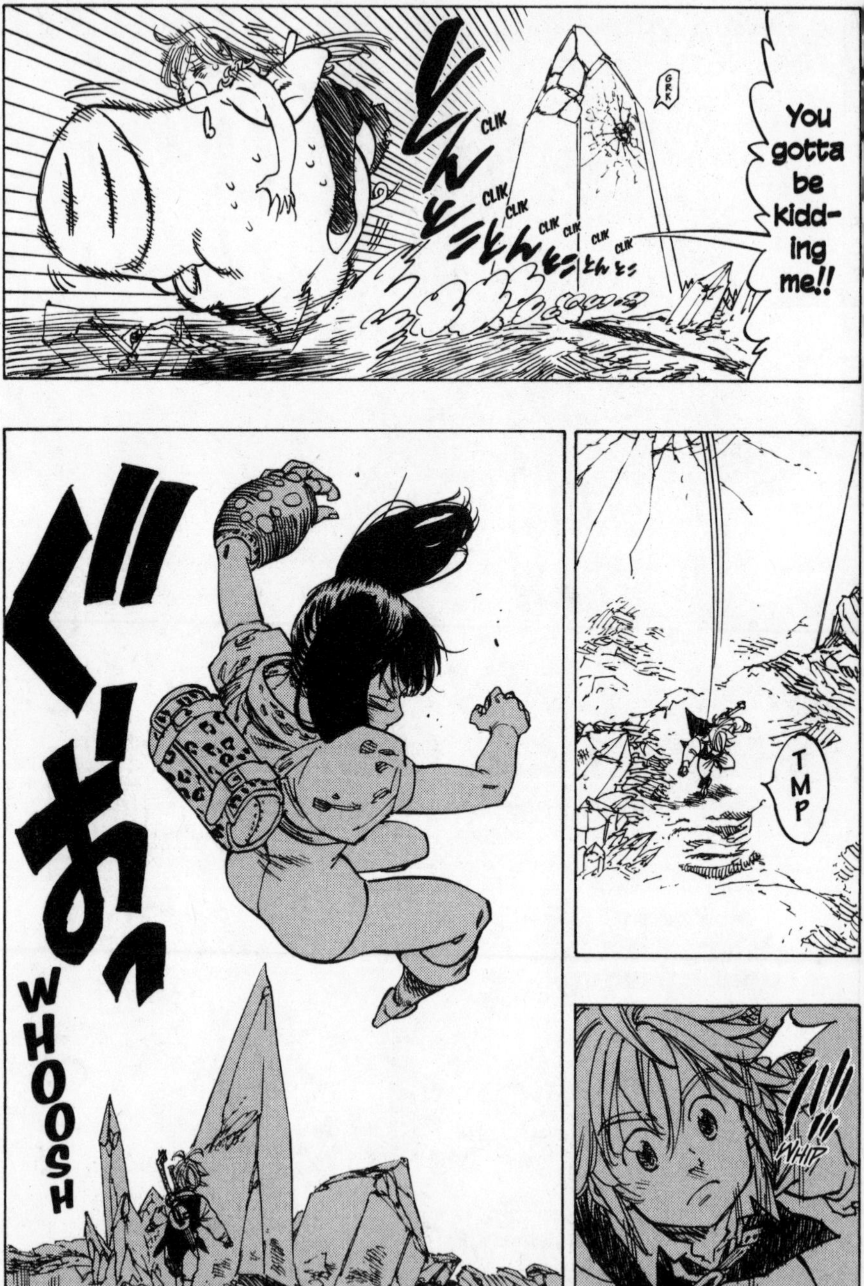
You gotta be kidd-ing me!!
GRK
CLIK CLIK CLIK CLIK CLIK CLIK CLIK
TMP
WHIP
WHOOSH

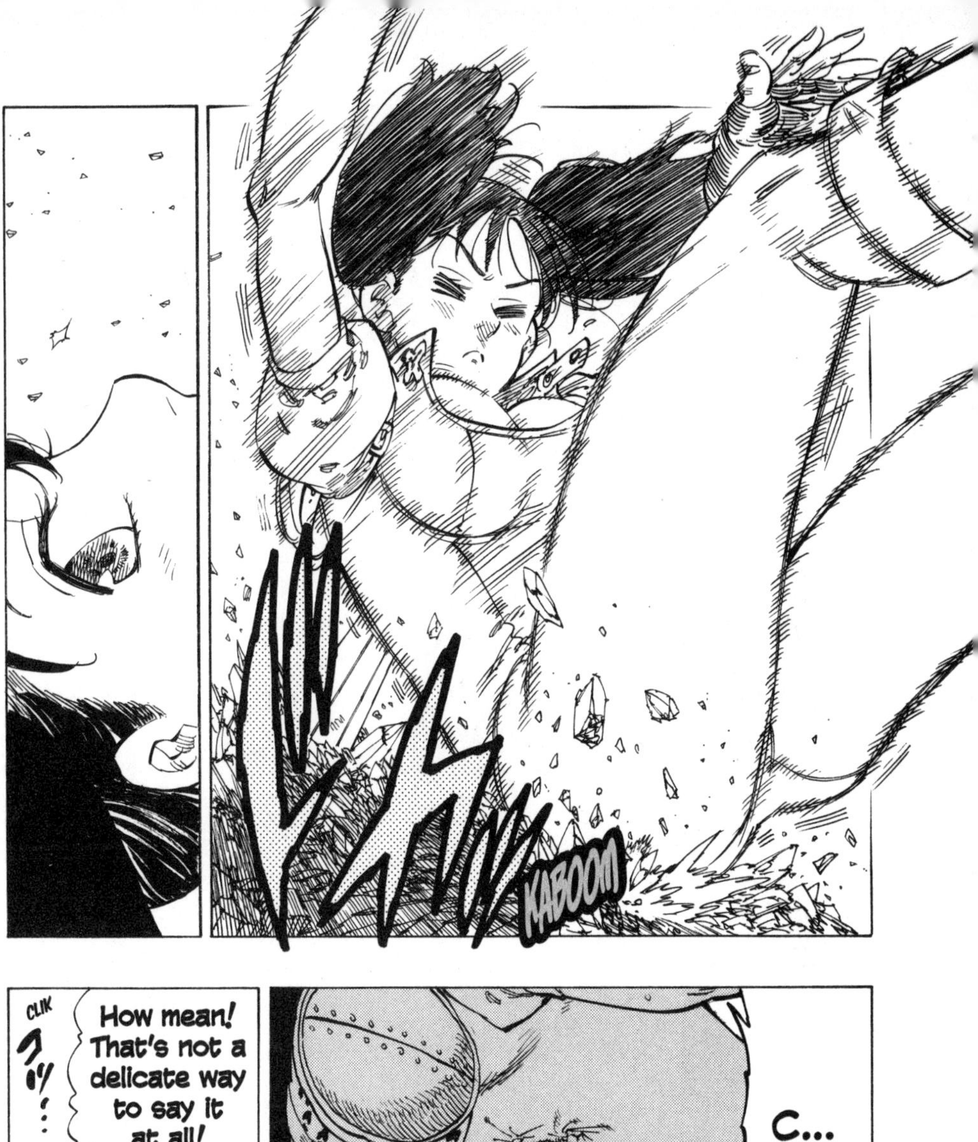
KABOOM
C... Cap-tain!
So heavy!
CRMBL
FLAKE
CRMBL
FLAKE
CLIK
How mean! That's not a delicate way to say it at all!
CLIK
Now is not the time!

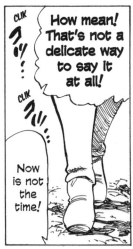

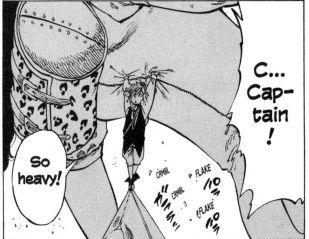

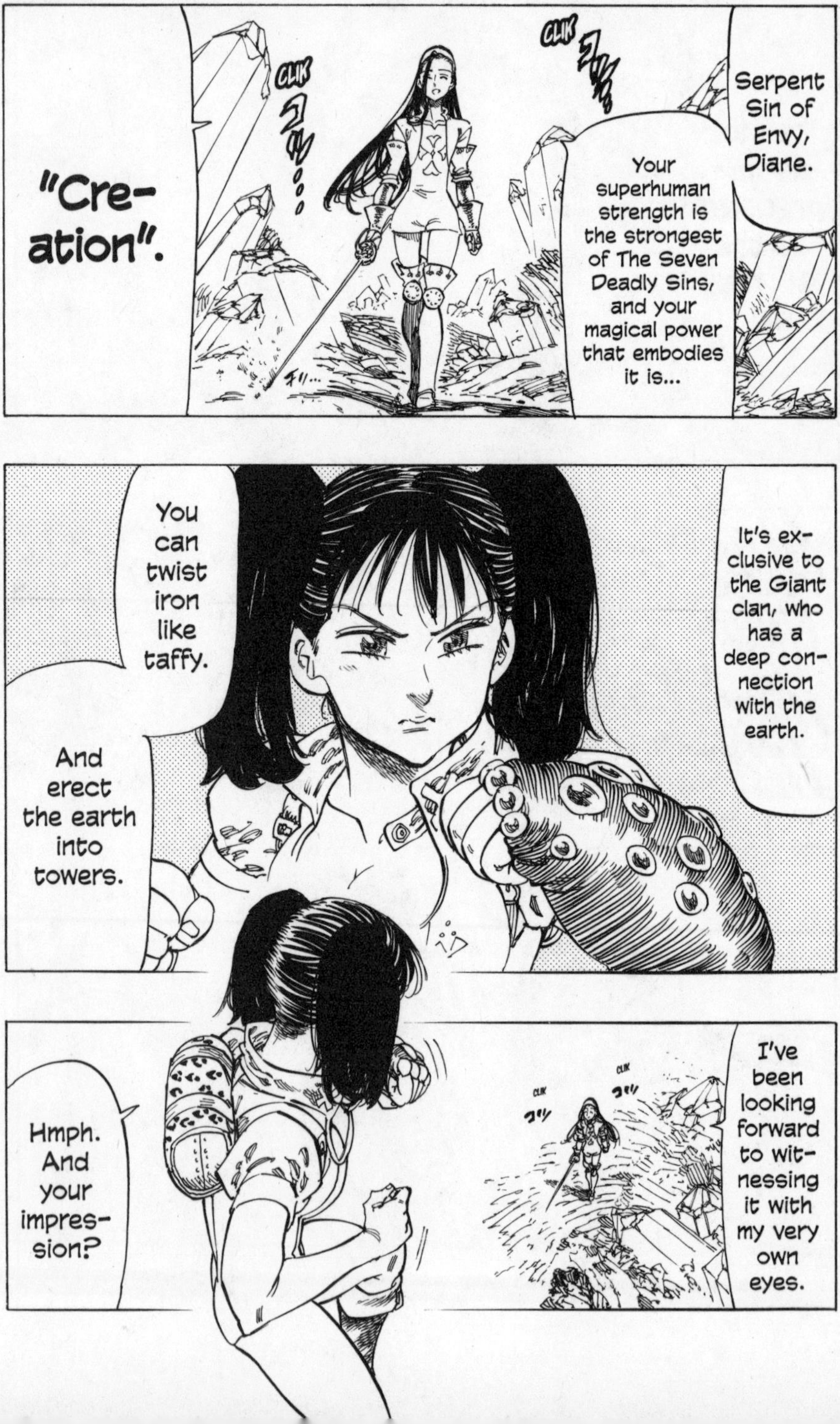
CLIK
CLIK
Serpent Sin of Envy, Diane.
Your superhuman strength is the strongest of The Seven Deadly Sins, and your magical power that embodies it is...
"Cre-ation".
It's ex-clusive to the Giant clan, who has a deep con-nection with the earth.
You can twist iron like taffy.
And erect the earth into towers.
CLIK
CLIK
I've been looking forward to wit-nessing it with my very own eyes.
Hmph. And your impres-sion?

Quite frankly, I'm disappointed.
It's not as impressive as the stories say.
Hmph.
In that case...
...how about this?
THWACK
FWIP
FWIP
FWIP
FWIP
CONK
REEL
!!

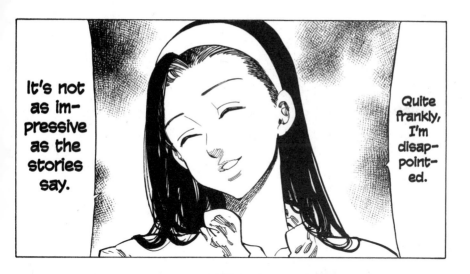

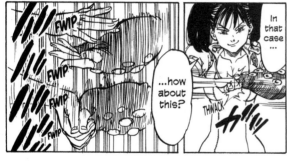

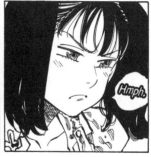

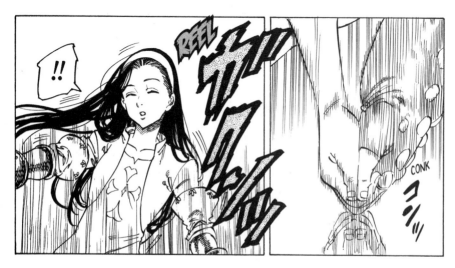

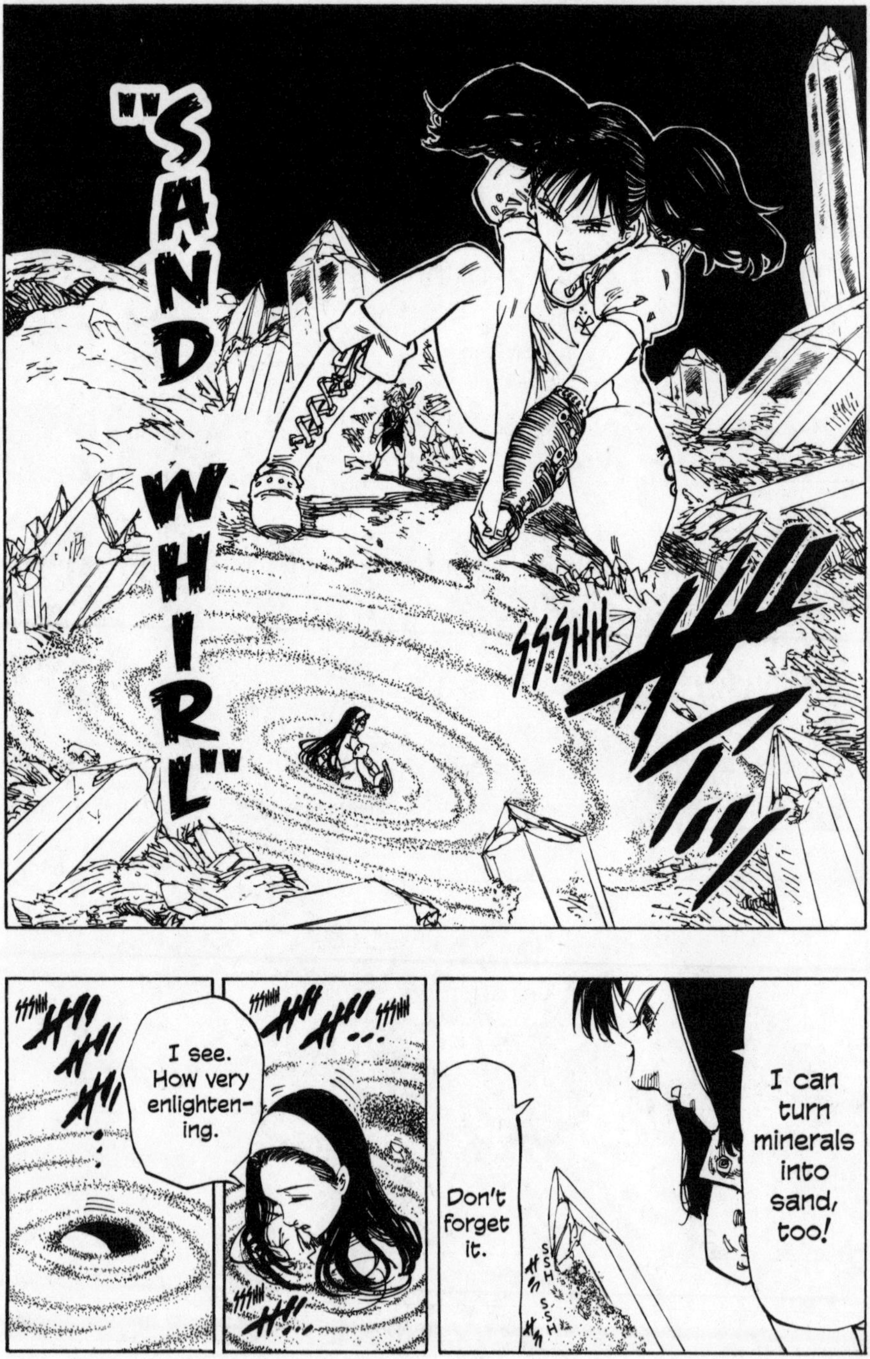
"SAND WHIRL"
SSSHH
I can turn minerals into sand, too!
Don't forget it.
SSH SSH
SSSHH SSSHH
I see. How very enlightening.
SSSHH
SSSHH

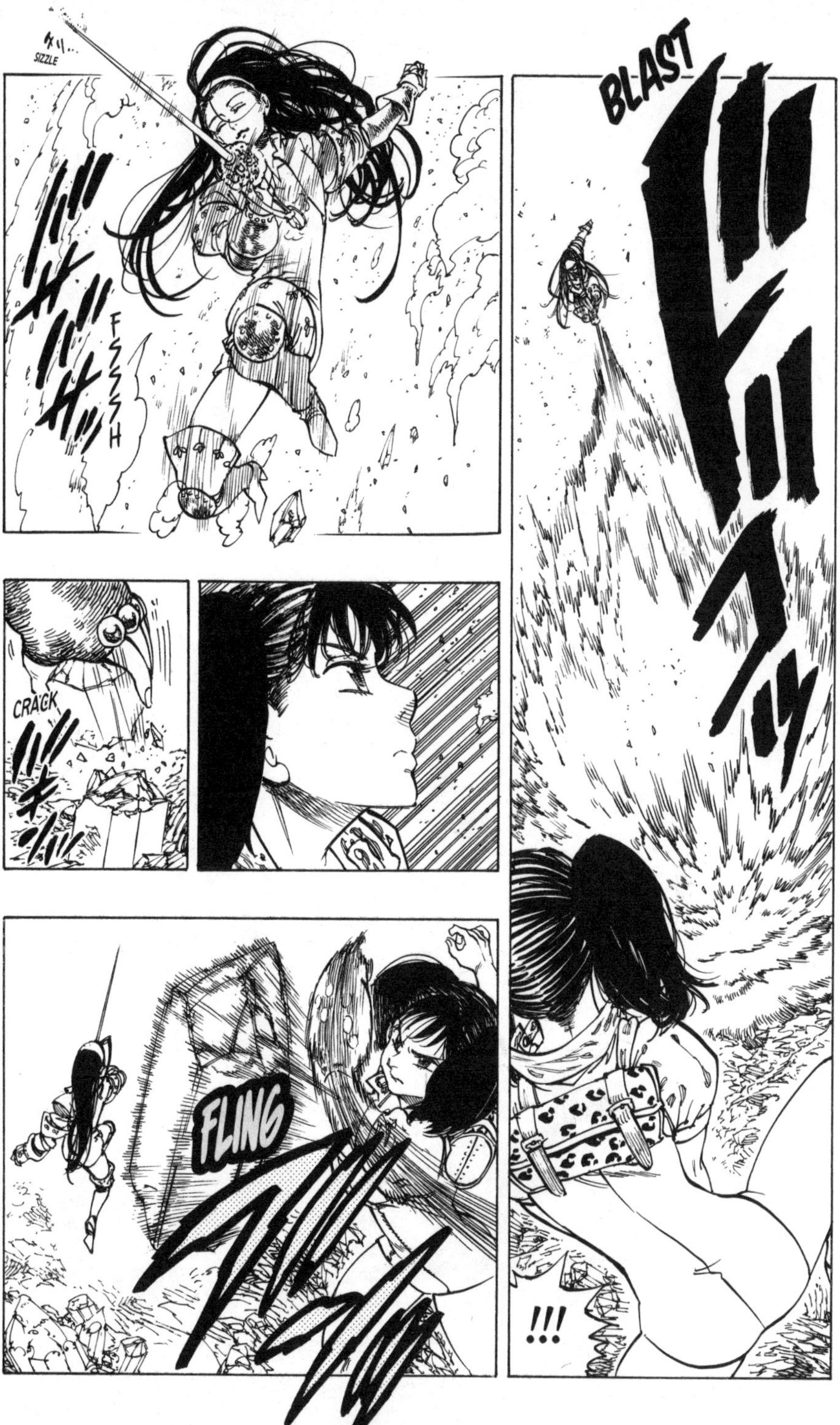
BLAST
!!!
SIZZLE
FSSSH
CRACK
FLING

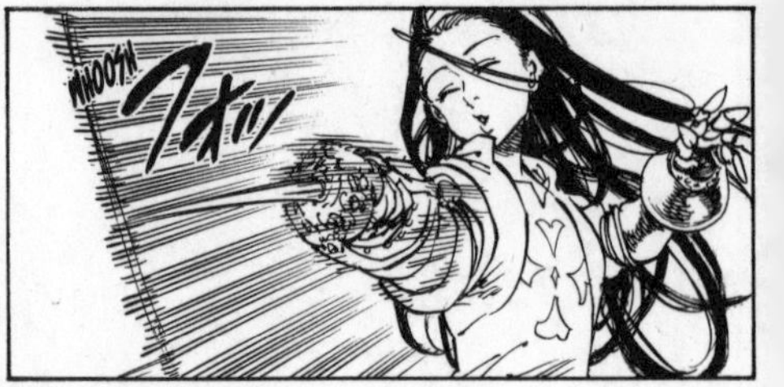
WHOOSH
フォッ

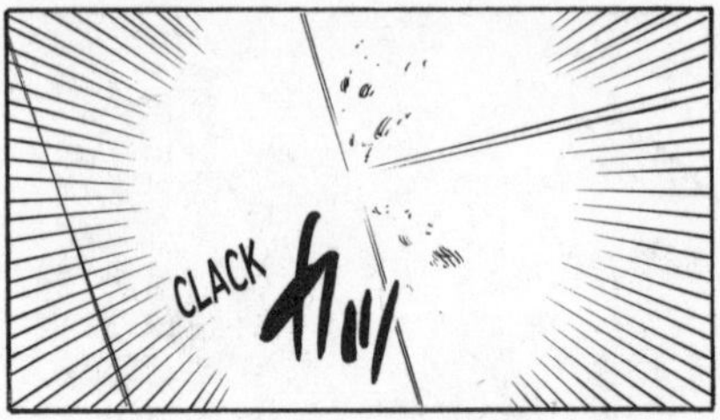
CLACK
カッ

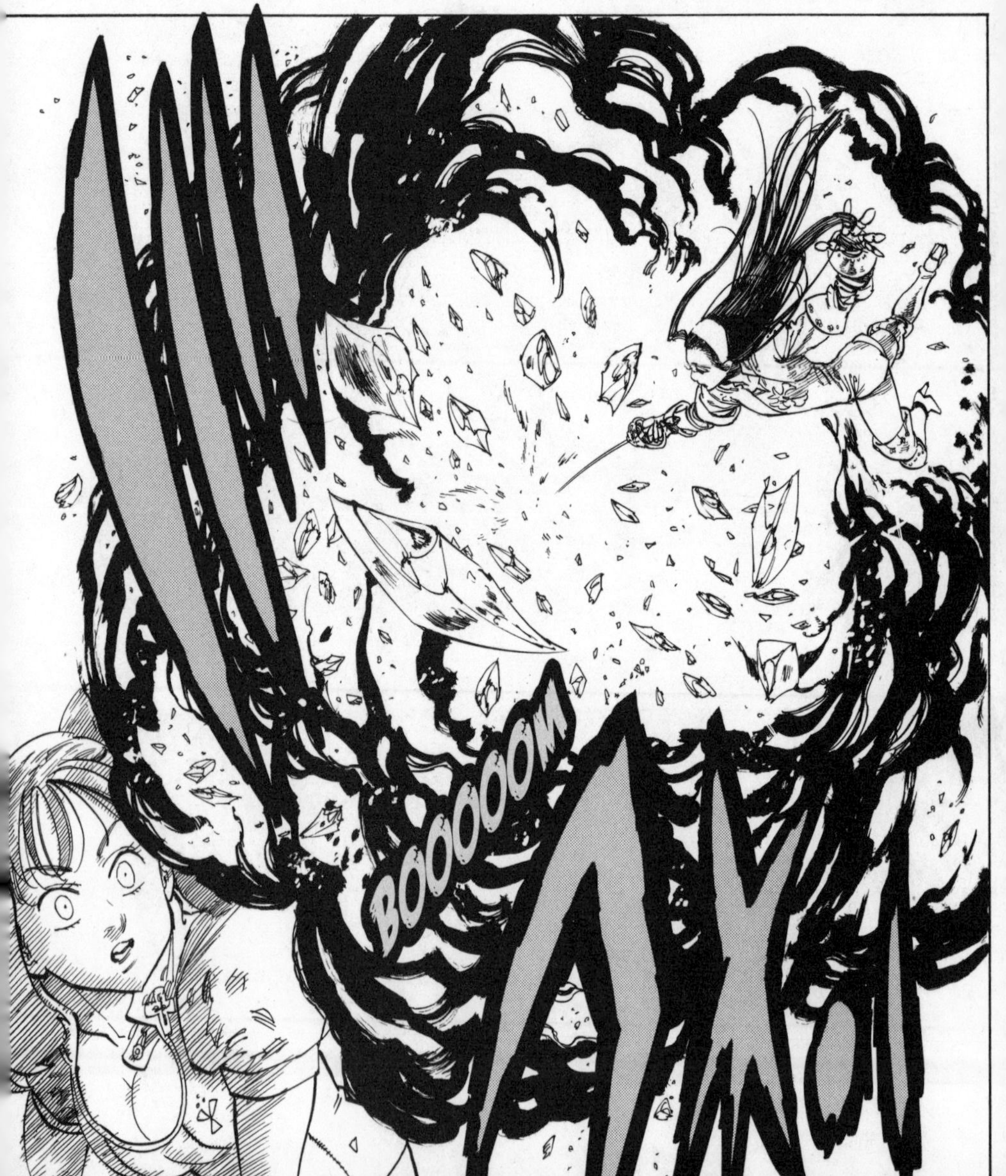
BOOOOOM

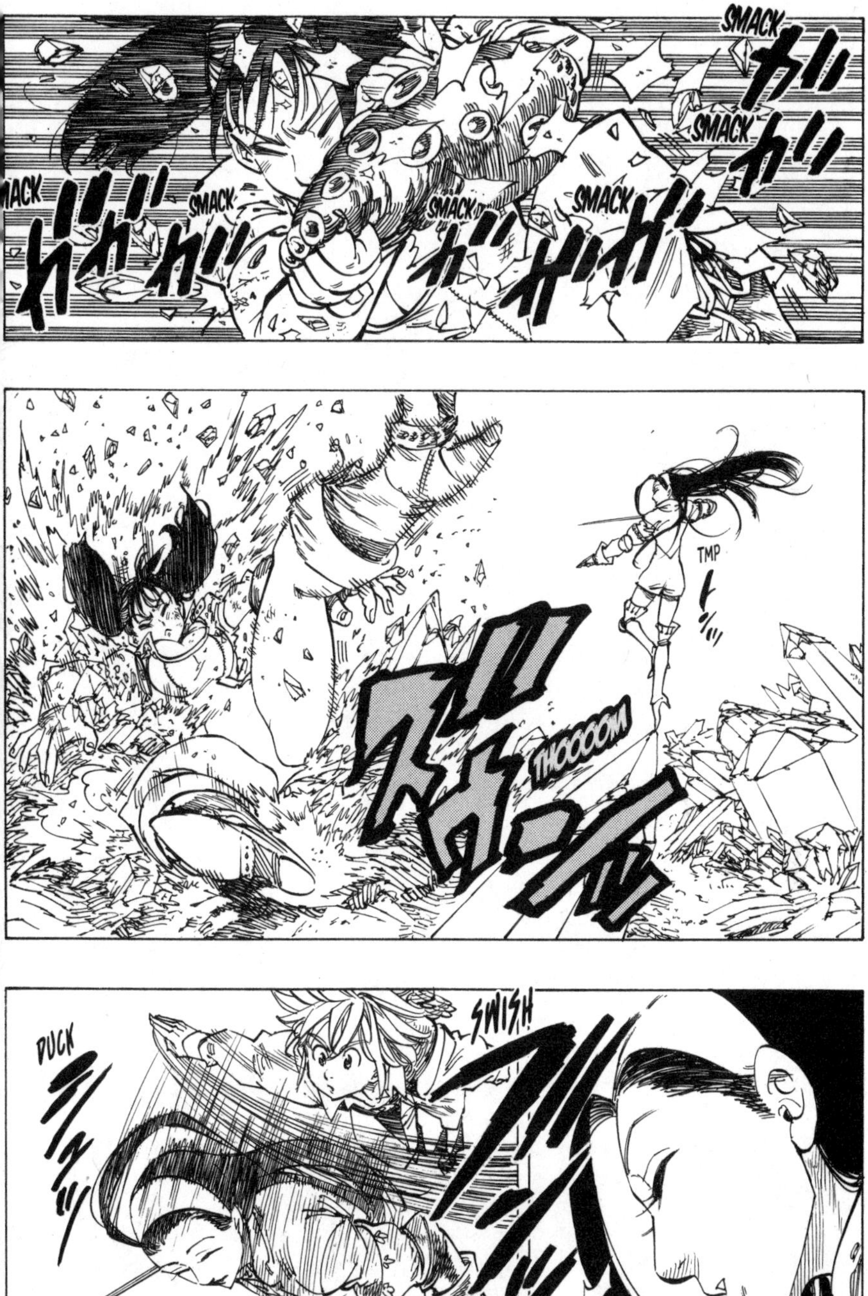
SMACK
SMACK
SMACK
SMACK
SMACK
TMP
THOOOOM
SWISH
DUCK

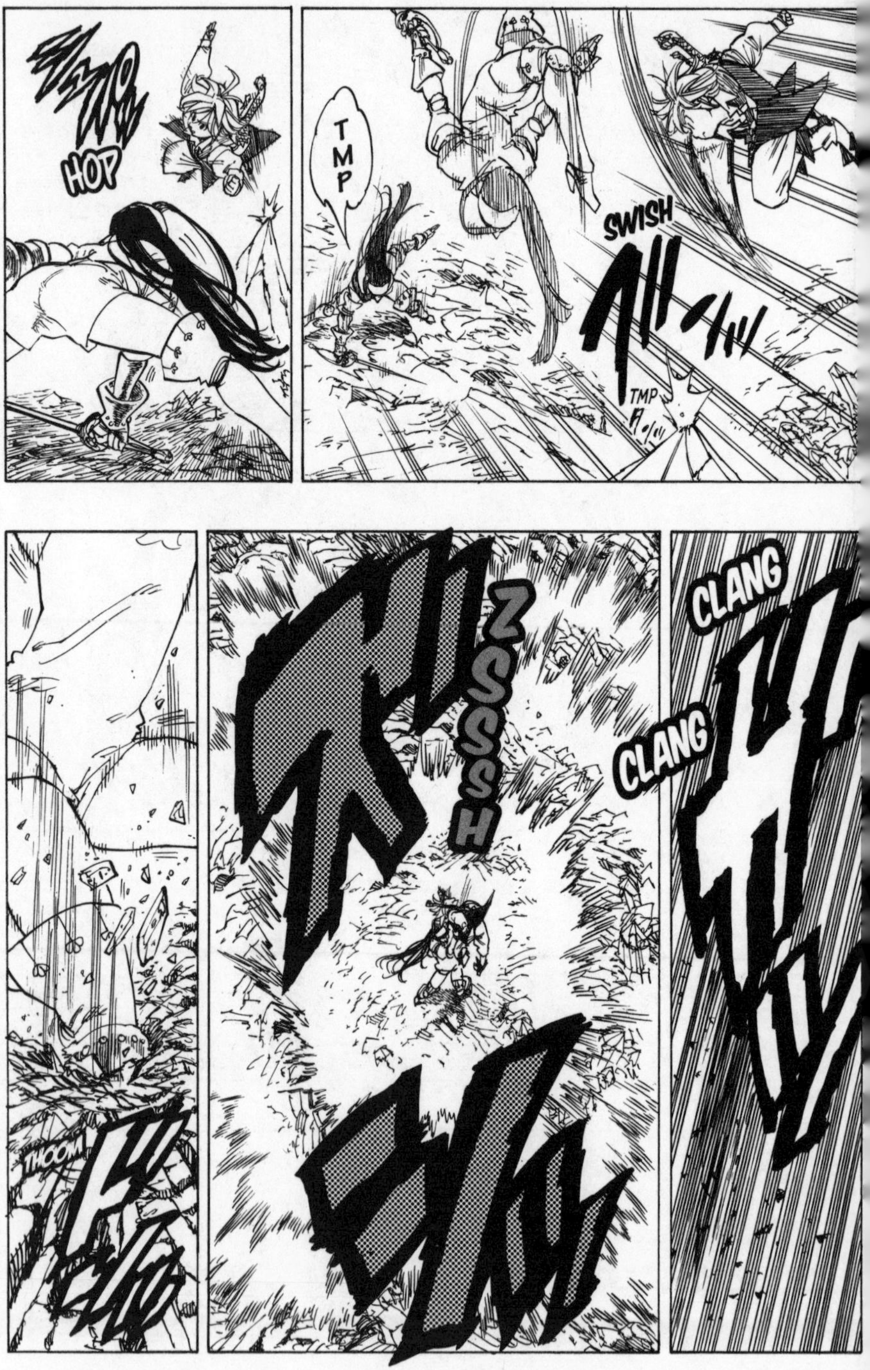
TMP
SWISH
TMP
HOP
CLANG
CLANG
ZSSSH
THOOM

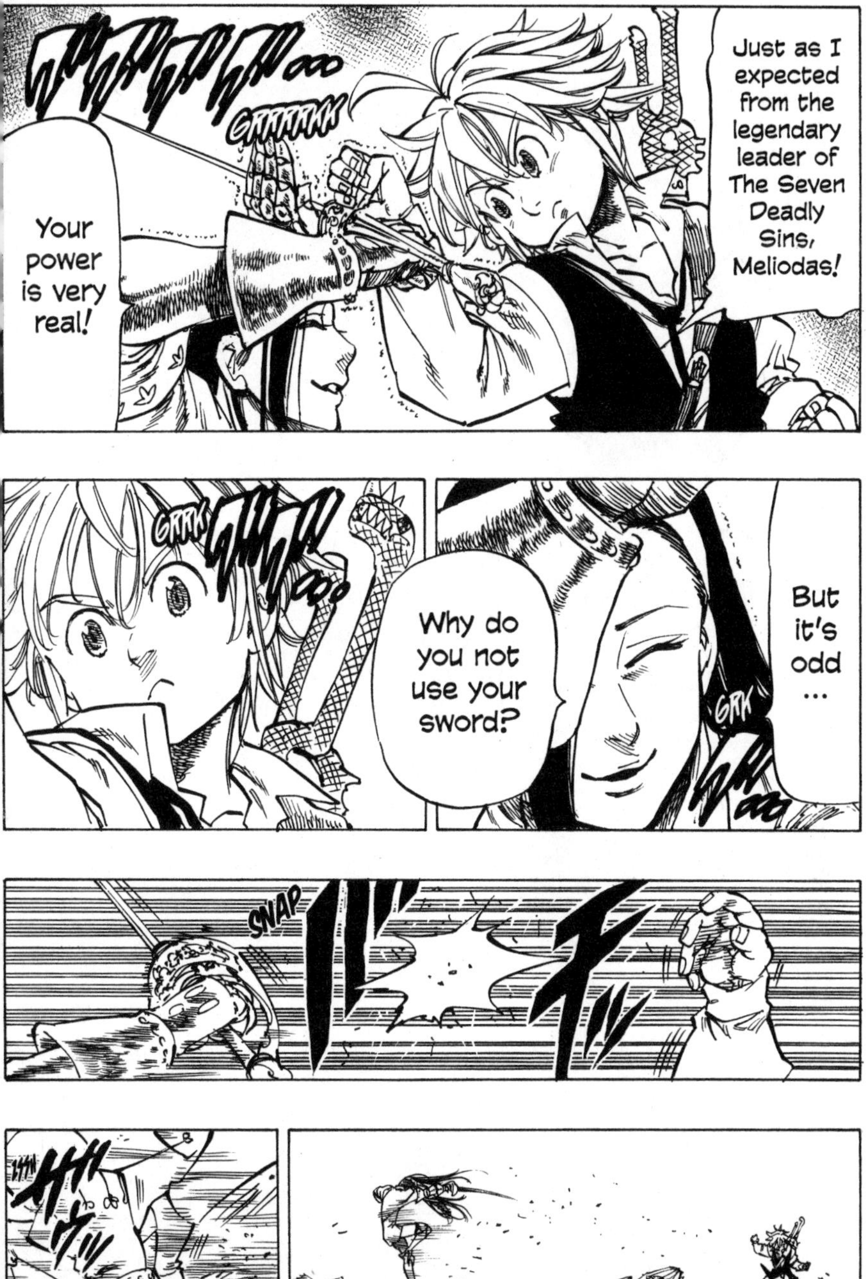
Just as I expected from the legendary leader of The Seven Deadly Sins, Meliodas!
GRRRRRK
Your power is very real!
But it's odd ...
Why do you not use your sword?
GRK
GRRK
SNAP

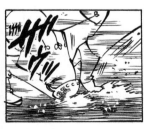

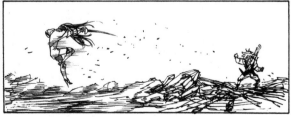

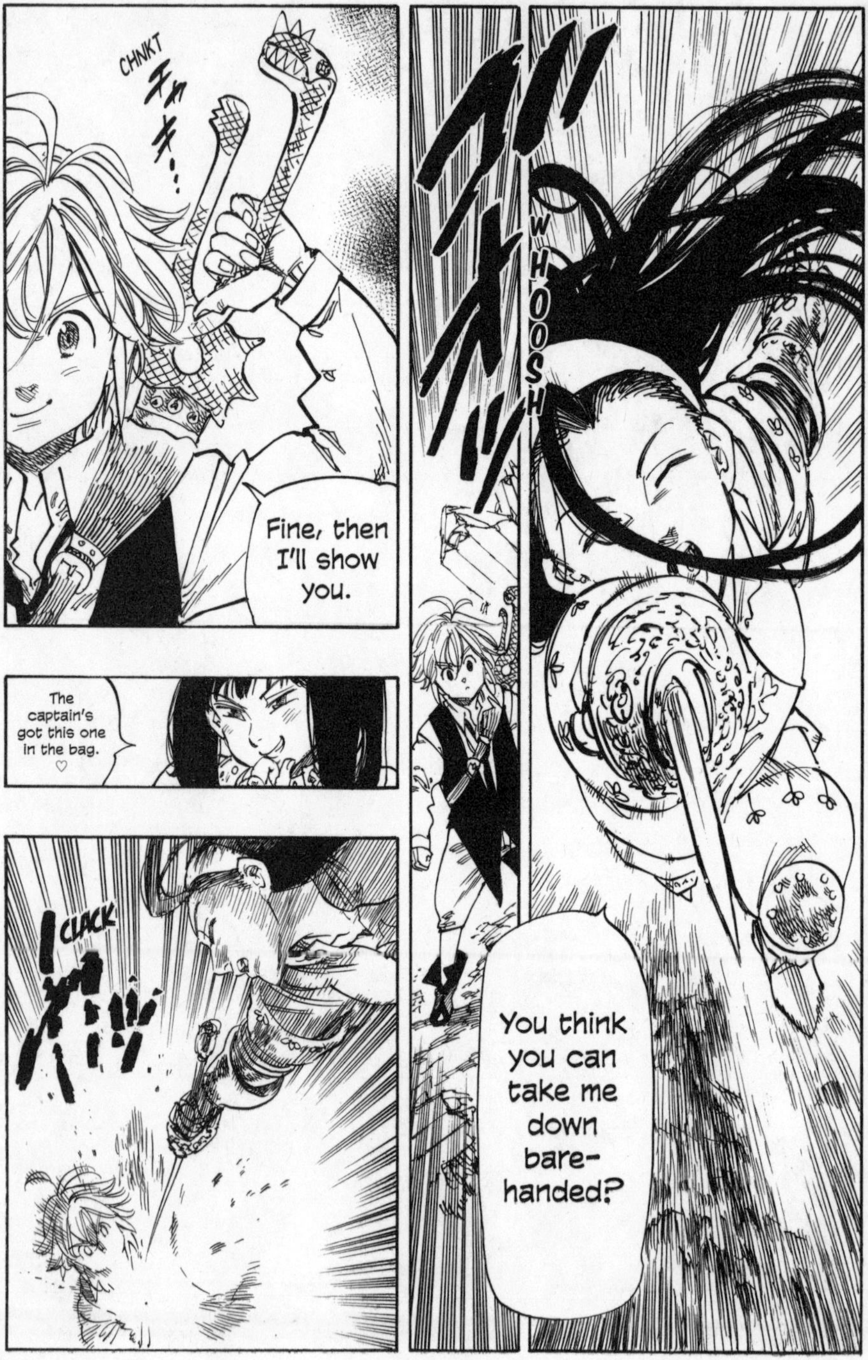
WHOOSH
You think you can take me down bare-handed?
CHNKT
チャキ…
Fine, then I'll show you.
The captain's got this one in the bag. ♡
CLACK

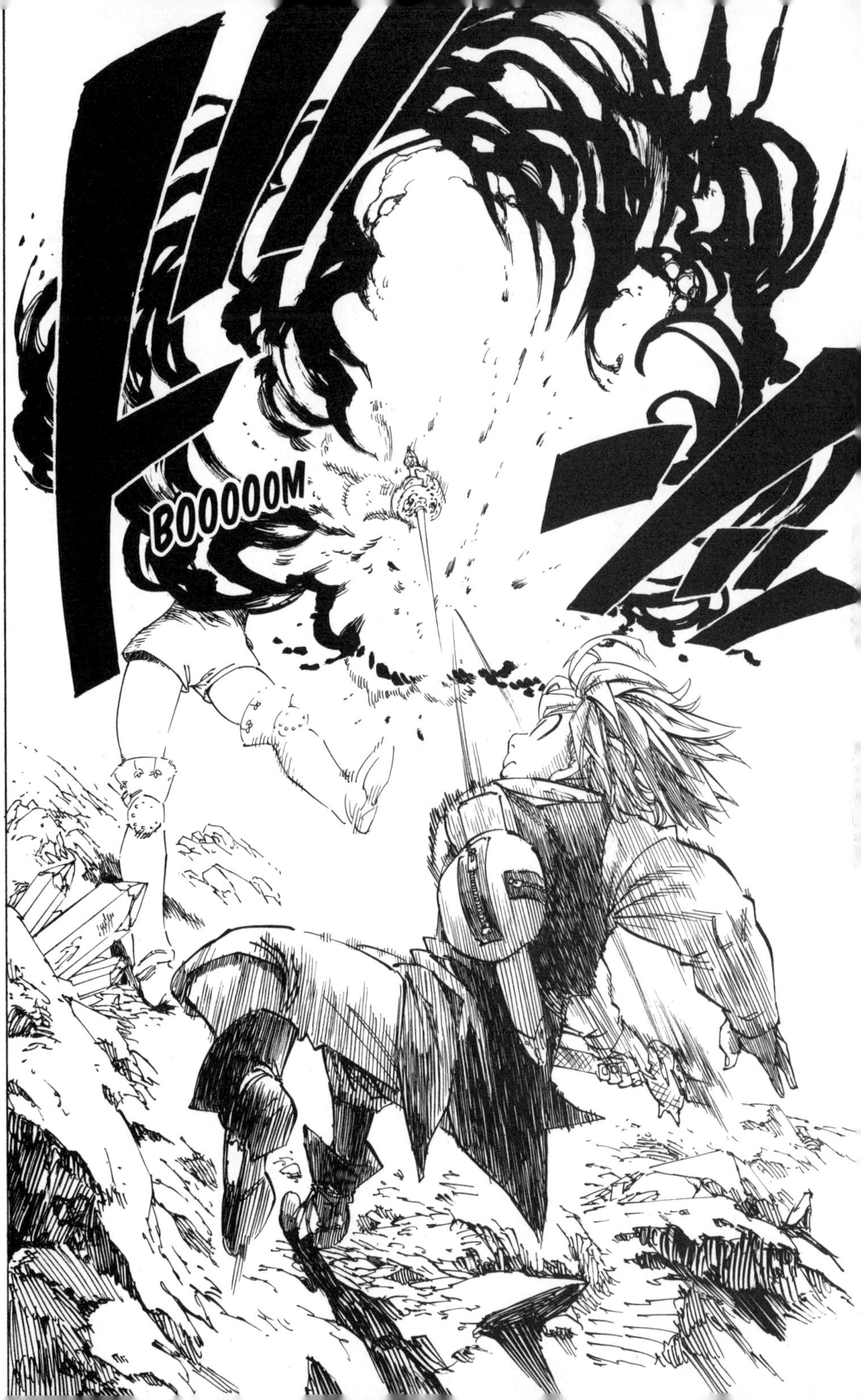
BOOOOOM

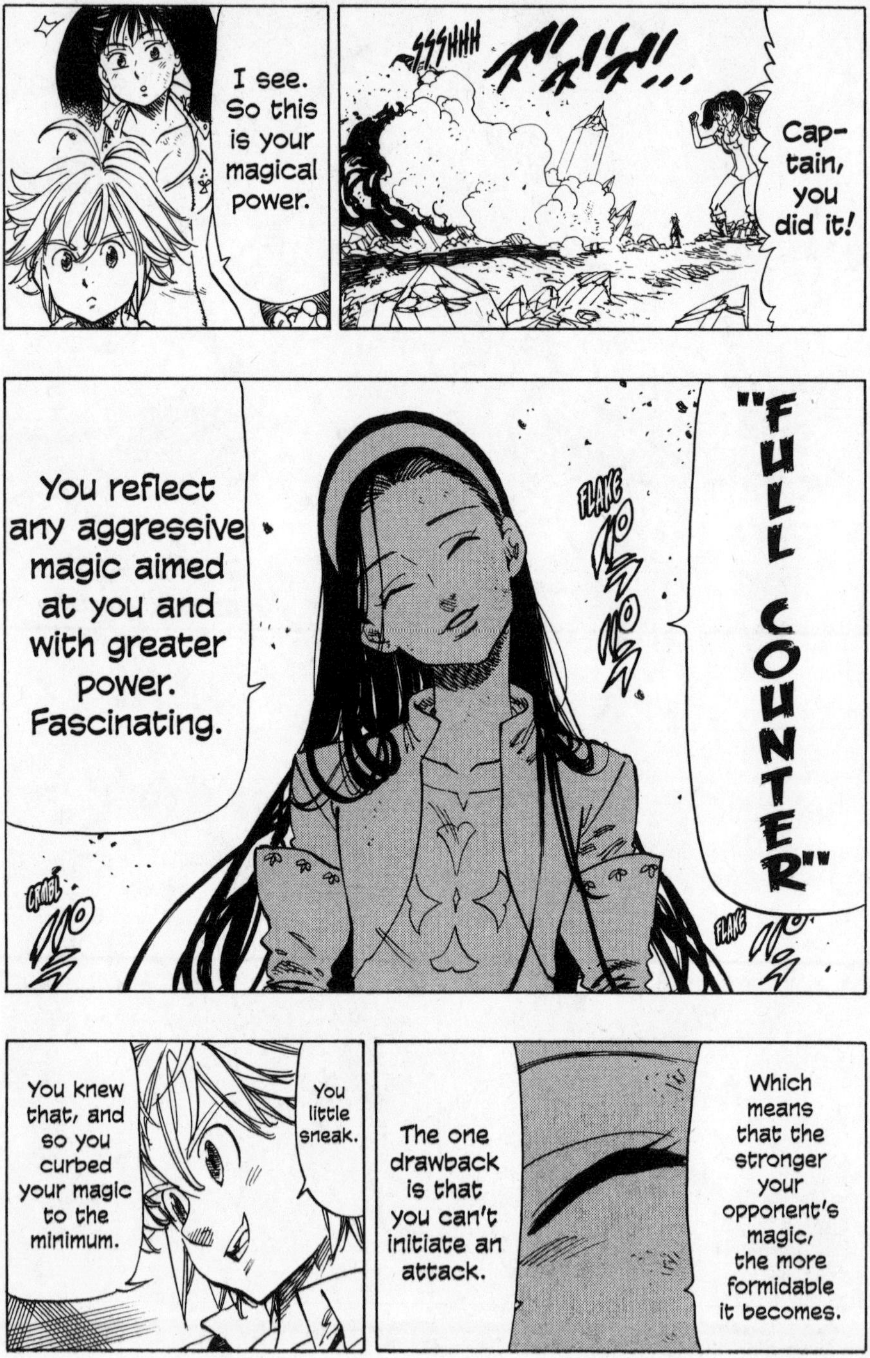
SSSHHH
Cap-tain, you did it!
I see. So this is your magical power.
"FULL COUNTER"
FLAKE
FLAKE
You reflect any aggressive magic aimed at you and with greater power. Fascinating.
CRMBL
Which means that the stronger your opponent's magic, the more formidable it becomes.
The one drawback is that you can't initiate an attack.
You little sneak.
You knew that, and so you curbed your magic to the minimum.

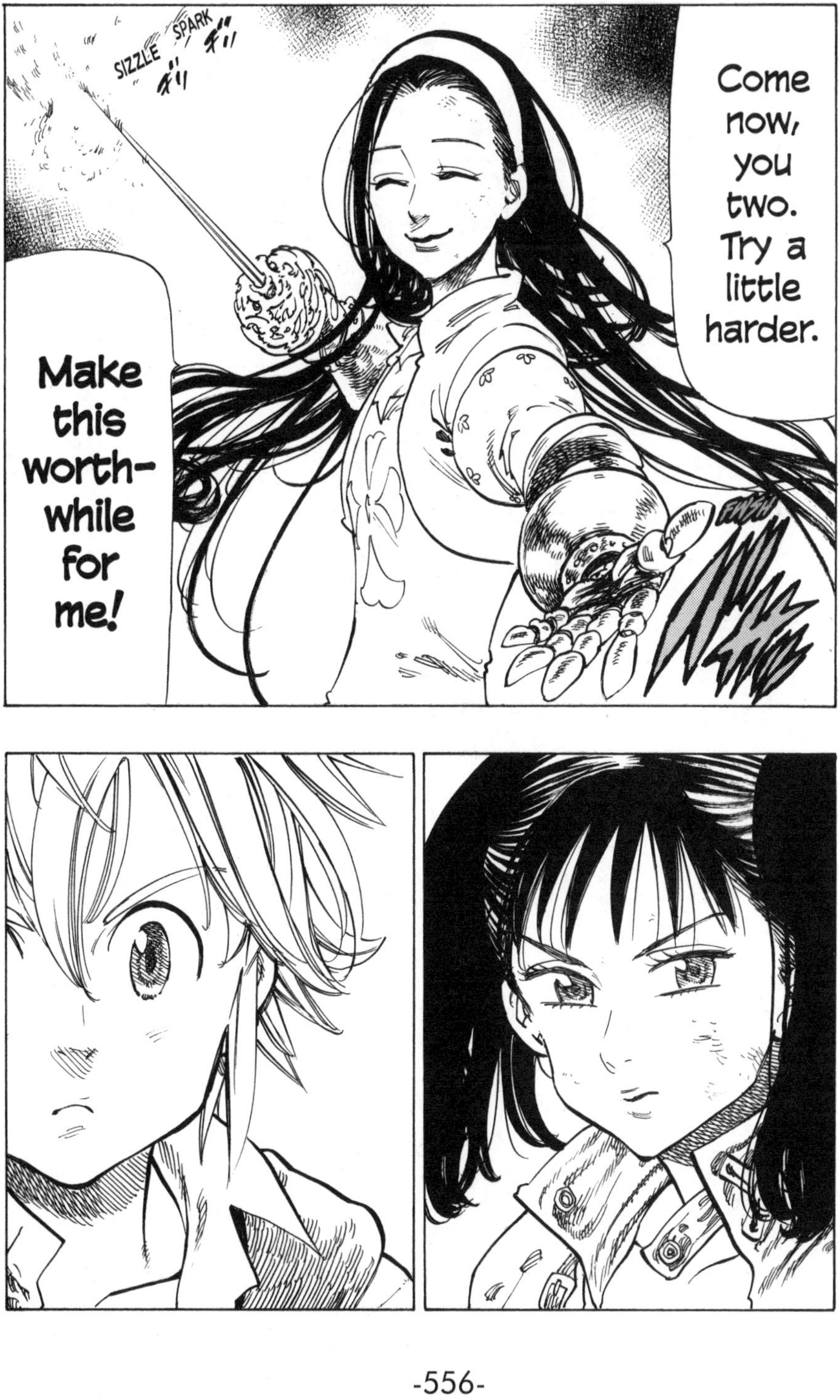
Come now, you two. Try a little harder.
SPARK
SIZZLE
Make this worth-while for me!
FWSH

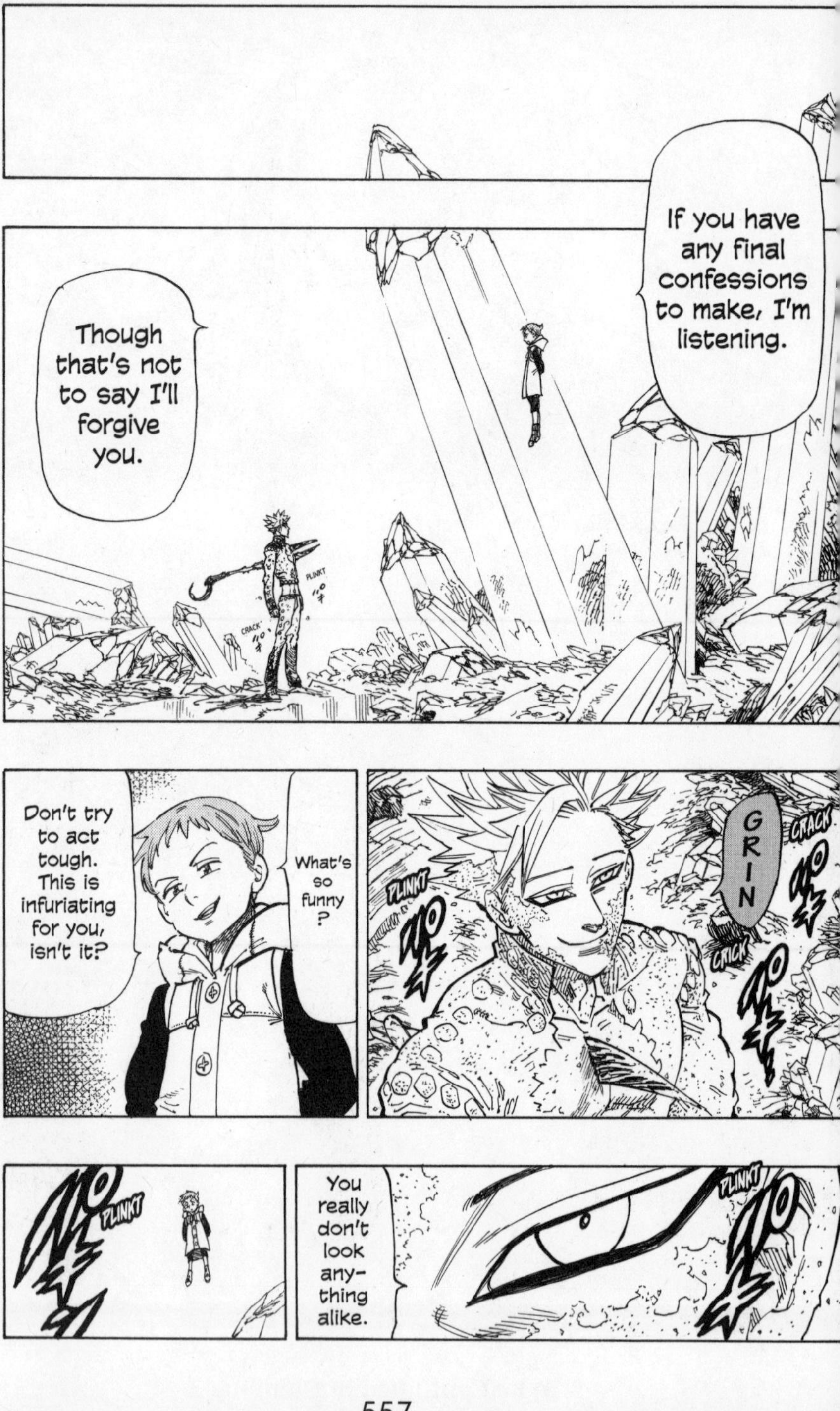
If you have any final confessions to make, I'm listening.
Though that's not to say I'll forgive you.
PLINK
CRACK
GRIN
CRACK
PLINK
CRICK
What's so funny?
Don't try to act tough. This is infuriating for you, isn't it?
PLINK
You really don't look anything alike.
PLINK

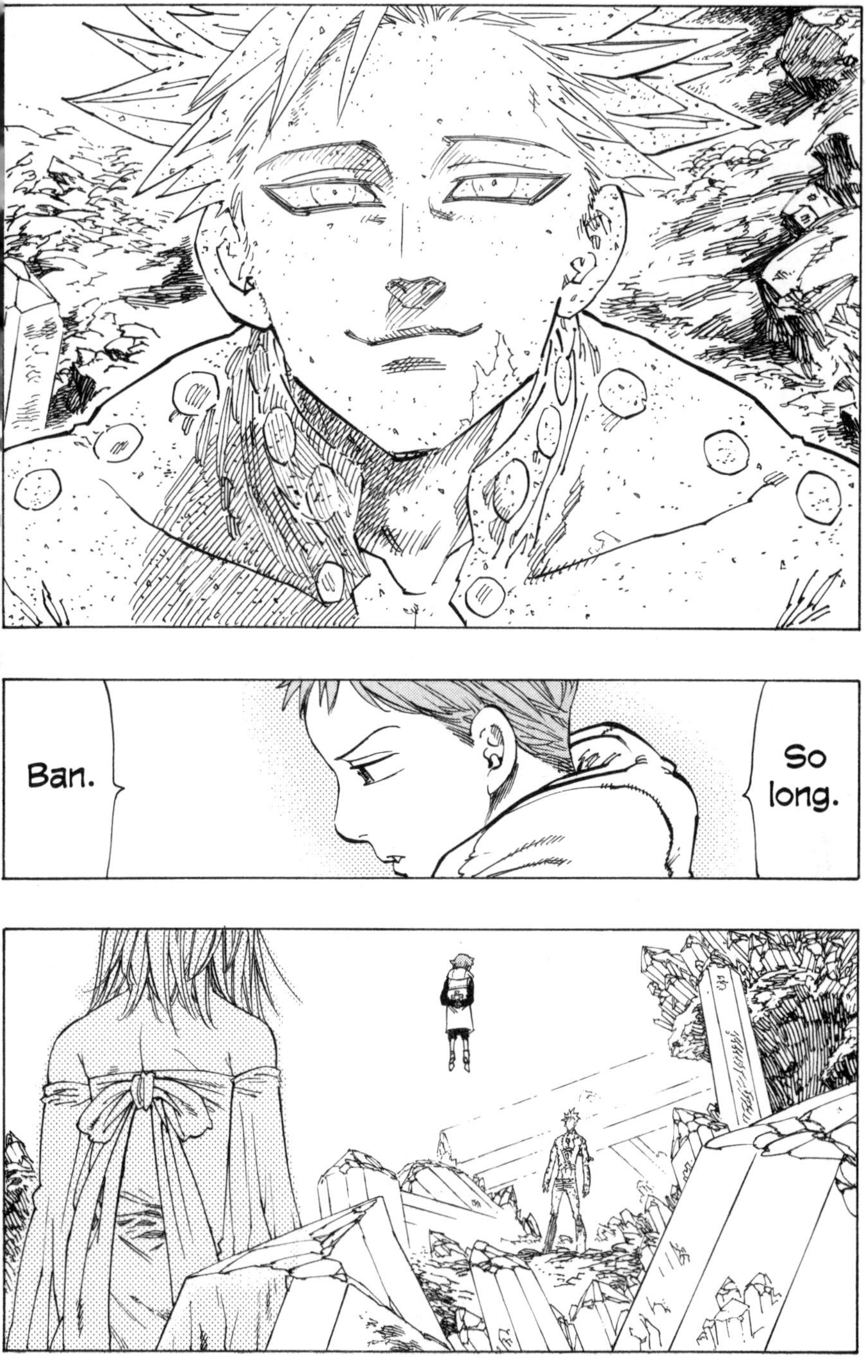
So long.
Ban.

To Be Continued in Omnibus 2

THE SEVEN DEADLY SINS

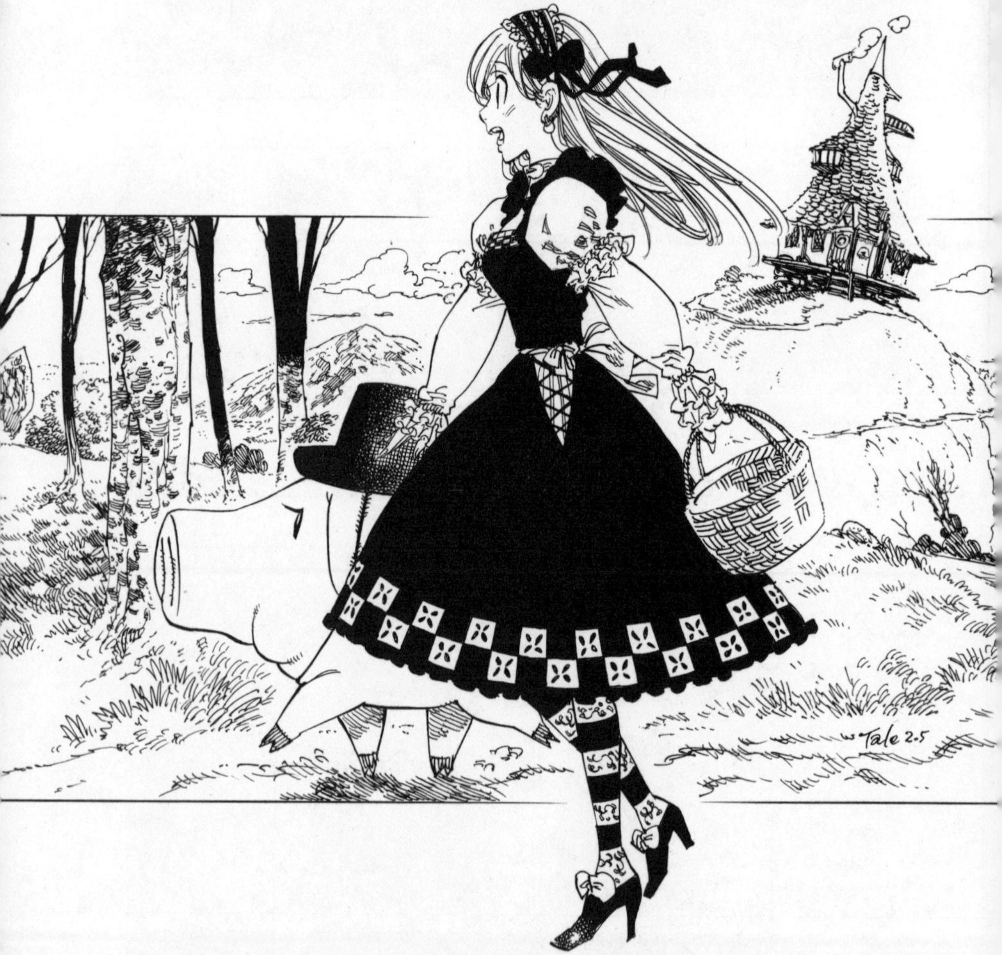

Bonus Chapter - Nothing Wasted

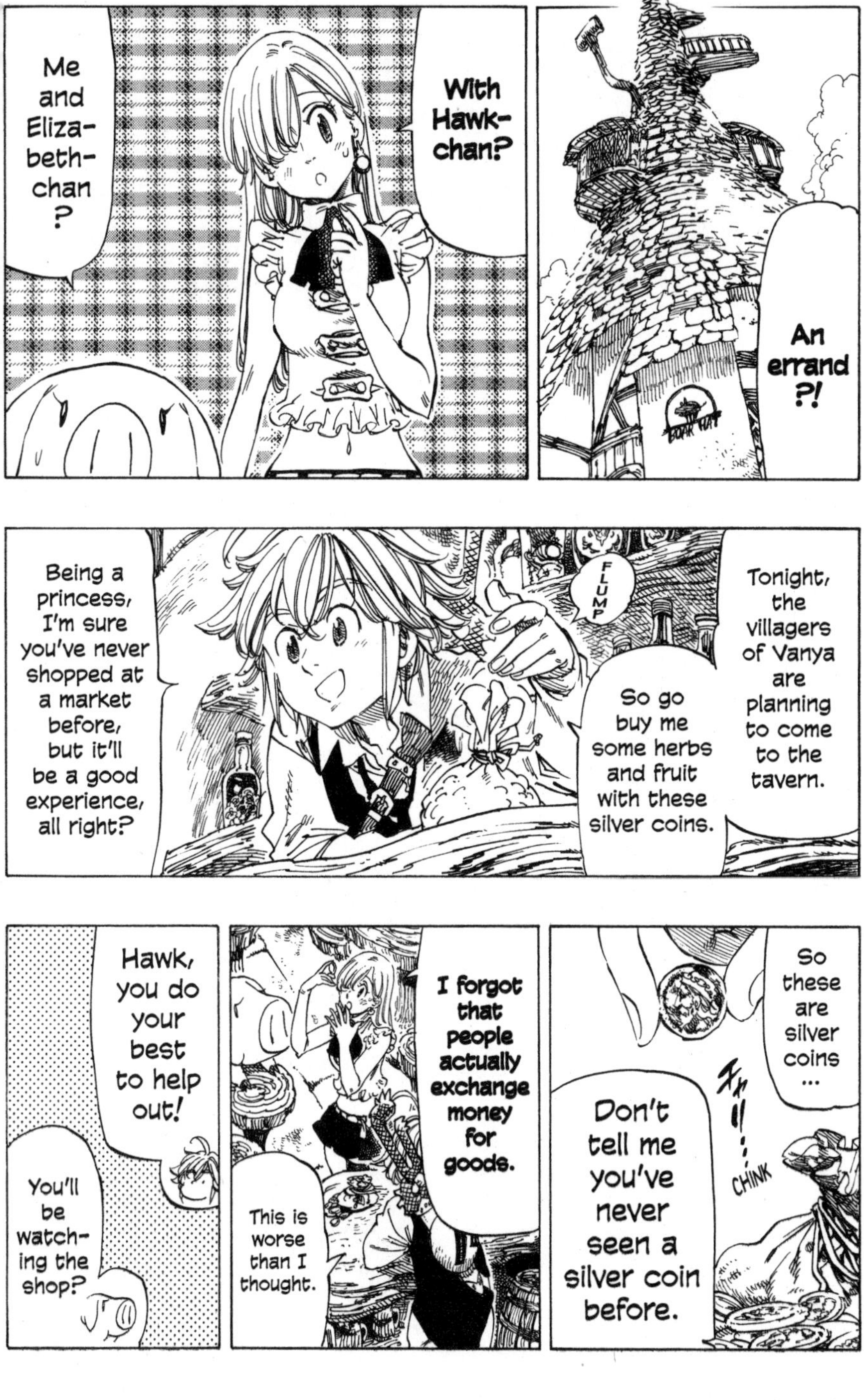
An errand?!
With Hawk-chan?
Me and Elizabeth-chan?
Tonight, the villagers of Vanya are planning to come to the tavern.
FLUMP
So go buy me some herbs and fruit with these silver coins.
Being a princess, I'm sure you've never shopped at a market before, but it'll be a good experience, all right?
So these are silver coins...
CHINK
Don't tell me you've never seen a silver coin before.
I forgot that people actually exchange money for goods.
This is worse than I thought.
Hawk, you do your best to help out!
You'll be watching the shop?

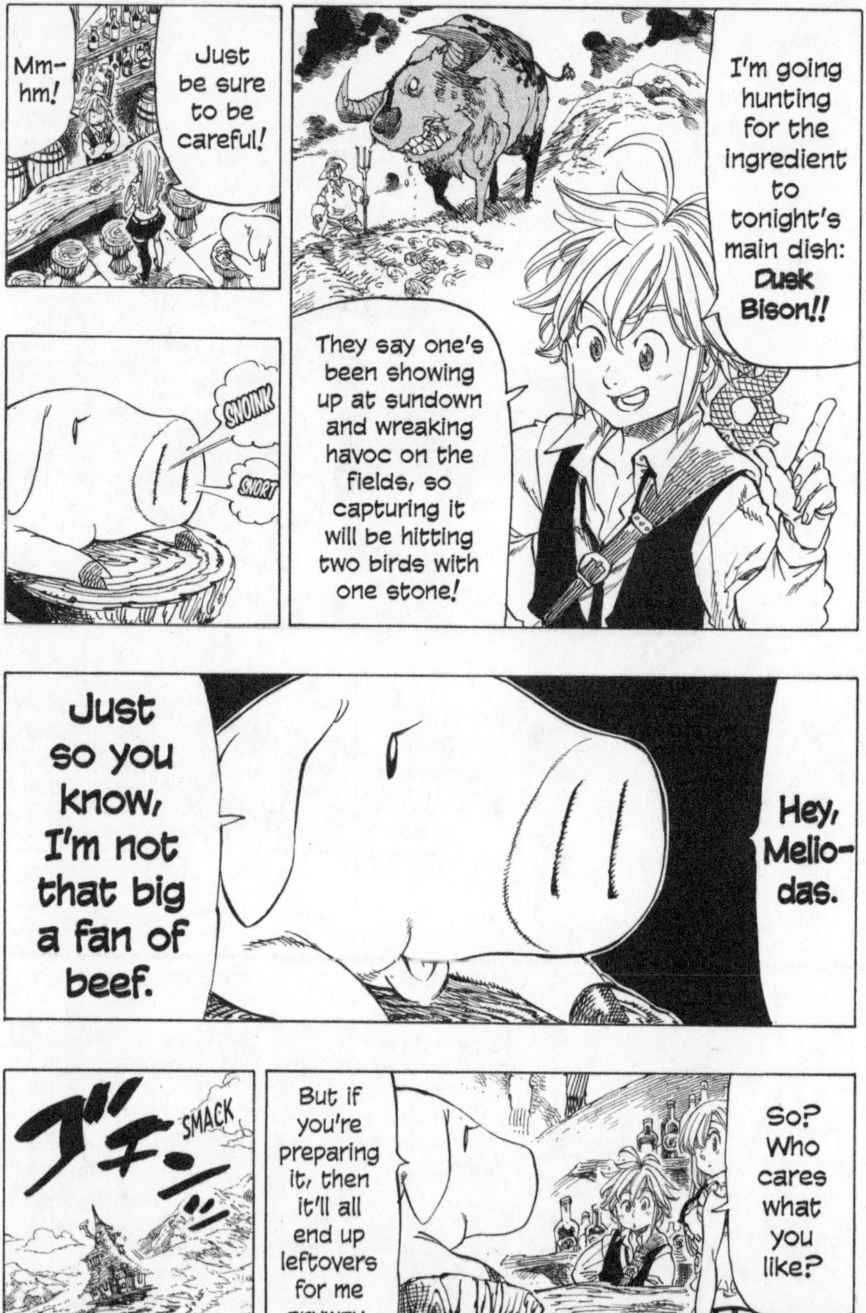

I'm going hunting for the ingredient to tonight's main dish: Dusk Bison!!
They say one's been showing up at sundown and wreaking havoc on the fields, so capturing it will be hitting two birds with one stone!
Just be sure to be careful!
Mm-hm!
SNOINK
SNORT
Hey, Meliodas.
Just so you know, I'm not that big a fan of beef.
So? Who cares what you like?
But if you're preparing it, then it'll all end up leftovers for me anyway.
ゴチンッ
SMACK

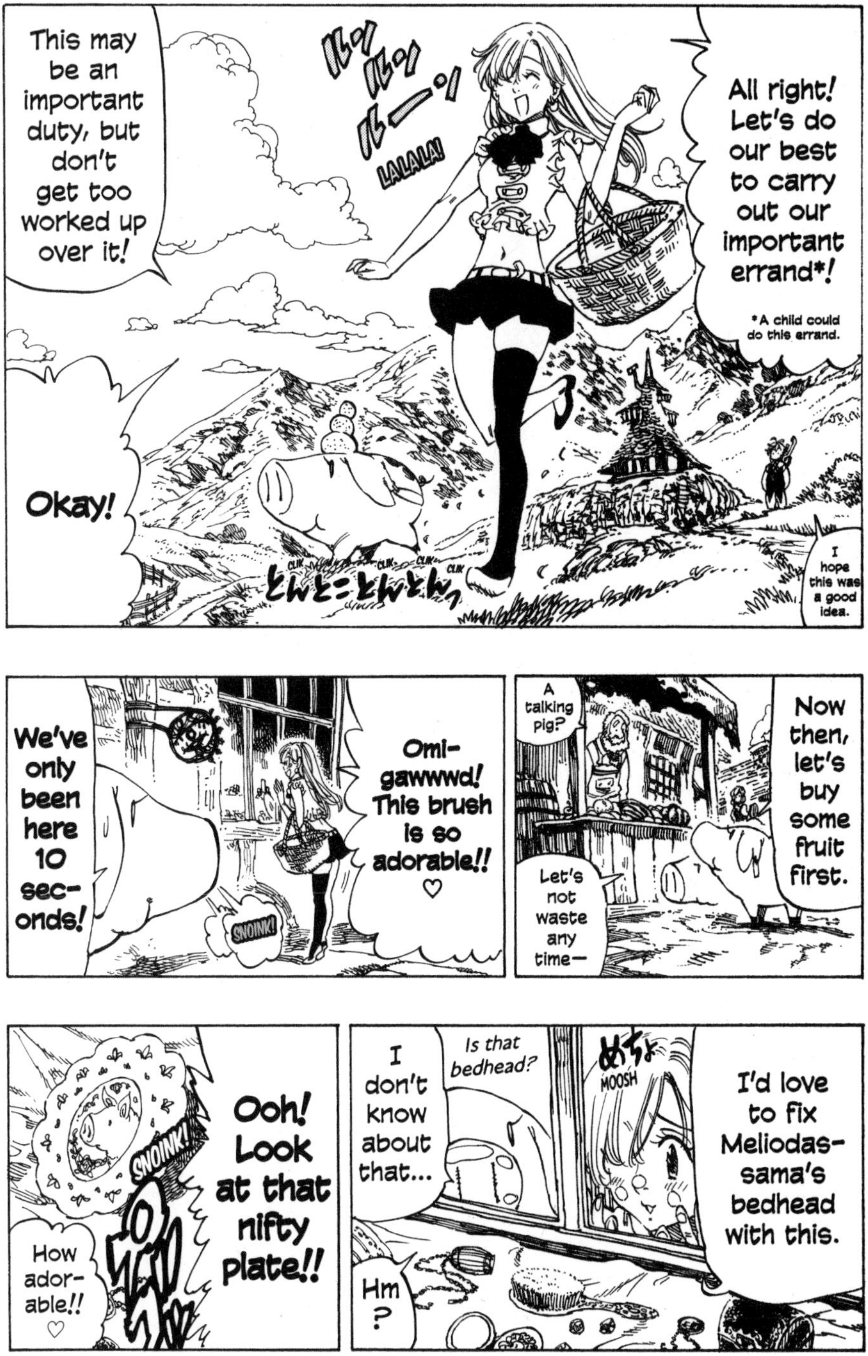

All right! Let's do our best to carry out our important errand*!
*A child could do this errand.
LALALA!
This may be an important duty, but don't get too worked up over it!
I hope this was a good idea.
Okay!
CLIK CLIK CLIK CLIK
Now then, let's buy some fruit first.
A talking pig?
Let's not waste any time—
Omi-gawwwd! This brush is so adorable!! ♡
We've only been here 10 seconds!
SNOINK!
I'd love to fix Meliodas-sama's bedhead with this.
MOOSH
Is that bedhead?
I don't know about that...
Hm ?
Ooh! Look at that nifty plate!!
SNOINK!
How adorable!! ♡

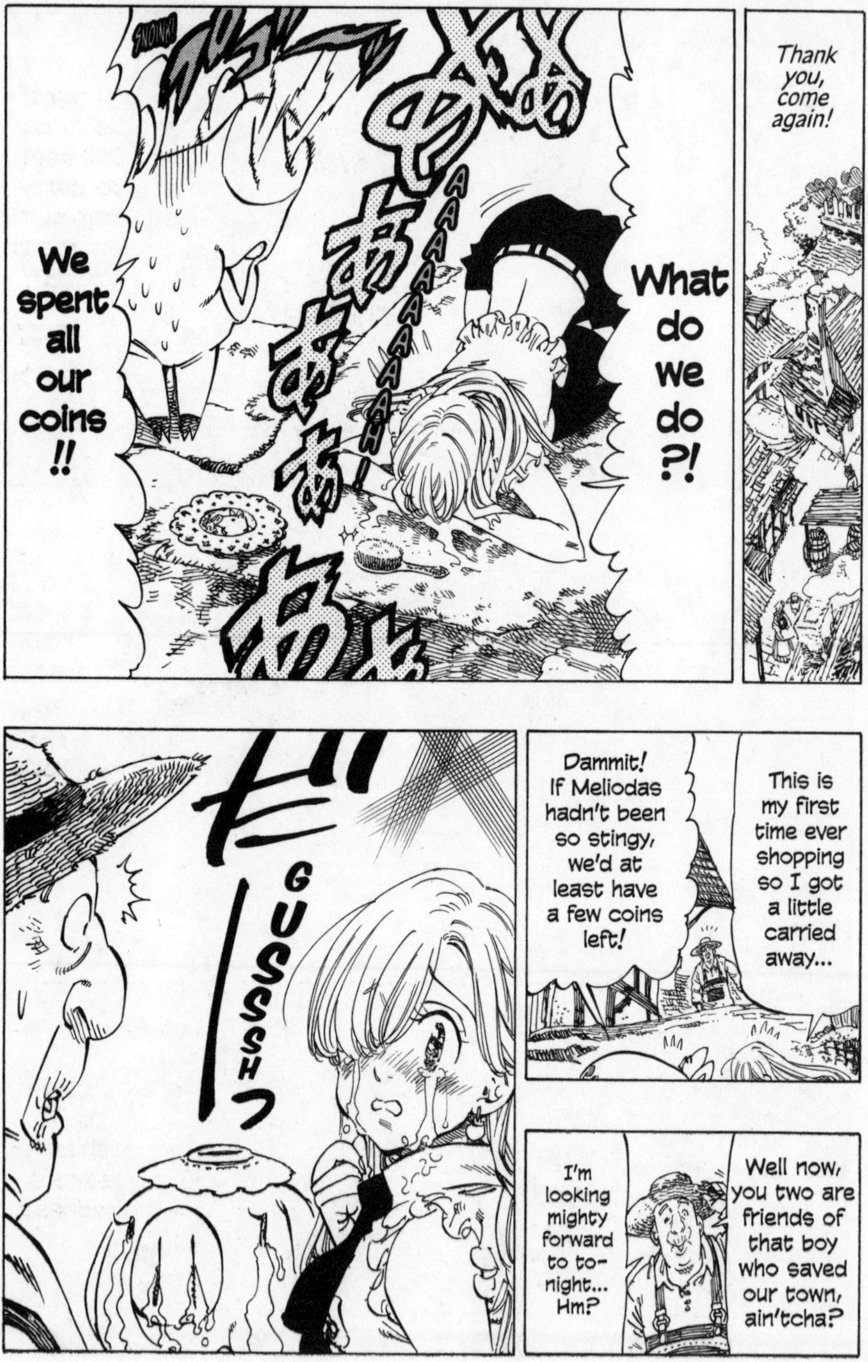
Thank you, come again!
What do we do?!
SNOINK!
AAAAAAAAAH!
We spent all our coins!!
This is my first time ever shopping so I got a little carried away...
Dammit! If Meliodas hadn't been so stingy, we'd at least have a few coins left!
Well now, you two are friends of that boy who saved our town, ain'tcha?
I'm looking mighty forward to to-night... Hm?
GUSSSH

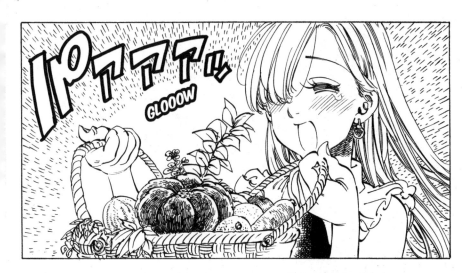

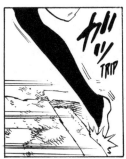

GLOOOW
I can't believe how much he shared with us!
LALA!
I can feel his kindness with my whole body!
CLIK
CLIK
CLIK
TRIP

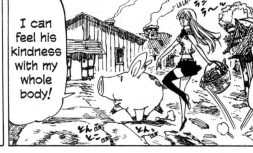

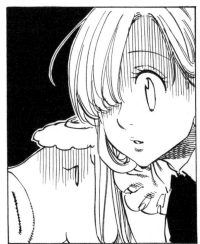

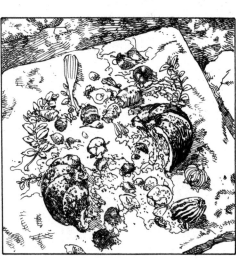

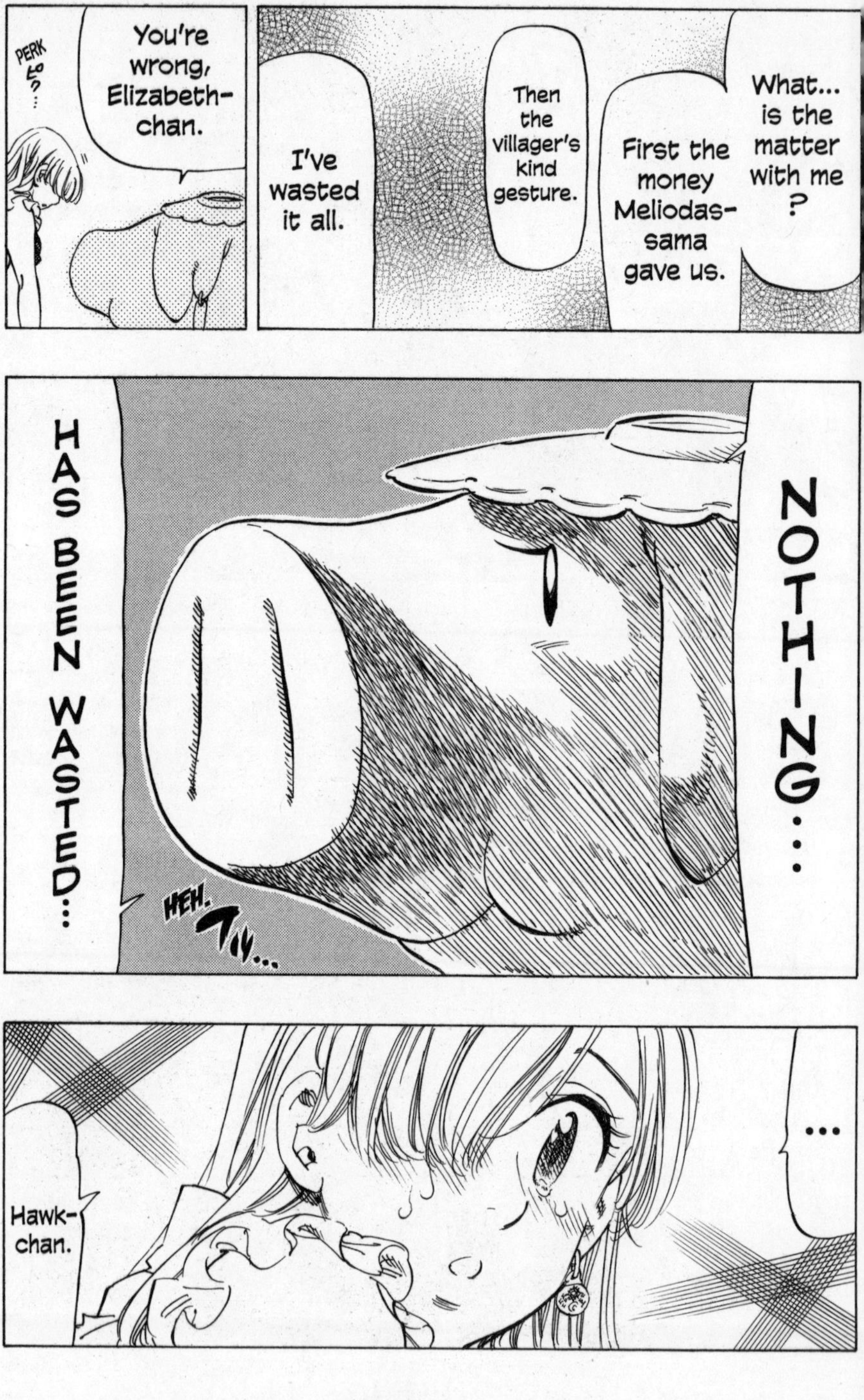
What... is the matter with me?
First the money Meliodas-sama gave us.
Then the villager's kind gesture.
I've wasted it all.
You're wrong, Elizabeth-chan.
PERK
NOTHING...
HAS BEEN WASTED...
HEH.
...
Hawk-chan.

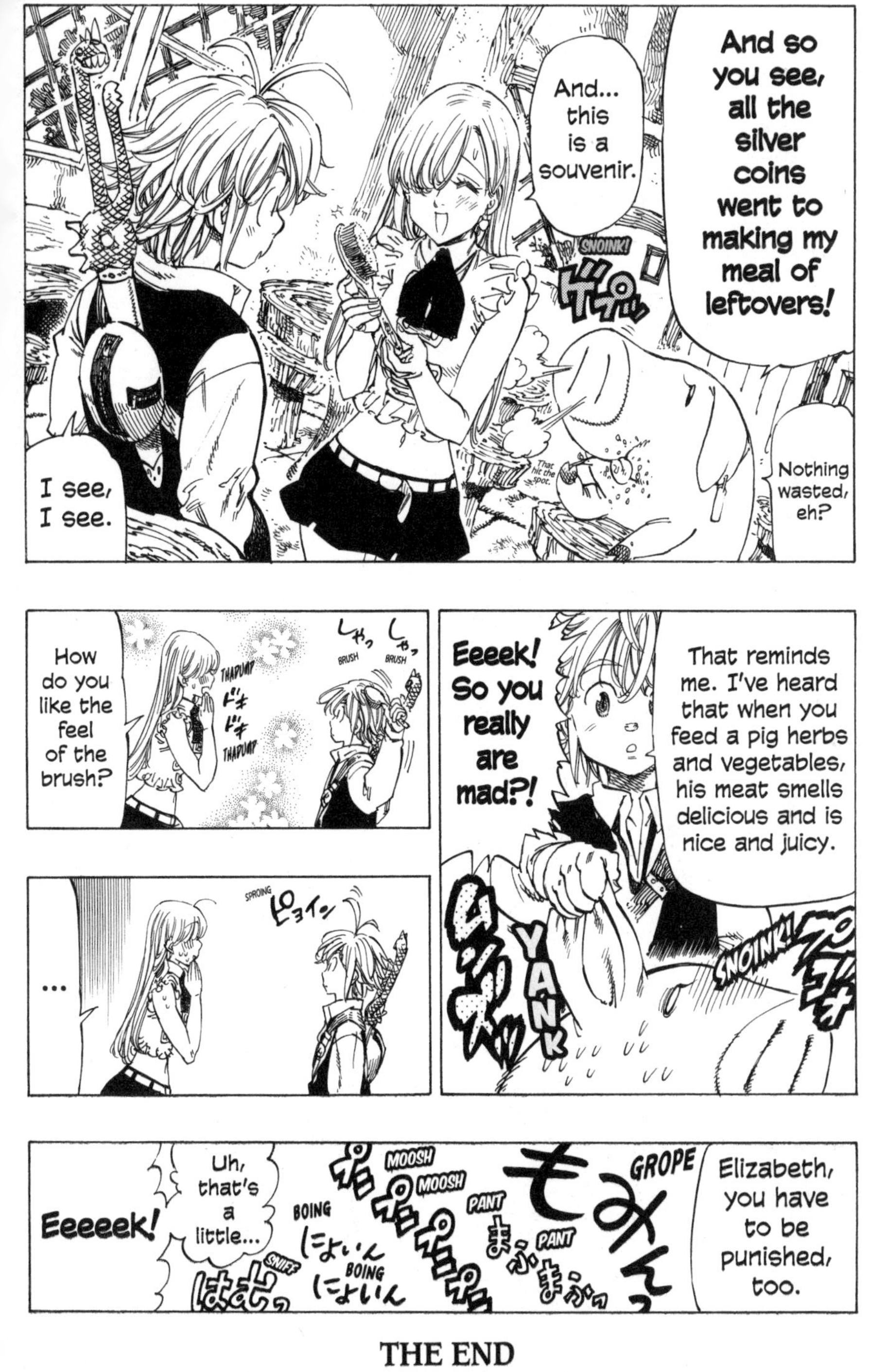
And so you see, all the silver coins went to making my meal of leftovers!
And... this is a souvenir.
SNOINK!
Nothing wasted, eh?
That hit the spot.
I see, I see.
That reminds me. I've heard that when you feed a pig herbs and vegetables, his meat smells delicious and is nice and juicy.
Eeeek! So you really are mad?!
SNOINK!
YANK
How do you like the feel of the brush?
BRUSH
BRUSH
THADUMP
ドキ
ドキ
THADUMP
SPROING
ピョイン
...
Elizabeth, you have to be punished, too.
GROPE
MOOSH
MOOSH
PANT
PANT
BOING
にょいん
BOING
にょいん
Uh, that's a little...
SNIFF
Eeeeek!

THE END

The one and only Deadly Sin who is immortal.

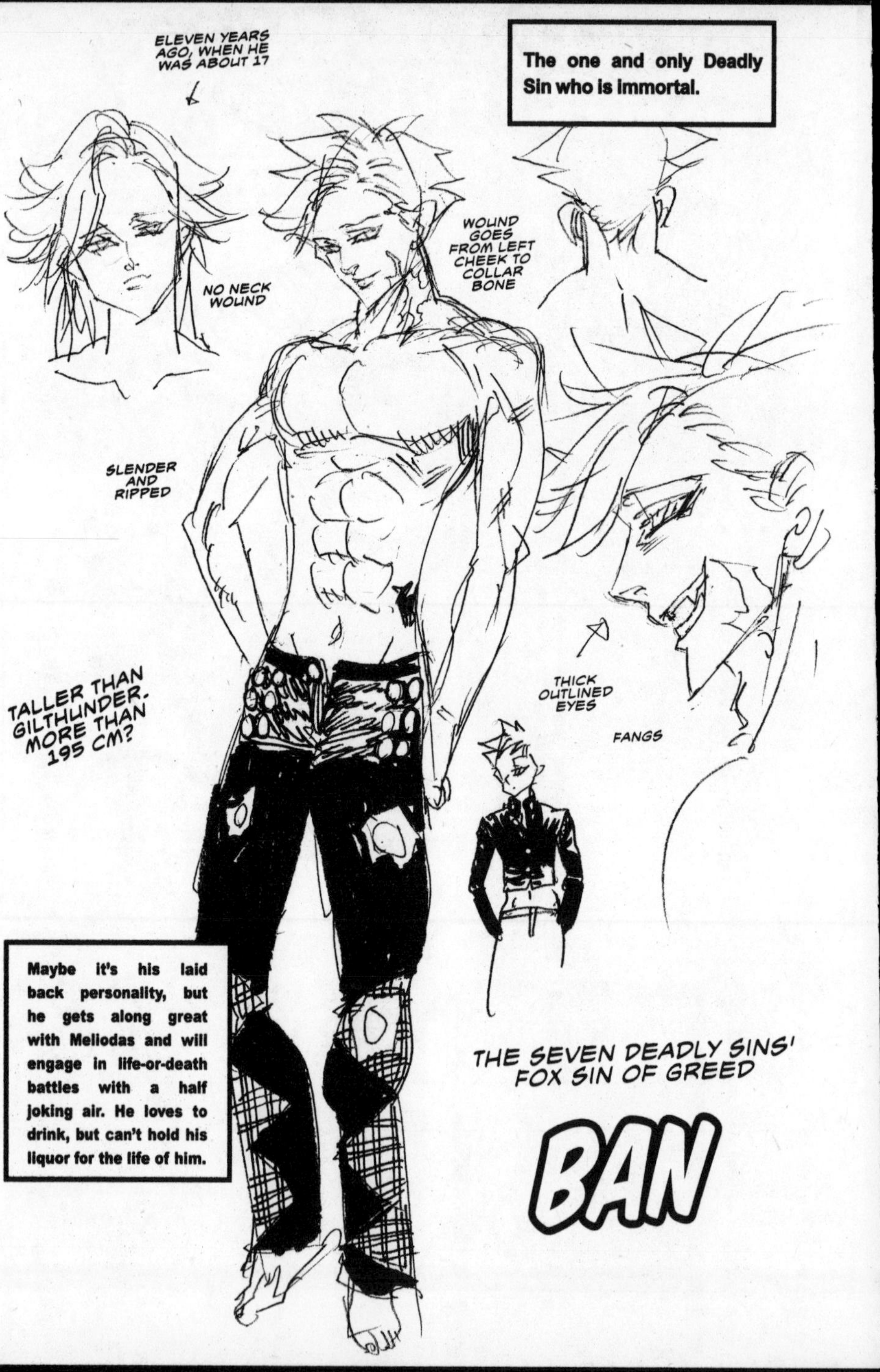
ELEVEN YEARS AGO, WHEN HE WAS ABOUT 17
NO NECK WOUND
WOUND GOES FROM LEFT CHEEK TO COLLAR BONE
SLENDER AND RIPPED
TALLER THAN GILTHUNDER. MORE THAN 195 CM?
THICK OUTLINED EYES
FANGS
THE SEVEN DEADLY SINS' FOX SIN OF GREED
BAN

Maybe it's his laid back personality, but he gets along great with Meliodas and will engage in life-or-death battles with a half joking air. He loves to drink, but can't hold his liquor for the life of him.

なな "THE SEVEN DEADLY SINS" ILLUSTRATION CORNER

"THE DRAWING KNIGHTHOOD" SPACE

Please include your name and location when submitting your postcard!!

M = H = E = D = B =

SPECIAL PRIZE

IWATE PREFECTURE, RION-SAN

祝！一巻発売★
STAR BOAR
これからも応援してます！

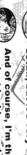

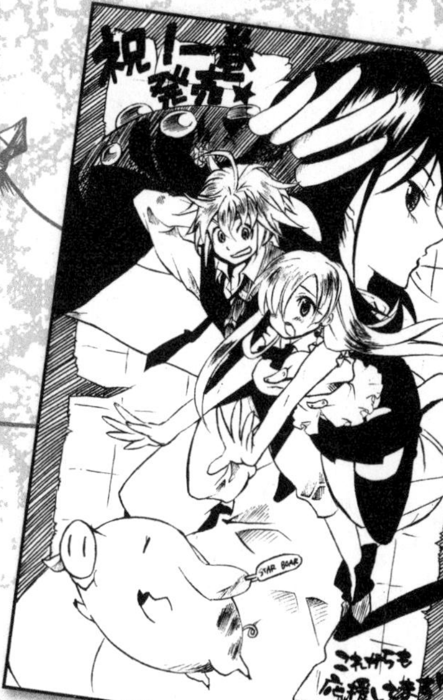

Not only is there a lot of attention to detail, but it's very dynamic. Wonderful!

And of course, I'm the coolest looking one!

Nah-uh, it's me. See?

Both of you, calm down! Say what you like, it's obviously me!

OSAKA, MAYU KURAHA-SAN

七つの大罪

D There's the Captain, being inappropriate again! Aargh!

M Mm-hm.

H Could you care any less?!

KANAGAWA PREFECTURE, AIO OBARA-SAN

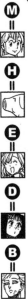

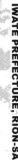

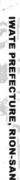

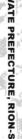

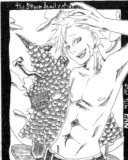

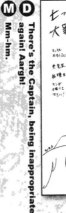

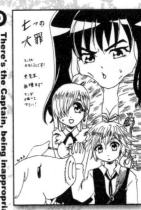

the Seven deadly sins
Fox Sin BAN

H Nice body!! ...Though not as nice as mine.

ALL ....

H Why're you all looking at me like that?!

Ooh, collage work!

Does that mean they love me most?!

Don't think too highly of yourself.

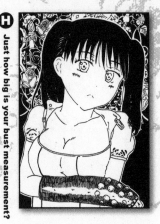

MIE PREFECTURE, HEAD-IN-THE-SAND-SAN

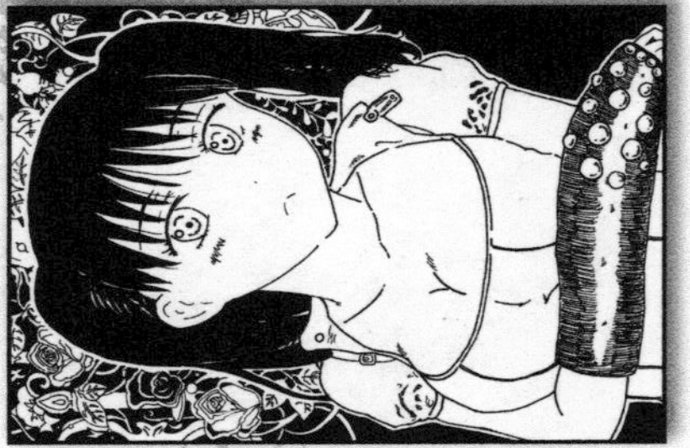

H Just how big is your bust measurement?

D You never ask a girl that!

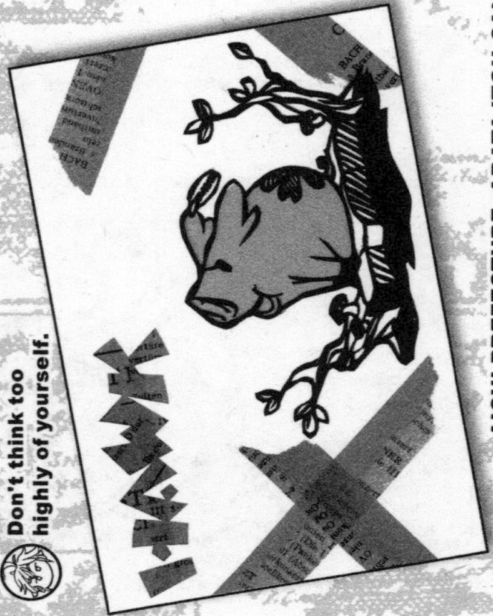

HAWK

AICHI PREFECTURE, ARATA ITOU-SAN

OSAKA, KOROMARU-SAN

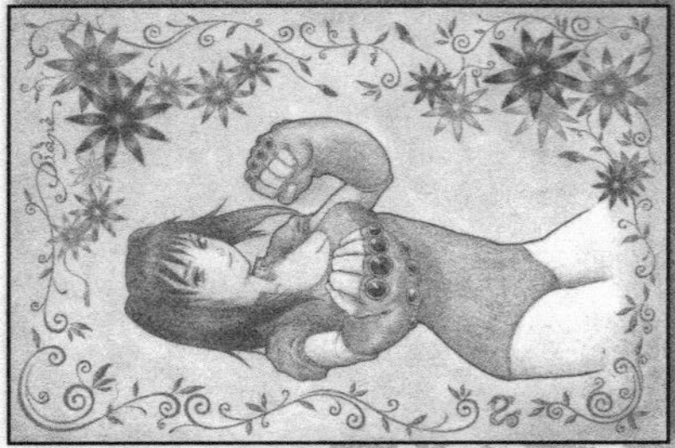

E It's a shame that we can't show the color version of this one!

D Wow, even the flowers were done by hand!

SAITAMA PREFECTURE, RIKU TAKENOYA-SAN

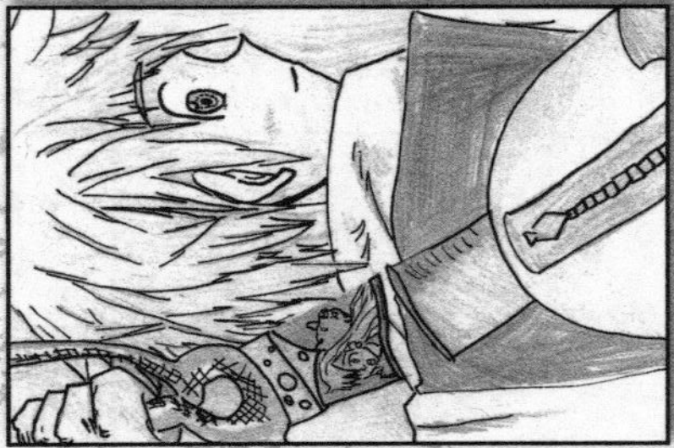

M Did you see how Elizabeth and the pig are reflected in the sword?

H ..."the pig"?

KANAGAWA PREFECTURE, TATSURIN-SAN

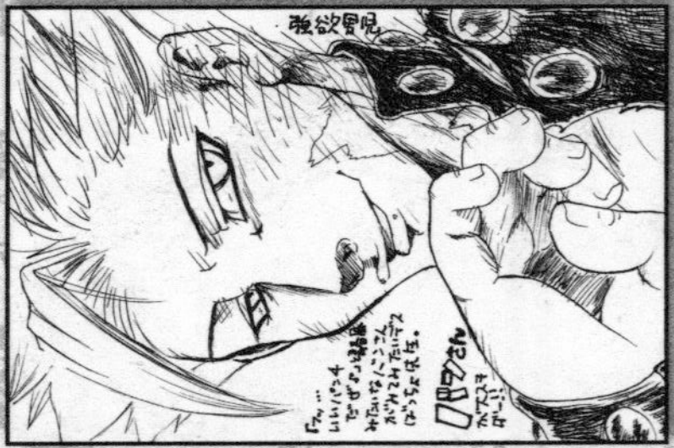

M It's got the smug look you always have on.

B Well, Cap'n♪ Maybe if you tried hitting puberty for once...

IBARAKI PREFECTURE, KAYOGAYO-SAN

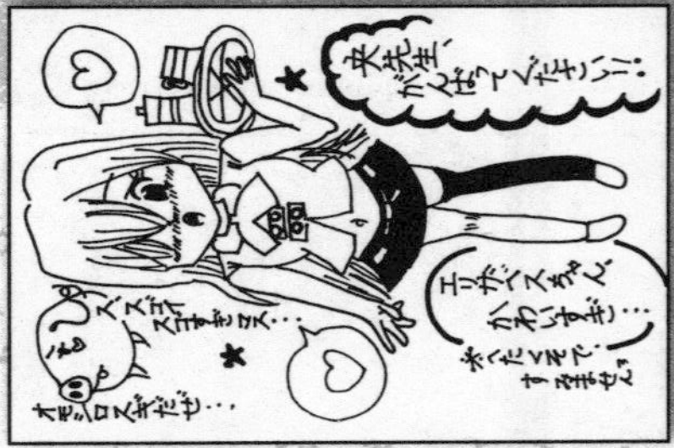

央先生、がんばってください!!
エリザベスちゃん、かわいすぎ…
※へたくそで、すみません

H Times like this, I'm so happy we've got such a great drawing card.

M And the uniform I chose for her has been quite a hit, don't you think?

OSAKA, AACHI SAKI-SAN

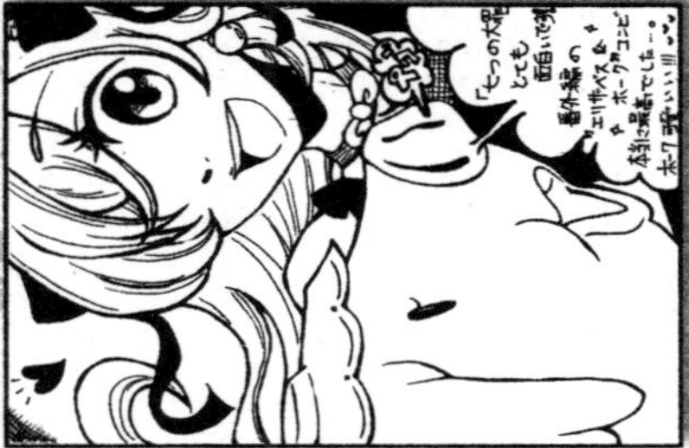

M You two really make a good team.

E Aaw...

M Why do you look so put out?

AICHI PREFECTURE, MADOKA KANEKO-SAN

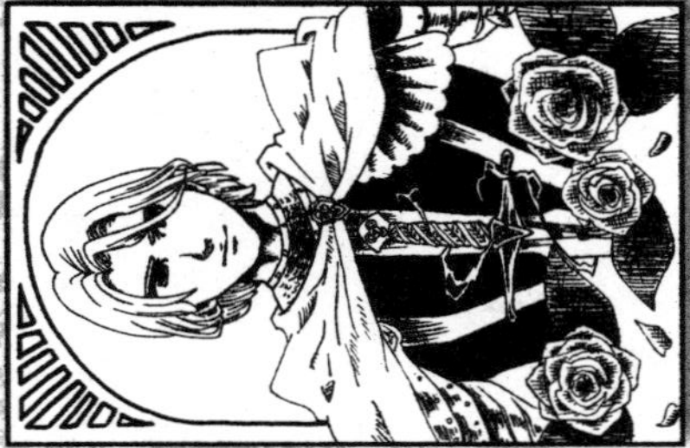

H Darn this pig jerk!! I'll pummel him next time I see him!

M ...You're only chance of winning would be if you attacked him in his sleep.

TOKYO, KEIKO KUROZAWA-SAN

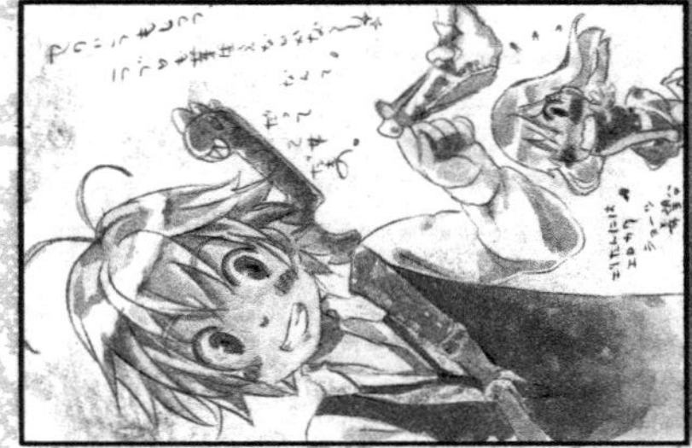

E M...Meliodas-sama!

M Meh.

H You perverted shopkeeper!

TOCHIGI PREFECTURE, RIRIKA YAMANAKA

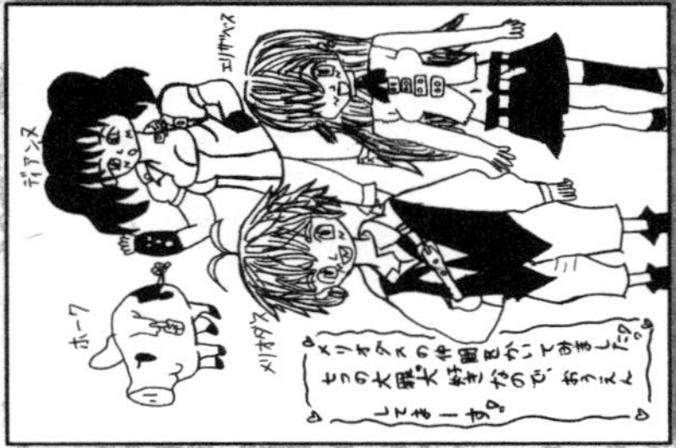
ディアンヌ
エリザベス
ホーク
メリオダス

M We've got to find the other Deadly Sins and fast.

D I wouldn't mind if it was just you and me.

NAGASAKI PREFECTURE, HIIKO-SAN

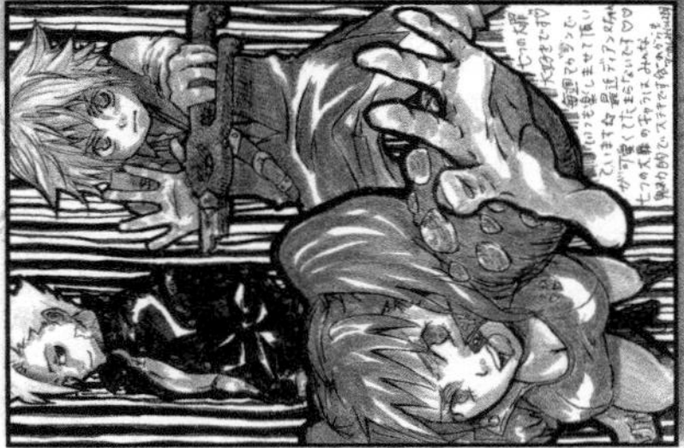

E This has a cool feel to it, like it's saying "the battle begins!"

H I wonder which of these three is the strongest.

FUKUOKA PREFECTURE, MINAKO MATSUO-SAN

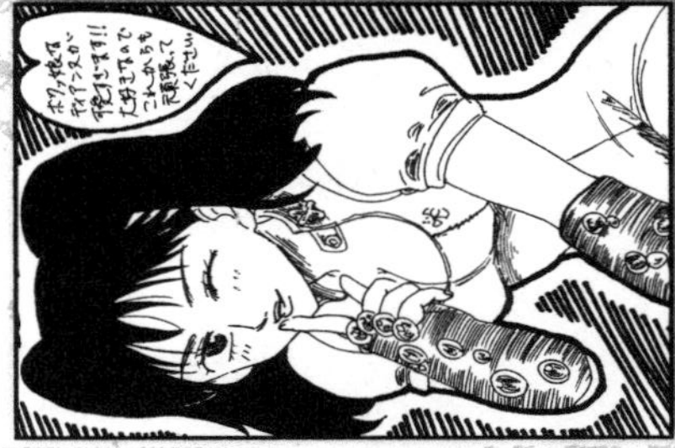

E I like how you look a little grown-up. It's a great look for you!

D Captain, does my sexiness make your head spin, too?

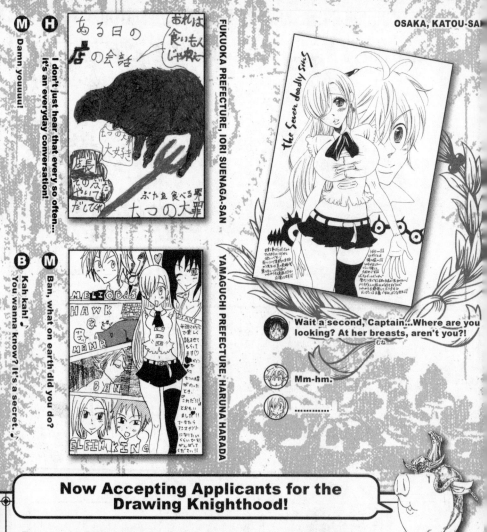

OSAKA, KATOU-SAN

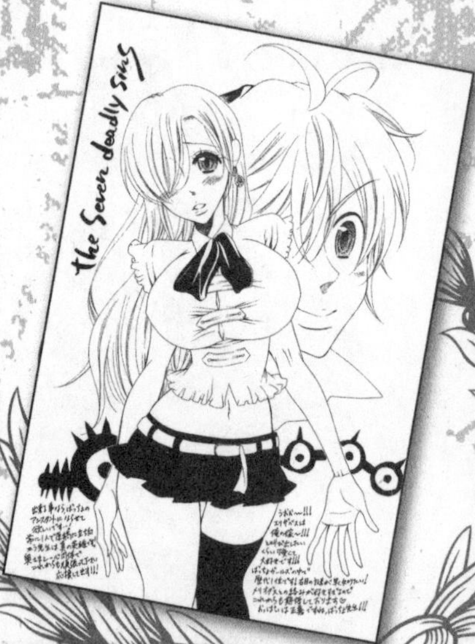
the Seven deadly sins

Wait a second, Captain...Where are you looking? At her breasts, aren't you?!

Mm-hm.

....

FUKUOKA PREFECTURE, IORI SUENAGA-SAN

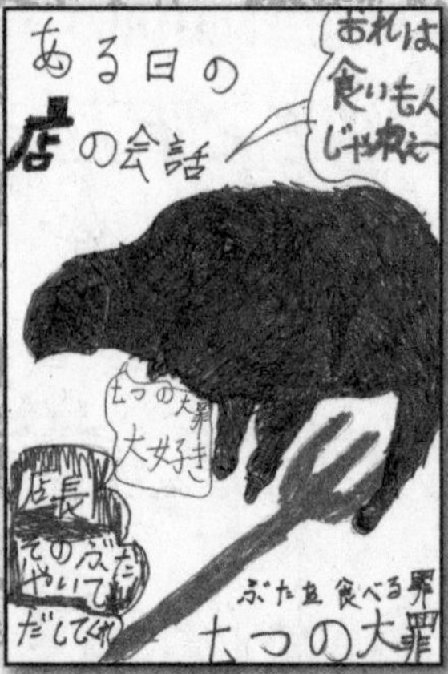
ある日の
店の会話
七つの大罪

H I don't just hear that every so often... it's an everyday conversation!

M Damn youuuu!

YAMAGUCHI PREFECTURE, HARUNA HARADA

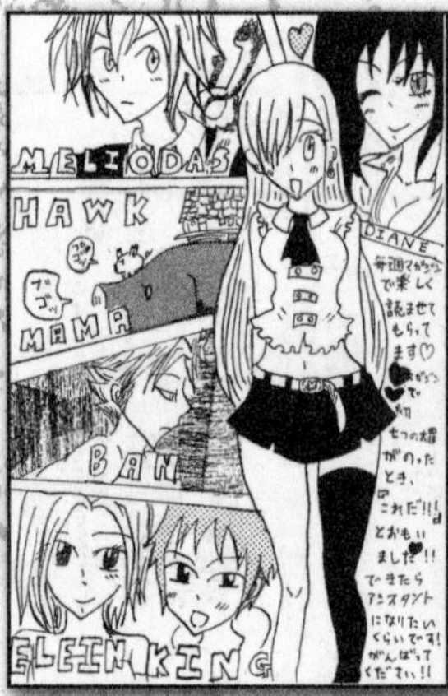
MELIODAS
HAWK
DIANE
MAMA
BAN
ELEIN
KING

M Ban, what on earth did you do?

B Kah kah! ♪ You wanna know? It's a secret. ♪

Now Accepting Applicants for the Drawing Knighthood!

- Draw your picture on a postcard, or paper no larger than a postcard, and send it in!
- Don't forget to write your name and location on the back of your picture!
- You can include comments or not. And colored illustrations will still only be displayed in black and white!
- The Drawing Knights whose pictures are particularly noteworthy and run in the print edition will be gifted with a signed specially made pencil board! And the best overall will be granted the special prize of a signed color drawing!!

Kodansha Weekly Shonen Magazine
Re: The Seven Deadly Sins Drawing Knighthood
2-12-21 Otowa Bukyo-ku, Tokyo 112-8001

* Submitted letters and postcards will be given to the artist. Please be aware that your name, address and other personal information included will be given as well.

Young characters and steampunk setting, like *Howl's Moving Castle* and *Battle Angel Alita*

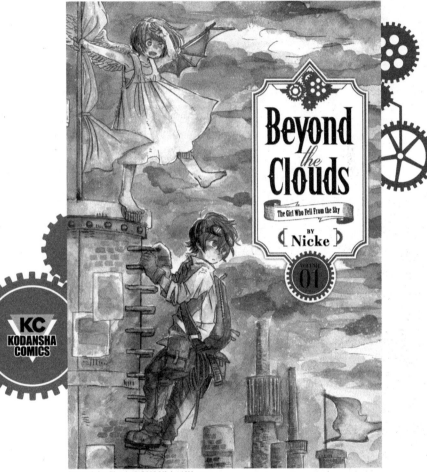

Beyond the Clouds © 2018 Nicke / Ki-oon

A boy with a talent for machines and a mysterious girl whose wings he's fixed will take you beyond the clouds! In the tradition of the high-flying, resonant adventure stories of Studio Ghibli comes a gorgeous tale about the longing of young hearts for adventure and friendship!

One of CLAMP's biggest hits returns
in this definitive, premium, hardcover
20th anniversary collector's edition!

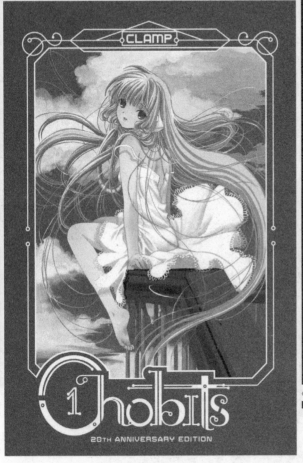

"A wonderfully
entertaining story
that would be a grea
installment in anyboc
manga collection."
— Anime News Network

"CLAMP is an all-femc
manga-creating
team whose feminine
touch shows in this
entertaining, sci-fi so
opera."
— Publishers Weekly

Poor college student Hideki is down on his luck. All he wants is a
good job, a girlfriend, and his very own "persocom"—the latest
and greatest in humanoid computer technology. Hideki's luck
changes one night when he finds Chi—a persocom thrown out in
a pile of trash. But Hideki soon discovers that there's much more
to his cute new persocom than meets the eye.

KC
KODANSHA
COMICS

The adorable new odd-couple cat comedy manga from the creator of the beloved *Chi's Sweet Home*, in full color!

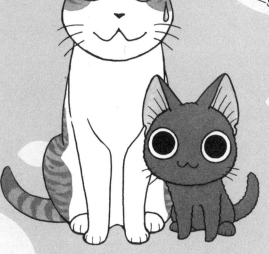

Sue & Tai-chan

Konami Kanata

Sue is an aging housecat who's looking forward to living out her life in peace... but her plans change when the mischievous black tomcat Tai-chan enters the picture! Hey! Sue never signed up to be a catsitter! *Sue & Tai-chan* is the latest from the reigning meow-narch of cute kitty comics, Konami Kanata.

KC KODANSHA COMICS

CUTE ANIMALS AND LIFE LESSONS, PERFECT FOR ASPIRING PET VETS OF ALL AGES!

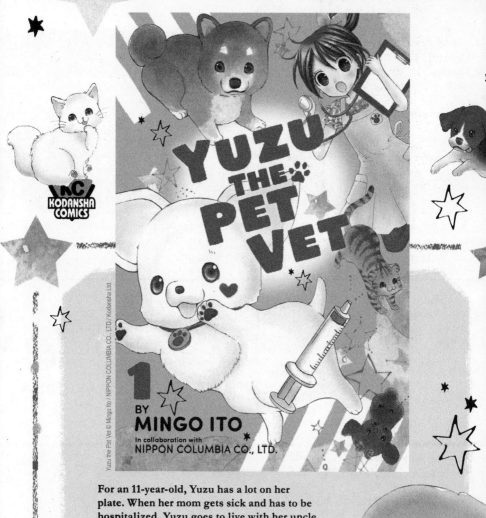

Yuzu the Pet Vet © Mingo Ito /NIPPON COLUMBIA CO., LTD./ Kodansha Ltd.

YUZU THE PET VET

1

BY **MINGO ITO**

In collaboration with
NIPPON COLUMBIA CO., LTD.

For an 11-year-old, Yuzu has a lot on her plate. When her mom gets sick and has to be hospitalized, Yuzu goes to live with her uncle who runs the local veterinary clinic. Yuzu's always been scared of animals, but she tries to help out. Through all the tough moments in her life, Yuzu realizes that she can help make things all right with a little help from her animal pals, peers, and kind grown-ups.

Every new patient is a furry friend in the making!

MW00777846

The Seven Deadly Sins Omnibus 1 is a work of fiction. Names, characters, places, and incidents are the products of the author's imagination or are used fictitiously. Any resemblance to actual events, locales, or persons, living or dead, is entirely coincidental.

A Kodansha Trade Paperback Original

Published in the United States by
Kodansha USA Publishing, LLC, New York.

Publication rights for this English edition arranged through
Kodansha Ltd., Tokyo.

First published in Japan in 2013 by Kodansha Ltd., Tokyo as
Nanatsu no taizai, vol. 1-3.

ISBN 978-1-64651-379-6

Printed in the United States of America.

9 8 7 6 5 4 3 2

Translation: Christine Dashiell
Lettering: James Dashiell
Editing: Julia(n) Leslie Guarch
Kodansha USA Publishing edition cover design by My Truong

Publisher: Kiichiro Sugawara

Director of Publishing Services: Ben Applegate
Associate Director of Operations: Stephen Pakula
Publishing Services Managing Editors: Madison Salters, Alanna Ruse
Production Managers: Emi Lotto, Angela Zurlo

KODANSHA.US

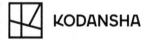